A HISTORY OF
CHRISTIANITY

A HISTORY OF CHRISTIANITY

KENNETH SCOTT LATOURETTE

STERLING PROFESSOR OF MISSIONS AND ORIENTAL HISTORY

AND FELLOW OF BERKELEY COLLEGE IN YALE UNIVERSITY

HARPER & ROW, PUBLISHERS

NEW YORK, EVANSTON, AND LONDON

To my colleagues past and present
of the faculty of the
Yale University Divinity School

CONTENTS

VIGOUR AMIDST STORM: BEGINNING IN A.D. 1914

BY WAY OF INCLUSIVE RETROSPECT

MAPS

xi

PREFACE

Here is both an old and a new story.

It is old. Repeatedly across its nineteen and a half centuries the history of Christianity has been told and retold. In one or another of its aspects it has called forth a voluminous and massive literature.

This is as it should be. Christianity has become the most widespread of all religious faiths. It is by no means dominant. It never ceases to be challenged. There have been times when it has seemed to be waning. Some of the major attacks on it have been made in our day. Its ideals have never been fully attained. Indeed, it at least is debatable whether they ever can be fully realized within the span of history, so high are they, and so far beyond anything actual, either in man's collective life, in small groups, or even in individuals. The one life in which they were fully embodied came to a cross, so contrary were they to current practice in religion and the state. Yet, measured by its effects, Christianity has become the most potent single force in the life of mankind.

Moreover, by its very genius, Christianity is a concern of the historian. If the Christian faith is true, it should be either central or at least be consciously kept as the setting and the point of reference for all the work of the historian. It had its inception in events and in a life which are part of the historical record. From the very first generation of Christians, there have been those who have believed that the clue to the perplexing and paradoxical human drama is to be found in Christ, that the whole of the created universe groans in travail waiting for the revealing of the sons of God, the sons of whom Christ is the first-born, and that it is the purpose of God to sum up all things in Christ, both in the heavens and upon the earth, and to put "all things in subjection under his feet." If this conviction arises from fact, to be seen in its proper perspective the entire course of mankind on the planet must be surveyed with reference to Christ, from the incarnation in Jesus of Nazareth, through his teaching, deeds, life, and resurrection, and it is no accident but of the very stuff of history that chronology is measured as B.C.—before Christ—and A.D., *Anno Domini,* the year of the Lord of men and of history.

It is not surprising that, equipped with this insight, again and again through the centuries Christian scholars have addressed themselves to the history of their faith and in the light of it have endeavoured to understand the nature of man and the course of mankind's pilgrimage. Examples can be instanced from the first to the twentieth century.

The story of Christianity is not only old: it is also ever new. In each age it must be told afresh. That is not merely because in every era a chapter is added by the ongoing current of events. It is also because at every stage of mankind's march fresh perspective is gained. Each generation of historians can say of its predecessors: "Without us they cannot be made perfect." That is partly for the reason that every historian can utilize the work of those of his craft who have gone before him. It is also because from the vantage of a later day and in the fresh setting of his times the historian can interpret anew the road which the race has thus far traversed. No historian can hope to give the final or definitive account of the course of Christianity. Those who come after him will presumably have the same advantages which he possesses over those who have earlier essayed the task. In each generation there must be those who will undertake to review for their fellows the scroll as it has thus far been unrolled.

Certain outstanding features of the mid-twentieth century make necessary now an attempt to resurvey the course of Christianity. These cannot be stated in logical order, for it is not clear that they are tied together in that fashion. One of them, probably the most pronounced at first glance, is the fact that the human race is bound together physically more closely than ever before. Decade by decade, almost year by year, rapid means of transportation and communication reduce the size of the globe in time-distances and make neighbours of people who only yesterday were remote from one another. Closely allied to the shrinkage of the planet is the emergence of what in some respects is a world culture. Civilization everywhere has been coming to have common features. These include machines, the scientific theories and processes which are closely allied with machines, nationalism, the trend towards socialism and democracy in one or another of their various forms, and the demand for universal primary education. Significantly, the immediate sources of the movements which have brought all mankind into close physical juxtaposition and of the outstanding features of the nascent world culture are to be found in the Occident, and the Occident has long been the main stronghold of Christianity, the major part of what traditionally has been called Christendom.

It is not surprising, therefore, that hand in hand with the spread of other features of the culture of the Occident, Christianity should be widely disseminated. That dissemination has not come automatically. Most of it has been achieved through the minority who have been deeply committed to the Christian faith. To be sure, much of it has been by emigration from Europe of those who have been Christians by heredity, but even of these the large majority have been Christians only in name and in the new environment have tended to drift away from the religious patterns of their fatherlands. It has been earnest Christians, usually from among the emigrants and their children, but sometimes missionaries from the mother countries who have kept the faith alive in the migrants as they have moved into a new setting. The spread of Christianity among non-Occidental peoples has been very infrequently through merchants or government officials from the Occident, but has been overwhelmingly by those giving their entire time as missionaries and by the converts of these missionaries. By whatever process, Christianity is today more widely distributed geographically and more deeply rooted among more peoples than it or any other faith has ever been.

By a strange and striking contrast, Christianity has never been as extensively challenged as in the mid-twentieth century. Not only have such traditional rivals as Islam, Hinduism, and Buddhism continued to prove resistant, but also, within "Christendom" great defections have been occurring and fresh rivals, sprung from Christendom, the chief of them Communism, have been spreading throughout the globe and have been threatening all historic religions, notably Christianity itself. Sometimes it seems that from Christianity have been issuing the forces of its own destruction.

It is against this background and from the coign of vantage which the present age affords that we will attempt to look backward and retell the history of Christianity from its beginning to our day.

Any history of Christianity, if it is to be comprehensive, must endeavour to survey the course of all the many features of the human story which can be traced in whole or even in part to Christ. We must strive to understand the fashion in which the impulses which issued from Christ have shaped the current of mankind's life.

Most of this will have to do with what we usually term Christianity. Christianity is a religion and as such is one of many religions. Its distinctive feature is that, as its name implies, it has Jesus Christ at its very heart. Yet Christianity is a synthesis of what the Christian regards as the Gospel, God's gift to man in Christ, and of the human response to it. Christianity centres about Christ but it is compounded of the faith, Judaism, from which Jesus sprang and which prepared the way for him; of Jesus himself, his birth, life, teachings, deeds, death, and resurrection; of the faith of his immediate disciples in him; and of the several aspects of the many environments into which it has moved.

Obviously a well-rounded account of the history of Christianity will narrate the story of its geographic spread, taking account of the forms of the faith which spread, the reasons for the expansion, and the methods, agents, and agencies through which the spread took place. Much of the history of Christianity will concern itself with the visible Church, the institutionalized fellow-ship, or, rather, the congeries of institutions which arose because of Christ. It must tell something of the character, the life, and the work of the outstanding creators and leaders of these institutions. It must narrate the story of the divisions within the Christian community and of the efforts to heal the divisions and to realize that unity in love which is of the essence of the Christian Gospel. It must cover the development of Christian thought, especially what is called doctrine, the attempts of Christians to give intellectual formulation to their faith. Such a survey must also recount the development of both corporate and private worship. It must tell of the means which Christians have used in their endeavour to live to the full the ideals of their faith and to encourage others to do so. To this end it must take cognizance of the methods and forms of instruction in the Christian faith, the course of Christian asceticism and mysticism both within and outside monastic movements, and the standards and processes of the discipline applied to their members by the churches. There must be accounts of some of the outstanding Christians, especially of those who have been regarded by their fellows as approaching the Christian ideal and of those who have been widely influential either within the Christian fellowship or outside it. A well-balanced narrative of the course of Christianity must also seek to disclose what the faith has meant to the rank and file of those who bear the Christian name and of those, unknown to wide fame, who in communities, most of them small and obscure, have been radiating centres of the faith. An inclusive history must say something of the effect of Christianity upon its environment, not alone individuals, although these are the goal and the test of the Christian Gospel, but also the many social and political institutions, movements, customs, and intellectual and emotional currents which shape individuals. Space must be assigned to the effect of the environment upon Christianity, for the two interact: Christianity both moulds and to some degree is moulded by the setting in which it operates.

If it is not to be distorted, the history of Christianity must include all the varieties of the faith. It must embrace not only those forms which have had a wide following, but also minority groups. It must mention not merely the numerous churches and movements which are features of the current scene in whatever part of the world they are found, but in addition those offshoots of Christianity which have disappeared.

From its very beginning, the course of Christianity must be viewed against the background of the entire human race. The necessity of this perspective should be obvious, yet often it has been ignored. Since Christians have claimed that Christ is essential to a comprehension of the meaning of history, since the outlook of Christianity is universal in its scope, and since from the outset the

ideal has been set before the followers of Jesus of winning all men to his discipleship, the historian must ask how far that understanding and that dream
have been realized. His canvass, therefore, must be all mankind from the beginning to the present. In every major stage of his narrative, he who would
survey the history of Christianity must strive to view it in its global setting.

This means, for example, that in those chapters in which we are telling the
story of the first five centuries of Christianity, when that faith was winning the
professed allegiance of the peoples of the Roman Empire and was developing
institutions, patterns of thought, and forms of worship which have been norma-
tive for the majority of Christians from that time to the present, we must make
it clear that most of mankind, both civilized and uncivilized, was not as yet so
much as touched by the Gospel and was not aware of even the name of Jesus
Christ. In the twelfth and thirteenth centuries, a period to which many are
inclined to look back as the heyday of Christianity, we must be aware of the
frequently forgotten fact that Europe, where the faith had its stronghold, and
especially Western Europe, where most of the vigour was displayed, was not
even as prominent in the total world scene as the Roman Empire had been a
thousand years earlier, and that the major centres of wealth, population, and
civilization were elsewhere. In that relatively brief span from the fifteenth
into the twentieth century, when so-called Christian peoples were spreading
throughout the globe and were bringing most of the human race under their
control, and when, in connexion with that expansion, Christianity was having
the greatest geographic extension which it had thus far enjoyed, we must
endeavour to take into account all the chief movements of the day, both within
and without "Christendom."

This perspective does not entail a comprehensive history of mankind. A
universal history might be written from the standpoint of the Christian faith.
Indeed, it has repeatedly been essayed, never more notably than by Augustine
in his *De Civitate Dei*. It does, however, mean that from the very outset the
effort must be made to place the story of Christianity in the setting of universal
history.

If the history of Christianity is surveyed with an awareness of the total
human drama, much more attention must be accorded the past few centuries
than has been usual in such accounts. During the past four hundred and fifty
years and especially in the last century and a half, Christianity has been more
influential in the life of the human race than at any previous time.

This is contrary to an impression which has wide currency. Generally it is
assumed that Christianity has been waning since the Renaissance and especially
since the eighteenth century. The secularism of the present age, the extensive
and often spectacular defections from the faith in so-called Christendom which

have occurred in the past two centuries, and the emergence of communism and other new challenges to Christianity have appeared to justify the dismissal of Christianity by many intellectuals as an interesting phenomenon which has had its day but is now dying. Even many Christians, among them some prominent in the churches, have shared in this appraisal and have occasionally spoken of the present as the "post-Christian era."

The picture is by no means so simple. It supports neither the pessimists nor the unqualified optimists. On the one hand are the adverse phases which undoubtedly exist and to which the prophets of gloom call attention. On the other hand are the wide geographic spread of Christianity, the many movements issuing from the faith, more numerous than in any other stretch of time of corresponding length and evidence of extraordinary vitality, and effects upon more branches of the human family than in any other period. If we are to seek to understand the fashion in which the Christian Gospel operates we must pay particular attention to these later centuries.

At the proper place we must take account of frankly anti-Christian interpretations of history and inquire into their significance. They have appeared within what has traditionally been known as Christendom and have entailed a repudiation of Christianity by much of the latter's hereditary constituency. The contrast between this trend and the fact that parallel with it Christianity has grown in influence in the world as a whole presents a seeming paradox in which there may be a clue to the correct understanding of history. It is partly because of the fact that in these later centuries this paradox, always present, has become especially vivid and has displayed itself on a world-wide scale that we must devote a large proportion of our space to the centuries which lie immediately back of us and particularly to the past four or five generations.

At the very outset we must notice the severe limitations under which all must labour who seek to recount the history of Christianity. We should be given pause by the warning in the Christian Scriptures that what from their viewpoint is the true perspective differs so radically from what is customary that to attain it requires a basic reorientation which is best described as a new birth. One of the ancient Hebrew prophets represents God as declaring: "My thoughts are not your thoughts, neither are my ways your ways. . . . As the heavens are higher than the earth so are my ways higher than your ways, and my thoughts than your thoughts." In the New Testament we find the forceful declaration on no less authority than that of Jesus himself that unless one receives it as a little child, learning afresh from the very beginning, he cannot enter the kingdom of God—that order in which God's will is known and done. Putting it even more bluntly, Jesus said that unless a man be born again, not only can he not enter into the kingdom of God but he cannot even see it, presumably meaning that he does not recognize it even when it is before his eyes. Similarly Jesus rejoiced that true insight had been hidden from the wise and the prudent and had been given to babes, and Paul insisted that God has made foolish the wisdom of this world and that through the wisdom of God the world through its wisdom has failed to know God. So contrary is the perspective given by the Gospel that those trained in the viewpoint of the Greeks tended scornfully to dismiss it as foolishness, and the Jews who were stoutly loyal to what they believed to be what God had given them in their national heritage were either puzzled or enraged by it.

All this would appear to mean that from the Christian standpoint those events, movements, and institutions which usually attract the attention of men and therefore find a place in the records of the past which survive are not nearly as significant as some which are scarcely noticed and of which either little or no trace remains or which, if it is there, is normally passed over by the historian. Yet it is to events and institutions which caught the eye, and to men and women who seemed important to their contemporaries that the historian is chiefly confined, even when he is aware that, judged by Christian standards, many of them are not as significant as others whose memory has so faded that when he seeks for them he cannot discover them.

Fortunately many individuals and movements have appealed to those whose insights have been born of their Christian faith. For them, accordingly, documents have been cherished. Because of their involvement in phases of the world about them which non-Christians deem important, some men and movements have been given a place in records made and preserved by those who did not sympathize with them. Then, too, many individuals and institutions which have borne the Christian name have compromised their Christian principles by mingling with the sub-Christian or anti-Christian world about them to such an extent that the latter has paid them the doubtful compliment of so noticing them that accounts of them have been kept.

Because of these factors, any history of Christianity, when viewed from the Christian perspective, while perhaps having something of true insight, cannot but be distorted and defective.

Moreover, even if his records gave all that he could desire and his own judgement were fully clarified by the Christian faith, the historian of Christianity would still be partly frustrated. Of the essence of his faith is the conviction that the Gospel was in the plan of God before He created man and thus before history began, and that the human drama, whether for individuals, for the Church, or for the race as a whole is not and cannot be complete within history, but moves on beyond this bourne of time and space. At best the historian can only record what has thus far occurred within history. If he could see in detail

what is to come and what and when the culmination is to be he could venture
on interpretation with greater assurance. As it is, the full pattern is not yet perceived and for much of it he can only offer conjectures. We are reminded that
both knowledge and prophecy shall be done away and that now we see as in a
mirror, darkly. A profound Christian conviction is that only faith, hope, and
love endure. These can be a matter of history, but we cannot understand the
past fully because not yet has history been completed nor the final outcome
seen of that love which the Christian believes to be the dominant characteristic
of God Who made all this vast universe and Who continues to work in it.

No one can hope to write history without presuppositions. The professional
historian of the nineteenth and twentieth centuries has aspired to be "objective"
and to tell "what actually happened." Yet every attempt to view the human
story, whether in some small segment or as a whole, involves a selection of
events from the stream which constitutes the crude stuff of history. Back of the
selection is a conviction of what is important. Governing this "value judgement" is, consciously or unconsciously, a philosophy. Underneath and condi-
tioning any endeavour to determine what happened also lies a theory of
knowledge, epistemology, with attempts to answer such questions as: Can we
know? If so how do we know? How valid and how complete is our knowledge? There have been and still are many theories of knowledge, many different answers to these questions. Many interpretations—"philosophies"—of
history have been or are held. Some are basically agnostic, declaring that there
may be no pattern in history, that if there is we cannot discover it, that all one
can confidently affirm about the various philosophies of history is that we cannot know which if any of them is true, and that we cannot be too sure even
of the validity of agnosticism. Others are cyclical, viewing history as endlessly
repeating itself. Others affirm progress in one form or another. The view associated with the name of Hegel is one of thesis, antithesis, and synthesis, the
synthesis becoming a new thesis, marked by a new antithesis, issuing in a fresh
synthesis, and so onwards, a combination of cycles and progress. The Hegelian
philosophy contributed to the emergence of the dialectical materialistic view of
history. The Hindu has traditionally regarded history, like human life itself, as
illusion. The nineteenth and twentieth century effort to determine what actually happened consciously or unconsciously has assumed that we can know
what happened. In general, historians of the various schools of that period have
believed that they could discover relationships between events—causes and effects. More and more they have assumed that history is universal, that the race has
a common origin, that increasingly mankind has become one, that what affects
the individual affects all, and that what the individual does concerns the whole.

Here is not the place to endeavor to determine which if any of the several philosophies is true, or even to seek for valid criteria by which they can be judged. That effort would necessitate a separate and large treatise. At the outset, however, we must say as clearly as we know how that underlying the pages which follow there is a profound conviction that the Christian Gospel is God's supreme act on man's behalf and that the history of Christianity is the history of what God has done for man through Christ and of man's response.

If it is complained that this is not an "objective" approach, it must be remembered that pure objectivity does not exist, even in the natural sciences. One is either for or against Christianity: there is no neutral or strictly "objective" ground. Reason has a legitimate place. We must employ it in testing what are presented to us as facts and in searching for other facts. But truth is not attained by reason alone. The insight that is born of faith can bring illumination. Faith is not credulity and if that which is called faith ignores reason it does so to its peril. But uncritical confidence in reason as the sole or final criterion is a blind act of credulity which may be even more dangerous than a faith which disdains reason. Throughout the chapters which follow is the conviction that the faith which is stimulated by contact with the Christian Gospel, the faith which is the commitment to God of the whole man, body, mind, and spirit, the commitment which is the response in love to God Who is love and Who in His love has revealed Himself in Jesus Christ, opens the mind towards the true understanding of history. That we fail to understand history is due to our lack of such a commitment. That we understand it partly but imperfectly arises from a commitment which is real but incomplete. No one of us has made a full commitment. If we are honest with ourselves we know how limited our commitment is. We should, therefore, never claim infallibility for our interpretation of history. Yet so far as the faith which follows commitment has been given to us, we must seek in its light to perceive the road which man has thus far traversed.

Limitations both in the records and in the historian are inescapable in narrating the history of Christianity. Yet we can attempt it, being aware in part of our handicaps. That is what is essayed in the work to which this is the preface.

In entering upon this adventure we must, as we have suggested, see the history of Christianity in its relation to the total story of mankind. We must endeavour to view it in the setting of human history as a whole. To segregate it from the rest of the course of mankind is to do it violence. Ours must be a purview as inclusive as all mankind and from the beginning to the present.

Obviously this purpose cannot be adequately fulfilled in one or two volumes: a multi-volume work would be too small for the total sweep of time and events. However, there may be some value in the effort to summarize the story

within the compass of a few hundred pages and in doing so to bring into
prominence the highlights in the record of Christianity. It is hoped that such
a survey will prove useful to the thoughtful student, whether he be clergyman
or layman, Christian or non-Christian, and that it will be helpful as a text-book
in colleges, universities, and theological schools.

The main outline of the book can be quickly discerned by reference to the
table of contents. It corresponds to what the author believes to be the main
divisions of the Christian story.

First of all is a section made up of three chapters which attempts to place
Christianity in its setting, to see it in the stream of history, to point out the
particular currents in that stream from which it had its rise, and to describe
the portion of the world in which it was born. Next is an account of the beginnings of Christianity. This must centre around Jesus. It may seem to be a
banality to say that Christianity cannot be understood apart from him. Yet
repeatedly through the centuries and in our own day there have been those
who have regarded Jesus as unimportant in the origin and initial growth of
Christianity. In contrast with this view, the author is convinced that without
Jesus Christianity is not only unintelligible: it would never have been. The
fashion in which Jesus Christ has shaped the faith which bears his name and
the degree to which his professed followers have embodied him or departed
from him never ceases to be both fascinating and significant.

After its origin, the course of Christianity is treated by what the author deems
to have been its major epochs. These, as he conceives them, are best seen as
pulsations in the life of Christianity as reflected in its vigour and its influence
upon the ongoing history of the race. The criteria which he believes to be valid
for discerning these pulsations are, in the main, three—the expansion or recession of the territory in which Christians are to be found, the new movements
issuing from Christianity, and the effect of Christianity as judged from the
perspective of mankind as a whole. Precise dates can seldom if ever be fixed
for the pulsations. The lines between the eras are fuzzy. One age has a way of
running over into its successor or of being foreshadowed before it is born. The
eras are realities, but there are no sharp breaks between them which can be
identified by particular years. Advance and retreat often begin at different
times in the several areas in which Christians are found and the first indications of revival are frequently seen before decline has been halted. Terminal
dates are, therefore, only approximations. Yet approximate dates can be named.

In treating each of these periods we will endeavour to sketch first of all the
contemporary world setting in which Christianity was found, with special
emphasis upon conditions in the areas in which Christianity was strong. We
will tell of the geographic spread of the faith, inquiring into the forms of

Christianity through which the expansion was effected, the reasons for the expansion, and the processes by which the spread took place. If there were territorial losses we will seek to describe them, their causes, and their extent. We will take account of the new movements in the institutional expressions of the faith, and will give brief accounts of the individuals who were more prominent in the Christian story. We will summarize the developments in the thought of Christians about their faith, in forms of worship, and in the means employed to mould the Christian constituency. We will also attempt to say something of the effect of Christianity on its environment and note, in turn, the effect of the environment on Christianity. Not always will these aspects be treated in precisely the order in which they are arranged in this paragraph but in one way or another they will be covered.

The first period or pulsation embraces roughly the initial five centuries. Within these years Christianity won the professed allegiance of the large majority of the population of the Roman Empire. During that time the Church came into being and its visible, institutional expressions took the forms which in their main outlines still characterize the churches in which the majority of Christians have their membership. The several books which compose the New Testament were written and assembled. Other literature was produced. Christians wrestled with the intellectual problems presented by their faith and in consequence Christian theology came into being. The main formulations then hammered out, together with the creeds in which they were summarized, have continued to be standard. Monasticism arose and spread. Forms of worship developed which have had lasting effects. Christianity made a marked impression upon the civilizations of the Mediterranean Basin but this was not as deep or as striking as was that upon other cultures in later periods. In these five centuries only a small fraction of the earth's surface and a minority of mankind were touched by the faith. The large majority of civilized mankind and almost all the uncivilized portions of the human race were not even aware of it. In consequence, Christianity became so closely associated as almost to be identified with a cultural tradition which was only one among several and it was threatened by the possibility of being a regional rather than the universal faith.

Between A.D. 500 and A.D. 950 Christianity suffered the greatest losses which it has ever encountered. Its very existence was threatened. The decay of the empire and the culture with which its phenomenal successes in its first five hundred years had almost identified it seemed to presage its demise. Christianity's very victory appeared to have become its doom. The invasion of the Mediterranean world by non-Christians, notably by Islam-bearing Arabs, tore from Christianity approximately half the areas which had been gained in the preceding period. The morale of the Christian communities declined to their lowest ebb. The story was not altogether one of loss. Additional peoples were brought to accept the faith, and outposts were established from Ireland to China and from Scotland and Scandinavia to Nubia. Some important developments occurred within the churches. Yet never again since those long, agonizing centuries has the prospect for Christianity appeared to be so bleak.

There followed, from A.D. 950 to A.D. 1350, four centuries of advance. The area across which Christianity was carried expanded. More significantly, striking developments occurred within the churches, the Christian faith produced outstanding personalities and important movements in thought and organization, and it helped to bring into being new cultures, notably in Western Europe.

Between A.D. 1350 and A.D. 1500 a decline was witnessed. Much territory was lost and disorganization and corruption appeared in the churches. Yet the recession was neither as prolonged nor as severe as the one between A.D. 500 and A.D. 950. A larger proportion of the territory covered was retained, a few advances into fresh areas were achieved, and vigorous movements issued from Christianity which were indications of vitality.

The two and a half centuries between A.D. 1500 and A.D. 1750 constituted an amazing epoch. A series of awakenings revitalized and largely altered the Christianity of Western Europe. That segment of the globe was entering a new era and Christianity had an important share in modifying the culture which emerged. To a less but still important extent changes were seen in some aspects of Eastern Christianity. Explorations, conquests, and intrepid missionaries carried Christianity over a larger proportion of the earth's surface than had previously been true of it or of any other religion.

From A.D. 1750 to A.D. 1815 a series of events and movements again menaced Christianity. The decay of Spain and Portugal, strong champions of the faith in the preceding two-and-a-half centuries, fresh intellectual movements, and a succession of wars and revolutions in Europe and America appeared to many to be about to bring Christianity to an end. However, viewed in retrospect, the years were more a pause than a recession. There were few actual losses of territory, and new movements, too small at their inception to attract general attention, were appearing and were later to bring Christianity to a new high level of vigour.

The century from A.D. 1815 to A.D. 1914 presented striking contrasts. Western civilization was again moving into a new age. Many of the forces which were moulding that civilization were either openly or tacitly hostile to Christianity. The faith was threatened in its chief strongholds. But new life in Christianity swelled to a flood. This was especially marked in the form of Christianity, Protestantism, which had come into being as recently as the sixteenth

century. It was also seen in what long had been the most active segment of
Christianity, the Roman Catholic Church. Christianity continued to be potent
in Occidental culture and among Occidental peoples. To an important degree
the Occident was still Christendom. Even more than between A.D. 1500 and
A.D. 1750 Christianity spread over the surface of the globe. It was an integral
feature of the new nations which were created by European peoples in the
Americas and Australasia. Especially through its share in shaping the United
States of America Christianity gained in the total world scene. For the first
time Christianity really penetrated Africa south of the Sahara and many of the
islands of the Pacific. It had an enlarging rôle in Asia. The fresh life within
Christianity had many expressions in various lands and wrought significant
changes in that religion. The faith also continued to shape the Occident and
had effects of varying importance upon the peoples and cultures to which it
was being carried.

The period which had its inception in A.D. 1914 and is still incomplete constitutes the latest division of our story. In spite of colossal threats and striking
losses, Christianity has moved forward. Never before at any one time have all
cultures been so shaken. The revolutions have centred in what was once termed
Christendom. Indeed, there is some reason for regarding them as the fruit,
directly or indirectly, of Christianity. Yet for the first time Christianity is
becoming really world-wide. It is entering into the lives of more peoples than
it or any other religion has ever done. Into the new and often terrifying stage
into which the human race, bewildered, is being ushered, Christianity is more
potent than in any earlier era. It is by no means dominant. Never has that
adjective been an accurate description of its place in the human scene. However, when the world is surveyed as a whole, it is more to be reckoned with
than at any previous time. It is an important factor in the world culture which
appears to be emerging.

Readers of *A History of the Expansion of Christianity* will be inclined to
regard the present work as a summary of the earlier one. The chronological pattern, already familiar to them through its volumes, will seem to confirm them
in that impression. Inevitably much that the author learned in the writing of
that survey has been carried over into the present one. But the book which
follows is by no means a condensation of its larger predecessor. It has a quite
different purpose. The one, as its title indicates, is an account of the spread of
Christianity. The chapters which follow endeavour to be a well-rounded
summary of the entire history of Christianity in all its phases and in its setting
in the human scene. In them expansion must have a place and at times be
prominent. However, it is only one aspect of a larger whole. It is a fresh effort
upon which we are embarked.

A bibliography will be attached to each chapter, usually with brief appraisals of the various titles cited. These bibliographies are by no means complete or exhaustive. To make them such would extend the book beyond all reasonable dimensions. Indeed, it would mean multiplying the work into many volumes, for the published material on the history of Christianity is enormous, and that in manuscript is even more extensive. What is attempted, rather, is a selection of the works which the reader or the student who wishes to go further in some of the subjects covered in the text may employ as references and as guides. Several of the books listed are original sources, or as near to original sources as can be obtained. More are secondary accounts based upon the sources or upon other secondary works. The larger proportion are in English, for this study is designed primarily for those who read that language. However, many are in other languages, partly because of their outstanding importance and partly because this book may be translated into other tongues and those who have it in those forms will not wish their reference material confined to English. Not every study consulted by the author in the preparation of this work has been listed. The author has, however, personally examined all those whose titles have been included in the bibliographies and the appraisals given are his own.

Specialists will probably wish that a larger documentation had been given for subjects in which they are particularly interested and may differ both from the estimates of individual books and from the presentation which has been made of the topics in which they are experts. The author can lay no claim to infallibility. He has attempted to avail himself of the best of the books, monographs, and articles of the specialists, to examine a fair proportion of the original sources, and by their use to make his pages as factually accurate as possible. He is painfully conscious, however, that he has not covered more than a small fraction of the pertinent material and that errors have almost certainly crept into what he has written. In questions of judgement and interpretation, moreover, many will almost certainly challenge much that is here put down. The author can only hope that what he has written will prove of some use to both general readers and specialists. He trusts that his survey may enable some who come after him to tell the story of Christianity with more accuracy and with greater insight than he has been able to command.

The author would express his gratitude to the many to whom he and this work are deeply indebted—to the thousands of scholars who have preceded him and from whose labours he has gleaned much of whatever of value these pages may contain, to students who have patiently submitted to having the material presented to them and by their questions have added much illumination, and to colleagues in Yale University and in many another institution of higher learning who have contributed of their knowledge. To no small degree they are in reality co-authors, although few if any of their exact words have been quoted. The title page would be quite too small to include all their names.

As again and again across the years, the author owes an incalculable debt to Mrs. Charles T. Lincoln for typing the manuscript and for suggestions in matters of style.

The author craves the privilege of dedicating this book to his colleagues, past and present, of the Yale University Divinity School. It seems almost invidious to single out any from that goodly company for special mention, for each has contributed, usually quite unwittingly, to these pages. However, the author is peculiarly under obligation to the three Deans under whom he has worked—Charles R. Brown, Luther A. Weigle, and Liston Pope—to Williston Walker, who first introduced him to the history of Christianity as a subject for serious study and whose writings have been of great assistance, to Roland H. Bainton, whose friendship and high standards of scholarship have been a continued inspiration and on whose vast erudition this book has again and again drawn, to Robert L. Calhoun, from whom the author has gained not a little of such knowledge of the history of Christian doctrine as he possesses, and to Raymond P. Morris, who as Librarian of the Yale University Divinity School has not only shown extraordinary skill and judgement in assembling and making accessible the pertinent literature but has also been unfailingly generous and wise in this counsel.

The author needs scarcely add that none of these many friends is to be held accountable for any errors which the book may contain or for any omissions of which it may be guilty.

THE PRE-CHRISTIAN COURSE
OF MANKIND

Chapter I

THE GENERAL SETTING OF CHRISTIANITY IN HISTORY

THE YOUTH OF CHRISTIANITY

Christianity is relatively young. Compared with the course of mankind on the earth, it began only a few moments ago. No one knows how old man is. That is because we cannot tell precisely when a creature which can safely be described as human first appeared. One estimate places the earliest presence of what may be called man about 1,200,000 years in the past. A being with a brain about the size of modern man may have lived approximately 500,000 years ago. In contrast with these vast reaches of time the less than two thousand years which Christianity has thus far had are very brief. If one accepts the perspective set forth in the New Testament that in Christ is the secret of God's plan for the entire creation, and that God purposes to "gather together in one all things in Christ, both which are in heaven and which are on earth," Christianity becomes relatively even more recent, for the few centuries since the coming of Christ are only an infinitesimal fraction of the time which has elapsed since the earth, not to speak of the vast universe, came into being.

When placed in the setting of human civilization Christianity is still youthful. Civilization is now regarded as having begun from ten to twelve thousand years ago, during the last retreat of the continental ice sheets. This means that Christianity has been present during only a fifth or a sixth of the brief span of civilized mankind.

Moreover, Christianity appeared late in the religious development of mankind. It may be something of this kind which was meant by Paul when he declared that "in the fullness of time God sent forth His son." We need not here take the space to sketch the main outlines of the history of religion. We must note, however, that of those faiths which have had an extensive and enduring geographic spread, Christianity is next to the latest to come to birth. Animism in one or another of its many forms seems to have antedated civilization. Polytheisms have been numerous, and some of them, mostly now merely

3

a memory, are very ancient. Hinduism in its earlier aspects antedates Christianity by more than a thousand years. Judaism, out of which Christianity sprang, is many hundreds of years older than the latter. Confucius, the dominant figure in the system which the Occident calls by his name, lived in the sixth and fifth centuries before Christ. The years of the founder of Buddhism, although debated, are commonly placed in the same centuries. Zarathustra, or, to give him the name by which English readers generally know him, Zoroaster, the major creator of the faith which was long official in Persia and which is still represented by the Parsees, is of much less certain date, but he seems to have been at least as old as Confucius and the Buddha and he may have been older by several centuries. Only Manichæism and Islam were of later origin than Christianity. Of these two, Manichæism has perished. Christianity is, therefore, the next to the youngest of the great religious systems extant in our day which have expanded widely among mankind.

That Christianity emerged in the midst of a period in which the major high religions of mankind were appearing gives food for thought. Most of these faiths came into being in the thirteen centuries between 650 B.C. and A.D. 650. Of those which survive only Judaism and Hinduism began before 650 B.C. Here was a religious ferment among civilized peoples which within a comparatively brief span issued in most of the main advanced religions which have since shaped the human race. This occurred with but little interaction of one upon another. Only Christianity and Islam are exceptions. Both of these were deeply indebted to Judaism, and Islam was influenced by both Judaism and Christianity.

The youth of Christianity may be highly important. It might conceivably mean that, as a relatively late phenomenon, Christianity will be transient. The other major religions have risen, flourished, reached their apex, and then have either entered upon a slow decline or have become stationary. Hinduism is not as widely extended as it was fifteen hundred years ago. Not for five centuries have important gains been registered by Buddhism and during that time serious losses have occurred. Confucianism has achieved no great geographic advance since it moved into Annam, Korea, and Japan many centuries ago, and at present it is disintegrating. Islam has suffered no significant surrender of territory since the reconversion of the Iberian Peninsula to Christianity, a process completed about four centuries ago, and in the present century has pushed its frontiers forward in some areas, notably in Africa south of the Sahara. Yet its advances have been much less marked than in the initial stages of its spread. It might be argued that Christianity is to have a similar fate and the fact of its youth may mean that for it the cycle of growth, maturity, and decay has not reached as advanced a stage as has that of other faiths. To this appraisal the fact of the emergence of the high religions, including Christianity, in the comparatively brief span of thirteen centuries may lend support. The grouping of their origins in one segment of time and the progressive weakening of so many of them might be interpreted as an indication that all religions, in the traditionally accepted use of that term, and including even Christianity, are a waning force in the life of mankind. Some, indeed, so interpret history and declare that the race is outgrowing religion. The losses in Europe in the present century might well appear to foreshadow the demise of Christianity.

On the other hand, the brief course of Christianity to date may be but a precursor to an indefinitely expanding future. The faith may be not far from the beginning of its history and only in the early stages of a growing influence upon mankind. As we are to see more extensively in subsequent chapters, the record of Christianity yields evidence which can be adduced in support of this view. As we hinted in the preface and will elaborate more at length later, the faith has displayed its greatest geographic extension in the past century and a half. As the twentieth century advances, and in spite of many adversaries and severe losses, it has become more deeply rooted among more peoples than it or any other faith has ever before been. It is also more widely influential in the affairs of men than any other religious system which mankind has known. The weight of evidence appears to be on the side of those who maintain that Christianity is still only in the first flush of its history and that it is to have a growing place in the life of mankind. In this Christianity is in striking contrast with other religions. Here are much of its uniqueness and a possible clue to its significance.

A third possible interpretation, and one to which many Christians subscribe, is that Christianity will neither disappear nor fully triumph within history, but that it will continue, sometimes waning, sometimes waxing in its influence upon individuals and mankind as a whole, until, perhaps early, perhaps millenniums hence, history comes to an end. To this view also much in the record appears to lend support.

The comparative youth of Christianity means that the history which is summarized in the subsequent chapters, complex and rich though it is, compasses only a small fragment of the total span of the story of the human race and, if mankind goes on, is merely an introduction to what later millenniums are to witness. If Christianity is only near the beginning of its course it may be that the forms which it has developed, whether institutional, intellectual, or ritual, are by no means to be final or continuously characteristic. This, however, is prophecy, and upon that dangerous road the historian ought not to venture.

THE LIMITED AREA OF EARLY CHRISTIANITY

The cultural area in which Christianity arose, that of the Mediterranean Basin, was merely one of the centres of contemporary civilization and embraced only a minority of mankind. It is important that this fact be recognized if we are to see the history of the faith in its true perspective. Since during the past four and a half centuries the Occident and its culture have been progressively dominant throughout the globe, and since in connection with it Christianity has had its world-wide spread, we are inclined to regard that condition as normal. In view of the circumstance that during its first five centuries Christianity won the professed allegiance of the Roman Empire, which then embraced the Occident, many have thought of it as having at this early date conquered the world. This is entirely mistaken. East of the Roman Empire was the Persian Empire which for centuries fought Rome to a stalemate. Its rulers regarded Christianity with hostile eye, partly because of its association with their chronic rival, and fought its entrance into their domains. India, although not united into one political realm, was the seat of a great culture which influenced the Mediterranean area but which, in spite of extensive commercial contacts, was but little affected religiously by the Occident. China had a civilization all its own. At the time when the Roman Empire was being formed, China was being welded into a political and cultural whole under the Ch'in and the Han dynasty. In area it was about as large as the Roman Empire. In wealth and population it may not have equalled its great Western contemporary, but in cultural achievements it needed to make no apology to India, Persia, or Rome. In the Americas were small beginnings of civilized states. In its first five centuries neither China nor America was reached by Christianity. These civilizations, even when taken together, occupied only a minority of the surface of the earth. Outside them were the vast masses of "primitive" mankind, almost untouched by Christianity until after its first five centuries were passed. It is against this background that we must see the rise and early development of Christianity. In its initial centuries the geographic scope of Christianity was distinctly limited.

THE UNPROMISING ROOTAGE OF CHRISTIANITY

When we come to the area in which Christianity began, we must remind ourselves that even there, in that geographically circumscribed region, the roots from which it sprang appeared to promise no very great future for the faith. It is one of the commonplaces of our story that Christianity was an outgrowth of the religion of Israel. Israel was never important politically. Only for a brief time, under David and Solomon, between nine hundred and a thousand years before Christ, did it achieve a domain of considerable dimensions. Even then it did not rank with the major empires. That realm soon broke up into two small states, the Northern and Southern Kingdoms, insignificant pawns in the contests among the great powers in the valleys of the Nile and of the Tigris and Euphrates Rivers. Except for what came through its religion, Israel was of slight consequence culturally. When contrasted with its neighbours in Mesopotamia and Egypt it occupied a small and infertile area in the Palestinian uplands. Its cities were diminutive and its buildings unimpressive. Its art was not distinguished. Today the monumental ruins of Egypt, Nineveh, Babylon, and even Syria dwarf those of Israel's past and make clear the relative insignificance, from the political and economic standpoint, of the land in which was the stock from which Christianity sprang.

In this respect Christianity was in striking contrast with those faiths which became its chief rivals. The polytheisms which it displaced in the Mediterranean Basin had the support of old and politically powerful cultures and states. Zoroastrianism was associated with Persia, for centuries one of the mightiest empires on the globe. Hinduism was indigenous to India, one of the major cultural centres of mankind. Buddhism was also a native of India and early won wide popularity in the land of its birth. Both Hinduism and Buddhism owed much of their extension outside India to the commerce and the cultural prestige of that land. Confucianism was for two thousand years so closely integrated with China, one of earth's mightiest civilizations, that its spread on the periphery of that realm seemed assured. Islam early brought unity to the Arabs and within a century of its origin was supported by one of the three largest and strongest empires of the day. At its outset Christianity had no such potent associations to commend it. Not until, after more than three centuries, it had, through its first amazing victories, become dominant in the Roman Empire did it achieve such an influential cultural and political alliance as these other faiths early possessed.

It is sometimes said that Israel owed its unique religious development to the fact that it was of the family of Semitic peoples and was on the land bridge between the great civilizations of Egypt and of Mesopotamia and so was stimulated by contributions from each of them. But there were other Semitic peoples who were in much the same favored position, the Phoenicians among them, and it was only in Israel that the religious development occurred which issued in Judaism and Christianity.

Moreover, it was in a minority, even within the comparatively obscure people of Israel, that the stream which issued in Christianity had its rise and its early course. The prophetic monotheism which was the source of Christianity long commanded the undivided support of only a small proportion of Israel.

The loyal minority were sufficiently numerous to cherish and hand down the writings of the prophets. Through them came the main contributions of Israel to the world. Within this minority we find the direct antecedents of Christianity. Yet the majority of Israel either rejected the prophets outright or devitalized their message by compromise. Even among the relatively insignificant people within which Christianity arose, only the numerically lesser part could be counted in the spiritual ancestry of the faith. Fully as significantly, it was largely those who believed themselves to be in the succession of that minority who so opposed Jesus that they brought him to the cross.

Christians have seen in this story the fashion in which God works. They have believed that always and everywhere God has been seeking man and has been confronting man with Himself and with the standard which He has set for man. Yet man, so they have held, persistently rebels against God and becomes corrupt. God, of His mercy and love, has wrought for man's redemption. This He has not done in the way which men would have predicted. Even those whom men have accounted wise have been so blinded by sin, especially by pride and self-confidence, that they could not clearly see or hear God. For reasons known only to Himself, so Christians have maintained, God chose as His channel for man's salvation a small, insignificant minority among the people of Israel, themselves of slight consequence in physical might. As the culmination of His revelation of Himself and His redemption of man, He sent His son, who, the heir of this humble minority and building on the foundations laid by them, became the centre of the Christian faith.

The story, as seen from a Christian standpoint, might also be put in the following fashion. God has always, from the beginning of the human race, been seeking to bring men into fellowship with Himself and into His likeness. He has respected man's free will and has not forced Himself on man. Only thus could He produce beings who are not automata, but are akin to Himself. In response to God's initiative, men everywhere were stimulated to grope for God. As a result of their seeking, various religions arose. All of these, clouded by man's sin, were imperfect and could not meet man's need or fulfil God's purpose. For some inscrutable reason, God found among the people of Israel a minority who responded to Him and, therefore, was able to disclose Himself fully through one who came out of that succession and through him made possible the salvation of man.

These interpretations, arising from Christian faith, might be suspect as biased. Yet, more than any others, as we are to see in a later stage in our story, they seem to make intelligible the facts presented by the course of Christianity on the planet.

BIBLIOGRAPHY

The literature on the history of religion is enormous. As good a comprehensive survey as any is G. F. Moore, *History of Religions* (New York, Charles Scribner's Sons, 2 vols., 1913–1919).

Chapter II

THE IMMEDIATE BACKGROUND OF
CHRISTIANITY: JUDAISM

It was from Judaism that Christianity sprang. Indeed, at the outset it appeared to be only one of several sects of Judaism.

THE RISE OF JUDAISM

Judaism arose out of the religion of Israel. It came through lawgivers, priests, and prophets and was the outgrowth of centuries of development.

For many generations, as we have suggested, the faith of which it was the fruitage obtained the undivided allegiance of only a minority of the folk who bore the name of Israel, but eventually it was held tenaciously by the majority of those who were called Jews. The disasters of the eighth and sixth centuries B.C. which erased the two small states that had been the political centres of the people led to a purification of the faith of the community which survived the debacle. The downfall of the Northern and Southern Kingdoms was the work of conquerors from the Tigris-Euphrates Valley and was accompanied and followed by the deportation of the leading elements and some of the masses. Others fled to Egypt. Only small and politically unimportant groups remained. Then, under the friendly tolerance of the Persian monarchs who brought Palestine within their boundaries, a new temple was built at Jerusalem which became the centre not only for the Jewish population of that region but also for the thousands of Jews who were scattered in other parts of Western Asia and of the Mediterranean Basin. The tie which held the Jews together was religious and the religion was Judaism.

The loyalty of the Jews to their religion was heightened by persecution. Antiochus Epiphanes, one of the Seleucids who in succession to Alexander the Great built a realm in Syria and adjacent lands, sought to force Greek culture and manners on the Jews. This was met by a revolt led by the Maccabees and was followed by the setting up of a small state in which the high priest was the central figure. It also intensified among many the zeal for their faith.

Later, in the first century before Christ, the Jewish state was brought within the growing power of Rome. Herod, of non-Jewish stock but married into the Maccabeean family, with the consent of Rome established himself over the little state and rebuilt the temple in Jerusalem. Here was a sad ending of the Maccabeean dream. That dream had envisioned a community in which God's will as expressed in the Jewish law and prophets was to be perfectly observed. The outcome was a state governed by an alien ruler whose chief ambition was his own power and the establishment of a dynasty. Yet it was during the reign of Herod that Jesus was born and under Herod's descendants that Christianity had its inception.

JEWISH BELIEFS AND LITERATURE

The Judaism of the centuries immediately before the birth of Christianity was strictly monotheistic and made much of the Law and the Prophets. Into the long story of its development we must not take the time to go, even in brief summary. For our purposes we must confine ourselves to such bare features of Judaism as are essential to an understanding of the beginnings of Christianity and the nature and characteristics of that faith.

Judaism regarded the Jews as especially favoured by God. Originally, at least for many, their god was a tribal deity, one of many gods, but choosing Israel for his own. With him Israel was believed to have entered into intimate covenant relations through which they were to be loyal to him and he, in return, was to aid them. Early, perhaps from the outset, some among Israel were monotheists. They regarded their god, Yahweh, a name mistakenly put into English as Jehovah, as the God of the universe, the maker and ruler of heaven and earth. Other peoples had their gods, but Yahweh was regarded by these monotheists as far more powerful than they. They were either false gods or were completely subordinate to him. To the Jew the core of his faith and the chief commandment were found in the declaration: "Hear, O Israel: The Lord our God is one Lord: and thou shalt love the Lord thy God with all thy heart, and with all thy soul, and with all thy might." God, so the devout Jew believed, had made man in His own image, but man had sinned against God and thereby had incurred His wrath. That sin, so the Jew held, began with the transgression of the first human couple, Adam and Eve. It was basically rebellion against God. God, however, of His great mercy chose Abraham, and of him and his descendants made a nation, His peculiar people. He also, the Jew maintained, gave him His law to control his conduct. That law had to do both with what are usually called morals and with ritual. It was briefly summarized in the Ten Commandments, but it had much more elaborate formulations. It included the regulation of food and diet and the observance of days, especially the Sabbath. The latter was to be kept with great strictness, free from the usual occupations of the rest of the week. Circumcision was universal and was regarded as a symbol of the covenant between Yahweh and His people.

The prophets were honoured as spokesmen for Yahweh. They not only foretold the future. The greatest of them also, and more especially, rebuked wickedness, both private and public, and, on occasion, sought to direct the policy of the community and the state and to encourage those who were obedient. They denounced the rich for oppressing the poor. Believing as they did that Yahweh is ruler of all the earth, they spoke out against the sins of the surrounding nations, but they were particularly vehement in their arraignment of Israel.

The law-givers and prophets were claimed by Christians as forerunners of Jesus. Their names and histories, as well as their teachings, became the property of Christianity and entered into its warp and woof. Outstanding were Moses, who led his people out of their captivity in Egypt, and through whom came the initial formulation of the Jewish law; Elijah, an heroic figure who stood as the champion of Yahweh and of the poor against the corruptions of the court of the Northern Kingdom and who captured the imagination of succeeding generations; Isaiah, who rebuked the wickedness of his people, especially those of the Southern Kingdom, called them to repentance, and heartened its king to withstand an Assyrian invasion; the latter part of the book which bears the name of Isaiah, with stirring chapters in which Christians have seen a prevision of Jesus and his vicarious sufferings; Amos, who sternly denounced the evils of the peoples of his world and especially of Israel; Hosea, who in his bitter experience with a faithless wife perceived something of the way in which Yahweh viewed a rebellious Israel; Jeremiah, who, in the last days of the Southern Kingdom, became an unpopular preacher of doom and in his own sufferings foreshadowed the experience of Jesus; and Ezekiel, the prophet of the exile, who spoke to those who had been carried to the Tigris-Euphrates Valley.

Judaism also gave rise to great poetry. The standard collection of its hymns, the Psalms, became the cherished possession of Christians and held and continues to hold a prominent place in their public and private worship. *The Book of Job,* with its wrestling with the problem of evil, passed over to the Christians. So also did *The Song of Songs,* which, allegorized, became a cherished treasure house of Christian mystics. What was known as the Wisdom literature of the Jews was also claimed by the Christians. Its proverbs and its glorification of Wisdom became a part of the Christian heritage.

Apocalypse, Eschatology, and Messiah

Prominent in the Jewish faith were apocalypses and a belief in the Messiah. The two were often associated but were by no means inseparable. The apocalypses were a kind of literature which flourished in Jewish circles in the centuries immediately preceding and following the time of Christ. The word meant to uncover or to reveal. An apocalypse claimed to be a divine revelation of the future. It arose from the Jewish conception of history. The Jews believed God to be at work in the affairs of men. Indeed, they held that He controlled all history. They saw much in life which was contrary to what they conceived to be the will of God. The wicked often lorded it over the righteous. Indeed, the righteous were repeatedly overwhelmed by the unrighteous. The disobedient appeared to prosper. Moreover, misfortunes of other kinds, such as sickness, overtook the good. The Jews were concerned to reconcile these uncomfortable facts with the sovereignty of God. They held that human history is a drama which begins with the creation of man, which early sees the rebellion of man against God, and which has its culmination in the victory of God in an era in which God's will is fully done. It was the future steps of this process which the apocalypses professed to reveal. They were based upon a profound conviction that God must ultimately triumph. They speak of "the age to come." This would be introduced by a great catastrophe with judgement beyond which would lie a new heaven and a new earth. They deal with what is technically known as eschatology, "last" or final things, at the end of history and beyond it, such as judgement and the life of the age to come.

As an agent for God's victory some of the Jews cherished the hope of a Messiah. Various views of the Messiah were held, but all agreed that he was the "anointed"—for that is what the word meant—a king who was to reign under divine commission. In the periods of subjugation to foreign rulers the Messiah was anticipated as the deliverer from the alien and as one who would set up the ideal realm in which God's will would be perfectly done. The Greek word used to translate Messiah was the one from which the English word Christ is derived.

The Synagogue

By the time of the birth of Christianity Judaism had developed an institution, the synagogue, which was to have a profound effect upon the nascent Christian Church. The synagogue had arisen between the revival of Judaism after the fall of the Northern and Southern Kingdoms and the time of Jesus. Synagogues were the chief centres of Jewish worship. Until its destruction a generation or so after the time of Jesus, the temple in Jerusalem was the main shrine of

Judaism. Yet both in Palestine and among the Jews of the "dispersion," scattered through much of the Mediterranean world and Western Asia, the synagogues were the places where most of the Jews worshipped and were taught. They had regular forms of service. In them the Law and the Prophets were read and expounded. Through them and the instruction given in them Judaism was perpetuated. Schools were associated with the synagogues and in them the Scriptures and the unwritten law were taught.

THE SCRIBE

A class which had developed by the time of Christ and which had great influence upon the Judaism of that period was the Scribes. The Scribes were professional teachers and scholars who concerned themselves with the Scriptures and particularly with the Jewish law, both in its written form and in its oral tradition. They might also be priests but most of them were laymen. They were by no means an hereditary caste, as were the priests, but any one through personal competence might enter their ranks.

VARIETIES OF JUDAISM

When Christianity came into being, Judaism was not all of one pattern. In it were to be found several trends, schools, and sects. Not all of them were important in the development of Christianity. We need notice, therefore, only those which were significant for the history of that faith.

A trend of primary importance was towards the penetration of Judaism by Hellenism. The Jews were widely scattered in the Mediterranean world. Here they fell under the influence of the Greek thought which was so potent in that region, especially after the conquests by Alexander the Great in the fourth century before Christ. Outstanding as a centre of Greek culture was Alexandria, in Egypt.

The preëminent representative of this trend was Philo, or Philo Judæus. An Alexandrian, born late in the first century before Christ and doing most of his work in the first century of the Christian Era, he was a contemporary of Jesus. He was profoundly influenced by Greek thought, especially by Platonism, but also by the Stoics and the Pythagoreans. Indeed, he knew Greek much better than he did Hebrew and could almost be counted as a Greek philosopher. He was of the Hellenistic world, that cultural atmosphere, a mixture of the Orient and Greece, which arose from the spread of Greek thought and manners into the Orient. It was Hellenism in which Philo was nurtured. Yet Philo was a loyal Jew by birth and religion and sought through his writings to commend his faith to the Hellenistic world. In interpreting the Jewish scriptures he employed the device of allegory, a method which he did not originate and which was to persist long after him, in Christian as well as in other circles. With the aid of allegory he sought to show that the profoundest speculations of Greek thought were to be found in Jewish law. He insisted that Moses was the source of much of Greek philosophy. This, too, became the attitude of some of the Christian writers of the first centuries of that faith.

The Hellenistic Judaism of which Philo was the leading representative at once found expression and was reinforced through what was known as the Septuagint. The Septuagint was made up of translations of Jewish sacred books into Greek. The name is derived from the tradition that the task of translation was accomplished in the third century B.C. in seventy-two days by seventy-two scholars sent from Jerusalem to Alexandria at the request of one of the Ptolemies. This tradition is found in a letter which is undoubtedly spurious. The translation was actually the work of many different hands. It was made piecemeal and in several centuries. It was obviously needed for the many Jews for whom Greek was the language of everyday life and to whom the Hebrew of the original was either unfamiliar or understood only with difficulty.

Hellenistic Judaism was varied. A certain amount of unity was given it by the synagogue and the use of the Septuagint in teaching and in the services of the synagogue. Yet the penetration of Judaism by Hellenism differed from community to community and even from individual to individual. Moreover, Hellenism itself was far from uniform. Hellenistic Judaism, therefore, had many aspects, most of which are now lost us through the ravages of time.

Through Hellenistic Judaism many converts were won from the surrounding non-Jewish communities. The Jews were profoundly convinced that theirs was the only true religion and that it would sometime become the faith of all mankind. They probably had few professional missionaries whose assignment it was to win the Gentiles, but in their intercourse with the non-Jews—the "Gentiles"—many Jews sought to bring the latter to their faith. Their synagogue services were open to all, whether Jew or Gentile. Many Gentiles were attracted to Judaism. Some of them partly adopted Judaism but did not become full members of the Jewish community. They abandoned idolatry and the worship of other gods, they observed the Sabbath and the Jewish regulations of clean and unclean foods, they attended the services of the synagogue, and, in general, observed Jewish ethics. Others went the whole way and became full proselytes. They not only conformed as did those who might be described as on the fringes of Judaism. In addition they were circumcised, were baptized (the baptism was by immersion), and offered a sacrifice in the temple in Jerusalem. They thus were accepted into the Jewish community as equals of those who were Jews by birth.

Many converts came from less than religious motives. Some were forced by the political authorities to accept Judaism. Numbers entered through marriage. Still others wished to share in the special privileges which were accorded the Jews in some regions and periods. However, many adopted Judaism from profound religious conviction.

Eventually, as we are to see, Christianity had much of its early spread through the circles of Hellenistic Judaism, both among those who were Jews by long heredity and those who had either become full proselytes or were on the fringes of the synagogue.

In general, the penetration of Judaism by Hellenism was less marked within Palestine than outside it. Some permeation there was, even in this traditional stronghold of the Jews. Many in its very home would have Judaism conform to Hellenism. However, as we have suggested, strong resistance was put up against the attempts at partial or complete conformity and especially against the efforts of Antiochus Epiphanes to assimilate the Jews to Hellenism.

Within Palestine the Hebrew religious heritage was shared by several groups. Some of these became significant for Christianity.

One of which we hear mention in the first century was the Samaritans. The Samaritans were not Jews. They were regarded by the latter as outsiders, partly akin and yet to be classed with the Gentiles. They were descendants of some of the Israelites who had composed the Northern Kingdom and who had not been carried away captive at the time of the downfall of that state. They accepted the Law as contained in the Pentateuch, the first five books of the Jewish scriptures, but they rejected Jerusalem as the centre of true worship and would not venerate some of the writings contained in the Jewish scriptures.

Another group of which we hear something in the New Testament was the Sadducees. They were aristocrats, a kind of hereditary caste, who entered into political life and for a time controlled the temple in Jerusalem. They tended to conform to Hellenism and to lead the Hellenistic party, so far as such a party could be said to exist. Yet in some ways they were, as are most aristocrats, conservatives. As such they held to the written and repudiated the oral Jewish Law. They also rejected personal immortality, judgement after death, angels, and devils. They displayed little deep religious conviction and did not have enduring influence.

Far more important for Christianity were the Pharisees. They wished to keep the inherited faith pure from alien contamination. They stood for the strict observance of the Law. Theirs was a personal as well as a national religion, for they showed a sense of sin, recognized the need for repentance, and made much of the grace and forgiveness of God. In contrast with the Sadducees they believed in a future life with rewards and punishments. They stressed oral tradition and by it elaborated and supplemented the written Law. The rank and file of the Palestinian populace were more influenced by them than by any other of the competing kinds of Judaism. It was with them that Jesus and the early Christians had their chief conflicts. In his teaching Jesus and the Pharisees seemed to have much in common, but in the contest with a school which it appeared so closely to resemble some of the essential characteristics of Christianity stood out. To these we are to recur later.

A form of Judaism which seems to have included only a comparatively few was the Essenes. They appear to have lived together in groups, holding all things in common. The majority were celibates. They possessed no slaves, hated war, and refused to hurt man either voluntarily or at the command of another. They were austere in both food and clothing, worked hard, and denied themselves pleasure. They prized honesty and, except for the vows which they assumed on entering the Essene fellowship, would not take oaths but simply give their unsupported word. They preferred agricultural occupations, but were also to be found in towns and villages. They gave generous assistance to the deserving poor. Much that we know of the Essenes is akin to Christian teaching. Yet there is no proof of Essene influence upon the Christian faith.

JUDAISM SUMMARIZED

This brief description of Judaism may seem to be a dry summary of bare facts. If it is no more than that it has failed to give a true picture of that religion. Perhaps no words can do Judaism justice or fully disclose the inwardness of the faith. The Jewish scriptures themselves do not attempt to compress all into a simple or brief formula. Indeed, words fail adequately to convey what a high religion, or perhaps any religion, means to those who have been really caught by it.

Yet certain passages out of the Jewish sacred writings, taken together, can serve to give at least an inkling of the genius of the faith. "In the beginning God created the heaven and the earth." "The heavens declare the glory of God and the firmament showeth His handiwork." "It is He . . . that stretcheth out the heavens as a curtain and spreadeth them out as a tent to dwell in; that bringeth the princes to nothing; he maketh the judges of the earth as vanity." "Thou shalt have no other gods before Me. Thou shalt not make unto thee any graven image . . . thou shalt not bow down thyself to them or serve them; for I the Lord thy God am a jealous God, visiting the iniquity of the fathers upon the children unto the third and the fourth generation of them that hate Me; and showing mercy unto thousands of them that love Me and keep My commandments." "Thou shalt not take the name of the Lord thy God in vain, for the Lord will not hold him guiltless that taketh His name in vain." "Remember the Sabbath day to keep it holy." "Honor thy father and thy mother."

"Thou shalt not kill." "Thou shalt not commit adultery." "Thou shalt not steal." "Thou shalt not bear false witness against thy neighbour." "Thou shalt not covet." "Thou shalt love thy neighbour as thyself." "Cease to do evil; learn to do well; seek judgement, relieve the oppressed, judge the fatherless, plead for the widow." "The feast of unleavened bread shalt thou keep." "Thou shalt not plow with an ox and an ass together." "Thou shalt not muzzle the ox when he treadeth out the corn." "Whatsoever parteth the hoof . . . and cheweth the cud . . . that shall ye eat. . . . The swine . . . is unclean to you." "You only have I known of all the families of the earth: therefore will I punish you for all your iniquities." "The Lord is merciful and gracious, slow to anger and plenteous in mercy. . . . He hath not dealt with us after our sins nor rewarded us according to our iniquities. . . . As far as the east is from the west so far hath He removed our transgressions from us." "The Lord is my shepherd; I shall not want." "They that wait upon the Lord shall renew their strength: they shall mount up on wings as eagles; they shall run, and not be weary; and they shall walk and not faint." "The fear of the Lord is the beginning of wisdom." "He hath showed thee, O man, what is good; and what doth the Lord require of thee, but to do justly, and to love mercy, and to walk humbly with thy God?" "The souls of the righteous are in the hands of God." "I know that my Redeemer liveth, and that He shall stand at the latter day upon the earth: and though after my skin, worms destroy my body, yet in my flesh shall I see God."

Here are God, the creator and governor of the universe; His choice of the Jewish people for His own, yet the responsibility which went with this favour; His requirements of the Jews, in worship, in morals, in the observance of days, and in food; His mercy and forgiveness; His protection and the strength which comes from Him; the reverence for Him which is the source of true wisdom; and the assurance of immortality, late in appearing and not universally held.

JUDAISM AND CHRISTIANITY

However, it was not Judaism which became the most widely influential of the faiths of mankind. It was Christianity. In one sense Christianity was the outgrowth of Judaism. Yet in a very real way it was not the offspring of Judaism but was new. It was the culmination of Judaism, but it was more. It regarded the lawgivers, psalmists, and prophets of Judaism as its own and as preparing the way for Christ. It was the fulfilment of Judaism, but it went beyond Judaism. At the outset it appeared to be another Jewish sect, although very small. Yet eventually it far outgrew in dimensions and influence all the Jewish sects combined. It did this because of distinctive qualities which at once related it to Judaism and distinguished it from Judaism. It was not just another

Jewish sect. It was a new and fresh faith. An understanding of Judaism is essential to a full knowledge of Christianity. But Judaism does not explain Christianity. Even a complete knowledge of Judaism would by no means ensure a knowledge of Christianity. Indeed, it might make difficult a real understanding of Christianity. Christianity was built on Jewish foundations, yet it was radically different. In this difference lies the secret of Christianity and of its phenomenal history.

Selected Bibliography

E. R. Goodenough, *Introduction to Philo Judæus* (Yale University Press, 1940, pp. xii, 223). By an outstanding specialist on Philo and Hellenistic Judaism.

G. H. C. MacGregor and A. C. Purdy, *Jew and Greek: Tutors Unto Christ. The Jewish and Hellenistic Background of the New Testament* (New York, Charles Scribner's Sons, 1936, pp. 366). A competent survey intended for non-specialists.

G. F. Moore, *Judaism in the First Centuries of the Christian Era. The Age of the Tannaim* (Harvard University Press, 3 vols., 1927–1930). A standard work of great erudition.

T. H. Robinson and W. O. E. Oesterley, *Hebrew Religion. Its Origin and Development* (New York, The Macmillan Co., 2 vols., 2d ed., 1937). One of the better of the many standard treatises, primarily for non-Jewish readers.

Chapter III

THE IMMEDIATE BACKGROUND OF CHRISTIANITY: THE GRÆCO-ROMAN WORLD

If Christianity was radically different from Judaism, the religion which in some degree was its parent, the gulf which separated it from the Græco-Roman world into which it was born was still wider. It was an alien environment into which Christianity came.

Yet much in that environment favoured the spread of Christianity. Moreover, the environment placed its stamp on Christianity. We must, therefore, seek to understand something of the main outline of the life and thought of the portion of the globe outside of Judaism in which Christianity had its beginning.

THE SCENE OF THE BIRTH OF CHRISTIANITY

First of all, we must remind ourselves again that the basin of the Mediterranean, the region in which Christianity came into being, in which it had its first great triumphs, and in which it long had most of its strength, embraced only a small fraction of the earth's surface. Moreover, when Christ was born it was the home of considerably less than half of civilized mankind. Culturally it presented a great variety, but in general it was dominated by two traditions, those of Greece and Rome. To the east lay Mesopotamia and Persia. Both made their contributions to the Græco-Roman world, but they were quite distinct from it. For centuries the Roman and Persian Empires were deadly rivals, with Mesopotamia, the scene of one of the oldest of the civilizations of mankind, as debated ground which was chiefly in possession of Persia. More remote was India, and still farther away was China. India exerted but little influence on Greece and Rome, and China still less.

Since it had its birth, its first triumphs, and its initial chief stronghold in the Græco-Roman world, Christianity was profoundly moulded by it. In organization and in thought it conformed in part to it. It came to be largely identified with what is called the Occident, that portion of mankind which is the heir of Greece, Roman, and itself. Only occasionally did it spread extensively among non-Occidental peoples. Not until recently has it gained substantial footing in all the other great cultural units and among the majority of the primitive groups of mankind. Only within the past few decades has it become actually world-wide. It still has its main centres in the Occident. While lately it has made tremendous strides towards becoming universal, it has not yet divested itself of the integuments which it acquired during its Occidental pilgrimage.

Conditions Favourable to the Spread of Religion

At the time when Christianity came into being, much in the basin of the Mediterranean favoured the spread of religions, either new or old. Jesus was was born in the reign of Augustus. After a long period of wars which had racked the Mediterranean and its shores, political unity had been achieved and the Roman Empire had become roughly coterminous with the Mediterranean Basin. Here and there it was soon to spread beyond it. Augustus was the first Emperor. Building on the foundations laid by his uncle, Julius Cæsar, he brought peace and under the guise of the chief citizen of a restored republic ruled the realm which for several generations Rome had been building. The internal peace and order which Augustus achieved endured, with occasional interruptions, for about two centuries. Never before had all the shores of the Mediterranean been under one rule and never had they enjoyed such prosperity. The *pax Romana* made for the spread of ideas and religions over the area where it prevailed.

With the *pax Romana* went the building of roads and the growth of commerce. Highways of solid construction traversed the Empire and made possible more extensive travel and trade than the region had ever known. The pirates had been curbed who had imperilled shipping in the Mediterranean. Roads, travel, and commerce facilitated cultural and religious as well as political unity.

Travel and trade were accompanied by the spread of two languages, Greek and Latin. Greek was spoken among one or more groups in most of the cities of the Empire where commerce was to be found. The Greek-speaking and Greek-reading groups were most numerous in the eastern part of the Mediterranean. Alexandria in Egypt was a particularly prominent focus of Greek culture. Yet those for whom Greek was a primary tongue were also present in Rome, in Sicily and the south of Italy, in some of the cities of the south of Gaul, and in several other centres in the western portions of the Mediterranean. The Greek was the *koine* in one or more of its varieties. Latin was more

prevalent in the West. In the first centuries of the Christian era, while Christianity was expanding in the Empire, it was increasingly the speech of much
of the population on the western borders of the Mediterranean. A religion
which employed Greek and Latin, and especially Greek, had advantages over
rivals which did not and might gain an Empire-wide hearing.

Important also was the religious and moral hunger which characterized
much of the populace of the basin of the Mediterranean in the centuries in
which Christianity was having its early development. The formation of an
all-embracing empire promoted the decay of the local religious cults of the
several states and cities which were brought within the inclusive political unity.
To be sure, many were maintained as a matter of custom or civic pride, but
the heart had largely gone out of them. Then, too, the advancing intelligence
and moral sensitivity of the times cast doubt upon the stories about the gods.
Many of these were both incredible to an educated mind and offensive to the
morally sensitive. The gods were not as good as the best men of the period
and could command respect only if the stories about them were treated as
myths and allegorized. The age had in it much of moral corruption. Yet it
also had consciences which revolted against the excesses of the day. A religion
which offered high moral standards and the power to attain them would be
welcomed by the more serious.

The times brought with them much of insecurity. In the comprehensive
political unity many individuals were uprooted from their accustomed environment and either as slaves, as soldiers, or by free choice found themselves unsupported by the social group in which they had been reared. While in part
outwardly preserved and even strengthened, the old city states which had
characterized the Mediterranean world and which gave their free citizens a
sense of community were basically weakened, absorbed in the large impersonal
Empire. Millions were disinherited and deracinated, slaves on the great landed
estates or in city mansions, many of them from distant parts of the Empire.
They were hungry for a faith which would bring them self-respect. They
sought sustaining companionship, many of them in fellowships which combined religious with social purposes. Longing for the assurance of personal
immortality was widespread and reached out wistfully for satisfaction through
religious faith and ceremonial. As cities multiplied and grew in size, made up
as many of them were of strangers and their children, and, like the Empire,
impersonal, they provided favourable environment for novel religious ideas
and for religious fellowships. They were melting pots into which many religions entered.

When, towards the close of the second century, disasters began to overtake the Roman Empire and society was threatened with progressive disintegration, many turned to religion for the remedy. Augustus and his successors had not solved the basic problems of the Mediterranean world. They had obscured them. For what appeared to be a failure in government they had substituted more government, and government was not the answer. Confidence in man's ability and reason was shaken. There was a widespread "loss of nerve." Religion was looked to for the sense of safety which had been lost. Moreover, there was a groping towards some kind of theism, towards a unifying principle or deity which could bring cohesion and in the confusion yield an inkling of a universe which would correspond to the political and economic unity which the Roman Empire had brought to the Mediterranean world. Distrusting themselves and their reason, men looked for the answer in antiquity and in religions which could claim the sanctions of the ancients and of long generations of believers.

Religious Rivals for the Allegiance of the Græco-Roman World

Although conditions in the Græco-Roman world favoured the spread of a faith, they did not necessarily mean that Christianity would be the religion which would triumph. The competitors were many. Several of these appeared to have a marked advantage over Christianity. Indeed, at its outset, Christianity seemed to be one of the least of many rivals and with no promise of success against the others. We cannot undertake here even to name all the contenders for the religious allegiance of the Mediterranean Basin. We must, however, say something concerning the more prominent of them.

Some cults were maintained by the state. These included the gods of Rome and those of the cities of the Empire. The Roman Empire was in part a congeries of city states. Many of these cities had existed before the formation of the Empire and had been autonomous. Each had felt itself dependent upon the favour of its gods and had seen to it that the worship of its official divinities was maintained. As we have suggested, the state religions were no longer believed in as strongly as formerly. However, the continuance of their rites was believed to be necessary for the welfare of society. They were, accordingly, kept up, often with great pomp.

Outstanding among the officially supported cults was that of the Emperor. The East had long been familiar with a ruler who was also a divinity. Alexander the Great had been accorded that rôle, as had many another potentate in the Orient. It was natural that Augustus, who had brought peace to the distraught Mediterranean world, should be hailed as an incarnation of divinity. Statues of him were erected and religious ceremonies were instituted for him.

An imperial cult followed. It might call forth little personal devotion. How-ever, it was regarded as a safeguard of law and order and important for the preservation and prosperity of the realm. Dissent from it might well be in-terpreted as treasonable and anarchistic.

[Prominent, too, were the mystery religions, but in a different way and with distinctive purposes. They were secret in many of their ceremonies and their members were under oath not to reveal their esoteric rites. Since after a few centuries they completely disappeared, we know them only imperfectly. They arose chiefly in the East—in Egypt, Syria, Anatolia, and Persia. Numbers of them centred about a saviour-god who had died and had risen again. The god and the story about him varied from cult to cult. As the cults spread within the Empire they copied from one another in the easy-going syncretism which characterized much of the religious life of that realm and age]

Several of the mysteries were built around Dionysus. According to the stories told about him, Zagreus, the son of Zeus by Persephone, was born in the form of a bull. He was destined to rule the world, but was torn apart and eaten by the jealous Titans. But Athena saved his heart, Zeus swallowed it, and when Semele bore Dionysus to Zeus, Dionysus was Zagreus reborn. He was also often given the name Bacchus. The reason for the association of the bull with fertility cults is obvious. In the cruder of Dionysiac mysteries, the devotees drank of the fruit of the vine, for Dionysus or Bacchus was the god of wine as well as of animal and vegetable life. They also ate of the flesh of a newly slain bull, still dripping blood, and thus partook of the life of the god. They engaged in sacred dances which induced ecstasy and in which they were sup-posedly possessed by the spirit of the god.

Various sects associated with the name of Orpheus, who by his playing charmed men and beasts, also had the Dionysus myth at their heart. Less orgiastic and more ethical than the crasser Dionysiac cults, they assumed as axiomatic a conviction widely held in the Hellenistic world that matter and flesh are evil and that the soul of man must be free from contamination with them. They also taught that men are born and reborn, in each reincarnation imprisoned in the flesh and subject to those ills to which flesh is heir, unless the soul can be freed from the body. That separation accomplished, the soul would live forever in bliss. The emancipation was to be achieved through initiation into the cult, with cleanliness and asceticism. After a ritualistic meal of raw meat, the votaries remained vegetarians. Thus they avoided further contamination with flesh.

Prominent among the mysteries were those associated with *Magna Mater,* the Great Mother, who loved the virgin-born shepherd Attis. Attis died, slain either by his enemies or by his own hand (if the latter, by emasculation).

Magna Mater mourned for him, effected his resurrection, and he became immortal. Postulants for full-fledged initiation mourned for Attis, and then, as the climax of a wild dance, emasculated themselves. This was followed by a day in which the resurrection of Attis was celebrated, and the devotees felt themselves united with Attis and so participants of his immortality. There was a lay membership of men and women which did not entail mutilation. Associated with this cult, but borrowed from elsewhere, was the *taurobolium*. In this a bull was killed and the devotees bathed in its blood as means of dying to the old life and being born again.

Somewhat similar cults had as their centre a young god whom the Greeks called Adonis and who died and rose again. In like manner another set of mysteries clustered around the myth of Osiris, a king who had been killed by his brother. His widow, Isis, mourning, sought him, until, finding his body, she revived it, and Osiris became the ruler of the dead. In the religion which developed around this myth, Serapis replaced Osiris and Isis was emphasized. The chief shrine was the Serapeum, obviously named for Serapis, in Alexandria. From that leading mart it spread by the trade routes to much of the Empire.

The Eleusinian mysteries, developed near Athens, had as their inspiring focus rites which dramatized the death of vegetation in the autumn and winter and the resurrection of life in the spring. This they did through the nature myth of Persephone, who was carried off by Hades to the underworld, was sought by her mourning mother, Demeter, was restored to the world of light, but was compelled to return to the underworld for part of each year.

Very widespread was the mystery religion which had Mithra for its main figure. Mithra, a god of Persian origin, was usually represented as bestriding a bull and slaying it. From the dying bull issued the seed of life for the world, and hence the act became the symbol of regeneration. The cult practised baptism and had a sacramental meal. Its membership was restricted to men and its places of worship, crypts or underground caverns, were too small to accommodate more than a very few at a time.

Almost all the mystery cults eventually made their way to Rome, the capital and chief city of the Empire. They also penetrated much of the Empire. Their appeal seems to have been the assurance of immortality which they gave to their members, combined with a fellowship which many craved in a world in which large numbers were uprooted individuals.

Akin to the mystery religions was Hermeticism, represented by a body of literature which claimed as its author Hermes Trismegistus. This literature presented a way of redemption of the spirit from the trammels of matter which issued in immortality. Like the mysteries and much of the thought of the day, it held as axiomatic a dualism which regarded matter as evil and spirit as good. Seeking to obtain emancipation from the flesh, it was strongly ascetic, inculcating abstinence from the pleasures of the flesh and opposing malice, envy, deceit, anger, and avarice. [Like so much of the religious life of the Græco-Roman world, it was syncretistic. It mixed polytheism, pantheism, and astrology.]

Hermeticism was representative of a religious strain known as Gnosticism which was greatly to influence Christianity in its earlier centuries. Although the majority of Christians ultimately rejected it, Gnosticism and the struggle with it had enduring effects upon Christianity. Pre-Christian in its origin, Gnosticism assumed, as did so much of Hellenistic thought, a sharp disjunction between matter and spirit. It offered a way of emancipation from the material world into the realm of pure spirit, and into freedom from the fatalistic control by the astral powers which underlay the current belief in astrology. It claimed possession of a secret *Gnosis,* or knowledge, through which this could be obtained, and made much af sacraments, ceremonial washings, and other rites. Like the mystery religions, it was for the privileged few who shared the knowledge through which emancipation was to be achieved. It took over from any source whatever it deemed of value.

Philosophy was popular in the Mediterranean world into which Christianity came. Very little which was fresh was being thought or said. The only major new school of philosophy which emerged after the birth of Jesus was Neoplatonism, and that, as its name indicates, was largely a development from Platonism and had in it little if anything that was basically original. Indeed, it represented a tendency which can be traced back at least as far as the first century of the Christian era. In its flowering it incorporated borrowings from more than one of the schools which had gone before it.

The philosophies which were most prominently represented in the world into which Christianity came were Stoicism, Epicureanism, the Peripatetics (carrying on the Aristotelian tradition), the Pythagoreans, the Platonists, and the Cynics.

Stoicism was very influential among many in high places. It drew much from Aristotle. It believed the universe to be a universe, an organic whole, with both body and soul, and governed by Reason which expresses itself in natural law. Stoicism was a pantheistic philosophy which regarded God as permeating all things but not being independent of them. Every man, it held, should live in accordance with the universal Reason which pervades nature. This would entail rational self-control and make one independent of outward circumstances. It meant self-discipline and, for those in public office, a high sense of responsibility. The Stoics held that a bit of the universal Reason is to be found in every man, that ideally men and gods are members of one society, the city of Zeus, and that all differences of nationality should be merged in the common brotherhood of man. They taught that all men are equal by divine right, declared that in the sight of God the slave is of as much value as the monarch, and maintained that all are entitled, as sons of God, indwelt by the universal Reason, to share in the good things of life. Stoicism was to have a marked effect upon many Christians and was to leave traces of its beliefs in some phases of Christianity.

Of the Epicureans and Pythagoreans we need say nothing except to mention them. Of the Peripatetics we may simply remark that Aristotle was later to have a striking influence on Christian thought, an influence which proved very persistent. Nor must the Cynics engage our attention. Unlike the Stoics and the Epicureans, who were largely aristocratic, they addressed themselves to the common folk. Rude of speech, living simply, often rebels against society and not above reproach morally, they harangued audiences wherever they could gather them, denouncing the objects for which men usually strive, including wealth and fame.

Platonism was of very great importance, partly because of the contributions which it made to some other schools through the borrowing which was common in the intellectual world, partly because of its contribution to Neoplatonism, and to no small degree because of the effect of its patterns of thought upon Christian theology.

Neoplatonism, while younger than Christianity, combined, as we have suggested, much from philosophies which had gone before it, including Platonism, Aristotelianism, Stoicism, and Neopythagoreanism. It had a deeply religious quality with a strong mystical trend. It sought through asceticism to curb the flesh and its desires, to purify the human soul of the taint acquired by its departure from its original estate, and by contemplation to attain union with God. Again and again through the centuries Christian mysticism was to be deeply indebted to it.

All these philosophies had a Greek rootage and were developed further in the Hellenistic world into which Christianity early moved. In one way or another they had a strain of dualism. Most of them tended to regard matter as evil, believed the soul of man to be contaminated by it, and sought the emancipation of the soul from its corrupting association.

While most of the philosophies appealed primarily to the educated, those who dabbled in the intellectual life were very numerous. Teachers of philosophy often enjoyed a large popular following and lecture halls for them and their listeners were widespread. The religious aspects of philosophy attracted many of those who suffered from the hunger for a satisfying faith which was so prominent in the Roman Empire.

Judaism must also be reckoned among the more formidable of the competitors for the religious allegiance of the peoples of the Roman Empire. In the preceding chapter we have said something about it. As a faith identified with one ethnic group and stressing its belief that Israel was a peculiar people, especially chosen by God, it could scarcely hope to win all the human race, even had it desired to do so. To be sure, some of its prophets had regarded it as having a universal mission and as destined to embrace all men in its fellowship and its blessings. Yet the majority of Jews did not follow them. However, as we have seen, Jewish communities were numerous and widely scattered, the Jewish scriptures had been translated into Greek, and thousands of non-Jews were attracted by the Jewish faith and either sought full incorporation into the Jewish people or constituted a fringe who had accepted many Jewish beliefs.

It was in this Roman Empire, newly formed, this portion of civilized mankind in which the heritages of Greece and Rome were dominant, that Christianity had its rise. It profited by the features of that world which made for the spread of religious faiths, but it faced the competition of many systems which appeared to have a much better prospect for survival and growth.

Selected Bibliography

A GENERAL PICTURE OF THE GRÆCO-ROMAN WORLD

S. Dill, *Roman Society from Nero to Marcus Aurelius* (London, Macmillan & Co., 1904, pp. xii, 639). Well-written and authoritative.

M. I. Rostovtzeff, *A History of the Ancient World,* translated from the Russian by J. D. Duff (Oxford, The Clarendon Press, 2 vols., 1930). By an eminent specialist.

M. I. Rostovtzeff, *The Social and Economic History of the Roman Empire* (Oxford, The Clarendon Press, pp. xxv, 695).

THE GENERAL RELIGIOUS PICTURE

C. N. Cochrane, *Christianity and Classical Culture. A Study in Thought and Action from Augustus to Augustine* (Oxford, The Clarendon Press, 1940, pp. vii, 523). Learned, with stimulating interpretations.

Franz Cumont, *Astrology and Religion Among the Greeks and Romans* (New York, G. P. Putnam's Sons, 1912, pp. xxvii, 208).

Franz Cumont, *The Oriental Religions in Roman Paganism,* translated from the 2d French ed. (Chicago, The Open Court Publishing Co., 1911, pp. xxiv, 298). By a distinguished specialist.

W. Warde Fowler, *The Religious Experience of the Roman People from the Earliest Times to the Age of Augustus* (London, Macmillan & Co., 1911, pp. xviii, 534). The Gifford Lectures for 1909–1910.

T. R. Glover, *The Conflict of Religions in the Early Roman Empire* (London, Methuen & Co., 1909, pp. vii, 309). Charmingly written, pro-Christian, based upon a wide knowledge of the sources.

Gilbert Murray, *Five Stages of Greek Religion* (Columbia University Press, 1925, pp. 276). By an eminent classicist.

A. D. Nock, *Conversion. The Old and the New in Religion from Alexander the Great to Augustine of Hippo* (Oxford University Press, 1933, pp. xii, 309). Competent, with some fresh points of view.

THE EMPEROR CULT

Kenneth Scott, *The Identification of Augustus with Romulus-Quirinus,* in *Transactions and Proceedings of the American Philological Association,* Vol. XLVI, pp. 82–105.

Lily Ross Taylor, *The Divinity of the Roman Emperor* (Middletown, Conn., American Philological Association, 1931, pp. xv, 296). Well done.

THE MYSTERY RELIGIONS

S. Angus, *The Religious Quests of the Græco-Roman World* (New York, Charles Scribner's Sons, 1929, pp. xx, 444). Scholarly, with a pro-Christian bias.

Franz Cumont, *The Mysteries of Mithra,* translated from the second revised French edition by T. J. McCormack (Chicago, The Open Court Publishing Co., 1903). Semi-popular lectures by an outstanding authority.

J. G. Frazer, *Adonis Attis Osiris* (Part IV of *The Golden Bough,* London, Macmillan & Co., 1907, pp. xix, 452).

W. K. C. Guthrie, *Orpheus and Greek Religion. A Study of the Orphic Movement* (London, Methuen & Co., 1935, pp. xix, 287). Excellent.

R. Reitzenstein, *Die hellenistischen Mysterienreligionen nach ihren Grundgedanken und Wirkungen* (Leipzig, B. G. Teubner, 3d ed., 1927, pp. viii, 438).

HERMETICISM

Jos. Kroll, *Die Lehren des Hermes Trismegistos,* in *Beiträge zur Geschichte der Philosophie des Mittelalters,* Vol. XII (Münster i.W., Aschendorffsche Verlagsbuchhandlung, 1914, pp. xii, 441).

Walter Scott, *Hermetica. The Greek and Latin Writings which Contain Religious or Philosophic Teachings Ascribed to Hermes Trismegistus, edited with English translations and notes* (Oxford, The Clarendon Press, 4 vols., 1924–1936). The standard work in English.

JUDAISM

G. F. Moore, *Judaism in the First Centuries of the Christian Era. The Age of the Tannaim* (Harvard University Press, 2 vols., 1927). By a distinguished specialist.

W. O. E. Oesterley and G. H. Box, *The Religion and Worship of the Synagogue* (London, Sir Isaac Pitman & Sons, 1907, pp. xv, 443). Scholarly, for non-Jewish readers.

E. Schürer, *Geschichte des judischen Volkes im Zeitalter Jesu Christi*, 4th ed. (Leipzig, Hinrichs, 3 vols., 1901–1911), translated as *History of the Jewish People in the time of Jesus Christ* (New York, Charles Scribner's Sons, 5 vols., 1891). Still a standard work.

JESUS AND THE GOSPEL

Chapter IV

JESUS AND THE GOSPEL: THE FOUNDATION OF CHRISTIANITY

Christianity had what looked like a most unpromising beginning. The contemporary observer outside the little inner group of the disciples of Jesus would have thought it impossible that within five centuries of its inception it would outstrip its competitors for the religious allegiance of the Roman Empire and become the professed faith of the rulers and of the overwhelming majority of the population of the realm. Still less would he have dreamed that within less than two thousand years it would become world-wide, with a more extensive geographic spread and a greater influence upon mankind than any other religion.

This failure of this hypothetical observer to foresee the future place of Christianity in the life of mankind can be readily understood. The faith appeared to begin as one of the many sects of Judaism. Although, as we have seen, the Jews were numerous and widely spread in the Roman Empire and here and there were found beyond its bounds, there seemed to be no possibility of their winning the realm to their faith. To be sure, Judaism was making many proselytes, but in spite of some tendencies to conform to the syncretistic trend of the times and adjust itself to the prevalent religious and intellectual patterns, basically it was exclusive and intolerant of its rivals and was too much the faith of one ethnic group ever to become universal. If that were true of Judaism as a whole, presumably it would also be true of its sects.

Even within Judaism Christianity seemed to have little future and still less did it give promise of outstripping Judaism. Jesus, the figure around whom Christianity centred, was of humble birth. At the very beginning of his public career he deliberately spurned as an unworthy temptation the suggestion that he seek to carry through his aims by political means. Although he performed many miracles, he always did so to meet an obvious human need, meticulously avoided any display of his power to call attention to himself or to prove his divine commission, and at times endeavoured to keep secret his astounding

33

works of healing. He chose for his intimates men from the humble walks of life and had few friends among the influential. His public career was brief, at most probably no more than three years and possibly compressed within a year. He wrote no book. As far as the surviving records show, he gave little or no thought to a continuing organization to perpetuate his teaching and his influence. He gathered about him a group of intimates, known to history as the Twelve Apostles, and he is reported as having declared that they were entrusted with large powers, but our earliest documents contain no certain proof (although this has been hotly debated, and the precise opposite has been and is held by the majority of Christians) that he intended these powers to be transmitted by them in a continuing succession that would make for a permanent, visible institution. Jesus appears not to have taught systematically, but to have spoken as the occasion required—at dinner parties, to a woman of dubious reputation whom he chanced to meet at a well, to a stranger who appealed to him to intervene in a family dispute, and to those who at the height of his brief popularity sought to join themselves to him and were told so sternly of the high requirements that, dismayed, they turned back. He came to an ignominious death which seemed to be not so much tragic as futile. The authentic records of his life and teachings are so brief that they could easily be printed in a single issue of one of our larger daily papers, and in these a substantial proportion of the space is devoted to the last few days of his life. No proper biography of him exists, if by that we mean a book which conforms to what in modern times are set as standards. So brief are our accounts that there have been scholars who have declared that we cannot really know Jesus and that he is not essential to Christianity. Even a thoughtful visitor in Jerusalem in the first few years of the Christian Church would scarcely have predicted that from such a beginning this Jesus, the centre of loyalty of this Jewish sect, would be long remembered.

Yet that life is the most influential ever lived on this planet and its effect continues to mount. Here is the most thought-provoking fact of human history.

Our Knowledge of Jesus

Although our accounts of Jesus are brief, they enable us to know him and his teachings as well as we can know any figure of like antiquity. He made so profound an impression upon those who were his intimates that their memories of him, some of them put into written form within a very few years after the events they record, enable us to have a vivid picture of him and his characteristics. His sayings, given as they were in pithy sentences or in stories of extraordinary beauty and imagery, could not fail to fasten themselves in the memories of the more thoughtful who heard them. They lent themselves to the kind of repetition which did not blur or distort them and were early collected in written form. Even if we did not have the four brief accounts which we call the Gospels we could gain a fairly adequate impression of him and of the salient points of his life, teachings, death, and resurrection from references in letters of his followers written within a generation of his death.

It seems almost presumptuous to attempt to compress what we know of the life and teachings of Jesus into a few pages and to expect within that short compass to give anything like an accurate and well-balanced summary of them. Yet that is what we must essay, for without such an account any sketch of the history of Christianity would lack the essential foundation for the entire story.

BIRTH, BOYHOOD AND YOUTH

Born in a manger in Bethlehem, the town associated with the name of David, the most glamorous of the Jewish kings, and reared in the village of Nazareth, Jesus grew up in a humble family. From the hills back of Nazareth a commanding view could be had of the plain of Esdraelon, crammed with history, and of snowy Hermon. From what we know of his later years, we may be fairly certain that Jesus often climbed these hills and, always sensitive and observing, fed his soul on the beauty around and below him and thought deeply on the life unrolled before him.

We catch very few glimpses of Jesus until, when about thirty years of age, he began his public career. From the names of his brothers which have come down to us, we gather that the family cherished the Maccabeean tradition and were loyal to the Jewish faith. That the household was deeply religious is borne out by many bits of evidence—the account of the conception and birth of Jesus in *The Gospel according to Luke,* much of which could only have come from his mother, Mary; the other narrative of his birth, in *The Gospel according to Matthew,* which was presumably, at least in part, from Joseph, his reputed father; the delicacy, beauty, and deep religious feeling of the nativity stories, especially those in Luke, which appear to reflect the character of Mary and Joseph, notably of the mother who, we are told, "kept all these things, pondering them in her heart"; the fact of the relationship of Mary to the mother of John the Baptist and to that earnest little household, dedicated completely to God; careful compliance with the Jewish law in circumcision and in the ceremony of consecrating Jesus to God in the temple, as Mary's first born; the welcome given the infant on that occasion by members of the circle of the devout who were looking for "the consolation of Israel" and the "redemption of Jerusalem," folk who were quietly waiting for God to bring about the consummation of history expected by faithful Jews; and the custom of Mary and Joseph to go every year, and not semi-occasionally, to Jerusalem to the feast of the Passover. We are not surprised that Jesus formed the habit of going to the synagogue, that he learned to read, that his chief reading was in the sacred books of his people, and that, even at the age of twelve, he had meditated profoundly on the issues raised by them. Since, after Jesus began his public career, we hear no mention of Joseph as living, we may assume that he had died and that Jesus had been left to earn the living for his mother and the younger brothers and sisters. It is, indeed, conceivable that the delay in entering upon his itinerant ministry was due to his feeling of responsibility for shelter and daily food for the dependent members of the family.

It was a stirring day and a stirring section of the world in which to live. The Roman Empire had only recently been established. It is part of the familiar Christmas story that Jesus was born during the rule of the first Roman Emperor, Augustus Cæsar. His own little corner of the earth was seething with unrest against Roman domination. Not far from Nazareth the city of Sepphoris was being rebuilt during his boyhood after its destruction by Roman forces to quell one of the recurrent uprisings. During the adult life of Jesus resentment against Rome was mounting and within the generation after his crucifixion it was to break out in a mad revolt which was to end in enormous slaughter and in the destruction of Jerusalem and its temple. The unrest was accentuated and in part was given direction by apocalyptic hopes with their accompanying expectation of direct intervention by God on behalf of the Jews. In these hopes the dream of a Messiah loomed prominently.

Now and again we can gain hints of what Jesus may have been thinking in those hidden years at Nazareth. The parables in which he couched so much of his teaching may have embodied some of his observations and reflections as he viewed the scene about him—farms which he knew as he watched from the hill-tops the clouds march inland from the Mediterranean and drop their rain regardless of whether the owners were good or bad, evidence to him of the impartial love of God for all men; a woman seeking for a lost coin; children playing in the market place; a king going to a far country to receive for himself a kingdom, perhaps an echo of the journey of the Herods to Rome to ask for confirmation of their claims; a pearl merchant; and the father and the two sons, the younger errant but appealing and the elder correct but forbidding. Then, too, must have been acquired the familiarity with the sacred books of his people which Jesus later displayed.

THE PUBLIC CAREER BEGINS

In whatever way they were occupied, the years of obscurity ended abruptly. Jesus' kinsman, John the Baptist, had become the centre of a religious awakening which deeply moved the region. An ascetic, he denounced the sins of those about him, spoke of imminent judgment with reward for the righteous and destruction for the wicked, urged repentance, and on the confession of their sins baptized the penitents in the Jordan. He gathered disciples about him, leading them in fasting and teaching them methods of prayer.

Jesus came to John and was baptized by him. The motive for that step is not clear, but John is represented as reluctant, declaring, perhaps on the basis of knowledge acquired through earlier contact, that he should be baptized by Jesus. Whatever his reason in seeking baptism, to Jesus the experience was profound. We can only conjecture its full meaning to him, but from the accounts which have come to us it at least brought a deepened realization of the significance of his sonship to God.

So soul-shaking was that day that immediately Jesus felt impelled to seek solitude, there to wrestle with the issues which it presented to him. So absorbed was he that, whether through preoccupation or deliberate choice, he did not eat. What seems to have been the climax were three urges which as he faced them he came to recognize as temptations. His mind was one which thought in pictures, as his parables witness, and these testings, as he narrated them later to his intimates—for they could have become known in no other way—were presented to him in that characteristic form. Should he use his power as God's son to meet his own physical needs? Should he seek in some startling fashion to test God's protecting power, expecting exemption from whatever disastrous results would normally follow foolhardy action, thereby seeking to convince the gaping multitude of his unique mission? Should he compromise his principles to gain earthly dominion and thus establish his righteous rule? He faced the urges, appraised them, and rejected them.

Again and again Jesus later met situations which confronted him with one or another of these issues in various forms, but at the outset of his public career he had seen once for all what was involved and he never wavered from the decisions then made. He refused to be an agent of the multitude's wishes for easy food, he rejected the repeated demand that he demonstrate the authenticity of his mission by a "sign" wrought especially for the purpose, and he would have nothing to do with political methods.

JESUS AND THE KINGDOM OF GOD

Returning to the haunts of men, Jesus began preaching and teaching. He believed that the kingdom of God was about to be inaugurated, and it was this which constituted the recurrent theme in his message. Obviously the kingdom of God meant a society in which God's will would prevail. As Jesus conceived it, the kingdom of God was to be the gift of God and was not to be achieved by men's striving. It was being inaugurated through Jesus and was both a present reality, already here, and a future hope. Like grain, it was to grow of itself and not by men's striving. Men were to prize it as the gem merchant would eagerly exchange all that he had for the exceptional pearl. While it was a society, men were to enter it one by one, and (although on this point some Christians have held otherwise and have identified it with the organized Church) it was not a visible institution but an inward possession.

Membership in the kingdom was not hereditary, for "the sons of the kingdom," presumably those born into it but having no other claim on it than birth, were to be "cast into outer darkness," while those who had been deemed aliens to it, "from the east and west," were to "sit down" in it. The kingdom of God was so important that men were "to seek it first," before food or clothing, and were to give up all that they possessed to obtain it. To Jesus the kingdom was "gospel" and "evangel"—great "good news." The terms "gospel" and "evangel," while technically correct as designations of the kingdom, have become so stereotyped by long pedestrian usage that in them the wonder and the exuberant joy which Jesus gave to them are often missed. To Jesus, men had not really begun to live until they had entered the kingdom of God, and to be in it was to have abounding, eternal life.

Jesus devoted much attention to describing the characteristics of those who had "entered the kingdom." If men were to enter the kingdom, or even to see it, they must gain a fresh perspective and make a new start. In the vivid, forceful language which was normal to him and which was an indication of one of his outstanding qualities, Jesus declared that men must "repent" (literally, "change their minds"), be "born anew," and "become as little children." It was those who were "poor in spirit," who recognized their inadequacies and who were painfully aware that they had fallen far short of the ideal which God had set for men, of whom it could be said that "theirs is the kingdom of heaven." The kingdom meant great joy; Jesus compared himself and his companions to a wedding party. Yet the joy was not incompatible with deep pain. Indeed, the former might not be possible except for the latter. He himself knew both and recognized that his disciples, as members of the kingdom, would also have both in their experience.

What Jesus called "the world" was obviously in opposition to the kingdom. It was for that reason that entrance to the kingdom entailed so drastic a re-orientation, a re-creation, of those who came into it from the world. Persecution would, therefore, be the lot of members of the kingdom. Such persecution, if it were for the sake of the righteousness which Jesus proclaimed, would be evidence of membership in the kingdom. However, Jesus is declared to have been sent by God into the world not to condemn the world, but that the world through him might be saved, and he said that those who had entered the kingdom were the light of the world.

Members of the kingdom were to strive to be examples of the life which God deemed ideal for men. They were to be single-minded—pure in heart. They were to be so eager for righteousness that their longing could be described as both hunger and thirst. They were to be clean in thought, to be so sincere that their word would require no adventitious support but would need only "yes" and "no." They were to be merciful, endeavouring to make peace, not seeking retaliation but returning good for evil, loving even their enemies. The word for "love" is not one meaning "liking" but one which involves an abandon in self-giving. They were never to seek the applause of men, but were to shun publicity in acts of mercy or in such religious exercises as praying and fasting. They were not to have anxious fear of what the morrow might bring, but were to seek first of all the kingdom and the kind of conduct approved by God, quietly confident that God would supply their physical needs.

Here was no asceticism, no condemnation of the body and of matter as evil, no attempt, as in the thought and religions so prevalent in the Hellenistic world and in much of the stricter side of current Judaism, to "free" the soul from what was deemed the contamination of the flesh and the material part of the universe. In contrast with John the Baptist who was clearly an ascetic and enjoined asceticism on his followers, Jesus and his intimate disciples both ate and drank and went freely to dinners, frankly enjoying them. While Jesus taught that men should never make their goal the accumulation of material possessions, that wealth imperilled the highest attainments of men, and that those who would follow him must be prepared to abandon all, whether property, home, or kindred, he embedded in the short model prayer which he gave his disciples, immediately after the petition for the coming of the kingdom and the accomplishment of God's will, a request for physical sustenance. Among the tests that he gave for character was the use that was made of money and the care that was either shown or denied to those in physical need.

Jesus' Concern for Individuals

Although Jesus had much to say of the kingdom of God, and in that must have meant, if not a visible social structure, at least the relations of men to one another, he was deeply and primarily interested in individuals and saw society, customs, and institutions only as they affected individuals. To him the Jewish respect for the Sabbath must not be permitted to stand in the way of helping individuals, whether that entailed healing them or relieving their hunger. He declared that he had "come to seek and to save that which was lost," and by that he meant individuals.

Some of the best remembered parables of Jesus centre about care for the individual. He compared his concern for "the lost" with the shepherd's leaving the ninety-nine in his flock who were safe in the fold and going into the wilderness to look for the one stray until he found it and with the woman sweeping her house meticulously in search of a missing coin and then, when she had discovered it, calling in her neighbours and friends to rejoice with her. He told of the father waiting for his wayward son and running to greet him when he saw him far off, returning. He commanded his disciples not to despise even one of "these little ones." He declared that God noted the fate of every sparrow, so that not one of them could fall to the ground without His will, and that since human beings are of more value than many sparrows, God must surely care for them. Again and again, although he talked collectively to multitudes and although on two memorable occasions he took care that they were fed, Jesus addressed himself to individuals and gave them of his best—the woman of the street, the short-statured tax-gatherer who had climbed a tree to see him, the Roman officer with a sick servant, the child who seemed to be lying dead and her distraught parents, many an unfortunate demoniac, the rich young ruler who came running to him and whom he loved at first glance. Almost all of his recorded healings, and there were many of them, were of individuals. Only once, in the case of a group of lepers, do we read of his healing as many as ten at a time, and what stands out in that incident was the gratitude of the one, a Samaritan, who returned to give him thanks.

JESUS AND MAN

Closely allied with his attitude towards the individual was the view which Jesus held of man. He was vividly aware of the strange mixture which is man. He fully recognized the depravity in man and declared that human fathers had to face the fact that they are evil. He saw and stated emphatically the tragic disaster that is the climax of the way of life which many, presumably most men pursue. Some of his sayings seem to disclose him as a hopeless pessimist. There would be many, he said, who would fail to respond to the invitation to enter the kingdom and when, all too tardily, they sought to retrieve their mistake would find that they were too late.

But Jesus held that men could enter into life, that men could, if they would, have a confident faith through which the seemingly impossible could become a reality. He appealed to men to think, sure that if they properly employed their reason it would lead them to correct conclusions. He believed that infinite possibilities were available to men if they would take the right way towards attaining them. His works of healing both body and spirit Jesus regarded as demonstrations of God's power, but he declared that this power was available to others if they would only reach out in faith and claim it. Life would be sheer wonder and joy if men would only enter the door which was there for them, the door into God's kingdom of light and love. Pain might also be there, but it was not incompatible with the fullness of life. Indeed, it could be made to contribute to a richer and a deeper harmony. Jesus never entered into the age-long debate of determinism as against indeterminism, of predestination and free will, but he quietly assumed that men had sufficient power of choice either to reject or to meet the conditions of entering upon the life which God had designed for them.

The Consummation of the Kingdom

Did Jesus expect the kingdom fully to come within history? Did he look for the transformation of society, either gradually or by progressive stages, until it would entirely conform to the will of God? Or did he expect history to be consummated abruptly in judgement to be followed by a display of the power of God in condemnation of the wicked and their separation from those who had conformed to God's will? The answer is not clear and appears to be a paradox.

Jesus obviously believed the kingdom to be already present. He saw his healings, especially his cure of those troubled by demon possession, as evidence that it had come. To him the forces of evil were intensely real and personal. He accepted Satan as an existent being, an enemy of God, and he addressed the demons whom he cast out, not as delusions of sick minds, but as actual. To him the fact that the demons were being deprived of their baleful power over men was clear proof that the kingdom of heaven, the rule of God, was beginning. Jesus taught his disciples to pray that God's will might be done on earth as it is in heaven and commanded them to make fellow-disciples of all nations, baptizing them, and teaching them to observe all that he had commanded the little inner group of his followers. By his comparison of the kingdom of God with "leaven which a woman took and hid in three measures of meal, till the whole was leavened" he might well be supposed to be implying that all human society would be fully transformed by a progressive process. There is, too, the confident statement by one who was very close to the mind of Jesus, that God sent his son into the world not to condemn the world but that the world might be saved through him.

On the other hand, Jesus declared that few find the way to life and that many follow the road which leads to destruction, that both good and evil grow until the harvest, apparently a sudden consummation, in which the wicked, their character fully revealed by the ripening of their course, will be dealt with as harvesters deal with noxious weeds, and the good be conserved as wheat is gathered into a granary.

Perhaps the paradox is insoluble within history. Certainly thus far in history it remains a paradox. What Jesus would have said had he been questioned about it we may not know. He certainly held that God is sovereign in the universe and that His will would be done. He also taught men to pray that it be done, as though God were dependent on their prayer.

Closely allied with the problem of whether Jesus believed that God's rule is to be acknowledged and complied with by all men within history is that other one of whether Jesus expected the consummation of history at an early date.

On the one hand is the well-known apocalypticism which pervaded the Jewish thought of the time and with which Jesus was clearly familiar. Much of it looked towards an early climax of history or at least a major, revolutionary crisis. Many sayings of Jesus can be interpreted as indicating that he shared this expectation. When speaking of what he seems to have intended to be interpreted as the end of history, he declared: "This generation shall not pass until all these things be done." He undoubtedly taught that history was to come to a climax in dramatic judgement and warned his disciples to watch, for their testing by their Lord's return might be at any time and would most certainly come when it was not expected. In this he was seemingly referring to the end of history.

Yet Jesus also most emphatically declared that the disciples were not to know precise times for the fulfilment of their expectation, and that not even he knew the day or the hour when the consummation was to come, but only God. Nor can we be sure to what extent his disciples, in remembering and handing on his sayings, expecting as they naturally did the early termination of history, misread the mind of Jesus and put together words of his which he had not intended to be interpreted in this fashion. We, too, may well misunderstand sayings in which imagery has a large part. A notable instance of this is the passage in which Jesus foretold the destruction of Jerusalem and appeared to conjoin it with the end of the world. That the destruction of Jerusalem was imminent any clear-headed man of the time must have seen. Seething resentment against Roman rule was obviously soon to break out in open revolt. Fanatics believed that God would intervene on behalf of his people, but Jesus was too much aware of the power of Rome, perhaps in part because of the ruthless and overwhelming fashion in which it had been displayed at Sepphoris, had too early in his public career come to the conclusion that it was not in accord with God's methods to step in miraculously to save even His own son if he presumed on His favour by recklessly jeopardizing his life, and was too sadly cognizant of the blind folly all about him to see anything but early doom for the people and the city that he loved. Jerusalem was rejecting the one way to peace, the way which he was offering it, and the end was tragically certain. He can be interpreted as having conjoined this with the end of history, and that has been a general understanding, especially among many recent scholars. Yet the interpreters may have failed to enter fully into his mind.

Certainly there are other sayings, so counter to current expectations that their preservation is evidence of correct reporting, which apparently imply a prolonged postponement of the final climax. Thought-provoking is the familiar parable of the five wise and the five foolish virgins who, anticipating being present at a wedding, were waiting for the coming of the bridegroom. The five who were condemned as foolish were those who, in expectation of the early arrival of the bridegroom, had come with insufficient oil in their lamps, and the five who were praised were those who were prepared for a prolonged delay, and, as the event proved, were right. It may well be that Jesus anticipated many successive crises, each a judgement, before the termination of history on this planet.

GOD IS CENTRAL AND SUPREME

Whatever Jesus may have believed about the future course of history, he had never a doubt of the power and the centrality of God. His belief in God underlay and shaped all his other convictions and his teachings. For him God's will was sovereign. But to Jesus God was no arbitrary despot. He was Father. Father was Jesus' characteristic name for God. God was, to Jesus, the ruler of all nature. He might be and, indeed, was often defied by hostile powers and beings, but He would prevail.

Jesus was not a philosopher dealing in abstract terms and concepts. He never talked about "the problem of evil." He frankly recognized the presence of evil; indeed, he was acutely aware of it, but he never asked why, if God were sovereign, evil was present. He faced squarely the tragedy in the world about him. He plainly stated that sparrows fall to the ground and that lilies, so beautiful and alive today, are tomorrow cast into the oven. Judgement, terrible and certain, awaits those who do not conform to God's will.

Yet as he looked out on the world of nature Jesus saw the heavenly Father so ordering it that the birds are fed and the flowers bloom in all their radiance. To those who would so acknowledge Him and conform their wills to His ways, God would show Himself as Father. Indeed, He was always seeking men, but, presumably because He respected their wills, He did not force Himself upon them. Perhaps it was for that reason that His will in a specific issue was not immediately clear. In employing his will to seek it, the child would make progress towards maturity. Like the father in Jesus' most famous parable,

God does not pursue the wayward into the far country, but waits. The prodigal is still His son, and when, disciplined by judgement, "he comes to himself," recognizes his course for what it is—sin against God's generosity—and knows his own complete unworthiness, but, instead of being overwhelmed by despair, trusts enough in the character which he has seen in the provision made for servants to turn again to his Father and ask only that he be treated as a servant, the Father, waiting and eagerly watching, not only welcomes him, but runs to him, cuts short his rehearsed speech, and insists that he is His son.

THE MAN JESUS

What manner of man was Jesus? No one can fully enter into the consciousness of another or completely understand him. No two human beings are exactly alike. The differences are often subtle and yet the very qualities which elude observation and precise description may be the most important. How impossible it must be, therefore, adequately to understand and to describe one who stood out so markedly from his contemporaries and from all men, both before and since. In the first century and through the generations that have followed opinions have sharply differed. It is evidence of his importance, of the effect that he has had upon history and, presumably, of the baffling mystery of his being that no other life ever lived on this planet has evoked so huge a volume of literature among so many peoples and languages, and that, far from ebbing, the flood continues to mount. More men notice Jesus than ever before, but appraisals have never been as varied or as numerous as in the past two centuries. This is the more extraordinary in view of the brevity of the records which have survived from the memories of his intimates. It is not his teachings which make Jesus so remarkable, although these would be enough to give him distinction. It is a combination of the teachings with the man himself. The two cannot be separated, but if they could the man would be the more important.

While all of this is true, some characteristics stand out so distinctly in the accounts which preserve the impressions of those who had an opportunity to know him best, that they are a guarantee of authenticity, so obviously are they from life and not invented or even seriously distorted. They also reveal to us much of the man himself and help to make clear something of the problems which confront those who seek a complete understanding.

Jesus was a great lover of nature. His sayings abound in references to the sun, the clouds, the rain, the birds, the flowers, seed-time and harvest, growth and decay. He was a minute observer, recognized the pain and the beauty about him, and with a few pregnant words could make vivid to others what he saw. In the technical sense of that term, he was, perhaps fortunately, not a philosopher, but he discerned the cosmic issues beneath the passing pageantry. The sharp contrast between grain and weeds posed for him the problem of good and evil, although he would never have put it in those abstract terms, and of how the sovereignty and righteousness of God in which he so profoundly believed could be compatible with the existence of what was bad. The seeming indifference of the weather to the moral qualities of men was to him evidence of the impartial love of God.

Jesus liked to be with people. He enjoyed social gatherings and good fellowship. He craved friendship. He quickly saw through the individuals whom he met. He was quick to discern and scorn insincerity, pomposity, and pride, but he was fully as prompt to penetrate beneath the surface into hidden and bewildered frustrations and timid longing for the good.

The sympathies of Jesus were as broad as the human race. To be sure, some incidents appear to belie this generalization. On one occasion Jesus seemed to put off the plea of a woman of another nation by saying that he was sent only to "the lost sheep of the house of Israel" and in dispatching his disciples on a mission of preaching and healing he instructed them not to go to non-Jews, whether Gentiles or Samaritans, but only to these same "lost sheep of the house of Israel." Yet in each instance there is another possible explanation than that of exclusiveness. In dealing with the Canaanitish woman he rejected the suggestion of the disciples that he send her away and did as she requested when she proved herself in earnest. The mission of the twelve was for a special purpose and did not imply a continuing exclusion of Gentiles from the Gospel. Again and again there are incidents and sayings which are clear evidence that Jesus went out of his way to reprove racial bigotry and believed his message to be as broad as humanity. Among these were his initial sermon at Nazareth in which he angered his fellow-townsmen by calling attention to occasions in the Scriptures in which Gentiles had been helped by the prophets when those of the house of Israel were apparently passed by, his selection of a Samaritan as the example of a good neighbour, his healing of the servant of the Roman centurion, and his commission to his apostles after his resurrection to make disciples of all nations.

Deeply religious himself, Jesus was impatient with professional or ostentatious religiosity. He challenged those about him to apply their minds to religion and morals. While honouring the past and the great prophets and lawgivers of his nation, he rejected blind and stubborn adherence to the letter of the law and of the writings which he revered, and treated the traditions of his people with a vigour and a freedom which in some aroused anger and in others were greeted with amazed admiration. While for almost all, and perhaps all of his moral and religious teachings parallels and precedents can be found in the writings of the Jewish sages, Jesus had about him a freshness and an originality which gave them such vivid expression and put them in such proportion and perspective that they were seen as both old and new.

Jesus had a keen sense of humour which again and again bubbles out irrepressibly, all the more strikingly because it is in contrast with the complete absence of humour in those writings of the Christians of the first century which have been preserved in the New Testament. He had a keen eye for the ridiculous and could make startling what he saw—the self-righteous man with the huge beam in his eye essaying to see and pluck out a mere speck in his neighbour's eye; the solemn and meticulous legalist who was so conscientious about details and yet so blind to great moral issues that he was like a man who, anxious lest he be contaminated by his food and drink, would painstakingly strain out the most minute gnat and then, without blinking, swallow an entire camel, hair, hoofs, humps, and offensive breath. He laughed at children playing in the market place, especially at those who, pouting, refused to join in the sport, even when their companions were quite willing to adjust the game to meet their wishes. His questions to the crowds about John the Baptist—"What went ye out into the wilderness to see? A reed shaken with the wind? . . . a man clothed in soft raiment?"—must have provoked laughter, so purposely contrary were they to what all of his hearers knew.

Jesus had the soul of a poet. While few of his recorded sayings are in poetic form, again and again his words breathe the spirit of poetry. His mind thought in terms of pictures and concrete scenes, not in abstract phrases. The parables and sententious sayings in which most of his teachings were couched were such that, once heard, they could not easily be forgotten. It is said that he chose that manner of speaking deliberately, but he could not have employed it so skilfully had it not reflected the quality of his mind. It is tantalizing to speculate whether he may not in part have acquired it from his mother, either by heredity or through long association, for the narratives in the first portions of The Gospel according to Luke which could have come only from her have much of the same quality, but with sufficient difference to make it clear that they and those sayings which are ascribed to him were not the invention of some one author.

There were about Jesus a quickness and a directness which no observing reader of the Gospel narratives can miss. Jesus could blaze forth in anger. Men remembered his glance. It is interesting to note how often, even in our brief accounts, Jesus is described as looking at a person. Here was a characteristic which stood out in the memories about him cherished by Jesus' intimates—his looking on the rich young ruler and loving him, his look at the time of Peter's denial which set that unhappy, loyal, puzzled soul to bitter, heart-broken weeping. Jesus enjoined decisive action—the cutting off of an offending hand or the plucking out of a wayward eye, striving (the Greek is the word from which our "agonizing" is derived) to enter in by the narrow door. He condemned the aimlessly drifting, un-thought-out life. He had no use for indecision—for those who said "I will follow thee, but"—and declared that he who put his hand to the plow and looked back was not fit for the kingdom of heaven. He who would become the disciple of Jesus—namely, learn of him—must renounce all that he had. He even had admiration for the vigorous action of the steward who, when his dishonesty had been disclosed, adopted a bold method of making his future secure.

Jesus could be very patient. He could see one in whom he had sensed possibilities for good and had enrolled among his intimates disintegrate morally and eventually betray him, and yet seek to hold onto him. For his other disciples, who often tried him by their slowness to understand what was obvious to him, he had a forbearance which must have been difficult for one of his quick and keen intelligence. Paul, who probably never knew Jesus personally, but who had heard much of him from those who did, was impressed by his meekness and gentleness, qualities in striking contrast with the quick anger which cruelty or callousness to human need evoked in him.

Another quality which has often been remarked was the absence of any sense of having committed sin or of a basic corruption in himself. The one possible exception is the reply to the inquirer who calls him "good master"— "Why callest thou me good? There is none good but one, that is God;" but another version of the incident gives a different phrasing which does not include a disavowal of goodness. It is highly significant that in one as sensitive morally as was Jesus and who taught his followers to ask for the forgiveness of their sins there is no hint of any need of forgiveness for himself, no asking of pardon, either from those about him or of God. Deep struggle of the spirit Jesus knew, but it seems to have been to discover what the will of God was and not from any inward division, any inability to follow what he knew to be right, such as Paul so poignantly describes in himself, or from any sense of recurring fault or of unconquered sinfulness such as the greatest of Christian saints have confessed.

Less important but still significant is the fact that we never hear of Jesus being ill. We read of his being weary, of his being grieved, of his suffering pain in spirit and in body, but the pain was inflicted by others and we have no hint that he knew what it was to be sick. He radiated confidence and health.

Fundamental in all of Jesus' life was his belief in God, his loyalty to Him, and his utter confidence in Him. Here was the fountain of his ethical convictions and teachings. He took time to be alone with God in prayer. When he instructed his followers in praying to go into a room, shut the door, and pray to their Father who is in secret, he was but telling them to do what he himself did. We read of his spending an entire night alone in prayer, and of his rising early in the morning after a crowded day to go into a desert place and there pray. Even on that night before his trial and death, when he asked the inner group of his disciples to watch with him in the agonizing hour in Gethsemane, he went a little apart from them for prayer.

THE UNIQUE RELATION TO GOD

One of the most difficult and mooted questions about Jesus is what he conceived himself to be. Did he regard himself as the Messiah? If so, what did that mean to him? Why did he so often call himself the Son of Man? Much ink has been spilled in the prolonged discussions of these issues. Across the centuries the relation of Jesus to God has engaged some of the best minds among his followers and is still a subject of debate. That is partly because of the paucity of our records, partly because of the difficulty of penetrating fully into the mind of another, but chiefly because we here have to do with a subject which stretches our minds and our comprehension to the limit and even then cannot be fully apprehended.

It must be obvious to any thoughtful reader of the Gospel records that Jesus regarded himself and his message as inseparable. He was a great teacher, but he was more. His teachings about the kingdom of God, about human conduct, and about God were important, but they could not be divorced from him without, from his standpoint, being vitiated.

It is clear that Jesus believed himself to have a relation to God such as no other human being has ever known. Even if we did not have the many statements in *The Gospel according to John,* such as those which describe him as the *Logos* (the "Word") become flesh, and in which Jesus declares that he and the Father are one, we would have the startling assertion by Jesus preserved in *The Gospel according to Matthew* that all things have been delivered to him by the Father, that no one knows the Son except the Father and that no one knows the Father except the Son and any one to whom the Son chooses to reveal him. This is corroborated by the conscious authority with which Jesus spoke. While declaring that he had not come to destroy the Law and the Prophets, he said emphatically that he came to fulfil them, thus assuming his authority to do so. By implication he also pronounced the Law to be imperfect and for the exact justice of an eye for an eye and a tooth for a tooth enjoined more than once in the inherited standards of his people he commanded his followers not to resist one who is evil. In contrast with the Jewish prophets who regarded themselves as but the mouthpieces of God and who either by implication or expressly supported their pronouncements by "thus saith the Lord," Jesus repeatedly used the words, "I say unto you," with the quiet assumption that he had the inherent right to speak in such fashion. This was among the reasons for the indignation which he aroused among the religious leaders of the Jews. They deemed him to be blaspheming, to be arrogating to himself the functions of God. With an air of authority which angered some about him, believing as they did that he was usurping the prerogatives of God, in more than one instance he declared an individual's sins forgiven.

Again and again Jesus made it clear that he regarded himself as both in the continuity of what had preceded him in the spiritual life of the Jewish people—the Law and the Prophets—and as inaugurating something which was radically new. He saw the Law and the Prophets as pointing forward to him and as culminating in him. As we have said, he insisted that he did not come to abolish the Law and the Prophets but to fulfil them. But in the fulfilling he contrasted what was said in them with what he declared to be right in such a striking manner, as in divorce, oath-taking, and retaliation, that he seems not so much to be completing as to be supplanting. In each instance a case can be made for the use of the word "fulfil" as a description of what he was doing, but the advance over the past is so great as to appear a revolutionary departure from it. Many of those who heard him exclaimed that his was a "new doctrine." He himself lent support to this reception by a saying about new wine in old wine-skins and of unshrunk cloth on an old garment with the frank statement that in each case the attempt to combine the old with the new would be disastrous to both. He believed that what he was beginning was strikingly different even from the movement of John the Baptist, for while he spoke of the latter in terms of high praise, saying that he was "more than a prophet," and that among those born of woman there was none greater than he, he was emphatic that "he that is least in the kingdom of God is greater than" John. To be sure, Jesus spoke of scribes (or scholars) who, "instructed unto the kingdom of heaven," brought out of the treasures of their learning what was both old and new: each could be better understood in light of the other. Moreover, no one of the sayings of Jesus, if taken by itself, is without precedent or parallel in the earlier or contemporary literature of his people. Yet in the forms of statement, especially in the parables, and in the synthesis and the emphasis given them there is a freshness which bears the stamp of conscious authority and of originality and genius.

So unique did Jesus believe his relationship to God to be that he seems to have found no designation in the scriptures of his people or in common usage which exactly described it. This may account for the reluctance which some of our accounts appear to reflect in him to allow himself to be called the Messiah.

That term was associated with a variety of stereotypes and to accept it would be to lay himself open to even more grave misunderstanding than he had to face. When he welcomed the burst of insight with which Peter declared that he was the Christ (Messiah), the son of the living God, and began to point out that for him, Jesus, that meant the cross and the resurrection, that disciple showed his complete lack of comprehension of what his Master believed the Messiahship to entail. He was presumably quite astonished and bewildered when Jesus turned and rebuked him. If, after months of intimacy, Peter did not understand, how much less the thousands who had not enjoyed that association. It was not until after the crucifixion and the resurrection that even his most intimate disciples began to see what was inseparable from his mission and to comprehend who and what Jesus really was.

Conflict with the Religious Leaders

This uniqueness of Jesus and the revolutionary contrast of his teaching with the traditions of his people were the source of much of the conflict which brought Jesus to his death.

The fashion in which Jesus brushed aside some of the customs and prohibitions most cherished by the Pharisees appeared to these self-constituted guardians of Judaism to threaten all for which they and their forefathers had fought against the surrounding world of paganism. What seemed to them to be his disregard of the Sabbath, his contempt for prescribed ablutions, and his willingness, even eagerness, to associate with those whom they regarded as sinners were in their eyes unforgivable breaches of religion and good morals.

In his turn Jesus believed the attitude of the Pharisees to be basically wrong, even blasphemous, and to be leading astray not only themselves but also those who looked to them for guidance. In characteristically vivid language, all the more biting because of its humour, he described them as blind leaders of the blind, with the ditch as their destination. Their error was their belief that they would earn God's favour by their deeds, or, to put it in another way, that they could accumulate merit with God by obedience to His law. This attitude, Jesus saw, bred meticulous care to conform to a set of ethical principles and of ritualistic acts, with a satisfaction in having approximated to them which nourished the deadliest of all sins, pride. Also contributing to pride was the satisfaction of recognition by other men with its associated striving for the approval of men and for place and position, a striving which might even lead one to pray, to undertake ascetic practices, and to perform deeds of mercy for the applause of men.

All this Jesus excoriated in trenchant phrase and apt illustration. He pictured the self-satisfied Pharisee praying in the temple "with himself" and, in a fashion which must have made the Pharisees writhe, placed in contrast and with approbation a member of that class which good Jews loathed as a symbol and instrument of the hated Roman rule, a tax-collector, who, conscious of his sin, pled humbly with God for mercy. To be sure, this portrait of the Pharisee was a caricature, probably deliberately so. At least some of that party were as unhappy as were the prophets whom they honoured over emphasis upon legalism to the neglect of just dealing, mercy, and humility before God. Yet there was that in Judaism which in practice so denied what Jesus was profoundly convinced to be the only correct view of man's relation to God that he believed that he must put the contrast as sharply as possible. In a parable which must have been puzzling on first hearing, Jesus told of the owner of a vineyard who in time of harvest gave exactly the same wage to those who laboured only one hour as to those who had been at it all day. The point, so disturbing to the Pharisee, was that one could not acquire merit with God by piling up good deeds, partly at least because, as Jesus said in another parable, even if we did all that is commanded by God we would only be doing our duty and would deserve no reward.

Jesus appeared to go out of his way to antagonize those in charge of the worship of God in the temple in Jerusalem. He held up for admiration as one who had fulfilled the law of love to one's neighbour a nameless representative of that group whom the Jews despised, the Samaritans, and pilloried a priest and a Levite as having been quite callous in their failure to observe it. His choice of the *dramatis personæ* must have been with an express purpose and not casual. It would bring out with crystal clearness the contrast between God's commands and the religion of the leaders of worship.

Jesus also appeared deliberately to challenge the Sadducees, the politically influential group which controlled the temple. He was scandalized by the fashion in which God's worship in this central shrine of his people's faith was being callously prostituted as a money-making device—in profit in the very courts of the temple from the exchange of money to the temple coinage and from selling pigeons and sheep and oxen for sacrifice. It may be significant that two of the accounts of this "cleansing of the temple" stress his indignation at those who dealt in pigeons. The sale of these for sacrifice by those who could not afford the more expensive sheep and oxen offered a way of making gain from the poorest of the devout and was especially abhorrent to one sensitive to injustice to those "who had no helper." It appears that for a time Jesus and his followers so took possession that "he would not suffer that any man should carry any vessel through the temple." This both angered and alarmed the Sadducean clique which controlled the shrine, for it threatened their revenues from their share in the proceeds of the money-changers and merchants and might bring down on them the Roman authorities, hyper-sensitive as the latter were in an occupied land which was seething with unrest to any move which might lead to a popular uprising.

By his teaching in Jerusalem in these parlous days Jesus did nothing to allay the enmity and fear of either Pharisees or Sadducees. In a peculiarly sobering parable he denounced them as faithless administrators of a trust. He also made it clear that he regarded them as the descendants of those who had killed the prophets.

Maddening to both Pharisees and Sadducees was Jesus' quiet attitude of authority. Jesus would not submit himself to be controlled by them, but challenged them and for a time appeared to have popular support. He was accused of making himself equal with God and of admitting that he was the Messiah. If he were permitted to continue, so these critics argued, he would jeopardize the law and order maintained by the classes which ruled in synagogue and temple. They could rationalize the offense he had given to their pride by saying that in the tense situation which existed in Palestine where they were like men sitting on top of a volcano which might explode at any moment, it would be the part of wisdom to eliminate Jesus rather than to risk his setting off an eruption.

CRUCIFIED, DEAD, AND BURIED

Under these circumstances it is not surprising that Jesus was arrested and executed. He himself had been expecting that outcome, for he was too clear-headed not to see that if carried through the course which he was pursuing could have no other climax. Indeed, he had declared that it was of the very essence of his mission, that apart from it his unique relationship to God could not be understood.

What is difficult and perhaps impossible fully to ascertain is the course of thought by which Jesus came to the deep conviction that he must bring the issue between himself and the dominant elements in his people to so sharp a focus at this particular time and then allow himself to be seized. The reasons for his challenge are fairly clear. Being sure as he was of God's goal for men, of God's purpose in Jewish history, law, and prophecy, confronted by entrenched privilege which, while professedly standing as the guardian of the Jewish heritage, was both blind to the true content of that heritage and was utilizing its championship to obtain for itself prestige, power, and wealth, he could no other than protest.

But why did he permit himself to be killed so soon after his public career had begun? Why did he not withdraw east of the Jordan to pursue a mission among the Jews there, or, perhaps, to the other Jewish communities which were scattered so widely within and to the east of the Roman Empire? He clearly saw that his disciples would be dismayed by his arrest and trial and, unnerved and not really understanding him and his mission, were most unlikely to become the nucleus of a growing movement to perpetuate his teachings. Why did he not take a longer time to instruct them, organize them, and add to their numbers, so that when death, whether peaceful or violent, should remove him they could continue with what he had begun?

From the viewpoint of worldly prudence the course Jesus was following was sheer madness. Having antagonized the Pharisees, both in Galilee and in Judea, by his procedure in the temple he now goaded their traditional rivals, the Sadducees, to side with them and take the initiative in eliminating him. After making his vivid demonstration in the temple and arraying the chief priests and the Sadducean clique against him, he took no measures to organize his followers permanently to support his reforms. Did he expect God to intervene on his behalf and thus to force Him to inaugurate the next stage in the kingdom of heaven? That would have been akin to what had presented itself to him months before in the wilderness when the suggestion came that he cast himself from a pinnacle of the temple that God might deliver him and thus dramatically demonstrate His Son's authority. Jesus had then dismissed it as a temptation of the evil one. It seems utterly unlikely that he would now have yielded to it.

Later, in looking back over their months with him, the disciples declared that they recalled that Jesus had foretold his death and resurrection and the proclamation of the Gospel throughout the entire world, but did they read back later events into dimly comprehended words? If their memories were correct, why the agony in the Garden of Gethsemane and the repeated petition, seemingly denied, that the cup might pass from him? Obviously here was no cowardice or weakness, for Jesus made no attempt at flight and showed no fear as he faced death. The mystery lies much deeper.

However, from our records, fragmentary though they are, it seems clear that for many months and perhaps longer Jesus had known that his course must lead him to Jerusalem and to death, that he saw it as foretold in the sacred writings of his people, and that his crucifixion was in the divine plan.

Whatever the processes by which Jesus arrived at his decision, some of the main outlines of the events of the days which are so important in the story of his life and for the future of Christianity are clear. Because from the beginning they were central in the consciousness and the faith of Christians, the accounts of the last few hours before the crucifixion, of the crucifixion itself, of the burial, and of the resurrection are fairly detailed, occupy a large proportion of each of the Four Gospels, and again and again are referred to in the others of the earliest Christian documents.

The time was the high Jewish feast of the year, that of the Passover, with its memories of the deliverance of the remote ancestors of the Jews from bondage in Egypt. On his way to Jerusalem for the feast Jesus tried to make it clear to his disciples both by his words and his attitude that a crisis was at hand. Yet the disciples were so obsessed with preconceived ideas of what the course of events must be for the Messiah and the kingdom of God that they misinterpreted him and were entirely unprepared intellectually and emotionally for what transpired.

Stimulated by the miracles which they had seen at his hands or by reports of them, an enthusiastic, spontaneous popular demonstration greeted Jesus as he rode into Jerusalem. His "cleansing of the temple" followed. Then came several days of teaching in the temple and of debates with those whom he had antagonized. The evening of his arrest Jesus had the meal with his twelve disciples which was to become famous in Christian history, art, and worship as "the Last Supper." The method of arranging for it which he took may well have been devised as a precaution against interruption by his enemies. The evening was marred by contentions among the disciples as to who was to be greatest, but Jesus himself set the example as one among them who served and demonstrated his attitude by washing their feet. As the eleven who survived after the defection and death of Judas looked back on the evening, they were aware that in the mind of Jesus it had peculiar significance. It was then that he took bread, gave thanks, broke it, and gave it to his disciples, saying that it was his body, and followed it with the cup, also giving thanks, having them drink from it, declaring that it was his blood of the new covenant. Something of fundamental importance was taking place. Around this was to develop the central rite of the Christian Church.

The group went from the supper room to Gethsemane on the Mount of Olives, perhaps to a spot looking out across the city. It was a place to which Jesus had been accustomed to go. From time to time through the months of his public career he had sought solitude for meditation and prayer, a practice which may well have been established during the years of obscurity. This night there ensued a time of agony which left an indelible mark upon the memory of his intimates, even though at the moment, heavy-eyed with sleep, they were only partly aware of it.

Into all that went on in the soul of Jesus during that bitter hour we cannot presume fully to enter. We can only venture conjectures from the imperfect record. Was it the consciousness of the seeming failure of his mission, apparently so soon to be terminated in pitiful futility? Was it the burden of the world's sin, the awful weight of man's blindness and depravity? Was it the apparent hopelessness of trying to make men realize the radiant vision of the reign of God which Jesus had endeavoured to share? Was it the seeming imminent triumph of evil, the victory within man himself of all that was ruining man, and the attendant defeat of God? Was it uncertainty, in the face of what looked like tragic frustration, of what God's will was?

Whatever the inward reason for that struggle, the hour was all the more dark because of the obtuseness of Jesus' most intimate friends. Those whom he had asked to share the watch with him were not so much indifferent as uncomprehending and slept except when, seeking fellowship, he roused them. His struggle had to be without the companionship of those upon whom, if it were to go on after his death, his mission would depend. Well-meaning enough though they were, they apparently completely failed to comprehend what he had been trying to do. His seeming failure must have been rendered all the more poignant by the realization that if the inner group with whom he had elected to share his vision were so far from comprehending it and only a few moments before had been disputing over who was to have priority in the kingdom which they were expecting, the great run of mankind would be even more blind. Yet, as he struggled alone with his burden, Jesus felt himself not alone, but in the presence of God, and like a refrain came the words, "Abba, Father, all things are possible unto Thee: take away this cup from me: nevertheless not what I will but what Thou wilt."

If there remained in the mind of Jesus any uncertainty as to what the will of God was, it was resolved by the appearance of the party who were seeking him for arrest. The cup from which only a few minutes ago he had prayed to be spared was being pressed to his lips and it was made the more bitter by the fact that the betrayer was one of the twelve intimates whom he had chosen. We shall never know why it was that Jesus picked Judas or the reason for Judas' treachery. Knowing his keen insight into character we can be sure that Jesus was never deceived in Judas. Moreover, Jesus would have been acting entirely out of character had he selected him with the deliberate purpose of having him become the betrayer and thus forever damning him. Jesus was always seeking to save men's lives and not to destroy them. It must have been that in Judas Jesus saw possibilities for great good as well as for sordid evil and had hoped by his love to evoke the one and discourage the other. If so, the outcome could only have added to the burden which was already his in the obtuseness of the other eleven and their failure to rise to the emergency. The eleven, dismayed by the unexpected turn of events, deserted Jesus. Poor, loyal Peter, in trying to keep within sight of his Master, stumbled into a triple denial.

There followed in quick and sickening succession the remaining scenes of the tragedy. Jesus was tried by the Jewish religious authorities and by the Roman Procurator, Pilate. To the informed and unprejudiced observer the charges were palpably false. They obviously seemed so to Pilate. Yet Pilate yielded to expediency and ordered that Jesus be crucified, with the inscription above him which showed his contempt for the accusers—"the King of the Jews." It is thought-provoking irony that, having deliberately refused to employ political methods and having rejected an interpretation of his mission which would make him a leader in the current unrest against Rome, Jesus should have been executed on the charge of planning revolt against Roman rule. It is in part a reflection of the complete failure of the leaders of his nation and of the representative of Rome to understand him. Their blindness made vivid the contrast to which Jesus had repeatedly called attention between their perspective and his, between them and the kingdom of God.

We read, almost as though we were seeing it ourselves, of scourging, of rough, derisive soldiers pressing a crown of thorns on his brow, of a purple robe, of mock homage, of blindfolding and smiting with the challenge to the erstwhile wonder-worker to indicate who struck him, of a blood-thirsty mob demanding crucifixion, of the procession to the place of crucifixion, of the nailing to the cross, and of the casting of lots by the executioners for his garments. Through all the excruciating hours Jesus bore himself with dignity and without wincing. He spoke a word of compassion for the women who bewailed him on his way to the cross. He prayed for those who crucified him, saying, what was undoubtedly true, that they did not know what they were doing. Therein was part of the tragedy. He gave a reassuring word to one of the two criminals who were crucified with him. He commended his mother to the care of one of his disciples. Once he gave evidence of the physical distress and spoke of his thirst. At what may have been an especially black moment he cried out: "My God, my God, why hast *Thou* forsaken me?" But those are the opening words of a psalm which, while recounting intense suffering at the hands of others so like that of Jesus in some of its details that by many it is regarded as prophecy and by others as a model on which the narrators of the crucifixion shaped their story, ends in a note of consolation, triumph, and praise, and Jesus may have had in mind the entire psalm and found strength in it in the long hours of pain.

When at last death brought oblivion to the sufferer it seemed that the drama had not been so much his failure as the failure of man and God.

The crucifixion was put through by the spokesman and official representatives of as high a religion as the world had thus far seen and by a magistrate of a government which was as good as any which man had produced. Yet in blindness, selfish fear, and stupid anger they had done to death the rarest spirit ever born of woman, who in his teachings and example had shown the only way by which his own nation could avoid destruction and by which mankind could attain fullness of life. The cross stood in judgement on all the men who had anything to do with it—not only upon the Jewish leaders who had engineered it, upon the mob who demanded it, upon the Roman official who ordered it, and upon the soldiers who carried it out, but also upon those Jews such as the one who gave him burial who, lamenting the execution, did nothing to prevent it, upon the disciples who had failed to understand Jesus and who, bewildered, deserted him, upon the government which had not made impossible such a miscarriage of justice, and even upon the Jewish religion which, while it had nurtured Jesus, had not prevented its own prostitution by its professed guardians. Since those immediately responsible for the crucifixion were a cross section of mankind, both good and bad, the cross was a condemnation of the entire race, vivid evidence of its stupid perversity and its impotence to save its noblest representative from rejection and humiliating death at the hands of man.

But had not God, if God exists, also failed? Is there a God at all? Or is the universe, if it be a universe, and not unintelligent and unintelligible confusion, morally indifferent and blind to what the high-minded among the race hold to be man's finest hopes and noblest aspirations? Is the universe playing sport with beings which it has produced or has it blindly given birth to men who are more intelligent than what has produced them, orphaned victims of unknowing chance? Had the Jewish prophets been correct in declaring that God is righteous and in setting forth a description of what that righteousness is? If so, is God, as the prophets and the psalmists had also declared, sovereign? In these beliefs Jesus had shared. He had even called God Father. He had declared that in him God was in some fresh fashion inaugurating His kingdom, His reign, and that he, Jesus, was in a unique sense the Son of God. Had the prophets and Jesus been tragically mistaken? Had they cherished beliefs which would not stand the test of fact? So the cross would have seemed to demonstrate.

RISEN, ASCENDED, EXPECTED, AND YET STILL PRESENT

The answer came on what Christians hail as the first Easter and in events which shortly followed that Easter. By it the judgement of man by the cross was not lightened or revoked, but Christians have been convinced that in it faith in God was vindicated, and God was seen not to have been defeated but to have triumphed and to have revealed the fashion in which His sovereignty is exercised.

The records which have reached us do not make clear the precise sequence of events on that first Easter. However, from them it is obvious that the disciples did not expect the resurrection and that it took them completely by surprise. The accounts also declare explicitly or by unmistakable inference that the body of Jesus which a few hours before had been reverently and sorrowfully laid in a rock-hewn tomb and carefully sealed in it by a huge stone was not to be found, but that the guardian boulder had been rolled away and that those who had come to anoint the body found the tomb empty. It is abundantly affirmed that the disciples were profoundly convinced that they had seen the risen Jesus, had talked with him, had watched him eat, and had viewed the wounds in his hands and his side, and that one of their number, incredulous, had had his doubts removed by the invitation to put his fingers on the marred hands and his hand into the wounded side. The accounts agree that the risen Jesus commissioned his disciples to go forth as his witnesses and representatives into all the earth. The biographer, almost certainly Luke and a companion of Paul, who tells us that he had taken pains to obtain all possible information from eyewitnesses and the narratives compiled from eyewitnesses and who probably wrote within less than a generation after the events he describes, declares that during forty days Jesus appeared to the apostles whom he had chosen, "speaking of . . . the kingdom of God"—the subject which had constituted the burden of his teaching before the crucifixion—giving them instructions for their mission, and promising them power to accomplish it. After forty days Jesus disappeared from their sight in such fashion that they knew that they were not to behold him again in that manner until a reappearance, his "second coming," which was to be their continuing and joyous expectation. Yet Paul believed that not many years afterwards Jesus had shown himself to him, and the disciples were convinced that Jesus had promised his continued presence with them and would make his abode in any one who loved him.

It seems significant that Paul is the only one of whom our early records tell us who had not been a disciple of Jesus before he met the risen Lord. To be sure, hundreds of these disciples saw him, but so far as our evidence permits us to know none other outside that circle of friends was won to belief by a vision of the glorified Christ. With the single exception of Paul, and the accounts of what happened to him on the Damascus road indicate that even he was not an entire exception, only those prepared by loyalty to Jesus actually saw him after the resurrection. Yet it is also significant and one of the compelling proofs of the resurrection is that the crucifixion left the disciples in despair and that, hopeless, they were transformed by their experience of the risen Jesus. The resurrection became essential in the faith of subsequent generations of Christians. It meant assurance that because Jesus lived they also would live. Even more important was the conviction nourished in Christians that by the resurrection Jesus had been vindicated and had been shown to be the Son of God with power.

THE COMING OF THE SPIRIT

The disciples, not only the eleven but also the larger circle who had been won by Jesus in the days of his flesh, were further strengthened and empowered by the fulfilment of a promise which had been given them by their risen Lord. On Pentecost, the Jewish feast which came fifty days after the second day of the Passover, there came upon the group in Jerusalem—a group which may have numbered slightly above a hundred—what they called the Holy Spirit. It was that occasion to which a large proportion of later Christians looked back as the birthday of the Christian Church. The continuing presence of the Holy Spirit was regarded by Christians as an essential feature of their life and faith.

Out of their experience with Jesus and with the Holy Spirit Christians found their conception of God enlarged and incalculably enriched. They continued to believe in one God and to name Him, as many pre-Christian Jews had done, Father. But they also believed that in Jesus they had seen God, that in Jesus the eternal *Logos* (a word which they found in current Hellenistic philosophic terminology) which was God Himself had become flesh. They likewise were convinced that the power which they found at work within them and within the Christian fellowship was also God. Jews as the early Christians were, nurtured on the great central affirmation of Judaism, "Hear, Oh Israel, the Lord thy God, the Lord is one," they were constrained, possibly to their surprise, to think of God as Father, Son, and Holy Spirit, Three in One. The intellectual issues raised by that illumination were to have perennial interest and became major subjects of thought, and, sad to relate, of controversy. The experience could never be adequately expressed in words, although some of the creeds or symbols which were devised in an attempt to do so gained wide, indeed, almost universal acceptance among those who bore the Christian name. Nor could all the questions about it be answered with entire satisfaction. Always there was mystery, yet belief in the Trinity, based upon early and continuing experience, became a distinguishing characteristic of Christianity.

The effects of the resurrection and the coming of the Holy Spirit upon the disciples were and are of major importance. From discouraged, disillusioned men and women who sadly looked back upon the days when they had hoped that Jesus "was he who should redeem Israel," they were made over into a company of enthusiastic witnesses. From them, as we are to see in the next chapter, faith in Jesus as Christ spread rapidly and spontaneously to many centres of the Græco-Roman world and even beyond it. They did not lose their individual characteristics nor were they immediately emancipated from their weaknesses. Most of the eleven apostles seem to have remained obscure. At least we do not have authentic reports of most of them after Pentecost. Except as names cherished in the memory of the Church and for stories about them which cannot be verified, the majority of them disappear from history. Indeed, we are not sure of the names of all of them, for the lists given do not fully agree. Peter, of whom we hear the most, for some time failed to grasp the full import of the universality of the Gospel which Jesus proclaimed and embodied and we read that on one occasion, either through lack of clarity of thought or cowardice, he compromised a principle which he had acknowledged. The disciples, like other men and Christians through the ages, remained human. Yet in them was a power, a life, which came to them through Jesus and which worked moral and spiritual transformation. That power, that life, proved contagious. The record of their operation in subsequent centuries is the history of Christianity.

How far were that power and that life to be effective? That they were potent within individual lives and groups is incontrovertible, but could the power displayed in the resurrection and at Pentecost remake the world which had crucified Jesus? Was history to prove that early Christian to be right when he declared that God sent not His Son into the world to condemn the world but that the world through him might be saved? That by the crucifixion the world, even at its seeming best, had been judged and found wanting is clear. But was the power that raised Jesus from the dead and which worked within the followers of Jesus completely to reshape that world and make it and all mankind to conform fully to the "high calling of God in Christ Jesus"? Could it lift even those who bore the Christian name "unto a perfect man, unto the measure of the stature of the fullness of Christ?" It is questions such as these that the history of Christianity should enable us to answer.

SELECTED BIBLIOGRAPHY

The literature on the subject of this chapter is enormous. No set of topics has more engaged the attention of scholars across the centuries. The flood of books and articles gives no indication of subsiding. Any selection from the available material lays itself open to legitimate criticism both for what is omitted and what is included. As will be readily seen from even a casual reading, the preceding pages are written from a conservative viewpoint. They have endeavoured to take account of recent as well as older scholarship, but they are frankly based upon an acceptance of the Gospel records as inspired and conveying accurate information. For instance, the virgin birth of Jesus is regarded as historical and John 21:24 is understood as confirming internal testimony for the Johannine source of the Fourth Gospel. Several of the books listed below, brilliant, reverent, able, and stimulating though they are, seem to the author to contain much of conjecture which, to say the least, is open to challenge, but which, unfortunately, is sometimes put forth with a dogmatic assurance which may mislead the unwary. Moreover, some of these books, like so many others written about Jesus, are so absorbed in the minutiæ of the various texts through which our knowledge of him has reached us, in discussions of the authenticity of particular incidents and sayings, of the factors which may have altered these in their transmission, and of the meanings of individual words and phrases that they obscure or entirely miss the main points and the central significance of the whole. They are like the scholars of Jesus' day—the "scribes"—who were condemned for their blindness. There is a kind of scholarship which is often praised but whose most highly esteemed qualities are its stumbling blocks. Yet Jesus himself said that it was possible for the "scribe"—the scholar—"to be instructed unto the kingdom of heaven." The viewpoints expressed in books which are the honest work of scholars must be taken into account by any who would delve deeply and comprehensively into a study of Jesus.

The sources of our knowledge of the life and teachings of Jesus are the Four Gospels and several of the letters in the New Testament, all of them written within seventy or at most a hundred years of the event and some of them clearly incorporating information and even fragments from still earlier sources.

Nine semi-popular and fairly recent books written by competent scholars are T. R. Glover, *The Jesus of History* (New York, Association Press, 1917, pp. xiv, 225), a sympathetic, brilliantly written interpretation; J. Knox, *The Man Christ Jesus* (New York, Harper & Brothers, 1942, pp. 100), a simple and moving summary based upon profound and extensive study; F. C. Burkitt, *Christian Beginnings* (University of London Press, 1924, pp. 152), three lectures by a distinguished authority of Cambridge University; F. C. Grant, *The Gospel of the Kingdom* (New York, The Macmillan Co., 1940, pp. xvii, 240), which reacts against the extreme eschatological view of Schweitzer; three little books by E. F. Scott, *The Gospel and Its Tributaries* (New York, Charles Scribner's Sons, 1930, pp. 295), *The Kingdom of God in the New Testament* (New York, The Macmillan Co., 1931, pp. 197), and *The Purpose of the Gospels* (New York, Charles Scribner's Sons, 1949, pp. vii, 171), by a Presbyterian, of Glasgow and Oxford training, long a teacher in the United States; C. H. Dodd, *The Parables of the Kingdom* (London, Nisbet & Co., 1935, pp. 214), persuasively putting forth a view called "realized eschatology"; and A. C. Headlam, *The Life and Teachings of Jesus the Christ* (Oxford University Press, 1923, pp. xiii, 336), a moderately conservative treatment by a bishop of the Church of England.

IN THE NATURE OF INTRODUCTORY HANDBOOKS FOR STUDENTS

C. T. Craig, *The Beginning of Christianity* (New York and Nashville, Abingdon-Cokesbury Press, 1943, pp. 366), with a comprehensive familiarity with modern scholarship and expressing positive views.

M. S. Enslin, *Christian Beginnings* (New York, Harper & Brothers, 1938, pp. ix, 533), fairly radical.

Somewhat technical and detailed is T. W. Manson, *The Teachings of Jesus. Studies of Its Form and Content* (Cambridge University Press, 1945, pp. xi, 352), by a competent and mature English scholar.

A SELECTION FROM A NUMBER OF RECENT AND CONTEMPORARY SPECIALISTS, CHIEFLY CONTINENTAL, ON THE LIFE AND TEACHINGS OF JESUS

R. Bultmann, *Jesus and the Word,* translated from the German by L. P. Smith and E. Huntress (New York, Charles Scribner's Sons, 1934, pp. xii, 226). Sympathetic with the crisis theology.

M. Goguel, *The Life of Jesus,* translated by Olive Wyon (New York, The Macmillan Co., 1933, pp. 591). By a French Protestant, written from the viewpoint of a fairly radical modern school of thought.

T. S. Kepler, *Contemporary Thinking About Jesus, An Anthology* (New York and Nashville, Abingdon-Cokesbury Press, 1944, pp. 429).

J. Klausner, *Jesus of Nazareth, His Life, Times, and Teaching,* translated from the original Hebrew by H. Danby (New York, The Macmillan Co., 1925, pp. 434). Mildly friendly to Jesus, by a Jewish scholar who attempts to show how Judaism differs from Christianity with the purpose of providing a history of Jesus in Hebrew for Hebrews.

H. A. A. Major, T. W. Manson, and C. J. Wright, *The Mission and Message of Jesus. An Exposition of the Gospels in the Light of Modern Research* (New York, E. P. Dutton & Co., 1938, pp. xxxi, 965), is a voluminous and useful statement of some modern views, with suggestive criticism of them, and also with decided views of its own.

C. G. Montefiore, *Rabbinic Literature and Gospel Teachings* (London, Macmillan & Co., 1930, pp. xxii, 442). By a liberal distinguished Jewish scholar.

A. Schweitzer, *The Quest of the Historical Jesus. A Critical Study of Its Progress from Reimarus to Wrede,* translated by W. Montgomery (London, Adam & Charles Black, 1910, pp. x, 410). Expresses extreme views of the place of eschatology in the teaching of Jesus.

Johannes Weiss, *The History of Primitive Christianity,* completed after the author's death by Rudolph Knopf, translated by four friends and edited by F. C. Grant (New York, Wilson-Erickson, 2 vols., 1937). Chiefly on Paul; approximately a third of the first volume on the Gospel narratives; makes many radical suggestions, brilliantly but often dogmatically expressed, and many of them at best hypotheses.

THE FIRST FIVE HUNDRED YEARS:
CHRISTIANITY WINS THE
ROMAN EMPIRE AND TAKES SHAPE

Chapter V

THE SWEEP OF CHRISTIANITY ACROSS THE GRÆCO-ROMAN WORLD

One of the most amazing and significant facts of history is that within five centuries of its birth Christianity won the professed allegiance of the overwhelming majority of the population of the Roman Empire and even the support of the Roman state. Beginning as a seemingly obscure sect of Judaism, one of scores, even hundreds of religions and religious groups which were competing within that realm, revering as its central figure one who had been put to death by the machinery of Rome, and in spite of having been long proscribed by that government and eventually having the full weight of the state thrown against it, Christianity proved so far the victor that the Empire sought alliance with it and to be a Roman citizen became almost identical with being a Christian. It is the steps by which this consummation came which are the subject of this chapter. The equally important questions of what happened to Christianity in the process, the degree to which Christianity conformed to the Græco-Roman world, and of how far it transformed it must engage us in subsequent chapters.

Our Fragmentary Knowledge

The complete story of the spread of Christianity in its first five centuries cannot be told, for we do not possess sufficient data to write it. Especially is our information for the early part of the period provokingly fragmentary. That need not surprise us. What should amaze us is that so much information has come down to us. Christianity began as one of the numerically smallest of the religions which, stemming from the Orient, were being carried across the Empire. Our knowledge of many aspects and persons of these centuries, even of those which loomed large in the eyes of their contemporaries and so would be prominently noticed, is notoriously imperfect. Most of such records as were made have long since disappeared. The circumstance that Christianity survived the Empire accounts for much of such information about its history as has remained, for some Christians treasured the memory of those of their faith who had gone before them and handed it on to posterity. Yet so small were the first Christian groups that most of them escaped the notice of those who were commenting on their times and all but a few of such documents and inscriptions as they themselves left have perished. Even he who would only sketch the main outlines of the history of the expansion of Christianity in and beyond the Roman Empire in these years again and again finds himself baffled.

The gaps in our knowledge are made the more tantalizing by hints that are given us of what a complete record would reveal. In the accounts of Jesus' life in the Gospels we are given glimpses of hundreds, perhaps thousands of followers in Galilee, yet we have only cursory mention of the early presence of Christians there which would give us ground for inferring that from the early disciples of Jesus there arose continuing Christian communities in that region. We are informed that throngs from Tyre, Sidon, and beyond the Jordan came to hear Jesus, and we hear of churches in these areas, but we do not know that they were founded by natives who had been born during the lifetime of Jesus. Through Paul's *Letters to the Romans* and what we read in *The Acts of the Apostles* we are aware of the existence of a strong Christian community in Rome within less than a generation after the resurrection. Precisely how it came to be we are not told. It was notorious that to Rome, the political centre and the largest city in the Mediterranean world in that day, came representatives of many cults and faiths, but who first brought Christianity to the Eternal City we cannot tell, and until shortly before the end of the first century we hear almost nothing about the church there. Yet Paul declared in his *Letter to the Romans,* written between twenty-five and thirty-five years after the crucifixion, that the faith of that church "is spoken of throughout the whole world," words which seem to mean that Christianity had been long enough in the capital for the fact to become very widely known. From the travel diary of a companion of Paul which has been incorporated in *The Acts of the Apostles* we learn that there were Christians at Puteoli, on the Bay of Naples, who greeted Paul on his fateful journey to Rome, between thirty and forty years after the resurrection. We may guess that they came there, as did Paul, by one of the most travelled of the trade routes, but as to who they were and when they first arrived we are not informed. There may have been Christians in Herculaneum and in Pompeii, not far from Puteoli, before the destruction of those cities in A.D. 79 by an eruption of Vesuvius, but we can only guess at the means by which, if it was present, the faith was brought to them. Although Mark is cautiously named as the Christian pioneer in Alexandria in Egypt and we know of a strong church there by the end of the second century, we cannot be sure of the date or the source of the Christian community in that great Hellenistic metropolis.

BEGINNING FROM JERUSALEM

The documents which have been preserved make much of the spread of the faith from the church in Jerusalem and especially of the missionary labours of Paul. It was natural that the initial centre of Christianity should be in Jerusalem. Here was the geographic focus of Judaism. Here Jesus had been crucified and raised from the dead, and here, at his express command, the main nucleus of his followers had waited until the Pentecost experience brought them a compelling dynamic. Peter was their acknowledged spokesman, but before many years, presumably as his missionary travels carried him ever more frequently away from Jerusalem, James the brother of Jesus became the head of the community. During at least part of Jesus' public ministry an unbeliever, James had been won somewhere along the way, possibly by the special appearance to him of the risen Christ. To their neighbours these early followers of Jesus, for they did not yet bear the distinctive designation of Christian, must have appeared another sect of Judaism, predominantly Galilean in membership, distinguished from other Jews by their belief that Jesus was the Messiah and by their expectation of the early return of their Lord. Their leader, James, appears to have been especially conservative in his loyalty to Jewish customs. They continued to use the temple as a place of worship and observed the Jewish law, including its ceremonies, circumcision, and the dietary regulations. Even some of the Pharisees joined them. So far as we know, their numbers were recruited entirely from Jews and proselytes to Judaism.

CHRISTIANITY BEGINS TO MOVE OUT INTO THE NON-JEWISH WORLD

The dream of universality in the teachings and life of Jesus would not down. Early there were those who believed that Jesus would render obsolete the temple and the distinctively Jewish customs. Of these we hear especially of Stephen. Stoned by the orthodox Jews for his views, views which outraged their complacent assumption that they were a people peculiarly chosen by God to the exclusion of others, Stephen became, significantly, the first Christian of whom we know to suffer death for the faith. His tragic end made it clear that his convictions, inherent as they were in the Gospel and soon to be shared by the majority of Christians, would render it impossible for Christianity to be confined within the boundaries of Judaism. The conflict was unavoidable, for some of the basic features of the Gospel made of Christianity, if it were to be true to its founder, a religion quite distinct from Judaism.

The persecution set off by the death of Stephen forced some Christians to realize as they had not done before the universalism which was of the essence of the Gospel and started a missionary wave which quickly carried Christianity permanently outside Judaism. Presumably this would have happened had Stephen not had his revolutionary views so tragically dramatized. Perhaps it was already occurring, but if so, our records are too fragmentary to tell us of its beginnings. Probably the experience which soon led Peter to see that non-Jews were "granted repentance unto life" without first becoming Jews would have come to him and to others had Stephen never lived. As it was, however, some of those who were forced to flee by the persecution in Jerusalem won converts in Samaria, and, what was even more important, still others preached to Greeks in Antioch, then the largest city in Syria and an important radiating centre of Hellenistic culture. Christianity was moving outside Judaism into that element of the Mediterranean world, Greek-speaking and Hellenistic, in which it was to have its greatest early growth. It was at Antioch, fittingly, that the followers of Jesus were first given the distinctive designation by which they have ever since been known, Christian. The word, itself Greek, symbolized the emergence of the new faith into the wider world.

PAUL, MISSIONARY AT LARGE

Outstanding in carrying the faith into the non-Jewish, and especially the Hellenistic world was a Jew whose conversion is closely associated with the death of Stephen. This was Saul, or, to use the name by which he is best remembered, Paul. We know more about Paul than we do of any other Christian of the first century. Not only does *The Acts of the Apostles* make him and his mission its main theme, but we also have, most fortunately, a number of his letters which give us intimate pictures of him. Yet, much as Paul tells us about himself, and much as Luke adds, there are great gaps in our information, both about what he did, and, still more tantalizingly, in our insight into his inner life.

It is clear that Paul was of pure Jewish stock, that his father had that highly prized privilege, Roman citizenship, that the son was born and reared at Tarsus, a Hellenistic city in what we now call Asia Minor, a stronghold of Greek learning. However, far from conforming to the Greek pattern, Paul had been carefully nurtured in Phariseeism. While probably not highly educated in Greek philosophy and literature, he was thoroughly at home in the Greek language, did not use it crudely, and was steeped in the Septuagint, the famous Greek translation of the Jewish scriptures. He also knew Aramaic and his training in Phariseeism made him think naturally in the methods of interpreting the sacred books which were current in that school of thought. Ardent by disposition, the young Paul may have been all the more loyal and dogmatic in the strict adherence to the Jewish law and customs entailed by his Phariseeism because of his consciousness of the paganism which was all about him in Tarsus. As a youth he went to Jerusalem, the citadel of his religion, to study at the feet of Gamaliel, one of the outstanding teachers in Pharisaic circles. Here he came in touch with the followers of Jesus and joined in persecuting them. He stood by when Stephen was stoned and was sent to Damascus with letters from the high priest to the synagogues in that city with instructions to have arrested and brought to Jerusalem for trial those who were adherents of the Nazarene heresy.

While on his way to Damascus, just as he was nearing that city, Paul was smitten by a vision which changed his life. He believed that the risen Jesus appeared to him and spoke with him, and was convinced that the experience was as authentic as those which had earlier come to Peter, James, and the others.

Into the inner history of the processes which led to this climax we can enter only through conjecture. Yet it is fascinating to make the attempt. We know from his letters that Paul was intense, sensitive, lacking in humour, given to moments of deep depression and of high, quivering exaltation, unquestioning in his belief in God and in the validity of the Jewish law. We also are aware that, by what seems to be a strange paradox, Paul regarded himself as blameless when measured by the Jewish law yet suffered from a deep sense of frustration and inner defeat. In some of the most poignant passages in literature, passages which because of their very vividness and obvious emotion seem to be autobiographical, he speaks of having been alive once "without the law," but that the commandment proved to be death to him, for sin, "taking occasion by the commandment," deceived him and by it killed him. He goes on to say, in moving words which reflect the experience of many conscientious and high-minded souls: "I am carnal, sold under sin. For that which I do I allow not, for what I would, that do I not, but what I hate, that do I. . . . O wretched man that I am, who shall deliver me from the body of this death?" By what he honestly believed to be God's will he felt driven to persecute the Christians, yet, perhaps because of the radiance which he had seen in the face of the dying Stephen, his inner turmoil was accentuated, for he here glimpsed a life which had found the inward victory and peace to which he was a stranger. He was set to wondering whether, after all, those whom he was hounding might not be right and he mistaken as to what God's will actually was.

Moreover, Paul may have been both repelled and attracted by the universality of the Gospel which he glimpsed in the burden of the message of Stephen. Reared a strict Jew in a Hellenistic, pagan city, he was all the more proud of his Hebrew heritage because he was a member of a minority. He held that his were the chosen people bound to God by a special covenant, and presumably he was contemptuous of Gentiles as being outside the pale. That the barrier between Jew and Gentile should be erased by Christ must have outraged much that he had held as axiomatic. Yet it may also have appealed to him.

The inner debate appears to have been going on during the long ride to Damascus, for in one account of the vision the risen Christ is quoted as saying to him: "It is hard for thee to kick against the pricks," implying that he had been fighting the trend in his mind which was leading him to be, as he later gladly described himself, "a slave" and a missionary ("apostle") of Christ. Certainly in that blinding instant Paul realized that it was not so much the Christians as Jesus whom he was persecuting.

It appears to be significant that the decisive moment came as Paul was nearing Damascus, where he would be compelled to act. Seeing the risen Christ and hearing his voice, he was stricken down, sightless. Restoration of sight did not come to him until he was comforted by a Christian who, in spite of his fears of the persecutor, obeying a compelling voice, came to him, declared himself a messenger of the Lord Jesus, and welcomed him into the Christian brotherhood.

By temperament a mystic, possessed of a usually quick, incisive mind, Paul was susceptible to the kind of experience which came to him on the road and in Damascus. Again and again later at crucial times he was to hear a divine command and obey it, but never again were the consequences to be so soul-shaking and revolutionary.

To suggest the background, disposition, and psychology which prepared Paul for what happened on the Damascus road is not to deny its reality or the truth of his profound conviction that through it Christ himself had spoken to him.

Here is one of the most important events in the entire course of Christianity. It gave to that faith one of its greatest instruments. As a missionary Paul was to have a leading rôle in the planting of Christian communities. As a thinker he was to place an indelible impress upon Christianity in its conceptions of God, Christ, the Holy Spirit, and the Church. His spectacular conversion after deep struggle was to be a prototype of the spiritual autobiographies of untold thousands of men and women, most of them obscure but some of them among the most prominent in the history of Christianity.

So great has been his influence that Paul is often said to have been the chief creator of what we now know as Christianity, and so to have altered what had been transmitted to him that it became quite different from the teachings of Jesus and transformed Jesus from the Galilean teacher and martyr into the cosmic Christ. That, so it seems to the present author, is a mistaken interpretation of the facts. Paul himself emphatically declared that he and those who had accepted the faith through him had "the mind of Christ." That is entirely true. While clearly not a colourless reproduction of Jesus or one who was slavishly bound to the strict letter of the sayings of his Master, and while giving evidence on almost every page of his letters of his own distinctive characteristics, Paul was so loyal to the mind of Jesus as we see it in the Four Gospels that did we not have these documents we would still be able to know what manner of person Jesus was, what were the essentials of his teachings, and his crucifixion, resurrection, and continued presence. Without the Gospels we would not have so many of the incidents or of the specific sayings of Jesus, nor would we be so much aware of his personal characteristics, such as his humour and his piercing glance, nor was the kingdom of heaven as prominent as in the sayings of Jesus as recorded in the Gospels, but if we were confined to Paul's letters we would not be led to a picture of Jesus essentially different from that which the Gospels give us.

This is all the more so because of Paul's devotion to Christ. It was of the essence of his new faith that the old Paul had been crucified with Christ, that the new Paul lived by faith in Christ, for Christ had loved him and given himself for him. Paul was profoundly convinced that Christ lived in him, and he expected after his physical death to be with Christ. Possessed by such a controlling passion, Paul would certainly seek to know all that he could of the teachings and earthly life of Jesus and to be true to what Jesus had said and been.

Moreover, although the phrase, "the kingdom of God" or "the kingdom of heaven," was not as frequently in the writings of Paul as it was on the lips of Jesus, the idea was often there. To Paul's mind, God had a purpose which includes the entire creation, God's plan for "the fullness of times" is "to gather together in one all things in Christ, both which are in heaven and which are on earth" and "the earnest expectation of the creation waiteth for the manifestation of the sons of God." Paul depicted the whole creation as groaning in travail and pain, "for the creature was made subject to vanity, not willingly, but by reason of him who hath subjected the same in hope. Because the creature itself shall be delivered from the bondage of corruption into the glorious liberty of the children of God." In this the kingdom or reign of God was interpreted, quite certainly as Jesus viewed it, as having a cosmic sweep including not only the human race and human history, but all the vast universe.

Of the precise chronology and detailed course of Paul's life after his conversion we are not fully informed. Yet we know much. For a time Paul remained in Damascus. There, to the amazement and discomfiture of the Jewish authorities, he, the recent persecutor of the new faith, boldly declared that Jesus was the Son of God and won some to his views. Not unnaturally, there were those among the Jews who sought to kill him, and he deemed it wise to leave the city, going by night and being let down in a basket from the top of the wall to escape those who were watching the gates for him. He then went to Arabia, to which part we do not know, but presumably a portion not far from Syria. Nor are we told what he did while in Arabia or how long he was there. He informs us that from Arabia he returned to Damascus.

"After three years," he goes on to say, but whether measured from his conversion or his return to Damascus seems not entirely clear, Paul went to Jerusalem and was with Peter for fifteen days and also saw James, the brother of Jesus. We may surmise, although we cannot prove, that through these contacts he learned much of the life, teachings, death, and resurrection of Jesus. To one of Paul's temperament this brief sojourn in Jerusalem must have been deeply moving. Memories of his student days and of the persecution in which he had an active part, and scenes associated with the life and death of his new Master must have stirred him to the depths. It is not surprising that in the temple he fell into a trance and seemed to see Jesus and talk with him, and that the burden of their conversation was Paul's future work. Nor is it strange that Paul wished to be a missionary to his own people. Indeed, he never outgrew his eager longing that all Jews might become as he was, a Christian. Perhaps it was in that hour of illumination that he could see that from his birth God had been preparing him to "reveal His Son" in him.

Yet the conviction came to Paul that his mission was to be to the Gentiles, the non-Jews. He was to be a pioneer. The universalism of the Gospel which may have been one of the causes of his original antagonism had gripped him. He declared that by special revelation the insight had come to him that through Christ the wall of partition between Jews and Gentiles had been broken down, that to both the way of life had been opened in Christ, and that the prerequisite of entering upon it was not heredity but faith, faith that was open to all men. He burned to preach the Gospel where no one else had taken it.

In going into a city for the first time Paul usually went to a synagogue and there declared Jesus to be the Christ. When, as generally happened, some heeded him but the majority, outraged, drove him out, he sought the Gentiles. Nor would he have his converts become Jews and conform to the ritualistic practices of the Jewish religion. To him the contrast between Judaism and the Christian message was sharp. His experience had taught him what from the teachings of Jesus should have been obvious to any one, that the radiant life which God desires for men is not to be had through the meticulous observance of the Law, for no one could ever fully keep the commands which God had given for men's instruction and guidance, or, if they attempted to win God's favour in that fashion, they would either be in despair or deceive themselves and be proud of having done so, and thus be guilty of the most deadly of all sins. That life is, rather, so Paul declared, to be received through simple faith, a full, trusting commitment of one's entire self to God in response to God's amazing love as seen in Christ.

Paul rang the changes on what was to him the astounding "Good News" of what God had done in Christ in sending the son of His love—that Christ had emptied himself, that he had submitted himself to being crucified by the very ones whom he had come to save, that in this God Himself had revealed His love for men, men who had so sinned against Him that, blinded, they had killed His Son, that in raising Jesus from the dead God had displayed His mighty power, and that through faith, faith which God Himself inspires, sinful man might be born anew and enter upon the eternal life of love which had been manifested in Christ, that kind of love which gives itself utterly to those who, far from deserving it, have no claim whatever upon it. Moved by this vision Paul preached Jesus in Jerusalem, but, as might have been expected, aroused intense opposition.

From Jerusalem, to escape from those who were seeking to compass his death, Paul went back to Tarsus. From there he was summoned to begin the missionary career of which our records give us many glimpses. First he was called upon by Barnabas, a representative of the Jerusalem church, to help with the young Christian community in Antioch which was drawing largely from non-Jews. He so won the confidence of the church in Antioch that he was sent by that body with Barnabas to carry relief to Christians in Judea who were suffering from a widespread famine. Returning from that errand, Barnabas and Paul were set apart by the Antioch church for a mission which led them to Cyprus and to parts of what we call Asia Minor.

Now ensued a number of years in which Paul, usually with one or more companions, carried the Christian message into much of Asia Minor and into Macedonia and Greece. Some of the details of these journeys have come down to us. Of others we have only hints. Paul gave his chief attention to cities. Much, perhaps most of the time he supported himself by working at his trade of tent-maker. He took satisfaction in not preaching where other men had preached and in not being dependent upon his converts for his livelihood. His was an arduous life. Celibate by conviction, Paul devoted himself entirely to his mission, untrammeled by family ties. We hear of his spending months in one or another of the larger centres. Much of the time he was travelling. He speaks of shipwreck, of perils from rivers and from robbers, of hunger and thirst, of beatings, and of being stoned. Upon him weighed the care of the many churches which he had helped to bring into being. He kept in touch with them by oral messages and by letters. A few of the latter survive and give evidence of the white heat and the pressure under which they were written. Although possessing enormous vitality and astounding powers of endurance, Paul had some persistent physical or nervous weakness which he described as a "thorn in the flesh" and which was to him a heavy burden. He met with bitter opposition, not only from Jews and other non-Christians, but also from other Christians and within some of the churches which he had nurtured. Yet after some years he could say that from Jerusalem as far as Illyricum, on the east coast of the Adriatic, he had "fully preached the Gospel of Christ."

Then came seeming disaster, and in an undertaking to which a sense of duty called him. For some time Paul had been gathering from his churches in the Gentile world a fund to give to the poor among the Christians in Jerusalem. He planned to go to Spain from Jerusalem, on the way visiting the Christians in Rome. It became clear that the mission to Jerusalem would be fraught with peril, for he was to be there at the Passover season and was regarded by many loyal Jews who would be flocking there at that high feast from many parts of the Empire as one who was threatening Judaism and the temple. Characteristically, Paul insisted on making the journey. While he was in the temple some Jews from Asia Minor who had been angered by what they had heard of his attitude towards Judaism aroused a tumult against him. A mob was seeking to kill him when the Roman guard intervened. There followed arrest, judicial hearings, detention of at least two years, an appeal by Paul to Cæsar, as was his right as a Roman citizen, the journey to Rome under guard, a shipwreck in which the prisoner took command, the survival of himself and the ship's company, the completion of the journey, and a stay of at least two years in Rome, presumably still technically as a prisoner, but with considerable freedom to receive visitors and to present to them the Christian message. Then the curtain falls and assured information fails. The fact of eventual martyrdom in Rome seems to be well established.

Further First Century Spread of the Faith

In those first early vigorous years Paul was by no means the only one who spread the faith through the Empire. We hear more about him than of any other, but in various ways we obtain glimpses of many. Peter travelled, for we hear of him in Antioch, and what seems to be reliable tradition speaks of him as being in Rome and dying there as a martyr. Not all its representatives agreed on the essence of the faith. We read of Apollos, who, as a missionary, differed in his message from that of Paul but who was willing to receive instruction from friends of Paul and, conforming, became one of Paul's valued colleagues. Others were so apart from Paul in their understanding of the Gospel that he believed that he must denounce them as bearing a false message. Some of those who spread the faith were professional missionaries, drawing their financial support from the churches, but others, like Paul and Barnabas, earned their livelihood by trade or a handicraft, and many witnessed while giving most of their attention to other occupations.

Christianity quickly moved out of the Jewish community and became prevailingly non-Jewish. As early as the time that Paul wrote his letter to it, a generation or less after the resurrection, the church in Rome was predominantly Gentile. This in itself was highly significant: Christianity had ceased to be a Jewish sect and, while having roots in Judaism, was clearly new and different from that faith.

In becoming non-Jewish in its following, Christianity was entering into the Hellenistic world. While one eminent scholar has attempted to prove that some of the books of the New Testament were first written in Aramaic and then translated into Greek, there can be no doubt that the form in which they gained their initial wide circulation was in Greek and it may well be that all of them were first written in that language. The Greek was the *koine,* the vernacular of that language which was current at the time. Even the church in Rome, at the heart of the Latin part of the Empire, employed the *koine.* This meant that Christianity, still relatively flexible in thought forms, would tend to find expression through the ideas abroad in Hellenism and perhaps would even be moulded by them. It first attracted those elements in the Hellenistic population which were influenced by Judaism and thus for at least a generation was less shaped by the Greek mind than if its initial converts had come straight from pure paganism.

Christianity did not become any more exclusively Hellenistic in constituency than it was Jewish. Early it numbered some whose speech was Syriac, and among those who are reported as hearing the Christian message at Pentecost were Parthians, dwellers in Mesopotamia, Medes, Elamites, as well as those from regions more clearly in the circle of Hellenistic culture. While they were, presumably, either Jews, Jewish proselytes, or enough interested in Judaism to have come to Jerusalem, it may well be that through some of the converts of that memorable day the faith was carried to non-Jewish, non-Hellenistic groups and individuals.

At the outset, Christianity was predominantly urban. It moved along the trade routes from city to city. By the second decade of its second century in at least some parts of Asia Minor it had spread widely into towns and even into the countryside, but its strength was in the cities which were so prominent a feature of the Roman Empire.

SECOND AND THIRD CENTURY SPREAD

We know even less of the spread of Christianity in the second century than we do of its propagation in the first century. Yet it is clear that it continued to grow in numbers of adherents and that before A.D. 200 Christians were found not only in all of the provinces of the Empire but also outside the Empire in Mesopotamia.

In the third century the expansion of Christianity was still more marked. It was gathering momentum. Moreover, in that century the illnesses of society which were later to bring about the disintegration of the Græco-Roman world were becoming palpable. Many, conscious of their insecurity, were seeking refuge in religion. Especially were those religions growing which stemmed from the Orient. Among them was Christianity.

By the close of the third century the chief numerical strength of Christianity was in the eastern part of the Empire. For reasons which will appear later, the church in Rome early took a leading position in the Christian fellowship, but most of the other main centres of the faith were in the eastern portions of the basin of the Mediterranean. Christianity was especially prominent in what we now term Asia Minor. Here Paul had spent many of his missionary years. Here were Greek cities and from them Hellenistic culture was permeating the countryside. Christianity, with a vital foothold in that culture, was spreading with it.

Through the accounts and writings of one of the leading Christians of Asia Minor of the third century, Gregory, later known as Thaumaturgos, or Worker of Wonders, we learn something of the propagation of the faith in Pontus, one portion of Asia Minor. A native of Pontus, born and reared a pagan, Gregory was from a wealthy and prominent family. Seeking an education to fit him for the duties of his station, in Palestine he came in touch with Origen, of whom we are to hear more in the next chapter. It was as a distinguished teacher of philosophy that Origen was sought out by the young Gregory. But Origen was more than a great teacher: he was also on fire with the Christian faith. Through him Gregory became a Christian. Returning to Pontus, Gregory was made bishop of his native city, somewhat against his will. This was about the year 240. He gave himself to completing the conversion of the populace of his diocese. When he died, about thirty years later, the overwhelming majority had accepted the Christian faith. It is said, somewhat rhetorically, that when he became bishop he found only seventeen Christians in his see and that at his death only seventeen remained pagan. In achieving this mass conversion, Gregory made the transition as easy as possible, substituting festivals in honour of the Christian martyrs for the feasts of the old gods.

In the great cities of the eastern part of the Mediterranean Basin, major centres as they were of Hellenistic culture, Christians became especially numerous. Antioch and Alexandria were notable for their strong Christian communities. Such smaller and yet important cities as Ephesus were also prominent in the early annals of the faith.

Most of those portions of the populations in the East which had been less penetrated by Hellenistic life were slow in adopting Christianity. Although, because of its historic importance, the church in Jerusalem was accorded respect in the Christian fellowship, the progress of Christianity in Palestine lagged. In Egypt Christianity was late in winning many adherents among the non-Greek-speaking elements of the population, the country folk whose tongue was the native Egyptian. Yet by the beginning of the fourth century parts of the Scriptures had been translated into more than one of the non-Greek vernaculars and the foundations had been laid of a native Egyptian (Coptic) church.

Although churches were found in some of its cities, especially in cosmopolitan Corinth, Greece as a whole delayed in becoming Christian. Athens especially, as the traditional centre for the study of Greek philosophy, long held to the old cults.

The northern shores of Africa, particularly in and around Carthage in the modern Tunis and Algeria, early had vigorous Christian churches. Here was produced the earliest extensive Latin Christian literature. It may be that the reasons are to be found partly in the conditions in that region. The Italians were immigrants or descendants of immigrants. Carthage had been a Punic or Phœnician city, the great rival of Rome. In a series of wars Rome had come out victor and Carthage had been destroyed. On the heels of the Roman conquest, Italians moved into the country, Carthage was rebuilt, largely as a Latin city, and a large Latin-speaking element came into being. Uprooted from their Italian environment, traditional Italian customs and religions may have had less hold on the immigrants and their children than in Italy and there may have been greater open-mindedness to the Christian message. Whatever the reason, Christianity became firmly planted in the Latin-using portions of the population and the church in Carthage was prominent in the Christian fellowship. With it were associated the names of such early prominent Latin writers as Tertullian and Cyprian, of whom we are to hear more later. Christianity also spread among the Punic elements, but probably more slowly, and still more slowly among the pre-Italian, pre-Punic elements, the Berber stock. This fact was to have tragic significance for the subsequent course of the faith in North Africa.

We know little of the details of the spread of Christianity in Italy outside of Rome, but by the middle of the third century the peninsula seems to have had about one hundred bishoprics, and, with the rapid growth of the faith in the second half of the third century, by A.D. 300 the number of dioceses must have greatly increased. Growth was more rapid in the Centre and the South than in the North, in the valley of the Po. Sicily had Christians in the third century and possibly in the second.

Almost nothing has survived about the planting of Christianity in Spain, but as early as the beginning of the third century the faith was well established in the South. Unfortunately some of our first pictures of Spanish Christianity are distinctly unfavourable—of bishops who absented themselves from their dioceses to engage in commerce, and of a Christian community which compromised with idolatry, homicide, and adultery. Yet, imperfect though it was, Spanish Christianity displayed more vitality than did its North African counterpart in surviving the Arab Moslem conquest of the eighth century.

In Gaul Christianity probably first entered directly from the East. In the Rhone Valley there were cities which long before the time of Christ possessed commercial connexions with Syria and the Hellenistic Orient. They were Greek colonies from Ionia, on the west coast of Asia Minor. In the second half of the second century, when we first catch authentic glimpses of it in that area, Christianity was fairly strong in the Greek-speaking communities in Lyons and Vienne. Irenæus, of whom we are to say more in a later chapter, and who flourished in the second half of the second century, was the first churchman in Gaul to achieve prominence. He was from Smyrna, in Asia Minor, where as a boy he had received instruction in the oral tradition which came to him only a generation removed from the original apostles. In Lyons, where he spent most of his working life, Irenæus learned the local vernacular and may have employed it to preach to the non-Hellenistic population. Before the end of the third century there were bishoprics in the northern parts of Gaul and in cities along the Rhine. Before that time, too, Christianity had won footholds in the Roman province of Britain, and early in the fourth century three bishops from Britain attended a council in Arles, in the south of Gaul.

CHRISTIANITY BEGINS TO OVERFLOW THE BORDERS OF THE EMPIRE

Well before the end of the third century Christianity had begun to gain adherents among peoples beyond the Roman Empire. As was to be expected, this was through contacts with Christians in the Roman Empire and was largely along the trade routes which irradiated from the chief commercial cities of that realm. Close commercial and cultural relations existed between the cities of Syria, such as Antioch and Damascus, where strong churches sprang up in the first century, and the Tigris-Euphrates Valley. It is not surprising, therefore, that by the end of the first quarter of the third century more than twenty bishoprics are known to have existed in the latter region and on the borders of Persia. They were found almost as far north as the Caspian Sea and as far south as the Bahrein Islands in the Persian Gulf. At Dura-Europos, on the Euphrates, on the great road between Antioch and Ctesiphon, twentieth century excavation has revealed a building which was used as a church at least as far back as the year 232. From the inscriptions on its walls it appears that the congregation was Greek-using. Syriac, however, became the major medium for the spread of Christianity in the Tigris-Euphrates Valley.

It was probably late in the third century that the mass conversion of Armenia was accomplished. A land the details of whose boundaries have varied with the vicissitudes of the years, Armenia is on the south slopes of the Caucasus and on the mountainous table-land north of the valley of the Tigris and Euphrates Rivers. Although its independence has been partially guarded by its topography, Armenia has had the disadvantage of being on the borders of much larger realms and has had to fight for its existence. In the first centuries of the Christian era it was a buffer state between the chronic rivals, the Roman and Persian Empires.

The precise course of the conversion of Armenia has been hopelessly be-clouded by legend. The great missionary was one Gregory, to whom the designation Illuminator was added because of his successful labours. Gregory seems to have been of the Armenian aristocracy and to have become a Christian while in exile in Cæsarea in Cappadocia, a region in which Christianity early made marked progress. Returning to Armenia and seeking to propagate his new faith, Gregory encountered persecution. Then he won the king, Tradt, Tirdat, or Tiridates by name. Why the king became a Christian we can only conjecture, but with the consent of his nobles he supported Gregory. The compliant population rapidly moved over to the new faith. Many of the shrines of the pre-Christian paganism were transferred, together with their endowments, to the service of Christianity, and numbers of pagan priests or their sons passed over into the body of Christian clergy. Some were made bishops. Gregory, obtaining episcopal consecration at Cæsarea, became the head of the Armenian Church and was followed in that post by his lineal descendants. To this day the Armenian Church has been known by his name and has been a symbol and bond of Armenian nationalism. Here was an instance of what was to be seen again and again, a group adoption of the Christian faith engineered by the accepted leaders and issuing in an ecclesiastical structure which became identified with a particular people, state, or nation.

By the end of the third century Christian communities may have been found on the northern and eastern shores of the Euxine, or Black Sea. This would be expected from the long-standing commerce of Hellenistic cities with that region and from the strength of Christianity in these cities.

Long before the end of the third century Christianity had gained adherents in Arabia. Some of them were in the parts of Arabia on the eastern borders of the Roman Empire and were presumably the fruits of commercial and cultural contacts. There were probably others in the South of Arabia, a region which had commercial intercourse with the Mediterranean world, especially through Alexandria, a city where, as we have seen, Christians were numerous.

Insistent tradition ascribes the introduction of Christianity to India to the Apostle Thomas, one of the original Twelve. Thus far this has been neither satisfactorily proved or disproved. Long before the time of Christ commerce was carried on between India and the Hellenistic world. Alexander invaded India's North-west and active Greek traders were familiar with the routes to that land. It may well have been that through some of the latter Christianity was carried to India before the end of the third century. It may even have made its way to one or more of the cities in Central Asia which had arisen in the wake of the conquests of Alexander and which were centres of semi-Hellenistic culture.

The Social Origins of the Early Christians

From what social and economic strata did the Christians of the first two or three centuries come? The only safe answer is that we do not know. As we have said, Christianity was at first primarily urban, at the outset among the Jews and the Gentiles interested in Judaism, and then among the Greek-speaking, Hellenistic sections of the cities, but also soon among the Syriac-using peoples of Syria and the Tigris-Euphrates Valley. It is often said that Christians were drawn from the dregs of the urban proletariat—the dispossessed, the slaves, and the freedmen. Christianity has even been described as an incentive and channel for the upsurge of the underprivileged, a social movement. For this appealing thesis some evidence can be adduced. Paul rejoiced that "not many wise men after the flesh, not many mighty, not many noble are called," and in the third century Celsus, the author of a trenchant attack on Christianity, declared that the faith had its chief hold among the ignorant. Yet we know that even in the first century numbers of men and women of wealth, education, and social prominence became Christians, and that in the original Christian group in Jerusalem there were not only poor but also those who had the means to aid their less fortunate fellows. It is possible that members of some of the most prominent families in Rome were among the early converts, and that a near relative of the Emperor Domitian was a Christian and, but for his death by execution, might himself have become Emperor. It may well have been that the proportion of the educated, the socially prominent, and the poor in the Christian communities was about that in the Empire as a whole. This would entail a predominance of the uneducated, but it would not necessarily mean that Christianity was associated with a movement to win more privileges for the proletarian elements in the great cities.

PERSISTENT OPPOSITION AND PERSECUTION

It is one of the commonplaces of history that in its first three centuries Christianity met persistent and often severe persecution, persecution which rose to a crescendo early in the fourth century, but that it spread in spite of opposition and was even strengthened by it. The tradition of martyrdom has entered deep into the Christian consciousness. The faith centres about one who was executed as an alleged threat to the established order and throughout its course it has been punctuated by forcible attempts to curb it. Indeed, with the possible exception of Judaism, Christianity has had more martyrs than has any other religion. Jesus warned those who would follow him that persecution would be their lot, that he would be a source of division and contention, and his words have been amply fulfilled. This is not strange. So radical are the claims of the Gospel, so sweeping are its demands on the faithful, so uncompromising does it render those who yield themselves fully to it, that opposition and even persecution are to be expected.

At the outset, as we have seen, the main persecutors of the Christians were those who held to Judaism and were antagonized by the fashion in which what superficially appeared to be a sect of Judaism was undermining institutions and convictions cherished by that religion. As the separation between Judaism and Christianity became more obvious and as the majority of Christian converts began to be drawn from the Gentiles, while antagonism between Jews and Christians did not decline, persecution of Christians by Jews was less frequent.

Christians had to face the dislike and active opposition of the pagan population about them. Criticisms were on several grounds but arose very largely on the one hand from the fact that they would not compromise with paganism, but held themselves apart from it and in so doing withdrew from much of current society, and on the other hand because they won converts from that society and could not but be noticed. To avoid unnecessary publicity and to escape so far as possible the notice of government officials, Christians held their services either secretly or without public announcement. In a broader and a deeper sense the dislike and the persecution which grew out of it and accompanied it were evidence that, as Jesus had said, in the Gospel something had entered the world with which the world was at enmity.

The accusations varied. (Because they refused to participate in pagan ceremonies the Christians were dubbed atheists. Through their abstention from much of the community life—the pagan festivals, the public amusements which to Christians were shot through and through with pagan beliefs, practices, and immoralities—they were derided as haters of the human race. They were popularly charged with perpetrating the grossest immoralities in their conventicles.) It was said that both sexes met together at night, that a dog was used to extinguish the lights, and that promiscuous intercourse followed. Garbled reports circulated of the central Christian rite, the Eucharist. The fact that it was celebrated only in the presence of believers fed the rumours that Christians regularly sacrificed an infant and consumed its blood and flesh. The circumstance that Christians called one another brother and sister and loved one another on the scantiest acquaintance was regarded as evidence of vice.

More sensible folk probably discounted these reports but were disturbed by the continued growth of an Empire-wide fellowship which, in an age when the political and economic order was obviously shaky, threatened the existing structure of society, for it not only withdrew itself from many of the customs which tied it together, but denounced them as stupid and wicked. Many pagans held that the neglect of the old gods who had made Rome strong was responsible for the disasters which were overtaking the Mediterranean world. Christians replied that they were law-abiding and moral, that they prayed for the Emperor, and that their prayers had reduced the misfortunes which had troubled mankind from long before the time of Christ, but their protestations did not remove the distrust.)

Crude and misinformed though many of the criticisms of Christianity were, here was an awareness that a force was entering the world which if given free scope would overturn the existing culture. Dimly, to be sure, and imperfectly, but with an appreciation of the actualities, non-Christians sensed that because of its revolutionary nature, its uncompromising character, and its claim on the allegiance of all mankind, Christianity was more to be feared by the established order than any of its many competitors, not even excepting Judaism.

Some of the educated were more acute in their criticisms on intellectual grounds, but whether they came as near to an appreciation of the central issues is doubtful. Celsus, whose charges written towards the latter part of the second century in his *True Discourse* we know through the lengthy reply by Origen, said that Christians defied the law by forming secret associations, that the ethical precepts which they taught were not new but were found in existing philosophies, that their attack on idolatry had in it nothing of novelty but had been long anticipated by one of the Greek philosophers, that Christians disparaged reason and taught: "Do not examine but believe," and that the supposed resurrection appearances of Jesus were in secret and only to those who were predisposed to believe in them. He ridiculed Christians for following the precedent set by Jesus and for saying: "Everyone . . . who is a sinner, who is devoid of understanding, who is a child, and . . . whoever is unfortunate, him will the kingdom of God receive." With something of an awareness of the central amazing message of the Gospel, he scoffed at Christians for asserting that God made all things for the sake of man, that men, created by Him, are like Him, as though bats or ants or worms had believed that God had become a citizen among them alone, that they were like God, and that all things existed for their sake. Porphyry, an early leader of Neoplatonism, pointed out what he held to be some of the discrepancies in the Christian Scriptures. How, he said, can the differences in the various accounts of the death and resurrection of Jesus be reconciled? Why, when Jesus foretold the martyr's fate for John and his brother, did John die a natural death? Was Paul not inconsistent when on the one hand he commanded his fellow-Christians to "bless and curse not," and on the other hand bitterly denounced his opponents? These are but typical of the embarrassing questions which the more sophisticated critics put to the Christians.

Christians replied to the attacks on their faith, but they did more. They counter-attacked, pointing out the weaknesses in the pagan religions and giving positive reasons for holding to Christianity. Numbers of the writings of these apologists have come down to us. How widely they were circulated among non-Christians and whether they won any converts we do not know, but at least they would confirm the faith of Christians. We find them in the second and third centuries and some were written as late as the fifth century. Of the most famous of the fifth century apologies, the *De Civitate Dei,* we shall have something more to say in a moment.

Few of the second and third century apologists devoted much attention to the Jews and Judaism. By the time that they wrote, the separation of the Christian community from Judaism was almost complete and Christians were being drawn primarily from paganism. Nor did the apologists pay much attention to the mystery religions. What was said about them was not complimentary, but apparently they did not loom as prominently as rivals of Christianity as has sometimes been supposed.

Negatively the apologists attacked the current paganism. They excoriated the immoralities ascribed to the gods by the current myths, pilloried the follies and inconsistencies in polytheistic worship, and poured scorn on the anthropomorphic conceptions and images of the gods. They did not hesitate to come to grips with the philosophies which were popular with the educated. Indeed, some of the apologists had once sought satisfaction in the study of philosophy and after being disillusioned had turned to Christianity. They pointed out the moral weaknesses of some of the leading philosophers, what they deemed the inconsistencies and contradictions in the writings of Plato, the lack of agreement among the philosophers, and what they believed to be errors in their teaching. Tertullian of Carthage, a lawyer who became a Christian in middle life, held reason, the reliance of the philosophers, to be a false guide to truth. Truth was to be found in the revelation of God in Christ. "It is by all means to be believed because it is absurd," he declared. To him the Gospel was, from the standpoint of philosophy, divine foolishness—as Paul had said long ago—but, as Paul had also implied, wiser than all the philosophers of Greece.

Positively the apologists made much of Jesus and of the Christian belief in God. In contrast with the syncretizing tendencies of the age, they did not attempt to gloss over the contrasts between the Gospel and the non-Christian faiths and philosophies or to suggest a working combination of Christianity with its rivals. Some declared that since Moses antedated the Greek philosophers and that since it fulfilled him and the prophets of Israel, Christianity had that sanction of antiquity for which many, despairing of reason, were asking of religion. They stressed the fashion in which the prophecies of the Jewish scriptures were confirmed by the teachings, life, death, and resurrection of Jesus. They also placed great weight on the moral transformation wrought by the Gospel and contrasted with the pagan society about them the high character of the Christian community, the fashion in which Christians helped one another, and the bringing together in one peaceable fellowship of those of different tribes and customs who had formerly hated one another. They pointed to the fact that Christians prayed for those who persecuted them and sought to share with those who hated them the Gospel and its promise to believers of a joyful reward from God.

In spite of the apologists, persecution by the Roman government was chronic and persistent. The Christian churches were associations which were not legally authorized, and the Roman authorities, always suspicious of organizations which might prove seditious, regarded them with jaundiced eye. Christians were haled before the courts as transgressors of the laws against treason, sacrilege, membership in a foreign cult, and the practice of magic. Since they would not share in the religious rites associated with the imperial cult, they were viewed as hostile to the state. The antagonism was particularly marked, since Christians, revering Christ as *Kurios,* or lord of the whole earth, often looked upon the Emperor, for whom the same claim was made, as Anti-Christ, while the imperial authorities were hostile to them as those who gave allegiance to a rival of the Emperor. Correspondence which has survived between the Emperor Trajan (reigned A.D. 98–117) and Pliny the Younger, who was serving as imperial legate in Bithynia, in the later Asia Minor, appears to indicate that Christianity was officially proscribed, that if Christians recanted they were to be spared, but that if they persisted in their faith they were to be executed.

Usually ten major persecutions are enumerated, beginning with Nero in the first century and culminating in the one which was inaugurated by Diocletian early in the fourth century. In general they fall into two main chronological groups, the first from Nero to the year 250, in which they were largely local and probably entailed no great loss of life, and the second Empire-wide, determined attempts to extirpate Christianity as a major threat to the common weal.

The most famous of the early persecutions was that in Rome in A.D. 64 associated with the name of the Emperor Nero. Our first detailed account is in the *Annals* of Tacitus, written perhaps fifty years after the event and therefore not to be accepted without question. It says that Nero, to meet the ugly rumour that a great fire in Rome had been set by his orders, sought to fasten the blame on the Christians. The latter were also accused of hatred of the human race. Some of the Christians, so Tacitus declares, were wrapped in the hides of wild beasts and were then torn to pieces by dogs. Others, fastened to crosses, were set on fire to illuminate a circus which Nero staged for the crowds in his own gardens. Indeed, the pity of the mob was said to have been aroused and turned to criticism of Nero. Tradition, probably reliable, reports that both Peter and Paul suffered death at Rome under Nero, although not necessarily at this time. Peter's remains are supposed now to lie under the high altar in the cathedral which bears his name in what were once the gardens of Nero. It may have been that the persecution of Nero spread to the provinces.

The last book of the New Testament, *The Revelation of John,* seems to have Rome in mind when it describes "Babylon the great, mother of harlots" as "drunk with the blood of the saints and the blood of the martyrs of Jesus." The date is uncertain and may well be much later than Nero. If so, it would appear to indicate that persecutions by the imperial government were sufficiently chronic to lead some Christians to regard with horror Rome and what it stood for.

It is only occasionally in the second century and the first half of the third century that we know of express instances of persecution. From early in the second century we have the letters of Ignatius of Antioch written on his way to Rome for execution as a Christian. From a little later in that century we have the famous martyrdom in Smyrna, in Asia Minor, of the aged Polycarp, who may have been the last survivor of those who had talked with the eyewitnesses of Jesus. Shortly before the middle of the second century a Bishop of Rome suffered martyrdom.

Some of the ablest and noblest of the Emperors were numbered among the persecutors. Hadrian (reigned 117–138), to be sure, insisted that those innocent of the charge of being Christians should be protected and commanded that those be punished who brought accusations which they could not prove against alleged Christians, but he did not forbid action against real Christians. Under Antoninus Pius (ruled 138–161) Christians suffered in Rome. One of the most high-minded and conscientious of all the Emperors, Marcus Aurelius (ruled 161–180), heartily disliked Christians, possibly because he thought of them as undermining the structure of civilization which he was labouring to maintain against domestic and foreign threats, and during his reign persecutions occurred, including one in Gaul. Under Commodus, the unworthy son of Marcus Aurelius, persecution, at first continued, was later relaxed because of the intervention of his favourite, Marcia. Indeed, through her intercession a number were released from hard labour in the mines to which they had been condemned for their faith. During the first part of his regime (193–211), Septimius Severus was not unfriendly towards Christians, had some of them in his household, and entrusted to a Christian nurse the rearing of his son, Caracalla. However, in 202 he issued an edict forbidding conversions to Judaism or Christianity, and a persecution followed of which we hear a good deal from North Africa and Egypt. It was then that the father of Origen perished in Alexandria, and Origen, in his adolescent ardour desiring to share his fate, was kept from it only by the resourceful action of his mother in hiding his clothes.

We are not certain that any of the persecutions of the first two centuries was Empire-wide. Presumably Christians were always in danger, for their legal status was at best precarious, a local or provincial official might at almost any time proceed against them, and some action of an Emperor might stiffen the backbone of otherwise lenient authorities. They were chronically regarded with suspicion by large elements in the populace and among the respectable citizens. Their peril was further accentuated by a procedure which gave their possessions to those who brought a successful accusation against them. Confiscation of goods, imprisonment, and torture might overtake them at any time, followed by hard labour in the mines or by execution. Some Christians courted martyrdom. This was partly because it brought honour from their fellow-Christians and was supposed to erase any sins which had been committed. It was also partly because of the devotion of those who were ambitious to share the fate of their Lord. The majority opinion of the Christians, while reverencing true martyrs, was against needlessly seeking arrest. We even read that some churches paid money to officials to insure freedom from molestation. It may well have been that, compared with the total number of Christians, the martyrs were very few.

A Breathing Space and Rapid Growth

In the first half of the third century after the brief outbreak under Septimius Severus the persecution of Christians almost entirely lapsed. It was sharply revived under Maximinus Thrax (reigned 235–238) but his rule was short. The time was one in which religions from the Orient were making rapid headway. Several of the Emperors were from the eastern part of the Empire and were not concerned to maintain the Roman tradition. They encouraged the existing trend towards syncretism and monotheism. One of them, Alexander Severus (ruled 222–235) is said to have had in his chapel statues of Orpheus, Abraham, Alexander the Great, several of the Roman Emperors, and Jesus. His mother asked Origen for instruction. Philip the Arabian (reigned 244–249) is sometimes named as the first Christian Emperor. He is reported to have shared in the pascal vigil and to have been assigned to the section which was prescribed for penitents for entrance to that service.

Certainly in the first half of the second century thousands were flocking into the churches. The Christian communities had long been growing, the uncertainties of the times were moving many to seek security in religion, especially in one which was giving rise to so inclusive and strong a fellowship as the Christian Church, and the weakening of existing patterns of society and the popularity of cults from the Orient which were esteemed as having the authority of hoary antiquity were easing the path to the Church.

THE SUDDEN STORMS UNDER DECIUS AND VALERIAN

In the year 250 the triumphant course of Christianity was brought to what appeared to be an abrupt and disastrous halt. The most severe general persecution which the faith had yet met broke out and, at imperial command, swept across the Empire. This was the act of the Emperor Decius. Decius came to the purple in the year 249. He was a native of Pannonia, north-west of Thrace, and may have represented a reaction in that region against the influences which had entered the Empire from the East. It may be significant that Maximinus Thrax, who was responsible for the brief persecution in the 230's, was from Thrace, and that Galerius, a notorious persecutor of the next century, was from the same general region.

We do not have the texts of the anti-Christian edicts of Decius, and we can only guess at the reasons for his action. Decius was acclaimed by his admirers as an embodiment of the old Roman virtues, and it may well have been that in the drift towards non-Roman religions under his immediate predecessors and in the attendant neglect of the Roman gods who, from his standpoint, had made Rome great, he believed the cause to lie of the calamities and decay which were palpably overtaking society.

Whatever the motives, in 249 imperial edicts were issued which presumably commanded all citizens of the Empire to sacrifice to the gods. Those who obeyed were given certificates as evidence that they had complied. Christians were not singled out but the sacrifices were to be made by all, of whatever faith. Obviously, however, Christians were the chief sufferers. In the easy-going syncretism of the times, pagans would not find their consciences troubled by compliance. They would simply be jarred temporarily out of any careless neglect of the traditional gods into which they might have fallen. For Christians, however, the issue was far more serious. To sacrifice would be apostasy and in current Christian belief apostasy was one of the sins for which no forgiveness was possible. Many Christians preferred their physical lives to spiritual death and fully complied. Numbers avoided so bald a departure from their faith by purchasing from venal officials certificates, or *libelli,* of compliance, without actually sacrificing. Others, how many we shall never know, braved the full displeasure of the state by failing to obey. Some of them were imprisoned, among them Origen, the Bishop of Rome, and the aged Bishop of Jerusalem. The two latter perished in prison. Others were killed outright. Some retired to places of comparative safety. Among the latter was Cyprian, the famous Bishop of Carthage of whom we are to hear more later.

Fortunately for the Christians, the persecution was of brief duration. In the year 251 Decius fell in battle with the Goths, "barbarians" against whom he was fighting to protect the Empire. In the months immediately before his death he had become too engrossed in the defence of the realm against the invaders to press his religious policy. Under his successor, Gallus (reigned 251–253), the anti-Christian measures were revived in at least some parts of the Empire, probably stimulated by a pestilence which drove terrified thousands to the altars of the old gods and led to hysteria against the Christians, who by their neglect of the gods were supposed to be accountable for the disaster. However, the persecution was not so protracted but that it proved salutary for the Church. It had been sharp enough to purge the Church of many of its weaker and more luke-warm members and yet had not been prolonged enough seriously to weaken it.

Under the Emperor Valerian (ruled 253–260) the anti-Christian storm broke out afresh and with redoubled fury. During the first few years of his reign Valerian appeared to be friendly to Christians and even had some of them in his household. Then his temper suddenly changed, possibly through the influence of one of his counsellors. The realm was still afflicted by foreign foes and domestic pestilence, and it may have been that Christians were again held responsible because of their antagonism to the gods who were believed to have made Rome strong.

The new persecution, which was begun in 257, seems to have been directed more astutely than was the one under Decius. The bishops, as the heads of the Church, were singled out and were commanded to do homage to the old gods under pain of exile. Christians were threatened with the death penalty if they so much as went to any of the meetings or services of the Church or even visited a Christian cemetery. Apparently the point of the measure against Christian conventicles was that they were still illegal, and the reason for action against Christian cemeteries was that, to have organizations which were within the law, Christians had formed themselves into burial associations, bodies which could obtain legal recognition.

In the year 258 a new and more drastic edict was promulgated. While, as in the case of its predecessor, we do not have the exact wording, presumably it ordered death for bishops, priests, and deacons; first confiscation of property and then, if this were not enough to induce apostasy, death for Christians of high rank in the state, confiscation of goods and banishment for Christian matrons, and slavery for Christian members of the imperial household. By hitting at the persons of prominence in the Church the latter would be deprived of its leadership.

Under these edicts the persecution was pressed in at least a majority of the provinces. In Rome the Bishop was taken while teaching seated in his chair in one of the catacombs and, with four of his seven deacons, was slain. The other three deacons were also soon caught and killed. One, Lawrence, is said to have been roasted on a gridiron. In Africa Cyprian was beheaded. A convert in middle life, as head of the church in Carthage Cyprian was one of the most honoured of the early bishops. In Spain a bishop who was reported to have been greatly beloved by both Christians and non-Christians was burned at a stake in an amphitheatre with two of his deacons.

The persecution ended abruptly in 260 when Valerian, at war with the Persians, was captured and disappeared from history. His son and successor, Gallienus, reversed his father's policy and either issued edicts of toleration for Christianity or rescripts to bishops which had much the same purport. Again a persecution which might have been disastrous had it been pressed over many years proved so short that the effect was rather to strengthen the Church than to injure it. The Church emerged with a fresh accretion of martyrs to reinforce its faith and courage.

A GENERATION OF PEACE AND PROSPERITY

Approximately a generation of relative peace and prosperity followed. Now and again we hear of martyrdoms, some of them in Rome and Italy, several in Gaul, others in Asia Minor, and still others in the Orient. There were efforts to purge the army of Christians, although, as we shall see, many, perhaps most of the early Christians had conscientious scruples against military service and presumably not many were in the legions. In the main, however, the

Christians were less molested by the state than they had been since the first
half of the century. Through the Church Christianity now presented the
strongest congeries of institutions in the Mediterranean world aside from the
imperial government. Many were attracted to it and Christians were prominent
even in the imperial household.

How many Christians there were at this time we have no way of knowing.
Estimates vary from about five in a hundred to about half the population.
The gain in two and a half centuries had been astounding.

CLIMAX OF STORM

Now, in the year 303, began the most severe persecution which Christianity
had yet experienced. On the imperial throne was Diocletian, one of the strongest
of the Emperors. He was from the vigorous peasant stock of Illyria, east of the
Adriatic, from which had sprung his three immediate predecessors. In the interests of greater effectiveness he had reorganized the administration of the
Empire.

Why Diocletian became a persecutor must be a matter of conjecture. He was
then in his late fifties, at a time when he might have been supposed to be past
undertaking any drastic change in programme. In addition to the Christians in
his household, his wife and his daughter, wife of Galerius, one of the two men
who, under the title of Cæsar, he had associated with himself and his imperial
colleague in the top ranks of the government, were either Christians or favourably disposed to Christianity. Galerius is generally supposed to have been the
instigator. An ardent pagan, he is said to have been ambitious to succeed
Diocletian and for this needed the support of the army, which was still predominantly non-Christian.

Whatever the motives, the persecution was instituted by a decree in 303
which ordered the destruction of the church buildings, the burning of the
sacred books, the demoting of Christians from places of honour, and the enslavement of Christian household servants who would not abjure their faith.
Other decrees followed which ordered the imprisonment of the rulers of the
churches, offered release to Christians who sacrificed to the old gods, and commanded torture for those who were obdurate. In 304 a fourth edict seems to
have been issued by Maximian, joint Emperor with Diocletian.

The storm was Empire-wide, from Britain to Arabia, but was particularly
severe in the East, where Christianity had its chief numerical strength. It lasted
more than a decade and endured longer in the East than in the West. Apparently the death penalty was inflicted only as a last resort, but torture was freely
applied to induce the victims to recant and through it many perished. It was
to this time that the martyrdom of Alban, not far from London, famous for

the fashion in which his memory was revered, is ascribed. On occasion there
was wholesale slaughter. Thus in Asia Minor a Christian town was surrounded
by soldiers and burned, together with its inhabitants. An eye witness declares
that he saw wild beasts leave unharmed the Christians who had been exposed
to them and turn upon those who were goading them on. In Rome the property
of the church was confiscated and many of the members perished. In Egypt,
Palestine, and Syria, the persecution was renewed again and again in the vicissitudes of the political situation and did not die out until the defeat (about
323) of the last of the persecutors.

As was to be expected, the response of the Christians varied. Some recanted
under pressure of torture and imprisonment. Some sent pagans or friends to
sacrifice for them. Others wavered, but eventually gave themselves to the
authorities. Still others sought martyrdom, and that in spite of the general
policy of the church officials which discouraged what was regarded as fanaticism. The courage of the victims made so great an impression on pagans that
we hear of at least two of the latter, educated men, becoming Christians.

CONSTANTINE ESPOUSES CHRISTIANITY

In what must have seemed an unequal contest between naked, ruthless force
and unarmed, passive resistance, it was not the imperial government but Christianity which emerged victor. Presumably this would have been the eventual
outcome, for Christianity was clearly proving itself the stronger. As it was, the
individual who was preëminent in the surrender of the state was Constantine.
Constantius Chlorus, the father of Constantine, was governing Britain, Gaul,
and Spain as Cæsar when the persecution broke out. He seems never to have
had any stomach for it and to have been at best half-hearted in his enforcement
of the anti-Christian edicts. When, after the abdication of his two superiors,
Diocletian and Maximian, he became one of their successors under the title of
Augustus, he appears to have allowed the anti-Christian measures to lapse. On
the death of Constantius Chlorus, in 306, Constantine, then in York in distant
Britain, already his father's known choice for the succession, was proclaimed
Emperor by his troops. He was confronted with rivals and a prolonged struggle followed. He did not become sole Emperor until 323, when he defeated
his last competitor, Licinius.

Constantine took the decisive step in his relation with Christianity in the
year 312. He had invaded Italy on his march towards Rome and was faced
with the army of his first formidable opponent, Maxentius. Apparently he
knew that Maxentius was relying on pagan magic and felt the need of a more
powerful supernatural force to offset it. Years later he told his friend, Bishop
Eusebius, the most eminent of early Church historians, that, after noon, as he

was praying, he had a vision of a cross of light in the heavens bearing the inscription, "Conquer by this," and that confirmation came in a dream in which God appeared to him with the same sign and commanded him to make a likeness of it and use it as a safeguard in all encounters with his enemies. How accurately Constantine remembered the experience we do not know, but Eusebius is usually discriminating in his evaluation of data, and he declares that he himself saw the standard which was made in response to the vision—a spear overlaid with gold, with a cross which was formed by a transverse bar and a wreath of gold and precious stones enclosing a monogram of the letters Chi and Rho for the name of Christ. The staff also had an embroidered cloth with the picture of Constantine and his children. Constantine was victor, the winning battle being at the Milvian Bridge, near Rome, and he therefore took possession of the capital. Presumably his faith in the efficacy of the Christian symbol was thus confirmed.

In the following year, 313, Constantine and Licinius, between whom the realm was temporarily divided, met at Milan and action was taken which was later looked back upon as having ensured toleration for the Christians through-out the Empire. Precisely what was done at Milan remains controversial. Some, including Eusebius, declare that an edict of toleration was issued. On the other hand it is contended that Constantine had already granted religious freedom and that whatever was done at Milan was by Licinius and was intended only for the eastern portions of the Empire where Licinius was in control. What-ever the details, it seems clear that important measures on behalf of the Christians were taken at Milan and that Constantine was consistently friendly.

The policy of Constantine was one of toleration. He did not make Christianity the sole religion of the state. That was to follow under later Emperors. He continued to support both paganism and Christianity. In 314, when the cross first appeared on his coins, it was accompanied by the figures of *Sol Invictus* and *Mars Conservator*. To the end of his days he bore the title of *pontifex maximus* as chief priest of the pagan state cult. The subservient Roman Senate followed the long-established custom and classed him among the gods. He did not persecute the old faiths.

As time passed, Constantine came out more and more pronouncedly in favour of Christianity. Whether he was a Christian from political motives only or from sincere religious conviction has been hotly debated. Perhaps he himself did not know. However, it is clear that he granted to members of the Christian clergy the freedom from all contributions to the state which had been the privilege of the priests of other religions which were accorded official recogni-tion. However, this soon led to so great an influx into the Christian priesthood of those from the curial class who wished relief from the heavy burdens which were crushing that once privileged stratum of society that another edict followed which limited ordination to those whose exemption would mean little loss to the government. Wills in favour of the Church were permitted. The Christian Sunday was ordered placed in the same legal position as the pagan feasts, and provincial governors were instructed to respect the days in memory of the martyrs and to honour the festivals of the churches. The manumission of slaves in churches in the presence of the bishop and clergy was legalized. Litigants might bring suit in a bishop's court and the decision rendered was to be respected by the civil authorities. Constantine forbade Jews to stone such of their co-religionists as chose to become Christians. He had his children instructed in the Christian faith and kept Christian bishops and clergy in his entourage. He built and enlarged churches and encouraged bishops to do likewise and to call on the help of civil officials. When he removed his headquarters to Byzantium, on the Bosporus, and enlarged that city and renamed it Constantinople, he built in it many churches. He prohibited the repair of ruined temples and the erection of new images of the gods. He forbade any attempt to force Christians to participate in non-Christian religious ceremonies. He took an active part in the affairs of the Church, thus establishing a precedent which was to be followed by his successors. The fashion in which he sought to promote Christian unity by calling the first general council of the Church and presiding at it will be noted in the next chapter. While Constantine did not receive baptism until the latter part of his life, the deferment of that rite seems not to have been from indifference to it, but from the conviction, then general, that it washed away all previous sins and, being unrepeatable, had best be postponed until as near death as possible.

THE CONTINUED GROWTH OF THE CHRISTIAN COMMUNITY UNDER THE SONS OF CONSTANTINE

The three sons of Constantine who followed him successively in the imperial purple were much more positive in furthering the Christian faith than their father had been. In 341 the second of them ordered that pagan sacrifices be abolished in Italy. The third, Constantius, commanded that "superstition cease and the folly of sacrifices be abolished" and removed from the Senate the statue of Victory which had been placed there by Augustus after the battle of Actium. He ordered temples closed. Yet of the pagan rites only sacrifices were forbidden, and processions, sacred feasts, and initiation to the mysteries, still permitted, presumably continued.

Under this prolonged patronage by the Emperors the Christian communities grew rapidly. The momentum acquired before Constantine was accelerated. Many now sought admission to the Church from other motives than purely religious conviction. Official favour and even wealth could be hoped for where formerly persecution, always in the background, tended to give pause to all but those impressed by the truth of the faith. Huge church structures were erected, some of which survive.

REACTION UNDER JULIAN AND THE COMPETITION OF OLD AND NEW FAITHS

The numerical triumph of Christianity in the Roman Empire was not yet fully accomplished. First came a brief attempt to restore paganism by Julian, one of the family of Constantine. There was also the continued competition of historic paganism, reinforced by the mounting disasters to the Empire. To this were added new religious faiths and the inroads of barbarians with their cults. As, from the vantage of the accomplished fact, we may think that the victory of Christianity in the Mediterranean world had long been assured, it did not necessarily so appear to contemporaries.

Julian, because of his record branded by Christians as "the apostate," is an extraordinarily appealing figure. Sensitive, able, studious, deeply religious, Julian had a youth which determined his scorn for Christianity and his nostalgic adherence to the traditional paganism. A scion of the Constantinian house and a cousin of the Emperor Constantius, he and his brother were left the only survivors of his branch of the family by a series of political murders which were designed to remove inconvenient rivals for the imperial purple. Kept under watchful ward by Constantius, he was instructed in the Christian faith and outwardly conformed to it. Indeed, for a time he may even have been a convinced Christian. However, reared under these unhappy circumstances, it is not surprising that Julian conceived an ardent admiration for the philosophies which were critical of Christianity and for the religions which that faith was supplanting.

Made Cæsar by Constantius and placed in command of an army on the frontier, Julian was proclaimed Augustus by his troops and was marching against Constantius when the latter's convenient death (361) left him undisputed lord of the Empire. On his march against Constantius, Julian threw off any remaining pretense of being Christian and openly acknowledged his paganism. He did not undertake a violent persecution of Christianity, but he deprived the Church and its clergy of some of the privileges accorded them by his recent predecessors, restored pagan temples, and in appointments to public office gave preference to pagans. He endeavoured to purge the revived paganism of its more palpable weaknesses and attempted to incorporate in it some of the institutional features of the Christian Church, such as a hierarchy, monasteries for meditation, penance, the sermon, and almonries. He wrote against the "Galileans," as he persisted in calling the Christians, and sought to annoy them by beginning the rebuilding of the Jewish temple in Jerusalem.

Julian failed. Paganism was too moribund to be revived by artificial stimulation. When, after a reign of about two years, he perished (363) in a war against the Persians, his troops elected in his place Jovian, of German descent. It is said that when Jovian at first demurred on the ground that he was a Christian, his troops declared that they too were Christians and refused to let him decline. Certainly Julian was the last Roman Emperor who openly avowed paganism. Some of the others were far from being Christians in character, but all of them outwardly conformed to the faith.

The ancient paganism was not yet dead. It held on in many places. It was strong in some of the rural districts and in remote mountain valleys. In the Eternal City the aristocracy, conservative as an aristocracy usually is, possibly resentful of the new Constantinople, cherished the pagan traditions associated with the days of Rome's glory. Especially in Italy, Gaul, and Spain paganism persisted, even in the cities, down into the fourth and fifth centuries)

The lament of the aristocracy seemed to be confirmed by the capture and sack of Rome by Alaric and his Goths in 410. To the Mediterranean world Rome was the symbol of civilization, order, and stability. Although Rome recovered very quickly physically, the experience further shook the morale of a portion of the globe which was being dealt many blows. Here, to the mind of the adherents of the old gods, was proof conclusive that the defection of the Christians from the ancient cults was the source of the illnesses of society.

The beginnings of the barbarian invasions which were to swell to major proportions in the fifth century often brought with them cults from beyond the borders of the Empire. As we are to see, some of the barbarians adopted Christianity before entering the Roman realms and all of those from the North were eventually to do so. However, for a time their religions brought fresh if fleeting resistance to Christianity.

New faiths were entering the lists against Christianity. One of these was Neoplatonism. An outgrowth of the ancient philosophies of Greece, especially Platonism, its first major creative figures, Ammonias Saccas and Plotinus, flourished in the third century. It was both a philosophy and a religion and in the fourth and fifth centuries was widely popular among the intellectuals. Julian was enamoured of it. It left a permanent impress upon Christianity, partly through Augustine of Hippo, partly through its share in shaping Christian thought in general, and especially in its contributions to Christian mysticism.

Formidable also was Manichæism. Manichæism had as its founder Mani, of the third century. Of Persian stock, with some of the blood of the Parthian Arsacids in his veins, Mani was reared in Seleucia-Ctesiphon, the chief city of Mesopotamia, where East and West met. Deeply religious, he was impressed by the many faiths with which he came in contact—the Zoroastrianism of his Persian ancestors, the ancient Babylonian beliefs, Judaism, and Christianity. He came to the conviction that he was commissioned by divine revelation to be a prophet. Opposed by the powerful Zoroastrianism, he was driven out of the Persian Empire and for many years was a wandering preacher of the new faith and is said to have travelled and taught widely in Central Asia and India. Returning to his native land, he is reported to have been favoured by the reigning monarch, but to have been killed under a successor. His followers went both westward and eastward and Manichæism was eventually represented from the Western Mediterranean to the China Sea. In the Mediterranean world especially it took on some Christian features. Mani is said to have begun his letters with "Mani, Apostle of Jesus Christ." He declared either that he was the Paraclete promised by Jesus or that the Paraclete spoke through him.

The Conversion of Augustine

The appeal of Neoplatonism and Manichæism as rivals of Christianity is vividly demonstrated in the spiritual pilgrimage of Augustine of Hippo (354–430). Born in North Africa of Latin stock, of a devoutly Christian mother, Monica, and a pagan father who became a Christian only late in life, as a youth Augustine was given Christian instruction. His mother did not have him baptized because, accepting the belief that baptism washed away sins committed before it was administered, she wished him to defer it until after the heat of youth was passed and with it the excesses of that ardent age. Brilliant, sensitive, intense, in his teens Augustine took a concubine who, before he was eighteen, bore him a son, named, perhaps conventionally, or deliberately by a strange perverseness, or from the religious feeling which characterized him, Adeodatus, "given by God." Unsatisfied religiously and seeking, Augustine dabbled with his inherited Christianity but was repelled by the crudity of the literary style of the Latin translation which was his only way to the Scriptures. For a time he tried Manichæism, but finding that it could not answer his intellectual questions, abandoned it. A teacher, first in North Africa, then in Rome, and eventually in Milan, he continued his religious quest. For a time his hunger seemed to be met by Neoplatonism, but that did not fully satisfy him and in Milan he came under the spell of Ambrose, the bishop of that city, a man of strong character and an impressive preacher, of whom we are to hear more in a moment. Suffering from conscious moral impotence and self-disgust because of his inability to control his sexual desires, a member of a small coterie who, with him, were searching, at the climax of his struggle Augustine rushed from his friends into a quiet nook in a garden, seemed to hear the voice of a child commanding "take, read," found before him a copy of Paul's *Letter to the Romans,* and his eye fell on the passage in the thirteenth chapter which includes the words: "not in rioting and drunkenness, not in chambering and wantonness, not in strife and envying, but put ye on the Lord Jesus Christ, and make not provision for the flesh, to fulfil the lusts thereof." This crisis precipitated conversion (386). He and Adeodatus were baptized by Ambrose at the same time (April 25, 387). While victory over the flesh was quickly achieved, Augustine later said that he still found pride a problem. He returned to Africa, became a prodigious writer, was the centre of what in effect was a monastic community, and died as Bishop of Hippo.

No other Christian after Paul was to have so wide, deep, and prolonged an influence upon the Christianity of Western Europe and those forms of the faith that stemmed from it as had Augustine. We are to recur to him again and again. Here we must simply pause to note that his *Confessions* became one of the most widely read autobiographies and maintains its place among the most moving and profound of the self-recorded records of a human soul and its struggles. His *De Civitate Dei*, written as an interpretation of history, originally as an answer to those who accused Christianity of being responsible for the fall of Rome to the Goths, remains one of the landmarks in the philosophy of history.

THE GEOGRAPHIC EXTENSION OF THE FAITH CONTINUES

In spite of the old and the new resistance, the spread of Christianity continued. By the close of its first five centuries Christianity had become the professed faith of the overwhelming majority of the population of the Roman Empire. The Jewish communities held to their ancestral religion, and here and there, usually in remote rural districts or mountain valleys, the ancient pagan cults lingered. In some groups and areas Christians were a smaller element than in others. Many of the nominal Christians paid only lip service to their ostensible faith and remained pagans at heart. Yet outwardly Christianity had triumphed. Moreover, Christianity continued to spill over the boundaries of the Roman Empire and was being carried to non-Roman peoples.

The spread of the faith within the Empire was furthered by more than one factor. As for several generations past, the momentum of early successes carried it forward. The Emperors were active in curbing the old faiths and in encouraging the acceptance of Christianity. Some were more zealous than others, but after Julian none sought to roll back the tide and the majority furthered it. There was no violent persecution of pagans comparable to that with which Christianity had formerly been confronted. Yet we hear of encouragement given by Theodosius I (reigned 379–395) to the demolition of temples. Theodosius proscribed not only sacrifices but also secret visits to pagan shrines and commanded that apostates from Christianity be deprived of all honours and of the right of inheritance and of conveying property by will. In many places temples were destroyed by Christians, often led by monks Early in the fifth century imperial edicts forbade making official holidays of the special days of the old cults, withdrew all privileges enjoyed by pagan priests, and commanded the destruction of temples still standing in rural districts. Later the incomes of temples were ordered diverted to the army, the destruction of pagan images was decreed, and surviving temples were to be given to some other public use. Pagans were commanded to go to the churches to receive Christian instruction, and exile and confiscation of property were made the penalties for refusing to be baptized.)

Jews were treated with lenience. Indeed, they were dealt with more mildly than were Christian heretics. Occasional sporadic outbreaks against them are recorded, but they were permitted to rear their children in the faith of their fathers and restrictive legislation against them was chiefly designed to estop them from what they were sometimes doing, winning Christians, usually Christian slaves in their possession, to Judaism.

Encouraged by the Emperors, bishops were active in the conversion of the non-Christians in their dioceses. Some required no incentive from the state, but were zealous on their own initiative, inspiring and directing missionaries. Thus in the fourth century Martin of Tours, whom we are to meet later as the leading pioneer of monasticism in Gaul, on becoming bishop of the see by which he is known seems to have found most of the surrounding countryside pagan. He led his monks in preaching, in destroying temples, and in baptizing. Victricius, Bishop of Rouen, a friend of Martin, established Christian outposts not far from the later Flanders. About the middle of the fifth century a synod meeting at Arles in the southern part of Gaul held that a bishop was derelict to his duty if he did not stamp out the worship of idols in his diocese.

Augustine was by no means the only convert of Ambrose of Milan. Son of a Prefect of Gaul, well educated according to the standards of the time, Ambrose (c. 340–397) was a civil official, Prefect of Upper Italy, when to his intense surprise and great reluctance and while still a layman and not yet baptized, he was constrained by the insistence of the populace to become Bishop of Milan. Entering upon a course of theological reading the better to fill his unsought post, he combined a Stoic background with Christian faith and became one of the most famous of bishops, administrators, and preachers. He was also a writer of hymns. He opposed the pagan party in Rome, won many non-Christians in his diocese, and encouraged missionaries in the Tyrol.

A contemporary of Ambrose, John Chrysostom ("the golden-mouthed," so called for his eloquence), whose dates were c.345–407, was originally headed for the career of advocate and was accordingly trained in oratory. Moved to seek Christian instruction, he was baptized in his mid-twenties, became a monk, and then, being ordained, rose to be the outstanding preacher in his native Antioch. Earnest, eloquent, he won widespread acclaim and at the instance of the Emperor was elevated to the episcopal see of Constantinople. In this post he sent missionaries to pagans, including the Goths on the borders of the Empire. Banished because of his courage in rebuking vice, he gave himself to winning non-Christians in the vicinity of his exile. He urged that the Christian owners of the great *latifundia* have chapels on their estates and work for the conversion of those who tilled their fields and vineyards. He held that the most effective means of conversion was the example of Christian living. "There would be no more heathen if we would be true Christians," he said.

In Alexandria late in the fourth century the bishop led in the destruction of temples and the Serapeum, the great shrine of Serapis which dominated the city from its hill, was turned into a church.

(Although by A.D. 500 the large majority of the population of the Empire were Christians, in some areas and groups, as we have hinted, the proportion was larger than in others. In Phœnicia and Palestine there were many pagans well after the close of the fifth century. Even in Antioch, one of the strongest Christian centres, at the end of the sixth century paganism still had a recognized head. Athens long remained a stubborn citadel of the pre-Christian philosophies and numbers of the Christian youths who flocked there as students had their faith weakened or destroyed. It was not until the year 529 that the Emperor, by closing the schools in Athens, formally put an end to that focus of pagan infection. Although the sack of Rome by the Goths in 410 dealt a severe blow to the pagan party in that city, it was not until the sixth and seventh centuries that some of the remaining temples were turned into churches. (At the close of the sixth century paganism survived in Sardinia and Sicily and missionary effort was still in progress in Corsica. In the seventh century there were pagans in the mountains between Genoa and Milan. At the end of the fifth century idolatry remained strong in Spain and the south of Gaul. While at the close of the fifth century paganism had by no means completely disappeared in the Roman Empire, its days seemed clearly to be numbered.)

The expansion of Christianity beyond the boundaries of the Roman Empire which had begun before the time of Constantine continued in the fourth and fifth centuries. Whether it was accelerated by the official espousal of the faith by the Emperors would be difficult to determine. In at least one area, the Persian Empire, support by the Roman Empire was a handicap. Rome and Persia were chronic and deadly enemies. The Persian rulers, Zoroastrian by religion, had their natural opposition to a growing, non-Zoroastrian faith heightened by the fear that Christians would be sympathetic with Rome. Their apprehension was not allayed by the fact that Constantine, posing as the protector of the Christians, protested against their persecution by the Persian state. In general, however, the continued adoption of the faith within the Roman Empire seems to have facilitated its spread outside the Empire.

This certainly was true of the barbarians who were invading the Empire from the North. They tended to conform to the culture of the Roman world, for it was the only civilization which most of them knew. Since Christianity was increasingly associated with that civilization, it was natural that they should adopt it.

The Goths were the first of the northern peoples among whom Christianity had a marked spread. That was because, being the earliest of the Teutonic peoples extensively to harass and invade the Roman provinces, they were also the first to be brought into continued intimate contact with the religion which was rapidly becoming the faith of that realm. It may have been that Christianity was first introduced among the Goths by Christians whom they had taken captive in raids in the third century. Two of the forms of Christianity with which we are to become familiar in the next chapter made headway among the Goths, the Arian and what came to be known as the Catholic. To these was added a third, that associated with Audius, a bishop of great purity of life who was banished for what were regarded as heretical doctrines and while in exile became a missionary among the Goths. However, most of the Gothic Christians were Arians.

The most famous missionary among the Goths was one of their own number, Ulfilas (c.311–c.380). When and how Ulfilas became a Christian we do not know. The usual conjecture is that it was while he was in Constantinople as a young man. It was a mild form of Arian Christianity with which he became acquainted and which he propagated. At about the age of thirty he was consecrated bishop of "the Christians in Gothia." What seem to have been his first missionary labours were north of the Danube. After a few years, seeking to protect his converts from persecution, he obtained permission to move them into Roman territory south of that river. Ulfilas translated part or all of the Scriptures into Gothic, presumably devising an alphabet for that purpose and thus for the first time giving Gothic a written form. It is an early instance of what was to be common in succeeding centuries, for more languages have been reduced to writing by Christian missionaries than by all other agencies put together.

Arian Christianity continued to spread among the Goths until most of them belonged to that branch of the faith. It was the Visigoths among whom Christianity was first strong and it was chiefly from them that it gained entrance among the Ostrogoths, the Gepidæ, and the Vandals. When these peoples settled within the Empire, as they did in the fourth century, a large proportion of them were already Christian. The fact that they were Arians while the bulk of the Roman population were Catholics reinforced a tendency to keep the two elements of the population separate. As, however, the inevitable acculturation and assimilation proceeded, Arianism gave way to the Catholic form of the faith. That process was not completed until late in the sixth century.

Others of the Teutonic peoples adopted the Catholic form of the faith from the very outset of their conversion. Thus the Burgundians, moving south of the Rhine early in the fifth century, accepted the Catholic Christianity of the provincial population among whom they settled. A little later the Burgundians who remained on the right bank of the Rhine became Catholic Christians. The Burgundians were thus the first predominantly Catholic Germanic people. Subsequently, when they established themselves in the Rhone Valley, they turned Arian, perhaps through contact with the Arian Visigoths.

More important for the future than the conversion of the Burgundians was that of the Franks. In the fifth century the Franks became dominant in the northern part of Gaul and the lower portions of the Rhine Valley. Late in that century their leader, Clovis, made himself master of much of Gaul and laid the foundations of what for the next four centuries and more was to be the most important state in Western Europe. He took to wife a Burgundian princess, a Catholic, and acceded to her request that the first of their children be baptized. He himself was eventually baptized, the traditional date being December 25, 496. He did not constrain his warriors to follow him, but eventually they did so. Clovis adopted the Catholic rather than the Arian form of Christianity, perhaps because he wished in that way to identify himself with the Roman provincials, Catholics, over whom he was ruling.

It was in the fifth century that we first hear certainly of Christianity in Ireland, that island beyond and yet near to the western bounds of the Roman Empire. The most famous of the missionaries to Ireland was Patrick. Patrick was a native of Roman Britain, but of what part we are not sure. He was at least a third generation Christian, for he speaks of his father as having been a deacon and his paternal grandfather a presbyter. We cannot be certain of the date of his birth, but the year most frequently given is 389. Presumably reared as a Christian in fairly comfortable circumstances, perhaps with a smattering of Latin, when about sixteen years old Patrick was carried away captive to Ireland by one of those raids which, breaking through the weakening defenses of the Roman borders, were harassing Britain. For at least six years he was a slave in Ireland and was set to tending flocks. There, perhaps through the solitude and hardships of his lot, his inherited faith deepened and he filled his days and nights with prayer. Dreams came which aroused in him hopes of seeing his homeland and which nerved him to seek and obtain passage on a ship. We are not certain of his life for the next few years. He may have wandered in Italy and perhaps spent some time in a monastery on an island off the southern coast of Gaul. It is clear that he eventually made his way back to Britain and was greeted with joy by his family as one risen from the dead.

Again there came dreams, now with what seemed to him a letter, "the voice of the Irish," with the appeal: "We beseech thee, holy youth, to come and walk with us once more." Heeding the call, Patrick returned to Ireland, but how soon and when we do not know. He was consecrated bishop, but again we cannot tell by whom or when. He seems to have had many years in Ireland, for he speaks of baptizing thousands and of ordaining clergy. Although he himself was not a monk, under his influence sons and daughters of chieftains adopted that way of life. His was both an arduous and a perilous missionary career, for he had to face opposition from fellow clergy and from armed foes. He seems to have reached a ripe old age. Other missionaries shared in the conversion of Ireland. That island became a centre from which, as we shall see, Christian influence was to radiate not only to Britain but also to much of Western Europe.

Christianity continued its spread among the peoples to the east of the Roman Empire, chiefly civilized folk along its eastern borders.

In Armenia the Christianity which had been adopted *en masse* by the population and its rulers became better understood and more identified with the nation's life. Before the end of the fifth century the Bible was put into Armenian and other Christian books were translated from Greek and Syriac. For many decades paganism survived in some of the mountain fastnesses, but towards the close of the fourth century a deepening and purification of the Christianity of the nation was effected under the leadership of Nerses, a descendant of Gregory the Illuminator. In the fifth century Armenia was dominated by the Persians and the overlords attempted to impose their religion, Zoroastrianism, upon the land. Numbers of the faithful suffered martyrdom, but by the end of the century the Church breathed more easily.

It was in the fourth century that Christianity seems to have been introduced among the Georgians, in the Caucasus, north of Armenia. Progress continued, apparently under the prospering encouragement of the ruling house. As in Armenia, a Persian invasion was accompanied by an attempt to force Zoroastrianism on the country, possibly to offset Christianity with its ties with the Roman Empire. In the fifth century, however, a king led a national uprising which purged the land of the fire cult and created bishoprics and erected many churches.

In Mesopotamia, on the debated border between the Roman and Persian

Empires, Christianity had its chief hold among the Syriac-using population. It made some headway among the Persians proper and a Christian literature arose in Pahlavi, or Middle Persian. But Zoroastrianism, the state cult, did not exhibit the weaknesses of the official paganism of the Roman Empire and offered more effective resistance to new religions, such as Manichæism and Christianity, than did the latter. In the first half of the third century, when Christianity was spreading fairly rapidly, a dynastic revolution which brought the Sassanids on the throne was accompanied by a revival of national feeling and of the associated Zoroastrianism. This dimmed the prospect for Christianity. From time to time, notably under Sapor II (reigned 310–379), persecution was especially severe: the number of Christian martyrs is said to have been as many as sixteen thousand. The fortunes of Christianity varied with the state of the political relations between Rome and Persia. During the recurring wars persecutions of the Christians, as suspected supporters of Rome, were intensified. The one exception was during the brief reign of Julian, when, in spite of hostilities between the two realms, Christians, out of favour with the Roman Empire, were regarded more leniently by the Persians. However, the wars with Rome brought Christian captives into the Sassanid realms and through them facilitated the spread of the faith. In the intervals of peace the restrictions on Christianity seem usually to have lightened. Some of the Persian nobility became Christians and one from that class is said to have been a zealous and successful missionary among his fellow-Persians and to have carried the faith even to the fierce Kurds in their mountain fastnesses.

Christianity was brought into Central Asia. By the end of the fifth century it counted converts among the Turks and the Hephthalite Huns and had bishoprics in the cities of Herat, Merv, and Meshed. From these centres irradiated caravan routes along which it might be conveyed to even more distant points. It may have been furthered by remnants of Hellenistic culture left in these cities in the wake of Alexander the Great.

A national organization was achieved for Christianity in the Sassanid realms. This was accomplished at a council held in 410. At the head was a Catholicos or Patriarch with his seat at Seleucia-Ctesiphon, the Sassanid capital. The state accorded him recognition and held him responsible for the conduct of his flock. Thus the Christians constituted a recognized minority enclave within the Persian domain. At times this led to state interference in the selection of bishops and there was the ever-present danger that unworthy aspirants for the office might obtain the post by bribery or political favouritism.

The distinctiveness of this Persian (or Assyrian) Church was further accentuated in the fourth century by doctrinal differences. The Persian Church was penetrated by the views of the relation of the human and the divine in

Jesus which are associated, somewhat inaccurately, with the name of Nestorius. We are to hear of this development more in detail in the next chapter. The views which were condemned by the Catholic Church in the Roman Empire are more accurately connected with the teachings of Theodore of Mopsuestia. They gained a strong foothold at Edessa. Expelled from that city, their exponents became teachers in Nisibis, the chief centre for the training of the clergy of the Persian (or Assyrian) Church. From Nisibis they spread throughout that church, but usually they were not extremely held.

In the fourth and fifth centuries the Christian communities in Arabia grew. Some of them were on the eastern borders of the Roman realms, some on the edge of Mesopotamia, some along the Arabian margin of the Persian Gulf, and others in the south of Arabia. They represented various strains of the faith, several of them far removed from orthodox or Catholic Christianity.

Christianity also obtained a foothold on the African side of the Red Sea, in Axum, from which the Christianity of the later Ethiopia or Abyssinia seems to have had its rise. The traditional account tells of a philosopher from Tyre who, taking with him two youths, one of them Frumentius, sailed for "India." On the return voyage they were seized by the inhabitants of one of the ports on the west coast of the Red Sea. All the ship's company were massacred except Frumentius and his fellow-youth. The two rose to high posts in the service of their captors and Frumentius set himself to the spiritual care of the Christian merchants from the Roman Empire whom he found there and built for them houses of worship. He went to Alexandria, asked the archbishop of that city, Athanasius, for a bishop, and Athanasius responded by consecrating him and sending him back to his flock. Whatever may be the truth of this story, it appears to be certain that Athanasius appointed one Frumentius Bishop of Axum. It seems probable that Frumentius won the king of Axum and that in consequence Christianity became the official faith of that state. This was in the first half of the fourth century. Thus was begun a connexion between the Christianity of Abyssinia and that of Egypt which was to persist into the twentieth century.

It is probable that in the fourth and fifth centuries Christians were to be found in India and Ceylon. Some doubt exists because of the uncertainty of the identification of geographic names and the confusion of the south of Arabia with India. If there were Christians in India, their associations were probably at least in part with the Tigris-Euphrates Valley.

WHY THE PHENOMENAL SPREAD OF CHRISTIANITY?

Why was it that Christianity had this amazing expansion? How shall we account for the fact that, beginning as what to the casual observer must have appeared a small and obscure sect of Judaism, before its first five centuries were out it had become the faith of the Roman state and of the vast majority of the population of that realm and had spread eastward as far as Central Asia and probably India and Ceylon and westward into far away Ireland? Why of all the many faiths which were competing for the allegiance of the Roman Empire, many of them with a much more promising outlook, did it emerge victor? Why, of all the Jewish sects, did it alone move outside the pale of Judaism and attract the millions of many races and cultures which composed the Mediterranean world?

The motives which led non-Christians to embrace the faith were many and varied. We hear of an entire family, headed by the grandfather, who became Christian because they knew of a case of demon possession which was cured by invoking the name of Christ. In the fifth century in one section of Gaul numbers of pagans were converted because, when a plague attacked the herds, the cattle of the Christians escaped or recovered and this was attributed to the use of the sign of the cross. On the other hand, we read of a son of pagan parents, also in Gaul, who later became a distinguished bishop, who was led to the Christian faith by struggling with the question: "What is the purpose of my life?" We are told of a fourth century Roman scholar and teacher of distinction who after prolonged and careful study asked for baptism. We have noted the fashion in which Augustine came through deep religious hunger and a sense of moral impotence. Augustine also said that he was impressed by the incarnation and the humility of Jesus, both of which he failed to find in the Neoplatonism in which he had sought an answer to his long yearning. Much earlier, in the second century, Justin Martyr, a native of Samaria, who wrote one of the more famous of the apologies for Christianity, and who won his sobriquet by his death for the faith, had sought wisdom through the philosophies of his day and became a convert when he found truth in Christ, Christ in whom the *Logos* had taken individual human-historical form.

One of the factors to which is attributed the triumph of Christianity is the endorsement of Constantine. But, as we have suggested, the faith was already so strong by the time when Constantine espoused it that it would probably have won without him. Indeed, one of the motives sometimes ascribed to his support is his supposed desire to enlist the coöperation of what had become the strongest element in the Empire, the Christian community.

Another cause was the disintegration of society, especially beginning with the last two decades of the second century, with the weakened opposition of old institutions to Christianity and a loss of nerve which led millions to seek security in religion. But why was it that of all the many religions which were competing and which offered to meet this need it was Christianity which was accepted?

It is clear that the institutions which Christianity possessed in the churches proved an attraction. In spite of the divisions which we are to describe in the next chapter, the Christian churches were the most inclusive and the strongest of all the various associations in the Roman world. They cared for their poor and for those of their number imprisoned for their faith. In times of distress churches would help one another by gifts of money or food. A Christian holding membership in a local unit of the Church would be among friends in whatever city or town he found others of his communion. The only fellowship approaching that of the Christians in solidarity was that of the Jews, and in contrast with the churches, which welcomed all, regardless of race, this was as much racial and cultural as religious. But what was the source of the churches and what gave them their strength?

Christianity was inclusive. More than any of its rivals it appealed to men and women from all races and classes. In contrast with the philosophies, which were primarily for the educated, Christianity had a message for the simple and the ignorant. It also won many of the keenest and most highly trained minds. Membership in the mysteries was expensive and therefore chiefly for the well to do. Christianity was for both rich and poor. Mithraism was only for men. The Gospel was proclaimed to both men and women. Why this inclusiveness? It was not in the parent Judaism.

In a combination of flexibility and uncompromising adherence to its basic convictions Christianity surpassed its rivals. Like the latter and to a much greater extent than Judaism it accommodated itself to the Græco-Roman world. It availed itself of Greek philosophy to think through its theology. It took over and adapted much from Judaism. In its organization it fitted into the patterns of the Empire. Yet, in striking contrast with the easy-going syncretism of an age in which one religion borrowed what it liked from its neighbours and all except Judaism permitted their adherents to share in the worship of the cults endorsed by the state, Christianity was adamant on what it regarded as basic principles. It held some sins to be unforgivable to Christians, among them any participation in non-Christian worship. As time passed, as we are to see, and the numbers of Christians multiplied, ways were found by the Catholic Church, the largest of the Christian communions, of declaring even the most serious of sins forgiven if there were true repentance, but severe penance was entailed. Some of the Christian groups broke from the Catholic Church in insisting on stricter procedures.

The constancy of the martyrs under torture impressed many non-Christians. As we have seen, by no means all Christians stood up under trial. Many wilted. Yet enough remained firm to give convincing evidence of a power which nerved children, old men, and weak women as well as stalwart youths to hold to their faith under gruelling and prolonged torment and to do so without bitterness towards their enemies. One of the apologists was obviously speaking truth when he declared that when reviled, the Christians blessed.

Moreover, Christianity worked the moral transformation which it demanded. Augustine was by no means the first or the only morally defeated individual who found victory in the Gospel. This was so frequent as to be almost normal. The apologists rang the changes on the welcome given by the Christian community to the tarnished, weak dregs of society and on the regenerating vigour of the faith.

It was not only to miracles of moral rebirth to which Christians could point. Pagans were also attracted by the miracles of healing wrought in the name of Christ.

Better than its rivals, Christianity gave to the Græco-Roman world what so many were craving from a religion. To those wishing immortality it pointed to the historic Jesus, risen from the dead, and to the promise that those who believed in him would share with him in glorified, eternal life. To those demanding high morality it offered standards beyond the full attainment of men and the power to grow towards them. To those craving fellowship it presented a community of worship and of mutual aid, with care for the poor, the infirm, and the aged. To those who, distrustful of reason, longed for a faith sanctioned by immemorial antiquity, it pointed to the long record preserved in what it termed the Old Testament, going back to Moses and beyond him and pointing forward to Christ. To those demanding intellectual satisfaction it could present literature prepared by some of the ablest minds of the day.

Whence came these qualities which won for Christianity its astounding victory? Careful and honest investigation can give but one answer, Jesus. It was faith in Jesus and his resurrection which gave birth to the Christian fellowship and which continued to be its inspiration and its common tie. It was the love displayed in Christ which was, ideally and to a marked extent in practice, the bond which held Christians together. The early disciples unite in declaring that it was from the command of Jesus that the Gospel was proclaimed to all, regardless of sex, race, or cultural background. The new life in Christ might express itself in many forms, but its authenticity was to be proved by high, uncompromising moral qualities as set forth by Jesus. Hence the combination of flexibility and inflexibility. As against the mystery religions, those cults which had so much superficial similarity to Christianity, it was partly belief in God, partly a theology, a metaphysic, which gave the latter its advantage, but it was chiefly that as against the mythical figures at the heart of the mysteries, Christians could point to Jesus, an historical fact. Through the Holy Spirit promised by Jesus came the moral transformations which were so marked in the Christian fellowship. The loyalty of the martyrs was to

Christ, and his example and the promise of eternal life through him were their sustaining strength. It was through the sign of his cross or by the use of his name that miracles were wrought. It was a true insight, even if exercised in derision, which named the members of the new faith Christians and in the city where non-Jews were first won in large numbers. Without Jesus Christianity would never have been and from him came the distinctive qualities which won it the victory.

We must not end this chapter without calling attention to what should be obvious, that in this victory of Christianity was also something of defeat. The victory had been accompanied by compromise, compromise with the world which had crucified Jesus, compromise often made so half-consciously or unconsciously that it was all the more serious a peril to the Gospel. In later chapters we must return to this more in detail and also to the attempts of Christians to meet the peril.

SELECTED BIBLIOGRAPHY

ON THE GENERAL SUBJECT OF THIS CHAPTER

For the pre-Constantinian period the standard work is A. Harnack, *Die Mission und Ausbreitung des Christentums in den ersten drei Jahrhunderten* (Leipzig, J. C. Hinrichs'sche Buchhandlung, 1902, pp. xii, 561), translated and edited by James Moffatt under the title, *The Mission and Expansion of Christianity in the First Three Centuries* (New York, G. P. Putnam's Sons, 2d ed., 2 vols., 1908).

For the entire period see K. S. Latourette, *A History of the Expansion of Christianity. Volume I, The First Five Centuries* (New York, Harper & Brothers, 1937, pp. xxiv, 412), with its footnote citations and its bibliographies. The present chapter is very largely a condensation and rearrangement of chapters III, IV, and V of this work.

For a Roman Catholic treatment see the pertinent sections in A. Fliche and V. Martin, *Histoire de l'Eglise depuis les Origines jusqu'a nos Jours,* Vols. I, II, III, IV (Paris, 1946–1948).

TEXTS OF THE SOURCES

J. P. Migne, *Patrologiæ . . . Latinæ* (Paris, 221 vols., 1844–1864) and J. P. Migne, *Patrologiæ . . . Græcæ* (Paris, 161 vols., 1857–1866).

ENGLISH TRANSLATIONS OF MANY OF THE EARLY CHRISTIAN DOCUMENTS

The Ante-Nicene Fathers (the American reprint and revision of the Edinburgh edition, Buffalo, The Christian Literature Publishing Co., 10 vols., 1885–1887).

The Church History of Eusebius, translated by A. C. McGiffert (New York, The Christian Literature Society, 1890, pp. x, 403). A translation of this most famous of early church histories, is especially valuable for its critical notes, although some of them are now out-dated.

See also a convenient collection, C. R. Haines, *Heathen Contact with Christianity during Its First Century and a Half, being All References to Christianity Recorded in Pagan Writings during that Period* (Cambridge, Deighton, Bell & Co., 1923, pp. 124).

Philip Schaff, editor, *A Select Library of Nicene and Post-Nicene Fathers of the Christian Church* (New York, The Christian Literature Co., first series, 14 vols., 1886–1890, second series, 14 vols., 1890–1900).

SECONDARY WORKS ON CERTAIN GENERAL ASPECTS

S. J. Case, *The Social Triumph of the Ancient Church* (New York, Harper & Brothers, 1933, pp. vii, 250). By a well-known expert, presenting stimulating, somewhat radical views.

C. N. Cochrane, *Christianity and Classical Culture. A Study in Thought and Action from Augustus to Augustine* (Oxford, The Clarendon Press, 1940, pp. vii, 523). A most stimulating discussion.

A. D. Nock, *Conversion. The Old and the New in Religion from Alexander the Great to Augustine of Hippo* (Oxford University Press, 1933, pp. xii, 309). Competent, with some fresh points of view.

G. Uhlhorn, *The Conflict of Christianity with Heathenism*, edited and translated by E. C. Smyth and C. J. H. Ropes (New York, Charles Scribner's Sons, 1879, pp. 508). Still useful although old and strongly Protestant and Christian in its bias.

PAUL

A. Deissmann, *Paul. A Study in Social and Religious History*, translated by W. E. Wilson (London, Hodder & Stoughton, 2d ed., 1926, pp. xv, 323). A standard work by an expert.

C. H. Dodd, *The Epistle of Paul to the Romans* (New York, Harper & Brothers, 1932, pp. xxxv, 246). With deep religious insight, by a thoroughly competent scholar.

T. R. Glover, *Paul of Tarsus* (New York, Harper & Brothers, 1925, pp. 256). A popular account by a competent scholar.

F. C. Porter, *The Mind of Christ in Paul* (New York, Charles Scribner's Sons, 1930, pp. xiii, 323). A work of ripe scholarship and mature religious insight, arguing the fidelity with which Paul reproduced and interpreted the mind of his Master.

FURTHER FIRST CENTURY SPREAD OF CHRISTIANITY

Hans Lietzmann, *Petrus und Paulus in Rom* (Berlin, Walter de Gruyter und Co., 2d ed., 1927, pp. viii, 315). Critical, careful, thorough.

A. C. McGiffert, *A History of Christianity in the Apostolic Age* (New York, Charles Scribner's Sons, 1897, pp. xii, 681). Standard, but partly out-dated by more recent scholarship.

SECOND, THIRD, FOURTH, AND FIFTH CENTURY SPREAD

A. Alföld, *The Conversion of Constantine and Pagan Rome,* translated by H. Mattingly (Oxford University Press, 1948, pp. vi, 140). A useful monograph.

A. Hauck, *Kirchengeschichte Deutschlands* (Leipzig, J. C. Hinrichs'sche Buchhandlung, 5 vols., 1922–1929). Standard.

T. Scott Holmes, *The Origin and Development of the Christian Church in Gaul during the First Six Centuries of the Christian Era* (London, Macmillan & Co., 1911, pp. xiv, 584). Carefully done.

H. Leclerq, *L'Afrique Chrétienne* (Paris, Librairie Victor Lecoffre, 2 vols., 1904). Competent.

H. Leclerq, *L'Espagne Chrétienne* (Paris, Librairie Victor Lecoffre, 1906, pp. xxxv, 396). Based upon careful research.

J. Mesnage, *Évangélisation de l'Afrique. Part que Certaines Familles Romano-Afriques y ont Prise* (Algiers, Adolphe Jourdan, 1914, pp. 98). Excellent, by a modern Roman Catholic missionary to Africa.

G. La Piana, *Foreign Groups in Rome during the First Centuries of the Empire* (*Harvard Theological Review,* Vol. XX, pp. 183–403).

W. M. Ramsey, *The Cities and Bishoprics of Phrygia, being an Essay on the Local History of Phrygia from the Earliest Times to the Turkish Conquest* (Oxford, The Clarendon Press, 2 vols., 1895, 1897). Based upon extensive archeological research.

AMBROSE

F. H. Dudden, *The Life and Times of St. Ambrose* (Oxford, The Clarendon Press, 2 vols., 1935).

CHRYSOSTOM

W. R. W. Stephens, *Saint Chrysostom, His Life and Times* (London, John Murray, 1872, pp. xiv, 474).

OUTSIDE THE EMPIRE

F. C. Burkitt, *Early Christianity Outside the Roman Empire* (Cambridge University Press, 1899, pp. 89).

F. C. Burkitt, *Early Eastern Christianity* (New York, E. P. Dutton & Co., 1904, pp. viii, 228). Popular lectures by an expert.

J. B. Bury, *The Life of St. Patrick and His Place in History* (London, Macmillan & Co., 1905, pp. xv, 404). The standard critical biography.

W. Germann, *Die Kirche der Thomaschristen* (Gütersloh, C. Bertelsmann, 1877, pp. x, 792). Scholarly, fairly critical.

J. Labourt, *Le Christianisme dans l'Empire Perse sous la Dynastie Perse* (Paris, Librairie Victor Lecoffre, pp. xix, 372). Standard.

Victor Langlois, *Collection des Historiens Anciens et Modernes de l'Armenie* (Paris, Librairie de Firmin Didot Frères, Fils et Cie, Vol. I, 1867, pp. xxxi, 421).

A. Mingana, *The Early Spread of Christianity in Central Asia and the Far East. A New Document* (Manchester University Press, 1925, pp. 80).

E. Sachau, *Zur Ausbreitung des Christentums in Asien* (*Abhandlungen der preus. Ak. der Wis. 1919 phil. hist. Klasse,* pp. 1–80). A scholarly summary.

C. A. Scott, *Ulfilas, Apostle to the Goths, together with an Account of the Gothic Churches and Their Decline* (Cambridge, Macmillan & Bowers, 1885, pp. xiv, 239). Excellent.

M. Tamarati, *L'Eglise Géorgienne des Origines jusqu'a nos Jours* (Rome, Imprimerie de la Société Typographico—Editrice Romaine, 1910, pp. xv, 710). Based upon extensive research.

W. A. Wigram, *An Introduction to the History of the Assyrian Church or the Church of the Sassanid Empire 100–640 A.D.* (London, Society for Promoting Christian Knowledge, 1910, pp. 318). By an English missionary to the Assyrians.

PERSECUTION

P. Allard, *Histoire des Persecutions pendant la Première Moitié du Troisième Siècle* (Paris, Librairie Victor Lecoffre, 1886, pp. xv, 524).

P. Allard, *Les Dernières Persécutions du Troisième Siècle* (*Gallus, Valérien, Aurélien*) *d'après les Documents Archéologiques* (Paris, Librairie Victor Lecoffre, 1887, pp. xvii, 411). Standard, by a Roman Catholic scholar.

L. H. Canfield, *The Early Persecutions of the Christians* (Columbia University Press, 1913, pp. 215). An excellent critical summary.

E. G. Hardy, *Christianity and the Roman Government. A Study in Imperial Administration* (London, George Allen & Unwin, 1905, reprint of 1894 ed., pp. xiii, 161). Carefully done with no extreme views.

K. J. Neumann, *Die römische Staat und die allgemeine Kirche bis auf Diocletian* (Leipzig, Veit und Co., 2 vols., 1890). Based upon the sources.

H. B. Workman, *Persecution in the Early Church* (Cincinnati, Jennings and Graham, 2d ed., preface 1906, pp. xx, 382). An excellent survey.

ATTITUDES AND ACTIONS OF THE EMPERORS

C. B. Bush, *Constantine the Great and Christianity* (Columbia University Press, 1914, pp. 258). Based upon extensive use of the sources.

The Life of Constantine by Eusebius . . . a revised translation by E. C. Richardson, in *Nicene and Post-Nicene Fathers of the Christian Church, Second Series,* Vol. I (New York, The Christian Literature Society, 1890).

E. J. Martin, *The Emperor Julian. An Essay on His Relations with the Christian Religion* (London, Society for Promoting Christian Knowledge, 1919, pp. 126). Objective, judicious.

W. C. Wright, *The Works of the Emperor Julian with an English translation* (London, William Heinemann, 3 vols., 1913–1923).

Chapter VI

CHRISTIANITY TAKES SHAPE IN ORGANIZATION AND DOCTRINE

Two of the most striking features of the history of Christianity in the first five hundred years of its existence were the development of visible organization and the intellectual formulation of belief. The two were so intimately interrelated that the course of their growth can best be treated together. By the time that the majority of the population of the Roman Empire had adopted the Christian name, the main features of the structure of the Christian community had appeared and the major verbal expressions of the Christian faith, including the Apostles' Creed and the Nicene Creed, which remained standard for the large majority of Christians from then onward, had been framed. While the faith was spreading and winning the population, the organization of the Church and the formulation of the intellectual statements of the faith were proceeding. Here were parallel, reciprocally interacting movements.

The Reticence of Jesus on Organization and Creed

So far as our records enable us to determine, Jesus gave little thought to a continuing organization and did not put the heart of his teaching in any single verbal formula which was to be binding upon his followers. To be sure, the word "church" is twice in the sayings of his which were remembered. Yet this is in only one of the Gospels, that according to Matthew, and it is not so much as mentioned in the other three. The one of these two sayings on which greatest stress has since been placed is that in which after Peter's declaration that Jesus was "the Christ, the Son of the living God," Jesus is reported as saying: "Thou art Peter, and upon this rock I will build my church, and the gates of hell shall not prevail against it. And I will give unto thee the keys of the kingdom of heaven: and whatsoever thou shalt bind on earth shall be bound in heaven; and whatsoever thou shalt loose on earth shall be loosed in heaven." Whatever else this passage may mean, it does not so much as hint that there was to be a series of successors to whom Peter was to have authority to transmit the "power of the keys." In the final chapter of *The Gospel according to John* we have the command of Jesus to Peter to tend and feed his sheep, but there is no indication that he meant this exclusively for Peter or that he gave Peter the authority to transmit the responsibility to others.

In still another passage, also in *The Gospel according to John,* the risen Christ is recorded as saying to "the disciples," presumably although not explicitly the eleven who survived the betrayal and suicide of Judas: "As the Father hath sent me, even so I send you. . . . Receive ye the Holy Ghost: whosoever sins ye remit, they are remitted unto them; and whosoever sins ye retain, they are retained." Yet here again there is not the slightest suggestion that the disciples to whom these words were uttered were given the right to hand on that dread power to successors. Here was no clear word of an organization which was to continue across the centuries. To be sure, on the night of his betrayal Jesus prayed that his disciples might be one and that all those who were to believe in him through their word might be one, as the Father was in him and he in the Father. This certainly implied a close and continuing fellowship, but it did not specify what visible structure, if any, that fellowship was to take. In choosing precisely twelve disciples for his intimates Jesus seems to have had in mind a community not unlike that of Israel, with its twelve tribes, a divinely chosen people. For this, however, he outlined no detailed structure nor did he sketch even its general outlines.

Still less did Jesus put the gist of his teachings into a compact statement which was to be remembered and repeated as final. The one set of words which he is recorded as giving to his disciples is what has been traditionally called the Lord's Prayer. That is a prayer and not a creed, and even it was not phrased as something which was to be held to with slavish accuracy, but as a suggested outline—"after this manner . . . pray," not "using these precise words pray."

THE NEW TESTAMENT IDEAL OF THE CHURCH

After his death and resurrection a fellowship of the followers of Jesus came into being which was called the Church. Beliefs about it arose almost immediately and it took a variety of visible forms.

The ideal of the Church appears again and again in the early Christian documents which compose the New Testament and which reflect the convictions of leaders in the primitive Christian fellowship. To these leaders the Church was to be inclusive and one. They shared the purpose of Jesus which was transmitted through *The Gospel according to John* that all believers in him should be as united as were he and the Father. More than once, carrying out this same conception, Paul spoke of the Church as the body of Christ. Obviously, as he saw it, it was to be one, knit together, each member contributing to the whole. *The Epistle to the Ephesians* declares that Christ is the head of the Church and dreams of the Church as ultimately being without spot, wrinkle, or blemish. The Christian fellowship, so the New Testament held, was to be a new Israel, a chosen people, but it was to be drawn from all mankind. In Christ both Jews and Gentiles were to be members of "the household of God," growing into "an holy temple." Not only was the Church to embrace both Jews and Gentiles, but in it there was also to be no distinction on the basis of race, nation, cultural status, servitude, freedom, or sex. It was to be gathered from every nation, and from all tribes, peoples, and tongues.

The Church As It Was

Actually, also as the writers of the New Testament clearly recognized, the Church was far from fully attaining this ideal. It was badly divided. On the very night of the prayer of Jesus for the unity of all Christians and only a few hours before that prayer was voiced, the disciples who were to be the nucleus of the Church were quarrelling over who of them should have precedence and one of them had gone out to complete his preparation for the betrayal of his Master. Even in the first generation of its existence the Church was torn by dissensions. In one local unit of the Church, in Corinth, there were factions between those who professed adherence respectively to Paul, Apollos, Peter, and Christ, and between rich and poor. As we are to see more particularly in a moment, the Church was deeply and bitterly divided between those who held that to become Christians Gentiles must adhere to Judaism through the symbolic act of circumcision and those who maintained, with Paul, that this was completely to misunderstand and pervert the Gospel. Before the first century of the Church was out, some were denying that Christ had come in the flesh, presumably foreshadowing movements, notably Gnosticism, which in the second century were to be major sources of division. Morally the Church was far from perfect. Some of those who wished to be regarded as Christians were adopting the attitude, technically called antinomianism, which was drawn from a misconception of man's response to God's grace and which was to recur again and again through the centuries, that the Christian need not be bound by any moral law. In at least one local congregation at the time of the common meal, some became drunk. We hear, too, of members of the Church being accused of fornication. In one congregation we have the spectacle, later to be almost chronic, of an outstanding member who was eager for power and control.

In this contrast between the ideal and the actual in the Church we have another example of the seeming paradoxes which are so familiar in the teachings of Jesus and in the New Testament in general. It is the setting up of perfection as the goal towards which Christians are to strive for themselves and for all men, paralleled by the frank recognition of the degree to which performance falls short of the goal.

THE ORGANIZATION OF THE EARLY CHURCH

The precise forms of the Christian community in the first century or so of its existence have been and remain a topic of debate. This is partly because in subsequent generations Christians sought in the organization of early Christianity the authority for the structure of their particular branch of the Church. It is also because the evidence is of such a fragmentary character that on many important issues it does not yield incontestable conclusions.

For the first two or three generations, the Christian community exhibited great variety. There was a consciousness, at least among some of the leaders, of the inclusive unity which, as we have seen, was the ideal set forth in the New Testament. Yet no central administration existed as the instrument for knitting together the many local units of the Church into a single articulated structure. The church in Jerusalem, as the initial centre of the Christian fellowship, endeavoured to exercise some measure of control, especially on the contested question of the degree to which Christians should conform to the Jewish law. To some extent it was heeded, perhaps after the pattern of the respect shown for the Jewish authorities in Jerusalem by the Jewish communities in various parts of the Gentile world, but it possessed no administrative machinery for extensive oversight. Its authority was more that of prestige than of precise canon law. Under these conditions, no comprehensive or uniform pattern of church practice and government existed.

Before the first century of its existence was out, the Church began to display certain organizational features which, developed, have persisted, with modifications, into the twentieth century. We hear of offices and officials. Prominent among them were deacons (from the Greek διάκονος meaning a servant or minister), elders (the English translation of the Greek πρεσβύτερος, from which the word presbyter is derived, and from which, in turn, comes the word priest), and bishops (from the Greek ἐπίσκοπος, with something of the meaning of overseer or superintendent).

It was early maintained that the precedent for the deacons was to be found in the seven who are described as having been appointed by the Twelve Apostles in the early days of the Jerusalem church to take charge of the daily distribution to the widows from the common store. While the historic continuity between the seven and the later diaconate has by no means been fully demonstrated, and in the New Testament we never have clear mention of deacons in the church in Jerusalem, it is indisputable that within a generation or two in some of the local units, or churches, deacons were regarded as characteristic officers, and it may have been that women as well as men served in that capacity.

The office of presbyter, or elder, may have been suggested by the organization of the synagogue, where elders were a regular part of the structure. In at least several of the local churches there was more than one bishop and the evidence seems to support the view that at the outset in some and perhaps all of the churches the designations of "elder" and "bishop" were used interchangeably for the same office.

Uniformity of structure was far from coming into being at once. In the earliest mention of what appear to be officers or leaders in the great Gentile church in Antioch, we hear of prophets and teachers, but not of deacons, elders, or bishops. In one of his letters to the church in Corinth, where he appears to be naming the offices in the church, Paul says nothing expressly of deacons, elders, or bishops, although some of his words can be so interpreted, but he speaks of apostles, prophets, and teachers. In his *Letter to the Romans* prophets, ministers, teachers, exhorters, givers (perhaps deacons), and rulers are named as what appears to be the order with which Paul is familiar. In another letter the list is apostles, prophets, evangelists, pastors, and teachers. In the first generation of the church in Jerusalem, James the brother of Jesus was regarded as its head, but not until later was the title of bishop attached to him. It is also clear that the church in Jerusalem had elders. It is likewise obvious that Paul exercised jurisdiction over the churches which he had founded. Whoever the author may be of the letters which bear the traditional designation of the first and second epistles of John, and this is much in dispute, he calls himself "the elder" and as such writes with acknowledged authority. He also speaks of a certain Diotrephes as loving preëminence in a church and refusing to recognize the power of the author.

In the fore part of the second century the picture began to change. While no single form of structure as yet prevailed, we now hear indisputably of what soon came to be the accepted pattern, a bishop governing a particular church and of at least one bishop, that of the church in Antioch, acting as though it were his acknowledged right to address himself with authority to other churches. In the first quarter of the second century Ignatius, bishop of the church in Antioch, while on a journey to Rome under guard for martyrdom, wrote letters to several churches, most of them in Asia Minor. In these is seen something of the organization of the churches and of the conception which Ignatius had of it. It is clear that in several of the churches which he addressed there was a single bishop. Presumably, although not certainly, there was only one bishop in a city. Ignatius enjoined obedience to the bishop. He spoke of presbyters and deacons as though they were the recognized officers in the church and commanded that they also be heeded. He declared that the bishop is representative of God the Father and that the presbyters are the sanhedrin of God, the assembly of the apostles. Nothing was to be done without the bishop and the Eucharist was to be administered either by the bishop or by some one to whom he had entrusted that function. Ignatius held that it was not lawful to baptize or to celebrate a love-feast without the bishop. He declared that he who honours the bishop shall be honoured by God. Ignatius writes as though the bishop, the presbyters, and the deacons had come to be essential to the existence of a church. Presumably that was true of such churches as he knew. These, naturally, were in Asia Minor and Syria. In his *Letter to the Romans* he does not mention any of these officers, but his silence does not necessarily argue that the church in Rome did not have them. The emphatic fashion in which he stressed these officers and respect for them may be evidence that the position which he advocated for them had not yet won general acceptance.

A letter from the church in Rome to the church in Corinth with which the name of Clement is associated and which may date from late in the first century and be earlier than the letters of Ignatius declares that Christ was sent forth by God, the apostles were sent by Christ, and the apostles, preaching through countries and cities, "appointed their first fruits . . . to be bishops and deacons of those who should afterwards believe." The letter also says that the apostles gave instructions that when these bishops and deacons appointed by them should "fall asleep, other approved men should succeed them in their ministry." The letter indicates that the bishops were appointed by the apostles "or afterwards by other eminent men, with the consent of the whole Church." It seems to imply that bishops were presbyters and that the church in Corinth had more than one of them. If this is true, the church in Corinth did not have the oversight of a single bishop as did the churches with which Ignatius was familiar. It may be that Clement himself, although the leader of the church in Rome, was only the chief of a group of presbyters in that city. In later lists he is given as one of the bishops of Rome in succession to Peter, but this may be reading back into the first century the institution as it existed before the close of the second century.

Another early Christian document, the *Didache ton Dodeka Apostolon*, or *Teaching of the Twelve Apostles*, describes a church organization which knew of travelling apostles and prophets and of resident prophets and teachers. It instructs the Christians to appoint for themselves bishops and deacons and to hold them in honour, along with the prophets and teachers. There were several bishops, not one, and no presbyters. It has been suggested that here was a transition from an earlier structure of the churches to the later one, either in communities apart from the main centres where old customs lingered, or perhaps mirroring the change in some of the larger urban churches.

In any event, the latter part of the first century and the fore part of the second century still saw variety in the forms of organization of the churches.

THE CHURCH OF ROME

Well before the end of the second century the Church of Rome was occupying an outstanding place in the total Christian fellowship. This was to be expected. Being in the capital and chief city of the Empire, if it were at all strong it would naturally be regarded with deference by a religious community which was found principally within that Empire. As we have seen, it appears to have been vigorous before Paul reached it. So important did Paul deem it that he felt it advisable when he had been hoping to come as a free man and not a prisoner to precede his visit by the most carefully thought out and deliberately written letter which we have from him. In addressing the Church of Rome, he declared that the news of its faith was already being "spoken of throughout the whole world." Presumably, since "all roads led to Rome," and the city was extraordinarily cosmopolitan and attracted representatives of most if not all of the many regions and races of the Empire, the Church of Rome would, through its members, have ties with many different portions of the realm. For several generations its language was Greek, the most generally used of the tongues of the Empire, and this would further its widely extended contacts. Although not founded by either, the Church of Rome enjoyed the prestige of the presence of both Peter and Paul, and what appears to be dependable information declares that Rome was the scene of the martyrdom both of the outstanding member of the original Twelve Apostles and of the chief missionary of the early Church. The epistle of Clement which we have already mentioned was written partly to ease a difficult situation in one of Paul's churches, that in the great commercial city of Corinth. It is evidence that the Church of Rome felt a responsibility for the peace of this sister church and that it believed that an expression of its concern would not be regarded at Corinth as an impertinence. It may well have been that it thought of itself as being under similar obligation to other churches. Certainly in the third quarter of the second century Irenæus, Bishop of Lyons, in Gaul, and who, coming from Asia, would not be biased by Roman origin, declared that "it is a matter of necessity that every church should agree with this church [i.e., of Rome] on account of its preëminent authority." This does not mean that the Church of Rome had the wide supervisory and directive functions which it later claimed and exercised through its bishops. However, the foundations for that eventual supremacy go back to the first century.

IDEAL UNITY AND ACTUAL DIVISION: THE CONTINUING PROBLEM

As we have suggested, Christianity early displayed one of the most striking features of its history, the contrast between the dream of complete unity, the unity of the kind of self-giving love seen in Christ, and division. No other religion has so high an ideal of an inclusive community of love. Yet, as we are to see again and again in the course of our story, no other religion has had as many divisions and as many bitter controversies between its adherents.

This contrast between dream and actuality was probably inevitable. It arose from the very essence of the Christian Gospel and was witness to the accuracy of the Christian insight into the nature of man and God's purpose. As the Christian faith sees it, man owes his nature to God's purpose and God's creative act, and God's purpose is to create man in his own image. If, as the Christian Gospel declares, God is love, the kind of love which is revealed in Jesus Christ and which is utterly self-giving, the Christian ideal must be the full realization of this love in individuals. Since to find its full expression this love must be both towards God and among individuals in their inter-relations, this love will give rise to a collective life of mankind which, if God's purpose is completely carried out, will be wholly controlled by love, love which arises from response to God's love. This is what is meant by the model prayer given by Jesus to his disciples: "Our Father which art in heaven, hallowed be Thy name. Thy kingdom come, Thy will be done on earth as it is in heaven." It is clearly implied in the commission to make disciples of all the nations, teaching them to observe all that Jesus commanded the inner group of his disciples. That love should be expressed first of all in the redeemed worshipping community of the disciples, and that community of faith and love is to seek to win the world. This is but a paraphrase of the well-known words of the Gospel that all who believe in Christ "may be one, even as thou, Father, art in me, and I in thee, that they also may be one in us: that the world may believe that thou hast sent me." This ideal has haunted the Church from the beginning.

The Gospel also frankly faces the sombre reality of man's sin, of the perversion of the free will with which God has endowed man, with its rebellion against God, its seeking to usurp the place of God, its self-centredness, and its basic corruption of man's nature. That sin, provoked by the unmerited love of God in Christ, is seen most dramatically and tragically in nailing Jesus Christ to the cross. By God's act in Christ, so the Gospel goes on to declare, his incarnation, his cross, and his resurrection, God has wrought the redemption of men and through His Holy Spirit is beginning to display its working in transformed lives gathered into a new community. But the individuals who compose that community are, as Paul so clearly saw, only in process of "being saved." They and the community which is the Church have not yet been entirely freed from sin, nor have they fully attained to the "high calling of God in Christ Jesus." The Church, as discerning Christians have long said, is still *in via* and not yet *in patria:* it is on the road, but has not yet reached its true home and goal and, presumably, will not do so within history, until that final culmination of history which is also the culmination of both God's judgement and His redeeming love.

Because of the compelling attraction of the ideal, compelling because it appeals to the nature with which man has been endowed by God, Christians are always lured by the dream of the complete unity of the Church and of its effective witness to mankind. By various roads they have endeavoured to attain it—usually by seeking to devise one organizational structure which will embrace all Christians, by verbal statements which will accurately and briefly put into words the Christian Gospel and to which all Christians will be induced to agree, by disciplinary measures to constrain all Christians to full conformity with the conduct to which the Gospel calls men, or by one form of worship. Yet so hampered have Christians been by the sin from which they have been only partially freed that each of these efforts has given rise to fresh divisions. The Lord's Supper, or Eucharist, which with its "table of the Lord" should be a symbol and bond of unity, by the very act of being made such a symbol has also become a symbol of division.

THE CONFLICT OVER THE RELATION TO JUDAISM

It was natural that the first major conflict within the Church should be over the issue of whether Christianity should remain within Judaism as one of the many sects of that faith, or whether its genius demanded that it become an independent and distinct religion. If Christianity were simply a variant of Judaism, Gentile converts to it should submit themselves to circumcision as an accepted initiatory step for admission to the Jewish community and as essential to sharing in the special covenant which Jews believed had been made between God and their progenitor. They should also observe all aspects of the Jewish law, including the Sabbath and the distinctions between clean and unclean foods. This was the conviction, held in moderation by their leaders but more extremely by others, of the majority of the Christian community which remained in Jerusalem after the persecution which began with the stoning of Stephen. On the other hand, an increasing number of Christians, of whom Paul was the outstanding spokesman, maintained that to insist that disciples of

Christ become members of the Jewish community and submit themselves to the Jewish law was utterly to fail to grasp the essence of the Gospel. They declared that in Christ and the Gospel God had done something quite new, foretold, to be sure, in the Jewish scriptures, but a fresh and unique act. They said that men were to enter into the fullness of life, not by earning it through the observance of God's commands as expressed in the Jewish law, but by faith in the love and forgiveness of God as seen in the death and the resurrection of Jesus. That faith would issue in gratitude and love towards God, and God's commands would be obeyed out of love and with no thought of winning a reward from Him. Many Christians in practice took positions between these two extremes.

Attempts were made to reach an agreement and maintain unity. Paul and his companion missionary, Barnabas, journeyed to Jerusalem to consult with the leaders of the Christians in that city, for that church, as the mother body, had, as we have seen, a degree of prestige. A compromise was reached which yielded most of what Paul had stood for. It did not demand circumcision.

The overwhelming majority of Christians took a view which claimed loyalty to Paul but which in practice had legalistic features and held to some aspects of Judaism. Indeed, for many of its adherents Christianity seemed to be primarily obedience to a moral code, a code which embraced some of the Jewish law, but which went beyond it and was, therefore, higher. Such, for instance, was the implication of *The Epistle of James* in the New Testament, of the *Didache,* and of other writings of the first generations of Christians.

Waning minorities, probably overwhelmingly Jewish in ancestry, clung to one or another variation of the conviction that disciples of Jesus should remain within the Jewish fold. The church in Jerusalem, headed by James the brother of Jesus, tended to do so. Indeed, early tradition declares him to have been highly regarded by the Jews. But he is said to have suffered martyrdom at the hands of the Jews in the year 62 and to have been succeeded in the leadership of the church at Jerusalem by another blood relation of Jesus. The church moved to Pella, a Gentile city east of the Jordan, and there survived for a time. Some of the Jewish Christians, referred to by one or more early Christian writers as Nazarenes, held that Jesus was the Messiah, the Son of God, and that his teachings are superior to those of Moses and the prophets, but that Christians of Jewish descent should observe the Jewish laws of circumcision, Sabbath observance, and foods. Others, called the Ebionites, maintained that Jesus was merely a man, a prophet, a spokesman for God, as were the great Hebrew prophets of the past. Although some of them accepted the virgin birth of Jesus, others are said to have taught that Jesus was the son of Joseph and Mary, that at his baptism Christ descended upon him in the form of a dove, that he then proclaimed the unknown Father, but that Christ, who could not suffer, departed from him before his crucifixion and resurrection. The Ebionites repudiated Paul, declaring him to be an apostate from the law. They used a Hebrew gospel of Matthew. There were several kinds of them. Some of these may have been continuations of pre-Christian varieties of Judaism. They persisted, as small minorities, until at least the latter part of the fourth century and perhaps much longer.

The waning and disappearance of the groups of Christians who sought to remain within Judaism made it clear that the radical newness of the Gospel was not to be obscured by reducing Christianity to a Jewish sect. Christianity was now unmistakably a separate religion, having rootage in Judaism and honouring the Jewish scriptures, but interpreting them as preparing for the basic and revolutionary novelty of Jesus and the Gospel.

THE GREEK MENACE

Scarcely had the course of events made it clear that Christianity was not to lose its distinctive message by absorption into the parent Judaism when the faith was confronted with an even greater menace. As it moved out into the non-Jewish world it was in danger of so far conforming to that environment that it would sacrifice the essential features of the Gospel. The threat was especially acute from Hellenism and the atmosphere of the Hellenistic world, for, as we have seen, it was in the portions of the population of the Empire where Hellenistic influences were especially strong that Christianity had its first major spread.

The danger was not conformity to polytheism, for against that Christians were quite adamant. It was more subtle and therefore more to be feared. It was the incorporation of some of the attitudes of the Hellenistic mind. One of these was the confidence in philosophy as the way to truth, or, in a less thorough-going conformity, the attempt to think through and present the Gospel in the categories of Greek philosophy. In the process the Gospel might be distorted or obscured. Another was the sharp disjunction between spirit and matter which was a basic assumption in much of Hellenism. This seemed to have come into Greek thought through the Orphic movement centuries before Christ. It was perpetuated through Platonism and Neoplatonism. By its presence in that cultural tradition, it had so moulded the thinking and the attitude of Christian converts from a Hellenistic background that it often came over with them. Through them and the continued study of Platonism and Neoplatonism it has persisted in the thought, practice, and worship of a large proportion of Christians.

In contrast with much of the Jewish tradition and, especially of Jesus himself, this attitude regarded matter, including flesh, as evil, and pure spirit as good. It conceived of man as a compound of flesh and spirit. To it, therefore, the goal of every man's striving must be salvation by the emancipation of the spirit from the contamination of the flesh. Here was a way of accounting for the presence of evil, that perennial problem for thoughtful and sensitive souls, which made a great appeal and had sufficient resemblance to the issue presented by the incarnation and the cross to attract many Christians. Again and again we shall find it as a recurring theme in the asceticism, thought, and mysticism of those who have borne the Christian name, among them some of the most devoted Christians, men and women who have been esteemed ideal exemplars of the Christian faith.

The Gnostic Threat

A somewhat related threat, Gnosticism, had wide vogue in the first few centuries of Christianity. Foreshadowings of it are recorded in the first century and in the second century it attained major proportions. As we saw earlier, Gnosticism was not a phenomenon which was to be found only in the guise of Christianity, but was widely prevalent in the Mediterranean world into which Christianity was ushered. This pagan Gnosticism was protean, taking many forms and drawing from a wide variety of sources. Into one or another of its varieties entered contributions from Orphic and Platonic dualism, other schools of Greek thought, Syrian conceptions, Persian dualism, the mystery cults, Mesopotamian astrology, and Egyptian religion. It was highly syncretistic. When combined with certain elements from Christianity, Gnosticism proved so attractive that, while no accurate figures are obtainable, the suggestion has been made that for a time the majority of those who regarded themselves as Christians adhered to one or another of its many forms.

The Gnosticism which essayed to knit Christ into its speculations included many different systems. Indeed, it is evidence of the power inherent in the Gospel and the excitement produced by it that it stimulated the formation of these multitudinous expressions.

Among the names that have come down to us as prominent in the creation of Gnosticism is Simon Magus, of whom we hear in *The Acts of the Apostles* as a magician in Samaria who professed conversion and was denounced by Peter for his attempt to buy the power to confer the Holy Spirit. Tradition, possibly authentic, declares that he was the father of several aberrant variants of Christianity. We also hear much, among others, of Basilides of Alexandria and of Valentinus, an Alexandrian who attained fame as a teacher in Rome and who had many disciples. Some of the Gnostics seem to have been men of better than average intellect and of deep religious feeling. We read of such schools as the Naassenes, who worshipped the serpent as the principle of generation, and their sub-groups, the Sethians and the Perates, the latter esteeming the serpent as midway between the Father and unformed matter.

In general the Gnostics believed in a *Gnosis,* which was not a philosophy which issued from man's striving, but a knowledge that had been revealed and was transmitted to those who were initiated into it. It had the fascination which for so many inheres in a secret disclosed to the privileged few. It professed to be universal, incorporating whatever of truth had been disclosed in any of the faiths to which mankind gave allegiance. It regarded pure spirit as good, but thought of that spirit as having become imprisoned in corrupt matter. Salvation was the freeing of spirit from matter. This salvation was to be attained by the teaching of revealed truth which was presented in the form of mysteries and which by stages was to emancipate the possessor and bring him back to the realm of pure spirit. Justification for the Gnostic beliefs was sought in the Christian and Jewish writings, allegorically interpreted, and in supposed teachings of Jesus which had not been committed to writing, but which had been handed down secretly through oral tradition.

To the modern mind the systems of which these were general characteristics seem complicated and even bizarre. In general they held that there exists a first Principle, the all-Father, unknowable, who is love, and who alone can generate other beings. Since love abhors dwelling alone, this first Principle brought into existence other beings, æons, which together with the first Principle constitute the Pleroma, "Fullness," true Reality. From this world of the spirit the present world appeared. According to one system this was through the work of one of the æons who, moved by pride, wished to do what the all-Father had done, and create something on her own. The present world was ascribed to a subordinate being, the Demiurge, who was identified with the God of the Old Testament. This present world, the world of matter, so this view held, has in it some traces of the spirit world. Men belong to this present world, and are compounded of spirit and matter, soul and flesh. Some have more of spirit than do others. Salvation, the freeing of spirit from the contamination of matter, is through Christ the redeemer. Many different accounts, conceptions, and interpretations were given of Christ. Some held that Christ was never associated with flesh, but that he merely seemed to be man and was really pure spirit. Another system conceived Christ as an æon. This view separated Christ from Jesus, but held the latter also to have been an æon in whom something of all the other æons was included. It also taught that another Jesus, sent to be the saviour of men, was born of the Virgin Mary. Not all men are saved, so the Gnostics went on to say, for many have little or nothing of spirit in them and in due time they will be destroyed. Others, having a portion of spirit in them, will be saved by being taught the hidden knowledge, or *Gnosis,* and through faith and works. They will be freed from the contamination of the flesh and mount to the Pleroma.

The Gnostics had no well knit, inclusive organization. They were too divided and too varied to be brought together. Some remained within the existing churches, teaching their doctrines, until they were cast out as heretics. Others formed themselves into separate congregations. These had special rites, distinct from those of the churches which did not hold their views, and some resembled the mystery cults which were widespread in the contemporary Roman Empire. Several were strictly ascetic in their morals. Others, claiming that, being predominantly spiritual by nature, they could not be corrupted, felt free to go to pagan festivals and to gladiatorial contests, and even to have irregular unions with women who had accepted their doctrines. Such at least were the accusations of their critics.

Obviously Gnosticism tended to minimize the historical element in Christianity and to divorce the faith from the life, acts, teaching, death, and resurrection of Jesus of Nazareth. It was a group of attempts at a universal religion which would take advantage of contributions from many sources, but which would hold as a basic assumption a sharp distinction between spirit and matter and would give to Christ a central place in achieving man's salvation. It was an effort, perhaps not consciously recognized as such, to acclimatize Christianity in a popular religious trend of the day and to show it to be consistent with it and a fulfilment of it. In doing so, by omission and interpretation it so badly distorted Jesus as to make him quite different from the Jesus recorded in the Gospels. Had Christianity come to be identified with Gnosticism, presumably it would have disappeared as the contemporary beliefs of non-Christian origin which were the outstanding features of Gnosticism ceased to have currency.

MARCION AND THE MARCIONITES

A movement sometimes classified, probably mistakenly, with Gnosticism, and even in starker contrast than the latter with Judaism, was that begun by Marcion. Marcion is said to have been a native of Sinope, a seaport in Pontus, on the south coast of the Black Sea, the country of the famous Cynic, Diogenes. He is reported to have been the son of a bishop and thus to have been reared a Christian. He came to Rome, a man of considerable wealth, about the year 138 or 139. He joined himself to the church in that city and made it a generous gift. He began teaching the distinctive views which brought him fame and attracted a large following in the church. However, he failed to win the majority and after a few years, probably about 144, he was cut off from the church's communion. Yet he carried with him a number of members and formed them into a separate church.

Marcion is reported to have been influenced by one of the Gnostics and Gnostic conceptions can be found in him, but much in his teachings was quite distinct from Gnosticism. To be sure, with the Gnostics he was a sharp dualist, but he drew the dualistic line in somewhat different fashion from them and his explanation of dualism was quite at variance from theirs. Unlike them he did not profess to possess a secret body of knowledge. Like them, and, indeed, like the Christian churches as a whole, he was deeply concerned with the salvation of men. This, however, he conceived to be not, as did the Gnostics, through initiation into a mystery, but by simple faith in what he believed to be the Gospel. He held that the Gospel had been lamentably distorted by the Church as he knew it, and he sought to recall the latter to what he was profoundly convinced was the simplicity and truth of the Good News.

Marcion insisted that the Church had obscured the Gospel by seeking to combine it with Judaism. He maintained that the God of the Old Testament and of the Jews is an evil God. Recalling the words of Jesus that a good tree cannot bring forth evil fruit, he argued that a world which contains the suffering and cruelty which we see all about us must be the work of some evil being and not of a good God. This God, whom he called by the Platonic term *Demiurgos,* a word also employed by the Gnostics, had created the world, with its revolting evils. This Demiurge, Marcion held, also created men, both their souls and their bodies. Marcion thus differed from the Gnostics in putting man's spirit as well as his body in the realm of evil. Yet, in a self-contradiction, perhaps as a result of his contacts with the Gnostics, he saw an antithesis between spirit and flesh. He also noted that the God of the Old Testament commanded bloody sacrifices to him, and, a God of battles, rejoiced in bloodshed and was vindictive. He taught that this God had given a stern and inflexible law for the governance of men, demanded obedience to it, was rigorous in his enforcement of it, and was arbitrary in his choice of favourites. "Good men," he held, were those who yielded obedience to the law of the Demiurge, but they, too, were the creation of that evil God. Marcion refused to evade the difficulties presented in the Jewish scriptures by the easy and popular device of regarding their text as allegory: he took them at their face value.

Marcion held that in contrast with the God of the Jews there is a second God, hidden until he revealed himself in Christ. This God is a God of love. Out of the pure mercy which is an essential part of his love, seeing the sad plight of men, he undertook to rescue them, beings for whom he had no responsibility, since they were not his, but were creatures of that other God, the Demiurge. This God of love, hitherto unknown to men, and perhaps even to the Demiurge, disclosed himself in Christ. Christ, so he taught, owed nothing to the Demiurge, and therefore was not born as men, the creatures of the Demiurge, are born, and only seemed to have a body. This view, technically dubbed docetism, from a Greek word meaning "to appear," that Christ was only a phantom who seemed to be a man, was, as we have noted, also found among the Gnostics. Nor was it limited to Marcion and the Gnostics, for it was a belief which was congenial to those who regarded flesh as evil and spirit as good and believed that the Redeemer, to be effective, must have nothing of the taint of the flesh about him.

Christ, so Marcion contended, came down from heaven and began teaching, proclaiming a new kingdom and deliverance from the rule of the malevolent Demiurge. However, those who were loyal to the Demiurge crucified Christ, thus unwittingly contributing to the defeat of the former, since the death of Christ was the price by which the God of love purchased men from the Demiurge and enabled them to escape from the latter's kingdom into his own. Christ also rescued from the under-world those who had previously died and who in their life-time had not been obedient to the Demiurge and thus from the standpoint of his law were wicked. All that the good God asks of men if they are to escape from the rule of the Demiurge is faith in response to his love. Men have been emancipated from the legalistic requirements of the Demiurge and of his creature, Judaism.

Marcion believed that Paul had understood this Gospel. In Paul he saw the sharp disjunction between law and grace, the grace which is the unmerited favour of God, which Marcion was passionately convinced was of the essence of the Gospel. He declared that the church of his day had obscured the Good News and he regarded himself as commissioned to proclaim the truth in its uncontaminated purity. To this end he made a collection of the letters of Paul, expurgating from them what he held to be the corrupting additions of later hands. He added to these *The Gospel according to Luke,* editing it in such fashion as to free it from what he viewed as accretions inconsistent with the Gospel. Here was an attempt to recall the Church to the primitive Gospel by summoning it to a restudy of the original sources. Marcion seems to have been the first to bring together an authoritative collection of the earliest documents of Christianity.

Marcion was also an organizer. He gathered his followers into churches. To the members of these churches all sexual union was forbidden. Husbands and wives were required to separate and chastity and celibacy were enjoined. Martyrdom was prized. Eloquent witness is borne to the compelling appeal of

Marcion and his teachings by the fact that the latter enjoyed a wide spread and persisted for centuries. Marcionite churches were especially numerous in the eastern part of the Empire. Although, because of the requirements of celibacy, they could be continued only by fresh conversions and not by heredity, they were to be found at least as late as the fifth century. Some of the Marcionites may have been absorbed into Manichæism and have contributed to the emphasis which in the West that religion gave to Christ.

THE MONTANIST MOVEMENT

A movement quite distinct from both the Gnostics and the Marcionites, but which had wide vogue in the latter part of the second century and persisted for more than two centuries and which brought division in the Church, took its name from Montanus, of Phrygia, in Asia Minor, who flourished in the second half of the second century. Because of the region of their origin, the Montanists were often referred to as Phrygians. They represented a revival of the prophets who were prominent in the first few decades of the Church, a call to Christians to stricter living, and a vivid belief in the early end of the world, in the second coming of Christ, and in the establishment of the ideal society in the New Jerusalem.

At his baptism Montanus "spoke with tongues" and began prophesying, declaring that the Paraclete, the Holy Spirit, promised in *The Gospel according to John,* was finding utterance through him. Two women, his disciples, were also believed to be prophets, mouthpieces of the Holy Spirit. The three taught that the Spirit had revealed to them the early end of the world, and that the New Jerusalem would "come down out of heaven from God," as had been foretold in *The Revelation of John,* and that it would be fixed in Phrygia.

The belief in the early second coming of Christ was not new nor was it exclusively a tenet of the Montanists. Ground for it was found in more than one of the Gospels and New Testament epistles and in *The Revelation of John.* Many held to the view that before the final end of history and the full accomplishment of God's purpose in the perfect doing of His will, a hope which was common to all Christians, Christ would return, set up his kingdom on earth and reign for a thousand years. The centre of this kingdom was often placed at Jerusalem. The return of Christ was associated with the resurrection and the last judgement. The conception of an age or ages of a thousand years' duration was not confined to Christians, but was also to be found in Judaism. Nor did all Christians who held the view agree upon the order of the events connected with the thousand year reign of Christ. The expectations associated with the millennial reign of Christ are technically known as chiliasm.

Not far from the time of Montanus at least two bishops, one in Pontus and one in Syria, were expecting the early return of Christ. The one declared that the last judgement would come in two years and those who believed him ceased to cultivate their fields and rid themselves of houses and goods. The other led his flock into the wilderness to meet Christ. Since the return of Christ and the last judgement were regarded as being so imminent, believers were urged to be strict in their living. Celibacy was encouraged, fasting was enjoined, and martyrdom was held in high honour.

The Montanist movement spread widely. It was especially popular in Asia Minor and persisted there and in Carthage into the fifth century. It was found in other sections of the Mediterranean world, including Rome, Gaul, and North Africa. It had itinerant preachers supported by the gifts of the faithful, and in time seems to have been fairly well organized, with a head living in Phrygia. It prized the records of the teachings of Christ and his apostles, but it believed, although not contradicting what had been said there, that the Holy Spirit continued to speak through prophets, and among these it included women. It stressed a high standard of Christian living among Christian communities into which laxity was beginning to creep.

The most eminent convert to Montanism was Tertullian. Born in Carthage not far from the middle of the second century, of wealthy pagan parents, he was widely read in philosophy and history, knew Greek well, and practised law in Rome. In early middle life he was converted and became a presbyter. Much of the remainder of his life he spent in his native city. There he wrote voluminously and was the first to employ Latin extensively on Christian subjects. Possibly because of the cast which his legal training had given to his mind, Tertullian's literary style was systematic, precise, and vigorously polemical. Pronouncedly orthodox, he composed an extensive treatise against Marcion. Early in the third century, in late middle life, he became a Montanist and remained critical of the majority church until his death, towards the close of the first quarter of the century.

The Development and Clarification of Catholic Organization and Doctrine by Competition

The popularity of Gnosticism, the teaching of Marcion, and the Montanist movement forced others who regarded themselves as Christians to develop a tighter organization and to give added attention to the clarification and formulation of their beliefs. At the outset, in the middle of the first century or earlier, all that was required for admission to the Christian fellowship represented by the Church was repentance, the affirmation that Jesus is Lord, baptism, and the reception of the Holy Spirit. The wide variety which was appearing in bodies which claimed the Christian name, especially the Gnostics and the Marcionites, seemed to call for a more detailed definition of the Gospel and additional tests for admission to the Church and continued membership in it. Thus came notable steps in the development of what was early called the Catholic Church and which soon, if it did not already do so, embraced the majority of those who thought themselves to be Christians.

The word Catholic as applied to the Church only gradually came into circulation. The earliest known use of the term is in the letter of Ignatius to the church in Smyrna. In this he declared that "wherever Jesus Christ is, there is the Catholic Church." We next find the term in a letter from the church in Smyrna written about the year 155, describing the martyrdom of Polycarp. There it is employed at least three times, twice where it might be taken to mean simply "universal," but once where it clearly has the connotation of orthodox. By the end of the second century the word Catholic was increasingly applied to the Church and in a technical manner, meaning both universal and orthodox. In the latter sense it was intended to distinguish the body which was regarded by its leaders as orthodox as against bodies and individuals which were thought of as heretics, in other words, professed Christians who were deviating from true Christianity.

In the development of the Catholic Church three motives were present. One was the desire to unite all Christians in conscious fellowship. A second was to preserve, transmit, and spread the Christian Gospel in its purity, that men may enter into the fullness of the life which it reveals and makes possible. The third was to bring all Christians together into a visible "body of Christ." In practice the three proved to be reciprocally contradictory, for in the process of defining the faith and of developing an organization bitternesses arose which were a palpable contradiction of the love which is the chief evidence of Christian unity. Those who regarded themselves as Christians separated into organizations which denounced one another and as an indication of their disagreement excommunicated, that is, refused to admit to the rite instituted by their professed Lord, those from whom they differed. They endeavoured to make of the Lord's Supper, the Eucharist, the memorial of Christ's sacrificial death, a sign and bond of unity, but by that very effort they rendered it an outstanding evidence of their divisions.

The claims of the Gnostics, the Marcionites, and the Montanists compelled those Christians who did not agree with them to seek to determine and make unmistakably clear what the Gospel is. To do this they sought, naturally, to go back to Christ himself. To determine what Christ had been, taught, and did they attempted, also quite understandably, to discover what had been said by the most intimate friends of Christ, the apostles, those who were believed to have been commissioned by him to perpetuate and spread his teachings.

They endeavoured to do this in three ways: (1) by ascertaining lines of bishops who were in direct and uninterrupted succession from the apostles and could therefore be assumed to be transmitters of the apostolic teachings, (2) by determining which writings were by the apostles or clearly contained their teachings and bringing them together in a fixed and authoritative collection, and (3) by formulating as clearly and briefly as possible the teachings of the apostles so that Christians, even the ordinary unlettered ones among them, might know what the Christian faith is, especially on the points in which the Catholic Church differed from Gnostics and Marcionites. Thus an impulse was given to what from that time to the present have been distinguishing marks of the churches in which the majority of those who profess and call themselves Christians have had membership—the apostolic succession of the episcopate, the New Testament, and the Apostles' Creed. These three features of the Catholic Church were by no means entirely due to the effort to ascertain what the true faith is: they were already present in embryo. However, their development was assisted and their form in part determined by the struggle to ensure that the Gospel should be preserved and transmitted in its pristine integrity.

APOSTOLIC SUCCESSION

In the fourth quarter of the second century, we have the case for the apostolic succession stated forcefully and clearly by Irenæus. A native of either Syria or Asia Minor, Irenæus had in his youth seen Polycarp, Bishop of Smyrna. Polycarp, he informs us, had been instructed by the apostles and had talked with many who had seen Christ. Coming to Gaul, Irenæus in time became Bishop of Lyons. Distressed by what he regarded as the errors and corruptions of the Gospel which he knew in Gaul and by the headway which he found on a visit to Rome was being made by them, he wrote an extensive treatise "against heresies," describing them and refuting them by setting forth what he believed to be the true faith. He insisted that the apostles had transmitted faithfully and accurately what had been taught them by Christ and had not, as the heretics asserted, intermingled with them extraneous ideas. He was emphatic that the apostles had appointed as successors bishops to whom they had committed the churches and in doing so had undoubtedly passed on to them what had been entrusted to the apostolic company by Christ. These bishops had been followed by others in unbroken line who were also guardians and guarantors of the apostolic teaching. He hints that he could, if there were space, give the lists of the bishops of all the churches, but he singles out that of the Church of Rome, which he holds to have been founded and organized by Peter and Paul. Peter and Paul, so he says, appointed Linus. Linus in turn, so Irenæus declared, was followed by others in unbroken line to the twelfth in the succession who was bishop when the book was being composed.

Writing in the first quarter of the fourth century, Eusebius, the most famous of the early historians of the Church, gave the lists of the bishops of several of the churches. We need not stop to enquire whether these were accurate. That they existed is evidence of the conviction which lay back of their compilation and preservation, that a succession of bishops from the apostles was assurance that the Gospel had been conserved and handed down and that it was one of the marks of the Catholic Church.

Bishops began coming together for consultation and common action. The first of these gatherings, or synods, of which we have record, although we are not entirely clear that it was made up of bishops or only of bishops, was held in Asia Minor to deal with Montanism. That movement was condemned as heretical and its adherents were expelled from the Church and debarred from the communion.

In its response to all three of these movements which it deemed heretical—Gnosticism, Marcionism, and Montanism—the Catholic Church quickened a process which was already in progress, the development of an administrative system which centred about its bishops. Gone were the days when in at least some churches presbyter and bishop were interchangeable terms and when there might be several bishops in a church, or, perhaps, a church without a bishop. Now bishops were becoming a characteristic feature of the Catholic Church, with a single bishop in a given city or area. If a city had more than one bishop, others beyond the one would be assistants.

The bishop was more than administrator. He also was in charge of the worship and supervised the entire life of the church within his territorial jurisdiction. As Christians increased the number of bishops grew. In some areas, notably in North Africa and Italy, every town had its bishop, and the bishops in one of these areas might number several hundred. However, another system was emerging, with territorial subdivisions, parishes, in charge of a resident presbyter or priest supervised by the bishop in the neighbouring city.

Whatever the organization, succession in direct line from the apostles was deemed of the essence of the episcopate. Even Tertullian, who became a Montanist, stoutly maintained that only those churches were valid which agreed in their teaching with those which had been founded by the apostles and where the faith had been kept pure by a succession of bishops going back to the apostles. Cyprian, Bishop of Carthage and a martyr in the third century, held that there was only one Church, that the episcopate founded upon the rock by Christ was in the Church and the Church in the bishop, and that if any were not with the bishop he was not in the Church. Moreover, Cyprian insisted that he who was not in the Church was not a Christian and that outside the

Church, authenticated by the presence of the episcopate, there was no salvation. The bishops were more and more becoming prominent as essential features of the Catholic Church.

As the third century wore on, and after the Gnostics, the Marcionites, and the Montanists had ceased to become a major menace, the Catholic Church continued to develop its structure. As early as the beginning of the second century a distinct cleavage had begun to appear between clergy and laity, and this in spite of the fact that in the first century every Christian was held to be a priest unto God. By the end of the second century the clergy had clearly become a separate "order," that designation having probably been derived from the designation given to Roman magistrates in a tightly stratified society. The election of a bishop was usually by the presbyters and other clergy of the city, was ratified by the congregation, and was approved by other bishops of the neighbourhood. When so chosen, the bishop was consecrated by other bishops. The bishop selected and ordained the subordinate clergy. Among the latter the chief ranks were presbyters and deacons. Below them were the minor orders, such as sub-deacons, acolytes, exorcists, readers, and janitors. Deaconesses were to be found in the eastern part of the Empire, with the responsibility of caring for members of their sex. In both East and West there were "widows," who were charged with the duty of prayer and nursing the sick. Cyprian, the famous Bishop of Carthage whom we have already met, while looking up to Rome as the chief church in dignity, regarded every bishop as having all the powers of the group and at most esteemed the Bishop of Rome as only the first among equals. But the Bishop of Rome claimed greater authority, and it was natural that the bishops of the larger cities, especially Rome, should be more prominent than those of the smaller cities and towns.

THE CANON OF THE NEW TESTAMENT IS DETERMINED

From the very beginning the Christians had revered the Jewish scriptures, had seen in them the preparation for Christ, and had read them in their services. Gradually, by common usage and consent, books of Christian authorship were also brought together. From a very early date several of the letters of Paul were read in the assemblies of Christians. The Four Gospels won acceptance, so that Irenæus, writing in the second half of the second century, while recognizing that some questioned the position of *The Gospel according to John,* stoutly maintained that there must be four Gospels, no more and no less. Marcion, as we have noted, seems to have been the first to assemble some of the Christian writings into a well-defined collection. This, as we have seen, included *The Gospel according to Luke* and some of the letters of Paul, edited to make them conform to Marcion's convictions.

It is possible that Marcion's initiative accelerated the formation of an authoritative collection by the Catholic Church. The Catholic Church obviously wished to have a recognized body of documents to which it could appeal as containing the records of the life and words of Jesus and what had been taught by the original apostles. As against Gnostics and Marcionites it could point to them for dependable data to determine what the Gospel was on which the Christian faith was based. The test for inclusion in the collection was authorship by an apostle or a close friend of an apostle.

Only gradually was universal assent given to the twenty-seven books which now comprise the New Testament. Some books were later than others in winning inclusion. *The Gospel according to John,* as Irenæus is evidence, was not accepted as quickly as were the first three Gospels. *The Revelation of John,* the only prophetic book to be admitted, was long questioned. The letters called *Hebrews, James, II Peter,* and *II* and *III John* were included in some lists but one or more of them were omitted in others. Several books not now among the twenty-seven were for a time here and there used in public reading as though they belonged in the canon. Among them were the letter of Clement to the Corinthians, already noted, the *Didache, The Shepherd of Hermas* (a series of revelations originating in Rome), the *Apocalypse of Peter,* and the *Epistle of Barnabas.*

It may be that *The Revelation of John* was viewed with suspicion and that the other writings of Christian prophets did not find a permanent place in the canon because of the distrust with which those prophets claiming to be the mouthpieces of the Holy Spirit were viewed by the bishops and their clergy. The Montanists, with their assertion that Spirit-inspired prophets continued to arise in the Christian community, were a challenge to the administrative regularity represented by the bishops, and their rejection by the Catholic Church may have accentuated the distrust for the prophets and their writings. Certainly prophets, accorded a place in the early Church next to the apostles, were no longer granted recognition by the Catholic Church. Inspiration through prophets was supposed to have ceased with the apostolic age.

The first list which has come down to us of the twenty-seven books which embraces only those which appear in our New Testament is in a letter written by Athanasius, Bishop of Alexandria, in the year 367. While it was not until long after that date that uniform agreement on the list was found among all teachers in the Catholic Church, by at least the end of the second century a body of writings embracing a majority of the present twenty-seven was being regarded in the Catholic Church as the New Testament and was being placed alongside the Jewish scriptures. The latter were thought of as the Old Testament and were interpreted in the light of the former.

It was, then, by the slow consensus of the Church that the New Testament was assembled and accorded recognition as especially inspired. It was not merely supposed actual apostolic authorship which ensured for a book inclusion in the New Testament. This had an important place. It was also by the test of experience through long use that the Christian community came to recognize in the writings which were admitted to the accepted canon a quality which distinguished them from those books which were rejected, a quality which to the Christian mind was and continues to be evidence of a peculiar degree of divine inspiration, the crown of the process of revelation recorded in the Old Testament.

THE APOSTLES' CREED

The present form of what we know as the Apostles' Creed probably did not exist before the sixth century. However, the essential core has a much earlier origin. It seems to be an elaboration of a primitive baptismal formula, the one given in the last chapter of *The Gospel according to Matthew*—"baptizing them in the name of the Father, and of the Son, and of the Holy Ghost." It may go back to an Eastern development of that formula, but more probably it had its inception in Rome. Certainly a briefer form, known as the Roman Symbol, was in use in the Church of Rome at least as far back as the fourth century. With the exception of two or three phrases it was known to Irenæus and Tertullian, and so was employed in the latter part of the second century.

The term "symbol" comes from a word which in one of its usages meant a watchword, or a password in a military camp. As applied to a creed, it was a sign or test of membership in the Church. Assent to the creed or symbol was required of those who were being baptized.

The Roman Symbol may well have been an elaboration of an earlier form which went back to the primitive baptismal formula, modified in such fashion as to make it clear that the candidate for baptism did not adhere to the beliefs in which Marcion, who had a strong following in Rome, differed from the Catholic Church. The opening affirmation, "I believe in God the Father almighty" (in the original Greek the word translated "almighty" means "all governing" or "all controlling," as one who governs all the universe), quite obviously rules out Marcion's contention that the world is the creation of the Demiurge and not of the loving Father. The phrases which follow, "and in Jesus Christ his son, who was born of Mary the Virgin, was crucified under Pontius Pilate, on the third day rose from the dead, ascended into Heaven, sitteth on the right hand of the Father, from which he cometh to judge the living and the dead," clearly do not permit the Marcionite teaching that Christ was a phantom, but assert positively that he was the Son, not of the previously unknown God, but of God who is also the Creator, that he was born of woman, and so from his conception shared man's flesh, that as sharing man's flesh as an individual human being he had a specific place in history, having been crucified and buried under a Roman official whose name is known. This, of course, does not deny that he is also the Son of God and so divine, but, as against Marcion, it asserts the fact that Jesus Christ was also fully human. The symbol likewise declares that the risen Christ is seated by the right hand of the Father, the God Who is the creator and ruler of the universe, so stressing the conviction that there is only one God, not two gods. By emphasizing the belief that Christ, the Son of the Father, is to be judge, the creed is repudiating, either deliberately or without that view explicitly in mind, the Marcionite contention that it is the Demiurge, not the Father of the Son, who is the judge. Of the concluding phrases, [I believe] "in the Holy Spirit, and the resurrection of flesh," the first was not in controversy and so was not amplified, but the second, an addition to the primitive formula, seems to have been intended as a protest against the view which counted flesh as evil.

Although the development was in part due to the conflict with the Marcionites and although several generations were still to elapse before all the phrases were added which make it as it stands today, it must not be forgotten that the Apostles' Creed had as its nucleus words going back to the first century and first explicitly stated in the post-resurrection command of Jesus to the apostles. It was meant to be simply a further interpretation to meet particular challenges as they arose. Thus it clearly is an expression of what was taught by the apostles, and the designation "Apostles' Creed" is not an accident or a mistake. Moreover, in those few words, "Father, Son, and Holy Spirit," is succinctly summarized the heart of the Christian Gospel—God Who is Father, Who once in history revealed Himself in one who was at once God and man and Who because of that continues to operate in the lives of men through His Spirit. In this is the uniqueness of Christianity.

The Continuation of Conflict within the Church

The methods to which resort was had against Gnostics, Marcionites, and Montanists to preserve the integrity of the Gospel and the efforts to further the unity of Christians in one fellowship were by no means entirely successful. To be sure, as organized bodies these three dissident groups eventually died out, although not until several centuries had elapsed. However, other causes of contention arose and, indeed, have continued to arise across the centuries. Some of them were healed without a visible breach in the Church, but others were so potent that the acceptance by all parties to the dispute of the apostolic succession of the episcopate, the authority of the New Testament, and the

Apostles' Creed did not estop formal and permanent division. Still less was the rupture prevented of that unity envisaged by Christ and such of his early exponents as Paul, that based upon love.

THE EASTER CONTROVERSY

An acute early controversy, one which ran concurrently with those aroused by Gnosticism, Marcionism, and Montanism, was over the time for the celebration of Easter. Although our first certain notice of Easter is from the middle of the second century, that festival, commemorating the resurrection of Christ, was presumably observed by at least some Christians from much earlier times.

Differences arose over the determination of the date. Should it be fixed by the Jewish passover and be governed by the day of the Jewish month on which that feast was set regardless of the day of the week on which it fell? This became the custom in many of the churches, especially in Asia Minor. In contrast, many churches, including that of Rome, celebrated Easter on the first day of the week, Sunday. It was the first day of the week when Christ rose from the dead and which because of that fact was early observed as the Lord's Day. Disputes also developed over the length of the fast which was to be observed preceding Easter in commemoration of the crucifixion and as to whether Christ's death occurred on the fourteenth or on the fifteenth day of the Jewish month of Nisan.

In various parts of the Empire, probably not far from the end of the second century, synods met to decide the issue. In general the consensus was for Sunday, but in Asia Minor the bishops held to the other method of reckoning. Thereupon Victor, Bishop of Rome in the last decade of the second century, sought to enforce uniformity by breaking off communion with the dissenting bishops and churches. Irenæus expostulated with Victor on the ground that the differences in practice had long existed without causing a breach in unity. Ultimately the observance of Easter on Sunday prevailed and probably the prestige of Rome was thereby enhanced. Yet the controversy, called Quartodecimanian from the fourteenth day of Nisan, long remained an unpleasant memory.

THE NOVATIAN AND DONATIST DIVISIONS

More serious were two schisms, one which began in the third century and which is usually given the name of Novatian, and the other which had its origin in the fourth century and is called Donatist. For both the primary source was dissatisfaction with what they regarded as the lax moral practices of the majority and both came into being as protests against the lenient treatment of those who had denied the faith in time of persecution.

In its earlier days the Church maintained rigorous standards for its membership. As we have seen, baptism was believed to wash away all sins committed before it was administered. After baptism, the Christian was supposed not to sin, and some sins, if indulged in after that rite had been administered, were regarded as unforgivable. Tertullian listed the "seven deadly sins" as "idolatry, blasphemy, murder, adultery, fornication, false-witness, and fraud." Both Hermas and Tertullian conceded that forgiveness might be had for one such sin committed after baptism, but allowed only one.

Modifications began to be made in this rigour. The guilty might obtain remission even for apostasy and sex offenses if they were truly repentant—although assurance of forgiveness and readmission into the full fellowship of the Church might be deferred until the penitent had demonstrated his sincerity by prolonged demonstration of sorrow for his sin. Pardon might be had through the officers of the Church. Those about to suffer death or who had endured imprisonment and torture for the faith were often looked upon as competent to assure forgiveness to the repentant, especially to those who had lapsed. The exercise of this function sometimes proved annoying to the bishops, among them to the Cyprian whom we have met as Bishop of Carthage. Again and again there were Christians who protested against this laxity. Part of the appeal of the Montanists was their insistence upon strict moral standards.

In the first quarter of the third century Callistus, Bishop of Rome, seems to have declared that no sin is unforgivable if the sinner is genuinely contrite. He is said to have appealed to Scripture for authority for his practice, finding as he did so ample precedent in the parables of the lost sheep and the prodigal son and in Paul's letters. He is also reported to have declared that the Church is like the field which has both wheat and tares and like Noah's ark, in which were many kinds of animals. In the next quarter of a century the principles of Callistus won wide although by no means universal acceptance in the Church.

In the middle of the third century the Decian persecution brought the issue starkly before the Church, for thousands yielded to pressure and compromised their faith. Many of them, terrified or deeply grieved by what they had done, sought readmission to the Church. In Rome the bishop, Cornelius by name, was prepared to permit the restoration of the lapsed. However, there was opposition led by Novatian, a presbyter of the Roman Church, no mean theologian, and of impeccable orthodoxy. Chosen bishop by critics of Cornelius, he gathered about him many who shared his convictions about exacting ethical requirements for church membership and rebaptized those who came to him from the Catholic Church. The movement spread and in part coalesced with the Montanists. Novatian appointed bishops for the emerging communities, and churches in sympathy with him arose in North Africa, the West, and especially the East. They persisted for several generations. In the fifth century there were three Novatian churches in Constantinople and even more in Rome. In the first half of the fifth century the Bishop of Rome took possession of their churches in that city and they could henceforth meet only secretly and in private homes. Yet their churches were still permitted in Constantinople.

The Donatist schism appeared after the persecution which began with Diocletian in the first quarter of the fourth century and had its main centre in North Africa. A Bishop of Carthage was consecrated in 311 by one whom the strict elements in the Church declared to have been a traitor during the persecution. These elements chose a counter bishop who in 316 was succeeded by Donatus, from whom the movement took its name. A number of factors combined to give the Donatists an extensive following in North Africa. It may have been that they were drawn largely from the non-Latin and the Catholics from the Latin elements in the population, and that the cleavage was in part racial and cultural. It is said that at one time they had 270 bishops. Synods called by Constantine at the request of the Donatists decided against the latter and for a time the Emperor sought to suppress them by force. Augustine endeavoured, without avail, to bring about a reconciliation. They regarded themselves as the true Catholic Church and continued at least until the Vandal invasion of the fifth century and possibly until the Moslem Arab invasion late in the seventh century.

Out of the controversy came the enunciation of the principle, formulated by one of the councils called to deal with the issues raised by the Donatists, that, contrary to the latters' contention, ordination and baptism are not dependent for their validity upon the moral character of the one through whose hands they are administered. This continued to be upheld by the Catholic Church.

A schism in Egypt about the same time as that of the Donatists and for a similar reason was that of the Meletians, named for the bishop who were their first leader. They, too, stood for a rigorous attitude towards those who had denied the faith.

As we have suggested, the majority in the Catholic Church took the attitude that no sin is beyond forgiveness if it is followed by true penitence. It may be that it was this conviction which led to the addition to the Roman Symbol of the phrase [I believe in] "the forgiveness of sins," now so familiar a part of the Apostles' Creed.

The Effort to Define the Trinity

A problem which long vexed the Church, and which even now has not been solved to the satisfaction of all who bear the Christian name, is that of the Trinity. As we hinted in an earlier chapter, through their deepest experiences the first Christians were confronted with the fact of Christ and of the Holy Spirit. How were Christ and the Holy Spirit related to God? The Christians were sure that God is one. Most of them were also convinced that in some unique way in Christ were both man and God and that the Holy Spirit was from God and is God. How could one hold to a belief in one God and make room for what had become known of Christ and of the Holy Spirit? The phases of the question which most engaged the attention of Christians were the relation of Christ to God and the work of Christ. This was as it should be, for Christianity had Christ as its central figure. Here, to the Christian, was the completely new and decisive fact in history. How could it be put adequately into the categories of existing human knowledge, thought, and speech? Inevitably Christians endeavoured to use terminology with which they were already familiar and sought analogies in existing philosophies and religious beliefs. Yet nothing which they found ready to their hands exactly met their needs. Christ was too novel to be fitted into what had been previously experienced without doing him violence. To Christians it was clear that he was fully man, an historical human individual, and that he was also God. How could these two convictions be reconciled?

As Christians wrestled with these problems differences arose which led to sharp controversies. The discussions and the controversies continued intermittently through the entire first five centuries and even beyond them. In their course the Catholic Church came officially to a common mind on most of the questions which had been raised and incorporated its conclusions in creeds and statements some of which to this day remain standard for the overwhelming majority of Christians. Yet the controversies led to fresh divisions, several of them of large proportions and some of which still survive.

Early Christian Views of Christ

The early Christians, including those who had been his most intimate companions, came to cherish very exalted views of Jesus. They named him Messiah, Christ, the anointed one. They called him *Kyrios* (Κύριος), "Lord." Indeed, the only creedal affirmation which seems to have been asked of the first converts was subscription to the declaration, "Jesus is Lord." While to those reared in a Greek or a non-Jewish Oriental background this term would bring to mind the many "lords" of the mystery religions with the assurance of immortality through being joined in union with the central figure of one or another of these cults, to those with a Jewish heritage the word *Kyrios* was the Greek term employed for the Hebrew *Adonai,* which meant God Himself, or, in one passage from the Psalms which Christians remembered, the Messiah as well as God. Sometimes Jesus was called the Wisdom of God, reminiscent of the *Sophia* ("Wisdom") in much of late Jewish thought which had been influenced by Hellenism, and in which Sophia had been almost personalized. Repeatedly he was called Son of God. In a famous passage in one of Paul's letters he is declared to have existed in the form of God but as empty-ing himself and being made in the likeness of man. In another well-known passage Christ is described as having been appointed by God to be "heir of all things, by whom also he made the worlds," and as "the brightness of his glory and the express image of his person." In the even more famous passage at the outset of *The Gospel according to John,* Jesus is identified with the *Logos* (Λόγος) or "Word," which "was in the beginning with God" and "was God," by whom all things were made. The *Logos* is described as having become flesh in Jesus.

Scholars are by no means agreed as to the source from which the term *Logos* came into this passage and, therefore, as to the precise meaning which it had for the author. Some maintain that it was from a strain in current Hellenistic thought to which several schools of Greek philosophy contributed, and which in Judaism had its outstanding exponent in Philo. This held that the God Who is far beyond man's knowing maintains His contact with the created world through the *Logos,* who is subordinate to God. Another view identifies the *Logos* with the Wisdom which is found in Hebrew literature. Still another conjecture sees the influence of religious conceptions in contemporary non-Christian Syria and Asia Minor and which stressed the unity of God and yet His nearness in the life forces.

What *The Gospel according to John* emphasized, and where it differs from all these other conceptions, is its declaration that the *Logos* became flesh, and became flesh in a particular man, Jesus of Nazareth. While in places it seems to view the *Logos* so incarnated as subordinate to God, it makes much of the intimacy of the incarnate Son with the Father and declares that the two are one.

The early Christians stated in various ways what they believed to be the specific work of Christ. "God was in Christ reconciling the world unto Himself"; "He hath made him to be sin for us who knew no sin that we might be made the righteousness of God in him"; "The blood of Jesus Christ his son cleanseth us from all sin"; "God commendeth his love towards us in that while we were yet sinners Christ died for us"; "Jesus Christ . . . the propitiation of our sins and not for ours only, but also for the sins of the whole world"; "God so loved the world that he gave his only begotten son,

that whosoever believeth in him should not perish but have everlasting life";
"For as in Adam all die, even so in Christ shall all be made alive"; he
"abolished death and brought life and immortality to light through the
Gospel"—these are some of the phrases which at once come to mind. Christ
was pictured as a judge. He was also named as saviour and as priest who
once for all had offered up himself as a sacrifice and continues to make intercession for the faithful to God "who spared not his own son but delivered
him up for us all." Jesus was also a prophet, speaking for God. He was king.
He was alpha and omega, the beginning and the end. As God had created all
things through him, so it was also the purpose of God to sum up all things in
him, whether in heaven or on earth.

These first century Christians did not attempt to make a complete orderly
statement of their beliefs about Christ. Here and there, as in *The Gospel according to John* and in Paul's *Letter to the Romans,* something of what they
believed to be the place of Christ in the human drama and in the universe is
set forth. Yet these early disciples were so carried away with the breath-taking
vision of what they believed Christ meant and of what God had done and
was doing in him that they could not put it in sober intellectual terms, nor
did they attempt to answer all the questions which Christians would inevitably
raise as they struggled with the problems presented by this unique and climactic
person whom they had come to know. In their writings were passages to
which appeal has been made to support divergent and even contradictory
views. Across the centuries Christians have continued to be moved by the
words in which the New Testament writers attempted to express what they
believed Christ to be and what God had wrought through him. Again and
again they have come back to them in the endeavour to enter fully into the
reality to which they bore witness.

CHRIST AND THE LOGOS

In the second and third centuries widely divergent views of the relation of
Jesus to God were put forward, even by those who regarded themselves as
being within the Catholic Church.

A group of these convictions centred on the identification of Christ with the
Logos. Not all those who made that identification agreed as to precisely what
it implied. Some, including the convert, Justin Martyr, whom we have earlier
mentioned, whose spiritual pilgrimage had led him through Greek philosophy
to Christ, and who had become acquainted with views of the *Logos* which
were akin to those taught by Philo, held the *Logos* to be "the second God."
To be sure, Justin Martyr's Christian faith led him to an affirmation which
was not to be found in Philo, that the *Logos* was incarnated in an historical

individual, Jesus Christ, for the salvation of men. Yet the *Logos* which had become flesh in Jesus Christ, while not different in kind from God the Father, was a second God.

On the other hand, Irenæus held that the *Logos* which became incarnate in Jesus Christ was the Son of God, the Mind of God, and was the Father Himself. In contrast with those against whom he especially argued, the Gnostics with their belief that Christ was a phantom, not man, and the Marcionites, with their particular form of dualism, Irenæus stressed his conviction that Jesus Christ was both man and God, fully man and from the beginning the incarnation of the *Logos,* that in Jesus God Himself suffered for men (who deserved nothing from Him), and that at the same time Jesus as man at every stage of his life, by what is known as *recapitulation,* or "summing up," perfectly fulfilled what God had intended man and His entire creation to be, and so, as representative of man, won for man the right to be recognized by God as having met His demands.

Irenæus is representative of a trend which, in reacting against the thinly veiled polytheism of the Gnostics and the two gods of the Marcionites, emphasized the unity of God. That trend, possibly reinforced by other factors, in some of its extreme forms known as Monarchianism, formulated a conception of the Trinity which was eventually condemned by the Catholic Church as untrue. Monarchianism was, in general, an attempt to stress monotheism against those who would make Jesus Christ, as the incarnation of the *Logos,* a second God, or would solve the problem presented to Christian thought by the belief in God the Father and Creator, the deity of Jesus Christ, and the action of the Holy Spirit by what was in effect tritheism, a belief in three Gods. While emphasizing the unity of God, the Monarchians also wished to honour Jesus and to explain the uniqueness of his life.

The Monarchians did not necessarily recognize a kinship among themselves, nor did they constitute a movement with a unified organization. While differing sharply from the Gnostics, they were, somewhat like the latter, diverse in the details of their views. Several of their leaders were expelled from the fellowship of the Catholic Church for their convictions, and others, more moderate, but with Monarchian tendencies, continued to be highly esteemed in that church.

In general, Monarchianism is usually said to have been of two types, dynamic (from the Greek *dynamis*—"power") and modalistic. The Dynamistic Monarchians believed that Jesus Christ was a man born of the Virgin Mary, and that in him was an impersonal power (*dynamis*) which issued from God. God's unity was thus preserved, for the power was not in any sense personal. Some of them have been styled Adoptionists, because they held that this power came upon Christ at his baptism, or, according to others, after his resurrection from the dead. This strain of thought was represented at Rome late in the second century and in the first half of the third century. Its leaders were excommunicated by the Bishop of Rome and attempted to found a separate church with their own bishop.

The most famous advocate of Dynamistic Monarchianism was Paul of Samosata, Bishop of Antioch in the third quarter of the third century, and also a civil official. Paul was accused by his enemies in the Church of loving pomp and power, of having acquired wealth by reprehensible means, of permitting in his entourage questionable relations with women, and of craving applause for his oratory. Whether these accusations were true we cannot know, for his critics were looking at him with jaundiced eyes. Apparently he sought to stress the humanity of Jesus. He held that in God are the *Logos* and Wisdom, but the *Logos* is not a distinct being and is what reason is in a man. The Wisdom dwelt in the prophets, but was uniquely in Christ as in a temple. Jesus was a man, but was sinless from his birth. The Holy Spirit was in him, he was united in will with God, by his struggles and sufferings he overcame the sin of Adam, and he grew in his intimacy with God. Three successive synods assembled to go into Paul's life and views and the third condemned and deposed him. However, he held on to his bishopric until, about 272, the Emperor Aurelian forced him to give up the church property, perhaps because he had been of the party of Zenobia, the famous queen in Palmyra, whom the Emperor had defeated.

Modalistic Monarchianism is also called Patripassianism, because it held that the Father suffered, and Sabellianism, from Sabellius, its most famous exponent. Noetus and Praxeas, who were early advocates, held that the Father was born as Jesus Christ, thus becoming the Son, and that He died and raised Himself from the dead. Sabellius held that Father, Son, and Holy Spirit are three modes or aspects of God, much as the sun is bright, hot, and round.

This form of Monarchianism made its way to Rome at the end of the first century and in the first quarter of the second century. It gained partial support from two Bishops of Rome, Zephyrinus (198–217) and Callistus (217–222). Although he excommunicated Sabellius, Callistus gave out a statement which declared that the Father and the Son are the same, and that the Spirit which became incarnate in the Virgin Mary is not different from the Father, but one and the same. While denying that the Father suffered, it asserted that the Father suffered along with the Son. It seems to have been a modified form of Modalistic Monarchianism. Hippolytus, a contemporary of Zephyrinus and Callistus in Rome, a prolific writer and a theologian of distinction, bitterly denounced the views of Callistus and, an uncompromising rigorist in morals, also accused him of being too lenient with sinners in the Church, since, as we have seen, he permitted the restoration to the fellowship of the Church of those who had been guilty of even the most serious offenses. Hippolytus, emphasizing the role of the *Logos,* was accused by Callistus of believing in two Gods. He would not recognize Callistus as bishop and for a time was set up by his followers as a rival bishop.

Monarchianism came to Rome from the East and here and there remained in Asia Minor, Syria, Libya, and Egypt for many years. It was especially persistent in Egypt. In the fifth century Augustine leaned towards Modalistic Monarchianism.

TERTULLIAN AND THE TRINITY

One who gave much thought to the problem presented by the relationship of Father, Son, and Holy Spirit, and who contributed substantially to the conception which became dominant, was Tertullian. With his legal mind, Tertullian had the gift of precise and clear statement. He also employed terms with which he was familiar in the law courts to give expression to Christian conceptions. He was polemical and, like an advocate, not always fair to his opponents. Often emphatic and startling, he was at times betrayed into inconsistencies. While pouring scorn on philosophy, he owed a great debt to the Stoicism in which he must have been nurtured in his youth, and his ideas were sometimes moulded by Stoic thought and expressed in Stoic terms. Yet he sought to base his beliefs squarely upon the Scriptures and argued from Scriptural passages and texts.

Like the Monarchians, whom he attacked, Tertullian believed in the *monarchia,* or sole government, of God. As to the Monarchians, so to him, God is one. In connection with God Tertullian employed the Latin word *substantia,* taken from Roman legal terminology and meaning a man's status in a community. He declared that in his *substantia,* or substance, God is one. Father, Son, and Holy Spirit, so Tertullian said, are three *personæ,* or persons. In *persona* Tertullian seemed to have in mind the use of that word in Roman law, where it meant a party in a legal action. These *personæ,* or parties, have their place in the οἰκονομία (economy), or administrative activity of God. They are seen in the government through which the *monarchia,* the rule of the one God, operates. Here is unity of *substantia,* but a unity distributed in a trinity, a unity of substance, but a trinity in form and in aspect. Before the world was created, Tertullian went on to say, God was alone, but always, since God is rational, there was in Him Reason, the Greek *Logos.* This Reason was God's own thought. The Reason expressed itself in Word, Word which consists of Reason. This Reason or Word is identical with what the Scriptures call Wisdom. Wisdom and Reason became also the Son of God. Yet there was a time when the Reason had not yet expressed itself in Word, when, namely, the Son was not. Here was a point which, as we are to see, later became a centre of contention. The Son was conceived by Tertullian as being subordinate to the Father, and the Holy Spirit proceeded from the Father through the Son.

In Jesus, so Tertullian averred, quoting *The Gospel according to John,* the Word became incarnate. Yet in Jesus the divine and the human did not fuse, as do gold and silver to form a new metal, *electrum,* for in that case Jesus would be a *tertium quid,* a third something which would be neither God nor man. Instead Jesus was both God and man. In Jesus Christ there is one *persona,* but two "substances" or natures, the divine and the human, the Spirit and the flesh. In the one "person," Jesus, the Spirit and the flesh exist together, without either the Spirit becoming flesh or flesh becoming Spirit. Yet, so Tertullian insisted, Jesus Christ was only one "person." Christ was merely a designation, meaning the anointed, and did not imply a person distinct from Jesus as the adoptionists had argued. Here, as in his use of *substantia* and *persona,* Tertullian contributed to later creeds through which the Catholic Church expressed its faith.

Tertullian aided in formulating and probably also in part expressed the theological convictions which prevailed in the western part of the Empire. Certainly that part of the Church was not so torn by the theological controversies of the fourth and fifth centuries as were the Eastern portions of the Church. This may have been because the Latin mind was less speculative and more practical and ethical than was the Hellenistic mind of the East. It may be significant that the greatest schisms over questions of morals and discipline, the Novatian and Donatist, had their rise in the West, while the main divisions over speculative theology, divisions which we are soon to describe, had their birth in the East.

THE GREAT ALEXANDRIANS: CLEMENT

While Tertullian was writing in Carthage there was beginning to flower in Alexandria a school of Christian thought which was to contribute even more than did he to the intellectual formulation of the Christian faith. Alexandria was one of the chief cities of the Roman Empire. Founded by Alexander the Great in the fourth century before Christ, it had become a cosmopolitan centre of commerce and of Hellenistic culture. Here was one of the great libraries of the world. Here Greek and Oriental philosophies met and here the latest of the Græco-Roman non-Christian philosophies, Neoplatonism, was born. Here the Jewish Philo had lived and had interpreted his hereditary faith in Greek forms. In the Museum was the equivalent of a university, famous throughout the Græco-Roman world. Before the end of the second century Christianity was represented by vigorous but divided communities. Alexandria was a stronghold of the Catholic Church and Gnosticism also flourished. In contrast with Tertullian, who, although influenced by Stoicism, professed to scorn philosophy, in Alexandria Christian thinkers regarded Greek philosophy as a tool to be used and the greatest of them became experts in it.

In Alexandria the main focus and stimulus to Christian intellectual life was in a catechetical school, made famous through two of its heads, Clement and Origen. This catechetical school was already in existence late in the second century. As its name indicates, its primary purpose was the instruction of candidates for Church membership in the principles of the Christian faith. Yet it also became a centre for advanced and creative thought and extensive literary activity. The first head of the school of whom we hear was Pantænus, a Stoic philosopher who had become a Christian. His most distinguished pupil was Titus Flavius Clement, a contemporary of Tertullian.

We do not know the precise year or place of Clement's birth or death. He may have been a native of Athens. It seems certain that he was born a pagan and that he was reared in the atmosphere of Hellenistic culture and thought. Possessed of an eager, inquiring mind, Clement appears to have conformed gladly to the eclectic temper of the Græco-Roman world of his day. He dipped into the various philosophical schools with which he came into contact and read extensively in some of them, notably in Platonism. Either before or after he became a Christian, he travelled widely in the eastern part of the Empire, seeking out those who could tell him what the apostles had taught. He was especially attracted by Pantænus and succeeded the latter as head of the catechetical school. Again exact dates are uncertain, but the last decade of the second century appears to have seen the height of Clement's Alexandrian career. He left Alexandria some time before the year 203, perhaps because of a persecution instituted by the Emperor Severus. We hear of him in Jerusalem and Antioch, called "the blessed presbyter," and praised by the Bishop of Jerusalem as having "built up and strengthened the Church of the Lord." When and where he died we cannot say.

Clement's three major surviving works are the *Protreptikos,* urging pagans to become Christians, the *Paidagogos,* translated, but not with entire accuracy, as the *Instructor,* intended to teach Christians the kind of conduct to be expected of those of their faith, and the *Stromateis,* or miscellanies, an admittedly poorly organized collection of notes, giving more advanced instruction in Christianity.

In these books Clement so far conceded to those Christians who cherished an aversion to philosophy as to agree with Paul that "the wisdom of the world is foolishness with God," and to admit that Jeremiah was right in insisting that the wise man is not to glory in his wisdom. Yet he contended that the philosophy of the Greeks was a preparation for the Gospel, to those who were familiar with it paving the way for perfection in Christ. He held that God is the source of all good things, of philosophy as well as of the Old and New Testaments. Indeed, he held that the Greek philosophers had learned much from Moses. It is possible, so he said, for one who is unlearned to became a Christian believer, but it is impossible for one without learning to comprehend fully what has been made known in the Christian faith. While he repudiated those who are usually called Gnostics, he held that there is a truly Christian *Gnosis,* or knowledge, a *Gnosis* which comes by faith and not through reason. He who has this *Gnosis,* so Clement declares, imitates God so far as possible, exercises self-restraint, loves God and his neighbour, and does good, not out of fear, but out of love. The Christian, Clement says, will gladly learn all that he can from all branches of human knowledge, whether music, mathematics, astronomy, dialectics, or Greek philosophy.

God, so Clement held, is knowable only through the *Logos,* His mind. The *Logos* has always existed and is the perfect mirror of God. The *Logos* is the face of God by whom God is manifested and made known. The *Logos* inspired the philosophers. Jesus is the *Logos,* the Word, who is holy God, the guide to all humanity, the *paidagogos,* or instructor, of Christians. Clement said that the *Logos* had shed his blood to save humanity. Yet Clement seems not to have thought of Jesus as really a man, but as merely in human form because he chose to appear so. Clement spoke of the Holy Spirit, but in such fashion that it is difficult to gain a clear picture of what he conceived the Spirit to be. He declared that "the universal Father is one, and one the universal Word" (*Logos*), "and the Holy Spirit is one and the same everywhere, and one is the only virgin mother . . . the Church." He affirmed that the Lord Jesus is the Word (*Logos*) of God, the Spirit made flesh.

Like Tertullian, Clement believed that every individual is free and is able to respond to God or to refuse to do so. Man may and does miss the mark, but he is capable of repentance. Yet, like Tertullian, he taught that after the initial repentance when one becomes a Christian only a single additional repentance is possible for a grievous sin.

THE GREAT ALEXANDRIANS: ORIGEN

Clement's successor as head of the catechetical school in Alexandria, Origen, was to be much more influential than he. His was, indeed, one of the greatest of Christian minds.

Origen was born of Christian parents, probably not far from the year 185.

A precocious child and the oldest of seven sons, he was instructed by his father in the Scriptures and in Greek learning. Possessed of an eager mind, he perplexed his father by questions about the deeper meanings which he believed lay behind the words of Holy Writ. When Origen was slightly less than seventeen years of age, his father was imprisoned and killed and the family's property was confiscated in the persecution by Severus which seems to have been the occasion for the termination of Clement's residence in Alexandria. In his youthful ardour, as we have seen, Origen wished martyrdom and was prevented only by his mother's firmness in hiding all his clothing and thus compelling him to remain at home. After his father's death, Origen continued his study of Greek literature and in part earned his living by teaching it.

Since, because of the persecution, no one was left in Alexandria to give instruction in the Christian faith to those who sought it, Origen began to undertake it and in his eighteenth year was in charge of the catechetical school, a post in which he was confirmed by the bishop. During the renewed persecution he boldly visited those imprisoned for their faith and accompanied some as they went to their death. He himself escaped only by shifting his home from house to house. He lived with extreme asceticism, curtailing his hours of sleep and giving himself exclusively to the catechetical school and to the continued study of the Scriptures and of Greek philosophy, including Neoplatonism. Partly to avoid the possibility of scandal in teaching women catechumens, he made himself a eunuch.

Origen visited Rome and Arabia and, later, Greece and Palestine. While in Palestine he was ordained a presbyter by two friendly bishops. The Bishop of Alexandria regarded this act as a flagrant disregard of his jurisdiction and had synods banish Origen from his see and, so far as possible, depose him from the priesthood.

Henceforward Origen made his headquarters in Cæsarea in Palestine. There he taught and wrote and from there he made occasional journeys. During the Decian persecution he was imprisoned and tortured. He was released, but his health was broken and not long after the persecution he died, in his seventieth year, and was buried at Tyre.

A superb teacher, he had a profound influence upon his students. From them and through his writings issued currents which were to help mould Christian thought for generations.

Origen was an indefatigable worker and wrote prodigiously. The better to study the Old Testament, he learned Hebrew, and in his *Hexapla* placed in parallel columns the Hebrew text and various Greek translations of the Old Testament. He wrote many commentaries on the Scriptures. Believing the Scriptures to be the word of God, he held that nothing in them was to be believed which is unworthy of God. He saw in the Scriptures three levels of meaning: first, the common or historical sense which is on the surface for even the simple-minded; second, the soul of the Scriptures which edifies those who perceive it; and third, for the perfect, a meaning hidden under what superficially is repugnant to the conscience or the intellect but which, discerned, can be expressed by allegory. The allegorical interpretation of the Scriptures was by no means new, but Origen gave it a fresh impetus. Origen's *Against Celsus* was evoked by the most penetrating criticism of Christianity produced in the Græco-Roman world of which we know and, in turn, was the ablest defense of Christianity which had thus far appeared. In his *Peri Archon* (*On First Principles*) which we have in full only in a Latin translation under the title *De Principiis,* and which somewhat altered the original, Origen gave to the Church its first orderly comprehensive statement of the Christian faith. In his literary labours he was assisted by a substantial body of amanuenses made possible by the generous financial aid of a friend.

Inevitably, like so many of the early Christian thinkers, nurtured as they were in Greek philosophy, and, indeed, like still others in succeeding centuries who were familiar with Greek thought, in his writings and in the formulation of his religious beliefs Origen bore the unmistakable impress of the Greek heritage. Yet Origen believed that he found the truth primarily in the Scriptures and in what had been transmitted in orderly succession from the apostles. The apostolic teaching, Origen held, is (1) that there is one God, the Father, just and good, the creator of all things; (2) that Jesus Christ, the God-man, was the incarnation of the *Logos* who is wisdom, word, light, and truth, coeternal with the Father, for since the Father is always Father there must always have been a Son, but who, since he is the image of the Father, is dependent upon the Father and subordinate to Him; Jesus Christ was not, as so many of the Gnostics held, a phantom, but was truly born of a virgin and the Holy Spirit, truly suffered, truly died, truly rose from the dead, conversed with his disciples, and was taken up into heaven; (3) that the Holy Spirit is associated in honour and dignity with the Father and the Son and that he is uncreated. Origen distinguished the Father, the Son, and the Holy Spirit from one another, although they constitute a unity. He taught that men derive their existence from the Father, their rational nature from the Son, and their holiness, or sanctification, from the Holy Spirit.

Origen held that there had been an earlier stage of the creation, a spiritual world, in which there were spiritual and rational beings to whom God had given free will. Some of these did not turn away from God, but others used their free will to do so. To punish and reform the fallen, God created the present visible world. Salvation was the work of the Son, the *Logos,* who in becoming man united with a human soul which had not sinned in its previous existence. The Saviour, the God-man, was the self-revelation of God, making evident to sinful men what God really is. The Saviour also gave himself as a ransom for the lost and by doing so conquered evil in the hearts of the fallen. He is a propitiatory offering to God. The Holy Spirit brings light to those who believe.

Origen taught that ultimately all the spirits who have fallen away from God will be restored to full harmony with Him. This can come about only with their coöperation, for they have freedom to accept or to reject the redemption wrought in Christ. Before their full restoration they will suffer punishment, but the punishment is intended to be educative, to purge them from the imperfections brought by their sin. After the end of the present age and its world another age and world will come, so Origen believed, in which those who have been born again will continue to grow and the unrepentant will be given further opportunity for repentance. Eventually all, even the devils, through repentance, learning, and growth, will be fully saved. Origen's conception of the drama of creation and redemption was breath-taking in its vast sweep and in its confident hope.

Influential though he was in the stream of Christian thought, some of Origen's views proved repugnant to the Catholic Church. Among these were his beliefs that the created world had always been, that human souls had existed from eternity before they came into these present bodies, that all souls, not only men but also demons, are ultimately to be saved, and that beyond this present existence the growth of souls through discipline is to continue until all are perfect. In the later years of the fourth century and in the fifth and sixth centuries controversy raged over Origen. In it monks, among them the scholarly and emphatic Jerome, and high ecclesiastics were involved. It entailed violent words and bitternesses. It contributed to the expulsion of John Chrysostom from Constantinople. Eventually, because of some of his teachings and also for others wrongly attributed to him, the Catholic Church in regional synods in Alexandria (399), Jerusalem, and Cyprus, and perhaps in one of its general or ecumenical councils, at Constantinople in 553, although this has been hotly debated, labelled him a heretic.

POST-ORIGENIST DEVELOPMENTS IN CHRISTIAN THOUGHT
AND THE RISE OF ARIANISM

Origen was so outstanding a mind, so radiant a spirit, and so stimulating a teacher and author, that for more than a century after his death he profoundly moulded the minds of Christian thinkers, especially in the eastern portions of the Roman Empire. From those who came after him and who were deeply indebted to him, two main streams of thought issued which came into conflict with each other and which late in the third and through much of the fourth and fifth centuries led to the most serious division which the Catholic Church had thus far experienced. The streams were not always clearly defined, and so abounding in energy was the rapidly expanding Church of the day that each had varied currents and branches which at times appeared to intermingle.

The two streams could both claim reinforcement from Origen. As we saw, Origen taught that Christ was the only-begotten Son of God, and that since God the Father had always existed, He could never have existed, even for a moment, without having generated the Son. The Son, therefore, is coeternal with the Father and existed before all worlds. Origen had taught that "his generation is as eternal and everlasting as the brilliancy which is produced by the sun." One of the two streams stressed the conviction that Christ is the Son of God, Wisdom and the *Logos* (Word) of God, and had always been, and that the *Logos* was, accordingly, equal with the Father. Yet, as we have said, Origen seemed also to say that Christ is a creature, and that as the image of the Father he is secondary to the latter and subordinate to Him. The other stream made much of this subordination of the Son to the Father.

The second of these streams was represented by a pupil of Origen, Dionysius, head of the catechetical school in Alexandria and bishop in that city around the middle of the third century. He seems to have been a man of scholarly competence, moderate and conciliatory. He found Sabellianism very influential in his diocese and preached against it. In making clear his dissent from that school of theology which, it will be recalled, regarded Father, Son, and Holy Spirit as aspects or modes of God, he stressed the distinctness of the Son as a person and in doing so used language which appeared to imply that the Father had created the Son, that there had been a time when the Son was not, and that the Son was subordinate to the Father. His friend, another Dionysius, Bishop of Rome, wrote him urging that he be more careful in his use of language and that he make it clear that the Son was (ὁμοούσιον) (*homoousion*), namely, of the same essential being or substance with the Father and not simply (ὁμοιούσιον) (*homoiousion*), of similar substance with Him. Dionysius of Alexandria answered that, while he did not find *homoousion* in the Scriptures, he was in agreement with the idea which it contained. The lines of controversy had not yet hardened.

The second of the streams also had an important channel through Antioch. At Antioch there was a presbyter, Lucian by name, a contemporary of Origen, who was an influential teacher and who perished in 312, a victim of the last great persecution before Constantine brought toleration. Among his students who became famous were Arius of Alexandria and Eusebius of Nicomedia (to be distinguished from Eusebius of Cæsarea, the Church historian). Lucian was an earnest student of the Bible and of theology and was one of those who saw in the *Logos* a way of expressing the relation of Christ to God. Yet he seems to have taken the position which was soon to make Arius a storm-centre.

Conflict between the two streams broke out over Arius. Arius was a presbyter in the Alexandrian Church. Tall, handsome, ascetic, earnestly religious, an eloquent preacher, he gave the impression of being arrogant. He protested against what he believed to be the Sabellianism of his bishop, Alexander. Alexander, so he said, taught that "God is always, the Son is always," and the Son "is the unbegotten begotten." In contrast, Arius maintained that "the Son has a beginning but that God is without beginning" and that the Son is not a part of God. The controversy between the two men became so sharp that Alexander called a synod in Alexandria and had Arius and his friends condemned and deposed. Arius sought and found refuge with his friend, Bishop Eusebius of Nicomedia, and carried on a correspondence maintaining his views, while Alexander wrote to numbers of his fellow bishops giving his side of the story. The conflict was chiefly in the eastern part of the Empire and seriously threatened to divide the Catholic Church in that region.

THE COUNCIL OF NICÆA

Then the Emperor Constantine stepped in. He had recently come over to the side of the Christians and, after a long, hard struggle had united the Empire politically under his rule. The dispute over Arius threatened the disruption of what, along with the Empire, was the strongest institution in the Mediterranean world, the Catholic Church. Constantine had already intervened in the affairs of the Church over the Donatist controversy. He now felt impelled to act in this much more serious division. To that end he first wrote to Alexander and Arius, sending the letter by his adviser in church matters, Hosius, Bishop of Cordova, calling on them to compose their differences and forgive each other. When this appeal did not succeed, Constantine had recourse to a council of the entire Catholic Church. He took the initiative, had the state pay the travel expenses of the bishops to the gathering, and, although only a catechumen, presided over its opening session, and was active in its deliberations.

Whether Constantine appreciated the niceties of the questions at issue is highly doubtful, for he was a layman, a warrior and administrator, not a philosopher or an expert theologian. In his letter to Alexander and Arius he said that having made "careful inquiry into the origin and foundation of these differences" he found "the cause to be of a truly insignificant character and quite unworthy of such fierce contention," and that the discussions should be "intended merely as an intellectual exercise . . . and not hastily produced in the popular assemblies, nor unadvisedly entrusted to the general ear." Constantine's words probably reflected the attitude of the average Christian layman. We read that one of these who had suffered for his faith in the persecutions which were of recent memory and who, hearing the pre-council disputes before the gathering at Nicæa, bluntly told the debaters that Christ did not "teach us dialectics, art, or vain subtilties, but simple-mindedness, which is preserved by faith and good works."

Constantine's action established a significant precedent for what were called ecumenical or general councils of the Catholic Church and for the frequent leadership of the civil power in them. Local and regional synods or councils were, as we have seen, not new. They may well have provided a conscious precedent for the council of the entire Catholic Church. Certainly the general or ecumenical council was to become an accepted method for seeking accord on major divisive issues and other urgent problems which concerned the whole Church.

The council met at Nicæa, in Asia Minor, in the year 325. To it came about three hundred bishops. Most of them were from the eastern part of the Empire. Because of his age the Bishop of Rome was unable to attend, but he was represented by two presbyters. While the overwhelming majority of the bishops were from within the Empire, there are said to have been one from Persia and perhaps one from among the Goths. Hundreds of lesser clergy and lay folk also came. After the formal opening of the council by an address by Constantine, and when the latter had given permission for the disputants to present their views, violent controversy broke out. The large majority had not yet taken a position, but Arius was supported by a small and vocal minority of whom the most prominent was Eusebius of Nicomedia, and another, equally determined minority upheld Alexander. With Alexander was one of his deacons, the able young Athanasius. Born not far from the year 300 of upper class parentage, from childhood Athanasius had shown a deep interest in the Church and, having come to the favourable notice of Alexander, had early been brought into the latter's official family. Athanasius was to succeed Alexander as Bishop of Alexandria and to become one of the outstanding figures in the entire history of Christianity.

The Arians presented a statement of their position, but this aroused violent opposition. Eusebius of Cæsarea, who took a middle position but was against any leaning towards Sabellianism and hence was inclined to favour the Arians, suggested as a statement to which all might agree the creed which was in use in his own see and which he said had come down from his predecessors in the Cæsarean episcopate and was taught catechumens and to which, presumably, assent was required at baptism. This seemed to win general assent, including the endorsement of the Emperor. It became, therefore, the basis of what has since been known as the Nicene Creed. The main body of the creed of Cæsarea read:

We believe in one God, the Father Almighty, maker of all things, visible and invisible, and in one Lord, Jesus Christ the word [*Logos*] of God, God from God, light from light, life from life, the only-begotten Son, first-born of all creatures, begotten of the Father before all ages, by whom also all things were made; who for our salvation was made flesh and dwelt among men; and who suffered and rose again on the third day, and ascended to the Father and shall come again in glory to judge the living and the dead. We believe also in one Holy Spirit.

To this creed was added, with the approval of the Emperor and perhaps at his suggestion, the word *homoousion,* applied to Christ. The term was adopted by the council and the creed proposed by Eusebius was altered to conform with it so that it was as follows:

We believe in one God, the Father Almighty, maker of all things visible and invisible, and in one Lord, Jesus Christ, the Son of God, the only-begotten of the Father, that is, of the substance [*ousias*] of the Father, God from God, light from light, true God from true God, begotten, not made, of one substance [*homoousion*] with the Father, through whom all things came to be, those things that are in heaven and those things that are on earth, who for us men and for our salvation came down and was made flesh, and was made man, suffered, rose the third day, ascended into the heavens, and will come to judge the living and the dead.

Even a cursory comparison of the two creeds will show the nature of the changes. For *Logos,* which the Arians could use, was substituted the word "Son," and that term was emphasized by keeping the word "only-begotten," that is, begotten in a way different from the sons of God who are adopted, and also by adding that the Son is of the substance of the Father. In place of "life from life," which might be interpreted in various ways, the phrase "true God from true God" was used to make more explicit "God from God." *Homoousion* was inserted. This was of central significance, for it stated emphatically a position which was the storm centre between the two extremes and was rapidly to become the crux of the difference between them. "Came down," another addition, implied that Christ had been with God and was not subordinate to Him, possibly the reason back of the substitution of "ascended into the heavens" for "ascended to the Father." "Was made man" was also inserted, perhaps to emphasize the belief that Jesus Christ was not only "true God" but also not merely "flesh," but true "man." This would serve to make clear that through the incarnation of the Son in Jesus Christ men could share in his sonship.

As in the Apostles' Creed, so in the Nicene Creed, painfully, slowly, and through controversies in which there was often lacking the love which is the major Christian virtue, Christians were working their way through to a clarification of what was presented to the world by the tremendous historical fact of Christ. At Nicæa it was more and more becoming apparent to them that the high God must also be the Redeemer and yet, by a seeming paradox, the Redeemer must also be man. The astounding central and distinguishing affirmation of Christianity, so they increasingly saw, and what made Christianity unique and compelling, was that Jesus Christ was "true God from true God," or, to put it in language more familiar to English readers, "very God of very God," who "was made man." Thus men could be reborn and become sons of God, but without losing their individual identity.

The words were not always wisely chosen, perhaps because words could not be found which would exactly stand for the reality. For instance, *ousia* had several different connotations in Greek philosophical usage and, although *substantia* was used in translation into Latin, and for one sense of *ousia*, accurately, the latter term had no precise Latin equivalent. Existing terminology was chosen which would come as nearly as possible to the fact and then would gradually be given the connotation which would convey what Christians meant by it.

To make the position of the council towards Arius unmistakable, it was declared that the Catholic Church anathematized, namely, cursed, those who say "there was a time when he [the Son of God] was not," or "that he did not exist before he was begotten," or "that he was made of nothing," or that "he is of other substance or essence from the Father," or that he was created, or mutable, or susceptible to change.

It will be noted that the creed which today bears the name of Nicene is a further development from the one which was adopted at Nicæa. Yet the latter's essential features were preserved.

The Council of Nicæa embraced the opportunity to settle some other issues which were troubling the Catholic Church. The time for the observance of Easter was agreed upon and made uniform, thus attempting to ensure accord on what had been a subject of controversy. Here, it may be remarked, the council was not entirely successful. Steps were also taken to end the Meletian schism which we mentioned earlier, but in vain, for the Meletians persisted for at least a century longer. Several canons, or rules, were adopted for the administration and discipline of the Church, among them one which required at least three bishops for the laying on of hands, namely, the consecration of a bishop, regulations for the treatment of those who had fallen away during the recent persecutions, for a uniform handling of the excommunicated, and for improving the morals of the clergy and the bishops by more care in admission to these orders, by prohibiting the clergy from exacting usury, and by keeping other women than near relatives from their homes. These canons shed much light on the quality of the lives of Christians in the fore part of the fourth century and on the means which were taken to maintain high moral standards and orderly procedures.

To enforce the decisions of the Council of Nicæa, Constantine commanded, with the death penalty for disobedience, the burning of all books composed by Arius, banished Arius and his closest supporters, and deposed from their sees Eusebius of Nicomedia and another bishop who had been active in the support of Arius.

THE RESURGENCE OF ARIANISM

The Council of Nicæa from which so much had been hoped did not bring enduring peace to the Catholic Church. Indeed, no council which has claimed to be inclusive or "ecumenical" has ever done so. Here and there a regional council has helped to restore unity in a particular area or in a segment of the Church, but many, perhaps most, of even these have failed. "Ecumenical" councils have either hardened old divisions or have led to new ones. They have usually been marked by bitterness and recriminations and, by bringing face to face those who have differed, have sharpened dissensions rather than healed them. However, like the Council of Nicæa, they have often contributed to a clarification of the thinking of Christians, have made more apparent what the issues were or are, and have enabled the majority to reach a common mind. In this paradox is seen something of the nature of the Church as it has actually operated in history.

While, viewed from the vantage of the centuries, it is quite clear that the Council of Nicæa was an important stage in the attainment of the Catholic Church of a consensus of conviction on the relation of Jesus Christ to God, for more than a generation it was not at all certain that the definitions arrived at by the council would prevail. Indeed, it looked as though Arius, although anathematized and exiled, would win. The debate continued, the Arians accusing those who adhered to the Nicene formula of being Sabellians, and the defenders of the Nicene Creed charging the Arians with making Christ a second and subordinate God. In a sense the Arians were seeking to fit Christ into the monotheism towards which much of pagan philosophy had been moving. In contrast the Nicene party was stressing the uniqueness of Christ and the Christian revelation with its conception of God.

The outstanding defender of the Nicene position was Athanasius. To him the real issue was the salvation of men. As he saw it, salvation is the rescue of men from the mortality which sin has brought upon them to participation in the divine nature. This, he held, can be accomplished only as "true God" is united with "true man." He declared that "He [Christ] was made man that we might be made God." A man of stalwart character and deep religious faith and insight, his intrepid and unwavering support contributed notably to the eventual triumph of the form of the faith which is associated with Nicæa.

As we have suggested, for years the tide appeared to be flowing against Athanasius and the Nicene findings. By the year 328 Eusebius of Nicomedia was back from disgrace and had become a trusted adviser of Constantine. In 330, only five years after Nicæa, Eustathius, bishop of the important see of Antioch and a leader of the anti-Arians, but one whose theological convictions were Monarchian, was haled before a synod, charged with various offenses, partly his theological teachings and partly his conduct, was deposed, and was exiled by the Emperor.

The friends of Arius urged upon the Emperor his rehabilitation. Arius presented to Constantine a confession of faith which, although it avoided the chief points at issue, appeared to the Emperor to be satisfactory. He was, accordingly, permitted to return from exile and, shortly before his death, was restored to communion. Indeed, it was the bishops, summoned again by Constantine, who, meeting in Nicæa in 327, readmitted to fellowship both Eusebius of Nicomedia and Arius.

Seeing Athanasius as their chief opponent, Eusebius of Nicomedia and his supporters sought by various means to have him put out of his office. In 335, at the summons of Constantine, who continued to be disturbed by the divisions in the Church, a council convened at Tyre. It heard charges against Athanasius, largely by the Meletians, accusing him of arbitrariness and cruelty in his treatment of them. Dominated by the Arians, it ordered him deposed. The Arians eventually succeeded in having Athanasius banished to Gaul. Just how they accomplished this is not entirely clear, but perhaps they convinced Constantine that he was a disturber of the peace of the Church. Marcellus, Bishop of Ancyra, in Asia Minor, also a staunch anti-Arian, was accused by the Arians of Sabellianism and was driven from his see.

Constantine died in 337. Shortly before, he was baptized by Eusebius of Nicomedia. He was succeeded by his three sons, Constantine II, Constans, and Constantius, and they divided the Empire among themselves. They permitted the exiled bishops to return and, in consequence, Athanasius was once more in Alexandria. The death of Constantine II, in 340, was followed by the division of the realm between the two survivors, Constans, who had the West, and Constantius, who ruled in the East. In the West the Catholic Church, supported by Constans, held to the Nicene decision, while in the East the majority of the bishops seem to have been against it. Constantius sympathized with them, and the anti-Nicene cause was strengthened when, in 339, Eusebius of Nicomedia was made Bishop of Constantinople. A synod in Antioch in which Eusebius had marked influence brought about a second expulsion of Athanasius from Alexandria and put another in his place.

Athanasius took refuge in Rome and was joined there by Marcellus. The then Bishop of Rome, the first of that line to bear the name Julius, took the side of Athanasius and Marcellus. Eusebius and his associates had written Julius, presenting their case and asking him to call a synod (or council) and be the judge. This Julius did, but the Eastern bishops did not come. The synod met in Rome in 340 or 341 and exonerated the two. Anti-Nicene bishops convening in Antioch drew up statements of the faith which they apparently hoped would bridge the widening chasm between them and the supporters of Nicæa, but these did not accomplish that result.

In a further attempt to heal the breach, the two Emperors, acting at the suggestion of Julius, called a council of the entire Church which met at Sardica, the later Sophia, near the border between East and West, probably in 343. Before the council had proceeded to business, the Eastern bishops, with Arian sympathies, protesting against the seating of Athanasius and Marcellus, withdrew, perhaps because they saw themselves outnumbered by their opponents. Bishop Hosius of Cordova presided. The council once more examined the charges against Athanasius and declared him innocent, adjudged Marcellus to be orthodox, and ordered the two, along with some others who had been ejected by the Eusebian party, reinstated in their posts. In 346 Athanasius returned in triumph to Alexandria. The Council of Sardica also issued a letter to all the bishops of the Catholic Church reporting its decisions, condemning the Arian views, and making a fresh statement of what it believed the Catholic faith to be. The council adopted a number of canons, largely disciplinary and administrative, for the regulation of the bishops. Among other acts the Council of Sardica decreed that if a bishop were deposed, he might appeal his case to the Bishop of Rome, who should take steps to see that it was heard and a decision given. Rome was forging ahead in its leadership in the Catholic Church.

Athanasius, as the outstanding champion of Nicene orthodoxy, was not allowed permanently to enjoy his victory. In 353 Constantius became the undisputed ruler of the entire Empire. His sympathies were clearly pro-Arian. He sought to achieve unity in the Church by bringing the Nicene party and the Western bishops to heel. Councils were called at Arles, in Gaul, in 353, and in Milan in 355. At the latter a tumultuous scene ensued. Yet the bishops were constrained to come into accord with their Eastern colleagues. Athanasius was again sent into exile (356), although this was spent chiefly in Egypt. For refusing to comply with the imperial wishes, Liberius, the Bishop of Rome, Hosius of Cordova, and one other were also exiled. At a council held in Sirmium, the imperial residence, in 357, the second to assemble there, the bishops, some of them clearly dominated by the Arian Emperor, put forward a creed which explicitly forbade the use of *ousia, homoousia,* or *homoiousia,* on the grounds, as was the customary reason advanced by the Arians, that these were not to be found in the Scriptures. Thus the distinctive phrase of the Nicene Creed was condemned. Apparently the extreme Arians were impatient with the long effort to dodge the basic issue between themselves and the Nicene party by the utilization of words which could be interpreted in more than one way and believed themselves to be strong enough to come out unequivocally with their own position and to force through its acceptance by the entire Catholic Church. Hosius, said now to be a centenarian, signed the creed, but, it is alleged, only after he had been brought to the council against his will and had been beaten and tortured. There is some ground for belief, although this has been warmly debated, that under the stress of exile Bishop Liberius of Rome also assented to the Arian position. Obedient councils held in several cities in the next few years concurred: outwardly the unity of the Church had been restored. The official term for the relation of the Son to the Father was *homois,* "similar," that is, "the Son is like the Father."

The issue was complicated by the relations between the Church and the state. The Arians would have the Church submit to the Emperor. The Nicene party insisted on the autonomy of the Church as against the Arian rulers.

The Defeat of the Arians

The seeming victory of Arianism, due as it had been to the Emperor Constantius, was illusory. However, the reversal of the tide did not come quickly. In 361 death removed Constantius. As we have seen, his successor, Julian, sought to restore paganism and was, accordingly, not averse to the weakening discord in the Church. Athanasius was able to return to Alexandria, but within the year Julian ordered him again into exile, his fourth, for his success in winning pagans to the Christian faith. On Julian's early death (363), Jovian, a Christian, was elevated to the purple, but was little interested in ecclesiastical disputes. Athanasius once more returned to Alexandria. Jovian was followed by Valentinian I, who soon made his brother Valens his colleague and put him in charge of the East. Valens was under the influence of the Arian clergy, for they were strongly intrenched in Constantinople, and Athanasius for the fifth time was exiled. Yet Valens was not as vigorous a supporter of the Arians as Constantius had been.

The Arians were weakened by internal divisions. Some took an extreme position. They would not say that the Son is like (*homois*) the Father, but frankly declared that he was unlike (*anomoios*) the Father, that he was fallible and might sin. They were known as the *anomoians*. In the middle were those who used the term *homois* and could be called the *homoians*. On the other extreme were those who approached the Nicene views and who eventually made common cause with the Nicene party. They have been called semi-Arians, but this probably is not accurate. They were reluctant to say that the Son is *homoousion* with the Father, apparently because they felt that this term meant Sabellianism, with the loss of individuality of the Son and, therefore, the un-reality of the incarnation and, accordingly, the failure to realize the wonder of the Gospel in making it possible for men to share in the nature of God without themselves being absorbed into God and losing their individual identity. They were, however, prepared to say that the Son was *homoiousion,* namely, of similar "substance" with the Father. These differences among the Arians had begun to appear before the death of Constantius. As we have seen, it was the middle of the road group, the *homoians,* who won out under him and who in synods controlled by them anathematized both the *anomoians* and the *homoiousians.* These differences continued and deepened.

In their views the adherents of the Nicene formula began to approach the "semi-Arians," or, better, *homoiousians.* At a council or synod held by Athanasius in Alexandria in 362, in an effort to win over the Meletians, who were numerous in Egypt and who were apparently *homoiousians,* a way to reciprocal understanding was sought, so we gather from a synodical letter which grew out of the gathering, by declaring that it is correct to hold that in God there is only one *ousia,* but that there the three *hypostases. Hypostasis* (ὑπόστασις) was a term found in both Platonic and Stoic philosophy and could be used as an alternative word for *ousia.* The Synod of Alexandria, indeed, seems to have regarded the two as interchangeable. However, in the development of the thought of the Nicene party, *ousia* came to be regarded as the equivalent of the Latin *substantia* ("substance") and *hypostasis* as translatable into Latin by *persona* ("person"). At Alexandria, it will be noted, the question of the Holy Spirit became more prominent than at Nicæa. At Alexandria it was made clear that the approved belief was that the Holy Spirit is not a creature, but is inseparable from the Father and the Son.

The formulation of the position that clearly distinguished between *ousia* and *hypostasis* and said that in God there is only one *ousia,* in which Father, Son, and Holy Spirit share, but that there are three *hypostases,* Father, Son, and Holy Spirit, was largely the work of what are often called the three great Cappadocians, Gregory of Nazianzus, Basil of Cæsarea, and Gregory of

Nyssa. It was they who led the way in so interpreting the Nicene Symbol that it won the support of the large majority of the Eastern bishops, including many of those who had been classed with the Arians. They represented what might be called right-wing Origenism, that stream of thought which had been reinforced by Origen and which held that the *Logos* has always been equal with the Father.

All three men were natives of Cappadocia, in what later was known as Asia Minor, immediately to the west of Armenia. All three have continued to be held in the highest esteem by those Eastern churches which bear the name Orthodox. Their dates of birth are somewhat uncertain, but all appear to have been born soon after the Council of Nicæa. They were younger contemporaries of Athanasius.

Gregory of Nazianzus was the son of a bishop. He studied in several centres, among them Alexandria and Athens, and so was familiar with Greek philosophy and the thought of Origen. The latter made a profound impression upon him. He was also much attracted by the monastic movement which, as we are to see in a subsequent chapter, was then in the first flush of its devotion and was making a strong appeal to the more earnest among the Christian youth. Late youth and early middle life were spent in comparative obscurity, but when he was not far from fifty he became a preacher in Constantinople and there by his conviction and eloquence did much to bring about the discomfiture of the Arians. Made Bishop of Constantinople not long thereafter, he held the post only a short time. Distressed by the criticism aroused by his promotion, he resigned and retired to the land of his birth.

Basil of Cæsarea, sometimes called the Great, and Gregory of Nyssa were brothers, the latter somewhat the younger. They were scions of a prominent family. A younger brother was also a bishop, an older brother a distinguished Christian jurist, and a sister was noted for her saintly life. Basil had an eager mind and was a fellow student in Athens with Gregory of Nazianzus. Like the latter, he was deeply influenced by Origen. The two joined in compiling a selection from Origen's writings. He was also strongly drawn to monasticism, for a time lived as a monk, and the rules for that life which are ascribed to him still constitute the basic guide for the monastic communities of the (Eastern) Orthodox Church. Not until middle life, however, was he ordained a priest. Naturally a leader and an eloquent preacher, he was made bishop of the important see of Cæsarea in Cappadocia and as such, imperious and vigorous, he did much to rout the Arians. He wrote extensively and improved the liturgy of his church.

Gregory, who was ordained by Basil as Bishop of Nyssa, a small town near Cæsarea, was not as able an administrator as his brother nor as eloquent a preacher as Gregory of Nazianzus, but he was a prolific writer and, like them stimulated by Origen, was a greater theologian than either.

Through long friendship and discussion the three Cappadocians worked out an interpretation of the Nicene formula which removed the doubts of many who had thus far questioned it. They were loyal to the wording of that formula, including *ousia* and *homoousion,* the words which were such a stumbling block to the Arians and which were regarded by the latter as smacking of Sabellianism, that is, as we may remind ourselves again, making Father, Son, and Holy Spirit modes or aspects of God. As we have suggested, they overcame this difficulty by saying that in God there is only one *ousia,* but that there are three *hypostases,* Father, Son, and Holy Spirit. They held that there are not three Gods, but only one, and that the one is to be found equally and identically in Father, Son, and Holy Spirit. For these three the Cappadocians preferred the term *hypostasis,* although they also gave as an alternative term *prosopon* (πρόσωπον).

The difficulty with the Cappadocian effort was that it tended to make God a somewhat vague, colourless abstraction. To one trained in the Platonic philosophy this might not seem alien or untenable, for Platonism held that ideas or forms are real. The generalized term "man," to use an example given by Gregory of Nyssa, has reality. Peter, James, and John seem to be three separate men, but they partake of a common humanity, a single *ousia,* "man." For one not schooled in Platonism, this conception of God might place an obstacle to that love of God which is both the primary obligation and high privilege of men. The Cappadocians did not entirely overcome the difficulty of finding words to compass the facts of Christian experience.

Although the Cappadocians did not fully succeed in making clear in language what Christians believed to be basic to their faith, they prepared the way for the final defeat of the Arians and the triumph in the Catholic Church of what was associated with the name of Nicæa. In the year 380 the Emperor Theodosius issued an edict on ecclesiastical affairs. Born in Spain and reared by parents who were attached to the orthodoxy of the West, he was anti-Arian by heredity and conviction. He ordered that all his subjects follow the faith which "Peter delivered to the Romans," "the deity of the Father and the Son and the Holy Spirit of equal majesty in a Holy Trinity." Congregations of those who varied from this faith were not to be recognized as churches and were to be prohibited. The following year, at his call, a council convened at Constantinople which confirmed the Nicene formula and anathematized those who would not accept it, naming specifically, among others, the *anomoians,* the Arians, and the semi-Arians.

The Nicene Creed

The gathering of 381 was eventually esteemed the Second Ecumenical Council, the first being that at Nicæa in 325. It is doubtful whether this rating can be fully justified. There came to be associated with it, mistakenly believed to have been adopted by it, the creed which today is given the name of Nicene and which is held as authoritative by the Roman Catholic, Orthodox, and several other communions. That creed seems to have been based, not directly upon the Nicene formula, but indirectly upon a fourth century creed which was in use in Jerusalem and which in turn was influenced by the Nicene formula. The major change from the latter were additions at the end. It read, in the form familiar in the Book of Common Prayer: "I believe in the Holy Ghost, the Lord, the Giver of Life, who proceedeth from the Father ['and the Son' was a later Western addition], who with the Father and the Son together is worshipped and glorified, who spake by the prophets. And I believe one Catholic and Apostolic Church. I acknowledge one baptism for the remission of sins. And I look for the resurrection of the dead, and the life of the world to come." The amplification of the clause about the Holy Spirit was put in to make it clear that the Spirit is not subordinate, for while the term *homoousion* was not applied to the Spirit, the intent is clear: the Father, Son, and Holy Spirit are uncreated and are to be worshipped together as one God.

This creed came into general use. The Arian cause was irretrievably lost. For several generations Arianism persisted as the faith of most of the Germanic peoples who, beginning with the latter part of the fourth century, were invading the Empire. Its adherents insisted that it was the true Catholic Church. But the overwhelming majority of Roman citizens held to the Nicene Creed, and Arianism eventually disappeared: its adherents died out or became Catholic (Nicene) Christians. By a slow and often stormy process the overwhelming majority of Christians had come to believe that the formula which bore the Nicene name contained the correct statement of the Christian faith on the questions which had been at issue. Today most of those who are called Christians continue to honour it, along with the Apostles' Creed, as the official authoritative formulation of their faith and as such employ it in public worship.

Further Christological Controversies: the Relation of the Divine and Human in Jesus: Apollinaris, Nestorius, Cyril

The general acceptance in the Catholic Church of what came to be called the Nicene Creed did not bring peace. That creed had been concerned primarily with the Trinity and with the relations within the Trinity of Father, Son, and Holy Spirit. There remained the problem of the relation of the divine and the human in Jesus Christ. Here was to be the storm centre of a controversy which was to continue into the seventh century. It was to issue in divisions some of which persist into the present. Here, as in the struggles over the inter-relations of the members of the Trinity, the majority came to the position which prevailed in the Western portion of the Church and in whose formulation the thought of Tertullian had been of marked assistance. Here, too, the dissensions were the most pronounced in the East. It was in the East that the enduring cleavages were seen.

In general, the participants in the controversy accepted the Nicene formula as authoritative. Within that pattern, however, with its declaration that "the only begotten Son of God . . . very God of very God . . . being of one substance with the Father . . . came down from heaven . . . and was made man," there was room for various interpretations of the fashion in which the Son of God and the human had been found in Jesus of Nazareth. One major trend, with its chief focus at Alexandria, stressed the divine element, at times apparently to the exclusion of the human. Another, strongly represented at Antioch, where the historical study of the Gospels had gone forward, emphasized the human element and tended to regard the divine and human as so distinct from each other that some of its representatives seemed to say that in Jesus there were two separate beings.

It was the first of these views which initially came to the fore. It was associated with Apollinaris, Bishop of Laodicea in Syria, a younger friend of Athanasius. Apollinaris felt that in one being, Christ, two complete and contrasting natures could not exist, namely, the divine, eternal, unchangeable, and perfect, and the human, temporal, corruptible, finite, and imperfect. Along with many others, he held each human being to be composed of body, soul, and mind or reason, the last being what distinguishes man from the lower animals. If the two natures were both in Jesus, the latter would really have in him two beings. Moreover, the human side of Jesus might sin, much as the extreme Arians declared to be possible. This, to Apollinaris, would make man's salvation impossible. He solved the problem of the relation of the divine and human in Jesus by saying that in him the divine *Logos* was the rational element. This, of course, would make Christ less than fully human and would leave the divine nature in him complete. Yet Apollinaris believed that he had remained true to Nicene orthodoxy, and that he had successfully solved one of the unresolved riddles.

The Cappadocians came out in opposition to Apollinaris. They saw that he had sacrificed the full humanity of Christ and said so. Gregory of Nazianzus insisted that only a Christ who had all the elements of human nature could redeem all of man, and that if every phase of man's nature were not redeemed, redemption would not be a fact. Those of the school of Antioch also vigorously disagreed. They held that the divine and human natures were both complete in Jesus and that the *Logos* dwelt in Jesus much as God dwells in a temple. God had thus been in the prophets and is in Christians, but the relation was unique in Jesus, for Jesus willed what God willed and in him the unity had become indissoluble. The school of Antioch was seemingly more affected by Aristotle than by Plato and made more of the historical facts of the life of Jesus. That of Alexandria, to which Apollinaris belonged, had been more under the influence of Plato. The Antioch school was concerned with the study of the historical accounts of the life of Christ. Diodorus of Tarsus was an outstanding teacher of these views and among his students were Theodore, Bishop of Mopsuestia from 392 to 428, John Chrysostom, and Nestorius, a presbyter and monk of Antioch who in 428 was called from his monastery to become Bishop of Constantinople.

Emphatic decisions against the views of Apollinaris were pronounced by various synods, among them ones in Rome in 374, 376, and 382, and in 381 by the Council of Constantinople which condemned the Arians.

Yet the struggle between the convictions represented by Alexandria and Antioch was not terminated by the anathemas against Apollinaris. It was kept up and out of it issued two extremes, on the one hand the several varieties of Monophysites and on the other that associated with the name of Nestorius. They failed to find favour with the Catholic Church and were ruled out and joined with geographic, political, and cultural factors in distinguishing churches which were separated from the Catholic Church and which have had a continuing existence.

The chief leader in the position associated with Alexandria was Cyril, bishop of that city from 412 to 444. He seems to have been moved not only by theological conviction but also, perhaps unconsciously or half-consciously, by ambition for leadership in the Catholic Church for himself and his see and by jealousy of the other great episcopal sees of the East, Antioch and Constantinople, both of them occupied by men who endorsed views from which he sharply dissented. Cyril shared in the refusal to accept the solution of Apollinaris, for he maintained that in Christ the divine and the human nature were both complete and that the latter included the rational element. But the unity in Christ, so Cyril held, was through the *Logos* who became incarnate in Christ, and who in becoming incarnate took on the general characteristics of man. The humanity in Christ was not so much an individual man as humanity in general. Salvation was accomplished by the personal *Logos* who assumed impersonal human nature, thus uniting it with the divine nature. It is thus, so Cyril taught, that human nature is enabled to become a partaker of God and of immortality. In this Cyril seemed to be following in the footsteps of Athanasius. He applied to the Virgin Mary a term which had long been in current use, *Theotokos* (Θεοτόκος), "God-bearing," or, as usually translated, "Mother of God," a term which, unfortunately, was to become a battle cry in as sharp and bitter a theological conflict as the Church had known.

As Bishop of Constantinople, Nestorius was zealous in attacking heresy, especially the remnants of the Arians. However, reared as he had been in the theological atmosphere of Antioch, he was reluctant to employ *Theotokos* in his sermons, but preferred instead *Christotokos* (Χριστοτόκος), "Christ-bearing," or "Mother of Christ," not "God-bearing," or "Mother of God." This aroused Cyril. Apparently he was all the more keen to scent heresy because his critics were complaining about him to the Emperor and to Nestorius. Nestorius had interested himself in the situation, and Cyril, partly moved by injured pride, welcomed an opportunity to shift attention from himself to the challengeable views of his rival. Nestorius was not always tactful, circulated his convictions widely, and dealt harshly with monks who dared to denounce him. Cyril came out in favour of *Theotokos* and a sharp exchange of letters took place between himself and Nestorius. Both men wrote to their fellow bishop, Celestine of Rome. Celestine found against Nestorius, possibly because the latter had not been as deferential to him as had Cyril and possibly also because Nestorius had displayed a certain degree of hospitality to some Pelagians, of whom we are to hear more a little later, who had fled to Constantinople. In 430 a synod at Rome ordered Nestorius either to recant or be excommunicated. Also in the year 430 Cyril convened a synod in Alexandria which condemned the positions which he maintained were those of Nestorius. Among them were the failure to use *Theotokos* and the separation of the divine and human nature in Christ in such fashion that Christ was viewed as a "God-bearing man," and that "Jesus is, as a man, energized by the *Logos* of God." Except for the reluctance to use *Theotokos,* Nestorius had not taught them.

The dispute waxed so warm that a general council was called—by imperial order—to deal with it. The bishops assembled at Ephesus in 431 (in what is usually called the Third Ecumenical Council). Cyril and his supporters reached the city first. Without waiting for the friends of Nestorius, a party of bishops from Antioch, the council convened under the presidency of Cyril and, when Nestorius declined to appear before it until the other bishops arrived, under the leadership of his chief accuser in a single long day's session it condemned and deposed him. Stirred up by their bishop, Memnon, the Ephesian populace committed acts of violence against Nestorius and his supporters. When, not long thereafter, John, the Bishop of Antioch, and the bishops with him came, they organized themselves, claiming to be the legitimate council, and condemned Cyril and Memnon as Arians and Apollinarians and deposed and excommunicated them. The bishops in Cyril's council numbered about two hundred and those in John's forty-three. A few days later, when the representatives of Bishop Celestine of Rome reached Ephesus, the majority council resumed its sessions and excommunicated Bishop John and his party.

Both sides appealed to the Emperor and the latter for the moment confirmed the deposition of Cyril, Memnon, and Nestorius and endeavoured to bring the two factions together and heal the breach. Nestorius was commanded henceforth to live in a monastery. A temporary peace was patched up when in 433 John of Antioch sent to Cyril a creed which declared Jesus Christ to be "true God and true man, consisting of a reasonable soul and a body," and the Virgin to be *Theotokos*. To this creed Cyril subscribed.

Nestorius remained in exile, most of the time, apparently, in Egypt, and often in great physical and mental distress. In his painful seclusion he wrote extensively in his own defense, setting forth his version of the unhappy controversy and elaborating a statement of his faith. From this it is not entirely clear whether he held the views which have been associated with his name—the presence of the divine and human in Jesus Christ in such fashion that there were in Him two distinct beings or persons rather than, as the majority view held, two natures concurring in one person (*prosopon*) and one substance (*hypostasis*).

One of the works written by Nestorius in exile bore the title *Tragedy*. That might be a description of the life of the author and of the group of which he was a central figure, and also be illustrative of one aspect of the course of the Gospel. In his youth giving himself completely to Christ and in pursuance of that dedication caught up in the monastic movement, in the prime of his manhood Nestorius was called to one of the most exalted positions in the Catholic Church, the leadership of the Church in the Empire's second capital, Constantinople. There in his zeal for Christ as he understood him Nestorius aroused the bitter enmity of fellow Christians who also believed themselves to be loyal to Christ and held that by his preaching Nestorius dishonoured him. The leader of the opposition, Cyril, in part confused allegiance to Christ with personal ambition. Scenes followed which were a denial of the love and therefore of the faith to which both parties were theoretically committed. Nestorius, defeated, languished long years in exile. Outraged and perhaps perplexed, he again and again went over the events and the convictions which had brought him to that pass. He believed himself to have been right, but his thinking appears either to have been too subtle or not clear cut. Dragging out his years in his banishment Nestorius perished in obscurity while his successful rival continued in office and died amidst the trappings of ecclesiastical splendour.

Neither man was perfect, either in his adherence to Christian moral standards or in his thinking. Through both the Church was further divided. Yet both had been, in their own eyes, sincere. In a sense they were typical of the entire Christian Church and epitomized the problem presented by the Gospel in the world.

"Nestorianism" Finds a Refuge in the Persian Empire

Nestorius was not entirely to fail. When once he was safely out of the way and John and Cyril were reconciled, the latter sought to bring about the condemnation of Diodorus of Tarsus and Theodore of Mopsuestia (now dead) whom he charged as authors of the Nestorian heresy. In this he was aided by the Bishop of Edessa. Moreover, Armenian monks with Monophysite tendencies came out vigorously against Theodore. John of Antioch, as might have been expected, rose to the defense of Theodore, and the Emperor, presumably at his instance, ordered that no one should be calumniated who had died in the communion of the Catholic Church—thus supporting John.

There were some, including bishops, who held views akin to those of Theodore and Nestorius who refused to subscribe to the creed through which Cyril and John had composed their differences. Because they were regarded by the imperial authorities as disturbers of the peace of the Church and thus of the realm, they were exiled. A number of them sought refuge in the Persian Empire. Among them were several who found a home at Nisibis, the chief training school for the clergy in the Persian domains. Eventually many of the leading ecclesiastical posts in that realm were filled by their students and, after something of a struggle, their doctrines became the accepted teaching of the Mesopotamian-Persian Church. That church now tended to regard the Catholic Church as heretical. This was of advantage to it, for ever since Constantine had espoused Christianity it had been looked at askance by the Persian monarchs as a possible supporter of their chronic enemies, the Roman Emperors. The Mesopotamian-Persian Church could now affirm that, since its ties with the church of the Roman Empire had been dissolved, that fear was baseless. It is said that on this ground one of the Sassanian monarchs of Persia decreed that Nestorian Christianity should be the only form of the faith granted official recognition in his possessions.

How far the teachers at Nisibis dissented from what was endorsed by the Catholic Church is debatable. The variation may not have been as great as has sometimes been said. Whatever the degree of the difference, the Mesopotamian-Persian Church came to be known as the Nestorian Church. As we have seen and are to see in later chapters, it was the means of an extensive eastward spread of the Christianity which in subsequent centuries carried the faith to the shores of the China Sea. The influence of Nestorius, therefore, did not disappear with his pitiful death, but was felt across the vast reaches of Asia.

THE CONTINUATION OF THE CHRISTOLOGICAL CONTROVERSY: "THE ROBBER SYNOD" OF EPHESUS AND THE COUNCIL AND CREED OF CHALCEDON

So long as Cyril of Alexandria and John of Antioch lived, the peace which had been effected between the theologies which they represented was fairly well preserved. However, that peace proved to be only a truce. After death had removed them from the scene the struggle broke out with renewed fury. Here were two tendencies which could scarcely be reconciled. The one, represented by the scholarship which had been strong at Antioch, stressed the historical study of the Gospel records of the life of Jesus and hence made much of his humanity. The other, with its traditional centre at Alexandria, interpreted the Scriptures allegorically, minimized the historical and therefore the human side of Christ, and gave great weight to the divine in him. It was in part an outgrowth of the position of Athanasius and had been carried further by Cyril, even though the latter had anathematized its extension in the form represented by Apollinaris. As we have suggested, the tension was heightened by rivalries between the great sees of the Orient, especially between Alexandria and the New Rome at Constantinople, for from the standpoint of the former the latter was an upstart. Moreover, Constantinople made itself conveniently obnoxious by drawing a large proportion of its bishops from men trained in the Antiochene tradition.

In 444 Cyril was succeeded at Alexandria by Dioscurus, a man fully as zealous as himself for the prestige and theology of his see and who went beyond Cyril in emphasizing the divine nature in Christ. In 446 Flavian, whose sympathies seem to have been with Antioch, was placed in the bishop's chair in Constantinople. Conflict soon arose over a monk of Constantinople, Eutyches. Eutyches denounced as Nestorian the creed of 433 in which John of Antioch and Cyril had reached agreement and declared that before the union (the incarnation) there were the two natures, divine and human, but that after the union (the incarnation) the two so blended that there was only one nature, and that was fully divine. In other words, Jesus Christ was *homoousion* with the Father but not with man. Eutyches was denounced at a synod in Constantinople in 448 over which Flavian presided, was excommunicated as a reviler of Christ, and was deposed from every priestly office. Eutyches presented his case to the Emperor and to a number of bishops, including the Bishop of Rome. Flavian also wrote to fellow bishops, as was the custom in the Catholic Church, among others to the Bishop of Rome.

The Bishop of Rome was one of the ablest men who have ever sat on the throne of Peter, Leo I, "the Great." Leo supported Flavian and sent him a long letter, known as the *Tome,* in which he set forth the view which had been generally held in the West and which had been clearly stated by Tertullian years before, that in Christ Jesus there was neither manhood without true Godhead nor the Godhead without true manhood, that in Christ two full and complete natures came together in one person, "without detracting from the properties of either nature and substance."

Dioscurus sided with Eutyches. The Emperor called a council of the whole Church to deal with the issue. The council convened at Ephesus in 449. Dioscurus presided and was dominant. Leo was not present but was represented by two legates. His *Tome* was denied a reading. The gathering professed allegiance to the creed of Nicæa, by a large majority declared Eutyches exonerated, and deposed Flavian and some of his supporters. Dioscurus excommunicated Leo and appointed an Alexandrian priest in his stead. It is not strange that in circles loyal to Rome the council was dubbed "the robber synod."

Leo was not to be so easily thwarted. He sought to have another council called, and in Italy. In 451 a council was indeed summoned by the Emperor, but it met, not in Italy, but at Chalcedon, immediately across the Bosporus from Constantinople, and was later known as the Fourth Ecumenical Council. About six hundred bishops were present, more than had previously come together at any one gathering, almost all of them from the East. Leo did not come, but was represented by legates. The latter were given the first place in the roll-calls. The imperial commissioners presided. Dioscurus was present, but was clearly out of favour. The *Tome* of Leo was approved and a creed was adopted which incorporated its views. The heart of it read:

Following the holy fathers we all, with one voice, define that there is to be confessed one and the same Son, our Lord Jesus Christ, perfect in Godhead and perfect in manhood, truly God and truly man, of rational soul and body, of the same substance [*homoousion*] with the Father according to the Godhead, and of the same substance [*homoousion*] with us according to the manhood, like to us in all respects, without sin, begotten of the Father before all time according to the Godhead, in these latter days, for us and for our salvation, born of the Virgin Mary, the Mother of God [*Theotokos*] according to the manhood, one and the same Christ, Son, Lord, Only-begotten, in two natures, inconfusedly, immutably, indivisibly, inseparately, the distinction of natures being by no means taken away by the union, but rather the peculiarity of each nature being preserved and concurring in one person [*prosopon*] and one substance [*hypostasis*], not parted or separated into two persons, but one and the same Son and Only-begotten, divine word [*Theon Logon*], the Lord Jesus Christ; as from the beginning the prophets declared concerning him, and the

Lord Jesus Christ has taught us, and the creed of the holy fathers has transmitted to us.

It will be seen that in this the distinctive views of Apollinaris, Eutyches, and those ascribed to Nestorius are condemned.

Flavian, now dead, was exonerated, Eutyches was denounced as a heretic, and Dioscurus was deposed and excommunicated.

In other legislation of the council, various regulations or canons were enacted for the administration of the Church. Moreover, the Bishop of Constantinople was placed second in precedence to the Bishop of Rome, thus promoting his see above the more ancient ones of Antioch, Alexandria, and Jerusalem.

THE FURTHER PROGRESS OF MONOPHYSITISM

In spite of Chalcedon, the view represented by Alexandria continued to spread. To be sure, the West, led by Rome, and such of the East as acknowledged Constantinople held by the decision of that council. But large elements in the East dissented. They were called Monophysites, for they stressed the divine nature in Christ, holding that it transformed the human nature in such fashion that the whole became divine, although with some human characteristics. The Monophysites varied in the degree to which they emphasized the divine in Christ, but they could not accept Chalcedon.

The division was largely regional. Most of Egypt, Ethiopia, and much of Syria became Monophysite, thus further breaking the unity of the Catholic Church and threatening that of the Empire. Armenia also tended in that direction. The Roman Empire, within which whatever unity the Catholic Church possessed had been achieved and to which it was deeply indebted, was already suffering from the disintegration which was to become permanent in the centuries after A.D. 500. In later chapters we shall see how the divisions in the Church and in the political structure interacted to reinforce one another. The efforts to achieve Christian unity through doctrinal statements, ecclesiastical organization, and the aid of the state were proving illusory.

Yet the state did not give up the struggle. In 476 the Emperor Basilicus in his *Encyclion* condemned the *Tome* of Leo and Chalcedon. In 482 the Emperor Zeno, in an attempt to heal the breach between Monophysites and the Chalcedonians, took a partly opposite tack and issued what was known as the *Henoticon,* a document which was purposely capable of various interpretations and which satisfied some of the moderate Monophysites. However, the more extreme of the Monophysites would not accept it, and the Bishop of Rome, believing it to be a rejection of Chalcedon, broke off communion with the Bishop of Constantinople, who supported it. To carry the story to its end would take us far into the period which followed the year 500. We must, accordingly, defer its completion to a later chapter.

AUGUSTINE AND PELAGIANISM

While the conflict over Nestorius and between the Alexandrian and Antiochene schools was raging in the eastern part of the Catholic Church, another struggle was being waged mainly in the Western portions of the Church. It seems to have been characteristic of the Latin West that this was primarily over the nature of man rather than, as in the Hellenistic East, over the relation of the human and the divine in Christ.

One of the striking facts of the history of Christianity is that after the fifth century creative, original thought became less and less frequent in the Eastern sections of the Church, but that it continued in the West and, with occasional sterile periods, has persisted into the present. This does not mean that thought and discussion on the great issues presented to the human mind ceased in the East. It was still to be found there, but except for some minority groups it took as final the conclusions reached in the "ecumenical" councils of the first eight and especially the first five centuries and it operated within the framework arrived at through those councils and raised few if any basically new questions.

Some reasons for this partial sterility are fairly obvious and will be pointed out in a subsequent chapter. Others must be largely conjectural and, therefore, debatable. It may be that they are to be found to some degree in the circumstance that the East addressed itself primarily to the relation of the divine and the human in Christ and was more concerned with the divine element in Christ and in the end, even beyond circles which were known as Monophysite, tended to stress the divine in him and to give less attention to his humanity. In contrast, the West, while agreeing in principle on the relation of the divine and the human in Christ as formulated in the findings of the councils in which it had joined with the Eastern portion of the Catholic Church, concerned itself also with problems of human nature and of the fashion in which the "grace"—the unmerited love of God in Christ—operated in relation to human nature.

This concern of the Western, or Latin, part of the Catholic Church with the nature of man and the manner in which God through Christ redeems and transforms it was vividly seen in the fifth century in Augustine.

In the preceding chapter we saw something of the early life and the conversion of Augustine. Here was a sensitive spirit and a first-class mind which, after a prolonged quest for moral victory, an answer to the riddle of life, and inner peace, first through Manichæism (which he hoped would satisfy him intellectually and give him moral power but which failed to do either) and then through Neoplatonism (which gave him a convincing intellectual framework from which he never long departed but could not meet his moral needs), at last found what he craved, in dramatic fashion, in the Gospel. In later years, through a long life, Augustine gave himself to a study of various aspects of the Christian faith.

No other single Christian thinker after Paul was to influence so profoundly the Christianity of Western European peoples. Individuals such as Thomas Aquinas, Luther, and Calvin were to have as great or greater effect on particular branches of the Christianity of the West, but no other after the apostolic age was so deeply to mould all the major forms of the Western wing of the faith. He combined deep personal Christian experience with an acute and disciplined intellect which had been quickened to profound activity by the Gospel and which was equipped with a knowledge of Neoplatonism, familiarity with the best Roman thought, and the Roman tradition of emphasis upon morals and action. Significantly, Augustine was to have little influence in Eastern Christianity. By helping to shape and by epitomizing much of Western Christianity, he contributed to the incipient divergence between the Christianity of the western and eastern portions of the Mediterranean world. His thought was dominant in Latin Christianity for at least eight centuries, has since remained prominent in the Roman Catholic Church, and was to make major contributions to Protestantism.

We have noted the conversion of Augustine at Milan in 385 and his baptism by Ambrose, the great Bishop of Milan, together with that of his son, Adeodatus, and a friend, at Easter, 387. Soon thereafter, Augustine, with his mother, Monica, Adeodatus, and some of his friends set out for his native place in Africa. On the way, while waiting at Ostia for their ship, Monica died. Adeodatus followed her a few months later, after the party's arrival in Africa. In Africa, at his family estate in Tagaste, the group lived in community in study and prayer. Within a little less than three years (in 391), while Augustine was visiting Hippo Regius, a port about two hundred miles west of Carthage, popular demand led to his ordination as presbyter. Four years later, after much hesitation on his part, at the insistence of the Bishop of Hippo he was consecrated bishop with the right of succession to that see. The following year, 396, on the demise of his predecessor, he became Bishop of Hippo and remained in that post until his death, August 28, 430.

At Hippo Augustine faithfully performed his episcopal duties—preaching, administering discipline, caring for the poor, and adjudicating disputes among his flock. He gathered clergy about him who lived together under a common rule. He also carried on an enormous correspondence and through this and his other writing made of the otherwise obscure port of Hippo one of the chief centres of Christian thought of his day. He was a prolific author. Although troubled with insomnia and often ill, he accomplished a prodigious amount of work.

In all his writing, although it bore the mark of his genius and contributed fresh insights, Augustine held to views which were already widely accepted in the Catholic Church. He had a high conception of the Catholic Church. He held that God's attitude towards man can be known only through faith, that faith is a guide to truth, and that faith is belief in what is taught by the Scriptures and the Church. He said that he would not have believed the Scriptures had the Church not declared them to be true. His youthful repugnance to them disappeared, partly because he had learned from Ambrose the method, so widespread in the Church, of interpreting allegorically passages, especially in the Old Testament, which had repelled him.

Although there were other important ones, including a treatise on the Trinity, Augustine's most distinctive works were on the interrelated subjects of human nature, the character of sin, the redemption of man, the attitude of the Church towards the sinner and the penitent, the Church within history, and history. His autobiography, the *Confessions,* is not so much narrative, although it contains it, as meditations on human nature as seen in himself and on the fashion in which God had dealt with him. His extensive polemics against the Donatists were on the burning issues on which the latter separated from the Catholic Church. These were not what are usually called doctrinal questions, for on such points as those on which Gnostics, Marcionites, Arians, and Monophysites differed from the Catholic Church Donatists were in accord with the latter. The contention, rather, as we have seen, was over the moral character of the priesthood and the treatment which the Church should accord to those Christians who, having been guilty of serious lapses, repented.

Augustine believed profoundly in the Catholic Church as a visible institution distributed throughout the world, continuous from the church of the apostles through its bishops, whom he esteemed the successors of the apostles. To be sure, Augustine held that bishops, including the Bishop of Rome, might err, but the Catholic Church, he maintained, was the Body of Christ, tangible, and outside it there was no salvation.

One of Augustine's most widely read works was the *City of God (De Civitate Dei).* Provoked by the sack of Rome by Alaric and his Goths in 410, and the insistence by the pagans that the fall of the Eternal City had been due to the abandonment by the growing body of Christians of the gods who had made Rome great, the *City of God* was not only an attempted refutation of that charge. It was also a positive and comprehensive philosophy of history, an interpretation of the entire human drama. In contrast with the Greek view which regarded history as a series of cycles, endlessly repeating itself, Augustine, in accordance with the Biblical view, maintained that it had a beginning and a culmination. Contradicting his non-Christian contemporaries who prized the Roman Empire as the citadel and guarantor of order in the midst of a chaotic world, a society held together by a divine ruler, and who viewed its decline with deep dismay, Augustine regarded the passing of the Empire with confident hope, believing that the Roman realm was to be replaced by an infinitely better order, that to be established by God. Augustine held that from the time of man's first rebellion against God two cities, the earthly and the heavenly, had existed, the first typified by Cain and the other by Abel. The earthly was formed by love of self and pride. It was not entirely bad, for Babylon and Rome, its highest representatives, and other governments had, out of regard for self-interest, brought peace and order. The heavenly city, on the other hand, is dominated "by the love of God even to the contempt of self." Men enter it here and now and it is represented by the Church, although not all in the Church are its citizens. The earthly city must fade as the heavenly city grows. As Augustine saw it, from its very inception all history has been directed and governed by God and moves to a climax in a society in which God's will is perfectly to be accomplished. Although his general conception of meaning in history was derived from the Scriptures, the boldness of his pattern, with its contrast between the city of the world and the city of God, and the fashion in which he fitted history into that framework was a striking contribution to the thought of mankind.

It is significant that the *City of God* concerned itself with man. To be sure, its subject was the dealings of God with man, but its emphasis was upon what happens to man. In this interest in man, visible institutions, and history Augustine differed from the thinkers of the Eastern sections of the Catholic Church. They focussed their attention upon God and tended to minimize man.

In his emphasis Augustine was more than an individual. He was typical of a major trend in the Western portions of the Catholic Church, of what might be called Latin Christianity. While this Latin Christianity fully assented to the creeds of Nicæa and Chalcedon and, indeed, as we have seen, contributed decisively to the latter, it was more concerned with historical man and human society than were the Greek and other branches of the Eastern sections of the Catholic Church. It was more activistic, more intent upon moulding society here and now than were these others. To be sure, Eastern Christianity had pronounced social effects and now and again had movements, such as that associated with the name of Joseph Volotsky in Russia in the sixteenth century, which sought to shape the entire life of a country, but in general, perhaps in part because of the practical Roman tradition, Western Christianity gave more thought and effort to man within history than did its Eastern counterpart. This may have been because of the Roman tradition, with its concern for empire and for the practical administration of human affairs.

The controversy of Augustine with Pelagius and the discussions over what was termed Pelagianism, were, characteristically, most marked in the Western or Latin portion of the Catholic Church. They were known in the East and Eastern synods dealt with them, but they were most pronounced and continued longest in the West.

The issue was the freedom of man's will and the manner in which the grace of God operates. In general the East, while by no means denying the grace of God, believed in the freedom of man's will and in the ability of the individual man to do what God commands. The great preacher of the Eastern Church, John Chrysostom, for example, insisted that men can choose the good and that when they do so grace comes to their aid to reinforce them in their effort to do what God commands. In the West, however, even before the time of Augustine, Tertullian, Cyprian, and Ambrose had declared for what is usually known as original sin. Ambrose, for instance, taught that through the sin of the first man, Adam, all Adam's descendants come into the world tainted with sin. "Adam perished and in him we all perished," he said. He held that no one is conceived without sin and that, therefore, the new-born infant has it. In contrast with Chrysostom, who maintained that man by his free will turns to God and that then God supports man's will, Ambrose believed that God's grace begins the work of salvation and that, when grace has initiated it, a man through his will coöperates.

Augustine went much further than Ambrose. That was probably in part because of his personal history of prolonged moral impotence against the sin which he believed had been with him from his conception and his infancy and because of his experience of having been sought by God's grace until he could not but yield to it. Augustine held that at the outset angels and men were created rational and free, the only created beings of which that could be said. In the beginning, moreover, so Augustine, true to his Neoplatonic background, taught, there was no evil anywhere. What we call evil, he said, is but the absence of good. In this he revolted from his Manichæan stage with its belief in a primal dualism, with an evil as well as a good principle in nature. Evil, as he saw it, is degradation, a decline from one's proper rank. His capacity for rational free choice, so Augustine went on to hold, is at once man's highest quality, a gift from God intended for his own good, and his chief peril. Only men and angels have rational free choice. They can exist without being wicked, but because they alone possess rational free will, only they can be wicked.

Employing his divinely given capacity for rational free choice, so Augustine further taught, the first man, Adam, fell into sin. This was not primarily a yielding to sub-rational instincts and emotional drives, as the Greeks would have held, but a choice made deliberately through the use of reason. Basically man's sin is pride, the desire of the creature to put himself in the centre rather than God, to do his will rather than God's will. Through his own bitter experience Augustine saw this degradation especially in sexual lust.

This falling away from man's God-given status into a lower level of being, so Augustine believed, is not one from which man can recover by his own effort. Every endeavour of man to restore himself to his primal rank is marred and made impotent by the degradation worked by that original sin. Man cannot raise himself by his own boot-straps. Having once put himself in the centre, his every effort to extricate himself is nullified by the fact that it arises from continuing concern for himself, and thus he is mired ever more deeply in the morass into which he has fallen. Man is still free, but only free to sin, to sink ever lower. He is not free to turn wholly to God. The sin of Adam and its resulting degradation are, so Augustine believed, passed on to all Adam's descendants, namely, all the human race. All of us have not only a tendency to sin, but through Adam's sin we share his loss of status, his self-centredness, his inability to choose God, and, therefore, his guilt in the sight of God. We can be rescued only through a second birth. This cannot be except by a fresh act of God.

Since by Adam's fall the wills of all Adam's descendants have been in bondage to sin and death, so Augustine said, freedom can come only by the grace of God. This grace of God was in Christ, Christ who was in God incarnate, fully God and yet fully man. The man Christ Jesus is the only mediator between God and man. Born of the Virgin Mary, he was not stained by the sin which accompanies ordinary human generation, and lived and died without sin. Christ is the second Adam, for in him God made a new start. Through the sin of the first Adam, Augustine declared, "the entire mass of our nature was ruined and fell into the possession of its destroyer. And from him no one—no, not one—has been delivered, or ever will be delivered, except by the grace of the Redeemer." Quoting Paul, to the effect that "the gift of God is eternal life through Jesus Christ our Lord," Augustine insisted that "a gift, unless it is wholly unearned, is not a gift at all," and that, therefore, even "man's good deserts are themselves the gift of God, so that when these obtain the recompense of eternal life, it is simply grace."

Augustine was profoundly convinced that all men share the sin of Adam and therefore deserve judgement. Of His great mercy, however, God has predestined some to salvation. The others He has predestined to the punishment which their sin deserves. All men, being stained by sin, deserve damnation, but God, of His grace, has by His free choice selected some to be saved and also has chosen those whom He will not save. Augustine, therefore, seemed to teach "double predestination," namely, the determination by God of those on whom He will have mercy and those on whom He will not have mercy. Augustine held that God has predetermined the exact number of those who are to receive His grace, and that that "number is so certain that one can neither be added to them nor taken from them . . . that the number of the elect is certain and neither to be increased nor diminished." Those who are of the elect will, accordingly, be saved. Of His grace God will accord them the gift of perseverance, so that even though they commit sins they will repent. Eventually those to whom perseverance has been assigned will not be able to sin. Before his fall Adam had been able not to sin, was able not to die, and might have persevered if he would. This was a blessing which was from God. The culminating blessing given to the elect will be that they will not be able to forsake good and not be able to die. This is the highest freedom of all. Here are convictions which we are to meet again and again in the course of Christianity in the West—"predestination," "irresistible grace," and "the perseverance of the saints."

No one can here certainly know, so Augustine taught, whether he is among the elect. He may be among the believers, for, quoting from one of the parables in the Gospels, "many are called." "But," to quote again from that parable, "few are chosen." Not all those who are "called" and "believe" will persevere. By baptism original sin and the sins committed before baptism are washed away. Augustine, indeed, advocated the baptism of infants on the ground that baptism is the prescribed way of washing away original sin—the sin inherited from Adam. Augustine taught that both baptism and the Lord's Supper are necessary to salvation. By God's grace men are enabled to do good works which God rewards as though they were theirs. A gradual transformation is wrought by His grace. Yet one may be baptized and partake of the communion, good works and spiritual growth may be seen, and still one may not be among those elected to receive the gift of perseverance and ultimate salvation. If one were to be confident of being among the elect, this might well lead to pride, a renewal of the basic sin. Therefore it is necessary that so long as a man is in this mortal flesh he shall be uncertain where he is "in the number of the predestined."

Some of these views of Augustine were elaborated and sharpened by his controversy with those known as the Pelagians, especially Pelagius and his associate, Cœlestius, and the Bishop of Eclanum, Julian. Pelagius was a British monk who came to Rome not far from the end of the fourth century and was there for several years. He was a layman, a man of some learning, and of austere and ascetic life. He was apparently scandalized by the loose living of many of the Roman populace and sought to persuade them to reform. He insisted that if they really desired to do so, they could keep the commandments of God. Among those whom he won was a younger man, Cœlestius, a lawyer and, like Pelagius, a layman. Cœlestius was more forthright and less tactful in expressing his views than was his teacher.

Shortly after 410 Augustine's *Confessions* was having a wide reading in Rome. In it Augustine had prayed: "Give what you command: command what you will." This seemed to Pelagius to lead to moral listlessness and he protested that man had sufficient free will to perform his duty to God and should exert himself to do so.

Not far from 411 Pelagius and Cœlestius came to North Africa, perhaps because of the sack of Rome by Alaric and his Goths. There Cœlestius applied for ordination as presbyter but was accused of heretical teachings and was excommunicated by a local synod (412). Among the teachings ascribed to him and which he did not deny holding were that Adam's sin injured himself only and not the human race, that every child is born as free as Adam was before his fall and can, if he chooses, do the right, that a man can fully keep God's commandments if he will, and that some before the time of Christ had been sinless.

Both Pelagius and Cœlestius went to the East, and the latter was ordained presbyter at Ephesus. In Palestine Pelagius attracted the attention of Jerome, who was living there, and aroused his ire. A synod at Jerusalem, to which the issue was referred, took no action except to refer the matter to Rome, and in 415 a synod at Diospolis (Lydda) in Palestine acquitted Pelagius. However, in 416 synods at Carthage, Mileve (in Numidia), and Rome took adverse action and the Bishop of Rome supported them. The next Bishop of Rome, Zosimus, first sided with Pelagius and Cœlestius, but, after the Emperor Honorius had exiled them (418), he also condemned them. In 418 a synod in Carthage came out against Pelagianism. In spite of these actions, Julian continued to argue the case and so brought against him the powerful pen of Augustine. Cœlestius, again going East, won the support of Nestorius, then Bishop of Constantinople. In 431 the Council of Ephesus which condemned Nestorius also acted against Pelagius, Cœlestius, and their associates, including Julian.

Those grouped under the category of Pelagians did not completely agree among themselves and held a variety of views. Julian, for example, seems to have been as much a Stoic as a Christian and was interested in the philosophical aspects of the issue, while Pelagius and Cœlestius appear to have been more concerned for religious and moral results.

In general Pelagians differed from Augustine in denying that the taint of Adam's sin and the impairment of the will brought by it have been transmitted to all Adam's descendants, but, in contrast, declared that each man at birth has the ability to choose the good. In other words, they denounced "original sin." Some seem to have held that Adam was created mortal and that his death was not due to his sin, that new-born children need not be baptized, for they have no original sin inherited from Adam which needs to be washed away, and that some men before and after Christ have so used their free will that they have been sinless. God's grace, so at least some Pelagians held, is seen in giving man free will at his creation, in giving man the law as a guide to his choice, and in sending Jesus Christ who by his teaching and good example assists men to do good. From Augustine's standpoint, this view made grace unnecessary and differed little from Stoic morality.

The struggle between Augustine and Pelagianism is a phase, within a Christian context, of the agelong controversy between determinism and indeterminism in which in many different cultures thoughtful men have engaged. To Christians with the experience of Paul and Augustine only one answer is possible, for in their own lives they have known the impotence of their wills and the power of victory which has come from outside themselves as the free gift of God through Jesus Christ. To them it is easy to regard the action of God as initiated solely by God and at His unfathomable discretion. Others, who have not known that deep inner conflict with its bitter frustration and the amazing joy of triumph through God's grace, have been inclined to hold to man's ability to attain, through his own effort, although perhaps aided by God, to the ideal life. In one form or another the issue has again and again been raised, especially in the Christianity of Western Europe.

SEMI-PELAGIANISM

Although Pelagianism had been officially condemned by the authorities of the Catholic Church, not all Catholics fully agreed with Augustine. Some thought that his doctrine of predestination, irresistible grace, and perseverance due entirely to God would undercut all moral effort, for if God chooses those who are to be saved and no sinner can take even the first step towards repentance and God without the impulse of God's grace, and if God will find a way of making His grace effective for the elect, why should any one trouble himself to attempt to do what is right?

This stage of the controversy over election as against free will was begun by John Cassian, a monk from the East who about 415 founded monasteries in the vicinity of Marseilles, in Gaul. He declared that God wishes all men, not merely some, to be saved, that He has not so made man that the latter neither wills nor is able to do good, and that when He sees in us even the smallest spark of a will towards goodness He strengthens it. Cassian was followed by his pupil, Vincent, a monk of Lerins, who declared that Augustine's teachings were novelties and that in the Catholic Church "all possible care should be taken" to "hold that faith which has been believed everywhere, always, and by all." (*Quod ubique, quod semper, quod ab omnibus.*)

Some in Gaul came to the support of the views of Augustine and in 529 the Bishop of Arles held a synod or council at Orange whose findings were approved by Bishop Boniface II, of Rome, and thus were accorded the support of that powerful see. The Synod of Orange affirmed original sin and declared that man has lost all power to turn to God and that turning to God is wholly through God's grace. It condemned those who affirmed that our will can anticipate God's action, that the beginning of faith and the desire to believe can come apart from the free gift of grace, and that apart from God's grace we can choose the good. Yet the findings of the synod said nothing of irresistible grace and condemned the teaching that some are predestined to evil. Moreover, the Synod of Orange did not speak of man as being totally depraved by Adam's sin. It said, rather, that by that sin free will is so inclined and weakened that "no one is able to love God as he ought, or believe in God, or do anything for God which is good, except the grace of divine mercy comes first to him." Moreover, the Synod of Orange ascribed more to baptism than did Augustine. To be sure, Augustine held that baptism is essential to the remission of sins, but the Synod of Orange declared that through the grace received at baptism "all who have been baptized can and ought, by the aid and support of Christ, to perform those things which belong to the salvation of the soul if they labour faithfully." The implication is that all, and not merely, as Augustine held, those of the limited number of the elect, can, if they are baptized, through the grace which comes through baptism, if they work at it faithfully, by the aid and support of Christ, be assured of salvation. They need not be distressed by the fear that they are not of those to whom, through grace, perseverance has not been given. Man's will has not been so impaired by Adam's fall but that, healed by grace and aided by Christ, it can achieve salvation. Here were semi-Augustinianism, a weakening of pure Augustinianism, and a view of baptism which were to characterize Latin or Roman Christianity in succeeding centuries.

THE CONTINUED DEVELOPMENT OF THE STRUCTURE OF THE CATHOLIC CHURCH

While these developments were taking place in the thought of Christians about their faith, and, as we have suggested, in part through the struggle to arrive at a common mind on the issues which were raised, the structure of the Catholic Church was continuing to grow. While this growth was in part from the effort to reach unanimity on central features of the Christian faith, it was profoundly affected by the patterns of the state and the society in which the Church found itself and by the relations of the Church to the state.

The Catholic Church was the majority Church of the Roman Empire. While it reached beyond that Empire and while there were minority Christian groups which excluded themselves from the Catholic Church or were excluded by it, in the main the Catholic Church was the Church of the Roman Empire. By the close of the fifth century the Catholic Church and the Roman state had become so intimately associated that the latter had placed an impress upon the former which was to prove indelible. The Catholic Church owed what might be called its structural unity as much to the fact that it had the support of the political unity which the Roman Empire had given to the Mediterranean Basin as to the love which theoretically should bind all Christians together. Indeed, when in the centuries which immediately followed the first five hundred years of the faith the Roman Empire fell apart, the unity which ideally should have existed in the Christian Church not only was too feeble to preserve the unity of the Mediterranean world: it also was not strong enough to hold the Catholic Church together. Yet so deeply had the Roman Empire placed its stamp on the Catholic Church that to this day the various fragments into which the latter broke have preserved many of the features, especially those of outward organization, which were acquired in the days of the Empire, and the largest fragment, the Roman Catholic Church, in many ways perpetuates the genius of pre-Christian Rome.

As we have suggested, increasingly the Church centred about the clergy led by the bishops and especially around the bishops. As early as the beginning of the second century a differentiation between clergy and laity began to be seen, and as time passed a priesthood developed which was regarded as the Christian counterpart of that of the ancient Jews. Leading the clergy and, therefore, the Church, were the bishops. As we have seen, the bishops were regarded as successors of the apostles. The development of the clergy and of ranks in the clergy may in part have been influenced by the example of the kind of officialdom which characterized the Roman Empire, especially during the later years of the period which we have been describing. We have also noted something of the theory of the episcopate held by the great Bishop of Carthage, Cyprian, who expounded it in letter after letter. He insisted that the bishops were necessary to the very existence (esse) of the Church and were not merely a form of administration found useful for the well-being (bene esse) of the Church. "The Church is in the bishop and the bishop in the Church," he said. He held that each bishop was the equal of every other bishop and that while a bishop might admonish one of his brothers no one had rightful administrative authority over any other. He declared that no bishop should "set himself up as a bishop of bishops," and that a bishop "can no more be judged by another than he himself can judge another." In this he was in conflict with the claims of the Bishops of Rome, claims to which we have already referred and to which we are to recur. The bishops tended to group themselves by the administrative divisions of the Empire, and for the election and consecration of a bishop the bishops of a particular province assembled. From very early days, bishops wrote letters to one another on matters which concerned the Church. Through them, Christians in one part of the Empire helped those in other sections who suffered from persecution or famine. Bishops prayed for one another, especially at the time of the Eucharistic services. Lists of bishops, emperors, and benefactors of the Church, both living and dead, were placed on tablets, called diptychs, for commemoration at the Eucharist. Removal of a bishop's name from the diptychs of another bishop was symbolic of excommunication.

After the time when, through Constantine, the government of the Roman Empire made its peace with the Church, the Church became increasingly associated with the state. Long before it had accepted the Church, the Roman state had insisted upon controlling the religion of its citizens. Its Emperor was *pontifex maximus,* the chief priest of the cults officially acknowledged by the state. It was, therefore, natural that when the Emperors were Christians they should insist upon having similar power in the Church. To be sure, they were not members of the hierarchy and did not perform the functions which by now had become exclusively assigned to the latter. The Church was never as fully subservient to the Emperor as the former pagan state cults had been, but to a degree maintained the autonomy which it had developed in the centuries when it had not been accorded legal recognition. In theory a Christian Emperor might be cut off from communion for his misdeeds like the humblest member of the Church. This was seldom done, but on a notable occasion in 390 Ambrose, as Bishop of Milan, remonstrated with the Emperor Theodosius for a massacre which the latter had ordered in Thessalonica and excluded him from the Church until he had proved his repentance by the acts prescribed for penitents. Yet the Emperors exercised great power in the Church. We have noted how Constantine and some of his successors sought to bring internal peace in the Church by calling councils of the Church. We have pointed out that some of the Emperors hastened the formal acceptance of Christianity by encouraging bishops in their missionary activities and by proscribing paganism and its ceremonies. Eventually, the Emperor himself, as we have reported, and as we are to see especially in the case of Justinian, declared what was sound doctrine. The Emperors enforced the decrees of councils against those condemned as heretics. They had a voice in appointments to high ecclesiastical office, especially in the East, near the main seat of their authority. As time passed, the assent of the Emperor was required even for the assumption of his powers by each successive Bishop of Rome. It was under the Emperors that what came to be called "ecumenical councils" became the voice of the entire Catholic Church.

In the course of the years the bishops in the larger cities began to exercise authority over the bishops in their vicinity. In 341 the Council of Antioch ordered that in each province the bishop in the chief city, or metropolis, should have precedence over the other bishops in the province, and that the other bishops should "do nothing extraordinary without him." In this the council believed that it was not making an innovation but was simply following a time-honoured custom. The metropolitan or archbishop was to take no common action without the concurrence of the other bishops in his province. Each bishop had authority in his own diocese, namely, "the whole district which is dependent upon his city; to ordain presbyters and deacons; and to settle everything with judgement." But he was "not to undertake anything further without the bishop of the metropolis," nor was the latter "to undertake anything further" without the consent of the other bishops of the province. Any bishop might have under him what were called chorepiscopoi, appointed by himself, to supervise the churches in villages and rural districts. The chorepiscopus had been ordained to the episcopate and could ordain those in the subordinate ranks of the clergy—readers, sub-deacons, and exorcists—but not presbyters or deacons.

The bishops in the chief cities of the Empire had positions of outstanding prestige, a prestige which, with modifications, has persisted into our own day. Especially prominent were those of Jerusalem, because of its historic associations with the beginning of Christianity, Antioch, the chief city of Syria and where the disciples were first called Christians, Alexandria, Constantinople, and, particularly, Rome. The bishops of these sees were eventually known as Patriarchs.

The Increasing Importance of the Church of Rome and Its Bishop, the Pope

As the centuries passed, the Church of Rome and its bishop, or the Pope as we must now begin to call him, became increasingly prominent in the Catholic Church. We have already noted the importance of the Church of Rome and the reasons why its bishops occupied a leading place. As time went on that position was accentuated. The removal of the main centre of the administration of the Empire to Constantinople, begun by Constantine, gave added importance to the Church of Rome and its head in the ancient capital and in the West, for they were no longer overshadowed by the Emperor and his court. As we have seen, the Popes usually took an active part in the controversies of the fourth and fifth centuries over the relation of the divine and human in Jesus Christ and between Augustinianism and Pelagianism and, with two possible and brief exceptions, were on the side which the majority eventually regarded as orthodox. Rome was more and more esteemed in the Catholic Church as the representative and champion of true Christianity. When, in the fifth century, the imperial power began to decline in the West, the Popes, by contrast, loomed larger in that region, especially in Rome and Italy. This was particularly the case when, after 404, the imperial residence in the West was taken from Rome to Ravenna.

To this prestige of their office some of the Popes made outstanding contributions. Fairly typical of the pontiffs of the fifth century was Innocent I, who held the post from 402 to 417. In spite of the fact that his tenure of the office saw the sack of Rome by Alaric (although Innocent was in Ravenna at the time on business of state), he was active in the affairs of the Catholic Church in Italy, Spain, Gaul, Illyricum, North Africa, Thessalonica, and the East. He championed, although unsuccessfully, the cause of his contemporary, John Chrysostom, when the latter was deprived of the see of Constantinople.

Far more important was Leo I, who held the office of Pope from 440 to 461, and who with Gregory I, whom we are to meet in a later chapter, is known by common consent as "the Great." None of his predecessors had been as forceful or had exercised so great an influence. He insisted that by Christ's decree Peter was the rock, the foundation, the doorkeeper of the kingdom of heaven, set to bind and loose, whose judgements retained their validity in heaven, and that through the Pope, as his successor, Peter continued to perform the assignment which had been entrusted to him. We have noted how Leo's Tome set forth the doctrinal position which was approved by the Council of Chalcedon. Leo declined to recognize as valid the canon enacted by that body which elevated the see of Constantinople to a position substantially equal with that of Rome, thus seeming to assert the right of his office to dissent from the decrees of a general or ecumenical council, but basing his opposition in part on the finality of what had been done earlier at Nicæa. Leo was a contemporary of the invasion of Italy by Attila and his Huns and was a bulwark of order in those troubled times. He interested himself in ecclesiastical questions throughout Italy, such as the qualifications of candidates for the episcopacy. In Gaul he successfully asserted the claims of the Church of Rome even as against metropolitans. He concerned himself with affairs in Spain and North

Africa. He obtained from the Emperor Valentinian III an edict which commanded all to obey the Bishop of Rome on the ground that the latter held the "primacy of St. Peter."

In 494 a successor of Leo, Gelasius, declared that the world is ruled by the Emperor and the priests, but that the latter are more important since they will have to give an account even for kings in the day of judgement, and that the Emperor must submit to prelates in divine matters. He also insisted that the Pope was of right preëminent over all priests. He declared that in view of the founding of the Church of Christ upon Peter and of the joint consecration by Peter and Paul of the Church of Rome, the latter "has been placed before the other churches" and hence depended for that position not on any decrees of synods, but upon Christ Himself. Moreover, by their presence and martyrdom Peter and Paul, so Gelasius said, had elevated the Roman Church "over all the others in the whole world."

Probably important for the contribution which the outstanding Popes made to the leading position of Rome was the fact that they embodied the skill in administration and the sense for law and order which were the characteristics of the great Romans.

SUMMARY

We do well to remember that the developments which we have described in the chapter of which the following lines are a brief summary were taking place concurrently with the amazing spread of the faith which we attempted to cover in the chapter that immediately preceded it. While Christianity was winning the professed allegiance of the overwhelming majority of the population of the Roman Empire and was being carried beyond the Roman borders, it was developing a visible, organized fellowship, the Church, and was seeking to define what Christians deemed the essential convictions of their faith. This was accomplished within the context of the Roman Empire and of Greek and Roman patterns of thought. Always there was the dream, going back to Christ himself, of a unity of love embracing all those who bore his name.

Never was that unity fully realized. Indeed, the history of the Church was—and has been throughout—chronically punctuated by dissension, often bitter and between outstanding leaders in the Church. Bishops, synods, and councils employed emphatic language in condemning individuals and views from which they differed. Never was there a single organization which was comprehensive of all who professed themselves Christians. The efforts to define the distinctive doctrines of the Christian faith invariably sharpened divisions among Christians. By the close of the fifth century several rival bodies were in existence, each regarding itself as representative of true Christianity and most of them calling themselves Catholic and denying that designation to the others. Such unity as existed had been furthered by the development of the Church within a single cohesive political structure, the Roman Empire. Moreover, again and again Roman Emperors had intervened in the affairs of the Church in an effort, usually futile or at best ephemeral, to achieve unity. In the process it often seemed as though Christ had died in vain, that his teachings were being hopelessly compromised and, while honoured in word, were denied in practice.

Yet, by a seeming paradox which we are to witness again and again in the history of Christianity, the failure to live up to the ideals set forth by Christ and his apostles was paralleled by prodigious vitality. From being one of the smallest of scores of rival religious groups, Christians had become numerically dominant, and that within less than five centuries. In a civilization which was dying and which was ceasing to say or to do anything new, Christianity had stimulated the emergence of the Church. This Church, to be sure, was really several churches rather than one, but the very divisions were evidence of vigour and of the power which had been released in the Gospel, and almost all branches, with the possible exception of the Gnostics, had common features of organization and belief.

The organization of the Church bore the indelible impress of the political framework within which it had arisen. However, it was not a pale reflection of that framework, but a fresh creation. The creeds and the discussions out of which they were formulated were influenced by Greek and Roman thought, but they were essentially new. Forced by the fact of living in a particular intellectual climate to use terms and employ ideas which were features of that climate, Christians were saying something quite novel and even revolutionary. They were handicapped by the only terminologies which lay to their hands and by the grandeur and originality of the Gospel. None of the words which they employed quite expressed what they were struggling to understand and to express, but what they said was, like the Gospel itself, fresh and striking. Christians had not yet rethought the whole range of human knowledge in terms of Christ, but some, notably Origen and Augustine, had attempted to see Christ in the setting of Greek philosophy, and in his *City of God* Augustine had endeavoured to discern the meaning of the entire human drama as disclosed in the Scriptures and Christ.

The Church and its faith were clearly a new creation. Their appearance and their spread were only the beginning of the story, for, as we are to see later, they were to continue to expand from the narrow confines of the Mediterranean world until by the middle of the twentieth century they had won footholds in almost every corner and among almost all the peoples of the globe.

SELECTED BIBLIOGRAPHY

GENERAL WORKS

J. C. Ayer, *A Source Book for Ancient Church History from the Apostolic Age to the Close of the Conciliar Period* (New York, Charles Scribner's Sons, 1913, pp. xxi, 707). A useful selection of translations with brief introductory comments, some of which are misleading.

L. Duchesne, *Early History of the Christian Church from Its Foundation to the End of the Fifth Century* (translated from the French. New York, Longmans, Green & Co., 3 vols., 1908–1924). By a liberal French Roman Catholic scholar.

The Church History of Eusebius, Translated with Prolegomena and Notes, by A. C. McGiffert, in *Nicene and Post-Nicene Fathers*, Second Series, Vol. I (New York, Charles Scribner's Sons, 1890). The standard translation into English of this most important of the early church histories, with extremely valuable notes.

Augustin Fliche and Victor Martin, editors, *Histoire de L'Église depuis les Origines jusqu'a Nos Jours* (Paris, Bloud & Gay, Vols. 1–4, 1947, 1948, cover the period to the election of Gregory the Great). By several Roman Catholic scholars.

H. M. Gwatkin, *Early Church History to A.D. 313* (London, Macmillan & Co., 2 vols., 1909). Readable, with references to the sources.

B. J. Kidd, *A History of the Christian Church to A.D. 461* (Oxford, The Clarendon Press, 3 vols., 1922). By a high Anglican. Valuable in part for its very extensive footnote references to the sources.

H. Lietzmann, *A History of the Early Church*. This comprehensive work, planned in German in five volumes, but left incomplete by the author's death in 1943, was brought down to the close of the fourth volume by a later hand. The first three volumes have been translated by B. L. Woolf as follows: *The Beginnings of the Christian Church* (New York, Charles Scribner's Sons, 1949, pp. 303), *The Founding of the Church Universal* (New York: Charles Scribner's Sons, 1938, pp. 432), and *From Constantine to Julian* (London, Lutterworth Press, 1950, pp. 340).

THE ORGANIZATION OF THE EARLY CHURCH

A. Harnack, *The Constitution and Law of the Church in the First Two Centuries,* translated by F. L. Pogson, edited by H. D. A. Major (New York, G. P. Putnam's Sons, 1910, pp. xiv, 349). A standard work.

J. B. Lightfoot, *Saint Paul's Epistle to the Philippians. A Revised Text with Introduction, Notes, and Dissertations* (London, Macmillan & Co., 1890, pp. xii, 350). Contains an important dissertation on the Christian ministry, by an Anglican bishop.

B. H. Streeter, *The Primitive Church, Studied with Special Reference to the Origins of the Christian Ministry* (New York, The Macmillan Co., 1929, pp. xii, 323). A thoroughly competent work by an Anglican.

Teaching of the Twelve Apostles, Edited with a Translation, Introduction and Notes by R. D. Hitchcock and F. Brown. New edition (New York, Charles Scribner's Sons, 1885, pp. cxv, 85).

THE RISE OF THE CHURCH OF ROME

J. T. Shotwell and L. R. Loomis, *The See of Peter* (Columbia University Press, 1927, pp. xxvi, 737). Translations of pertinent sources for the first four centuries.

GNOSTICISM

The major contemporary description of the various Gnostic teachers and groups which, while an anti-Gnostic polemic, contains much information nowhere else obtainable, is by Irenæus, translated under the title *Against Heresies* in *The Ante-Nicene Fathers,* Vol. I, pp. 309 ff. (Buffalo, The Christian Literature Publishing Co., 1885).

A semi-popular summary treatment of Gnosticism by an expert is F. C. Burkitt, *Church and Gnosis. A Study of Christian Thought and Speculation in the Second Century* (Cambridge University Press, 1932, pp. ix, 153).

More technical and detailed is E. de Faye, *Gnostiques et Gnosticisme* (Paris, Paul Geuthner, 1925, pp. 547).

THE MARCIONITES

The standard treatment is Adolf von Harnack, *Marcion: Das Evangelium von fremden Gott. Ein Monographie zur Geschichte der Grundlegung der katholischen Kirche* (Leipzig, J. C. Hinrichs'sche Buchhandlung, 1921, pp. xv, 357).

E. C. Blackman, *Marcion and His Influence* (London, Society for Promoting Christian Knowledge, 1948, pp. x, 181), appreciates Harnack but holds that he has overestimated Marcion's influence on the formation of the New Testament canon and the Apostles' Creed.

MONTANISM

Bonwetsch, *Die Geschichte des Montanismus* (Erlangen, Andreas Deichert, 1881, pp. viii, 210).

J. de Soyres, *Montanism and the Primitive Church* (Cambridge, Deighton, Bell & Co., 1878, pp. viii, 167).

THE FORMATION OF THE NEW TESTAMENT

Two popular accounts, both by specialists, are B. W. Bacon, *The Making of the New Testament* (*The Home University Library of Modern Knowledge,* New York, Henry Holt and Co., 1912, pp. 256), and E. J. Goodspeed, *The Story of the New Testament* (The University of Chicago Press, 1916, pp. xiii, 150).

THE DONATISTS

W. H. C. Frend, *The Donatist Church. A Movement of Protest in Roman North Africa* (Oxford, The Clarendon Press, 1952, pp. xvi, 360). A very important study, carefully done.

GENERAL WORKS ON THE HISTORY OF CHRISTIAN DOCTRINE

A. von Harnack, *History of Dogma,* translated from the third German edition by E. B. Speirs, J. Millar, *et alii* (London, Williams & Norgate, 7 vols., 1894–1899). Marked by the well-known conviction of the author that the historical Jesus, the Jesus disclosed in the first three Gospels, and the conceptions of him held by Christians, were profoundly altered by Greek thought and especially by Neoplatonic philosophy and the identification of Christ with the *Logos.* Brilliant and erudite, Harnack has proved provocative, convincing to some, controverted by others, and always stimulating.

A. C. McGiffert, *A History of Christian Thought. Volume I, Early and Eastern from Jesus to John of Damascus* (New York, Charles Scribner's Sons, 1932, pp. x, 352). Written in late life by a distinguished scholar, embodying a course which he had taught for many years, much briefer than Harnack's work, somewhat less technical, but still with extensive references to the sources. The viewpoint is that of the liberalism of the latter part of the nineteenth and the fore part of the twentieth century.

R. Seeberg, *Text-Book of the History of Doctrines.* Revised, 1904, by the author, translated by C. E. Hay (Philadelphia, The United Lutheran Publishing House, 2 vols., 1905). *Volume I. History of Doctrines in the Ancient Church,* pp. xviii, 413. Not as brilliant as Harnack, and more detailed and technical than McGiffert, but probably the best comprehensive summary.

THE APOSTLES' CREED

A. C. McGiffert, *The Apostles' Creed* (New York, Charles Scribner's Sons, 1902, pp. vi, 206).

TERTULLIAN

Translations of the works of Tertullian are to be found in *The Ante-Nicene Fathers,* Vols. III and IV (New York, Charles Scribner's Sons, 1899).

CLEMENT OF ALEXANDRIA

A translation of the works of Clement of Alexandria is in *The Ante-Nicene Fathers,* Vol. II, pp. 163–605 (New York, Charles Scribner's Sons, 1899).

ORIGEN

Translations of Origen's chief surviving works are in *The Ante-Nicene Fathers,* Vol. IV, pp. 221–669 (New York, Charles Scribner's Sons, 1899).

On Clement and Origen see C. Bigg, *The Christian Platonists of Alexandria* (New York, The Macmillan Co., 1886, pp. xxvii, 304).

THE COUNCILS

C. J. Hefele, *A History of the Christian Councils,* translated from the German by W. R. Clark. The first four volumes (Edinburgh, T. & T. Clark, 1872–1895) carry the story down to A.D. 680. By a Roman Catholic scholar, more extensive than any other treatment available in English.

E. H. Landon, *A Manual of Councils of the Holy Catholic Church* (Edinburgh, rev. ed., John Grant, 2 vols., 1909). A much briefer compendium than Hefele, arranged alphabetically by councils rather than chronologically.

ATHANASIUS

Select Writings and Letters of Athanasius, Bishop of Alexandria, edited, with prolegomena, by A. Robertson in *A Select Library of Nicene and Post-Nicene Fathers of the Christian Church.* Second Series, edited by P. Schaff and H. Wace, Vol. IV (New York, Charles Scribner's Sons, 1903, pp. xci, 605).

NESTORIANISM

J. F. Bethune-Baker, *Nestorius and His Teaching. A Fresh Examination of the Evidence* (Cambridge University Press, 1908, pp. xviii, 232). Carefully done.

F. Loofs, *Nestorius and His Place in the History of Christian Doctrine* (Cambridge University Press, 1914, pp. vii, 132). A careful study by an expert, differing from Bethune-Baker in some of its conclusions.

F. Loofs, *Nestoriana. Die Fragmente des Nestorius gesammelt, untersucht und herausgeben* (Halle, Max Niemeyer, 1905, pp. x, 407). Competent.

Nestorius. The Bazaar of Heraclides. Newly translated from the Syriac and edited with an Introduction, Notes & Appendices by G. R. Driver and Leonard Hodgson (Oxford, The Clarendon Press, 1925, pp. xxxv, 425). The joint editorship of a specialist in the language and a theologian.

AUGUSTINE

Saint Augustin's The City of God, translated by Marcus Dods, and *On Christian Doctrine in Four Books,* translated by J. F. Shaw, in *A Select Library of the Nicene and Post-Nicene Fathers of the Christian Church,* edited by P. Schaff, Vol. II, pp. vi, 621 (New York, Charles Scribner's Sons, 1887).

St. Augustin: On the Holy Trinity. Doctrinal Treatises. Moral Treatises, translated by various authors, in *A Select Library of the Nicene and Post-Nicene Fathers of the Christian Church,* edited by P. Schaff, Vol. III, pp. iv, 578 (New York, Charles Scribner's Sons, 1900). This also includes the *Enchiridion.*

Saint Augustin's Anti-Pelagian Works, translated by P. Holmes and R. E. Wallis, revised by B. B. Warfield, in *A Select Library of the Nicene and Post-Nicene Fathers of the Christian Church,* edited by P. Schaff, Vol. V, pp. lxxii, 567 (New York, Charles Scribner's Sons, 1902).

L. Bertrand, *Saint Augustin,* translated by V. O'Sullivan (New York, Appleton-Century-Crofts, 1914, pp. viii, 396). A popularly, well-written biography.

C. N. Cochrane, *Christianity and Classical Culture: a Study of Thought and Action from Augustus to Augustine* (Oxford, The Clarendon Press, 1940, pp. vii, 523). A competent survey with stimulating conclusions.

Chapter VII

ADMISSION, WORSHIP, AND DISCIPLINE IN
THE CHRISTIAN COMMUNITY

While Christianity was spreading and while the Christian Church was coming into being, developing its organizations, thinking through its faith, and experiencing divisions, other aspects of the Christian community were taking shape. Processes and standards were being worked out for admission to the Church, forms of worship were developing, and methods were being devised for achieving and maintaining Christian ideals of life. They are of importance not only in themselves but also because they shed light on the effect of the Christian Gospel and because many of the customs and forms which then emerged have either persisted through the centuries and characterize the churches to which the majority of Christians now belong or form the foundation for current practices. To them we now turn.

ADMISSION TO THE CHURCH

As we have seen, admission to the Church was through baptism. In the first few decades of the Church, baptism might be administered on a simple profession of faith in Christ. Thus on the famous day of Pentecost, often regarded as the birthday of the Church, when about three thousand are reported to have been added to the fellowship of the disciples, the injunction was to repent and be baptized in the name of Jesus Christ. Whether all were baptized on that day is not explicitly stated, but we hear of the Ethiopian Eunuch being baptized after only brief instruction and of a jailer at Philippi receiving the rite, with all that were in his house, on the very night in which he seems first to have heard of Christ, with the simple requirement of belief "in the Lord Jesus Christ." An early baptismal formula, in accordance with the command in the closing words of *The Gospel according to Matthew,* was "in the name of the Father and of the Son and of the Holy Ghost." Baptism seems to have been by immersion, at least normally. Whether it was by immersion only has been a matter of debate and on it no unanimity has been realized. Immersion appears to have been implied in the symbolism of death and burial to the old life and the resurrection to the new life of which Paul spoke so graphically. Baptism seems to have been regarded as requisite for the "remission of sins" and for the new birth through which alone one could enter the Kingdom of God. It was often, perhaps regularly, followed by the laying on of hands by one of the apostles, although not necessarily by one of the Twelve, and through this the Holy Spirit was held to be imparted.

By the time that the *Didache* was written, baptism, at least as that document knew it, was still comparatively simple. It was preceded by instruction. Both he who administered baptism and such other Christians as could do so were to fast before the rite was given to a neophyte. Baptism was to be "in the name of the Father, and of the Son, and of the Holy Ghost." It was normally to be in "living," that is, running cold water, but if that were not available it might be in other and even in warm water. If immersion were impossible, water was to be poured upon the head three times "into the name of the Father and Son and Holy Ghost." Another early custom was to have the candidate anointed with oil both before and after baptism.

Tertullian, writing not far from the end of the second or the beginning of the third century, describes baptism. Evidently it had been further elaborated. The rite was to be administered by a bishop or a presbyter or deacon designated by him, or, in the absence of these, by a layman. It was generally given at Easter or during the fifty days after Easter. Candidates were to prepare for it by prayer, fasting, vigils through entire nights, and the confession of all past sins. Immediately before baptism, which was in water that had previously been blessed, the convert formally renounced the devil, his pomps, and his angels. He was also anointed with oil to drive out evil spirits. After the rite the newly baptized candidate was given a mixture of milk and honey to taste and was again anointed with oil. Then a hand, preferably that of the bishop, was laid on him, invoking the Holy Spirit, and he was signed on his forehead with oil. He refrained from the daily bath for a week after having received the rite.

Baptism was by a thrice-repeated immersion, preferably in water running through the baptistry. The first immersion was preceded by a confession of faith in God the Father, the second by a confession of faith in Christ Jesus, the Son of God, and the third by a confession of faith in the Holy Spirit. In at least some churches, so we must note in passing, the candidate was baptized naked, the children first, then the men, and finally the women. No one was to take into the water anything except his body.

The post-baptismal laying on of hands for the reception of the Holy Spirit was the rudimentary form of what later came to be esteemed one of the sacraments, confirmation. In Rome by the end of the fifth century this was regularly done by the Pope, as Bishop of Rome, in a special chapel behind the baptistry. There the newly baptized were brought. Then the Pope prayed to God to send His Holy Spirit on them, and, dipping his thumb in the consecrated oil, made the sign of the cross on the forehead of each saying "In the name of the Father, and the Son, and the Holy Spirit, Peace to you."

Tertullian appears to have believed that he was describing baptism as it was generally practised in his day, but it may well have been that no such uniformity existed as he supposed. For instance, according to another early account, the bishop anointed the candidate before rather than after immersion. Tertullian vigorously opposed teaching and the administration of baptism by women, because there were Christians who advocated both.

By Tertullian's day the baptism of infants seems to have been common, so much so that he spoke of it as though all Christians were familiar with it. At baptism the children had sponsors who took vows, apparently on behalf of the children. Tertullian favoured the deferring of baptism for infants until they themselves knew Christ and asked for baptism. He also advocated that for the unmarried baptism be delayed either until they married or until the habit of continence had been established.

Some baptized infants eight days after birth, but Cyprian objected even to this postponement. In this he was supported by Augustine, who held that baptism removed the taint of original sin derived through Adam.

As we have seen in the case of Augustine, baptism was regarded as washing away previous sins and, since it could not be repeated (although martyrdom, being interpreted as a baptism by blood, might count instead of baptism by water or be a second baptism), it was by many deemed the part of wisdom to postpone it until the first heat of youth was passed or until one's final illness. Some authorities in the Church might discourage such delay, but numbers, even of eminent laymen, including more than one of the Emperors, judged it safe and adopted it.

In the years when Christianity was spreading rapidly and thousands of converts were coming from paganism, baptism was preceded by a period of instruction and probation as a catechumen. Admission to the catechumenate was eventually by a ceremony in which the priest blew on the face of the aspirant, signed his forehead with the cross, and put a grain of salt in his mouth. Catechumens were counted as Christians and were admitted to the services of the Church, but were required to leave when a certain stage in the ritual was reached, before the celebration of the Eucharist. In some places the catechumenate was for three years.

The question began to be raised in the Catholic Church of the efficacy of baptism if it were administered by one who was regarded as a heretic. Tertullian and Cyprian of Carthage stoutly maintained that such baptism was not valid. This view was held in some other sections of the Church, especially in Syria and Asia Minor. On the other hand, Rome and Alexandria regarded baptism as authentic no matter by whom it had been given, provided only that it had been with water and with the essential forms.

Early Christian Worship

What was done in the assemblies of the early Christians? In what did their meetings consist? In what manner did they worship? So far as we know, no single pattern was followed. There was much spontaneity, and the Holy Spirit was believed to be impelling and guiding. Here and there we have hints of what took place, but nowhere do we have a complete picture. We are told that in the first days of the Church in Jerusalem the initial large influx of converts, those who came out of the stirring events of Pentecost, "continued steadfastly in the apostles' doctrine and fellowship, in the breaking of bread and in prayers." Here were instruction, presumably a rehearsal of the sayings, deeds, death, and resurrection of Christ; fellowship or community, the "breaking of bread," which may mean the supper which had been instituted by Christ; and "prayers," as though these were already customary. We hear, too, of meetings of the Jerusalem Christians on special occasions for thanksgiving or petition. In the church in Antioch in its earliest days there were prophets and teachers, and this may have implied gatherings at which they spoke.

From Paul's first letter to the church in Corinth we have as nearly a detailed picture of the assemblies of a church of the first generation of Christians as has come down to us. Apparently there were meetings in which both men and women spoke, although Paul declared that in all the churches it was the rule that women should keep silent. Paul implies that the assemblies were open to non-Christians as well as Christians, and that they were often noisy and confusing. Several might simultaneously "speak with tongues." At the same time two or more might be "prophesying," that is, voicing a message which they believed had been given them by the Spirit, perhaps in the form of a "revelation." There were some who were gifted with the ability to "interpret tongues," or to put into the common speech the meaning of what had been spoken in an unknown tongue. There were those who broke out in spontaneous prayer in a "tongue" or in the vernacular. Apparently it was the custom for the hearers to say "Amen"—"so be it"—a sign of emphatic agreement, at the end of a prayer, especially if that were one of thanksgiving. There was singing, perhaps at times in a "tongue," at other times with a psalm. Paul strove to bring some kind of order into these gatherings. Although he himself had the gift of "tongues," he held it to be far inferior to speaking in a fashion which others could understand, so that all might profit. He would limit these speeches in a "tongue" to two or three, and one at a time, with some one on hand to interpret. If there was no one to interpret he who felt impelled to use an unknown tongue was to keep silence. He commanded the "prophets" to speak one at a time, and only two or three at one meeting.

At Corinth the Supper of the Lord was prominent in the common life of the church. It seems to have been associated with a meal, the *agape,* or "love feast." To Paul's distress, to this meal each brought his own food and drink and the better supplied did not share their provisions with those who had little or nothing, with the result that some became drunk and others went away hungry. Paul recounted the original institution of the Lord's Supper as he declared that he had "received" it "of the Lord," presumably by direct revelation, and insisted that he who partook of the Lord's Supper in an unworthy manner was guilty of the body and blood of the Lord, as though he were among those who had crucified Christ. Paul believed that in some real sense, while the bread was eaten and the wine was drunk in memory of Christ, the wine and the bread were also the blood and the body of Christ. Said he: "The cup of blessing which we bless, is it not a communion in [or participation in] the blood of Christ? The bread which we break, is it not a communion in [or participation in] the body of Christ." The meaning of the Lord's Supper and the character of the presence in it of Christ were eventually to become two of the most controversial questions among Christians.

From the beginning the example and forms of worship of the Jewish synagogue had a marked influence upon Christian worship. The Christians were familiar with the Jewish scriptures, presumably in part because they were read in their services. The *Trisagion,* "Holy, Holy, Holy, Lord God of Sabaoth, heaven and earth are full of His glory. Blessed be He for ever," was used in Christian worship, probably from a very early date, and was a direct contribution from the synagogue. So, too, was the congregational response, "Amen."

LATER DEVELOPMENTS IN WORSHIP

As from the second century we gain further glimpses of the worship of the churches, we find that it was built about the Lord's Supper. This was coming to be called the Eucharist, from a Greek word meaning the giving of thanks. The Eucharist was being clearly separated from the *agape.* The emphasis upon the Lord's Supper was to be expected, for it perpetually focussed attention upon the source of the Church's origin and vigour—Christ, his death, his resurrection, his continuing life, and the new and eternal life given to the Christian through him. It was with the narrative of the death and resurrection of Christ, if we may judge from the proportion of space given it in all

Four Gospels and from the emphasis upon it in the other writings in the New Testament, that the instruction of catechumens was largely concerned and on it the thought and faith of Christians were centred.

One of the earliest descriptions of the Eucharist, that by Justin Martyr, not far from the middle of the second century, recognizes the similarity to what was seen in one of the mystery cults, Mithraism, but holds that this was because the latter had imitated the Christians. Latterly it has been repeatedly asserted that in baptism and the Eucharist Christians borrowed from the mysteries and that Christianity was simply another one of these cults, with Christ as its hero-god, slain by his enemies and raised from the dead, and, like them, drawing its appeal and power from the assurance to the initiates that through its rites the believers would share in the death and in the resurrection and immortality of its god. The similarity is striking.

Yet fully as striking are the differences. None of the others could point to a clearly historical figure, nor could the other figures begin to match Christ in teachings and character. It was in retaining their belief in Jesus Christ as fully man as well as fully God that the majority of Christians rightly discerned that the uniqueness of their faith consisted, against the Gnostics who would minimize or reject Jesus as a particular man who lived at a particular date in history, or the Marcionites who held that he was not truly flesh, but only seemed to be man, or those who maintained that he was merely an ordinary man who somewhere in the course of his life had been adopted by the Divine Spirit.

There is no proof of either conscious or unconscious copying from the mystery religions by Christians. Indeed, the voluminous writings of Christian apologists of the early centuries which have survived make very little mention of the mystery religions. Their attacks are directed, rather, against the Greek and Roman polytheism with its pantheon and its stories of the gods, or against the Greek philosophies, as though the mystery cults did not count. Presumably many Christians were aware of the latter and might even once have been adherents of them. They may have carried over into Christianity some of the conceptions of religion derived from them. This, however, has yet to be demonstrated. Certainly Christianity was essentially different from what we know of these cults, and the similarities are only superficial.

Already in the second century the chief day of worship and of the celebration of the Eucharist was Sunday, and the reason given was that it was on this first day of the week, "the Lord's Day," that Christ had been raised from the dead. In choosing that day instead of the Jewish Sabbath (although for centuries even many Gentile Christians also observed the seventh day, or Sabbath) or of Friday, the day of their Lord's crucifixion, Christians were giving further evidence that their faith was primarily in the risen Christ.

Two somewhat detailed descriptions of the fashion in which the Lord's Supper was celebrated in the second century have come down to us. The one, in the *Didache,* was intended primarily for Christians. The other, in one of the apologies of Justin Martyr, was designed to be read by non-Christians. The two show variations from each other, an indication that uniformity had by no means been attained, but they also display striking similarities. Both, for example, speak of the rite as the Eucharist, evidence that this designation had become very widespread.

In the *Didache* the direction is given that only the baptized shall share in the Eucharist. First the cup was given, with the prayer of thanksgiving, apparently already fixed and ritualistic:

We thank Thee, our Father, for the holy vine of David Thy servant, which Thou hast made known to us through Jesus Thy servant; to Thee be the glory forever.

Then came the broken bread with the prayer:

We thank Thee, our Father, for the life and knowledge which Thou hast made known to us through Jesus Thy servant; to Thee be the glory forever. Just as this broken bread was scattered over the hills and having been gathered together became one, so let Thy church be gathered together from the ends of the earth into Thy kingdom; for Thine is the glory and the power through Jesus Christ forever.

After the communicants had been "filled" there was another prayer of thanksgiving:

We thank Thee, holy Father, for Thy holy name, which Thou hast caused to dwell in our hearts, and for the knowledge and faith and immortality which Thou hast made known to us through Jesus Thy servant; to Thee be the glory forever. Thou, Master Almighty, didst create all things for Thy name's sake; both food and drink Thou didst give to men for enjoyment, in order that they might give thanks to Thee; but to us Thou hast graciously given spiritual food and drink and eternal life through Thy servant. Before all things, we thank Thee that Thou art mighty; to Thee be the glory forever. Remember, Lord, Thy church, to deliver it from every evil and to make it perfect in Thy love, and gather it from the four winds, it, the sanctified, into Thy kingdom, which Thou hast prepared for it; for Thine is the power and the glory forever. Let grace come and let this world pass away. Hosanna to the son of David. Whoever is holy, let him come; whoever is not, let him repent. Maranatha. Amen.

Maranatha, it will be noted, appears to have been one of the earliest expressions of Christians, for we find it in Paul's first letter to the Corinthians. It seems to have been an Aramaic word meaning either the affirmation "our

Lord has come" or, as a prayer for Christ's second coming, "Our Lord, come."

There was also the instruction to "permit the prophets to give thanks as much as they will," presumably making a place for spontaneous prayers by the "prophets," either itinerant or resident, who were a feature of the Christian communities which the *Didache* depicts.

Justin Martyr, describing the Eucharist as he knew it not far from the middle of the second century and presumably in the cities of Asia Minor, among them Ephesus, says that immediately after he had been baptized, which Justin calls "illumination," the new Christian was brought to the assembly of the "brethren," for prayers in behalf of themselves, the freshly baptized, and "for all others in every place," that they might be counted worthy, by their works, and that they might "be saved with an everlasting salvation." After the prayers, the Christians saluted one another with a kiss, a custom enjoined by Paul and perhaps of even earlier origin. There was then brought to the one of the brethren who was presiding bread and a cup of wine mixed with water. He took them and gave thanks to "the Father of the universe, through the name of the Son and of the Holy Spirit," usually at considerable length, and presumably "free prayer," without prescribed form, that the communicants were counted worthy to receive these things at his hands. When he had finished, the congregation said "Amen," and the deacons gave to those present the bread and the water mixed with wine and carried portions to those who were absent.

Justin Martyr goes on to say that the bread and the wine so blessed were not received as common bread and drink, but "as the flesh and blood of that Jesus who was made flesh." He also reports that the Eucharist was observed regularly on Sunday, presumably in addition to these special celebrations for the newly baptized. On Sundays it was preceded by readings from "the memoirs of the apostles or the writings of the prophets" "as long as time permits." After the reader had ceased, he who was presiding "instructs and exhorts to the imitation of these good things." Then all rose together and prayed and there followed the service of the Eucharist in the manner described above. Justin also said that contributions made by the well to do, apparently in connexion with the Eucharist, were deposited with the presiding officer, and the latter used the fund to succour widows, orphans, the sick, prisoners, strangers visiting the Christians, and others who were in need.

The Eucharist as described by both the *Didache* and Justin was open only to the baptized, in it thanksgiving was made, and the bread and the wine were consumed. Yet there are differences, although some of these may be due to failure of one or the other account to give all the details. In the *Didache* the wine came first, the bread second, and in Justin the reverse was the case.

In the *Didache* there was place for a fixed form of prayer as well as free prayer; in the service as known to Justin only free prayer. Justin regards the bread and the wine as the body and blood of Christ, while the *Didache* does not so describe them. The former speaks of the wine as mixed with water, the latter knows nothing of water with the wine. The former tells of portions of the consecrated bread and wine being taken to the absent, of a presiding officer, and of deacons who do the distributing; the latter makes no mention of any of these. Justin describes a Sunday observance of the Eucharist as preceded by reading from what we would now call the Old Testament and the New Testament and a discourse by the one who was presiding, but the *Didache* speaks of neither. In contrast with Justin, the *Didache* tells of a prayer of thanksgiving after the bread and the wine. It also knows prayers for the unity of all Christians, while Justin mentions prayers for all Christians only in connexion with the Eucharist as it was celebrated for the newly baptized.

Hippolytus, of Rome, writing in the first half of the third century, says that immediately after baptism the neophytes were given the Eucharist. The bread came first, and then, in order, they tasted of three cups—of water, of milk mixed with honey, and of wine. Here were variations, but still a simplicity which in succeeding centuries was superseded by more elaborate forms.

DEVELOPING LITURGIES FOR THE EUCHARIST

Well before the end of the fifth century, the Eucharistic rite and the liturgy connected with it had been greatly enlarged. The clergy had become quite distinct from the laity and the presbyters and bishops had become priests patterned consciously after the Jewish priesthood of pre-Christian times and offering a bloodless sacrifice at an altar. The stately, huge church buildings which were erected, especially after Constantine espoused the faith, probably made for an elaboration of a ritual which would be in keeping with them. In at least some sections of the Empire, the sanctuary, which contained the altar, the bishop's throne, and the seats of the clergy, was separated from the laity by a screen and the laity were not supposed to enter it. The altar might be of wood or be a stone slab supported on pillars. The fore part of the liturgy seems to have been an adaptation of the worship in the Jewish synagogue. Variations there still were, but in the chief churches, such as Rome and Alexandria, forms had been developed which had spread widely from these centres and had become associated with particular regions, notably Syria, Egypt, and Gaul.

In general, the following appears to have been approximately the procedure common to all the varieties of the liturgy. When the congregation gathered, the men were on one side of the church and the women on the other. The clergy were in the apse, where was the altar. The youths were by themselves, sitting or standing. The older people were to sit and the mothers with children had a special place. The deacons were to see that all took their proper places and that no one whispered, laughed, nodded, or slept.

The service began with several selections from the Scriptures, by "readers" who took their stand in the ambo, a kind of pulpit or desk raised above the congregation about the middle of the church where they could be heard by all. The readings were interspersed with Psalms chanted by another of the clergy and taken up at the end by the congregation. The last of the readings was from one of the Gospels and all the congregation rose for it. Then one or more of the priests spoke, the custom apparently being that such of the priests present as desired to do so might address a homily to the assembly.

After the homilies those who were not entitled to be present at the Eucharist were dismissed. First the catechumens left, having first offered up a silent prayer at the invitation of the deacon, while the congregation joined in a prayer offered on their behalf by the deacon by answering with *"Kyrie Eleison"*—"Lord have mercy"—followed by a prayer which the catechumens offered in a form suggested by the deacon and by a blessing from the bishop. Next, after the same form, those catechumens were dismissed who were preparing for baptism. Then the penitents who had not yet been received back into communion were sent away, with similar prayers and an episcopal blessing.

The communicants alone being left, they responded to a litany led by the deacon with the words *"Kyrie Eleison."* Then came the Eucharist proper, with the bishop officiating, clad in a festal garment, with the priests around him. There were prayers by the bishop, with responses from the congregation. Among the latter was the *Trisagion, Tersanctus* or *Sanctus*—"Holy, holy, holy . . ."—in which the choir of angels was believed to join. Early in the service, at the outset of the liturgy proper, the bishop gave the kiss of peace to the clergy, and the faithful interchanged it with one another, the men to the men and the women to the women.

There was then the consecration of the bread and the wine, modelled on the account in the Gospel of the institution of the Lord's Supper. This was followed by a prayer for the Church throughout the world, the Lord's Prayer, a litany led by the deacon, and the blessing by the bishop. Somewhere in the course of the centuries there was added to the liturgy the invocation of the Holy Spirit to descend upon the bread and the wine to make of them the body of Christ.

Then came the communion, the clergy first partaking of the elements in the order of their rank, followed by the members of the congregation. The bread and the wine were given to all. During the partaking of the communion, singers chanted some of the Psalms.

After the communion the bishop again offered prayer and gave his blessing and the deacon dismissed the congregation with the words "depart in peace."

This was the Eucharist substantially as it was celebrated in the fourth century. Changes continued to be made in it. For instance, as the conversion of the Empire was completed, the catechumens diminished in numbers and their dismissal either disappeared or became, in at least one of the liturgies, purely vestigial and formal.

OTHER TIMES AND FORMS OF WORSHIP

The Eucharist was the central and chief form of Christian worship developed in these early centuries of the faith. However, it was by no means the only occasion for worship. Some practices were private, by individuals, and others were by groups or congregations. Several of the customs and forms were taken over from Judaism, often with modifications: others were of purely Christian origin.

The most frequently repeated prayer was that given by Christ himself, the Lord's Prayer. This was used both by congregations and by individuals. The *Didache* held that it should be said three times a day. In his treatise on prayer Tertullian gave first importance to it.

The times of prayer were frequent. In the second century it was the custom, presumably held up as the ideal to all the faithful, to pray at daybreak and nightfall when normally Christians came together for prayers and the singing of psalms, and at three other hours of the day—at mid-forenoon, at noon, and at mid-afternoon. We also hear of prayers being enjoined at midnight. Bible reading was commended for the individual Christian if there were no communal services on that day.

Sunday was the chief day of worship. Then the first service, at least at some places and in the second century, was before the dawn, with readings from the Scriptures, chants, homilies, and prayers. After it came the Eucharist in the early hours of the morning. As we have seen, the common meal, the *Agape* or love feast, which in Paul's day seems to have been held in connexion with the Eucharist, was eventually separated from it and held later in the day. It was soon dropped completely, but for what reason is not entirely clear.

The Eucharist was observed on other days than Sunday. Partly after the Jewish custom, two days in the week were marked by fasting and prayer, but they were not those set apart by the Jews, namely, Mondays and Thursdays, but Wednesdays and Fridays. In Latin the word "station" was applied either to these days or to the fasts connected with them. In many places these two days were occasions for the Eucharist, but some Christians felt that they would be breaking their fast if they took communion on them. The Wednesday and Friday fasts were usually concluded by mid-afternoon, and some had the bread and the wine of the Eucharist reserved for them until that hour. In numbers of churches Saturday also became a fast day, or the Friday fast was prolonged into Saturday, and in some churches the Eucharist was not celebrated on that day.

We must note that prayer was commanded before dinner in the form of a brief thanksgiving, with a petition and a dedication to "every good work." The blessing on the meal could not be given by a layman, but only by the bishop or, in his absence, by a presbyter or deacon.

First-fruits were offered to the bishop, who gave thanks for them and presented them to God.

In addition to these regular times of worship, there were special occasions which entailed Christian ceremonies. Among them were ordination, the consecration of virgins, the dedication of churches, and the blessing of marriages. Ordination to the lower ranks of the clergy was by very simple ceremonies. Even that for priests and deacons was not elaborate, but usually consisted of prayers by the congregation and the bishop, the laying of the bishop's hands on the heads of those ordained, and the kiss of peace from the bishop. The consecration of bishops was more extended. The bishop was supposed to be the choice of his flock, including his clergy, and in his consecration all were recognized. The Eucharist was part of the ceremony. The consecration was normally by at least three bishops, but in times of persecution one bishop was held to be sufficient if the act was with the permission of other bishops, and by the sixth century the Pope might officiate alone. As we are to see later, the setting apart of women to virginity and to the service of the Church went back to the first century, and long before the close of the fifth century this was by formal ceremony, often celebrated with great pomp, and always presided over by a bishop, in which the virgin was given the veil as the bride of Christ.

In the fourth century we begin to hear of the dedication of edifices for Christian worship. Buildings erected especially for that purpose multiplied after the cessation of the persecutions in the fore part of the fourth century. Many of these were constructed near or over the tomb of a martyr. Martyrs were held in veneration and either the tomb or some relic of a martyr was so highly prized that eventually, although not until after the fifth century, the presence of a relic in the altar was held to be essential to a church. Until about the close of the fifth century all that usually seems to have been considered necessary for the consecration of a church building was the celebration in it of the Eucharist. Not far from that time special services of dedication increased.

Christians were not required to seek the blessing of the Church to give validity to their marriage. However, by the time of Tertullian it seems to have become customary to have a Christian ceremony in which the Church cemented the marriage, confirmed it with an oblation, and sealed it with a benediction.

CHRISTIAN FESTIVALS AND THE BEGINNING OF "THE CHRISTIAN YEAR"

Either from the beginning or from near the beginning Christians held some days and seasons as sacred. A few of these were taken over from the Jews, such as the observance of one day in seven for special worship and Pentecost. Several other Jewish feasts were completely disregarded, such as the Day of Atonement and the Feast of Tabernacles. Because of its association with the crucifixion and the resurrection of Christ, connected as they were with it, the Passover became central in the Christian calendar, although with a quite altered connotation.

Easter, the day of rejoicing, was preceded by a fast. The pre-Easter fast varied in duration. In some sections, in the second century it was for only one or two days, although in others it was prolonged to several days. In the third century the church in Alexandria fasted for the week preceding Easter. Montanists had a pre-Easter fast of two weeks. In the fourth century the forty days before Easter, *Quadragesima* (although it might be six weeks), became common as a period of special observance, but for many the fast was only for Holy Week, and for others possibly three weeks. We also read of *Quadragesima* being kept distinct from Holy Week, separating its fast from the fast of the latter. In Antioch and much of the East the addition of Holy Week to *Quadragesima* made a fast of seven weeks. In some places Sunday and in others Saturdays and Sundays were exempted from the Lenten fasting. The observance of the Sunday before Easter, commemorating the triumphal entry of Jesus to Jerusalem, seems to have begun at Jerusalem at least as early as the fourth century and to have spread gradually from there. Maundy Thursday, the Thursday before Easter, was observed as the anniversary of the institution of the Lord's Supper and in North Africa late in the fourth century the Eucharist was celebrated on the evening of that day, rather than in the morning, which, as we have seen, had become customary. Good Friday, quite naturally, was carefully observed, although in varying manner. The lighting of the Paschal or Easter candle became common in some sections before the end of the fifth century, and the formal blessing of the candle was fairly general as a pre-Easter custom.

By the end of the fourth century two other festivals had become widespread, the Epiphany, originating in the East, and the twenty-fifth of December, radiating from the West. The Epiphany, at first celebrated on the sixth and tenth of January, but eventually only on the former date, commemorated the birth of

Jesus, the adoration of Jesus by the Wise Men, and the baptism of Jesus. Christmas, the observance of the twenty-fifth of December as the birthday of Christ, appears to have begun at Rome. The New Testament, it is scarcely necessary to say, gives no clue to the precise days of any of these events, but they were obviously of importance to Christians, and Epiphany and Christmas, although fixed conventionally, became outstanding.

The festival of the Presentation of Christ in the Temple, or the Purification of the Virgin, was observed in Jerusalem as early as the fourth century. That of the Holy Cross, commemorating the alleged discovery of the cross on which Jesus was suspended and the dedication of churches in Jerusalem erected by Constantine, began at Jerusalem and gradually spread. There were also feasts in honour of the apostles and others who were revered as saints, one for the Maccabees, and, at least as early as the sixth century, one for the Angel Michael. In different places various days were observed in memory of local martyrs. Some of the great episcopal sees had special periods of fasting which did not gain universal acceptance.

CUSTOMS OF PRAYER

The manner of public prayer developed or took over certain forms. The custom early arose of facing the East in prayer. In public prayer one attitude was that of standing with arms outstretched or upraised. Another was lying prone, face downwards. To Tertullian's disgust, some sat down after a prayer had been completed. Tertullian declared that fasting or kneeling in worship on the Lord's Day and between Easter and Whitsunday (Pentecost) was improper.

PSALMS, HYMNS, MUSIC

The Epistle to the Ephesians enjoins the use of "psalms, and hymns, and spiritual songs." Some of these hymns are to be found in the New Testament itself, imbedded in its text. From a very early date, perhaps from the beginning, Christians employed in their services the psalms found in the Jewish Scriptures, the Christian Old Testament. Since the first Christians were predominantly Greek-speaking, these psalms were in a Greek translation. We hear of at least one form of service in which, after the reading from the Old Testament, the "hymns of David" were sung. This was done as a solo, presumably as a chant. At the end of each verse the congregation would join, taking up the final words in a short refrain. Later the responses might be by a choir. In Rome the custom arose of singing a psalm from the ambo, or *gradus,* and hence this psalm was called the *gradualis,* or the gradual. Another psalm was called the *tractus,* or tract. Some distinctly Christian hymns were early written in Greek, but in prose form, conforming to the pattern of the psalms as put into Greek. At least as early as the fourth century it became customary to follow the psalm with the *Gloria*—in one of its forms translated into the familiar "Glory be to the Father and to the Son and to the Holy Ghost, as it was in the beginning is now and ever shall be, world without end. Amen."

In Gnostic circles religious poetry arose to compete with the Old Testament Psalms. Some Catholics therefore distrusted the composition of hymns after this pattern, on the ground that they might smack of heresy. Yet from at least the second century hymns were written by the orthodox which, like their Gnostic counterparts, employed the forms of Greek poetry. Clement of Alexandria concluded one of his works with a hymn to Christ in Greek classical metre. Until near the end of the fourth century, in the services of the Catholic Church only the Old Testament Psalms and the hymns or canticles from the New Testament were sung: the other hymns were for personal, family, or private use. Gradually there were prepared versical paraphrases of the Psalms, hymns with lines of equal length, and hymns which were acrostics.

In Constantinople in the days when John Chrysostom was its bishop, the Arians are said to have congregated in the city squares and around the gates, or to have paraded through the streets at night, going to their meetings outside the walls, chanting antiphonally songs which denounced the Catholic views. To counter their efforts, John encouraged some of the Catholics to chant their own hymns in nocturnal processions. As a result violent conflicts between the two factions arose, and several on both sides were killed.

Just when the custom of antiphonal singing arose is not clear. One church historian of the fifth century ascribes it to Antioch not far from the beginning of the second century. Another church historian, also of the fifth century, declares that it began in Antioch in the fourth century, when two of the laity divided the choirs into two parts to sing the psalms of David antiphonally, and that from Antioch the custom spread in all directions. It is from the antiphon that the word "anthem" is derived.

Great writers of hymns began to emerge as early as the second century. Thus Bardaisan (Bardesanes), suspected of heresy late in that century, had a collection of one hundred and fifty hymns in Syriac. In the fourth century, Ephraim, clearly orthodox, a powerful preacher, wrote many hymns in Syriac for liturgical purposes, some of which are said still to be in use. Also in the fourth century, Hilary of Poitiers, in Gaul, during a sojourn in Asia Minor was so inspired by the Greek hymns which he heard there in the churches that on his return to Gaul he began writing hymns in Latin, some of them acrostics, and others in the rhythm of the marching songs of the Roman legionaries. It was in this century that one of the most widely used hymns of the Church, the *Te Deum,* seems to have been composed. The authorship and date have been disputed, but the majority opinion appears to credit Niceta, a bishop in Dacia (north of the Danube), with the authorship. Niceta is said to have employed hymns in the winning of the pagan barbarians in his diocese. Quite undisputed is the fact that Ambrose, the great Bishop of Milan, composed hymns which he taught his flock to sing. His most famous convert, Augustine, has recorded how deeply moved he was by them. They proved extremely popular and for many centuries were the inspiration of other Latin hymns, written, as were they, in eight stanzas. A Spanish contemporary of Ambrose, Prudentius, developed what seems to have been a new type of hymn, having more warmth and glow than those of Ambrose, but for personal and domestic use and not for liturgical purposes. The so-called Athanasian Creed, beginning with the words *quicumque vult,* has by some been classified with hymns. Its precise date, author, and place of origin have not been indisputably determined, but it appears to have originated in the West, perhaps in Gaul, and possibly as early as the fifth or the beginning of the sixth century. Like the *Te Deum* it put into verbal form what were held as central convictions and was widely employed in public worship. Late in the fifth century the Nestorian Narsai (Narses) wrote many hymns, some of them for use in church services. Roughly contemporary with him was Romanus, a pioneer in Byzantine hymnody, whose compositions were to come into extensive use in Constantinople in the sixth century.

Numbers of these Christian hymns, like the *Te Deum,* were what might be termed with accuracy but still in misleading fashion, theological. They put into verbal expression either for congregational worship or for the individual, the central and distinctive convictions of the Christian faith. They were, accordingly, a witness to the effect of Christ on the human spirit. As the worship of the Christian communities centred around the Eucharist, with its commemoration of the sacrificial death of Christ, so the hymns of the Christians of the first five centuries concerned themselves chiefly with Christ and with what God was believed to have done through him.

THE EMERGENCE OF POPULAR CULTS AND FORMS OF WORSHIP WITHIN THE CHURCH

Before the end of the fifth century subsidiary cults and forms of worship began to appear within the Catholic Church. We have noted that Christian worship stressed the Eucharist and that the Eucharist had to do primarily with the central distinctive features of Christianity—Christ himself, his incarnation, death, and redemption and eternal life through him. We have seen that the great creeds of the Church focussed on them their attention, and that the hymns made much of them. Yet side by side with this emphasis upon Christ, although subordinate to it and in theory associated with it, there were emerging special reverence for other beings and practices of worship which were reminiscent of the non-Christian religions of the Mediterranean world.

Martyrs were held in high honour. This had been true as far back as the first and second centuries, as is vividly attested by the last book in the New Testament. Their cults grew rapidly in the fourth and fifth centuries. The last great wave of persecutions which began with Diocletian added many to their ranks. The events of those tragic days were read back into the earlier centuries when those who had suffered death for the faith were actually relatively few. Their numbers were exaggerated and their sufferings were magnified, until the Church of the first three centuries was viewed in retrospect, mistakenly, as a church of martyrs. When, in the fourth and fifth centuries, after the last persecutions, converts flooded into the Church, they tended to transfer to the martyrs some of the reverence they had given and the attributes and powers which they had ascribed to the gods of paganism. The relics of martyrs were cherished, their tombs became the goals of pious pilgrimages, and they were appealed to in prayer to intercede with God on behalf of their votaries. They were believed to work miracles and were esteemed as healers of disease, guardians of cities, and patrons of trades.

Angels, especially Michael, were also revered, and to the martyrs were added Christians of exemplary lives, especially ascetics, as among those through whom prayer could be made. The process of canonization was to wait for regularization until later centuries, but it was already in being through the consensus of the faithful in particular localities or in the Church at large.

The Virgin Mary was early viewed with great respect, but in the fourth and fifth centuries the importance accorded her rapidly mounted and her cult increased. As we have seen, she was acclaimed as the "Mother of God." In Ephesus something of the worship paid to Diana may have been transferred to the Virgin Mary and she is said to have taken possession of the Sicilian sanctuaries of Ceres and Venus.

Here and there sites sacred to pagan divinities were appropriated by Christians and were still regarded as hallowed, but by Christian saints rather than by the gods. In at least one place the temple of a non-Christian god was transformed into a Christian church and the latter was devoted to that god thinly disguised by prefixing the title "Saint" before his name.

Beliefs and practices which were either magic or closely akin to magic had wide vogue among Christians. Even the highly intellectual Origen held that the repetition of the name of Jesus, if made in faith, would expel demons. In pagan days the ill had been taken to the temples to sleep in them in the hope that in their dreams directions would be given them by the god for treatment which would heal their disease. The practice was transferred to Christian churches and became so common that the ecclesiastical authorities felt constrained to take action against it. Spells and charms, blessed in the name of Christ or one of the saints, were much used. In one recorded instance the sign of the cross was employed in Gaul to protect cattle against an epidemic and was believed to have proved efficacious.

DIONYSIUS THE AREOPAGITE

By the end of the fifth century Christian mysticism was beginning to be profoundly moulded by Neoplatonism, an influence which has persisted into our own day. Very potent were the writings ascribed to Dionysius the Areopagite, mentioned in *The Acts of the Apostles* as a convert of Paul at Athens. Dionysius was not their author, for they seem to have been composed either in the last quarter of the fifth century or the first half of the sixth century, perhaps by a monk or a bishop. Some of the terminology is Christian, but the basic conceptions are primarily Neoplatonic. God, Who is supra-personal, supra-essential Essence, above either time or eternity, Who is the source of the universe and Who pervades it, from Whom constantly issue emanations, exercises His power through nine orders of celestial beings and does so on earth through the hierarchy of the Church, which corresponds to the celestial hierarchy and which begins with bishops as the highest rank, has priests in the second rank, and deacons in the third and lowest rank. Every hierarchy culminates in Jesus Christ. The sacraments, administered by the ecclesiastical hierarchy, are the channel of the divine operation of grace. Perhaps in an effort to escape the extreme dualism in the widely prevalent Manichæism, the Pseudo-Dionysius, stressing what had come down from Platonism and Neoplatonism, held that sin is largely negative, that there is nothing that is inherently evil, and that in all evil is some good. Salvation is regarded as the deification of the saved, and deification is the highest possible resemblance to God and union with Him. It is to be sought in moral and intellectual discipline, with the sacraments as an aid and a means, and through contemplation which carries one outside of oneself, above reason, to the vision which realizes that the individual is never really separated from God. Yet the self continues to exist, even when merged with God.

Here were views which either did not emphasize or were contrary to such basic Christian convictions as the creation of the world by the will of God, the corruption of man through man's voluntary rebellion against God, the redemption of man through the self-giving of God in the incarnation, the costly sacrifice on the cross, and the new birth through the Holy Spirit.

Yet the writings of the Pseudo-Dionysius carried great weight, partly because they were believed to be by a close intimate of Paul, and were to be a handbook of Christian mysticism in both the East and the West, a major channel of a strong Platonic and Neoplatonic strain in Christian piety.

It was not only in Christian mysticism that the writings of Dionysius the Areopagite were influential. They also made an impression on Christian thought. For instance, the outstanding Western theologian of the Middle Ages, Thomas Aquinas, quoted from them extensively.

OTHER FORMS OF PRIVATE WORSHIP AND DEVOTION

It was not only or even chiefly through the Pseudo-Dionysius that the spirit of contemplation and prayer was nourished among Christians. There was much family and private reading of religious books. This was true of the writings included in the Scriptures. Books were expensive, for printing was still centuries in the future, and literacy was by no means universal, but many individuals and families had copies of the Scriptures and the temper of the Church encouraged Bible reading by individuals and groups. Translations of all or parts of the Bible were made into several of the vernaculars. Many Christian books not included in the Canon were also widely circulated. Works of a devotional nature continued to be written. Famous among these was Augustine's *Confessions*. Late in the fifth or early in the sixth century there appeared in Gaul *De Vita Contemplativa* ("The Contemplative Life") by Julianus Pomerius, who had Augustine as his model. These were only two among many from both the Western and the Eastern sections of the Church on which contemporaries and later generations nourished their faith.

THE DRESS OF THE CLERGY

How early the members of the clergy were distinguished from the laity by special garb is not clear. At the outset there seems to have been no difference in dress. Indeed, so long as persecutions lasted, such a distinction would have made the clergy conspicuous and would have singled them out for arrest. Even after persecutions ceased, in the fifth century one of the Popes expressly forbade any special ecclesiastical dress, but the fact that he found it necessary to issue this prohibition may be evidence that such costumes were beginning to be worn elsewhere and that Rome was holding to an earlier custom. At that time the outdoor dress of Roman civil officials was an undergarment, a tunic, with or without sleeves, and an immense sleeveless cloak which was without an opening in the front and was passed over the head. The undergarment might be bound around the waist by a girdle. Presumably this was the fourth and fifth century dress of the Roman clergy. In later centuries these garments, perpetuated and conventionalized, became part of the specialized clerical dress. By the end of the fifth century a second tunic, with large sleeves, called the dalmatic, worn over the undergarment and under the cloak, became a distinguishing mark of the Pope and his clergy and might have been in use elsewhere.

From at least the first half of the fifth century, and perhaps earlier, what was known as the *pallium* was regarded as a badge of the bishop's office. The *pallium* was of white wool and was a kind of scarf worn over the shoulders. It seems also to have been a mark of civil service in the Roman Empire of the time, perhaps derived from a short mantle introduced by the Greeks. The privilege of wearing the *pallium* may have been granted the bishops by the Emperors in connexion with the special recognition accorded the clergy after the Emperors had become Christians. Certainly the Emperors are known specifically to have granted to individual bishops the privilege of wearing the *pallium.* Some time after the fifth century, in the West the *pallium* came to be regarded as part of the garb of the Popes and the Pope granted it to bishops as a symbol of his approval of their election and therefore of his authority over them. It was esteemed as a kind of duplicate of the mantle of Peter and so as a token of the power of his successors, the Bishops of Rome. In the East, as early as the fourth century, bishops, priests, and deacons had the *orarium,* a conventionalized form of a handkerchief or neckcloth. It was of linen and was worn as a stole, draped over the shoulder. In the fourth century a council in Phrygia deemed it necessary to forbid its use by sub-deacons and other minor clergy, presumably because they were adopting it.

FINANCING THE CHURCH

How were the churches maintained financially? From the very outset the churches cared for the poor and the widows. This was true not only in the immediate circle of each congregation, but churches also came to the rescue of other churches which were suffering from special or chronic stress. Moreover, some of the apostles drew their support from their fellow-Christians. For a brief time in the first church in Jerusalem all the Christians shared in a community of goods. In that church the widows were given especial help. The Jerusalem church charged the Gentile churches to remember the poor, and in this the great missionary to the Gentiles, Paul, heartily concurred. Paul took pride in labouring with his own hands for his support, but seems to say that other apostles, including Peter, and the brothers of Jesus were maintained by the churches. Paul raised a substantial sum from the Gentile churches to aid the Christians in Judea, and directed that this was to be done by Christians setting aside something on the first day of the week, obviously, a form of systematic giving.

In the fourth century, following the precedent of the Old Testament and harking back in part to earlier Christian practice, we find the command to bring the first-fruits of the winepress, the threshing-floor, the oxen, the sheep, and other things to the priests, and to devote a tenth of one's increase to the widows, the poor, and strangers. We also read that every true prophet or teacher who came to a Christian community was to be maintained. These instructions were at least current in the East.

When, beginning with Constantine, the Church began to be shown special favour by the state, clergy were exempted from the public obligations which had become a burden on many, and donations to the Catholic Church through legacies were permitted. Constantine erected numerous church buildings in various parts of the Empire and endowed them. Later Emperors also erected churches. Before long, some of the clergy were being accused of using unworthy means to obtain legacies from the well-to-do. Before the close of the fifth century, whether through legacies or other channels, some of the churches, notably that of Rome, became the owners of large possessions, the management of which became a major problem of administration, and the income from which went in large part to the support of widows, orphans, and the poor.

ETHICAL IDEALS AND MORAL DISCIPLINE IN THE CHURCH

Throughout the first five centuries, as through their successors, the records disclose a marked gulf in Christians and the Christian communities between professed ethical ideals and motivation for moral action on the one hand, and performance on the other, together with continuing efforts to close the gulf either by bringing the ideals down to a level attainable in performance or by inducing performance to conform to the ideals.

In the New Testament, the motive and basic principle of action is *agape,* love, love of God and love of man, inspired by the love of God, especially as seen in His self-giving in Christ and in the death of Christ for rebellious, sinful men on the cross. The Gospel is not a new law, a fresh and higher set of moral standards through obedience to which men are to find salvation and enter into life.

To be sure, in penetrating fashion Jesus laid bare the springs of action and placed the emphasis upon the governing, inward thought and motive rather than on the outward deed. He declared that the ideal was to act like God, to be "perfect, as your heavenly Father is perfect." Here was a standard so high that it seemed impossible of attainment, and yet in it discerning souls recognized what men must be if they are to realize to the full the purpose for which

God had created them. Jesus seemed to believe that it was theoretically possible for all to reach the goal, yet he also perceived clearly and frankly the evil in men, held that men must strive (the Greek word is that from which the English word "agonize" is derived) to enter the gate to true life, and declared that only a very few find the gate and pursue the path into which it opens.

Paul recognized the impossibility of obeying entirely the moral law, the law of God, and saw in that law and the sense of moral impotence and frustration bred by its acceptance "our schoolmaster to bring us unto Christ that we might be justified by faith." When confronted by the law, especially as interpreted by Jesus, sensitive spirits were brought to see how far short of it they fell. Across the centuries one of the fruits of Christianity has been the quickening and deepening of the consciences of men. Indeed, the more discerning have recognized the basic sin to be self-sufficiency, pride, and rebellion against God, have appreciated something of the depth of man's depravity as they have seen representatives of the highest religion and the noblest of man's governments nail the Son of God to the cross, and have stood in amazed awe at the wonder of God's love and forgiveness in giving His Son thus to die for man's redemption. It is men's response in humble faith and love to God's love in Christ, so the New Testament says, which should be the well-spring of Christian living. No man can perfectly attain to God's ideal for him in this life, but accepting this as a fact, Paul declared that he pressed on to lay hold on that for which he had been laid hold on by Christ Jesus, striving "toward the mark for the prize of the high calling of God in Christ Jesus." In his *Confessions*, as he looked back over his spiritual pilgrimage, Augustine clearly recognized that, while he had been freed by the Gospel from slavery to the grosser sins of the flesh, he had not yet completely overcome man's fundamental sin, pride.

Here is not a set of commands through obedience to which men can earn anything from God. Men, so the New Testament sees, can never fully comply with God's commands, and even if they could and did they would deserve nothing from Him, but would only, like good servants, have done what it is their duty to do. The Christian Gospel is, rather, the good news of God's love and of that kingdom of God which is God's free gift to men and into which men can enter here and now by accepting that gift. Christians are to determine their actions, not by legalistic rules, but by the love of God which itself is the gift of God through His Holy Spirit and by its inevitable corollary, love for their neighbours. As the *Epistle of James* says, "Thou shalt love thy neighbour as thyself" is the "royal law." As Paul emphatically states: "Love worketh no ill to his neighbour, therefore love is the fulfilling of the law."

Yet from the outset this conviction about conduct has been confronted by two perils. On the one hand, there has been what is technically known as antinomianism, the assumption that the Christian, by being emancipated from legalism, the meticulous observance of rules, is free from all moral law and can with impunity disregard it. The other, often more subtle and in one form or another much more widely held, is the conviction that the Gospel is a new and higher law, that being a Christian primarily entails obedience to moral maxims, some of them ancient and to be found in the Old Testament and some of them new and seen in the New Testament, and that one's salvation is to be earned by that obedience. This tendency, even though only a tendency and not carried to its logical conclusion, is found in some books which were greatly prized by Christians of the first five centuries, among them the *Didache*, *The Shepherd of Hermas,* and extensive portions of the *Paidagogos* of Clement of Alexandria. Indeed, *The Shepherd of Hermas* declares that it is possible to do more than God commands and by so doing to gain more abundant glory.

Fully as serious as these two perils has been the failure of Christians even to approximate in practice to the high standards set forth in the New Testament. This is seen again and again in the pages of the New Testament, where the sins of professing Christians are frankly described and condemned. It is also apparent in such records as we have of succeeding generations of Christians. Sometimes these sins were excoriated and at other times, as in the language of the participants in the controversies which distressed the Church and which we described in the preceding chapter, were unrecognized or unacknowledged by those who were guilty of them, sad evidence of self-righteousness and lack of love even in some of those who were later revered as saints. Lapses multiplied as multitudes poured into the Church, especially after persecutions ceased and the Emperors espoused the faith.

The Church had early to face the problem of what should be done with those of its members who sinned. Baptism, we have noted, was regarded as washing away all offenses committed before it. But what of those sins committed after baptism? Some of these were held to be especially serious, or "deadly." Tertullian, as we have hinted, said that they were seven in number—idolatry, blasphemy, murder, adultery, fornication, false-witness, and fraud. To the early Christians the most heinous of sins were the denial of the faith, murder, and gross sexual offenses. *The Shepherd of Hermas* allowed the possibility of one repentance after baptism, a possibility in which, as we have seen, Clement of Alexandria concurred, but Hermas held that beyond that one post-baptismal repentance no other was possible. This appears to have been the view of Clement. Clement said that if allowed continual and successive repentings for sins, Christians would differ nothing from those who never have been Christians, except only in the consciousness of having sinned. Yet he repeated approvingly a story about the Apostle John who in his old age sought and won to penitence a man who as a youth had been baptized and then, falling away, had committed many sins and had become the leader of a band of robbers. Thus he at least recognized as possible repentance for a multitude of sins committed after baptism.

In the preceding chapter we have seen that some groups broke from the Catholic Church in part or entirely in protest against what they held to be too great leniency of the latter towards moral lapses, especially apostasy. Among these were the Montanists, the Novatians, and the Donatists.

In this rigour, whether in the Catholic or in other Christian bodies, there was grave danger of legalism, of equating Christianity with morality, all the more so since outward acts were more readily detected than inner motives, pride, and the failure to respond with love to God's love. Moreover, while the New Testament has severe words for those who sin against the Holy Spirit or who lapse from the faith, and while, as some early Christian writers soberly recognized, even those who have long been seemingly exemplary Christians may come to moral shipwreck in their later years, it is perfectly clear that Jesus taught that no matter how often a man sins, if in genuine repentance he turns to God, God will forgive him. The issue is not God's readiness, even eagerness to forgive, but man's ability and willingness to repent. That should be obvious from the most frequently repeated of Christian prayers, the Lord's Prayer, and from assurances given again and again in the New Testament.

The Catholic Church increasingly made provision for the restoration of the genuinely penitent. Not far from the end of the second century, Tertullian described the practice of the single repentance which was permitted after baptism. The penitents were required to fast, living on plain food, to dress in mourning garb, to lie in sackcloth and ashes, to pray, to weep, to bow before the presbyters, and to kneel before the faithful and ask their prayers. How far Tertullian was describing the customary procedure and how far he was holding up an ideal which was seldom attained is not clear.

Those who had suffered for the faith as martyrs and had survived were believed to have the power to declare sins forgiven. They were besieged by penitents and, as we have noted, their leniency was a source of embarrassment to the stricter souls and to the bishops and other clergy. We have seen that early in the third century a Bishop of Rome, Callistus (Calixtus I), permitted the restoration of those guilty of fornication and adultery if they fulfilled the conditions for pentitents. After the Decian persecution, a synod in Carthage under Cyprian ruled that to those who had denied the faith hope of restoration must be held out to keep them from reverting to paganism, but that a long penance must be imposed on them. This stand was confirmed by a synod in Rome in 251 and by another in Carthage in 252. The severe persecutions which began with that of Diocletian early in the fourth century led to many apostasies. The Council of Nicæa found it necessary to define the conditions of the readmission of those who had thus lapsed. None who was penitent was to be forbidden the communion on his death bed, but the others might be kept waiting for from two to ten years. For them, as for other penitents for grave offenses, there were grades through which they passed before readmission to full communion. Some were dismissed at particular points in the service—some after the sermon and the reading from the Scriptures, some after the prayers—while others might remain through the Eucharist.

Penance and penitents were under the direction of the bishop, and restoration was usually not easy and was only with the consent of the bishop. If the sin had been publicly known, restoration must also be public. In the churches in the West, especially in Rome, a place was appointed in which penitents stood and mourned until the completion of the service. They then cast themselves prostrate on the ground with groans and lamentations. The bishop, weeping, also cast himself on the ground, and the congregation wept and groaned. The bishop then arose, offered a prayer for the penitents, and dismissed them. The penitents were also required to fast, or to abstain from bathing, or to suffer some other deprivation for a period fixed by the bishop.

In the East, after the persecution by Decius in the middle of the third century, it became customary for the bishop to designate a special priest to hear the confessions of those who had sinned, to fix the penance, and to grant absolution. Late in the fourth century, because of a scandalous incident, this office was abolished in Constantinople and the decision of whether he should partake of the communion was left to the conscience of each Christian. From Constantinople the cessation of the appointment of a priest to hear confessions spread widely, and the result was increasing laxity in maintaining moral standards among the members of the Church. Against this laxity monasticism, of which we are to read in the next chapter, was a reaction and a protest.

The growing laxity which contributed to the monastic reaction was also seen in the clergy, both high and low. Especially beginning with Constantine and the friendship of the state, self-seeking, pomp, and luxury began to appear among them. Some of the bishops, particularly in the larger sees, lived like magnates, and the priests and deacons sought wealth. Thus in the latter part of the fourth century the Bishops of Rome kept a large establishment and set a princely table, and some of the clergy fawned on wealthy women, hoping for gifts or legacies. At least one contest for the Papal throne was accompanied by brawling and bloodshed.

Easy-going though much of the Catholic Church had become in its enforcement of moral standards, in its recognition of the inexhaustible mercy and love of God to the truly penitent it was holding to a central affirmation of the primitive Christian faith. It was also doing this in preserving baptism, with its witness to the new birth, the complete transformation which is of the essence of Christian faith and experience as taught at the outset of Christianity, and in putting at the heart of Christian worship the Eucharist, with its thanksgiving for the incarnation, the sacrificial death of Christ, and the power of the new life which has issued from them. In baptism, worship, and discipline the Church was seeking to preserve and to stress what was strikingly distinctive of Jesus Christ and the teaching of the apostles. Nor did all the bishops and clergy succumb to the pomp and circumstance which accompanied their posts.

Selected Bibliography

BAPTISM, WORSHIP, AND THE EUCHARIST

A competent survey, from the Roman Catholic viewpoint and stressing the practices in the Church of Rome, is by the distinguished Roman Catholic scholar, L. Duchesne, translated by M. L. McClure, *Christian Worship, Its Origin and Evolution. A Study of the Latin Liturgy up to the Time of Charlemagne* (London, Society for Promoting Christian Knowledge, 1931, pp. xx, 593).

G. Dix, *The Shape of the Liturgy* (Westminster, Dacre Press, 1945, pp. xix, 764). Another excellent survey, of a somewhat different kind, by a staunch Anglo-Catholic.

For the *Didache* see *Teaching of the Twelve Apostles . . . edited with a translation, introduction and notes* by R. D. Hitchcock and F. Brown (New York, Charles Scribner's Sons, 1885, pp. cxv, 85).

For Tertullian, *On Baptism,* see a translation by S. Thelwall in *The Ante-Nicene Fathers,* Vol. III, pp. 669–679 (New York, Charles Scribner's Sons, 1899).

Justin Martyr's description of the Eucharist is in his *First Apology,* translated in *The Ante-Nicene Fathers,* Vol. I, pp. 185, 186 (Buffalo, The Christian Literature Co., 1885).

See also an early document on the catechumenate, baptism, the Eucharist, and other forms of worship, in *Constitutions of the Holy Apostles,* Book II, Section VII, in *The Ante-Nicene Fathers,* Vol. VII, pp. 421, 422, 465–478, 483–491 (New York, The Christian Literature Co., 1896).

Still another early document, of the third century, with a description of the Eucharist, ordinations, the catechumenate, baptism, widows, prayers, and other church customs is *The Apostolic Tradition of Hippolytus,* of which a useful translation, under that title, accompanied by an extensive introduction and notes, is by B. S. Easton (New York, The Macmillan Co., 1934, pp. 112).

On the Jewish influence on the forms of Christian worship, see W. O. E. Oesterley, *The Jewish Background of the Christian Liturgy* (Oxford, The Clarendon Press, 1925, pp. 243). Carefully done, well documented.

Also very carefully done, broader in its geographic scope than Duchesne, is J. H.

Srawley, *The Early History of the Liturgy* (Cambridge University Press, 2d ed., 1947, pp. xviii, 240), semi-technical, with an excellent bibliography and footnotes.

Translations of some of the early liturgies are in *The Liturgies of SS. Mark, James, Clement, Chrysostom, and Basil, and the Church of Malabar,* by J. M. Neale and R. F. Littledale (London, Griffith Farran & Co., 7th ed., no date, pp. xl, 256), with an introduction and notes.

Excellent, and on a limited phase of the liturgy is W. H. Frere, *The Anaphora or Great Eucharistic Prayer, An Eirenical Study in Liturgical History* (London, Society for Promoting Christian Knowledge, 1938, pp. vi, 212).

EARLY CHRISTIAN POETRY AND HYMNS

Excellent, compact articles by A. Baumstark, A. J. Maclean, and G. M. Dreves are in J. Hastings, editor, *Encyclopædia of Religion and Ethics,* Vol. VII, pp. 5–24 (New York, Charles Scribner's Sons, 1915).

A survey more limited geographically, based upon careful research and sound judgment, is F. J. E. Raby, *A History of Christian-Latin Poetry from the Beginnings to the Close of the Middle Ages* (Oxford, The Clarendon Press, 1927, pp. viii, 491). The section covering the first five centuries is pp. 1–120.

CLERICAL DRESS

In addition to a section in Duchesne, *Christian Worship,* see G. S. Tyack, *Historic Dress of the Clergy* (London, William Andrews & Co., 1897, pp. 134).

DIONYSIUS THE AREOPAGITE

C. E. Rolt, *Dionysius the Areopagite on the Divine Names and the Mystical Theology* (London, Society for Promoting Christian Knowledge, 1920, pp. viii, 223). Contains a valuable introduction and translations.

OTHER DEVOTIONAL READING

A. Harnack, *Bible Reading in the Early Church* (London, Williams & Norgate, 1912, pp. x, 159).

Julianus Pomerius, *The Contemplative Life,* translated and annotated by Mary Josephine Suelser (Westminster, Md., The Newman Bookshop, 1947, pp. 220).

P. Pourrat, *Christian Spirituality from the Time of Our Lord till the Dawn of the Middle Ages,* translated by W. H. Mitchell and S. P. Jacques (London, Burns, Oates & Washbourne, 1922, pp. x, 312). The first volume of a comprehensive survey by a Roman Catholic. An excellent introduction.

SIN, PENANCE, FORGIVENESS

Clement of Alexandria, *The Stromata,* Book II, Chap. XIII, in *The Ante-Nicene Fathers,* Vol. II, pp. 360, 361 (New York, Charles Scribner's Sons, 1899); *Who Is the Rich Man that Shall be Saved,* XLII, in *The Ante-Nicene Fathers,* Vol. II, pp. 603, 604.

C. J. Hefele, translated by W. R. Clark, *A History of the Christian Councils* (Edinburgh, T. & T. Clark, 2d ed., 1872), Vol. I, pp. 415–423. Valuable for its citations from the original documents.

The Pastor of Hermas, Book II, Commandment 4, Chap. 3, in *The Ante-Nicene Fathers,* Vol. II, p. 22 (New York, Charles Scribner's Sons, 1899).

Sozomen, *Ecclesiastical History,* Book VII, Chap. 16, in *A Select Library of Nicene and Post-Nicene Fathers of the Christian Church, Second Series,* Vol. II, pp. 386, 387 (New York, The Christian Literature Society, 1890).

Tertullian, *Against Marcion,* Book IV, Chap. X, in *The Ante-Nicene Fathers,* Vol. III, p. 356 (New York, Charles Scribner's Sons, 1899); *On Repentance,* IX–XII, in *The Ante-Nicene Fathers,* Vol. III, pp. 664, 665; *On Modesty,* in *The Ante-Nicene Fathers,* Vol. IV, pp. 74–101 (New York, Charles Scribner's Sons, 1899).

O. D. Watkins, *A History of Penance* (London, Longmans Green and Co., 2 vols., 1920). Volume I is to A.D. 450.

Chapter VIII

THE RISE OF MONASTICISM

What is the perfect Christian life? Can it be lived? If so, how? Does it entail the transformation of all human society? Can individuals be immersed in a prevailingly or partially un-Christian society without compromising their principles and be fully Christian? To be fully Christian, is it necessary to withdraw from society? If so, must one live alone, or must those intent on the complete Christian life seek it in community with others? If life in community is necessary, can there be a community, a human society, which will fully embody the Christian ideal? In one form or another these questions have been raised by Christians from the outset and have been recurrent across the centuries. Beginning in the third century they became insistent and in the following two centuries were increasingly clamant.

As we have seen, the early Christians were a small minority of the population of the Roman Empire and to a large degree held aloof from the society about them, seeking to realize the ideal in the small communities which then made up the Church. By the middle of the third century thousands were pouring into the Church. The great persecutions of the second half of the third century and the first quarter of the fourth century only temporarily checked the flood and by their failure eventually accelerated it. Before the close of the fifth century the overwhelming majority of the citizens of the Roman Empire were professing themselves to be Christians, had been baptized, and were members of one or another of the bodies which bore the Christian name. As we saw at the end of the last chapter, with the progress of the mass conversion the discipline of the Church was being relaxed and the gap between the ideal and the performance of the average Christian widened.

It was partially as a reaction against this laxity and partly because of the dissatisfaction which the teachings of Jesus and the apostles aroused with anything short of perfection that monasticism arose. At first it was primarily a lay movement, not within the hierarchical structure of the clergy. To some degree it was a rebellion of the individual against the organization of the Catholic

Church, regimented as that was under the bishops and clergy. Indeed, at times its members were quite unsubmissive to the bishops and were insubordinate, even tumultuously so, against a particular bishop. Many bishops looked with unfriendly eyes on the monks. In the initial decades of monasticism numbers of monks, laymen living alone, seldom partook of the Eucharist. Yet by the end of the fifth century monasticism had spread so widely that it had become characteristic of the Catholic Church. It was being regarded as the preferred way towards the perfect Christian life and as such it was attracting many of the most ardent Christian youth. Henceforward it was to be an accepted feature of the Catholic Church and of most of the churches into which that church divided. At present, while rejected by most of Protestantism, it is found in the churches which embrace a majority of those who regard themselves as Christians. It so captured the churches that in the East eventually the bishops were normally, indeed almost if not quite universally, drawn from the monasteries. In the West many of the bishops were monks. Before the end of the sixth century Pope Gregory I, one of the strongest men to sit on the throne of Peter, was drawn, reluctant, from his monastery—although it is not certain that he ever took monastic vows—and since then many monks have been numbered among his successors.

Monasticism has displayed many variations and has been one of the chief ways in which the vitality of the Christian faith has found expression. We are, accordingly, not only to trace its beginnings, but in later chapters we are again and again to recur to it to sketch its successive stages.

To a certain degree monasticism represented the triumph of ideas which the Catholic Church had denounced as heretical. Into it crept something of the legalism, the belief that salvation can be earned and deserved, which is opposed to grace and which had been theoretically rejected when the Ebionites were appraised as untrue to the Gospel. In it was still more of the conviction that flesh and matter are evil which had been so prominent in Gnosticism, the Marcionites, and Manichæism. In the triumph of monasticism, therefore, basic attitudes and beliefs won acceptance which in other forms the Catholic Church had branded as contrary to the genius of the Christian faith.

Moreover, at its inception, and to some degree in its later history, monasticism had much in it which was in contrast with the Gospel. At the outset, for the most part it was not missionary, in the sense that it did not endeavour to win non-Christians. It did not seek to save the world but to flee from it. The primary objective of the monk was his own salvation, not that of others.

We must also note that, again in opposition to what is found in the New Testament, where all Christians are called upon to be saints and a holy priesthood, monasticism tended to divide Christians into two groups—those aspiring to perfection and those content to compromise with sub-Christian or non-Christian practices.

Yet distinctively Christian elements were in the monastic movement. On renouncing their possessions the aspirants to the monastic life distributed them among the poor. Hundreds of monks, including the most famous of the pioneers, gave spiritual counsel to those who came to them. In later centuries, especially in the West, many monastic organizations became missionary or devoted themselves to the service of others. Indeed, from the sixth century onward most of the missionaries of the Roman Catholic and Eastern Churches were men or women who had taken monastic vows.

PRE-MONASTIC CHRISTIAN ASCETICISM

Although it has been prominent in the churches in which the majority of Christians have been enrolled, monasticism was unknown in the first two centuries of Christianity. Later generations believed that they found commands and precedent for the ascetic life in the teachings and example of Jesus and in other writings in the New Testament, but the accuracy of their interpretation is at least open to question. To be sure, Jesus declared that he who would become his disciple must surrender all that he had, in one notable instance commanded a wealthy young man to sell all that he possessed and give to the poor, and by saying that there were some who had made themselves eunuchs for the kingdom of heaven's sake appeared to commend celibacy. Yet, in marked contrast with John the Baptist, who was clearly an ascetic, Jesus, as he himself remarked, came both "eating and drinking" and neither he nor his disciples fasted during his lifetime. His leading disciple, Peter, and some others of the apostles, even after the resurrection continued to live with their wives. Paul, who favoured celibacy, knew of no express command from Jesus to support him in it and said in effect that matrimony might be as much a gift of God as the unmarried state. While community of goods was practised for a time in the early days of the original Christian church in Jerusalem, the giving of one's possessions to the common store was voluntary and not compulsory, and from the very beginning private ownership of property seems to have been normal among Christians. In at least one place in the New Testament those who forbade Christians to marry and commanded them to abstain from some kinds of food were deemed untrue to the faith. While widows were accorded special recognition, no one was enrolled as such before sixty years of age and the younger widows were commanded to marry and rear children.

However, long before monasticism, and, indeed, from the first days of the Church, fasting was an accepted discipline. Widows who did not remarry and who devoted themselves to prayer and the service of the Church became customary. Moreover, celibacy was early prized by the Church. *The Shepherd of Hermas* held that while it was not wrong for Christian widows or widowers to remarry, they would "gain greater honour and glory of the Lord" if they refrained from doing so. As we have seen, the Marcionites forbade marriage. While the Catholic Church did not have that requirement for membership, in 305 a synod in Elvira, in Spain, demanded celibacy of the bishops and other clergy. Even earlier the custom had been established that a bishop, a priest, or a deacon should not marry if he had been unmarried before his ordination, and that if his wife died there was to be no remarriage. The official decrees of synods, councils, and Popes enjoining celibacy on the clergy seem to have arisen out of a growing custom and to have reinforced it rather than to have initiated it.

Gradually the tradition was developing which was later to become fixed, in the West for the celibacy of deacons, priests, and bishops, and in the East celibacy for the bishops, but marriage before ordination for deacons and priests. In 385 Pope Siricius enjoined chastity upon all priests, saying that their daily offering of the sacrifice of the Eucharist made this necessary. In 390 a council at Carthage commanded chastity for bishops, priests, and deacons. Not far from the middle of the fifth century Pope Leo the Great extended to subdeacons the rule of clerical celibacy. In the second half of the fourth century a council in the East condemned those who regarded as unlawful receiving the Eucharist from the hands of a married priest. Late in the seventh century, in 692, a council which was esteemed ecumenical by the Eastern but not by the Western section of the Catholic Church declared that any who wished might be married before ordination as subdeacon, deacon, or priest, but no one should do so after ordination, and a married man who was raised to the episcopate must separate from his wife and provide for her in a monastery.

The Beginning of Monasticism

These trends in Christianity prepared a fertile seed bed for monasticism. On the one hand, the level of the morality of the average Christian appeared to be sinking and the ardent, their consciences quickened by the high standards of the New Testament, were not content. On the other hand, Christians had long honoured and many of them had practised voluntary poverty, fasting, and celibacy. But why should it have been monasticism rather than other forms of asceticism which arose and flourished on this soil?

It was in the third century and in Egypt that monasticism sprang up on the ground so prepared. Attempts have been made to find its source in Indian, Greek, pagan Egyptian, or Jewish roots, but none of these has been supported by conclusive proof. Indeed, from the outset Christian monasticism has differed markedly from any previous asceticism or religious community. It seems probable that the impulse which led to its emergence was predominantly and perhaps entirely from the Gospel. Origen, a native of Alexandria, gave an example of extreme asceticism in self-mutilation and in austerity in food, drink, sleep, and bodily comforts, and he had a profound influence upon many of his pupils who became prominent in the Church in Egypt. Ascetic Gnostics, Marcionites, and Montanists were found in Egypt and may have contributed to the later developments.

Yet factors other than those of Christian provenance may have been responsible for the birth of monasticism in Egypt rather than in some other land. Mysticism and the contemplative life were in non-Christian circles in Egypt, including the Neoplatonism which had its origin there, and they may have stimulated that phase of the monastic life. It is possible that influences may have entered from India. Manichæism may have contributed, although probably, if at all, later. Political and economic disorders in Egypt in the third and fourth centuries may have bred a sense of insecurity which impelled many to seek escape from the world. It is conceivable that a desire to be rid of the growing burden of civic obligations contributed to the flight of some from ordinary society. Probably, too, monasteries arose in part from disgust with city life, with its dust, crowds, noise, and moral corruption. That motive certainly made a strong appeal to some in other lands when the monastic movement had spread to them. The geography and climate of Egypt favoured the life of the monk, whether solitary or in community. The fertile valley of the Nile was a ribbon flanked on either side by the desert, rain was infrequent, and the ascetic could live alone and with little shelter, with such slight food as he needed from villages near at hand or raised on his own little plot of ground. Before the third century was out, Christian hermits were beginning to be seen in Egypt. Some of these had fled to the desert to escape the Decian persecution and remained there after it was over. Others, probably more numerous, began living in solitude as ascetics near villages in huts built by themselves and there gave themselves to prayer and contemplation.

The most famous of the early monks was Anthony. We know of him chiefly from a biography which is attributed to Athanasius, the great Bishop of Alexandria, noted for his part in the Arian controversy, and which by its early and wide circulation did much to stimulate the spread of the monastic life. The account which this biography gives of Anthony can be briefly summarized. Anthony was born, of Egyptian ancestry, probably not far from the year 250, of well-to-do Christian parents, and was reared in their faith. When he was about eighteen or twenty years of age his parents died, leaving him with the care of a younger sister. One day, while in church, he heard, in the reading of the

Gospel, the command of Jesus to the rich young ruler: "If thou wilt be perfect, go and sell what thou hast and give to the poor, and thou shalt have treasure in heaven, and come, follow me." Going out from the church, he immediately gave his inherited acres to the villagers, sold his movable possessions, and distributed the proceeds among the poor, reserving only enough for the care of his sister. Later hearing in church the injunction of Jesus, "be not anxious for tomorrow," he turned over even this remaining fund to the poor and placed his sister in the care of a community of virgins. He took up his abode outside the village, working with his hands, spending part of the return for food and giving the rest to the poor, visiting the hermits of whom he had heard, and learning from one or another of them graciousness, love, kindness, endurance, meekness, freedom from anger, and the art of prayer. He fought temptation in many forms, ate and drank sparingly and only of bread, salt, and water once a day after sunset, often went without food for from two to four days, slept but little and then usually on the bare ground, and to harden his body would not anoint it with oil. Later he withdrew to a ruined fort on a mountain and there dwelt alone for nearly twenty years, seldom seen by any. His fame eventually attracted disciples who built themselves cells in the mountains and emulated him in the solitary life. With him they formed a kind of community. Demons and the Devil were very real to him and he had many a bout with them. During one of the persecutions early in the fourth century he went to Alexandria, ministering to those condemned for the faith to the mines and the prisons, and hoping for martyrdom for himself. After the persecution ceased, he increased his austerities—fasting, giving up bathing, and wearing a skin garment with the hair next to his flesh. He withdrew again to solitude. There many sought him out, some for spiritual counsel and others for the miraculous healing of their diseases. He was strongly opposed to the Arians, and, going to Alexandria, denounced their views. As his fame spread, the Emperor Constantine and two of the latter's sons wrote to him, asking and receiving his counsel. He is said to have died in 356 at the age of 105 years. Although without formal education, he possessed a vigorous mind and a retentive memory. He was humble, cheerful, with a radiant love for God and with sympathy and well-mannered courtesy for the individuals who came to him.

Anthony represented two types of monasticism. One of these was that of hermit, the eremitical life, where each monk lived in solitude. The other was a modification of the way of the hermit, in which the monks had individual dwellings—a cell, a cave, a hut, or some other shelter—yet sufficiently near one another to make fellowship possible. They might even have over them a fellow-monk as a kind of director. Such a collection of monks was known as a *laura*.

A third type of monasticism was the cenobitic, in which the monks lived in a community, or monastery, governed by a head monk and by rules. He who was looked back to as the great pioneer of that kind of life was Pachomius, a younger contemporary of Anthony, who was born c.285 or c.292 and who died in 346. The son of pagan parents in Egypt, at the age of twenty Pachomius was for a short time in the imperial army. There he was impressed with the thoughtful kindness of Christians in bringing food and drink to the soldiers. Leaving the army, he was given instruction in the faith, was baptized, and joined himself to an ascetic. Some time afterwards he began a monastery, and it became so popular that several others arose. Pachomius ruled over them from a central monastery. As he was dying he appointed a successor and the latter eventually chose a coadjutor who succeeded him in his office.

Rules were gradually developed for the operation of the community. By the end of the fourth century the Pachomian system was fairly mature and stabilized. Each monastery was surrounded by a wall. Within this wall there were the houses in which the monks dwelt, twenty-two to forty to a house, and each with his own private cell. Every house had a common room for meetings. Within each enclosure there were also a church, a refectory, a library, a kitchen, a bakery, a store house for food, various workshops, and an infirmary. All the monasteries were under a superior-general or archimandrite who appointed his own successor. He visited them, made rules for them, and to each named one of the monks as resident head. In each house were placed, so far as possible, those with the same type of work. In every house the monks were ranked by order of seniority. Dress was prescribed and was very simple. All who applied were admitted if they were willing to keep the rules, but full membership was given only after a probation of three years. Each day had its regular times for group prayers by houses. The Eucharist was celebrated twice a week. Twice a year there were assemblies of all the monks, and at one of these the custom was for each to forgive any of the others who had done him an injury. Monks slept three in a cell and in a sitting, not a recumbent position. Study and memorization of passages from the Bible were required of all and the illiterate were taught to read. Manual labour was also compulsory, partly in the weaving of rushes into mats and baskets for sale and partly for the supply of the physical needs of the community. Extreme asceticism was discouraged, although some of the monks followed a very austere diet or might greatly curtail their hours of sleep. There were two meals a day, and flesh and wine were forbidden. Twice a week there were community fasts. Strict obedience to their superiors was required of all, and there were punishments for the disorderly. Chastity and poverty were compulsory. Gossip was forbidden and conversation was supposed to be limited to spiritual subjects. Each monastery had between two and three hundred monks and the total by the time of the death of Pachomius is said to have been three thousand.

Mary, the sister of Pachomius, gathered a nunnery about her which was put under the control of the Pachomian superior-general. Soon after the death of Pachomius, two other nunneries were formed. Although they were also in the comprehensive organization, precautions were taken to keep the men and women from meeting.

The Further Development of Monasticism

In the fourth and fifth centuries monasticism spread widely and monks multiplied. Monks and monasteries were especially numerous in the East, notably in Egypt, Mesopotamia, Palestine, and Syria, partly because in the latter two countries pre-monastic asceticism had been strong in Christian circles. In Mesopotamia they seem to have had beginnings which were quite independent of influences from Egypt. They may have been indebted to Manichæan monasticism and through that to Buddhist and Hindu asceticism. Monks and monasteries were also present in the West. All three kinds of monks were found—the solitaries (who were especially numerous in Palestine), those whose cells were grouped into a loose community, a *laura,* and those dwelling in the highly organized groups of which Pachomius had been a pioneer.

Some of the monks practised extreme austerities. There were the "pillar saints," those who lived on the top of pillars. One of the earliest and quite the most famous of them was Simeon Stylites, who died in 459. He dwelt on his pillar east of Antioch for thirty-six years, is said to have touched his feet with his forehead more than 1244 times in succession, and to have dripped with vermin. His fame spread, and multitudes, including some high state officials, came to see him. Other monks were immured in cells, some of them so small that they could neither lie at full length nor stand at full height. In one group the monks are reported to have subsisted on grass which they cut with sickles. Some monks passed many nights without sleep. Others went for days without food. The extreme ascetics were popularly esteemed "athletes of God." Many were said to work miracles of healing.

More numerous than these individualistic ascetics were the monks who lived in communities according to rule. After Pachomius, the most famous pioneer in the East of this form of monasticism was Basil of Cæsarea, whom we have already met as a scion of a wealthy, earnestly Christian family and as one of the three great Cappadocian champions and interpreters of Nicene orthodoxy. In 358, then in his late twenties, Basil visited Egypt and was profoundly impressed by what he saw there of the Pachomian monasteries. During their student days at Athens he and Gregory of Nazianzus agreed to join in living the ascetic life.

The ascetic life had appeared among the Christians in his native country some time before Basil's return home, and Eustathius, Bishop of Sebaste, north-east of Cæsarea, had already founded monasteries. Although later separated on questions of doctrine, Basil and Eustathius were for a time close friends. Moreover, Basil's mother, one of his sisters, Macrina, and a younger brother began in Pontus the nucleus of a community for simple Christian living which later was to develop into a nunnery. Indeed, Macrina was looked back to as the founder of women's conventual life in the Greek portion of the Catholic Church. Basil distributed part of his property among the poor and embarked on the monastic life in a secluded spot across the river from this establishment. Others joined him. He did not condemn Christians who married, but he believed celibacy and asceticism to be the higher way.

Basil was not long permitted to give himself exclusively to the monastic discipline, for he was drawn into the general life of the Church—into its theological controversies and eventually into its administration as a bishop. In this he was a prototype of many outstanding monks, both in the East and the West. They found that they could not withdraw completely from the world or from the Church as a whole, but must participate in them. Yet in the intervals which he devoted to the monastic life Basil worked out a set of rules which helped to shape monasticism in the Catholic Church, both in the East and the West. These were not in one formal piece of legislation, but were directions for the ascetic life contained in several writings, especially what are known as *The Longer Rules* and *The Shorter Rules*.

Here is not the place for a full description or even an adequate summary of these directions. In them Basil was deeply indebted to what he had seen in the Pachomian monasteries in Egypt. Yet he was no slavish imitator but was, rather, a creator. He knit the monastery into more of a community than had Pachomius. In general Basil advocated that the ascetics dwell together in communities rather than in solitude, declaring that association with others was necessary to the full Christian life, such as the practice of the law of love to one's neighbour. In the community room was to be found for both work and prayer. Extreme austerity was to be avoided, for after testing it in his first years of the ascetic life Basil had found it unfruitful. Food was to be simple and inexpensive and during the common meal a book was to be read. Work was for the supplying of the needs of the monastery and was varied, with preference given to agriculture and chief honour paid to intellectual labour, especially the study of the Scriptures. The monastery had its officers, with a superior over them all, chosen by the heads of neighbouring monasteries and after a period of probation accepted by his brethren. The superior was to seek the counsel of senior brethren. The obedience of the monk was to be absolute and the commitment was for life. Entrance to a monastery did not necessarily entail the renunciation of all the postulant's property, but he was to distribute at least part of it to the poor, taking care to do so with wisdom, remembering that he held it in trust from God. The monks were to make frequent confession of their sins, probably to one or another of the more mature of their brethren and not necessarily to a priest. After entering the monastery, the monks were to have as little contact as possible with their families, for this would embroil them with the world and its affairs. The monastery as a whole, through its official almoner, gave aid to the poor outside its walls, more especially to those who were dedicated to God. Boys were received to be educated in a religious manner, but were largely kept separate from the monks. The monasteries did not form a closely knit order, but constituted a kind of loose federation, and in time of need the richer were supposed to come to the assistance of the poorer. The monks were mostly laymen and the bishops seem to have had no control over them or the monasteries except that the formal admission to the monastic life was in the presence of a bishop. Yet Basil himself, as we have seen, became a bishop, and he made important contributions towards bringing the monastic life into the life of the Catholic Church as a whole. He and his monks became champions of orthodoxy and he set the example of a man of learning and outstanding gifts of organization giving himself both to the ascetic life and to the Church.

As we have suggested, Basil had a profound influence upon later monasticism, in both the East and the West. The great leader and organizer in the revival of Byzantine monasticism, Theodore the Studite, whom we are to meet in the eighth century, and whose reformed monastery, an outgrowth of a church and centre of monasticism founded in Constantinople in the late fifth century by Studius, became a model throughout the Eastern or Greek wing of the Catholic Church, drew his inspiration largely from the writings of Basil. In the West, Cassian, a fifth century pioneer in developing monasticism in Gaul, was aware of the work of Basil. Basil's precedent was formative in the rules devised by Benedict of Nursia, whom we are to meet in the sixth century. Benedict took over the Basilian pattern, although not slavishly or to the neglect of other earlier forms of the monastic life, and modified it to suit the needs of himself and of the community which he founded. For centuries his rule was dominant in the monasticism of the West.

An older contemporary of Basil and apparently quite unaffected by him, but a pioneer of the monastic movement in the West, and especially in Gaul, was Martin of Tours. We have already met him as a bishop who was active in spreading the faith in his diocese. Martin was born in the first half of the fourth century, the son of pagan parents. Since his father had been a military officer, Martin, complying with the requirement which made that occupation hereditary, entered the army in his teens. He was then already a catechumen. It was while serving in northern Gaul that the most famous incident of his life is said to have occurred. He is reported to have divided his coat with a beggar on a cold winter day and that night, in a dream, to have seen Christ clothed with the half which he had given away and saying that it was he with whom the young soldier had shared his garment. Baptized and resigning from the army two years later, Martin joined himself to Hilary of Poitiers, a famous champion of Nicene orthodoxy, journeyed to his parents to try to win them to the Christian faith and, returning to Gaul, established himself as a hermit. Others were attracted to him and a community arose which became the beginning of a monastery. The Christians of Tours wished him for their bishop and, luring him into the city, constrained him to accept the post. While performing with distinction the duties of his office, he remained humble, refusing to sit on the bishop's throne but using instead a rude stool, and continued to live as a hermit in a cell outside the city and there was joined by admirers who became the nucleus of another monastery. Many miracles were attributed to him. He was active in winning non-Christians and travelled extensively outside his diocese on various errands in the interests of the faith. He believed that no one was so depraved that he was beyond the scope of God's pardon. Himself impeccably orthodox, he protested against the persecution of heretics. He died in 397 or 400, probably in his seventies or eighties, exhausted by a journey which he had undertaken to restore harmony among the clergy in a town in his diocese. A younger contemporary admirer who wrote his biography declared that "he judged none and condemned none and never returned evil for evil. No one ever saw him angry, or annoyed, or mournful, or laughing. He was always the same and presented to everyone a joy of countenance and manner which seemed to those who saw it beyond the nature of man. Nothing was in his mouth except Christ, nothing in his heart but piety, peace, and pity." This biography early had a wide circulation and helped to shape the general religious life as well as monasticism in the West. The large number of churches in Western Europe which were dedicated to Martin were evidence of the impress which he made upon the Christianity of that region.

Another, but very different Western pioneer of monasticism was Eusebius Hieronimus Sophronius, better known as Jerome. A gifted and diligent scholar, enormously erudite, a master of languages, a lover of books, wielding a facile, vigorous, and often vitriolic pen, Jerome was an eloquent advocate of the monastic life. A contemporary of Martin of Tours, Ambrose of Milan, Augustine of Hippo, John Chrysostom, and the great Cappadocians, Jerome was born about the year 342 of devout Christian parents, near Aquileia, not far from the head of the Adriatic. As a youth he studied in Rome and there his ardent nature caused him on the one hand to be moved by the churches and the cata-combs and on the other to succumb to some of the vices which abounded in that capital. Baptized in Rome in his mid-twenties, he was attracted to the ascetic life. This had already entered Rome, perhaps stimulated by the descriptions given of the monks of Egypt by Athanasius when, exiled from his see, he took refuge with his fellow bishop, the Pope. It had won women from some of the wealthiest circles of Roman society. Returning to Aquileia, Jerome became one of a group of young men who gave themselves to the ascetic life. From Aquileia Jerome journeyed east and for three years lived as a solitary ascetic on the borders of Chalcis, southeast of Antioch, devoting himself to austerities, correspondence with his friends, and study in the library which he had brought with him. Restless by disposition, he lived for a time in Antioch, was there, reluctant, ordained priest, travelled to Palestine to visit the holy places of his faith, and then made his residence in Constantinople, where he formed a friendship with Gregory of Nazianzus. Journeying again to Rome, he was secretary of a council which aspired to be ecumenical, from 382 was secretary to Pope Damasus until the latter's death in December, 384, and, with the encouragement of the latter, began the work on a Latin translation of the Scriptures which was to be one of his chief claims to fame. While in Rome he continued to wear the dress and follow the abstemious discipline of the hermit and became spiritual director and teacher to the circle of wealthy women who were interested in the ascetic life. With one of these, Paula, he formed an especially close friendship. Against bitter opposition, Jerome eloquently advocated the ascetic life, praised virginity, and excoriated the luxurious and wealth-seeking among the clergy of the city.

After the death of Damasus Jerome left Rome, perhaps because of disappointment at not being elected Pope or because of the opposition and criticism which he had aroused. A few months later he was followed by Paula. Together they visited the places associated with the life of Jesus, among them Jerusalem, Bethlehem, and Egypt. Returning to Bethlehem, Jerome built a monastery and established himself in a cave close to the reputed site of the nativity, while Paula erected convents and a hospice for pilgrims. There Jerome gave himself to the routine of the monk, with its prayers, austere meals, and work. His chief labours were literary, and in them he had the encouragement of Paula and the assistance of scribes who wrote at his dictation. He composed commentaries on the Bible, engaged in theological polemics, and carried on a voluminous correspondence. His chief accomplishment was a fresh translation of the Bible into Latin from the original tongues. Because of its merit, both in its scholarship and its felicitous Latin style, this translation won its way among Latin-using peoples and eventually became standard for the Roman Catholic Church. However, the text which circulated under the name of the Vulgate, namely, the Latin vernacular version of the Bible, did not preserve the work of Jerome in its purity. It incorporated an older version of the Psalms, in part revised by Jerome, and some of its other sections were from older translations, partly unrevised or partially revised. It was a late sixteenth century revision of the Vulgate which was eventually made standard by Papal decree. Jerome lived on until 420, surviving the death of Paula and several of his closest friends, and dying where he had spent the last thirty-four years, in Bethlehem. His was a tempestuous career, but by his ardent advocacy of monasticism he had given a great impetus to that movement, especially in the West.

Martin of Tours and Jerome were by no means the only ones responsible for the growth of the monastic movement in the West. Ambrose of Milan furthered it. In the fourth century Bishop Eusebius of Vercellæ in Italy had the clergy of his cathedral live together according to a rule. Augustine of Hippo gathered his clerical household into a community. At least two Popes of the fifth century founded monasteries in Rome. Early in the fifth century John Cassian began monasteries in Marseilles and Lérins in the south of Gaul which soon enrolled thousands.

By the end of the fifth century monasticism had become firmly established in the Catholic Church in both East and West and had begun to take on the forms which were to characterize it through the centuries. It was to undergo many modifications, but in its numerous ramifications it was to be the main channel through which bursts of new life were to find expression in the various churches which conserved the traditions of the Catholic Church of the Roman Empire. One of the best gauges of the vitality of these churches, and especially of the Roman Catholic Church, is to be found in the numbers and strength of the reforms of existing monastic houses and of the new monastic or near-monastic movements which emerge in any one era. When vigour has been at a low ebb, the monastic life has languished and become sluggish or corrupt. In times of revival, the monastic life has attracted ardent souls who wish to give themselves unreservedly to the faith and has taken on fresh variety and new forms.

Here was effort after effort to create communities which would completely realize the Christian ideal and also, in the case of increasing numbers of variations of the monastic patterns, dream after dream of making these communities centres from which the Christian faith would irradiate and transform the non-Christian world about them. Never did the effort fully reach its goal nor was the dream ever entirely fulfilled. Most monastic institutions, if they survived, fell away from the purposes of their founders and became lethargic or worse.

Yet the vision would not die. Its constraining appeal persisted and was never more compelling than in the nineteenth and twentieth centuries.

SELECTED BIBLIOGRAPHY

GENERAL WORKS

A. Harnack, *Monasticism: Its Ideals and History and the Confessions of St. Augustine. Two Lectures.* Translated into English by E. E. Kellett and F. H. Marseille (London, Williams & Norgate, 1901, pp. 171). The lecture on monasticism is a general, interpretative essay.

W. H. Mackean, *Christian Monasticism in Egypt to the Close of the Fourth Century* (London, Society for Promoting Christian Knowledge, 1920, pp. 120). Soundly based upon the sources.

I. G. Smith, *Christian Monasticism from the Fourth to the Ninth Centuries of the Christian Era* (London, A. D. Innes & Co., 1892, pp. viii, 351). A competent, well-documented survey.

H. B. Workman, *The Evolution of the Monastic Ideal from the Earliest Times to the Coming of the Friars* (London, The Epworth Press, 1913, pp. xxi, 368). A well-written, scholarly survey, of which a little more than a third is devoted to the period covered by this chapter.

ANTHONY

Athanasius, *Life of Antony (vita Antoni)*, translated by H. Ellershaw, with notes by A. Robertson, in *A Select Library of Nicene and Post-Nicene Fathers of the Christian Church,* Second Series, Vol. IV (New York, Charles Scribner's Sons, 1903), pp. 188–221.

BASIL

Saint Basil. The Letters, with an English Translation, by R. J. Deferrari (London, William Heinemann, 4 vols., 1926–1934). Greek text, English translation, and notes.

W. K. L. Clarke, *St. Basil the Great, A Study in Monasticism* (Cambridge University Press, 1913, pp. lx, 176). Carefully done, by a specialist.

W. K. L. Clarke, *The Ascetic Works of Saint Basil, Translated into English with Introduction and Notes* (London, Society for Promoting Christian Knowledge, 1925, pp. 362).

E. F. Morison, *St. Basil and His Rule. A Study in Early Monasticism* (Oxford University Press, 1912, pp. xii, 150). Carefully done, based upon the sources.

M. G. Murphy, *St. Basil and Monasticism* (Washington, The Catholic University of America, 1930, pp. xix, 112). A doctoral dissertation.

MARTIN OF TOURS

E.-Ch. Babut, *Saint Martin de Tours* (Paris, Librairie Ancienne H. Champion, no date, pp. viii, 320). Objective, carefully done.

L. Foley, *The Greatest Saint of France* (Milwaukee, Morehouse-Gorham Co., 1931, pp. xi, 321). Popularly written, based upon careful research, with critical notes.

Sulpicii Severi Vita Sancti Martini, in *Corpus Scriptorum Ecclesiasticorum,* Vol. I, pp. 109–141.

JEROME

E. L. Cutts, *Saint Jerome* (London, Society for Promoting Christian Knowledge, 1897, pp. ix, 230). Popularly written, based upon careful scholarship.

Largent, *Saint Jerome,* translated by H. Davenport (New York, Benziger Brothers, 1913, pp. x, 196).

Select Letters of St. Jerome, with an English translation by F. A. Wright (London, William Heinemann, 1933, pp. xvi, 510). Parallel Latin text and English translation.

Chapter IX

EARTHEN VESSELS . . . THE EXCEEDING GREATNESS OF THE POWER

In one of his most famous passages, Paul declares that "we have this treasure in earthen vessels, that the excellency [or exceeding greatness] of the power may be of God, and not of us." In another letter he speaks of "the exceeding greatness of His power to us-ward who believe, according to the working of his mighty power which he wrought in Christ, when he raised him from the dead and set him at his own right hand . . . far above all principality and power, and might, and dominion, and every name that is named, not only in this world, but also in that which is to come; and hath put all things under his feet."

As we come to the end in the initial period in the history of Christianity we would do well to ask just what effect the Christian Gospel was having. By the year 500, as we have seen, the overwhelming majority of the population of the Roman Empire were calling themselves Christians and the faith had begun to be carried beyond the borders of that realm. It was but a small proportion of the earth's surface which had been touched by Christianity. Only here and there had the peoples of primitive cultures who thinly occupied most of the world been reached, and of civilized mankind less than half had even so much as heard the name of Christ. Most of the Persians and the Indians and all the Chinese were as yet ignorant of it. Long before the end of the fifth century the Roman Empire had been showing signs of internal weakness and the invasions had begun which were to hasten its disintegration and, as they became more pronounced, were to usher in for Christianity an agonizing period of decline.

What was Christianity doing to the peoples who had accepted it and to their culture? Was the "exceeding greatness of His power" to be seen, and if so how? Had it been true of Christ that God had "put all things under his feet"? Had "the earthen vessels" to which "the treasure," "the light of the

236

glorious Gospel of Christ," been entrusted so hampered it that it had been nullified or at least weakened, or had the fact that "the treasure" was in "earthen vessels" made more vivid, as Paul had declared, that there was in the Gospel a unique power, something so in contrast with human nature that it was obviously not man's creation, but from outside man, so demonstrably from Christ that it was clear that the Catholic Church was right in affirming that Jesus Christ, while fully man, was also God incarnate, the Word become flesh? Would the power prove so potent that it would survive the centuries of adversity and break out with renewed vigour, or would it be dissipated through the corruption of the earthen vessels?

It was not merely a question of striking changes, but of what kind of changes. Sweeping changes there had been before in the Mediterranean world and in other cultures, as in the wake of Alexander the Great and of Gautama Buddha, and changes there were to be again. Fully as important was the quality of the changes. How far were these to reflect the kind of life which was disclosed in Christ? Were men being transformed into likeness to Christ?

An even deeper question, one at which we cannot more than hint in this place, was that raised by Paul's confident affirmation that God had "foreordained" "them that love God . . . to be conformed to the image of His Son." Was this true? Was Christ, as the author of *The Epistle to the Hebrews* declared, "the brightness of His [God's] glory, and the express image of His [God's] person"? In the changes which were taking place was the Creator of the universe at work, fulfilling His purpose for man, and could this purpose be seen in the kind of individuals and the characteristics of the communities which were emerging?

These questions are not of antiquarian interest. It was in these five centuries that Christianity first moved out into the world. It was then that it created a literature and developed organizational features, intellectual statements of belief, and forms of worship which for the majority of those bearing the Christian name have remained standard to this day. The experience of these initial centuries should shed important, perhaps decisive light upon the questions which we raised at the close of our fourth chapter, just before we embarked upon this period, about the place of the Gospel in human history, the query as to whether in it is to be found the clue to the enigma which the universe presents to man and which man presents to himself. They should be of assistance in determining whether, to use another affirmation of Paul, "God was in Christ, reconciling the world unto himself," and, if so, just how that reconciliation has operated.

The Power Creates the Church, Christian Literature, and Christian Theology

From what has been said in the preceding chapters it must be apparent that power of extraordinary magnitude was at work. Into a civilization which had ceased to say or to do much that was new a dynamic force had entered which had brought into being a vast new literature, of which the New Testament was only a small portion, inspired by a compelling creative message, centred about Christ. This force was also responsible for the emergence of the Christian Church, a structure without parallel in history, which, while arising within the Roman Empire and in part owing its unity to that Empire, was spreading beyond the borders of that realm and with an inner vitality which enabled it to survive the breakup of that state. In connexion with the Church a new profession had arisen, the clergy. The clergyman was in part priest, modeled consciously on the pattern of the Jewish priesthood and perhaps unconsciously showing the influence of the pagan priesthood. Yet the clergyman was far more than a priest, officiating at the public services of the Church. He was also a pastor, a shepherd and guide of souls. That function was to grow as the centuries passed and was to make the profession of the Christian clergyman quite unique.

This power had stimulated the conventionalized mind of the Græco-Roman world to wrestle with the baffling new intellectual problems presented by the birth, life, death, and resurrection of Christ and to reach answers which were novel in the history of human thought. It had created new forms of worship and in monasticism had brought into being a movement which, like the Church, was to outlast the society within which it arose and against which it was a protest. Moreover, the Christian Gospel had worked moral and spiritual transformations in the lives of individuals. In some, as in Paul and Augustine, these were spectacular. In others, such as Ambrose and Tertullian, they were not as cataclysmic but were no less real. In still others, such as Origen, Anthony, and Basil of Cæsarea, reared as Christians from infancy, the product was also distinctive and contagious.

Yet No Attempt Was Made to Reshape Civilization

In addition to the effects which we have already noted, there were others which must be taken into account if anything like satisfactory answers are to be given to the questions which we have propounded.

It is significant that no thoroughgoing remaking of Græco-Roman society was achieved. Indeed, none was attempted. For the first two centuries Christians constituted a small minority. At the outset many of them expected the early visible return of their Lord, bringing with him the abrupt end of history. For several generations, as we have seen, substantial numbers of Christians continued to reassert that hope. For the most part the Church was concerned for the salvation of the individual. It sought to gather these individuals into its fellowship and it constituted a community, divided to be sure, but fairly distinct from the world about it. Their critics charged Christians with being enemies of society, but Christian apologists protested the loyalty of their co-believers to the Empire. Tertullian, for instance, declared that Christians regarded the existence of the Roman Empire as a bulwark against chaos, held that God had appointed the Emperors, and that, as commanded by the New Testament, Christians prayed for their temporal rulers, the Emperors and their ministers, and even for those who persecuted them. Against those who charged Christians and their neglect of the gods with the responsibility for the ills which were overtaking society, Tertullian boldly insisted that because of its sins the human race had always deserved ill at God's hands, that God's judgements had brought misfortunes upon mankind in pre-Christian days, and that calamities had actually declined since the advent of Christianity, for, so he said, from that time onward virtue had placed some restraint upon the wickedness of the world and men had begun to pray for the averting of God's wrath. Christians were far from attempting the overthrow and reconstruction of Græco-Roman society. To be sure, they were attacking certain features of that society—its polytheism, its immoralities, its gladiatorial contests, the indecencies of its theatre, its infanticide, and its sexual irregularities—but in doing so they believed that they were conserving and not destroying the Empire and its civilization.

When, beginning with Constantine, the Empire made its peace with the Church, it sought to control the latter and to use it as a bulwark against the mounting threats to the stability of the realm. In this the leaders of the Church acquiesced. Indeed, when the sack of Rome by Alaric and his Goths in 410 made apparent the mortal weakness of the Empire, Augustine stoutly declared that the presence of churches as sanctuaries and the Christian profession of some of the Goths had mitigated the disaster.

With the numerical triumph of Christianity through the winning of the overwhelming majority of the population of the Roman Empire to the Christian faith, it might have seemed that the Church would at last undertake the reshaping of civilization. However, the emergence of monasticism served further to preclude even the formulation of such a programme. The monks sought to withdraw from the world and either to live completely apart from society or to set up communities of their own which would perfectly embody the Christian ideal.

Although Christians did not attempt the complete remaking of Græco-Roman civilization, they attacked some of the constituent elements of the life about them and in other ways their attitudes were in stark contrast with the culture in which they were immersed and wrought not only negative but also positive changes in the Mediterranean world. Moreover, there was a striking difference between Græco-Roman civilization and the Roman state on the one hand and on the other the faith set forth in Christ and by his apostles. There were basic differences in values—what was deemed most worth while—and in conceptions of the nature and destiny of man, of the universe, of the course of history, and of power—between the kind of power seen in the cross and the resurrection and that which formed and sustained the Roman Empire. These could scarcely be reconciled. Here, as in Judaism, the parable of Jesus of the new wine in old wineskins was pertinent, perhaps tragically so. In trying to put the one into the other both might be lost.

THE PROFOUND EFFECT ON THE RELIGIOUS LIFE

As was to be expected, Christianity had a profound effect upon the religious life of the Roman Empire and its people. Christian apologists devoted much of their energy to denouncing the pagan cults in which the Empire abounded and would have no compromise with them. As we have suggested, there was some carry over from paganism in the attitudes and practices of many Christians, but there was not the deliberate and easygoing syncretism which was so marked a feature of the contemporary religious life outside of Christianity and Judaism. The Church was officially intransigent. It held that through itself alone was salvation, the true goal of human life, to be attained. By the year 500 the pagan cults had all but disappeared. They survived chiefly in backward rural districts and remote mountain valleys, or among the barbarian invaders.

So sweeping a religious revolution had never before been seen in the Mediterranean world. It was not unique. It was later to be paralleled by the supplanting of religions, some of them "higher" than the paganism of the Roman Empire, by Islam, and by the elimination and absorption in most of India of Buddhism, also a "high" religion, by Hinduism. Yet in some ways the victory of Christianity was a more notable achievement than either of these. In contrast with Islam, the triumph of Christianity, which had really been won before Constantine espoused the faith, had been accomplished without the use of arms or the support of the state, and, unlike the success of Hinduism in India as against Buddhism, it was not the resurgence of the hereditary religion against what the latter regarded as an heretical variant from itself.

The religious effects of Christianity were not alone negative, the destruction of rival cults. Christianity contributed to new religious movements. It was a potent element in Manichæism, and in the various forms of Gnosticism. It may have had some influence on the rise and growth of Neoplatonism. Even more significant were the positive results in the conceptions of God and of human nature, in the kind of worship, and in the quality of living which the victor produced. On the conceptions of God and of human nature and on the kind of worship associated with Christianity, we have already said as much as the limitations of our space will wisely permit. However, we must add something about the basic convictions concerning the relation of the Christian community to the society in which it was immersed, convictions concerning the goal of history, and the sort of behaviour and character which issued from the religious beliefs of Christians. Here were tensions and reciprocal contradictions. While they were partially resolved as Christian thinkers achieved an uneasy reconciliation and as membership in the Church came to be almost identical with citizenship in the Empire, they never fully disappeared, but persisted, a source both of weakness and strength in the society with which Christianity had become associated.

The Tension between the Early Christians and "the World"

From the beginning, Christians felt themselves in opposition to what they called "the world." They recognized the antagonism between Jesus on the one hand and, on the other hand, the state in which they were set and which had brought about the crucifixion of Jesus and the chronic persecution of his followers. This contrast found dramatic expression in Augustine's *City of God* with its sharply drawn distinction between the city of the world and the city of God, but that famous book was the more important because it was an amplification by a first-class mind of views already cherished by Christians.

Many tended to identify the Church with the city of God. Even Augustine seemed at times to do so. Certainly as it grew the Catholic Church became a distinct society, within the Empire but not fully of it, a kind of *imperium in imperio*. It had its rules and laws, the beginnings of its canon law, administered by its own officers, the clergy, alongside the state. This contributed to the contrast between Christians and the society in which they were immersed.

Moreover, as we pointed out in a previous chapter, the Christian view of human history differed radically from that of the Græco-Roman world. It was the contrast between fate and destiny. The Greeks, and in this Roman thinkers followed them, regarded history as endlessly repeating itself in a series of cycles, so that what is now had been in some earlier stage of man's career and would be again in later eras. Blind fate determined it. Here was a weary, pessimistic appraisal of man's course. To the Christian, in striking contrast, human history has God as its sovereign, begins with God's creation of man, and will go on to a climax in which God will still be master. Christians saw in history a cosmic drama, centring about man's creation with freedom of will, man's sin, and the redemption of man through the incarnation, the cross, the resurrection, and the coming of the Holy Spirit. Through Christ, so Christians believed, fallen, sinful man could be transformed and grow into fellowship with God and in likeness to Him. This gave to man a dignity and a worth and to history a meaning which Græco-Roman thought had not known.

Christians differed as to when the climax to history would arrive and as to its precise nature. Yet the early Christians held that God was even now master, that, while the climax had not yet come, it was near. Paul said that "the day is at hand" and that Christians should even now "walk honestly as in the day" where God's will is perfectly done. Jesus seemed to say that here and now men could enter that kingdom where God's will is the rule, in a "realized eschatology," the end of history, which for them had already dawned. Many believed that the climax would be in a second coming of Christ. Some sought to discover the precise date of that coming, while others, while convinced that it would be, held that no man could know the day or the hour. Origen was convinced that the Word, the *Logos,* would "prevail over the entire rational creation, and change every soul into His own perfection" and that "the consummation of all things is the destruction of evil, although as to the question whether it shall be so destroyed that it can never anywhere arise again, it is beyond our present purpose to say." Many, among whom was Augustine, taught that perfection could never be realized within history, but only beyond it, in heaven.

The opposition between Christians and "the world" was partially allayed, as we have suggested, as the centuries wore on. Leaders of the Church held the latter to be like Noah's ark, in which were all, both good and bad. Christianity tended to fuse with Platonism and Stoicism. Stoicism was utilized by Christian thinkers to afford a theoretical foundation to ethics. To the Stoic there was in the universe a dominant Divine Reason from which came a moral natural law. Some of the Christian intellectuals held that this natural law of the Stoics was identical with Christian moral law. Yet this convenient accommodation did not entirely erase the contrast between Christianity and "the world" in which it had to operate.

CHRISTIANS AND WAR

One of the issues on which the early Christians were at variance with the Græco-Roman world was participation in war. For the first three centuries no Christian writing which has survived to our time condoned Christian participation in war. Some Christians held that for them all bloodshed, whether as soldiers or as executioners, was unlawful. At one stage in its history the influential Church of Alexandria seems to have looked askance upon receiving soldiers into its membership and to have permitted enlistment in the legions only in exceptional circumstances. Hippolytus, prominent in Rome, in putting down in writing what he believed to be the apostolic tradition and so the authentic Christian teaching, maintained that when he applied for admission to the Christian fellowship a soldier must refuse to kill men even if he were commanded by his superiors to do so and must also not take an oath, and that military commanders must resign if they were to continue as catechumens. A catechumen or baptized person, so Hippolytus said, who sought to enlist as a soldier must be cut off from the Church. Tertullian argued against Christians being members of the Roman armies on the ground that this brought one under a master other than Christ, that it entailed taking the sword, and that, even when the army was used for police purposes in peace time, it made necessary the infliction of punishment, when all revenge was forbidden to the Christian. He said that in disarming Peter Christ ungirded every soldier. Another consideration which weighed against service in the armies was the strong possibility that as a soldier the Christian would be required to take part in idolatrous rites. Some Christians would permit service in the legions in times or areas of peace when the function of the army was that of the police, but frowned upon it in war.

So clear was the opposition of the early Christians to bearing arms that Celsus, in his famous attack on them, declared that if all were to do as did the Christians the Empire would fall victim to the wildest and most lawless barbarians. In replying, Origen did not deny that Christians were pacifists. Indeed, he said that Christians do not fight under the Emperor "although he require it." Instead he argued that if all were to become Christians, the barbarians would also be Christian, and that even now, when Christians were in the minority, their love, labour, and prayers were doing more than Roman arms to preserve the realm.

For the early Christians, pacifism was largely theoretical, for they were chiefly from groups other than those from which the legions were recruited and they did not have the responsibility for formulating state policy.

In spite of the general trend among Christians towards pacifism, in the third century the numbers of Christians serving in the legions seem to have increased. This was especially the case on the frontiers, menaced as they were by invasion, and in the West.

Moreover, after the Emperors had espoused Christianity and they and Christian officials were charged with the responsibility for the body politic and for making decisions for the government, the attitude of the majority of Christians towards war changed. Christians now began to believe that some wars are just. That was the position taken by Ambrose. Augustine elaborated the theoretical basis for a just war. He held that wickedness must be restrained, by force if necessary, and that the sword of the magistrate is divinely commissioned. Not all wars are just. To be just, so Augustine said, a war must be waged under the authority of the prince, it must have as its object the punishment of injustice and the restoration of peace, and it must be fought without vindictiveness and without unnecessary violence. It must also be carried on with inward love. Yet without the authority of the prince, Augustine taught, the civilian must not use force to defend even his own life. The clergy and the monks were to be entirely exempt from military service. It was this principle of a righteous or just war which was held by a large proportion of Christians in subsequent centuries.

CHRISTIANS AND PUBLIC AMUSEMENTS

On amusements Christians also set themselves against the prevailing mores of Græco-Roman life. The theatre, gladiatorial combats, and contests between men and beasts were almost universal. Every city of consequence had prominent structures for them. The pagan Emperors, even such noble spirits among them as Marcus Aurelius, considered it part of their public duty to give gladiatorial shows and to attend them, and the crowd demanded them. Yet leading Christians unhesitatingly condemned the theatre and the sports of the amphitheatre. The theatre was opposed because of the lewdness of its plays and its hypocrisy—its simulation of love, wrath, fear, and sorrow. Tertullian gave as reasons for the prohibition to Christians of attendance at the public spectacles the fact that the games and the gladiatorial contests were in honour of the pagan gods, that they stirred up rage, bitterness, and grief, that the accompanying betting was too agitating to be wholesome, and that through them crime was not only committed but also taught. Another of the early Christian writers denounced the gladiatorial shows as "a cannibal banquet for the soul," and still another as inculcating murder. Some, including Clement of Alexandria, forbade Christians to frequent the race course. Hippolytus declared that early Christian tradition did not countenance attending or taking part in chariot races. Augustine described and condemned the blood lust aroused by witnessing the gladiatorial combats. For a time the Church refused baptism to a professional gladiator unless he would renounce that occupation and excluded from the communion those who frequented the games. Under the influence of his new faith, the Emperor Constantine forbade gladiatorial shows and abolished the legal penalties which required criminals to become gladiators. John Chrysostom, like many a lesser bishop and preacher, took up the verbal cudgels against horse-racing, popular farces, and pantomimes.

Yet these amusements were continued even after the majority of the population of the Empire had become professed Christians and when many, perhaps most of their patrons bore the Christian name. We are told that the gladiatorial combats persisted in Rome until, in the fifth century, a monk, Telemachus, leaped into the arena to stop the combatants and the mob, presumably nominally Christian, stoned him to death for interfering with their pleasure. Thereupon the Emperor ordered that the spectacles be stopped and Telemachus enrolled among the martyrs. Probably, however, the end of the gladiatorial combats and of contests in the arena between men and beasts was due as much to the growing poverty of the declining Empire and the dearth of recruits for the ranks of the gladiators as to the Christian conscience.

CHRISTIANS AND SLAVERY

Christians carried on no organized campaign against slavery. That was to wait until the nineteenth and twentieth centuries. Yet here, also, although by no means so markedly as in the case of amusements, the trend of the Christian conscience and of Christian practice was against a basic, generally accepted institution of the Græco-Roman world and mitigated its harshness.

Even the casual student of Græco-Roman culture cannot but be aware of the prominence in it of slavery. The Greek democracies had slavery, and the leisure of their free citizens for the affairs of the state was made possible by the labour of slaves. In the Roman Empire the great landed estates were worked by slaves, and slaves also did much of the urban labour and performed most of the domestic service in households which could afford them. The lot of the slaves was often unhappy and public opinion condoned the use of the lash on them, the killing of them when their usefulness was past, and the selling of them at a low price when they became old.

Few Christians condemned slavery outright, many Christians owned slaves, and some Christian masters treated their slaves harshly. Yet Christian teaching ameliorated the lot of slaves. While Paul commanded slaves to obey their masters as slaves of Christ, doing their work as unto him and not unto men, he also exhorted masters to forbear "threatening" their slaves, remembering that there is no "respect of persons" with Him who is in heaven, the Master of both earthly masters and slaves. In a very touching letter Paul returned a fugitive slave to his master, pleading with the latter to receive the runaway as a brother in the Lord. Paul also declared that in the Christian fellowship there is neither bond nor free, but that "all are one in Christ Jesus." More than once in later centuries Christian writers reminded those of their faith that in

God's sight the master has no higher status than the slave, but that both are to be judged. Ambrose said that the slave might be superior in character to his master and be really more free than he. Augustine declared that God did not create rational man to lord it over his rational fellows. In this attitude both Ambrose and Augustine may have been influenced by Stoicism, but they believed it to be in accord with Christian principles. In many places slaves might hold office in the Church. It was not unusual for pagans to free their slaves, but many Christians did likewise. That they believed that a connexion existed between their faith and this act is seen from the fact that manumission was often solemnized in a church and on one of the great festival days, especially Easter. Near the end of the first century we hear of Christians who voluntarily became slaves to ransom others from bondage.

Christianity undercut slavery by giving dignity to work, no matter how seemingly menial that might be. Traditionally, labour which might be performed by slaves was despised as degrading to the freeman. Christian teachers said that all should work and that labour should be done as to Christ as master and as to God and in the sight of God. Work became a Christian duty.

Before the end of the fifth century slavery was declining. This was not due entirely and perhaps not even chiefly to the influence of Christianity, but the latter contributed to it.

The Christian Attitude Towards Property

Could a man of wealth become and remain a Christian? Did the Christian ethic make for a revolution in the attitude towards property and the industrial and commercial structure of life? Some passages in the New Testament brought disquiet to tender consciences. Notable was the statement of Jesus to the rich young ruler that if he would be perfect he must sell all that he had and give to the poor, and his further comment that it was extremely difficult for a rich man to enter the kingdom of heaven. As we have seen, the early church in Jerusalem for a time practised community of goods. With some partial exceptions poverty was one of the rules for those who sought to be fully Christian by following the way of the monk. Christian teachers tended to regard agriculture and manual labour as preferable to trade and frowned upon the latter for those of their faith. Clement of Alexandria did not proscribe trade, but said that the Christian merchant should seek to determine what would be a just price to ask for his wares and to demand no more and accept no less.

Yet Christian teachers did not forbid private property. They held that luxury was contrary to Christian principles and commended simplicity in clothing and in eating and drinking, but they also enjoined labour and did not require the full surrender of the fruits of labour. The Church became the owner of large estates and even monasteries possessed property collectively and sold on the market the products of the work of the monks.

CHRISTIAN PHILANTHROPY

Gifts of individuals to the public weal were not a Christian innovation. Many non-Christians had been very generous. Indeed, in the Roman Empire benefactions by private individuals and public officials were a commonplace. Through them baths, temples, theatres, roads, bridges, aqueducts, markets, schools, and libraries were constructed and games and other public amusements were provided.

However, in the use of money for the general welfare, Christianity brought five significant innovations. It made giving the obligation of its adherents, poor as well as rich, for it was held that all should contribute, each according to his ability, and this was symbolized by the collection which was early part of the Eucharistic ritual. The motive that was stressed was also new: it was love in grateful response to the love of Christ, who, though he was rich, yet for the sake of those who were to follow him became poor, that they through his poverty might become rich. The objects of beneficence were also changed, at least in part. The Christian community stressed the support of its widows, orphans, sick, and disabled, and of those who because of their faith were thrown out of employment or were imprisoned. It ransomed many who were put to servile labour for their faith. It entertained travellers. One church would send aid to another church whose members were suffering from famine or persecution. In theory and to no small degree in practice, the Christian community was a brotherhood, bound together in love, in which reciprocal material help was the rule. This was more easily carried out in the years when Christians were a minority, but something of the same spirit, even though attenuated and institutionalized, carried over into the days when Christians became a majority.

Christian love and service were not restricted to members of the Church. They were also extended to non-Christians. The command to love one's neighbour was not forgotten, nor the parable by which Jesus had illustrated that command, of care for a nameless stranger upon whom misfortune had fallen. In one of the New Testament writings Christians were enjoined, as they had opportunity, to do good unto all men. We read that later, when pestilence swept great cities such as Carthage and Alexandria, and when the pagans had fled to escape it, Christians remained and cared for the sick and dying. After persecutions ceased, wealthy Christians founded hospitals.

We must note that, as a fifth innovation, Christian giving was personalized.

Springing as it did from love, it was not impersonal service to masses of men, although often, as in times of famine, it dealt with large numbers, but it poured itself out to individuals, valuing each as having distinct worth in the sight of God, one "for whom Christ died."

Sex, Women, Children, Marriage, and the Family

In that important realm of human life which embraces the relations between the sexes, the status of women and children, marriage, and the family, Christianity wrought significant modifications.

Women were prominently and favourably mentioned in the cherished records of the life of Christ. While Paul would not allow them to speak in the meetings of the churches, he declared that in Christ Jesus there could be neither male nor female, and in the churches of the first generation women were honoured as prophetesses. Women seem also to have served as deaconesses, although this is not certain. As we have seen, from the very early days of the Church widows and virgins were held in high respect.

We have noted that at least from the time of Paul virginity was esteemed above the married state. Yet, except in some of the minority groups, such as the Marcionites, marriage was not proscribed. In the case of the death of one partner, a second marriage was forbidden by the stricter elements in the Church, but was eventually permitted by the more lenient. A third marriage was regarded as evil. Sexual intercourse outside of marriage was sternly interdicted and within marriage was permitted only for the procreation of children. Divorce was not allowed, except after the violation of the marriage bond by one of its partners. Sexual offenses were by no means unknown among Christians, but they were long held to exclude the offender from the Church. Later, as we have noted, restoration was permitted after due repentance and discipline. Civil law forbade a woman of high degree to marry a man of lower social rank, a freedman, or a slave, and decreed that if she disobeyed she would sink to the status of her spouse. Yet society in general winked at such unions. Early in the third century, although he was sharply criticized for it, Pope Callistus (Calixtus I), who relaxed the rule for sexual offenses, also pronounced such marriages legal from the standpoint of the Church.

Children were to be held in tender regard. Jesus himself had set the example and Paul, while enjoining them to obey their parents, commanded that the fathers should not provoke them to wrath but rear them in the "nurture and admonition of the Lord." The destruction of young life, either by abortion or infanticide, was forbidden.

In its first few centuries, within the Church which it had called into being Christianity had not only largely drawn the sting of slavery, given dignity to labour, and abolished beggary. It had also elevated the status of women and given new worth to childhood.

CHRISTIANS AND PAGAN LITERATURE

Should Christians study and teach the non-Christian literature—the Greek and Roman philosophers, poets, and dramatists—held in such high regard by the pagans about them, or were these writings so in contrast with the Gospel that to read them would contaminate the faith of Christians?

Here Christians did not fully agree. We have noted that such outstanding moulders of Christian thought as Clement of Alexandria and Origen were students of the Greek philosophers and, while not uncritical of them, levied tribute on them in forming their own conceptions of the Christian faith. They were by no means alone in this. We have remarked the fashion in which Ambrose was indebted to Stoicism and Augustine to Neoplatonism. The list could be lengthened. Moreover, it was through Christians that such of Greek and Roman literature as has survived to our day was preserved and transmitted. Yet Jerome came to believe that he must give up his passion for the Greek and Roman classics as a kind of idolatry. Many Christian writers poured scorn on the philosophers and denounced the accounts of the gods in the literature of the day for their immoralities and puerilities. Numbers of Christians, moreover, feared to have any contact with Greek and Roman literature, holding that the Scriptures were sufficient.

We must remind ourselves that between the Christian and the Greek approach to the intellectual life a great gulf existed, a gulf which helps to explain the distrust of many Christians for pagan philosophy. The Greeks relied on reason as the primary way to truth, but underneath that reason they had, consciously or unconsciously, certain presuppositions to which they applied reason. Among many Christians the non-Christian use of reason and its presuppositions were rejected. Jesus had thanked God that He had hid the Gospel from the wise and prudent and had revealed it unto babes, and Paul had declared that in the wisdom of God the world through wisdom had not known God. The road to the truth most important for man was held to be the acceptance by faith of what God had done in the incarnation, the cross, and the resurrection. Augustine declared: "Believe in order that you may understand." By the fifth century a loss of confidence in the Greek use of reason was fairly widespread in the Roman Empire, outside as well as within Christian circles.

Yet reason in itself was not universally disavowed either among non-Christians or Christians. In succeeding centuries the effort to determine the relation of reason to faith was to constitute a continuing problem in Christian circles. Jesus himself appealed to men to use their minds. Leading Christians, including Paul and Augustine, applied reason to the data derived through faith. In rejecting the Greek use of reason they did not reject reason itself. They maintained that through reason men could attain to an understanding of some aspects of truth. But they held that in the Gospel fresh and essential data had been given by God, of which reason must take account, that in Christ God had assumed the initiative, that it was through faith, the faith which is a full commitment of themselves to God in Christ, that men gain the central insights into the meaning of life, lay hold on true life, and enable God to lay hold of them, and that, having made this commitment and having gained these insights, they can apply reason to what has thus come to them.

CHRISTIANITY AND LANGUAGE

A phase of the influence of Christianity, although only in part in contrast with the culture in which the faith was set, was its effects on language. This was seen in a variety of ways.

One which was little short of revolutionary was the new meaning which Christianity gave to certain words, some of them in familiar use. In attempts to express their deepest convictions and central beliefs, Christians sometimes coined new terms. Often, however, they took over existing words, such as *deus* in Latin and *theos* (θεòς) in Greek, and endeavoured to fill them with distinctively Christian content. They were not entirely successful, for many of the terms carried over with them to those who employed them something of their pre-Christian and even anti-Christian connotations. Yet in varying degrees Christians gave peculiarly Christian meanings to the words which they adopted.

In some regions Christianity assisted in the spread of a language or creating for it literary form. In Asia Minor Christianity was probably responsible for the supplanting of the numerous local tongues by Greek, and in Gaul the disappearance of the Celtic vernaculars and the triumph of Latin seem to have been closely associated with the spread of Christianity. Yet in Armenia the golden age of native literature came through the translation and composition of Christian books through an alphabet formed for that purpose. In Egypt it was the successful effort to provide the masses of the population with a literature in the speech of everyday life which halted the exclusive use of the alien Greek for the written page and which stimulated the development of an alphabet which could be quickly and easily learned by the multitude in place of the ancient hieroglyphics which could be the property only of the few. Through this medium Coptic Christian literature came into being, largely the work of monks. Its major creative period was in the latter part of the fourth and in the fifth century. Similarly, the use of Syriac in literature which had been cramped by the spread of Greek through the Hellenizing of Syria after the conquests of Alexander the Great was stimulated by the conversion of Syriac-speaking peoples to the Christian faith. The flowering of Syriac literature went hand in hand with the spread of Christianity among those for whom Syriac was the vernacular and was a concomitant to the effort to make Christian literature accessible to the rank and file. Gothic was first given a written form, so far as we know, by the Christian missionary, Ulfilas, and the Georgians owed at least two alphabets to Christians.

CHRISTIANITY AND ART

The effect of Christianity upon art was not immediately revolutionary or startling, either negatively or positively. To be sure, under the influence of the faith the construction of pagan temples and the making of images of the gods ceased, and some temples were destroyed. However, it was not until after the first five centuries that distinctively Christian forms of art and architecture began to be prominent.

Long before the year 500 paintings inspired by the Christian faith had begun to appear, and a few surviving specimens can still be seen, notably in the catacombs. The catacombs themselves represented a modification in funeral customs. Christians disapproved of cremation, the form of disposing of the dead normally followed by pagans, and held that the body should be buried intact. In Rome until the fifth century Christian burial was prevailingly in niches in the subterranean passages in the volcanic material which underlay the city, passages whose prototypes were the galleries left by excavators of building materials. In these catacombs and upon some of the Christian sarcophagi Christian scenes were often depicted, among them the nativity, and Jesus as the Good Shepherd.

However, the catacomb as a burial place was not a Christian invention, for the Jews also employed it. Moreover, the Christian scenes normally used non-Christian art forms. Thus at least some of the portrayals of the Good Shepherd are clearly modelled after pagan pictures in which Orpheus was the central figure: with some modifications a representation of Jesus was substituted for that of Orpheus. Beginning with the age of Constantine and the full toleration of Christianity, large church edifices were erected, but these generally adopted existing architectural traditions, modifying them to meet the purposes of Christian worship. It was not until the sixth century that revolutionary forms of church architecture began to appear.

CHRISTIANS AND THE STATE

What attitude did Christians take towards the state, especially towards the Roman Empire in which their faith arose and in which the large majority of them had their home? We have seen that they did not set out deliberately to supplant the Roman state or to remake the structure of society of which it was an essential part. However, did they weaken or strengthen it?

The attitude of Jesus towards the state was not one either of unqualified disapproval or approval. He certainly did not head a movement of his people to throw off the Roman yoke, although there were some who wished him to do so and he was crucified on the charge of setting himself up as a king in opposition to the Emperor. He commanded obedience to the men in authority in the Jewish community and to the law of Moses which presumably governed that community, paid his taxes, in a somewhat cryptic saying enjoined rendering unto Cæsar the things that were Cæsar's, and as a part of what has been called his teaching of non-violence directed that no resistance was to be offered if by due process of law one's cloak were taken away, even unjustly. He refused for himself or his cause to employ political methods and never advocated rebellion. Indeed, although he declared that his followers would be haled before representatives of the state, he did not advocate denial of the jurisdiction or disobedience to the findings of the courts, but, rather, commanded those so arrested to state their case and trust God to suggest to them what to say. Yet Jesus had scorn for Herod as a person, and stood in no awe of rulers, not even of Solomon, so revered in Jewish history. Moreover, his teaching and example of refusing to rely upon the power represented by the state and his dependence upon a radically different kind of power, that seen in the apparent weakness of the cross and vindicated by the resurrection, if fully carried out would make unnecessary the sort of state represented by the Roman Empire.

The attitude of the Christians of the first three centuries towards the state seems contradictory. Paul declared that government derived its authority from God and instructed Christians to be obedient to its officers and to pay their taxes. *The First Epistle of Peter* commanded Christians to honour the Emperor. Yet *The Revelation of John* regarded the Roman Empire as evil and diametrically opposed to the Christian faith. Paul forbade Christians to take disputes among themselves to the Roman courts and characterized the Roman magistrates as "those least esteemed in the Church." While Christians bore the persecutions by the state passively and, so far as we know, without opposing them with violence, and although they offered prayers for the Emperor, they regarded as apostasy participation in the cult which gave divine honours to the Emperor, and at least some of them refused to take oaths and looked upon government officials in general as evil and the state as hostile to God. Christians held that for them loyalty to God must be given priority over loyalty to the state and that on occasion the one might require disobedience to the other. Striking wholesale examples of this were seen in the thousands of Christians who refused, even at the cost of their lives, to comply with the imperial decrees to sacrifice to the gods. Although there were some Christians in public posts, there was a conviction widely held among Christians that none of their number should hold office under the state, for to do so might entail participation in pagan ceremonies or the taking of life through the infliction of the death sentence. As late as the beginning of the third century Hippolytus said that historic Christian custom required a civic magistrate to resign his office as a condition of joining the Church. As we have seen, usually Christians regarded service in the army as wrong for them. Yet where compliance with the laws of the state did not mean disloyalty to what they believed to be their allegiance to God, Christians endeavoured to be model citizens. They paid their taxes and in other ways complied with the demands of the government. Moreover, as Christians multiplied, as they did in the third century, increasing numbers of them were in public posts.

When, beginning with Constantine, the Emperors became professing Christians, and when, in the course of the next two centuries, the overwhelming majority of the population of the Empire were brought into the Church, the latter, as we have seen, entered into a kind of alliance with the state. Except for the brief interlude of Julian, the magistrates were predominantly Christians and even under Julian the majority in the legions regarded themselves as of that faith. It is probable that the state gained by that alliance, for, in spite of its internal divisions, the Catholic Church was, next to the government, the most comprehensive and well articulated body in the Roman Empire and served to reinforce a political regime which was already displaying symptoms of disintegration. Moreover, leading Christians hailed Constantine as appointed by God and by Christians the Emperor now was accorded peculiar honour and added authority as a bulwark against anarchy. Some generations later, the Emperors were crowned by representatives of the Church in a religious ceremony.

Yet the alliance of Church and state was by no means an unqualified advantage to the Roman imperial government. The internal dissensions of the Church threatened, as we have seen, to rend not only the Church but also the Empire. Indeed, in the next period they were to contribute to the break-up of the Empire. The rapid growth of monasticism in the fourth and fifth centuries withdrew thousands from ordinary society either to the solitary life of the anchorite or to communities which were virtually autonomous. Here may have been a source of weakness for the state.

Beginning with Constantine, Christianity seems to have had some influence upon the laws of the realm. Constantine appears to have endeavoured to rule as a Christian, to make the Empire safe for Christianity, and to create a world fit for Christians to live in. This is reflected in some of his modifications of the laws and additions to them. Constantine's legislation against gladiatorial combats seems to have been inspired by the Christian faith. So do his edicts in behalf of widows, orphans, and the poor, and against immorality, the separation by sale of a slave and his wife, infanticide, the selling of children into slavery, prostitution, immoral religious rites, and the ancient right of a father to kill his child. The profession of an actress normally entailed prostitution, and in the third century, by imperial decree, apparently at the instance of the Church, it was commanded that if an actress at the point of death asked for and was given the last sacraments, and then recovered, she was not to be forced to resume her former way of life.

NEW WINE IN OLD WINESKINS: THE POWER OF CHRIST AND THE POWER OF CÆSAR

The relation of Christianity to the Roman state poses even deeper questions than those raised in the preceding paragraphs. As we have hinted, we see here two powers, the power of Christ and the power of Cæsar. In one of his parables Jesus declared that new wine could not safely be put into old wineskins, for if it were, the skins would break and the wine would be lost. Did that prove to be true in the case of the Roman Empire and the Christian Gospel? Would "the exceeding greatness of the power" destroy the "earthen vessels" and in the process itself be dissipated or be gravely and perhaps irreparably weakened?

To what extent, if at all, were the "decline and fall of the Roman Empire" due to Christianity? Again and again, as we have seen, while Christianity was spreading, the accusation was made that it was bringing mortal illness to the Empire and to the structure of Græco-Roman society. Repeatedly the Christian apologists addressed themselves to answering that charge. Outstanding was the *City of God* of Augustine, but this was not by any means the only work evoked by the complaint, nor the last. The accusation has more than once been renewed in modern times.

The Christian apologists, far from admitting the truth of the indictment, insisted that, instead of weakening the Empire, Christians were actually strengthening it. Thus in the first half of the second century *The Epistle to Diognetus* declared: "What the soul is to the body, that are Christians to the world. . . . The Soul is imprisoned in the body, yet preserves that very body;

and Christians are confined in the world as in a prison, yet they hold the world together." As we have seen, Tertullian insisted that Christians did more than pagans for the Emperor, that they regarded him as appointed by God, and held that chaos was prevented only by the continued existence of the Roman Empire. Origen said that by their prayers Christians were of more service to the realm than if they had fought for it in the legions, for by their petitions they "vanquish all demons who stir up war . . . and [who] disturb the peace." Which were right, the critics or the apologists?

In attempting to find the answer to this question, we must bear in mind several facts. First we must recall that the symptoms of mortal illness were present in the Græco-Roman world before Christ was born. Precisely what were all of the causes scholars have never agreed, but as to the sickness of that region in the first century before Christ there can be no debate. To be sure, in every culture, even at the height of its prosperity, evidences of serious weakness can be found and are by no means conclusive proof of impending collapse.

However, in the second place, in the century before Christ was born the evidences of disintegration were so palpable in wars, in the passing of the old order, and in moral corruption, that the thoughtful feared early collapse. From this disaster the Mediterranean Basin was saved by Julius Cæsar and Augustus Cæsar, especially the latter. Through the structure devised by Augustus with the Emperor as its head, peace, the *pax Romana,* was established almost coincidently with the coming of Christ. Then followed a period of material prosperity hitherto unequalled in the Mediterranean world—although paralleled by a somewhat similar era in the contemporary China under the Han dynasty. No wonder that Rome and the Empire were regarded as the bulwarks of civilization against anarchy.

Yet, in the third place, we must note that the principate devised by Augustus did not cure but only temporarily halted the course of the disease from which Græco-Roman culture was suffering. Except for the political structure given it by Augustus, that culture was ceasing to say or to do anything substantially new. In philosophy the only fresh system of consequence which emerged in the first two centuries of the Empire, so prosperous materially, was Neoplatonism, and that was chiefly a development from the earlier Platonism and may possibly have in part owed to Christianity the stimulus which brought it into being. After the first century with its Augustan Age and the generation which followed it, no contributions of first class importance were made in literature or art. It was only through Christianity that a major impulse was at work to stir spirits in a jaded world to fresh creation. By the end of the second century the remedies applied by Augustus had begun to fail. Indeed, they may have aggravated the malady. Certainly the disease was breaking out afresh.

As a fourth fact we must note that the disease could not accurately be traced to Christianity. It had appeared before that faith had been born. Its fresh outbreak in the closing decades of the second century was before Christians were sufficiently numerous to have become its inciting cause.

A fifth consideration is the fact that Christianity did not prevent the disease from running its course and bringing the demise of the Roman Empire. Christianity did not save the Græco-Roman stage of civilization. If it was not the source of the disease from which Græco-Roman culture suffered, neither did it heal that culture of its illness.

As a closely related fact we do well also to recall that at its very outset Christianity had not saved the Jewish community from which it sprang nor had it brought even a temporary pause in the mad, headlong course which led that community to futile rebellion against Roman rule and to the destruction of Jerusalem and of the temple which had been the centre of Jewish worship. Jesus had clearly foreseen the tragic climax towards which events were heading, had offered an alternative course through which the catastrophe could have been avoided, but had the heart-breaking experience of meeting blind rejection.

A seventh observation is not so much a fact as a comment. It may be that Christianity could not save either Græco-Roman civilization or the Jewish society which centred in and found its symbol in Jerusalem and the temple. Both may have been founded on presuppositions so contrary to the Christian Gospel that they had to pass before the Gospel could begin to find free expression. We do well to remind ourselves again and again that it was official representatives of Judaism and the Roman Empire who brought Jesus to his death, because they sensed more or less clearly that if he were loyally and consistently followed the religious structure and the political system of which they were the respective custodians and to which they were bound by self-interest would disappear. Certainly Jesus, as Stephen and others of the early Christians clearly discerned, rendered the temple and its elaborate sacrifices unnecessary, and, as Paul declared, had made it obvious that the legal road of earning the favour of God was worse than a blind alley and led away from the path to true life. As Augustine saw, what he called the earthly city, based upon force, pride, the love of human praise, the desire for domination, and the self-interest represented by the Roman Empire, had value in the restraint of wickedness and the preservation of order, but was basically different from the city of God, for the latter was built upon quite other foundations. The kind of power which had brought the Roman Empire into being was diametrically opposite to the power of God dramatically and decisively displayed in the cross. When Paul said that Christ crucified was a stumbling-block to the Jews and sheer folly to the Gentiles, namely, the Greeks and the Romans, and that the ways through which the Greeks were seeking wisdom did not bring them to the wisdom of God as revealed in the cross, he was stating unvarnished fact. If the Gospel was not to be obscured, Christianity had to break free from Judaism and the Roman Empire would have to pass.

An eighth set of facts is one which we are to see somewhat elaborated in our account of the next major period in the history of Christianity, but which we must briefly summarize here to enable us to give a tentative answer to the question posed to us by the coincidence of the progressive decline of Rome with the seeming triumph of Christianity. It was in the western portions of Europe, where the collapse of the Roman Empire was most marked, that Christianity was to display its greatest vigour in succeeding centuries. Indeed, the near disappearance of Græco-Roman culture in that region gave to Christianity one of its greatest opportunities. By being largely freed from the incubus of the Roman state and of the closely associated cultural heritage of Greece and Rome, the kind of power which was of the essence of the Gospel was given freer course than it had been accorded under the professedly Christian Emperors. This was akin to the fashion in which that power displayed itself in great might in that wing of Christianity which broke through its Jewish integuments and ceased to be a Jewish sect in contrast with the nervelessness of the strain of Christianity represented by the Ebionites and which attempted to remain within Judaism.

In this connexion we must also anticipate the next chronological sections of our story by noting that Christianity was the means by which the remnants of Græco-Roman civilization were transmitted to Western Europe and that in the East, where the dwindling Roman Empire continued and passed over into the Greek Byzantine Empire, it was Christianity which reinforced the state, helped to give it cohesion, and put spirit in its defense against the onslaughts of its enemies.

We shall also be recording, when that stage of our narrative is reached, that on the southern and eastern shores of the Mediterranean the conquering force, Arabic Islam, which overthrew Roman rule in those areas, proved too strong for the kind of power represented in Christianity, and the churches slowly faded out.

May we now attempt to summarize in a few words what the evidence seems to show of the relation of Christianity to the decline of the Roman Empire and of the civilization associated with it? Christianity was not the basic cause of the "fall of Rome." Yet it did not prevent that "fall." Whether it retarded or hastened it we cannot certainly know. In the segment of the Empire which continued with Constantinople as its nucleus Christianity undoubtedly prolonged the life of the Empire and later it was to aid in what purported to be a revival of that Empire in the West. In the West it became the vehicle by which much of Græco-Roman culture was transmitted to a subsequent age. Christians also were a major instrument in passing on much of that culture to the Arabs who overwhelmed the eastern and southern portions of the Empire. While Christianity helped to perpetuate more or less extensive elements of Græco-Roman civilization, it placed those elements in a new context. Where, in the West, the disintegration of the old came in such fashion that Christianity was partially emancipated, that faith had a much larger share in moulding life than the Roman Empire had permitted it.

What Happened to the New Wine?

If the old wineskins were broken by agents other than the new wine of Christianity and that wine actually preserved something of the wineskins, what happened to the wine? Was it lost or fatally denatured? Or, to change the metaphor, was the "exceeding greatness of the power" weakened by the "earthen vessels" in which it was at work? To put the question less figuratively, how far, if at all, was the Gospel compromised by elements in the culture, in many ways so in contradiction with it, into which it moved and in which it appeared to be victorious?

That the Gospel was in grave danger of being lost among those who professed to adhere to it must be obvious. It was launched into a hostile world with none of the safeguards which human prudence would have counselled. As we have more than once reminded ourselves, Jesus wrote no book, but trusted his teachings and the record of his deeds to the memories of men and women who, though loyal, while he was with them in the flesh failed really to understand him. He did not utter his words in systematic form, but spoke as the occasion seemed to demand. So far as our evidence goes, he gave almost no thought to an organization to perpetuate his mission. Certainly he did not create an elaborate organization. Under these circumstances it would have been natural to expect that, coming into a world which was either misunderstanding or hostile, or both, the Gospel, as it spread, would be hopelessly distorted and lost. That this happened, indeed, has repeatedly been said. There have been many, some of them of great erudition, who have declared that Jesus is at best a shadowy figure, early obscured by his reporters and interpreters, and that we can be certain of almost none of his deeds and sayings. They see him hidden by layers of tradition and believe the Christianity of the fifth century to have been compounded of Judaism, Græco-Roman polytheism, appropriations from the mystery cults, and Greek thought.

That Christianity was influenced by all these phases of its environment is indubitable. We have had occasion to note some of the contributions from these several sources. But that it remained distinct and owed its outstanding qualities to Jesus is both certain and important.

From Judaism issued the larger part of the Scriptures which Christians revered as the inspired word of God. From Judaism came also the belief in one God, much of the ethical standards, the seven day week with its day of rest and worship, portions of the early forms of worship, the conviction of being a chosen community distinct from the world about it, something of the dream of becoming the universal religion of mankind, baptism, much of the conception of history, and the precedents for a priesthood and of regarding Christ's death as a sacrifice which became outstanding characteristics of Christianity.

Yet it is one of the striking features of these Jewish legacies that they were thought through in the light of the life, death, and resurrection of Jesus and were interpreted in terms of these and of the teachings of Jesus. The temptation to become simply a variant of Judaism was successfully resisted and those groups which most nearly conformed to Judaism dwindled and perished. Moreover, the figure of Jesus, his teachings, and the main events of his life, death, and resurrection stand out so clearly in the records contained in the New Testament as to preclude any possibility of their invention or serious distortion.

Although some striking similarities to the mystery religions are seen in the story of a divine being slain and risen again, of immortality acquired by sharing symbolically in his death and resurrection, of initiatory rites, and of a sacred meal, there is, as we have suggested, no proof of conscious or even unconscious copying and the differences between Christianity and the mystery cults are greater than the similarities. We have also seen that Catholic Christianity fought free of absorption into the current non-Christian Gnosticism. While here and there some transfer from Greek and Roman polytheism may have occurred, as in the cults of some of the saints and in a few of the festivals, all of these contributions were profoundly altered to conform with Christian convictions. A major peril was one of attitude, for converts were inclined to expect Christianity to do for them what they had demanded of their pre-Christian gods but to do it better. Yet the trend of the teaching of the Church was towards the progressive weakening of these attitudes and the inculcation of conceptions more nearly in accord with the Gospel.

In some ways, more serious than any of these threats to Christianity from its environment was the belief in the sharp disjunction between the material and the spiritual world, or, in human terms, between flesh and spirit, which was prevalent and which appeared axiomatic to many, perhaps the majority, in those elements of the population in which Christianity first made its chief gains. In some of its most extreme forms, notably those represented by the Marcionites, the Gnostics, and the Manichæans, it was rejected by the Catholic Church. Yet it made itself felt in theology and in the attitude of the rank and file of Christians, notably in the East, and was particularly potent in monasticism and in clerical celibacy. Through these channels, especially through the last two, it has remained a permanent feature of the churches in which the majority of Christians have been members. As we have noted, it distorted the teachings of Jesus. Yet, as we have seen and are to see repeatedly in later chapters, among many of those who espoused it, Christian monasticism was not merely the negative denial of the flesh but also carried with it the propulsion to go out into the world in an effort to serve and transform individuals and society.

Probably an even greater peril came from Greek philosophy. This was the temptation to regard Christianity as a philosophy, better than that of the Greeks, but not essentially different, truth to be arrived at by the application of the human mind and of man's rational processes. Fully to yield would be to ignore the fundamental contrast which we have noted and to denature the Christian faith. Fortunately for Christianity its intellectuals who most profoundly influenced the future course of the faith never entirely succumbed to this tendency. For example, Augustine, while retaining much of the Neoplatonism which had once captivated him, held it to be basically defective in not taking cognizance of the incarnation. Moreover, as we have said, Augustine, in his famous "believe in order that you may understand," while by no means repudiating reason, was giving to it a different place than that accorded it in Greek philosophy, and, along with other Christian thinkers, was taking account of data which were unknown to the pre-Christian Greeks and which were rejected as "foolishness" by those who continued to adhere to Greek philosophy.

Yet Christians made substantial appropriations from Greek philosophy. Clement of Alexandria and Ambrose of Milan based much of their ethics on what they had learned from Stoicism. The writings of the Stoic Epictetus, somewhat modified to make them more palatable, had a wide circulation in Christian circles. To be sure, Christians took over from Stoicism only what they believed to be consistent with their faith and would have nothing to do with the basic pantheism of that philosophy which would deny the opposition of God to sin, and looked forward to the consummation of the kingdom of God, rather than backward to a Golden Age, as did the Stoics. But Christian ethics were long to give evidence of Stoic contributions. Platonism had a marked influence on Christianity. It entered from many channels, among them the Hellenistic Jew Philo, who was utilized by some early Christian writers, and through Justin Martyr, Clement of Alexandria, Origen, Augustine, and the writings which bore the name of Dionysius the Areopagite. The term *Logos,* which was extensively employed by Christians as they thought about the relation of Christ to God, came from Greek philosophy, perhaps by way of both Stoicism and Platonism. We have seen how the Christian creeds employed technical terms from Greek and Latin. With these, as with the word *Logos,* pre-Christian connotations would inevitably enter.

However, as we earlier suggested, the creeds never became really Greek. They sought to express convictions which were central in the Gospel and peculiar to it. They were distinctively Christian and not Hellenistic. Moreover, it has been suggested that Christian thinkers solved the problems of order and change, reason and emotion, the physical and the intellectual with which classical philosophy had wrestled, and did so without denying the validity of the changing, the emotional, or the physical. They thereby provided a basis for individual salvation in a world of dislocated individuals and a principle on which a stable but not a rigid society might be based.

What in many ways proved the menace which was most nearly disastrous was that presented by the kind of power on which the Roman Empire was founded, a kind of power, as we have seen, which was in complete contradiction to that seen in the cross. From the very beginning, pride of place and the desire for control in the Christian community were chronic temptations. On the very eve of the crucifixion, first on the way to Jerusalem and then at the final supper, in the inner circle, among those who were to be the apostles of the Good News, there were some who sought superior rank and recognition as "the greatest," incidents which led to characteristically vivid sayings from Jesus and which may have been the reason for the assumption by him of the menial role of washing the disciples' feet. By word and by deed Jesus put in stark contrast the two kinds of greatness, that esteemed by the "kings of the Gentiles," namely, the one in vogue in the Roman Empire, and that which should characterize his disciples. It was the contrast between those who from the vantage of visible power established and maintained by crude force professed to seek to do good and were called benefactors and those who humbly served in tasks which were despised in the other kind of society.

In one of the letters preserved in the New Testament there is evidence, as we have said, of sharp conflict between the author, who believed himself vested with authority in one of the churches, and another "who loveth . . . preëminence." Again and again, even in the brief summary of the preceding pages, we have caught glimpses of similar incidents. The various churches, including the Catholic Church, creations of Christianity and the visible vehicles by which it was transmitted, were clearly institutions. Even before Christianity was accorded toleration by the state and while it was still subject to chronic or intermittent persecutions, not a few of its bishops were accused of striving for prestige and were entering into intrigues and exerting the kind of power which was akin to that of the dignitaries of the state. Some of the bishops were surrounded by pomp and maintained households and a manner of life which rivalled those of civil officials. Indeed, it is a question whether any visible institution, especially if it becomes large, can avoid falling victim in part to trends in the direction of the power which crucified Jesus.

The danger to Christianity was augmented when the state made its peace with the Church. Until then, as we have seen, Christians tended to keep aloof from government and many, perhaps the majority of the Christians believed that loyalty to Christ was inconsistent with holding civil or military office or serving in the army. Beginning with Constantine, that attitude was weakened. The Emperors and an increasing proportion of the officials and of the troops assumed the Christian name. In these positions they, perforce, exercised the sort of power on which the state rested. Christian officials had to make choices for the state among courses none of which was in full conformity with Christian principles and to take action which entailed the use of the kind of force on which the state was built. Emperors exercised their power to interfere in the affairs of the Church. To be sure, they did this primarily in an effort to bring unity to the Church and through the prestige of their position more than through naked force, and in this may be seen something of the ameliorative influence of Christianity. Yet here was still power which was in contrast with that vividly displayed in the cross.

This peril, as we are to see, became more marked in the succeeding centuries. In the West as the Roman Empire declined, the Catholic Church took over many of the functions previously performed by the state. In the East in the area where the Empire continued, the tie between Church and state was very close and the Church was in large degree controlled by the state and was used to serve the latter's purposes.

It is clear that the Church was the product of the Gospel. It is also clear that the visible, institutionalized church, whether Catholic or one of the bodies which dissented, was shot through and through with contradictions to the Gospel. As Augustine frankly recognized, the two cities, the earthly and the heavenly, are intermingled. He held that they are to continue to be entangled until the last judgement effects their separation.

In view of these facts, necessarily succinctly stated, was the new wine being dissipated? Where was the exceeding greatness of the power? It will be remembered that the power was characterized as that which, having faced seeming defeat in the cross, was displayed in the resurrection of Christ from the dead. It is a power which is associated with seeming weakness. It is a power which does not at once destroy the religion or the state which nailed Christ to the cross, but which, by a kind of paradox, achieves a victory which would have been impossible without defeat. It is a basic Christian conviction that Christ was glorified through his death and resurrection and became far more potent than he had been in the days of his flesh.

The exceeding greatness of the power was displayed primarily in the transformation of those men and women who became followers of Christ, who put their trust in him. Even now, so Jesus had said, men might enter the kingdom of God, and, indeed, were entering it. To use other figures employed in the New Testament, men could be born again, they could die to sin and, by the same power which raised Jesus from the dead, they could be raised to walk in newness of life. The proof that they had experienced this new birth, this resurrection to a new life, was to be seen in their "fruits," in the "fruits of the Spirit." These fruits were described in one place as "love" (the Greek word is *agape,* namely, the kind of love displayed by God in Christ and by Christ in his self-giving), "joy, peace, longsuffering, gentleness, goodness, faith, meekness, temperance." Paul, who coined this list, was quite aware that these qualities would not at once be realized in any one life in their perfection and said of himself that he had not fully attained. Years after his conversion, as we have more than once said, Augustine made a similar confession. They are qualities which are not susceptible to precise measurement, at least not by men. They do not achieve complete expression in any visible institution or organization. Perhaps it was something like this which Jesus had in mind when he declared that the kingdom of God was not to come in such fashion that it can be seen or in such a manner that men could point to it and say, "Lo here or lo there" and yet that "the kingdom of God is among you" (or, in an alternative translation, "within you"). As Jesus saw it, the kingdom of God is both present now and is also a future hope. Part of the Good News is, so the New Testament documents disclose, that the exceeding greatness of the power is in the fresh creation of sinful men and the dying to sin, the sin which through man's perverse misuse of the free will with which he is endowed has brought on him, individually and collectively, the tragic aspects of human history. This fresh creation issues in the beginning of a new life.

Although that new life cannot be measured, its presence can be observed. Even in the fragmentary documents which have reached us from the first five centuries of Christianity, it is clear that the fruits of the Spirit were to be seen in many individual lives. We have pointed to a few outstanding examples, such as Paul and Augustine. Were there space, we could name many more. From the few the records of whose lives have been preserved across the wreckage of the centuries we are on safe ground in assuming that for every one of whom we know there were hundreds, perhaps thousands, of whom we do not know, for most of them were very humble folk who left no written documents behind them. The testimony of the apologists, although given with a pro-Christian bias, bears this out. They appeal to what is to them obvious fact, the moral and spiritual changes wrought through conversion. Even though in the majority of those bearing the Christian name the alteration was either slight or had not occurred, the honour accorded by the Church to the minority in whom the fruits of the Spirit were seen was indicative of a persistently held ideal and of the reality of the new life in those who had experienced it.

It was chiefly through such lives that the creative impulse was released which produced the Church and Christian literature, theology, and worship, which swept away the pagan cults of the Roman Empire, which wrestled with the problems of war and with the relation to the state, property, marriage, and the popular amusements. It was through these lives that within the Church the position of women and children was lifted, dignity was given to labour, and much of the sting was taken from slavery. No individual attained fully to the "high calling of God in Christ." The churches were by no means identical with the city of God: there was in them much of the earthly city. Yet here, in earthen vessels, was a power at work which, in spite of what looked like chronic frustration, out of human material apparently hopelessly and basically marred and twisted, was achieving the seemingly impossible, the re-creation of thousands of men and women until they displayed something of the quality of life which was seen in Jesus Christ.

It was these men and women who were, to use the language of Jesus, "the salt of the earth" and "the light of the world." In the succeeding sections of this work we will see that, as Christians have multiplied and converts have been won from more and more peoples, these characterizations have been increasingly demonstrated to be true. They do not hold for all who have borne the Christian name, but they are valid for a minority in whom "the exceeding greatness of the power" has been palpably at work.

Selected Bibliography

WORKS WHICH COVER MOST OF THE TOPICS DEALT WITH IN THIS CHAPTER

C. J. Cadoux, *The Early Church and the World. A History of the Christian Attitude to Pagan Society and the State down to the Time of Constantius* (Edinburgh, T. & T. Clark, 1925, pp. li, 675). A comprehensive, careful work based on the sources.

C. N. Cochrane, *Christianity and Classical Culture. A Study of Thought and Action from Augustus to Augustine* (Oxford, The Clarendon Press, 1940, pp. vii, 523). A thought-provoking analysis based upon extensive reading in the sources.

I. Giordani, *The Social Message of the Early Church Fathers,* translated from the Italian by A. I. Zizzamia (Paterson, N. J., St. Anthony Guild Press, 1944, pp. x, 356). Based upon an extensive use of the sources, by a Roman Catholic, and decidedly pro-Christian.

Hippolytus, *The Apostolic Tradition of Hippolytus,* translated into English with introduction and notes by B. S. Easton (Cambridge University Press, 1934, pp. 112).

K. S. Latourette, *A History of the Expansion of Christianity. Volume I, The First Five Centuries* (New York, Harper & Brothers, 1937, pp. xxiv, 412). Chapters VI and VII deal with the subjects covered in this chapter.

E. H. Oliver, *The Social Achievements of the Christian Church* (Toronto, Board of Evangelism and Social Service of the United Church of Canada, 1930, pp. 192). Meant for class use, decidedly pro-Christian, containing excellent bibliographies.

E. Troeltsch, *The Social Teachings of the Christian Churches,* translated by Olive Wyon (New York, The Macmillan Co., 2 vols., 1931). Approximately the first half of this well known work is given to the period covered in this chapter.

CHRISTIANS AND WAR

R. H. Bainton, *The Early Church and War,* in R. M. Jones, editor, *The Church, The Gospel, and War,* pp. 75–92 (New York, Harper & Brothers, 1948, pp. xii, 169). A competent summary.

C. J. Cadoux, *The Early Christian Attitude to War. A Contribution to the History of Christian Ethics* (London, Headley Bros., Publishers, 1919, pp. xxxii, 272). A careful, well-documented study which stresses the refusal of the early Christians to sanction war or to serve in the armed forces.

A. Harnack, *Militia Christi. Die christliche Religion und der Soldatenstand in den ersten drei Jahrhunderten* (Tübingen, J. C. B. Mohr, 1905, pp. vii, 129). Marked by the scholarship for which the author is famous.

U. Lee, *The Historic Church and Modern Pacifism* (New York and Nashville, Abingdon-Cokesbury Press, 1943, pp. 249). Argues against the pacifist position.

G. H. C. Macgregor, *The New Testament Basis of Pacifism* (London, J. Clarke & Co., 1936, pp. 159). Supports the pacifist's position.

J. Moffatt, *War,* in J. Hastings, editor, *Dictionary of the Apostolic Church,* Vol. II, pp. 646–673 (New York, Charles Scribner's Sons, 1918).

CHRISTIANS AND SLAVERY

R. H. Barrow, *Slavery in the Roman Empire* (London, Methuen & Co., 1928, pp. xvi, 259). Carefully done; well documented.

SEX, CHILDREN, MARRIAGE, AND THE FAMILY

R. H. Bainton, *Marriage and Love in Christian History,* in *Religion in Life,* Vol. XVII, pp. 391–403). Has an excellent bibliography.

R. S. T. Haslehurst, *Some Account of the Penitential Discipline of the Early Church* (London, Society for Promoting Christian Knowledge, 1921, pp. vii, 162). Quotes extensively from the sources.

CHRISTIANS AND THE STATE

The Epistle to Diognetus is translated in *The Ante-Nicene Fathers,* Vol. I, pp. 25-30 (Buffalo, The Christian Publishing Co., 1885).

C. H. McIlwain, *The Growth of Political Thought in the West from the Greeks to the End of the Middle Ages* (New York, The Macmillan Co., 1933, pp. vii, 244). Excellent.

WHAT HAPPENED TO THE NEW WINE? THE INFLUENCE OF THE
ENVIRONMENT ON CHRISTIANITY

S. Angus, *The Religious Quests of the Græco-Roman World* (New York, Charles Scribner's Sons, 1929, pp. xx, 444). Carefully done, with a pro-Christian bias.

C. Clemen, *Primitive Christianity and Its Non-Jewish Sources,* translated by R. G. Nisbet (Edinburgh, T. & T. Clark, 1912, pp. xiii, 403). Careful, conservative in its judgements, employing the sources.

S. Dill, *Roman Society in the Last Century of the Western Empire* (London, Macmillan & Co., 2d ed., 1906, pp. xxviii, 459). Readable, scholarly.

F. Gavin, *The Jewish Antecedents of the Christian Sacraments* (London, Society for Promoting Christian Knowledge, 1928, pp. viii, 120).

E. Hatch, *The Influence of Greek Ideas and Usages upon the Christian Church,* edited by A. M. Fairbairn (London, Williams & Norgate, 1890, pp. xxiii, 359). The Hibbert Lectures for 1888.

C. N. Moody, *The Mind of the Early Converts* (London, Hodder & Stoughton, 1920, pp. xii, 310). A stimulating comparison between the Early Church and what the author has known about converts in Formosa.

E. F. Scott, *The Gospel and Its Tributaries* (New York, Charles Scribner's Sons, 1930, pp. 295). By a competent New Testament scholar.

THE DARKEST HOURS:
THE GREAT RECESSION,
A.D. 500 — A.D. 950

MAP TO ILLUSTRATE THE
HISTORY OF CHRISTIANITY
IN
WESTERN AND CENTRAL EUROPE
A.D. 500-1500

Scale of Miles
0   100   200   300   400

Chapter X

THE SETTING OF THE GREAT RECESSION

The seeming triumph of Christianity in winning the professed allegiance of the Roman Empire carried with it a major threat. In the preceding chapters we noted the fashion in which Christianity was imperilled by the extent to which a large proportion of those who bore the Christian name were compromising with the non-Christian environment in which they were immersed. We also saw the manner in which the Church was being interpenetrated by ideals which were quite contrary to the Gospel, especially the conception and use of power which were in stark contrast to the kind of power exhibited in the life and teachings of Jesus and in the cross and the resurrection. A nearly related but somewhat different danger was the close association with the Roman Empire and Græco-Roman culture which that victory brought. Although before it had completed the first five centuries of its course Christianity had begun to spill over the boundaries of the Roman Empire, by the end of that period it had become almost identified with that realm and its civilization. The overwhelming majority of Roman citizens thought of themselves as Christians and the large majority of those who bore the Christian name were Roman citizens. The Catholic Church, which embraced most of those who counted themselves as Christians, had grown up within the area which had been given political unity by the Roman Empire and in its structure reflected the pattern of that Empire. While strikingly original in its essence, Christian theology had perforce employed Greek and Roman terms and had utilized concepts drawn from Greek philosophy. By the year 500 the Roman Empire and Græco-Roman culture were in decline. Christianity had both weakened them and prolonged their life. In succeeding centuries their disintegration was accelerated. Could Christianity survive their demise or would it share their growing debility and ultimate death?

That Christianity was seriously affected by the fatal sickness of the Roman Empire is one of the most palpable facts of history. For more than four centuries the outcome was by no means clear. In the numbers of those who called

269

themselves Christian, in apparent inner vitality as expressed in fresh movements inspired by the faith, in the moral and spiritual quality of the churches which were the official vehicles of the Gospel, and in its prominence in the total human scene, Christianity lost ground.

The Roman Empire suffered from both internal weaknesses and external pressures. We have already noted that the weaknesses in part ante-dated the coming of Christianity, that they were for a time allayed by the imperial system inaugurated by Augustus Cæsar, but that from the end of the second century they began again to be apparent, were aggravated, and multiplied. The external pressures were by invaders who took advantage of the internal decay to overrun most of the Empire. Their inroads accelerated Rome's decline. The main incursions were from two directions, from the north and north-east on the one hand and from the south-east on the other. Those from the north and north-east were by peoples who were thought of as barbarians and whose cultures were of a "lower" and more nearly "primitive" stage than that of the Romans. Their cultures, including their religions, disintegrated under contacts with what was left of Græco-Roman civilization and by the year 1000 most of the northern invaders who had settled in what had once been the Roman Empire had taken on the Christian name and were in part conforming to the remnants of Græco-Roman culture which had survived their conquests. Those from the south-west, the Arabs, were the bearers of a new and vigorous religion, Islam. While in some ways they, too, were "barbarians" and took over much of the cultures of the peoples of "high" civilizations whom they subdued, their religion almost entirely supplanted the faiths of the conquered populations. From the seventh into the tenth century the Moslem Arabs mastered about half of the lands which had been ruled by Rome. This segment also embraced about half of what might be denominated Christendom. In it the Christian churches dwindled more or less rapidly. With the possible exception of Judaism, Christianity proved more resistant to Islam than the faith of any other people whom the Arabs overran, and in two regions, the Iberian Peninsula and Sicily, it did what no other religion accomplished: it eventually won back extensive areas and populations from the Prophet. However, this did not come at once. For several centuries the record was one of progressive losses of the Cross to the Crescent.

Christianity not only survived these disasters. Eventually it forged ahead to fresh advances which carried it farther geographically than it had gone in the first days of its might. Some of the gains were made while major losses were being suffered on other fronts, but most of them were not to be achieved until much later centuries. Christianity even proved to have profited by the break-up of the Roman Empire, for, in the West, largely freed from the latter, it eventually displayed renewed vigour and a long series of fresh, creative movements.

In this recovery from the disintegration of the closely allied Roman Empire and in this subsequent spread Christianity surpassed the record of any other religion. A religion is often an integral part of a particular culture. When a culture disappears the religion associated with it also tends to die out. Some religions prove to have more vitality than the cultures with which their early development had been connected and outlast them. In its ability to survive the passing of cultures with which it has been intimately related, to win back territories in which it has experienced grave losses, and to gain peoples of other cultures, Christianity has been unequalled. Buddhism, absorbed by Hinduism in its native land, India, lived on outside of India and was reintroduced into India by immigrants. Yet most of its geographic spread was prior to the assimilation of its Indian constituency by Hinduism and since then it has thrown out few new movements. Islam survived the decay of the Arab Empire through which it had its initial spread and, capturing other peoples, notably the Turks, enjoyed fresh geographic expansion through them. In Persia, partly divorced from Arab culture, it gave rise to fresh developments. Yet in general Islam has been closely tied to the Arabic language and to Arab culture and apart from that connexion it has not displayed much vitality. Judaism did not perish with the disappearance of the little Jewish state which centred in Jerusalem, but compared with Buddhism, Islam, and Christianity it has won relatively few converts outside of its own community, a community which has never been able to break away from its narrowly ethnic traditions and become universal. Hinduism and Indian culture have been inseparable and Confucianism has been identified with the particular form of Chinese civilization of which it has been the core. Christianity continues to bear the imprint of its Jewish heritage and of the Græco-Roman world into which it first moved, but more than any other of the faiths of mankind it has proved its capacity to outlast cultures with which it has seemed to be identified and some of which it has helped to create. Freed in part from the crippling compromises of the Gospel which that association entailed, it has inspired fresh movements within itself and in its milieu, it has resumed its expansion, and more and more it has approached the universality which has been of its essence.

The dates of the beginning and the end of the great recession cannot be precisely determined. We have named the end of the fifth century as the climax of the first great period of advance and as ushering in the decline, but by selecting a round number, A.D. 500, we are wishing to convey the suggestion that no single year can be pointed to as a sharply marked divide between the one era and the other. The conquest of the Roman Empire by the northern invaders is sometimes said to have begun in 378, for in that year the Goths defeated the legions and slew the Emperor Valens in the battle of Adrianople, not far from Constantinople, the capital which Constantine had created only a few decades earlier. The capture and sack of Rome in 410 was even more spectacular. However, Rome as a city was not seriously damaged and soon recovered, and while in the fifth century various Germanic peoples established kingdoms in the West—the Visigoths in Spain, the Ostrogoths in Italy, the Burgundians in the south of Gaul, the Vandals in North Africa, the Angles and Saxons in Britain, and the Franks in the north of Gaul—most of them still thought of themselves as within the Roman Empire and several of their rulers accepted titles from the Roman government.

Not far from the year 500 came various events which may be regarded as marking both the peak of the triumphal course of Christianity in the Roman Empire and the beginning of the decline and of a new age. In the year 476 Romulus Augustulus, commonly viewed as the last of the Emperors in the West, was deposed by the Herulian Odovacar (Odoacer), and while the event was not regarded as of outstanding importance by contemporaries and the Empire continued, the centre was now indisputably in Constantinople and the date has been traditionally given as marking the end of the Western Empire. In 496 Clovis, King of the Franks, was baptized, both a landmark in the conversion of the Germanic invaders and an indication that a new era had begun in which not the Roman Empire, but Germanic rulers were to become champions of the faith in the West. One era was passing and another was beginning. In the year 529 the Emperor Justinian I closed the ancient schools at Athens in which philosophy had been taught, an act symbolic of the triumph of Christianity in the very citadel of the non-Christian philosophies which had once been dominant in the Roman Empire. Not far from that same year Benedict of Nursia and a small band of his followers established themselves on Monte Cassino, the centre from which was to spread the rule which for centuries was to shape the monastic life of the West.

The decline of Christianity was not rapid nor without spurts of revival. In the second and third quarters of the sixth century, as we are to see, the generals of Justinian I renewed Roman administration in much of the West and in North Africa and Justinian himself, as an earnest Christian, added to the prestige of the Church in the East. In that century Christianity spread up the Nile into what is now called the Sudan. It also was carried eastward and early in the seventh century was planted in China. In the West in the latter part of the sixth century Pope Gregory the Great greatly added to the power of the Church of Rome, and through missionaries, some of them from Rome and some from Ireland, a beginning was made towards the conversion of the Germanic peoples who had settled in Britain and of other pagans on that island. In the seventh century the reconversion of Britain was practically completed.

Yet the seventh century also saw the spectacular and rapid Arab conquests. It is from A.D. 622 that the Moslems date the beginning of their era. Mohammed died in 632. Before A.D. 651 the Arabs had conquered Palestine, Syria, Mesopotamia, Persia, and most of Egypt. In 697 they took Carthage, the capital of North Africa, and by 715 they had overrun most of Spain. The political victories of the Arabs were accompanied by the spread of Islam and the beginning of the slow decline of the Christian communities in the Arab domains. In the meantime, in the sixth and seventh centuries, the Slavs, pagans, were moving into the regions north of Greece, filling most of the Balkan Peninsula and even much of Greece itself, and the pagan Avars effected settlements in the Balkans and raided Greece. In consequence, substantial portions of these areas were being de-Christianized. In 680 the Bulgars, an Asiatic folk, moved south across the Danube and established a non-Christian state at the expense of the eastern remnants of the Christian Roman Empire. Never again was Christianity to lose so large a proportion of the territory in which it was the dominant religion.

The eighth century witnessed a marked revival of the faith and an improvement in the morale of the Church in the West under the Carolingians, rulers of the Franks, and the conversion of much of Germany. Yet the ninth and tenth centuries saw new waves of invasions of the West by pagans. The Carolingian Empire broke up and could offer them but feeble resistance. The Scandinavians ravaged the shores of most of Europe, and established themselves in much of Britain, in the part of France, Normandy, to which they gave their name, and in the western portion of the later Russia. Wherever they went they plundered churches and monasteries. They dealt mortal blows to the flourishing monasteries of Ireland in which had been centred the Christianity of that island. Late in the ninth century the pagan Magyars made themselves masters of Hungary, to the detriment of whatever churches were found in that region.

The decline of the Carolingians and the renewed invasions were followed by decay in the quality of the life of the Church in the West. Monasteries became lax in the observance of their rules, bishops tended to be secular magnates, and the morals of the clergy deteriorated. In the middle of the tenth century, the Papacy, deprived of the support of the Carolingians, became the victim of local factions in Rome and reached an all time nadir.

In the eighth and ninth centuries the section of the Church which had its centre in Constantinople was torn by a prolonged controversy over the use of images. In the ninth century, moreover, the Moslem Arabs conquered Sicily, established strongholds in the southern parts of Italy, and took Crete. The Arab successes made for fresh advances of Islam in territories which were traditionally Christian. In China a severe outburst of persecution in 845 seriously weakened the small Christian communities in that Empire.

In spite of the disasters the ninth century was also a time when in Central Europe, the Balkans, and Constantinople the tide seemed to have turned. Notable advances of the faith were being achieved among the Slavs and Bulgars and the patriarchal throne in Constantinople was held by Photius, outstanding as scholar and churchman. From our tantalizingly imperfect knowledge of early Christianity in India comes evidence which may indicate a growth in the eighth and ninth centuries. In the West the upswing was beginning to be seen even in some of the darkest hours. The monastery of Cluny, both a centre and a symbol of renewed life, was founded in 910. In the East the Byzantine Empire, the leading champion of Christianity in that region, was enjoying a revival in the latter part of the ninth and in the fore part of the tenth century. The end of the recession might, therefore, be placed as early as 850 or 900.

On the other hand, because of events which we are to see later, such as the spread of the Cluny reforms and the revival of the Roman Empire in the West under Otto I (he was crowned Roman Emperor in 962), and the beginning of the conversion of Russia (which may be dated from the baptism of Olga c.954, or, better, from the baptism of her grandson, Vladimir, c.987), A.D. 950 seems preferable. The upswing was not sharp or sudden. By that year it was distinctly noticeable in some quarters, but in others the decline appeared to be continuing and not yet quite to have reached its lowest point. For instance, in spite of the persecution which followed an imperial edict of 845, Christians were still reported in some of the ports of China in 877–878, while not far from 987 Nestorian monks sent to China to assist the Church there declared that they could find no Christians in that land.

In A.D. 950 Christianity was far less prominent in the total human scene than it had been in A.D. 500. In A.D. 500 the Roman Empire, while tottering, was still outwardly the mightiest realm on the planet and Christianity was its professed faith. In extent and culture the Roman Empire was then rivalled only by its chronic enemy, the Persian Empire, and by the Gupta Empire in India. Neither of these controlled as much territory as was still nominally in the Roman domains, and the Gupta Dynasty was showing signs of disintegration. China was in a long period of division, civil strife, and foreign invasion.

During the first five centuries of the Christian era the expansion of Christianity was paralleled by that of Buddhism. Approximately five centuries older than Christianity, by the time of the birth of Christ Buddhism had already spread through much of India and Ceylon and had penetrated into Central Asia and China. In A.D. 500 its geographic extent was probably wider than that of Christianity. Like Christianity, but for other causes, by A.D. 950 it had fallen on evil days. In India, the land of its birth, it was decadent and was in process of the absorption and elimination by Hinduism which were to bring about the severe decline of which we have already spoken. Before A.D. 950 it had entered upon the slow decay in China which is still in progress. It was never as widely spread as was Christianity in the seventh century or as Christianity ultimately became. In the seventh century Christianity was represented by communities from Ireland in the west to China in the east, and from Scotland and Germany in the north to the Sudan and possibly South India in the south. Yet between A.D. 500 and A.D. 950 Buddhism was also spreading —in South-east Asia, the East Indies, Korea, and Japan—and in A.D. 950 it was probably more prominent in the total world scene than it had been in A.D. 500.

The four and a half centuries between A.D. 500 and A.D. 950 also witnessed the emergence of Islam, vigorous and younger than Christianity, and by the latter of those years Islam, after only three centuries, was almost as widely spread geographically as Christianity and was the official faith of states which were more powerful, in the sense in which that term is applied to states, than were any of those which were professedly Christian. During most of the period, moreover, China was ruled by the T'ang Dynasty which, during its heyday, was, along with the Arab Empire, the mightiest realm on the planet, and Confucianism, which provided the ideological foundation of Chinese culture, was on the eve of a great revival.

In A.D. 950 a religiously neutral world traveller or the hypothetical visitor from Mars might have given it as his opinion that Christianity was to share the fate of Manichæism, which, also after an extensive geographic spread, was waning. Manichæism, it will be recalled, was younger than Christianity but older than Islam. Like the latter, it was indebted to Christianity but it never had as powerful political support as that accorded Christianity through the Roman Empire or Islam through the Arabs. After a rapid expansion which carried it as far west as Carthage and as far east as the China Sea it slowly died out, although its last remnants lingered on in China at least to the beginning of the seventeenth century.

In these centuries of its great decline Christianity was espoused by a few kingdoms in Western and Southern Europe which, compared with the major empires of the day, seemed insignificant, by the Byzantine remnant of the Roman Empire, and by such minor states as Armenia and Ethiopia. Culturally Christianity seemed to be of dwindling significance. Italy had not recovered from the "barbarian" invasions and the "Christian" peoples of Western Europe, while vigorous, were crude. Constantinople was wealthy and its upper classes were polished, luxurious, and sophisticated, but were ceasing to do or say much that was new. The Nestorians in Mesopotamia had tutored their Arab conquerors in Hellenistic culture, and in the process had put some of the Greek philosophers into Arabic, but the Arabs had proved apt pupils of the Nestorians and other subject peoples and were producing a culture which appeared to be fully as "high" as that of Constantinople and "higher" than that of the Franks or others of the Germanic peoples who had been converted to Christianity. To the thoughtful non-Christian tourist Hindu and Buddhist India, although politically divided, would have seemed to be on a more advanced cultural level than any "Christian" land except the Byzantine Empire, and under the glorious T'ang Dynasty the great cities of China would have been far ahead even of Constantinople. From the standpoint of Augustine's earthly city, by A.D. 950 the political and cultural associates of Christianity had decidedly declined since the days of Constantine and his immediate successors and even since Justinian I. If its future depended upon the kind of power embodied in the earthly city and its affiliated cultures, the outlook for Christianity was grim.

The break-up of the Roman Empire was accompanied and followed by divisions in the Catholic Church. As we have seen, the Catholic Church arose within the framework of unity provided by the Roman state. When that framework fell apart, the bond of love which ideally characterizes Christians did not have sufficient strength to hold the Church together. The ostensible grounds for the divisions which emerged were doctrinal and administrative, and these intensified the divisions. However, the cleavages were largely along the cultural, racial, and national seams in the fabric which Rome had once held together. Arian Christianity became identified with some of the Germanic conquerors; the descendants of the ancient Egyptians, the Copts, found in Monophysitism reinforcement of their antipathy to the Byzantine tie. Somewhat similarly Monophysitism was the bond of a Syrian Christianity and, in another form, of the national church of Armenia as against the orthodox Greeks. Nestorianism continued to be the faith of the majority of the Christians in Mesopotamia and the regions to the east, although both Monophysites and Orthodox also had communities in Mesopotamia and the lands which lay eastward of that fertile valley.

In point of numbers the major cleavage was between the portions of the Catholic Church which centred respectively at Rome and Constantinople, the one predominantly Latin and Roman by tradition and temper, and the other Greek and Byzantine. The separation cannot be given a precise date. The two main wings of the Catholic Church drifted away from each other partly because of cultural traditions, partly because of rivalry between the two great sees, and partly because of the obstacle presented to communications by the widening of time-distances and the difficulty brought by the disruption of political unity to preserving intimate physical contact. Now and again the breach seemed to be healed, but across the centuries it deepened and widened. While various dates have been given for the final break, the ones usually offered come after this period and none of them has won universal acceptance by historians.

As we endeavour to cover the years of what we have called the great recession, it seems best to do so by summarizing the course of Christianity in each of the main divisions of the Church. First we will survey the history during these centuries of that branch which had its main centre in Constantinople, for it was here that the tradition of the relation of the Catholic Church and the Roman Empire which had been inaugurated by Constantine went on without interruption and was strengthened. Constantinople was the capital from which the Roman Empire was carried on without a lapse and by almost insensible stages became what is commonly called the Byzantine or Greek Empire. The branch of the Catholic Church officially espoused by the continuing Empire regarded itself as the Orthodox Church. Eventually, by processes which are to be discerned in this period but which matured centuries later, the Orthodox Church became a family whose main members were national churches. We will then move on to the several smaller churches in the East, especially to those of Monophysite complexion, including the Coptic, Ethiopian, Jacobite, and Armenian bodies, and to the Nestorians. Finally we will survey the course of that branch of the Catholic Church which found its cohesion in Rome and the Roman Pontiff, the Pope, for it was from this section of the Church that Christianity was to have its chief developments in the next three major periods of its history.

Here again we shall wish to ask how far the kind of power seen in the cross and the resurrection was compromised by the sort of power that expressed itself in the earthly city and where and to what degree it made the Gospel effective in particular individuals, in institutions, in regions, in cultures, and in the entire human scene. Viewed against the background of all mankind, was it really waning? The Christian faith holds that God was in Christ reconciling the world to Himself. In what fashion and to what degree, so far as the surviving records enable us to discern it, was that reconciliation working during these four and a half centuries? Was the decline as great as it might have appeared to the Martian observer who employed the criteria suggested by citizens of the earthly city and who, supposedly, would have been his chief channels of information? Or was there evidence which, assessed by the criteria set up in the New Testament, would give other results?

Chapter XI

THE BYZANTINE CONTINUATION

As we have suggested, it seems fitting that in carrying our story into the period which follows the first five hundred years we should begin with that portion of the narrative which centres about Constantinople and which leads into an account of what may be designated as the Greek or Byzantine segment of Christianity. It was through the administrative structure which had its headquarters at Constantinople that the Roman Empire persisted without a break. Through it, accordingly, the relationship between Church and state which had its inception under Constantine continued its most characteristic development. We have seen that Christianity had its first extensive spread in the Hellenistic, Greek-using elements in the Mediterranean world. It was through Greek that all of the early Christian writings incorporated in the New Testament were given their permanent and authoritative form. Greek was the language of most of the oldest leaders in Christian thought. In the course of the centuries with which this chapter is to deal Greek became the prevailing language of that continuation of the Roman Empire which, dominated by Constantinople, is usually called Byzantine, from Byzantium, the pre-Constantinian designation of that city. Through extensive geographic expansion in subsequent centuries this Greek or Byzantine Christianity was to become the faith of the majority in Eastern Europe and the Balkan Peninsula and as such was to remain one of the numerically major forms of Christianity.

THE JUSTINIAN ERA

The decline of the Roman Empire which had been so marked in the fifth century seemed to be halted in the sixth century and for a brief time that realm flowered again. The central figure in the revival was the Emperor Justinian I, who reigned from 527 to 565, dying in his eighties. A nephew of his predecessor, Justin I, an Illyrian peasant who had come to Constantinople in his youth to seek his fortune and had risen to the throne in 518 at the age of sixty-six, Justinian had been the real power during much of his uncle's tenure of the high office. Justinian was highly intelligent, enormously hard-working, paying great attention to details, friendly, usually in control of his temper, vain, autocratic, ambitious, sometimes vacillating, temperate in his private life almost to asceticism, and deeply religious. He cherished the dream of restoring the Roman domains to their former extent and of bringing unity to the Church. This last he sought to achieve by obtaining the triumph of the orthodox faith of Chalcedon over its rivals, especially the Arian Christianity held by many of the Germanic invaders and the varied kinds of Monophysitism.

Thanks very largely to able generals, during the reign of Justinian Italy, North Africa, and part of Spain were brought back under Roman, or perhaps we should now say, Byzantine rule. Wars were waged against the chronic enemy, Persia. Under Justinian this revived Roman Empire was probably the mightiest realm on the planet, for the period was one of decline for the major contemporary kingdom in India, that of the Gupta, and China had not yet emerged from the political division which had come upon that land in the third century and which had been aggravated by invasions from the north and west.

Justinian's Empress was Theodora. Theodora, like Justinian's family, was of humble origin. A contemporary, Procopius, who wrote a *Secret History* defaming both Emperor and Empress, tells scandalous stories of her youth. These may have been exaggerated, but it is regarded as certain that before her union with Justinian she had had an illegitimate child. She was indisputably a woman of great resolution, charm, beauty, ability, and force. After she was raised to the throne she seems to have remained true to Justinian, who, in turn, was devoted to her. The two differed religiously, for while Justinian was staunch in his Chalcedonian orthodoxy, Theodora was a warm supporter of the Monophysites. She was energetic in redressing wrongs, and she is given the credit for stringent legislation suppressing the sale of girls into prostitution and for founding a convent in which the unfortunates were given an opportunity to begin a better life.

Under Justinian and Theodora, perhaps because of the latter's love of luxury and display, the imperial court took on additional pomp and those coming into the imperial presence were required to prostrate themselves. This was in accord with the lavish ornateness which was to characterize Byzantine life, both secular and religious.

It was partly in this spirit that Justinian became a great builder. At his command towns came into being, extensive fortifications, roads, bridges, baths, and palaces were constructed, and many churches and monasteries were erected. His most famous architectural achievement was Saint Sophia, the cathedral church of Constantinople. Saint Sophia was the climax of a new style of architecture which made outstanding use of the dome and which was inspired by the Christian faith and had as its purpose a worthy setting for Christian worship.

Justinian was deeply interested in theology. Almost inevitably, therefore, he took a leading part in the controversies which were still raging over the relation of the divine and human in Christ. We have seen how in 482 the Emperor Zeno had attempted to compose the differences between the Chalcedonians and the Monophysites by his *Henoticon*. This had not brought peace, for while some Monophysites accepted it, others of them rejected it, and, on the other extreme, the Pope would have none of it and excommunicated the Patriarch of Constantinople for being associated with it.

Into all the complicated details of the disputes and the attempted settlements during the reign of Justinian we must not take the time to go. In general, Justinian, who was no mean theologian in his own right, endeavoured to bring about agreement on the basis of ostensibly holding to the decrees of Chalcedon but slanting the latter in the direction of the views of Cyril of Alexandria. These, it will be recalled, while conceding the human element in Christ, subordinated it to the divine. Justinian seems to have hoped that by this policy he would draw together the adherents of Chalcedon and the more moderate among the Monophysites. The latter, it will be remembered, represented varying shades of theological conviction, some leaving less room for the human in Christ than others. In this effort Justinian found support in the writings of a contemporary monk, Leo of Byzantium, who, employing Aristotelian categories, held that one could affirm two natures in Christ without going to the extreme associated with what was regarded as Nestorianism, and that, while the two natures, the human and the divine, might remain, they could be regarded as so commingled and united that in Christ there would be but one *hypostasis,* that of the *Logos.*

In 544 Justinian issued an edict in which by his own fiat he condemned three writings or groups of writings (sometimes known, not with entire accuracy, as "the three chapters"), including those of Theodore of Mopsuestia, who had had much to do with shaping the views of the two natures in Christ which had been associated with the name of Nestorius and had been rejected by the Catholic Church, and of a Theodoret who had come out against Cyril and in behalf of Nestorius. However, this edict, far from making for harmony, stirred up fresh dissension. In the West some of the bishops regarded it as an iniquitous action against men who, being dead, could not defend themselves, as a repudiation of Chalcedon, and as an endorsement of the Monophysites. The resulting controversy is known as that of "the three chapters."

In the ensuing struggle the Pope, Vigilius, came through with a record of vacillation and self-contradiction. At first he opposed the imperial edict and broke off communion with the Patriarch of Constantinople, who supported it. Then, arriving in Constantinople, he executed an about face and issued a

Iudicatum in which, while careful to support Chalcedon and not to concede to the Emperor the right to determine matters of doctrine, he independently condemned the writings which had been anathematized in the imperial edict. The *Iudicatum* met with sharp criticism from many bishops in Gaul, North Africa, Scythia, Dalmatia, and Illyria, as compromising Chalcedon, and in 550 Vigilius withdrew it. Vigilius also reversed himself in other decisions. Yet on occasion he showed courage, refused to yield to the Emperor, and stood up for the authority of the Papal see.

Eventually, after many discussions among the bishops and with Justinian, the latter called a synod of the entire Catholic Church, usually known as the Fifth Ecumenical Council. This met in Constantinople in 553. Vigilius refused to attend and insisted on giving an independent judgement on the points at issue. The gathering confirmed the condemnations of the imperial decree of 544, and, at the command of the Emperor, probably had the name of Vigilius as an individual struck from the diptychs, but without breaking off communion with Rome. The Emperor banished Vigilius, but the latter was freed when he had conceded the legitimacy of the council. This Vigilius did, condemning "the three chapters" and their defenders. Thus the Cyrillic interpretation of Chalcedon, with its leaning towards Monophysitism, was made official for the Catholic Church.

Yet the Fifth Ecumenical Council did not, as Justinian had hoped, restore unity in the Church. In spite of its endorsement by Vigilius and his successor, numbers of the bishops in Italy and Gaul refused to recognize it as authoritative and for more than a century part of the West was divided from the main body of the Catholic Church. Moreover, Justinian's dream of providing a *via media* which would win back the Monophysites was by no means entirely fulfilled. The more extreme among the latter believed that assent would mean compromise of jealously held convictions. In some areas, notably Egypt, Ethiopia, Syria, and Armenia, Monophysite views were becoming identified with a regionalism which, to use a nineteenth and twentieth century term, was a kind of nationalism. It resented control by the Greeks and from Constantinople.

What Justinian was unable to accomplish by negotiation, persuasion, and a council of all the Church he endeavoured to bring about by force. He wished an empire which would be solidly Christian and orthodox. He sought to extirpate what survived of paganism. In its formal cults, paganism was clearly dying. Yet many continued to be pagans at heart and held to the pre-Christian Greek philosophies. To rid the realm of these remnants Justinian enacted fresh legislation. He commanded both civil officials and bishops to seek out pagan superstitions and forbade any persons "infected with the madness of the unholy Hellenes" to teach any subject. There were prosecutions and confiscations of property and, as we have seen, Justinian closed the schools of philosophy in Athens. Yet many, among them some in high office, remained pagans and usually were not molested if they were not ostentatious in their faith. Justinian also placed the Samaritans under heavy disabilities and ruthlessly suppressed the revolts which his measures provoked.) He was somewhat more lenient towards the Jews, but essayed to regulate their worship. He decreed the death penalty for Manichæans and for heretics who, after recanting, fell back into their former beliefs. He tried to argue with Manichæans, and, when he failed to convert them, had numbers of them killed, among them nobles and senators. He took vigorous measures against heretics, and was especially zealous against the Montanists, who after nearly four centuries still persisted in Phrygia, the region of their origin. He took action against some who, professing to follow Origen, used the name of that famous teacher to justify a pantheistic mysticism which was enjoying something of a vogue, especially in Palestinian monasteries. He labelled Origen as a heretic and either the Fifth Ecumenical Council or an earlier synod in Constantinople in 543 condemned some of the teachings ascribed to that great Alexandrian.

Justinian did not act as emphatically and consistently against the Monophysites as against other heretics. As we have seen, he sought to woo the more moderate of them and Theodora's known advocacy of their views may have softened his rigour towards them. In his last years he attempted to force on the Church a form of Monophysitism known as Aphthartodocetism. This held that Christ's body, being divine, had undergone no change from the time of its conception in the womb of Mary, and was incorruptible, incapable of suffering or of the natural and blameless passions. It thus distinctly limited Christ's humanity. Justinian tried to impose this view on the bishops of the Catholic Church, and, since the orthodox among them resisted, he was preparing to apply physical violence when death removed him.

Not only did Monophysitism continue. It also spread. Its most active missionary was a younger contemporary of Justinian, Jacob Baradæus. Born about 490, of well-to-do parents, Jacob was given a good education and had fluent use of Greek, Arabic, and Syriac. From his early youth he was committed to the ascetic life. During an episcopate of nearly a generation, from 542 to 578, he roved from Nisibis in Mesopotamia to Alexandria in Egypt, usually on foot and garbed only in a ragged horse cloth, and is said to have consecrated two patriarchs, eighty-nine bishops, and a hundred thousand priests. He extended Monophysitism, strengthened it, and did something towards giving it a sense of unity. The term Jacobite applied to a large wing of the Monophysites either perpetuates his memory or was intended to indicate the claim of the group to be the true Church, the custodians of the faith of James, or Jacob, the brother of Jesus.

In spite of the labours of Jacob Baradæus, the Monophysites were badly divided. They differed from one another in doctrine and had no comprehensive organization. Towards the end of the sixth century there were said to be twenty Monophysite sects in Egypt alone. One form was tritheism, which held that in the Trinity there are really three Gods, each with a substance and a nature different from the others.

After the death of Justinian there were attempts to unite the Monophysites. In 575 the Monophysites of Egypt chose a Patriarch of Syrian origin, but he was not generally accepted. Not far from 580, about two years after the death of Jacob Baradæus, partly through the efforts of an Arab Christian prince, a council was held which seemed for a brief time to have brought a semblance of accord. Yet that also failed. The two leading Monophysite sees were the Patriarchates of Antioch and Alexandria.

In Alexandria there was also an orthodox Patriarch, but loyalty to him was confined chiefly to Greek residents and imperial functionaries. In spite of the use of force to obtain conformity with the Catholic faith, most of the Egyptians adhered to Monophysitism in one or another of its expressions.

Justinian was not content with seeking the doctrinal unity of his realm. He also enacted a large number of laws which dealt with various aspects of the life of the Church—the election of bishops, the appointment of the heads of monasteries, the ordination of clergy, public worship, the management of church property, and the morals of the clergy (legislation which, by forbidding simony—the sale and purchase of ecclesiastical office—and the attendance of the clergy at the theatre and horse-races, is an indication that some of the clergy were given to these practices). Justinian increased the functions of bishops in the administration of civic and social matters, such as the overseeing of public works, the enforcement of legislation against gambling, and the rearing of exposed infants. In some matters they acted in place of the governors.

It will be seen that Justinian greatly accelerated a movement which had begun with Constantine for the domination of the Church by the Emperor and which made the Church an instrument of the state. This control of the Church by the Emperor, known as cæsaropapism, was so characteristic of the eastern continuation of the Roman Empire that it was also called Byzantinism. As we have suggested earlier, it was the continuation of the tradition of the pre-Constantinian Roman Empire by which the Emperor, among other titles, bore that of *pontifex maximus,* or chief priest.

It is not surprising that under Justinian, with the renewed vigour displayed by the Roman Empire, Christianity continued to spread in the outlying sections and on the borders of the realm. The re-conquest of North Africa was followed not only by the strengthening of the Catholic Church against the Arians and Donatists who flourished in that region under the Vandals. It also led to the conversion of some of the pagan Berbers, a process which continued after the death of Justinian. During the reign of Justinian Christianity was carried further up the valley of the Nile, into Nubia, in both its Catholic and Monophysite forms. Through the encouragement and initiative of Justinian at least one people in the Caucasus and a barbarian folk who crossed the Danube into Roman territory adopted the Christian faith.

THE FINAL STAGES OF THE CHRISTOLOGICAL CONTROVERSY: MONOTHELETISM

The lack of unity among Christians, and especially between Monophysites and the majority, which Justinian had failed to eliminate, continued to pose a major problem to both Church and state, and Emperor after Emperor wrestled with it. The issue became urgent when, in the seventh century, Arab invaders bearing a new religion, Islam, began their conquests. The Emperors believed it imperative to have Christians and the Empire present a common front against the invader. A fresh approach was made towards bringing Orthodox and Monophysites together, but, far from attaining its goal, it brought another wave of controversy.

The new approach was suggested by the Patriarch Sergius of Constantinople to the Emperor Heraclius and found support in the writings, then relatively new, which were attributed to Dionysius the Areopagite. These had said that the selfsame Christ and Son works divine and human deeds by one divine-human operation (*energeia*). For a time the statement that Christ acted through one *energeia* brought about union in Egypt of Orthodox and Monophysites, but it drew attack. Sergius, in an attempt to by-pass a divisive debate, suggested that the discussion of whether Christ acted through one or more than one *energeia* be dropped, but that surely all would agree that in Christ there was only one will (*thelema*). To this Pope Honorius, to whom Sergius had written, assented. Seemingly backed by the bishops of the two most eminent sees in the Church, in 638 the Emperor Heraclius issued an edict containing the views of Sergius, forbidding the discussion of one or two energies, and declaring that Christ had one will. This seemed to win the assent of the legates of the successor of Pope Honorius, but in 641 a later Pope came out against Monotheletism, the statement that there was only one will in Christ, and declared that his had really been the view of Honorius. Subsequent Popes also affirmed that there were two wills, divine and human, in Christ, and this in general was the conviction in the West. It was argued that if Christ is truly man as well as truly God, he must have a human as well as a divine will. To deny him a human will is to deprive him of his full humanity. It was, of course, held that the divine and the human will were always in accord and never in disagreement.

Since the discussion was a menace to the unity of the Church and was producing fresh division and weakness, in 648 the Emperor Constans II forbade
further debate of the questions of one or two energies and of one or two wills.
In defiance of this order, in 649 Pope Martin I held a synod at Rome which
declared for two wills in Christ, condemned the Patriarch of Constantinople for
taking the opposite view, and also came out against the imperial edicts of 638
and 648. For what he deemed the Pope's contumacy the Emperor had Martin
brought to Constantinople as a prisoner, treated him cruelly, and exiled him to
the Crimea. There Martin died. The Greek monk Maximus, known to later
generations as the Confessor, who had been an able and outspoken opponent of
Monotheletism, was imprisoned, tortured, mutilated, and exiled.

By this time most of the provinces where the Monophysites were strongest
had been lost to the Arabs, and, apparently from a desire to bring peace in such
of the Church as remained within the Roman Empire, the successor of Constans II called what is usually known as the Sixth Ecumenical Council. This
met in Constantinople in 680 and 681. It pilloried the advocates of the Monothelete position, naming among them several Patriarchs of Constantinople
and Pope Honorius as instruments of the Devil, and came out flatly for two
wills and two energies in Christ, as "concurring most fitly in him for the
salvation of the human race." In its distinctive findings the council declared
that it was following the suggestions of the reigning Pope, Agatho, and of the
synod of a hundred and twenty-five bishops which had been held under him in
Rome the preceding year.

The Sixth Ecumenical Council is generally said to mark the end of the
centuries-long debate over the relation of Jesus Christ to God and over the
fashion in which the divine and human were to be found in him. To be sure,
the issue was revived by a Byzantine Emperor early in the eighth century and
a large group in the Lebanon, the Maronites, held to Monotheletism until the
twelfth century, when they made their peace with Rome. Moreover, the
Nestorians and various branches of the Monophysites continued their independent existence. Yet by the eighth century Arianism, the first major dissent on
the issue, had largely disappeared, and for the main bodies of Christians in the
West and for those in the East who had their chief centre in Constantinople
the discussion had ceased and a common mind had been reached.

The positions defined in the course of the debate have since been deemed
final by the churches which together embrace the large majority of Christians.
Roman Catholics, Orthodox, and most Protestants hold to them. The various
branches of the Monophysites cling to the findings of their spiritual ancestors
of the fifth and sixth centuries. It has been mainly among some Protestants, and
they small minorities of that wing of the faith, that the ancient questions have

been raised afresh and answers given which differ from those of the first six ecumenical councils.

The Western and Eastern Sections of the Catholic Church Continue to Drift Apart

Although for them agreement had been reached over the nature of Christ and the relation of the divine and human in him, the Western and Eastern sections of the Catholic Church were drifting apart, the one looking to Rome and the other to Constantinople.

A stage in the separation was a council held in Constantinople in 692. It was summoned by the Emperor, but, while the East regarded it as supplementary to the Sixth Ecumenical Council and really a continuation of that body, its membership was purely from that section of the Empire. It dealt with matters of organization and discipline rather than doctrine. Its enactments have been regarded as binding by the portion of the Church led by the See of Constantinople but have never been fully accepted by Rome or by the section of the Church which has looked to Rome for guidance. The council reaffirmed the position of Chalcedon that "the See of Constantinople shall enjoy equal privilege with the see of Old Rome . . . and second after it." In open opposition to Rome it permitted the marriage of deacons and presbyters, forbade the Roman custom of fasting on Saturdays during Lent, prohibited the representation of Christ as a lamb, as was customary in the West, and ordered that Christ be depicted in human form. The final division had not yet come and East and West were usually in communion with each other. Indeed, while the then Pope refused to assent to the decisions of the council of 692, a few years later another Pope signed them with some qualifications. Yet a gulf was appearing and was widening.

The Coming of the Arabs and Islam

The disintegration of the Roman Empire which had been seemingly halted by Justinian was hastened, as we have more than once suggested, by the spectacular irruption of peoples from the south-east, the Arabs, the bearers of a new religion, Islam. Moslems reckon their era as beginning with the Hegira, A.D. 622, the traditional (but erroneous) date of Mohammed's flight from Mecca to Medina. Within a century of that year the Arabs had overrun about half of what had once been the Roman Empire and were the political masters of approximately half of what might be called Christendom, or the Christian world. The story is a familiar one, but to put it in its proper perspective in the history of Christianity we must summarize it afresh.

Islam owes its birth to Mohammed, whose years were 570–632. Deeply and sincerely religious, Mohammed believed himself to be the mouth-piece of God. By his followers, the Moslems (properly Muslims), he is revered as the Prophet, and the revelations which they believe to have been given to him by God, whom he called Allah, have been assembled preëminently in the Koran, a book which Moslems hold in fully as high esteem as Christians do the Bible. Mohammed knew much of Judaism and something of Christianity and was influenced by them both. He honoured Jesus as a prophet but emphatically denied that God could have a son, for this seemed to him to be derogatory to the greatness and uniqueness of God. Here Islam differed and still differs basically from Christianity. It declares that the gulf between God and man is too great to be bridged, while the fundamental conviction of Christianity is that the gulf, although undoubtedly great, has been bridged by God's initiative in Christ, Christ who is both God and man. Some, including especially many Christians in the early Moslem centuries, regarded Islam as a Christian heresy, but Islam is held by its adherents to be a fresh revelation from God, the final religion, and not a reinterpretation of Christianity.

The sweep of Islam across much of Western Asia and North Africa and into Europe was facilitated by the power vacuum which had been created by the chronic wars between the Roman and the Persian Empire. On the eve of the Arab invasion these two realms had recently come through a stage of their hereditary struggle which had exhausted them both. In the second decade of the seventh century, beginning in 611, when they took Antioch, the Persians had torn Syria and Palestine from the Roman Empire and had pillaged Jerusalem, looting and burning churches, killing thousands of Christians, and carrying off what the latter revered as the Holy Cross on which Christ was believed to have suffered. They also captured Alexandria, probably in 618 or 619, and thus put themselves in control of Egypt. They marched through Asia Minor, seized Chalcedon on the Sea of Marmora near the Bosporus, and encamped just opposite Constantinople. In the meantime, Avars and Slavs came in from the north and one of their raids even broke through the walls of Constantinople. The Persian successes were probably facilitated by the apathy or even hostility of the Mesopotamian Nestorians and the Monophysite Syrians and Egyptians towards the Byzantine rule, identified as that was with the Greeks and Catholic orthodoxy. Then, in the 620's, by one of the striking reverses of history, the Byzantine Empire, led by the Emperor Heraclius, reasserted its power, bought off the Avars, and, in what it deemed a holy war, retook Syria, Palestine (including Jerusalem and its sacred sites), and Egypt, invaded Persia, and extracted a peace, including the Holy Cross, from the demoralized Persians. But the struggle had impoverished and weakened both realms and had rendered them vulnerable to the new invaders.

The Arab advance was spectacular. Mohammed died in 632. He was followed in the leadership of the Moslems by a succession of men who bore the title Caliph, meaning "successor," "viceregent," or "vicar" (of Mohammed). Under the Caliphs the Arabs, although by no means all of these at first accepted Islam, moved into Byzantine and then into Persian territory. In 635 they took Damascus, in 636 all of Syria fell to them, and in 638, after a siege of two years, they captured Jerusalem, although the Holy Cross escaped them and was carried to Constantinople. In 641 or 642 Alexandria capitulated and the Arabs were thus assured of the possession of all Egypt. Their rapid conquests were facilitated not only by the near-exhaustion of the Byzantine realm through the recent Persian wars, but also, as had been the Persian advance, by resentment against the imperial efforts to establish Catholic orthodoxy against the prevailing Monophysitism. In Egypt, moreover, the Byzantine forces were poorly organized and ineptly led. By 650 Mesopotamia had been conquered and the heart of Persia had been overrun. Thus the traditional eastern rival of Roman and Byzantine power was eliminated, only to be replaced by a more dangerous foe. By 650, too, parts of Asia Minor and North Africa were under Arab sway.

The Arabs became a naval as well as a land power, occupied part of Cyprus, captured the island of Rhodes, and raided Sicily and Southern Italy. In the 670's they repeatedly attacked Constantinople itself from a nearby base and were beaten off partly through the use of "Greek fire," a new invention the formula of which was a carefully guarded Byzantine secret.

In 697 Carthage, the centre of Byzantine power in North Africa, fell to the Arabs. For a time the Berbers in that area proved a knotty problem, but by 715, with the assistance of Berber forces, the Straits of Gibraltar had been passed (indeed, they have that name from Tarik, the general who commanded the crossing) and the Visigothic rule in Spain had been overthrown. Arab arms were carried across the Pyrenees and the Moslem call to prayer was heard in southern Gaul. There the Arab Moslem tide was not halted until 732 when, in the battle of Tours (or Poitiers) the Franks, in a decisive victory, stemmed it and began the slow process of rolling it back. Early in the eighth century the Arabs penetrated the Punjab in India and far into Central Asia.

In 717–718, taking advantage of a rapid change of rulers, mutinies, and a near approach to anarchy in the Byzantine Empire, the Arabs again attacked Constantinople, but were repulsed by the able Leo III, the first Emperor of the Isaurian line. Near the middle of the eighth century the Byzantine Empire recovered Cyprus and pushed the Arabs out of Asia Minor. Not for many centuries was the Moslem threat to Constantinople renewed. Yet in the ninth century Crete was taken, Sicily fell to the Moslems, Moslems established posts on the Italian coast, and Rome was attacked more than once and on at least one occasion saved itself only by paying a ransom.

The Arabs did not remain united politically and bitter wars among them were frequent. The strongest and most brilliant of the states established by them was that of the Abbasid Caliphs, descended from Abbas, uncle of Mohammed, with its capital at Baghdad.

The conquests of the Arabs by no means meant the early extinction of the Christian communities in the realms of the Caliphs. Arab Christians, of whom there were many, were in theory required to become Moslems, for Mohammed is said to have declared that there could not be any other religion in Arabia than Islam. Yet many Arab Christians were allowed to retain their faith, and in return were heavily taxed. In principle, the Moslems regarded Christians, like the Jews, as "people of the book" and tolerated them. Indeed, for a time the Arabs looked askance at the adoption by them of Islam, for conversion would give the privileges of Moslems and deprive the Arab rulers of the proceeds of the discriminatory taxes levied against Christians. At the outset in Egypt and Syria non-Catholic Christians were better off than they had been under Byzantine rulers, for the latter had attempted to force their faith upon them. So, too, in the former Persian realms Christians, notably those who were most numerous there, the Nestorians, were freer than they had been under the Zoroastrian princes. Encouraged by their new masters, they taught the latter, as we have suggested, much of Greek civilization, translating in Arabic some of the writings of the Greek philosophers.

However, in Moslem realms Christianity was under handicaps which made for a decline of the numbers of its adherents, sometimes rapid. At the time of the Arab conquest many, particularly in North Africa where the prevailing faith of Christians was not Monophysite or Nestorian, but Catholic, took refuge with their fellow Catholics in Sicily and the south of Italy. They thereby reinforced the Greek element, already strong in those traditionally Greek regions, in the churches in these areas. Others went to Spain, Greece, Gaul, and even Germany. This exodus dealt what proved to be a fatal blow to the Christianity of North Africa. As was to be expected, nearly everywhere the Arab conquests were followed by extensive defections to Islam. Occasionally, but infrequently, these were accomplished by force. Some were from the conviction that the Moslems were right in proclaiming Mohammed to be the true prophet of God and to have a later and higher revelation than Christianity. The conviction was reinforced by the military victories, for they appeared to prove that Islam was under the peculiar favour of God. Many moved over to Islam from quite mundane reasons: from the worldly standpoint it was better to be identified with the ruling class.

Then, too, Christians were under legal disabilities which made accessions to the churches, except by birth, all but impossible, placed their worship under restrictions, and laid other galling disabilities upon them. In lands where Moslem law prevailed, unrepentant apostasy from Islam was punishable by death. Conversions to Christianity, therefore, were very rare and converts usually disappeared. Christians might retain their churches, although some of these were turned into mosques, but in theory they could not build new ones. They were prohibited from displaying their faith through public religious processions or by loud church bells. Possibly following the precedent of the Zoroastrian Persians with religious minorities, the Moslem Arabs required Christians to wear a distinctive badge or garb. Christians were not allowed to serve in the armies, but instead a special head tax was levied on men who normally would have been able to bear arms.

For purposes of administration, another device was taken over from the Zoroastrian Persians. Each of the Christian communions was treated as a distinct community and was placed under its ecclesiastical head. The latter was given authority over the members of his flock and was held responsible for them. In later centuries these communities were called *melets* or *millets*. Catholic Christians in communion with Constantinople were, quite understandably, regarded by the Arabs with especial suspicion and for many years were not allowed to have a community organization under their own head. They were known generally as Melchites or Malkites, from a Syriac word meaning "king," for they were the ones who were obedient to the imperial commands and therefore belonged to the "king's" church.

The effect of these regulations and of this administrative system was to place the churches on the defensive and to render them static, encysted minorities. They resisted change and held to the patterns which had come down to them from their fathers. They feared that any departure from the traditions of the past would be followed by the disintegration of their entire life and their faith. This meant that churches in the Arab realms were extremely conservative.

Under these circumstances, the churches in the Moslem domains, those of the Arabs and their Moslem successors of later centuries, many of them Turks, were tenaciously persistent, but slowly lost ground. The rate of decline varied from country to country. In Arabia most of the Christian communities seem to have died out before the tenth century. In North Africa the decay was marked but somewhat less rapid. In the eleventh century there were still five bishops, but late in that century the three bishops necessary for the consecration of an archbishop were not to be found and the man elected to the post by the Christians in 1074 was sent by the Moslem ruler to Rome for that rite. In Nubia, south of Egypt, Christianity persisted well beyond the thirteenth century, but eventually disappeared, not to be renewed until in the nineteenth century and then by missionaries from Western Europe. Elsewhere the churches continued but, even in the twentieth century, were still dwindling.

The Slowing Down of Theological Creativity in the Church of the Byzantine Empire

It is understandable that in those churches which were encircled by Moslems, embedded in Moslem states, and perpetually on the defensive, fresh thinking on theological issues would cease or, if it appeared, would be quashed by the ecclesiastical authorities. Any innovation would seem perilous. It is possible that this necessity of passive defense contributed to a somewhat similar absence of creative thought in that portion of the Catholic Church which centred about Constantinople. Theological activity did not disappear in this Byzantine, or, as we must also now call it, Greek Church. Theology remained a major concern in the intellectual circles, especially in the wealthy and highly cultured capital. Yet vigorous, fresh thinking such as was to revive and continue in the Christianity of Western Europe was not found. Certainly the successive blows dealt by the Arabs and then, centuries later, as we are to see in later chapters, the even more disastrous experiences with Christian Crusaders from the West and, after them, with the Moslem Turks, must be part of the explanation.

Whatever the cause, the Byzantine Church displayed no such theological ferment as did Western Europe. It held to what had been done in the Catholic Church in the first seven and especially the first five centuries. It regarded itself as the guardian of the true Christian faith taught by Christ and his apostles. Indeed, that to this day is the attitude of the family of Orthodox Churches in which the Patriarch of Constantinople, his effective authority and the flock over which he immediately presides sadly dwindled, is still theoretically the ranking bishop.

The Last Great Figure in Greek Theology, John of Damascus

He who is usually regarded as the last great figure in the theology of the Greek wing of the Catholic Church was John of Damascus. It is significant that he is important, not for original thought, but for his systematization of that which had gone before him. John belongs to the first half of the eighth century. He was born in Damascus, the son of a high official in the court of the Caliph, then located in that city. He succeeded to his father's position, but resigned it and entered the monastery of St. Sabas, near Jerusalem. He was deeply religious, as can be seen from the important share that he had in the hymn-writing which helped to shape that part of Byzantine worship.

John's main theological work was *The Fountain of Knowledge*. In this there were three parts, first an exposition and application to theology of Aristotle's Dialectic, second a description of heresies, reproducing and bringing down to date an earlier work by Epiphanius, and, third and most important, "An Accurate Exposition of the Orthodox Faith." Here was a complete theological system based on the teachings of the fathers and the findings of the councils of the Catholic Church.

John thought of the Christian faith in its orthodox or Catholic form as having already been defined. What he attempted to do was to make a comprehensive synthesis of what had been established. In this he did not differ substantially from the great Cappadocians, Basil of Cæsarea and Gregory of Nyssa. To be sure, they had Platonic assumptions and arrived at the idea of the unity in the Trinity after stressing first the fact of Three, Father, Son, and Holy Spirit, and then coming to the insight of unity, while John, inclined to Aristotelianism, started off with the unity of the Godhead and then discerned in it the Trinity. John began with the nature of God, went on to the creation, the nature of man, providence, foreknowledge, predestination, and the salvation of man, and concluded with the resurrection and speculations as to what would develop as the entire purpose of God in the universe is disclosed.

The work was so comprehensive, so clearly written, and stated so well what was believed in the Greek wing of the Catholic Church, that it became standard in its field for that branch of the Church and through a twelfth century Latin translation also influenced the Western section of the Church, including notably Peter Lombard and Thomas Aquinas.

The Iconoclastic Controversy

The major dispute in the Greek or Byzantine wing of the Catholic Church after the seventh century was not over the nature of Christ, but over the use of images in Christian worship. In this the West also became involved, although it was not as badly divided as were the Greeks. The controversy broke out in 726 and raged, with intervals of comparative quiet, for over a century, until 843. It was concomitant with the recovery of the Byzantine Empire from the internal disorder from which the realm suffered near the beginning of the eighth century and was the result of the religious policy of the Emperor Leo III, who brought a fresh access of strength to the waning Byzantine power.

Objections by Christians to the use of images and pictures—icons as they are technically known—were by no means new. We have seen that pictures of Christian subjects, even of Christ himself, had been made long before the sixth century. Yet there had also been opposition to them on the ground that they smacked of paganism. In the sixth century, before his consecration a Syrian bishop denounced the veneration of the representations of Christ, the Virgin

Mary, the apostles, and other saints. In that same century, moreover, a bishop of Massilia (Marseilles) was reprimanded by the Pope for ordering the destruction of the images in the churches in his diocese, for that pontiff, while agreeing that they should not be adored, held that they were a valuable means of instructing illiterate Christians in the faith.

Yet icons became increasingly numerous. Christ, his mother, the apostles, saints, and scenes from the Old and New Testaments were pictured in mosaics, frescoes, bronze, and carvings in ivory. They were characteristic of churches and chapels and were in private homes.

Why the Emperor Leo decided to open a campaign against them is not entirely clear and has been much debated. It is noted that he was not a Greek but was from the East and it has been suggested that, having been faced with the taunts of Moslems and Jews that Christians were idolaters, he wished to remove the ground for that charge and thus to facilitate winning the support of Moslems and Jews for the Empire. It is also said that he hoped to reconcile the Montanists and other Christians who dissented from the Catholic Church. Leo is reported to have been moved as well by the desire to make the throne master of the Church, to reduce the power of the monks, and to eliminate the control of education by the Church. His is likewise conjectured to have been a revolt of the non-Greek elements in the Empire against the Greek dominance, for, in general, the Greeks were for the icons and Leo and the other Emperors who led in the attacks against them were of non-Greek stocks and cultures. Some have seen in the iconoclastic movement primarily an effort at religious reform.

Whatever the motives which originally actuated Leo, the struggle became complicated by many factors. In it were on the one hand abhorrence of the use of icons as idolatry and on the other popular emotional devotion to them, including veneration of some of the particular images which were singled out for destruction. The contest was in part from the conviction of many churchmen and especially of monks that the Church should be independent of the state, at least in matters of faith and religious practice, and the equally determined purpose of Emperors to assert their authority over the Church. Monks, who had separated themselves from the world, were particularly active in their opposition to the icon-forbidding Emperors. The Emperors may have wished to curb the monasteries because the latter drew so many men from the service of the state and, tax-exempt, reduced the imperial revenues. The army often sided with the iconoclasts, apparently because it wished its head, the Emperor, to be supreme and to be reverenced without the rivalry of veneration for the icons. Women were prominent in the defense of icons, perhaps because of emotionally religious temperaments. In general, as we have suggested, the Greek constituency in the Church was committed to the icons, and much of the attack on the icons came from non-Greek elements. Yet the iconoclasts tended to favour the revived study of the pre-Christian Greek literature while the monks opposed it as tending towards paganism. Personal ambitions and rivalries were always present and at times were very strong. Partisan strife in Constantinople had long been rife. Until the reforms of the Emperor Heraclius in the first half of the seventh century it had centred about the two major parties in the circus, the Blues and the Greens. It had entered into theological disputes. While the Blues and the Greens were now in the past the party spirit was still strong. At one point the putting away by an iconoclastic Emperor of his wife and the marrying of another woman gave occasion for the charge of adultery by those who favoured the icons and also was used by them to insist that an Emperor must be as obedient to the laws of the Church as the lowliest commoner. Theological issues were raised. It is said that the controversy was a split with Hellenism, that those who favoured the icons stood for the historical element in Christianity and that those who opposed them were of the Origenist, Platonic strain who were critical of efforts to confine Christianity to history.

The iconoclasts pled the prohibition of the second commandment to make "the likeness of anything" and held that to do so "draws down the spirit of man from the lofty worship of God to the low and material worship of the creature." They declared that "the only admissible figure of the humanity of Christ . . . is the bread and wine in the Holy Supper." They took a variety of attitudes towards the icons. Some were completely intolerant. The more extreme among them condemned the popular veneration of the saints and of the Virgin. Others would compromise.

To be sure, the iconoclasts did not forbid art. They encouraged pictures of birds, musical instruments, clusters of fruit and flowers, hunting scenes, chariot races, and donors to the Church, and substituted the Emperor's head on the coins for Christ or the Virgin. Some of these motifs resembled and may have been consciously drawn from early Christian art, such as is still to be seen in the catacombs in Rome. The opponents of the iconoclasts held this art to be of the Devil. They argued, too, that the iconoclasts were really Monophysites, denying the reality of the incarnation and of the humanity of Christ, for by refusing to depict the human form of Christ they laid themselves open to the charge that they were affirming that he was God but were denying that he had ever really become man.

Two important figures, both against the iconoclasts, claim special notice. One was John of Damascus. In the early days of the controversy, before he entered a monastery and while he was still a civil servant in the Caliph's government, he came forward against the iconoclast position. In the ninth century, in the later stages of the dispute, an outstanding defender of the use of icons was Theodore of Studius. Born in Constantinople of a well-to-do family, when he was twenty-two Theodore entered a monastery on Mt. Olympus, in Bithynia in Asia Minor, under the tutelage of his uncle. Eventually he succeeded the latter as abbot. Later he and some of his monks moved to Constantinople and entered a large monastery which had been founded in 463 by Studius. Under his leadership that house soon attained prominence and the Studite monks became famous.

There Theodore further developed a rule which he had received from his uncle and made it into a meticulous organization of the monastic life with a rigorous discipline. Among the features which he took over from his uncle was the prohibition of receiving not only women but also female animals into the monastery, probably to discourage the breeding of animals for sale and the accompanying employment of non-monks as servants to assist in this profit-producing activity. Theodore's changes had a wide influence in Byzantine monasticism and in the lands to which Byzantine Christianity spread.

Theodore took an uncompromising attitude in favour of the icons and he and his monks were prominent in the opposition to the imperial policy. Probably this was both out of conviction that the imperial position was wrong on that particular issue and partly from opposition to the domination of the Church by the state. Theodore was persecuted, banished, and imprisoned, but the rigours to which he was subjected did not break his spirit. A scholar, a gentleman, a leader, he attracted both men and women. Uncompromising, at times gloating over the disasters to the enemies of the causes which he espoused, he was also a writer of hymns and a spiritual counsellor to members of both sexes.

The details of the long attempt to be rid of the icons need not long detain us. The issue was raised, as we have seen, by Leo III not many years after he came to the throne. He is said to have been urged to this course by some of the bishops. An edict against the use of icons was issued in 725 or 726 and was followed by the destruction by imperial order of an image of Christ which had enjoyed great popular veneration. That act provoked a riot. In 730 a council convoked by the Emperor took further measures against the icons. The Patriarch of Constantinople was deposed for refusing to concur and one who was opposed to the icons was elevated to the see. The Popes set themselves against the imperial policy and Gregory III, the last Bishop of Rome to have his election confirmed by a Byzantine Emperor, called a council which excommunicated the iconoclasts. In retaliation for the hostility of Rome and to the great annoyance of the Popes, the Emperor transferred Greek bishoprics in Italy and Sicily from the supervision of the latter to that of the Patriarch of

Constantinople. The son and successor of Leo, Constantine V, was even more adamant against the icons than his father had been. In 753 or 754 he called a council of more than three hundred bishops which obediently condemned the icons but in which, significantly, neither the Pope nor the patriarchs of Antioch, Jerusalem, and Alexandria were represented. Severe persecutions of those who held to the icons followed, but under Constantine's son, Leo IV, icons were tolerated outside Constantinople.

On the death of Leo IV, in 780, his widow, Irene, became regent for his infant son. She favoured icons and promoted to the patriarchate Tarasius, a sympathetic civil official who, in conformity with ecclesiastical tradition, took monastic vows and so became eligible for the office. A council of the entire church was called which met in 787, for the most part at Nicæa. Tarasius presided rather than the Emperor or a civil official delegated by the Emperor. He was eager to solve the relations between Church and state by having the Church recognized as supreme in matters of dogma and by according to the Emperor authority in ecclesiastical law and administration. The Pope was represented and the gathering is generally regarded as the Seventh Ecumenical Council. The council approved the use of icons, but regulated the manner in which they should be honoured. The council also forbade the appointment of bishops by the lay power and ordered that in each ecclesiastical province an annual synod be held.

The decisions of the council did not immediately win universal acceptance. Many in the East held to their iconoclastic convictions. On the other hand, some who favoured the icons, notably Theodore of Studius and his monks, were unhappy because those bishops who renounced iconoclastic views were treated leniently and were permitted to retain their posts. Even in the West, where the Popes had consistently stood for the icons, in the Frankish domains a council at Frankfort (794), while allowing images to be set up in the churches, forbade their veneration and denounced the findings of the Council of Nicæa. In 825 a synod in Paris condemned the Pope for assenting to the findings at Nicæa. Not until the eleventh century did Northern Europe accept the Nicæan gathering as the Seventh Ecumenical Council.

Early in the ninth century, in 813, Leo V, the Armenian, came to the imperial throne and revived iconoclasm. However, he was much milder in his enforcement of the ban than had been some of his predecessors and the attack was not so much on icons in general as upon some of the uses of them, especially in worship in private houses. The veneration of icons seems to have continued outside the capital, especially in Greece, the islands, and much of Asia Minor.

In 842 another woman, Theodora, came to power as regent for an infant son, this time Michael III. Like Irene, she favoured the icons and in 843 she restored them. That act really terminated the struggle, although echoes of it were still heard and there were some who held to iconoclastic views. The day in which the icons were formally reinstated, the first Sunday in Lent, is still celebrated in the Greek Church as the Feast of Orthodoxy.

While icons were finally legitimatized, the long protest was not without lasting effect. By tacit consent, in practice after 843 in the Greek portion of the Catholic Church sculptured figures were no longer employed, and icons were confined to pictures. Yet, for good or for ill, they were permanently established in the life and worship of the Catholic Church in both East and West.

In the important and intimately related problem of relations between the Church and the state, the controversy ended in a compromise. The Emperor and the army, who wished the Emperor supreme, did not have their full way. The icons were retained, and this was a victory for the monks and those who wished to have the Church less subservient to the state. Yet in the final settlement it was the crown and not the Church which took the initiative.

The Continued Monasticism of the Byzantine Church

We have had occasion more than once to note the prominence and something of the place which monasticism held in the Byzantine branch of the Catholic Church. That monasticism had been partly shaped by Basil. Theodore the Studite had added to it. Monks were prominent in the life of the Church and the community and were much less susceptible to control by the cæsaropapist state than was the ecclesiastical hierarchy, even though technically the bishops were drawn from the monasteries. The contrast may have been accentuated by the practice begun in the eighth century of appointing to the Patriarchate of Constantinople men who had risen through the civil bureaucracy and were thus seasoned in practical, secular administration and who in their mature years had gone through the form of assuming monastic vows. To this the more radical monks, among them the Studites, were vigorously opposed. They wished strict compliance with the canons of the Church. The monks were quite the most independent section in the official church of the Byzantine Empire.

More and more the course and the characteristics of this Eastern monasticism and those of the West diverged. Eastern monasticism tended towards contemplation and away from activism. Western monasticism displayed much greater variety. Some groups emphasized worship and contemplation, others activism, and still others combined the two. In the East, rather more than in the West, monasteries tended to be grouped together on holy mountains. They were also in the cities, but the mountain monastic communities were either without exact parallel or were more prominent than in the West. Several of the holy mountains were in Asia Minor. What came to be the most famous of all was in Europe, Athos, a rugged promontory jutting southward from the mainland into the Ægean. Mount Athos first attained prominence in years immediately preceding 950 through the exodus to it of monks from Constantinople in protest against the election to the Patriarchate of one whom they had opposed.

Hermits were revered in both East and West and were sought out by both the lowly and the eminent, and on mundane as well as spiritual questions. In the East, although they seem not to have persisted but to have been a fad that passed before many generations, "pillar saints" were prominent, those who had Simeon Stylites as their most famous prototype and inspiration. One of them was Daniel (409–493), whose years of fame were on the eve of the period with which we are now concerned. He entered a monastery at the age of twelve and spent the next twenty-five years there. For five years he visited some of the most famous of the ascetic "athletes of God" of his day, at forty-two he came to Constantinople and, after living for nine years in what had been a pagan temple, he mounted a pillar and passed his last thirty-three years on it. He was visited by multitudes, including officials, Emperors, and Patriarchs, at imperial command was ordained priest by one of the latter, and is said to have prophesied the fate of Emperors and to have been consulted not only on personal problems, but also on weighty matters of state. Many miracles were attributed to him.

A hermit, but not one of the pillar saints, was Theodore of Sykeon, of the latter part of the sixth and the first part of the seventh century. Born in Galatia in Asia Minor, the son of a prostitute, from early childhood he was very devout and began following the ascetic road. So early did he commend himself by his singleness of purpose that he was ordained priest at the age of eighteen. He journeyed to the holy places in and near Jerusalem and at his request was given the monk's habit near the Jordan. Returning to his home country, he led a life of extreme asceticism, much of the time in a narrow cage suspended from a rock, where he was exposed to the storms of winter, had himself loaded with irons, undertook prolonged fasts, and followed a severe regimen of psalm-singing. Others were attracted to him and he became the centre and the head of a monastery. He was famed for his miracles of healing, of expelling demons, and of ending a curse of locusts by killing the locusts, and for inducing repentance of sin. At the insistence of the populace of a neighbouring city he was made their bishop. After eleven years, troubled by the burdens of administration which interrupted his prayers and contemplation and prevented him from giving due attention to his monasteries, he resigned his episcopate. He was sought by many, some for physical healing and others for spiritual and moral advice. Even high officials and Emperors honoured him and asked his counsel.

We must note another trend which in subsequent centuries was to give rise to a memorable controversy. That was towards contemplation and the way of the mystic. Known technically as Hesychasm, it went back to the beginning of monasticism. It was to have many aspects, some of them bizarre, as we are to see in a later period, was to persist into modern times, and was to be very important in that child of Byzantine Christianity, the Russian Orthodox Church.

MINORITY MOVEMENTS BRANDED AS HERETICAL BY THE ORTHODOX

Not all the religious life of the Byzantine Empire inspired by the Christian faith was contained within the official church. Before the decline in vigour which marked these centuries had reached a nadir, there emerged awakenings which from the beginning were quite outside the Catholic Church. At least one of them flourished for centuries. Since they were often persecuted and eventually died out, only fragmentary information about them has survived and about some we know very little.

The most prominent and persistent of these separate groups was the Paulicians. Possibly a primitive form of Christianity cut off from later developments by geographic isolation, they are first heard of early in the second half of the seventh century on the eastern borders of the Empire, south of Armenia. They called themselves simply Christians and the designation Paulician was given them by their enemies. The first leader of whom we know was Constantine-Silvanus who, set on fire by reading the Gospels and the letters of Paul, became an itinerant preacher and eventually was stoned to death.

The Paulicians developed many leaders and divisions. Like the Marcionites, they were dualists, holding that matter, including this world and the flesh, is the creation of an evil power, the imperfect God of the Old Testament, while spirit and souls are the work of the good God. The "perfect" among them abstained from sexual intercourse and from some kinds of meats. They rejected infant baptism and, taking Jesus as their model, were baptized at the age of thirty, in a river. The "hearers," or adherents, were not required to follow this hard road, but hoped to be baptized and undertake it sometime before their death. The Paulicians rejected the honours paid by the Catholics to the Virgin Mary, the invocation of the saints, icons, incense, candles, and all material symbols. Maintaining the Eucharist and the Agape, they observed the former at night and used in it water, not wine. They would have none of the Catholic hierarchy and had only one grade of ministry. They accepted most of the New Testament. Christ was regarded as born of the good God, but as passing through his mother's body like water through a pipe and deriving nothing from her flesh. To them both his birth and his death were unreal, and his work was that of a teacher.

The Paulicians were severely persecuted, but, in resisting, they became excellent soldiers and won respect for their fighting abilities. The iconoclastic Emperors were generally tolerant of them and one of them moved Paulician colonies to the Balkan peninsula to fend off the Bulgars. They experienced a revival at the beginning of the ninth century through Sergius who, like Constantine-Silvanus, had been won by reading the Gospels and Paul's epistles. Sergius became a travelling preacher, supporting himself by working at his trade as a carpenter. In the ninth century, persecuted, some of the Paulicians took refuge in Moslem territory and from there harassed the borders of the Empire.

Still more of the Paulicians moved into the Balkans in the tenth century, especially into Bulgaria. Here they seem to have contributed to a dissident movement, Bogomilism, which continued for many centuries.

Early in the ninth century we hear of another heresy, that of the Athingani. The Athingani were in Phrygia, in Asia Minor, and may have been a branch of the Paulicians. They, too, were persecuted by the state at the instance of the official church.

THE REVIVAL OF THE BYZANTINE CHURCH AND RENEWED STRAINS IN RELATIONS WITH ROME

As we have suggested, recovery to Christianity from the disasters which accompanied the disintegration of the Roman Empire began in the Eastern branch of the Catholic Church in the ninth century. It was well under way by 950, when the decisive upswing in the Western branch of the Catholic Church was about to become noticeable. The revival in the Byzantine Church was associated with the period which was spanned by the Macedonian dynasty, 867 to 1056, a period of about two centuries. The iconoclastic controversy which had so long wrought internal turmoil in the Church was ended, and external foes were less of a menace than they had been or were to be later. The capital of the Caliphate had been moved from Damascus to Baghdad, so that the threat from the Arabs to Asia Minor was not as acute as formerly. On the eastern border, Armenia, a professedly Christian state, was under strong rulers and was having its golden age. To be sure, external dangers had not passed, for in 904 the second city in the Empire, Salonika, was sacked by Moslem corsairs from Crete, in 910 a Byzantine expedition against Crete was defeated, and in the fore part of the tenth century Bulgaria, a near rival, had its great day. But, as we are to see, the height of Bulgarian power was under a Christian ruler and was evidence of the triumph of Christianity in that realm. In the second half of the tenth and the first half of the eleventh century Byzantine power attained its highest point since the beginning of the Arab conquests. The Church shared in the prosperity.

In the first half of the tenth century, that is, the last fifty years of the period with which we are here dealing, before the rise of the Holy Roman Empire of the German nation, the Byzantine Empire was the strongest state in Europe. However, neither it nor that German state which bore the Roman name was nearly as wealthy or as extensive as the Roman Empire had been in its prime, and in territory and population both were very minor powers as compared with China, united as that great land was by the Sung dynasty which came into being in 960.

The resurgence of the Byzantine realm and church was accompanied by renewed strains between the Eastern and Western wings of the Catholic Church.

An outstanding figure in the vigorous life of the Byzantine Church in the second half of the ninth century and one who became a storm centre in the relations between the Eastern and Western wings of the Catholic Church was Photius. Photius came from an eminent Byzantine family of ancient Greek stock and was related to Emperors. During the iconoclastic controversy his father had suffered persecution because of his loyalty to the icons. His uncle, Tarasius, had been the Patriarch who presided at the Council of Nicæa in 787. Photius was a distinguished scholar, the centre of the intellectual renaissance which was one of the features of the revival in Byzantine life. In his house the intelligentsia gathered for the reading and discussion of ancient and recent Greek literature, pagan and Christian. He was a favourite at court and, a civil official, was president of the imperial chancellery when, in 858, he was made Patriarch of Constantinople in succession to Ignatius, who had resigned. Like Tarasius, therefore, he came to the post from civil office.

Ignatius, the son of an Emperor and made a eunuch in his youth by political enemies, had been brought to power in the midst of bitter division in the Church by Theodora, whose part in the restoration of the icons we have already noted. Ignatius was almost immediately a centre of controversy. Honest and zealous, revered by later generations as a saint, he seems to have proved tactless and not to have been worldly-wise. Certainly he alienated many and was regarded by the intellectuals as both ignorant and contemptuous of Greek philosophy. Soon after being made Patriarch he committed, perhaps out of ignorance, the serious *faux pas* of sending a pallium to the Pope, implying that he had the right to invest the latter with that symbol of his office. The Pope, quite understandably, replied that he gave the pallium to bishops but did not receive it from others.

In the controversies between Ignatius and his opponents appeal was made to Rome by both parties, for in theory the Latin and the Greek Church were both in the Catholic Church and the Pope was recognized as having great even if not supreme authority. Among others, Ignatius had as antagonists the young

Emperor, Michael III, and the latter's uncle and most influential minister, Bardas, the successful rival of Theodora for the control of that pleasure-loving monarch. Ignatius publicly refused the communion to Bardas, alleging, perhaps on insufficient grounds, that the latter was guilty of incest. Bardas had Ignatius deported to a convenient island and the latter abdicated and urged his friends to join in electing a new Patriarch.

Photius seems to have been chosen because he was acceptable both to the opponents and to the friends of Ignatius. He was regularly elected by a synod of bishops called for that purpose. A layman, he was hurried through all the degrees of the priesthood in one week. This was contrary to canon law, but for it there was much precedent. Bishops from both the friends and opponents of Ignatius joined in consecrating the new Patriarch. His elevation seemed to have brought peace to the Church.

The concord had lasted only a few weeks when the conflict between the parties in the Church broke out more furiously than ever. Some of the prelates revolted against Photius, Bardas, and Michael III and insisted on the restoration of Ignatius. They were replaced by men who were friendly to Photius, but the vast majority of the monks would not recognize the latter's authority. The monastery of Studius, so active in advocacy of the icons, led in the opposition. In 861 a synod was held in Constantinople at which Papal legates were present, instructed by their master to investigate. Here Ignatius appeared, denied that he had appealed to Rome, and challenged the competence of the Roman representatives. The latter ratified the deposition of Ignatius. The action of Rome was based on the claim that, as recognized by a much earlier council at Sardica, the Pope had the right to re-try a case against any bishop. The synod also passed acts designed to control some of the abuses in the monasteries, and thus confirmed the enmity of many monks against Photius and his supporters.

The Pope, who was the vigorous Nicholas I, while not at first repudiating his legates in joining in the confirmation of the deposition of Ignatius, did not yet recognize Photius or enter into communion with him. He was eager to extend the control of Rome over the Bulgarians who, as we are to see, were about to be converted, and also to restore to his direct jurisdiction Illyricum, which had been transferred to the Patriarch of Constantinople by Byzantine monarchs who, as Roman Emperors, claimed that right. The Pope, presumably, would have recognized Photius had the latter acceded to his territorial desires, but this Photius would not do. In 863 the Pope held a synod in Rome which, acting on the conviction that the Papal legates had exceeded their authority in 861, stripped Photius of all ecclesiastical dignity and restored Ignatius to the

Patriarchate. The Emperor, Michael III, refused to admit the competence of Rome in such matters and said so frankly to the Pope.

In replying, Nicholas I asserted in no uncertain terms what he held to be the prerogatives of the Papal see and declared that through the clear words of Christ himself the Popes had power "over all the earth, that is, over the entire Church" and insisted that no council of the Church could be called without the Pope's consent—conveniently disregarding the fact that earlier ecumenical councils had been called by the Emperor and had been presided over either by him or his representative. Here was an assertion by the Pope of the Church's independence of the power of the state and of his authority in the Church. The latter was not new and practice, even in Constantinople, had been tending in the direction of the former.

The situation was still further complicated by developments in Bulgaria. There the king, Boris, under pressure from Constantinople, had accepted baptism from the hands of Greek clergy sent by Photius. Greeks, Armenians, and Paulicians poured into the country instructing the populace in the new faith. Boris wished to have his church free from both Rome and Constantinople, and in an effort to gain as favourable terms as possible played off each against the other. He wished a patriarch of his own but might compromise on an archbishop. Rome sent two bishops who engaged in instruction and baptism. Missionaries also came from the Franks, who adhered to the Latin form of Christianity.

The close juxtaposition of missionaries from the two wings of the Church brought into sharp relief the differences which had developed across the years. The Latins had a celibate clergy and confirmation was only by a bishop. The Greek priests were married (to them, as we have noted, the Roman insistence on a celibate clergy smacked of Manichæism) and confirmation was by the priest. Moreover, the Latins were putting *filioque* into the creed which is usually called Nicene, saying that the Holy Spirit proceeds from the Father and the Son, whereas the original of the formula spoke of the Holy Spirit only as proceeding from the Father. The insertion had developed in the West in conflict with Arian Christianity, the faith of the Goths who ruled in Spain and part of Italy. To state their position as against the Arians the Catholic Latin clergy had framed a creed (possibly, as we have seen, originally a hymn) which was commonly given the name of Athanasius, because the Arians called the Catholics Athanasians. That creed had *filioque*. The Latins added the phrase to the Nicene Symbol, presumably to bring that and the Athanasian Symbol into accord. This seems to have been done first at Toledo in Spain in 589 or 653 to signalize the conversion of the Visigoths from Arianism to Catholicism. While in St. Peter's in Rome the Popes did not use *filioque* until early in the eleventh century, the custom had gradually spread through the West and in 809 under Charlemagne a synod at Aachen had given its approval. The Greeks were not averse to saying that the Holy Spirit proceeds from the Father through the Son, but objected to saying "and the Son." Then, too, in contrast with Greek custom, the Latins fasted on Saturdays and used milk, butter, and cheese in Lent.

The struggle for Bulgaria continued. At first Boris seemed to have been won by the Pope's envoys. Partly to offset this success, in 867 Photius called a synod in Constantinople which condemned Pope Nicholas and tried to wean the Franks from him by acclaiming, with the consent of Michael and Bardas, the Carolingian Louis II of that people as joint Emperor.

Then came a sudden reversal. Basil "the Macedonian," of humble Armenian origin, murdered Bardas (866), was made joint Emperor with Michael, and in 867 had the latter assassinated while drunk. These deaths deprived Photius of his two most powerful backers and freed Ignatius, who was still living, from his most influential enemies. Basil had the support of the party of Ignatius. Under the circumstances, Photius resigned and Ignatius was reinstated as Patriarch.

Hoping to bring unity in the Byzantine Church, Basil now referred to the Pope the whole tangled issue of Ignatius and Photius. A new pontiff, Hadrian II, was now on the chair of Peter. At a synod in Rome in 869 Hadrian decided against Photius and for Ignatius. In 869-870 a poorly attended synod was held in Constantinople, some members of which assented to the Papal condemnation of Photius. However, there was no enthusiasm for conforming with Rome and in spite of the protest of the Pope's representatives, by action of Basil, to whom the synod referred the question, Bulgaria was placed under the Patriarch of Constantinople. Ignatius then consecrated an archbishop and several bishops for Bulgaria. This angered the Pope, who held that his recognition of Ignatius had been conditional upon the latter's assent to the Roman claims in Bulgaria.

A reconciliation was effected between Basil and Photius and the latter returned to court as a tutor to the Emperor's sons. Ignatius and Photius also seem to have made peace with each other. When the former died, in 877, the latter quietly succeeded him as Patriarch. From then until 886 his influence in Church and state was at its height.

In 879-880 a largely attended council met in Constantinople. Photius presided. The Papal legates, in the name of the Pope, John VIII, joined with the council and the representatives of the three other Patriarchs—Jerusalem, Antioch, and Alexandria—in recognizing Photius as the legitimate and canonically elected Patriarch. The action taken against Photius by Pope Hadrian II was repudiated by Pope John's representative. Nothing was said about *filioque*, for in Rome that had not yet been added to the creed. Pope John VIII, although admonishing Photius for his lack of humility, confirmed his reinstatement. The breach between the Western and Eastern wings of the Catholic Church was technically healed. Yet differences remained and were to come again to the fore.

As to Photius, some of the partisans of Ignatius remained recalcitrant. On the death of the Emperor Basil, in 886, the latter's son, Leo, who came to the throne, was hostile and Photius resigned. He lived on, but how long we do not know. Within a few decades after his death he was canonized by the Byzantine Church.

We have devoted to Photius and the events associated with him a much larger amount of space than may at first sight seem warranted. We have done so for several reasons. Photius himself is important, for he was one of the ablest ecclesiastics produced by the Byzantine Church. His career provides a window by which we may gain insight into that church, its politics, the fashion in which it was related to the state, and a little of its life. From it we can also glean some understanding of the state of the Catholic Church in the ninth century. We see it as continuing to think of itself as one and as intimately related to the Roman Empire. That Empire, although sadly diminished in area since the days of Constantine or even Justinian, was still regarded as inseparable from the Catholic Church. In theory there was a Christian society of which the Roman Empire was the civil phase and the Catholic Church, which included all true Christians, cared for what might be called the religious side. The Emperor had power in the Church, although that was being challenged in the West and now and then was being questioned in the East. In the Catholic Church the Pope asserted his primacy and to some degree was so acknowledged in both East and West. Yet East and West were continuing to drift apart. Even before Photius, in 781, the Popes had ceased to date their documents by the regnal years of the Emperors in Constantinople and in 800 a Pope had crowned Charlemagne as Roman Emperor. This was followed in the ninth century by the coronation by the Popes of some of the successors of Charlemagne. Carolingian Emperors regarded themselves as the Western colleagues of the Eastern monarchs and held the Empire to be still one. Towards the end of the reign of Charlemagne the Emperors in Constantinople assented to that claim. In actuality division was in progress. Not only were strains chronic, but from time to time they became so acute that actual schisms appeared. Thus far these schisms were temporary, but from the vantage of the perspective of a later age we can now see that they would eventually become permanent.

In spite of protestations to the contrary, the only true Christian unity, that of love, was largely lacking and from time to time the administrative structure which presented to the world an impressive façade and provided an opportunity for unity broke down and at best only partially hid the basic conflicts. These were primarily in sectional loyalties, in ecclesiastical customs, and in the rivalry between the sees of Rome and Constantinople. Popes and Patriarchs stood up for the authority of their respective offices and, perhaps unconsciously, under the guise of adherence to principle were jealous for their personal prestige and power. As we have seen, the Catholic Church had grown up within the inclusive political framework provided by the Roman Empire. It survived that realm, but after the scaffolding of the Empire fell away its inherent cohesion was not strong enough to hold it permanently together.

The Northward Expansion of Byzantine Christianity

The expansion of the Byzantine wing of the Catholic Church to the east was long estopped by the chronic warfare between the Roman Empire and the Zoroastrian Sassanian dynasty which ruled in Mesopotamia and Persia. Beginning with the seventh century expansion to both east and south was effectively blocked by Islam.

However, to the north the situation was not so forbidding. To be sure, pagans, largely Slavs, Avars, and Bulgars, had broken through the imperial defenses and had settled in what had once been imperial and Christian territory. Slavs had infiltrated into Macedonia, Epirus, Greece, and Asia Minor. Scandinavians, the Northmen, moving southward, had taken possession of part of what was later to be Russia and were raiding the Byzantine coasts. In 860, for example, they attacked Constantinople itself. In the 890's the pagan Magyars established themselves in the modern Hungary. Yet these invaders were of a "lower" stage of "civilization" than were the Christian Greeks and tended to adopt the latter's culture and religion. Before the middle of the tenth century the conversion of all of these except the Northmen—the Varangians—north of the Black Sea was well under way. Moreover, through contacts made possible by commerce, Byzantine Christianity was spreading among the peoples of the Caucasus.

Beginning with the reconquest of North Africa, under Justinian, as we have seen, Catholic Christianity resumed the expansion in that region which had been interrupted by the Vandal occupation in the preceding century. Numbers of the Berbers were converted. However, the Arab conquest brought that to an end and, as we have noted, Christianity rapidly lost ground.

In lands which remained under the administration of the Byzantine continuation of the Roman Empire the conversion of the invaders was part of the assimilation to "Christian" Greek culture. Following Roman practice, the imperial armies were in part recruited from "barbarian" peoples. Since the state was officially Christian, festivals were regularly observed among the troops in honour of the Virgin Mary and the saints, and the armies were deemed to be fighting in behalf of the Catholic faith. Those who came into the ranks as pagans would, therefore, speedily conform. In Asia Minor, Greece, Macedonia, and Epirus, conversions seem to have come about unspectacularly and through the ordinary machinery of the diocesan organization. We hear of the monks of Mt. Athos baptizing a large body of Slavs. The Patriarch of Constantinople appointed inspectors to oversee the work of conversion in the European provinces. We read of men of Slavic blood high in the Church, among them at least one Patriarch of Constantinople.

The conversion of the Slavs outside the areas which were continuously under the political control of Constantinople proceeded more slowly, but made rapid progress in the second half of the ninth century. Some of it, as we are to see, was through German missionaries and to the Latin wing of the Catholic Church. Some, however, usually that in the regions nearest Constantinople, was by missionaries from the Greek Church.

The most famous of the early missionaries to the Slavs from the Eastern wing of the Catholic Church were the two brothers, Constantine (also known as Cyril from the name which he assumed late in life) and Methodius. Shortly before the year 852 the Moravians were won to a nominal profession of the Christian faith. Precisely how that was accomplished we do not know, but within a few years Italian, German, and Greek missionaries were said to be labouring among them. Sometime in the years 861, 862, or 863 the prince of the Moravians, Rastislav, himself a Christian, asked the Byzantine Emperor for missionaries to instruct his people. That Emperor was Michael III whom we have already met in connexion with the end of the iconoclastic controversy and with Photius. Michael, often contemptuously known as "the drunkard," was more noted for his dissipations than his piety. However, in his name and perhaps at the instance of his minister, Bardas, and on the recommendation of Photius, then in the first period of his patriarchate, the brothers were appointed.

Methodius and Constantine are said to have been sons of a prominent citizen of Salonika, an officer in the army. Methodius was the older and may have been a civil official before entering the monastic life. Constantine, the younger, is reported to have gained distinction as a teacher and philosopher and to have been a missionary to the Khazars in what is now Russia. Tradition has it that before the brothers left Constantinople Constantine had devised a script for the writing of Slavonic and had begun the translation of the Gospels into that tongue. Whether this was the first reduction of Slavonic to writing we do not know, nor are we sure which of the ancient Slavonic alphabets, the Cyrillic or the Glagolithic, was his work.

Rastislav received the brothers with honour and they began the instruction for which they had come. Constantine continued his translation and put the liturgy and some other religious literature into Slavonic. In doing this he was following the custom of the East, where the Bible and the services of the Church were customarily in the vernacular. However, in Moravia he met opposition. This was probably from German clergy who were penetrating that region. Jealous of Byzantine influence, they maintained that the only languages permissible in the Eucharist were the three which were alleged to have been in Pilate's placard on the cross of Christ—Hebrew, Greek, and Latin. This became a cause of controversy with the Germans which was to plague the lives of both brothers.

Methodius and Cyril went to Rome (868), thus acknowledging the authority of the see of Peter. This must have been balm to the soul of the Pope, then Hadrian II, as recognition of his authority by Greek priests in his dispute for jurisdiction with the Patriarch of Constantinople. Yet the Pope wished to avoid giving unnecessary offense to the powerful Germans. He is said to have received the brothers cordially, to have given approval to the Slavonic service books, to have permitted the use of Slavonic in the Eucharist in some of the churches in Rome, and to have made arrangements for the ordination of several of the candidates for the priesthood who had come to Rome with the missionaries. Constantine died in Rome (February 14, 869).

Heeding a last wish of his brother, Methodius continued the mission to the Slavs. Possibly at the request of one of the Slavic princes, the Pope revived an ancient bishopric in Illyricum and appointed Methodius to it, presumably welcoming this opportunity to strengthen, through a Greek, the jurisdiction which he claimed in that area. The Germans were offended. Methodius was tried and condemned by a synod of Germans and for two years and a half was confined in a German monastery. The Pope eventually obtained his release, rebuked two German bishops who were involved, and ordered his restoration to his see. Yet Rome compromised with the Germans and Pope John VIII, he who confirmed the reinstatement of Photius, ordered Methodius not to use Slavonic. Perhaps, in view of the needs of the mission in Bulgaria, John later relented and permitted Slavonic in the services of the Church. John (c.879) made Methodius archbishop and head of the hierarchy for the Moravians. Methodius is said to have visited Constantinople in 882 and to have been received cordially by Photius. Photius established in Constantinople a school for Slavonic studies. This became a refuge for Slavonic priests who had been sold into slavery by a hostile prince and had then been freed by Venetians and sent to Constantinople. Methodius died in 884 or 885.

The course of the pupils of Methodius continued to be troubled. Probably at the instance of German clergy, Rome again withdrew its permission for the use of Slavonic. In the year 900 the pagan Magyars crossed the Danube, soon made themselves the masters of much of the area in which Constantine and Methodius had laboured, and Christianity suffered. Yet the work of translating Christian literature into Slavonic went on and contributed greatly to the spread and nourishment of the Christian faith in Bulgaria and, after 950, in Russia.

It was through the Byzantine wing of the Catholic Church that Christianity made its chief gains among the Serbs. The Emperor Heraclius (reigned 610–641), whom we have already met in connexion with the Monothelete controversy and the Persian and Arab invasions, sent missionaries who baptized some of the Serbs. In the second half of the ninth century Basil I attacked the Serbian pirates who were preying on commerce, swept them off the seas, laid waste their strongholds, and, sending them priests, compelled them to accept baptism.

We have already had occasion to say something of the conversion of Bulgaria. That, however, is so important that it demands a more comprehensive statement. The Bulgars were a people of Asiatic origin and of Turkish or Hunnish stock. In the second half of the seventh century they had made themselves masters of extensive territories north of Constantinople. They were so near that capital that they repeatedly threatened it, especially in those perilous decades when the Arabs were making great gains. They were a minority who ruled over a population which was predominantly Slav.

As we have seen, the Khagan or King of the Bulgars, Boris, was baptized in 864 or 865. Boris seems to have been considering that step for some time. One of the Carolingians, Louis the German, whom Boris had defeated, believed that he had persuaded him to receive the rite. While the Bulgarian army was out of the country assisting Louis, the Byzantine forces invaded the country and Boris purchased peace by ceding some territory, promising to withdraw from his alliance with Louis, acknowledging the suzerainty of Michael III, and accepting baptism. Envoys of his were baptized in Constantinople and a mission of Greek clergy sent by Photius went to Bulgaria and baptized the prince himself.

This act of Boris precipitated a rebellion of the Bulgar aristocracy. It may be that Boris wished to use his new faith as a means towards introducing European civilization and of strengthening his own power as against that of the nobles. We shall see that happening in more than one kingdom in succeeding centuries. To this the nobles would quite understandably object. Boris put down the rebellion and furthered the instruction and baptism of his subjects. As we have noted, missionaries came from the Byzantine Empire—Greeks,

Armenians, and Paulicians—and a mass conversion was soon in progress. Missionaries also entered from the West.

We have remarked that Boris wished to have a patriarch of his own for Bulgaria. It may be that his motive was in part to make certain that the Bulgarian church would not be used to further the political designs of either the Byzantines or the Germans. It is probable that he at least wished to have his realm and his church on a full equality with Constantinople. We have reported how he bargained with both the Pope and the Patriarch of Constantinople to attain this ambition and took advantage of the rivalry between the two sees to gain his end. Boris did not at once obtain a patriarch, but in 870 Ignatius consecrated a Bulgar as archbishop and sent him with ten bishops and many priests to his new see. In spite of the surrender by Photius in 879–880, as part of his peace-making with Rome, of his patriarchal powers in Bulgaria, Boris continued relations with Constantinople. This was natural, for that city was much nearer than Rome. He sent a younger son, Simeon, to Constantinople to be educated as a monk, presumably with the hope that he would return to head the church in Bulgaria, thus keeping both state and church in the hands of one family.

Some of the Slavonic clergy who had been trained by Constantine and Methodius and who had found their old homes impossible were welcomed by Boris. The latter was trying to bring about an amalgamation of the Bulgars with the subject Slav majority and to that end was encouraging Slavonic literature. One of the exiles, Clement of Ochrid, probably a Byzantine Slav, was sent by Boris to Macedonia and there established a school for training clergy and translating sacred books. Later he became a bishop.

In 889 Boris resigned his throne and retired to a monastery which he had founded near his capital as a centre of Slavic Christian culture and was succeeded by his eldest son, Vladimir. However, Vladimir led a pagan reaction. Around him gathered the nobles who were opposed to the innovations of Boris—Christianity, the new customs associated with that faith, and the centralizing of authority in the monarch. After a few years Boris, thoroughly aroused, emerged from his retirement, deposed Vladimir, had him blinded and placed in confinement, called a national council, and had Simeon chosen for the vacancy. He also induced the assembly to substitute Slavonic for Greek as the language of the Bulgarian church. Feeling his life work now to be secure, Boris once more retired to his monastery.

Under Simeon Bulgaria enjoyed its golden age. Simeon renounced the monastic life for which he had been trained, but he furthered the growth of Bulgarian literature. This was in Slavonic and was made up mostly of translations from Greek. It was from Bulgaria that Slavonic literature spread to other

Slavic peoples. Under Simeon the formal conversion of the land to Christianity was completed. He also fulfilled his father's vision of a realm legally on an equality with the Byzantine Empire. He surrounded himself with the splendour and ceremonial which he had seen in Constantinople, assumed the title of "the Tsar and Autocrat of all Bulgarians," thus giving his crown a title on a par with that of the Macedonian dynasty in Constantinople, and had the Bulgarian bishops declare (918) the Bulgarian Church fully independent (autocephalous) and place a patriarch at its head. The patriarch crowned Simeon, hailing him with the imperial title. At first the Patriarch of Constantinople was unreconciled to these changes, but Rome seems to have accepted them, and in 927, the year of Simeon's death, Constantinople also assented. The Bulgarian Church was orthodox in doctrine, but independent in administration. By Simeon's initiative it was the first to establish the tradition, later characteristic of the family of Orthodox Churches, of being reciprocally independent of one another administratively, but of agreeing in doctrine and regarding the Patriarch of Constantinople as a kind of *primus inter pares* among their heads. In the first half of the eleventh century, less than a century after Simeon's death, the Byzantine Emperor Basil II conquered the country, made it a Byzantine province, and cancelled the Bulgarian patriarchate. But Bulgaria continued to be professedly Christian.

Just when and how the peoples of the Caucasus became Christians we do not know. Conversion began well before the sixth century, but it continued after that time and seems largely to have been through Byzantine influence. Some of it was in the reign of Justinian. The conversion of the Alans is said to have been in the eighth century. Contacts with Byzantine commerce and culture by way of the Black Sea, long a Greek lake, furthered the process. The birth of the largest offshoot of the Byzantine Church, that of Russia, was not to come until shortly after 950.

THE EFFECT OF THE BYZANTINE ENVIRONMENT ON CHRISTIANITY

What effects did the Byzantine environment have upon the Christianity which was so closely associated with it? We have seen that the Eastern and Western wings of the Catholic Church tended to drift apart and we have noted some of the differences which were the ostensible causes of the friction between Latin and Greek Christianity. But were there other characteristics, perhaps permeating more deeply the genius of the Eastern wing, which can be attributed to the Greek and Byzantine influence?

We must say at the outset that the Byzantine Church was Catholic. That is to say, it inherited those features of the Catholic Church which had been developed in the first five centuries. Its administrative structure, with its bishops and patriarchs, was that which had arisen in the Roman Empire and in its main outlines it remained much as we have already met it. It accepted the creeds and the doctrine which are associated with the first four ecumenical councils and assented to the findings of the three councils held in the period covered by this chapter. Its liturgy, its sacraments, and its monasticism were a continuation and outgrowth of those of the earlier centuries. Indeed, it thought of itself, as do its successors, the Orthodox Churches of today, as the guardian of true Christianity, the possessor and custodian of the Catholic faith.

Yet this Byzantine Christianity displayed features which were peculiar to it and which must be attributed in part to the milieu in which it inescapably had its existence. These were not in formal dogmas, for those remained substantially unaltered, but were, rather, in practices and in temper.

First of all we must remind ourselves of what we have again and again had occasion to notice, the effect upon the Church of the close relation with the state. Beginning with Constantine, the first formally to accept the Christian faith, the Emperors sought to control the Church and to make it serve the state and society as they had the non-Christian official cults. That tradition was strengthened in the sixth and seventh centuries by Justinian and other strong Emperors, and was what has been termed cæsaropapism. The Emperors called church councils and presided at them either in person or by deputies. They issued decrees on ecclesiastical matters. Although technically they had only the right of nomination, they often virtually appointed the Patriarch of Constantinople. No Patriarch could hold office without their consent. Until late in the eighth century elections to the Papacy were confirmed by them. The subordination of Church to state persisted and today is seen in the family of Orthodox Churches.

Yet the Church was not as fully mastered by the state as the pre-Christian official cults had been. From time to time individuals and groups within the Church protested, and by the middle of the tenth century a partial independence had been achieved. At times the Church forced the Emperor to make concessions. We have noted that the monks, who in theory had given themselves fully to the Christian faith, repeatedly refused to conform to the orders of the state. This was seen especially under the iconoclastic Emperors, when they spear-headed the opposition to the government's efforts to remove the images. The Studites, led by their most famous member, Theodore, were particularly uncompromising in the later stages of the struggle. After the controversy had been decided in their favour, they opposed the imperial policy on some other issues. The Patriarch Tarasius rather than the Emperor or one of the latter's representatives from among the civil officials presided over the Seventh Ecumenical Council, in 787. From time to time a Patriarch or some other spokesman for the Church insisted that the Emperor and other high officials must in morals be fully as subject to the discipline of the Church as the humblest Christian. The principle came to be recognized that to be valid the coronation of the Emperor must be by the Patriarch of Constantinople as the ranking bishop in the Eastern wing of the Church. A strong Patriarch might exact promises from a compliant Emperor as a condition for officiating. Thus early in the ninth century the Patriarch obtained from the incoming Emperor a written pledge to preserve the orthodox faith, not to shed the blood of Christians, and not to scourge ecclesiastics.

A second characteristic was the growing sterility in theological thought. Theology continued to be a major subject of study and writing. The Patriarch Photius, for example, was deeply learned in that field as in so many others. Yet, as we have seen, the most famous theological work of this period, *The Fountain of Knowledge* by John of Damascus, had in it little that was new, but owed its fame to its competent and comprehensive summary of views already endorsed by the Catholic Church.

Why this sterility? We do not know. As we have suggested, it may have been because of the fact that the Byzantine realm was prevailingly on the defensive, fighting to preserve its waning remnant of the Roman Empire against encroaching invaders and that this made it conservative, hostile to major change of any kind. This was especially the case after Justinian, and notably so after the beginning of the Arab invasions.

A third characteristic was the emphasis upon the public services and especially upon the liturgy through which the Eucharist was celebrated. They were marked by ornate pomp. Much of this may have been because of the prosperity of Constantinople. The Byzantine Empire centred about that city and was dominated by it. As the metropolis of Europe, living primarily by its commerce, it was wealthy and its upper classes were luxurious. The imperial court was noted for its splendour. To this Justinian had added. It was to be expected that the great church built by him, Saint Sophia, would be rich in mosaics and that ceremonies in it would match those in the imperial court. Since it was the cathedral church of the Patriarch and the leading ecclesiastical structure of the realm, in the other church edifices so far as possible efforts were made to duplicate what was done in it.

From this emphasis upon the formal public worship of the Church may have come the tendency to regard religion as primarily the correct performance of the liturgy. Religion was by no means completely divorced from ethics, nor were morals regarded as purely private. The state was supposed to follow Christian principles and ascetic anchorites gave spiritual and moral counsel, not only to private individuals on matters of faith and conduct, but also to high officials, including Emperors, on policies of state. Yet there was in this Byzantine Christianity less of activism and more of other-worldliness than in its Latin counterpart.

This other-worldliness may also have been seen in the stress on Easter and the resurrection. The Latin wing, while by no means belittling that festival, made more of the crucifixion and the atonement. This may have reflected the tendency in the Greek tradition as it developed in Hellenistic times to emphasize the distinction between matter and spirit, to regard the former as evil and the latter as good, and to think of salvation and immortality as the emancipation of spirit from flesh. Latin Christianity, on the other hand, may have reflected the Roman regard for law and administration, with the desire to realize an ideal society here and now and the conviction that conformity to good morals is one of the essential features of such a society.

A fourth characteristic of Byzantine religion, and especially of Byzantine monasticism, seemingly related to this last, was the trend towards ascetic withdrawal from the world, with mysticism and contemplation. This can easily be exaggerated. The same characteristic was to be found in the Christianity of the West. Yet as the centuries passed, the activist element in Latin monasticism became increasingly prominent and the contemplative, non-resisting, non-activist, mystical strain in Byzantine monasticism and especially in its most numerous offspring, Russian monks and monasteries, became more marked. It is significant that for centuries the most widely used writings on mysticism in Christian circles were those ascribed to Dionysius the Areopagite and that they were written in the East and were profoundly shaped by Neoplatonism.

The Effect of Christianity upon Byzantine Life and Culture

Fully as important as the question of the effect of the Byzantine environment upon Christianity is that of the influence of Christianity upon those peoples and individuals who lived under Byzantine rule.

First it must be noted that Christianity contributed markedly to the unity of the Byzantine Empire. Christianity was the official faith of that realm. Closely associated as it was from near its outset with Hellenism, it furthered the assimilation of the non-Hellenistic elements in the Empire. Especially after the Teutonic and Arab conquests lopped from the Empire most of its non-Hellenistic provinces, that realm was a Greek Christian state. The remaining non-Hellenistic constituencies were absorbed, together with those northern invaders who settled within the imperial domains. Wars against the Zoroastrian Persians and the Moslem Arabs were regarded as holy, and religious enthusiasm contributed to the resolution with which they were waged.

In the second place, Christian influence was increasingly seen in the laws of the Byzantine Empire. When the famous Institutes of Justinian are compared with those of the non-Christian Gaius of the second century, they are seen to have alterations in the laws of marriage and succession, in regard to chastity, and concerning the exposure of infants which reflect the Christian convictions of the later rulers. In the *Ecloga,* promulgated in the eighth century, after Christianity had a longer time in which to make itself felt, the marks of that faith are even more evident. References to the Scriptures for confirmation for legal principles are numerous, every concubine was made a wife, and punishment for fornication, formerly left to the Church, was included. In the *Basilics,* issued in the latter part of the ninth century, Christianity is still more prominent. The first book is devoted to the Holy Trinity and the Catholic faith, and three books are given to ecclesiastical law.

In the third place, the Christian impress on Byzantine architecture and art was profound and creative. Byzantine architecture had its most glorious expression in Saint Sophia, built, as we have seen, at the command of Justinian. It embodied a pattern which appears to have had one of its roots in the churches in Syria, Mesopotamia, and Armenia and which was developed primarily for the purposes of Christian worship. Much of pre-Christian art persisted, including pagan themes, but the mosaics and frescoes for which Byzantine churches are famous were inspired primarily by Christ, his mother, and Christian saints and stories. Manuscripts were illuminated, often with Christian scenes.

Byzantine literature was to a large degree religious and concerned itself with Christian subjects. Theology, the devotional life, hymns, lives of the saints, and sermons were obviously from Christian sources and made up a large proportion of Byzantine libraries. The hymns of Romanos of the sixth century, of Andrew of Crete of the seventh and eighth centuries, and of John of Damascus are especially memorable. Romanos developed the form of hymn which became characteristic of the Byzantine Church.

The effects of Christianity in individual lives were marked and varied. We have seen it in a few outstanding figures, some of them Patriarchs and others of them monks. Always it is difficult to measure precisely. Perhaps it is best observed in the ideals portrayed in the biographies of those who were regarded as saints. Even when men did not conform to them these standards reveal what was believed to be Christian.

We must frankly recognize, however, that Byzantine culture fell far short of the full realization of the new life stressed by Christ. There was much study of the pre-Christian Greek philosophers and many of the Byzantine scholars were basically pagan with only a superficial and quite perfunctory conformity with the official Christianity. Something of a revival of classical studies came in the ninth and tenth centuries, and this in spite of the opposition of monks who condemned it as a reversion to heathenism and associated it with the iconoclasm which was so repugnant to them. The centuries-long absorption with doctrine controversy led to an emphasis upon orthodoxy in intellectual belief and verbal profession, but tended to belittle ethical practice. Constantinople was a commercial city and its inhabitants were noted for suavity and a trickery in trade which their professed faith did little to amend. There was also much of perfidy and cruelty. Now and again an ascetic or a Patriarch would admonish an Emperor not to take life, but this seems to have had little effect upon the behaviour of the rulers or their officials.

Yet not all teaching and preaching was purely doctrinal. In the writings of the period we come across emphasis upon following the example of Christ in gentleness, humility, pardoning the sinner, not repaying evil for evil, and forgiving one's enemies. Theodore of Studius taught that the true Christian is a copy or impression of Christ. Here and there, too, comes a gleam in an individual in high ecclesiastical position. Thus, at the time of the Byzantine-Persian wars of the early years of the seventh century, the Catholic Patriarch of Alexandria was John, who was known as the Almsgiver. From an eminent family in Cyprus, a devout layman whose wife and children had died, he had been chosen for the post at the desire of the Emperor Heraclius. A prelate who refused compromising presents, he lived simply, almost austerely, and devoted the revenues of his see chiefly to the poor and to the refugees from the Persian conquest of Palestine. He humbly sought reconciliation with one of his clergy who had become alienated from him, endeavoured to enforce uniformity in weights and measures in that commercial city where variable standards had made for much dishonesty, and increased the salaries of his stewards to render it unnecessary for them to eke out their stipends by receiving bribes. The fact that his biography, recounting his deeds of virtue, could be written in popular literary style and have a wide circulation is evidence that when such a life appeared it was recognized as Christian and was held up for emulation. Presumably to every record of one such individual which has been preserved, there were hundreds, perhaps thousands of lives which bore the impress of Christ which have not left any written evidence of their existence.

SELECTED BIBLIOGRAPHY

GENERAL WORKS WHICH INCLUDE IMPORTANT SECTIONS OF THE RELIGIOUS ASPECTS OF BYZANTINE HISTORY

H. H. Baynes and H. St. L. B. Moss, editors, *Byzantium. An Introduction to East Roman Civilization* (Oxford, The Clarendon Press, 1948, pp. xxxi, 436). Chapters by several experts, an extensive bibliography, and a sheaf of illustrations.

J. B. Bury, *History of the Later Roman Empire from the Death of Theodosius I to the Death of Justinian* (A.D. 395 to A.D. 565). Vol. II (London, Macmillan & Co.,

1923, pp. lx, 494). Covers the sixth century to the death of Justinian. By a master of the subject.

J. B. Bury, *A History of the Eastern Roman Empire from the Fall of Irene to the Accession of Basil I* (A.D. *802–867*) (London, Macmillan & Co., 1912, pp. xv, 530). By the same master hand as the above.

A. A. Vasiliev, *History of the Byzantine Empire. Vol. I, From Constantine the Great to the Epoch of the Crusades* (A.D. *1081*) (*University of Wisconsin Studies in the Social Sciences and History, Number 13,* Madison, 1928, pp. 457). An excellent summary, especially important for its use of Russian works.

A. A. Vasiliev, *Justin the First. An Introduction to the Epoch of Justinian the Great* (Harvard University Press, 1950, pp. viii, 439). Contains an important chapter on Justin's religious policy.

SOURCES

The writings of several of the important figures of the period are in the multi-volume J. P. Migne, *Patrologiæ . . . Græca.* For instance, those of Theodore of Studius comprise Vol. 99 and those of Photius fill Vols. 101, 102, 103, and part of 104. The Greek text is given with a Latin translation.

SPECIALIZED WORKS ON VARIOUS ASPECTS OF THE STORY

E. Dawes and N. H. Baynes, *Three Byzantine Saints. Contemporary Biographies Translated from the Greek* (Oxford, Basil Blackwell, 1948, pp. xiv, 275). Not only translations illustrating Byzantine popular Christianity, but also excellent introductions.

F. Dvornik, *Les Slaves, Byzance et Rome au IXe Siècle* (Paris, Ancienne Honoré Champion, 1926, pp. v, 360). Based on a careful study of the sources.

F. Dvornik, *The Photian Schism. History and Legend* (Cambridge University Press, 1948, pp. xiv, 504). A very important detailed critical study.

G. Every, *The Byzantine Patriarchate, 451–1204* (London, Society for Promoting Christian Knowledge, 1947, pp. 212). An excellent survey, especially good on relations with Rome.

A. Gardner, *Theodore of Studium. His Life and Times* (London, Edward Arnold, 1905, pp. xiii, 284). Carefully done.

C. J. Hefele, *A History of the Councils of the Church. Volume IV* (A.D. *451 to* A.D. *680*), translated by W. R. Clark (Edinburgh, T. & T. Clark, 1895, pp. x, 498). Standard on the Fifth Ecumenical Council, Constantinople 553, and the events immediately before and after.

K. S. Latourette, *A History of the Expansion of Christianity. Volume II, The Thousand Years of Uncertainty,* pp. 158–166, 223–249, 286–307 (New York, Harper & Brothers, 1938).

M. Spinka, *A History of Christianity in the Balkans. A Study of the Spread of Byzantine Culture among the Slavs* (Chicago, The American Society of Church History, 1933, pp. 202). Thorough and competent.

Chapter XII

THE SMALLER EASTERN CHURCHES

We have repeatedly noticed the existence of churches which had broken away from the Catholic Church and had ceased to be in communion with it. Until well after the year 950, indeed until the sixteenth century, many more of these were to be found in the East than in the West. Some of these bodies completely died out and we have only fragmentary information about them. Most of that which has reached us has come down from their critics. Such were the Paulicians. Some of the movements which have disappeared differed radically from the Catholic Church not only in doctrine but also in forms of worship and in organization. However, several of the dissident bodies have survived into our own day, although with greatly diminished numbers. As we have suggested, they separated from the Catholic Church ostensibly on questions of doctrine but in reality as much from regional, national, or racial opposition to the dominance of the Byzantine Empire and the Greeks as on creedal grounds. At the outset they were larger than the more drastic dissenters. Beginning with the seventh century, all had to face Islam. Sooner or later, although for some not until after 950, almost all the territories in which they existed were subjugated by Moslems. Identified with national or racial units, they held out against the politically dominant Islam. However, eventually all dwindled in numbers and today none is as strong as it was in the era with which this chapter deals. All that have survived have preserved, with variations, the structure and forms of worship which were theirs before they separated from the Catholic Church. All have a distinct clergy with the main orders of priests and bishops. All have monks and monasteries. All have baptism and the Eucharist, and the latter is usually observed with an elaborate liturgy. Each has its creed. Each regards itself as preserving the Gospel in its purity and looks upon other churches as heretical.

In several of the lands in which these bodies enrolled the majority of those bearing the Christian name, the Catholics were to be found under their own clergy but as minorities for whom a customary designation was Melchite.

There were, as we have seen, "Melchite" or Catholic Patriarchs of Jerusalem, Antioch, and Alexandria.

It was a divided Church which faced the expanding and dominant Islam and the common danger from that rival faith did not bring its severed branches together. Indeed, by removing the common bond of political unity under a professedly Christian state, the Byzantine continuation of the Roman Empire, the Arab conquests led to an accentuation of the gulfs which kept the bodies apart. In Baghdad, for instance, the capital of the Abbasid Caliphs, there were Nestorian, Jacobite, and Melchite communities. There resided the Catholicos or Patriarch of the Nestorians. On at least one occasion when the Melchite Patriarch of Antioch appointed a metropolitan for the Melchites in Baghdad, the Nestorian Catholicos strongly objected to the action as an infringement on his see. But the Jacobites also had a bishop there.

During the earlier centuries of the period from A.D. 500 to A.D. 950, even after the Arab conquests, several of these churches displayed geographic expansion. By A.D. 950, however, and this becomes one reason for fixing that year as the terminal date of the era of the great recession, almost all and perhaps all were losing ground.

We must now take up the chief of these churches one by one and say something of their history. At best we can give them only brief mention. That is partly because the records of some of them are not available to us, but chiefly because, even as early as this period, the main stream of Christianity as measured by inner vitality and the effect upon mankind as a whole did not flow through them. We will begin in the south-west of the areas in which they were present and move northward and eastward.

Monophysites of Egypt, Nubia, and Ethiopia

We have already had occasion to note the winning of the peoples of Egypt to Christianity. We have seen that the faith seems first to have found rootage in Alexandria in the Greek-speaking elements of that cosmopolitan Hellenistic city and that the head of its Christian community became one of the chief patriarchs in the Catholic Church. We have noted that before the end of the fifth century the faith became rooted among the native Egyptian stock and in time was the dominant religion of the land. To facilitate the integration of the faith in the lives of the masses the Scriptures were translated and other Christian literature was prepared in the vernacular and the services of the Church were carried on in that tongue. We have remarked, too, that this Coptic population followed its leaders in refusing to accept the decisions of the Council of Chalcedon and held to Monophysite views. Monophysites by no means entirely agreed among themselves, and their dissensions, theological and personal, troubled the Coptic Church, but opposition to the Chalcedonian theology was associated with nationalistic resistance to Byzantine rule and in general only the minority, Greeks and those loyal to the Emperor, held to the Catholic faith. On the eve of the Arab conquest the imperial government, represented by the Melchite Patriarch, was taking severe measures to suppress Monophysitism.

At the outset the Arab victories brought relief to the Coptic Christians, for the latter were freed from persecution by Byzantine officials. The Arabs tolerated all the varieties of Christianity and prevented the Copts from taking vengeance on the Catholics. Under Arab rule, therefore, both Copts and Melchites continued. To be sure, Christians were placed under the disabilities which we have already noted as general under the Moslem Arabs, including a discriminatory tax. Within a generation of the conquest a large proportion of the Christian population, both Coptic and Melchite, went over to Islam. Yet Arabs employed many Christians in the government. They utilized Christian artists and architects. Indeed, what we often call Arab architecture seems to have been at least in part the creation of these Christian employees.

As the years passed, Moslem restrictions on Christians were tightened. Early in the eighth century additional financial burdens were placed on the Christians and in that same century persecutions were instituted which led to the apostasy of many, even of several of the bishops, and which were countered by futile revolts that were sternly suppressed. By at least the tenth century Christians were forbidden to attempt to convert Moslems, to marry Moslem women, to speak disparagingly of the Prophet or the Koran, to display crosses, to ring church bells or in other ways to obtrude their faith on Moslems, to erect houses higher than those of Moslems, to ride thoroughbred horses, or to drink wine in public or to allow swine to be seen, since both of these were abhorrent to good Moslems. Now and again Christians won converts from Islam, but such defections from the dominant faith were usually visited with severe penalties.

Yet Christianity persisted. Monasteries, of which Egypt had been the chief early centre, continued and were the main strongholds of the faith. From them, as was general in the Eastern Churches, the bishops were recruited. Although, in their resistance to Islam, the churches tended to hold to the Coptic language in their services, even when Arabic became the vernacular of the masses, some Christian literature was prepared in the latter tongue.

We have noted how, from Egypt, beginning chiefly in the sixth century, the Christian faith spread southward into Nubia, roughly the present Sudan, and became very strong, apparently the prevailing faith in that region. Naturally the dominant form of Nubian Christianity was that of Egypt, Monophysite.

We have also seen that Ethiopia, which we associate with the present Abyssinia, had Christian communities before the end of the fifth century. Early in the sixth century an Ethiopian prince led an expedition to South-western Arabia which had as at least one of its objects the relief of Christians who were being persecuted by rulers of Jewish faith. In the sixth and seventh centuries the Ethiopian Church continued to prosper and was in close touch with the Coptic Church and its monasteries. From the seventh to the thirteenth century we know little of the history of Ethiopian Christianity. There were attacks by pagans and Moslem Arabs and in the tenth century a princess who was zealous for Judaism instituted a severe persecution. Yet the Church lived on, obviously Monophysite.

Syrian Monophysites

We need add little to what has already been said about Monophysitism in Syria. Jacob Baradæus was active in spreading it, but it did not owe its strength primarily to him. Syrian Jacobites travelled eastward as merchants and perhaps to escape persecution by the Catholic Byzantine rulers. Presumably they were the chief means of the wide extension of that form of the faith as the religion of some of the Christian minorities in Mesopotamia and east of that region. They had an ecclesiastical organization in Persia, but were not as numerous there as the Nestorians.

Armenian (Gregorian) Christianity

Armenia, won to Christianity in the third century chiefly through the efforts of Gregory the Illuminator, owed much of its cohesion to that faith. Christianity was the national religion and had a national organization. A border state, between the two great empires of the Romans and the Zoroastrian Sassanid Persians and then between the Byzantine successor of Rome and the Arab Caliphs, Armenia was repeatedly invaded and threatened by conquest from both sides. Inhabiting a rugged country, the Armenians relied for their independence upon their armies and the fortified hilltop strongholds of their nobility. The Sassanids succeeded in extending their suzerainty over the country, and in the fifth century, perhaps to ensure complete submission, attempted to force Zoroastrianism on the land. This led to revolt and late in the fifth century the Sassanian monarch gave up the effort to de-Christianize Armenia by force and granted religious liberty.

The Armenian Church held to the faith of Nicæa as against Arianism, but it rejected Chalcedon and remained Monophysite. The definite rupture with the Catholic Church was in 491. This may have been in part from the desire to preserve the independence of the land against Byzantine rule. Chalcedon was anathematized twice in the sixth century by synods of the Armenian Church, first in 524 or 527 and then in 552. In the latter part of the sixth century an occasional Armenian prelate conformed to the Catholic faith, but brought with him no large proportion of his flock. Late in the sixth century Persia was constrained to cede part of Armenia to the Byzantine Emperor Maurice. In the portion which he controlled, Maurice had a council of Armenian bishops called which gave its adherence to Chalcedon and named an Orthodox Catholicos, or head, of the Armenian Church. Since the bishops who were in the part of the country not under Byzantine control would not assent to this action, a schism took place. In general, the Armenians held to their Monophysitism and as a symbol of their political independence of Constantinople.

The coming of the Arabs meant a new threat to Armenian political and religious freedom. After fighting which lasted from 639 to 859 the Armenians granted the Arabs the same kind of suzerainty which the Sassanids had enjoyed. This permitted the Armenians a considerable degree of autonomy. In general, the Arabs conceded to the Armenians liberty to hold to their faith. Late in the seventh and early in the eighth century there were further Byzantine efforts to bring conformity with the Catholic Church, but for the most part the Armenians remained aloof and in 719 a national council again declared itself against the Chalcedonian position. The Christianity of Armenia differed in some of its practices from that of Constantinople. Its clergy were largely hereditary, perhaps going back for precedent to the hereditary priesthood of pagan days. In the mass it used wine unmixed with water. The Armenian Church had its own literature in the language of the country and made contributions in architecture which appear to be one source of the Byzantine ecclesiastical style. It had strong monasteries, prosperous schools, and distinctive art. It spread east of the Euphrates, largely through Armenian colonies and merchants.

NESTORIAN CHRISTIANITY AND ITS EASTWARD EXTENSION

The form of Christianity which had the widest geographic spread in this period was the one which is usually given the name Nestorian. To be sure, it did not win the official adherence of any important state and with the possible exception of a few tribes in Central Asia and perhaps an occasional section and city of the Tigris-Euphrates Valley was never more than the faith of a minority. Yet it had some important effects and its course is of great interest.

Nestorianism owed its prominence to the fact that it constituted the major church in the realms of the Persian monarchs and then of the Abbasid Caliphs. We have seen something of the early history of Christianity in the Persian realms, of its persecution, of the introduction of doctrines associated, perhaps mistakenly, with the name of Nestorius, and of the fashion in which separation from the Catholic Church occurred and a distinct organization was set up with its Patriarch or Catholicos, at the Persian capital, Seleucia-Ctesiphon.

In their structure and customs the Nestorians were very similar to the other Eastern Churches and seem not to have stressed in their teaching the differences in their beliefs about the relation of the human and divine in Christ. They had monasteries and in the period with which we are here concerned they insisted that the bishops and Catholicos must be unmarried. They had the Eucharist. They had images of Christ and of the saints and held in reverence the relics of martyrs and other outstanding Christians.

The coming of the Arabs brought the Nestorians some relief from the chronic and occasionally severe persecutions from which they had suffered under the Zoroastrian Sassanids. To be sure, they were required to pay a special head tax, as were other Christians in Moslem realms. From time to time, especially during wars with the Byzantine Empire, church buildings of Nestorians as well as of other Christans were destroyed, particularly those which had been erected contrary to the laws which forbade fresh construction. Yet many Nestorians were employed by the Arabs and were given high places in the Arab court. Some Christians were exempted from the head tax. During the first few generations of Arab rule, before the new masters had acquired the arts of the high civilization in which they had settled, the Nestorians provided accountants for the government, and physicians, astrologers, and philosophers for the realm. Nestorians were prominent as bankers and merchants. As we have more than once noted, it was Christians who first translated into Arabic some of the works of the ancient Greek philosophers. Much that the Christians of Western Europe were later to learn from the Moslem Arabs had first been taught the latter by Nestorians.

The Nestorians engaged in extensive missionary activity. In spite of prohibitory laws they won numbers of converts from the Persian Zoroastrians, more than they were later to gain from the Moslem Arabs. South and East of the Caspian, in Central Asia, they had many communities and missionaries. There were Nestorian churches and bishops and even metropolitans in some of the caravan cities of Central Asia, among them Merv, Herat, and Samarqand. Before the Arab conquests Christianity seems to have spread widely among the non-Christian peoples of this area, notably among the Turks and the Hephthalite Huns. Until the coming of Islam its chief rival in Central Asia appears to have been Manichæism. After the military advances of the Arabs, Islam became the major competitor, but the issue of the contest between the Cross and the Crescent was not decided until well after 950, when, as we are to see, the Cross lost.

Nestorian Christianity was planted in India. Our knowledge of how and when that was done is tantalizingly fragmentary. We know that there were Christians in India before the rise of the distinctive Nestorian beliefs and that these may have come through commercial contacts with the Christians of Mesopotamia, Syria, and Egypt. As we have said, tradition even ascribes the first Christian preaching to the Apostle Thomas. In the thirteenth and fourteenth centuries travellers from Western Europe found well established Christian communities on the coasts of South India and Ceylon. The more detailed reports of Western Europeans of the sixteenth century make it clear that the ecclesiastical language of these communities was Syriac, indicating that they had been nourished and perhaps planted by Syriac-using peoples, and their church connexion was with the Nestorians of Mesopotamia. Inscriptions concerning Christians found in South India dating from the seventh into the ninth century are in Pahlavi, or Middle Persian. All of this seems to point to the growth and perhaps the introduction of Christianity in India through contacts, from the sixth century onward, with the Christians, primarily Nestorians, of Persia, Mesopotamia, and Syria. From what we know of the history of trade, it is natural to assume that the contacts were made largely through commerce, for the Christian communities were on or near the coast and in or near cities and from as far back as pre-Christian times there had been maritime trade between India and the lands to the west. The Nestorian communities in India, however, seem not to have been primarily the descendants of immigrants, but to have been of Indian stocks. This would appear to point either to extensive intermarriage of Christian immigrants with indigenous peoples or to active missions as their source, probably in association with the Christian mercantile communities.

It was through Nestorians that Christianity was introduced to China. The year of the first known coming of Christianity to that vast land was 635. At that time the T'ang dynasty had recently risen to power and T'ai Tsung, the ablest monarch of that line, was on the throne. China was entering on one of the glorious epochs of its history and for two centuries or more was the most powerful and perhaps the wealthiest realm on the planet, rivalled only by the Arab Empire, and that did not long remain as united as did China. The first missionary, A-lo-pên, came to the capital, Ch'ang-an, the present Hsianfu. Ch'ang-an, possibly the largest city in the world of that day, attracted representatives of many races and faiths. T'ai Tsung is said to have given A-lo-pên a cordial welcome and, after he had examined translations of the books which the latter brought with him, to have ordered the preaching of their contents. He may have done this because he was fairly tolerant of all religions. In succeeding years Christian monasteries were founded in several centres, Christian literature in Chinese was produced, and a metropolitanate was created for

China. Some converts were won, but the core of the Christian communities and perhaps their membership was predominantly foreign. Buddhism, then in its heyday in China, Taoism, and a reviving Confucianism were the prevailing religious systems of the Empire. Christians were a very small minority, perhaps not as numerous as Moslems, Manichæans, or Zoroastrians. Late in the ninth century there were still Christians in China, but an imperial edict of 845 which was directed primarily against the Buddhists and which also included Christians in its proscription seems to have brought a sharp reduction in the numbers of the latter. The disorders which accompanied the end of the T'ang dynasty late in the ninth and early in the tenth century may have contributed to a further decline. Monks sent in 980 to put the Church in order could find no traces of Christians in the land.

SUMMARY COMMENT

We must note that in the vast area covered by this brief chapter and especially in Mesopotamia, Syria, Palestine, and Egypt, we appear to see one of the striking failures of Christianity. Here was a major reverse, indeed, the major territorial reverse of all the history of the faith. Here Christ had lived, died, and risen again. Here the Gospel was first preached, here the original Christian churches came into being, and here the name Christian was coined. Here were three of the five great patriarchal sees of the Catholic Church—Jerusalem, Antioch, and Alexandria—and the earliest creative theological thinking. It was here that monasticism arose, with its daring and resolute dream of the complete attainment of the Christian ideal. Yet here Christians were more divided than anywhere else in the first thousand years of the faith and fell further short of the ideal of the unity of love than elsewhere. In some areas the majority adopted the Christian name but much of this was superficial and could not stand the test of adversity. When Islam came, borne by conquering Arabs, the churches shrank and slowly became fossilized and sterile. To be sure, some converts were made to the east of the Arab domains, notably by the Nestorians, but they were usually small minorities. Yet more than any other religion in Islam-dominated lands, Christianity displayed the ability to survive and to reach out into new areas and propagate itself.

SELECTED BIBLIOGRAPHY

W. F. Adeney, *The Greek and Eastern Churches* (New York, Charles Scribner's Sons, 1928 [preface 1908], pp. xiv, 634). A fairly good survey.

W. Barthold, *Zur Geschichte des Christentums in Mittel-Asien bis zur mongolischen Eroberung. Berichtige und vermerhte deutsche Bearbeitung nach dem rus-*

sischen Original herausgegeben von Dr. Rudolf Stübe (Tübingen, J. C. B. Mohr, 1901, pp. vii, 74). Excellent.

L. E. Browne, *The Eclipse of Christianity in Asia from the Time of Mohammed till the Fourteenth Century* (Cambridge University Press, 1933, pp. 198). Based upon extensive reading in the sources and secondary works.

L. Duchesne, *Les Missions Chrétiennes au Sud de l'Empire Romain* (Ecole Française de Rome, *Mélanges d'Archeologie et d'Histoire,* 1896, pp. 79–122).

J. Labourt, *Le Christianisme dans L'Empire Perse sous la Dynastie Sassanide* (Paris, Librairie Victor Lecoffre, 1904, pp. xix, 372). A standard work.

A. Mingana, *The Early Spread of Christianity in Central Asia and the Far East: A New Document* (Manchester University Press, 1925, pp. 80).

A. Mingana, *The Early Spread of Christianity in India* (Manchester University Press, 1926, pp. 82).

A. C. Moule, *Christians in China before the Year 1550* (London, Society for Promoting Christian Knowledge, 1930, pp. xvi, 293). Translations of all the known sources, with notes.

E. Sachau, *Zur Ausbreitung des Christentums in Asien* (*Abhandlungen der preuss. Ak. der Wissenschaften, phil. hist. Klasse,* 1919, pp. 1–80). A scholarly summary.

W. A. Wigram, *An Introduction to the History of the Assyrian Church or the Church of the Sassanid Persian Empire 100–640 A.D.* (London, Society for Promoting Christian Knowledge, 1910, pp. 318). By an English missionary.

Chapter XIII

THE COURSE IN WESTERN EUROPE

As we move into the West we find a story which in some significant ways differs from that in the East. Here the disintegration of the Roman Empire began earlier than it did in the East and was much more marked than in the areas which remained under the Eastern continuation of that realm, the Byzantine Empire. Yet in the West Christianity eventually most strikingly proved its vitality. From the West it had its broadest geographic expansion, in the West arose the large majority of the vigorous new movements after the ninth century, and from the West came the widest and deepest influences upon mankind as a whole.

Why was this? How are we to account for the fact that in the region in which the collapse of the Empire with whose life Christianity had become so closely interrelated first became most apparent and where the earliest sweeping conquests by invaders occurred, Christianity displayed not only its most pronounced recovery but also its greatest vigour? Had an intelligent traveller from China or India journeyed through the Mediterranean world at the end of the sixth century he probably would have given a quite contrary forecast and would have looked for the revival and the renewed spread of Christianity, if they came at all, from the East. Here, with the exception of Rome, were all the most ancient and the strongest churches. Here the existing patterns of life had been far less disturbed. Here the larger part of the theological thinking and discussion had taken place and was still in progress. Here monasticism, that potent new movement in protest against the growing laxity of life in the Church, had arisen and had shown its most extensive development.

The answers to this question must be in part conjectural. Yet some factors can be pointed to as offering possible clues. One of these seems to have been that the collapse of the Empire freed Christianity from the restrictions placed on it by its close association with that regime and gave greater opportunity for its inherent genius to express itself than was true in the East, where the Roman state persisted.

Nearly allied to this factor is a second. The threat to Christianity in the West brought by the disintegration of the Empire and the inroads of invaders, while serious, was not overwhelming. Indeed, it was not as ominous as in much of the East. Situated as it was at the extreme tip of Eurasia, Western Europe was either not reached by many of the invasions which the East had to meet, arising as most of them did from the heartland of the continent, or, in the case of the Arabs, in the south-east, or it had to face them only after they had spent their main force. Thus the invasion which was most disastrous for the Christianity of the East, that of the Arabs, bringing with it a new faith, Islam, against which few counter gains have been made by Christianity or any other religion, was rolled back soon after it crossed the Pyrenees and never overwhelmed the churches of Gaul, the Iberian Peninsula, or Sicily to the extent that it did those nearer Arabia. Eventually the churches of these areas reëmerged and won or expelled all Moslems. The Bulgars, the Mongols, and the Turks penetrated effectively only to the eastern edges of Western Europe. What might have been the future of Christianity in Western Europe had invasions continued may be surmised from the fact that not until the last, that of the Scandinavians, had ended, did the recession cease which they helped bring and the resurging vitality emerge which issued in fresh advance. In contrast with the East where the major incursion, that of the Moslem Arabs, brought with it a "high" religion, Islam, all the invasions of the West were either by "barbarians" who were already in part converts to Christianity or who had more nearly "primitive" religions. It is a generalization borne out by universal human experience that a "primitive" religion yields more readily to a "high" religion than does a "high" religion to another "high" religion. Christianity won back none of the ground lost by it in the East to Islam, but, in contrast, it not only regained all of the territory in the West which it lost but pressed out beyond its former frontiers and gathered into its fold pagan peoples of "primitive" faiths and cultures.

THE MAIN FEATURES OF THE WESTERN EUROPE IN WHICH CHRISTIANITY WAS SET (A.D. 500–A.D. 950)

The first few generations after the fifth century witnessed a progressive disintegration of what remained of the Roman Empire and of Græco-Roman civilization in the West. The invaders established themselves in various parts of the Roman domains. At the outset their rulers usually prized Roman titles conferred on them by the Emperors and regarded themselves as still within the Empire. Actually, however, they were heads of kingdoms which for most practical purposes were independent. In Italy the Ostrogoths were masters of much of the country from the latter part of the fifth century until Justinian's generals overthrew them about the middle of the sixth century. Then came the Lombards who founded a kingdom which survived until 774. For centuries after the downfall of that kingdom Lombard nobles ruled parts of Italy. The Visigoths controlled much of the Iberian Peninsula until, in the eighth century, they gave way to the Arabs. The Burgundians were in the Rhone Valley. Germanic folk, mostly Angles and Saxons, colonized Britain and founded a number of small states.

The Franks proved to be the major power. At the outset of the sixth century they were in control of much of Gaul, especially its northern portions, and of a large part of the Rhine Valley. The ruling line, the most prominent of whom was Clovis, of whose conversion in 496 we have spoken, were known as the Merovingians. In the first half of the seventh century the authority of the Merovingians declined and that of local magnates increased. In the fore part of the eighth century the Merovingians, now become purely nominal monarchs, *rois fainéants,* were gradually replaced by a new dynasty, the Carolingians. The Carolingians had emerged in the seventh century. Near the close of that century Pepin (or Pippin) of Heristal became the virtual ruler. Charles Martel, his illegitimate son who succeeded him, exercised even more power and in 732 won lasting fame by checking the Arab advance into Gaul at the decisive battle near Tours. In 751 a son of Charles Martel, Pepin (or Pippin) the Short was crowned King of the Franks and relegated the last of the Merovingians to a monastery. Pepin the Short (died 768) was succeeded by his son, another Charles, better known as Charles the Great or Charlemagne (742–814), who brought the power of his house to its apex and was crowned Roman Emperor on Christmas Day, 800. Under the Carolingians and especially under Charlemagne the Frankish state reached its height. Compared with the Chinese Empire under the contemporary T'ang dynasty it was a small affair. Yet through it, as we are to see, Christianity displayed a new surge of life.

After Charlemagne the Frankish power declined. Although for a time it was still formidable, by the end of the ninth century the Carolingians, with whom it was closely allied, had ceased to be of major importance in the West and their disintegration left a power vacuum which was not to be filled until the second half of the tenth century. The invasions of the Scandinavians—the Northmen or Vikings—added to the confusion and brought civilization in Western Europe to a further low ebb.

Parallel with the political changes came other profound alterations in the life of Western Europe. The chronic disorder made for a decline in commerce and industry. The Roman roads fell into disrepair. Travel, whether by land or sea, was rendered perilous by robbers, either singly or in bands. Cities and towns dwindled in population and wealth. Education and the arts languished.

Crude agriculture became the main productive occupation and wealth was chiefly in land. Feudalism began to emerge, a structure by which power became fragmented into hundreds of units, large and small, and the authority of the kings suffered. Warriors were the rulers and the chief occupation of the aristocracy was fighting.

In spite of the advantages which geographic location gave it over the branches of the faith in the lands farther east, could the Christianity of the West seize the opportunity? Could it win these roistering warrior tribesmen even to a nominal allegiance? If it gained their professed adherence, could it bring them to an understanding of the Gospel and to conformity with it? Could that church which, in the course of drawing into its ample fold the majority of those bearing the Roman name, had compromised with non-Christian living, preserve enough vitality really to propagate the Gospel? Here was the challenge. It was not fully met. Perhaps, given the nature of man and of the Gospel, it could not be. Yet to an amazing degree Christianity rose to it and had a more profound effect upon the peoples of Western Europe and their culture than it had exerted upon the Roman Empire in the first five centuries.

The General Course of Christianity in Western Europe

For a time the quality of Christian living declined and the very existence of Christianity was threatened. The danger was not the immediate disappearance of a formal profession of that religion. Indeed, as we are to see, the majority of the pagan invaders were fairly quickly brought to an outward adoption of Christianity and the faith was even carried beyond what, in the year 500, had been its northern borders. The peril, rather, was the progressive denaturing of what bore the Christian name by secularization and corruption of many kinds. The decline was not sudden nor was it continuous. Numerous attempts were made to stem the trend, many individuals and groups were bright gleams in the night, and here and there partial recovery was effected. Yet by the middle of the tenth century Christianity in Western Europe was at a lower ebb than it was ever again to be.

As we attempt to picture a scene which has many details and which is very confusing, we can best do it by broad strokes, bringing out some of the main features and sketching in several of the more prominent individuals who figured in it.

The Victory of the Catholic Church over Arianism

One of the features which marked the earlier portions of these centuries was the disappearance of Arian Christianity and the bringing into the Catholic

Church of those who had professed it. Arianism had been the form of Christianity which had won a large proportion of the Germanic peoples who had settled in the Roman Empire. This was true of most of the Goths, including the Ostrogoths who ruled in much of Italy and the Visigoths who were dominant in Spain. In so far as they were Christians, the majority of the Lombards who followed the Ostrogoths as masters of much of Italy were Arians. Many of the Burgundians were of that faith. So were a large proportion of the Vandals who controlled North Africa. The Arians regarded themselves as the true Christians and their churches as the Catholic Church. However, the overwhelming majority of the Latinized Roman provincials over whom the invaders ruled were loyal to Nicæa. It was to be expected that the invaders, a minority, although the ruling minority, and of more nearly "primitive" culture, would eventually conform to the language, manners, and customs of the majority. As they did so, quite understandably they accepted Nicene Catholic Christianity.

By the end of the seventh century most of the Arian Lombards had become Catholics. In Spain the transition was earlier. Recared, the Visigothic king, near the end of the sixth century apparently decided that his realm must have one religion and that that had best be the faith of the majority. Accordingly, at a synod at Toledo he formally became a Catholic and was quickly followed by a number of Arian bishops and nobles. In Gaul the Arians among the Burgundians were beginning to turn Catholic before the end of the sixth century. The fact that Clovis, the ruler of the people who became dominant in Gaul, accepted the Nicene rather than the Arian form of the faith, was decisive in the victory of the Catholic Church in that area. The Goths who had ruled in the south of Gaul were conquered by the Franks and that meant the elimination of their Arianism. The reconquest of North Africa by the Romans under Justinian in the first half of the sixth century made for the triumph of the Catholic Church in that region.

The disappearance of Arianism facilitated the religious and cultural unity in Western Europe. Had the Arians prevailed or even persisted as a strong factor with their national churches and lack of any generally acknowledged centre of orthodoxy and administration such as the Catholics possessed in Rome, that all pervasive cohesion which the Catholic Church gave to an otherwise divided Europe might not have been achieved.

THE EMERGENCE OF WESTERN FORMS OF MONASTICISM

One of the major features of the Europe of these centuries was the extensive spread of monasticism and the development of forms of that movement peculiar to the West.

An important figure was Cassiodorus. Born late in the fifth century, his long life spanned most of the sixth century. Of noble ancestors from Antioch but a native of Italy, he served as a high official under the Ostrogoths. In his later years, when the armies of Justinian had overthrown the Ostrogothic kingdom, Cassiodorus retired to his estates in the south of Italy and there founded two monasteries. One was for those who wished to follow a solitary, ascetic life. The other he made a house of learning. He had it pleasantly equipped, collected for it a library of theology and classical literature, and encouraged the transcription of existing books and the composition of new ones. He himself wrote and compiled a number of works. In an age in which wars were bringing the neglect of learning, he strove to create a centre for the study and propagation under Christian auspices of all products of the human mind. His example may have helped to inspire scholarly pursuits in other monasteries. Certainly some of his writings were widely used in later centuries.

More influential than Cassiodorus was Ireland. Remote in its western sea, Ireland was spared most of the invasions of the sixth, seventh, and eighth centuries. Not until the Northmen came was it to suffer as severely as the rest of Western Europe. Between the time of Patrick and the sixth century we know little of the history of Christianity in the island. When our information again begins to be dependable, we see an Ireland which was the home of a vigorous monasticism. The Church did not have the kind of territorial diocesan organization under the administration of bishops which, influenced by the forms of civil government, prevailed in areas which had been in the Roman Empire. In creed, the Irish Church was in accord with the Catholic faith. In some particulars, especially the date for celebrating Easter and the form of the tonsure, it differed from the customs sponsored by Rome, but in theology it was orthodox. In contrast with that of the continent, the Christianity of Ireland was organized around the monastery. This may have been because of the prominence of the tribe in Ireland and a partial reproduction of it in the Church, where the monasteries may have been a Christian substitute for it. Whatever the reason, in Ireland monasticism was dominant. The important administrative officers were the abbots. Unless, as was sometimes the case, the abbot was also a bishop, the bishop's only distinctive function was that of ordination.

Irish monasteries were centres of learning. The chief subject of study was the Scriptures. Latin was the main language through which this was carried on, and some of the works of Latin Christian scholars were also cherished. Much attention was paid to the copying of manuscripts and their illumination.

An outstanding feature of Irish monasticism, one which we shall have occasion to note more at length later, was the migration of Irish monks to other countries. What moved them we cannot certainly know. Ostensibly they went for the "love of God," "in order to win the heavenly fatherland," "for the love of the name of Christ," and after the example of Abraham who, at the divine call, left his country and his kindred for a strange land. Compounded with this religious urge may also have been a desire to see other peoples, a kind of *wanderlust*.

The Irish *peregrini* went far. They voyaged to the Orkneys, the Faroes, the rough coasts of Scotland, and perhaps even to Iceland. They were in the forests of Germany, the rugged hills of Gaul, the foothills of the Alps, the valleys of the Rhine and the Danube, and the cities and remote valleys of Italy. Sometimes they went singly and became hermits. Often they formed groups, frequently of thirteen in imitation of Christ and the apostles. Some of them were missionaries to pagans. Others sought to elevate the morals of the nominally Christian populations near whom they settled. Often they were an irritation to the churchmen of the Continent, for they did not readily fit into the diocesan pattern and their "wandering bishops" and their individualistic hermits did not prove amenable to customary ecclesiastical discipline. Yet they were numerous and were a characteristic feature of Western Europe through most of the period from 500 to 950. Here was an extensive movement of a people, akin to the migrations which were flooding Europe, but transformed by a Christian purpose.

Much more widely influential than Cassiodorus and than even the Irish monks was Benedict of Nursia. A contemporary of Cassiodorus, he also was an Italian. He was born about the year 480 at Nursia, among the Apennines northeast of Rome, and was of good family. As a youth he went to Rome to study, but the scholastic life held no attractions for him. He was distressed and disgusted by the vices and frivolities of the city, and, when about fifteen or twenty years of age, he took up the life of the hermit. Fame began to come and the monks of a neighbouring monastery urged him to become their abbot. He proved too strict for them and returned to his hermit's routine. High and low sought him, eager to share with him what was deemed the complete Christian life, or brought their sons to have him train them in it. There, at Subiaco, up a valley east of Rome, twelve monasteries arose, each with twelve monks and a superior. About 528 or 529, when he was not far from fifty years of age, Benedict moved to Monte Cassino, not quite half way between Naples and Rome, and there, on its summit, destroying a pagan temple where worship to Apollo was still maintained, he established a monastery. The monastery grew and, although he remained a layman, bishops and priests as well as the laity came to consult him. He seemed to carry with him an atmosphere of quiet peace. He died some time after 542, preceded shortly by the twin sister who had also adopted the monastic life and lived in a convent not far from his own.

Benedict's great contribution was the rule which he gave to his monastery. In devising it he learned what he could from predecessors, especially Basil of Cæsarea but also John Cassian, founder of a famous monastery near Marseilles, and other monks. However, he was not a slavish borrower, for his rule bears indelibly the mark of his own experience as monk and abbot. He was aware of the various kinds of monks, some anchorites, some wanderers, some living by twos and threes but without wise guidance. He believed the best form of the life of a monk to be the cenobitic, that of the community, and it was for this that he devised his rule. In it he displayed that genius for order and administration which we associate with those who created and governed the Roman Empire.

That it was Benedict who had never had the experience of civil administration rather than the seasoned Roman statesman, Cassiodorus, who devised a rule which embodied the qualities which we regard as characteristic of Rome is surprising and seems to belie that comment. Yet Benedict, with his background of Roman culture and probably without at all being aware of the significance of what he was doing, worked out a monastic organization which stood the test of the centuries.

As Benedict envisaged it, the monastery was to be self-contained and self-supporting, with its fields and workshops. Over it was the abbot, chosen by the entire community. He was to have complete authority, but was to remember that his title meant father and that he was ultimately accountable to God. The monastery was to have other officers, especially if it were large—among them a prior (or provost), deans (each over ten monks), a cellarer, a novice-master, and a porter. Monks were to be admitted first for a novitiate of one year. After that time their decision was irrevocable. Upon entry the monk was to surrender all his property, either distributing it to the poor or giving it to the monastery. He was to think of nothing as being his own. The nobles and wealthy who brought their sons to be entered in the monasteries, even though they made large gifts to the foundation, were to expect no special favours. The ideal was a kind of Christian communism, like that of the early Christians in Jerusalem, whom Benedict cited for his precedent, where no one called anything his own, but all shared in the common stock.

The life was orderly but was not unduly severe and was probably more comfortable than was that of the great masses of the population. Clothing and meals were simple but adequate, and special provision was made for the ill, the aged, the very young, and those doing heavy manual labour. There was to be fasting at regular times, but this was not of the kind practised by the extreme ascetics whom we have met. Much weight was given to humility. Provision was made for various degrees of discipline, from private admonition to physical punishment, excommunication, and, as a last resort, expulsion. Idleness was declared "an enemy of the soul." The entire round of the twenty-four hours was provided for, with eight services, one every three hours, and with periods for sleep, including a rest early in the afternoon, for eating, and for labour. The labour might be in the fields or in the library, according to the aptitude of the monk. There was also time for directed and supervised reading and for meditation and private prayer. Silence was encouraged and was the rule at meals and after compline, the last of the services of the day. Joking and laughter were frowned upon. There was reading aloud at meals from religious books by those assigned to that function. Stress was placed on worship by the entire community and directions were given for the services. These were to include the Psalms, so that the whole of the Psalter was recited each week, reading from the Old and New Testaments with accepted commentaries on them, hymns, prayers, among them the Lord's Prayer, and the frequent use of the *Gloria,* the *kyrie eleison,* and the canticle *Benedictus.* Although hospitality was enjoined and practised, provision was made for keeping the monks from having more contact with the outside world than was absolutely necessary. There was a place for priests, for they were needed to say mass, but they were to obey the rule as fully as the lay monks.

The rule was wisely designed for a group of men of various ages living together in worship and in work for the cultivation of the full Christian life as that was conceived by the monk.

The rule of Benedict became standard in the West, probably because of its intrinsic worth. Pope Gregory the Great did much to give it popularity. It was taken to Britain by missionaries sent by Gregory from Rome and of whom we are to hear more in a moment. In the seventh century it began to gain in Gaul. Charlemagne admired it and furthered its adoption. By the latter part of the eighth century it was generally accepted. No central organization existed for its enforcement and to bring uniformity: each monastery was independent of every other. Modifications might and often were made in the rule by individual houses. Yet it became the model from which many other rules stemmed.

In an age of disorder the Benedictine monasteries were centres of quiet and orderly living, communities where prayer, work, and study were the custom, and that in a society where prayer was ignored or was regarded as magic to be practised for selfish ends, where work was despised as servile, where even princes were illiterate, and where war was chronic. Like other monastic establishments, Benedictine foundations tended to decline from the high ideals set by the rule. Many were heavily endowed and in numbers of them life became easy and at times scandalous. When awakenings occurred, they often took the form of a return to the rule or its modification in the direction of greater austerity. Even when the rule was strictly obeyed, the monasteries were self-centred and were not concerned with the salvation of the society about them, except to draw individuals from it into their fellowship. However, as we are to see, the missionaries of the Western Church were predominantly monks. It was chiefly through them, although often at the initiative and under the protection of lay princes, that the faith was carried beyond its existing frontiers. Later, moreover, monks of the Benedictine rule became prominent in the general life of the Church and of the community as a whole.

Even when the rule of Benedict was not adopted or where the full monastic way was not followed, the dream of Christian community life often made itself felt. It was seen, for example, in what were known as canons regular. A number of clergy attached to a particular church, perhaps a cathedral, would live together according to rule (*regula*). Not technically monks, these canons regular became a feature of the Catholic Church in the West. The parish churches to which they were attached were known, accordingly, as collegiate churches. The designation canon came from the term *vita canonica* which was given to this custom. The place in which the canons gathered for their official meetings was known as the *capitulam* or chapter, a name also used for the collective group of the canons. Augustine of Hippo had some such arrangement in his episcopal household. Further impetus was given to the development by Bishop Chrodegang of Metz not far from the year 760 and the custom spread under the encouragement of Charlemagne.

The Growing Power of the Church in an Age of Disorder

As the structure of the Roman Empire disintegrated, invasions multiplied, wars and disorder increased, and life and property became progressively unsafe, the Church stepped into the breach and took over some of the functions for which society had been accustomed to look to the state. It emerged as the protector of the weak, the poor, the widows, and the orphans. That was notably the case in Gaul. Here in the fifth and sixth centuries the bishops were largely recruited from the Gallo-Roman aristocracy. Drawn as they were from the wealthy, educated, Latinized provincials, they stood for the old order, but it was an order of comparative justice and stability in a day of an approach towards anarchy.

As time passed, in Western Europe, especially north of the Alps, bishops tended to become magnates not differing greatly from secular lords except in their titles and some of their functions. As the power of the central government declined and much of it passed into the hands of feudal lords, the Church, caught in the trends of the day, also in part conformed and its chief officials, notably its bishops, had their armies and bore arms. There were splendid exceptions, but we hear of bishops who were unchaste, gluttonous, and bibulous. Power of the secular kind entailed perils to true Christian living, and many there were who succumbed.

THE AUGMENTED POWER OF THE PAPACY AND GREGORY THE GREAT

In the general disorder, the Papacy, under some very able men, markedly increased its power and extended the geographical range of its authority. In principle, as we have seen, even before the year 500 its claims were sweeping. Whether those claims would be implemented depended upon the opportunity and upon the ability of the individuals in the Papal chair. The political disorders offered the challenge. Some Popes were weak and did not rise to the occasion. Indeed, as we are to see, towards the end of the period the Papacy fell victim for a time to the turbulence of the surrounding political scene and sank to an all-time low in its power. Yet it also had some very able and devoted men.

Of the Popes of this period the strongest was Gregory I, by common consent called the Great. Significantly, too, he was canonized by the Catholic Church and esteemed a saint, an exemplar of Christian faith and life. Occupying the throne of Peter from 590 to his death in 604, or for only fourteen years, he packed into that brief period a prodigious amount of work and achievement.

Gregory came from a prominent Roman house and had a Pope among his ancestors. The family was deeply religious. Three of his father's sisters dedicated themselves as virgins and two of them were eventually enrolled as saints. After his father's death his mother adopted the monastic life and later was canonized. Gregory was born about the year 540 and was given as good an education as the Rome of his day could provide. That city had been sacked again and again, it was greatly reduced in population, its aqueducts were no longer functioning, and many of the huge public buildings of imperial days were falling into ruins. Gregory knew no Greek and cared little for the classical pre-Christian Latin authors or for philosophy, astronomy, or mathematics. He early showed marked administrative ability and was appointed by the Emperor to head the civil administration of the city. Through the death of his father he inherited large wealth. Much of that wealth was in Sicily and with it he founded and endowed six monasteries on that island. He also turned his ancestral home in Rome into a monastery. The remainder of his fortune he gave to the poor. Whether he ever became technically a monk is in debate, but he was undoubtedly attracted to the monastery, frequented the one which he had founded in Rome, led an ascetic life, and was a warm admirer of Benedict. Indeed, most of our authentic information about the latter comes through him. The Pope appointed him one of the seven regionary deacons of the city, officers whose duty it was to look after the administration of alms. For six years he served in Constantinople as the Papal representative at the imperial court. When he arrived, Justinian had been dead for less than fifteen years, much of Italy, including Rome, was still in the Empire, and the Christological controversies had not yet been finally resolved. Always strictly and gravely orthodox, he was grieved by the large number of Monophysites who were separated from the Catholic Church. While in Constantinople he wrote voluminously in the clear but unadorned Latin which was characteristic of him. Returning to Rome about 585 or 586, he became secretary to the Pope.

In 590, through the popular acclaim of the clergy and people of Rome, Gregory was elected Pope. He was most reluctant to assume the duties of the office and is said to have written to Constantinople asking that the necessary imperial confirmation not be given. As Pope he faced a combination of problems which would have appalled and baffled a less able and resolute man, and he had to meet them under the handicap of physical frailty and recurrent attacks of indigestion, gout, and fever. His was the responsibility for seeing that the population of Rome was fed. Shortly before his accession the city had suffered from an inundation of the Tiber and the ensuing pestilence, and this aggravated his problem. The Lombards were expanding their power in Italy. In addition to the military threat of their arms and to the ruthless pillaging which is associated with invasions, they presented a religious challenge, for, to the extent that they were Christians, they were Arians. Gregory had the responsibility for the very large physical possessions of the Church of Rome, including its buildings in Rome and its endowments, chiefly in lands, in Italy, Sicily, Gaul, and North Africa. He held to the traditional claims of his see for priority in the Catholic Church, and as Patriarch in the West felt especial responsibility for Italy, Gaul, and Spain. At the outset he may almost have despaired of saving from shipwreck what he called "the rotten old vessel of which God had given" him "the charge."

Gregory rose to all the manifold obligations and reached out beyond them to new enterprises. He saw that Rome's poor were fed and that the church fabrics of the city were repaired and maintained. He managed the estates of the church so successfully that their revenues were increased, but with humane treatment of those who cultivated their lands. He raised armies, kept Rome inviolate from Lombard attacks, negotiated with both Lombards and imperial officials, and on his own authority made peace with the Lombards. During his pontificate he was the outstanding figure in Italy, in its political as well as its ecclesiastical life. He exercised authority in Gaul and Spain, attempted to reform abuses in the church in the Frankish domains, reached out into Illyricum, and inaugurated the Roman mission to Britain of which we are to hear more in a moment. He maintained contacts with the other patriarchs of the Catholic Church and insisted on the primacy of Rome, especially against the claims of the Patriarch of Constantinople.

Gregory preached frequently. He also gave thought and effort to the public services of the Church, including its liturgy and music. He introduced changes in the liturgy. The type of music called Gregorian and which attained wide and prolonged popularity has been attributed to him. Just how much, if anything, he had to do with it has been in dispute, but it is clear that he was interested in the music of the Church and it is probable that he at least made decisive modifications by editing what had come down from the past. He maintained strict discipline among the clergy, sought to enforce the rule of clerical celibacy which had long been the ideal in the West, and gave especial oversight to the bishops who were in the ecclesiastical province of which the Bishop of Rome was metropolitan. He was greatly interested in monasteries, gave them increased liberty from the supervision of the bishops to govern their internal secular affairs, and was zealous in reforming those foundations which had lapsed morally and spiritually. He deposed unworthy abbots, sought to prevent monks from wandering about from one monastery to another, and, to obviate causes for scandal, decreed that women's convents be kept far apart from men's monasteries.

While one of his favorite designations of himself, *servus servorum Dei* ("servant of the servants of God") had been employed before him, and not exclusively by Popes, it seems peculiarly appropriate for him. When, in the ninth century, it began to be used only by the Popes, it may have been in part because of his example. There was fully as great aptness in a phrase which was on an epitaph of Gregory, *consul dei* ("God's consul"), for to a pre-eminent degree Gregory brought to the Church the administrative gifts which characterized the great Romans. Like the more eminent consuls he was a builder of empire, an empire centred in Rome. It was an empire, too, which like that of the consuls and the Cæsars who bore the title of consul guarded the heritage of Græco-Roman civilization, *Romanitas*. Yet Gregory was not just another consul: he was a consul of God and the empire which he sought to strengthen was, as he saw it, the kingdom of God in which Christ was ruler and the Pope, as Peter's successor, Christ's vicegerent. In an age of mounting chaos that empire of Christ's Church stood for decency, order, justice, and the high values of the spirit. More than any other one man, Gregory laid the foundations for the power which the Church of Rome was to exercise in the Western Europe of the next nine centuries.

The contrast with the Eastern wing of the Catholic Church is significant. The latter developed no such able administrators as did the Papacy. In this respect it had no one to compare with Leo the Great or with Gregory the Great. The obvious reason for the difference is that in the West the Empire waned and the Popes stepped in to take its place in preserving order while in the East the Empire continued and the leading Patriarch of that region, he of Constantinople, was overshadowed by the Emperor and the state. Even when men came to that Patriarchate from the civil service, as did Photius, they had been subordinates and not rulers and tended to conform to the tradition of cæsaropapism. There may be deeper but more subtle reasons, such as the distinction between the Roman and the Greek genius, the one practical, the other, in its later Neoplatonic form, stressing spirit at the expense of flesh. It will be recalled that Monophysitism, belittling the human element in Christ, had much greater vogue in the East than in the West. Whatever the reasons, the contrast was real.

This trend towards regarding the Popes as the successors of the Cæsars and the Papacy as the exponent and protector of *Romanitas* brought with it both beneficent results and perils. On the one hand it gave to the Church of the West a structural unity, helped to hold Europe together, and made for civilization. On the other, it substituted, perhaps fatally, visible organizational unity for the unity of love and mixed the kind of power represented by the Roman Empire with that of the Cross and the resurrection. The latter was not completely lost, but it suffered by its conjunction with *Romanitas*.

Gregory was not only an administrator. For centuries he was even more famous as a theologian. Here he was not an originator, for his primary talents were not those of the scholar. His preaching was simple and practical. In common with his times, he employed the allegorical interpretation of the Scriptures, held the relics of the saints in great reverence, and believed in and emphasized miracles. He was intimately familiar with the text of the Bible and made much use of it. He was a warm admirer of Augustine and it was to a large degree the latter's thought that he endeavoured to transmit. Gregory did not exactly reproduce Augustine. While, with the latter, he held that the number of the elect is fixed, he seemed to make less of predestination by God than of God's foreknowledge. He believed in the divine initiative in the salvation of the individual, but held that once grace had begun to act, enabled by it, the individual could coöperate with it. To him sin was more weakness than the basic corruption of man's nature which Augustine stressed. He was substantially in accord with the modified Augustinianism of the Council of Orange.

Gregory put into written form much of the popular Christianity that had been growing up. He had more to say of purgatory than Augustine and was more certain of it than was the latter. Purgatory, so Gregory taught, is a state, a fire, in which Christians are purged of light sins before the final judgement.

Men must repent of sins committed after baptism. He held that God's forgiveness is conditioned solely on men's contrition for their sins, but that works of penance lighten the load which would otherwise have to be borne in purgatory as disciplinary and cleansing, and that masses for the souls in purgatory are a help. For Christians this side the gate of death masses and the aid of the martyrs and saints are also to be sought, not that they ensure forgiveness, but because they aid in the discipline which the Church prescribes for those who repent of post-baptismal sins. Gregory also wrote extensively on angels and demons, systematizing what was generally believed in the circles of his day. He gave to both an hierarchical arrangement. He thought that the end of the world was at hand.

The writings of Gregory became standard and were much read in succeeding centuries. He was regarded as the last of the great fathers of the Latin Church and did much to fix its beliefs.

OTHER CONTEMPORARY THEOLOGICAL ACTIVITY

Contemporary with Gregory was Isidore, Archbishop of Seville and head of the Church in Spain from about 600 to 636. His brief summary of Christian doctrine incorporated in his *Book of Sentences* was to be studied for centuries in the West as a text-book in theology. His *Origins* or *Etymologies,* a kind of compact collection of the secular and ecclesiastical knowledge of his age, was also widely used in the Middle Ages as a *vade mecum* to theology and the wisdom of Græco-Roman antiquity. Isidore, like Gregory, was not original. In the storms of the age theological activity was dying and, except for a brief revival in the heyday of the Carolingians, was not again to awaken until the eleventh century.

THE DONATION OF CONSTANTINE AND THE PSEUDO-ISIDORIAN DECRETALS

Two other literary creations of this era need to be noted, for, while largely forgeries, they were made to strengthen the authority of the Papacy in an age when the Church in Western Europe was in danger of falling apart into a welter of tribal, royal, and feudal churches, dominated by secular princes, and when the unity provided by the See of Peter afforded cohesion. One of these was the Donation of Constantine. Probably written about the middle of the eighth century, it purported to be from early in the fourth century and by the Emperor Constantine. It described the latter's conversion, baptism, and miraculous healing from leprosy through Pope Sylvester I, and said that out of gratitude he was making over to the Pope and his successors his palace in Rome and "the city of Rome and all the provinces, districts, and cities of Italy or of the Western regions."

About the middle of the ninth century there arose, from the region around Rheims, the *Decretals of Isidore,* professing to have been compiled by one Isidore Mercator and to be a collection of decisions of councils and Popes from Clement of Rome late in the first or early in the second century to the eighth century. They included the Donation of Constantine. Some of the material was genuine, but much was spurious. The *Decretals* depicted the Popes as claiming supreme authority from the beginning, permitted all bishops to appeal directly to the Pope, thus limiting the authority of archbishops, and regarded bishops and Popes as free from secular control. In an uncritical age it was accepted as genuine and, although not the work of the Popes, was used to reinforce their claims.

The Spread of Christianity in the West

One of the striking features of these centuries of disorder in Western Europe is the fashion in which, in spite of the near-anarchy, Christianity continued to spread. While many factors contributed to this expansion, it would not have been except for the inner vitality of the faith.

In Italy, Spain, and Gaul the native pagan cults which survived at the end of the fifth century disappeared and those imported by the invaders, except for Islam, were replaced by Christianity.

More serious than overt paganism were the sag in morals and the increase in superstition of those who bore the Christian name. In Gaul the later Merovingians were a sorry lot, weak and vicious. Under them the quality of living of laity and clergy deteriorated.

A gleam in the growing darkness issued from Ireland. The Irish *peregrini* who came to the Frankish domains were distressed by the low level of morals which they found among professing Christians and struggled manfully to raise it and to win to the faith such openly avowed heathen as remained. They encouraged the laity to come to them to confess their sins and as a means of discipline worked out penitentials, with penances prescribed for specific sins.

The most famous of the Irish missionaries in the Frankish domains was Columban. He was a contemporary of Gregory the Great, perhaps born in the same year. Handsome, full-blooded, attracted by and attracted to the opposite sex, as a youth, against his mother's tears, he entered the monastic life. From the famous monastic community of Bangor, in what is now County Down, he led a band of twelve across the sea and preached in the Merovingian realms more earnest faith and living. In the Vosges Mountains he founded monasteries which attracted many and to which he gave a more austere rule than that of Benedict. Eventually he aroused the ire of the Merovingian rulers, partly because of his frank speaking against the king's habit of taking concubines, and perhaps because of his unwillingness to submit to the bishops of the Frankish realm on the date for the celebration of Easter. To avoid deportation he left the Frankish domains and resumed his wanderings. These took him to a monastic community in the mountains between Milan and Genoa and there he died, probably in 615. Monasteries which followed his rule multiplied in the lands of the Franks.

The Irish *peregrini* were not an unalloyed asset to the religious life of the Continent. Unaccustomed to the diocesan form of church organization which they found there, they tended to disregard it. Their bishops wandered about as they pleased, ordaining whom they would. Their monasteries were reluctant or entirely unwilling to accord jurisdiction to the diocesan bishops. Some of the *peregrini* were accused of holding and teaching erratic and heretical doctrines. Yet in the main the Irish made important contributions through their missionary labours among Christians and non-Christians.

One of the most striking and important territorial gains of Christianity during this period, both in its immediate and its long-term results, was the conversion of the pagan peoples of the island of Great Britain. We have noted that Britain was part of the Roman Empire and that before the end of the fifth century the large majority of the population who had conformed to Latin culture had also accepted the Christian faith. It was in this Christian Britain that Patrick had been reared and from it that he went as a missionary to Ireland. However, not all the population of the island had adopted the Christian name. North of the Roman *limes,* in the later Scotland, were areas which had not been won to the faith and perhaps had not even been touched by it. Moreover, and more significantly, Germanic peoples, mainly Angles and Saxons, all of them pagans, had settled in the eastern portions of the island and had been formed into a number of petty kingdoms. The descendants of the Roman provincials, Christians, had moved to the western parts of the island or to Britanny or had been killed off.

In the sixth and seventh centuries within the span of approximately a hundred years the conversion of these Germanic settlers, the English as we had best call them, was accomplished. In it the British Christians in the west of the island had little or no part. Presumably their clergy were not concerned to give the Gospel to these invaders and chronic enemies. The missionaries were from two sources, Ireland and Rome. Both began their labours late in the sixth century. These gain added significance from the fact that in the seventh and eighth centuries English missionaries had a large share in the conversion of Germany and in the improvement of the Christianity of the Carolingian realms and that in recent centuries British Christianity, mainly that of England and Scotland, has been carried to much of the world.

The Irish missionaries to the English were largely associated with the names of Columba (also known as Columcille) and Iona. Columba was born in Ireland, of royal blood, probably in 521, and so was an older contemporary of Gregory and Columban. He seems early to have dedicated himself to the monastic life and in due time was ordained deacon and priest. He was never a bishop. In 562 or 563, when in the full vigour of middle life, moved, so his friend and biographer says, by "the love of Christ," he left Ireland with twelve companions and established his headquarters on Iona, a rocky island about three miles long and about a mile and a half wide off the west coast of Scotland. He was a man of striking personality, a born leader, forceful, with quick wrath for injustice to the weak, with tenderness for the poor and for the brute creation, and with a simple and deep faith in God. He is said always to have been occupied—with study, prayer, writing, fasting, and watching. Iona was his centre and there he was head of the monastic community which he founded. From Iona he made frequent journeys, some to Ireland, but more in what is now the mainland of Scotland. In Scotland there were immigrant Scots from Ireland, Celtic and probably largely Christian. There, too, were other Celtic folk, Picts, many of them pagans. The Christian faith had already been planted among these Celts, partly by Ninian, a younger contemporary and warm admirer of Martin of Tours, in the fore part of the fifth century. Kentigern, probably the same as Mungo, a shadowy figure about whom little certain information has survived and whose headquarters are said to have been at Glasgow, had been active as a missionary in the north of Great Britain in the sixth century. Columba also won some of the Celtic folk of Scotland. His disciples told of miracles performed through him which had much to do with gaining respect for his teaching.

Long after Columba, the community at Iona carried on his tradition. It was from Iona, a generation or so after the death of the founder, that a notable contribution was begun towards the conversion of some of the English. In a struggle for power in Northumbria, one of the Anglo-Saxon kingdoms in the north of England, two princes of the blood royal took refuge on Iona and there were baptized. When one of them, Oswald, came into control in Northumbria, he asked Iona for a missionary for his people. Christianity had already been introduced into the kingdom by the Roman mission of which we are soon to speak, but it was to Iona that Oswald turned for a bishop. The first to be sent proved poorly adapted to the assignment, but the second, Aidan, was remarkably successful. To him Oswald gave headquarters on the island of Lindisfarne, off the east coast, larger than Iona but, like the latter, a convenient centre. Aidan travelled through the little kingdom mainly on foot, winning pagans, confirming believers, caring for the poor, ransoming slaves, and educating and ordaining priests. Aidan's successor, Finan, also from Iona, baptized the king and royal entourage of Mercia, an Anglo-Saxon kingdom in the heart of England, and aided in the conversion of the East Saxons. Cuthbert, later Bishop of Lindisfarne, famous as a saint, had much to do with extending the work of conversion in the North. It was the English Bishop Wilfrid, educated on Lindisfarne, who was instrumental in bringing the South Saxons to the baptismal font and who directed the conversion of the Isle of Wight, said to have been the last of the "provinces" of Britain to be brought to the faith.

Quite apart from the stream which issued from Iona, there were other Irish who aided in the conversion of the English. To the monasteries of Ireland, too, went many English boys for education and training in the ascetic life.

The inauguration and initial direction of the Roman mission to the English were part of the enormous labours of Pope Gregory the Great. The members of this mission did not effect the conversion of as many of the English as did the Irish, but they brought the English Church into close fellowship with Rome and were the means of organizing it into the pattern of territorial dioceses and parishes which prevailed on the Continent.

How Gregory first became interested in the English we do not know. Oral tradition declares that before he became Pope he saw some lads in the slave market in Rome who attracted him by their fair bodies, fine hair, and winsome features. On inquiring, he was told that they came from Britain, that the population was pagan, and that the boys were Angles. "Right," he said, "for they have an angelic face and it becomes such to be co-heirs with the angels in heaven." When he learned that they were from the province of Deiri, he exclaimed, "Truly are they *De ira,* withdrawn from wrath and called to the mercy of Christ." When told that their king's name was Ælla he exclaimed, "hallelujah, the praise of God the Creator must be sung in those parts." The tradition went on to declare that Gregory offered himself to the Pope as a missionary to Britain, but that the Roman populace would not let him go.

Whether or not this story is true, Britain was traditionally within the patriarchate over which Gregory presided and, as we have seen, he sought to fulfil what he deemed his responsibility in various parts of that vast area. It is not strange that with his devotion and wide-ranging vision, as Pope he endeavoured to win its pagans to the faith and to give the church there an ecclesiastical organization. He seems to have redeemed some English slaves with the funds of the Church and he expressed himself as grieved that the British bishops were doing nothing for the conversion of their pagan neighbours.

To inaugurate the mission, Gregory chose men from the monastery which he had founded in his paternal mansion in Rome. It was a small company. Headed by Augustine, not to be confused with the famous Bishop of Hippo, it set out from Rome in 596, a century after the baptism of Clovis and thirty-nine years before A-lo-pên brought the faith to China, at the other extreme of Eurasia. Here was to be a new kind of conquest of Britain from Rome. The contrast with that earlier one was striking. Across a valley from the monastery rose the Palatine Hill, with the remains of the palaces of the Cæsars from which Britain had once been ruled. As a physical power Rome was now feeble. Yet this little band, unsupported by arms, was to inaugurate a conquest which was to continue centuries longer and have more enduring effects than had that which had been achieved and maintained by the legions. When the group reached Gaul they became terrified by the dangers in the way and Augustine returned to Rome to ask permission to discontinue the enterprise. Gregory sent him back with a kind but firm letter ordering them on.

Augustine and his band landed on the coast of the Kingdom of Kent, just across the English channel from the Continent. The King of Kent had a Christian wife, a Frankish princess, and with her was a Frankish bishop. After a little hesitation, the king gave the mission his consent to establish themselves in his capital, Canterbury, and turned over to them an existing church building, named for Martin of Tours. Before long he was baptized and thousands of his subjects followed him to the baptismal font. Augustine went to Arles, in the south of Gaul, for consecration as archbishop, and thus became the first Archbishop of Canterbury. At Canterbury Augustine began a monastery, using a pagan temple which had been given him by the King. Following the Benedictine rule, it became the prototype of many Benedictine houses in England.

Gregory kept in touch with the mission, sent it reinforcements, and counselled it through letters. He authorized Augustine to appoint twelve diocesan bishops and to place a bishop at York who, as the Christians increased in that region, should also become an archbishop and ordain twelve bishops. Thus was extended to England the diocesan system which had been developed on the Continent after the pattern of the Roman Empire. To this day Canterbury and York have remained the seats of the two metropolitans of the Church of England. Gregory advised the adaptation of ritual to local circumstances and counselled that pagan temples be transformed into churches rather than destroyed. With occasional reverses, the Roman mission was carried into portions of the east and north of England. While, as we have said, it did not win as many converts as did the Irish, it effectively forged a connexion between the Church in England with the Papacy which was not to be severed until the sixteenth century and then not completely.

Not at first did all the Christians in Great Britain submit to the hierarchy connected with Rome. Through tactlessness or ignorance Augustine antagonized the British bishops in the west of the island, sensitive as they already were because of the gulf between the Britons and the English and their long isolation from Rome. Differences in customs between those who received their faith through the Roman mission and those who obtained it through Ireland and Iona also caused divisions. Only gradually were these healed.

The English Church owed a great debt to Theodore of Tarsus. As his name indicates, he was from Asia Minor. He was in Rome when the death of an Englishman who had been sent there by the Kings of Kent and Northumbria for consecration as Archbishop of Canterbury left that post in urgent need of an occupant. Although then sixty-six years of age, he accepted the appointment (668), went to England and put the church in order. He was well educated in Greek and Latin and in secular and ecclesiastical literature. He found the church in a bad way, for a recent pestilence had carried off many of the clergy and populace and only three bishops were left. He travelled widely, "the first bishop whom all the English Church consented to obey," created new dioceses, consecrated bishops, established a parish system, held synods which brought increasing conformity with Rome, spread the church music of Rome, trained men in Greek, Latin, the Bible, astronomy, and mathematics, and brought in stricter moral discipline. He lived until 690, or to the great age of eighty-eight. In his later years the Celts made a determined effort to regain control, for a time with some success, but his work had been well done and he is remembered as the real organizer of the Church in England.

Within less than a century after the arrival of Augustine, missionaries from the recently converted English were going to the Continent. There for several generations they led in the conversion of much of what are now Holland and Germany. They organized the Church there and tied it up solidly with Rome. Thus they justified the efforts which Rome had put forth on behalf of England. Two names stand out in the story, Willibrord and Winfrith or, as he is better known, Boniface.

Willibrord laboured in what is now Holland with his headquarters at Utrecht. He was by no means the first missionary in the later Belgium and Holland. Part of what is now Belgium had been in the Roman Empire and had been reached by missionaries before the fifth century. Irish *peregrini* and missionaries from the Frankish domains had been there and with much success. The English Bishop Wilfrid had preached among the Frisians while on one of his trips to Rome and had baptized many. Willibrord came from a devout English family and had his early training in a monastery at Ripon of which Wilfrid was the founder. When about twenty years of age he went to Ireland. In 690, then in his thirty-third year, he embarked for Frisia, after the Irish fashion with eleven companions, and established himself at Utrecht, by which the Rhine then flowed. He sought the aid of Pepin of Heristal and the latter, eager to extend Frankish power in that region, gave it to him. He also asked Papal support and in 695 or 696 was given archiepiscopal consecration in Rome, almost exactly a hundred years after Augustine had set out from the Eternal City on his hesitant mission to England. Quite understandably the Frisians connected Willibrord with Frankish imperialism and associated baptism with submission to Frankish rule. Baptisms decreased or increased with the ebb and flow of Frankish power. Yet until he was eighty-one Willibrord continued at his difficult task. He was aided by other missionaries from England, and while success was slow, by the time of his death he saw Christianity well established in the southern part of what is now the Netherlands.

Winfrith first came to the Continent to aid Willibrord. The precise year and place of his birth are not known, but the date was possibly 672 or 675 and the place not far from Exeter. In early childhood he expressed a wish to enter the monastic life, but only tardily won his father's consent. He received his training in monasteries near Exeter and Winchester and there displayed qualities of scholarship, Christian character, teaching ability, sound judgement, and administrative skill which marked him out for distinction. In 716 he went as a missionary to the Frisians and for a time was at Utrecht. Because of unfavourable political conditions the door seemed closed and for a year and a half he was back in England. In 718 he once more left for the Continent and was never again to see his native land. He went first to Rome to obtain Papal approval for his mission. Winning it and now with the Latin name of Boniface, in 719 he went north, first to Germany and then, because of a change for the better for missions in Frisia, for three years he served under Willibrord, destroying pagan temples and building churches. Willibrord wished him for his successor, but Boniface declined, pleading as a reason his commission from the Pope and his conviction that only the Pope could appoint to the episcopate. He then went back to Germany. There he organized and purified the existing Christian communities and also won pagans to the faith. In Hesse he had the most spectacular success of his career. At Geismar, in the presence of a large number of hostile pagans, he began cutting down an ancient oak which was sacred to the god Thor. Before he had quite felled the tree a powerful blast of wind completed the demolition and the hoary giant, crashing, broke into four fragments. The pagan bystanders were convinced of the power of the new faith and from the timber Boniface erected an oratory to St. Peter.

Boniface commanded the confidence of successive Popes and by them was made bishop and then archbishop. By accepting appointment as bishop and archbishop from Rome and swearing allegiance to the Pope he strengthened the authority of the Papal see in the North. As archbishop Boniface was authorized by the Pope to found new episcopal sees. Through him these could also be tied to Rome.

The Carolingians committed to Boniface the task of reforming the Church in the Frankish domains. He kept in touch by letter with his friends in England and from that land and on the Continent recruited many helpers. He made much use of women. He was an indefatigable traveller, teaching, organizing, founding monasteries. Chief of his monastic foundations was Fulda, in the initiation of which he was aided by his disciple, Sturm. It followed the rule of Benedict and became the main centre of learning and theological education for much of Germany. Boniface was appointed Archbishop of Mainz. Under his leadership synods were held in the Frankish domains which sought to enforce the celibacy of the priests, to reduce the worldliness of the clergy, and to exalt the authority of diocesan bishops and reduce that of wandering bishops. Working under the authority of the Popes, Boniface did much to extend the Papal power in the Frankish domains. He reformed not only the Frankish Church but also the Church in Bavaria and in Thuringia. Boniface longed to go as a missionary to the Saxons who remained on the Continent.

Finally, in his old age, and by his own wish, Boniface returned to the Frisians, among whom he had spent his first missionary years, and there baptized thousands, destroyed temples, and erected churches. The end came, probably in June, 754, and as he would have wished. He had set a day for the confirmation of neophytes and had summoned them from far and wide to meet him on the banks of a river. There a band of pagans, apparently intent on plunder, fell upon him and his companions. Enjoining non-resistance on those about him, he was killed by the attackers. Humble, a man of prayer, self-sacrificing, courageous, steeped in the Scriptures, a born leader of men, affectionate, a superb organizer and administrator, he was at once a great Christian, a great missionary, and a great bishop. The Church in Germany owed him an incalculable debt. By the end of the eighth century the remainder of the pagan Frisians, for whom Boniface had given his life, had accepted Christian baptism.

Except the Scandinavians, the last of the Germanic peoples to be drawn into the Christian fold were the Saxons who had remained on the Continent after so many of their number had migrated to Great Britain. This was not strange. Their lands lay north of the Frisians and the Hessians and it was late when the Frankish boundaries were extended to include them. They long resisted conversion, for they associated it with Carolingian imperialism. Several English missionaries laboured among them, and Boniface, armed with Papal authority to proclaim the Gospel to them, pled for helpers from England. Due largely to English efforts, by the last quarter of the eighth century a small minority among the Saxons had been won.

The conversion of the bulk of the Saxons was through the vigorous use of armed force by Charlemagne. Charlemagne was determined to bring the Saxons into his realm and in 772 reduced much of the region to ostensible submission. As part of the process of integration under his rule he insisted upon baptism. He could not always be in the Saxon territories and during his absences repeated revolts broke out. As often as they occurred he returned with fire and sword. He did not depend entirely upon armed force. Many of the recalcitrant he moved into the Rhineland among a professedly Christian population, thus to facilitate their assimilation. He encouraged missionaries, many of them Anglo-Saxons, to come to these kinsfolk of theirs and baptize and instruct them. He divided the land into dioceses and had bishops set over them, thus giving the area a comprehensive ecclesiastical organization.

Here was the most naked use of armed force for the spread of the faith which Christianity had yet seen. It is pleasant to record that it did not go unprotested and that the boldest critic of whom we know was Alcuin, the English scholar who had been brought to court by Charlemagne to aid in the revival of learning of which we are to hear in a moment. He spoke out quite fearlessly and pled that adults be not baptized until they had been properly instructed and that tithes be not exacted of the newly converted.

Whether by force or by quiet instruction by missionaries, the Saxons became staunch adherents of their Christian profession. In the next period they were to become bulwarks of the faith.

Before the year 950 beginnings had been made in the conversion of the Scandinavians, that last wave of pagan invasion which was to scourge Western Europe. Willibrord made an effort to plant the faith in Denmark, but without success. The most notable pioneer among the Scandinavians was Anskar (or Ansgar) (801–865), who was a native of Flanders and is said to have been of Saxon stock. Anskar began his mission at the instance of the son and successor of Charlemagne, Louis, whose usual designation, the Pious, is evidence of his deep interest in Christianity. Like his father before him, but without his exuberant energy, Louis wished to extend the Frankish domains and to do so in close association with the spread of Christianity. To further his purpose, he had an archiepiscopal see created with Hamburg as its centre, later associated with Bremen, and had Anskar appointed to it and given Papal confirmation and the title of Papal legate for the North. Anskar was courageous, travelled widely, had some missionaries as helpers, and won a few converts. However, the majority of the Scandinavians were not as yet minded to become Christians. Independent, they especially spurned the suggestion of accepting the faith from agents of the Carolingians, for that would imply and might actually entail submission to rulers whose realms they were raiding. When, late in the tenth and in succeeding centuries, Scandinavia received baptism, it was under the leadership of its own princes and through missionaries from subject England from which nothing was to be feared politically.

Before 950 some of the Scandinavians who settled within "Christendom" accepted baptism. This was the case in England. It was also true in what came to be known as Normandy. Here the first Duke, known variously as Rollo, Hrolf, and Hrolfr, concluded a treaty with the Carolingian king in 911 by which his holdings were given legal status and in return he and some of his followers agreed to be baptized. It was not until after 950, however, that the conversion of most of the Scandinavians was accomplished.

From the preceding summary, all too brief, of the conversion of the peoples of Western Europe, it will be seen how largely it was by mass movements of entire tribes or peoples, led by the chieftains or kings. As the numerical triumph of Christianity in the Roman Empire had been completed by mass conversion encouraged and latterly enforced by the Emperors, so in these much smaller units which made up Western Europe in this period, that faith was adopted as the religion of the community, usually at the command or at least with the energetic assistance of the prince.

Here we must note the contrast between the theology officially held in the Church in the West and the practice, a contrast which was to continue down to our own day, not only in the Catholic Church of the West, but also in large wings of its major offshoot, Protestantism. The theology was Augustinian and in theory held that only through God's grace could any one be saved, that the recipients of grace were predestined and that presumably, as Augustine had held, their number was infallibly fixed. As a corollary of predestination all chosen by God would be saved through irresistible grace and the perseverance of the saints. Those not chosen would not be saved, regardless of what they or others, such as missionaries, might attempt to do. In apparent contradiction of that conviction, whole tribes and peoples were baptized and given Christian instruction and the other ministries of the Church.

There seems to be no evidence that any of the missionaries were troubled by the paradox. If they were, they might have taken refuge in the findings of the Synod of Orange in 529, findings which had Papal approval and which held that by the grace transmitted through baptism all who had received that rite can, if they labour faithfully, do those things which "belong to the salvation of the soul." Since through mass conversions baptism was practically universal and was given in infancy to successive generations, it followed that all might be saved if they worked together with God, performing those things which were held to be commanded by Him through the Church.

That the Catholic Church acted on the assumption that this could be accomplished was evidence of a basic optimism which we are to see persisting in the West, both in that Church and in Protestantism. It was also in the Eastern Churches and particularly in the Greek wing of the Catholic Church. But here it was not so marked. That it was no stronger in the East may have been due to the greater obstacles which the churches there faced, nearer as they were to the heartland of Eurasia and to the vast populations of Asia. Especially did the prospect seem hopeless for those Christians who were confronted by Islam.

How far in these conversions in the West was the Gospel understood and really accepted? Could the professedly Christian communities be knit together into an inclusive fellowship exemplifying the basic Christian tie of love? Much of the alleged Christianity was obviously very superficial and quite without comprehension of the real import of the Gospel. However, most of the missionaries through whom the instruction was given were monks. That meant that they were in principle fully committed to the Christian faith and to carrying out thoroughly its precepts in their own lives. It is significant, moreover, that often second and even first generation converts became noted exemplars of the faith and that the nominal winning of the Anglo-Saxons had scarcely been completed before missionaries from England were going to the Continent. We find such characters as Willibrord and Boniface and scores of others whom we have not the space so much as to name who bear unmistakably the distinctive marks of Christian character and who as such were revered by many of their contemporaries, even though but few sought to emulate them.

These many tribal, embryonic national Christian communities possessed a common tie in the Church of Rome. The Popes were increasingly acknowledged as the visible head of the Church and to a greater or less extent exercised supervision. Rome was a centre of pilgrimage. From all over Western Europe the devout flocked to its churches and shrines. It was sadly shrunken from the days of its imperial splendour, but now was a period when nowhere in Western Europe were there cities of any size. Rome was impressive even in its ruins and it still possessed imposing churches and shrines sacred to the memories of the two greatest of the apostles, Peter and Paul. Here also were to be had miracle-working relics of saints and martyrs, to be carried back to the monasteries and churches of the several lands of Western Europe.

The Carolingian Revival

Christian living and the inner life and unity of the Church were furthered by the great Carolingians. For about two centuries the Carolingians brought under their sway much of Western Europe including at the widest extent of their realms the larger portions of what are now France, Belgium, the Netherlands, Western and Southern Germany, Switzerland, and Austria, perhaps half of Italy, slight footholds south of the Pyrenees, and much of the east coast of the Adriatic. Their rule stretched from the Elbe to Barcelona and from the North Sea to south of Rome. Their power reached its apex under Charlemagne and was symbolized by his coronation as Roman Emperor by the Pope in Rome in 800. Compared with that of the Cæsars of the second and third centuries Charlemagne's empire was a small, impoverished, and semi-barbarous affair. In splendour it was far inferior to the contemporary Byzantine Empire, the Abbasid Caliphate, and the waning T'ang dynasty in China. Yet its glories dazzled Western Europeans. The Carolingians assisted the Christianity of Western Europe by giving a measure of peace and political unity to a fairly large area, by actively furthering improvements in the Church, and by an alliance with the Papacy which gave protection to the Roman Pontiffs against local enemies in Italy, especially the Lombards and unruly factions in the city.

The earliest of the Carolingians who rose to prominence, Pepin of Heristal and Charles Martel, had no very deep religious interest. Indeed, in his pressing financial needs, the latter appropriated some of the property of the Church, a move which is not surprising in view of the fact that in his day, through the gifts of generations of benefactors, about a third of the land of the realm is said to have been in the possession of ecclesiastical institutions. However, Pepin of Heristal and Charles Martel were quite willing to give moral support to Willibrord and Boniface in their missionary labours, for these would aid in the extension of Frankish political power.

The two sons of Charles Martel, Carloman and Pepin the Short, who succeeded their father on his death in 741, were more religiously minded. Indeed, after six years Carloman retired to the monastery of Monte Cassino, leaving Pepin in undivided control. They reinforced Boniface in his efforts to reform the Frankish Church and much of his success was due to their aid. Beginning with Clovis, the Frankish rulers had exercised a large degree of authority over the Church in their realms, and Pepin wielded this to improve the quality of the clergy and to strengthen the Church's discipline. In the age of disorder the custom of holding annual synods of the bishops, summoned by the king, had almost lapsed. Synods now became more numerous and acted vigorously to improve the morals of the Frankish domains. After Boniface retired to resume his mission among the Frisians, Chrodegang, Bishop and later Archbishop of Metz, continued his reformatory labours. Outstanding among the Frankish bishops of his day, he was zealous in cleansing the Church.

Pepin the Short also established relations with the Papacy which accrued to the benefit of himself and the See of Peter. For several years the Popes had been in a very difficult situation. They were threatened by the Lombards. At the same time they had broken off relations with the Emperors at Constantinople over the iconoclastic issue. Under Pope Gregory III, who held the chair of Peter from 731 to 741, or, in other words, during the later years of Charles Martel, a Roman synod had excommunicated the opponents of the icons and in retaliation the Byzantine Emperor, an ardent iconoclast, had exercised his authority to remove Sicily and such portions of Italy as he could command from Papal jurisdiction. In theory Rome had been under the Emperor, but the breach now severed that connexion and Gregory III was the last Pope to seek and be given the approval of the Byzantine Emperor for his election. Gregory turned to Charles Martel, as the most powerful Christian political figure in the West, for aid against the Lombards, but in vain.

Pepin the Short was more friendly to the Church and the Papacy. He asked of Pope Zacharias, who succeeded Gregory III, approval for relegating the last of the Merovingian *rois fainéants* to a monastery and the assumption by himself of the royal title. He thus seemed to say that the Pope had the right both to depose monarchs and to grant crowns, a principle which was to be of enormous importance in succeeding centuries. Pope Zacharias gave the requested assent. In 752 Zacharias was followed in the Papal chair by Stephen II. The Lombards were a growing menace. In 751 they had taken Ravenna, long the seat of the Exarch, the chief representative in Italy of the Emperor, and were threatening Rome. Stephen journeyed north to seek the aid of Pepin and was housed in a monastery at St. Denis, near Paris. There he crowned and anointed Pepin, confirming the earlier coronation, said, somewhat debatably, to have been by the hands of Boniface. He also anointed Pepin's queen and the king's two sons, Carloman and the future Charlemagne. In return, Pepin waged two campaigns in Italy against the Lombards and compelled the latter to turn over to the Pope their recent conquests from the Emperor, including Ravenna.

In granting these lands to the Pope Pepin the Short is usually regarded as having inaugurated the temporal power of the Papacy and the Estates of the Church. This status the Popes have claimed from that day to this, although it was to be sadly weakened in the nineteenth century.

The step was not as revolutionary as might at first sight appear. As we noted when we spoke of Gregory the Great, the Church of Rome had long held vast properties which it administered, widely scattered in Italy, Sicily, Sardinia, Corsica, and Gaul. To be sure, in theory these were within the structure of the Roman Empire and thus were subject to the Emperors. In practice, however, the Popes had managed them through an elaborate bureaucracy almost as though they were independent. Because of the decline of the imperial power in Italy, the Popes had been the chief defenders of the city of Rome. Gregory the

Great, for example, had raised armies for protection against the Lombards. Even with these qualifications, the action of Pepin was highly significant.

Pepin the Short died in 768 and was succeeded by his sons Charles and Carloman. The latter followed his father to the grave in 771 leaving Charles, whom we best know as Charlemagne, "Charles the Great," as sole ruler. In Charlemagne the Carolingian power reached its height. His was a long reign, for he died in 814 and thus was on the throne for nearly half a century, for more than forty years without a colleague. A bold and skilful warrior, he greatly extended the borders of his realm. He was also an able administrator whose organizing and directing genius actively concerned itself with all aspects of the life of his domains. Under his vigorous hand important political and ecclesiastical innovations were made and for a time it seemed that permanent recovery had been effected from the disorders which had followed the decay of the Roman Empire. By his coronation as Roman Emperor on Christmas Day, in the year 800, and in Rome itself, it might almost have seemed that the preceding centuries had been a bad dream and that the glories of the Cæsars were not only to be revived but also enriched and transfigured by the Christian faith of ruler and people. The act was not regarded as an innovation, for Rome still held the imagination of the peoples of Europe, civilization was thought of as inseparable from it, the Roman Empire continued, even if with diminished borders and from Constantinople, and there was ample precedent for two Emperors, one in the East and one in the West. Eventually Charlemagne was recognized by two successive Byzantine rulers as entitled, with themselves, to the designation of Emperor.

Charlemagne was deeply and genuinely religious and conceived of himself as ruling by Christian principles. He was masterful, autocratic, cruel in at least some of his wars, and notoriously lax in his marital relations, but he was moderate in his eating and drinking. He could not write (although in his mature life he made some pretense of trying) and while he could read he preferred to be read to. He was fond of the history of antiquity but he took especial delight in the writings of Augustine, particularly his *De Civitate Dei*. This work gave him his political and social philosophy and he set himself so far as possible to making his realm the City of God.

Possessed of this masterful energy and this religious motive, Charlemagne continued the reformation and improvement of the Church which was already under way. In the newly conquered lands won from paganism he created bishoprics, established monasteries, and appointed the men who were their heads. In the older parts of his domains, where the bishops were elected by the chapters with the consent of the people, his license was necessary. As the tradition of elections was weakened, he used his authority to place in episcopal chairs men whom he believed to be suitable and to endow them with the revenues of abbeys. He encouraged the regular holding of synods. He himself presided at important synods which dealt with theological doctrines and had the major voice in the decisions.

Charlemagne concerned himself with improving the structure of the Church. The parish system had long been spreading in the Frankish domains and the countryside had been divided into parishes, each with its clergy. Many of the parishes and chapels had been endowed with lands by local magnates for "the salvation of their souls," but the donors retained to themselves and their heirs the privilege of naming the pastors. These rights could be transferred by sale, gift, or bequest. Under these circumstances the bishop, beyond his function of ordination, might be permitted very little if any control. Charlemagne insisted that the bishops have the power of discipline over the clergy in their respective dioceses. The bishops also had political and civil functions.

Charlemagne's measures did not prevent many ecclesiastical endowments being allocated for the support of his favourites, even laymen. Thus his biographer, Einhard, an intimate at his court and that of his son, Louis the Pious, enjoyed the income of several important abbeys and, although married and living with his wife, seems to have been an abbot.

Further to raise the level of the Church, Charlemagne revived and strengthened the existing system of archbishops. He increased their number. Each was in theory to supervise the bishops in his province. The *missi dominici* sent out to enforce the king's decrees had authority in matters ecclesiastical as well as civil and military.

Charlemagne perfected a system of tithes for the support of the bishops and the parish clergy. For authority for the principle the clergy cited the Mosaic Law. The custom had spread gradually. In 585 a synod of Frankish prelates asked that it be regularized. Pepin the Short gave tithes legal status as a recognized tax and Charlemagne further endorsed them. In the Frankish domains and elsewhere in the Western Church, the support of the clergy and the care of the poor also came from offerings, many of them mass stipends in return for which masses were said for the donors or for those whom they designated.

Charlemagne encouraged the repair, embellishment, and construction of churches and the improvement of public worship. Pepin the Short had already furthered the spread of the "Gregorian chant." Charlemagne sought to make universal the form of the liturgy which had developed at Rome.

He endeavoured to raise the morals of the laity and to improve the acquaintance of the common man with the main principles of the faith. To this end he commanded the clergy to preach on the Creed, prayer, and the Ten Commandments. In theory all Christians were to know the Lord's Prayer and the Creed.

Through ecclesiastical legislation he strove to inculcate and enforce the sanctity of the marriage tie, and that in spite of his own errant example.

Charlemagne also stressed the education of the clergy. Even after the reforms of Boniface and Chrodegang, great room remained for improvement. In many monasteries learning had lapsed and idleness and ignorance abounded. His purpose was the advancement of religion and the Church, but as a foundation the study of the great authors of Roman antiquity was stimulated. Indeed, that we have the works of these pagan writers is in many instances due to the copies made in this period of literary revival. The form of Latin script was encouraged, a vast improvement over what had immediately gone before it, which became standard in succeeding centuries and is familiar in our printed books of today.

To aid in this educational programme Charlemagne drew scholars from wherever he could find them. They came from Ireland, Spain, Italy, Gaul, and, notably, England. In the seventh and eighth centuries some of the Anglo-Saxon monasteries had become centres of learning. Most famous of all their scholars was Bede. Reared in a monastery in Northumbria in the present County Durham, he was diligent in his religious duties and in his studies. He used Latin easily, knew some Greek, and was master of such of the learning of the day as was available to him. He wrote voluminously and on many subjects, but is best remembered for his *Ecclesiastical History of England,* our fullest source for the conversion of the Anglo-Saxons and the early years of the English Church. Alcuin, the most distinguished of the savants at the court of Charlemagne, a scion of a noble family, related to Willibrord, and a younger contemporary of Boniface, had been educated at York under the direction of one of the disciples of Bede. He had headed the school in that city. A trusted intimate of Charlemagne, with no great originality, he was immensely learned, taught in the palace school which his royal master had set up, wrote extensively, and died (804), ripe in years and honours, as head of the monastery of St. Martin of Tours.

Charlemagne was not especially interested in furthering asceticism. He founded a few monasteries, but to him they were not important for the practice of the full Christian life, but rather as centres of education and civilization.

Charlemagne concerned himself with the Papacy. He renewed his father's grants to the see of Peter and treated the Popes with respect. However, he made it clear that he expected them to support him with their prayers while leaving to him practical matters of political action and administration. He may not have been entirely happy when the Pope took the initiative of crowning him Roman Emperor as he was kneeling at the high altar on that memorable Christmas Day. That act, however, had fully as far-reaching significance as the

Papal sanction to the assumption of the royal power by Pepin. It established the precedent that the imperial coronation of the Western successors to the Cæsars must be by the Pope and thereby accorded that pontiff an enhanced position.

THE DECLINE OF THE CAROLINGIANS

With the death of Charlemagne (814) the Carolingian power entered upon a decline. It was not sudden, but none of his line who followed Charlemagne had his ability and the Carolingian structure depended so largely upon the quality of the monarch that as the latter deteriorated the fabric fell apart.

Charlemagne's immediate successor, Louis the Pious, who reigned from 814 to 840, was deeply religious in a monastic rather than his father's lay fashion but he did not possess the force and administrative gifts of his sire. The impetus given by his predecessors carried the realm forward and he was crowned as Roman Emperor. As was to be expected, he was active in ecclesiastical affairs, and synods continued the reform movement.

True to his convictions, Louis was especially concerned with improving the quality of monastic life. To this end he called to his assistance Witiza, better known as Benedict of Aniane. Born about the year 750, Benedict was now in his mid-sixties. The son of a Gothic count, he had served in the court under Pepin the Short and Charlemagne. Then, in his twenties, he had renounced the world and entered a monastery. Disturbed by the laxity in the house which he had chosen, he founded a monastery of his own at Aniane in which he sought to restore the observance of the rule of Benedict in its full strictness, and with especial emphasis upon worship and self denial. His example proved contagious and by the time of Charlemagne's death many other houses were adhering closely to the Benedictine ideal. Louis made Benedict of Aniane his adviser on monastic affairs and the order went forth that all monasteries in the realm must follow the Benedictine rule as interpreted by him.

The death of Louis the Pious (840) was followed, in 843, by the division of the realm between his three sons, Lothair I, who was given the imperial title and who received the region which included the Frankish portions of Italy and the valley of the Rhone, Louis, because of his assignment known as "the German," to whom went the area east of the Rhone, and Charles the Bald, who was apportioned most of the modern France and who was eventually (875), exactly seventy-five years after that had happened to his grandfather, to be crowned Roman Emperor by the Pope on Christmas Day in St. Peter's. This division, the civil strife which followed, and continued quarrels among the subsequent scions of the Carolingian line brought added internal weakness.

Not immediately, however, did collapse come. The intellectual and religious activity which had been encouraged by the great Carolingians went on well into the ninth century. Charles the Bald was abler than his father and his court was a centre of learning. It was not until the latter part of the ninth and the fore part of the tenth century that the darkness became intense.

Renewed Theological Activity Under the Carolingians

The intellectual and religious revival made possible by the Carolingians was accompanied by fresh theological activity and controversies over doctrine. Indeed, as at so many other periods in the history of the faith, innovations in Christian belief and the consequent debates were evidences of vitality.

One of the controversies centred in Spain. For a time after the Arab conquest the churches which survived south of the Pyrenees, and they were many and strong, were in part cut off from Rome. In the second half of the eighth century an archbishop, Wilchair, came in from the Frankish domains, apparently charged by the Papacy with carrying out reforms analogous to those which Boniface was working north of the Pyrenees. A bishop consecrated by him as a kind of Papal legate attempted to bring the date for celebrating Easter in accord with that of Rome, to introduce other Roman customs, and to prevent mixed marriages of Christians with Moslems. The vigorous methods of one of his subordinates aroused resentment among Spanish churchmen.

More serious was a dispute over the nature of the Trinity. Here the Pope stepped in and reproved not only the extreme views of one of the most outspoken partisans of the Roman Church, but also those of Elipand, Archbishop of Toledo and as such the ranking ecclesiastic in the Spanish Church. Elipand held to a conviction about the relation of the divine to the human in Jesus Christ which may have come down from early Latin Christian thinkers and have persisted, distorted, because of the isolation of Spain from the theological discussions which had issued in Chalcedon. In an attempt to insist upon the full humanity of Jesus Christ, it held that though in his divine nature he was the Son of God, the human Jesus was only a son by adoption. To this doctrine Felix, Bishop of Urgel, also adhered, and Urgel was in the portion of Spain which late in the eighth century was brought under Frankish rule. Summoned to a synod at Regensburg in 792, Felix renounced the Spanish view. Out of deference to the Pope, Charlemagne sent him to Rome, where again he repeated his rejection of adoptionist views. He then returned to his diocese.

However, the bishops in Spain maintained their position. Thereupon Charlemagne summoned a synod which met at Frankfort in 794 and in which were represented most of the Latin Church except that in the part of Spain controlled by the Moslems. The synod condemned the Spanish christology and to the documents embodying its findings Charlemagne added a letter of his own to the Spanish bishops, urging them to comply with the Frankfort decisions. Like some of the Roman and Byzantine Emperors, he was setting himself up as competent on theological issues. Moreover, although he was not yet a Roman Emperor and so had no ground for a legitimate claim of jurisdiction in most of Spain, he was assuming the right to speak to the churches of all Spain. He pled as a reason a request from the Christians of that land.

Incidentally, it was this Council of Frankfort which condemned the pronouncement of the Council of Nicæa of 787 for its permission to pay reverence to images and regarded it not as an ecumenical gathering, but as one simply of the Greeks.

The Council of Frankfort did not end the controversy over Spanish adoptionism. Even before the council had met, Felix, in spite of his solemn rejection of that position, had entered into an epistolatory controversy with Alcuin on the issue and the two continued the debate after Frankfort. In 798 a council at Rome called by the Pope condemned Felix's adoptionism. In the year 800 Alcuin and Felix met in a theological joust in the presence of Charlemagne at Aachen (Aix-la-Chapelle). Felix professed himself convinced and forswore adoptionist terminology, but the authorities did not trust him and he was kept in confinement in Lyons until his death (818). Through lengthy letters Alcuin attempted to bring Elipand to renounce adoptionism, but the latter was obdurate and he and the other bishops in the Spain which was under Moslem rule continued to hold to it.

In one respect the Frankish Church agreed with the Spanish Church. We have seen that in 809 a synod at Aachen approved the custom which had originated in Spain of adding *filioque* to the creed.

More far-reaching in its consequences than the adoptionist controversy was a development of views over the nature of the Eucharist and the emergence of the conception of that central rite of the Church which was later called transubstantiation. Not far from 831 Radbert, or Radbertus, a monk in the famous monastery of Corbie, near Amiens, to whose name Paschasius is usually prefixed, a scholar widely read in Latin and Greek theology, wrote an extensive treatise on the Eucharist, which later, in a revised form, he dedicated to Charles the Bald. He held that while to the senses the bread and the wine in the sacrament remain unaltered, by a miracle the *substantia* of the body and blood of Christ, the very body which was his on the earth, is present in them. However, this change takes place only for those who believe it and accept it in faith, and it is not effective for the unbeliever. To the believer, as had been said centuries earlier, it is the medicine of immortality.

This view did not win immediate acceptance. A distinguished teacher, author, and scholar, Raban Maur (Hrabanus Maurus), a pupil of Alcuin and abbot of the famous monastery of Fulda, denied that "the sacrament of the altar is truly the body of Christ which was born of the Virgin, suffered on the cross, and was raised from the tomb," but he held that the body of the risen Lord is present, even though not physically, and that to receive the body of Christ is to be united with Christ by faith in such a manner as to form with him a single body. Gottschalk, a former monk of Fulda, now imprisoned in a monastery for views which we are to note in a moment, indignantly rejected the suggestion of Radbert that the Christ on the altar suffers anew and dies anew, but he also differed from Raban Maur who seemed to say that the Eucharist was only a sign of grace, and maintained that the body and blood of Christ are mysteriously present as an objective reality, quite independent of the faith of the communicant. Ratramnus, like Radbert a monk of Corbie, in a brief treatise written at the request of Charles the Bald, held that the view of Radbert worked harm to the religious life, for since the effects of partaking of the Eucharist are spiritual, the bread of the Eucharist must be spiritually and not physically the body of Christ. To hold that Christ is physically present would negate the spiritual power and healing which are the true fruits of the sacrament. In spite of these criticisms, the position set forth by Radbert was nearer to that which was eventually endorsed by the Roman Catholic Church than was that of his opponents. Final official action, however, was to wait until the thirteenth century.

Gottschalk was the centre of another controversy, that over predestination. As a child, the son of a Saxon count, he had been dedicated to the monastic life in Fulda. When he reached adolescence, he sought and obtained release on the ground that this had not been with his assent. Yet he did not return to the secular life and, although he left Fulda, was ordained to the priesthood and became one of the numerous itinerant monks of the time. He was a diligent student of the writings of Augustine and, attempting to support his position by quotations from that saint, held that, for reasons which we cannot fathom, God predestines some to eternal life and that those so predestined cannot fail of that life, while, on the other hand—and here was the chief point of debate—those who are not predestined to eternal life are predestined to eternal death.

Obviously this was contrary to the official view which had been set forth in 529 at the Council of Orange. It will be recalled that the Orange gathering, while affirming original sin, declaring that turning to God is wholly through God's grace, and anathematizing those who declare that our will can anticipate God's action, also condemned the teaching that some are predestined to evil and said that if they labour faithfully all the baptized can perform those things which are necessary to salvation.

Powerful opposition was ranged against Gottschalk. In it were the abbot of his old monastery, Raban Maur, and the aggressive and skilful controversialist, Hincmar, Archbishop of Rheims. They were willing to say that God foreknows the sin of those who are not elected to salvation, but they denied that He fore-ordains it. In 848 Raban Maur, now Archbishop of Mainz, had Gottschalk expelled from the realms of Louis the German. That action threw the unfortunate monk into the province of Hincmar and in 849 the latter caused him to be deposed from the priesthood and imprisoned in a monastery.

This did not end the controversy. Gottschalk had powerful friends who rose to his defense. They came out vigorously against Hincmar and some councils took their side. However, in a council in 860 in which most of the Frankish domains were represented, it was Hincmar who triumphed, with slight verbal concessions to his opponents. An attempt was made to take the case to Rome, but a few years later the unfortunate Gottschalk died in his monastic prison, unreconciled to the Church.

More radical than Gottschalk, but in another way, was Claudius, Bishop of Turin, who flourished under Louis the Pious. Said to have been a pupil of Felix of Urgel, he was an earnest student of Augustine. He vigorously denounced the reverence of images and the cross. In this he was in agreement with the general convictions in the Frankish Church. However, he also came out against the current practice of asking for the intercession of the saints. Even more striking was his attitude towards the Papacy. He was critical of the Pope, declaring that he is not to be called apostolic who sits in the seat of the apostle, but he who does the work of an apostle.

The most eminent intellectual figure of the reign of Charles the Bald, John Scotus Eriugena (also called Johannes Scotus), was drawn into the controversies over the Eucharist and predestination. An Irish scholar, he was familiar with the great Greek theologians and translated the works of some of them into Latin, including especially Dionysius the Areopagite. In his intellectual position he was more of a Neoplatonist than a Christian, but in words and perhaps sincerely, he subscribed to the Christian faith. Some questioned his orthodoxy but he was protected by the friendship of Charles the Bald and by his superior scholarship, equipped as he was with a knowledge of the Greek as well as the Latin writings to which the Church looked as authoritative. His was a powerful and philosophically subtle mind and in the disputes of the day he undercut both parties. For instance, in the issue of predestination and foreknowledge, he declared that from God's standpoint there is neither past nor future, for, since He is eternal, He sees all of us and at once. He declared the disjunction between foreknowledge and foreordination to be false, because God can know only what He does. He also held that evil has no real being. Eriugena was too formidable to be tried for heresy by his Frankish contemporaries, but in 855 and 859 his views were condemned by synods.

DEVELOPMENTS IN CHURCH DISCIPLINE

The Carolingian age saw not only intellectual activity but also important developments in the means which the Church employed to further Christian living. It will be remembered that the rule for forgiveness of post-baptismal sins had been public confession, exclusion from the communion, and, after the ecclesiastical authorities were satisfied with the penitent's sincerity as shown by the performance of prescribed acts, public and formal restoration. This custom had been maintained in the West after it had been given up in the East.

In the disorders attendant upon the breakup of the Roman Empire and the invasions, this form of discipline had been weakened or allowed to lapse. In place of it there had come, as we have suggested, largely from Ireland and the Irish *peregrini,* the practice of private confession to a priest. The latter prescribed to the sinner the works of penance which must be performed before restoration to communion. The Irish penitentials, with their instructions to those hearing confessions, probably did much to regulate morals in a stormy age.

However, early in the ninth century the reformers in the Frankish realms began to condemn these penitentials as too much dependent upon the whims of the priest and as being unregulated by ecclesiastical authority. They sought, therefore, to renew public confession and restoration, and councils, bishops, and theologians pronounced in favour of them. Since great difficulty was encountered in persuading the guilty to undergo this prolonged and humiliating ordeal, efforts were made to improve the procedure of private confession. Private confession and penance were continued, but with more careful episcopal supervision. Books of directions for priests hearing confessions were prepared by bishops or under episcopal supervision which sought to embody as much as possible of the earlier standards and practices of the Church.

DECLINING CAROLINGIAN AND GROWING PAPAL POWER

We have noted the fashion in which from the time of Gregory the Great the powers of the Popes north of the Alps had markedly increased. This was due to several factors, among them the great ability of Gregory himself, the success of the Roman mission in England culminating in Theodore of Tarsus, the Anglo-Saxon missionaries on the Continent, loyal as they were to Rome, and the support accorded these missionaries by the early Carolingians.

Pepin the Short and Charlemagne had protected the Popes from the Lombards and local disorders in Italy and had thereby enhanced their position.

However, they two, and especially Charlemagne, were such powerful figures that they overshadowed the Popes. While paying them deference, they used them for their purposes.

When, after Louis the Pious, the power of the Carolingians declined, for a time that of the Popes increased. This was partly because the Carolingians no longer dominated the Popes. It was also because the bishops in the Carolingian domains looked to Rome for protection against the archbishops. We have seen how the numbers and authority of the archbishops had been augmented as a phase of the Carolingian reforms. So long as the throne was in the hands of Charlemagne it was able to keep these functionaries in check. However, under the weaker rulers who followed, some of the archbishops seemed to the bishops to be overbearing and to be treating them as subordinate officials. Hincmar of Rheims, aggressive and masterful as he was, especially aroused opposition. The bishops called upon the Popes for protection against their metropolitans. Then, too, as the authority of the Carolingian monarchs declined, lay lords infringed upon what many of the clergy held to be the rights of the Church and the tendency was to look to Rome for support. It was at this time and from the domains of Charles the Bald, perhaps from Mainz or possibly from Rheims, that the Isidorian Decretals were assembled. Partly genuine and partly spurious, this collection of documents was designed to curb the power of the metropolitans and the lay nobility by stressing the position of the Papacy.

The Papal chair also had the advantage of being occupied by some very able men. The most eminent of these, Nicholas I, who was Pope from 858 to 867, we have already met in the conflict with the Byzantine wing of the Catholic Church, and have noted how vigorously he acted in that complex situation. In the West he was appealed to by several of the Carolingians in their conflicts with one another. Like Charlemagne, but in a different manner, he sought to realize in history what he conceived to have been set forth in Augustine's *De Civitate Dei*. He held that the Church was superior to all secular rulers, that the Pope is the ruler of the Church, and that the bishops are his subordinates through whom he carries out his divinely commissioned functions. Nor were these convictions empty theories. Appealed to by a bishop whom Hincmar, as Archbishop of Rheims, had deposed, he compelled the latter to restore him. In a notorious divorce case in which Lothair II, son of Lothair I and greatgrandson of Charlemagne, had obtained the consent of a synod in Metz to put away his wife, Thietberga, that he might marry a concubine, Nicholas forced Lothair to take back Thietberga and excommunicated two archbishops for siding with the king. He also made his will felt against an archbishop of Ravenna who claimed independence of the See of Peter.

The Descent of Darkness

The last decades of the ninth century and the first half of the tenth century were for Western Europe and the Western wing of the Catholic Church years of deep darkness. The Carolingian realms were hopelessly divided among quarreling, weak scions of that famous line. Charles the Fat, the son of Louis the German and greatgrandson of Charlemagne, bore the imperial title and for a time most of the Carolingian domains were reunited under him, but he was deposed in 887 and died the following year. What had been the Frankish kingdom broke up finally into a number of fragments.

Feudalism rapidly developed. Its roots went back before the time of Charlemagne but it now began to flourish. It was partly the result of the weakening of the monarchy and the desire for security in an age of disorder. It was also in part the outgrowth of an agricultural economy in which commerce had dwindled, towns were few and small, and money was scarce. The weaker landowners put themselves under the protection of the stronger and in return made contributions to their lord in the form of contingents for his armed forces and in other forms of service. The system was based upon land which was usually cultivated by serfs who were half free and half slave and who could not be sold from the soil which they tilled but who could not leave it. The major occupation of the feudal lords was fighting and war among them was chronic. This warfare made commerce and other peaceful pursuits difficult and produced a sag in morals.

The internal disorder in Western Europe was augmented by foreign invasion. This was from several directions. From the North came the Scandinavians, sea raiders in long boats. They landed on the coasts and swarmed up the rivers, burning, murdering, and pillaging. Pagans, they did not spare churches or monasteries. Indeed, they found them easy and attractive prey. Here and there they effected permanent settlements, especially in the British Isles, Normandy, Iceland, and the western parts of the later Russia. They brought ruin to the monasteries of Ireland, which, hitherto all but immune from invasion on that far western isle, had been a centre of peaceful Christian living and a source of light to Western Europe. They dealt severe blows to that Anglo-Saxon Christianity from which so many missionaries and scholars had issued to convert the pagans and raise the level of Christian living on the Continent. Up the Seine they came and besieged Paris, up the Loire to Orleans, along the Garonne to Toulouse, and by the Rhone as far as Valence. In Italy a number of cities, including Pisa, fell to their arms. In the 890's the Magyars, a pagan people from the East, poured over the Carpathians and established permanent colonies in the later Hungary. Moslem raiders harassed the shores of Italy and in 846 even plundered the famous churches, St. Peter's and St. Paul's, in Rome itself, for both shrines were outside the then city walls. On the East the Slavs were a menace.

In this approach to anarchy the Church and its institutions suffered and the quality of Christian living declined. Feudal lords appropriated monasteries and churches and either named their incumbents or seized their properties. Bishops and abbots became feudal lords and had little to distinguish them from their lay neighbours except their titles and some of their functions. Bishops and clergy perished or were killed outright in the invasions. Thus in 882 Hincmar, the famous Archbishop of Rheims, died while fleeing from Norman raiders. An Archbishop of Canterbury, taken by the Danes and held for ransom, had no way of raising the sum demanded by his captors except by despoiling his people and courageously chose death.

Unprotected and caught in the welter of the chaotic Italian political scene, the Papacy sank to its lowest ebb. Some Popes of the fifteenth and sixteenth centuries may have been greater sinners, but they were men of force who counted in Europe and the Western Church as a whole. In the latter part of the ninth and the fore part of the tenth century the Popes were either vicious or too weak to cope with the overwhelming odds against them. The tenure of office of many was brief: between 897 and 955 seventeen followed in rapid succession. One, John VIII, who died in 882, is said, on evidence that is not entirely uncontestable, to have been poisoned by his attendants and, when the drug took effect too slowly, to have had his skull crushed by a mallet. In 897 the corpse of the ambitious Pope Formosus, who had died the previous year, was taken from its sarcophagus, tried before a council over which his successor presided, condemned, despoiled of its vestments, and cast into an unconsecrated tomb for strangers and then taken by the populace and thrown into the Tiber. But Formosus had friends and the conflict between them and his enemies continued. Within a few months another Pope salvaged the body of Formosus which, having been rescued and buried by a hermit, he gave honourable sepulchre among the tombs of the ancient Popes and had a synod reverse the condemnatory acts of the anti-Formosus council. In 903 a partisan of Formosus was Pope for about two months and was then thrown into prison by a palace revolution which put another on the Papal throne. This new occupant, in turn, was replaced by a Pope supported by an armed escort, was degraded, and was sent to the prison where his victim was incarcerated.

For more than a generation after 904 the city of Rome and the Papacy were controlled by one local family, whose most prominent members were Theophylact, his daughter Marozia, her husband Alberic, and a younger Alberic, the son of Marozia and Alberic. We have varying estimates of the moral quality of the family. Marozia especially has been given a bad name. They controlled the choice of the Popes. One of these, John XI, who held the post from 931 to 935, was reputed to have been the son of Marozia and Pope Sergius III, who had reigned from 904 to 911. Another Pope, John X, who was on the throne from 914 to 928, fell out of favour with Marozia. It is said that because of his opposition to her proposed marriage with Guy, Marquis of Tuscany (the elder Alberic had died) she had his brother slain before his eyes and then had him imprisoned and killed. In 932 the younger Alberic seized the control from his mother, Marozia, and confined her and John XI in the Castle of St. Angelo. Alberic, called "the glorious prince and senator of all the Romans," was now in power. He seems to have wished to reform the Church and to have put fairly sincere and religious men on the Fisherman's throne. However, they were his creatures and apparently feared to take important action without his consent.

With such conditions in Rome, the Popes could not wield the influence in European affairs or in the Church of the West that had been exerted by some of their great predecessors. Certainly they could not give the moral and religious leadership that would lift the Church and the Christianity of the West from the slough into which they had fallen.

Faint Gleams of Light

Here and there in the darkness were gleams of light which, as the event proved, were harbingers of a better day. As we are to see again and again, often in what have appeared to be the darkest hours for the Christian faith movements have begun which, at the time affecting only small minorities, have later assumed major proportions and have brought revival and advance. In England, in a remote corner of the then Christendom, in the last three decades of the ninth century a king, Alfred the Great, established his rule over much of the country, compelled one of the Viking leaders to accept baptism, and brought about a religious and intellectual revival which on a smaller territorial scale was not unlike the earlier one on the Continent under the Carolingians. While his death was followed by something of a relapse, the darkness was never again as intense as it had been before him and, as we shall see, England became the chief source of the missionaries who won the peoples of Scandinavia to the Christian faith and instructed them in it. In the year 910, when Sergius, one of the creatures of the notorious Marozia, was on the Papal throne, the monastery of Cluny was founded which, as we are to hear later, became a radiating centre and symbol of a renewed life that was to bring the Christianity of Western Europe to a fresh high level.

EFFECT OF THE ENVIRONMENT

What effects did the environment in Italy and the west of Europe have upon Christianity in that region in the four and a half centuries from 500 to 950? How different did the Christianity of the West become from that of the Eastern wing of the Catholic Church? Because of the political division and the difficulty of physical communication the two were drifting apart. Cultural and other factors were working for separation, and in the West there were conditions which were placing their imprint on the Catholic Church of that area.

One striking contrast was that Byzantine Christianity was Greek, while the Christianity of the West was dominated by Rome. In spite of its weakness in the last half of the ninth and the first half of the tenth century, the Bishopric of Rome, the Papacy, exerted an influence over almost all Western Christendom. Over only the far periphery, especially Ireland, and Spain under the Arabs did it have little control. The Papacy stood for *Romanitas,* the tradition of imperial Rome, partly Christianized but still unmistakably Roman in its administrative genius, its insistence on law and order, and its comprehensive organization.

The claims and the power of the Papacy were furthered by the absence in the West of a strong competing civil state headed by an autocratic monarch such as the Greek Church faced in the Byzantine continuation of the Roman Empire. Even Justinian did not possess as much power in the West or in Italy as he exercised in the neighbourhood of Constantinople. Increasingly the authority of his successors waned. It was not recognized beyond Italy, Sicily, and the east coast of the Adriatic, and even there it was dwindling. The restoration of the imperial title in the West by Charlemagne did not bring the same degree of control over the Papacy by the state as the Byzantine Emperors wielded over the Patriarchate of Constantinople, for strong though he was, Charlemagne spent most of his time north of the Alps, a precedent followed by his successors, and Rome was never his or their capital. Occasionally, as in the decades immediately preceding 950, the absence of adequate civil protection injured the Papacy, but at other times, under strong Popes, notably Gregory the Great, it was an advantage.

In the West the Catholic Church became the Roman Catholic Church and, with some relapses, the administrative power of the Bishops of Rome over that Church mounted. The tendency to split up into national, tribal, and ethnic churches which in the East proved so divisive was also present in the West, but the growing power of the Papacy partly nullified it and gave a degree of unity to Western Christendom which was in striking contrast with the increasing and enduring schisms in the East.

The Roman temperament was seen in monasticism. It was the rule of Benedict, developed only a short distance from Rome and with the moderation, the sense of practical possibilities, and the organization which were typical of the Roman spirit, which prevailed in the West.

As Rome and other cities in the West declined in population, Christianity in that area adapted itself to the prevailing rural life and economy. That was in contrast with the Greek wing of the Catholic Church, increasingly dominated as it was by a commercial city, Constantinople.

Towards the end of the period Christianity was beginning to conform to feudalism in its organization and thought as it was never to do in the East.

The thought of Augustine, an influence which grew in the West, gave to that branch of the Catholic Church a distinct character, especially since Augustine had little or no currency in the East.

In a confidence in miracles, both West and East were in accord. How far that can be ascribed to the environment, especially to the environment peculiar to this period, may be debatable. It is clear, however, that while from the very beginning Christians had believed in the miraculous and the power of the Christian faith to work miracles was one of the factors in the conversion of the Roman Empire, in the years after 500 miracles loom more prominently in the writings of the educated leaders of the Church in the West than in the centuries before that dividing line. Gregory the Great had very much more to say of them than did the pre-sixth century fathers of the Church. The same is true of Bede. It is also significant that Einhard, the intimate and biographer of Charlemagne and possessing a classical Latin style which was the fruit of the Carolingian intellectual revival and of familiarity with the writings of pagan Latin antiquity, sent agents to Rome who after prayer robbed one of the chief churches of highly prized relics and brought them back for one of his foundations and that he recorded the miracles wrought through them after they had come into his possession.

THE EFFECT OF CHRISTIANITY ON THE WEST

What effect did Christianity have upon Western Europe? Here were the descendants of the Roman provincials, religiously the products of the mass conversions of the fourth and fifth centuries. Here, too, were the scions of the barbarian invaders who also had come into the Church by community movements. Could Christianity raise the life of this population so that it would approximate to the standards set forth by Christ? The odds seemed overwhelmingly against success. Not only did Christianity face the obstacle of human nature, basically corrupted by sin, as Augustine had so clearly pointed out, but it also was confronted by the remnants of Græco-Roman civilization, that civilization which had crucified Jesus and which Augustine had seen as in stark contrast with the City of God. Within the borders of Western "Christendom" there were chronic fighting and rapine, and on its borders were the aggressive Moslem and frankly pagan peoples who were constantly seeking to press into a partially and superficially Christianized area.

Among the effects we must first of all remind ourselves of what we have summarized in the preceding pages, the continued adherence to the Christian name of most of the descendants of the Roman provincials and the professed acceptance of the Christian faith by the overwhelming majority of the invaders. Although in Spain and Sicily there were substantial Moslem elements, some of them invaders and others converts from the traditionally Christian population, in the North Christianity had not only won those pagans who had settled within what had once been the boundaries of the Roman Empire, but it had also been carried beyond those borders and had been firmly established in Ireland, Scotland, and the lands of the Frisians and the Saxons. In Spain and Sicily strong churches survived the Moslem conquests and in later centuries were again to embrace the entire population.

An effect which has often been noted was the preservation through the Church and the monasteries of much of the civilization of the Roman Empire and its transmission to later generations. From the standpoint of the Gospel this was not an unmixed blessing, for, as we must never allow ourselves to forget, that civilization was basically antagonistic to Christ and his message and in utilizing it the Christian community might be preparing the way for its triumph over the Gospel. Here, as we are to see, has again and again been a major peril, notably beginning with the Renaissance and continuing into our own day. Could Christianity, while perpetuating much of Græco-Roman culture, so select from it and transmute it that it could be made to serve the Gospel? That, whether or not they were aware of it, was what outstanding Christians were attempting. That was the dream of some of the great Popes and was seen in the Carolingian revival. Men like Charlemagne and Pope Nicholas I were seeking to make actual the City of God in the regions where their influence could reach. That they did not completely succeed is obvious.

That they and others less outstanding than they did not entirely fail must also be recognized. In the new stage of culture which was emerging in Western Europe there was more conscious effort to bring all of human life into submission to Christ than there had been under the pre-sixth century Christian Roman Emperors. The effort fell far short of the goal. The visible Church was penetrated and at times seemingly captured by irreconcilably hostile forces. The majority of the laity had at best only a faint insight into the meaning of the Christian message. Large portions of the clergy were corrupt.

Prominent administrative posts, including the episcopate, tended to be captured by men ambitious for place and power in a fashion which quite contradicted the Gospel. The designation "servant of the servants of God" employed by some of the Popes and taken from the memorable words of Jesus that they who wished to be greatest among his disciples must be servants of all became in the mouths of some of the occupants of the throne of Peter sheer hypocrisy. The property owned by the Church, theoretically to be used for the welfare of men, became a major menace to the true genius of the Church. Even the monasteries, dedicated as they were in principle to the full realization of the Christian life, almost always departed from the ideals of men like Benedict of Nursia and Benedict of Aniane. Presumably this was unavoidable. At least in one way or another and to a greater or less extent it has been seen in all institutions which bear the Christian name. Yet Western Europe after 500 and especially, as a result of what had been achieved between the year 500 and the year 950, in the centuries which immediately followed the latter date, was more nearly moulded by the Gospel than it had been before the disintegration of the Roman Empire and the great invasions. This was seen in almost every phase of its life. It was also apparent in individual after individual. Even when the majority fell so far short of Christian ideals that they seemed not to deserve the Christian name, they recognized and honoured those rare men and women who unmistakably displayed the fruits of the Spirit. These they called saints, cults arose in their honour, their physical relics were venerated, and they were regarded as worthy of emulation by all Christians.

SELECTED BIBLIOGRAPHY

GENERAL WORKS

A. Fliche and V. Martin, editors, *Histoire de L'Eglise depuis les Origines jusqu'à nos Jours.* Vol. IV, *De la mort de Théodose à l'élection de Grégoire le Grand,* by P. Labriolle, G. Bardy, L. Bréhier, G. de Plinval (Paris, Bloud & Gay, 1948, pp. 612); Vol. V, *Grégoire le Grand les États Barbares et la Conquête Arabe* (590-757), by L. Bréhier, R. Aigrain (Bloud & Gay, 1947, pp. 576); Vol. VI, *L'Époque Carolingiene,* by E. Amann (Bloud & Gay, 1947, pp. 511); Vol. VII, *L'Église au Pouvoir des Laïques* (888-1057), by E. Amann and A. Dumas (Bloud & Gay, 1948, pp. 544). By Roman Catholic authors, scholarly, and with their major interest in the Roman Catholic Church.

A. Hauck, *Kirchengeschichte Deutschlands,* Vols. I and II (Leipzig, J. C. Hinrichs'sche Buchhandlung, 1887, 1890) cover the period dealt with in this chapter. A standard work, with copious footnote references.

H. von Schubert, *Geschichte der christlicher Kirche im Frühmittelalter* (Tübingen, J. C. B. Mohr, 1921, pp. xxiv, 808). Confessedly a handbook, it is very useful as such.

IRISH MONASTICISM

L. Gougaud, *Christianity in Celtic Lands* (London, Sheed & Ward, 1932, pp. vii, 530). A translation of an enlarged revision of the author's *Les Chrétientés Celtiques,* it contains excellent footnotes and is the best single volume survey of the subject.

W. A. Phillips, *A History of the Church of Ireland from the Earliest Times to the Present Day* (Oxford University Press, 3 vols., 1933–1934). By various members of the clergy.

BENEDICT OF NURSIA AND HIS RULE

The Rule of Saint Benedict. Translated with an Introduction by Cardinal Gasquet (London, Chatto & Windus, 1925, pp. xxviii, 150).

J. McCann, *Saint Benedict* (New York, Sheed & Ward, 1937, pp. 301). Semi-popular, scholarly, with official Benedictine approval.

GREGORY THE GREAT

F. H. Dudden, *Gregory the Great. His place in History and Thought* (London, Longmans, Green & Co., 2 vols., 1905). The standard life in English.

H. H. Howorth, *Saint Gregory the Great* (New York, E. P. Dutton & Co., 1912, pp. lvii, 340). Semi-popular, scholarly, depending in part on Dudden, but based upon independent research.

THE SPREAD OF CHRISTIANITY IN THE WEST

Adamnan, *Life of Saint Columba, Founder of Hy,* edited by W. Reeves, in *The Historians of Scotland,* Vol. VI (Edinburgh, Edmonston & Douglas, 1874, pp. clxxxiv, 385).

J. T. Addison, *The Medieval Missionary. A Study of the Conversion of Northern Europe* (New York, The International Missionary Council, 1936, pp. xiv, 176). A careful survey and interpretation.

Bede, *Historia Ecclesiastica.* A standard translation is by C. Plummer (Oxford, The Clarendon Press, 1896). Another is J. A. Giles, *Bede's Ecclesiastical History of England; also the Anglo-Saxon Chronicle* (London, George Bell & Sons, 1907, pp. xliv, 515).

A. Grieve, *Willibrord. Missionary to the Netherlands, 691–739, Including a Translation of the Vita Willibrord by Alcuin of York* (London, The Society for the Propagation of the Gospel in Foreign Parts, 1923, pp. 139). Chiefly important for its translation of this standard early source by Alcuin.

K. S. Latourette, *A History of the Expansion of Christianity. Volume II, The Thousand Years of Uncertainty* (New York, Harper & Brothers, 1938, pp. ix, 492).

G. W. Robinson, *The Life of St. Boniface by Willibald* (Harvard University Press, 1916, pp. 114). The standard biography which was written at the request of Boniface's successor.

THE CAROLINGIAN REVIVAL; THE ENGLISH BACKGROUND

T. Allison, *English Religious Life in the Eighth Century as Illustrated by Contemporary Letters* (London, Society for Promoting Christian Knowledge, 1929, pp. xvi, 154).

E. S. Duckett, *Anglo-Saxon Saints and Scholars* (New York, The Macmillan Co., 1948, pp. viii, 488). Well written, scholarly.

The Life of Bishop Wilfrid by Eddius Stephanus, Text, Translation, & Notes, by B. Colgrave (Cambridge University Press, 1927, pp. xvii, 192). By an intimate associate of Wilfrid.

THE CAROLINGIAN REVIVAL

H. Bett, *Johannes Scotus Erigena*. A Study in Mediæval Philosophy (Cambridge University Press, 1925, pp. 204).

E. S. Duckett, *Alcuin, Friend of Charlemagne* (New York, The Macmillan Co., 1951, pp. xii, 337). A standard, charmingly written account.

Einhard's Life of Charlemagne. The Latin Text Edited, with Introduction and Notes, by H. W. Garrod and R. B. Mowat (Oxford, The Clarendon Press, 1915, pp. lix, 82).

A. Gardner, *Studies in John the Scot (Erigena). A Philosopher of the Dark Ages* (London, Henry Frowde, 1900, pp. xi, 145).

Chapter XIV

RETROSPECT AND PROSPECT

The four and a half centuries covered in the preceding four chapters may seem
disheartening for any who would share the dream of Jesus for the coming of
the kingdom of God. What had happened to that vision with its confident
assertion that the reign of God was at hand? Any student who seeks to understand the nature and the course of human history and especially any Christian
who is concerned with the fashion in which the God in Whom he believes
deals with men and with what can be expected in history from the Christian
Gospel must take this period into his total purview.

In trenchant phrases and vivid parables Jesus had pictured the characteristics
of the kingdom of God and of those who are its members. All men of goodwill must gladly, or perhaps sadly, admit that if mankind were to conform to
the ideals which he set forth, men would no longer hate one another and be
obsessed with the competitive struggle for food, clothing, and shelter, but
would live in friendly coöperation and in that living would find an abundance
for their physical needs in humble, glad service to one another. Yet Jesus had
been crucified. His disciples were convinced that he had risen from the dead
in conquering, radiant life, and that through the Spirit which issued from the
Father and Jesus men could be born into that life. They were impelled by the
faith that ultimately God's gracious will would be fully done and all creation
would be freed from bondage, entering into the glorious liberty of the children
of God, and that God would sum up all things in Christ, whether in heaven
or on earth.

In that faith the early Christians had gone forth. They had shared it with
others. The seemingly incredible had happened. Although beginning as one of
the numerically smallest of hundreds of competing religious groups in the
Græco-Roman world, within five centuries Christianity, the religion which
arose out of their faith, had won the professed allegiance of the vast majority
within that world, a world which then embraced the largest single aggregation
of civilized mankind. Out of that faith had grown the Christian churches, the

largest of them the Catholic Church. By an amazing burst of vitality within a culture which had ceased to think or to say much that was new, that faith had given birth to creative thinking in theology, to new forms of worship, to an Empire-wide ecclesiastical organization, and, even more significantly, had transformed thousands of individuals and had started them on the road towards the goal "of the high calling of God in Christ Jesus."

Then decline, slow but prolonged, had set in. In winning the professed allegiance of the peoples of the basin of the Mediterranean the process had been completed by a mass conversion which watered down the quality of living. Swamped by these millions, the Catholic Church had relaxed its discipline and in some areas had apparently all but given up attempts to enforce it. Efforts of growing minorities to a full attainment of the Christian ideal had issued in monasticism, with its communities and its solitaries. But many of the latter had gone to revolting extremes, sometimes of bizarre exhibitionism quite contrary to the Gospel ideal, and after the first burst of enthusiasm and devotion in their founding, the former tended to run down and to become characterized by uninspired routine or even by indolent self-indulgence.

Then the Roman Empire and with it the Græco-Roman world had disintegrated. Christianity had not saved it or brought it into conformity with the ideals set forth in the Gospels or the epistles of the early apostles. The Church itself was divided by bitter dissensions and the prey of power-loving ecclesiastics and princes. The invasion of the Moslem Arabs flooded about half of the territory which might be called "Christendom" and within it the churches dwindled and ceased to put forth new expressions of vitality. North of the Mediterranean, in regions unconquered by the Arabs, floods of barbarians poured in, most of them at the outset non-Christians and most of their Christians Arians and so bringing weakening division to the Christian ranks. These invaders from the north and north-east came in successive waves, and recovery, conversion, and partial assimilation had not been completed for one until another arrived and the level of Christian living was again lowered.

Christianity persisted, but the creative activity which it had shown in the first five centuries in fresh movements and in thought declined and in large areas disappeared. To be sure, it gave stability to the Byzantine realms and strengthened their resistance against invasions. Partly under its ægis much of Græco-Roman culture went on, and Christians were the chief channels through which it was transmitted to the Arabs. However, that achievement, as we have suggested, did not ensure the preservation of the Gospel, but rather might obscure and weaken it, for in its basic assumptions and convictions that culture contradicted the Gospel. Christianity had not brought into the likeness of the Gospel the remnants of the urban life of the Mediterranean world. The largest

"Christian" city was Constantinople, and in spite of its many churches and the disappearance of the pagan cults, one may question whether it more nearly approximated the ideals of the Gospel than had pre-Christian Rome. "Christian" Rome of the year 950, although it was the religious capital of Western Europe and was kept alive by its churches and the pilgrims who flocked to them, was very much smaller than the burgeoning metropolis of the early Emperors and probably was as iniquitous, even if not in all the same ways. Nor, although it was theoretically dominant in them, did Christianity bring to its high standards rural Asia Minor and Greece or the predominantly agricultural Western Europe of these dark centuries. Indeed, in chronic wars with their accompaniment of cruelty, callousness, robbery, sexual laxity, and the glorification of brute force, the Western Europe of the middle of the tenth century may have been further from the standards of the Gospel than was the same area five hundred years earlier. In its numerical strength Christianity was not nearly as important in the year 950 as it had been in the year 500, and the states which professed allegiance to it did not loom as large in the total world scene in the middle of the tenth century as they had at the close of the fifth.

Where, then, was the "exceeding greatness of the power"? The vessels were still palpably earthen: had they proved too much so for "the power"? Was the weakness of God as seen on the cross actually stronger than men as Paul had declared, or had the sin of man proved too much for it? We must frankly recognize the plain historical facts which we have summarized in the preceding paragraphs and the equally certain fact that Christianity has never regained most of the territory which it lost to Islam.

We may not be able to discern the full answer to the questions which the story raises. However, we must note that Christianity had won to a professed allegiance the earlier invaders from the North who had settled within what had been the boundaries of the Roman Empire and was even moving beyond the former Roman *limes* into fresh territories. We must recall the fashion in which many Christians protested against the non-Christian conduct of their fellows in both East and West and the forms of instruction and discipline which the Church in the West adopted to bring into partial conformity to its standards the rude barbarians of that region. We must remember that in much of the West in some of the darkest days the Church had endeavoured, not always unsuccessfully, to protect the weak and had preserved and furthered education and orderly living. We must, moreover, remind ourselves that even in this brief survey we have met individuals of outstanding and wide influence, such as John of Damascus, John the Almsgiver, Columba, Gregory the Great, and Boniface, who clearly bore the impress of the Gospel and were admired, and rightly so, as its exemplars. For every one whose memory our scanty records have preserved, presumably there were many thousands, also exemplars of Christian faith and life, of whom no trace survives. In them the kingdom of God was present and they were both light and salt. Through them the faith was spread and nourished. Always there continued to be darkness and decay but had it not been for them the darkness would have been more intense and the decay more noisome.

We must also call attention to the fact that although to a large degree the kind of power seen in governments and in institutions, including even those of the Church, was in contrast with that seen in the incarnation, the cross, and the resurrection, some governments proved less of an obstacle to the Gospel than did others. The Sassanid and the Arab states, for example, the one dominated by Zoroastrianism and the other by Islam, made the course of Christianity very difficult. The Christian Roman Emperors were both an aid and a hindrance. The order which they gave and their protection to the Church were of assistance, but their efforts at the control of the Church often compromised the Gospel and their friendship encouraged in the Church a kind of power which was the opposite of that seen in the Gospel. Much depended on the character of the monarch. Those who, like Alfred the Great, were earnestly endeavouring to rule as Christians were of more help than those who were not. The great Carolingians by their patronage, in spite of their use of armed force, facilitated the spread of Christianity and the reform of the Church by deeply Christian churchmen.

Moreover, as we have hinted, already, even in the darkest hours at the end of the ninth and the beginning of the tenth century, a fresh resurgence of vitality was evident in Christianity. It was fairly obvious in Byzantine realms but was also present in Western Europe. In the next four centuries it was to carry Christianity over a larger proportion of the earth's surface than until then had been true of it or any other one religion, it was to issue in more fresh movements than had been seen since the first three centuries of the faith, and it was to stamp far more deeply the civilization of Europe than it had that of the Roman Empire. These results were especially marked in Western Europe, but to a less degree they were also seen in parts of Eastern Europe. To that stage of our story we must now turn.

FOUR CENTURIES OF
RESURGENCE AND ADVANCE
A.D. 950 — A.D. 1350

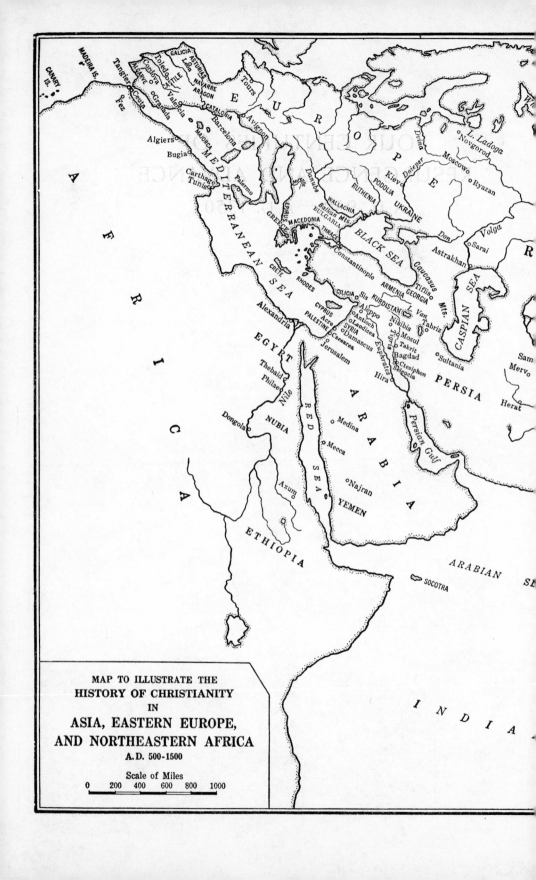

MAP TO ILLUSTRATE THE
HISTORY OF CHRISTIANITY
IN
**ASIA, EASTERN EUROPE,
AND NORTHEASTERN AFRICA**
A.D. 500-1500

Scale of Miles
0 200 400 600 800 1000

R   S   S   I   A

A

MTS.

L. Baikal

Amur

A   S   S   I   A

L. Balkash

JAPAN
SEA

Karakorum

MONGOLIA

JAPAN

STAN

Almalik

Ili

Tunhuang

Cambaluc

TIEN SHAN

ashgar

Tarim

Yellow

YELLOW
SEA

Changan

Yang-chow

PUNJAB

C   H   I   N   A

Nanking

Chinkiang

Chengtu

Hang-chow

Ganges

Yangtze Kiang

Zaitun

PACIFIC

I   N   D   I   A

BURMA

OCEAN

TTE I.

ranor

BAY OF

Annam

CHINA

MALABAR

Mailapur

BENGAL

SEA

NCORE

on

Champa

CEYLON

BORNEO

O   C   E   A   N

SUMATRA

JAVA

Chapter XV

THE MAIN FEATURES AND THE WORLD
SETTING OF CHRISTIANITY

Not far from the year 950 a fresh surge of life was seen in Christianity which was to continue until about the year 1350. No precise dates can be set for either its beginning or its end. As we have seen, it commenced earlier in Byzantine or Greek Christianity than it did in Western or Latin Christianity. It was most marked in Western Europe but in some of its aspects, notably in the geographic extension of the faith, it had striking manifestations in the East, in Byzantine and Nestorian Christianity.

In these four centuries Christianity won the formal allegiance of most of such of the peoples of North-western and Central Europe as had not previously accepted it. It expanded into what is now Russia. It regained from Islam most of the Iberian Peninsula. On the north and west it was planted in Iceland and Greenland and possibly was carried to North America. It was professed by minorities in Central, East, and South Asia. By the year 1350 Christians were scattered from Greenland on the extreme north and west to the China Sea on the east, and to India on the south.

The main strength and the most abounding vigour of Christianity were in Western Europe. Here were most of the new movements which were expressions of the resurging life. From here the chief territorial spread of the faith was achieved. Here Christianity was more potent in shaping civilization than it had previously been anywhere, more even than in the Roman Empire after the formal conversion of that realm. In Western Europe it was so vital and so influential that in later centuries it was there and among peoples who migrated from Western Europe that it continued to display its greatest power.

Why this resurgence of Christianity and in these particular centuries? We do not know. We can recognize some of the contributing factors but we cannot be certain that they were the most important.

As we suggested in the last chapter, a revival of strength was seen in the Byzantine Empire in the second half of the ninth and the first half of the tenth century. It continued in the second half of the tenth and in the fore part of the eleventh century. At the end of the first quarter of the eleventh century the Byzantine Empire had reached an apogee which it was never again to attain.

In Western Europe, as we also saw, near the end of the tenth century the invasions which had racked that section from the fifth century ceased. There were still movements of peoples and chronic war, but not again were there major incursions of non-Christians into Western Christendom which left large deposits of settlers. The Northmen were the last of such waves to submerge much of Western Europe. Later invasions of non-Christians, notably of the Mongols and the Ottoman Turks, might threaten the region, but they did not penetrate effectively beyond its eastern and southern borders.

The cessation of the invasions was accompanied and followed in Western Europe by a growth of wealth, the beginnings of modern states, the inception of that expansion of its peoples which by the middle of the twentieth century was to revolutionize most of mankind, and the emergence of a fresh aspect of civilization.

Commerce revived and with it, both aided by it and aiding it, cities increased in numbers and population. This was first notable in Italy, where was the capital of Western Christianity, Rome.

In Western Europe kingdoms, nascent nations, began to emerge from the welter of feudalism. In 987 the feudal princes chose as King of France one of their number, Hugh Capet, Duke of France, with his capital at Paris. Although at the outset possessing one of the weaker of the feudal principalities, under successive heads the Capetian family gradually added to their domains and made of France a strong state. In 911, on the death of Louis the Child, the last of the Carolingians to rule in Germany, the great tribal princes of that area together with the chief clergy elected Conrad of Franconia king. The title of King of the Germans did not remain permanently in the Franconian house as did that of King of France in the Capetian family. In 919 it passed to a line of Saxon dukes. In 962 one of that dynasty, Otto I, who had been made King of the Germans in 936, was crowned Roman Emperor. The ablest of Western rulers since Charlemagne to gain that title, he had already driven off the Danes, had defeated the Hungarians, had established his effective power over the great dukes of Germany, had put men whom he trusted at the head of the main bishoprics and monasteries, and had made himself master of much of Italy. His coronation as Emperor by the Pope is often regarded as beginning what was known as the Holy Roman Empire of the German Nation, an institution which was to persist until 1806. At the time the step was not looked upon as an innovation, for by his coronation Otto was regarded as having come into the succession of Roman Emperors. The term "Holy" was meant to indicate that the Roman Empire was Christian and the words "of the German Nation" were intended to convey the principle that normally the imperial throne would be filled by a German. In this fashion the political leadership of Western Christendom passed to a Saxon, one of that people who less than two centuries earlier had been brought forcibly by Charlemagne to accept the Christian faith. In 1066 William the Conqueror began a strong state in England. The gradual expulsion of Moslem political rule from the Iberian Peninsula was accompanied by the rise of professedly Christian kingdoms, chief of which were Castile, Leon, Aragon, Navarre, and Portugal. There emerged other Christian kingdoms in Western Europe, among them Denmark, Norway, Sweden, Scotland, Poland, and Hungary.

The expansion of Western Europe may be said to have dated from the first of the Crusades, in 1096. Through the long line of subsequent Crusades and the commerce of the Italian cities, before 1350 it had touched not only Western Asia but also India and China.

These political and economic developments were paralleled by the coming in Western Europe of a distinctive stage of civilization. Many-sided, embodying fresh achievements of the peoples of that region and contributions from Græco-Roman culture, in every phase it bore the imprint of the revived Christianity of the era.

Expanding and vigorous though it unquestionably was, in these four centuries Western Europe and even all Christendom did not loom as prominently in the total world scene as had the Roman Empire from the first to the fifth century. Far richer, more populous, and more sophisticated was China of the Sung Dynasty (960–1279). Although, like Europe, divided politically, India was probably wealthier than the former and contained more people. The Arab realms were now in fragments, but the Moslem world stretched from Spain through Western Asia and Persia into Central Asia and India. In most of this area Islam was dominant. Moslem civilization reached a high level, and its thought, especially that of Averroes (1126–1198), exerted a marked influence on the intellectual life of Christian Europe. In the eleventh century the Seljuk Turks, Moslems, created a realm in Persia and Western Asia which was larger than that of any Christian state of that day. While it soon broke up, some of its fragments continued to be important.

In the latter part of the twelfth and in the thirteenth century there blazed forth in meteoric fashion an empire, that of the Mongols, which ruled over a larger area and over more people than any which up to that time had been created by man. It was not Christian. Although some of its princes had Christian mothers and were baptized as infants, it was frankly pagan. Its founder, best known by his later designation, Jenghiz Khan, "Universal Emperor," was the son of the head of a confederation of some of the tribes in Mongolia. After his father's death he fought his way to the headship which had been held by his sire. He extended his rule over several of his neighbours and before his death (1227) he had begun the conquest of China and Central Asia. Under the sons and grandsons of Jenghiz Khan the victorious sweep of the Mongol arms continued. By the close of the thirteenth century the Mongols were masters of China, Korea, most of Central Asia, Persia, Mesopotamia, Armenia, Georgia, and the south of Russia. Beyond the borders of that vast area their armies had been seen in Poland, Hungary, Moravia, North-west India, Burma, Annam, and Champa, and their fleets attacked Japan and Java. While within a century and a half of the death of Jenghiz Khan the Mongol realm had broken up and the Mongols had been expelled from China, large fragments of Eurasia were much longer under Mongol rule, notably in Central Asia and Russia, and in the sixteenth century conquerors of Mongol stock subdued much of India and founded a dynasty which lasted into the nineteenth century. Compared with the Mongol Empire as it was in the thirteenth and fourteenth centuries the Christian kingdoms and the remnants of the Byzantine Empire were petty principalities which escaped incorporation only because they were sufficiently on the periphery not to feel the full impact of the Mongol armies.

Although in 1350 Christians were more widely scattered geographically than in 500 or 950, they may not have been as numerous as in the former year. In the year 1350 Europe had been more profoundly shaped by Christianity than in the year 950 or than had the Roman Empire in the year 500. Yet the portions of the world which called themselves Christian were by no means as prominent in the total world scene as had been the professedly Christian Roman Empire in the year 400 or even, after an additional century of decline, in the year 500. In the year 1350, to the hypothetical visitor from Mars Christianity would probably not have appeared as much a factor in the life of mankind as Islam or Buddhism and possibly no more so than Hinduism or Confucianism. However, it had proved its ability to survive the demise of the realm and the culture in which it had achieved its first triumphs and with which it had seemed to be identified, and, winning the barbarian invaders from the North, it had been a major stimulus in stirring them to produce an advanced civilization.

As we pursue the narrative of Christianity in these centuries, we will first tell of the progress towards the conversion of the peoples of Europe. We will then trace the course of Christianity in Western Europe, for it was here, rather than in the waning Byzantine realms, that the faith was to have its chief centre into the twentieth century. Finally we will move eastward, to tell of what was transpiring there in the Christian communities.

Chapter XVI

RENEWED AND CONTINUED PROGRESS IN THE EXPANSION OF CHRISTIANITY

The century which was bounded by A.D. 950 and A.D. 1050 saw as wide a geographic advance of Christianity as any in the history of the faith until after A.D. 1500. It witnessed the conversion of those pagans who so recently had been a scourge of Christendom, the Scandinavians, in some of their homelands—Denmark, Norway, and, incompletely, in Sweden—and in lands beyond the earlier borders of "Christendom" in which they had effected settlements—Iceland, Greenland, and, more notably, Kiev, the nucleus of the later Russia. It was the time when many of the Slavs of Central Europe came to the faith—some of those east of the Elbe through the efforts of Otto I, but especially the Czechs and Poles. During that period the Magyars were converted and Hungary joined the ranks of professedly Christian nations. In Spain the Christian reconquest of the peninsula made extensive strides. In Sicily the occupation by Christian Normans spelled the doom of Islam in that island. In Mesopotamia an Arab tribe accepted the faith. Thus those pagans who had threatened the very existence of Christianity were being won, and, as nowhere else by any other religion, the tide of Islam was being rolled back. In that same hundred years in Central Asia the Keraïts, who were later to be conquered by the Mongols and to be the means of the infiltration of Christianity into the ruling line of that masterful people, adopted the Nestorian form of the faith.

The following two centuries were to witness a further geographic extension, but nothing as spectacular as this.

THE CONVERSION OF THE SCANDINAVIANS

We have noted the fashion in which the Scandinavians, the "Northmen," had ravaged much of Europe in the ninth and tenth centuries. We have also seen that their conversion had begun before the year 950. At the instance of Louis the Pious the Archbishopric of Hamburg had been created as a mis-

385

sionary outpost for that purpose and Anskar had been appointed to it, had travelled widely in the northlands, and had made some converts. After the death of Anskar (865) the prospect seemed so unfavourable for winning Scandinavia that late in the ninth century it was suggested that the see of Hamburg-Bremen be discontinued and it was only the reluctance of the Pope which prevented the step from being taken. However, some of the Northmen who settled in Great Britain and Ireland and the portion of the Frankish domains which later had its name, Normandy, from them, accepted baptism. Indeed, before the last quarter of the tenth century they had provided three archbishops for the Church in England. Under their contacts with the peoples whom they were attacking, the inherited religion of the Vikings was disintegrating and they were adopting both the faith and much of the culture of the conquered.

It was in the second half of the tenth century that Christianity began to make rapid headway in the three Scandinavian lands—Denmark, Norway, and Sweden. In each conversion was accomplished as a community affair by a kind of mass movement. In each the eventual triumph of Christianity came through royal initiative. In at least one of these lands, Norway, the kings took advantage of it to extend their authority over recalcitrant nobles. In each, as had been true in other states, the kings insisted upon controlling the church in their respective realms. Each obtained the creation of an archbishopric to head the church in his domains.

The actual instruction, baptism, and difficult nurturing of the infant churches was chiefly by missionaries from England. This appears to have been for two reasons. In the first place, through the repeated invasions and ultimately through the Danish conquest of England, close contacts had been established between the Scandinavians and that land. In the second place, since the English were a subject people, the Scandinavians had nothing to fear from them politically. Had missionaries been accepted from the Carolingian realms or from the archiepiscopal see of Hamburg-Bremen, they might have been the means of establishing Carolingian and then German political power in Scandinavia. As we have seen, missionaries were used by the Carolingians to extend their control over much of Germany. It would not have been surprising if a similar sequel had followed had the Church been founded in Scandinavia by missionaries from Carolingian and German territories. Since most of the missionaries were from England, the dream of Louis the Pious and Anskar that the Archbishopric of Bremen-Hamburg would be the radiating centre for Christianity in the North was largely although by no means entirely frustrated.

Denmark and Norway were brought to the Christian faith almost simultaneously, but the process of conversion began in Denmark slightly earlier than in Norway. That was probably to be expected because of the nearer proximity of Denmark to Christendom and the smaller size of the country. Not long before the year 950 a King of Denmark, Harald Bluetooth, was baptized. His son claimed for him that he had "made the Danes Christian," and we hear of bishops among that people. In the succeeding reign, that of Sweyn (Svend I), the conqueror of the larger part of England, a pagan reaction occurred. It was under Sweyn's son, Canute, that Denmark finally came into the family of professedly Christian states. From 1019 until his death in 1035, Canute was king in both England and Denmark and for a time he was also master of Norway. Canute was a Christian and beginning with 1020 he vigorously supported the Christian cause. He made a pilgrimage to Rome and is said to have commanded that all his subjects learn the Lord's Prayer and go to communion three times a year. Many missionaries came from England, but it was not until early in the twelfth century that Denmark was removed from the jurisdiction of the Archbishop of Hamburg and was given an archbishopric of its own.

In Norway the course of conversion was more spectacular than in Denmark. Harald Fairhair (died 933), a pagan, by much fighting had made himself master of most of Norway and had begun the establishment of a monarchy which would rule over that land. His son and successor, Haakon "the Good," had been reared in the English court as a Christian. He tried to win his people to his faith, but the opposition of the landowners proved too strong for him. Not many years after Haakon's death Harald Bluetooth of Denmark made himself lord of Norway and sought to spread Christianity in the land, but without much success. More effective were the brief efforts of a greatgrandson of Harald Fairhair, Olaf Tryggvason. A posthumous child, born about 963 or 964, from boyhood Olaf led an adventurous and colourful life. Early captured by the Vikings and sold as a slave, he was rescued by an uncle, adopted the life of a Viking, raided England, was baptized by a hermit on the Scilly Islands off the south-west coast of that land, and was confirmed by the Bishop of Winchester. Handsome, huge of stature, daring, fearless, he was the embodiment of the Viking ideal. In 995 he returned to Norway and there was elected king. He set about bringing all the Norwegians to acknowledge him and to receive baptism. The two processes seem to have gone hand in hand. He accomplished them by persuasion where possible and by force where necessary. Now and again he destroyed pagan temples and slew members of the opposition. Most of the land was nominally Christian when, in the year 1000, he perished in a great naval battle with the Danes, Swedes, and his Norwegian opponents.

The conversion of Norway was completed and the Church firmly planted by another Olaf—Olaf Haraldsson, or St. Olaf. Like the other Olaf, a posthumous child, he was also of the lineage of Harald Fairhair. Stocky, strong, skilful in sports, good to look upon, fair of hair, ruddy of face, keen of mind, with eyes before which, when they lighted up in anger, strong men quailed, he was a born leader of men. At the age of twelve he began his Viking career. He fought in England and France and raided the shores of Sweden. In his early twenties (in 1015) he went to Norway to claim the throne, defeated his enemies, and was rapidly acknowledged by *thing* after *thing,* the *thing* being the local assembly.

Once securely in power, Olaf sought to make his realm Christian not only in name but also in fact. Priests and bishops from England aided him in instructing his people, but not all these were strictly foreigners, for from their names it appears that three of the four bishops from England had Scandinavian blood in their veins. He travelled through the land to see that churches were built and priests set over them. He framed laws on what he believed to be Christian principles, proscribing paganism and customs which were contrary to Christian morals. Yet even he did not bring about the baptism of all his subjects. Many local magnates opposed him, partly because of his attempt to increase the royal power at the expense of their authority and partly because of his suppression of the pagan shrines which were their property and from which came much of their revenues and prestige. Aided by Canute of Denmark, they rose in rebellion and in a battle in 1030 Olaf was slain. A revulsion of popular feeling swept Olaf to canonization. Miracles were soon reported to have been wrought at his tomb, churches were erected in his honour, and he became the patron saint of the realm.

Although the formal conversion of Norway may be said to have been completed by the time of Olaf's death, the instruction of the populace in the tenets of the faith and the development of an organization for the Church required many decades. Monks and secular priests from England were of assistance. The *scald,* the bard who was an accepted feature of the old order, spread the message through his songs, and respected laymen who were committed to the new faith gave it prestige. By the latter part of the eleventh century the country had a diocesan organization. The division of the area into parishes and the provision of local clergy proceeded, although only gradually. Diocesan boundaries usually conformed to pre-Christian political divisions. The Archbishop of Hamburg attempted to exercise jurisdiction, but the king angrily objected and insisted on having his bishops consecrated in France or England. In 1152 Norway was given an archiepiscopal see of its own and its church thereby achieved the kind of national status which prevailed in several other kingdoms of Europe. Technically this was within the structure of the Catholic Church of the West over which the Pope was supreme, but Rome was far away and its power not so effective as in nearer lands.

The last of the three Scandinavian kingdoms fully to enter the Christian fold was Sweden. Christians were to be found there at least as early as the ninth century, and Anskar visited the land more than once. By 936 such Christian communities as had existed seem to have disappeared, but the faith was soon renewed. Many Swedes who had been in England as merchants or soldiers and had been baptized there returned home. In the second half of the tenth century there were bishops in Sweden. Early in the eleventh century a Swedish king, Olof Skötkonung, was baptized and inaugurated a bishopric, under the jurisdiction of the see of Hamburg-Bremen. Although most of the land was still pagan and the main shrine of the old worship was maintained as formerly at Uppsala, missionaries from England were preaching the new faith. As was to be expected and as was true in Norway, Christianity triumphed first in the South, nearer to Christendom, and paganism lingered longest in the North. It was not until the first decades of the twelfth century that Christianity was dominant. Monasticism entered through the Cistercians who, as we are to see, represented a revival in that movement. When, in 1164, Sweden was given its own archiepiscopal see, its first incumbent was a Cistercian, its seat was placed at Uppsala, and the cathedral was erected on the site of the head temple of the pre-Christian pagan cult. Thus was Christianity clearly victor and not in a lax form but headed by a member of that order, then young, which represented one of the latest and strictest attempts to conform fully to the Christian ideal.

THE SPREAD OF CHRISTIANITY IN SCANDINAVIAN OUTPOSTS
IN THE ATLANTIC

The Viking explosion of the ninth and tenth centuries planted Scandinavian colonies, largely Norwegian, on westward-lying islands as far away as Greenland. In the latter part of the tenth and the fore part of the eleventh century Christianity was carried to them and their populations accepted it, but in some instances not without hesitation and with divided counsels.

The Orkney, the Faroe, and the Shetland Islands had something of a Christian population before the coming of the Vikings. The latter represented a pagan influx. Olaf Tryggvason is credited with the conversion of the populations of the Faroes and the Shetlands and with the forcible baptism of the head man of the Orkneys. Olaf Haraldsson helped to confirm and deepen the change.

The first settlers of Iceland seem to have been Irish monks, but, obviously, they did not give rise to a continuing population. The first large immigration appears to have been by Norwegians who disliked the centralizing measures of Harald Fairhair. Some effort at their conversion was made in the 980's. More vigorous and outwardly successful measures were taken at the instance of Olaf Tryggvason during his brief and stormy reign. Many were baptized and for a time civil war threatened between Christians and pagans. This was avoided by a compromise suggested by one of the leading men. It was agreed that all were to accept baptism, but that secret sacrifices to the old gods were to be met with only minor penalties. A few years later paganism was officially abolished. Olaf Haraldsson sent at least one bishop and a bell and timber for a church. The island long suffered from a shortage of clergy. This was partly met by training local boys and by a line of native bishops. The lads so prepared remained in subjection to the chiefs, and the bishops, while sent to the Continent for consecration, were elected by the island assembly, the *Althing*.

The first Norse settlement of Greenland was on the less insalubrious west coast and from Iceland, near the end of the tenth century. The leader was a pagan, Eric the Red. Christianity was introduced by his son, Leif, who had been won to the faith by Olaf Tryggvason and who, to his father's disgust, brought a priest to the island. The Norse population was never large, probably not much over two thousand. Churches and a cathedral were eventually erected and in the fore part of the twelfth century a bishop was consecrated. The bishop was henceforth the civil as well as the ecclesiastical head of the colony.

It was by the Norse that Christianity reached America. Leif Ericson himself is said to have been the first to touch the continent. How many Norse came in succeeding years we do not know. Nor do we know where they went, how many if any of them were Christians, or whether they made any converts among the Eskimoes and Indians.

THE WINNING OF THE SCANDINAVIANS IN RUSSIA AND THE BEGINNINGS OF RUSSIAN CHRISTIANITY

It was not only in Western and North-western Europe and in islands in the North Atlantic that the Scandinavians became Christians. Almost simultaneously there was a movement towards the faith led by the Scandinavian rulers of a state which centred in Kiev, on the Dnieper, and which is usually regarded as the beginning of one of the numerically largest bodies of Christians, that of Russia. As was natural from the geographic location, this was not through the Latin but through the Byzantine or Greek wing of the Catholic Church.

In the ninth century in the great Viking movement, Scandinavians, most of them Swedes, made their way southward across the plains and along the rivers of what was later western Russia and became masters of the local, largely

Slavic, populations. They were known as Varangians or Rus and their chief settlements were Novgorod in the north and Kiev in the south, in the later Ukraine. Never more than a minority of the population, eventually they adopted the Slavonic tongue of the subject majority.

Christianity had long been present on the northern shores of the Euxine or Black Sea. Christians were there at least as early as the fourth and fifth centuries. To be sure, in the south of what is now Russia the rulers of the dominant people, the Khazars, had adopted Judaism, but in the second half of the ninth century the famous Patriarch of Constantinople, Photius, of whom we heard in an earlier chapter, organized a mission for the Russians which was so far successful that the latter asked for a bishop. Slightly later, also in that century, the Emperor Basil I, "the Macedonian," and the Patriarch Ignatius, whom we have also met, sent as a missionary to the Russians a bishop who is said to have made many converts.

Through these or other channels, by the middle of the tenth century Christianity had entered Kiev and at least one church building had been erected in that city. In the 950's, Olga, the dowager regent, was baptized and sent to Otto I of Germany for missionaries. These seem to have had no very marked success.

It was under Vladimir, the grandson of Olga, that the mass conversion of Kiev and the territory which was dependent on it began. Precisely when and how Vladimir became a Christian we do not know. An oft-repeated story declares that he was visited by representatives of Islam, Judaism, Latin Christianity, and Greek Christianity, each of whom sought to win him. It is further said that of all the delegations that of the Greeks made the greatest impression on him and that he took the decisive step after a deputation appointed by him had visited Constantinople and had reported the overwhelming splendour of a service in the cathedral of Saint Sophia at which they had been present. While this story is almost certainly a later fabrication, it at least reflects the choice which faced Vladimir as he saw the disintegration of the inherited religion of the Varangians and cast about for a faith to take its place. Islam, Judaism (popular among his neighbours, the Khazars), and the Latin and Greek forms of Christianity were the viable possibilities. The last may have won his support because it was the faith of the most powerful, the wealthiest, and the most civilized of the states which bordered on his domains. It will be recalled that the Byzantine Empire was not only near by but at that time was also approaching one of the heights of its might. Vladimir received delegates from the Pope and sent representatives to Rome, but it was to the Greek wing of the Catholic Church that he adhered.

In accepting Greek Christianity, Vladimir seems deliberately to have made it clear that for him baptism was not a token of submission to the then expanding Byzantine realm. He captured a Byzantine town in the Crimea and as a price of peace exacted the hand of a Byzantine princess to add to his collection of wives and concubines. It was after his return from the Crimea that he actively undertook the conversion of his people. The exact date is uncertain, but it was towards the close of the tenth century. It has been said, but this is questioned, that he required the populace of Kiev to betake themselves to the river for collective baptism and that he ordered the destruction of all the idols in the city. It is certain that he encouraged baptisms, built churches, founded monasteries, and sent clergy to other centres to spread what had been begun at Kiev. It was in 991 that the population of Novgorod was baptized by the bishop of the Crimean town which Vladimir had seized. By the end of his reign (1015) there were three bishoprics in his domains, but with characteristic independence he would not submit to ecclesiastical control from Constantinople.

After Vladimir and under the impulse given by him and with the encouragement of his successor, Christianity continued to spread in Russia. Still later it was carried to new areas. In the twelfth century, for example, monks from Novgorod planted it on the upper reaches of the Volga.

As in Western Europe, most of the active missionaries were monks and it was monastic Christianity which was held up as the ideal. Fully as much as in Western Europe, the Christianity of the masses was very superficial. Several generations passed before the majority would sufficiently conform even to so slight a degree as to attend the services of the Church and receive the sacraments. The dioceses were huge, the Metropolitan of Kiev, for centuries the head of the administrative structure, was appointed by the Patriarch of Constantinople and was usually a Greek and unfamiliar with local conditions, and a substantial minority of the bishops were from abroad and understood little of the customs or language of their flocks. The clergy were poorly trained and at best were too few for the size of the country. They were usually chosen by their parishioners and the bishops were selected by the local princes.

Superficial though much of this early Russian Christianity undoubtedly was, it began to take root. An extensive Christian literature was made available in Slavonic, the speech of the majority. This was partly through fresh translations from the Greek and partly by utilizing translations which had already been made for Bulgaria and which, as we have seen, were indebted to the initiative of Constantine (Cyril) and Methodius in the second half of the ninth century. A majority of the bishops and presumably almost all the parish priests were of the indigenous stock. Monasteries multiplied and from the outset were a normal part of the life of the Church. A famous one on the outskirts of Kiev had a profound influence.

THE CONVERSION OF BOHEMIA

Simultaneously with the rapid progress of conversion among the Scandinavians some of the largest groups of Slavs were being incorporated into Christendom. We have noted the labours of Constantine and Methodius in the second half of the ninth century, the winning of Bulgaria with its predominantly Slavic population, also in that fifty years, and have hinted at the activities of German missionaries among the Slavs of Central Europe. By the year 900 Christianity was strong in Moravia. The hundred years between 950 and 1050 witnessed the adherence to the faith of the two largest Slavic states in Central Europe, Bohemia and Poland.

The conversion of Bohemia was in part through the impulses which stemmed from Constantine and Methodius, but was chiefly from Germany. Famous near the beginnings of the Church in Bohemia was Václav, better known to most of us as Wenceslas, who came to the throne about 923–924 at the age of eighteen. A Christian, profoundly religious, he is said to have been a builder of churches, generous to the poor, ardent in his personal religious devotions, to have worn a rough shirt under his royal robes, and to have remained a virgin. He was a tributary of the German King and under him German missionaries entered. In 929 while on his way to mass he was murdered by his brother, Boleslav I, and an anti-German, anti-Christian reaction ensued. The combination of his piety and his tragic end made of Václav the national saint.

In the latter part of the century the climate again changed in favour of Christianity. Boleslav II, the son of the murderer of Václav, reigned from 967 to 999. In contrast with his father, he actively encouraged the spread of the faith. It was under him that the nominal conversion of Bohemia was substantially completed. He founded monasteries and built churches. Otto I was a power with whom to reckon and it seems to have been at his instance that the initial bishopric in Bohemia, that of Prague, was created. The first bishop was a Saxon and the second, Adalbert, although of Czech blood, was related to the family of Otto I, had been educated at Magdeburg, the seat of the bishopric which that German ruler had created as a centre for missions among the Slavs, and was strongly committed to the Cluny movement, with its strict standards of Christian living. He made himself unpopular by attempting to raise the semi-pagan life of his flock to the level advocated by the Cluny reformers, and was martyred (997) as a missionary to the pagan Prussians south of the Baltic. By that time Bohemia was regarded as a Christian kingdom.

THE CONVERSION OF POLAND

To the north of Bohemia lay Poland, that region whose absence of clearly defined geographic boundaries has rendered it the tragic victim of its strong neighbours. Here, as in Bohemia, Christianity entered partly under pressure from the Germans. Also, as in several of the lands which we have noted, its progress was associated with the growth of centralized political control by a king and was opposed by those local magnates who wished to preserve their independence and who associated it with the pre-Christian order.

We do not know exactly when the first conversions were made among the Slavs of the region which we know as Poland. In the second half of the tenth century a Slavic prince who ruled over part of the area accepted baptism, perhaps through the influence of his wife, the sister of Boleslav II of Bohemia. He was forced to recognize the overlordship of Otto I. In 968 a bishopric was created for the Poles at Poznań (Posen) and its first two incumbents were Germans.

The great growth of Christianity in Poland was under a son of this prince, Boleslaw Chrobry ("the Brave"), who reigned from 992 to 1025. Boleslaw brought together one of the largest states of the Europe of his day and sought to strengthen the royal authority at the expense of the local magnates. He encouraged missionaries. When Adalbert was martyred by the Prussians he had the body brought to Gniezno (Gnesen). That city was soon (1000) made the seat of an archbishopric, the brother of the martyr was put at its head, and three suffragan sees were created under it. Thus the Church in Poland was given a hierarchy, even though that might be inadequate for so large a realm. The creation of these bishoprics was at the initiative of the imaginative young Holy Roman Emperor, Otto III, grandson of Otto I, but the suggestion may have come from Boleslaw, for the act made the Polish Church almost independent of that of Germany.

After the death of Boleslaw what might have been anticipated took place. A revulsion set in against the royal authority and the faith which was so closely associated with it. For a time the Kingdom of Poland broke apart. Churches and monasteries were burned and bishops and priests were either driven out or killed. While the work of Boleslaw was never completely undone, for several generations the Christianity of the country was on a low level. Bishops were too few and their dioceses too large for adequate administration.

THE CONVERSION OF THE MAGYARS

It was late in the ninth century, while the Viking invasions of Europe were in full flood and the measure of order given by the Carolingians was declining, that the Magyars effected settlements in the modern Hungary. From there they repeatedly raided Italy and Western Europe as far as the North Sea. Pagans, they burned churches, plundered monasteries, killed some priests before the altars and carried others into captivity. They contributed to the low ebb of Christianity in the first half of the tenth century.

Rising German power checked the Magyar advance and in 955 Otto I inflicted a stunning defeat which freed Western Europe from the Magyar terror. Germans, Christians, moved eastward and colonized regions on the Danube on the Magyar borders. On the south-east the Bulgars had become Christians and the faith, as we have seen, was spreading in Bohemia and Poland on the Magyars' north. It is not strange that Christianity began making headway among the Magyars themselves.

The mass conversion of Magyars came late in the tenth and early in the eleventh century. It was chiefly accomplished through the royal family and especially by Vajk, better known as Stephen, who made of Hungary a monarchy of the type that was emerging in Western Europe.

It is said that two Magyar princes were baptized in Constantinople while on a political errand and that they brought back a bishop with them. However, it was to the West rather than to Constantinople that the leaders turned for their culture and their religion. In 973 Magyar envoys appeared at the court of Otto I and not far from that time German missionaries began to penetrate into Magyar lands. A Magyar prince, Geisa, was making himself master of the country and compelled many of his subjects to accept baptism. Baptism and submission to his authority appear to have gone hand in hand.

Geisa's labours were brought to a culmination by his son Vajk (Stephen). Stephen succeeded his father in 997 and continued the latter's measures for the unification of the realm and the adoption of Christianity. He himself preached to his subjects, urging them to accept the new faith. Although some question has been raised about the authenticity of the Papal letter which is our chief source of information, it is said that in the year 1000 Stephen asked of the Pope and received the royal title, a crown, and a hierarchy for his realm, with an archbishop and subordinate bishops. It is certain that many missionaries entered, a large proportion of them Slavs, and that by legislation Stephen enjoined respect for Sunday, decorum during church services, and the payment of tithes for the support of the Church. He also gave bishops judicial powers in matrimonial and ecclesiastical questions much as was customary in the West.

Stephen's innovations met stubborn resistance which from time to time flared up in open rebellion. When death removed his strong hand (1038) the almost inevitable reaction revived pagan rites and brought violence against the clergy. However, after a generation of internal dissensions and foreign wars and invasions, late in the eleventh century a succession of strong monarchs gave renewed support to Christianity and the Church.

CHRISTIAN COUNTER-GAINS AGAINST ISLAM IN SPAIN AND SICILY

As we have suggested, the four centuries which followed the year 950 witnessed a substantial reclamation of territories lost to Islam in Spain and Sicily.

In Spain the Moslem Arab conquest had no sooner reached its high-water-mark than the small states which survived in the North under Christian leadership began to regain the lost territory. This, like the Arab domination, was achieved by armed force. The first stage of the Moslem retreat is usually dated from a battle in 718 in which the Christians were victors. Various Christian states arose—Aragon, León, Navarre, Castile, Portugal, and in the Asturias, Galicia, and Catalonia. These states often fought among themselves and thereby gave breathing spaces to the waning Moslem power. In the latter part of the tenth century Almanzor, the great minister and general of the Caliphate of Cordova, inflicted defeat after defeat on the Christian armies. However, in 1034 the Caliphate of Cordova came to an end and with it disappeared what had been the main centre and rallying point of Moslem power. The tide of battle ebbed and flowed, but by the middle of the thirteenth century the Moslem political power had been reduced to the small state of Granada, in the extreme south-east.

In the territories reconquered by Christian from Moslem princes little force was employed to bring about conversion from Islam. As in the Moorish states Christians had been tolerated and Christian bishops and clergy had continued to minister to their flocks, so now, under Christian rulers, such of the Moslems as chose to do so were permitted the free practice of their religion and were left in possession of their mosques, houses, and estates and for a time had magistrates of their own faith. Similarly as under Moslem rule Christians had been subjected to certain disabilities and special taxation, so Christian princes required Moslems to live in segregated districts and to pay tithes to the Church and a special tribute to the state.

Under these circumstances Islam declined in the Iberian Peninsula. Some of its adherents migrated to Africa to be under Moslem rulers. Others deemed it expedient to conform to the religion of their new masters. Active missionary effort was directed to the Moslems, especially beginning in the thirteenth century with the rise of the great missionary orders, the Franciscans and the Dominicans, of whom we are later to hear much. On at least one occasion an over-zealous bishop said mass in a mosque in violation of a pledge given by the Christian conqueror at the time of the surrender. It was long after 1350 that the last remnants of Islam disappeared from the Iberian Peninsula, but by that year the outcome was fairly well assured.

The extinction of Islam in Sicily was the result of the Norman conquest of that island in the second half of the eleventh century. The Normans, as their name indicates, were the descendants of Northmen who had settled in the area, Normandy, which took its name from them. In Normandy they had become Christians. The religious motive seems either to have been absent or distinctly secondary in their invasion of Sicily. A minority, they deemed it the part of wisdom to grant religious freedom to the diverse faiths of their subjects. Jews, Moslems, Greek Orthodox, and Roman Catholics enjoyed equal rights. Towards the end of the twelfth century, after a hundred years of Norman rule, Moslems were still numerous and influential and held high posts at court. However, the early Norman magnates strengthened the Church and founded additional bishoprics, thus in part undoing the damage which had accompanied Moslem dominance. Islam, never represented by more than a minority, declined. By the middle of the thirteenth century it had almost disappeared.

The Slow Completion of the Conversion of North-western Europe

The remarkable spread of Christianity in the hundred years after 950 brought into nominal adherence to the faith most of the major peoples of Western Europe who had thus far been outside its fold. The one important exception was the Moors in the Iberian Peninsula and these, as we have seen, were dwindling. Yet in 1050 by no means all those who dwelt in Western and Central Europe thought of themselves as Christians. In addition to the Moslems in the Iberian Peninsula and Sicily and the Jews, a small and widely scattered minority, there were still frankly pagan enclaves. They were principally along the southern and eastern shores of the Baltic. Chief among them were the Slavs north and east of the Elbe (Wends the Germans called them), the Pomeranians, the Lithuanians, the Prussians, the Estonians or Ests, the Letts, the Finns, and, in the extreme North, the Lapps.

After the middle of the eleventh century the geographic advance of Christianity in Western and Central Europe continued but at a much less marked pace. As we have repeatedly reminded ourselves, the effect of nominal conversion upon the majority of the peoples who had been won in the preceding hundred years was slight and the deepening of the faith through instruction, the recruiting and training of clergy, the development of dioceses and parishes, and the administration of the Church's sacraments was slow. In some lands, notably in Poland and Hungary, the first wave of conversion, associated as it was with vigorous and sometimes violent and ruthless expansion of the royal power, was followed by a pagan revival. Recovery always came, but it might be retarded. By the year 1350 conversion had been accomplished in all Western and Central Europe except for the Lithuanians, the Finns, the Jews, and the Moslem remnants in Spain. Beginnings had been made in all these and before long the Lithuanian pagan majority was to accept baptism.

Efforts for the conversion of the Wends commenced in a large way in the first half of the tenth century. Divided into many tribes, the Wends then occupied most of the later Germany east and north of the Elbe. The German rulers attempted to extend their control over them and their territories. This led to chronic warfare which was often waged with savage cruelty. Since the Germans professed to be Christians, both they and the Wends regarded baptism as a symbol of submission to German authority and the issue was compounded by racial bitterness. Otto I extended his domains, somewhat super-ficially, eastward to the Oder. He sought the conversion of his newly acquired Wend subjects. To this end he founded two bishoprics in Wendland and placed them under the Archbishopric of Magdeburg, inaugurated for this very purpose, on the left bank of the Elbe, looking across the river into Wend terri-tory. After death had removed his strong hand, the Wends revolted and directed part of their spleen against the bishops, symbols as they were of Ger-man rule. German authority was later restored, but when it declined the Wends once more rose. Again and again the cycle was repeated. Some of the Wends were baptized, but the territory which had been theirs became solidly com-mitted to Christianity only through the immigration of Germans, a process which required centuries.

The conversion of the Pomeranians, a Slavic people on the Baltic with their capital at Stettin, was accomplished during the twelfth and the fore part of the thirteenth century. In it Poles, Danes, and Germans had a part, but Germans were the chief agents. In the first quarter of the twelfth century a king of Poland invaded the region, captured some of the cities, and as a price of peace required the populace to pay him tribute and to accept baptism. His chief emissary for inducing the Pomeranians to fulfil their promise to be baptized was a German, Bishop Otto of Bamberg.

Otto was an organizer, a man of affairs, who had been Chancellor of the Holy Roman Empire. At this time probably in his sixties, he had the fearless-ness and energy of youth. Twice he journeyed into Pomerania, both times in the 1120's, taking with him a band of assistants. He went unarmed, but with impressive pomp, with the endorsement of the Pope, and the second time with the authority of the German king. Under him numbers were baptized, but not until the close of the century do there seem to have been many Pomeranian priests. German and Danish monastic communities and the German farmers whom they encouraged to come to till their lands did much to complete the assimilation of the Pomeranians to the Christian faith.

It was in the latter part of the twelfth and the fore part of the thirteenth century that Christianity was firmly established among the Finns. This was largely through the Swedes, but it was an Englishman, Bishop Henry of the Swedish see of Uppsala, who, martyred, is esteemed the founder of the Finnish church. It was, however, a Swedish conquest which began in 1249 that led the majority to an outward conformity to the Christian faith. The Swedes also had missions among the Lapps, in the extreme north of the Scandinavian Peninsula, but by the middle of the fourteenth century only a minority had been won.

Late in the twelfth and early in the thirteenth century the Danes were especially strong in the Baltic. Through them conversions were made among the Ests, south of the Gulf of Finland. The Swedes and the Russians from Novgorod also had a part in bringing the Ests to accept the Christian faith. Indeed, there was unseemly rivalry among these nationalities in using baptism as a means of gaining support for their interests.

Except for the Lithuanians, the majority among the Baltic peoples south of the Gulf of Finland became Christians through the Germans. Early contacts with Germans were commercial. German merchants frequented the Baltic ports. Accounts brought by merchants led an elderly German monk, Meinhard, to go to the lower Dvina and preach to any who would listen. He was soon consecrated bishop for that area. The second of his successors, Albert, founded the city of Riga near the mouth of the Dvina and inaugurated (1202) a crusading order with the name, singularly inappropriate for Christian missionaries, Knights of the Sword, officially and slightly less offensively, *Fratres Militiae Christi*. By this time Crusades, of which we will have more to say in the next chapter, had become an honoured phase of the activities of Western Christendom and orders which combined monastic vows with the career of the soldier had come into being to further them. The Knights of the Sword conquered a fairly extensive area and required of pagans a pledge to accept baptism as a symbol of submission.

The Prussians, a non-Germanic people, were very resistant. Late in the tenth and early in the eleventh century they killed several missionaries. Undiscouraged, other missionaries came and baptisms followed. In the first half of the thirteenth century the Teutonic Knights undertook the task. They, too, had arisen from the Crusades, originally for the purpose of serving Christians in Syria and Palestine. In 1225–1226 they were called by a Pole for aid against a tribe of Prussians. Here they found their main field of endeavour. After a half century of fighting they conquered the land. They then ruled it for several centuries. Under them the Prussians outwardly conformed to the Christian faith.

The Teutonic Knights attempted to subjugate the Lithuanians, but the latter resisted both them and their religion. It was not until 1386 that as the price of an alliance with the Poles against the Knights the Lithuanians agreed to mass baptism and the destruction of their pagan temples. Obviously even then the conversion was superficial and pagan practices survived at least as late as the seventeenth century.

The Jews in Western Europe

Through most of Western Europe the Jews remained an unassimilated minority, largely city dwellers and keeping to their ancestral faith. There was much popular feeling against them and from time to time mobs attacked them. Some of the Crusaders on their way to the Holy Land slaughtered men, women, and children. Through the centuries there was a trickle of conversions which occasionally became a substantial stream. Many of these were forced and some were from motives of prudence, but others were from religious conviction. In general the Popes condemned the use of violence to bring conversions, but declared that if a Jew had been baptized he had thereby been made a member of the Church and was subject to its discipline if he reverted to the religion of his forefathers.

Jews were especially numerous in Spain. Throughout most of these centuries, with the exception of occasional spasms of persecution, they were treated with leniency by both Moslem and Christian rulers. Indeed, in the twelfth, thirteenth, and fourteenth centuries they often rose to high positions in the government and the administration of the finances of the Christian states was largely in their hands. Gradually, in the thirteenth and fourteenth centuries prejudice against them mounted and official measures were taken to compel them to attend sermons presenting the Christian faith. Presumably some baptisms followed. Not until 1391, however, does toleration seem to have ended.

The Further Spread of Christianity in Russia

In the first half of the thirteenth century Christianity in Russia entered upon grim days. The Mongols swept into the land and made themselves masters of the area north of the Caspian and Black Seas. They were pagans and the immediate effect of their conquest was adverse for the Church. Many Christians perished, numbers of church buildings were laid in ruins, and service books and vestments were destroyed. Eventually the dominant groups among the Golden Horde—the Russian Mongols—embraced Islam. It would not have been surprising if Russian Christianity, by the majority very superficially and unintelligently held, had disappeared.

However, the net effect of the Mongol conquest was to deepen the hold of Christianity on the Russians and to spread the faith into areas hitherto untouched. In general the Mongol rulers were friendly to the Church and did not attempt to force their Christian subjects to abandon their faith. The Church was given authority over its members in moral and religious questions, especially in marriage, sex offenses, inheritance, and the duties of children to parents. It was accorded immunity from some forms of taxation. The Church was regarded by Russians as the one institution which was peculiarly their own and became a symbol of what might be called Russian nationalism. It was the tie of Russian unity.

To escape the Mongol yoke many Russians migrated northward, beyond the border of Mongol rule. Numbers also sought release by abandoning the world and adopting the monastic life. Hermits made their way to the northern forests. In other places in the North monastic communities were established. Around many of the latter towns sprang up and the monasteries became schools in agriculture and the Christian faith. Through them pagans were converted, lands cleared, roads and canals built, marshes drained, and improved methods of cattle breeding and cultivating the soil were introduced. By them the Russian language was spread and various Finnish tribes were assimilated to the Russian church and Russian culture.

THE GROWTH OF CHRISTIAN MINORITIES IN ASIA

Between 950 and 1350 more and more of the peoples of the western end of the continent of Eurasia made Christianity their official faith. Simultaneously, immersed in the dominant Islam, the churches on the north shore of Africa and in Western Asia east and south of Asia Minor slowly dwindled. Europe and Christendom were becoming synonymous.

For a time in these four centuries it seemed that Christianity, balked in the Moslem world, might not be so largely confined to an area which was on the periphery of civilization, but might win in Central and Eastern Asia. Converts were made in Central Asia and China and strong churches existed in India and on even one island, Socotra, in the Arabian Sea. At the outset of their conquests the hope was cherished by some that the Mongols themselves would be converted. If they, the rulers of the mightiest and most extensive empire that mankind had yet known, were to become Christians, all of the civilized and much of the uncivilized world might follow. Here was a major opportunity and challenge. The opportunity was not seized. Probably it could not have been. Yet during these centuries Christian communities, most of them small, multiplied in the regions in Central and East Asia which were subject to the Moslems. This was chiefly through the Nestorians but it was also in part through Catholics from Western Europe.

We have seen that Nestorians had won some of the Turkish peoples of Central Asia and were represented in the caravan cities of that region, radiating points of cultural influence. We have also noted that, carried to China in the seventh century by Nestorians, by the latter part of the tenth century Christianity had died out in that realm.

Early in the eleventh century Nestorian Christianity began to make fresh gains. Not far from the year 1000 the prince of the Keraïts, a Turkish folk in Central Asia, is said to have asked for baptism. In the thirteenth century that people were professing Christians. In that same century the Onguts, a Tartar folk dwelling to the north of the great northern bend of the Yellow River, also called themselves Christians, and among the Uighurs, a people long prominent in the area through which ran the trade routes from China to the West, were some of that faith. When or how they became Christians we do not know. In the thirteenth and fourteenth centuries European travellers found strong Christian communities in South India.

The Mongol advance seemed at first to favour Christianity. Among the early conquests of Jenghiz Khan was that of the Keraïts and in what seems to have been an attempt to strengthen his power he married one of his sons to a princess from the Keraït ruling family. She was a Christian and the mother of two of the most prominent of Jenghiz Khan's grandsons, Khubilai Khan and Hulagu. Hulagu's favourite wife was a Christian. Mangu, Grand Khan of the Mongols from 1251 to 1259, is said to have been baptized by an Armenian bishop. The inherited faith of the Mongols was a form of shamanism, a kind of "primitive" religion which yields easily to a "higher" religion. There was substantial ground for the hope that the Mongols might become Christians.

Under the Mongols Christianity once more appeared in China. At the Mongol capital, Cambaluc, the later Peking, the Nestorians had an archbishop. A native of North China, but probably not a Chinese, journeyed westward with an older companion and eventually became head of the entire Nestorian Church. Nestorian communities, presumably all foreign, were found in several Chinese cities. A Nestorian was governor of one of these cities and built several monasteries. Alans, Christians from the Caucasus, constituted a contingent of the Mongol garrison in Cambaluc.

The Mongol Empire opened the doors to wide-flung missions from the Catholics of Western Europe. In general the Mongols were fairly tolerant religiously and when once their rule had been established—although that was often by wholesale slaughter—they brought in a degree of peace and order. They accorded security to the east-west land trade routes across Asia. Many European merchants, mostly from the flourishing Italian cities, journeyed by them as far as China—which they knew as Cathay. They also went by sea to India and to the great marts of the China coast.

When the Mongol storm broke across Eurasia, two of the chief missionary orders of the Catholic Church, the Franciscans and Dominicans, were in the first flush of their enthusiastic youth. They took advantage of the new day to plant missions which were scattered from Russia to the China Sea. In the Mongol domains in Russia the rulers, as we have seen, were religiously tolerant.

The Pope assigned the region to the Franciscans and here, about 1300, the Brothers Minor had seventeen stations, including a monastery in the capital. Converts were made, among them members of the reigning family. The friars accompanied the nomads on their wanderings, preaching and administering the sacraments. Several bishoprics and two archbishoprics were created.

In Persia under the Mongols both Franciscans and Dominicans, principally the latter, were present. There were a Latin archbishopric and several bishoprics. These Western Catholics devoted their chief efforts to bringing to allegiance to Rome members of the other churches in the region—Nestorians, Jacobites, Armenians, Georgians, and Greek Orthodox.

In Central Asia Franciscans sought to establish missions and we hear of martyrdoms of Brothers Minor but also of baptisms and of at least one church building.

Both Franciscans and Dominicans were in India. Some suffered martyrdom, but some won converts and there was at least one Latin bishopric.

The most spectacular as well as the most remote of the missions of Western Christians which arose in the wake of the Mongol conquests was in China. China was the most populous and the richest of all the lands under Mongol rule. Its largest cities were said to surpass any in the rest of the world. To them came many merchants from Western Europe, the most famous, because of a narrative left by one of them, the Polos. In 1269 two Polos, brothers, arrived from Cathay at Acre, on the east shore of the Mediterranean, with letters from Khubilai Khan, then ruling all the Mongol domains from Cambaluc, asking for teachers of the science and religion of Europe. After a delay, two Dominicans started on the return trip with the Polos, who now had with them young Marco, the son of one of the latter, who was eventually to write the book at which we have hinted. Before they had gone far the friars took alarm at rumoured dangers and turned back, but the Polos kept on. In 1278 a report that Khubilai Khan had been baptized stimulated the Pope to start a group of five Franciscans towards China, but what happened to them we are not told.

So far as our records enable us to know, the first Catholic missionary to reach China was an Italian Franciscan, John of Montecorvino. He arrived in Cambaluc in 1294, bearing a letter from the Pope to Khubilai Khan. The latter had recently died, but his successor received John courteously. John encountered bitter opposition from the Nestorians, who were powerful at court, but he remained and by 1305 had built a church, had won about 6,000 converts, and had translated the New Testament and Psalter into what he described as "the language and character which is in most general use among the Tartars." By 1306 he had completed a second church at Cambaluc.

Letters from John telling of these successes reached the Papal court and caused something of a sensation. To reinforce him the Pope appointed seven Franciscans and created them bishops with authority to consecrate John as archbishop. Of the seven, one either did not leave Europe or soon turned back and three died on the way, so long was the journey and so formidable the hardships. From time to time other Brothers Minor came and missions were established in several cities. So far as we know, the last medieval missionaries to reach China were a party led by a Papal legate which arrived at Cambaluc in 1342 and reported to the Papal court on its return trip in 1353.

Missions to Moslems in North Africa and Western Asia

The Latin Catholics were not content with seeking to convert the Moslems in the Iberian Peninsula and Sicily or with turning the flank of the Moslem advance by taking advantage of the Mongol conquests to carry their faith into Russia, Central Asia, India, and the Far East. They also sought to win Moslems in those areas in North Africa and Western Asia which had been torn from Christendom by Islam and to bring into unity with Rome the Christian communities in these regions, chiefly in Western Asia, which had survived the Arab conquests. Much of this was in connexion with the Crusades. Most of the active missions were by Franciscans and Dominicans.

However, one of the most far-ranging in his dreams for missions, including the conversion of the Moslems, Raymond Lull, was disliked by the Dominicans and only late in life connected himself with the Franciscans. Born about 1232 on the island of Majorca, Raymond Lull was reared in aristocratic circles and until he had passed his first youth his was the life of a dissolute courtier. Then, converted by recurring visions of Christ on the cross, he made provision for his wife and family, gave the rest of his property to the poor, and devoted himself to religion. He wrote prodigiously. A mystic, some of his works were in that field. His chief concern was to see all men won to the Christian faith. He urged that the Mongols be reached before they accepted Islam or Judaism. He travelled extensively, pressing upon Popes and cardinals the founding of monasteries for the preparation of missionaries. He devised a system of presenting the Christian faith to non-Christians and lectured on it in some of the main centres of theological learning. It was on the Moslems that he concentrated most of his missionary zeal. He made three missionary journeys to North Africa. On the first two he was arrested and deported and on the third, in 1315 or 1316, when he was probably past eighty years of age, he was stoned so severely that he died.

Between them the Franciscans and Dominicans covered most of the Moslem world. In this they were supported by Papal letters to Moslem princes.

Both orders were in North Africa, seeking to serve the Christian sailors, merchants, and captives in that area and to revive the Christian cause which once had had a chief stronghold there but under the Moslem rule had all but disappeared. Bishoprics were created. In the twelfth and thirteenth centuries two other orders were formed to ransom or otherwise rescue the Christians who had been carried captive to that region.

Franciscans and Dominicans were widely scattered in Western Asia. Many were in cities which had been captured by the Crusaders. Others went beyond these centres. Their chief numerical successes were among the churches which were not in communion with Rome. One entire group, the Maronites, was drawn permanently into the Roman fold. From the others only minorities were gathered. Usually these became Uniates, that is, they were permitted to retain their ancient rites, customs, and languages, but brought their creeds into conformity with those of Rome and acknowledged the supremacy of the Pope.

Summary

As we have pursued our rapid way through this condensed account of the conversion of much of Europe, inevitably the question has again and again arisen to perplex us, as it has in earlier sections on the spread of the faith: to what extent, if at all, did these converts understand the Gospel, really commit themselves to it, and know its power? How far, from the standpoint of the true spirit of the faith, were mass conversions desirable? Was it true, as some one was later to put it, that Europe was inoculated with a mild form of Christianity in such fashion that it was immune to the real thing?

Probably full definitive answers are impossible. Yet certain facts are clear. At the outset the vast majority of the nominal Christians were quite unaware of the nature of the Gospel or of the kind of life entailed through the new birth wrought by it. Most of them were baptized either in response to a command from some ruler, their own or a foreign conqueror, or because those about them were receiving the rite. Traditionally religion had been a community affair. As peoples professed to exchange their former faiths for Christianity, it continued to be so. If they thought about it at all, the majority probably expected the new religion to do for them what they had asked of the old, but to do it better.

However, from the outset there were some who caught at least a faint glimmer of what was meant by the Gospel. We must remember that the active missionaries were usually monks and that monks were those who, in theory, had committed themselves fully to the commands of Christ as they understood them. As time passed, moreover, ethical standards that were believed to be Christian were accepted by almost all as ideal, even when they were far from being fully obeyed. Progressively in most lands of "Christendom" instruction was given which involved as a minimum familiarity with the creed, the Lord's Prayer, and something of the meaning of the sacraments.

Probably in the professedly Christian countries of Europe there was quite as much understanding of what was recorded in the New Testament and as much whole-hearted acceptance of it as in the minorities of Asia, whether these were recent converts who had come one by one or were ancient churches, encysted within the dominant Moslem or Hindu communities. Indeed, from Europe there issued, to a much greater degree than from these minorities, movements which we are to meet intermittently through the remainder of our narrative, some of them monastic and some of them from the Catholic standpoint heretical, which sprang from a deep desire to be fully Christian. It would seem that where either the overwhelming majority or a substantial minority profess to be Christian, fresh efforts for the perfect realization of the wonder of the Gospel have been more frequent than where Christians have been minorities which have been primarily on the defensive, seeking to hand down their faith from generation to generation to their children and grandchildren, set consciously in a hostile world, but despairing of winning that world to the faith.

SELECTED BIBLIOGRAPHY

GENERAL WORKS

K. S. Latourette, *A History of the Expansion of Christianity. Volume II, The Thousand Years of Uncertainty* (New York, Harper & Brothers, 1938, pp. ix, 492). A survey of the years from 500 to 1500, with extensive footnote references.

J. T. Addison, *The Medieval Missionary, A Study of the Conversion of Northern Europe A.D. 500-1300* (New York, International Missionary Council, 1936, pp. xiv, 176). A careful and accurate study of missionary methods.

The Cambridge Medieval History (Cambridge University Press, 1911 ff.) has several chapters which are pertinent to the subject of the conversion of Europe.

A. Hauck, *Kirchengeschichte Deutschlands* (Leipzig, J. C. Hinrichs'sche Buchhandlung, 5 vols., 1922-1929). Invaluable and has large sections which fall within the range of several of the areas and subjects treated in this chapter.

THE SCANDINAVIANS

Saxo Grammaticus, *Gesta Danorum* (edited by A. Holder, Strassburg, Karl J. Trübner, 1886, pp. lxxxviii, 724). Composed in the last quarter of the twelfth and the first quarter of the thirteenth century and least undependable when it deals with events of those years.

K. Lübeck, *Die Christianisierung Russlands* (Aachen, Xaveriusverlagsbuchhandlung, 1922, pp. 118). By a Roman Catholic, objective, scholarly, using Russian and Western European material.

POLAND

J. X. Seppelt, *Zur Einführung des Christentums in Polen* (in *Zeitschrift für Missionswissenschaft,* Vol. X, 1920, pp. 86–93). An excellent summary.

SPAIN AND PORTUGAL

C. R. Haines, *Christianity and Islam in Spain* A.D. *756–1030* (London, Kegan Paul, Trench, Trübner & Co., 1889, pp. viii, 182). Scholarly, based largely on original sources.

THE WENDS AND BALTIC PEOPLES

J. W. Thompson, *Feudal Germany* (University of Chicago Press, 1928, pp. xxiii, 710). Specializes on the northern and eastern expansion of the Germans and their culture, but has marked prejudices.

F. J. Tschan, *The Chronicle of the Slavs by Helmold, Priest of Bosau* (Columbia University Press, 1935, pp. xii, 321). A translation of a very useful twelfth century source.

ASIA AND NORTH AFRICA

W. F. Adeney, *The Greek and Eastern Churches* (New York, Charles Scribner's Sons, preface 1908, pp. xiv, 634).

B. Altaner, *Die Dominikanermission des 13 Jahrhundert* (Habelschwerdt, Frankes Buchhandlung, 1924, pp. xxiii, 247). Carefully done, with extensive footnotes.

L. E. Browne, *The Eclipse of Christianity in Asia* (Cambridge University Press, 1933, pp. 198). Useful.

E. A. Wallace Budge, *The Monks of Kûblâi Khân* (London, The Religious Tract Society, 1928, pp. xvi, 335). The best English translation of an important document.

L. Lemmens, *Die Hiedenmission des Spätmittelalters* (Münster, Aschendorffsche Verlagsbuchhandlung, 1919, pp. x, 112). Primarily concerned with Franciscan missions.

A. C. Moule, *Christians in China before the Year 1550* (London, Society for Promoting Christian Knowledge, 1930, pp. xix, 293). Translations, with excellent notes, of pertinent sources.

E. A. Peers, *Ramon Lull, a Biography* (London, Society for Promoting Christian Knowledge, 1929, pp. xviii, 454). By a specialist on the Spanish mystics.

E. A. Peers, *A Fool of Love. The Life of Ramon Lull* (London, Student Christian Movement Press, 1946, pp. 127).

H. Yule, *Cathay and the Way Thither: Being a Collection of Medieval Notices of China,* revised by H. Cordier (London, The Hakluyt Society, 4 vols., 1925, 1926). Long a standard.

Chapter XVII

EXPANSION THROUGH THE CRUSADES

A phase of the life of Europe which loomed large through at least half of the four hundred years from 950 to 1350 was the Crusades. In spite of their name, they were not entirely religious movements. Indeed, they were a phase of the beginning of the expansion of Europe which, after a pause, was to be of major importance for the world and for Christianity in the ensuing generations and not least in the twentieth century. Ostensibly they had a Christian motive, they were with the authorization and in no small degree at the initiative of the Roman branch of the Catholic Church, they were permeated by religious, if not purely Christian, devotion, and they had marked effect upon the Christian communities, both in the West and in the East. However, important though they were, this is not the place for more than a brief summary of them. Our interest in them is primarily in their bearing upon our subject, the history of Christianity. From that standpoint they are significant partly because through them Western Christianity was projected into the Eastern Mediterranean, partly because of the effects, largely disastrous, on relations between the Western and Eastern wings of the Catholic Church, and partly because of the repercussions on Latin Christianity.

THE ROOTS OF THE CRUSADES

Why were the Crusades? The causes were mixed and varied. They were in part that *wanderlust* which seems to have been one of the factors in the invasions of the Roman Empire and its successors in Europe of which we have had much to say in earlier chapters. They were in part economic. In the generation or more preceding the First Crusade Western Europe had repeatedly suffered from famine. To the thoughtful of that time Europe, sparsely settled by twentieth century standards, appeared to be overpopulated. It had more mouths than the economy of the time could feed and observers were not wanting who believed the land to be groaning under the weight of its inhabitants. Many sought release in these expeditions to the East. The Italian cities, now beginning to grow and looking eastward for trade, encouraged the Crusades as a means of furthering their commercial enterprises. There was the personal factor. Ambitious men saw in the Crusades opportunity for adventure, fame, and power.

At the outset the desire of the Byzantine Emperors for aid against the Moslem Seljuk Turks contributed to the Crusades. In the eleventh century the Byzantine Empire fell on evil days. These began in 1025 with the death of the Emperor Basil II and were accentuated when in 1056 the Macedonian dynasty which had brought to the realm large accessions of territory and of power came to an end. Internal dissensions combined with foreign invasions to threaten the very existence of the realm. In the West the Normans conquered Southern Italy, long a Byzantine possession. From the north barbarians forced their way to the very walls of Constantinople. Even more formidable were the Seljuk Turks. Originally from Central Asia, converts to Islam, in the eleventh century they built an empire which included Persia, Mesopotamia, Syria, Palestine, and Egypt. They fought their way into Asia Minor and in 1071, the year of a decisive victory of the Normans in Southern Italy, inflicted a stunning defeat on the Byzantine army in Armenia, near Lake Van, and overran much of Asia Minor. The accession (1081) to the imperial throne of Alexius Comnenus brought vigorous leadership to Constantinople. This was continued by his immediate descendants. Some territory was regained, but only by what proved to be a reprieve.

It is the religious factors which are here chiefly our concern. They were undoubtedly potent. First of all in the minds of many was the rescue from the Moslem of the places in Palestine, especially Jerusalem, which were sacred to the Christian. For centuries Christians from the West, like those from other regions, had been making them the goal of pious pilgrimages. To bring them into Christian hands and keep them was ostensibly the chief objective of the Crusades.

Another phase of the religious motive was the protection of the Byzantine Empire against the Moslem Turks. As we have said, the Turks were threatening this historic bulwark of Christendom. The Byzantine Emperors appealed to the Christians of the West for assistance and the Popes were disposed to give it.

Intimately related to this second religious motive was a third, the desire of the Popes to heal the breach between the Western and Eastern wings of the Catholic Church and to restore Christian unity. In the tenth and eleventh centuries relations between East and West had deteriorated. Greek Catholics were scandalized, perhaps not unwillingly, by the state of the Church in the West—by the weak Popes of that period of Papal decline, by the spectacle of bishops leading armies, something which their wing of the Church did not know, and by reports of the generally low state of the faith in the West before the reforms which were beginning to get under way in the latter part of the tenth century. With some of these reforms they were not in accord, notably the emphasis upon the celibacy of the priesthood. There remained, too, the chronic sources of irritation which we have repeatedly noted. In 1054 the friction had reached an acute point when, in negotiations between the Papacy and the Patriarchate of Constantinople, the Papal legates laid on the altar of Saint Sophia at the hour of solemn service a sentence of excommunication of the Patriarch. The latter replied with a strong denunciation of the Latin position. The rupture was not necessarily final, for there had been earlier ones which in principle had been healed, but it was serious, and the Popes wished to remove it.

THE FIRST CRUSADE

What is called the First Crusade began in 1096, the immediate outgrowth of an appeal by Pope Urban II in a stirring sermon at a synod at Clermont, in France, in November of the preceding year. The congregation, deeply moved, is said to have boomed out: *"Deus vult"* ("God wills it") and this was made the slogan of the enterprise. The Pope had been asked by the Eastern Emperor for aid against the Seljuk Turks. He was not the first Byzantine Emperor to seek such help. A predecessor had made a similar plea to Gregory VII, whom we are to meet again, as we also are Urban II, as a leader in reform in the Western Church and in seeking to enhance the power of the Church in the affairs of men. Urban called on the Christians of Western Europe to go to the succour of their Eastern brethren and also to free the holy places from the hands of the infidels. "Plenary indulgence," of which we are to hear more later, was promised to all who took part and eternal life to those who lost their physical lives in the enterprise. The cross was worn as a symbol by those who responded.

Preachers, conspicuous among them Peter the Hermit, spread the message through much of Western Europe. Popular enthusiasm mounted. Throngs, poorly organized, set forth, some of them attacking the Jews or pillaging fellow Christians as they went. Most of this wave perished, some before reaching Constantinople and others not long after they had crossed into Asia. Much better organized armies left in the summer of 1096, arrived in Constantinople that winter and the next spring, fought their way through Asia Minor, captured Antioch in June, 1098, with great slaughter, and the following year took Jerusalem, putting many of its inhabitants to the sword.

The most respected of the crusading leaders, Godfrey of Bouillon, was made Protector of the Holy Sepulchre. After his early death he was succeeded by a brother who had the title King of Jerusalem. Crusaders established themselves in various centres in Syria and Palestine, where the ruins of their strongholds can still be seen. Their political structure was feudal, as was natural for those coming from the Western Europe of that day. Rome appointed a Patriarch of Jerusalem and several bishoprics and archbishoprics were set up. Although reunion of all the Eastern Churches had not been accomplished under the ægis of Rome, the Western Church had largely extended its holdings, and in the East. The Crusaders were far from being ideal exemplars of the faith which they professed and few if any willing conversions from Islam were made by them.

THE LATER CRUSADES

The fall of Edessa in 1144 stimulated what was known as the Second Crusade, for Edessa was a key city in the defenses of the Crusaders' kingdom. That Crusade was preached by Bernard of Clairvaux, esteemed a model Christian by his own and later generations. It was, however, a failure, for many of its contingents perished before reaching Syria and it broke down in its attempt to take Damascus.

Moslem divisions had been one cause for the success of the First Crusade. Now the Kurdish Saladin built a strong Moslem state which enveloped the Latin kingdom on its land frontiers. In 1187 in a memorable and decisive battle at Hattin the European forces were cut to pieces. Jerusalem and most of the Crusaders' centres soon fell to the triumphant Islam.

It was to retrieve these losses that the Third Crusade was launched (1189). Three armies set out, led respectively by the Holy Roman Emperor Frederick Barbarossa, one of the most eminent of that long line, the scheming King Philip Augustus of France, and the adventurous King Richard, "the lion-hearted," of England. The Emperor came to his death in Asia Minor, the kings of England and France quarrelled, and the recapture of Acre was the chief tangible achievement of the costly expedition.

The dream of retaking the Holy Places would not be quieted, and in 1202 the Fourth Crusade set forth, stimulated by Pope Innocent III, whose tenure of that high office, as we are to see, marked the apex of the medieval Papacy. It was aimed at Egypt, where was Saladin's chief strength, for crushing him was believed to be a strategic prerequisite to the retaking and holding of Palestine. The Crusaders were dependent upon Venice for ships. Venetian influence turned the expedition to Constantinople. Venice had extensive commercial interests in the Eastern Mediterranean, wished an Eastern Emperor who would be compliant to its wishes, and supported a candidate for the post. The Crusaders stormed Constantinople (1204), plundered it, divided the

Eastern Empire's possessions, and placed one of their number, Count Baldwin of Flanders, on the imperial throne. Venice was given large possessions, chiefly islands which were important for her commerce. A Latin Patriarch of Constantinople was appointed. For the moment it seemed that the long cherished Papal ambition had been realized and that the Eastern and Western wings of the Catholic Church had been united under the undisputed rule of the Bishop of Rome.

The Crusading conquest of Constantinople was a major disaster for the Christian cause in the East. The Byzantine Empire, already enfeebled, was dealt a blow from which it never really recovered and which contributed to the weakness that ultimately (1453) put Constantinople into the hands of the Moslem Ottoman Turks. Except where overwhelming Latin military power compelled it to do so, the Greek Church did not submit to Rome but continued under its own Patriarch. The Greek masses loathed the Latins and the rift between the two wings of the Catholic Church was widened and deepened. The Byzantine Empire continued with headquarters at Nicæa, the city in Asia not far from Constantinople famous in the history of the councils of the Church. In 1261 it retook Constantinople and the Latin state came to an ignominious end.

Of the rest of the Crusades we need say very little. The distressful Children's Crusade of 1212 was the fruit of emotional appeals, chiefly notable as a vivid example of one phase of the religious temper of Western Europe of the day. Many of the youths who responded to it ended in slavery in Egypt. The sceptical Holy Roman Emperor Frederick II, whose stormy relations with the Papacy are one of the complicated sets of episodes of the Middle Ages, through negotiations and a treaty with Egypt obtained possession (1229) of Jerusalem, Bethlehem, Nazareth, and the roadstead of Jaffa and was crowned King of Jerusalem. In 1244 Jerusalem once more fell to the Moslems and was not again to be in "Christian" hands until the twentieth century.

Sacred alike to Jews, Christians, and Moslems, Jerusalem was desired by all three. Henceforth, for more than six centuries it was to be held by a succession of Moslem rulers. In the thirteenth century other efforts were made by Christians to regain it, but none as formidable as the earlier Crusades. Louis IX of France, the ideal Christian knight, led an expedition to Egypt in which he was taken prisoner. He died of disease in an attack on Tunis in 1270, where he had gone on his way to Palestine in the hope of baptizing the local ruler. Prince Edward, later King Edward I of England, took over the leadership, went to Palestine, stormed Nazareth, but did not capture Jerusalem. In 1291 Acre was lost and with it the last of the Crusaders' strongholds in Western Asia. Although the hope of renewing the attempt to seize Jerusalem was not surrendered for several generations, as expeditions with that objective the Crusades were over.

THE CRUSADING SPIRIT

The crusading idea, of a holy war commanded and blessed by the Church, had become deeply implanted in the Western European mind. Crusades were not confined to expeditions to retake or protect the Holy Places in Palestine. They were waged against Moslems in the Iberian Peninsula, against the pagan Wends and Prussians, against the heretical Cathari, and against still others, some of them Christians, whom the Popes adjudged enemies of the faith.

MILITARY MONASTIC ORDERS

Military orders arose from the Crusades. Their members took the standard monastic vows of poverty, chastity, and obedience, but were warriors who had dedicated their lives and their arms to the service of Christ. We have already noted the Knights of the Sword and the Teutonic Knights. More famous were the Templars and Hospitallers. The former were founded in 1119 with head-quarters near the temple site in Jerusalem. Their purpose was to protect pilgrims and fight in defense of the Holy Land. They were popular as symbols and guardians of the Holy Places and became wealthy through the gifts of the pious. Wealth brought them enemies and their independence of the bishops aroused the dislike of these ecclesiastics. In 1312 the Pope suppressed the order and much of its property went to the Hospitallers. The Hospitallers, or Knights of St. John, were based upon a hospital in Jerusalem near the church of St. John Baptist which had been originally founded by Charlemagne. As their name indicates, the first purpose of the Hospitallers was to care for the sick, but in the twelfth century they were made into a military order. They long maintained headquarters on the island of Rhodes and then (until 1798) on Malta. There were other crusading orders, among them one in Portugal, the Order of Christ, which succeeded to the property of the Templars in that kingdom. One of its Grand Masters, Prince Henry the Navigator, in the fifteenth century directed the exploring expeditions along the west coast of Africa which were to outflank the Moslem world and prepare the way for the extensive spread of Christianity in the South and East of Asia.

THE CRUSADING HERITAGE

The Crusades constitute one of the most striking and thought-provoking features of the history of Christianity. While in spirit many of the wars of the Eastern Empire were closely akin to them, they were primarily an outgrowth of the Latin or Western wing of the Catholic Church. They may be regarded as a phase of the activist temper of much of Western Christianity. Here was an effort to achieve the kingdom of God on earth by the methods of that world which the New Testament declares to be at enmity with the Gospel. To put it in Augustinian terms, it was the employment of the instruments of the earthly city to further the City of God. Arising from a mixture of motives, they enlisted much devotion. Here and there were Christians who questioned whether basically they were true to the Gospel and many more deplored the cruelty, immorality, and pride which went with them. However, the great majority of the Christians of Western Europe accepted them and endorsed them. In this the Papacy, the head of the Western Church, led.

The Crusades constituted a complete reversal of the attitude of the early Christians towards war. As we have seen, that was predominantly one of condemnation. By the majority, participation in it as a soldier was deemed inconsistent with the Christian ideal. Later the theory was developed that wars could be just. Now some wars were regarded as holy and in fulfilment of the purposes of God. *Deus vult* ("God wills it") was the cry.

The Crusades had important consequences. They stimulated the growth, already beginning, of the commerce of the Italian cities. They brought Western Europe into intimate contact with the high civilizations of the Near East. Yet they failed in their primary objectives. They did not put the Holy Places permanently into the possession of Christians. They weakened rather than strengthened the Greek Church and the Eastern Empire in their resistance to aggressive Islam. Minorities from the Eastern Churches were won to fellowship with Rome, but the Crusades deepened rather than bridged the widening rift between the Western and Eastern wings of the Catholic Church. Probably they intensified the hatred and the scorn of Moslems for the Christian name. The Crusades aided somewhat in the geographic spread of Christianity, principally along the south and east shores of the Baltic and to a lesser extent in the ephemeral Franciscan and Dominican missions in Central Asia and the Far East. However, they may actually have retarded the understanding of the Gospel. They were an aspect of the partial capture of the Church by the warrior tradition and habits of the barbarian peoples who had mastered Western Europe and had given their professed allegiance to the Christian faith.

SELECTED BIBLIOGRAPHY

Ambroise, *The Crusade of Richard Lion-Heart,* translated by M. J. Hubert, with notes and documentation by J. L. La Monte (Columbia University Press, 1941, pp. xi, 478).

T. A. Archer and C. L. Kingsford, *The Crusades* (New York, G. P. Putnam's Sons, 1894, pp. xxx, 467).

M. W. Baldwin, *Raymond III of Tripolis and the Fall of Jerusalem* (*1140-1187*) (Princeton University Press, 1936, pp. viii, 177).

The Cambridge Medieval History, Vol. V (Cambridge University Press, 1929).

Villehardouin and DeJoinville, *Memoirs of the Crusades* (Everyman's Library No. 333, New York, E. P. Dutton & Co., 1908, pp. xli, 340).

Chapter XVIII

REVIVAL THROUGH MONASTICISM: THE RICH AND VARIED DEVELOPMENT OF THE MONASTIC IDEAL IN WESTERN EUROPE

Recovery from the decline which Christianity had suffered in Western Europe between the years 500 and 950 found expression and was furthered through fresh monastic movements. These became more numerous and took on greater variety than ever before. Indeed, in diversity they were much more marked than in the Eastern wing of the Catholic Church or than in any of the Eastern Churches.

Here, we may note, is one of the criteria of vitality in the Christian community. At the times when the tide of life is running low, few new movements appear. When the Christian faith is coursing with vigour through its visible manifestations, old movements are rejuvenated and new ones are born. In the Catholic Church some of the major manifestations of these revivals have been in monasticism. Seeking to attain to the Christian standard of perfection and so to obtain eternal life in heaven, men and women reared in the Catholic Church quite understandably turn to the monastic ideal and either enter existing orders or form fresh ones. In their zeal they may create novel forms of monasticism.

It is, therefore, one of the chief evidences of the awakening that came in the Western wing of the Catholic Church that in the second half of the century many existing monasteries were reformed and that new monastic communities sprang up. Closely associated with these movements were others which sought to embody the Gospel and to win nominal Christians to conform to it but which the Catholic Church deemed heretical. More intimately related than the latter were efforts to purge the whole Church of the corruption that was so obvious and so tragic, to bring all of Western Christendom to a closer approximation to Christian standards, and to spread the Western faith to peoples who had not yet accepted it. Monastic movements continued to multiply throughout the four centuries from 950 to 1350 and reached a crest in the thirteenth century.

As we have seen, monastic life had fallen to a low level in the latter part of the ninth and the fore part of the tenth century. The invasions of Northmen, Moslems, and Magyars had laid many monasteries in ruins. Countless monks had been killed or driven into the cities. In numbers of monasteries secular princes had diverted the endowments to their own purposes. They turned over to the monasteries only part of the revenues and allowed the enrolment of monks to fall off. In many others lay patrons had appointed as abbots men who valued the post as a means of livelihood, who were married, and who brought to the monasteries their families, their warriors, their horses, and their hunting dogs. Numbers of monks married and dwelt in the monastic buildings with their wives and children. The canons, members of the groups of clergy who lived by a semi-monastic rule in collegiate churches and cathedrals, conformed even more easily to the world than did the monks. In some monasteries canons were substituted for monks, for they did not have to hold as closely to the Benedictine rule as did the latter.

FIRST HINTS OF AWAKENINGS

A generation or more before 950 there had been stirrings of reform. Now and again synods deplored the decay of monastic life but did little to effect a change. Some monasteries, but how many we do not know, maintained a fairly strict observance of the Benedictine rule. Here and there new ones were founded. The influence of Benedict of Aniane waned but did not die. Thus (c.933) John of Gorze refounded the abbey by which he is known. It was near Metz and its influence made itself felt from Cologne to Toul. Near Namur Gerhard inaugurated the monastery of Brogne and gave a stimulus to better monastic life in Flanders. Both Gorze and Brogne followed in part the lead of Benedict of Aniane with his emphasis upon liturgical prayer, his lengthening of the services, and his tendency to discourage both agricultural labour by the monks and the teaching of those not of the monastic community.

THE CLUNY MOVEMENT

The revival was given conspicuous leadership by the monastery of Cluny and its abbots. Cluny was north of Lyons, not far from Macon and the Rhone River. Its first abbot and real founder was Berno. A Burgundian, Berno had already made a record as abbot of another monastery where he had held to the strict observance of the Benedictine rule. So many youths were attracted by his zeal that he deemed it necessary to begin an additional house. This he did in 910 at Cluny on land given by William the Pious, Duke of Aquitaine. To prevent his successors from corrupting the foundation and diverting it from its original purpose, as lay princes had done with many other monasteries, Duke William placed it directly under the protection of the Pope. Like Gorze and Brogne, Cluny was profoundly affected by what had been done by Benedict of Aniane in his modifications of monastic life and ceremonies.

Many were hungry for the type of leadership given by Berno. As we have suggested, Christians of the day believed, as had many before and have many since, that the salvation of their souls was to be best attained by the monastic road. Men and women denied themselves here that they might win heaven hereafter. It was this impulse that constituted the wellspring of monasticism. Many entered upon the life from other motives, such as ease and physical security, or were committed to it by parents who wished to provide for their offspring, but had monasticism rested on these foundations it would not have endured. It was the urge for the attainment of wholeness of life, of meaning to life that would endure through eternity, which was the persistent source of recurring monastic revivals. To those who were impelled by it Cluny made a profound appeal.

Cluny grew in its enrollment and attracted gifts. Devout lay lords who had the nomination to abbacies asked Berno to accept the post and to undertake the reform of their houses. He acquiesced. On his retirement (926) because of age, he transferred most of his abbacies, including that of Cluny, to Odo.

Odo, who was abbot from 926 to 942, travelled extensively in France and Italy to promote the reform of monasteries. Of some he was made abbot. In others those in charge asked his advice. In the monasteries which he visited for that purpose he usually left one or more monks who had been trained at Cluny and whom he could trust to inculcate the spirit of that house.

For about two and a half centuries, with one exception, Cluny had a notable succession of able and devoted abbots. Scions of noble families, well educated according to the standards of the time, they gave themselves unstintedly to the work of their office, some of them refusing high ecclesiastical position to do so, and made their weight felt in Church and state. Under the fifth of the line, Odilo, who held the post for about fifty years (994–1048), the number of monasteries affiliated with Cluny rose from thirty-seven to sixty-nine. In addition, there were still more smaller groups, cellae, "cells," affiliated with the larger units. Although he was slight in build, short of stature, and nervous, Odilo inspired respect and was a forceful leader. Yet in discipline he inclined to mercy. By the beginning of the twelfth century the number of associated monasteries had risen to more than three hundred. Hugh the Great, who was abbot for approximately sixty years, from 1049 to 1109, ruling as he did eventually over more than three hundred widely scattered monasteries, was for years an efficient ally of the reforming Popes and was canonized a little over a century after his death. He had an unworthy successor who held the post for thirteen years, but the latter was followed by Peter the Venerable who was abbot from 1122 to 1157, or for thirty-five years, and who did much to restore the discipline of Cluny and its affiliated houses.

Cluny thus became the centre of a "congregation" of monasteries, the precursor of such orders as the Franciscans, Dominicans, and Jesuits. Heretofore each monastery had been independent of every other. Through Cluny a family of monasteries arose.

In theory Cluny held to the rule of Benedict of Nursia. In practice it modified it. It stressed silence, except in group worship. As had Benedict of Aniane, it lengthened and elaborated the services. No longer did the monks work with their hands in the fields. That labour was left to serfs while the monks devoted themselves to prayer. Their abbey churches tended to be huge. That of Cluny, begun late in the eleventh and completed in the first half of the twelfth century and dedicated by the Pope himself, was said to have been at the time the largest church in Western Europe. Scholarship was not encouraged and the study of the non-Christian authors of classical antiquity was either forbidden or deprecated.

The influence of Cluny spread widely beyond the monasteries which were closely associated with it. Many existing houses were made to accord with its practice. That was true even of the mother Benedictine house on Monte Cassino. Numbers of new foundations were on the model or under the inspiration of Cluny. Moreover, as we shall see in a later chapter, from it came bishops and Popes who led in the reform of the Western Church.

THE RISING TIDE OF MONASTIC LIFE

In the tenth and eleventh centuries, partly but by no means entirely through the inspiration and example of Cluny, the tide of the monastic life continued to mount.

In England there was Dunstan (c.909–988). Of noble Saxon stock, monk and abbot of Glastonbury, later Archbishop of Canterbury, he and some of his friends who became bishops led in the improvement of the monasteries and of the Church as a whole in that land. There were similar movements in France, Italy, and Germany which in the last two countries were encouraged by some of the Holy Roman Emperors.

More and more it became the practice, somewhat after the manner of Cluny, for monasteries to be put in the ownership or under the control of some famous abbey. This was partly to escape the debilitating influence of a lay proprietor and partly to insure the strict observance of the monastic rule in the subordinate houses. Thus the abbey devoutly named Chaise Dieu (Casa Dei, the House of

God), founded in Auvergne in 1046, eventually had about three hundred dependent priories.

Fleeing from the Turkish invasions, Greek monks brought their traditions, chiefly to Italy but also to France.

In Italy new foundations were made, several of them through devoted scions of noble stock who had abandoned the world for the life of prayer and asceticism. Famous was Romuald (c.950–1027) of the ducal family of Ravenna who turned monk to expiate a crime of his father. He soon left the Cluniac Benedictine monastery which he had entered and became a hermit. An extreme ascetic, he was a wanderer and inspired many by his example. From him there arose a type of hermit community in which the members were strenuously ascetic and dwelt in separate houses, but had some of their liturgical services and meals together. From time to time they went forth as preachers. From this eventually came the Camaldulian Order, named for its centre at Camaldoli.

Peter Damian (c.1007–1072) was also of Ravenna, but from a lowly, poverty-stricken family. Through hard labour he acquired an education and taught at Parma. Then, from an inward urge to the perfect Christian life, he entered a monastery, became a hermit noted for extreme austerity, eventually was made abbot, and, inspired by the example of Romuald, whose biography he wrote, organized monasteries which were affiliated with his own. As were so many others of this new burst of monastic devotion, he was deeply concerned for the purification of the Church as a whole and urged the Popes to further it. One of the latter made him Cardinal Bishop of Ostia, the ancient seaport of Rome, and he became prominent in the inner circles of the Papal entourage, where we shall meet him again, labouring to carry out his dreams.

John Gualbert (c.990–1073) as a youth also came under the influence of Romuald. He was for a time at Camaldoli and then founded a monastery at Vallombrosa near Florence which soon became the head of a family of monastic houses. In them perpetual silence was the rule. The manual labour was performed by *conversi,* lay brothers, to leave the "choir monks" free for prayer. The choir monks were those who devoted themselves to the services in the chapel.

Noted, but in a somewhat different way, was Bernard of Menthon (923–1008). Born in a rich family of noble blood, he refused an honourable marriage to which his family urged him, entered the ranks of the clergy, and in his mid-forties was Archdeacon of Aosta, near the southern outlet of the famous pass across the Alps which now bears his name. Distressed by the savagery and poverty of the folk who dwelt in the mountains and who robbed travellers crossing the pass, he gave himself to them, won them, and then at the head of the pass founded a monastery and dedicated it to the care of those who journeyed by its doors. In 1213 Pope Innocent III put it under the rule of the Augustinian canons.

Still different was the Monastery of Bec, in Normandy. Like Cluny, it was to be a wellspring of vitality for large areas, especially Normandy and England. In contrast with Cluny, it was a centre of intellectual life and theological activity. It was begun in the fore part of the eleventh century by Herluin. Herluin was of noble birth, a warrior who in his late thirties turned to religion. He learned to read, was ordained priest, and gathered a small monastic community. To this in 1042 came Lanfranc. Lanfranc was from the North of Italy. He had been a teacher of law and letters and in his late thirties, after having taught in the cathedral school of Avranches, on the south-west coast of Normandy, he turned monk and entered Bec. Somewhat later, in the 1050's, Anselm joined the community. He was of Lombard stock and was born in a valley in the Italian Alps. Studious and deeply religious, he had long wished to adopt the monastic life, but in this met the bitter opposition of his father. It was not until he had crossed the Alps that he felt free to take the step. He proved to be the greatest theological intellect between Augustine and Thomas Aquinas and in this capacity we shall meet him again. Lanfranc and he were successively Archbishops of Canterbury and we shall also find him courageously standing for the purity and independence of the Church as against rulers who wished to use the Church for their own purposes. Lanfranc and Anselm gave Bec its distinctive character—the combination of deep religious devotion, in which they reinforced what came through Herluin, with scholarly pursuits. Bec became famous as a school, wealth poured in, and many subordinate priories were attached to it, notably in England.

THE MONASTERIES GAIN SPECIAL PRIVILEGES

Part of the tenth and eleventh century revival was a movement, largely successful, to free the monasteries from the control of lay lords and diocesan bishops. The power of lay lords had been one of the sources of the decay in the monastic life. To circumvent it, increasingly monasteries were removed from the power of the feudal nobility and were placed directly under the Pope. Theoretically the Pope could not divert their properties to other uses than those prescribed by the founder and was the guardian rather than the proprietor. Nor could he legally use the income from the endowments for himself or his favourites. The proportion to be given to him was usually fixed by the donor in the founding charter.

The diocesan bishops had proved a source of annoyance to the monasteries. In principle each bishop had extensive powers over all the ecclesiastical activities and institutions in his diocese. In monasteries he could hold services, consecrate altars, ordain such of the monks as were raised to the priesthood, and exercise discipline through excommunicating the obdurate or interdicting services.

Restrictions on these functions had been begun as early as the sixth or seventh century. In the tenth and eleventh centuries on behalf of house after house the episcopal authority was further reduced or annulled by Papal action. In many instances even the right of ordination was taken from the diocesan bishop. While episcopal ordination was still necessary, the monastery might ask any bishop whom it chose to administer the rite.

The kings also increasingly granted to monasteries immunity from the jurisdiction of royal officials and took the houses under their special protection.

This movement to free monasteries from all local secular or ecclesiastical interference and so to ensure them liberty to pursue the full Christian life was to continue into at least the thirteenth century. Thus there arose autonomous communities each with its own endowments in land, independent of the secular order and from the economic structure about it, for unhampered and full conformity to the Christian ideal in individual and group living as the monks and other Catholic Christians of the time understood it.

Here were centres of life from which issued impulses which helped to raise the level of the Christianity of almost all of Western Europe. The rude barbarians who had been converted in mass were taught something of the meaning of the faith which they had professed to accept. They were challenged by it. Many did not respond or responded only to react against it. Indeed, the grossness, superstition, stark depravity, cruelty, and callous self-seeking of millions in medieval Europe is one of the striking features of the age. On the other hand, thousands rose to the appeal. Never has the contrast between sinner and saint been greater. Not all life was transformed, but all aspects of Western Europe were profoundly affected.

The Cistercian Movement

In the twelfth century the leadership in creative, vigorous monastic life passed to the Cistercians. As we have suggested more than once, each great revival of the monastic life tended to be followed by decline. A leader of flaming devotion and high idealism would attract youth, and austerity would characterize the first years of the new house or houses. Then would come popularity and wealth, either through the labour of the monks themselves or by gifts from devout admirers, zeal would wane, and the quality of life would sink to mediocrity and uninspired routine or worse. In the twelfth century this began to happen to Cluny. The number of its affiliated monasteries continued to mount, although more slowly than earlier, but it was no longer in the van.

Other and younger movements took its place as pioneers. Chief of these were the Cistercians.

The Cistercians began with Robert, a Benedictine monk who by his zeal for reform and strict observance of the monastic ideal attracted a number of hermits. After being an abbot of a new community at Molesme in Burgundy in huts made of boughs (begun c.1075), eventually, as that foundation fell away from its first fervour, he removed (1098) to a new centre at Citeaux, not far from Dijon, in the eastern part of what is now France. Citeaux became the mother house of what were soon to be the Cistercians (from the Latin name, Cistercium, for Citeaux). The basic features of the Cistercian movement were given it by Robert, and especially by the second and third abbots of Citeaux, Alberic and Stephen Harding, the latter an Englishman.

In general the Cistercians held to the Benedictine rule. However, they had five distinct characteristics which set them off from other monks. First, and least important, was their garb. Instead of the black habit of the Benedictines, they wore greyish white, and are often referred to as the "white monks."

Second was an attempt, quite usual in new monastic movements, to observe the rule of strict poverty. This the Cistercians sought to accomplish by reducing to a minimum the physical accompaniments of their common worship. In contrast with the great churches and elaborate and costly liturgical vestments and ornaments of the Cluniacs, they had crucifixes of painted wood, chalices of silver rather than gold, and unadorned vestments of linen or fustian rather than of silk. They refused to derive the income for their houses from tithes, offerings, altar and burial dues, or from estates worked by serfs. Their clothing and food were to be of the simplest.

In the third place, in contrast with many of the foundations of the black monks which were near the cities, the Cistercians established their houses far from other habitations. Their lands were to be cleared and tilled by their own labour and not that of serfs. Some of this was done by the choir monks. Most of it was by the more numerous *conversi,* or lay brothers. The *conversi* were illiterate, they memorized only the creed and a few of the prayers, their prayers at the canonical hours were brief, and they were allowed more sleep and food than the choir monks. They followed the rule of silence except such exchange of words as was necessary for their work. The use of lay brothers made servants unnecessary.

A fourth feature was the reduction of the time spent in the liturgical services, for it will be remembered that these had been lengthened by Cluny and had become the chief occupation of the monks. Instead, room was made for more private prayer. There was to be no school for oblate children, namely, those of tender years who had been dedicated by their elders to the monastic life. No novices were to be accepted who were less than sixteen years of age. Thus all the monks were supposed to come by their own choice and from a sense of divine vocation.

The fifth distinct characteristic of the Cistercians was the provision for welding all the houses together into an integrated order, the first of its kind and the precursor of many others. The Cluniac houses were under the theoretical supervision of the abbot of the mother house, but they early became too numerous for effective oversight by one man. In the Cistercian system each monastery retained a large degree of autonomy, but identical service books were provided for all, each abbey was visited annually by the abbot of Citeaux or the abbot of one of the four other oldest foundations, and every year all the abbots of all the houses assembled at Citeaux in a general chapter to maintain fellowship and to take such legislative and disciplinary measures as might be necessary. Citeaux itself was visited and inspected regularly by representatives of its four eldest daughter houses.

The Cistercians quickly achieved wide popularity. Ardent youths were attracted by their devotion. In country after country their houses arose in desolate places. Forests were cleared, swamps were drained, and the necessary monastic buildings were erected.

BERNARD OF CLAIRVAUX

The early popularity of the Cistercians was due in no small degree to Bernard of Clairvaux. Bernard was the most influential individual in the religious life of Western Europe of his generation. The first half of the twelfth century was marked by many men eminent in the Latin Church, but in the weight which he carried with his contemporaries Bernard stood head and shoulders above them all.

Bernard of Clairvaux was born in 1090 about two miles from Dijon and therefore not far from Citeaux. He was of Burgundian noble stock and of devout parents. At their birth his mother dedicated each of her children to God. Frail of physique, charming, from boyhood Bernard was deeply religious. It was probably in 1112, when he was about twenty-two years of age, that Bernard became a monk of Citeaux. With him he brought about thirty friends and relatives, including five of his brothers, who had been won by his ardent persuasiveness. The last remaining brother, the youngest, followed them later. In 1115, at the age of twenty-five, Bernard became abbot of a new foundation, the fourth of the Cistercian houses, at Clairvaux, in a rugged mountain valley near some of his own kinfolk and about a hundred miles from Citeaux. He was to remain head of that house until his death, in 1153.

Combining the qualities of both the mystic and the man of action, Bernard rose fairly steadily to his position of preëminence. As a mystic, his devotion was to the Virgin Mary and especially to Christ. He was moved by the love of Christ and was committed to him not only as God but also as man. He did much to promote a revival of adoration of Jesus in his humanity. This is seen in the hymn which is usually ascribed to him, *Jesu, dulcis memoria,* portions of which in their English translations are the hymns which begin with the lines "Jesus the very thought of thee with sweetness fills my breast" and "Jesus thou joy of loving hearts." If not written by Bernard, *Jesu, dulcis memoria* is akin to his spirit. Humble and yet bold and on occasion caustic, Bernard became the mentor of Western Europe. Eloquent and persuasive as a preacher and orator, he was a major force, as we have seen, in promoting the Second Crusade. He carried on a prodigious correspondence and travelled seemingly incessantly. He was the author of several books. He interested himself in the affairs of the Church at large and was the major influence in healing a schism which had been produced by the nearly simultaneous election of two Popes. In striving to maintain what he deemed orthodoxy, he sought to win heretics by preaching and was a vigorous and persistent critic of Abélard, whom we are to meet later as a leading intellectual figure in Western Europe in the twelfth century. One of his own monks from Clairvaux became Pope. Bernard's great popularity attracted hundreds and possibly thousands to the Cistercian way of life. Largely because of him, the Cistercians became active in reforming and elevating the quality of the Church.

OTHER TWELFTH CENTURY MONASTIC MOVEMENTS

The Cistercians were the leading but by no means the only new monastic movement which rose to prominence in the twelfth century.

Next to the Cistercians, the most prominent were the Carthusians. They were founded in 1084 by Bruno, who had been a canon and a distinguished teacher at Rheims and who four years earlier had abandoned the world for the monastic life. He and a small group established themselves in a wild spot, Chartreuse, later to be called the Grande Chartreuse, approximately twelve miles north of Grenoble in a mountain valley of about 3000 feet elevation. It was from Chartreuse that the order took its name, and from it were derived the English designation, Charterhouse, and the Italian title of its houses, Certosa.

Bruno soon moved on to found other colonies of hermits and the chief impulse to the order was given by the fifth prior of the Grande Chartreuse, Guigo I, a friend of Peter the Venerable and Bernard of Clairvaux. Guigo founded additional houses, attracted men to them, and put into detailed writing the customs of the mother monastery.

The Carthusians were profoundly influenced by the early monasticism of Egypt. Their way was one of great austerity. Those who followed it lived in separate little houses, wore hair shirts, fasted rigorously, and gave themselves to reading, prayer, and labour, especially the copying of manuscripts. Each community met together for worship in a common chapel, for some of their meals, and occasionally for conversation. Never nearly as numerous as the Cistercians, the Carthusians were to persist with rules which were not to be basically altered.

Less numerous and prominent than the Carthusians and much less so than the Cistercians were several other movements which in origin were roughly contemporary with these two. One was the order of Grandmont, begun about the year 1074 or 1100 by Stephen of Muret near Limoges, in what is now the west central part of France. Stephen was of French aristocratic stock and had been a hermit in the south of Italy before returning to his native land. Grandmont carried the rule of poverty even further than did the Cistercians or the Carthusians. Its monasteries were not permitted to own churches, tithes, lands, animals, or fixed revenues. It required its monks never to leave the monastic enclosure. To free the choir monks for their spiritual duties, Grandmont entrusted to its lay brothers all responsibility for the material side of the community's life.

An order which spread widely through France was that of Fontevrault. It was founded about 1101 by Robert of Arbrissel. Robert as a priest in Rennes had vigorously attacked abuses in the Church, had then become a hermit, and later had recruited many, both men and women, for the monastic life. The mother house, at Fontevrault, near Saumur, in the west of France, was ruled by an abbess and was primarily for women. It also contained men who had dedicated themselves to the service of the nuns. It especially attracted the daughters of the royal family and the high nobility.

Another family of monasteries sprang from a foundation at Tiron made by one Bernard in 1109. Like the Cistercians, it reduced the time given to liturgical services that the monks might devote more of their hours to labour.

Vitalis, who died in 1122, founded a monastery in the forest of Savigny, in France. It inspired the formation of a number of houses in the north of France and in England. Their programme closely resembled the Cistercians and in 1147 they were absorbed by the latter.

The eleventh and twelfth centuries also saw the development of canons regular who took their inspiration and some of their rule of life from Augustine of Hippo. It will be remembered that Augustine and the clergy who lived with him formed a community which followed a discipline devised by him. We have noted that in Carolingian times groups of clergy attached to churches had begun to govern their fellowship by semi-monastic rules. In the revivals of the eleventh and twelfth centuries the Augustinian Canons multiplied in France, England, and Germany. In the twelfth century some of these communities of canons came to be very much like monasteries, and differed from the latter chiefly in leaving their members free to exercise their ministry, especially that of preaching, outside the walls of their houses.

An order of the Augustinian Canons which spread widely was the Premonstratensians. Its founder was Norbert, who was a great friend of Bernard of Clairvaux, was later Archbishop of Magdeburg, and had wide influence in the Church. The mother house, begun in 1120, was at Premontre, in the northwest of France. Norbert at first thought of affiliating it with the Cistercians. To give its members greater freedom to move about in the world preaching than the rules of Citeaux permitted, he made it into a house of canons regular, but the austerity of the mother and daughter houses resembled closely that of the Cistercians.

Late in the twelfth century an order, the Trinitarians, much like the Augustinian Canons, came into being. The purpose was the ransom of Christians who had been taken captive by Moslems. Usually the ransom was effected by the payment of money, but in extreme instances individual Trinitarians offered themselves as substitutes for those whose release they sought.

We must also recall that in the twelfth century the monastic ideal was both sufficiently potent and flexible to give rise to the Templars, the Hospitallers, and the Teutonic Knights. In Spain and Portugal, partly out of the long wars for the Christian reconquest of the Iberian Peninsula, crusading orders arose, the chief of them in Spain being that of Santiago and that of Calatrava, and in Portugal, as we have seen, the Order of Christ.

THE COMING OF THE FRIARS

As Western Europe passed on into the thirteenth century, new forms of monasticism emerged. Many of the old ones continued. The Benedictine rule was still standard. However, the impulse which produced monasticism gave evidence of its amazing creativity in bringing into being a new type of movement which, while clearly in the monastic stream and deeply indebted to the past, had in it much that was novel. This displayed itself in what are called the friars or the mendicant orders. They are usually thought of as four in number, the Franciscans, the Dominicans, the Carmelites, and the Augustinians. These were known respectively as the Brothers Minor or Grey Friars, the Preachers or Black Friars, the White Friars, and the Austin Friars. To these four were added a few similar but much smaller bodies. They all combined the monastic life and its ideals of poverty, chastity, obedience, and community living with preaching to those outside their fellowship. They were missionaries both to the nominal Christians of Western Europe and to non-Christians in various parts of the globe. This was especially true of the two largest, the Franciscans and Dominicans. To this day these two orders have had a leading part in the world-wide extension of the Roman Catholic form of the faith. The Franciscans have vied with a much younger order, the Society of Jesus, in providing the Roman Catholic Church with a larger number of missionaries than has any other of the orders and societies.

The emergence of the mendicant orders was associated with the growth of cities in Western Europe. By the thirteenth century that part of the world was beginning to move out of the almost exclusively agricultural economy which had followed the decline of the Roman Empire and the disappearance of the urban civilization which had characterized that realm. Cities were once more appearing. It was to deepening the religious life of the populace of the cities and towns that the friars devoted much of their energy. Most of the earlier monasteries had chosen solitude and centres remote from the contaminating influences of the world. In contrast, the mendicant orders sought the places where men congregated and endeavoured to bring the Gospel to them there. The older monasteries were associated with a prevailing rural and feudal milieu. The medicant orders flourished in the rapidly growing urban populations.

Here was a striking enlargement of the monastic movement. It had been foreshadowed by the participation of outstanding monks, among them Lanfranc, Anselm, and Bernard of Clairvaux, in the affairs of the Church and of the secular world. Some Benedictine monasteries had conducted schools for youths who did not take their vows and through their guest rooms had given hospitality to many from the world. The Templars and Hospitallers were examples of orders which did not remain within their cloisters but instead gave themselves to the physical care of others. Bernard of Menthon had inaugurated a community which served travellers across the Alpine pass which bears his name. The Trinitarians were ransoming captives. The Augustinian Canons and especially the Premonstratensians had been moving in the direction of service to the world outside monastic walls. The friars were a further and substantial stage. The trend was to be continued. In subsequent centuries, as we are to see, monastic orders and congregations arose, either of men or of women, who gave themselves primarily to teaching and nursing. Yet several orders whose houses cut themselves off from the world persisted and from time to time new ones like them came into being. Much more than in the Eastern Churches, in the West monasticism developed many and varied forms. Here was evidence of the amazing vitality and of the ability of Christianity to adapt itself to fresh environments.

THE FRANCISCANS

As we have suggested, what was eventually the largest of the mendicant orders in its numerous branches was what officially is designated as the Order of Little Brothers or Friars Minor (*Ordo Fratrum Minorum,* abbreviated as O.F.M.), but popularly is known as the Franciscans. The name Franciscan is appropriate, for not only was the order begun by Francis of Assisi, but it has never ceased to be challenged by the ideals of its founder. From time to time efforts, often stormy, have been made to bring its practice to conform to the difficult standards of that compelling genius.

Francis is one of the most winsome figures of Christian history. He was born in 1181 or 1182 in Assisi, an ancient town on heights overlooking the gorge through which the Tiber emerges from the mountains. His father was Pietro Bernardone, a well-to-do cloth merchant. He had little formal education, but he knew a little Latin and could read and write. He also knew French. His baptismal name was Giovanni, but the nickname of Francesco—Francis—was given him and was the one by which he was best known and remembered. He was ardent, charming, and sensitive. At first he was a play-boy, a boon companion of the gay young scions of the local aristocracy, and a leader among them in their revelries. Yet he seems to have possessed an innate refinement and is said not to have succumbed to grossness in speech or act.

The conversion of Francis to the life of religion was not a sudden dedication, but came as the result of a spiritual pilgrimage of many months which began in late adolescence. It was partly induced by illnesses and disappointments and was marked by painful and intense struggles of the spirit and in its earlier stages by relapses into the former way of life. Francis began giving himself to the service of the poor and in spite of his loathing for their disease, visited lepers and cared for them. He spent much time in solitude in the fields and hills. He was inspired by the love of Christ which had been driven home to him in the contemplation of a crucifix in a nearby chapel. His fellow-townsmen at first thought him insane. His father, enraged, kept him in confinement at home until his mother released him. Finally his father took him before the bishop to disinherit him and Francis, stripping himself of the clothing which he had had from his sire and standing naked before the bishop, declared that henceforth he desired to serve only "our Father which art in heaven." He set himself to repairing with his own hands the chapel where was the crucifix which had come to mean so much to him, begging stones and also his food. That task completed, he addressed himself to the restoration of other chapels.

Among these his favourite was Santa Maria degli Angeli, the Portiuncula, a humble affair which after Francis became famous was enclosed by a large but gaudy church.

It was in 1209 at the Portiuncula during the reading of the Gospel at the mass that Francis, then in his upper twenties, heard the call which sent him forth on his life mission. He felt impelled to become a travelling preacher, proclaiming the kingdom of God and calling men to repentance, doing so in complete poverty, subsisting on whatever food might be given him, and radiating the love of Christ. He sought to imitate Jesus and to obey him to the letter.

Francis at once set about preaching in his native town. Others, attracted, joined themselves to him. As their rule he gave them the command of Jesus to sell all and give to the poor and to go forth without staff, food, money, or a second coat, preaching the kingdom of God and healing the sick. They called themselves the penitents of Assisi. They made the Portiuncula their headquarters and built near it huts of boughs. For a habit, they wore tunics of the brown coarse cloth from which peasants made clothing. They went about, barefooted, two by two, preaching and helping the peasants in the work of the fields.

These early days were marked by mingled opposition and cordial response. Many deemed the brothers mad, pelted them with mud, insulted them, and tore off their clothing. Others were impressed by their patent sincerity and by their joyousness under persecution and in their espousal of their Lady Poverty.

Francis and his companions were not entirely unique. The time was one of religious ferment. There were numerous wandering preachers, many of them ascetics and some of them frowned upon by the Church as disobedient heretics. Contemporary Italy also had many bands or guilds whose members went about together singing hymns of penitence and praise.

Francis was no heretic. A humble son of the Church and a layman, he submitted himself to the constituted ecclesiastical authorities. In 1210 he and eleven companions went to Rome to seek Papal permission to pursue their manner of life. Innocent III, one of the greatest of the Popes, was then on the throne of Peter. After some hesitation and a careful investigation by members of his *curia,* for he professed fear that their manner of life was too severe, Innocent gave them tentative approval and permitted them to continue preaching. However, he made the quite natural condition that in each diocese where they preached they must first obtain the consent of the bishop and that they elect a superior who could be held responsible for their conduct. Francis was the inevitable choice for the headship of the group. Thus the Penitents of Assisi, a few years later called by Francis in characteristic fashion the Minor, or Humbler Brethren, became an order.

Returning to Assisi, Francis, now reinforced by Papal approval, was received with acclaim and throngs flocked to his preaching. He sought, with success, to heal civil strife in his home city between the feudal nobility and the townsfolk. His followers multiplied and obtained from the proprietors, a Benedictine monastery, the Portiuncula as permanent headquarters.

In these early days of the order, the Brothers Minor worked with their hands for their livelihood, supplementing the labour with begging when food was not otherwise to be had. Francis insisted upon absolute poverty, would not permit any of the brethren to have money, and is said on one occasion to have forbidden a brother to own even a psalter, saying that if he possessed one he would wish for a breviary, and that if he owned a breviary he would soon be haughtily commanding one of his fellows to bring it to him.

The Brothers Minor not only preached but also sang. Some of their hymns were improvised by Francis, for his was always the soul of a poet. Especially famous was his *Praises of the Creatures,* better known as the *Canticle of the Sun.*

Closely related to the poetic strain in Francis was a love for all creation and a joy in it. One of the stories which his early disciples cherished was that of a sermon which he preached to the birds, exhorting them to praise and love their Creator. They also declared that once when Francis was preaching the swallows made so much noise that he could not be heard and that on his charging them to be quiet until he had finished they meekly subsided. At another time he made nests for turtle doves that they might lay eggs and rear their young under the protection of the brethren. This love of nature seems to have increased with the years and never to have been more keen than in his last months when his body was racked by pain.

The preaching of Francis and his associates was unstudied and direct. It stressed the adoration of God, repentance, generosity, and the forgiveness of wrongs done to one by others. It made much of love for one's neighbours and one's enemies, humility, and abstention from vices, including especially the vices of the flesh. It advocated fasting and encouraged the confession of one's sins to a priest.

By his sincerity, joyousness, earnestness, and radiant love Francis rapidly won an increasing number to the Brothers Minor. At first he admitted those who applied without the novitiate customary in the older orders. Among those who sought entrance was Clara, a girl of sixteen, twelve years younger than Francis, a scion of the Sciffi, one of the noble houses of Assisi. He welcomed her with great affection and in 1212, three years after the decisive call had come to him, received her into the order. In spite of the bitter opposition of her father, she persisted. To her father's even greater wrath, a younger sister followed her. Other women came and a house was found for them in Assisi. Thus a second order, a woman's branch of the Franciscans, the Poor Ladies or Poor Clares, came into being.

Early, although not formally until 1221, there also sprang up what is usually known as the Third Order, or, more accurately, the Order of Penitents. Its members were not fully to follow the way of Francis and were to remain in the world and hold property, but they were to be sparing in food and drink, give alms, abstain from vice, accept the sacraments, and remain loyal members of the Catholic Church. One of its earliest members north of the Alps was Elizabeth of Hungary (c.1207–1231). The daughter of a king of Hungary, devout from her childhood, she was early betrothed in one of the dynastic matrimonial alliances which were common and at fourteen was married to the Landgrave of Thuringia. Her husband perished in a crusade and in the later years of her brief life she gave much of her fortune to the poor, founded a hospital, and in Marburg with her own hands cared for the sick.

Francis was enthusiastically missionary in purpose and practice. He himself traversed much of Italy, preaching. He wished also to go to the Moslems. He sought to journey to the Holy Land, but was thwarted by shipwreck. He went to Spain to open a way to Morocco, there to reach Moslems who had recently been defeated by a coalition of Christian princes and had taken refuge in that land. Illness stopped him and compelled him to return to Italy. Eventually, in 1219, he went to Egypt, in company with what is usually called the Fifth Crusade. He was deeply grieved by the lack of discipline and the vicious lives of many of these champions of the Cross. Yet from among them he won some who helped to spread the Franciscan movement to Northern Europe. He also presented the faith to the Sultan and seems to have gained the latter's respect. He returned to Italy (1220) by way of Palestine and Syria. Not content with himself going on missions he sent out his friars to various parts of Europe and to Morocco.

Francis quickly ran his course. October 3, 1226, when only in his mid-forties, he breathed his last in the church of Portiuncula where, seventeen years earlier, he had heard the call which had sent him forth preaching. In his later years he had been increasingly frail and had more and more withdrawn from the management of the order. His ardent devotion to Christ and his meditation of Christ's passion were crowned by the appearance of the *stigmata,* the wounds of his Master, on his own body. Death came peacefully and in the end painlessly. Two years later, in 1228, he was formally proclaimed to be a saint by his friend and the patron of the order, the former Cardinal Ugolino of Ostia, now Pope Gregory IX.

Before death claimed him, Francis had the mingled joy and pain of seeing the Order of Brothers Minor quite outgrow him and the deep grief of knowing that it was already beginning to depart from the simplicity and poverty of its first days. In his last months he sought to stem the tide by dictating his will. In this he commanded all the brothers to work at some honourable occupation, not for gain but for a good example, and to flee idleness. Only when they were not paid for their work were they to beg. They were not to receive churches or habitations. The will expressly forbade the brothers to seek a bull which would relax this interdiction or to introduce glosses or modifications in the rule or the will.

Yet before and after the will was dictated the worldly wisdom of Innocent III in declaring the primitive Franciscan ideal too severe for human flesh and blood had been confirmed by the event. Organization proved necessary. Early the Brothers Minor assembled annually at Portiuncula. In 1216 at the request of Francis, Ugolino became the protector of the brotherhood. His guidance had much to do with shaping the next stages of organization. In 1220 a Papal bull prescribed a novitiate of one year as a prerequisite for full membership, fixed the garb, and declared the vows to be irrevocable. In 1221 the order was given a new rule, much longer than the original one. Francis was not an organizer or an administrator. He was too impulsive, too subject to changes of mood, too unpredictable, to carry the load of running a great organization. The actual management passed into the hands of others, within a few months to one of the first companions of Francis, Brother Elias, whom Francis, as minister general, appointed his vicar. In 1223 another rule was adopted which made begging rather than labour with the hands the normal method of support. To the intense indignation of Francis, Brothers Minor were beginning to establish themselves in the universities which were arising in Europe. Francis distrusted scholarship as a perversion of the original purpose. Preaching was not being given its former primary place, but Brothers Minor were becoming advisers in the Papal *curia*. No longer was the marriage to Lady Poverty being strictly observed, but collectively property was beginning to be acquired. Theoretically the property was not held by the order, but by friends or by the Pope in behalf of the order. Structurally the order had become fairly elaborate. Every group had its *custos,* or head. The groups were organized by territorial provinces, each of which had its minister and its chapter. Over all was a general chapter and a minister general.

After the death of Francis further relaxation of the primitive ideals entered and a sharp division disrupted the pristine brotherhood of love. On the one extreme were those who wished to hold to the manner of life which had been followed by Francis in the initial years of the fellowship, with its absolute poverty and its itinerant preaching. This group, a minority, who came to be known as the Zealots or Spirituals, were given prestige by the presence of several of the earliest companions of Francis. On the other extreme were those who desired a complete relaxation of the rule of poverty. In the middle were the majority, moderates, who would maintain something of the primitive poverty, but who wished the order to establish itself in the universities, develop scholars, and acquire influence in the Church. The conflict between these strains was acute. Indeed, no large order of the Catholic Church has had so explosive a history or has been rent by so many schisms.

It was the moderates who before many years obtained control. The first minister general after Francis, John Parenti, who served from 1227 to 1232, favoured strict conformity to the wishes of the founder. Yet it was under him that Pope Gregory IX declared (1230) that the will of Francis was not binding. In 1232 John retired under pressure, and Elias was elected in his stead. Although he had had the confidence of Francis, Elias departed from the strict observance of the latter's wishes. He was an extraordinarily able promoter and administrator. Before his election as minister general he had, with the support of the order's great patron, Pope Gregory IX, begun the erection of a huge church in Assisi as a memorial to Francis, a structure which was a visible denial of the ideals of the Poverello. For it Elias gathered funds from many quarters. Under him the order grew rapidly, its missions were extended, new provinces were organized, and its strength was augmented in the universities, institutions which then were in the first flush of their youthful popularity. He encouraged scholarship. Elias was autocratic and the pressure which he employed to raise the huge sums for the memorial church provoked criticism. Opposition arose, not only from the Zealots, against whom he had taken stern measures, but also from the moderates, especially in some of the universities. In a dramatic session of the general chapter in the presence of Gregory IX in 1239 Elias was deposed. Under his immediate successors further relaxation in the rule of poverty was effected. John of Parma, who became minister general in 1247, although of aristocratic stock and an accomplished scholar, was of the Zealots and insisted upon a strict observance of the will of Francis. However, after a decade he resigned and was followed by Bonaventura. Bonaventura was a philosopher and mystic, was known as the Seraphic Doctor, and was eventually canonized. He held the post for more than a quarter of a century, until in 1273, having been made a cardinal, he also resigned. A man of action, courteous, humble, cheerful, tactful, courageous, a stirring preacher, he has been called the second founder of the order. A moderate, he brought the Brothers Minor more and more into conformity with the monastic tradition. He took action against the Zealots and during his administration some of the more extreme of them were imprisoned.

The Spirituals or Zealots did not tamely submit to the trend towards moderation. In a variety of ways they protested. Some of them were profoundly influenced by the writings of Joachim of Flora (or Fiore).

Joachim was born in 1130 in Calabria in the extreme south of Italy and except for his wanderings spent his life there. He early began preaching, then entered a Cistercian monastery, eventually was ordained priest, and, reluctantly, was made abbot. Desiring a stricter way of life than he had found there, he left that post. Disciples came to him and he founded a monastery, that of St. John of Flora (Fiore). He was released from his obedience to the Cistercians and in 1196 the new order, that of Flora (Fiore), obtained Papal approval. It never became large. Joachim himself died in 1202. He was, then, an older contemporary of Francis of Assisi.

Through his writings Joachim exerted a wide influence. He was esteemed a prophet. He gave an interpretation of the human drama for which he claimed Biblical foundation. To his mind history had three ages, or dispensations, that of the Father, the Son, and the Holy Spirit. He complicated this pattern by others, three of them of five ages each, another of seven ages, and still another of eight ages. The three ages, of Father, Son, and Holy Spirit received his chief emphasis. They overlapped. That of God the Father began in Adam and ended in Christ. In it men followed a carnal life, marrying and giving in marriage. The second age, that of God the Son, began with Uzziah and was to be consummated in the year 1260. In it life was a mixture of flesh and spirit and it was the age of the clerics. The third age, that of God the Spirit, is that of the monks. In it men are to live a purely spiritual life. It was inaugurated with Benedict of Nursia and is to last until the end of the world. The third age is to be marked by a gift of the Holy Spirit, that of contemplation, and in it the whole Church is to become a contemplative society. The first period was one of law, fear, labour, and slavery. The second was one of grace, humility, truth, discipline, and filial service. The third is to be one of love, liberty, happiness, and contemplation. Here is to be the culmination of history.

It can readily be seen that this bold scheme of history would have an appeal for many, including those of the tradition of Francis of Assisi. The teachings of Joachim profoundly shaped the thought of the Spirituals and also of many outside Franciscan ranks. They reinforced those who attacked the corruption in the Church and the Papacy. Quite understandably the latter hit back. In 1225 one of Joachim's books and in 1259 his other works were officially condemned by the Church. Any who favoured his views, including the Spirituals, were under suspicion and some of them fell afoul of the Inquisition and were killed.

The Spirituals were eventually in several schools and in various parts of Europe. Fascinating though their story is, we must not take the space to recount it. Some were in Ancona, others in that hotbed of heresies, Provence, and still others in Tuscany. Some completely withdrew from the Order of Brothers Minor. The extremists among the seceders were known as the Fraticelli, or "Little Brothers." They exalted the ideal of poverty and the mission of Francis of Assisi. Some of their groups were protected by one or another member of the nobility.

Fairly typical of the Spirituals—if anyone can be called typical of so diverse a set of movements and of men—and also of the sharp contrasts and the religious ferment seen in Italy in the thirteenth century, was Jacopone da Todi (c.1230–1306). A scion of the nobility, wilful, high-spirited, extravagant, vain, arrogant, perhaps a Doctor of Laws from the University of Bologna, disdainful of religion, a brilliant intellectual, in his late thirties he was shocked into the religious life, perhaps by the death of his young wife. He revolted against his earlier habits, gave his goods to the poor, and, dressed meanly, seemingly half-mad, urged his fellow-townsmen to repentance and fought his besetting sin of pride. He joined the Franciscans and became a leader of the Spirituals. Mystic, poet, drinking of that fountain of mediæval mysticism, Dionysius the Areopagite, a wandering lay missionary, he became involved in Italian politics, for five years languished in prison at the command of the Pope, was released by a new Pope, and spent his later years in contemplation and in communion with the "Infinite Light."

Various attempts were made to restore unity in the Order of Brothers Minor. For a time a Papal bull following the Council of Vienne, in 1312, seemed to give promise of success. However, the vigorous measures against the Spirituals taken by John XXII, who came to the Papal throne in 1316 and who instituted a severe persecution of them, drove some of the extremists to declare that the Pope was Antichrist or the forerunner of Antichrist, that the Roman Church was the harlot of Babylon described in the Apocalypse, and that the sacraments of the Church were obsolete. The tension was heightened when, in flat contradiction of the findings of the general chapter of the Franciscans in 1322 which declared that Jesus and the apostles had stood for absolute poverty, John XXII, in a bull in 1323, denounced this view as false and heretical. In 1322 John ended the fiction by which the Pope held property for the use of the Franciscans and turned it over directly to the order.

In spite of these internal difficulties and secessions and its departure from strict adherence to the ideals of Francis, the Order of Brothers Minor continued and never ceased to play an important role in the Church.

THE DOMINICANS

The Dominicans, officially the Order of Preachers (*Ordo praedicatorum*) or the Preaching Brothers (*Fratres Praedicatores*), like the Franciscans, arose early in the thirteenth century. The two had many similarities. They also displayed marked differences. At times they were unfriendly rivals. In contrast with the Franciscans, whose founder was deeply distressed by the drift towards the universities, from the outset the Dominicans were dedicated to teaching and scholarship as well as to preaching. It was no accident that from them came Thomas Aquinas, whom Roman Catholics were eventually to regard as having made the authoritative systematic intellectual statement of their faith. Moreover, while committed to poverty, the Dominicans were not as haunted by the ideal of complete abnegation of all worldly goods as were Francis and some of his followers. With notable exceptions they tended to be recruited from the aristocracy. Also with outstanding exceptions the Franciscans were from the humble classes. Nor did the sons of Dominic have about them the explosive quality which so punctuated the early centuries of the Brothers Minor. From them issued no movement comparable with the Spirituals or the Fraticelli.

Of Dominic, the founder of the Order of Preachers, we have a far less vivid picture than we do of Francis of Assisi. He seems not to have been nearly so colourful a figure. Yet he appears to have been even more the creator of the order which is usually known by his name than was Francis of the Brothers Minor. He was born in Castile about the year 1170. He was, therefore, an older contemporary of Francis. In his youth and until his mid-twenties he was for several years a student in one of the cathedral schools of Spain. Then he became an Augustinian canon in the cathedral of his native bishopric and eventually under a reforming bishop rose to be prior of the chapter. In other words, his was the somewhat conventional course of an able, scholarly clergyman who was committed to the conscientious pursuit of his calling. He was humble, for he later refused two bishoprics and shortly before his death attempted to resign from the headship of the order of which he was the chief creator. He was stern with himself in his strict asceticism. He gave himself to prolonged prayer. He was gentle, and in spite of his austerities left the impression of always being joyful.

Dominic might have passed his life in comparative obscurity had he not been confronted by a major challenge. This was the defection from the Catholic Church of a large proportion of the population in what is now the south of France. That region had not yet been assimilated to the rising kingdom of France and was largely distinct in culture. In the latter part of the twelfth and in the thirteenth century the Catholic Church in that area was weak and was represented by a body of clergy who were predominantly ignorant and corrupt. As we are to see more at length in the next chapter, what the Church deemed heresy was rife. The major movement was that of the Cathari, and the leaders of that sect seem to have been better morally than the rank and file of the Catholic clergy. In Dominic's lifetime, as we are also to say later, the Inquisition and armed force in the form of a crusade were being brought to bear on them. Heresy was being wiped out by blood. Early in the thirteenth century, when he was in his thirties, Dominic travelled in the south of France with his bishop, Diego d'Azévédo, and was stirred to the depths by what was to him the appalling religious state of the populace.

It seems to have been Diego who took the lead in devising and carrying through the first stages a peaceful method of bringing into the Church those who had revolted from it. This was to be by bands of missionaries who in poverty, ascetic holiness, love, and intellectual calibre were to win respect for the Catholic faith and converts to it. A nunnery was founded at Prouille, near Toulouse, in 1206. It eventually grew to large proportions and in a sense was the mother house of the future order.

When Diego returned to his diocese, Dominic took over the leadership of the enterprise. The first few years were difficult and discouraging. Yet, with characteristic determination, he persisted. Kindly, winsome, possessed of deep convictions, he persevered, driven by a love of souls and sustained by a life of prayer. In 1214 or 1215 a citizen of Toulouse gave him a house and he gathered about him a small company of men who lived in community. In 1215 Dominic went to Rome to the Fourth Lateran Council, a gathering to the importance of which we are to recur in a later chapter. He sought from Pope Innocent III approval of the new order. The Pope was reluctant, partly because the Lateran Council, alarmed at the multiplication of novel monastic movements, had ordered that any one who wished to found a new religious house must accept its rule from one which had already been approved. The Pope gave his consent, but on condition that Dominic would adopt the rule of some established order. In conformity with this command, Dominic chose the rule of the Augustinian Canons. He may have been moved to do this by the fact that he had already been a member of a community which was of this pattern. In framing the constitution of his order, Dominic was especially influenced by the structure and experience of the Premonstratensians who, it will be remembered, were a widely spread development from the Augustinian Canons. Late in 1216 and early in 1217, at the request of Dominic, Pope Honorius III confirmed the order. The name, Friars Preachers, seems to have been suggested by Innocent III.

Dominic was profoundly moved by his contacts with Francis and the Franciscans. He met Francis in Rome in 1218 and attended the general chapter of the Brothers Minor at Portiuncula in that year. At their general chapter in 1220 the Dominicans decided to wed Lady Poverty. How far this was in imitation of the Franciscans is a matter of debate. That the Franciscans were an important influence in the step seems certain. Precisely how determinative they were we cannot tell. Like the Brothers Minor, the Dominicans became mendicants, begging their daily bread from door to door.

The Dominicans spread almost as rapidly and widely as the Franciscans. Dominic spent most of his later months in Rome. He died in 1221, shortly after presiding at the second general chapter of the Order. By that time the Dominicans are said to have had sixty houses. They were already represented at the new university centres of Paris and Bologna. The number of houses is reported to have grown to 404 in 1277, a little more than fifty years later.

The Franciscans and the Dominicans resembled each other not only in being "begging friars." In organization each had territorial provinces with chapters and a head, a general chapter of the entire order, and a single head of the whole. Each had a second order for women, and each a third order for the laity. Both were intensely missionary and by widely flung enterprises in Europe, Asia, and Africa sought to bring nominal Christians to a deeper faith and to win non-Christians. Both established themselves in the universities and the members of both did much preaching.

However, in contrast with the Franciscans, who sought the moral conversion of their hearers by the witness of untutored simplicity and a life of absolute poverty and self-giving love, the Dominicans strove to overcome ignorance and error through all the skills of trained minds. They stressed the education of their members. Each of their houses was a school and each must have at least one doctor of theology to direct the study of that subject. Scholarship was given an honoured place. But scholarship was for the purpose of preparing preachers who were to become missionaries to the masses.

THE CARMELITES

The Franciscans and the Dominicans were by far the largest of the mendicant orders. So popular did they become and so mightily did they stir the imagination of earnest Christians in Western Europe that they stimulated the development of similar bodies. Of these the most prominent were the Carmelites and the Augustinian Hermits or Friars.

The Carmelites ascribed their origin to Elijah who, it was said, founded a community of hermits on Mt. Carmel which continued to the time of Christ. Some of its members, so it was claimed, were then converted to the Christian faith and enrolled the Virgin Mary and the apostles as members. The order, it was maintained, then persisted unbroken as a Christian fellowship.

Actually, what became the Order of Our Lady of Mount Carmel can be traced only to the twelfth century. At that time a few pilgrims who took advantage of the Crusades to go to Palestine established themselves as a company of hermits on Mt. Carmel. About the year 1210, namely, while the Franciscans and Dominicans were taking shape, they were given a rule by the Latin Patriarch of Jerusalem. They were not unlike the Carthusians and and the Camaldulians. They were to live in silence and retirement far from other human habitation and were to meet only at specified times but not for meals. Eventually several other affiliated groups arose in Palestine.

The reconquest of Palestine by the Moslems constrained the Carmelites to scatter. They went to Cyprus and to several countries in the south and west of Europe. In 1229 they won Papal recognition as mendicants. Many were attracted to their ranks. The younger group found the old way of the hermit unfitted to conditions in Europe and wished, like the other friars, to preach and in preparation for that mission to frequent the universities. A crisis arose which threatened the existence of the order. Rescue from this outcome was chiefly by some of its English members, led by Simon Stock, who became general of the order in 1247. He obtained modifications which brought the order more nearly into the pattern of life of the Franciscans and Dominicans. In spite of protests Simon's ideas eventually prevailed and at a chapter general in London in 1281 closer approximation to the programme of studies of the Dominicans was achieved. The Carmelites established themselves in the universities. Yet the love of the older type of life, that of the hermit, persisted among some of the members.

The Augustinian Hermits

The Friars Hermits of St. Augustine or the Augustinian Order sprang from several communities in Italy which early in the thirteenth century sent colonies into Germany, Spain, and the south of France. They were among those movements towards the semi-hermit life which abounded in Italy late in the twelfth and in the fore part of the thirteenth century and were expressions of the religious awakening of those decades. In general they followed the rule ascribed to Augustine of Hippo, for, as we have hinted, this had become common among non-monastic groups devoted to religion.

It was largely through the initiative of the Papacy that a number of these bodies were brought together under a common organization. The Popes were disturbed by the multitude of new movements, some of which smacked of heresy or were in danger of becoming heretical. Quite understandably, they sought to draw them together into a structure which could meet Rome's approval and through which they could serve the Church. In 1243 Pope Innocent IV brought hermits in Tuscany under the Augustinian rule and appointed Cardinal Richard Annibaldi as their supervisor. More than any other one man, Annibaldi was responsible for the growth of the order. A Papal bull of 1256 which merged several bands of hermits into a closer union is usually regarded as the decisive landmark in making the Austin Friars an order. Before the close to the thirteenth century the Augustinians had conformed to the pattern of the Dominicans. They became a preaching order and based that preaching upon theological training and scholarship.

OTHER MENDICANT ORDERS

The popularity of the great medicant orders contributed to the creation of still other bodies which resembled them. Most of them were ephemeral, partly because the Council of Lyons (1274) sought to discourage them. However, some persisted. Prominent were the Servants of Mary, usually known as the Servites. They were founded in 1233 by seven youths from aristocratic families of Florence who, giving up their wealth, established themselves on a mountain near that city. The community grew and in 1240 became an order which followed the Augustinian rule and also consciously borrowed from the constitutions of the Dominicans. In the 1240's the Servites received Papal approval but not until 1304 was that made final. Eventually they were ranked with the four great mendicant orders. We hear as well of the Friars of the Cross, also called the Crutched Friars. There were several bodies known as Fratres Cruciferi, one of which went back at least to the twelfth century and another to the thirteenth century.

THE FRIARS MULTIPLY AND CLASH WITH THE SECULAR CLERGY

As we have suggested, the movements represented by the friars quickly attracted large numbers of members and spread rapidly through Western Europe. Why this was so is not entirely clear. It may have been because they combined the sort of complete devotion to the Christian ideal that was seen in the traditional monasticism with service to others in the form of missions to nominal Christians and to non-Christians. Whatever the reason, they became one of the most familiar features of the Europe of the thirteenth century and continued to grow.

This growth brought the mendicant orders into repeated conflicts with the secular clergy. By the term "secular clergy" or "seculars" is meant those clergy who are not members of monastic bodies but who live *in sæculum,* namely, in the world. Before the end of the thirteenth century, the Popes had, by successive steps, made the friars independent of the bishops and responsible only to their own superiors and to the Holy See. While older orders had also enjoyed this immunity from control by diocesan bishops and were directly subject to the Pope, this status made the friars unusually irritating to the episcopacy, for, unlike most of the earlier monks, they did not live apart from the world, but went everywhere preaching, hearing confessions, and saying mass. Preaching had been a prerogative of the bishops and hearing confessions and giving the communion were among the functions of the parish clergy. Many bishops and parish priests, accordingly, felt aggrieved. In 1254 Pope Innocent IV, yielding to the complaints which had come to him, especially from the University of Paris, where the Dominicans were in open conflict with the university authorities, forbade religious orders to receive into their churches on Sundays or feast days the parishioners of others, to preach even in their own churches before mass, to preach in parish churches, or to hear confessions without the consent of the parish priest. Before the year was out, this edict had been revoked by Innocent's successor and the mendicants continued to flourish. Many of them also rose to high office in the Church. Here was a new and permanent element in the Catholic Church of the West.

OTHER THIRTEENTH AND FOURTEENTH CENTURY MONASTIC MOVEMENTS

The popularity of the friars did not fully eclipse the older monastic orders. In the thirteenth and fourteenth centuries, as we have hinted, while the former were coming into being and catching the imagination of Western Catholics, the older forms of monasticism persisted. The Benedictines, the Cluniacs, the Cistercians, the Carthusians, and others still constituted an important feature of the religious life in Western Europe. Indeed, a few new orders arose on the older patterns.

Thus in 1231 the Sylvestrines were founded by Sylvester Gozzolini. They followed the primitive form of the rule of Benedict and went beyond it in austerity and the practice of poverty. Italian in origin, they did not spread extensively beyond that peninsula. Although never numerous, they survived into the twentieth century.

In 1319 the Olivetans were officially constituted, taking their name from their original hermitage on Monte Oliveto and in memory of Christ's agony on the Mount of Olives. They sprang from a small group of aristocrats of Siena who in 1313 went to a mountain fastness to follow the ascetic life as hermits. The bishop whom the Pope appointed to direct them gave them the rule of Benedict. To this they adhered with great strictness. Their houses multiplied and were formed into an order with a general chapter and a superior general.

SUMMARY

This rapid survey of the development of the monasticism in Western Europe in the four centuries between 950 and 1350 will at least give evidence of the abounding vitality of the Christianity of that region in these years. As we look back across the story eight generalizations stand out.

1. For a large proportion of Christians the monastic way seemed to be the road through which to pursue the perfect Christian life and to attain the goal of the salvation of one's soul.

2. All the efforts to attain the Christian ideal through monasticism tended to spend their force and the institutions to which they gave rise to become prosaic and even corrupt.

3. From time to time, often in protest against this laxity, new monastic movements sprang up and flourished.

4. These fresh movements displayed increasing variety. Some of them, like the earlier ones, sought complete separation from the society about them, there to live uncontaminated by the evil which seemed an integral part of the world. On the other hand, a mounting trend was towards active participation in the world in an effort to save it and to win more and more men and women to the Christian faith.

5. The overwhelming majority of the new monastic movements had their origin in Italy and in what had once been Gaul, areas which had long been professedly Christian. Few arose in regions such as England, Scotland, the north of Germany, and Scandinavia, which had recently been won to the Christian faith, or in Spain, where Islam had not yet been fully vanquished. To this there were a few exceptions. One of them was Bec, where the founder was from Norman stock which only two or three generations earlier had been pagan, but even in Bec Lanfranc and Anselm, the leaders who did most to give the foundation distinction, were from Italy. It may be noted, by way of anticipation, that in subsequent centuries most of the new monastic movements had their birth in Latin Europe, while in contrast the movements which issued in Protestantism were especially strong outside Latin Europe.

6. The initiators of the new orders were chiefly from the aristocracy. Francis of Assisi was an outstanding exception, but even he was from the merchant class and not from the peasantry.

7. Here was a swelling tide seeking to deepen and make more intelligent and effective the loyalty to the Christian faith which had become nominal through the mass conversions of the earlier centuries.

8. Finally, we must note what we have already suggested and what will become more apparent in the next two chapters, that the monastic develop-

ments were but one phase of an even more inclusive mounting wave of religious life. This was concurrently making itself felt in other movements, some of them within the Church and some denounced by the latter as heretical, in efforts to purify the Church and with it to lift to a higher level the entire population which bore the Christian name.

SELECTED BIBLIOGRAPHY

GENERAL WORKS

G. G. Coulton, *Five Centuries of Religion* (Cambridge University Press, 4 vols., 1923, 1927, 1936, 1950). The first three volumes cover this period. Voluminous, enormously erudite, they are unsympathetic with monasticism.

D. Knowles, *The Monastic Order in England. A History of Its Development from the Times of St. Dunstan to the Fourth Lateran Council 943–1216* (Cambridge University Press, 1940, pp. xix, 764). Valuable not only for its description of conditions in England, but also for its account of monasticism on the Continent of Europe. By a Roman Catholic, singularly objective.

D. Knowles, *The Religious Orders in England* (Cambridge University Press, 1948, pp. xvi, 348). Carries the story of the preceding volume from 1216 to 1340. Like its predecessor, it contains valuable summaries of the course of Continental monasticism.

H. B. Workman, *The Evolution of the Monastic Ideal from the Earliest Times down to the Coming of the Friars* (London, The Epworth Press, 1927, pp. xxi, 368). Approximately the last third of this general, semi-popular survey covers the period of this chapter.

CLUNY

J. Evans, *Monastic Life at Cluny 910–1157* (Oxford University Press, 1931, pp. xii, 137). Carefully done.

L. M. Smith, *The Early History of the Monastery of Cluny* (Oxford University Press, 1920, pp. x, 225). Based upon extensive use of the sources.

L. M. Smith, *Cluny in the Eleventh and Twelfth Centuries* (London, Philip Allan & Co., 1930, pp. xxviii, 348). Like the earlier volume by the same author, carefully done and based upon the sources.

THE CISTERCIANS AND BERNARD OF CLAIRVAUX

M. H. d'Arbois de Jubainville, *Études sur l'État Interieur des Abbayes Cisterciennes et principalement de Clairvaux au XII*e *et au XIII*e *Siècle* (Paris, Aug. Durand, 1858, pp. xviii, 489).

Life and Works of Saint Bernard, Abbot of Clairvaux, edited by J. Mabillon, translated and edited with additional notes by S. J. Eales. (2d ed., London, Burns, Oates, & Washbourne, no date, 2 vols.). Made up chiefly of the letters of Bernard.

Cæsarius of Heisterbach, *The Dialogue of Miracles,* translated by H. von E. Scott and C. C. Swinton Bland, with an introduction by G. G. Coulton (London, George Routledge Sons, 2 vols., 1929). Stories told by a Cistercian in the first half of the thirteenth century which throw light on the religious life of the times and especially on that of one Cistercian abbey.

R. S. Storrs, *Bernard of Clairvaux, the Times, the Man, and His Work* (New York, Charles Scribner's Sons, 1907, pp. xvi, 598). Semi-popular, well-written lectures, based upon the sources.

W. W. Williams, *Studies in St. Bernard of Clairvaux* (London, Society for Promoting Christian Knowledge, 1927, pp. vi, 160). A well-written, sympathetic account of Bernard, with special emphasis upon his early years and the first part of his career, with extensive footnote quotations from the sources.

THE CARTHUSIANS

E. M. Thompson, *The Carthusian Order in England* (London, Society for Promoting Christian Knowledge, Part I, 1930, pp. x, 550). About a fourth of the whole is on the history of the order outside of England.

FRANCIS OF ASSISI AND THE FRANCISCANS

Out of the enormous amount that has been written on the subject, the following will be found useful.

T. S. R. Boase, *St. Francis of Assisi* (London, Gerald Duckworth & Co., 1936, pp. 137). A popular, well-written account.

P. Cowley, *Franciscan Rise and Fall* (London, J. M. Dent & Sons, 1933, pp. x, 212). A popular account, chiefly on Francis and the order until his death, with a brief summary of later developments—"the fall"—by a warm admirer of Francis.

P. Robinson, *The Writings of Saint Francis of Assisi Newly Translated into English with an Introduction and Notes* (London, J. M. Dent & Sons, 1906, pp. xxxii, 208). By a Franciscan.

"The Little Flowers" & the Life of St. Francis with the "Mirror of Perfection" (London, J. M. Dent & Sons, 1910, pp. xxii, 397. In *Everyman's Library*). *The Little Flowers* (*Fioretti*) and *the Mirror of Perfection* (*Speculum*) record the memories of Francis transmitted orally or in writing, as cherished by the saint's intimate friends. They have much of the miraculous and are told with the bias of the Spiritual Franciscans. The *Life* is the official one by Bonaventura, not as colourful as the other two books in this volume.

R. M. Huber, *A Documented History of the Franciscan Order* (*1182–1517*) (Milwaukee, The Nowiny Publishing Apostolate, 1944, pp. xxxiv, 1028). A useful summary by a Franciscan, of the history of the Franciscans, based upon the documents and with extensive references to them.

A. G. Little, *Guide to Franciscan Studies* (London, Society for Promoting Christian Knowledge, 1920, pp. v, 63). A useful introduction to the sources.

J. R. H. Moorman, *The Sources for the Life of S. Francis of Assisi* (Manchester

University Press, 1940, pp. xiv, 176). A critical description and evaluation of the various sources.

P. Sabatier, *Life of St. Francis of Assisi* (New York, Charles Scribner's Sons, 1909, pp. xxxv, 448). A standard life by a Protestant who was a warm admirer of Francis.

THE SPIRITUAL FRANCISCANS

D. M. Douie, *The Nature and the Effect of the Heresy of the Fraticelli* (Manchester University Press, 1932, pp. xix, 292). A scholarly study which, while specializing on the Fraticelli, embraces the entire movement of the Spirituals.

H. C. Lea, *A History of the Inquisition of the Middle Ages* (Vol. III, New York, Harper & Brothers, 1888, pp. ix, 736).

D. S. Muzzey, *The Spiritual Franciscans* (New York, American Historical Association, 1907, pp. 75). A prize essay, in the form of a brief, comprehensive summary with excellent references to the sources.

V. D. Scudder, *The Franciscan Adventure. A Study in the First Hundred Years of the Order of St. Francis of Assisi* (London, J. M. Dent & Sons, 1931, pp. 432). Well written, scholarly, with special emphasis upon the internal struggles in the order and the development of the Spirituals.

E. Underhill, *Jacopone da Todi, Poet and Mystic 1228–1306: a Spiritual Biography* (London, J. M. Dent & Sons, 1919, pp. xi, 521). A careful study by a distinguished specialist in mysticism.

JOACHIM OF FLORA

H. Bett, *Joachim of Flora* (London, Methuen & Co., 1931). Brief, but an excellent comprehensive summary conscientiously based on wide use of the sources and pertinent secondary works.

DOMINIC AND THE DOMINICANS

R. F. Bennett, *The Early Dominicans. Studies in Thirteenth-Century Dominican History* (Cambridge University Press, 1937, pp. xii, 189). An important survey, treating phase by phase various aspects of the Dominican life, practice, and achievement.

A. F. Drane, *The History of St. Dominic, Founder of the Order of Preachers* (London, Longmans, Green & Co., 1891, pp. xvii, 485).

G. R. Galbraith, *The Constitution of the Dominican Order 1216 to 1360* (Manchester University Press, 1925, pp. xvi, 286). A carefully documented study of the Dominican organization.

P. Mandonnet, *St. Dominic and His Work,* translated by M. B. Larkin (St. Louis, B. Herder Book Co., 1945, pp. xviii, 487). A comprehensive account, by a Dominican, with chief emphasis upon the order in its early years, and its varied activities and achievements.

Chapter XIX

POPULAR RELIGIOUS MOVEMENTS:
MOVEMENTS OTHER THAN MONASTIC
FOR THE FULL PRACTICE OF THE
CHRISTIAN LIFE BOTH INSIDE
AND OUTSIDE THE CHURCH

The abounding vitality of Christianity in Western Europe in the four centuries between the years 950 and 1350 did not find its only expression through monasticism, vigorous and increasingly rich in its variety though that was. It also displayed itself in many minority movements which arose, like monasticism, from a desire for a more thoroughgoing commitment to the Christian faith. Some of them were ardently missionary, seeking to win others from the nominally Christian population. Many remained within the Catholic Church. Others were outside it, either by their own choice or because they were expelled for what that Church deemed their heresies. These movements are the subject of this chapter. In the following chapter we shall deal with the efforts to raise the entire Church in the West, which meant practically all of Western Europe, to a higher plane of life, and to do this through a comprehensive ecclesiastical structure.

As we enter upon these extra-monastic minority movements, we must remind ourselves again of the general situation in Western Europe during these centuries. Here was an area, still sparsely settled when compared with the Europe of the nineteenth and twentieth centuries, or even with the China and India of that day, but which was emerging from a prolonged series of foreign invasions. Cities, though small and unsanitary, were growing, commerce was increasing, distinctive art, architecture, and literature were appearing, and the first beginnings were being seen of that expansion of European peoples which was to be so outstanding a feature of the history of the world after the fifteenth century.

There had been a mass conversion of this Europe to Christianity. Much of it had been while the Roman Empire was still intact, well before the year 500. Some of it had been that of the barbarian invaders as they settled within the former borders of the Roman Empire. Several of the mass conversions, especially in the period after 950, either had carried or were carrying the boundaries of Christendom far beyond those of the Roman Empire at its widest extent. Could this mass conversion become more than nominal? Could either the entire body of these professed Christians, together with their collective life, be lifted to an approximation to the high standards set forth by Christ, or, if not, could substantial elements be brought towards those standards? We have seen how the effort was made through monasticism first to draw minorities from this mass of ostensible Christians into ideal Christian communities and then, increasingly, especially beginning with the thirteenth century through the friars, groups presumably completely dedicated to Christ, to lift all of Western Christendom to a higher level and to carry the Christian message to other parts of the world. In the next few pages we will go on to the non-monastic movements at which we have hinted.

Popular Movements Which Remained within the Church

Movements of laymen outside monasteries which in one way or another sought a more earnest practice of the Christian faith multiplied during these centuries.

Prominent among them were the third orders of the various bodies of friars, to which we have already referred.

Confraternities, associations of lay folk, bound together by rules and vows under the authorization of a bishop, were a growing feature of the life of the Church. One is said to have been founded not far from the beginning of the thirteenth century.

Earlier we have noted the singing guilds which began in Italy in the twelfth century. In the second half of the thirteenth century they became organized, with chapels and other meeting places and with written constitutions. They went in procession through towns, or met in the evenings on piazzas or before some shrine to sing hymns of penitence and adoration. Their singing was in the vernacular.

A movement which is said to have begun in Perugia in 1259 was that of the Flagellants. By a kind of mass contagion men, women, and children bewailed their sins and many of them marched through the streets, naked except for loin cloths, crying to God for mercy, and scourging themselves until the blood ran. Old enmities were forgiven and enemies were reconciled. Criminals confessed their misdeeds and where possible made restitution. Murderers asked pardon of the relatives of those whom they had killed. In some places priests headed the processions and led them to churches where the penitents prostrated themselves before the altars. The Flagellants spread beyond Italy to Germany and Bohemia, but subsided almost as quickly as they arose.

The beguines comprised a variety of lay groups which seem not to have been confined to any specific set of forms and to have displayed wide variety. They were made up originally of women, but the designation later was also given to men. The origin of the name is in dispute. At the outset and to a certain extent for some centuries, the term appears to have been applied to an unmarried woman who followed the life of virginity while living in the world. The beguines wore a distinguishing garb. Some of them lived alone or with their families. Others had a collective life in beguine houses. These houses were not monasteries. No vows of poverty were taken. Some beguines were wealthy and others were from the poorer classes. Occasionally widows were in the houses. Many of the beguines were assimilated to the third orders of the friars. Indeed, the growth of the beguines seems to have been stimulated by the example of the Franciscans and Dominicans and some of the beguine houses were associated with houses of the Franciscans. In 1311 the Council of Vienne under Pope Clement V took action against the beguines on the ground that they were channels for the spread of heresy. However, in one form or another they survived into the sixteenth century.

HERETICAL MOVEMENTS

In centuries which saw so much ferment in the religious life of Western Europe, it is not surprising that movements arose which could not be reconciled with the Catholic Church. We shall probably never learn even the names of all of them. Of those which we know, we must take the space to mention only the more prominent. We hear of heresies in the tenth and eleventh centuries, but in the twelfth century they reached more formidable dimensions.

As we enter upon their description it is well to note a feature which most of them had in common. The leadership and the bulk of the membership were not from the aristocracy but were primarily from the urban populations, merchants and artisans, and, to a less extent, from the peasants. In contrast, most of the monastic movements were initiated and led by members of the landed aristocracy. The striking exception was the Brothers Minor, who, as we have more than once reminded ourselves, were begun by a scion of the city merchant class. Yet it will be remembered that the extreme wing of the Franciscans, composed of those who deemed themselves most loyal to the ideals of their founder, tended to be critical of the Catholic Church and many of them broke with it. In this contrast is possibly to be seen the beginning of the rootage of the Christian faith among the masses and the consequent stimulation to independent thought and action. The governing groups, on the other hand, as is true of most aristocracies, were conservative and held to the established order.

One of the movements which was frowned upon by the Catholic Church had as its leader Tanchelm. He began to preach in the diocese of Utrecht and early in the twelfth century his views had fairly wide currency in the Low Countries and the Rhine Valley. He attacked the entire structure of the Catholic Church, denied the authority of the Church and of the Pope, and held that at least some of the sacraments were valueless. He was accused of teaching that irregular relations between the sexes affect only the body and not the soul and so are permissible, but this may have been a complete misrepresentation by his enemies. For a time he was imprisoned by the Archbishop of Cologne. In 1115, after his escape, he was killed, allegedly by a priest.

Not far from the same time, early in the twelfth century, Peter of Bruys, himself following a strictly ascetic way of life, rejected the baptism of infants, the Eucharist, church buildings, ecclesiastical ceremonies, prayers for the dead, and the veneration of the cross. He held that the cross, as the instrument of Christ's death, should be despised rather than honoured. He burned crosses and himself is said to have been burned by an infuriated mob. His followers are sometimes called Petrobrusians. They re-baptized those who joined them, profaned churches, burned crosses, and overthrew altars.

Sometimes classed with Peter of Bruys, but perhaps mistakenly, was Henry of Lausanne. Like the former he preached in what is now France and in the first half of the twelfth century. Before his death in 1145 he is said to have attracted a wide following, called Henricians. He taught that the sacraments were valid only when administered by priests who led a life of asceticism and poverty. He condemned the clergy of the day for their love of wealth and power. He was a contemporary of Bernard of Clairvaux. The latter, quick to attack all that he regarded as heresy and so endangering the salvation of souls, preached against Henry and his views in the areas in which they had gained currency.

ARNOLD OF BRESCIA

Roughly contemporary with Peter of Bruys and Henry of Lausanne was Arnold of Brescia. Born in the city in the north of Italy by which he is known, he studied theology at Paris. Returning to Brescia, he was ordained priest and became the head of a community of canons regular. From his youth he had been noted for his purity of life and his espousal of poverty. He was earnestly eager to see the Church conform fully to the Christian ideal. Believing that this could not be so long as its leaders compromised with the world, he attacked the bishops for their cupidity, dishonest gains, and frequent irregularity of life and urged that the clergy renounce all property and political and physical power. Ardent by temperament and uncompromising, he aroused the antagonism of his bishop, and was ordered by Pope Innocent II to leave Italy and not to preach without Papal consent. A friend of Abélard, a distinguished scholar and teacher and a centre of controversy whom we are to meet later, he was lumped with the latter by Bernard of Clairvaux and was vigorously attacked. Bernard obtained his condemnation by the Council of Sens (1140). In 1145 or 1146, after protracted wanderings, Arnold was given absolution by Pope Eugene III. Soon, however, he again broke with the Pope. He denounced the temporal power of the Papacy and sided with a republic which had been set up in Rome under the local aristocracy and which had driven the Pope out of the city. The effort at a republic collapsed. Eugene III returned to Rome, and his successor, the able Hadrian IV (Nicholas Breakspear, the only Englishman to occupy the Papal throne), had Arnold expelled from the city. At the instance of Hadrian Arnold was seized by order of the Holy Roman Emperor Frederick I (Barbarossa), was delivered to the civil authorities of Rome, and in 1155 he was hanged, his body was burned, and his ashes were thrown into the Tiber. Some of his followers survived him and, a dissident sect, like him lived chastely and austerely and denounced the clergy and the Pope.

THE WALDENSEES

More numerous than the followers of Arnold of Brescia and more lasting as a fellowship were those who were known as the Waldensees or the Vaudois. The origin of the name is in debate. It is said to have been from the *vaux* or valleys or *vallis densa,* shaded valley, in which the Waldensees long persisted. It is also conjectured to have come from Peter Waldo, or Valdez.

Peter Waldo, a rich merchant of Lyons, became impressed with the brevity and insecurity of life and went to a theologian to ask the way to heaven. In reply, he was given the injunction of Jesus to the rich young ruler: "If thou wilt be perfect, go sell that thou hast, and give to the poor." Waldo proceeded resolutely (1176) to carry out the command. Paying his creditors and providing for his wife and children, he distributed the rest of his property among the poor and began begging his daily bread. He made a diligent study of the New Testament through a translation into his native tongue. Inspired by it, he undertook to imitate Christ. Garbed as Christ had commanded his apostles to be in their special missions during his lifetime, and, like them, taking no purse, he preached in city and countryside.

Peter Waldo soon attracted followers. They called themselves the "Poor in Spirit" or the "Poor Men of Lyons." Imitating him, they dressed as he did and went about preaching. So far they resembled the movement which Francis of Assisi was to inaugurate three decades or so later. When the Archbishop of Lyons forbade them to preach, Peter Waldo appealed to the Pope. The Pope at first looked favourably on their vow of poverty and gave them permission in dioceses where the bishops would allow them. Soon they found this restriction too hampering and disregarded it. They asked authorization of the Third Lateran Council (1179) but were denied it. Still they persisted and in 1184 the Pope excommunicated them. Believing that they ought to obey God rather than men, they continued to preach. Their numbers multiplied and they were joined by many of the Humiliati, who had arisen in and near Milan and in that same year (1184) had come under Papal prohibition.

In their tenets and practices the followers of Waldo continued to seek to conform to the New Testament. They memorized large portions of its vernacular translations. Following what they believed it commanded them, they went about two and two, preaching, simply clad, barefoot or wearing sandals, and subsisting on what was given them by those who listened to them. They refused to heed Pope or bishop and taught that the Church of Rome was not the head of the Catholic Church but was corrupt. They held that women and laymen could preach, that masses and prayers for the dead were without warrant, that purgatory is the troubles which come to us in this life, and that to be efficacious prayer need not be confined to churches. They criticized prayers in Latin on the ground that they were not understood by the people, and derided church music and the canonical hours. They declared that while priests and bishops who lived as had the apostles were to be obeyed, sacraments administered by unworthy priests were invalid and that a layman was as competent as a priest to hear confessions. They taught that every lie is a deadly sin, that oaths, even in law courts, are contrary to Christ's commands, and believed that all taking of human life is against God's law. They observed the Eucharist together and held that, if necessary, any layman might administer it. Their only forms of prayer were the "Our Father" and grace at meals. They had their own clergy, with bishops, priests, and deacons, and a head of their fellowship.

The Poor Men of Lyons spread rapidly and widely and were soon to be found in Spain, Italy, Germany, and Bohemia, as well as in their native France. Internal conflicts developed, partly because Peter Waldo, the first head, was deemed arbitrary in his rule, and in 1210 many in the north of Italy withdrew. Other variations developed in organization and doctrine. Many continued to think of themselves as members of the Catholic Church.

Pope Innocent III sought to take advantage of their differences to win the Poor Men back to the Church. He encouraged (1208) the formation and spread of *Pauperes Catholici* ("Poor Catholics") who under ecclesiastical direction would follow such of the practices of the Waldensees as the Church could approve. By this means many who had been attracted by the Poor Men were held or won back.

For the most part the Waldensees were humble folk. Even their enemies described them as dressing simply, industrious, labouring with their hands, chaste, temperate in eating and drinking, refusing to frequent taverns and dances, sober and truthful in speech, avoiding anger, and regarding the accumulation of wealth as evil.

Yet, branding them as heretics, the Catholic Church and the civil authorities sought to eliminate them, by persuasion if possible and if not by force. Such Waldensees as survived persecution sought refuge in the valleys of the Italian Alps, where we are to meet them again at the time of the Reformation.

The Cathari or Albigenses

A movement further removed from the faith of the Catholic Church than the Waldensees was that of the Cathari ("Pure") or, as they were known from one of their chief centres, Albi, in the south of France, Albigensees. In some places they also were called Patarini or Patarenes, although that appellation was not confined to them and was sometimes made to include all heretics. Like the Waldensees, they flourished in the twelfth century and were most numerous in Northern Spain, Southern France, and Northern Italy. Indeed, the two movements had much in common and seem to have interacted upon each other.

It is interesting and perhaps significant that the major new monastic order of the twelfth century, the Cistercians, originated in the same general region, although slightly farther north and east, and that the two chief monastic movements of the thirteenth century, the Franciscans and Dominicans, also had their rise and early growth in that geographic belt. The Cathari were but one expression of the religious ferment, chiefly Christian in its forms, which profoundly moved the Latin South of Europe in these centuries.

Yet the Cathari were not confined to Latin Europe. They were also found east of the Adriatic, among the Slavs. There they enjoyed an advantage over the Catholic Church in their use of the vernacular in their services. We also hear of them in Constantinople, where they had both a Greek and a Latin church.

What is now southern France, where the Waldensees and the Cathari had their chief strength, was fertile soil for such a movement. As we know from the statements of some of its own leaders, the Catholic Church in that region was unusually corrupt and had forfeited the respect of earnest souls. Some of the clergy compiled indecent books and permitted immodest songs to be sung in church. Many priests were luxury-loving, illiterate, indolent, profane, and tolerated simony and clerical concubinage. In such a situation a religion with high moral appeal and practice would gain a ready hearing.

The Cathari were dualists, believing that there are two eternal powers, the one good and the other evil, that the visible world is the creation of the evil power, and that the spiritual world is the work of the good power. They were, quite understandably, accused by their enemies of being Manichæans. Some later scholars have asserted and others have as vigorously denied the Manichæan origin. It is less debatable that they were influenced by the Paulicians and the Bogomils, dualists whom we have already met in the Eastern Church and who were strong in Bulgaria and the Balkans. Whether they owed their beginnings to contacts with these groups we do not know. As early as the first half of the eleventh century there were those in the south of what is now France who were arraigned by the ecclesiastical authorities for holding a dualistic heresy. In the twelfth century their numbers mounted.

The Cathari claimed to find in the Bible support for their convictions. Some of them rejected parts of the Old Testament, holding that they were the work of the Devil, but they all stressed the New Testament and gave especial weight to *The Gospel according to John.* Their views were by no means uniform, but on several they seem to have been agreed. They held, as we have suggested, that there are two powers, the one evil and responsible for the material world and the other good and the maker of the immaterial world. Some put forth a variant of this dualism, saying that the good God had two sons, one of whom, Satanal, rebelled, and the other, Christ, became the redeemer. All maintained that there were two churches, the one their own, that of Jesus Christ, good, and the other that of Rome, evil. Accordingly, they rejected the orders and laws of the Roman Catholic Church and taught that its sacraments were quite useless. As dualists, believing flesh to be evil, they endeavoured to shun all that had to do with the reproduction of animal life.

The Cathari were of two grades. Those who had fully embraced their way of life were called the "perfect" (*perfecti*). Admission to the "perfect" was by a kind of spiritual baptism, called "consolation." It was administered by one who had already received it and through it forgiveness of sins and entrance into the kingdom of the good power were obtained. The perfect must remain continent. If unmarried they must continue celibate, and if married, husband must separate from wife and the man must never again so much as touch a woman. They were never to eat meat, milk, or eggs, since these were the fruits of reproduction. They were not to engage in war or to own property. "Believers" (*credenti*) who had not yet become "perfect" might marry, hold property, and even outwardly remain members of the Roman Catholic Church and share in its sacraments. "Believers" looked forward to salvation through "consolation," although that step might be postponed until old age or fatal illness. At least some of the Cathari believed in the transmigration of souls and taught that Christ came to redeem those who had fallen and to enable them to return to their Creator.

In their communal worship the Cathari followed very simple forms. They had no church buildings. They held that since flesh is evil, Christ could not have had a real body or have died a real death. Accordingly they had no use for crosses or crucifixes. They read from the Scriptures, heard sermons, and shared a common meal from bread which, held in the hands, was blessed, broken, and distributed to the seated believers. We hear of other forms of the common meal in which bread, fish, and wine were used, and which was preceded by the washing of the feet of the participants by the "major" who presided. There seems to have been another form, on Easter, in which bread and wine were the elements.

In organization the "perfect" corresponded to the clergy of the Catholic Church. The Cathari were said to have majors (bishops), presbyters, and deacons, but they appear to have been without a comprehensive ecclesiastical structure.

As is so often true of persecuted groups with secret meetings, tales gained popular credence which accused the Cathari of the grossest immoralities. However, some of their most caustic critics bore witness to their high moral character. They were ardent missionaries. They seem to have been recruited largely from peasants and artisans, but they included some scholars and produced an extensive literature in the vernacular, including translations of the Bible. While, as we have said, strongest in Northern Italy, Southern France, and the north of Spain, the Cathari also won converts in Northern France and Flanders, chiefly in the cities.

THE SUPPRESSION OF THE HERESIES

One of the striking features of the movements of these centuries which the Catholic Church branded as heresies was that they either completely died out or, in the case of the Waldensees, dwindled to small groups. This disappearance appears to have been due in part to inherent weakness and the lack of an effective organization and in part to measures adopted by the Catholics.

It is of the actions taken by Catholics of which we hear most. In spite of the corruption within its ranks, the Catholic Church possessed striking advantages. In its system of parishes and dioceses directed from one common centre, Rome, reinforced by monastic orders and supported by secular rulers, it had a comprehensive structure which could operate on a wide front and from varied angles. Several Popes and councils of the Church formally condemned the heretics. Numbers of preachers, among them, as we have seen, Bernard of Clairvaux, Dominic, and the original group which the latter gathered about him, used eloquence and persuasion. The ecclesiastical combined with the civil arm to arrest heretics and punish them. In 1179 the Third Lateran Council proclaimed a crusade against them. This is said to have been the first occasion in which that device was employed against those who called themselves Christians. Recruited and led by a Papal legate, in 1181 a crusading army appeared to have some success, but it was soon disbanded and the Cathari once more raised their heads. In the ensuing quarter of a century, both the Cathari and the Waldensees multiplied, especially in Southern France.

It was Innocent III who initiated measures which dealt the decisive blows against the dissidents. At first his efforts seemed to meet with as little success as had those of his predecessors. The outstanding lord in Southern France, Count Raymond VI of Toulouse, evaded Papal efforts to induce him to take positive action and Philip Augustus, the King of France, hesitated further to complicate his own difficult problems, including his chronic troubles with England, by risking a prolonged internal war to enforce the Papal commands. Then, in 1208, the Papal Legate, Peter of Castelnau, was murdered in Raymond's domains and perhaps at his court. Innocent took advantage of the widespread horror evoked by the crime to call forth a crusading army. Religious zeal represented in an outstanding leader of the crusading armies, Simon de Montfort, combined with quite secular motives, sectional jealousies, and the desire of the nobles of Northern France to reduce the power of the South and to profit by its wealth.

Years of warfare followed, with wholesale destruction. It is said that when one of the first cities to be taken, Beziers, was entered, and the Papal Legate was asked whether the Catholics should be spared, the latter, fearing that the heretics would feign orthodoxy to save their lives, commanded: "Kill them all, for God knows His own." Louis VIII of France (reigned 1223–1226), the son of Philip Augustus, pressed the crusade against the Albigenses. He was followed by Louis IX, who reigned from 1226 to 1270. Deeply religious, esteemed by the Middle Ages the ideal Christian monarch, Louis IX regarded himself as the champion of the Catholic faith and was quite willing to press the campaigns against heretics.

By the Treaty of Paris, in 1229, Count Raymond VII of Toulouse promised loyalty to the Catholic Church and to give his daughter in marriage to one of the king's brothers. This ended the crusade. In that same year, to make certain that the peace was effective, an ecclesiastical council at Toulouse outlined a stern procedure for the eradication of heresy in the South. Among other measures, the council forbade to the laity the possession of copies of the Bible, except the Psalms and such passages as were in the breviary, and condemned vernacular translations. It thus sought to remove one of the prevalent sources of heresy.

To aid in the suppression of the heresies resort was had not only to crusades but also to the Inquisition. In principle the Inquisition was not new. The very words *inquisitio* and *inquisitor* came from Roman law and, like so much else in canon law, were taken over from the Roman Empire. Now and again in earlier centuries persons accused of heresy had been tried by ecclesiastical or secular authorities and on some the death penalty had been inflicted. In theory the bishops had jurisdiction in detecting and punishing heretics, but in practice many, perhaps most, had been lax or indifferent. Opinion within the Church was not uniform nor were all civil rulers content to commit to the Church full jurisdiction over their subjects on such issues. To complete the work begun by the crusades and to eradicate whatever heresy remained, the Council of Toulouse of 1229 systematized and elaborated the inquisitorial process. Further developments were due to the then reigning Pope, Gregory IX, and additions and modifications were made by later Pontiffs. In other words, the trend, then marked, of strengthening the administrative and judicial control of the Papacy over the entire Western Church was extended to the systematic eradication of heresy. Early inquisitors were chosen largely from the Dominicans. Soon members of other mendicant orders, especially the Franciscans, were used.

In contrast with what had been the custom under the Roman civil law, in the practice of the Inquisition the accused was regarded as guilty until proved innocent and was not confronted with the witnesses against him. Torture might be employed. Eventually the system spread to most countries in Western Europe and usually had the support of the kings as well as of the ecclesiastical authorities.

As a result of the internal weaknesses and lack of cohesion of the heretical movements and of the action of the Catholics through the state, crusades, the preaching and teaching of the mendicant orders, the activities of some of the bishops, and the measures taken by the Inquisition, by the middle of the fourteenth century the heresies which had flourished in the twelfth and thirteenth centuries had largely died out.

We shall see how in the fourteenth and fifteenth centuries and especially in the sixteenth century fresh bursts of life in Western Europe led to the emergence of other movements which could not be contained within the Catholic Church. At the appropriate place we must raise and seek to answer the question why, in contrast with the earlier dissenting movements, those of the sixteenth century persisted and for the most part increased until in the nineteenth and twentieth centuries a major spread of the Christian faith was through them. To enter into that problem at this point would be premature, but we must not pass on from the "heresies" of the twelfth and thirteenth centuries without pausing to note it and to call attention to its importance.

SELECTED BIBLIOGRAPHY

E. Comba, *Waldo and the Waldensians before the Reformation,* translated by T. E. Comba (New York, Robert Carter & Brothers, 1880, pp. 69). Contains extensive footnote references to the sources.

G. G. Coulton, *Inquisition and Liberty* (London, William Heinemann, 1938, pp. xiii, 354). Enormously learned, with a strong anti-Catholic slant.

D. L. Douie, *The Nature and Effect of the Heresy of the Fraticelli* (Manchester University Press, 1932, pp. xviii, 292). A scholarly study.

R. W. Emery, *Heresy and Inquisition in Narbonne* (Columbia University Press, 1941, pp. 184). Based largely upon local manuscript archives.

E. Holmes, *The Albigensian or Catharist Heresy. A Story and a Study* (London, Williams & Norgate, 1925, pp. 138). A popular survey.

H. C. Lea, *A History of the Inquisition of the Middle Ages* (New York, Harper & Brothers, 3 vols., 1888). A standard work of prodigious scholarship.

A. L. Maycock, *The Inquisition from Its Establishment to the Great Schism* (London, Constable & Company, 1927, pp. xxiii, 276). A Roman Catholic account, somewhat apologetic and defensive.

A. Monastier, *Histoire de l'Eglise Vaudoise depuis son Origine et des Vaudois du Piédmont jusqu'a Nos Jours* (Paris, Delay, 2 vols., 1847). By a Waldensian pastor.

A. Muston, *The Israel of the Alps. A Complete History of the Waldensees and Their Colonies; Prepared in Great Part from Unpublished Documents.* Translated by J. Montgomery (London, Blackie & Son, 2 vols., 1875). By a French Protestant pastor.

H. Nickerson, *The Inquisition. A Political and Military Study of Its Establishment* (Boston, Houghton Mifflin Co., 1923, pp. xvii, 258). A semi-popular, serious account, chiefly of the Albigensees and the Crusade and Inquisition invoked against them.

D. Phillips, *Beguines in Medieval Strasburg. A Study of the Social Aspect of Beguine Life* (Stanford University Press, 1941, pp. ix, 252). A doctoral dissertation.

A. S. Turberville, *Mediaeval Heresy & the Inquisition* (London, George Allen & Unwin, 1920, pp. vi, 264). The earlier part of the volume deals with this period.

E. Vacandard, *The Inquisition. A Critical and Historical Study of the Coercive Power of the Church.* Translated by B. L. Conway (New York, Longmans, Green & Co., 1926, pp. xiv, 195). By a Roman Catholic.

H. J. Warner, *The Albigensian Heresy* (London, Society for Promoting Christian Knowledge, 2 vols., 1922, 1928). Especially valuable for its extensive translations from the sources.

Chapter XX

THE EFFORT TO PURIFY THE ENTIRE
CHURCH, ESPECIALLY THROUGH
THE PAPACY

Could all Western Christendom be really Christian? More than once we have called attention to the problem. Western Europe had adopted the Christian name by mass action, usually tribe by tribe. Baptism had become a social convention. A vast distance separated the living of the ordinary Christian from the high demands of Jesus for discipleship. Could that distance be narrowed?

In the preceding two chapters we have noted efforts which deepened the living of minorities. Some were monastic. Others were non-monastic. Some remained within the Catholic Church. Others denounced the Catholic Church or were expelled from it as heretical. As the centuries passed these several kinds of movements increased in numbers and endeavoured to reach a larger proportion of the population. The earlier ones were primarily monastic, despaired of the world at large, and sought salvation by withdrawal from it. Those caught up in them lived either as hermits or in communities apart from the other dwellings of men. They regarded themselves as good Catholics and asked the approval of the Pope but were largely independent of the normal ecclesiastical structure of parishes and dioceses. Increasingly monastic movements appeared, notably but by no means exclusively the Franciscans and Dominicans, which strove to combine distinctive Christian living in communities with reaching and serving the entire population. They were paralleled by non-monastic movements, some of them heretical, which also endeavoured to win others to what they deemed conformity to the standards of Christ.

Contemporaneous with these minority efforts were men who hoped to raise the level of all Western Christendom through the geographically inclusive structure of the Catholic Church. With its parishes and their priests, its dioceses and bishops, all heading up in the Roman Pontiff, the Catholic Church could touch all those in Western Europe who called themselves Christians. There were those who strove to utilize this inclusive organism to produce a society

459

which would fully conform to the Christian ideal and which would eventually embrace all mankind. Some of these dreamers were humble folk. Others were bishops whose efforts were confined chiefly to their own dioceses. Numbers were monks. Others were laymen or members of the secular clergy. Many sought to operate through synods, either regional or universal, or endeavoured to make of the Papacy an instrument for attaining this goal. Among the latter were some who occupied the Papal throne. Often secular rulers took a hand in the effort. But, as we are to see, repeatedly the ecclesiastical authorities clashed with nobles, kings, and emperors.

The dreamers worked against mountainous handicaps. As we have more than once noted, in the five or six centuries before the year 950, invasion had succeeded invasion and each wave had interrupted the recovery from its predecessor and had brought fresh disorder. Fighting was chronic. Commerce had dwindled. Crude agriculture was the major means of livelihood. After the hopeful Carolingian revival, learning had again declined. The emerging feudalism was dividing Europe into a multitude of political entities which combined with the wars and the bad state of the roads, piracy, and banditry to render an inclusive Christian fellowship extraordinarily difficult. That unity faced an additional obstacle in the existence of what were in effect tribal churches, in each of which the chieftain, whether under the title of king, count, or duke, strove for control and to that end sought to appoint to its leading positions men whom he could dominate. In one fashion or another, offices in the Church were bought and sold. The practice was called *simony,* from Simon Magus, who, according to *The Acts of the Apostles,* had offered to purchase of Peter the power to confer the Holy Spirit. A large proportion of the clergy were notoriously lax in their sex relations and were married or kept concubines. This was known as *nicolaitanism,* from a practice denounced in *The Revelation of John.*

The efforts of the reformers were directed in large part to the purification of the clergy from these abuses, for it was hopeless to seek to improve the quality of the spiritual and moral life of the masses if the pastors were corrupt. Many looked to the Papacy for leadership and to advance the reform sought to place worthy men upon the chair of Peter. They conceived of the Catholic Church as embracing all true Christians and as finding its unity by conforming to the Church of Rome and by submitting to the head of that church. Periodically, indeed almost chronically, Popes and many of the bishops and archbishops strove to free the Church from the control of lay lords. The most ambitious of the Popes endeavoured to dominate not only the ecclesiastical but also all other aspects of life, including especially the political.

The battle for the cleansing of the Catholic Church and the achievement of an ideal society was always being fought but was never won. The vision of making the Church worthy of the designation *Corpus Christi,* the body of Christ, and of Christendom a society which could be described as the *Corpus Christianum,* was not to be fully realized. Probably it could not be. The ideals set forth by Christ are too high to be reached within history. Throughout this period, as both before it and after it, the struggle was a continuing thread in the history of Christianity. Sometimes it was pushed with vigour and gains seemed to be made. At other times it was allowed to lag. Yet always consciences made sensitive by the demands of Christ were grieved by the gap between the ideal and the actual. Nearly always there were those who were nerved by their faith to seek to close it.

The movements for reform through the reinvigoration of the existing monastic institutions or the creation of new ones were usually closely interrelated with those for the improvement of Church and society as a whole. In its effects the Cluny revival spread far beyond the Cluny houses. The same was true of the Cistercians. As we have seen, Bernard of Clairvaux was outstanding in the affairs of the Church and one of his protégés from Clairvaux became Pope. It was not long after the birth of the Franciscans and Dominicans before members of those orders were occupying high places in the Church.

EARLY REFORM EFFORTS BY BISHOPS

Here is not the place even to name all the bishops who were active in trying to lift the level of Christian living in their dioceses. To enumerate them would extend these pages far beyond any reasonable length. As fairly typical of many we must pause to speak briefly of a few who were active early in this period. We must especially name two who, although in different countries, were contemporaries.

In England in the tenth century that recovery continued from the destruction from the Viking invasions which had been begun under Alfred the Great. To be sure, the land was later to be ruled from Denmark and in 1066 it was conquered by descendants of the Vikings, the Normans, but these alien monarchs did not deal the severe blows to orderly life and to the Church that had been given by their pagan predecessors. Part of the recovery was seen in the improvement of the religious life of the realm. This was through the reinvigoration of old monastic houses, the founding of new ones, and efforts to purify the life of the entire nation. Of the many who were both the children of the revival and aided it, Dunstan was outstanding. We have already met him as a leader in monastic reform.

Dunstan was born about 909 in the south of England. He was related to the royal house and members of his family had occupied important episcopal sees. He is a controversial figure, but from his youth until extreme old age, for he died in 988, when he was nearly eighty, he was influential in the Church, and in his maturity he was also outstanding in affairs of state. He was one of the most learned men in the realm. Indeed, as was so often the case in Western Europe in that age, the repute of his scholarship and mechanical skill led to a popular report that he was an adept in the black arts. He had force of character and initiative which aroused opposition but which also had the capacity to inspire others and to win their veneration and love. There was about him, too, an aura of authentic sanctity which made a profound impression on many.

In his youth, as a result of a severe illness, Dunstan became a monk. In his mid-thirties he was made Abbot of Glastonbury and the monastery which he built there became the centre of a religious awakening. He attracted able followers, some of whom in time became leaders in the Church. An unfriendly king exiled him to the Continent and there he came in touch with some of the new tides of life. Brought back to England in 957 by a new and devout young monarch, Dunstan became a leader in a widespread monastic revival which seems to have been modelled in part upon what he had seen on the Continent but which was also distinctively English. Appointed to the see of Worcester, he was soon transferred, or, to use a later technical term, "translated," to the see of London and then, as Archbishop of Canterbury, to the primacy of the entire Church in England. He did much for the political unification of England, strove to improve the administration of justice, and sought to win the Scandinavian elements. In the more strictly religious aspects of life he endeavoured to eradicate what was left of paganism, to improve the quality of the secular clergy, and to bring the entire body of laity to a higher moral and spiritual level. He was supported and supplemented by two other extraordinarily able and devoted monks who were made bishops. One of them, Oswald, of Danish ancestry, who lived on until 992, as Bishop of Worcester and then as Archbishop of York strove not only to further the monastic movement but also to be a father of all in his dioceses.

While the awakening in England was taking place, a somewhat similar advance was being registered in Germany. As we have seen, in 911, when the Carolingian line died out in that land, Conrad of Franconia was elected king, and was followed in 919 by Henry the Fowler, Duke of Saxony. Conrad was in close alliance with the Church, for an archbishop had been chiefly responsible for putting him on the throne and a bishop was his chief adviser. Henry the Fowler had little use for the Church. Henry the Fowler in turn was succeeded by his son, Otto I, "the Great," who was descended from Charlemagne in the female line and who, as we have recorded, reigned from 936 to 973 and in 962 was crowned Roman Emperor. Otto made extensive use of the Church. He strengthened the great bishoprics. Since they were non-hereditary, he could control the elections to them and make their incumbents his allies to offset the power of the hereditary lay nobility. He also used frontier dioceses to push forward German rule over the Slavs east of the Elbe. Under him there was a literary revival which centred at his court and which was led by Irish and English monks and by Greek and Italian scholars. Next came Otto II, son of Otto I. He reigned from 973 to 983 and died before he was thirty. Otto III, son of Otto II and a Byzantine princess, was brought to the throne at the age of three by his father's death and died in 1002 in his early twenties. Reared by his mother and under ecclesiastical influence, he purposed restoring the glory of the Roman Empire and was also very devout and deeply concerned for the welfare and purity of the Church. Henry II, who reigned from 1002 to 1024, was also genuinely religious. He was eventually canonized, along with his queen. While firm with the clergy he was generous with them and was an ardent furtherer of reform. Conrad II (reigned 1024–1039), a strong ruler, was politically rather than religiously minded. He was followed by Henry III (reigned 1039–1056), an extremely able monarch. Earnestly Christian, he was reinforced by a queen of similar convictions. Thoroughly committed to the Cluniac reforms, he fought simony, went on pilgrimages, and in 1043 proclaimed the Day of Indulgence, using it to announce forgiveness to his foes and to urge that his subjects follow his example. With such a succession of monarchs, several of them vigorous and seeking to strengthen the Church, and a few of them ardent reformers, it is not surprising that movements for improving the quality of Christian living should be making headway. To this also contributed the cessation of the destructive incursions of barbarians.

Revival in the Church did not come entirely or even primarily by the initiative of the monarchs. Nor, at the outset, was it from the movement which was associated with Cluny. In the first half of the tenth century, as we have seen, Gerhard as founder and abbot of a monastery at Brogne, south of Namur, in what is now Belgium, was the outstanding pioneer of an awakening which spread through much of Lotharingia, a territory which was roughly the region of the Rhine Valley. Reinforcement came, as we have also noted, especially from the monastery of Gorze, in the diocese of Metz, a centre in which the new life sprang up quite independently of both Brogne and Cluny. But it was not long before Cluny was also making its influence felt.

In the second half of the tenth century and the first half of the eleventh century this German reform movement was augmented by the enhanced position given the bishops by Otto I and by the zeal of Henry II and Henry III. Great prelates cleansed monasteries, built churches, promoted education, fostered art, and in other ways strove to improve the spiritual and moral life in their dioceses.

Among the best of these bishops was Bernward of Hildesheim, who, born about the year 960 and dying in 1022, was a contemporary of Dunstan. He was of noble Saxon stock, from a family which had provided several prominent Church officials. As a younger son he was reared for a high post in the Church and seems from the beginning to have had a genuine religious interest. Educated in the cathedral school at Hildesheim, the seat of a bishopric which had been planned by Charlemagne nearly two centuries earlier as part of his programme for pacifying and giving religious training to the Saxons, Bernward became a tutor of Otto III and was later a trusted friend of the zealous Henry II. He was made Bishop of Hildesheim and in that post built churches, fought nicolaitanism among his clergy, gathered relics, and promoted art and education. He was canonized in the century after his death.

THE REFORMING SPIRIT CAPTURES THE PAPACY

It was largely through the initiative of the German monarchs of the tenth and eleventh centuries that the Papacy was rescued from the low state into which it had fallen in the latter part of the ninth and the fore part of the tenth century. Like the Carolingians before him, Otto the Great succumbed to the lure of restoring the glories of the Roman Empire. Three times he led an expedition across the mountains. He assumed the throne of Italy and, as we have more than once reminded ourselves, in 962 was crowned Roman Emperor by the Pope. For centuries this imperial will-o'-the-wisp, this *ignis fatuus,* was to lure German monarchs to dissipate their strength south of the Alps and was to keep them from constructing a unified Germany comparable to the kingdoms of more limited territorial ambitions which were built by royal houses in other parts of Europe.

These German Holy Roman Emperors were a recurring and, indeed, a fairly constant factor in Papal affairs. In theory Christendom was to have two heads, both divinely commissioned, the one civil, the Emperor, and the other spiritual, the Pope. In practice it was the Papacy which exerted the geographically more extensive influence, but for nearly a century it was Otto the Great and those who followed him in the imperial office who were responsible for putting on the Papal throne most of the worthy Pontiffs of that period and who eventually made the revival dominant at the Papal court. However, that control was not quickly achieved. Not until Pope Leo IX, who held office from 1049 to 1054, was reform firmly seated. In the preceding ten decades the record was very chequered.

The details of the story of the steps by which, with the vigorous support of the German Holy Roman Emperors, the new element obtained control of the Papacy are confusing. We need not here attempt to recount them all. However, some of the more important features and incidents, together with a few of the main figures, must claim our attention.

When, in 961, Otto the Great made his second expedition into Italy, it was said to have been in response to an appeal from Pope John XII. John wished the protection of Otto against Berengar II, who as titular King of Italy constituted a threat. John XII was the son of Alberic and the grandson of Marozia, whom we have met earlier as prominent members of a family which for some time had controlled Rome and the Papacy. John XII was only in his teens when he became the head of the Church of Rome and was more devoted to the chase and to pandering to his passions than he was to the duties of the supposed head of Western Christendom. It was John XII who in 962 crowned Otto Roman Emperor. The two concluded an agreement, the *Privilegium Ottonis,* whereby Otto conceded to the Pope temporal jurisdiction over about three-fourths of Italy and the Romans were not to consecrate any one as Pope who did not take an oath of fealty to the Emperor. John XII soon fell out with Otto and the latter had him deposed and another elected in his place.

There ensued a struggle for the Papacy between the Romans on the one hand and successive German Emperors on the other. The former insisted on their traditional right to elect their bishop. The latter, impatient with the quality of the men so chosen, especially since it was by a populace now shrunk to small dimensions and swayed by local leaders who had scant regard for the Emperors, strove to put their own nominees on the Papal throne. For a time the Roman family Crescentius dominated the city and sought to have their creatures made Popes.

The contest lasted for several reigns with Popes and anti-Popes each claiming to be legitimate. In 985 he who went by the title of Boniface VII died suddenly, perhaps poisoned, and his body was dragged through the streets of Rome and left naked and unburied. In 996 the youthful and ardently religious Otto III had one of his relatives placed on the Papal throne as Gregory V, the first German to hold the office. On the latter's death, in 999, Otto obtained the election of his tutor, Gerbert, a Frenchman, reputed to be the most learned man of his age. As Sylvester II Gerbert laboured to eradicate simony and clerical marriage and concubinage, but the demise of his imperial patron (1002) left him without powerful support and within a few months he too was dead.

After two Crescentian Popes, a faction headed by the nearby Counts of Tusculum was in control in Rome and had its nominees placed in the See of Peter. One of these, Benedict VIII (reigned 1012–1024), who was of the family of the Counts of Tusculum, was a friend of the Abbot of Cluny and favoured reform. Indeed, he and the Holy Roman Emperor Henry II collaborated to that end. However, another of the Tusculan Pontiffs, Benedict IX, nephew of his two predecessors and who became Pope in 1032, is said to have been one of the most profligate ever to occupy the post and degradation seemed again to triumph. Opposition to him arose, partly through the Crescentian faction, and for a time there were three rivals in Rome, each claiming to be the lawful Pope. It is not surprising that earnest leaders in the monastic revival, such as Peter Damian, were scandalized and longed for a cleansing of the Augean stables.

Decisive change came through the intervention of Henry III, soon to be crowned Holy Roman Emperor. As we have seen, Henry III was deeply religious. In 1046 synods held at his instance and under his direction deposed two of the competing Popes and constrained the third to resign. Neither of the first two men whom Henry caused to be placed successively on the Papal throne lived long. The next whose election he obtained was Leo IX, who held the post from 1049 to 1054. Under Leo IX the tide of reform swept into the Papacy and held it.

Leo IX, elected in his mid-forties, was of a noble family of Alsace. As Bishop of Toul in Lorraine, he had already made a record as administrator, organizer, and reformer. The integrity of his character is attested by his eventual canonization. Chosen at an assembly at Worms, in Germany, at the instance of Henry III and with the concurrence of delegates from Rome, he would not assume the title and functions of Pope until, after reaching Rome, garbed as a humble pilgrim, his election was confirmed, as long custom required, by the people and clergy of the Eternal City. In other words, he would not consent to the Pope being a mere creature of the Emperor. A friend of the Abbot of Cluny and of Peter Damian, he could be counted on for vigorous measures. He travelled extensively in Italy and beyond the Alps, holding synods which took action against the purchase and sale of Church offices, insisted that bishops should not be appointed by lay lords but be elected by clergy and people, and commanded clerical celibacy. He did much to restore the prestige of the Papal see.

Leo IX broadened the scope of the Roman cardinalate by appointing to its ranks men of reforming zeal from outside the environs of Rome. He thus made it more representative of the Western Church as a whole and surrounded himself with men whom he could trust. The "cardinals" had been, as the name indicates, the leading clergy in and near Rome. They included the priests in the chief or "title" churches in Rome, the deacons in charge of the districts into which Rome had been divided in the third century for the administration of poor relief, and the bishops in the immediate neighborhood of the city. From them, quite naturally, had come the Pope's advisers. Originally the designation cardinal had not been confined to Rome but had been given to outstanding clergy anywhere in the Catholic Church. The action of Leo IX enhanced the position of the Roman cardinals in the Church at large, for it established the precedent of drawing into the inner circle of the Papal entourage and the central administration men of ability from any part of the Church regardless of their country.

Leo IX had difficulties with the Patriarch of Constantinople of which we are to speak later and which, in 1054, led to another stage in the separation of the Eastern and Western wings of the Catholic Church. He died in 1054 and was soon followed, in 1056, by the Emperor Henry III. The latter's six-year-old son came to the throne as Henry IV under a regency.

THE RISING POWER OF THE REFORMED PAPACY

The new spirit could not tolerate with complacency the continued control of the Papacy by the Holy Roman Emperors. Even though the latter had been largely responsible for putting strong men on the Papal throne, their action represented a domination by lay lords which threatened the secularization of the Church. To the ardent among the reformers this was simony. Their dream was a Christian society in which Church and secular rulers would coöperate, but in which the Church would be independent of the latter and, in case of a conflict of authority, would be supreme. To them this seemed inevitable logic, for, as they saw it, the Church was the custodian of the Gospel, its officers were accountable for the eternal welfare of the souls of their flocks, and in a social structure ordered by Christian principles theirs must be the decisive voice.

A struggle was to ensue, one in which the leaders of the Church, operating in the name of the power displayed in the crucifixion and resurrection of Christ, were to utilize the kind of power represented by the state. In so doing, although they acted from what seemed to them the highest of motives, they were to make of the Roman Catholic Church an hierarchical structure which was so nearly captured by this other kind of power that it became an enemy to the power seen in the cross and the empty tomb. Because of the methods which the reformers employed to purify the Church the evils against which they laboured came back with redoubled force. However, we are anticipating our story.

Following Leo IX there came two Popes, both favouring reform but both with too brief a tenure of office to make their purpose effective. On the death of the second, in 1058, the Tusculan faction attempted to reassert their control of the Papacy and put up a Pope of their own.

The return of the old subserviency of the Papacy to one or another of the coteries of Roman families was prevented by the decisive courage of a man who was to be the chief actor in the Papal scene for nearly three decades. This was Hildebrand.

HILDEBRAND EXALTS THE PAPACY

Hildebrand was born about the year 1025, possibly not far from Rome, and was reared in Rome. His ancestry is not clearly established, but he seems to have had aristocratic blood from both sides of his house. His mother was related to a family of bankers and had him educated in a monastery in Rome of which her brother was abbot and where the rule of Cluny was partly in force. In late youth he continued his education in the Lateran Palace, closely associated with the Papacy. He therefore knew Rome and the Papal curia intimately and in some of its most corrupt years. Although educated in a monastery, he did not become a monk until he was in his early twenties. He may have taken the step at Cluny. Also while in his early twenties he was for a time in Germany. He returned to Rome in the train of Leo IX. Leo admitted him to minor orders. He was likewise a friend of the earnest Peter Damian. His rise was not sudden. Swarthy, small of stature, slightly deformed, only his piercing glance gave physical evidence of the genius which lay within. A practical man of affairs, he was also deeply devout. We know very little of his inner life, but he clearly belonged with those who wished to purify the Church. By the time he was thirty-five he was being noted as a young man of promise.

In 1059 it was Hildebrand who was largely instrumental in obtaining the election of Nicholas II, thus defeating the efforts of the Roman nobility to revive their earlier control of the Papacy.

The brief pontificate of Nicholas II, for it lasted only from 1059 to 1061, was marked by momentous steps. In the chief of these, the enactment of highly important legislation determining the procedure for elections to the Papacy, Hildebrand appears to have had little part. Indeed, it was Humbert, a cardinal-bishop, who seems to have been chiefly responsible for them. A monk from the diocese of Toul and an exponent of the Lotharingian revival, he had written a treatise, *Adversus simonaicos,* in which he outlined a programme for the purging of the Church.

This new legislation was in the form of a Papal decree of 1059. It has come down to us in two different versions. The two agree that in the election the cardinals were to take the initiative, that in case disorders in Rome made a meeting in that city inadvisable, they might hold the election elsewhere, that if a suitable man could not be found in the Roman Church the Pope might be chosen from any other church, and that if war or intrigue prevented the Pope from being enthroned according to custom he might nevertheless exercise all the functions of his office. The two forms differed chiefly in that one required the cardinal-bishops to take the lead and gave little recognition to the Emperor, while the other made no distinction among the cardinals and required imperial consent to the person chosen. With modifications, the principles expressed in the decree still govern elections to the Papacy, namely, that the choice is to be by the cardinals, that the cardinals are not required to meet in Rome, that the Pope need not be a Roman, and that, in case of necessity, he may exercise his functions from some other centre than Rome. Although still the Bishop of Rome and holding his place in the Catholic Church because of that fact, he was made more representative of the Western wing of the Catholic Church as a whole and was not as subject to the factional strife in the city of Rome as had been all too often the case in the preceding three or four generations. The reform wave had captured the Papacy.

The death of Nicholas II in 1061, preceded as it was by a few weeks by that of Cardinal Humbert, deprived the reformers of two outstanding leaders. Hildebrand now stepped into the breach. Utilizing the procedure for Papal elections which had been promulgated in 1059, he brought together in Rome the cardinals and other leading churchmen. At his instance and by his prompt action, they elected to the Papacy a friend of Peter Damian, who took the title of Alexander II and held the post from 1061 to his death in 1073. The Roman nobles, wishing to revive their control of the Papacy, collaborated with the bishops of Lombardy, who disliked the reform movement, and sent a delegation to Germany to ask Henry IV, still a child of eleven years, to appoint one of their friends, an Italian bishop, Cadalus, to the post. The regency, glad of an opportunity to assert the traditional practice of the German kings in controlling the Papal succession, had the young Henry give his approval. Thus the Roman nobles and the German monarchy combined to frustrate the reformers' efforts for the independence of the Papacy of the secular arm. For almost the entire reign of Alexander II Cadulus was an annoying rival. Part of the battle was fought in Rome itself with the use of arms on both sides. Tortuous and complicated diplomacy was involved, with the lavish use of money by both sides to purchase the favour of the Roman populace. In the struggle Hildebrand was deeply involved. Thanks in part to him, Alexander II maintained his authority.

Alexander II proved to be an able Pope, and while he owed much to Hildebrand, his achievements were by no means due entirely to the latter. Nor was Peter Damian, who was also one of his advisers, to be credited with more than a fraction of the advances made under this pontificate. Indeed, Damian, fiery advocate of reform though he was, did not prove to be as wise in counsel as Hildebrand. Under Alexander II substantial progress was registered towards the realization of the dream of rendering the Papal power effective in all aspects of the life of Western Europe. In the political realm Alexander II compelled young Henry IV, potentially the mightiest monarch in that region, to surrender his purpose to divorce his wife. He gave his approval to William the Conqueror's conquest of England and to the invasion of Sicily by the Normans of Southern Italy. In each instance he sent a gonfalon, or standard, which he blessed, to be carried by the army. In the ecclesiastical realm he deposed the Bishop of Florence on the charge of simony, he aided William the Conqueror in putting Norman bishops in English sees, he induced the mighty Lanfranc, now Archbishop of Canterbury, to come to Rome to receive the *pallium* instead of sending it to him, as Lanfranc had requested, and he humbled the proud Archbishop of Cologne by compelling him to enter Rome walking, and barefooted. Legates appointed by the Holy See intervened again and again in ecclesiastical affairs in various countries. Appeals to Rome were encouraged from the wide reaches of the Church. Alexander II made his power felt in Denmark, only recently won to the Christian faith. In portions of Spain under Christian rulers he obtained action against simony and clerical marriage and encouraged the substitution of the Roman liturgy for the local Mozarabic liturgy which had long been in use in the peninsula. Alexander II was engaged in a head-on conflict with Henry IV over the control of the appointment to the important Archbishopric of Milan when death removed him from the scene and bequeathed that contest to his successor.

HILDEBRAND AS POPE GREGORY VII

That successor was Hildebrand. Hildebrand was the sole survivor of the band of able reformers who had gathered about Leo IX, for Peter Damian had died a few weeks before. At the funeral of Alexander II in the great church of St. John Lateran the crowd began to shout "Hildebrand for our Bishop." The mob carried him forcibly across the city to St. Peter's and there, with scant regard for the procedure which had been prescribed by Nicholas II and which he himself had supported, the cardinals hurried through the election with the consent of the bishops, abbots, monks, and laity, and, although only a deacon, Hildebrand was enthroned and took the title of Gregory VII. Not as great a man as Pope Gregory I, of whom he was a student and ardent admirer, he was to make the Papal power more widely felt and more potent in Church and state than had that distinguished predecessor. His reign, which, lasting as it did from 1073 to 1085, was only two years less than that of the latter, was like that other, one of the high-water marks of the Papacy.

Gregory VII's conception of the Papal office was sweeping. In its most inclusive form it is expressed in the *Dictatus Papae,* which was probably his own work, although it has sometimes been ascribed to others. Whether or not it had Gregory as its author, that document undoubtedly reflected his mind. It defined the Papal position in twenty-seven affirmations. Among them the following stand out: the Roman Church was founded by God; the Roman Pontiff alone deserves the title "universal"; he alone can depose or reinstate bishops; he alone may use the imperial insignia; he is the only man whose feet princes must kiss; he can depose emperors; he may transfer a bishop from one see to another; he may divide rich bishoprics and unite the poor ones; he has the power to ordain a cleric of any church and he who is ordained by him may not receive a higher grade from any other bishop; no synod can be called general without his authorization; a sentence passed by him cannot be reversed by any one except himself; he may be judged by no one; to him should be referred the important cases of every church; the Roman Church has never erred, nor will it err to all eternity; he who is not at peace with the Roman Church shall not be considered Catholic; the Roman Pontiff may absolve subjects from their allegiance to wicked men. Many of these claims were not new, but never had they been expressed in more positive fashion.

It is important and significant that these and the others of the twenty-seven points dealt with what in the broadest sense of that term was the administrative and disciplinary position of the Pope. In other words, in promoting the health of the Catholic Church the Papacy's function was to ensure correctness of doctrine and effective executive and judicial action. The tides of life upon which, in the last analysis, the vitality of the Church, as of any religious body, depended must be looked for elsewhere. We have seen them coming through monasticism, which the Pope and hierarchy accepted, and through movements which the Papacy and the hierarchy deemed subversive. Some of the Popes, including Hildebrand, were regarded as exemplary Christians and were eventually canonized. Presumably they would be channels for renewals of vigour in the Church. However, they constituted a minority of the Popes and a very small minority of the officially recognized saints. Administration, by an autocratic hierarchy heading up in the Pope, could not produce that vigour. At the most it could remove handicaps to it by the negative procedure of purging the Church of such moral abuses and doctrinal aberrations as were amenable to executive and judicial action.

Gregory put the Papal claims into effect. He compelled archbishops to come to Rome to receive the *pallium* as the mark of their office and to maintain contact with the Holy See. He strove to keep all bishops dependent on the Pope and stood against their appointment and investiture by lay princes. He not only sent out legates on special missions, as had his predecessors, but he also appointed some men to be his resident representatives in particular regions and countries, thus ensuring closer supervision from Rome and the enforcement of the Papal edicts. He held frequent councils in Rome and through legates encouraged and supervised provincial councils to enforce his measures. He sought to stamp out simony and clerical marriage and concubinage. He ruled the Papal states in Italy. He claimed suzerainty, in the feudal sense of that term, over some of the Norman princes in Italy, over Aragon in Spain, Hungary, the kingdom of Kiev, and the kingdom of Croatia-Dalmatia. In some instances this suzerainty was created at the request of princes who thereby sought legal recognition for their position. He endeavoured to bring under the control of Rome the churches in the newly converted countries of Denmark, Norway, Poland, Bohemia, and Hungary.

Gregory's greatest and most famous struggle was with Henry IV. It was prolonged and intricate. We must not take the space to go into it in detail, but it was so important that we must note its outstanding features. The issue was central in the programme of the reformers, the independence of the Church from the control of the laity. Its focus was the right of investiture. In Germany, thanks largely to the policy initiated by Otto the Great to offset the power of the hereditary lay princes, the bishops and archbishops had become great territorial magnates. To control them, the monarch insisted upon the right of appointing them and of compelling them to swear fealty to him. This the reformers would not tolerate, for it seemed to them to be diverting the bishops from their proper functions, the spiritual oversight of their flocks, and to make of them secular princes with predominantly secular interests.

The issue between Gregory VII and Henry IV was first joined over the Archbishopric of Milan, a dispute which had begun under Gregory's predecessor. In the spring of 1075 a synod at Rome had come out afresh against lay investiture, thus denying Henry any part in creating bishops. Later in that year Henry made an appointment to the Archbishopric of Milan. In December, 1075, Gregory took him to task not only for this act but also for some other episcopal appointments. In January, 1076, Henry IV, after a council of German nobles and bishops at Worms, denounced Gregory as "not Pope, but false monk," and demanded that he descend from the Papal throne. In this he was joined by a number of German and Italian prelates, who declared that Gregory had perjured himself by not abiding by an oath which he was said to have given to Henry III not to ascend the Papal throne or permit any one else to do so without the consent of that monarch or his son. Accordingly, they renounced their allegiance to him.

Gregory countered, in February, 1076, by deposing Henry, forbidding any one to serve him as king, and anathematizing him. Here was the most drastic step which any Pope had thus far taken in the political realm, the attempted dethroning of the mightiest monarch of Western Christendom. Henry's enemies in Germany seized the occasion to ask Gregory to preside at an assembly of the German notables at Augsburg in February, 1077, for either the condemnation or absolution of Henry. Pope Gregory accepted and prepared to go to Germany. To forestall Gregory and the proposed assembly, Henry hastened to Italy in the dead of winter, sought out the Pope, who, for fear of violence from Henry, had taken refuge in the friendly fortress of Canossa, and there for three days stood barefoot, in a penitent's garb, before the castle gate, asking mercy. Pressed by some of his supporters, including the Abbot of Cluny, Gregory relented and granted Henry absolution in return for the latter's solemn oath to do justice according to the Pope's judgement or to conclude peace according to his counsels. Henry had won a tactical victory, but the memory of his abject submission at Canossa remained as a vivid demonstration of Papal power.

In spite and in part because of the startling episode of Canossa, Henry IV emerged victor. To be sure, Henry's enemies in Germany rose in revolt and elected a rival king, and in 1080 Gregory, reluctantly taking sides, again declared Henry deposed. But Henry had a synod pronounce Hildebrand deposed and elect a Pope in his place, invaded Italy, entered Rome, and had him whom he had made Pope crown him Emperor (1084), while Gregory VII, still unyielding, helplessly kept within the walls of the castle of San Angelo in Rome. Normans from the south came to Gregory's relief, took Rome, and carried him off with them (1084). The following year (1085) Hildebrand died in exile at Salerno, apparently a beaten man.

HILDEBRAND'S SUCCESSORS CONTINUE THE BATTLE FOR REFORM

Hildebrand's seeming defeat did not halt the work of reform. His immediate successors continued in the path which he had followed. This was not without opposition. Henry IV insisted on controlling the bishops until his forced abdication, in 1105. Some of the bishops came out for the imperial position. From time to time rival Popes were set up.

The son of Henry IV continued his father's struggle until what proved to be a working compromise was reached, in 1122, a generation after the death of Hildebrand, in the Concordat of Worms, between Henry V and Pope Calixtus II. By that agreement elections of bishops and abbots in Germany were to take place in the presence of the Emperor, but according to church law and without simony or violence. In case of dispute the Emperor was to give his judgement after consultation with the metropolitan and other bishops of the ecclesiastical province. Nothing was said about the imperial presence being necessary at elections in Italy. Investiture with ring and staff, the symbols of spiritual authority, was relinquished by the Emperor to the Church. In return, the Pope agreed that investiture with the temporal possessions attached to the office was to be by the Emperor and should carry with it such obligations to the Emperor as legally went with it. The Concordat of Worms did not end the conflict between Popes and Emperors. We shall meet it again later in the twelfth century.

In spite of the chronic friction between the two centralizing powers of Western Europe, the Pope and the Emperor, Roman Pontiffs, inspired by the purpose of raising the moral and spiritual level of all Christendom, continued to labour to make the dream a reality. This was true of Pope Urban II, who came to the Papal throne in 1088, only three years after the death of Hildebrand, and held it until 1099. A scion of a noble family, he had been educated under the direction of Bruno, the founder of the Carthusians, had been a monk at Cluny, and had been made Cardinal Bishop of Ostia by Gregory VII. Deeply religious, thoroughly committed to reform, experienced in administration, he was fully as courageous as Gregory VII and as convinced of the right of the See of Peter to supremacy, but was less tactless. Nourished as he had been in the Cluny tradition, he vigorously and persistently fought the purchase and sale of church offices, condemned admitting to major orders any who were not celibates, and opposed the lay investiture of church offices. By extending the Papal control over monasteries he augmented the power of the Holy See as against the bishops and lay princes. He excommunicated King Philip I of France for putting aside his wife to marry the wife of one of his vassals. In his struggle with Henry IV inherited from Gregory VII, he excommunicated the Emperor. In initiating the First Crusade as an enterprise of all Western Christendom he added to the prestige of the Papacy. The Council of Clermont, held in 1095, over which Urban II presided, and which was the scene of the launching of the Crusade, also took other important actions. It renewed earlier Papal decrees against simony, nicolaitanism, and lay investiture. It ordered deposed all non-celibate priests, deacons, and sub-deacons. No fees were to be asked for confirmation, extreme unction, or burials. No one was to receive any ecclesiastical office from a layman. No bishop or other cleric was to take a feudal oath of loyalty to a king or any other lay lord.

We must pause to remark that one result of the First Crusade and its successors was the enhancement of the prestige and power of the Popes. The Crusades were begun by the Papacy. No Crusade was valid without Papal endorsement. The Crusades were an additional and important channel through which the Popes asserted, and often effectively, their leadership of Christendom.

One other action of the Council of Clermont requires special note, not because it was new but because it is illustrative of a persistent attempt by the Church to bring society to a closer approximation to Christian standards. That was to enforce the Peace of God. The Peace of God and the Truce of God were efforts by the ecclesiastical authorities to reduce the destructiveness of the wars between feudal lords which were chronic during these centuries.

The Peace of God had been first attempted towards the end of the tenth century as a local project in France. At the outset it sought to exempt from attack by the combatants all persons and places consecrated by the Church—clergy, monks, virgins, churches, and monasteries—and to estop fighting on Sundays. Exemption was later also claimed for all those protected by the Church, such as the poor, pilgrims, crusaders, and merchants on their journeys. The Peace of God spread and had the endorsement of many synods and bishops. To enforce it numbers of dioceses formed what were known as confederations of peace.

The Truce of God dated from early in the eleventh century. At first it forbade fighting from Saturday night to Monday morning. Later it was extended to the days of the week connected with central events in the life of Christ, to Thursday as ascension day, to Friday as the day of the crucifixion, to Saturday, when Christ's body lay in the tomb, and to Advent and Lent. The penalty for violation of the Truce of God was excommunication. Like the Peace of God, the Truce of God spread from France to Germany and Italy. Never fully enforced, it exercised some restraint upon the disorders of the times.

In an attempt to curb war, the Church also endeavoured to eliminate jousts and tournaments, since these gave popularity to private feuds and the shedding of blood. For instance, in 1139 the Second Lateran Council (called the tenth ecumenical council by the Western Church) forbade them.

THE REFORM MOVEMENT SPREADS IN VARIOUS COUNTRIES

As we have again and again said or hinted, it was not only through the Papacy that efforts were made to bring the rank and file of Western Christendom to a closer approximation to the standards set forth by the Christ and the apostles. We have seen how in the early years of the reform movement, before it had captured the Papacy, it was being carried forward by bishops, usually bishops who were monks or who had been profoundly influenced by monastic revivals. Similarly, as the reform gathered momentum, it found expression on the national level, partly through Papal legates, partly through outstanding bishops, and partly through monasteries and local or regional synods. We must here take a moment to hint at some of the reforms in particular regions and nations.

Early in the twelfth century, substantial advance was made in France in curbing simony, the violation of clerical celibacy, and the control of the Church by lay lords. At times the king, in his struggle to increase the royal power at the expense of the nobility, while himself insisting on a voice in the naming of bishops, endeavoured to restrain the domination of the Church by his great vassals. Many of the feudal gentry, moreover, surrendered, apparently voluntarily, the authority which they had possessed to name the priests for the parishes in their domains. Here and there better bishops appeared, more devoted than their immediate predecessors to the spiritual and moral care of their clergy and their laity.

In Germany and North Italy the prolonged struggle between Popes and Emperors militated against reforms. In Germany, however, we read of bishops who were diligent in preaching and who encouraged the parish priests to visit the sick among their flocks, faithfully administer the sacraments, and give religious instruction to their flocks. In Germany diocesan synods seem to have been frequent. We also hear of religious literature in German for the masses— hymns, long poems setting forth Biblical stories and the drama of salvation, and translations of Latin works of theology. In Germany, as elsewhere, painting and sculpture were employed to depict themes from the Bible and the lives of the saints, thus making them vivid to the illiterate who could not have access to them through the written page.

Hungary, only recently the scene of the conversion of the Magyars and the emergence of a Christian monarchy, saw several reforming councils in the early years of the eleventh century.

The measures associated with the name of Hildebrand also penetrated to England. Here the Norman kings had insisted upon controlling the Church. William the Conqueror had endeavoured to use his authority to improve the quality of the Church and had seen to it that the ranking archbishopric of England, that of Canterbury, was filled by Lanfranc, who had become outstanding as a teacher in the monastery of Bec and who was a champion of the Cluniac reforms. Lanfranc pushed those reforms in England. Wulfstan or Wulstan (c.1007 or c.1012–1095), who as Bishop of Worcester was the one pre-Conquest prelate who was permitted to retain his see under the Normans, was a spiritual child of the Dunstan movement and was canonized by Pope Innocent III. Anselm, also of Bec, who on the insistence of King William II succeeded Lanfranc as Archbishop of Canterbury and held the post from 1093 to 1109, had a prolonged struggle with William II and Henry I in an effort, mixed in its outcome, to achieve the independence of the Church from royal domination and to insist upon its close subordination to the Pope. Under the civil strife which marked the reign of the weak Stephen the Church wrested concessions from the king. Henry II attempted to restore the royal authority over the Church and in doing so came into conflict with Thomas Becket whom he himself had placed in the Archbishopric of Canterbury. The contest reached its climax in 1170, in the murder of Becket. That tragedy made of the latter

England's most popular saint of the period and enabled the Pope to obtain recognition of the claims of the Church for which Becket had died.

The Improvement in Various Aspects of the Morals of the Laity

Through education and legislation the ecclesiastical authorities endeavoured to lift the various aspects of life more nearly to the Christian ideal. We have already noted the attempt to reduce the destructiveness of war by the Peace of God and the Truce of God. The reform movement of the tenth and eleventh centuries also sought to induce the warrior to govern his conduct by Christian principles. Thus when the young noble reached his majority and formally assumed his arms, the Church blessed his sword with the prayer that he would use it to defend churches, the widows, the orphans, and all the servants of God. Thus arose chivalry, the code of the Christian warrior of gentle birth. Additions were made to it as the years passed. It demanded that the knight keep his plighted word and be loyal to his lord. He was to fight against the infidel and when death came was to make his confession and receive the communion. The *Chanson de Roland,* composed in the first half of the eleventh century, was a poetic form of a legend of a much earlier struggle against the Moslem in Spain which helped the wide circulation of some phases of the ideal. Even more striking were the accounts of Arthur and his Knights of the Round Table which in the dress that they were given late in the twelfth century idealized Christian chivalry. The story of Parzival (Perceval), an ancient folk tale, as it was put into poetry by Wolfram von Eschenbach late in the twelfth or early in the thirteenth century centered around the Holy Grail (the platter or the cup used by Christ at the last supper), suffering, atonement, and the knightly virtues, and was a notable expression of the standard set up for the Christian knight.

The Church sought to purify marriage and sex relations for the laity at large. In feudal society, not yet recovered from the demoralization of the centuries-long series of invasions and plagued by chronic fighting, sex relations were notoriously lax. Kings and nobles divorced their wives almost with impunity and spawned illegitimate children. With such examples at the top, the masses could not be expected to be much better. At the end of the eleventh and the fore part of the twelfth century, as a part of the general wave of reform, synods and canon lawyers sought, so far as legislation could do it, to enforce continence and render divorce difficult. Here and there efforts were made to give stability to the families of slaves.

The Church also strove to bring the economic phase of society to conform with what it deemed Christian standards. For instance, it forbade the taking of interest.

The Papacy Attains Its Height as a Comprehensive Legislative and Administrative Structure

In the last half of the twelfth and the fore part of the thirteenth century the Papacy reached the high point of its power in Western Europe. Never before had its influence been so strong in so many aspects of the life of that region. Never again did it make its weight felt so potently in so many phases of the culture of that area.

This apex of Papal might came as a climax to the religious revival which had captured the Holy See. It also paralleled the crest of the urge to attain the perfect Christian life which had expressed itself both through monasticism and in movements which the Church deemed heretical and which had culminated on the one hand in the emergence of the mendicant orders and on the other hand in the Albigensees and Waldensees. With it, too, were associated the growth of commerce and intellectual developments, including the rise of universities and the flowering of scholastic theology of which we are to speak in the next chapter. This coincidence of several movements seems to have been more than fortuitous. Precisely what was cause and what was effect we may not know, but that all were closely allied features of a particular stage in the history of Europe is certain.

It seems also significant that the Papacy and the Holy Roman Empire reached a climax not far from the same time. The struggle between Pope and Emperor continued and in some respects was intensified. Both contestants were reinforced by the revival of scholarship and with it the study of law.

The development of canon law attained a high point in the *Decretum* of Gratian, compiled about the middle of the twelfth century. Canon law, or the law of the Church, had its roots in the first century, but has been the product of a development which has been in progress from then until the present. Gratian's was by no means the first treatise on it. Many collections had been made, notably in the tenth and eleventh centuries. The *Decretum* of Gratian was in part a compilation, but it was more. It embodied the considered opinions of the author. Since Gratian had his spiritual fellowship with one of the strictest groups of the revival of the Benedictine rule with its passion for the reform of the Church, it was natural that he should exalt the position of the Pope. He was a master of his subject, did his work at Bologna, the main centre of the awakening interest in both canon and civil law, and his *magnum opus* was long regarded as standard.

On the other hand, the renewed study of Roman law, especially in the compilations made under Justinian which had been introduced to Bologna early in the twelfth century and which had spread to other centres, exalted the position of the Emperor. It was the Emperor as absolute monarch who was prominent in the Justinian code, and Justinian and the stronger among his Christian predecessors had often been dominant in ecclesiastical affairs. Civil lawyers, therefore, would tend to declare that any imperial edict, even in Church matters, should be obeyed.

Italy was deeply divided by the struggle. Two parties, Guelphs and Ghibellines, were prominent in Italian politics and civil strife between them was chronic. The Guelphs upheld the independence of the Church as against the Emperor and also stood for the autonomy of Italian cities, since these had less to fear from the Pope than from the Emperor. The Ghibellines supported the authority of the Emperor.

By the close of the thirteenth century both the Papacy and the Holy Roman Empire had passed the crest of their power. Neither was ever fully to recover the position which it had held in Western Europe. For the Empire the decline was to be permanent. Technically the Holy Roman Empire survived until early in the nineteenth century. The title of Emperor long added prestige to him who held it. Yet the time of its glory had passed. The efforts of the German monarchs who held it to make it effective south of the Alps was long to prevent the unification of Germany and Italy. After more than two centuries of decline, under new conditions the Papacy was to rise to a far wider geographic influence than at any earlier time. Yet that influence was exerted in a fashion different from that which had been seen in its great era which followed the triumph of the eleventh and twelfth century reformers and never again was it to achieve a full recovery in North-western Europe.

Even after the medieval Papacy and Empire had passed their peak, the contest between the two did not immediately cease. Indeed, as the authority of the Emperors waned, some of the most forceful and intellectually powerful treatises in its defense appeared. Thus early in the fourteenth century Dante Alighieri, the greatest poet of his age, wrote his *Monarchia,* in which he maintained that a universal monarchy is necessary for the peace and welfare of mankind, that this had been conferred upon the people of Rome, and that the Emperor held his authority directly from God and not through the Pope. While Dante declared that the Emperor must reverence the Pope, it is not surprising that the latter placed the *Monarchia* upon the index of forbidden books.

In the opening years of the fourteenth century John of Paris, a Dominican, wrote a treatise on the relationship between royal and Papal powers in which he placed restrictions on the latter but sought a balance between the two.

Much more radical and devastating was the *Defensor Pacis,* completed in 1324 by Marsilius of Padua and John of Jandun. Marsilius (Marsiglio Mainardino), an Italian physician and for a brief time Rector of the University of

Paris, was an ardent Ghibelline. John of Jandun, a Frenchman, was an out-standing teacher in the University of Paris. The *Defensor Pacis* attacked the claims of the Papacy to supremacy in state and Church. It had no use for the idea of a universal Christian empire. It held that there must be many states, each based upon the law inherent in nature, and that the Church should not have jurisdiction over them. The law for the several states was to be made by assemblies of all male adult citizens. The executive, which might be either one man or a council, was to be elected by the assembly and was to have authority over all other executive and judicial authorities. The *Defensor Pacis* maintained that since Christ did not claim temporal power but submitted himself and his property to the state and since, in accordance with his commands, the apostles did likewise, the clergy must hold to that example. It taught that the clergy must follow the way of absolute poverty, and that they and the Church must have no temporal authority. It came out sharply against the claims of the Papacy. It held that in the early Church there was no distinction between priests and bishops, and that all the bishops were equal and were all successors of the apostles. To obtain united action in the Church, the *Defensor Pacis* ad-vocated the holding of general councils made up of priests and laymen elected by the voting assemblies of each of the states, assemblies which, as we have seen, were to be composed of all adult male citizens. Papal supremacy was attacked, with its emphasis upon the privileges of the clergy and its claim of suzerainty over the Holy Roman Empire. The canon law was denounced. It is not surprising that the Pope condemned the book even more emphatically than he did Dante's *Monarchia*. The *Defensor Pacis* was quite impracticable, but it was not without effect.

In the first half of the fourteenth century an earnest Franciscan, William of Ockham (Occam), whom we shall meet again as an outstanding theologian, advocated the independence of the state from the Church. He held as un-necessary Papal confirmation of the election of an Emperor or the investiture of an Emperor by a Pope. The Pope, he said, should be subject to the Emperor in secular matters. Ockham also insisted that the Papacy is not a necessary form of government for the Church. He declared that the Scriptures do not teach that Christ appointed Peter as the prince of the apostles. He held that not the Pope but only the Scriptures are infallible and that Popes may fall into error and be deposed. He taught that even the college of cardinals or a general council of the Church may err.

GREAT POPES OF THE TWELFTH CENTURY

Here is not the place for a complete list of the Pontiffs under whom the Papacy attained its greatest power. We must, however, pause to mention those who were outstanding. Some of them reigned in the twelfth century.

Innocent II (1130–1143), supported by Bernard of Clairvaux, was dominant as against the Holy Roman Emperors of his reign and triumphed over two rivals who claimed the Papacy. He told the bishops that they held their sees of him as vassals held their fiefs of their sovereigns and that they could not retain them without his consent.

Eugene III, a pupil of Bernard of Clairvaux, was in office from 1145 to 1153. It was he who appointed Bernard to preach the Second Crusade. He demonstrated the authority of the Papacy over the Church by deposing the powerful Archbishops of York, Mainz, and Rheims for disobedience. He strengthened the prestige of the Pope in distant Scandinavia. He reformed abuses in France. Yet for a time he was driven from Rome by the republic which had as one of its officials that Arnold of Brescia who had denounced the temporal power of the Papacy.

Adrian IV (1154–1159), who, as we have seen, was the only Englishman to sit on the Papal throne, was able to expel Arnold from Rome and was stout in his maintenance of Papal authority against the mighty Frederick Barbarossa. Frederick I (Barbarossa), who was German King from 1152 to his drowning on a Crusade in 1190, had been crowned Emperor in 1155, emulated Charlemagne, and was one of the strongest of the Holy Roman Emperors. He sought to make good the claims of the Emperors as against the Popes and during much of his reign carried on the traditional struggle.

Alexander III, Pope from 1159 to 1181, was an expert in canon law, and further augmented the power of the Holy See over secular princes and the Church. This he did in spite of the fact that during almost all his reign he had to contend with a succession of rivals who were set up by the opposition and that he came into head on collision with the ambitious and able Frederick Barbarossa. The latter was defeated and in a memorable scene at Venice in 1177 knelt and kissed Alexander's feet. Alexander took advantage of the murder of Thomas Becket to obtain recognition from Henry II of England of some of the Church's claims. Appeals to Rome increased, together with the nomination by the Papal Curia of bishops and holders of benefices in many parts of Europe. At the third Lateran Council (counted as the eleventh ecumenical council by the Western Church), held in Rome in 1179, further measures were taken for reform.

It was Alexander III who commanded that in the future canonization should be only with the authority of the Roman Church. Earlier, individual bishops had formally recognized the cults which had arisen around particular individuals who because of their character, their virtues, and the miracles believed to have been performed through them had become those by whose intercession God was approached. Abuses had crept in, and Alexander decreed that henceforward none should be officially enrolled among the saints without Papal consent. Not all the bishops obeyed and it was the seventeenth century before a Papal bull finally succeeded in reserving canonization to the Holy See.

INNOCENT III

The climax of the Papacy is usually regarded as having been reached under Lotario de' Conti di Segni who under the title Innocent III reigned 1198 to 1216. Of aristocratic Lombard lineage on his father's side and of the Roman nobility on his mother's side, he was born not far from Rome in 1160 or 1161. Educated in Paris, the main centre for the study of philosophy and theology, and at Bologna, noted for its emphasis on law, Innocent III was one of the most learned men of his day and was equipped in both theology and canon law. Made a cardinal-deacon at the age of twenty-nine by Pope Clement III, who is said to have been his uncle, he was early in the central administrative machinery of the Holy See. Because the next Pope, Celestine III, was of a rival Roman family, the young cardinal was out of favour for seven years. On the very day of the death and funeral of Celestine III, although not yet forty years of age and only in deacon's orders, he was hurriedly but unanimously elected to the vacant see by his fellow-cardinals and was enthusiastically acclaimed by the clergy and people of Rome. After a decent interval he was ordained priest and consecrated bishop.

A man of singleness of purpose, iron will, and great executive and diplomatic ability, Innocent III brought the Papacy to the apex of its influence in the political life of Europe and markedly extended its administrative control of the Church. A prodigious worker, he drove his own body mercilessly. To curb a fever he is said to have subsisted for some time chiefly on lemons. It may be significant, however, that in contrast with such predecessors as Leo I, Gregory I, and Gregory VII, who were, like himself, distinguished for enlarging the power of the Papacy, he has never been canonized. Nor, unlike the first two, has the designation "Great" ever been associated with his name. Perhaps that was because he was too prone to use the worldly tools in his effort to make actual the City of God. Yet he clearly recognized the distinctive Christian virtues and could speak most feelingly of them and of the life of the spirit.

Innocent III had an exalted conception of the position and mission of the Papacy. There seems to have been in it little if anything that was really new or that had not been asserted by some among his predecessors. Yet in letters, sermons, and other pronouncements he gave it forcible expression. He dreamed of Christendom as a community in which the Christian ideal was to be attained under Papal guidance. As the successor of Peter, the Pope, so Innocent held, had authority over all the churches. On at least one occasion, moreover, he declared that as Pope he was the vicar of him of whom it had been affirmed that he was king of kings and lord of lords. He wrote that Christ "left to Peter the governance not of the Church only but of the whole world." He also said that Peter was the vicar of Him whose is the earth and the fullness thereof, the world and they that dwell therein. How far he believed this to mean that the Pope should be a temporal ruler is in dispute. He certainly made his weight felt in affairs of state, especially but by no means exclusively in Italy. He conceded that kings were given certain functions by divine commission, but he held that God had ordained both the pontifical and the royal power, as he had the sun and the moon, and that as the latter draws its light from the former, so the royal power derives its dignity and splendour from the pontifical. Moreover, as a true successor of the great reforming Popes, Innocent insisted that the power of the secular ruler did not extend to the clergy, but that the clergy were to be independent of the law of the state and subject only to the Church.

Several features of the times combined to facilitate or to call forth by their challenge the exercise of the powers claimed by Innocent III for the Papacy. As we have earlier seen, his tenure of that office coincided with a swelling tide of religious life which displayed itself in the emergence of the Franciscans, the Dominicans, and other mendicant orders and in the prevalence of the Waldensees and the Cathari. The wealth of Europe was mounting. The Holy Roman Empire was declining. The Emperor Henry VI, the able son and successor of Frederick Barbarossa, had been a serious threat to the Papacy, for by his marriage with the heiress of the Norman kings who had ruled in Sicily and South Italy he controlled both the north and the south of that land and made it difficult for the Roman Pontiff to play off the one against the other as he had long been able to do. However, Henry VI died the year before Innocent III became Pope, leaving as his heir an infant son, Frederick II. The lad's mother died the year that Innocent ascended the throne of Peter and left the Pope as guardian of her son and regent of Sicily. A contested succession to the throne of Germany gave Innocent the opportunity to mix in the affairs of that distracted country. The kingdoms which were already in existence in Western Europe were assuming larger stature in comparison with the Empire but were not yet supported by a national sentiment which was strong enough successfully to defy Rome. Under these favouring and challenging circumstances Innocent III made good the claims of the Papacy to a greater degree than had any of his predecessors.

Innocent III further extended the Papal control over the Church. It was under his Pontificate that the Crusaders captured Constantinople. Although the diversion of the Crusade from its supposed purpose, the retaking of Jerusa-

lem, had been made against the wish of Innocent, the conquest of Constantinople had been followed by the setting up of a Latin hierarchy and a Patriarch
for that city and the other Byzantine territories which were subservient to
Rome. Latin rule in Constantinople enabled Innocent to extend the control of
Rome over the churches in Illyria, Bulgaria, and Wallachia which had formerly
been orientated towards the Byzantine wing of the Church. He also used the
occasion to bring the Church in Armenia within the Roman orbit. The
Maronites in the Lebanon, who had been monothelites, were won to conformity with Rome. No Pope had previously brought so much of the Church
in the East under the administrative control of the See of Peter. While most of
the gains proved to be only temporary, that they were achieved at all was
noteworthy. Innocent III authorized a crusade against the pagans on the south
and east shores of the Baltic, sent missionaries to the Prussians, and brought
the newly converted in that region under Papal direction. He reformed the
Church in Poland. He asserted the right of the Pope to give the decision in
all disputed elections to the episcopacy. He insisted that the Pope alone could
authorize the transfer of a bishop from one see to another. He declared that
only the Holy See could create new dioceses or change the boundaries between
existing dioceses. He was emphatic in seeking to further the high moral
character of the episcopate and the priesthood and continued the struggle to
enforce the celibacy of the clergy. To strengthen and purify the Church he
ordered that tithes for the support of the Church be given precedence over all
other taxes, he excluded all lay interference in ecclesiastical affairs, and he
prohibited any one man from drawing the income from more than one church
office. He affirmed the right of Rome to review important cases and thus added
to the trend to take appeals to the Holy See. He gave the Papal chancery the
best organization that it had thus far had.

In his effort to raise the level of Christian life in Europe, Innocent fought
what he deemed heresy. To this end he employed various means. Among them
was the Crusade against the Cathari.

It was Innocent III who called and dominated the most important of the
assemblies of the Church of the Middle Ages, the Fourth Lateran Council,
regarded by the Roman Catholic Church as the twelfth ecumenical council.
This convened late in 1215 and addressed itself to a wide range of problems.
It enacted a more comprehensive body of legislation than did any succeeding
council until that of Trent, nearly three hundred and fifty years later. It sought
not only the reform of the Church but also the improvement of the life of
the general Christian community. It laid down rules for the better education
of the clergy. It gave more precise definitions to several Christian doctrines.
Among them were a formula on the Trinity, transubstantiation, and the con-

demnation of what were deemed the errors of some of the heresies of the day. It sought to further the union with the Greek wing of the Catholic Church, then seemingly facilitated by the Latin conquest of Constantinople. It endorsed the new crusade which was a dream of Innocent III. It sought to raise the level of marriage and family life. It condemned the taking of interest and to prevent Jews from exacting it of Christians it forbade the latter to have any commerce with the former.

An act of the Fourth Lateran Council which was of major importance in the effort to raise the level of the rank and file of the laity was that which enjoined upon all Christians the duty of making their confession to a priest at least once each year. The early practice of penance, as we have seen, was public penalty and public restoration. Gradually in the Western wing of the Catholic Church the custom had spread of private confession to a priest, the private prescription by the priest of discipline, and the reconciliation of the penitent by the priest, also private. We have pointed out that as far back as the previous period penitentials, or books of directions to priests for examining penitents, had gained circulation. The custom of private oral confession had grown. Now a council representing the entire Western Church declared it to be obligatory upon every Christian.

It was especially in political affairs and in his dealings with kings and other princes that Innocent III exercised more power than any of his predecessors or successors. Here especially he seemed to be rendering effective the purpose of making the Papacy the instrument for bringing all the life of Christendom into conformity with Christian standards. He brought Papal dominance in much of Italy. In Rome itself he required the civil officials to acknowledge him rather than the Emperor as their sovereign and substituted his own appointees for the imperial judges. He won from the Tuscan cities acknowledgement of his suzerainty and obtained from the Emperor Otto IV the cession of lands claimed by the Papacy as grants from earlier rulers. In Germany he became the arbiter between two claimants to the throne and in return for his favour exacted from one of them, Otto IV, a promise to protect the possessions of the Church of Rome. Insisting that the Pope had the right to pass on the validity of elections to the imperial office, Innocent III crowned Otto IV Roman Emperor, but later, when Otto proved obdurate, excommunicated him and played a significant part in stirring up the opposition which cost him his throne. When he turned against Otto, Innocent gave his support to Frederick II, obtained his election as King of the Romans and King of the Germans, and wrung from him the freedom of the Church in Germany to elect its bishops and the concession of the right of appeal to Rome. So long as Innocent III lived, Frederick, able and ruthless though he was and quite sceptical religiously, was largely dominated by him. Innocent insisted upon the Papal overlordship of Sicily.

In France Innocent compelled Philip Augustus, as strong a monarch as Western Europe of that day knew, to take back the wife whom he had divorced and to restore to the Church lands which he had confiscated. Innocent was active in Spanish affairs. He crowned the King of Aragon at Rome as his vassal. He compelled the King of Leon to put away the wife whom he had married despite prohibitory canon law. He induced the Kings of Navarre and Castile to make peace and unite to fight the Moors. Portugal, Poland, Hungary, and Serbia became Papal vassals. In Norway he intervened to bring to time a priest who, having slain the king, had compelled the bishops to crown him.

Especially notable was the triumph in England. Here Innocent came into conflict with the notorious King John by insisting that the latter accept as Archbishop of Canterbury the able Stephen Langton in place of one whose election John had sponsored. John, furious, seized church property and drove many of the bishops into exile. Innocent excommunicated John, deposed him, and transferred the crown to Philip Augustus. To save his throne, John abjectly submitted, surrendered his kingdom to the Pope, and received it back as a Papal vassal. For many years thereafter, and under several Popes, Papal legates were prominent in the government of England.

THE SLOW DECLINE OF THE PAPACY

Never again, as we have suggested, was the Papacy to be so potent in so many phases of the life of Europe. After Innocent III a decline set in which slightly less than two centuries later was to bring the See of Peter to a nadir that, while not as low as that of the tenth century, was in sad contrast with the purposes cherished for it by the great Popes of the eleventh and twelfth centuries.

The decline was not sudden. The thirteenth century saw several strong and high-minded Pontiffs, and some of them continued to make their office a force in Christendom. Thus the successor of Innocent, Honorius III, who held the post from 1216 to 1227, took measures to improve the education of the clergy and through his legates had great weight in the affairs of England during the minority of John's son, Henry III.

Yet even some of the strong Popes met serious reverses. Honorius III was followed by Gregory IX, a nephew of Innocent III. Although he came to the Papal throne in his early eighties and held it for fourteen years (1227–1241), until his mid-nineties, Gregory IX acted with vigour in a prolonged contest with the Emperor Frederick II, fostered learning, canonized Francis of Assisi and Dominic, strengthened the Inquisition, and sought to bring about the reunion of the Western and Eastern wings of the Church. But his excommunication of the Emperor failed to bring the latter to terms. Although Innocent IV (Pope from 1243 to 1254) had a general council of the Church excommunicate and depose Frederick II, he was unable to unseat that Emperor. Alexander IV (Pope from 1254 to 1261), nephew of Gregory IX, failed to dislodge the illegitimate son of Frederick II from his rule in Sicily and Southern Italy or to unite Europe against the threatened invasion of the Mongols.

The growing weakness of the Papacy was vividly demonstrated in 1294 when, after a Papal interregnum of two years caused by the rivalry of two powerful families and dissensions among the cardinals which prevented an election, the latter placed on the Papal throne a Benedictine monk, the organizer of a monastic congregation, who had the title of Celestine V. Although he was acclaimed by idealists and the Roman populace, Celestine, inexperienced in ecclesiastical politics and nearly eighty years of age, proved quite unable to meet the administrative demands of the post and after a few months resigned. In spite of the fact that less than twenty years after his death he was canonized, Dante pilloried him as he who had made the great refusal.

The decline of the Papacy became even more marked during the reign of Celestine's successor, Boniface VIII (Benedict Gaetani), who held the See of Peter from 1294 to 1303. Related to several Popes, among them probably Innocent III, with long experience in the Papal curia and as Papal legate, he brought scholarship and undoubted ability to the post. He was a lover of learning and promoted the founding of universities. He made as great claims for Papal authority as were ever promulgated. In his bull *Unam Sanctam,* issued in 1299, he declared "that it is altogether necessary to salvation for every human creature to be subject to the Roman Pontiff." He sought to make good this sweeping assertion. But, tactless, quick-tempered, lordly, and a lover of magnificence, he was far from being the equal of the greatest of his predecessors in ability or character and was defeated in his chief efforts to enforce his will. In spite of a Papal excommunication and interdict, a prince whom he opposed became ruler of Sicily. In the bull *Clericos Laicos,* promulgated in 1296, Boniface emphatically condemned the taxation of the clergy and Church property in France for royal purposes. A prolonged struggle followed between him and Philip IV of France, and at one point the Pope prepared to excommunicate and depose the king. A band of mercenaries instigated by the Pope's enemies seized the Pontiff at Anagni and held him prisoner. Although the burghers of Anagni rescued him and returned him in seeming triumph to Rome, within less than a month, an aged and broken man, he died of chagrin and melancholy.

WHY THE DECLINE OF THE PAPACY?

The reasons for the decline of the Papacy were complex. Among them, however, was the growth of monarchies reinforced by a rising tide of a sentiment akin to nationalism. Kingdoms were not new but they were becoming stronger. As communications improved and cities and commerce grew, Western Europe began to emerge from its exclusively agricultural economy and endless division into large and small units associated with one another through feudal ties. Yet the dream of drawing together all Christendom into one unit dominated by the Holy Roman Empire and the Papacy was not fulfilled. Instead, Western Europe remained divided into numbers of states, large and small. Each monarch sought to control that portion of the Church which was within his domains and resented Papal interference. In this he was supported by the majority of his subjects, for they were averse to seeing foreigners placed in ecclesiastical posts by Papal appointment and were especially angered by the taxes imposed through the Church for the support of the Papal curia.

The debilitating conflict between Empire and Papacy was another source of the decline of the Papacy. The efforts of the reformers to free the Church from secularism by making it independent of the state and the vision which sustained the great Popes of a society in which the Christian purpose would be predominant through the guidance of the Bishops of Rome as Vicars of Christ had led to prolonged internecine strife in which Popes resorted to measures which were quite inconsistent with Christian standards of conduct. The Empire suffered more than the Papacy, but the latter was weakened, especially in moral stature.

Furthermore, the very machinery which the reforming Popes developed to make their power effective in purifying the Church and raising the moral and spiritual level of society proved a source of weakness. Their measures entailed the multiplication of officials, many of them at Rome and others scattered throughout Christendom, an elaborate and expensive bureaucracy. Positions in that bureaucracy were sought by ambitious men, for they brought prestige, physical comfort, even luxury, and a kind of power which was antithetical to that of the Gospel. Here, in the name of the Gospel, was a perversion of the Gospel which eventually became a noisome scandal. The taxes required for the support of the bureaucracy aroused resentment which challenged, often successfully, the authority of the Papacy to impose and collect them.

THE PAPACY GOES INTO CAPTIVITY AT AVIGNON

The decline of the Papacy became vivid in what is often called the Babylonian Captivity. From 1309 to 1377 the Popes resided at Avignon, and although that city was not in France, it was overshadowed by that realm. All the Popes of the period were Frenchmen and were subject to French influence which at times became domination by the King of France. The Papacy was almost a French institution. This weakened its prestige in nations and regions at enmity with France and after 1350 issued in the Great Schism which, as we are to see, weakened not only the Papacy but also the Western Church.

It was under Clement V, Pope from 1305 to 1314 and the second after Boniface VIII, that the headquarters of the Papacy were removed to Avignon. Clement had been Archbishop of Bordeaux which, although under the King of England, was French soil. Under pressure from the King of France he annulled the acts which had been directed against that monarch by his two predecessors. He was noted for appointing his relatives to high office in the Church, including six whom he made cardinals. All but two of the twenty-four cardinals whom he created were French, a precedent which was to be followed by his Avignon successors.

The longest reign of the Avignon Pontiffs was that of John XXII, from 1316 to 1334. Coming to the office when he was sixty-seven, John XXII lived into his eighty-fifth year. In spite of his advanced age, his was a vigorous rule. Austere and simple in his private life, he left behind him a large personal fortune. He was involved in extensive wars over German and imperial affairs, for the struggle between Popes and Emperors continued to plague both lines of potentates. Possessing outstanding organizing and executive gifts, he increased the centralization of the affairs of the Church in the Papal curia and departmentalized the administration. He faced serious financial problems, for the removal to Avignon had cost the Papacy some of its Italian revenues and his extensive participation in war consumed almost two-thirds of his budget. Yet he proved to be something of a financial genius in augmenting the Papal funds and in introducing an efficient financial system. Among other measures he reserved for his treasury the income for three years of all minor benefices which fell vacant in the Western branch of the Church and also claimed the personal property of bishops on their death.

In general, the Avignon years were marked by luxury in the Papal entourage and the enlargement of varied forms of Papal taxation and exaction. Palatial residences for Pope and cardinals were erected. These and the style of living maintained within them were costly. The Papal bureaucracy and the Papal ventures in politics also demanded large expenditures. Among the sources of funds were what were technically known as Papal reservation and provision. By reservation was meant the right of nomination to a vacant benefice. Provision was appointment to a benefice before it fell vacant. From each new appointee the Pope expected the annate, approximately one year's revenue of the post. The income from vacant benefices the nomination to which was in Papal hands was also an increasing source of revenue, especially since the posts might be deliberately kept unfilled. In their effort to control the moral and religious life of Western Christendom the Popes, as we have seen, had encouraged or required appeal to their court. Under the Avignon Pontiffs the fees exacted for such appeals were another source of funds.

These enlargements of Papal powers and taxes aroused widespread resentment. In England, for example, in 1351 there was enacted the Statute of Provisors which forbade Papal interference in elections to ecclesiastical posts. This was followed, in 1353, by a law, *Praemunire,* which prohibited appeals to courts outside the kingdom. Although the Pope was not specifically named in the act, the intent was clear.

Some of the Avignon Pontiffs were upright men who strove to correct abuses and to improve the life of the Church, but the tide was against them. The Papacy was in a decline which in the next period was to be a scandal to the Christian name, first because of a prolonged and bitter division of Western Europe among rival claimants of the see and then because men of quite unworthy character manœuvred themselves into Peter's Chair.

SUMMARY

It is a record of contrasts, frustrations and triumphs, this effort through the hierarchy to bring all Western Christendom to a near approximation to the Christian ideal. Here was a noble ambition. With the exception of small minorities, the peoples of Western Europe either had been won or were being won to an avowed acceptance of the Christian faith. Yet the majority had only a vague conception of the nature of the religion whose name they had taken. The habit of war was strong. Injustice and immorality were rife. At the outset of the period all too frequently even the monasteries, supposed conservers and exemplars of Christian living, had departed from their professed standards, and the clergy, by profession the guardians and shepherds of the masses, were notoriously corrupt.

In the course of the centuries between the years 950 and 1350 potent impulses had raised the level of Christian living in the monasteries and in some of the movements which were branded as heretical by the Catholic Church. In spite of the fact that they were zealously missionary, the mendicant orders and such bodies as the Waldensees succeeded in reaching only minorities. On the other hand, great dreamers, some of them monks and some of them of the secular clergy, strove to bring the entire body of mass converts and their descendants to what Paul had called "the high calling of God in Christ Jesus." To accomplish this purpose they strove to cleanse the vast body of clergy from the parish priests to the Pope and through this purified hierarchy to reach not minorities but all who bore the Christian name.

The struggle proved unending. Successes were registered, some of them striking. Many among the bishops and parish priests were exemplary Christians. More and more of the laity were being brought to an intelligent appreciation of the faith and to a disciplined observance of it. The reformers captured the Papacy. Yet abuses, even in the hierarchy, were never fully eliminated. At times they seemed to mount and the age-long efforts of the reformers to be vain. Indeed, in time the very machinery which had been developed by the dreamers to make their vision a reality proved an obstacle to the realization of the purposes of its creators. Increasingly Europe was ostensibly Christian. For the majority the Christian faith was at best nominal and in actual practice they denied it. That majority included many of the clergy and even bishops and Popes. Yet increasingly Europe numbered individuals and groups which were earnestly committed to the Christian faith. Nor can we say that the efforts of those who strove for a fully Christian society were entirely fruitless. As we are to see in a later chapter, more phases of the life of Western Europe were profoundly influenced by Christianity than was true in the Roman Empire after the seeming triumph of the faith in that realm. But for the dreamers that would not have occurred.

Selected Bibliography

GENERAL WORKS

A. Fliche and V. Martin, editors, *Histoire de l'Église depuis les Origines jusqu'à Nos Jours*. Carefully done, by Roman Catholics and from the Roman Catholic standpoint, stressing the role of the Papacy, but with an honest attempt at objectivity and with helpful references to the sources and the literature. The volumes which cover this period are E. Amann, *L'Église au Pouvoir des Laïques (888–1057)* (Paris, Bloud & Gay, 1948, pp. 544); A. Fliche, *La Réforme Grégorienne et la Reconquete Chrétienne (1057–1125)* (Bloud & Gay, 1946, pp. 502); A. Fliche, R. Foreville, and J. Rousset, *Du Premier Concile du Lateran a l'Avènement d'Innocent III (1123–1198)* (Bloud & Gay, 1948, pp. 204); and A. Fliche, C. Thouzellier, and Y. Azais, *La Chrétienté Romaine (1198–1274)* (Bloud & Gay, pp. 512).

A. C. Flick, *The Rise of the Mediaeval Church and Its Influence on the Civilization of Western Europe from the First to the Thirteenth Century* (New York, G. P. Putnam's Sons, 1909, pp. xiii, 623). Approximately the second half of the volume deals with this period. Valuable as a summary and for its bibliographies.

A. Hauck, *Kirchengeschichte Deutschlands*. Of this standard work, dependable and with extensive references to the sources, Vols. 3, 4, and 5 (Leipzig, J. C. Hinrichs'sche Buchhandlung, 1920, 1913, 1920) cover this period.

A. Lagarde, *The Latin Church of the Middle Ages,* translated by A. Alexander (New York, Charles Scribner's Sons, 1915, pp. vi, 600). A standard summary.

H. K. Mann, *The Lives of the Popes in the Middle Ages* (London, Kegan Paul, Trench, Trübner & Co., 2d Ed., 18 vols., 1925–1932). Vols. IV–XVIII cover this period and go through the year 1304. Enormously learned, the work is by a Roman Catholic priest and tends to give a favourable picture of the Popes.

J. McCabe, *Crises in the History of the Papacy* (New York, G. P. Putnam's Sons, 1916, pp. xiv, 459). A history of the Papacy centering on outstanding figures, of whom three fall within this period.

THE EFFORT TO ENFORCE THE CELIBACY OF THE CLERGY

H. C. Lea, *History of Sacerdotal Celibacy in the Christian Church* (New York, The Macmillan Co., 3d ed., rev., 2 vols., 1907). Of this standard work more than half of Vol. I deals with this period.

DUNSTAN

J. A. Robinson, *The Times of Saint Dunstan* (Oxford University Press, 1923, pp. 188).

BERNWARD

F. J. Tschan, *Bernward of Hildesheim* (University of Notre Dame, Vol. I, 1942, pp. vii, 235).

HILDEBRAND

S. Gregorii VII Romani Pontificis Epistolæ et Diplomata Pontificia, being Vol. CXLVIII of J. P. Migne, *Patrologia Latina* (Paris, 1853, columns 1472).

A. J. Macdonald, *Hildebrand: A Life of Gregory VII* (London, Methuen & Co., 1932, pp. ix, 254). Well written, semi-popular, with frequent references to the sources.

A. H. Mathew, *The Life and Times of Hildebrand Pope Gregory VII* (London, Francis Griffiths, 1910, pp. xi, 308). Semi-popular, based upon the sources, but with almost no footnote references to them.

LANFRANC

A. J. Macdonald, *Lanfranc. A Study of His Life, Work and Writing* (Oxford University Press, 1926, pp. vii, 307). Based upon a careful and critical use of the sources.

WULFSTAN

J. W. Lamb, *Saint Wulfstan, Prelate and Patriot: a Study of His Life and Times* (London, Society for Promoting Christian Knowledge, 1933, pp. xiii, 218).

THOMAS BECKET

W. H. Hutton, *Thomas Becket, Archbishop of Canterbury* (Cambridge University Press, 1926, pp. vii, 315).

LAW, WAR, MARRIAGE, ECONOMIC LIFE

B. Jarrett, *Social Theories of the Middle Ages* (Westminster, Md., The Newman Bookshop, 1942, pp. ix, 280). A semi-popular survey, by a Dominican.

E. Troeltsch, *The Social Teachings of the Christian Churches,* translated by Olive Wyon (Vol. I, New York, The Macmillan Co., 1931, pp. 445). Slightly more than half of this volume is on medieval Catholicism.

JOHN OF PARIS

J. Leclercq, *Jean de Paris et l'Ecclésiologie du XIII*ᵉ *Siècle* (Paris, Librairie Philosophique J. Vrin, 1942, pp. 268). By a Dominican. Contains the text of *De Potestate Regio et Papali.*

MARSILIUS OF PADUA

The Defensor Pacis of Marsilius of Padua, edited by C. W. Previté-Orton (Cambridge University Press, 1928, pp. xlvii, 517). The Latin text with an extensive introduction.

E. Emerton, *The Defensor Pacis of Marsiglio of Padua. A Critical Study* (Harvard University Press, 1920, pp. 81). By a distinguished specialist in Church history.

INNOCENT III

L. Elliott-Binns, *Innocent III* (London, Methuen & Co., 1931, pp. xi, 212). Popularly written.

A. Luchaire, *Innocent III* (Paris, Hachette et C ᵢₑ, 6 vols., 1905–1908). Extensive, but weak in its lack of footnote references to the sources.

BONIFACE VIII

T. S. R. Bose, Boniface VIII (London, Constable & Co., 1933, pp. xv, 397). Very well done.

L. Tosti, *Pope Boniface VIII and His Times,* translated by E. J. Bonnelly (New York, S. R. Leland, 1933, pp. 546). By a Roman Catholic strongly biased in favour of Boniface VIII.

CONFESSION AND PENANCE

H. C. Lea, *A History of Auricular Confession and Indulgences in the Latin Church* (Philadelphia, Lea Brothers & Co., 3 vols., 1896). A standard survey.

O. D. Watkins, *A History of Penance. Being a Study of the Authorities* (London, Longmans, Green & Co., 2 vols., 1920). Valuable for its extensive citations from the sources and its excellent summaries. The latter part of Vol. II deals with this period.

THE BABYLONIAN CAPTIVITY

A. C. Flick, *The Decline of the Medieval Church* (New York, Alfred A. Knopf, 2 vols., 1930). Nearly two-thirds of Vol. I is devoted to the Babylonian Captivity. An objective account based upon the sources and secondary works.

Chapter XXI

CREATIVE THOUGHT IN THE WESTERN CHURCH

One of the most striking features of the Christianity of Western Europe in the four centuries from 950 to 1350 was intense intellectual activity. The vitality which was seen in the geographic spread of the faith, the creation of many new forms of monasticism, the emergence of movements deemed heretical by the Catholic Church, and the efforts through the hierarchy led by the Papacy to render the faith dominant in all aspects of life also gave rise to theological ferment. A large proportion of the intelligentsia of Western Christendom directed their attention to the problems presented by the Gospel. Theology became a major subject of study, "the queen of the sciences." Some of the ablest minds that mankind has ever known were stimulated by it to profound thought. Thousands of lesser minds were engaged by it. What the Roman Catholic Church of the twentieth century adjudged the standard formulation of theology was by Thomas Aquinas, of the thirteenth century, but it was the culmination of three centuries of discussion and debate.

As order began to reappear in the West after the centuries of invasions and cultural decay, it was not strange that men applied their minds to the faith which was part of their heritage. They availed themselves of what had been written in the years before the darkness had descended. They addressed themselves to the New Testament, to the scholars of the early Church, and especially to Augustine and Gregory the Great. We have noted the rebirth of theological activity under the peace and security given by the great Carolingians, a revival which the decay of that line and the coming of the Vikings made abortive. Now the tide of thought once more rose.

As in other expressions of Christianity, in this period there was much more of vigour and creativity in the Western wing of the Catholic Church than in the churches of the East. The reasons for the contrast in the intellectual realm are probably those which accounted for it in the other aspects of the faith. We have already sought to discover them and we will recur to them in a later chapter.

THE RISE OF SCHOLASTICISM

Thought about Christianity in Western Europe in this period was closely associated with what is usually called scholasticism. Scholasticism was the achievement of the school men. It arose from the schools of the period and found its most marked development in connexion with them. Its inception was in the intellectual and religious revival under the Carolingians and its first great figure was John Scotus Eriugena. It was renewed in the eleventh century in some of the monasteries, notably Bec, in Normandy, and in schools maintained under the auspices of cathedrals. It continued in the universities which arose late in the twelfth and in the thirteenth century. Paris was the chief but by no means the only centre of scholastic theology. Near or associated with its cathedral were schools made famous by great teachers. Here sprang up the institution which was to be the type for numbers of universities in the north of Europe. An association or guild of teachers, it made theology its major subject. The other outstanding early university, Bologna, was, as we have seen, especially famous for law. Universities multiplied in the thirteenth and fourteenth centuries. They were chiefly ecclesiastical foundations, obtaining their charters from the Pope. While one might be best known for law and another for medicine, normally theology was an honoured subject in them all.

An outstanding objective of the school men was to ascertain the relation of faith and reason. It was a problem which had confronted Christian thinkers long before the school men and which continued to challenge them long after scholasticism was considered by many to be outmoded. Is what the Christian believes to have been given by God in the long process of revelation which culminated in Christ consistent with reason or are the two contradictory? If they are compatible, which should have priority, the faith by which the Christian accepts and commits himself fully to what has been given in the divine revelation and transmitted through the Church, or man's reason? Can reason demonstrate as true what the Christian believes about God? If it cannot, does what is received by faith complement what is reached by reason or do the two contradict each other? If reason seems to deny what the Christian accepts on faith as given by God, shall the Christian accord his reason priority and throw over as false what he has received through faith or can he find some way of holding to both? These were among the basic questions with which scholasticism wrestled.

In addressing itself to its task scholasticism employed the intellectual apparatus which it had inherited from the pre-Christian Græco-Roman world.

This was Greek philosophy, and especially what had been written by Plato and Aristotle. At the outset few of the school men could read Greek. Their lectures and discussions were carried on in Latin. Only portions of the works of Aristotle and of those in the Platonic tradition were available to them in that language. However, enough of Aristotle was accessible to enable them to employ Aristotelian logic. It was by means of this logic or dialectic with its syllogisms that they engaged in intellectual activity. They also were familiar with a work by the Neoplatonic Porphyry.

As the centuries wore on, more of the writings of Greek philosophers reached the school men. Especially notable was the influence of additional works of Aristotle. Some of these came in Arabic translations. The Moslem Arabs had first made contact with the Greek philosophers through the Nestorians, especially through Nisibis, that centre of Nestorian theological education. Nestorian scholars possessed Syriac translations of the Greek originals. By them translations were made into Arabic for their new rulers. Jewish philosophers were also seeking to work through their faith in terms of Greek thought. In the portions of Spain ruled by Moslems were schools controlled by the Arabs in which Christians and Jews as well as Moslems studied. Partly through them more of Greek thought became available to the Christian scholars of Western Europe.

Western Christendom also became acquainted with Jewish and Moslem Arab thinkers who had been influenced by Greek philosophy. Among the Jews Maimonides (1135–1204), a warm admirer of Aristotle, was especially read. Among the Moslems were Alfarabi, Algazel, and particularly Avicenna. Outstanding in his effect upon later scholasticism was Averroes or Averrhoes, a daring and prolific native of Cordova of the twelfth century. By the end of the twelfth century much of his work was available in Latin translations.

Under the impact of this Greek thought, either coming directly or through Moslem Arab intermediaries, the active and eager minds of the Christian scholars of Western Europe were stimulated and shaped as they addressed themselves to theology.

As we describe the theological activity of these centuries it will become apparent that it differed markedly from that of the first five centuries of Christianity. In general it took as settled the issues around which had centered that earlier period of creative Christian debate. Gnosticism had disappeared. The stark dualism represented by Marcion was present in the Cathari but for the majority of Christians in the West it was no longer an open question. The relationship of Christ to the Father and of the balance of the divine and human in Jesus were accepted as defined in the historic creeds of the Catholic Church.

At times, indeed, the school men seemed to be following slavishly what had come to them from the first centuries of their faith. They quoted as authoritative the Scriptures and the Christian thinkers whom they esteemed as the fathers.

Yet the greatest of the school men were far from being parrots. Men like Anselm and Thomas Aquinas had as acute and powerful intellects as had Origen or Augustine. In inquiring into the relation between faith and reason they were wrestling with issues quite as basic as those presented by the Gnostics, the Marcionites, the Arians, and the Monophysites. Although using the thought forms of Greek philosophy which were at their hands, the best of them were bringing to bear as keen, courageous, and honest minds as had either the pre-Christian or the Christian predecessors whom they revered. Building on the answers given by earlier generations, they were either asking whether these could be validated afresh or were putting in new ways old questions, such as the meaning of the death of Christ. Moreover, they were concerned more with the nature and attributes of God than had been their predecessors in the first five centuries.

REALISM AND NOMINALISM

An issue which appeared early in scholasticism and continued throughout its course was that between realism and nominalism. The division led to vigorous and often bitter debates. Philosophical in its origin, it had important religious implications.

Realism, which went back to its early formulator, Plato, declared that universals have an existence which is independent of the mind of the thinker. According to this view, general terms represent reality. Species and genera exist apart from the individual units embraced by them. For instance, "man" is not a figment of the imagination which the mind constructs to lump together the millions of beings called men, but in itself is an entity. Among other things, when applied to theology this means that man or mankind has a unity which has been corrupted by the sin of the first man, Adam. The saving work of Christ is for all mankind and not for isolated individual men, and the Church is more than the sum of individual Christians or local congregations. We can more readily believe in the Trinity if we regard as real a divine inclusive essence which is in Father, Son, and Holy Spirit. The realist held that the idea of the universals in the mind of God becomes the ground for the existence of individual things and beings.

Nominalism, on the other hand, maintained that only particular things are real, and that universals are merely words coined by the intellect. To put it in another way, such terms as man, city, nation, animal, and Church are concepts of the mind and only individual objects and events exist. Men, seeing what they believe to be resemblances between objects, invent abstract terms and group individual objects under them.

Between extreme realists and nominalists gradations were found. For example, some moderate realists held that the idea in God's mind is not precisely reproduced in the characteristics of a species and that the concept which is nourished in a man's mind of what constitutes a species is not entirely the same as the actual characteristics of the species. To give one illustration: the species "cow" does not exactly reflect what was in the mind of God; and what man perceives in the species "cow" is not altogether what is in that species.

GREAT LANDMARKS IN SCHOLASTICISM: ANSELM

It would be aside from our purpose to give a detailed account of the history of scholastic theology. We must content ourselves with saying something of its outstanding figures, individuals who loom up as landmarks. Of these the first to draw our attention is Anselm (c.1033 or c.1034–1109).

We have had occasion to mention Anselm more than once. Coming from Italy, he joined the monastic community of Bec in Normandy and became the outstanding intellectual light in an early expression of the monastic revival. Called by the execrable William Rufus in a moment of panic-stricken remorse to succeed Lanfranc as Archbishop of Canterbury, Anselm took the post only from a sense of duty. In it he had a prolonged conflict with the difficult William and with the latter's successor, the much stronger Henry I, over the issue of the lay control of the Church. His whole-souled committal to the reform movement is attested by the welcome given him at Cluny during his exile from his see. Through reluctant necessity Anselm was an administrator. He was also, but not unwillingly, a man of prayer who left behind him a guide for meditation and spiritual self-examination. He was, moreover, a pastor who as prior, abbot, and archbishop had much at heart the welfare of his flock. He cared for them one by one as individuals as well as in groups.

Anselm combined charm with firmness, gentleness with strength, sanctity with sagacity. Humble in spirit, without ambition for personal power or preferment, he was painfully conscious of his unworthiness in the sight of God. A contemporary of Hildebrand, he left as deep an impress upon Christian theology as the great Pope did on the See of Peter. Highly disciplined, penetrating, careful, and precise, much of Anselm's writing on theology was packed into small compass and yet is amazingly clear. Some of it was done in his days at Bec. Much of it was accomplished during his sojourns on the Continent, exiled because of his conflicts with the monarchs of England. Steeped in Augustine, Anselm did not slavishly reproduce that great master, but did his own thinking. He was a realist in philosophy and theology. Seeing no conflict between faith and reason, he took the familiar position of believing that he might understand and accepted through faith what was taught by the Church, but he held that the truth of what was thus received could be demonstrated by the processes of the intellect and could be supported by reason. Indeed, he maintained that the major tenets of Christianity, such as belief in God, the nature of God, the Trinity, immortality, and the incarnation, death, and resurrection of Christ, could be reached by reason and were the inescapable accompaniments of a rational view of the universe. His most famous theological works were his *Monologium* (*A Soliloquy*), *Proslogium* (*A Discourse*), and *Cur Deus Homo* (*Why God-man*).

The *Monologium* was composed at the insistent request of students. In it Anselm engaged in a meditation on the being of God. He was keenly aware of Augustine's writings and believed that he was not setting forth anything which was contrary to them. He held that there is a Being which is the best, the greatest, and the highest of all existing beings; that whatever is, exists through Something; that this Something, this Nature, derives existence from Itself, not from something else, and all beings derive existence through this Nature; and that this Nature created all things out of nothing, but that before their creation the idea of them existed in the mind of the Creator. Thence Anselm goes on to deduce by rational processes the main features of this Nature, this Supreme Being. Without appealing to the Bible he seeks to prove and describe the Trinity, the Father, the Son, and the Holy Spirit proceeding from the Father and the Son, and to arrive at the conclusions set forth in the great creeds of the Catholic Church.

The *Proslogium* seems to have come to Anselm as the culmination of long mental and spiritual struggle with the problem which it sets forth. The agony was so intense that it deprived him of appetite and sleep and robbed him of peace in his devotions. Then, suddenly, in the night, light broke and he quickly wrote down what it brought to him. Here, in a treatise of only a few pages, Anselm set forth what is often called the ontological argument for the existence of God. Anselm held that God is that Being than which nothing greater can be conceived to exist. This Being is obviously greater than one which can be conceived not to exist. God must exist in reality and not only in man's thought, for if he were merely a figment of the imagination, a Being which has actual being as well as being pictured in man's mind could be conceived of as existing. The latter must be true. To put it in still other words, reason demands the idea of a perfect Being, lacking in nothing; the idea of a perfect Being is of necessity the idea of Being which has existence, for a Being which lacks existence would not be perfect. God, so Anselm held, is not only that Being than which nothing greater can be conceived, but is greater than can be conceived. From this point Anselm went on to develop the characteristics, or attributes of God much as in the *Monologium*. In subsequent centuries, it must be noted, several of the most acute philosophical minds of the Occident, among them Descartes and Kant, examined Anselm's argument for the existence of God, some to refute it and some to affirm it.

In *Cur Deus Homo* Anselm dealt with the incarnation and the atonement. To put it in somewhat different language from that which he employed, Anselm held that since by his sin man had flaunted the will of God, God whose will governs the universe, God could not disregard that sin without upsetting the moral order of the entire creation. Even though in His mercy He might wish to overlook man's transgression He could not do so without being immoral, and this would be contrary to His nature. To maintain the moral order satisfaction must be given. That satisfaction must be fully equal to the offense. Since the sin is man's, satisfaction must be given by man. Yet man has nothing which he can offer to God over and above what he already owes to God, for even if he always perfectly conformed to God's will he would be but doing his duty. However, if man were not to be redeemed from his sin, God would be frustrated, for in creating man God intended him to choose and enjoy the supreme good, which is God Himself. While none but man can make the satisfaction to compensate for man's sin, only God can make that satisfaction, for the satisfaction must be greater than anything in the universe except God. That satisfaction, therefore, must be made by one who is both God and man. For that reason God became incarnate in Jesus. God did not under-take a fresh creation of man, for a fresh creation could not have made satis- faction for the descendants of sinful Adam. He was born, therefore, of Mary, of the seed of Adam. Of the three persons of the Trinity, only the Son, begotten of the Father before all worlds, could be incarnate, for if one of the other persons had been born of Mary there would have been two sons. By the incar-nation, Jesus Christ, fully God and fully man, and only he, could make the needed satisfaction and enable God to forgive man without doing violence to the moral balance of the universe.

It has often been suggested that in his view of the atonement Anselm was influenced by the legal patterns of his day. These permitted the substitution of a money payment for the return of an eye for an eye or a life for a life. Anselm, so it is said, regarded the God-man, Jesus Christ, as making that substitution by his sufferings and death. It may be that Anselm thought in these terms. However, his insight was more penetrating and his view more comprehensive than the conventions of feudal society and their Teutonic background. There are hints of similar insights in Gregory the Great, with his rootage in Roman law, and, still further back, in the Old and New Testaments.

Anselm's theological contributions were not limited to the three treatises which we have summarized, important though these were. He opposed the doctrine of the Trinity as set forth by John Roscelin, who seems to have been a nominalist, denying the reality of universals, and thus to have thought of the Trinity as Three Gods. Anselm so forcefully argued against him that for several generations nominalism was discredited in the Catholic Church. He cogently presented the argument for the procession of the Holy Spirit from the Father and the Son, justifying the *filioque* clause as against the Eastern wing of the Catholic Church. In his very last hours he was wrestling with the age-long problem of how to reconcile the freedom of man's will with the omniscient foreknowledge and the predetermination of God. To these as to the other problems with which he dealt, Anselm brought the clarity of thought and the facility for verbal expression which were characteristic of him.

Great Landmarks in Scholasticism: Abélard

From Anselm we move on to one of his younger contemporaries, Peter Abélard (or Abailard). Probably born in 1079, Abélard was about thirty years of age and in the flush of his fame and his stormy career when the great archbishop breathed his last. Dying in 1142, he lived a third of a century after Anselm had been gathered to his fathers. Also a contemporary of Bernard of Clairvaux, with whom he was to have unhappy relations, his life was set at a time and in a country in which great tides of spiritual awakening were flowing. It was a period of intellectual ferment when students were thronging the schools which, flourishing, were the precursors of the university movement of a generation or two later. Daring architects were venturing from the inherited heavy Romanesque into the soaring Gothic. Here was an era to stir the pulses of sensitive, intellectually alert spirits.

Abélard both shared and contributed to the brilliance of the age. He was a striking and somewhat contradictory figure. Possessed of a rapier-like intellect, he thrived on debate. Charming, keen, a stimulating teacher to whom the atmosphere of the lecture room was as the breath of life, he attracted throngs of students. Intellectually eager and inquiring, but also arrogant, he rejoiced in challenging accepted beliefs and in worsting rivals in debate, including his own elders and teachers. Yet there was in him a deep strain of religious sensitivity and insight and from him came one of the most influential interpretations of the atonement. In spite of his questioning, he was a sincere Christian and held it to be the function of reason using Aristotelian logic to refute error and illumine the truth which comes through divine revelation and is apprehended by faith.

Abélard was born in Brittany not far from Nantes and of aristocratic stock.

His father had a bent towards learning and since both parents later adopted the monastic life, supposedly they were more than conventionally religious and surrounded their son's infancy with a devout atmosphere. Abélard early developed a hunger for learning. He went to various centres, in some places worsting his teachers, and eventually became the most popular of the lecturers in Paris. At first primarily a student and teacher of philosophy, later he gave himself more to theology.

At the height of his early fame Abélard was attracted by the beautiful and educated Héloïse, niece of a canon of the cathedral in Paris, sought her companionship by becoming her tutor and an inmate of her uncle's home, and won her love. Then came heartbreak. He had a child by her and against her protests, for she wished not to hamper his career by the more formal bond, was secretly married to her. Her uncle, infuriated by the entire affair, had ruffians break in on him and emasculate him. At Abélard's desire Héloïse became a nun. She declared that she had ever wished to please him more than God. He became a monk and had a tempestuous time in the monastic houses of which he became successively a member. Some of the letters of Abélard to Héloïse after their separation are among the most poignant in literature.

Students continued to flock to Abélard. He wrote extensively. One of his more famous books was *Sic et Non* (*Yes and No*). Intended for beginners, it listed several scores of questions on science, ethics, and theology, and for each gave quotations from the Scriptures and the Fathers which seemed to support contradictory answers. The book was meant to be provocative and to stimulate independent thinking. Yet Abélard never made reason supreme. To him faith and reason went hand in hand.

Abélard antagonized many. His enemies had him haled before a council at Soissons in 1121 for heresy. In 1140, largely at the instance of Bernard of Clairvaux, who regarded as subversive to the faith some of his teachings, including his views on the Trinity, the atonement, free will, and original sin, Abélard was condemned by a council at Sens. The two men were opposites in temperament. Abélard, while honestly Christian and conforming and submitting to the Catholic Church, was the intellectual, daring, acute, not content to accept conventional phraseology. Moreover, in reacting against nominalism which tended to think of the Trinity as three Gods, Abélard took a position which verged on monarchianism and laid himself open to the charge of Sabellianism. Bernard was a mystic, stressing the divine love, and was not a speculative theologian. Intensely committed to the historic formulas of the faith and the generally accepted views, he regarded Abélard as a dangerous rationalist. Since both were prominent, they could not but clash. Bernard, more forceful and more influential in ecclesiastical circles, carried the authorities with him. Abélard appealed to Rome, the Pope confirmed the condemnation, and he was excommunicated. Cluny gave him refuge, he and Bernard were reconciled, and his last months were spent in prayer and reading.

In philosophy, in his penetrating fashion Abélard pointed out weaknesses in both nominalism and realism. In addition to his *Sic et Non* and his remarkable stimulus to individual pupils, Abélard's distinctive contributions to theology were chiefly his teaching about ethics and the atonement.

In ethics Abélard held that sin is not alone in the overt act but primarily in the motive. He rejected the view of original sin which was found in Augustine. He held that mankind does not share in the guilt of Adam's sin, but that all, through the sin of Adam, share in the punishment meted out to Adam. However, so he maintained, every human being can coöperate with the grace of God and by good works escape that punishment. To be sure, men have weaknesses which incline them to sin, but in themselves these do not bring guilt to men. Men also have tendencies to good. By reason, which is the gift of God to man, individuals can discover what is good. They can then employ their wills to follow the good. Sin or the absence of sin lies in the motive, the intention, with which men act. The growing practice of auricular confession to a priest, Abélard held, could not be for the purpose of obtaining absolution, for the power to retain or remit sins which Christ gave his apostles was not transmitted to the bishops, and unless the verdict of the bishop accorded with divine justice it would possess no validity.

Abélard's view of the atonement is usually called, but not with precise accuracy, the moral influence theory. He rejected the position set forth by Anselm that the satisfaction made by Jesus Christ was necessary for the forgiveness of sins, for, he pointed out, God had forgiven sins before Christ came. If, he argued, forgiveness is an act of grace, it must be free and without demand for compensation for sin. In contrast, Abélard declared, God is love and has voluntarily assumed the burden of suffering brought on by man's sin. This act of God's grace, taken freely and without the necessity of making satisfaction for sin, awakens in men gratitude and love for God. In Jesus Christ, who is both man and God, men see what men should be, by contrast are brought to a realization of their sin, and by God's love seen in Christ are won to a response which releases new springs of love which issue in right conduct. In this fashion the sinner becomes a new creation, a different self.

Opinions differ as to the effect which Abélard had on later theological thought. Some hold it to have been transient. Others believe it to have been marked and continuing. Without attempting to determine which of these estimates is correct, we can at least be certain that here was an outstanding figure in the theological activity of the Europe of that period.

Great Landmarks in Scholasticism: Hugo of St. Victor

A contemporary of Abélard and Bernard of Clairvaux, a critic of the former and a friend of the latter, was Hugo (or Hugh) of St. Victor (1096–1141). Son of a Saxon count and educated in Germany, he spent most of his adult life as a member of the community of Augustinian canons of St. Victor, in Paris. This community had a school which was famous at the time. Hugo taught in it and wrote extensively. His works included commentaries on several books of the Bible and the rule of Augustine, and disquisitions on the moral life, the way of the mystic, and various questions of theology. By far his largest treatise was *De Sacramentis Fidei Christianae*. Although this work had the sacraments as its title, it was actually a comprehensive survey of theology, beginning with the creation, God, and the Trinity, going on to the fall of man, original sin, and the incarnation, and then dealing more at length with the sacraments. Hugo divided knowledge into two branches, theology and philosophy. He saw no necessary conflict between them. Some truths in theology, so he held, are to be proved by reason; some, while not demonstrable through reason, are in accord with reason, while still others cannot be discerned through unaided reason but come through revelation apprehended by faith. Man has three gates or organs through which knowledge comes to him—his physical eye, the eye of the mind, and the eye of the spirit. Hugo was a mystic, and he valued highly what entered through the eye of the spirit by what he called contemplation.

We are to say more of the sacraments in the next chapter, but we must pause to notice that Hugo defined a sacrament as a "physical or material element presented clearly to the senses, by similitude representing, by institution signifying, and by consecration containing an invisible and spiritual grace." In other words, a sacrament is not only a sign or symbol of a sacred thing but it is the physical medium through which grace operates. Hugo came out clearly for transubstantiation in the Eucharist. This view was by no means novel, but it had recently been a subject of vigorous debate. Berengar, head of the cathedral school at Tours, had fairly recently denounced transubstantiation and in doing so had aroused Lanfranc to step forward in its defense. Within less than a century after the death of Hugo, the Fourth Lateran Council, as we have seen, made it the official position of the Western wing of the Catholic Church.

Great Landmarks in Scholasticism: Peter Lombard

Peter Lombard was chiefly distinguished as the author of the *Sentences,* the most widely used text-book in theology in Western Europe during the Middle Ages. Because of that fact he was often known as the Master of the Sentences or just the Master. A contemporary of Abélard, Bernard of Clairvaux, and Hugo of St. Victor, he was a native of Novara, a few miles west of Milan, then regarded as being in Lombardy. Educated at Bologna, he went to Paris, taught there in the cathedral school, and for a brief time in his later years was Archbishop of Paris. Although critical of him, he was influenced by Abélard. Hugo of St. Victor also made an impression on him. He was deeply indebted to Augustine, John of Damascus, and Gratian the canonist.

The *Quatuor Libri Sententiarum* is briefly described by its title. It was made up of four books. The first treated of God, His nature, the Trinity, the attributes of God, and predestination. The second was devoted to God's creation, including angels, but principally man, sin, free-will, and the need of redemption. The third dealt mainly with the work of redemption through Christ, including the question of whether Christ had not only love for man but also faith and hope, in other words, whether Christ was fully human. The fruits of the Spirit were covered, and the seven cardinal virtues. The fourth book was chiefly concerned with the sacraments and eschatology. The method of treatment was to assemble pertinent quotations from the fathers revered by the Catholic Church.

In a certain sense the *Sentences* were pedestrian and not a work of creative thought. However, had they been merely pedestrian they would not have enjoyed the popularity and prolonged and extensive use that was theirs. They were extraordinarily comprehensive and skilfully compiled. They covered the field of Christian theology and the subjects which were of interest to the teachers and students of the time. They raised the pertinent questions, and, employing the prevalent dialectic method, explained and interpreted them and brought together passages from the outstanding authorities which would best throw light on them. In the day before printing had reduced the cost and when teachers and students could own few books, the Bible and Peter's Lombard's *Sentences* provided what were deemed the essentials for a theological education.

THE HIGH TIDE OF SCHOLASTICISM

In the latter part of the twelfth and in the thirteenth century scholasticism reached the peak of its popularity and creativity. Commerce was increasing, towns and cities were growing, new ideas were flooding in from abroad through Jewish and Arab scholars and contacts with the East by way of merchants and Crusaders. More works of the great Greek philosophers were becoming available in Latin, partly through translations from Arabic, and partly through the Latin occupation of Constantinople, bringing as it did Western Europe into intimate touch with that centre of Greek learning. Especially was more of Aristotle becoming known. He was often called the

Philosopher, so head and shoulders above the other masters of thought was he regarded. Universities were springing up and were covering a wider range of knowledge than had the earlier monastic and cathedral schools. At the same time the mendicant orders were coming into being, both stimulants and products of the religious awakening. As we have seen, the Dominicans and Franciscans early attached themselves to the rising universities, the one through the deliberate plan and the other in spite of the protest of the founder. Among the many caught up in these two orders were some minds of high quality. Inspired by their faith and having their energies channeled through it by their dedication to the religious life, they devoted themselves to theology. From these orders came the men who in the thirteenth and fourteenth centuries brought scholastic theology to its apex.

We can simply make brief mention of a few of the outstanding names. In general, the Franciscans tended to hold the traditional Platonic and Augustinian views and, while not unfamiliar with him, were less committed to Aristotle than were most of the Dominicans and at times were very critical of him.

Prominent among their great scholars was John of Fidanza (1221–1274), better known as Bonaventura and called the *doctor seraphicus*. We have already met him as a head of the Franciscans. He refused the Archbishopric of York but towards the end of his life, reluctantly and at the insistence of the Pope, became Bishop of Albano and cardinal. A mystic, influenced by Neoplatonism through Augustine and the writings ascribed to Dionysius the Areopagite, he held that the highest knowledge comes through union with God, a union which is to be reached through meditation and prayer. For him Aristotelianism was anathema, an error on which to pass judgement. He knew and used the scholastic dialectic and his theological writings won respect.

Bonaventura had as one of his teachers an Englishman, Alexander of Hales, who in his mid-fifties became a Franciscan and was known as the *doctor irrefragabilis*. Alexander of Hales was familiar with Aristotle and sought to reconcile Augustinianism with it. Robert Grosseteste, who died in 1253, while not a Franciscan, was friendly to the members of the order and was their first teacher of theology when they established a house at Oxford. A great scholar, he was expert in the mathematics and natural sciences of the day. He wrote commentaries on Aristotle and helped to give currency in Western Europe to that philosophy. But he also knew Neoplatonism, John of Damascus, and the writings of the pseudo-Dionysius, and tried to bring Augustinianism into accord with Aristotle. As Bishop of Lincoln from 1235 to his death in 1253, Grosseteste was known as a leader in reforming the clergy and stood out for the independence of the bishops from royal control. He also protested against the financial exactions of the Pope and the Papal curia.

· At the outset of the growing interest in Aristotle, many of the bishops feared it as a threat to the inherited faith, coming as that had so largely through Augustine and those influenced by Augustine and hence with a Platonic slant. Moreover, the additional works of Aristotle had first become known through the Spanish schools and were interpreted with an Averroist slant, a trend which was subversive to historic Christian teachings. For instance, Averroes denied personal immortality. Averroism held that reason is supreme as a way to truth and there were Averroists who maintained that some things are true when reached by faith but false when tested by reason. Even more basically the Averroists believed that the material world is without beginning or end, that all the universe, including God and man, is governed by immutable necessity, and that far from having free will and reaching out to discover truth, we receive it passively from the cosmic mind. In this cosmic mind with its denial of persons who are free agents lay the ground for the rejection of individual immortality. In the light of such views, it is quite understandable that the authorities of the Catholic Church took alarm at the popularity of Aristotle as interpreted by Averroes. Here was a heresy which might lure the intellectuals from the Christian faith and be even more of a peril than the Cathari and Waldensees. Good churchmen were, accordingly, critical of those who attempted to reconcile Christian theology with Aristotle.

Yet the great Dominican theologians boldly thought through the Christian faith in terms of Aristotelian patterns. Their work was facilitated by fresh translations of Aristotle made directly into Latin which removed some of the fears of the conservatives. The two most prominent of the Dominican school men were Albert of Cologne, better known as Albertus Magnus and called *doctor universalis,* and Thomas Aquinas.

Albertus Magnus (c.1193 or c.1206–1280) was born in Germany, possibly of aristocratic and certainly of wealthy stock. He studied at various centres, among them some Italian cities. In his youth, while in Italy, he was caught up in the enthusiasm of the early days of the Order of Preachers and joined himself to it. He taught in several places in Germany and became famous as a lecturer in Paris. He later taught at Cologne, was head of the German province of his order, for a brief time was Bishop of Ratisbon, a post which he took reluctantly at Papal behest that he might work a reformation in the diocese, and then, that task accomplished, at his own request was permitted to lay down the burden. Later he travelled widely in Germany, preaching. He spent most of his last years in Cologne.

Although actively engaged in the affairs of his order and of the Church for much of his life, Albertus Magnus was a scholar of no mean dimensions. He did much to popularize Aristotle among the learned circles of Western Europe. Deeply interested in wide ranges of natural science, he studied those portions of Aristotle which were devoted to that subject and added the fruits of his own independent observations. Some of the latter anticipated the results of nineteenth and twentieth century science. He was also intimately familiar with the Bible and wrote commentaries on it. He was, too, a distinguished theologian. He was not unacquainted with Neoplatonic thought. However, he systematically employed Aristotle in his approach to theology and attempted to make this great pre-Christian Greek an aid to Christian thought.

THE PRINCE OF THE SCHOOL MEN: THOMAS AQUINAS

One of the major contributions of Albertus Magnus was to the thought of Thomas Aquinas. In Thomas Aquinas we come to the high point in the achievement of scholasticism. Endowed with a penetrating and synthesizing mind, he applied the methods of the school men to theology and employed Aristotle in such fashion that he produced what the Roman Catholic Church was eventually to regard as its standard formulation of theology. A close student of Aristotle, he made full use of that philosopher in his attempt to think through and set forth in systematic fashion the whole range of Christian theology. Yet he did not follow him slavishly.

Thomas Aquinas, known also as *doctor angelicus* and *doctor communis,* was born at the end of the year 1224 or at the beginning of 1225, at Roccasecca, not far from Monte Cassino. His father was Count of Aquino and was related to the imperial house of Hohenstaufen. At a tender age Thomas was placed in the monastery of Monte Cassino, the mother house of the Benedictines, there to be educated under the supervision of his uncle, the abbot. He early showed an inquiring mind and an aptitude for study. At about the age of nineteen he was attracted, as were so many others of the high born young intellectuals of the day, to the Order of Preachers. His mother and brothers, angered by this step, seized him and kept him in confinement for over a year, hoping to dissuade him. However, he persevered, made his escape, went to Paris, and there studied with Albertus Magnus. He was in Paris midway in the reign of Louis IX, the Saint, when the university was in the heyday of its youth. After about three years he went to Cologne, there to continue his education under the direction of Albertus Magnus. For a time he was known as the "dumb ox," so quiet was he and so large of frame. Yet before long his unusual mental capacity became apparent. In his mid-twenties he declined appointment to be Abbot of Monte Cassino. Back once more in the University of Paris, he was a friend of Bonaventura. He began teaching at an early age and soon rose to distinction,

Years of teaching and writing followed, some of them in Paris, some in Spain, many of them in several centres in Italy, then again in Paris, and at the last in Naples. Several of his years in Italy were spent as a member of the Papal court. On one occasion he refused the Archbishopric of Naples urged on him by one of the Popes.

Thomas Aquinas regarded his vocation as that of the scholar, teacher, and writer. To this he gave himself with single-minded commitment. His labours were prodigious and his literary output enormous. Calm, kindly, quietly charming, chary of words except in the line of duty, he concentrated on thought. Yet he was primarily and deeply religious. He wrote hymns and commentaries on the Scriptures as well as philosophy and theology and assisted in the inauguration of the feast of Corpus Christi. Although unusually tall and bulky, his body was frail and could not indefinitely stand up under the strain to which his devotion to study subjected it. He died when about forty-nine years of age, deeply mourned, especially by his fellow Dominican and former teacher, Albertus Magnus.

Almost unfailingly calm and modest, Thomas Aquinas was from time to time drawn into controversy. In the struggle of the secular clergy to oust the friars from the University of Paris he came out boldly and eventually successfully on behalf of the Dominicans. He entered into debate with Averroists who were prominent in the University of Paris and argued that their distinctive views which were giving offense to the orthodox were based upon a false interpretation of Aristotle. An Aristotelian, intimately familiar with that scholar's work, he contended for the Philosopher against the conservatives who feared him as endangering the Augustinian theology which had been dominant in the Western Church. Among his opponents were a few in his own order but especially some of the Franciscans, for the members of that order, as we have seen, were inclined more towards Augustine and his Platonism.

Thomas Aquinas had the gift not only of clarity of mind, but also of facility of statement and a comprehensive intellect. Deeply indebted to Albertus Magnus, he put into orderly form what the latter had given him. He was by no means a slavish transmitter and on some points differed from his great teacher. He was not as much interested in natural science as was Albert, for he was exclusively a philosopher and theologian. Here he surpassed his mentor in range and inclusiveness of thought and systematic statement.

The great achievement of Thomas Aquinas was setting forth the relation of reason and faith in such fashion that those to whom the Aristotelian philosophy was definitive could feel that they might consistently remain Christians. As we have seen, the introduction to the full range of Aristotle's thought by the translation of his works into Latin had brought stimulus to the minds of

Western Europeans. In the thirteenth century he enjoyed a great vogue among a large proportion of the intellectuals of Western Europe. The task to which Aquinas set himself was the reconciliation of Aristotle with the Christian faith. He did this from profound conviction, especially since he believed that Plato, whom many were following, did not have the correct answers to man's quest.

Of the many works which came from the pen of Thomas Aquinas, the two which present his thought most comprehensively are his *Summa Contra Gentiles,* designed to equip missionaries to the Moslems with arguments in the presentation of their faith, and his *Summa* or *Summa Theologiae* (less correctly *Summa Theologica,* a form legitimatized by long usage), a massive work left uncompleted by his early death.

As we have said, Aquinas was critical of Plato. To Plato ideas or forms were real. Aquinas rejected this position. He was not a realist in the scholastic meaning of that term. He therefore also differed from Augustine and his Neoplatonic framework. To him, as to Aristotle, knowledge is based upon what the senses perceive. The data provided through the senses when interpreted by reason are a road to knowledge. Yet, while holding to the principles of Aristotle, Aquinas went beyond Aristotle, for the latter was not a Christian and Aquinas was preëminently held by that faith. To Aquinas faith is also a road to truth. Much of truth is not to be reached by reason. It comes by way of revelation from God and is to be appropriated by faith, that is, by feeling and will. As part of nature, man can know nature through his senses and reason, so Aquinas held. But Aquinas believed that man is also supernatural, and that man's ultimate happiness consists in contemplating God. That goal, so he declared, is not to be fully attained in this life, nor can it be reached by man's unaided intellect. The vision of God which is man's highest goal can come only through the outpouring of the divine goodness. Through that vision man is made a partaker of eternal life. However, so Aquinas taught, since God is the origin of both nature and revelation, both reason and faith are from Him and cannot be in conflict with each other, nor can the knowledge reached through the senses and reason contradict the truth which is given through revelation and apprehended through faith.

Aquinas held that the existence of God can be demonstrated on the basis of the knowledge which we obtain through our senses and our reason. He rejected both the view that the existence of God is self-evident, as Anselm had maintained, and that it cannot be proved but must be accepted on faith alone. He also taught that the attributes of God, such as that He is one, good, and infinite, can be confidently affirmed, partly through reason and partly through faith, and that God can be known by man. Aquinas went on to maintain that everything which exists has been created and is sustained by God. God creates what is out of what is not.

Having dealt extensively with God, Thomas Aquinas proceeded to speak of man. He described his soul and the various powers of the soul. Aquinas was to a certain degree a determinist, although in a somewhat masked form. To be sure, the will, so he held, is moved only by itself and not by its environment. But, he taught, God moves all His creatures, including man, in accordance with their natures. Yet Aquinas was not a determinist in the Moslem Averroist sense of that term. In stressing the competence of human reason he went far towards free will, even though he believed it to be limited.

As we have said, to Aquinas the end of man is the vision of God. All beings, including man, are subject to the law of God. This law has eternally existed in the mind of God. In the created world it is reflected in the law of nature, or the natural law. To assist man in knowing that law, God gave the divine law as it is seen in the Old Testament. That law was meant to guide man. Man, through his will, can conform to the law of nature, but partly through ignorance and partly through the misuse of his will he has failed to do so. Although marred by sin, man can still cultivate the four natural virtues—prudence, justice, courage, and self-control. However, it is only through God's grace that the distinctively Christian virtues, faith, hope, and love, can come to man. Only by God's grace, which man can never earn, can man be changed and attain to the vision of God. Grace, according to Aquinas, is both the divine act of God, undeserved by man, and its effect in "a certain supernatural thing in man coming into existence from God." He agreed with Augustine that "without grace men can do no good whatever" and that by its light they know what to do and by its help do what they know. Grace is a new birth wrought in the Christian by the creative act of God. Aquinas regarded grace as prevenient, that is, it is what stirs a man to the repentance on which the new birth is conditioned, and it enables man to repent. When the new birth has been wrought, grace continues to enable the Christian both to will and to work in such fashion as to please God.

Because man sinned, so Aquinas said, God became incarnate in Christ, the God-man. Christ was born of the Virgin Mary. Aquinas could not go as far as the Franciscans, who held to the immaculate conception, that is, that Mary was herself conceived without the taint of original sin, a view which in the nineteenth century the Roman Catholic Church explicitly and formally endorsed. He declared that it is proper to venerate Mary as the mother of Christ, but he did not believe it to be necessary to hold that she was miraculously conceived. It is primarily through Jesus Christ, so Aquinas said, that God's grace is mediated to man. Jesus Christ is teacher, Messiah, priest, and sacrifice.

Through the sufferings and death of Christ man is freed from the power of evil and from the penalty for sin and is reconciled to God. Aquinas combined the views of Anselm and Abélard on the atonement, holding that Christ both made satisfaction for man's sin and moved men to love.

Grace, so Aquinas maintained, comes to man through the sacraments. The sacraments derive their efficacy from the passion of Christ. The sacraments are means through which the grace operates which comes through Christ. God works through them. They are dependent for their power upon God and not upon the attitudes of those to whom they are administered. Their effect, so Aquinas declared, is *ex opere operato,* namely, from the act of performing them.

THE SIGNIFICANCE OF AQUINAS

How significant was Thomas Aquinas? Why is it that we have called him the prince of the school men? He was not an innovator in Christian doctrine. That must be apparent even in the brief summary which we have given of his teachings. What he wished to do was to present the historic Christian faith as held by the Catholic Church. We have seen that in his treatment of the immaculate conception of Mary he differed from what became the accepted teaching of the Church. However, he kept so closely to the central core of Catholic teaching that even now, as we have seen, his work is basic in the study of Roman Catholic theology.

Indeed, much of his significance lies in just that achievement. He lived in a day when Western Europe seemed to be in danger of departing from the Christian faith. Although they were being stamped out, the Cathari had only recently passed the apex of their spread. Professing to be Christians, probably sincerely so, and prizing the New Testament, they had rejected some of the most fundamental of the apostolic teachings. In the University of Paris, the chief centre for the study of Christian theology, Averroism, with its contradiction of some of the central Christian convictions, was gaining in popularity. The Aristotelian vogue and the use being made by the Averroists of him whom the scholars of the day called the Philosopher was a further threat. By employing Aristotle and by doing so in such fashion as to make him a bulwark of the Christian faith, and by presenting that faith comprehensively and clearly, Aquinas, more than any one else of the four centuries between 950 and 1350, provided Christianity with a firm intellectual foundation.

Moreover, by his use of reason and in delimiting the boundaries between reason and faith, Aquinas gave to reason an honourable place in Christian thought. To him there was no conflict between the two. Both are from God.

In this conviction he was not alone, nor was he a pioneer. However, he mightily reinforced it. In another chapter we will recur to the contribution which, in the use of reason and confidence in an orderly universe, Aquinas and other school men made to the general intellectual development of Western Europe.

We must also see Aquinas in relation to the other religious movements in Western Europe in the thirteenth century. The climax of scholasticism of which he was the outstanding representative was paralleled by a flood tide in other currents in the religious life in that part of the world. The amazing deepening of the Christian faith of the masses which was stimulated by the mendicant orders and which found part of its expression in them was still in the first flush of its pristine power. Indeed, Aquinas was in no small degree its product. It is one facet of his significance that he, as a Dominican, carried out the purpose of the founder of his order to devote scholarship to the cogent presentation of the Christian faith. We must also remember those popular movements, the most extensive being the Albigensees and the Waldensees, which, although condemned by the Catholic Church, were efforts to bring to a better understanding of the Gospel and a full commitment to it some of the millions who through the mass conversions of earlier generations had inherited a professed allegiance to it. The heyday of these movements had been not far from the boyhood of Aquinas. So, too, the effort to purify the hierarchy of the Catholic Church from parish priest to bishop, archbishop, and Pope, and through it to make of Christendom the *Corpus Christianum,* a truly Christian society, attained its climax under Innocent III, only a decade before the birth of Aquinas. To no small degree the significance of Aquinas was in the fact of this synchronization. He was a part of one of the great waves of Christian advance. In him the spirit which was pulsing through all these related movements had seized and stimulated a first-class mind to notable achievement.

THE BEGINNING OF THE DECLINE OF SCHOLASTICISM

Scholasticism never again attained the heights that it reached in Aquinas. After him there were able minds which devoted themselves to its dialectic. However, they did not use it as successfully to solve the intellectual problems presented by Christianity as had such men as Anselm and Aquinas. In them there appeared a gulf between reason and faith, a gulf which might prove disastrous to both. Why this was so is not entirely clear. Then, too, the intellectual life of Europe began to turn away from the methods and the interests of the school men. The latter continued, but new currents were passing them by, currents which were to be especially potent after 1350.

Aquinas did not at once attain to the preëminence which was later accorded him. He had vigorous critics among his contemporaries and in the centuries immediately after him.

Among the more severe critics of Aquinas, but himself not merely a negative but also an independent and positive thinker, was John Duns Scotus, who is also called the *doctor subtilis*. About the biographical data of Duns Scotus there has been much uncertainty. He seems to have been born in the south of Scotland not far from the English border, perhaps in 1265 or 1266, and to have become a Franciscan when in his early or middle teens. He was, then, a younger contemporary of Albertus Magnus and Aquinas, being a child at the time of the latter's death and having become a Franciscan in the former's last years. He studied in Paris and perhaps in Oxford, briefly taught in Oxford, took his doctorate of theology in Paris, and died in Cologne in 1308, when still in his early forties. As a Franciscan, he was eventually accorded a position in theology in his order akin to that held by Aquinas among the Dominicans. The controversies between the two schools of thought were accentuated by jealousy between the two orders, for rivalry, sometimes bitter, has been chronic among the various monastic bodies of the Catholic Church. The inclusive structure of that church, whether in the West or in the East, has not ensured the bond of love which is central in Christian unity as conceived in the New Testament. Being a Franciscan from early adolescence, Duns Scotus was predisposed to dissent from Aquinas.

The differences between the theologies of Aquinas and Duns Scotus went deep. Like the former, the latter had a first-class mind and was inspired by his Christian faith to use it. He was in the Franciscan tradition which made much of Augustine, but he was more influenced by Aristotle than Bonaventura had been. In Duns Scotus there was a trend towards a disjunction between reason and faith which was to become acute in the next century in another Franciscan, William of Ockham, and which was to mark a breakdown in the scholastic attempt to bring the two into a consistent synthesis. Anselm and Aquinas had attempted to show that Christian beliefs were at least not inconsistent with reason and that some of them could be established through reason. Duns Scotus entered a path which, when followed further, issued in the denial that the major Christian convictions can be demonstrated by reason or are even consistent with it, and in the affirmation that they must be believed simply on the authority of the Church or of the Scriptures. We must note, however, that a degree of doubt is thrown on the thought of Dun Scotus by the uncertainty which exists as to whether some of the works attributed to him were written by him, at least in the form in which they have come down to us.

The path which Duns Scotus entered but which he did not follow to its end was the one into which he was led by his emphasis upon the freedom of God's will. Aquinas held that God's will acts in accordance with reason. To put it more extremely than Aquinas would state it, God is bound by reason, and the very nature of God is such that He does not act in a way that is not consistent with reason. This means, therefore, that since human reason is derived from God, nothing which God is or does is out of accord with man's reason. Through the use of his reason man can know much about God, and even though some of God's acts, notably the incarnation and the work of Christ, could not have been discovered through reason, they are not contrary to reason. In contrast, Duns Scotus viewed God as being completely free and not bound by reason. As he saw it, God is not under the necessity of conforming to reason. His acts, therefore, by implication, may even be contrary to reason. Yet Duns Scotus did not think of God as capricious or as making for chaos. But it was God's will and not His reason or His mind which brought the world into being.

Duns Scotus also regarded man as having more freedom of will than had either Augustine or Aquinas. He believed in original sin, but held that by it men have not lost the power of free decision. He had no thought of denying the incarnation or the atonement. Indeed, along with his fellow-Franciscans, he taught that Mary was without original sin. Yet he did not believe, as had Anselm and some others, that if God wished to forgive man He was bound to become incarnate and to be crucified that the moral order of the universe might be preserved. He did not hold that the incarnation and crucifixion were the wisest way to achieve man's salvation, as had Aquinas, for that would limit God's freedom. All he would say was that they were the way chosen by God.

Duns Scotus stressed the authority of the Church and the duty to believe what the Church teaches and to conform to what it commands. What the Church teaches may not be supported by reason and may even seem irrational, but is to be accepted because the Church says so.

Duns Scotus differed from Aquinas and others of his predecessors in the value which he gave to what is technically known as attrition. By attrition is meant sorrow for sin from fear of the punishment which follows sin. Aquinas maintained that this was not the true repentance which is prerequisite to the forgiveness of God, but that really to be repentant one must have contrition, that is, sorrow born of love of God for having slighted God's love. In contrast, Duns Scotus held that attrition is a sufficient starting-point towards God's forgiveness. This is not because through it a man deserves forgiveness, but because God wills it so.

THE BREAKDOWN OF SCHOLASTICISM: WILLIAM OF OCKHAM: THE COMPLETION OF THE DIVORCE OF FAITH AND REASON

A symbol and a decisive contributor to the decline of scholasticism was the Englishman William of Ockham (or Occam), known as *doctor invincibilis* and *venerabilis inceptor*. Born about 1300, at Ockham, in Surrey, he early became a student at Oxford and there joined the Franciscans. A radical, rebel, and controversialist by temperament and conviction, he eventually identified himself with the Spirituals of his order. He championed the cause of the Emperor as against the Pope. As we saw in the preceding chapter, he held highly unconventional views of the structure and authority of the Church.

Given such a character, it is not strange that William of Ockham was daring, provocative, and argumentative in theology. In philosophy, in contrast with Duns Scotus, who held to a modified form of realism, he was a nominalist, although not in an extreme sense, and a vigorous critic of realism. He emphatically rejected the universals which were essential in realism. All that we can know, he held, are individual things. These we know by what he called intuition. Intuition is caused by objects, but even it can give incorrect information. We know not only external objects through our senses. We also know, and even more convincingly and immediately, our inner experiences such as joy and sorrow. An Aristotelian, he attempted to apply the principles of the Philosopher fearlessly and ruthlessly.

Turning from philosophy to theology, Ockham maintained that none of the Christian beliefs can be proved through reason by the logic employed by the school men. Even the existence of God, he held, cannot be demonstrated, and he found inconclusive all the arguments which Aquinas had adduced to support it. He declared that we must accept the tenets of Christianity, including such basic ones as the existence of God and the immortality of the soul, because the Church teaches them and because they are contained in the Bible. They cannot be proved but are to be accepted only on faith.

Here was the complete divorce between reason and faith. Scholasticism had come to the point where it had accepted defeat in the struggle towards what had been its great objective, to employ the tools given by the Greek pre-Christian philosophers to demonstrate by reason the validity of the great Christian affirmations.

William of Ockham and those who agreed with him had given up hope of reconciling the wisdom of man with the wisdom of God. To them, as to Paul, the cross and all that was involved in it were foolishness when judged by the wisdom of the Greeks, and man through his wisdom had not known God. They might not go as far as Paul and declare that God had made foolish the wisdom of the world, but they would insist that between truth as reached by the methods of logic derived from the Greeks and the truth made known through the Gospel a gulf existed which reason could not bridge.

Ockham's views did not win universal acceptance among the school men. The debate went on, often acrimoniously, but in scholastic circles Ockham's theology gained wide popularity.

It seems significant that the decline of scholastic theology which was evidenced by its progressive failure to support Christian faith by reason paralleled the ebbing of vitality in other phases of the Catholic Church of the West. As in these other aspects of the Church's life, it began to be seen in the later decades of the thirteenth century but did not become pronounced until the second half of the fourteenth century. As the climax of scholasticism attained in Thomas Aquinas was roughly coincident with the peak reached in monasticism with the emergence and early growth of the mendicant orders and in the Papacy in Innocent III but was slightly later, so the first indications of decay in scholasticism approximated in time the early hints that the ecclesiastical structure of Western Europe was to suffer from the changes in the on-going stream of history but lagged slightly behind them. No new monastic orders comparable in power and extent with the Franciscans and Dominicans appeared between the first quarter of the thirteenth century and the first half of the sixteenth century and no Pope after Innocent III (who died in 1216) was to wield as much power as he in so many facets of the life of Europe. Yet, as in these other expressions of the vigour of the Catholic Church, the decay in the intellectual approach did not become spectacular until the second half of the fourteenth century. Although William of Ockham not only registered the sharp disjunction between reason and faith which gave evidence of the breakdown of scholasticism but also was a leader in the attack on the political power of the Papacy, his was a vigorous mind and he was still within the scholastic tradition. It appears to be more than a coincidence that he died late in the 1340's and that he may have been a victim of the plague, that Black Death whose scourge, which first became striking in 1347 and 1348, was to speed up the passing of the old order in Europe and was to contribute to the next period of sharp recession in the course of Christianity.

Summary

The problem of the school men was not new. From their very early days Christians had been struggling with the relation between philosophy, the search of man for truth by his rational processes on the one hand, and the Gospel on the other. Could the affirmations of the Christian faith be supported by reason? Indeed, might they be reached concomitantly but independently of revelation? In seeking the answer, the school men took advantage of the tools provided them by the pre-Christian Greek philosophers, especially Plato and Aristotle. The answers at which they arrived were varied. It is significant and sobering that the longer the scholastic method was employed the greater was the tendency to conclude that the truth of the basic Christian convictions could not be proved by the dialectical apparatus. Anselm had proceeded on the confident conviction that through reason implemented by logic man could demonstrate at least some and perhaps all of the major tenets of Christianity. Aquinas held that some of the truths affirmed by Christianity could be supported by reason and that while others could be arrived at only by the path of faith, none was inconsistent with reason. William of Ockham taught that none of the essential features of Christian belief could be proved to the satisfaction of man's reason but that they must be accepted on the authority of the Church and of the Scriptures. To be sure, not all Catholic scholars agreed with him. Many held to those who taught the contrary, especially to Anselm and Aquinas. As the centuries passed, Aquinas was more and more honoured. Yet in 1350, the trend was away from him. Here was poor preparation for meeting the intellectual challenges which the age into which Western Europe was moving posed to Christianity.

SELECTED BIBLIOGRAPHY

GENERAL WORKS

M. H. Carré, *Realists and Nominalists* (Oxford University Press, 1946, pp. vi, 128). Four essays which cover Augustine, Abélard, Thomas Aquinas, and William of Ockham.

F. Copleston, *A History of Philosophy. Volume II. Mediæval Philosophy Augustine to Scotus* (London, Burns, Oates & Washbourne, 1950, pp. x, 614). A competent, objective survey by a Jesuit.

R. Seeberg, *Text-Book of the History of Doctrines. Volume II, History of Doctrines in the Middle and Modern Ages,* revised, 1904, by the author, translated by C. E. Hay (Philadelphia, The United Lutheran Publishing House, 1905, pp. xii, 492). A standard treatment by a Lutheran, of which about the first third covers this period.

B. Smalley, *The Study of the Bible in the Middle Ages* (Oxford, Basil Blackwell, 2d ed., 1952, pp. xxii, 406). Carefully done.

LANFRANC

A. J. Macdonald, *Lanfranc. A Study of His Life Work & Writing* (Oxford University Press, 1926, pp. vii, 307). Carefully done.

ANSELM

Texts of Anselm's works are in J. P. Migne, *Patrologia Latina,* Vols. CLVIII and CLIX (Paris, 1853, 1903).

St. Anselm, *Proslogium; Monologium; an Appendix in Behalf of the Fool by Gaunilon; and Cur Deus Homo,* translated from the Latin by S. N. Deane (Chicago, The Open Court Publishing Co., 1903, pp. xxxv, 288).

St. Anselm's Book of Meditations and Prayers. Translated from the Latin by M. R. (London, Burns, Oates & Washbourne, 1872, pp. xvi, 294).

Eadmeri Historia Novorum in Anglia et Opuscula duo de Vita Sancti Anselmi et Quibusdam Miraculis Ejus, edited by M. Rule in *The Chronicles and Memorials of Great Britain and Ireland during the Middle Ages* (London, Longmans, Green & Co., 1884, pp. cxxvii, 460). By a friend and admirer of Anselm.

J. M. Rigg, *St. Anselm of Canterbury. A Chapter in the History of Religion* (London, Methuen & Co., 1896, pp. 294).

ABÉLARD

Petri Abælardi Abbatis Rugensis Opera Omnia juxta editionem Parisiensem anni 1626, suppletis quæ in ea desiderabantur opusculis accedunt Hilarii et Berengarii Abælardi Discipulorum Opuscula et Epistolæ, in J.-P. Migne, *Patrologia Latina,* Vol. CLXXVIII (Paris, 1885).

Abailard's Ethics. Translated with an introduction by J. R. McCallum (Oxford, Basil Blackwell, 1935, pp. x, 93).

Abélard, Peter, *Historia Calamitatum. The Story of My Misfortunes. An Autobiography,* translated by H. A. Bellows (St. Paul, Thomas A. Boyd, 1922, pp. xxi, 96).

The Letters of Abélard and Heloise, translated from the Latin by C. K. S. Moncrieff (New York, Alfred A. Knopf, 1942, pp. xiii, 264).

J. McCabe, *Peter Abélard* (New York, G. P. Putnam's Sons, 1901, pp. vii, 402). A semi-popular account.

J. K. Sikes, *Peter Abailard* (Cambridge University Press, 1932, pp. xvi, 282). A careful study based upon an extensive use of the sources.

HUGO OF ST. VICTOR

Hugonis de S. Victoris . . . Opera Omnia in J.-P. Migne, *Patrologia Latina,* Vols. CLXXV, CLXXVI, CLXXVII (Paris, 1879).

Hugh of St. Victor, *Explanation of the Rule of St. Augustine,* translated by A. Smith (London, Sands & Company, 1911, pp. xi, 121).

PETER LOMBARD

P. Lombardi . . . Opera Omnia . . . Accedunt Magistri Bandini . . . Sententiarum Libri Quatuor, in J.-P. Migne, *Patrologia Latina,* Vols. CXCI, CXCII (Paris, 1879, 1880).

BONAVENTURA

Breviloquium by St. Bonaventure, translated by E. E. Nemmers (St. Louis, B. Herder Book Co., 1946, pp. xxii, 248).

The Franciscan Union. Translation of St. Bonaventure's Itinerarium Mentis in Deum (London, Burns, Oates & Washbourne, 1937, pp. ix, 74).

Holiness of Life. Being St. Bonaventure's Treatise de Perfectione Vitae ad Sorores, translated by L. Costello (St. Louis, B. Herder Book Co., 2d ed., 1928, pp. xxxi, 103).

E. Gilson, *The Philosophy of St. Bonaventure,* translated by I. Trethowan (New York, Sheed & Ward, 1938, pp. xiii, 551). A modern expert treatise by a Roman Catholic.

ROBERT GROSSETESTE

F. S. Stevenson, *Robert Grosseteste Bishop of Lincoln* (London, Macmillan & Co., 1899, pp. xvi, 348). Well done.

ALBERTUS MAGNUS

H. Wilms, *Albert the Great: Saint and Doctor of the Church* (London, Burns, Oates & Washbourne, 1933, pp. xxi, 226). Based upon extensive research and sympathetic with Albertus Magnus.

THOMAS AQUINAS

Sancti Thomae Aquinatis Doctoris Angelici Ordinis Praedicatorum Opera Omnia secundum impressionem Petri Fiaccadori Parmae 1852–1873 photolithographice reimpressa (New York, Musurgia Publishers, 25 vols., 1948–1950).

The Summa Contra Gentiles of Saint Thomas Aquinas, Literally Translated by the English Dominican Fathers from the latest Leonine edition (London, Burns, Oates & Washbourne, and New York, Benziger Brothers, 4 vols., vol. 3 being in two parts, 1924–1929).

The Summa Theologica of St. Thomas Aquinas, Literally Translated by Fathers of the English Dominican Province (London, Burns, Oates & Washbourne, 2nd and rev. ed., 19 vols., 1920–1922).

Introduction to Saint Thomas Aquinas, edited with introduction by A. C. Pegis (New York, Random House, 1948, pp. xxx, 690). A useful volume, made up principally of translations from Aquinas.

R. Garrigou-Lagrange, *The One God. A Commentary on the First Part of St. Thomas' Theological Summa,* translated by B. Rose (St. Louis, B. Herder Book Co., 1943, pp. viii, 736). By a competent scholar.

E. Gilson, *The Philosophy of St. Thomas Aquinas,* translated by E. Bullough, edited by G. A. Elrington (Cambridge, W. Heffer & Sons, 1929, pp. xv, 372). A standard work.

M. Grabmann, *Thomas Aquinas. His Personality and Thought,* translated by V. Michel (New York, Longmans, Green & Co., 1928, pp. ix, 190). A brief, semi-popular account.

R. L. Patterson, *The Conception of God in the Philosophy of Aquinas* (London, George Allen & Unwin, 1933, pp. 508).

A. D. Sertillanges, *Saint Thomas Aquinas and His Work,* translated by G. Anstruther (London, Burns, Oates & Washbourne, 1932, pp. ix, 150). A popular, sympathetic account.

DUNS SCOTUS

M. Heidegger, *Die Kategorien- und Bedeutungslehre des Duns Scotus* (Tübingen, J. C. B. Mohr, 1916, pp. 241).

R. Seeberg, *Die Theologie des Johannes Duns Scotus* (Leipzig, Dieterich'sche Verlags-Buchhandlung, 1900, pp. vi, 705). Very carefully done.

P. Vignaux, *Justification et Predestination au XIVe Siècle. Duns Scot, Pierre d'Auriole, Guillaume d'Occam, Gregoire de Rimini* (Paris, Ernest Leroux, 1934, pp. viii, 189).

WILLIAM OF OCKHAM

The De Sacramento Altaris of William of Ockham, edited, Latin text, and English translation by T. B. Birch (Burlington, Iowa, The Lutheran Literary Board, 1930, pp. xlvii, 576).

Le Tractatus de Principiis Theologiæ attribué a G. d'Occam, édition critique, L. Baudry (Paris, Librairie Philosophique J. Vrin, 1936, pp. 159).

R. Guelluy, *Philosophie et Théologie chez Guillaume d'Ockham* (Louvain, E. Nauwelærts, 1947, pp. xxiv, 383). Based upon extensive research.

Chapter XXII

PARISH LIFE, PUBLIC WORSHIP, DISCIPLINE, AND PRIVATE WORSHIP AND DEVOTION IN WESTERN EUROPE

How did the Christian faith operate among the masses of the people in Western Europe during the four centuries between 950 and 1350? We have had much to say of the monastic movements, but they centered their efforts upon the small minority of the population who were their members. To be sure, their effects were felt in much wider circles. As the centuries wore on, especially after the rise of the mendicant orders with their missionary zeal, the influence of those fully committed to the Christian life affected more and more of the common run of mankind about them. But we have thus far said little of the commonalty and of its religion and morals. We have spoken of the movements which the Catholic Church condemned as heretical, but except in certain sections these did not reach beyond minorities. We have told of the efforts of the reformers to make of the Catholic Church an instrument for raising all of Christendom to a nearer approximation to the Christian ideal, but in doing so we have focussed our attention on the directing centre, the Papacy and the councils of the entire Church, with here and there an excursus to outstanding bishops and archbishops. Only incidentally have we hinted at the fashion in which these struggles at the top had repercussions among the multitude. We have recounted in summary the intellectual approach to the Christian faith, but this also directly affected only the small minority who were scholars. We have not stopped to ask how far if at all echoes of the discussions were heard by the illiterate who constituted the bulk of Western Europeans.

We must now pause to inquire the way in which Christianity was mediated to the rank and file and the nature and features of the response. This will lead us to say something of the structure of diocesan and parish organization and life, of worship, both public and private, of the methods employed to acquaint the ordinary Christian with the tenets and practices of his faith, and of the

523

discipline applied to guide or constrain the millions of individuals who were the supposed concern of the Church. The scene with which we have to deal is extraordinarily varied and generalizations are correspondingly perilous, but if we are to essay to paint the picture at all we can do so only with broad strokes, with here and there an illustrative detail.

THE DIOCESAN AND PARISH STRUCTURE

In reaching the masses with the Christian faith the chief channel of Christianity was the Catholic Church. That Church inherited the ecclesiastical structure which had evolved in the Roman Empire. It continued this, but with important modifications. That structure, it will be recalled, was territorially comprehensive and its main divisions reflected roughly the administrative units of the Empire. It had its dioceses, each with its bishop. Dioceses were grouped by provinces, and in each of these the bishops might meet in synods and the bishop in the leading city had a kind of preëminence and came to be known as the metropolitan. The bishops in the outstanding cities of the Empire, of which the chief were Rome, Antioch, Alexandria, Constantinople, and, because of its historic significance for the faith, Jerusalem, were termed patriarchs and exercised their authority over a still wider area. In the course of time parishes, much smaller divisions than the dioceses, developed for the care of the faithful in the local scene. This form of organization carried over into the period with which we have been dealing.

Important modifications were made. In the early days of the episcopate, vacancies were filled on nomination by neighbouring bishops and were approved by the clergy and laity of the diocese. As metropolitans emerged, each usually supervised the election and consecrated and installed the bishops in his province. Beginning with the sixth century in the West the assent of the king was generally required and the king often controlled the appointment. In theory the choice of the bishop was by the clergy and people of the diocese. By the middle of the twelfth century the election in most of Western Europe was by the canons, the clergy attached to the cathedral, the bishop's church. As we have seen, between 950 and 1350 a major struggle developed for the determination of the succession to the episcopate between the Pope on the one hand and the kings on the other. Under the great Popes the Roman See was an increasing power, but the conflict was not fully resolved.

Parishes multiplied. Especially did they do so as cities declined and Western Europe became prevailingly rural. In principle each had its resident priest or priests who administered the sacraments. This priest was called *presbyter* or *rector*. Because he had as his charge the *cura animarum,* the care of the souls in his parish, in time he might also be known as *curatus,* from whence comes the French *curé*. The priest might be known as the *parson,* or the *person* (from Latin *persona*), the most important man in the parish. At least in England, the resident clergyman might be called *vicar*. In this case the income from the parish had been assigned to a monastery or had been appropriated in some other way, perhaps by the bishop. The *vicar,* who was a *vicarius* or substitute for the parish priest, and who might not be in full priest's orders, was employed for a fraction of the revenues, to give spiritual care to the parish. In principle the parish priest was responsible to the bishop of the diocese and was supervised by him. In practice the chief layman in the parish, the local lord within whose domain the parish lay, was often more to be reckoned with than the bishop. It was he or his predecessors who had founded and endowed the parish. He therefore often made the appointment and controlled the appointee.

The clergy constituted a special class. They had their own courts and stoutly maintained that they could not be called to account by the civil courts or be taxed by the secular rulers. Here, as we have seen, was a source of chronic conflict between the state and the Church.

The Parish and Its Life

The parish was the unit around which revolved many of the community activities of the local population, especially in rural districts. The parish church and its services were a focus where baptisms were administered, marriages were consecrated, and the dead buried. Mass was supposed to be said daily and it might be preceded, especially on Sundays, by matins and succeeded by evensong. Sunday masses were well attended, but were often poorly conducted and scarcely listened to by the congregation. Parish churches and church yards were used for community dancing, games, banquets, sports, buffoonery, festivals, fairs, and markets.

Presumably the quality of Christian life in the parish depended primarily upon the parish priest or his substitute. He it was who gave religious instruction, administered the sacraments, and looked after the spiritual and moral welfare of his flock. In theory the priest was celibate and had been trained for his calling in the cathedral church of the diocese. From there he was supposed to go to the cathedral church of the metropolitan of the province for additional instruction and the Fourth Lateran Council ordered that in each of the latter there should be a chair of theology.

In practice the ideal was not fully attained. That there were some worthy priests is certain. How large a percentage of the whole they constituted cannot be determined and probably varied from region to region and from time to time. Many were palpably unworthy. There were periods and areas in which the majority are said to have been married or to have had concubines. Some had irregular relations with the women of the parish. Many frequented taverns. A large proportion were avaricious. Indeed, avarice was one of the main charges leveled against them. Numbers eked out their incomes by keeping taverns, buying and selling, and lending money.

Support of the parish clergy was partly through tithes levied on the fruits of the field, on merchandise, and on handicrafts. From the tithes not only were the clergy supported, but aid also came for the poor of the parish and for the maintenance and repair of parish buildings. Offerings were made at the mass, baptisms, marriages, and funerals. Technically voluntary, in practice they became obligatory fees paid for services rendered by the priest. Obviously they lent themselves to exactions and disputes.

Investigations made from time to time by reforming bishops and archbishops showed that substantial numbers of the parish priests did not understand the Latin of the services which they conducted, not even that of the mass. Very few were familiar with the Bible. The rise and multiplication of the universities in the thirteenth and fourteenth centuries might have been supposed to bring improvement, especially since in some of them the major subject was theology. However, canon law seems to have been more studied than theology, for it was a better road to preferment. Then, too, not many parish priests were university graduates. University men tended to go into the higher ranks of the clergy or into teaching, or to be absorbed in the central administrative structure of dioceses and the Papacy. Not all metropolitan cathedrals had occupants for the chairs of theology which were required in principle.

As we have suggested, the revenues from the parish might be diverted to absentees, individuals or monasteries, and the actual work be done by substitutes who were not always priests or even deacons. They were usually poorly trained men hired for a pittance, and that in spite of the protests of reforming bishops. Pluralism was widespread. By this was meant that one man might draw the revenues of several parishes and, an absentee incumbent, live in luxury and employ a *locum tenens*. This was regarded as so usual that many men, otherwise excellent, connived with it to their own profit. Thus we hear of one thirteenth century English bishop, later canonized, who, before he was elevated to the episcopate, held the rectorship of at least ten parishes in addition to other stipends.

The situation was complicated, both for worse and for better, by other factors. There were wandering priests, ordained, but not adequately controlled by bishops, who intruded in parishes, administering the sacraments in disregard of the resident priest. There were assistant clergy, deacons or sub-deacons. There were the parish clerks. There were chantry priests. These last said masses on behalf of the souls of the dead and were supported by endowments left by pious benefactors for that purpose. Frequently they had other duties and were really assistants to the *rector*. All too often their time outside that spent in saying mass was frittered away in idleness or worse. In some parishes there were also chaplains in charge of chapels which were erected to serve those who lived at inconvenient distances from the parish church. Again and again members of the mendicant orders disregarded parish boundaries and conflicts ensued with the secular clergy. However, by their preaching and example, especially during the first flush of devotion in the early days of the orders, the friars helped to raise the level of intelligence and living of the rank and file of the laity. This they did both as the result of their direct impact upon them and indirectly by stimulating the seculars to be more faithful in their ministry.

The instruction given the great body of the laity seems to have increased as the centuries passed. Much of this was through preaching. Originally chiefly the function of bishops, preaching was more and more by parish priests and, after the mendicant orders came into being, by the friars. In a day when books were few and expensive and illiteracy was the rule and literacy the exception, the oral word through the preacher was very important not only for exhortation but also for imparting the basic tenets of the faith. Some energetic bishops commanded the priests of their dioceses to preach and outlined the contents of the sermons. Thus in 1281, John Peckham, a highly educated Franciscan, Archbishop of Canterbury, had his provincial synod command the priests to preach each quarter, instructing their parishioners in the articles of the faith, the Ten Commandments, the seven deadly sins, the seven principal virtues, and the seven sacraments. In more than one country books of sermons were prepared and circulated to assist the priests in their preaching. Instruction also came through the religious plays that were given in churches and churchyards. It was furthered through paintings on the walls of churches, sculpture, and stained-glass windows.

EPISCOPAL SUPERVISION

Ideally the life of the parish was the concern not only of the priest but also of the bishop. Some bishops were too much caught up in the administration of the kingdom to give much care to their dioceses. That was especially the case since such posts as chancellor of the realm were often filled by them. Many bishops were too worldly to trouble themselves much with the details of their official responsibilities. Yet there were bishops who took their duties seriously. Their number multiplied through the mounting religious devotion and the reforming zeal of the age. They made regular journeys of visitation, carefully inspecting the parishes of their dioceses, recording what they found, and seeking to encourage the faithful among the clergy and to discipline the negligent or corrupt.

THE SACRAMENTS

Much of the religious life of the laity centered in the sacraments. In the last chapter we said something of the developing beliefs about them. It was not until 1439 that their number was finally officially fixed. Some authors revered by the Church had spoken of only two, baptism and the Eucharist. Peter Damian had enumerated twelve and Hugo of St. Victor thirty. Peter Lombard seems to have been the first to limit them to seven and to give the list which the Roman Catholic Church eventually made final. By the fourteenth century these had gained general acceptance. They were baptism, confirmation, penance, the Eucharist, extreme unction, marriage, and ordination.

BAPTISM

Baptism of infants had become universal for the offspring of Christian parents. It was believed to effect the new birth. It was, therefore, necessary for salvation. Infants dying unbaptized, so it was held, being still tainted with original sin, could never enjoy that beatific vision of God which is heaven. Popular belief had it that they went to hell. Children were, accordingly, to be baptized as soon after birth as possible. Water was to be used and the ceremony might be by immersion or by affusion, namely, pouring water over the child as the sponsor held it over the font. If the newly born child was in danger of dying, water must be cast on it "in the name of the Father, and of the Son, and of the Holy Ghost." Even though the words were uttered in the vernacular rather than Latin, and imperfectly, the intention was believed to make them effective. It was said, however, that many adults were uncertain whether they had been baptized and that baptism was often neglected.

CONFIRMATION

Confirmation was by the bishop. In at least one region it was to be administered in the child's fifth year. By it the child was supposed to become "God's champion." From various countries come reports that through indifference large numbers had not been given the rite.

PENANCE

Penance had, as we have repeatedly hinted, developed from the forms in use in the first five centuries of the Church. No longer was confession made in public to the congregation nor was the bishop the usual officer of the Church who declared the penitent forgiven and received him back into communion.

Public penance persisted for a time alongside private confession, but it gradually disappeared, especially after the eleventh century. The practice of private confession to a priest with the accompanying penance is usually said to have spread from the Irish monasteries, but the way for it seems to have been prepared quite independently of them.

Penance now entailed contrition for sin, oral private confession to a priest (inviolate secrecy was only slowly observed), the performance of whatever work of satisfaction was commanded by the priest, and the declaration of forgiveness or absolution by the priest. It was recognized that forgiveness rested ultimately with God and that it was conditioned upon the true repentance of the sinner. But it was held that God had granted to Peter and the apostles and through them to the priests the power to remit sins.

In one way or another instructions were developed for the priests to enable them to probe the consciences of those who came to confession. These involved questions of conduct, both of omission and commission—for example, whether things had been borrowed and not returned, whether the children had been taught good manners, the creed and the Lord's Prayer, and whether the churchyard gate had been left open so that animals wandered in. Then there were what were known as the mortal or deadly sins, declared to be seven in number—pride, covetousness, lust, anger, gluttony, envy, and sloth.

The priest prescribed good works to be done as discipline and in satisfaction for sins and graded according to the seriousness of the offense. These might be fasting, the giving of alms, pilgrimages, gifts to the Church, self-flagellation, or some other specific act. Absolution was conditioned upon the performance of these works. In principle, reinforced by the Fourth Lateran Council in 1215, every Christian was to go to confession at least once a year. Thus all the baptized were to come under the disciplinary ministrations of the Church.

INDULGENCES

In connexion with penance there developed the theory and practice of indulgences and of the treasury of the Church. At first indulgences seem to have been of a limited kind, and were the remission of some of the prescribed works of penance in return for some other act, such as gifts to a monastery or a church. It was also held that if the "temporal" penalties for sin were not met in this life, they would be required after death, in purgatory, before the soul was cleansed from its sin and was capable of the beatific vision of God. In the eleventh century the custom began, at first not widely, of granting plenary indulgences, that is, remission of all the temporal penalties for sins. True repentance was, of course, still a prerequisite to forgiveness, but the Church claimed the power to remit the temporal penalties. This was done by local bishops and the Popes. One of the early instances of plenary indulgence was the granting of it by Pope Urban II to those who enlisted in the First Crusade. Later plenary indulgence was extended to those who enabled others to go on a crusade or who performed some other specified good work.

In support of the practice of indulgences the school men, among them notably Alexander of Hales, Albertus Magnus, and Thomas Aquinas, elaborated the principle of the treasury of the Church. It was held that the apostles and saints had done far more than was necessary to assure themselves of heaven and had thereby added to a surplus of merit already enriched by what Christ had done. It was maintained that the Church had been granted the power to transfer some of it to reduce or cancel the good works required of penitent sinners in satisfaction for their offenses. In 1343 Pope Clement VI gave official endorsement to the principle.

Some of the school men, although clear that the Church could remit such penalties in this life, were not convinced that indulgences could accomplish more for the souls now in purgatory than encouragement to pray that the penalties in that state might be lightened. Others held that indulgences granted by Popes and bishops were effective not only in this life but also in purgatory. In the thirteenth century the belief spread that one person could obtain an indulgence for another, and that the living might even obtain indulgences for the souls in purgatory. Here, in the sixteenth century, was to be one of the moot points between Protestants and Catholics.

Indulgences, we must note, were not permissions to commit sin. Nor could they release souls from hell, where the punishment for sin was not temporal, that is, limited in time, but was eternal. Nor did they make repentance unnecessary. They presupposed genuine penitence. Yet here was a growing practice which later was to be grossly abused.

The Eucharist

As in the earlier centuries, so in this period, the Eucharist, which we may also call the Lord's Supper, holy communion, or the mass, was the high point and centre of Christian worship. In the Catholic Church the liturgy of the mass underwent no drastic change in this period. He who had known it in the year 500 in Rome, had he come back to the Eternal City in the year 1350 and gone to mass, would have noticed some modifications but would quickly have felt at home. The Roman rite spread through much of Western Europe, but was adapted to incorporate elements from local or regional usages. Variations existed in several areas. In England, for example, the missal according to the Use of Sarum (Salisbury) differed somewhat from that of Rome and became widespread in the British Isles.

The major developments in the Eucharist during these four centuries were not in the liturgy but in the affirmation of transubstantiation, the withdrawal of the cup from the laity in the communion, the extensive use of excommunication, the feast of Corpus Christi, and the adoration of the reserved sacrament.

We have already seen that in 1215 the Fourth Lateran Council expressly declared transubstantiation to be the teaching of the Church. While in theory the dogma was not new but went back to Christ himself in his institution of the Lord's Supper, the formulation made binding in 1215 had been developed in terms of scholastic philosophy. It had been a subject of debate among the school men and had on occasion provoked acrimonious controversy. Now that what the Western Church regarded as an ecumenical council had spoken, only heretics would dare openly to challenge the decision.

The denial of the cup to the laity came slowly and was a natural concomitant of the growing acceptance of transubstantiation. If through the words of consecration by the priest the bread and the wine in the Eucharist actually become the body and blood of Christ, great care must be taken to prevent any profanation of these elements. Particularly was there danger of spilling some of the wine as the cup was given to the laity. Gradually, therefore, the custom arose of giving only the bread or wafer to the laity and having only the priest take of the cup.

Excommunication was not new. We have met it from the early days of the Church. In the first five centuries it was invoked against those Christians who became flagrant sinners or in ecclesiastical disputes over doctrine or jurisdiction. It continued to be so employed. In addition it was now used as a weapon in contests between the clergy on the one hand and princes on the other. It was also increasingly resorted to by the clergy to coerce the laity in such matters as the observance of feasts and the payment of tithes. Theoretically intended to bring the sinner to repentance, it became a means of constraining the unwilling to compliance with the wishes of those who had the power to exclude from the Eucharist.

Related to excommunication and, indeed, called that until the time of Innocent III, who gave it the designation by which it was afterwards known, was the interdict. Employed at least as early as the ninth century, it became a potent instrument in the hands of the great Popes of the latter part of this era. In its broadest application it was the prohibition of the public administration of the sacraments and of the services of the Church in a given area. Private marriages and the baptism of infants were usually permitted, but most of the ministrations of the Church were suspended until the offending prince or city submitted. For example, Innocent III made effective use of it against John of England in placing under it all of the latter's kingdom.

The feast of Corpus Christi arose in the thirteenth century to commemorate the institution of the Eucharist. It is said to have been begun at the instance of Juliana, a nun, who urged it upon the Bishop of Liege and upon him who in 1261 became Pope Urban IV. In 1246 the Bishop of Liege ordered its observance in his diocese and in 1264 Urban IV instructed the entire Church to honour it. It was placed on the Thursday after Trinity Sunday, of which we are to say more in a moment. The office for it, composed by Thomas Aquinas, was of singular beauty. In spite of Papal endorsement, the feast made but slow headway. However, by the middle of the fourteenth century it was fairly general in Western Europe.

Another custom which arose from the emphasis on transubstantiation and which spread widely in the latter part of the period was the worship of the consecrated bread and wine. They were reserved or exposed all day on the altar in a transparent receptacle called a monstrance and the faithful would come individually or in groups and adore them.

Ideally the Eucharist was to be celebrated reverently and with great dignity. This was often observed, as in the Cluniac houses, with much pomp, and at other times, as in the Cistercian monasteries, with studied austerity. All too often, however, especially in parish churches, the mass was performed perfunctorily and carelessly, and neither the priest nor the congregation took it very seriously.

We must note that the fact that mass was said in Latin, a language understood by fewer and fewer of the laity in Latin Europe as the vernacular departed further from it, and never by more than a handful among the laity in Northern Europe, tended to remove it from the multitude. In the early centuries it was in the vernacular and the congregation understood it and shared in the responses. As its language became unintelligible to the laity and even to some of the priests, it was a spectacle which at best was staged with impressive beauty and at the worst was hurried through in slovenly fashion, with ragged vestments and dirty or tarnished altar furnishings.

EXTREME UNCTION

Pastors were strongly encouraged to give the communion to the sick who were in danger of death and to administer to them extreme unction. Scriptural authority for extreme unction was sought in Mark vi:13, where the apostles are described as anointing the sick with oil and healing them, and in James v. 14, 15, where the sick is instructed to call upon the presbyters of the Church, who are to pray over him, anoint him with oil in the name of the Lord, with the promise that the prayer of faith will save him that was sick, and that if he had committed sins they will be forgiven him.

Anointing with oil had a long history in Christian practice. It
for physical healing, and its use had often been abused. It was also conn
with penance, for the forgiveness of sins. In this period it came to be separated
from penance and was regarded as the distinct sacrament. Down to the twelfth
century the practice in the West was to give it to all the ill who asked for it,
except those who were doing public penance, but in the twelfth and thirteenth
centuries it came to be regarded as only for those believed to be dying. The oil,
properly consecrated, was held to make for mental and possibly bodily health,
and to work pardon for sins. The priest was to be available day or night to
administer it.

Marriage

Marriage was now esteemed one of the sacraments. Here the Christian conscience and the Church faced a difficult and complex problem. Could the strong
urge of sex be directed and controlled by the Christian ideal? Could customs
of betrothal and marriage, some of them of pre-Christian origin and many of
them, even of post-Christian development, with little of the Christian in them,
be made to conform to Christian standards? What were Christian standards?
Much of marriage was governed by property or power interests, such as the
desire for an heir to inherit the estate or the union of two families to strengthen
the position of each. A marriage might be arranged with scant regard to the
personal wishes of the bride or the groom. Often betrothals were entered into
apart from the Church and cohabitation begun, perhaps to see whether the
union would be fertile and produce the wished for heir, before the blessing of
the priest was asked. Under what circumstances could a marriage be annulled?
These were some of the problems which perplexed the canon lawyers. In this
period the Catholic Church in the West was struggling to find the answers
and to enforce the regulations which it developed. On by no means all issues
was a common mind attained. It was held, probably with increasing emphasis,
that marriage was a sacrament, that the formal blessing by the Church through
a priest was obligatory upon Christians when they entered into matrimony,
and that questions of the validity of a particular union and possible termination were for ecclesiastical and not for civil decision. However, on many details
and concrete applications there was as yet no agreement.

Ordination

We must not take the space to say much about ordination. It was regarded
as a sacrament and was normally administered by a bishop, as one of the
successors of the apostles. In very exceptional circumstances a priest might be
delegated to serve for the bishop.

FUNERALS

...ng the sacraments. However, it was attended by Chris-
...nally mass was celebrated. Eventually what was known
...dead was said. Masses and prayers for the dead did not
...ut were continued, and petitions for the dead were part of
...es.

THE FESTIVALS OF THE CHURCH

For the rank and file of Christians, as for the clergy, the Christian year, with its holy days and festivals, was of major importance. It entered into the warp and woof of every-day life and the observances connected with its special days did much to give instruction and to stimulate worship and devotion. Long before the tenth century the main structure of the Christian calendar had come into being. Sunday, Lent, Easter, Christmas, Pentecost, and some other days gave it rhythm and helped to remind even the careless of the main events in the life of Christ and of the Church.

In this period additions were made. They came largely out of the rising tide of Christian faith which marked these centuries. We have seen that in the thirteenth century the feast of Corpus Christi was inaugurated. Pentecost, or Whitsunday, commemorating the coming of the Holy Spirit, was the seventh Sunday after Easter. Its observance went back to early Christian times, but it was not until the eleventh century and later, possibly as a concomitant of the deepening religious life of the area, that it became generally prominent in Western Europe. It was known as Whitsunday because of the white garments worn by those coming to baptism in the days when Europe was being converted and because those not baptized on Easter were given the rite at Pentecost. The observance of Trinity Sunday, the first Sunday after Pentecost, in honour of the Trinity, seems to have originated early in the tenth century. It spread gradually, partly through the influence of Cluny, but was not made obligatory on the whole Church until the first half of the fourteenth century.

Feasts in honour of the Virgin Mary were largely of Eastern origin. This seems to have been especially true of the feast of the Conception of the Virgin (although it may have been of Irish provenance). Its extension in Western Europe appears to have begun in the eleventh century and to have been furthered by the Benedictine monks, but Bernard of Clairvaux was critical and it was long in being accepted at Rome.

When a saint was canonized, a day was set for his or her commemoration. As the centuries passed the numbers of the official saints multiplied and the days for the most notable of them also increased. A day for prayers for all of the dead, eventually known as All Souls' Day, was slow in developing. Late in the tenth century an abbot of a distinguished monastery spoke of it as being of long standing in his house. Early in the eleventh century Odilo, an abbot of Cluny, ordered a day for the annual commemoration of all the departed. Backed by the prestige of Cluny, the custom spread widely among other families of monasteries.

The Popularity of the Saints and the Virgin Mary

To Christians of that age the unseen world of spirits was very real. The Devil and his hosts were believed to be the source of many and perhaps most of the ills which beset the human race. Stories were abroad of those who had sold their souls to the Devil. Equally vivid were those forces and spirits which were opposed to evil. Indeed, a major contribution of Christianity was the confidence that men need not be subject to the demons but that they could be protected from them and, if their victims, could be delivered from them. Since in his crucifixion Christ had triumphed, the sign of the cross was believed to be effective against the machinations of the allies of darkness and many stories were told of its potency as a guard against them. The angels of God were also real to believers. The saints, in whom grace had triumphed, were revered. Not only by their good works had they added to the treasury from which the Church might draw to reduce the temporal punishments for the penitent. They also could be invoked and their aid obtained as intercessors.

Especially was the Virgin Mary honoured. It was a man's world, this era that we call the Middle Ages of Europe. Men controlled state and Church. In a time of warfare they did the fighting. The majority of the saints were men. Men were the theologians and the founders of the great monastic orders. Yet the Virgin Mary was exalted, perhaps partly in semi-conscious appreciation of the imbalance of the masculine and the hunger for the ideal which womanhood could supply. As we have seen, the Virgin Mary had early been accorded a high place and her designation, Mother of God, had been a battle cry in theological controversies in the Eastern wing of the Catholic Church. In this era of religious revival the devotion paid her in the West mounted. Special chapels for her were a normal feature of the churches. The faithful in all walks of life, confident in her mercy and concern, pled with her to intercede for them with her Son and also to give them her direct aid. In the early years of the twelfth century collections of legends gathering around the Virgin began to be made.

It was in the eleventh century, not far from 1050, that we first begin to hear of the prayer to the Virgin, the *Ave Maria,* or the Hail Mary. Made up in part of a portion of the angelic salutation at the time of the Annunciation, in part of the greeting of Elizabeth to Mary, with the addition of a plea that the Virgin pray for the petitioners, its origin is obscure and not all of even its brief length appeared at once. Like so much of the religious devotion of the age, it seems to have originated in the monasteries. However, before the end of the eleventh century at least one bishop and local synod enjoined the clergy to see that their parishioners knew it, and in the thirteenth century, encouraged by bishops and synods, it spread rapidly to many countries in Western Europe.

Connected with the *Ave Maria* was the Angelus. The Angelus was in honour of the incarnation. In later centuries the faithful were summoned to it three times a day, at morning, noon, and evening, by the ringing of a bell, and were to respond with a triple repetition of the *Ave Maria*. In this period the Angelus seems to have been only in the evening. Its origin is obscure, but we begin to hear of it as early as the thirteenth century. It spread rapidly as a parish custom and was a means of increasing the devotion of the rank and file of the laity, reminding them of the incarnation and drawing them to prayer to the Virgin. In the first half of the fourteenth century, John XXII, one of the ablest of the Avignon Popes, recommended it and gave an added impetus to its spread throughout the Church.

Many hymns were written in honour of the Virgin. One of them, *Ave Maris Stella,* is probably much older than this period, but it was popular during these centuries and in that era several other hymns were founded on it.

A GREAT SURGE OF CHRISTIAN POETRY

The four centuries from 950 to 1350 were marked by a luxurious flowering of religious poetry, including hymns. In view of the rising tide of devotion and enthusiasm, this was to be expected. A large proportion of the composition was by members of the new monastic orders which sprang from the religious awakenings of the period. As we have seen, hymns were not new, and many of those most widely used, including the *Te Deum Laudamus,* dated from much earlier centuries. Now, however, in contrast with the Greek wing of the Catholic Church, where hymn writing had passed its zenith, in the Latin portion of the Church religious poetry flourished, its forms became richer and more varied, its rhythm more regular, and its rhyme purer. Much was in Latin. Many hymns were also in the vernacular and were popular among the laity. We have noted the guilds of singers who in the twelfth and thirteenth centuries were widespread in Italy.

Hymn writers were numerous and some of the greatest of the school men were among them. Thus Peter Abélard prepared a hymn-book for Héloïse and her nuns. Thomas Aquinas and Bonaventura were notable composers. In the Abbey of St. Victor in Paris, an outstanding centre of scholastic theology,

Adam, who died in 1142, is said by some to mark the zenith of medieval hymnody. It was to be expected that Cluny, with its earnest life of devotion and worship, would give rise to hymns. One of the most famous poems to come from it was the lengthy *De Contemptu Mundi,* said to have been written by Bernard (not to be confused with Bernard of Clairvaux), about the middle of the twelfth century. Sections from it translated into English in the nineteenth century by the Anglican, Neale, have gained popularity in English-speaking Protestantism under the titles, "For thee oh dear, dear country" and "Jerusalem the Golden."

The Breviary Is Collected, Standardized, and Attains Wide Circulation

A type of work which originally had its formulation and chief use among monks, but which eventually spread to the secular clergy and had wide influence upon the laity, was the breviary. It had its major development in this period.

As the name indicates, the breviary was an abridgement. It was also and primarily a compilation. Its purpose was to put in convenient form what the monks and the clergy needed in their collective services and their private devotions.

Earlier (Chapter VII) we have noted that long before this period the custom had arisen in the Church of praying six or seven times a day at specified intervals. The services connected with these "canonical hours" came to be known as offices. In time patterns for them were developed, with Psalms, readings from the Scriptures, hymns, antiphonaries, and prayers. They varied from place to place and from age to age. Special days, such as the great festivals and those in honour of the saints, had offices appropriate to them. As was natural, the offices were assembled in books for the use of the clergy.

Before the end of the sixth century what was known as the Roman usage had been elaborated. In the time of Charlemagne we hear of an abbreviation, or breviary, of the offices for the canonical hours prepared for lay folk. With their emphasis upon the offices for the canonical hours, various monasteries developed set forms. Some monks recited all the Psalms daily, but this was excessively time-consuming. Many monasteries, accordingly, arranged to spread the recitation of the entire Psalter over a week, and assigned to each of the seven daily services its appropriate Psalms. The oldest known breviary which contained all the canonical offices is said to date from 1099 and to have been in use at Monte Cassino. Under Pope Innocent III the breviary began to spread beyond Benedictine circles.

It was the Franciscans who developed the breviary which, with modifications, came into general circulation in much of the Western Church. Travelling as they did, they wished books with the offices for the canonical hours in such compact form that they would not be a handicap on their journeys, made as these usually were on foot. They wished, not large tomes for choirs who were resident in particular churches and monasteries, but a light volume from which the offices could be recited as they tramped the roads. The Franciscan breviary, regarded as the "modern office," became the chief basis for a breviary which had the endorsement of Rome. To the Franciscan breviary were added features which had been traditional at Rome. The Franciscan breviary thus modified gained wide currency among the secular as well as the regular clergy and through the clergy could not but have an effect upon the laity.

Charitable Lay Enterprises

An expression of the Christian faith of the laity which was seen in hundreds of parishes was care for the unfortunate. With the deepening of the religious life of Western Europe through the revivals, especially those of the twelfth and thirteenth centuries, and with the growth of cities and the increase in wealth, works of Christian charity multiplied. Many bishops, clergy, and monks had long made it part of their duty to care for the sick and the afflicted. Now the laity increasingly shared in this labour. Sometimes they formed associations and confraternities for this purpose. Hospitals and asylums for the ill, the crippled, and the aged were founded and maintained. Sufferers from leprosy, a disease which was especially feared by Europeans of the day, aroused compassion and houses for them were created, often under the protection of St. Lazarus or St. Magdalen. Hospices were also conducted for pilgrims and travellers.

Pilgrimages Were Popular

One of the most widespread accompaniments of the religious life of the period was pilgrimages. Like so many other practices, these were by no means new. They were present from the early days of the Christian faith. Nor are pilgrimages an exclusively Christian phenomenon. They are found in many other religions. Back of them lies not only the religious impulse but also the desire to travel. The Christians of Medieval Europe were not behind the faithful of other ages in their zeal to visit sites esteemed sacred to their faith. Palestine, the Holy Land par excellence, associated with the scenes of the birth, life, death, and resurrection of Christ, attracted thousands. Rome with its churches and its memories of Peter and Paul lured other thousands. Tombs of saints, like that of Thomas Becket at Canterbury, were the goal of many.

Relics of saints were prized as highly as they had been in earlier centuries and shrines which housed them were the objectives of countless pilgrimages.

THE WIDENING AND DEEPENING OF THE APPEAL OF THE WAY OF THE MYSTIC

It was inevitable that the rising tide of religious life in Western Christendom should have as one of its outlets the way of the mystic and the life of private prayer. The first flush of enthusiasm in the early stages of each new monastic order invariably gave rise to a deepening mysticism, the cultivation of the sense of the presence of God. We have already said something of the impetus to mysticism given by Bernard of Clairvaux and Francis of Assisi, especially through their emphasis upon the human side of Christ and the events in his life. There was much of the mystic in Thomas Aquinas and, as we have noted, he held the crown of human existence to be the vision of God. His contemporary and friend, Bonaventura, was a notable mystic as well as an outstanding theologian, and his *Itinerarium Mentis in Deum* (*The Soul's Journey to God*) is evidence of the depth of his experience and insight. The Franciscan tertiate, Raymond Lull, whom we have already met as a missionary to the Moslems, was known equally well for writings which were expressions of Christian mysticism.

There were women among the mystics. Famous among them was Hildegarde (1098–1179). At the tender age of three she began to see visions and increasingly she felt the light of God enveloping her soul. At eight she was given as an oblate to a Benedictine monastery and when nearly fifty she founded a monastery of her own. Like many mystics, she concerned herself actively with the affairs of her time in Church and state. She carried on an extensive correspondence with Popes, Emperors, princes, princesses, bishops, and saints. Her visions were often in the form of allegories. She also prophesied, admonishing those in authority and speaking of Antichrist and the end of the world.

The Cistercian foundation for women at Helfta, near Eisleben, in Saxony, was a school of mysticism. Among its daughters was she who is known as Gertrude the Great (1256–c.1302). Reared from childhood in the monastery, she came under the spell of the writings of Bernard of Clairvaux and had such a special devotion to the heart of Jesus that on one Christmas night she felt her heart united to that of the Child Jesus. She had an abiding sense of the presence of God and had felt the imprint of the Trinity. On one occasion in the mass she believed that she saw Christ face to face. With Gertrude the Great are often grouped Mechtilde of Hackborn (died 1310) and Mechtilde (1217–1282), a beguine of Magdeburg who was a Dominican tertiate.

Also renowned was Bridget or Birgitta of Sweden (c.1303–1373). A daughter of the high aristocracy, the wife of a prominent noble, she was the mother of eight children. From her childhood she had been devout and had had visions in which she believed she talked with Christ and the Virgin. In her maturity these increased, especially after the death of her husband (1344). She had what she was convinced were revelations, she prophesied, and she felt impelled to rebuke the King of Sweden for onerous taxation and injustice to the humble among his subjects. Like some others among the mystics, especially in the West, she had marked organizing and administrative ability. She founded an order, at first associated by the ecclesiastical authorities with the Augustinian Canons, but eventually distinct, that of Our Most Holy Saviour, better known as the Bridgettines, which was carried on by her daughter Katherine and which expanded to other lands.

There were notable mystics among those at whom the Catholic Church looked askance or condemned outright as heretics. Among them were Joachim of Flora, of whom we have already spoken, and his contemporary, Amaury of Bena, in the diocese of Chartres, who, like Joachim, believed that the age of the Holy Spirit had come. In spite of the efforts of the Inquisition to root it out, Amaury's influence long persisted.

In the Abbey of St. Victor the writings ascribed to Dionysius the Areopagite had a profound influence. The house was a famous centre not only of scholasticism and hymnody but also of mystical piety. The philosophy and theology of St. Victor were shot through and through with it. The Victorines looked upon the universe as a book written by the hand of God and as a mirror in which the thought of God is reflected. They taught that that thought is expressed in the Scriptures and that these are to be read as allegories. To discover the mind of God, the method of dialectical logic is not enough and may even be misleading. It may be sought and reached through intuition and meditation. This approach is crowned by contemplation with its insight into truth and by ecstasy. The divine light which shines through contemplation enables us to know truth which cannot be attained by the path of reason and which may even be contradicted by reason. Thus said the men of St. Victor. Outstanding among the Victorines were Hugo or Hugh (1096–1141) of whom we have already spoken because of his prominence in scholastic theology, Richard, who died in 1173 and was the leading mystic of the house, and Adam, his contemporary (died 1177), the chief poet and hymn-writer.

Early in the fourteenth century there was a notable mystical movement in Germany which had Dominicans among its outstanding leaders and which was to persist into the latter part of the fourteenth century where we are to meet it again in the work, *Theologia Germanica,* which was to have a profound influence on many, including Martin Luther. Indeed, in this movement and others contemporary with it, we see a transition from the high tide of the period of 950 to 1350 through the ebb of 1350 to 1500 to the resurgence of the tide after 1500. In it Neoplatonism, partly mediated through Dionysius the Areopagite, was to be influential, a strange contrast with the Aristotelianism which was so potent in much of Dominican theology.

The strain which was channeled through the Dominicans was paralleled by that of the beguines and their male counterparts, the beghards, whom we have already come to know and who persisted into the fourteenth century. They were especially strong in Germany. So, too, were the Brethren of the Free Spirit, mystics, who formed themselves into secret associations, notably in Cologne, and, proscribed by the ecclesiastical authorities, were hunted out by the Inquisition. The Friends of God, as they were known, were less subject to suspicion by the hierarchy. Grouping themselves in circles whose member-ship was made up of both clergy and laymen, they sought to foster the mystical life in themselves and others, followed a course of strict asceticism, and tended to be critical of the majority of the clergy. Some of the Dominican mystics had close contacts with the Friends of God. Indeed, the greatest among the former, John Eckhart, is sometimes regarded as their father.

Why this movement should have come at this time and in this region we do not know. The period was one of distress, with civil strife and recurrent epidemics of the Black Death, but the mystics had begun to emerge before the environment reached its nadir and they were not necessarily a reaction from the sufferings of the age. Yet the insecurity and fears of the day may have contributed to them.

John ("Meister") Eckhart (c.1260–c.1327) was the chief founder of the four-teenth century German Dominican mysticism. Born in Thuringia, he early entered the Order of Preachers, then studied in the University of Paris, and, returning to Germany, was prior of at least two monasteries, was for a time head of the Saxon province of his order, was vicar-general of his order for Bohemia charged with reforming its houses, taught, was a notable preacher in the vernacular, with a clear, simple style, and, late in life, while professor of theology at Cologne, partly because of the anti-Dominican animus of the Franciscans, was accused of heresy. He appealed to the Pope, and died before verdict was given.

Eckhart protested, sincerely, that he was orthodox. Yet he verged on pan-theism. He knew scholastic theology but at times seemed to scorn it. He showed the influence of Dionysius the Areopagite, Eriugena, Hugo of St. Victor, Averroes, and Avicenna, as well as Aristotle. He held that in the human soul there is a spark, a light, which is of the same nature as God and that nowhere is God so really God as in the soul. It can be seen how he laid himself open to the charge of erasing individuality in men. In 1329 Pope John XXII branded as heretical seventeen propositions drawn from his works.

Eckhart had what he believed to be direct experience of God. His preaching grew out of his own profound religious life and he wished to help others to share it. He did not prize ecstatic emotion, but calmness and quiet. Yet he lived an active life and believed that to have peace in a life of pain was far better than to have a life of rest and peace in God. His writings were popular with some of the leading German intellectuals of the nineteenth and twentieth centuries and may have helped to shape their ideas, even if only by confirming them, especially those of Hegel.

John Tauler (died 1361), also a Dominican, was profoundly influenced by Eckhart. An earnest preacher, he was not a great scholar, but sought to strengthen ordinary folk to bear the distresses of the day. Another disciple of Eckhart was Henry Suso (c.1295 or 1300–1365), a native of Constance, who entered the Dominican Order at the age of thirteen. Deeply religious and highly imaginative from his youth, frail of body and often ill, sternly ascetic in self-flagellations and abstinence from food, he was subject to moods of deep depression and long periods of intense mental suffering. He also knew moments of high ecstasy. Not an original genius, he showed in his writings a capacity for a sentimental but surging love of God. In his later years many were drawn to him for spiritual counsel.

Ranking with Eckhart was one of the high peaks of the mysticism of the fourteenth century was John Ruysbroeck (1293–1381). A Fleming, born near Brussels, at the age of eleven he came under the instruction of his uncle, a canon in a church in Brussels, and was reared by that uncle and the latter's colleague. Educated by them, he became familiar with the works of Augustine, Dionysius the Areopagite, Gregory the Great, Bernard of Clairvaux, the Victorines, Bonaventura, and Aquinas. Ordained when he was twenty-four, he became chaplain to his uncle. In mature life the latter had a sudden soul-shaking experience which made him over from a somewhat conventional priest into a completely devoted spirit. Caught by the contagion of that dedication, the uncle's colleague and Ruysbroeck began a more austere way of life. Ruysbroeck, too, grew in his knowledge of God's love, a love which flooded his heart, and sought to present what was to him the true way of God's lovers against some of the local mysticism which seemed to him to be departing from the faith.

When he was fifty, Ruysbroeck and his two older companions withdrew to Groenendael, or Green Valley, in a forest near Brussels, and formed the nucleus of a community which eventually adopted the rule of the Augustinian Canons. There to an advanced age he gave himself to contemplation, prayer, the humble manual work of the community, joy in the birds and the animals of the wild-wood, and writing. The fruits of his pen were to have a wide influence. Tauler may have visited him and some of his books became the familiar prop-erty of many among the Friends of God. We are later to note his contribution to the early years of the Brethren of the Common Life. The best known of his works is *De Ornatu Spiritualium Nuptiarum* (*The Adornment of the Spiritual Marriage*), in which he developed the three stages of the life of the Christian mystic. His great stress was upon love.

Contemporaneous with this fourteenth century flowering of mysticism in Ger-many and Flanders was a somewhat similar movement in England. Whether it was the fruit of the Continental mystics we do not know. Like them it carried over beyond 1350 and we are to see it again. Its chief figure in the first half of the century was Richard Rolle, who was born in Yorkshire somewhere between 1290 and 1300 and died, perhaps of the Black Death, in 1349. He seems to have come from a well-to-do family but, restless with a longing which was unsatisfied by the pleasures which money made possible, he found peace only when he gave himself to following Christ in poverty. He was educated in Oxford and perhaps in Paris. Fleeing the world, he lived for a time as a hermit, but moved about, alternating between solitude and giving spiritual counsel and service. He was possessed by the love of God and devotion to Christ. He wrote extensively, put the Psalms into English, and poured out his soul in lyric poetry of praise.

SUMMARY

As the centuries passed, Christianity more and more became the conscious property of increasing elements in the population of Western Europe. The religious awakenings which in part expressed themselves in the succession of new monastic orders and in lay movements, some of them branded as heretical by the Catholic Church, were paralleled by tides which spread in ever widen-ing circles among the rank and file. By no means all in Western Europe were profoundly affected. The majority were probably touched only superficially. The period was characterized by depths of depravity and heights of sanctity. The pessimist and the cynic have much to support their claim that by and large the clergy were ignorant, slovenly, and greedy, and followed their profession as a livelihood and not a vocation, and that the laity were irreverent and looked upon the ritual of the Church as at best a form of magic by which what they wished in this life and hereafter could be wrung from a hostile or indifferent universe. Yet the impression which one gets from the records is not only one of this side of the picture, indubitably dark and real though it was, but is also one of a growing and more intelligent commitment to the Christian faith by an enlarging proportion of Western Europeans. The attempt of the earnest idealists to effect this result through the inclusive hierarchical structure of the Church had given rise to a vast ecclesiastical machinery which was already in danger of defeating the purpose which the reformers had in bringing it into being. Yet, partly through that machinery and partly in spite of it, Christianity was making an ever deeper impress upon the rank and file of the population.

SELECTED BIBLIOGRAPHY

PARISH LIFE, THE SACRAMENTS, AND THE CULT OF THE VIRGIN MARY
AND THE SAINTS

G. G. Coulton, *Ten Medieval Studies* (Cambridge University Press, 1930, pp. xi, 297). Readable, erudite, and critical of Catholicism.

G. G. Coulton, *Life in the Middle Ages: Selected, Translated & Annotated* (Cambridge University Press, 4 vols., 1928–1930). Selections from original sources.

E. L. Cutts, *Parish Priests and Their People in the Middle Ages in England* (London, Society for Promoting Christian Knowledge, 1898, pp. xvii, 579). Readable, with extensive translations from the sources.

H. Gasquet, *Parish Life in Mediaeval England* (London, Methuen & Co., 1906, pp. xix, 279). A semi-popular account.

A. Hauck, *Kirchengeschichte Deutschlands,* Vol. IV (Leipzig, J. C. Hinrichs'sche Buchhandlung, 1913, pp. viii, 1070). The initial chapter has material bearing on this topic.

H. C. Lea, *A History of Auricular Confession and Indulgences in the Latin Church* (Philadelphia, Lea Brothers & Co., 3 vols., 1896). Very useful.

J. A. MacCulloch, *Medieval Faith and Fable* (Boston, Marshall-Jones Co., 1932, pp. 345). A somewhat disparaging view.

A. J. Macdonald, *Berengar and the Reform of Sacramental Doctrine* (London, Longmans, Green & Co., 1930, pp. xii, 444). Carefully done.

J. T. McNeill and H. M. Gamer, *Medical Handbooks of Penance. A Translation of the Principal Libri Poenitentiales and Selections from Related Documents* (Columbia University Press, 1938, pp. xiv, 476). A useful compilation.

J. R. H. Moorman, *Church Life in England in the Thirteenth Century* (Cambridge University Press, 1945, pp. xxviii, 444). A thoroughly competent study, with extensive references to the sources and an important bibliography.

R. C. Mortimer, *The Origins of Private Penance in the Western Church* (Oxford University Press, 1939, pp. 195). A competent study.

B. Smalley, *The Study of the Bible in the Middle Ages* (Oxford, Basil Blackwell, 2d ed., 1952, pp. xxii, 406). Based upon extensive research. Declares that "the Bible was the most studied book of the Middle Ages" and that its language and content permeated medieval thought.

O. D. Watkins, *A History of Penance* (London, Longmans, Green & Co., 2 vols., 1920). Comprehensive.

THE BREVIARY

P. Batifol, *History of the Roman Breviary,* translated by A. M. Y. Baylay (London, Longmans, Green & Co., 1912, pp. xiv, 340). Erudite, with a strong bias in favour of the older Roman offices.

THE MYSTICS

C. Butler, *Western Mysticism. The Teaching of SS Augustine Gregory and Bernard on Contemplation and the Contemplative Life* (New York, E. P. Dutton & Company, 1923, pp. xiii, 344). Contains stimulating but debatable generalizations.

T. W. Coleman, *English Mystics of the Fourteenth Century* (London, Epworth Press, 1938, pp. 175). An excellent survey.

M. M. Comper, *The Life of Richard Rolle Together with an Edition of His English Lyrics (Now for the first time published)* (London, J. M. Dent & Sons, 1928, pp. xx, 340).

Meister Eckhart. A Modern Translation, by R. B. Blakney (New York, Harper & Brothers, 1941, pp. xxviii, 333). The translation preserves something of the easy colloquialism of the original.

R. M. Jones, *The Flowering of Mysticism. The Friends of God in the Fourteenth Century* (New York, The Macmillan Co., 1939, pp. 270). The best brief survey in English. By a distinguished American Quaker, it is sympathetic, well written, and based upon prolonged research into the sources and the pertinent secondary works, including especially Denifle.

P. Pourrat, *Christian Spirituality in the Middle Ages,* translated by S. P. Jacques (London, Burns, Oates & Washbourne, 1924, pp. xiii, 341). The second volume of a three-volume comprehensive survey by a Roman Catholic.

H. M. D. Redpath, *God's Ambassador: St. Bridget of Sweden* (Milwaukee, The Bruce Publishing Co., 1946, pp. xv, 216). A popularly written account by a Bridgettine nun.

Yorkshire Writers. Richard Rolle of Hampole, an English Father of the Church and His Followers, edited by C. Horstman (London, Swan Sonnenschein & Co., 1895, pp. xiv, 442). A useful collection of texts.

John of Ruysbroeck, *The Adornment of the Spiritual Marriage, The Sparkling Stone, The Book of Supreme Truth,* translated from the Flemish by C. A. Wynschenk Dom (London, J. M. Dent & Sons, 1916, pp. xxii, 259).

A. G. Seesholtz, *Friends of God. Practical Mystics of the Fourteenth Century* (Columbia University Press, 1934, pp. viii, 247). An excellent survey.

The Life of Blessed Henry Suso by Himself, translated from the original German by T. F. Knox, with an introduction by W. R. Inge (London, Methuen & Co., 1913, pp. xxxviii, 254). A poignant self-revelation.

E. Underhill, *Ruysbroeck* (London, G. Bell & Sons, 1914, pp. viii, 193). By an outstanding specialist on mysticism.

Chapter XXIII

THE SHAPING OF WESTERN EUROPE

When we shall have completed the chapter on which we are now embarking we will have devoted almost as many pages to the course of Christianity in Western Europe in the four centuries between 950 and 1350 as we did to the entire range of Christianity in the first five centuries of its history. Why have we done this? At first sight it may seem to be a strangely disproportionate allotment of our space, a space all too limited for the narration of so vast and important a story as the entire course of Christianity in the first nineteen and a half centuries.

It was natural that we should spend so much time on the first five hundred years. It was then that Christianity inspired the writings which comprise the New Testament, formulated its basic creeds, produced a vast body of literature, developed its organizational structure, gave rise to the monastic life, and inaugurated forms of worship which, with modifications and additions, have been standard for the large majority of Christians from that time to this. It was then, too, that Christianity achieved the seemingly impossible. From being what looked like an obscure sect of Judaism, competing with scores of other cults, it won the professed allegiance of the overwhelming majority of the population of the most powerful and the wealthiest state of that day, the Roman Empire.

In contrast, Western Europe from 950 to 1350 was by no means as populous as had been the Roman Empire at its height and was far less prominent in the total world scene than that realm had been in its heyday.

Yet the apparent distortion of perspective can be amply justified. That is partly because of the intrinsic interest of the developments in Western Europe, for here, as we have seen, Christianity displayed an amazing vitality which expressed itself in a wide variety of creative achievements. It was also because, in the face of untoward conditions, different from those which confronted it in the Roman Empire, but in their way fully as difficult, Christianity profoundly influenced more aspects of the life of Western Europe in these four centuries

546

than of the Roman Empire in five centuries. More important still, within the next six centuries the peoples of Western Europe, so largely shaped by Christianity, were to dominate all of the human race to a degree that has never been true of any other segment of mankind. This they did partly by vast migrations, partly by political and economic mastery, but even more in ideas and cultural patterns. Those nations who in the twentieth century revolted against the political and economic imperialism of the West paid Western Europeans the largely unconscious homage of adopting the science and the machines which were first developed by them, and Communism, the ideology which through Russia sought to supplant the dominion of Western civilization, had its origin in Western Europe and was deeply indebted to Christianity. It was chiefly through Western European peoples that after A.D. 1500 Christianity had an astounding geographic spread, more extensive than that of any other religion in all history.

In the next few pages we must attempt to summarize the effect of Christianity upon Western Europe during the four centuries between 950 and 1350. We need not give much space to the topic, for, important though it is, not a little has already been hinted at or covered piecemeal in the preceding seven chapters. However, we must endeavour to draw together what has been scattered through those pages, here and there adding to it, and interpreting it. This is especially important, because in that effect lies part of the answer to the questions which are a major concern of this survey, the fashion in which the Christian Gospel has operated in history and the way in which, through it, God works—if, as the Christian faith declares, God exists and interests Himself in mankind.

At the outset we must note the contrast between the situation which confronted Christianity in the Roman Empire in the first five centuries of the faith and that which it faced in Western Europe from 950 to 1350. In the Roman Empire Christianity entered a high civilization which in material wealth and power was approaching its zenith but at a time when the creative genius of Græco-Roman civilization had about spent its force and when, except for Christianity itself and in the political realm, little that was basically new was being thought or done. Many were hungry for a dependable word on the questions which men ask about the nature of the universe and the meaning and possible destiny of human life. Christianity was only one of many systems which were offering answers. It came into the scene with a minimum of institutional and creedal equipment. Such of that as it possessed it inherited mainly from Judaism. Its compelling attraction was unique, "Jesus Christ and him crucified," "risen from the dead," and to him it owed its ultimate victory, but at the outset there were no fixed forms of organization or worship and only simple, if profound and breath-taking, affirmations. As we have seen, Christianity's most striking effect upon the Roman Empire was in the realm of religion. There it eliminated most of its rivals or, as in the case of the Greek philosophies, utilized them for its purposes. With a sense of the community and unity of all the followers of Christ, it brought into being the churches, especially the Catholic Church, an extensive literature, and formidable and largely original theologies. However, upon other aspects of civilization the influence of Christianity, while noticeable, could scarcely be called revolutionary. Græco-Roman culture was by no means completely reshaped.

The situation with which Christianity had to do in Western Europe between 950 and 1350 differed strikingly from that which it met before the year 500. In name the Roman Empire still existed and stirred the imagination of the peoples of both Western and Eastern Europe. Actually it had disappeared, although the Byzantine realm claimed the designation and was in the unbroken succession, and the German kings sought added prestige in the imperial title. In Western Europe internal decay and a series of barbarian invasions which continued for more than six centuries had brought civilization to a low ebb. Near-anarchy prevailed, learning and morals had sunk to a low level, and superstition was rife. The cessation of the invasions not far from the middle of the tenth century gave opportunity to create a new civilization. In its shaping Christianity had a very large share. From the beginning it was an integral part of the whole, challenging it and entering into the warp and woof of every aspect of the newly emerging culture.

The Christianity which so profoundly moulded Western European civilization was not that which in the first century had begun its victorious course in the Græco-Roman world. It still centered about Jesus Christ and drew its inspiration from him. However, it had become all but identified with a great institution which, far more than the realm which had its capital at Constantinople or what was called the Holy Roman Empire, was the heir of the Eternal City. Much more inclusive geographically than either, more nearly than they it perpetuated the Roman genius of universality, administrative skill, and justice based on law. Its capital was Rome and its greatest Popes were born in or near Rome and had something of the political sagacity of the ablest of the Cæsars— yet partly transformed and shot through and through with what had come from the Christian heritage. As we have seen, increasingly the Church of Rome controlled the Catholic Church in Western Europe. The word Roman prefixed to Catholic in the designation of that church is accurate, both because of the growing domination by the Church of Rome and the genius which that church imparted to the whole.

The Roman Catholic Church was the major means of the transmission to this new culture of Western Europe of what went into it from the Græco-Roman past. It was not the only channel. Much came through the Greek East, much by way of the Arab world (although it was through Christians of the East that the Arabs learned most of what they acquired from the earlier Mediterranean world), some through Irish monasticism which at most had only slight ties with Rome, and some survived in Italy apart from the Church. Yet for better or for worse it was mainly to the Catholic Church that Western Europe was indebted for whatever it inherited from Greece and Rome.

We have said for better or for worse, because from the standpoint of Christ and the Gospel the Græco-Roman heritage was by no means an unmixed blessing. In many ways the Gospel and Græco-Roman culture were reciprocally contradictory. From the time that an official representative of Rome had crucified Jesus a basic tension had existed between the Gospel and that culture. As Paul so clearly declared, to Greek philosophy the cross and what it stood for were stark foolishness. It is not surprising that the attempt to reconcile the two which was undertaken by the school men began to break down before the Middle Ages were spent. Here, however, was more than a conflict between the Gospel and a particular culture. It was a symptom and a symbol of a tension between the Gospel and all civilization, between the two cities of Augustine's famous survey of history.

Something of the effect of Christianity upon the newly forming civilization of Western Europe can be seen if we take up briefly one by one the major phases of that culture.

The Christianizing of Religion

First of all we naturally place the religious aspects of Western Europe. Here Christianity faced an appalling array of problems. It had to try to bring more nearly to its standards the nominally Christian descendants of the population of the western sections of what had been the Roman Empire. For the large majority of these peoples conversion had been very superficial and the Church had great difficulty in making its discipline effective. The long series of invasions with their attendant disorder made for the deterioration of even the shoddy quality of what went by the name of Christianity. To the offspring of the Roman provincials were added the invaders and their progeny. Those from the North came with a crude polytheism, a disorderly array of many gods, and a belief in innumerable spirits, many of them malignant. While before many generations they accepted baptism, they did so largely *en masse,* by group action led by their tribal chieftains, and were loosely fitted into the fellowship of a church which was already embarrassed by the sub-Christian level of its existing constituency. In the Iberian Peninsula and Sicily, moreover, Christianity was confronted by an aggressive Islam and when it slowly won back territories which it had lost and effected the outward conversion of the former Moslems, it found that these accessions, even when their pre-Islamic ancestors had been Christians, carried over some of their Islamic beliefs and practices. It is not surprising that under these circumstances the religious life of Western Europe fell far short of the high standards set forth in the New Testament and that it had in it so many contradictions.

Yet the Gospel was making headway. This was seen in part in the many movements which we have described in the preceding chapters—in the appeal which it made to the ardent spirits who founded the new monastic orders; in individuals and groups and societies among lay folk, some of them accepted and others rejected by the Catholic Church, who sought to live the full Christian life; and in the many efforts by princes, Popes, bishops, and humble priests to make of the Catholic Church an agency for shaping all of Western Europe into a *Corpus Christianum,* a true Christendom. When only these aspects are viewed, enthusiasts hail the age as preëminently Christian, look back on it with nostalgic admiration, and regard all that followed as departure from the faith and as the progressive de-Christianization of Europe.

There is another side of the picture at which we have more than once hinted. Undoubtedly there were many lives which reflected the power of the Gospel and are rightly viewed as exemplars of Christian faith and virtue. In appalling contrast there were depths of human depravity. Among high and low, in city, village, and country, among clergy, laity, and even monks, there were flagrant brutality, gross sensuality, and unrelieved arrogance and self-seeking. To be sure, nominal assent was almost universally given to the Christian faith. There was little overt denial of what was ostensibly the community religion. In practice, however, Christian ethical standards were widely denied, and the most sacred rites of the Church were repeatedly and even habitually performed carelessly. At times they were parodied. Church offices were bought and sold and their incomes diverted to purely selfish luxury, and to gratify their lust for power ambitious men strove for place and position in the Church. Even the ablest of the Popes who had at heart the reform of the Church sought to attain that end by measures which contradicted the Gospel and therefore eventually brought frustration. Here and there, notably in the brilliant circle which surrounded the extraordinarily learned, intellectually curious, charming, arrogant, and pitiless Emperor Frederick II, while there was a half-mocking prudential conformity with the faith, there were also cynicism and the use of the Church and the faith for purposes which were in complete denial of the Gospel. Notorious scoffers were found in high places. Among the devout as well as the merely conventionally religious there were superstition, con-

fidence in astrology, and customs and beliefs which employed Christian ceremonies, sacraments, and symbols as magical means to avert disaster or to attain
desired objectives.

Indeed, here was a vivid example of what has so often been seen in the history of Christianity. The Gospel accentuates contrasts. Beginning with the
opposition aroused by Jesus which led to his crucifixion by official representatives of as high a religion and as good a government as man had thus far
known, down into the nineteenth and twentieth centuries, in periods and
regions in which the Gospel has especially displayed its power and Christianity
has been the most vigorous, that very vitality has been paralleled by heightened
opposition. At times, as in the first centuries of Christianity, that has shown
itself in persecutions; in other times, as in the one with which we are here
dealing, it has been by outward assent but by denial in practice; in still other
eras, notably the nineteenth and twentieth centuries, it has been by frank rejection by large elements in traditionally Christian lands and by the adoption of
methods by presumably Christian nations which have contradicted Christian
principles.

CHALLENGING MORALS WITH CHRISTIAN STANDARDS

Intimately associated with religion were morals. Here, as we have repeatedly
seen, Christianity was the chief means of disciplining the population. This was
done in many ways, partly through sermons, partly through the teaching of
the Ten Commandments, partly through story and drama, and partly through
the sacrament of penance with its confession, prescription of penalties, and
absolution. A major deterrant from sin was the fear of hell and the Devil and
his hosts, for these were very vivid to the peoples of the period. Scoffers who
professed not to believe in them might on their death beds turn in terror to
the priest. Yet in principle the chief motive for repentance and righteous living
was the love of God. There is no denying the vast gulf between the ideal held
up in the Gospel and the behaviour of a large proportion of the population. It
was a robustious age in which life was cheap, warfare chronic, and for many,
perhaps the majority, the daily routine drab and sordid. Yet the Gospel did
not allow to go unchallenged the degradation accentuated by centuries of disorder. It created a tension. Thousands responded to it and other thousands
who fell lamentably short of the ideal paid homage to the characters of those
who to their minds approximated it.

Adequately to appraise the effect of Christianity on the religious and moral
character of Europe we must recall the honour paid men and women like
Bernard of Clairvaux, Francis of Assisi, Clara, Elizabeth of Hungary, Dominic,
Bonaventura, and Aquinas. Many were canonized by popular acclaim before

the Catholic Church gave its official imprimatur. Thousands who did not attain to their standards either sought to emulate them or felt themselves rebuked by them. Numbers of those labelled heretics but who sought to embody the Gospel were revered by the rank and file of their followers.

SHAPING THE INTELLECTUAL LIFE

One of the striking features of the period is the close association of religious and intellectual awakenings. We have seen that in the dark ages between the years 500 and 950 in large areas the only schools were the ones maintained in monasteries, those islands of orderly living in a time when civilization was at a low ebb. We have also noted that as the invasions subsided and the shadows began to lift, monasteries and cathedrals were the main centres of study and teaching. Some of the new monastic houses distrusted the pagan authors whose writings were regarded as a normal basis of education and not all cathedrals had significant schools. However, in contrast there were such houses as that of Bec, founded out of deep religious conviction, which within a generation became a major seat of intellectual creativity. St. Victor, the famous community of Augustinian Canons, was noted both for its earnest spiritual life which brought it fame for its mystics and for its philosophers and theologians. Some of the schools maintained in connexion with cathedrals for the preparation of clergy attracted great teachers and were thronged by eager students. The universities which began to appear at the end of the twelfth century and which multiplied in the thirteenth century were largely church foundations. As we have said, that of Paris, the model for most of the universities for Northern Europe, developed from a cathedral school. The rise of the universities coincided with the revival which found expression in the mendicant orders. The Dominicans, with the emphasis placed on scholarship by their founder, gravitated towards them almost automatically. It is significant that, in spite of the opposition of Francis, the Brothers Minor also early established themselves in the universities. There seems to have been something in the Christian faith which inspired many of those who committed themselves fully to it to intellectual inquiry and adventure. Thus Roger Bacon, a first-class mind, caught by the enthusiasm and devotion of the first flush of the Franciscans and sharing the somewhat stormy and unconventional character of that order, became a forerunner of modern science. We have already seen something of the wide range of the intellectual inquiries of the Dominican Albertus Magnus.

This stimulus by Christianity to fearless intellectual activity should not surprise us. We have already met it in such outstanding minds in the earlier centuries as Origen, Augustine, and Eriugena. We shall run across it increasingly as the centuries pass. To the northern peoples who had invaded Western

Europe and to whom the world about them had neither order nor meaning, the Christian faith brought the conception of a universe created by One Whose august purpose is shot through and through with love and Who governs the worlds by uniform law. In that universe the Christian must move reverently but he can also move confidently. History, so Christianity teaches, is not sound and fury, signifying nothing, as the barbarians had believed, nor is it a weary repetition of cycles as the Greeks had regarded it. It had a beginning in the creative act of God and moves towards a culmination determined by Him. It is not strange, therefore, that the beginnings of the science and the machines of Western Europe are found in this period and among those whose spirits and minds had been gripped by the Christian faith. It has been said that the first machines were the clocks developed in monasteries in connexion with the canonical hours. Whether or not this is true, it was to those who were moved by the Christian faith that the beginnings of the scientific outlook and method in Western Europe must be traced.

Moreover, we must remind ourselves that much of the literature of the period concerned itself with Christian themes. This was true of philosophy and theology. It was also true of the poets. Walther von der Vogelweide (c.1170–c.1230), the prince of the Minnesingers, from the beginning had a serious moral and religious strain which deepened with the years. That most famous of all the European poets of the period, Dante (1265–1321), wove his greatest work, the *Commedia,* around the Christian faith. The popular tales which centered about the Holy Grail and which later were given literary dignity are evidence of the fashion in which the Christian drama of redemption had taken possession of the imagination of large circles in Europe.

CHRISTIANITY AND ART

Any who travel widely in Western Europe cannot but be aware of the fashion in which the religious awakenings of these centuries were contemporary with striking outbursts of artistic creativity. The evidence is still there for all who will to see, in monasteries, churches, cathedrals, and museums. Only a fraction of what was produced has survived wars, revolutions, and the tooth of time. Yet even the remnants are impressive. Not all art and architecture was religious. Castles reflected the place of the king and the feudal noble, and town halls bore witness to the communal spirit of the growing cities. Yet most of the largest structures were churches. Some of them were monastic, and it is thought-provoking that they do not owe their size to the desire to accommodate large congregations. They were for use by the monks, and seldom were those in any one house numerous enough to fill more than what was called the choir. They were for the worship of God and to enshrine the

Eucharist with its mystery and wonder. To be sure, the abbots who directed the building were probably often moved as much by ambition to promote their own fame or the prestige of their monastery as by the desire to glorify God, but the latter was at least the ostensible purpose. So with parish churches and cathedrals: priests, benefactors, and bishops may have urged on the building from ambition to perpetuate their own memory or from the sheer joy of achievement. Yet the theme was Christian. The Biblical story was told in sculpture, mosaic, painting, and stained glass, and the altar with its bloodless sacrifice was the focus of the whole. The wish to equip the altar and its services in a fashion which would honour the Presence so confidently affirmed inspired the lavish expenditure of imaginative skill on vessels, furnishings, and vestments. Most of the painting of the period had Christian subjects. Monkish devotion found expression in the painstaking and often beautiful illumination of the manuscripts whose transcription was part of the labour prescribed by the monastic rule.

This is not the place to tell the story of the architecture of the age, with its accomplishments in various forms of the Romanesque, developed, as the name indicates, from Roman antecedents, and in its most notable examples not a debasement of its prototypes, but a fresh and stirring creation, or in the Gothic with its ingenious flying buttresses which made possible its great windows and soaring pinnacles and towers. Nor can we do more than mention the stiff and stylized painting and sculpture, seemingly fearful of distracting the attention from their religious purpose by obtruding fleshly beauty. Even the multitudes of figures and carvings which ornamented the Gothic structures and which often were faithful pictures of forms from everyday life or else grotesque or humorous expressions of the imagination could be interpreted as the consecration of all of His creatures to the service of God. Here was an overflowing, exuberant genius which gave itself to divine themes and which was at least in part evoked by them.

RUTHLESS POWER AND THE CHRISTIAN FAITH

One of the notable groups of effects of Christianity in this period was in the political realm. It was in this area of life that at the outset power seemed most ruthless. Governments were set up and dominated by strong men who had won their position by intrigue and war. The class with the most prestige was not the scholars, as in theory in China, or the priests, as in Hindu India, but the warriors. The clergy were tempted to ape them. The Roman Empire had been welded together by conquest and diplomacy which relied on arms. Its head, Emperor (Imperator), by his very title was commander-in-chief and depended upon the legions for his position. Western Europe added to that tradition the many states which were carved out by war. Its dynasties were founded by successful warriors and its kings and nobles felt themselves compelled to resort to battle to hold their possessions and to extend them. This was true not only in the centuries of the invasions but also after the invasions had ceased.

As Christianity spread and members of the ruling class accepted it, it had an effect upon the theory and practice of government and upon the conduct of war and the manners of the warrior. As we have seen, most of the new monastic movements were begun by members of the nobility. There were even kings who divested themselves of their crowns to enter a monastery. Yet this was withdrawing from the burdens of civil office and had little direct effect on government. However, there were many who retained their titles and positions and who attempted to bring to them Christian insight. Coronations were normally by Christian rites. No one could be Holy Roman Emperor except through coronation by the Pope. Kings and Holy Roman Emperors were in theory bound to conduct themselves as Christians and to rule for the benefit of their subjects. For many, perhaps the majority, this was only a matter of form. Some, however, took the obligation seriously. For example, we have seen that the Emperor Henry III proclaimed a Day of Indulgence in which he professed to forgive his enemies and urged his subjects to emulate him.

We have noted something of the manner in which the Christian conscience attempted to deal with war by initiating the Truce of God and the Peace of God and by developing and inculcating chivalry, the code of conduct for warriors of gentle birth. We read, too, that in 1119 the Council of Rheims instructed chaplains to discontinue religious ministrations in castles to which booty from unjust wars was carried. A much more pretentious proposal was made in the twelfth century for Papal prohibition of all wars between princes, for Papal arbitration of all disputes, for the excommunication and deposition of any ruler who failed to observe a decision when it was once rendered, and for armed assistance by the clergy and lay rulers to one who was attacked after submitting to the Papal verdict. Obviously this was not adopted. However, the sense of being part of Christendom, of membership in a family of nations, laid the foundations for a body of law designed to govern the relations among princes.

Christian scholars elaborated political theory in the light of their faith. They held that both Church and state, Papacy and Empire, were founded by God and in the last analysis were responsible to Him. Aquinas taught that a ruler exercises his power as a divine trust and that a monarch who has betrayed that trust has lost his right to the obedience of his subjects. Some radicals, notably the Dominican John of Paris and Marsilius of Padua, maintained that the powers of both the civil and ecclesiastical officials are based upon the sovereignty of the people. There were dreamers who, like Dante in his *Monarchia,* envisioned a mankind-embracing Christian society in which the Pope and the Emperor were to be the leaders.

The conviction was widely held that the state is a divine concession to human weakness, but that its purpose is the maintenance of righteousness; that law, as the embodiment of justice, is above the king and must be obeyed by him; and that the relation between the king and his subjects is based upon a reciprocal obligation to maintain peace and justice. Some of the concepts of the Roman law which became influential in much of Europe were rethought in Christian terms. Thus the term *justitia* might be employed where the purpose was the salvation of the soul rather than the ownership of tangible property.

Christian conviction strove to eliminate some of the crude methods of determining justice which had been inherited from a pre-Christian Teutonic past. Prominent among them were trial by fire and water and by battle. Some bishops might defend and even advocate them. However, again and again Church councils and Popes condemned them.

To be sure, many official spokesmen for Christianity conformed to the tradition of resorting to intrigue and armed force. Popes fomented wars, summoned armies to their aid, sought to offset one monarch by calling another to their assistance, and preached Crusades. The Crusading orders attempted to combine the calling of the monk with the profession of the soldier. Yet there was a persistent conviction that members of the clergy should not bear arms. Here, as in so many aspects of life, the Christian ideal created a tension by challenging men to attain what was seemingly impossible, but what, prodded by Christian teaching, they knew to be right.

CHRISTIANITY AND ECONOMICS

In the keen competition for livelihood, how far was Christianity effective?

It is clear that through monasticism Christianity did something to give dignity to labour and added greatly to agriculture and so to the increase in the supply of food. Under the Benedictine rule work was obligatory. Although in many of the Benedictine houses food and clothing came from estates cultivated by serfs and while in several monastic orders manual work in the fields was assigned to lay brothers and the choir monks gave themselves to prayer and study, in others all the monks, even those of aristocratic birth, toiled in their gardens or on the lands of the monastery. Whether by all members of the community or only by the lay brothers, monasteries did much to clear land, bring it under cultivation, and develop improved crops and methods of tillage.

The first use of marl to enrich the soil is attributed to them and they were noted for their vineyards and their wines.

In industry and trade the impact of Christianity was uneven. In principle all taking of interest was strictly condemned and absolution could be had only by full restitution of the sums so acquired. In practice the Knights Templar became famous as bankers. In theory the ideal was believed to be communal ownership and individual use, for God was held to be the supreme owner and the world to be for the benefit of mankind. From the common store each should have whatever he needed. There were those who maintained that Christ and his apostles had followed the way of absolute poverty and insisted that those who fully gave themselves to him, especially the clergy and the monks, should follow their example. The official Church condemned this view and it was argued that because of the taint of sin in man community of property was impossible and private property permissible. Yet in practice, as we have seen, the monasteries held their property as a community possession. There were, moreover, many non-monastic communities of lay folk, among them beguines and beghards, who owned their property in common or adopted apostolic poverty.

Much of the trade and commerce of the age was carried on through guilds. Guilds had religious features and supposedly were guided by Christian standards. The ideal of a just price was generally acknowledged, that is, that a merchant or artisan should ask for his goods only what was fair. Theorists attempted to determine the principles for ascertaining it. The just price was applied to wages as well as to the sale of the products of labour.

THE CHRISTIAN IMPRESS ON WIDE RANGES OF THE IDEALS AND LIFE OF THE COMMUNITY

In addition to those aspects of life which were religious, moral, intellectual, æsthetic, political, and economic, Christianity affected profoundly the ideals and to a large extent other phases of the practice of the society and civilization of Western Europe. More and more as the period wore on it made itself felt in all ranges of the life of the community.

This was seen in the growing value placed on the individual as possessing an eternal soul for whose salvation the Son of God had given his life. Thus Meister Eckhart said that authorities usually taught that all persons are of equal rank by nature and went beyond this and held that the meaning of the incarnation is that by becoming man God meant to lift not just a few, as might have been the case had Jesus Christ been merely a man chosen from his fellows to be exalted, but entire human nature and with it all men into His likeness and His fellowship. We may recall that Bridget dared to rebuke the King of

Sweden for his callous exploitation of the poor. Centuries earlier, King Olaf Haraldsson of Norway, who was largely responsible for the conversion of his country, forbade the exposure of infants (except monstrosities) and decreed that at the opening of the national *thing* (the assembly of notables of the realm) a slave should not be sacrificed as heretofore, but freed. These instances could be multiplied many fold.

Socially Western Europe of the Middle Ages, as later, was a fairly tightly stratified society. At the lowest level were the slaves and the half-free serfs. Yet with the growing permeation of society by Christian ideals, consciences were becoming uneasy. No one could hear, day after day or Sunday after Sunday, the *Magnificat,* with its affirmation that God had put down the mighty from their seats and exalted them of low degree and that He had filled the hungry with good things and had sent the rich empty away, without sometime becoming aware of its contradiction of what he saw about him. The Christian teaching was that slaves had souls and equally with their masters could be heirs of eternal salvation.

Manumission of slaves was frequent and was often done by the master shortly before his death as a service which would work for the salvation of his soul. Significantly, the motives assigned in the formal documents which implemented the act were the brotherhood of man, the example of Christ, love for God, and the hope of salvation. In 1102 a Church council in London forbade the slave trade. In 1179 the Third Lateran Council, theoretically acting for all the Catholic Church, declared that no Christian should be subjected to slavery. When in the thirteenth century Bologna emancipated its serfs, it professed to have derived from Christianity the motive which prompted the act. While in political life it was practically impossible for one of lowly birth to rise to high position, the Church was much more flexible. Although scions of the nobility had a better opportunity for advancement in office than those of low degree, instances were not wanting of sons of humble parentage becoming bishops. To mention only one instance out of many, Robert Grosseteste, scholar and reforming Bishop of Lincoln, was of very obscure birth. Some of the canons of his cathedral were disgruntled by his elevation, but the fact that this was possible for sheer ability and character is evidence that in the Church these could win recognition.

The Christian faith also stimulated care for the sick, the poor, and the stranger. In a society where strife was chronic and survival seemed to depend on ruthless struggle which had no use for the weak, monasteries regularly entertained travellers, parishes cared for the indigent, and in the name of Christ hospitals were founded and maintained for the ill and the aged.

The position of women was affected. To be sure, as we have said, it was a man's world. In an age and a society in which warfare was chronic and the aristocracy were bred to arms, women were subordinate and men played fast and loose with them. However, it is evidence of the growing influence of Christianity that in the thirteenth and fourteenth centuries there were numbers of women who were eventually canonized, thus being recognized by the Church as worthy of emulation by all Christians. The cult of the Virgin Mary could not but make for reverence for womanhood and motherhood. Chivalry extolled loyalty to the lady who had won the devotion of the knight. There may be more than a coincidence in the fact that the accentuation of the cult of the Virgin and the development of chivalry were features of the same centuries. Closely associated with chivalry were the troubadours and the minnesingers, poets who extolled love. It may have been because of the impact of the Christian ideal that they sang of the objects of their affection not only for their physical charms but also for the beauty of their souls.

Here, as in so much of life, especially where it was challenged by the Christian faith, there were striking contrasts. Within the Church these were represented by Eve, subordinate to man and an agent of his fall, and the Virgin Mary and some of the women saints, and between the monastic conception, on the one hand, which viewed woman as a temptation and prized celibacy and, on the other hand, the teaching that marriage is a sacrament and therefore a channel of grace. In courtly lay circles there was the exaltation of the kind of love found in the poems of the pagan Ovid, and also the inculcation of loyalty to God and to one's lady in such fashion that these two were believed not to be contradictory.

As we have seen, marriage was regarded by the Church as a sacrament. In the midst of a society made chaotic by repeated invasions and chronic war and where for millions abject poverty was normal, the sex urge, always a problem with possibilities either for degradation or for noble achievement, often gave rise to grave irregularities among high and low. Here the Christian faith continued to point to the possibility of worthy direction and the Catholic Church by both negative prohibitions and the positive investing of the marriage tie with sanctity sought to make the Christian ideal a reality. While for multitudes, probably the majority, practice fell far short of what the Church taught, thousands, whether those who voluntarily chose the road of celibacy as a divine vocation or those who entered into the marriage tie, demonstrated that sex could be a blessing and not a curse. Marriages were normally arranged by the parents and were without romantic love. The latter was widely sought outside the marriage bond, although it did not necessarily go beyond what the Christian ideal could permit. Yet perhaps more often than not, between husband and wife there were, if not love, genuine affection and respect.

The effort was made to keep Sundays and other holy days free from the ordinary occupations of the week. Stories were told of the dire calamities which descended upon those who persisted in labouring or in holding or going to markets and fairs on these days. Some of the great festivals of the Christian year were the occasion for drunkenness and rowdyism, but the attempt was made to stress their religious significance.

Among the themes of sermons, including those of the friars, was the denunciation of extravagance and luxury in dress, of gambling, of dancing, and of masques, and at times the preachers had such effect that bonfires were built into which women cast what were pilloried as the instruments of sinful frivolities. Hunting and gaming were also condemned, but some writers and preachers held these to be contrary to the Christian profession only if carried to excess.

CONTRASTS AND AN UNRESOLVED QUESTION

On the area where once the Roman Empire had flourished there arose three civilizations, the Byzantine Greek, the Arab, and the Western European. Each was an heir of Greece and Rome and incorporated much from these great predecessors. To each distinctive features were added. Of the three that of Western Europe proved by far the most dynamic. By the twentieth century it was to spread over all the earth and by the mid-twentieth century varying elements from it were to be adopted by every people and tribe. Why was this? Why was it the civilization of Western Europe rather than that of the Byzantine Empire or the Arabs which was to prove so creative and potent? Presumably the world traveller of the middle of the tenth century would not have predicted that outcome. Probably he would have chosen Arab civilization first, Byzantine culture second, and Western Europe last as the one carrying with it the wave of the future. What made the difference? Was it race? That is too mixed a factor to be separated out and proved to be the cause. Was it natural resources? In these, if all natural endowments are included, the three seem to have been too nearly equal to account for the contrast. Was it climate? There, again, the three were too nearly alike to warrant regarding it as the decisive element.

Was the cause to be found in religion? As between the Byzantine and Western European civilization on the one hand and the Arab civilization on the other, here was a clear-cut and striking contrast. In the one Christianity was the professed faith and in the other Islam. Moreover, it may be significant that it was largely through Christians that the Arabs were introduced to Greek thought, that in the centuries of greatest Arab creativity the Christian communities in the Arab realms were still large, and that as they dwindled the cultural ferment in the Arab world declined. Yet Western Europe proved to be far more continuously creative than did Byzantine Greek culture, and both were adherents of Christianity and, indeed, of Catholic Christianity.

May it be that the answer is to be found primarily in a combination of the contrast in religions and in the conditions under which the religions operated? May the decisive factor in the dynamic in Western Europe have been Christianity and the conditions by which it was surrounded? Can it be that Western Europe forged to the fore because in it, largely through history and geography, Christianity had freer course than in the Byzantine realms? By history we mean the fact that the Roman Empire more nearly disintegrated in Western Europe than in the Byzantine continuation and that therefore Christianity was less shackled by the state. The geographic element is seen in the circumstance that, being on the Western tip of Eurasia, Western Europe was less subject to the pressure of non-Christian invaders, and especially of the Moslem invaders, than was the Byzantine Empire, and that therefore Christianity was less handicapped by being constantly on the defense and ultimately being subject to Moslem rulers.

We cannot be sure of the answer. Probably it is not to be found solely in one factor. However, that the presence of Christianity was the major cause is at least an arguable hypothesis. It is certain that it was in this period which we have been covering that Western Europe began to give indications of its future dynamic and prominence, for it was then that a distinctively Western European culture began to emerge. It was then, as we have seen, that Western Europeans first began the expansion which later, after a pause between the middle of the fourteenth century and the latter part of the fifteenth century, was to carry them all over the globe. Even between 950 and 1350 they had penetrated from North America to the Far East and from Greenland to South India and the Malay Peninsula, over more of the planet than had any other group of mankind. It was also precisely in these centuries that a striking revival in Christianity occurred and that the faith was increasingly moulding every aspect of the newly emerging culture.

Again and again we shall have occasion to remind ourselves that Western European civilization has by no means been an unqualified blessing to mankind. Indeed, in it and through it some of mankind's chronic evils have had their most colossally destructive effects. Outstanding are the wars, the materialism, and the exploitation of men by their fellows which have followed the development of science and machines. If Christianity is even partially responsible for the creativity and dynamic of Western civilization, it may have contributed to the phenomenal and tragic growth of these evils, evils which are direct contradictions of the Christian ideal for men. Has, then, Christianity miscarried? Has it been twisted to curse rather than to bless mankind? Can we gain here any inkling of the fashion in which God works in history? To this question we will recur again and again.

Before we seek to suggest more in detail, as we hope to do later, a possible answer to this searching and sobering query we will do well to remind ourselves that Christianity began in seeming weakness in a homeless birth in an inn, and that its most frequent symbol, a cross, records apparent frustration and defeat. Yet even by the year 1350 that faith had spread more widely than had any religion up to that time and in Western Europe it was entering deeply into a culture which was throbbing with vitality, a culture which presented stark contrasts and striking tensions which were accentuated and to no small degree due to the challenge of the Christian ideal.

SELECTED BIBLIOGRAPHY

The Art of Courtly Love by Andreas Capellanus with introduction, translation, and notes by J. J. Parry (Columbia University Press, 1941, pp. xi, 218). A twelfth century author.

G. G. Coulton, *Five Centuries of Religion* (Cambridge University Press, 4 vols., 1923–1950). Of this monumental work, with its constant reference to the sources and its sturdy debunking of the idealization of the Christianity of the Middle Ages, *Volume III, Getting and Spending* bears more upon this chapter than does any of the others.

G. G. Coulton, *Life in the Middle Ages Selected Translated & Annotated* (Cambridge University Press, 4 vols., 1928–1930). Selections from the primary sources.

C. G. Crump and E. F. Jacobs, editors, *The Legacy of the Middle Ages* (Oxford University Press, 1926, pp. xii, 549). Essays by various experts covering a wide range of aspects of the life of Western Europe in the Middle Ages.

C. Dawson, *Religion and the Rise of Western Culture* (New York, Sheed & Ward, 1950, pp. xvi, 286). Gifford Lectures by a scholarly Roman Catholic layman.

S. C. Easton, *Roger Bacon and His Search for a Universal Science. A Reconsideration of the Life and Work of Roger Bacon in the Light of His Own Stated Purposes* (Oxford, Basil Blackwell, 1952, pp. vii, 255). Excellent. Based upon extensive research.

Bede Jarrett, *Social Theories of the Middle Ages 1200–1500* (Westminster, Md., The Newman Bookshop, 1942, pp. ix, 280). By a Dominican.

J. A. MacCulloch, *Medieval Faith and Fable* (Boston, Marshall-Jones Co., 1932, pp. 345). A somewhat disparaging view.

H. Rashdall, *The Universities of Europe in the Middle Ages*, rev. ed., edited by F. M. Powicke and A. B. Emden (Oxford University Press, 3 vols., 1936). The standard account.

H. O. Taylor, *The Mediæval Mind. A History of the Development of Thought and Emotion in the Middle Ages* (London, Macmillan & Co., 2 vols., 1911). A standard survey from the barbarian invasions to and including Duns Scotus, Ockham, and Dante.

E. Troeltsch, *The Social Teaching of the Christian Churches,* translated by Olive Wyon (New York, the Macmillan Co., 2 vols., 1931). The second half of the first volume of this standard work covers this period.

Chapter XXIV

THE EASTERN CHURCHES FROM A.D. 950
TO A.D. 1350

While the developments in Western Europe which we have been describing were in progress, what was happening in the churches in the East? Here Christianity had begun. Here it had its earliest numerical strength. Here had lived most of its creative minds of the first five centuries, and here monasticism had arisen. Yet these churches were more exposed to Islam than was the Christianity of Western Europe. They were nearer to the sources of the successive waves of invasion from the heart-land of Eurasia, in this period chiefly Turks and Mongols, and they were more divided by cultural, racial, and regional barriers, by ancient feuds, and by theological controversies than were the Christians of Western Europe.

We have seen the threat and the opportunity which came to them through the Mongol conquests and we have said something of their geographic expansion. We have noted how through the Byzantine wing of the Catholic Church the faith spread into Russia. We have watched the wide extension of Nestorian Christianity among minorities scattered across Asia from Mesopotamia into India and to the China Sea and have noted that through one of these minorities, the Keraïts, some of the Mongol princes were baptized as infants and there seemed some possibility that the rank and file of the Mongols might follow. Here was a geographic expansion of vast extent which for the time being appeared to hold promise of a further growth that might embrace Eastern Europe and most of Asia. When taken together with the contemporary vigour in the Christianity of Western Europe and the even greater areas traversed by missionaries of that branch of the faith, they constituted a forward surge in the Christian tide which was astonishing after the recession which accompanied the decline and disintegration of the Roman Empire. We have also recorded how through the Crusades the leaders of the Western wing of the Catholic Church were hopeful for the reunion of the severed branches of

564

that comprehensive Catholic Church which had arisen in the Roman Empire but which had broken apart as that realm went to pieces. It was an era of achievement and of even greater possibilities.

We must now take up these Eastern Churches one by one and tell briefly the story of each.

THE BYZANTINE WING OF THE CATHOLIC CHURCH

First of all we must turn to the largest of these bodies, the Greek or Byzantine wing of the Catholic Church. Here there was high tragedy. We have seen that recovery from the blows given by the decline of Rome and the great invasions appeared to have begun earlier than in the West. Here the period 950–1350 opened hopefully with the conversion of the state which centered about Kiev, the nucleus of the future Russia, the empire where the largest member of the family of Orthodox churches was to arise. Yet the mother church, that of Constantinople, was to be dealt a nearly fatal blow by its fellow-Catholics of the West, a blow much more weakening than any thus far suffered from that traditional foe, Islam.

It was not until the period was far along that tragedy came. The advance which had been begun in the ninth century continued into the first half of the eleventh century. From the standpoint of geographic extent and economic power the Byzantine Empire expanded and reached a high point not far from the middle of the eleventh century. Under various rulers of what was called the Macedonian Dynasty Byzantine prestige was enhanced and partial control was renewed in South Italy and along the Adriatic, Bulgaria was subdued, the Crimea was an important outpost, the peoples of the Caucasus were tied to Constantinople by heavy subsidies to their rulers, much of Armenia was annexed, and Byzantine might was acknowledged in Northern Syria. Won by commercial concessions, the Venetians added their fleets to Byzantine naval power. In spite of the drain of the wars of conquest, the imperial treasury was replenished by taxes on industry and trade and by revenues from the newly annexed lands. Constantinople, the cultural and political centre of the realm, was the wealthiest city in Christendom. Although by no means as extensive or as rich as was China under the contemporary Sung Dynasty, or as the Roman Empire had been even as late as Justinian, this Byzantine Greek successor of the Roman name was staging a notable recovery.

Then, in dramatic fashion, came a series of political reverses. The death of Basil II in 1025 after a long reign marked the removal of the monarch under whom the realm had reached its apex. The Macedonian Dynasty faded out in a succession of mediocre Emperors. Domestic anarchy was paralleled by the successful advance of the Seljuk Turks, folk from Central Asia who, converted to Islam, had made themselves masters of the decaying Abbasid Caliphs at Baghdad. By 1081 the Turks were dominant in most of Armenia and Asia Minor. In South Italy by 1071 Byzantine rule was erased by the Norman conquest and there were revolts on the east shore of the Adriatic.

In 1081 Alexius Comnenus founded a dynasty, that of the Comneni, which lasted until 1185. Under Alexius Comnenus, who reigned from 1081 to 1118, and under his son, John II Comnenus, who followed him and died in 1143, a partial recovery was achieved. Partly through the aid of the First Crusade, Byzantine suzerainty was again established over much of Asia Minor and even over Antioch. Late in the dynasty Byzantine troops once more landed in Italy, but at the expense of alienating Venice, whose friendship was already waning. But within a few years Byzantine forces finally left Italy, never to return. Moreover, the interior of Asia Minor was again lost to the Seljuk Turks.

However, under the later Comneni there was something of a cultural renaissance. Art and letters flowered again and the great literature of pre-Christian Greece still had its students.

We have already spoken (Chapter XVII) of the conquest of Constantinople in 1204 by the Fourth Crusade and the setting up of a Latin empire in that city. That event was a culmination of encroachments from the aggressive West which had long been in process. From the time of the First Crusade, warriors from Western Europe ostensibly on their way to the Holy Land, although at times a help, had been an embarrassment to the Byzantine rulers. In South Italy the Normans advanced on the traditionally Greek areas and in time expelled the Byzantine forces. In 1147 the Normans had invaded Greece, even more an integral part of the Byzantine realms. The rising tide of anti-Western nationalist feeling in Constantinople had come to a climax in the slaughter of the Latins in that city in 1182. Partly in retaliation, in 1185 the Normans had sacked Salonika.

By no means all the Byzantine territories were incorporated into the Latin empire. In them an aroused Greek nationalism supported princes who claimed to be the legitimate Roman Emperors. In 1261 one of these, Michael Paleologus, took Constantinople and ended the feeble Latin regime. From the Paleologi were to come Byzantine Emperors until the capture of Constantinople by the Turks in 1453 established the Moslems in that Christian capital. Yet never was their empire to approach in size that of the Macedonian Dynasty. Western Europeans, among them Venetians and Genoese, were long to retain parts of what had been Byzantine territory, including Athens, some of the islands in the Ægean, Crete, and a section of Asia Minor. It was fellow-Christians from the West quite as much as the Moslem Turks who were responsible for the final collapse of Christian Byzantium.

These political disasters could not but affect the Eastern wing of the Catholic Church and deepen the widening gulf between it and the Western wing of that church.

OUTSTANDING FEATURES OF THE BYZANTINE CHURCH

Several features must be noted of that branch of the Catholic Church which looked to the Patriarch of Constantinople as its ranking bishop. Most, if not all of them, had appeared earlier but were now intensified.

One of them was the lack of creative movements comparable to those which were surging in the Christianity of Western Europe. No new monastic orders appeared which could be regarded as counterparts of those in the West. Nor were there dissident movements—"heresies"—which were as vigorous as those in the West, unless it was the Bogomils, and these were Slavic rather than Byzantine. Much attention was paid to theology, but no fresh approaches were made which equalled those of the school men. While occasionally, as we shall see, showing a critical and independent attitude towards the state, the Byzantine Church had no such numerous and determined succession as had the West of men who sought through the hierarchy to purify the Church, to make it an instrument for raising the spiritual and moral level of all society, and to that end to free the Church from the control of the civil authorities.

Somewhat and perhaps closely related to this characteristic was the conviction of the Eastern wing of the Catholic Church that it was the champion and guardian of the true Christian faith as that had been taught by the early apostles. It regarded itself as orthodox, so much so, indeed, that Orthodox eventually became the designation by which it distinguished itself from other churches. The family of national churches whose major member in these centuries was that of the Byzantine Empire regarded as of its essence the conservation of the Christian faith, changeless, and looked askance not only on those churches in the East which earlier had separated from the Catholic Church, but also at what it deemed the innovations of the Western wing of the Catholic Church.

The reasons for this relative absence of fresh movements and for this sturdy adherence to what was deemed orthodox Christianity were probably complex. The chief of them, however, may have been the fact that the Byzantine Empire was chronically on the defensive. That realm was the waning continuation of the Roman Empire and of the Græco-Roman and especially the Greek heritage. It was a major bulwark of Christendom against Islam. Like the other churches of the East which geography compelled to face a triumphant Islam, it sought to preserve its existence by holding uncompromisingly to what had come down to it from the fathers and to distrust all variation as enervating disloyalty which would be productive of divisions and so of weakness. In contrast, the Christianity of Western Europe was not so immediately under pressure from Islam and, when in the tenth century the barbarian invasions subsided, it began a vigorous territorial expansion and was freer to reach out in new ways to meet the challenges in its central domains.

Another and a very striking characteristic of this Eastern wing of the Catholic Church was the fact that it possessed sufficient vitality to survive the state with which it had been intimately associated. This was seen more clearly in the next period when the Byzantine Empire finally succumbed to the conquering Turk. However, it was also true of the eleventh, twelfth, and thirteenth centuries when, as we have seen, that realm was shrinking. As the Byzantine state tottered towards its slow death the Church survived and in Greek areas became the refuge of Greek nationality. Moreover, as we are to say more at length a little later, even during these centuries of the fatal illness of the Byzantine Empire, the Christianity which looked to the capital as its main centre was spreading and showing renewed vitality on some of its geographic frontiers.

LIMITED CÆSAROPAPISM

We must call attention to the fact that the Church was not always tamely subservient to the Byzantine or Eastern Roman Emperors. In earlier chapters we have noted how from the time of Constantine in the fore part of the fourth century the Emperors had taken an active part in the affairs of the Church. Continuing the pre-Christian tradition that religion and religious cults must be subservient to the state, they had sought, usually successfully, to dominate the Church. They called general councils, expressed themselves on theological issues, and controlled the election of the Patriarchs of Constantinople. Here was preëminently what was known as Cæsaropapism, the kind of control of the Church and its hierarchy by the prince to which the lay rulers of Western Europe aspired but which they were not uniformly able to achieve.

Yet even in Constantinople the Emperors did not always fully have their way. Earlier (Chapter XI) we have seen how in the case of the Patriarchs Photius and Ignatius the Emperors met determined opposition in their attempts to control the Church. The able Nicephorus II, who reigned from 963 to 969, ordered that the bishops reach no decision and make no nominations or promotions without imperial consent. Yet the Patriarch refused to crown the next monarch, John Tzimisces (reigned 969–976), ostensibly because he had murdered his predecessor, until he had abrogated this command. Nicephorus II also attempted to curb the power of the Church and of the monasteries by forbidding the creation of new religious foundations or the enlargement and enrichment of those already in existence. But in 988 pressure from the Church and the monks was sufficiently strong to bring about the rescinding of this edict. Michael Cerularius, Patriarch 1043–1058, sought to make the Church independent of the state somewhat in the fashion that the contemporary reformers in Western Europe were endeavouring to do, but by no means necessarily in imitation of them. For a time he appeared to be succeeding, but the Emperor whom he had helped put on the throne turned against him, he was deposed near the end of 1058 and, exiled, died a few days later. However, almost immediately he was canonized by popular acclaim, the Emperor was compelled by public opinion to give him an elaborate funeral, and the next Patriarch instituted an annual feast in his honour. The Patriarch Arsen Autorianus had the courage to refuse pardon to the powerful Emperor Michael Paleologus, who had restored the Byzantine rule at Constantinople, because that monarch had blinded his rival for the throne. Arsen's act cost him his post, but a loyal minority, presumably as much for political as religious motives, refused to concede the validity of the ordinations of the Patriarch who was put in his place and for a time constituted a dissident sect.

BYZANTINE MONASTICISM

Still another feature of the Eastern wing of the Catholic Church was the distinctive character of Byzantine monasticism. Monasticism continued to be prominent. The monastery of Studius, in Constantinople, long exerted a large influence in both Church and state. The communities on Mt. Athos grew and became famous. There were other mountains noted for their monastic establishments. Some of the latter had been founded before 950 and others were inaugurated after that year. Houses existed for women as well as for men. No orders existed comparable to those which arose in the West during these centuries, such as the Cistercians, Franciscans, and Dominicans, in which numbers of houses were brought within the structure of a single organization and under a common rule. The reforms carried through in the preceding period by Theodore of Studius had a wide influence, but Studius did not become the mother house of an order. Nor did monks give themselves to widespread preaching and to the care of parishes as was increasingly true of the friars of the West. Monasteries were primarily for the perfection of their members by prayer and ascetic practices. Some monks, usually a minority in any one house, were hermits and lived a life of solitude. However, the monasteries often were associated with philanthropic enterprises and had hospices for the aged and the poor and hospitals for the care of the sick. Usually they were self-governing and in at least some instances efforts were made by the founders to prevent any outsider, even the Patriarch or the Emperor, from taking possession of them.

As in Western Europe, so in the Byzantine realms, monasteries tended to depart from the high ideals of their founders and the enthusiasm and devotion of their initial years. Numbers entered them for the purpose of obtaining an easy livelihood. Many monks were ignorant, indifferent to their religious duties, and morally reprehensible. Some retained their personal property instead of holding all in common. Several of the monasteries sought to add to their collective wealth. Many came into the possession of laymen. Originally this was done on the condition that the lay proprietor repair or rebuild the physical plant. Eventually, however, this became only a pretext or might not be honoured even nominally. The one to whom the monastery had been granted appropriated the revenues for his own ends and gave only a pittance for the support of the monks. From time to time efforts were made to correct these abuses, but no such sweeping waves of reform were seen as were common in these centuries in the West.

HESYCHASTIC MYSTICISM

In the Eastern as in the Western wing of the Catholic Church there was mysticism. In the Eastern branch this took distinct forms. There were, as we have noted, monks who gave themselves to solitary contemplation. A special form of contemplation arose which is known as Hesychasm. It seems to have had as its father Simeon Neotheologus (or "New Theologian"), a Studite monk of the eleventh century. In the fourteenth century it flourished especially on Mt. Athos. It sought through special practices to attain the beatific vision of God. It held that the divine light can be attained and that it is of grace, bringing justification, joy, and peace. The Hesychasts claimed that by holding their breath, fixing their eyes upon their navels, and making the spirit reënter the soul, they could be enveloped by the light which shone around Christ at the time of his transfiguration on Mt. Tabor.

Hesychasm led to violent controversy. In its defense it was urged that the light was not the divine essence, for God Himself could never be seen by man, but that it was an operation or agency of God, divine grace. The critics contended that such a light could only be of the essence of God and that to separate the essence from the operation was to be guilty of falling into the error of believing in two Gods. The champion of the Hesychasts was Palamas, a monk on Mt. Athos, later (1349–c.1360) Archbishop of Thessalonica. The chief opponent was Barlaam, a native of Calabria, in Italy, a monk who had sought the union of the two wings of the Catholic Church. The issue was complicated by the widening gulf between the Latin and Byzantine Churches. The Roman Catholics held with Barlaam. The Byzantine Church, at first divided, eventually came out emphatically for the Hesychasts. In 1341 a synod in Constantinople supported them and this decision was confirmed by a second. A third synod sided with the adherents of Barlaam's views, but a fourth, in 1351, approved the Hesychasts and excommunicated Barlaam and his chief supporter, the Archbishop of Ephesus. Its decision was final and Hesychasm had the official endorsement of the Byzantine Church. We shall see that it persisted and that in the nineteenth century it enjoyed something of a revival, especially in the largest member of the family of Orthodox churches, that of Russia.

The fact that Hesychasm, with its quietism, loomed so prominently in the Orthodox Church is evidence of still another feature of that wing of Christianity. Here was a meditative, passive, non-activistic faith which specialized on the interior life. It had parallels in the West and in some respects resembled the mysticism which was prominent in various sections of Latin Christianity in the fourteenth century. However, Orthodox monasticism was not as varied in its expressions as was that of Western Europe.

THE WIDENING RIFT BETWEEN EAST AND WEST

Probably it was to be expected that the Eastern and Western wings of the Catholic Church would drift farther apart. Here was one of the outstanding features of the history of Christianity in the four centuries between 950 and 1350.

The causes were many. The ostensible reasons were such differences as the *filioque* clause in the Nicene Creed, the contrast between the Western custom of clean-shaven clergy and the Eastern bearded clergy, the Latin tradition of fasting Saturdays in Lent, the singing of the Alleluia only on Easter, the eating of animals strangled and of blood, the celibacy of the parish clergy in the West as against the married clergy in the East (a cause of friction which became more marked as the reformers in the West sought to enforce the rule of celibacy within their jurisdiction), the use in the West of unleavened bread (azyme) in the Eucharist instead of the leavened bread which was employed in the East, and the custom in the Greek Church of rebaptizing Latins who wished to come into its fellowship.

Vigorously and often bitterly though these issues were debated, in reality they were superficial. Underneath were far more weighty and basic factors. The enveloping structure of the Roman Empire within which the Catholic Church had arisen and which facilitated its unity had further disintegrated. While both claimed to be heirs of the Roman Empire, the Holy Roman Empire and the Byzantine Empire had become clearly separate and the fiction that they were the Western and Eastern wings of the same realm was progressively more difficult to maintain. Rivalry between the Roman Pontiffs and the Patriarchs of Constantinople continued. The East resented the claims of the Popes to universal dominion over the Church. The encroachments of Western Euro-peans upon the Byzantine realms which culminated in the capture of Constan-tinople and the setting up of a Latin Patriarchate in that city aroused hot resentment among the masses of the Greeks which their leaders, eager for political reasons to effect a reconciliation, could not successfully over-ride. Then, too, the Greeks looked upon the Latins as barbarians.

In addition to these sources of friction there were differences which went far back into the history and outlook of the Latin and Greek wings of the Catholic Church and which had been sharpened with the years. To be sure, both repeated the Nicene Creed as standard and in theory held to the Chalce-donian theology. However, the Greek wing tended to emphasize the divine side of Christ and to give a truncated view of his humanity. In its long struggle with Monophysitism it had come to verge on that position. Its typical picture of Christ, which may have been adapted from the pre-Christian representations of Zeus, portrayed him as Pantocrator, the Lord Omnipotent. In contrast, the West stressed not only the full deity of Christ but also his full humanity and at times may have seemed almost Nestorian in its tendency. In the twelfth century there developed in the West, partly through the stimulus given by Bernard of Clairvaux, a devotion which while not denying the incarnation, dwelt on the man Jesus. It has been said that Byzantine Christianity tended to minimize the Christ of the Gospels and to act as though its faith was in a mythical heavenly saviour. In contrast the West did not forget the Jesus of the Gospels. Perhaps for this reason and possibly because of the Roman tradition, Western Christianity was activist and ethical. It tended to believe that the moral stand-ards of the faith could be met and through auricular confession and penance sought to bring the masses to them. Christianity did not mould Byzantine cul-ture as deeply as it did the civilization of Western Europe. Eastern Catholicism was not so intent upon reshaping all of life as was its Western counterpart. The Byzantine liturgy was much more elaborate and the Eucharist more re-moved from the congregation than was usually true in the West. The iconos-tasis, a partition, separated the congregation from the altar and what the priest did at the altar to a much greater degree than did altar screens in the West.

The rupture between East and West did not come at once and not until after 1350 was it clearly final. Important incidents marked its course. Of these some were in the Patriarchate of the able and vigorous Michael Cerularius. Cerularius was alarmed by the conquest of Southern Italy by the Normans and the prospect of the transfer of the ecclesiastical supervision of that area and of Sicily from Constantinople to Rome. Moreover, at the time when Cerularius came to the Patriarchate (1043) the utterly unworthy Benedict IX was on the Papal throne. It may have been for this reason that at the outset he did not notify the

Pope of his election or have the Pope's name on his diptych, namely, that he did not make mention of him in the prayers at the Eucharist. However, in 1049 a very different man became Pope, the able and reforming Leo IX, who held the post until 1054. Leo IX endeavoured to extend the sway of Rome to Sicily and Southern Italy and campaigned against the clergy who, in accordance with the Greek custom, were married. This aroused Cerularius and in retalia- tion he and Leo of Ochrida, the Metropolitan of Bulgaria, closed the churches and monasteries of the Latin rite in their territories. At the same time Leo of Ochrida wrote to a bishop in Southern Italy warning him against what he held to be the errors of Rome and the churches in the West.

Cardinal Humbert, a monk who was a leader in the reform in the West, a sturdy opponent of lay investiture, translated the letter from Greek into Latin and was empowered by the Pope to reply. In that letter the commission given to the Roman See through Peter was emphatically asserted, together with the promise that the faith of Peter and so of the Church of Rome should not fail, the spurious Donation of Constantine, then accepted as genuine, was quoted to uphold the Papal claims in Italy, and the fact was stressed that in contrast with Rome's record of orthodoxy some of the Patriarchs of Constantinople had been heretics. The letter also pointed out that in his clemency the Pope had permitted churches and monasteries of the Greek rite to continue in Rome. For political reasons the Byzantine Emperor wished to have harmonious rela- tions with the Pope. Presumably at his instance Cerularius returned a moderate reply. The Emperor also wrote in the same vein. Both expressed the desire to maintain the unity of the Church. Leo IX was not conciliatory. He protested to the Emperor the arrogance of Cerularius and in a letter to the Patriarch set forth strong strictures on the latter's conduct. Thus the Pope asserted the claim of the See of Peter to supremacy over the entire Catholic Church and held that this was incompatible with the autonomy of national churches.

Leo IX appointed a delegation to carry these letters to Constantinople. On it were three high ecclesiastics, one of them the uncompromising Cardinal Humbert and another the future Pope Stephen IX who, like Humbert, was an ardent reformer and an advocate of the authority of the Roman See. The Emperor was still conciliatory, for he wished an alliance with the Pope to restore and maintain Byzantine influence in Italy. However, Cerularius, noted for his independence of imperial domination, was obdurate and on July 16, 1054, the Papal legates dramatically laid on the altar of St. Sophia, as it stood ready for the Eucharist, a sentence of excommunication of the Patriarch and his supporters and left the cathedral, shaking the dust off their feet. In his turn, within a few days, at a solemn synod Cerularius excommunicated the legates,

These acts of the Papal legates and of Michael Cerularius and his synod by no means effected a final breach between the Roman and the Orthodox churches. The Catholic Church was still regarded as one. The Patriarch of Antioch, as a leading figure in the Catholic Church, sought to mediate between the disputants. In the ensuing centuries when Crusaders and pilgrims from Western Europe were numerous in the East, coöperation between members of the hierarchy in the East and the Latins was not uncommon and from time to time the latter were given the communion by Eastern clergy. Although at one time the Byzantine Emperor Alexius Comnenus was excommunicated by the Pope and in return forbade the Latin churches in Constantinople to use unleavened bread in the Eucharist, in 1089 Pope Urban II, who was deeply concerned to heal the breach, removed the excommunication and the Emperor advised the synod of his church provisionally to place the Pope's name on the diptychs. Urban had as a chief motive in promoting the First Crusade the reunion of the churches, and in 1098, while the Crusade was in progress, he convened a Council at Bari, in the south of Italy, of both Latin and Greek bishops. The Greek bishops, however, were only from Italy and possibly Sicily and not from the Byzantine Empire, for the purpose was primarily local, to make Papal power effective in the domains recently conquered by the Normans. The main point of discussion seems to have been the *filioque* phrase. Anselm was the chief advocate of the Papal position and the Greeks are said to have been won over by him.

In spite of the hopes of Urban II, the First Crusade and its successors widened rather than bridged the gulf between the Western Church on the one hand and the Eastern churches on the other. The Crusaders tended to regard the Greeks as well as the other Eastern Christians as heretics. Latin clergy supplanted the Eastern clergy or were placed alongside them. Some Eastern Christians were won to union with Rome, but the majority held aloof and their antipathy was accentuated by the behaviour of the Crusaders. The conquest of Cyprus by Western Europeans late in the twelfth century and the creation of a Latin hierarchy with special privileges as against other Christians accentuated the tension, for the island had long been under the Greek wing of the Church. The Latin conquest of Constantinople in 1204 and the setting up of a Latin Patriarch in that city heightened popular resentment. Greek nationalism rallied around the Byzantine Church and made it a symbol of resistance. The conquest was effected during the high tide of Papal power under Innocent III. At the time it looked as though reunion was about to be accomplished under that great Pontiff, but the majority of the Greeks kept aloof. They could not bring themselves to concede the supremacy of the Pope.

Yet efforts for reunion continued to be made. During the Latin occupation of Constantinople John III (Ducas Vatatzes), one of the Byzantine Emperors who maintained a capital at Nicæa, in an effort to regain territories which had been lost to the Latins, hoped for peace between the two churches. At his request made through the Byzantine Patriarch Pope Gregory IX sent envoys to see whether an accord could be reached. No agreement followed; each side stated (1234) its grievances against the other and would not yield on crucial issues. Negotiations were resumed not far from 1250, this time between John III and Pope Innocent IV. They dragged out for three years or more and when they seemed about to succeed they were terminated by the death (1254) of both the Emperor and the Pope.

Discussions over reunion were resumed under the Emperor Michael VIII Paleologus, the first of his dynasty, who in 1261 restored the Byzantine rule in Constantinople. Michael's object appears to have been the security of his throne, for he was faced by internal as well as foreign enemies and felt himself in need of Papal support. He was especially afraid of Charles of Anjou who from his base in Sicily and Italy was attempting to build an empire in the Mediterranean. Eventually, in May, 1274, at the Second Council of Lyons, regarded by the Roman Catholic Church as the Fourteenth Ecumenical Council, the goal seemed to have been attained. The Greek delegation conceded all that was asked by the Pope and unity was declared to have been restored. However, the overwhelming majority of the constituency of the Byzantine Church would not assent. Nationalism ran high and with it resentment against any hint of submission to the hated Latins. Yet the Emperor Michael attained his purpose of security for his throne. In 1282, a revolt against Charles of Anjou, known as the Sicilian Vespers, removed the menace from that prince. After Michael's death his son and successor felt himself strong enough to renounce the arrangement made at Lyons and the breach between the churches was deepened.

The advances of the Ottoman Turks led some of the Byzantine Emperors to seek accord with Rome in the hope of obtaining military help from the West. Suggestions were put forward that a general council of the severed branches of the Catholic Church be held, to include the Papal representatives and the Patriarchs of Constantinople, Antioch, Jerusalem, and Alexander. The conversations came to nought. In 1369 the Byzantine Emperor John V while on a visit to Rome made his submission to the Pope, but he could not carry his tottering empire with him. As we shall see, another effort, at the time seemingly successful, was essayed in 1439, but it, too, proved futile. The once outwardly united Catholic Church was fractured, presumably beyond repair.

NON-BYZANTINE MEMBERS OF THE FAMILY OF ORTHODOX
CHURCHES: THE BULGARIANS

The story so briefly summarized on the preceding pages of this chapter may give the impression that for Byzantine in contrast with Latin Christianity the period from 950 to 1350 was one not of advance but of almost unrelieved recession, especially after the middle of the eleventh century. That, however, would be far from the truth. To be sure, politically the Byzantine succession of the Roman Empire was in a fatal decline which was only partly interrupted by the brilliant rulers of the Macedonian Dynasty. Moreover, the churches within its borders were suffering, both from the conquests of the Moslem Turks and the incursions of the Crusading Christians from the West. Yet the northward geographic spread of Christianity from the Byzantine nucleus which had begun before 950 continued. By it the faith was carried far beyond the boundaries which it had reached before the barbarian invasions. Through it new national bodies were added to the family of Orthodox churches which looked towards Constantinople and its Patriarch as their centre.

First of all we must note briefly the somewhat sadly chequered course of the faith in Bulgaria. We have already seen (Chapter XI) how in the second half of the ninth century and the fore part of the tenth century, under the royal leadership of Boris and his son Simeon, the Bulgars and their Slavic subjects had been brought to accept Christianity and how under the latter Bulgaria had enjoyed a golden age, with Simeon adopting the designation Tsar and having the bishops of his realm declare their church independent with one of their number at its head as patriarch.

However, after death had removed the strong hand of Simeon (927) a decline set in which lasted until 1186. The great Emperors of the Macedonian Dynasty extended their sway, first over the eastern and then over the western part of the country, and the church lost its independence and was dominated by Greek bishops and clergy. The heads of the church were appointed from Constantinople and Greek was enforced as the ecclesiastical language.

The Bulgarian Church was also troubled by a religious movement which we know as Bogomilism. This seems to have arisen in the tenth century. Its origin is obscure. It is said to have been begun by a Bulgarian Orthodox Christian priest named Bogomil or at least to have found an early leader in him. It is also declared to have been indebted to the Paulicians and even to have been a continuation of them—that set of sturdy religious groups whom we met earlier (Chapter XI) and who were condemned by the Orthodox as heretics. There had been active Paulician settlements in the Balkan Peninsula from at least the eighth century and contagion from them is quite within the range of possibility.

Bogomilism had in it Christian elements which were set in a basic context of dualism such as we have repeatedly seen in our story. It rejected the Old Testament, for the latter told of the creation of this present evil world by God. It accepted the New Testament, but rejected the miracles of healing by Christ since these had to do with the flesh, and held them to be parables of healing from sin. The Bogomils maintained that all branches of the Christian Church were in error and would have nothing to do with their doctrines, rites, sacraments, orders, holy days, crosses, icons, and saints. They repeated the Lord's Prayer four times each day and four times each night. While disapproving of marriage, they enjoined abstention from it only on "the perfect" and permitted it for the rank and file, "the hearers." "The perfect" were active missionaries and spread their faith against severe persecution. We have already noted the similarity between the Cathari and the Bogomils, a resemblance which may indicate that the former were derived from contact with the latter.

Bogomilism was associated with a Slavic particularism and reinforced the revolt against the domination of the Byzantine Empire and the Greeks, including the Orthodox Church, associated as that was with Byzantine and Greek imperialism. It also seems to have championed the cause of the oppressed slaves and serfs against their masters, who were largely Greeks.

In the weakness which fell upon the Byzantine Empire after the disappearance of the Macedonian Dynasty and especially after the divisions brought by the Latin conquest of Constantinople, the Bulgarians rose and threw off the Greek yoke. The first effective revolt was in 1186. Bulgarian bishops were gradually substituted for Greek prelates. To obtain recognition of the legitimacy of the new order, the Bulgarian ruler entered into long negotiations with the powerful Pope Innocent III, whose prestige in the East had been heightened by the setting up of the Latin empire on the Bosporus. As a result, the Bulgarian prince, Kaloyan, acknowledged himself to be subject to the Roman See and was crowned by a Papal legate. The Bulgarian hierarchy, including its primate, accepted the supremacy of the Pope. This, however, seems to have made little difference in the life and internal organization of the Bulgarian Church.

As under a later ruler the renewed Bulgarian empire continued to expand, the Byzantine Emperor, in the hope of assistance against his Latin rival, recognized the Bulgarian monarch as Tsar or Emperor, and therefore on a legal equality with himself, and in 1235 the Greek Patriarch, with the consent of the other three Patriarchs of the Greek Orthodox Church (namely, those of Antioch, Alexandria, and Jerusalem) conceded patriarchal rank to the head of the Bul-

garian Church. Yet the latter, who three years earlier had deserted the Roman
allegiance and had recognized the authority of the Greek Patriarch of Constantinople, continued to be subordinate to him. The Popes attempted to
assert their suzerainty over Bulgaria, but in vain. The reunion of the Roman
and Greek churches officially effected at the Second Council of Lyons included
the Bulgarian Church. However, as we have seen, that act, which ignored the
rank and file of the constituency, was rejected by popular clamour in the
Greek domains. For most practical purposes it was also ignored in Bulgaria.

In the fore part of the fourteenth century Hesychasm was carried into Bulgarian monasticism and gained an influential following.

In the latter half of the thirteenth century Bulgaria entered upon another
period of political decline. In the fore part of the following century this was
accentuated by invasions of the Serbs and the Turks. In the half century after
1350, as we are to see in the next period of our story, the Turks eliminated the
Bulgarian state and brought fresh problems to the Christianity of that unhappy
land.

Non-Byzantine Members of the Family of Orthodox Churches: the Serbs

We have already noted (Chapter XI) the introduction of Christianity among
the western neighbours of the Bulgarians, the Serbs, in the seventh and ninth
centuries. This was under Byzantine auspices and in the ninth century was by
compulsion. In the latter part of the ninth century a marked impulse was given
to the acceptance of Christianity by the indirect influence of Constantine
(Cyril) and Methodius through the Christian literature prepared in Slavonic
by them and their pupils. During the latter part of the ninth and into the
eleventh century Byzantine, Bulgarian, and then Byzantine power dominated
most of the Serbs. This tied the Serbian churches to the Orthodox wing of the
faith.

However, since the Serbian territory was a border land between Rome and
Constantinople, some of the Serbs and especially their neighbouring Slavs, the
Croats, adhered ecclesiastically to Rome. In 1076 the mighty Hildebrand as
Pope Gregory VII conferred the royal dignity upon a Croatian chieftain and
the following year granted it to Michael, a Serbian chieftain, in return for the
latter's recognition of Papal suzerainty. This, of course, meant that ecclesiastically Michael's growing realm passed into the Roman orbit. A few years later
the Pope raised the bishopric of Antivari to archiepiscopal rank, giving the
church among the Serbs a degree of administrative unity.

The realm which Michael had erected proved ephemeral. After the death of his son and successor (1101) the domains which had been assembled fell apart. For a time Byzantine influence mounted. However, the decline of the Byzantine Empire in the latter part of the twelfth century and the added weakness brought by the Latin conquest of Constantinople enabled a Serbian prince, Stephen Nemanya, who ruled from 1168 to 1195, to bring most of the Serbs under his sway—with the notable exception of Bosnia and Hum. Religiously the domains of Stephen Nemanya were divided. Part adhered to Rome, part to Constantinople, and Bogomils were numerous. Stephen had been baptized in the Latin rite, but he was enthusiastically Orthodox. While he tolerated the churches of the Latin rite, he gave his support to the Orthodox wing of the Church. Moreover, he conducted a crusade against the Bogomils and drove most of them out of the country. They found refuge in Bosnia and Hum. Stephen Nemanya founded a dynasty which consolidated Serbia into a kingdom and survived until 1371. It was Stephen Nemanya's son, also Stephen, who assumed the title of king.

The creation of a Serbian national church was the work of a younger son of the first Stephen, Rastko (1174–1236). Rastko was reared at the court of his father. When in his impressionable mid-adolescence, not far from the age of eighteen, he was won to the monastic life by a Russian monk from Mt. Athos. Fearing parental opposition, he fled secretly to Mt. Athos and there took monastic vows and the name of a famous Serbian saint, Sava, by which he is best remembered. Not many years thereafter (1195) his father left his throne to become a monk and his queen became a nun. Stephen, now known as Simeon, founded the monastery Studenitsa and joined his son Sava on Mt. Athos. There the two built and richly equipped a monastery which soon became the major Serbian literary centre and the school in which the leaders of the Serbian Church were trained.

Simeon's death in 1200 seemed to throw the Serbs into the Roman camp. Civil strife over the succession broke out between two of his sons, brothers of Sava. The then Pope, Innocent III, used the opportunity to extend Roman influence over the land. To obtain the help of Hungary one of the rivals, through the astute diplomacy of Innocent, was compelled to acknowledge Roman supremacy. In his turn, to win Papal support, the other rival, the second Stephen, divorced his wife, the daughter of the Byzantine Emperor, married a Venetian, received from Innocent's successor a royal crown, and vowed obedience to the Pope. The Papal legate proceeded to set up a Latin hierarchy.

However, Sava, loyal to his Orthodox convictions, was not to be frustrated. He had returned to Serbia in 1208 and the clergy, many of whom had been trained by him, stood by him. Moreover, popular opinion was with him.

He had travelled the length and breadth of the land, reforming the Church and raising the level of its life. The people knew him and supported him. Sava went to Nicæa, then the capital of the Byzantine Empire, obtained from the Emperor, Patriarch, and synod recognition of the independence of the Serbian Church, and was consecrated archbishop to head the new autocephalous hierarchy. Returning home, he easily gained from his brother recognition as head of the national church, for the king presumably welcomed an arrangement by which that body would be autonomous and under the control of a member of his family. The Papal legate withdrew, together with his Latin clergy, and Sava set about the ecclesiastical organization of the country. He established schools, one of them in connexion with Studenitsa. He resumed his journeys over the realm, supervising, inspiring, and when necessary disciplining the clergy. He adjusted inherited pre-Christian customs to Christian purposes. After the death of his brother, the king, he crowned the latter's son, his nephew. Eventually he passed on his own office to a man whom he had trained. More than any other one man Sava shaped the Christianity of Serbia. That Christianity perpetuated the Byzantine tradition of the close association of Church and state, a national church, and the type of monasticism which had its chief exemplars on Mt. Athos. Under Sava Greek Christianity, adapted to Serbian traditions, became firmly rooted.

We must here pause to note the important place which that variant of Christianity, Bogomilism, came to have in Bosnia and the adjoining Hum, later known as Herzegovina. Both areas bordered on Serbia, to which they were closely related in race. The Bogomils, or Patarenes as they were known in this region, had found a refuge there after their expulsion from Serbia. They multiplied and spread into the nearby Croatia, Slavonia, Hungary, and Dalmatia. One reason for the strength of Bogomilism in Bosnia and Hum seems to have been that, being neither Greek Orthodox nor Roman Catholic, it reinforced local particularism against the Orthodox Serbs on the east and the Roman Catholic Hungarians on the north, peoples who sought to extend their control over these two districts. Apparently from a politic desire to divert Hungarian aggression, in 1204, in the Pontificate of Innocent III, the ruler in Bosnia and some of the leading Patarenes formally abjured their heresy in the presence of Papal representatives. However, when the danger lapsed, Bogomilism revived and in the third quarter of the thirteenth century the majority of the Bosnians and their nobles are said to have been Patarenes. Even the Catholic bishop was reported to have been one of them. In spite of persecutions, a crusade, the Inquisition, and the labours of Dominican and Franciscan missionaries, until long after 1350 Patarenism continued to flourish in both Bosnia and Hum.

Non-Byzantine Members of the Family of Orthodox Churches: the Russians

It was in Russia that Greek Orthodox Christianity made its most extensive gains during this period. Earlier (Chapter XVI) we told of the introduction of Christianity to the state which centered around Kiev, the historic nucleus of the later Russia. We also saw that the invasion and conquest by the non-Christian Mongols, at first destructive, actually deepened the hold of Christianity on the Russians, partly because the Church, as the one institution which was clearly theirs, was the symbol and bulwark of Russian nationalism. Moreover, during the centuries of the Mongol occupation, Christianity was carried north of the Mongol domains. Between 950 and 1350 this Greek Christianity which had Constantinople as its focus, through the conversions to it effected in Russia, approximately doubled the area in which it was the religion of the majority. There was no proportionate increase in the number of its adherents, for Russia was still sparsely settled. However, it probably added far more to its fold than in the same centuries it lost to Islam through the Turkish encroachments on its traditional territories.

Since we have already summarized the geographic spread of Christianity in Russia we must here content ourselves with saying something of the internal developments which contributed to the distinctive characteristics which the faith in that land eventually presented.

Contributions to Russian Christianity came through a number of channels. The major foreign source was the Eastern wing of the Catholic Church. Much of the Christian literature was translations from the Greek into Slavonic which entered by way of Bulgaria, for the vernaculars of the two regions were sufficiently akin to make this possible.

The fact that these translations into the vernacular were available had a negative effect. For centuries few of the Russian clergy and monks troubled themselves to learn Greek, for what they wished was at hand in their native tongue. This meant that the vast treasures of pre-Christian Greek literature and philosophy were closed to them. Russian literature of these centuries centered on practical, moral, and ascetic ends. This was in contrast with Western Europe in this period. Here the language of the liturgy and the Church was Latin. Priests and monks learned it and in doing so they acquired a key which unlocked to them the wide range of pre-Christian Latin literature and thought.

The Pechersk or Caves Monastery at Kiev was the most famous pioneer foundation and so had a large share in shaping the future monasticism of Russia. Hilarion, the first Metropolitan of Russian origin, a noted scholar and preacher, in his earlier days had dug a cave for himself near Kiev and there had practised meditation. A precursor of the later community of the Caves was Anthony, who had been a monk at Mt. Athos. The Caves Monastery eventually followed the rule of the monastery of Studius in Constantinople in the development of which Theodore the Studite had had so important a part. That rule became the norm for subsequent Russian houses. Through travellers and pilgrims contacts were made and maintained with other centres in Constantinople and with Mt. Athos. A Russian monastery was developed on that holy mountain and from it a fairly constant stream flowed into Russia.

For the first half century or so after the baptism of Vladimir (c.988) the church in his domains, thanks to his insistence, was autocephalous and so practically independent of the Patriarch of Constantinople. However, beginning with 1037, most of the Metropolitans of Kiev were selected by the Patriarch. Although in the twelfth century the Russian princes nominated the bishops, through the Metropolitans the tie with Constantinople was very close. The rich Byzantine liturgy was adopted by the Russian Church and made a profound impression on the Russian spirit.

Another channel through which influences from abroad came to Russian Christianity was Palestinian monasticism. Theodosius, who with his teacher Anthony was the founder of the Caves Monastery and so of Russian monasticism, was a warm admirer of the monks of Palestine. True to what he had heard of his Palestinian models, he avoided extreme asceticism, placed limits on silence, and sought a balance between the active and the contemplative life.

Still another medium through which Christianity came to Russia was the Catholicism of the Latin West. When the first conversions of Russians were being made the rift between the Eastern and Western wings of the Catholic Church was not nearly as great as it was to become in the eleventh century. The sense of unity, although weakened, was still strong. Therefore it was not deemed improper for lessons to come from both directions. We saw that it was to Germany that Vladimir's grandmother Olga had sent for missionaries. Missionaries from the West helped in the conversion of the Russians under Vladimir. Intermittent contacts with Rome existed in the eleventh century. It is possible that the system of levying tithes for the support of the Church which Vladimir adopted was suggested by Western practice. The Mongol conquest damaged the Kievan culture which, near to the West, had some elements from the Latin wing of the Church and separated Great Russia, that which later clustered around Moscow, from the West while enabling contacts to be maintained with Constantinople. However, some intercourse was continued through Dominican and Franciscan missionaries. Both, but especially the latter, were in Kiev in the thirteenth century. At the beginning of the fourteenth century the Brothers Minor had seventeen stations in the portions of Russia ruled by the Mongols, with several bishoprics and two archbishoprics. Some of the converts were Mongols. Presumably repercussions were felt in the Russian Church.

To these contributions from abroad the Russians added distinctive ones of their own. One was kenoticism, the emptying of self in humility. It is significant that the first to be canonized by the Russian Church and for centuries esteemed the patron saints of the land were Boris and Gleb, sons of Vladimir, who, without offering armed resistance, were killed by henchmen of their brother in the latter's desire to rid himself of them as possible rivals to the succession. The older of the two, Boris, is said to have spent the night before his death in prayer, waiting for his murderers. In the legends which recounted the tragedy, he is reported to have been moved by humility and love and a realization of the vanity of the kind of power represented by the state. Whether or not the reports are true, the fact that they were formulated and treasured gives insight into what was valued by many Russian Christians. The multitude esteemed the two brothers as saints because they were innocent sufferers. They were honoured in liturgical offices for having "forsaken the perishable glory of this world" and for "hating the kingdom of the world and loving purity."

Theodosius, or Feodosi (died 1074, and so an older contemporary of Hildebrand and Abbot Hugh of Cluny), the first Russian monk to be canonized (Boris and Gleb were not monks), the real organizer of the Caves Monastery, the chief pioneer and inspirer of Russian monasticism, was also noted for kenoticism. It is said that from childhood he was marked by humility, in spite of the pleas of his wealthy parents wore uncouth and patched clothing, and later worked with the slaves in the fields. He ran away from his mother to enter the monastery. Eventually, relenting, she yielded to his entreaties and herself became a nun. As head of the monastery he is reported always to have been merciful and mild, to have been loth to resort to punishment to discipline his monks, and to have welcomed back the wayward who had fled the cloister.

Theodosius made another contribution to Russian monasticism. He sought to have the monastery serve the world. From its income he supported a hospice for the beggars and the sick and sent food to the prisoners in the city jail. He was the spiritual counsellor of many and seems to have been responsible for the inauguration of a Russian tradition that monks should be the confessors and guides to lay folk. He went out into the world to make contacts with individuals and to rebuke and exhort the erring.

Kenoticism and practical service to the world were not the only trends in Russian monasticism. Even in the Caves Monastery there was a grim strain of extreme asceticism and fear of demons which was in partial contrast with Theodosius.

Another Russian monk, not canonized until the mid-sixteenth century, was

Abraham of Smolensk, of the second half of the twelfth and the fore part of the thirteenth century. It was after the death of his parents that he distributed his inherited goods among the poor and entered a monastery on the outskirts of Smolensk. He became an ardent student of the writings of the Fathers of the Church, was sternly ascetic, warned all who would listen of the impending wrath of God, and in his prayers implored God to have mercy on the people. The laity thronged to him, but the clergy and monks were hostile and for a time had him confined in a monastery and forbidden to say mass, why is not entirely clear. Eventually released, he became the head of a monastery, and there until his death at a ripe age taught and counselled those who came to him.

Much more influential was Sergius, the patron saint of Russia and the most widely beloved of her holy men. He was born sometime between 1314 and 1323 and died in 1392. He lived, then, after the Mongol conquest. He was the outstanding example of a new type of monasticism which arose after that event. Pre-Mongol Russian monasteries had been either in towns or near them. After the Mongol inroads, many monks settled in the northern forests, away from human habitation and Mongol rule. In many ways Sergius resembled Theodosius. He was marked by kenotic humility. He worked with his hands and even in the days of his greatest fame tended the monastic garden. He protected and comforted the oppressed. Unlike Theodosius, he was first a hermit. Then others began to gather around him, each dwelling in a separate cell. Eventually, against his will, for he feared the temptation to pride, he was ordained priest and was made abbot of the community. A monastery founded by him, the Troitsa (Trinity), about forty miles from Moscow, became famous and was the mother of many other houses. Also unlike Theodosius, Sergius was a mystic, a pioneer in Russia of that type of religious experience and devotion. He seems to have been affected by the Hesychast movement, newly arrived from Mt. Athos. But his was not only a life of prayer. He encouraged the prince of Moscow to resist the Mongols by force of arms. He gave his blessing to the force sent out to meet the Mongols and the notable victory which followed was attributed by the prince to his prayers.

It was only gradually that the Christian faith really penetrated to the masses of the population of Russia. Accepted first in the upper circles, it was slow in making its way to the rank and file. Paganism long survived. It seems significant that the *Tale of Igor's Campaign,* written at the end of the twelfth century by a professed Christian, and unique in early Russian literature for its intentionally artistic form, has in it almost nothing distinctively Christian but is prevailingly pagan and secular. As late as the eleventh century pagan magicians, *volkhvi*, had sufficient influence to stir up a popular anti-Christian uprising in Novgorod, the leading centre of Christianity in the North-west.

The Bible, read in Slavonic in the services of the Church, eventually became familiar to monks and the lay folk who attended the liturgy. Of the Old Testament the Psalms were the most prized. The New Testament was especially valued.

The Gospels made a great impression upon the early Russian saints. Here they got behind Christ the Pantocrator who had come to them in the Byzantine tradition and rediscovered the human aspects of Jesus. Through the Gospels and the saints the voluntary suffering and humility of Jesus contributed markedly to the kenotic quality in the Russian religious ideal.

By way of a Slavonic translation the Pseudo-Dionysius (Dionysius the Areopagite) became the possession of the Russians and, as in East and West, made its Neoplatonic contribution to mysticism.

Slow though the process was, Russian life was being moulded by Christianity. In contrast with Slavic paganism which did not inculcate responsibility, Christianity with its ethical teaching, reinforced by a belief in the future life and the last judgement, nurtured in individuals a sense of accountability for their deeds. It brought an awareness of sin and an urge to repentance and so introduced the element of struggle for moral perfection. As in Western Europe, it quickened men's social conscience. Some of the leaders of the Church objected to slavery, and monasteries had hospitals and asylums for the aged. Christianity stimulated legislation to end class feuds and bloody revenge. Rulers as well as subjects were held to be under the judgement of God. Good princes were praised and bad ones condemned.

Eventually Christianity became the conscious possession of the masses. Many flocked to outstanding monks for counsel. There was no formally regularized confession to priests as in the West, but there was preaching with practical instruction in Christian virtues. The emphasis was upon the love of God and one's neighbours and upon repentance, even with tears, and fasting. There were also the fear of God and humility.

By the middle of the fourteenth century Christianity in Russia, as in Western Europe, was in a new milieu.

When Christianity was being adopted Russia was composed of a congeries of loosely related political units. In the eleventh century the state which had centered in Kiev and in which the Russian hierarchy had its head tended to disintegrate. Then, in the middle of the thirteenth century, came the Mongol conquest. The Kievan culture largely disappeared. It was chiefly the Church which survived. Remnants of independence persisted in the South-west, in the North-west around the cities of Novgorod and Pskov, and in the forests in the North-east. In the North-west there were threats from the Swedes and the Teutonic Knights. Had either or both of these succeeded, the Church in that region might have been assimilated to the Latin Christianity of the West. However, Alexander Nevski, the Prince of Novgorod, defeated the Swedes (1240) and the Teutonic Knights (1242) and the Mongols made him Grand Prince of Kiev. In the following century he was canonized. In the South-west in the mid-thirteenth century a local prince, in an effort to obtain assistance from the West against the Mongols, accepted a crown from the Pope and permitted Roman Catholic missionaries to enter. The latter seem to have made little headway. In the first half of the thirteenth century, Lithuanians, still pagan, pressed southward and took Kiev. They were friendly to the Orthodox Church, some of them were baptized, and in their capital, Vilna, numbers of Orthodox churches and monasteries were erected.

It was neither in the North-west nor the South-west that the centre of the Russia of the future was to emerge, but in Moscow. Here Daniel, a son of Alexander Nevski, ruled. Daniel's son, Ivan, extended his domains, but as subordinate to the Mongols and accepted his title from them. He called himself Grand Prince of Moscow and of all Russia. He supported the Orthodox Church and under him Moscow became the seat of the Metropolitan of Russia. Through the influence of the Mongol pattern, the Grand Prince of Moscow became autocratic, insisted upon full control of all aspects of life, and demanded unquestioning obedience of his subjects. Here was arising the later Russia, with its centralized autocracy. In the next period it was profoundly to affect the course of Russian Christianity.

The Monophysites of Egypt, Nubia, and Ethiopia

In contrast with Western Europe, the Balkans, and Russia, the period from 950 to 1350 cannot be said to have been one of renewed vigour in the Monophysite Christianity of Egypt, Nubia, and Ethiopia. In the third quarter of the tenth century a new line of rulers, the Fatimids, Shiah Moslems, took possession of Egypt and separated it from the Abbasid Caliphs of Baghdad. At first Christians hoped that the change would give them relief. To the south, in the upper part of the Nile Valley, in the tenth century most of Nubia held to the Christian faith and resisted the infiltration of Islam and the threatened conquest of the Moslem Arabs of Egypt. Yet the four centuries were, in general, marked by progressive gains of Islam at the expense of the churches and by deterioration in the quality of life in the surviving Christian communities.

During the first generation of the Fatimite rule restrictions against Christians were eased and there were conversions from Islam. Christians were in high places at court and at least one of the Caliphs had a Christian wife.

However, for a decade in the first quarter of the eleventh century there was severe persecution from the Caliph Hakim, who is said to have been insane. He was clearly a religious fanatic. He ordered the destruction of churches and put Christians under extreme disabilities. In succeeding generations times of relative toleration alternated at irregular intervals with more or less severe persecutions. In the first half of the fourteenth century the latter became unusually acute.

The Coptic Church, which had the majority of the Christians of Egypt, suffered chronically from corruption. Many bishops and Patriarchs charged fees for ordinations and consecrations and the practice bred abuses. Now and again reformers arose, some of them in high office in the Church, who sought to end the custom, but they were only temporarily successful. The ecclesiastical authorities found it wise to keep on good terms with the Moslem rulers. Repeatedly this led to the interference of these non-Christians in the affairs of the Church and at times to unseemly attempts by aspirants for ecclesiastical position to obtain the endorsement of the state.

There seem to have been no new creative currents in life or thought in the Coptic Church. Nor were there fresh monastic movements. Presumably this was because the Church was of necessity on the defensive, since conversions to it from Islam entailed the strong possibility of death to the convert and an accentuation of persecution for the Church. Innovations were feared as possible sources of division and weakness.

In the second half of the twelfth century controversy arose over a practice which was modifying the method of confession. The custom of the Coptic Church had been that confession of sin was to be either publicly and collectively in the congregation or privately to a priest. If made while in a congregation, the penitents were invited to confess their sins silently to God while a censer was being carried around the church. Eventually the Patriarch gave permission to the individual to make his confession on his knees in the privacy of his chamber, not to a priest, but in the presence of a lighted censer. To this a certain priest, Mark, objected. An eloquent preacher, he urged on thronging congregations that confession to a priest and absolution through him were necessary to salvation. Excommunicated, Mark continued to preach and also declaimed against the custom of circumcision which had long been a custom in the Church in Egypt. Facing deposition, he went over to the Melchites, taking some of his followers with him. This, however, cost him his popularity. Returning to his mother church, he died in obscurity.

As we have hinted, there were other Christians in Egypt. Melchites, that is, those who adhered to the Greek Orthodox Church, had a Patriarch, but were relatively few. Armenians came to escape intolerable conditions in their native land and kept their own ecclesiastical organization. They, too, were not numerous.

In Nubia Christianity remained the prevailing religion much longer than in Egypt. We hear that in the eleventh century a king in that region erected monasteries and churches. However, Islam, dominant as it was in the Egyptian part of the Nile Valley, almost inevitably gained ground in Nubia. In the thirteenth century mosques were being built and Christianity was waning. Yet it was to continue for centuries longer. Ecclesiastically it seems to have been subordinate to the Coptic Church in Egypt.

The Church in Ethiopia was also dependent upon that in Egypt. We know little of the course of Christianity in the country between the sixth and the twelfth century. Christian literature seems largely to have disappeared. Late in the tenth or early in the eleventh century a princess of the Jewish faith sought to stamp out Christianity. She was followed by Christian rulers and in the twelfth century a monarch attempted to increase the number of bishops and so make the Church independent of Egypt. In this, however, he failed. In the second half of that century a prince is said to have carried forward the frontiers of the faith in the South against paganism. In the thirteenth century Coptic monks translated the New Testament into one of the languages of the land and additional Christian literature came from Egypt. Islam was pushed back by successful military campaigns by the rulers (of the Solomonic dynasty which claimed descent from Solomon and the Queen of Sheba), monks increased in number, and some of them won converts from paganism on the frontiers of the country and within Ethiopia itself. Attempts by reformers among the monks to raise the level of morality at the court and among the nobility aroused opposition in high quarters. As an incident of the conflict, but important as an indication of vitality in the Church, the abbot of a leading monastery excommunicated the king and the latter took vigorous measures against the abbot.

The Jacobite Syrians

The Monophysites, or Jacobites, of Syria possessed an ecclesiastical structure which was headed by a Patriarch of Antioch. While in most places constituting only a minority of the population, they had a fairly wide geographic extension eastward into Persia and northward and westward into Asia Minor and Cyprus. In the twelfth century they are said to have had about twenty metropolitans and a hundred bishops. That same century and the fore part of the thirteenth century saw marked literary activity among them, including an outstanding work on the liturgy. Their most notable figure is reported to have been Barhebræus (1226–1286), famous as a scholar in several fields and reputed to have been one of the most learned men of his age. He was broad in his ecclesiastical contacts and on his death was honoured by Orthodox, Nestorians, and Armenians as well as Jacobites. A much smaller body than their fellow-Monophysites, the Copts, they were normally in communion with the latter and looked up to them with respect. At times the two churches were separated. Moreover, from time to time the Jacobites were troubled by internal dissensions. In the fourteenth century these and persecutions by Moslems reduced their morale and their numbers.

ARMENIAN (GREGORIAN) CHRISTIANITY

We have seen (Chapter XII) that the Armenians, a distinct people in the mountainous regions north of Mesopotamia, had a national church, Monophysite in its creed, and a bond and symbol of Armenian nationality. Pressed by strong peoples and states on its borders, the Orthodox Romans to the west and south-west, and the Zoroastrian Persians, then the Moslem Arabs, later the Turks, still later the Mongols, and eventually the Turks again from the east and south, the Armenians struggled to maintain their political and ecclesiastical independence. Not always were they successful, but their church proved more effectively resistant than their state.

The struggle continued during the four centuries between 950 and 1350 and with varying fortunes. From the second half of the ninth to the third quarter of the eleventh century a dynasty, the Bagratid, governed the country, but only semi-independent and under the suzerainty of the Caliph at Baghdad. Soon after the middle of the eleventh century the Bagratid rule disintegrated. That was due partly to Byzantine victories but chiefly to Turkish invasions. Because of the latter, the country split into several principalities under rulers who were either Turks or Kurds. About 1235 the Mongol invasion brought fresh disorders.

In the last quarter of the eleventh century an Armenian kingdom was set up in Cilicia, in Asia Minor, to the west of Armenia proper. That realm became the main centre of the Armenian Church and endured into the second half of the fourteenth century. The westward move of the Armenian Church brought it into more intimate contact with the Greek Orthodox. The coming of Crusaders from the West and the establishment by the Crusaders of strongholds in the adjacent Syria made for contacts with the Catholics of Western Europe and the Popes. Negotiations with the Byzantine Church failed to bring union. Latin influence was stronger. The Cicilian Armenian rulers sought support from the Crusaders and the West. Negotiations with the Papacy led to close relations between the Armenian and Roman Churches. Many of the Cicilian Armenian Christians submitted to Rome. Although they tended to maintain their traditional ecclesiastical customs, Latin contacts brought modifications. There were Italian colonies in Cilicia as well as Latin missionaries, and there were Armenian groups in Italy.

The decay and disappearance of the Crusaders and their principalities in Syria and Palestine were followed by the weakening of the Latin influence among the Cicilian Armenians and the collapse of the Cicilian Armenian state.

The Turkish invasions and rule in the main historic centre of their nation led many Armenians to emigrate. They went in various directions—eastward, westward, and southward. They constituted colonies, mainly in the cities, and maintained themselves by handicrafts and trade. Usually they preserved their language and customs and held to their church as a bulwark of their distinctiveness. In these respects they were not unlike the Jews, although differing markedly from the latter in many ways, including religion.

In Armenia the national church was troubled by separatists, most of whom seem to have been Paulicians. The Paulicians were not all of one kind, but they appear to have had strong resemblances to one another. Many of them were active in spreading their faith. From time to time there were also disputes with Nestorians and Jacobites who were on the fringes of the main strongholds of the Armenians.

In spite of conquests by non-Christians, pressures from Greek and Latin Christians, and secessions to the Paulicians, the majority of the Armenians held to their historic church. Moreover, these centuries were fairly fertile in the production of Christian literature in Armenian. This included the *Book of Lamentations,* or *Nareg,* written by one Gregory, a monk, early in the eleventh century, a widely read book of meditations and prayers of penitence and aspiration, and a lengthy prayer and many hymns by Nerses, Catholicos in the third quarter of the twelfth century. They are evidence of vitality in the Armenian Christianity of these centuries.

THE NESTORIANS

In our account of the geographic spread of Christianity in the period between 950 and 1350 (Chapter XVI) we have seen the amazing extent of territory covered by that easternmost of the Christian communions, the one to which the name of Nestorian is usually but probably mistakenly given. It will be recalled that this was the church which arose in the Persian Empire, which had its main centres of numerical strength in the Tigris-Euphrates Valley, which persisted under Arab rule, and which during these centuries had its headquarters at Baghdad. It will also be remembered that in the thirteenth and the first half of the fourteenth century there were Nestorian communities, most of them small, in Central Asia and China, and that through intermarriage with the ruling family of the Keraïts, who were Nestorian Christians, some of the Mongol princes, descendants of Jenghiz Khan, had been baptized in infancy. That there were Christian communities on the west and east coasts of South India during these years we know from the reports of Western Europeans who found them there on their journeys to and from China. We have almost no information on their internal history in these centuries, but it seems clear that, although claiming to have been founded by Thomas of the original apostles, their ecclesiastical connexions were with the Nestorians in Persia and Mesopotamia. For several centuries, as we have said, the population of Socotra, an island near the eastern entrance to the Gulf of Aden, called themselves Christians, but whether they were originally Monophysites or Nestorians we do not know. In the fifteenth century they were reported to be predominantly Nestorians. Not far from 1350 there were said to have been Nestorian metropolitans in China, India, Samarqand, Turkestan, Kashgar, and two other centres, each with from six to twelve suffragan bishops.

Early in the fourteenth century the Nestorian Patriarch is reported to have had a hierarchy of twenty-five metropolitans and from two hundred to two hundred and fifty bishops. Under the Caliphs at Baghdad Nestorians had been prominent as officials and physicians, so much so that Moslems accused them of being arrogant. From time to time new church buildings were erected. When about the middle of the thirteenth century the Mongols supplanted the Caliphs, the Christians basked in the favour of the new rulers. Hulagu, the first of the Mongol conquerors in Western Asia, was believed by at least some of the Nestorians to have been baptized. He may have favoured the Christians to offset the Moslems. His successor was also friendly. As the Mongol power began to wane, Moslems took their revenge on the Christians. Yet in the middle of the fourteenth century Nestorianism seems to have been spread over more territory and to have been more prosperous than ever before.

SUMMARY

In general, the four centuries between 950 and 1350 saw a very considerable extension of the eastern frontiers of Christianity, with especially wide expansion in the thirteenth and fourteenth centuries. The faith had become firmly rooted among the Slavs of the Balkan Peninsula. It had spread to the plains of Russia and by 1350 was being carried northward into the forests on the edge and beyond the fringes of the Mongol occupation. Christian communities were to be found clear across Eurasia from the Atlantic and the western and eastern shores of the Mediterranean to the China coast and from Scandinavia and north of Moscow to South India. Some of the eastward extension was through Franciscan and Dominican missionaries, fruits of the great awakenings in the

Christianity of Western Europe. Most of it was through the Eastern Churches, especially the Greek Orthodox wing of the Catholic Church and the Nestorians.

Yet the Christianity of the East was in an extraordinarily precarious situation. The Byzantine Empire, its main political bulwark, was clearly waning. Almost everywhere in Asia Christianity was represented by minorities, many of which were slowly yielding ground to an aggressive and politically and socially dominant Islam. In few of these Christian communities were tides of fresh life showing themselves in fresh creative movements. Here was nothing comparable to the surging vitality in the Christianity of Western Europe. It is not surprising that it was in the East that the losses suffered after 1350 were the most sweeping.

Selected Bibliography

GENERAL WORKS

A. Fortescue, *The Lesser Eastern Churches* (London, Catholic Truth Society, 1913, pp. xv, 468). By a Roman Catholic, but not polemical.

B. J. Kidd, *The Churches of Eastern Christendom from A.D. 451 to the Present Time* (London, The Faith Press, preface 1927, pp. 541). Chiefly valuable for extensive information and footnote references to the sources and secondary literature.

THE BYZANTINE CHURCH

W. F. Adeney, *The Greek and Eastern Churches* (New York, Charles Scribner's Sons, 1908, pp. xiv, 634). A comprehensive survey of the history of these churches.

N. Baynes and H. St. L. B. Moss, editors, *Byzantium. An Introduction to East Roman Civilization* (Oxford University Press, 1948, pp. xxxi, 436). Contains excellent summary chapters by experts and an extensive bibliography.

G. Every, *The Byzantine Patriarchate 451–1204* (London, Society for Promoting Christian Knowledge, 1947, pp. 212). Stresses the history of the relations between Rome and Constantinople and argues that the rupture of 1054 was not as important or as final as is often said.

A. Fortescue, *The Orthodox Eastern Church* (London, Catholic Truth Society, 3d ed., preface 1911, pp. xxxiii, 451). Historical and descriptive, by a Roman Catholic.

A. Fortescue, edited by G. D. Smith, *The Uniate Eastern Churches. The Byzantine Rite in Italy, Sicily, Syria and Egypt* (London, Burns, Oates & Washbourne, 1923, pp. xxiii, 244). Deals chiefly with the Italo-Greeks, their history and recent status. From a Roman Catholic point of view.

A. Michel, *Humbert and Kerullarios Studien* (Paderborn, Ferdinand Schöningh, 2 vols., 1924, 1930 (*Quellen und Forschungen . . . herausgegeben von der Görres-Gesellschaft*). Contains a good many texts of the original documents.

CHRISTIANITY IN BULGARIA AND SERBIA

M. Spinka, *A History of Christianity in the Balkans. A Study in the Spread of Byzantine Culture among the Slavs* (Chicago, The American Society of Church History, 1933, pp. 202). A competent survey based upon the sources.

CHRISTIANITY AMONG THE RUSSIANS

G. P. Fedotov, *The Russian Religious Mind* (Harvard University Press, 1946, pp. xvi, 438). By an outstanding expert, covering the Kievan period, from the tenth to the thirteenth century.

F. P. Fedotov, compiler and editor, *A Treasury of Russian Spirituality* (New York, Sheed & Ward, 1948, pp. xvi, 501). Translations of standard biographies or autobiographies of eight Russian saints, together with some of their works, from the eleventh to the thirteenth century.

G. Vernadsky, *Kievan Russia* (Yale University Press, 1948, pp. xii, 412). Contains important sections, by a thorough scholar, on the conversion of Russia and the religious life of the country.

G. Vernadsky, *Relations byzantino-russes au XIIe siècle* (*Byzantion,* Vol. IV, 1927–1928, pp. 269–276). By an expert.

G. Vernadsky, *The Status of the Russian Church during the First Half-Century following Vladimir's Conversion* (*The Slavonic and East European Review,* Vol. XX (1941), pp. 294–314).

N. Zernov, *The Russians and Their Church* (London, Society for Promoting Christian Knowledge, 1945, pp. v, 193). A semi-popular historical survey.

CHRISTIANITY IN EGYPT, NUBIA, AND ETHIOPIA

E. A. W. Budge, *The Egyptian Sûdân, Its History and Monuments* (London, Kegan Paul, Trench, Trübner & Co., 2 vols., 1907). By a distinguished specialist.

E. A. W. Budge, *A History of Ethiopia, Nubia, and Abyssinia* (London, Methuen & Co., 2 vols., 1928).

E. L. Butcher, *The Story of the Church of Egypt. Being an Outline of the History of the Egyptians under Their Successive Masters from the Roman Conquest until Now* (London, Smith, Elder & Co., 2 vols., 1897). An extensive but somewhat uncritical assemblage of material.

THE JACOBITES OF SYRIA

Chronique de Michel le Syrien Patriarche Jacobite d'Antioche (*1166–1199*), edited and translated into French by J.-B. Chabot (Paris, Ernest Leroux, 4 vols.). The portions of this history which deal with the period which here engages us are in Vols. I and II (1901, 1905). The work is valuable both for the Jacobites and the Nestorians.

ARMENIA

L. Arpee, *A History of Armenian Christianity* (New York, The Armenian Missionary Association of America, 1946, pp. xii, 386). Written by an Armenian Evangelical, it is warmly pro-Armenian and vigorously anti-Roman Catholic.

M. Ormanian, *The Church of Armenia. Her History, Doctrine, Rule, Discipline, Liturgy, Literature, and Existing Conditions,* translated from the French by G. M. Gregory (London, A. R. Mowbray & Co., preface 1910, pp. xxxiii, 271). By a former Armenian Patriarch of Constantinople.

THE NESTORIANS

The History of Yaballaha III Nestorian Patriarch and of His Vicar Bar Sauma Mongol Ambassador to the Frankish Courts at the End of the Thirteenth Century, translated from the Syriac and annotated by J. A. Montgomery (Columbia University Press, 1927, pp. 82). A fascinating contemporary picture of the Nestorian Church.

Chapter XXV

RETROSPECT AND PROSPECT

In these four centuries between 950 and 1350, what had happened to the dream of the kingdom of God which had been proclaimed and cherished by Jesus? We have called the period one of resurgence and advance. In it Christianity had been carried over a wider reach of territory than even in those great first five centuries of accomplishment which had inaugurated its course. To be sure, Christianity had rewon only a small proportion of the territory which it had been forced to yield to Islam, but except in Asia Minor it had suffered no major fresh losses to that faith and it was in process of regaining the Iberian Peninsula and Sicily. In the lands in Western Europe which for centuries had been swept by successive waves of invasion, mostly of pagans, it had brought the conquerors to professed obedience. As with a rising tide, it had stimulated the emergence of movement after movement which made for a deepening of this nominal allegiance. It had entered significantly into every major phase of the new culture which was emerging in this formerly devastated area. It continued to be the professed religion of the waning remnant of the empire which still claimed the Roman name but was Byzantine and Greek. From that core it was spreading in the Balkans and Eastern Europe north of the Black Sea and there was beginning to affect cultures, although as yet not as profoundly as it was in Western Europe. In all this how far was the kingdom of God being realized? To what degree, if at all, were men and women rising to what Paul called "the measure of the stature of the fulness of Christ"? How far and in what ways was God's will being "done on earth as it is in heaven"?

Obviously God's will was not yet fully done. "The exceeding greatness of his power" was still in "earthen vessels." Even the institutions called churches and which were presumably both the expressions and the vehicles of that power were far from complete conformity with it. Indeed, the most imposing of those institutions, the section of the Catholic Church which had the Pope as its head, from the efforts of great dreamers to make God's will dominant had in part succumbed to another kind of power, the kind which had crucified Christ.

Monastic movements which had sprung from the ambition to embody fully the commands of Christ were never perfect expressions of those commands and as they grew older tended to depart further from them.

But the Gospel was not without effect. God's word was not returning to Him void. As in earlier centuries, lives were emerging which palpably bore the impress of Christ. Whether they were more numerous than earlier it is impossible to determine. They would have been the first to acknowledge, as had Paul so many generations before, that they had not fully attained nor were already made perfect. "The power" did not render even the greatest of the Christians infallible. Bernard of Clairvaux preached Crusades. Hildebrand helped to create a Papal organization which was corrupted by a kind of power which was opposed to Christ. They and others of those regarded as model Christians were evidence that "the power" did not overrule the freedom of man's will and thereby make men incapable of sin or error.

Yet out of the crude stuff of roistering and ruthless barbarian ancestry and descendants from the Roman provincial stock, most of it only superficially converted, men and women were appearing who were regarded by those about them as exemplars of the Christian ideal, products of the transforming power which had gripped Paul and the other apostles. The very fact that they were so esteemed was evidence that the masses of professing Christians, even when they themselves did not seriously attempt to emulate them, were sufficiently responsive to the Gospel to recognize its fruits and pay reverence to those who bore them.

Moreover, more than in the first five centuries and to a much larger degree than in the discouraging four and a half centuries of the great recession, the "power" was entering into those customs, institutions, and standards of conduct generally accepted in much of Europe, especially Western Europe, which were shaping the majority of the population. By no means all Europe was even nominally Christian. Such portions as bore the Christian name were palpably far short of deserving that designation. Those called Christians were as yet only a small minority of mankind. Yet the "power" was at work, irradiating some of the crude stuff of the "earthen vessels." It was sensitizing consciences, making them uneasy and ill content with anything short of the seemingly impossible "high calling of God in Christ Jesus" to be perfect as God is perfect and to be "filled with all the fullness of God." The "exceeding greatness of his power" was enabling men and women to approach that goal. It was also inspiring them to seek to raise the level of entire communities and of all human society towards the performance of God's will on earth. The contrasts between ideals and performance were striking, sometimes in individuals, more frequently in society. This, however, was evidence of the challenge given by Christ and an indication of the fashion in which the "power" worked.

Now followed another period when it seemed that the "power" was fading from the human scene. For something more than the century and a half between 1350 and 1500 Christianity was losing ground. As in the earlier periods, precise dates for the beginning and the end of the era cannot be fixed. In some areas of geography and of life the recession began before 1350. Here and there it was being overcome before 1500. In other places recovery either never came or was retarded until after 1500. Yet these dates can serve roughly as boundaries. In these fifteen decades the geographic frontiers of Christianity shrank alarmingly. The faith vanished from most of Asia and was hard-bested in Asia Minor and the Balkan Peninsula. Loss of morale and decay were apparent in Western Europe, the area in which Christianity had been the most potent in the preceding four and a half centuries. Yet the recession was not as severe or as prolonged as had been that between 500 and 950. Incipient recovery, too, was more marked and the ensuing advance more striking and far-reaching. To that recession, the second of major proportions in the history of Christianity, we must now turn.

GEOGRAPHIC LOSS
AND INTERNAL LASSITUDE,
CONFUSION, AND CORRUPTION,
PARTLY OFFSET BY VIGOROUS LIFE
A.D. 1350 — A.D. 1500

Chapter XXVI

THE SETTING OF THE SECOND RECESSION

Not far from the middle of the thirteenth century a number of important developments occurred in Europe and Asia which worked adversely for Christianity. They were not as nearly disastrous for the faith as had been those which brought the great recession that marked the four and a half centuries between A.D. 500 and A.D. 950. Yet they were serious and to the hypothetical traveller from Mars might have seemed to presage the disappearance of Christianity from the world scene. As in the great recession from the close of the fifth to the middle of the tenth century the menace came from two directions, namely, through pressures external to lands where Christianity had become rooted and through the disintegration of the political and cultural structure with which Christianity had become associated, so now in Eurasia at large events were transpiring which brought losses, and developments in Christendom itself spelled peril.

One of the most momentous and widespread of the changes was the disintegration of the Mongol Empire and the accompaniments and aftermath of that series of events. This took place in the second half of the fourteenth century. Presumably that wide-flung realm could not be long held together after the impulse given by the initial wave of conquest had been spent. It broke up into a number of fragments, large and small, and some of these soon disappeared. In 1368 the Mongol Dynasty in China came to an end and was succeeded by the Ming Dynasty, founded by a Chinese and brought to power in part by anti-foreign sentiment. This meant the expulsion, the assimilation, or the dying out of the minor foreign communities in China, among them those which professed the Christian faith. Indeed, so completely did Christianity disappear in China that we do not know either the date or the manner of its demise. The bulk of the Mongols became Buddhists, and this placed fresh obstacles to any possible conversion to Christianity. Islam became firmly established in the north-west of China and in what later was known as Sinkiang. It may well have been that some of the nominal Christians in that area went over to that faith. In Persia and Central Asia the Mongols turned Moslem, thus effectively precluding the spread of Christianity among them. The end of the Mongol Empire entailed difficulties for the trans-continental trade which had mounted under the relative security given the heart-land of Asia by the comprehensive Mongol rule. This rendered perilous if not impossible the journeys of missionaries from Western Europe to that region and thus helped to terminate the enterprises of the Franciscans and Dominicans in Persia and Central Asia. Timur (Tamerlane), the fanatical Moslem of Mongol stock whose life (1336–1405) spanned the second half of the fourteenth century, carried on extensive wars of conquest which radiated from his capital at Samarqand into Central Asia, Persia, Mesopotamia, and North-west India. They seem to have borne hard on the Christian minorities, mostly Nestorians, which were in Central Asia. Certainly these perished, leaving behind them only grave stones.

One phase of the aftermath of the Mongol Empire favoured the spread of Christianity. The decline of Mongol rule in Russia and the growing extent and power of the state which had its capital in Moscow made for the extension of Christianity in that region and for the emergence of a Russian Church which had distinct characteristics that we are to note in the following chapter.

Ominous for the future of Christianity was the continued advance of the Ottoman Turks. We have seen that this had begun before the middle of the thirteenth century and by 1350 had wrested much of Asia Minor from Christian rulers. In 1329 Nicæa was taken. Between 1350 and 1400 the Turks established themselves in Europe, mastered Adrianople, and conquered Bulgaria. In 1453 Constantinople fell to their arms. It became their capital. This meant the subjection of the Christian population to Moslem rule. The triumph of the Crescent over the Cross was dramatized by the conversion into a mosque of Saint Sophia, that great church which had been erected by Justinian and which for over nine centuries had been the chief cathedral of Greek Christianity. The Ottoman Turks swept on into Europe, reduced Greece and the Balkan Peninsula, conquered much of Hungary, besieged Vienna, and threatened Western Europe. In 1500 the Turkish tide had not quite reached its height. A politically divided Western Europe was unable to unite against it, and that in spite of the repeated and frantic appeals of the Popes. The age of the Crusades had passed. Once more the Crescent was in the ascendant. In the next chapter we are to see more at length the problems which this brought to Christianity.

In what had become the chief stronghold of Christianity, Western Europe, a new age was coming to birth which carried with it grave threats to the faith. Beginning a few years before 1350, successive epidemics of bubonic plague, the

"Black Death," swept over the region and are said to have reduced the population of Northern Europe by as much as a third and that of England by a half. By decimating the ranks of the Franciscans and Dominicans, the "Black Death" dealt severe blows to the missions and the quality of these orders. In recruiting their ranks to make good their losses the friars accepted men who fell below the earlier high standards. By reducing the labour supply the Black Death hastened social changes, including the decline of serfdom.

Even more serious were developments which were ushering in a new Europe. Nation states were emerging under the leadership of absolute monarchs. Gun powder was making more deadly the wars between them. The Holy Roman Empire, that combination of institution and dream which had given a measure of unity to Western Europe, was in hopeless decline. Its great rival for the mastery of Western Europe, the Papacy, survived, but with weakened political and moral influence. The vast machinery which great Popes had built up to implement their purpose of fulfilling what they believed to be Christ's commission to the See of Peter either proved beyond the capacity of well-meaning but mediocre Pontiffs or fell prey to ambitious men who employed it for selfish purposes. Popes still sought to be effective in the life of Western Europe, but their political activities were chiefly restricted to Italy. More and more the absolute monarchs who were strengthening their power over nation states were extending their control over the Church in their realms, a control which was to be augmented after 1500.

Feudalism, an expression of a predominantly rural economy, was passing. Commerce, banking, and cities were continuing the growth which had been prominent since the eleventh and twelfth centuries. In the *bourgeoisie* monarchs were finding allies, often restless and independent, in their efforts to increase their power at the expense of the feudal aristocracy. In its ambition to reach all men and transform society in Western Europe the Church had become closely associated with the feudal structure. Many of the endowments of churches and monasteries were in land and were integrated with the feudal economy. Now that feudalism was passing, the Church was handicapped by its earlier achievements. As the victory of Christianity in the Roman Empire had wrought an intimate tie between the faith and that realm which had proved embarrassing when the latter decayed, so the efforts of Christians, to a large degree successful, to make their faith effective in the feudal stage of Europe proved a liability when, in its turn, feudalism became moribund. Could "the exceeding greatness of the power" which Paul declared to be inherent in the Christian Gospel prove itself potent in this new Europe of commerce, cities, and aggressive, fighting nation states ruled by ruthless absolute monarchs?

Intellectually and spiritually Western Europe was moving into a new day. Here was an even more serious, if less immediately obvious threat to Christianity. Scholasticism, with which the theology of the Church had been closely associated, was decaying. It still dominated the universities and the monastic orders, including the Franciscans and Dominicans, but the main new currents of intellectual life were flowing in other channels. This seemed to augur ill of Christianity and the Church.

The Renaissance was in progress with its companion, humanism. No one date can be assigned for the beginning of the Renaissance. Preparation for the Renaissance went back before 1350, but not until the fifteenth century did it come to its flood tide. Literally Renaissance means new birth, as though during the Middle Ages Europe had been dead and had now again become alive. The term Revival of Learning is also employed for one phase of the Renaissance, as though the Middle Ages had been intellectually sterile. The designations are evidence of the pride of the age, somewhat narrowly self-conscious, and of its contempt for its immediate predecessor. Actually, as we have seen, the Middle Ages had been pulsing with life and intellectually had been highly creative. Indeed, to no small degree the Renaissance was the child of the Middle Ages and would not have been but for what had been accomplished through Christianity.

The Renaissance was multiform and complex. In its broadest sense it embraced most of the currents which were shaping Western Europe in the fourteenth, fifteenth, and sixteenth centuries. It ran parallel with discoveries in geography and astronomy, with growth in commerce, and with fresh movements in literature and art. It was intimately related to an enthusiasm for the pre-Christian literature of Greece and Rome and to an increased study of Greek.

Humanism was an accompaniment and manifestation of the Renaissance. An outstanding early humanist was Petrarch (1304–1374) who left behind him a large number of admirers and disciples. In contrast with the asceticism and contempt for the world in which the Middle Ages had professed to see the road to the goal of man's course, eternal life, Petrarch and humanists in general had an exuberant appreciation of life in this present world. They were attracted by what they saw in Virgil, Cicero, and Horace. Increasingly they became expert in the great poets, historians, essayists, and philosophers of Greece and Rome. They rejoiced in verbal expression and prized literature for the skill and grace which it displayed and the present enjoyment which it afforded. The men of the Renaissance took pleasure in nature and sought to explore and understand it. They were fascinated by the beauty of the human body and endeavoured to study its anatomy and to reproduce it in art. They waxed enthusiastic over the surviving examples of the sculpture of pre-Christian Greece and Rome with their faithful portrayal of the body in bronze or stone. They were self-confident, believing in themselves and man. They took joy in their critical faculties, and especially in challenging what had been accepted in the Middle Ages. They poured scorn on scholasticism and the school men. Admiring and reviving the architecture of Rome and Greece, they despised the architecture of the Middle Ages, contemptuously calling it Gothic, by which they meant barbarous. They sought satisfaction in human achievement and believed in man's power to understand the world and to master it. They thought of man as the competent architect of his own future. While paying lip service to the Christian faith, they tended to rule out God, the need of redemption, and the incarnation, and to ignore life beyond the grave. Often they flaunted Christian morality.

In a very real sense the Renaissance and humanism were an outgrowth of the Middle Ages and of the Christian faith which had so large a share in shaping the culture of that era. The confidence in the orderliness of the natural world, the belief that man and his environment constitute a universe and are not unintelligible chaos had been drilled into the mind of Western Europe by the school men, nurtured as they were in the Church and committed to the Christian faith. To be sure, the intellectual tools which they employed had been devised in pre-Christian Greece and increasingly they came to the conclusion that these would not enable man to demonstrate the truth of the main Christian affirmations. Yet they were confident that God had created and continued to govern the universe, and that, although He made high and inexorable demands, His purpose for man was beneficent. The Psalms, which were a large part of the services of the Church and the monasteries, took pleasure in the world of nature and overflowed with gratitude for it. The sayings of Jesus throbbed with the beauty, mystery, and tragedy of growing things, birds, sunshine and rain, and human joys and sorrows. Some of the greatest of the school men, among them Albertus Magnus, the teacher of Thomas Aquinas, had inquiring minds which ranged widely over nature.

As in so many others of the contributions which have come to mankind through the Christian faith, humanism, in part the product of Christianity, could be either an aid or an enemy of that faith and, in fact, was both. The typical humanist of the Renaissance was a member of the Catholic Church. Many, like Petrarch, held office in the Church and were supported by it. Humanists might and often did attack certain features of the Church of the day. Petrarch, for example, was very critical of the monks. Yet ostensibly in creed they remained orthodox. Numbers of humanists were not only nominal but also devout and sincere in their Christian faith. They combined their humanist enthusiasms with Christian devotion. While by no means entirely lacking in Italy, humanists of this stamp were especially prominent north of the Alps. On the other hand, humanism could and in many instances did lead to what in effect even though not overtly was a denial of the Christian Gospel. Perhaps it was more dangerous because it was not openly in opposition. It often passed over into an arrogance which had no deep sense of sin or of creatureliness and which felt no need for the forgiving grace of God. To a large proportion of the humanists heaven and hell were either non-existent or unimportant. This present life was what counted. Some might be personally humble but were convinced of man's self-sufficiency to solve his problems. More were vain, self-seeking individualists, nominally Christian, but patent contradictions of the Christian ideal. There was much scoffing at Christianity. This phase of the humanistic strain was to contribute to the secularism which then and in later centuries was to be one of the most serious threats to Christianity.

The intellectual life of Western Europe was given added impetus by the invention of printing by movable type. This occurred not far from the middle of the fourteenth century. The device spread rapidly and, replacing the slow and costly multiplication of books by manual transcription, vastly facilitated the circulation of ideas. It was furthered by the use of paper in place of the more expensive parchment. The manufacture of paper, probably derived indirectly from China, became common in Europe in the thirteenth and fourteenth centuries.

Towards the close of the fifteenth century came the renewal of that expansion of Europe which had been begun in the Crusades and the eastern commerce of the Italian cities and which had been halted by the Black Death, the break-up of the Mongol Empire, and the growth of the Ottoman Empire. It was furthered by the increase in the use of the mariner's compass. It was to continue into the twentieth century. Could the Christianity of Western Europe, handicapped by so many internal weaknesses, respond to the opportunity and the challenge given by that expansion, move into the lands opened to Western Europeans, and make the impact of the Occident a blessing and not a curse?

As we move on into the century and a half between 1350 and 1500 we will find the Eastern and Western wings of what had been the Catholic Church drifting farther and farther apart. We will see the effort at reunion break down, apparently with finality. Each wing was henceforth largely to go its own way. Much of the Orthodox Church was under Turkish domination. What became the largest member of the family of Orthodox Churches, that of Russia, was more and more separated by geography and genius from the Roman Catholic Church. While occasionally influenced from Western Europe, Russian Christianity was distinct from it. The other Eastern Churches dwindled and without repair. It was in the Christianity of Western Europe that the currents of life were chiefly pulsing. We shall deal first, but briefly, with Christianity in the East and then turn, and more nearly in detail, to that of Western Europe.

Dort
Münster
Magdeburg BRANDENBURG Berlin
GERMANY
Ypres
Brussels
Dortmund
Eisleben
Wittenberg
Douai Louvain
Marburg Halle Leipzig
Cambrai Cologne
WESTPHALIA Wartburg Erfurt
PICARDY Fulda Schmalkalden Dresden
Rheims LUX. Frankfort Herrnhut
Meaux Trier Mainz HESSE Zwickau
Paris Metz NASSAU Darmstadt
Verdun Worms Prague
PALA- Speier Nuremberg BOHEMIA
Toul TINATE
Vézelay Strasburg BAVARIA
LORRAINE Ulm Ingolstadt
BURGUNDY Augsburg
Basel Constance
FRANCE Zürich St. Gall
Bern Einsiedeln
Laussane SWITZERLAND
Geneva THE GRISSONS

Main map:

NORWAY
SWEDEN
Trondhjem
Bergen
Strangnäs
SCOTLAND NORTH SEA
Aberdeen
St. Andrews
Glasgow Edinburgh
ULSTER DENMARK Copenhagen
IRELAND Drogheda BALT
Dublin HOLSTEIN
ATLANTIC WALES NETHERLANDS Bremen Hamburg Berlin
OCEAN ENGLAND Leiden GERMANY SILESIA
London Münster
Canterbury SEE BELGIUM Cologne Leipzig Dresden
INSET Brussels Frankfort Prague
Brest NORMANDY PICARDY LUX. HESSE BOHEMIA
Paris Metz BAVARIA MORAV
Strasburg Augsburg Vienna
La Rochelle Basel AUSTRIA
Bay of Bern
Biscay FRANCE SWITZERLAND THE GRISSONS
Vienne Geneva
Trent
LEÓN Montpellier Avignon Bologna Venice BOSNIA
GUIPUZCOA PYRENEES Vienne
NAVARRE Chieti
Lisbon Pamplona Manresa Barcelona CORSICA Rome ADRIATIC SEA
PORTUGAL Salamanca Montserat Naples
Madrid SPAIN ITALY
Alcala SARDINIA
Granada Somassi
Strait of Gibraltar SICILY
Tangier Gibraltar MEDITERRANE
Algiers
MOROCCO ALGERIA Tunis TUNIS
Tripoli
TRIPO

EUROPE 1500-1750

Chapter XXVII

CHRISTIANITY IN THE EAST
A.D. 1350 - A.D. 1500

For all the Eastern Churches except that of Russia the decades between 1350 and 1500 were marked by losses of territory and numbers, some of them extensive. Nowhere, with the exception of Russia and, to a less extent, the Balkans, were there significant new movements in Christianity. It was a dark and discouraging era.

The Lesser Eastern Churches

Outside the family of the Orthodox Church, among what numerically were the lesser Eastern Churches, the gloom of recession was unrelieved by any ray of light or hope.

As we have hinted, the Nestorians suffered more than any of the others. With the expulsion of the Mongols from China the Nestorian as well as the Roman Catholic communities in that realm completely died out, whether rapidly or slowly we do not know. The conversion of Mongolia to Buddhism precluded any hope of the spread of Christianity in that region. The coming over to Islam of the Mongols in Persia meant the end of such slight traces of Christianity as were found among them in that land. The disorders attendant upon the disintegration of Mongol power in Persia and the Tigris-Euphrates Valley seem to have borne heavily upon all varieties of Christians in these regions, and especially upon the Nestorians, the most numerous of the Mesopotamian Christian bodies. The campaigns of Timur in the last quarter of the fourteenth century were attended by widespread destruction of life. The Nestorians suffered greatly and dwindled to remnants, some in Mesopotamia and some which took refuge in the highlands of Kurdistan. Their Patriarchs found no abode in which they could long settle. In the fifteenth century the custom arose of transmitting that office from uncle to nephew. This made it as nearly hereditary as possible under the rule which required that the post be filled by a celibate.

Christian communities with Nestorian connexions survived in South India. We hear that in 1490 some of them sent to the Nestorian Patriarch for bishops, with the information that they had long been without episcopal ministrations. The lapse may have been due to persecution.

The island of Socotra ceased to be Christian, but how and by what stages we do not know.

From the reverses encountered in this period the Nestorians were never to recover. They persisted, but as small enclaves. Those in or on the edge of Kurdistan were subject to recurrent raids by the Kurds, a vigorous, rough independent mountain folk with a religion which was compounded of Islam, the professed faith, with non-Moslem elements. Few though they were, in the centuries after 1500 the Nestorians were divided, partly by internal schisms and partly by efforts of other Christians, Roman Catholic and Protestant, to win their allegiance.

The Monophysite Jacobites, with a Patriarch of Antioch as their ranking bishop, also suffered. Small communities, presumably largely merchants and handicraftsmen, had been scattered widely in Persia, Mesopotamia, and Central Asia. Like the Nestorians, they were at a grave disadvantage when the Mongols turned Moslem, in the disorders which accompanied the break-up of Mongol rule, and during the wars of Timur. They, too, died out completely in Central Asia and most of Persia and dwindled in Mesopotamia. In Syria, the major centre of their strength, they also fell on evil days. From 1292 to 1495 they were divided among themselves by rival Patriarchs. Much as in the latter part of the fourteenth and in the fifteenth century the Roman Catholic Church was weakened by the Great Schism between rival Popes, so in this much smaller body internal dissensions among claimants for the headship of the church brought sad enervation. Persecutions by Moslems added to the distress. By the time the schism was healed (1495) and one Patriarch, at least theoretically, had the allegiance of the entire body, the constituency is said to have shrunk to approximately fifty thousand poor families.

Between 1350 and 1500 Armenian Christianity did not meet as many or as grievous disasters as did the Nestorians and Jacobites. However, it, too, experienced reverses and, like the Jacobites, divisions. The Armenian kingdom which had arisen in Cilicia in Asia Minor in the eleventh century continued to 1375. It had been closely associated with the Crusaders and its last dynasty, that of Lusignan, was a Latin family. Through that association many Armenians had come into union with Rome. The Cilician kingdom declined and the *coup de grâce* was given by Egyptian forces in 1375. In the meantime, following the break-up of Mongol rule, much of the historic Armenia was divided into many principalities under Armenians, Turkomans, and Kurds. In the last two decades of the fourteenth century and in the opening years of the fifteenth century Timur and his armies repeatedly invaded Armenia, bringing their customary destruction. To escape them many Armenians migrated to other regions. After the death of Timur much of Armenia was ruled by a family of Turkomans until, early in the sixteenth century, it was supplanted by the Persians.

Largely in consequence of these vicissitudes, Armenian Christianity was divided. Some Armenians were kept in union with Rome as Uniates, that is, they preserved many of their customs but acknowledged the supremacy of the Pope and brought their creeds into conformity with those of Rome. Franciscan and Dominican missionaries laboured valiantly to bring this about. Armenian bishops were present at the Council at Florence when, in 1439, as we are shortly to see, the Pope seemed to have achieved the reunion of the Orthodox Church with Rome, and the union of the Armenians with the See of Peter was solemnly proclaimed. However, the majority of the Armenian Christians held aloof. Their church, in turn, presented a sorry spectacle of dissension and violence. It is said that each of the last six of its Patriarchs (1377–1432) who ostensibly had their headquarters at Sis, the capital of the Cilician Armenian kingdom, had obtained the post through bribery and the assassination of his predecessor. There were efforts, only partially successful, to reëstablish the Armenian Patriarchate at Etchmiadzin, near the foot of Mt. Ararat. Various claimants for the post came forward. A symbol of legitimacy was what was believed to be the right arm of Gregory the Illuminator, under whom the conversion of the land had been successfully begun late in the third century and who was regarded as the great saint of the church. Encased in a silver reliquary this grisly object was used in consecrations, thus in physical form conveying apostolic succession. During these decades it passed now to one Patriarch and now to another. Indeed, there were at least two which were asserted to be genuine.

After Constantinople became the capital of the Ottoman Turks, the conqueror, wishing an administrative head for the Armenians in his realm, gave to their bishop civil jurisdiction over all of their nation in the Turkish Empire and made him their sole representative to the government. This was in accordance with the pattern adopted for other Christian bodies in that realm. This bishop had the title of Patriarch, but was subordinate to the one in Etchmiadzin.

In spite of these many hardships, so debilitating to the inner life of the Church, Armenian Christianity continued. Clergy were trained and ordained and bishops were consecrated. Many Armenians of the dispersion remained loyal to their mother church. Indeed, the church produced a notable theologian.

Gregory of Datev (c.1346–1410) taught and wrote during troubled years and in the latter part of his life was forced to flee to escape the disorders which followed the death of Timur. A monk and a teacher of theology, he was a loyal Monophysite who wrote vigorously against those who sought to bring the Armenian Church into union with Rome. His *Book of Questions,* completed in 1397 during the invasions by the armies of Timur, was an outline of theology in which he sought to set forth the Christian faith in comprehensive fashion. He was familiar with the outstanding early writers of the Catholic Church, both East and West, including Augustine. He also knew the more recent theologians of the West, among them Albertus Magnus and Thomas Aquinas. Not a creative thinker, he presented the historic Christian tradition, but from a Monophysite angle. His work was to be cherished by his church as a standard.

The dates 1350 and 1500 had no especial significance in the history of the Coptic Church. To be sure, the 1350's were marked by a severe anti-Christian outbreak and in 1517 Egypt was taken by the Ottoman Turks. Yet persecutions were no new experience and the coming of the Turks, Moslems like their predecessors, a succession of Mameluke rulers, was by no means revolutionary for the Church. As often heretofore Moslem feeling against the Christians was aggravated by resentment at the prominence of Christians in official circles. The Moslem rulers found it to their advantage to employ them as clerks and administrators. Some Christians used their favoured position to ignore the discriminatory regulations against those of their faith. Many were wealthy and also seemed to the Moslems to be arrogant instead of humble as beseemed members of a minority religion. From time to time persecution broke out, accompanied by mob violence. Some Christians renounced their faith. We hear that in 1389 large numbers of these apostates marched through the streets of Cairo, lamenting that they had abandoned the religion of their fathers from fear of persecution and denouncing Islam. They were beheaded, both men and women, and a fresh persecution of Christians followed.

In Nubia Christianity was waning. Early in the period it was sufficiently strong to embolden a Nubian prince to protest against the persecution of his fellow-believers in Egypt. He seized Moslem merchants in his realm and would not release them until the Coptic Patriarch, incarcerated for his faith, had been given his liberty. However, by 1500 the Moslem rulers of Egypt were extending their influence in Nubia and Moslem merchants were bringing in their faith. Nubian Christianity was on the way out.

Little information has come to us of the history of Christianity in Ethiopia (Abyssinia) during this period. Presumably the connexion was maintained with the Coptic Church. It is probable, too, that the head of the Ethiopian

Church was still appointed from Egypt. That Christianity survived is clear, for we are to hear more of its history when we come to the next period.

The fact that, in the face of extraordinarily unfavourable conditions, the churches in the East survived is evidence of marked vitality. From within them came a succession of priests and bishops and men to staff the monasteries. To what extent if at all they produced men and women who were exemplars of Christian living we cannot know. That the majority fell far short of the ideal is clear. That some approached it is probable.

THE TURKISH CONQUEST OF THE BALKAN PENINSULA

The years between 1350 and 1500 witnessed the conquest by the Ottoman Turks of most of the Balkan Peninsula. It was not until after the larger part of the Balkan Peninsula had succumbed that Constantinople fell.

The Turkish conquest brought fresh problems and some changes to the Christianity of the region. In 1349 the Byzantine Emperor called on his son-in-law, the emir of the Ottoman Turks—for he had given his daughter in marriage to this magnate—to aid him against the Bulgars who were besieging Salonica. The Turks responded and thus began their widening incursions into Europe. In 1356 several thousands of them settled permanently in the Balkan Peninsula. The Balkan peoples were weakened by internal divisions and could not offer effective resistance. Early in the 1360's the Turks shifted the centre of their power to Europe and transferred their capital to Adrianople. Late in the 1360's they began the systematic reduction of Bulgaria. In 1389 at a decisive battle at Kosovo Polye the Turks defeated a Serbian-Bulgarian-Croatian coalition and reduced the several princes to a position of vassalage.

In spite of the Turkish advance the religious life of the Balkans did not at once decline. Indeed, in the second half of the fourteenth century the Bulgarian Church experienced a notable revival. The outstanding figures of the awakening were Theodosius of Trnovo (died 1367 or 1368) who, a monk and an ardent Hesychast, took a leading part in fighting the widespread Bogomilism, and Euthymius, a disciple of Theodosius and in the last quarter of the century Patriarch of the Bulgarian Church. A marked increase in the preparation of Christian literature was seen. Extensive revisions were made of works already existing in Slavonic, fresh translations were prepared from the Greek originals, and new books were written. Under Euthymius the Hesychast movement seems to have captured the Bulgarian Church.

However, the revival was short-lived. Towards the close of the fourteenth century, the loss of Bulgarian political independence was followed by the end of its ecclesiastical independence. The Bulgarian Church was brought under the Patriarch of Constantinople.

The mid-fourteenth century mark saw the Orthodox Church in Serbia on an upward surge. The great ruler of the country, Dushan, assumed the title of Emperor and a council made its archbishopric a patriarchate. The Patriarch of Constantinople was unreconciled to a step which seemed to threaten his preëminence in the Orthodox communion and retaliated by anathematizing the Serbian Church and its Patriarch. Yet under Dushan's vigorous regime the Church ignored the displeasure of Constantinople, improved its internal life, and took action against Bogomilism. In the second half of the fourteenth century a new monastery, the Great Meteoron, was inaugurated on a high crag in Thessaly in a region of hermits known as the Thebaïd of Staghi. Its founder was Athanasius, who had been trained on Mt. Athos. With the mounting of the Turkish menace a reconciliation was effected (1375) between the churches of Serbia and Constantinople by which the title of Patriarch was confirmed for the head of the former. When, in the second half of the fifteenth century, almost all Serbia was brought under Turkish administration, the Church became the symbol and the tie of Serbian nationalism.

In spite of the Turkish conquest of the Balkan Peninsula, in only one area, Albania, was there extensive conversion of the Christian population to Islam. In Albania, in contrast with Bulgaria and Serbia, the Slavs were in a minority. The dominant groups were descendants of peoples who had inhabited the region since the dawn of history. Protected by a mountainous terrain, they had maintained themselves against all invaders. They were chronically opposed to the Slavs. For centuries before the Turkish conquest they had been Christians, divided between the Latin and Greek wings of the Catholic Church. It was not until the fifteenth century that the Turkish conquest began. It was only slowly accomplished and Turkish rule was never firmly established over the sturdy highlanders. Yet eventually, probably not until the sixteenth and seventeenth centuries, the majority of the Albanians became Moslems. It has been suggested that the motives were the desire to be accepted as equals of the Turks and animosity against the Slavs, since most of the latter were of the Orthodox Christian faith.

The Turks Erase the Byzantine Empire and Use the Orthodox Church for Their Purposes

In 1453 Constantinople, long a bulwark of Christendom against the Moslem advance, fell to the Ottoman Turks. The night before the final assault the defenders—Emperor, Patriarch, and nobles, together with their Latin allies—knowing that this was the end, partook of the communion in Saint Sophia. The next day the Emperor died fighting in the breach. On May 30 the Turkish ruler, by fitting coincidence with the title Mohammed II, entered the city and held a Moslem service of thanksgiving in Saint Sophia. Mohammed seemed at last to have supplanted Christ in the capital of that state and Church which had prided themselves on being the perpetuators and champions of the faith, unadulterated, that had been proclaimed by the apostles. Constantinople became the Turkish capital, Saint Sophia was transformed into a mosque, early in the sixteenth century the Turkish Sultans obtained from the last of the Abbasids the title of Caliph, the successor of the Prophet and the religious head of Moslems the world over, and the quondam citadel of Eastern Christianity became the seat of the titular head of the Moslem faithful.

In the closing years of the fifteenth century and in the sixteenth century the Turkish Empire continued to expand. At its height, under Suleiman the Magnificent (1520–1566), it included all the Balkan Peninsula, except rugged Montenegro and a strip of the Dalmatian coast, it reached into Hungary, made the Black Sea a Turkish lake, and embraced Asia Minor, Armenia, Georgia, the Euphrates Valley, Syria, Palestine, Egypt, and the north coast of Africa as far as Morocco. Italy was threatened and a foothold, temporary as it proved, was obtained in that peninsula. Western Europe shivered in fear, but, divided, gave scant heed to the frantic appeals of the Popes for a crusade to stem the Turkish tide.

The Turkish conquest brought many accessions to Islam. As we have said, they were numerous in Albania. They were even more prevalent in Asia Minor. That region, the earliest large area in which Christianity had been the faith of the majority, now became predominantly Moslem. Christian communities survived, but chiefly in the historic Greek cities on the coast and among the Armenians. The motives for conversion varied. Wishing to be identified with the new rulers, some of the upper classes made the shift. Many Christian slaves of Moslem masters conformed to the faith of their owners. In the Balkan Peninsula, some of the Bogomils became Moslems to escape persecution by Orthodox and Catholic Christians. Systematic and compulsory conversion to Islam was common. Thousands of sons of Christians were torn from their parents, reared as Moslems, and enrolled in the armies. Out of the choicest of these converts recruits were chosen for the Janizaries, the picked fighting core of the Turkish forces. Many churches were transformed into mosques.

Yet Christianity did not perish. The Orthodox Church survived the Empire. Mohammed II had a synod elect a Patriarch and invested him with the insignia of his authority. As part of the administrative system by which the Turks governed their realms, the major divisions of Christians were regarded as distinct nations, or millets, each with its own laws and with an ecclesiastic at its head. The Orthodox were called the Rum Millet, or Roman Nation, and had their Patriarch as their responsible official. He exercised far more authority over his flock than had his predecessors under the Christian Emperors. He maintained his courts in which some categories of cases of the Orthodox were tried. Other Orthodox bishops and patriarchs in the Turkish realms were made subject to him.

This new status of the Orthodox had serious handicaps. The Patriarchs were chosen and held office at the pleasure of the Sultan. Frequently they were deposed after a brief term. They had to make heavy payments to the Sultan for the post and received from him the symbols of their office. In return they exacted fees, often onerous, from their bishops and clergy. What in the West was called simony became the rule. Under such circumstances numbers of the Patriarchs and bishops were unworthy men. Many of the wealthy and influential members of the Greek Orthodox community had their homes near the seat of the Patriarch, in the Phanar district of Constantinople. They tended to control the Church and to exercise a monopoly of its chief offices. The rule of the Phanariots had in it much of special privilege and corruption. Moreover, Christians were put under the disabilities which from early in the Arab conquests had been common in lands with Moslem rulers. In principle at least they were specially taxed, were required to wear a distinctive garb, and were to make no public display of their religion. Now and again fanatical sultans instituted persecutions and threatened to compel all Christians to accept Islam and either to destroy the churches or transform them into mosques.

In spite of these handicaps the Orthodox Church still had its clergy, its services, and its monks. It produced few if any great theologians and no major new movements issued from it. But it lived on, an expression not only of the Christian faith but also of Greek nationalism.

RUSSIAN CHRISTIANITY FINDS A CENTRE IN MOSCOW, EXPANDS, AND IS MODIFIED

In one region, Russia, the Orthodox Church continued to spread. Not only was there territorial expansion but there were also movements in Christianity which gave evidence of marked vitality. The Mongol occupation seems to have deepened the attachment of its Russian subjects to the Church. The Church became a tie of Russian unity, so far as that existed, and of Russian distinctiveness as against the conqueror. There was, too, the progressive permeation of the masses by Christianity due to the continued presence of the Church, its priesthood, and its services.

Much of this was in the Russia which centered about Moscow. The Grand Princes of Moscow, as they were styled, influenced by what they had seen in the Mongol regime, became autocrats with absolute rule over their domains. Supported by the Church, they brought under their control the free cities and

the many local lords who had been part of a decentralization of power somewhat akin to the feudalism of Western Europe. Some Mongol princes also
accepted their rule. In 1480 the Grand Duke of Moscow, Ivan III, threw off
the last vestiges of the Mongol yoke and became fully independent.

Ivan III claimed to be the legitimate successor of the Byzantine Emperors.
While he was still in his early teens Constantinople fell to the Turks. After the
death of his first wife he married a daughter of the nearest relative of the
last Byzantine Emperor. He adopted the double-headed eagle, symbol of imperial power, and the elaborate ceremonial of the Byzantine court, and demanded that his nobles be completely subject to him.

The older Russia, that which in later centuries was known as the Ukraine
and which centered about Kiev, was not quickly drawn into the Muscovite
orbit. In the middle of the fifteenth century, for instance, the Metropolitan of
Kiev was independent of Moscow and was directly under the Patriarch of
Constantinople.

Monks continued to be pioneers of the north-eastward expansion of Russia
and its religion and culture. Many, moved in part by the desire to escape
foreign rule, went beyond the Mongol frontiers into the forests and either
singly or with a handful of disciples built cells. If a monk was of outstanding
sanctity others joined him, the cell became a monastery, and around it a village
might arise, at the outset made up of lay folk who came for spiritual counsel
but later attracting merchants and artisans. The monasteries became schools,
hospitals, and inns for travellers. Some had libraries and to them princes and
nobles turned for information. Monasteries had a large part in shaping the culture of the state which centered about Moscow. More than before the Mongol
invasion they were directing the intellectual and artistic phases of Russian life.
They were noted for the skill which some in their communities displayed in
painting icons. Most distinguished of these painters was the monk Andrew
Rublev, who died about 1427.

In this fourteenth and fifteenth century Russian monasticism of the north-
eastern frontiers were many who, regarded as model Christians, were canonized. Sergius, whom we have already met, was one of the earliest as well as
the most famous of them.

Two forms of monastic life developed which were to come into sharp conflict shortly after 1500. One of these had as its pioneer and outstanding exemplar
Joseph of Volokolamsk, or Joseph Volotsky. Born in 1440 of a noble family,
Joseph early became a monk and persuaded his parents and brothers to follow
him. He eventually founded a monastery near Volokolamsk. This he made a
model in protest against a relaxation of the monastic life which had become
prevalent. The custom had been developing for the wealthy to enter a monas-

tery in their old age, keeping their property, living on its proceeds, and leaving it to the community on their death. Monasteries were reluctant to accept any one as a novice unless he brought with him a substantial sum. They became comfortable places in which to spend one's years supported by the labour of serfs. Against this trend Joseph inveighed. In his monastery near Volokolamsk he enforced a strict rule which demanded severe fasts, hard work, and diligence in study. Learned, an eloquent preacher, he entered actively into the life of Russia. Although firmly insisting that the individual monk have no property of his own, he saw no sin in the collective possession of wealth by the monastery. Indeed, he encouraged the erection of great monastic buildings and espoused long services and gorgeous vestments, vessels, and altars. He made his monastery a school for the education of prelates, attracted to it the scions of the aristocracy, and encouraged the bishops and abbots who came from it to take part in public affairs. They could thus render Christianity a force in various aspects of the life of the nation. Before many years men trained in his tradition became outstanding in the Russian Church. Strict in their discipline, firmly orthodox in doctrine, strenuously opposed to all heresy, insisting upon the punctilious observance of traditional rites, they had little of the mystic about them and minimized meditation and the inner life of prayer. They were known as Josephites.

In striking contrast was a widespread trend in monasticism which had as its chief representative a contemporary of Joseph, Nilus (Nil) Sorsky (c.1433–1508). Monks of this kind were numerous in the North, beyond the Volga, and were known as the Transvolgians, the Transvolga "elders" (*startzi*), or the Non-possessors. They preferred to live alone and to have no property, either singly or collectively. They devoted themselves to solitary meditation and prayer, supported themselves by the labour of their hands, wrote few if any books, and beyond giving spiritual counsel to laymen did not mix in the affairs of the world. They may have been influenced by Hesychasm. They also perpetuated the kenotic tradition.

Probably of peasant stock and with the surname Maikov, as a young monk Nilus had journeyed to Palestine and Greece, had there known the Hesychast movement, and probably had acquired some competence in the Greek language. He was deeply learned in the literature of his church. Returning to Russia, for a time he was a member of a monastery founded by Cyril, a disciple of Sergius, in Northern Russia. In a spot in the forest a few miles from there he undertook the life of a hermit. A small group of his friends and disciples settled about him.

Nilus advocated a combination of the way of the hermit with that of the cenobite. He believed the religious life to be best nurtured in a small group, a *skete,* not exceeding twelve members, under the spiritual direction of a *starets* ("elder"), their superior. The members were to live far from the habitations of other men. They were to practice complete poverty and the greatest simplicity, owning no land and working with their hands for the bare necessities of existence. They were not to be averse to accepting alms, but always in moderation, and were never to obtain anything by force.

True to the kenotic tradition, while orthodox himself and permitting excommunication for heretics and apostates, Nilus opposed capital punishment for them and advocated a degree of tolerance. To him the goal of the religious life was the union with God of the soul which had fully given itself to the love of God. The road of that union could not be taught: it must be shared. He wished not to be called teacher but simply to be a friend. Even devout conversations might divert the soul from its true road. Any appeal to the senses through elaborate church services and beautiful and rich accoutrements of worship was a snare to be shunned. He advocated the repetition of short prayers to Jesus followed by interior prayer of the spirit, with no audible expression.

Probably it was inevitable that the Josephites and the Non-possessors should clash. The conflict seems first to have come to a head in 1503, in the later years of Nilus. At a council held at Moscow Nilus lifted his voice against the severe measures which were being proposed against the Judaizers, heretics of whom we are to speak in a moment. As might have been expected, the Non-possessors, with their kenotic principles of non-resistance, were defeated by the activist, zealous Josephites. Yet among them were many who were eventually canonized as ideal Christians and the tradition which they represented was again and again to make itself felt in Russian Christianity. The victory of the Josephites, advocating as they did the participation by monks in public life, furthered the close association of Church and state which, in part inherited from Constantinople, was to be a marked feature of Russian Christianity.

Two movements, branded as heresies, appeared in Russian Christianity in the fourteenth and fifteenth centuries. One of these was that of the Strigolniks or "barbers," seemingly so called because their outstanding leader, a deacon of Pskov named Karp, was barber to the clergy. Some of the Russian clergy felt the practice to be wrong of charging fees for the sacraments. They found a spokesman in a bishop who protested to the Patriarch of Constantinople against the Metropolitan of Moscow for upholding the custom. The Patriarch supported the Metropolitan. But Karp was not satisfied. He listened sympathetically to candidates for ordination as they complained of the charges made by the Archbishop of Novgorod. He came to believe that ordinations made in this fashion, being tainted with simony, were invalid. From that it was an easy step to the conviction that all sacraments administered by clergy who were guilty of simony were worthless and that to receive them would be condoning the sin and so would be sharing in it. Since simoniacal fees were universal, all the sacraments of the Church must be shunned by sincere Christians. Accordingly the Strigolniks left the Church and formed separate congregations which were served by laymen. The attempt was made to conform to the manner of life of the Christians of the first century and to have nothing to do with what they believed to be the apostate official church, with its wealth and formalism. The lay readers refused any financial remuneration, interpreted the Bible to their flocks, and set an example of humble, earnest living. The only sacrament which was observed by them was that of penance. Prayers for the dead were denounced as contrary to the Scriptures. Strict moral standards are said to have been observed. The conjecture has been offered that the Strigolniks were influenced by Bogomilism, but this appears to be unproved.

It was to be expected that the bishops and clergy would be opposed to a movement which was so critical of them. Two deacons who were the leaders, one of them Karp, were executed in Novgorod in 1375. Vigorous action against the Strigolniks continued until they seemed to have been stamped out. It may have been, however, that they were simply driven into a secret existence.

The other outstanding Russian heretical movement of this period was that of the Judaizers. This is said to have begun in the 1470's with the conversion to Judaism of two priests in Novgorod by a Lithuanian Jew. They kept their new faith secret and continued in the Church. They proved to be ardent missionaries. Through them Judaism spread and numbered among its adherents clergy who were high in Church and state or who, remaining crypto-Jews, attained high office, one of them as primate of the Russian Church and another as chancellor of the Grand Prince of Moscow. They did not go over completely to Judaism but showed the influence of that faith in various ways, some in opposition to the use of icons, and others in an interest in Jewish philosophy and science, especially in astrology and Kabbalah. If, as seems usual, they adopted some of the dogmas of Judaism they were not circumcised nor did they conform to the Jewish ritual.

In 1487 the Archbishop of Novgorod learned of the movement. At his request a church council was called, but the friends of the Judaizers and men who, like Nilus, objected to capital punishment, prevented stern measures from being enacted. The Grand Duke Ivan III seemed to favour the movement in his desire to curb the monasteries and seize their lands. His daughter-in-law went over to it. However, in 1503 another council met at Moscow and after prolonged debate, in which, as we have seen, Nilus again opposed harsh treatment, those who advocated drastic treatment triumphed. Several of the heretics were burned and others were sent to prison for life. That seems to have ended the movement, although it may simply have gone into hiding.

From these various movements, those within the Church and those branded as heretical, it was clear that Christianity had taken firm root in Russia. It was giving rise to indigenous expressions of the faith and was strong enough to cope successfully with serious defections. It was still emphatically loyal to what had come to it from Constantinople. Indeed, Moscow was beginning to be viewed by good Russians as the successor to that city as the headquarters of Orthodoxy. Sometime late in the fifteenth or in the fore part of the sixteenth century a Russian monk wrote a fulsome letter to the Moscow ruler in which he declared that since Rome had become heretical and Constantinople had fallen to the infidel Moscow had succeeded them as the third seat of the guardian of the apostolic faith and was never to be followed by a fourth. Indeed, the Russian Church probably better represented the Greek Orthodox Church as it was before the Turkish conquest than did the Greek Church of later centuries. The latter was to be influenced by the Roman Catholic Church in its scholastic forms and was less flexible. Yet modifications in the Russian Church were being made in practice though not in formal doctrine and at least one independent effort at basic reform, that of the Strigolniks, had appeared.

PAPAL EFFORTS TO WIN THE EASTERN CHRISTIANS

In spite of the weaknesses which, as we are to see, were afflicting it during the century and a half between 1350 and 1500, the Papacy did not give up the hope of bringing about the visible union under its control of all who bore the Christian name. In this it was aided by many ardent supporters.

We have noted the recurring attempts before 1350 to bring this about and have recounted how some of them had been made in connexion with the Crusaders and their footholds in the East. They had given rise to Uniate bodies, that is, as we have suggested, those drawn from Eastern dissident churches who submitted to the Pope but who kept their traditional liturgies and many of their inherited customs.

One of these, brought into union during the Crusades, was that of the Maronites, who seem to have had their origin in the Monothelite controversy in the seventh century and to have held to that position until their accession to Rome. Others were Greeks of the Byzantine rite. They had a complex history complicated by the relations between Rome and Constantinople and the breaks and the attempts at the reunion of those who held to these two sees. In Italy there had long been Greek-speaking churches and monasteries who observed the Basilian rule. The Greek rite was preserved, notably in the monastery of the Mother of God at Grottaferrata, a house founded early in the eleventh

century on the Alban Hills not far from Rome and continued across the years
into the twentieth century. There were also Greek Uniates in various cities in
the East, including Constantinople itself. Some of the Armenians became
Uniates before 1350 and a Uniate Armenian church persisted. Latin influence
contended with Greek in the Balkan Peninsula, especially on the east coast of
the Adriatic and in the North-west near to Austria and Hungary. It also
penetrated into Russia. Between 1350 and 1500 it entered Russia chiefly by way
of Poland and Lithuania. It was late in the fourteenth century (beginning in
1386) that the conversion of the upper classes of Lithuania was accomplished.
This came about through an alliance which Lithuania sought with Poland
against the Teutonic Knights. Since the Poles adhered to Rome, it was Latin
Christianity which the Lithuanian aristocracy adopted. The Lithuanians extended their rule over part of Western Russia and some of the Russian nobility
conformed to the Roman Catholicism of their new masters. However, the bulk
of the Russian population, even under the Lithuanians, held to the Orthodox
form of the faith.

The last great and seemingly successful effort of the Papacy to bring the
Eastern Christians into union with it was through a council, regarded as
ecumenical by the Church of Rome, at Ferrara and then at Florence in 1438
and 1439. The Byzantine Emperors, in desperate straits because of the advance
of the Turk, had been seeking help from the West and to obtain it sent
embassies to its courts and offered to enter into negotiations with the Pope.
Pope Eugenius IV (reigned 1431–1447) was eager to assert his authority in the
Church in his struggle with the councils of which we are to speak in the next
chapter and to win the prestige which would accrue from the consummation of
reunion under his auspices. To Ferrara came the Byzantine Emperor, the
Patriarch of Constantinople, representatives of the Patriarchs of Antioch,
Alexandria, and Jerusalem, and a score or more of Eastern bishops. Among the
latter was Isidore, Metropolitan of Kiev, and thus, in a sense, a representative
of the Russian Church. Another was Bessarion, Metropolitan of Nicæa.
Prolonged discussions followed on the traditional and familiar points at issue
and on questions of procedure and precedence. Agreement was reached, partly
through compromises. The most thorny question of all, the authority of the
Pope, was assented to in the ambiguous statement: "We recognize the Pope
as Sovereign Pontiff, Vice-gerent and Vicar of Christ, Shepherd of all Christians, Ruler of the Church of God; saving the privileges and rights of the
Patriarchs of the East." These "privileges and rights" were left undefined and
vague, presumably intentionally so, for only thus could both Latins and Greeks
be satisfied. The decree proclaiming the union was published in July, 1439.
Most of the Greeks signed it with reluctance and one refused his assent.

As was true of the accord reached at the Council of Lyons in 1274, the union ostensibly effected at Florence was rejected by the overwhelming majority of the constituency of the Greek Orthodox Church. In spite of the Turkish peril, they were quite unreconciled to the arrangement even though it was intended to bring them military help. Moreover, the Patriarchs of Antioch, Alexandria, and Jerusalem jointly repudiated the acts of the Ferrara-Florence Council. On returning to his see, Isidore was promptly clapped into jail by his irate flock. Escaping, he made his way to Rome, was created cardinal, and was appointed Papal Legate to Constantinople. The Pope was able to send only a handful of troops to that beleaguered city. Some of these perished in the last desperate and fruitless stand against the Turks.

Officially the union stood until after the fall of Constantinople. Quite understandably, for he wished as little connexion as possible of the church in his realms with his enemies in the West, the victorious Turk sided with the foes of union. In 1472 a synod in Constantinople speaking for the Orthodox Church formally repudiated the action at Florence and anathematized those who adhered to it.

Yet gains there were for Rome. Some of the Greeks remained in communion with the Pope. Bessarion held true to the Ferrara-Florence agreements, made his home in Rome, became a cardinal, was a leader in the Renaissance, helped to encourage the study of Greek and Plato, was a benefactor of the Greek scholars who took refuge in Rome after the fall of Constantinople, and led in the reform of the Greek monasteries in South Italy. More important still, some of the other Eastern Churches had spokesmen at the Council of Florence. The head of the Armenian Uniates appointed legates to renew the accord of himself and his group and late in 1439 the appropriate decree was issued. The Coptic Patriarch of Alexander sent as a representative an abbot who also had authority to speak for the ruler of Ethiopia. Later, when the Pope transferred the council to Rome, delegates arrived from one of the factions of the Syrian Jacobites. A Nestorian bishop and delegates from those of the Maronites who had not yet submitted to Rome also came. Through the council, then, which the Church of Rome counted as clearly ecumenical, with representatives from almost all the severed branches of the Catholic Church, larger or smaller sections from these bodies which it regarded as dissident submitted to the Pope and brought their creeds into accord with his.

Although the Papacy registered gains in the East, the large majority of the Christians in that region remained aloof. The Roman programme for achieving the unity of all Christians had not proved successful. After 1500 it was to be dealt another major blow by its inability to hold the majority in Great Britain and North-western Europe who had heretofore accepted it. The section of the

Church headed by the Bishop of Rome continued to insist that conformity with it was the way which Christ had appointed for that unity of all who believed in him for which he had prayed. However, it was to be increasingly clear that the Papal pattern was an ecclesiastical continuation of the imperial dream of pre-Christian Rome and that great and growing numbers of those who bore the Christian name would not assent to it.

SELECTED BIBLIOGRAPHY

L. Arpee, *A History of Armenian Christianity* (New York, The Armenian Missionary Association, 1946, pp. xii, 386). By an Armenian Evangelical, warmly pro-Armenian and anti-Roman Catholic.

S. Bolshakoff, *Russian Nonconformity* (Philadelphia, The Westminster Press, 1950, pp. 192). A useful, comprehensive historical sketch, with an excellent bibliography.

L. E. Browne, *The Eclipse of Christianity in Asia from the time of Muhammed till the Fourteenth Century* (Cambridge University Press, 1933, pp. 198). Only the last few pages of this excellent survey fall within the period covered by this chapter.

E. L. Butcher, *The Story of the Church of Egypt* (London, Smith, Elder & Co., 2 vols., 1897). An extensive assemblage of material.

G. P. Fedotov, compiler and editor, *A Treasury of Russian Spirituality* (New York, Sheed & Ward, 1948, pp. xvi, 501). Useful translations of sources with excellent introductions.

A. Fortescue, *The Orthodox Eastern Church* (London, Catholic Truth Society, 1929, pp. xxxiii, 451). A good survey, in spite of a strong Roman Catholic bias.

A. Fortescue, *The Uniate Eastern Churches. The Byzantine Rite in Italy, Sicily, Syria, and Egypt* (London, Burns, Oates & Washbourne, 1923, pp. xxiii, 244). This careful, well-written Roman Catholic study deals almost exclusively with the Greeks who were in union with Rome. Most of it has to do with Italy.

A. H. Hore, *Eighteen Centuries of the Orthodox Greek Church* (London, James Parker & Co., 1899, pp. vi, 706). By a sympathetic Anglican.

B. J. Kidd, *The Churches of Eastern Christendom from A.D. 451 to the Present Time* (London, Faith Press, preface 1927, pp. 541). Not very readable but packed with data.

M. Spinka, *A History of Christianity in the Balkans. A Study in the Spread of Byzantine Culture among the Slavs* (Chicago, The American Society of Church History, 1933, pp. 202). An excellent survey based upon the sources.

G. Vernadsky, *The Heresy of the Judaizers and Ivan III* (*Speculum*, Vol. VIII, pp. 436–454).

Chapter XXVIII

WESTERN EUROPE: DECLINE AND VITALITY

Increasingly after 1350 Western Europe became the main centre of Christianity. Here was the chief hope of that faith. Due to the several factors which we have noted in the preceding chapter, the Eastern Churches were waning in numbers and vigour. In spite of the mounting vitality shown by the Orthodox Church in Russia, the gains registered in that land, and the claim that Moscow had become the Third Rome, the citadel and guardian of the true faith, Eastern Europe was still on the periphery of Christendom. Moreover, in Western Europe Christianity had plowed more deeply into the entire life of the population than it had elsewhere. Entering the partial vacuum left by the collapse of Græco-Roman culture in that region, a collapse more profound and a vacuum more striking than in the area controlled by the Byzantine Empire, it held to its allegiance the descendants of the Latinized peoples and won the invaders from the North. Being the most nearly stable element in the culturally fluid society which followed, and containing a powerful spiritual and moral dynamic, it helped to mould every phase of the civilization which emerged.

Now that civilization was passing, to no small degree because of currents which issued from Christianity. In the new age into which Western culture was being hurried, there were forces which were threatening Christianity in both old and new ways. As a result, in Western Europe that faith appeared to be declining. For centuries there had been a struggle in the various institutions which bore the Christian name between lethargy and corruption on the one hand and reform and renewal on the other. Between 950 and 1350 the latter appeared to be winning. Now, in the period bounded roughly by the years 1350 and 1500 the former seemed uppermost. In aspect after aspect of the life of Western Europe, including especially the Church, deterioration, as judged by Christian standards, was under way. Yet it did not become as marked as in the dark centuries between 500 and 950. There was also evidence of sound

624

life, some of it old and much of it new. Here and there were indications that the ebb would not always continue, that the tide was turning, and that eventually it would come to the flood. We must first sketch the grim side of the picture. We will then turn to the brighter side and point out the sound life that remained and the fresh expressions of "the greatness of the power."

THE DECLINE OF THE PAPACY AS A POLITICAL, MORAL, AND SPIRITUAL FORCE

The most striking of the symptoms of the malady which was afflicting the Christianity of Western Europe was the decline of the Papacy. In the preceding centuries great reformers had envisioned the See of Peter as the directing agency through which all Christians could be held to the true faith, all the universal Church be unified and kept firm in its mission, all of Christendom brought towards the high ideal of God proclaimed in Christ, and ultimately all mankind governed. The occupants of the Fisherman's throne had varied in ability and achievement, but the most outstanding of them had made their office a force in the major aspects of the life of Western Europe and one to be reckoned with in the Byzantine Empire and Western Asia. In their efforts to implement their dream the Popes had developed an ecclesiastical structure which reached throughout most of Western Europe and which made necessary an elaborate bureaucracy at its centre. In addition to the Pope the chief figures in the bureaucracy were the cardinals.

One of the striking indications that decline had begun was, as we have noted, the removal in 1309 of the seat of the Papacy to Avignon. Claiming their place as head of the Catholic Church by virtue of the fact that they held the post of Bishop of the Church of Rome, because of the disorder in Italy for which the centuries-long conflict between their predecessors and the Holy Roman Emperors was largely responsible, the Popes found residence in that city dangerous if not intolerable. The first Avignon Pope, Clement V, was subservient to Philip IV, "the Fair," King of France. That powerful monarch had been responsible for the death of Boniface VIII in a contest between the two over the taxation of the clergy and Church property in the former's domains in which the Pope had lost.

The Papacy remained at Avignon until 1377. Although technically that city was not then in France, during most of its years there the Papacy was under French influence. As we have seen (Chapter XX) life was luxurious for the cardinals and their dependents and the financial devices used to support them bore heavily on Western Europe and provoked much criticism. Seven Popes made Avignon their residence. None was as evil as some who were to follow.

All were university-trained and three were monks. At least half of them were upright, pious, and wished to give worthy leadership to Christendom. Most of them were able and several struggled to reform the Church, including Avignon with its throngs of idle benefice-seekers. Usually they were skilful administrators. In theory they held to the claims of Papal authority put forward by their great predecessors and some made their weight felt in European politics. Indeed, the Avignon Popes were the most powerful potentates in Western Europe in their day. So long as the Papacy was there, Avignon was more cosmopolitan and international than any other city in fourteenth century Europe.

Yet the system was too much for the Popes. Several of them succumbed, at least to the extent of putting their relatives in lucrative and important posts. The very complexity and weight of the machinery which had been constructed with the ostensible welfare of Christendom and of the millions of individuals who constituted its population as its purpose entailed abuses which even the strongest and most high-minded of the Avignon Pontiffs could not eliminate and could scarcely check. The Papacy was paying the price for having utilized the kind of power which seemed essential to the realization of its objectives but which entailed contradictions of Christian ethical and spiritual principles. Conditions continued to deteriorate and permeated the entire church of which the Papacy was the head. Pluralism (the holding of two or more benefices and drawing the incomes from them), absenteeism (not living in the post the income from which came to the titular holder), self-seeking greed, and loose-living among the clergy mounted.

Worse was to follow. Many, especially but not exclusively in Italy, were distressed by the prolonged absence from Rome. Some of the noblest spirits of the day, notably Catherine of Siena, of whom we are to hear more in a moment, pled with successive Popes to return to their proper place in the city from which they took their title and which was their immediate responsibility. The next to the last of the Avignon Popes, Urban V, went to Rome in 1367 and was there about three years. He found the city sadly dwindled in population and its churches and palaces almost in ruins. He set about repairing the churches, but conditions proved discouraging and he retreated to comfortable Avignon. His successor, Gregory XI, made it one of his purposes to move his seat to Rome and accomplished it early in 1377. The "Babylonian Captivity" had ended. Yet out of that return, so fervently desired by some of the most earnestly Christian spirits of that day, came what was remembered as the Great Schism of the West. For a generation, from 1378 to 1417, Western Europe was divided between rival Popes, always at least two, and latterly three, each supported by a section of the Church.

The Great Schism Begins

The Great Schism began soon after the death of Gregory XI, in 1378. The Roman populace were insistent that a Roman, or at least an Italian, be his successor. Although two-thirds of the cardinals who composed the electing conclave were French and would have preferred one from their own nation who would have led them back to Avignon, they were divided over which Frenchman to choose. Moreover, they were in Rome and were subjected to the clamour of the mob. Under pressure they selected a Neapolitan who took the title of Urban VI. A university graduate, an archbishop, and in charge of the Papal chancery, Urban was sixty years of age when he was put in the chair of Peter. He proved an unhappy choice. Although a scholar, an experienced administrator, austere in his private morals, and zealous for reform, he was tactless, obstinate, quick-tempered, and, so his enemies said, arrogant. He soon antagonized the cardinals, especially since he flatly refused even to consider going back to luxurious Avignon, publicly rebuked them for their worldliness, was peremptory in forbidding them their profitable pluralism and simony, and commanded them to live in the sees whose episcopal titles they bore.

The cardinals, some of whom were of noble blood, took umbrage at such treatment from a Pope whom they considered low-born. Moreover, at Avignon they had had the growing tradition of dominating the Pope and would not brook this new independence. Within a few months they left Rome. Declaring that Urban VI's election had been obtained under duress from the Roman mob and hence was illegal, they demanded that he resign. The overwhelming majority denounced him as an apostate and Antichrist. They insisted that they had the power to depose as well as to appoint and declared the post vacant. The French majority in the college of cardinals thereupon elected another Pope, one of their own number and a prince related to the King of France. A soldier, a shrewd politician, and not above reproach in his private life, he took the inconsistent title of Clement VII. Soon, with his cardinals, he had settled in Avignon. Urban VI, indignant, refused to recognize the legitimacy of the action and appointed a new group of cardinals but without deposing the old.

The countries of Europe now lined up on one or the other side. Spain, France and her satellite, Scotland, and part of Germany supported the Avignon Pope. Northern and Central Italy, most of Germany, England, Scandinavia, Bohemia, Poland, Flanders, and Portugal remained with Urban VI. Thus the growing nationalism was showing itself. Often before there had been two men who simultaneously claimed the Papal title. Never before had Western Europe been so nearly evenly divided between them by sharp territorial lines.

The Resort to a General Council

Pained by this rupture of visible unity, many strove both to heal the breach and to purge the Catholic Church of corroding evils. Devout souls, scholars, the University of Paris, whose voice carried great weight in Europe, and some monarchs struggled with the problem. Eventually they had recourse to that instrument, a general council, which since the initial one at Nicæa early in the fourth century had been regarded as the means by which the mind of the Church could be expressed and appropriate action taken. Indeed, now that the Papacy was divided and had proved incapable of stamping out the grievous abuses which crippled the Church, many hoped that by gaining recognition of the authority of a general or ecumenical council as superior to that of the Pope, not only would unity be restored but the Church would be cleansed. This, in brief, was the conciliar theory. There followed what is sometimes known as the conciliar movement. Obviously it was entirely counter to the theory which had prevailed in the West for the past several centuries and which insisted that the Pope alone could call a general council, that either he or his representative must preside, and that none of its actions was valid without his approval. The movement succeeded in ending the schism, but not in making the council supreme as against the Pope or in purging the Church of the corruption which was threatening its life.

Several years elapsed before the proposal that a general council meet became a reality. To be sure, in 1324, half a century before the Great Schism, the *Defensor Pacis* had advocated a general council which would be above the Popes. In 1379 and 1380, soon after the two rival Popes had been elected, a specialist on canon law, then in Paris, proposed that the King of France invite other princes to join with him in calling a council. A similar suggestion was made in 1381 by a scholar at the University of Paris. When Urban VI died a successor was chosen who continued the Roman line. Clement VII carried on an inglorious course at Avignon for sixteen years and was followed by a much abler and more upright man, Benedict XIII, who held the post for more than a quarter of a century. Efforts were made to induce the Pontiffs of both lines to resign and permit the choice of a new one on whom the whole Church could unite. That was suggested, among others, by the University of Paris. At one time both Popes had agreed to abdicate. However, each found ways of evading his promise. Eventually cardinals from both Rome and Avignon jointly tried their hands at ending the schism and called a general council. This met at Pisa in 1409. It was attended by several hundred cardinals, patriarchs, archbishops, bishops, abbots, heads of religious orders, scholars, and representatives of universities and of kings and princes. It deposed both Popes and, without waiting to hear whether either would heed the decree, authorized the cardinals to elect a new one. This the cardinals did. Since neither the Avignon nor the Roman Pontiff would comply, there were now three who claimed the chair of Peter. Each had the support of one or another of the states of Europe.

More and more leaders among the European intellectuals were advocating the holding of a general council and, scandalized by the schism and because of it losing faith in Papal supremacy, were maintaining that such a body was superior to the Pope in the government of the Church. Among them were Peter d'Ailly (1350–1420), theologian, philosopher, chancellor of the University of Paris, confessor to the King of France, and eventually Archbishop of Cambrai, cardinal, and papal legate; and John Gerson (1363–1429), a pupil of d'Ailly, chancellor of the University of Paris, pamphleteer, and writer of books of devotion. These, with many others, laboured mightily for union and were earnest advocates of a general council. The idea spread, endorsed by clergy, synods, universities, and even cities, and promoted by a flood of pamphlets.

The Council of Pisa was an inauspicious beginning. Not only did it fail to heal the schism: it enhanced it. Moreover, it did not bring the reforms in the Church at large which had been hoped from it. The second Pope chosen by the cardinals to continue the Pisan line after the death of the first incumbent was Baldassare Cossa, John XXIII. Undoubtedly able and a commanding personality, he was an aristocrat who had led a wild youth, was more of a statesman and general than a spiritual leader, and was accused, probably with some ground, of being deceitful, cruel, tyrannous, and debauched in his private life. He had dominated the Council of Pisa and the first Pope chosen by that body. That the conciliar movement had put him in the chair of Peter could scarcely commend it to the conscientious and thoughtful spirits in Europe.

THE COUNCIL OF CONSTANCE

The Council of Pisa is not officially regarded as having been representative of the entire Church. A much larger council was held at Constance from 1414 to 1418. Unlike that of Pisa, it is counted as ecumenical by the Roman Catholic Church and is reckoned as the sixteenth in the series. While by no means accomplishing all that had been hoped from it, it ended the Great Schism. In doing so it prepared the way for the death of the conciliar movement, for by placing the Catholic Church under one Pontiff rather than two or three, it facilitated the triumph of the Pope over the council.

The Council of Constance was called by the newly elected German King and King of the Romans, Sigismund, who eventually (1433) was to be crowned Holy Roman Emperor. Thus Sigismund renewed the earlier tradition in which ecumenical councils had been convened by the Roman Emperor rather than by any bishop or group of bishops. He induced John XXIII to coöperate with him in summoning the council. Yet his call was sent out first and that of John XXIII went out soon afterward, and independently. Even more than Pisa, the gathering brought together a notable assembly of cardinals, archbishops, bishops, abbots, scholars, clergy, and lay folk. Indeed, it was the most widely representative of the Church that had ever met in Western Europe. Its first task was to end the Great Schism. In this Peter d'Ailly was prominent. Largely at his suggestion, the voting in the council was by nations, thus preventing it from being dominated by the large party which John XXIII had succeeded in drawing together to support his claims. This was a procedure without precedent in the history of the councils and was evidence of the place which nations were coming to have in Western Europe. By it the universities and laity were given a voice, for they were in the national delegations.

The council found it no easy matter to end the Great Schism. Under pressure, John XXIII, the only one of the three Popes present, solemnly promised to abdicate if the other two would do likewise. Soon thereafter, as sentiment in the gathering swung against him, he fled from Constance in disguise, pleading ill health. Some question arose as to whether the council could proceed without him. Sigismund saved the day by insisting that it continue and Gerson preached a sermon in which he declared that a general council was representative of the entire Church, that it might be called without the authorization of a Pope, and that it might require a Pope to abdicate. After futile negotiations, John XXIII was charged with a long list of misdeeds and immoralities and was formally deposed. The Roman Pope, Gregory XII, resigned, was made a cardinal and, honoured, died two years later at the age of ninety. The remaining Pope, he of Avignon, Benedict XIII, refused to abdicate, although a committee headed by Sigismund himself journeyed to him in Narbonne, in the south of France, to urge him to comply. The council thereupon declared him a perjurer, a heretic, an obstacle to the union of the Church, and deposed him. Until his death, c.1423, Benedict continued to insist that he was the rightful Pope. He was followed by two successors in the Avignon line but they attracted only a negligible following. Deputies from the five nations into which the council had been divided for voting purposes joined with the cardinals and elected as Pope Cardinal Oddone Colonna, a member of an old Roman family and a man of unblemished reputation. He took the title of Martin V and presided over the subsequent sessions of the council. The Great Schism of the West had been ended.

The council addressed itself to the reform of the abuses in the Church which were so clamant. However, it was too badly divided to accomplish much, especially since many of its members would have lost valued privileges had some of the measures advocated been adopted. Indeed, it was probably hoping too much to expect that a council made up predominantly of men who were profiting by the abuses which it was proposed to eliminate would consent to drastic measures. Some decrees were passed which were designed to check simony, to reduce the financial exactions of the Papacy, to end one form of conferring the income of several benefices on a single individual, and to prevent benefices being awarded to men who because they were unordained or uncon-secrated were given dispensations excusing them from fulfilling the duties attached to them. In other ways the power of the Pope was abridged and the attempt was made to curtail some of the evils which had grown up in con-nexion with indulgences. The German delegation obtained from the new Pope a concordat, but one which was to run only for five years, placing restraints on some of the revenues drawn from their country by the Pope, cardinals, and Papal curia. The French delegation negotiated a somewhat similar agreement. The English also got a concordat, more limited in its scope but unrestricted in time. The cardinals were at most to be twenty-four in number and were to be more equitably distributed among the nations, and not, as had been the case, predominantly from one nation.

More important were decrees which were designed to ensure the implementa-tion of the conciliar theory. Another general council was to meet in five years, a second after another seven years, and thereafter councils were to convene at least every ten years. Before the close of each council the place of the next meeting was to be set by the Pope with the consent of the council. Thus the general council of the Church was always to be either in session or to be expected at the end of a definite interval. It might be called more frequently in case of an emergency, but the time between councils could not be lengthened beyond the five, seven, and ten year spans set forth in the decree. It was declared that the council drew its power immediately from Christ, and that all, even the Pope himself, were "bound to obey it in all those things which pertain to the faith, to the healing of the schism, and to the general reformation of the Church."

There was one action of the Council of Constance, the condemnation and burning of John Hus, to which we are to recur later in this chapter. We must mention it here, however, as part of the effort to extirpate heresy. The Council was concerned not only with the administrative unity and moral reform of the Catholic Church. It was also intent upon preserving doctrinal unity and was resolved to root out all that smacked of heresy. In its eyes Hus stood out as the most dangerous contemporary heretic and it took vigorous action against him.

The Pope elected by the Council of Constance, Martin V, set himself to restore the damaged power and prestige of his office. Himself from a distinguished Roman family, he returned to Rome and repaired the city, its neglected churches and fortifications. He sought to bring order into the turbulent states of the Church, which were presumably directly under the government of the Pope. Comparatively modest in his own manner of living, he celebrated with great pomp the public occasions in which he officially appeared. He made his weight felt in ecclesiastical affairs in several countries in Europe. However, he was accused, justly, of favouring members of his family. Moreover, he was not disposed to concede the authority to the general council which had been enacted at Constance but wished to renew the prerogatives which had been claimed by his great predecessors. Nor did he do much to carry through even the limited reforms which had been outlined at Constance.

The Failure of the Conciliar Movement

Yet, in obedience to the command laid on him by the Council of Constance and prodded by that centre of the conciliar theory, the University of Paris, Martin V called a general council to meet at Pavia in 1423. The gathering had barely convened when an outbreak of the plague caused it to move to Siena. Attendance was slim and the Pope, never enthusiastic about the meeting, did not attend but contented himself with sending representatives to preside in his name. Measures for reform, which was one of the professed purposes of the gathering, were blocked by the Pope's supporters. After efforts lasting a little over a year the council was dissolved.

Martin V did little to effect the reforms which were so urgently demanded by widespread elements in the Church. To be sure, he appointed a commission of cardinals to suggest reforms in the Papal curia. They reported and, following their recommendations, in 1425 he ordered some changes. Among them were injunctions to bishops and archbishops to reside in their dioceses, to hold provincial synods three times a year to correct abuses, to set an example of Christian living, and to shun heavy financial exactions. However, little seems to have been done to enforce the decree. The old abuses continued and complaints were still loud.

When, in 1431, Martin V died, the cardinals, before electing a successor, drew up a document called a capitulation to which the new Pope was to be required to subscribe. It demanded, among other things, that the Pope respect the rights, the persons, and the property of the cardinals and turn over to them half the revenues of the Church of Rome, reform the Papal curia "root and branch," and call a general council.

The man chosen took the title of Eugene IV and held the post from 1431 to 1447. Of aristocratic Venetian stock, he was austere in his private life, deeply religious, simple in his tastes, vigorously opposed to nepotism, generous to a fault with money, dignified, and with an imposing presence. He is chiefly remembered for the fashion in which he made the Papacy master of the general council.

In accordance with the instructions of Martin V given on the eve of his death, the general council met in Basel in 1431. The Roman Catholic Church officially regards it as the seventeenth ecumenical council. The Pope appointed as the presiding officer in his stead Cardinal Cesarini (1389–1444), a man of humble birth who had risen to high office by sheer ability and character. Scholar, humanist, ascetic, devout, punctilious in his religious duties, affable, Cesarini made an ideal Papal legate. Members of the council were tardy in arriving and the sessions were slow in getting under way. Late in 1431 Eugene IV, made fearful by what he had heard of the gathering, ordered it dissolved and another council held at Bologna a year and a half thence. Cesarini wrote a strong letter protesting the unwisdom of this action. Sigismund advised the council to stand firm. Nicholas of Cusa (1401–1464), scholar, philosopher, theologian, mystic, and reformer, although later a firm supporter of Papal supremacy and a cardinal, at this point came out strongly for the authority of the council, maintaining that the Pope was simply one member of the Church, that the Church alone was infallible but could transfer that prerogative to a general council, and that the council was superior to the Pope and could depose him.

In February, 1432, the council pronounced itself legally assembled and declared that its authority rested upon acts of the Council of Constance and that any proceedings against its members were null. It organized itself by committees and gave seats and votes to members of the lower as well as the higher ranks of the clergy. It was thus widely representative. It told Eugene IV to withdraw his bull of dissolution and to appear with his cardinals before it within three months, either in person or through representatives. When they did not come the council held them guilty of contempt.

With so much opinion against him in the Church and in Europe at large, Eugene IV seemed to yield. He recognized the council as legal and sent four legates to represent him. When the legates, arriving, attempted to take charge of the council in the Pope's name, they were told that the Pope was subordinate to the council and must obey it. Early in 1434 the Pope made what appeared to be a complete capitulation, annulled all his bulls against the council, and gave it his support. That year a rebellion in Rome forced him to flee from the city. Papal prestige was at a low ebb. The council seemed to have won and the conciliar idea to be clearly in the ascendant.

The Papal cause was further handicapped by the disclosure during the Papacy of Eugene IV that the Donation of Constantine which had so long been important in the foundation on which claims for Papal civil sovereignty had been erected was a forgery. The spuriousness of the document was demonstrated independently by the critical acumen of two scholars of the new age, Nicholas of Cusa in 1433 and Laurentius Valla in 1440.

In another realm the Council of Basel appeared to have justified the principle on which it was acting. By negotiation and compromise it made peace with the moderate wing of the followers of Hus and thus seemed to have brought back into the bosom of the Catholic Church a numerous element who had been condemned as heretics.

When it came to the reform of the Church the Council of Basel failed, and failed conspicuously and lamentably. This was chiefly because thoroughgoing reform would mean sacrifices, some of them serious, by the majority or all the members of the council. Some measures were passed, among them ones to forbid simony, to enforce the celibacy of the clergy, and to forbid theatricals and other secular amusements in churches and churchyards.

Since the council was anti-Papal it was relatively easy to decree the abolishment of some of the sources of the revenue of the Popes and the cardinals which had long been a source of complaint, among them the annates, for this entailed no privation on any but a very few members of the council. So, too, legislation was put through to restore the election of the higher clergy by the chapters as against Papal appointment and to regulate the age and composition of the cardinalate and the election of Popes. In its antagonism to the Pope the council over-reached itself. Among other prerogatives, it claimed the right to grant indulgences. Some who had hitherto supported it, including the powerful and high-minded Cesarini and most of the Italians and later Nicholas of Cusa, disillusioned by what they believed to be its excesses, went over to the supporters of the Papacy.

The seeming success of the Council of Basel in limiting the power of the Papacy encouraged the French and the Germans to take similar steps and thus to reduce the administrative control and the financial exactions of Rome within their borders. In 1438 in the Pragmatic Sanction of Bourges the King of France recognized the supremacy of the general council, with the provision that it should convene once a decade, abolished annates and first-fruits, ordered that vacancies to the larger benefices be filled by election rather than by Papal appointment, and limited the number of cardinals to twenty-four. Less sweeping measures were taken in Germany and agreed to by the Pope.

The major crisis in the Council of Basel and one which issued in its final undoing came in connexion with the effort for the reunion of the Latin and Greek wings of the Catholic Church. In the last chapter we saw that the threat of the Ottoman Turk constrained the Byzantine Emperor and Patriarch to seek reconciliation with Rome in the forlorn hope of obtaining military assistance from the West. The majority of the council wished the Eastern delegation to come to Avignon. The Pope suggested an Italian city, and this the Greeks preferred as being more convenient. The Pope ordered the council transferred to Ferrara and a minority of its members, including Cesarini, complied. They convened at Ferrara and then at Florence. There, as we have noted, they met the Greeks and what appeared to be striking success crowned their efforts. Enormous prestige accrued to the Pope.

The departure of the moderate and pro-Papal minority left the Council of Basel in the hands of the radicals who wished further to curb the power of the Pope. In the spring and summer of 1439 a decree was enacted which declared a general council to be supreme in matters of faith. Another decree deposed Eugene IV, released all Christians from allegiance to him, and pronounced his acts null and void. In the autumn of 1439 it chose as Pope Duke Amadeus of Savoy. The latter took the title of Felix V. He was able to attract very little support and ten years later resigned. The small remnant of the Council of Basel, now in Lausanne, put the best face possible on the adverse situation. Eugene IV was now dead and had been succeeded at Rome by Nicholas V. The council voted to recognize him as the true Pope.

With that act of virtual abdication the conciliar movement may be said to have come to an end. It had failed to curb the power of the Papacy. Indeed, by ending the Great Schism of the West, itself no mean accomplishment and its major achievement, it had dug its own grave. When once the Church in Western Europe was reunited under one Pope, the Pontiffs, asserting the traditional claims of their predecessors, made their power effective against the councils, divided as these were and without adequate leadership. Moreover, like the Papacy, members of the councils were too deeply involved in the abuses against which much of Europe was complaining to work the sweeping reforms which the situation demanded.

The conciliar idea did not quickly die. Again and again in the fifteenth century, even after the Council of Basel had ended in a fiasco, there were those who wished to have recourse to a general council of the Church. Sometimes these were Popes who hoped to use it to rally Europe against the Turk. Now and again a monarch invoked the spectre of a general council to wrest some concession from the Pope. Many of those longing for the reform of the Church hoped against the hard facts that a council could accomplish it. We shall meet the idea again in the sixteenth century. Yet, whether or not men realized it, the councils had proved themselves unable to purify the Church or to construct machinery for its administration.

The Further Moral Decline of the Papacy

Still worse was to come. Administrative unity had been restored to the Catholic Church in Western Europe under the direction of the Papacy but the basic moral reforms for which sensitive souls had struggled had not been achieved. The ecclesiastical structure through which they should have been accomplished had in it so many in positions of authority whose comfort would have been compromised by basic changes that in spite of the labours of some earnest souls in high places the purging in "root and branch" which had been promised was not accomplished. Now that there was only one Pope and the effort to control him through a council representative of the entire Church had failed, the Papacy became even more a centre of corruption. It was captured by the Renaissance and secularistic humanism. Men ambitious for ostentatious luxury and for power and prestige of a kind which was entirely contrary to the genius of the Christian Gospel worked their way into the Papal curia and even into the college of cardinals and the Papacy itself. This did not come all at once. It was not until the close of the fifteenth century that the Papacy reached its lowest depths of moral degradation. Then it did so on a tragically grand scale in an individual of outstanding ability and force of character, but who was as nearly the opposite of the Christian ideal as it is possible for man to be.

The first of the Popes to represent the Renaissance was Nicholas V, who held the post from 1447 to 1455. He had struggled up from humble origins and in his student days in Florence, that centre of Renaissance art and letters, had caught much of the spirit of the new day. He combined humanism with earnest Christian purpose. Temperate in his personal habits, he was a collector of manuscripts, is credited with having founded the Vatican Library, and, a patron of artists, scholars, and men of letters, made Rome a centre of the new humanism and art. It was he who adopted the plans for the new St. Peter's. Although a lover of peace and genuinely religious, he was not the one to lead in the urgently needed reformation of the Church. He even attracted to Rome and gave support to humanists who were essentially pagan.

Callistus III, a Spaniard, who was Pope from 1455 to 1458, was chiefly memorable for the fashion in which he advanced the members of his family, the Borgias, including especially his nephew, Rodrigo, whom we are to meet again in a moment as the infamous Alexander VI.

Æneas Sylvius Piccolomini who with the Papal title of Pius II held the post from 1458 to 1464, had had a humanistic training, was late in seeking ordination, in youth and middle age had led a life which was far from blameless, had an illegitimate son, and was noted for promoting his interests by astute diplomacy. He had written much, some of it in the clever but low moral tone characteristic of the Renaissance. However, he confessed his faults and professed, perhaps somewhat theatrically, to have had a conversion comparable to that of Paul and Augustine. An indefatigable traveller, he was a true son of the Renaissance in his love of natural scenery and his glowing descriptions of it. His energy was largely spent in attempting to rally a divided Europe against the advancing Turk.

Paul II, who reigned from 1464 to 1471, represented an anti-humanist reaction. A nephew of Eugene IV, he was from Venice. Vain, a lover of pomp, charming, imposing, dignified, open-handed to the poor, he sought to expel from Rome those of the humanists who were thinly veiled pagans, and attempted to curb simony and to bring order in the Papal states. Yet he, too, could scarcely be expected to cleanse the Church.

Although he was the General of the Franciscans, the successor of Paul II, Sixtus IV (1471–1484), was more interested in making the Papacy the centre of a strong Italian state than in rendering it an effective moral and spiritual force in Europe. Of blameless personal life, a scholar, a distinguished teacher in various universities, as Pope he found himself surrounded by a turbulent Italy confronted by the threatening Turk. Italy was divided into many states. The largest were Venice, Milan, Florence, Naples (called the Kingdom of the Two Sicilies), and the States of the Church, the latter directly under the Pope. There were many lesser states, and complicated intrigue and war engrossed the attention of rulers and peoples and blocked all efforts to present a united front against the aggressive foreign foe.

True to the traditions of his predecessors of an earlier age, Sixtus IV strove to unite Western Europe in a crusade against the Turk. To that end he assembled a fleet which saw inconclusive action. Embroiled in the maze of Italian politics, he was more than once engaged in wars with cities and states. Vying with Italian princes who were patrons of Renaissance art and literature, he accorded support to humanists, enlarged the Vatican Library, built the chapel (Sistine) which fittingly bears his name, and spent large sums on new streets and building projects in Rome. In other words, he sought to make Rome the literary and artistic capital of Renaissance Europe. He lavished offices on members of his family.

All this, it need scarcely be pointed out, was in striking and utter contrast with the ideals and purposes of the founder of the order of which Sixtus IV had been the head. That contrast was symbolic of the fashion in which the Roman Catholic Church and the Papacy were succumbing to trends, seemingly dominant, which were threatening to de-Christianize Christendom. One observer, obviously unfriendly, dated the period of Papal decadence from Sixtus IV. While clearly an exaggeration, it is significant of the deflection of the Papacy from its professed status of Vicar of Christ that this could be said of that office when it was held by the successor of Francis of Assisi.

The Papacy Reaches a Nadir

He who had the title of Innocent VIII (1484–1492) owed his elevation to the Papacy in part to unseemly factional strife among the cardinals at the time of his election and to the powerful support of a nephew of his predecessor, Sixtus IV. Before ordination he had been married and had had a son by his wife and two illegitimate children. While in his private morals this widower seems to have reformed after being made a priest, he proved to be an amiable but weak administrator. He was largely under the influence of the corrupt nephew of Sixtus IV to whom he owed his promotion, and under him the morals of the Papal curia from the cardinals down were lamentable. In urgent need of income, partly because of his embroilment in Italian politics, Innocent VIII sold church offices and created new ones, also to be sold. Some of his appointees to the cardinalate were worthy men, but one was the illegitimate son of his brother and another was Giovanni de' Medici, the thirteen-year-old son of the powerful Florentine, Lorenzo de' Medici. Before he was eight years old that favoured child, designated for ecclesiastical preferment, had been given, with the consent of Sixtus IV, an abbacy, and before he was twelve he had two more, including that of Monte Cassino, the mother house of the Benedictines—that appointment in itself being evidence of the deterioration of both the Papacy and monasticism. To be sure, when under importunate pressure from the lad's father he designated him cardinal, Innocent VIII insisted that he be not formally installed for three years and that in the interval he give himself to the study of theology and canon law, but even then he was only sixteen when he undertook his full duties.

Several of the cardinals lived in luxury in the style of secular princes, hunted, gambled, entertained lavishly, and had mistresses. Outstanding among them was Rodrigo Borgia, nephew of Calixtus III. Handsome, able, genial, an orator, forceful, compellingly attractive to women, possessing a huge income from the benefices lavished upon him, he had been elevated to the cardinalate when he was still under thirty years of age and served prominently under five Popes. By his acknowledged mistress, married successively to three other men, he had four children, and by other mothers had two more children. For all of his off-spring he sought position and wealth. One of them, Cæsar Borgia, was designed by his father for a career in the Church. At the age of seven he was given benefices. Later he was made bishop and when his father became Pope he was made archbishop and then cardinal.

In 1492 Rodrigo Borgia was elected Pope and, taking the title of Alexander

VI, he held the post until his death in 1503. It was charged that he obtained the election by wholesale bribery of the cardinals. Yet in many quarters the choice was welcomed. He proved to be an able and strong administrator. He was hardworking and was expert in the business and etiquette of the Vatican. At one time he appeared to give himself to much needed reforms in the Church. He encouraged some of the religious orders. Like Sixtus IV, he was clearly on the side of those who, in the current disputes on the subject, held to the immaculate conception of the Virgin Mary. He gave his support to the Angelus which, as we have seen, was in honour of the Virgin and of the incarnation. He defended the prerogatives of the Church in the Low Countries against those who were encroaching on them.

Yet Alexander VI is chiefly remembered for his preoccupation with European and especially with Italian politics and for the shameless way in which he sought to further the advancement of members of his own family. Particularly notorious were the adventures of Cæsar Borgia and the Pope's support of them. Cæsar Borgia was obviously unfitted for an ecclesiastical career. Formally released by his father from his clerical obligations, he married and set about carving out for himself a state in Italy. In an age of unbridled ambition and intrigue in Italian politics, he was outstanding in courage, daring, calculating self-interest, utter perfidy, and cold-blooded cruelty to all who stood in his way. Deprived of Papal support by his father's death, his projects came to nought.

The exploits of Cæsar Borgia and the evil deeds of Alexander VI lost nothing in the telling. Both men had enemies who cared as little for the truth as did they. There have been those who have sought to defend their memory, especially that of the father. But while there have been exaggerations and although both were charged by contemporaries with crimes of which they have not been conclusively proved guilty, the evil characters of both are well established. While Alexander VI was certainly not as weak and may not have been as depraved as the worst of his predecessors, notably some of the tenth and the fore part of the eleventh century, under him the Renaissance Papacy sank to a nadir in morality. When the sixteenth century dawned the outlook for moral and spiritual leadership by the Popes in bringing Christendom to a high level such as had been envisioned by Hildebrand and other reformers of the Middle Ages was extremely grim. The Papacy was a liability rather than an asset.

Monarchs Curtail Papal Control

Not only did the Papacy sacrifice much of its moral leadership. It also had its administrative powers restricted. It was losing the struggle to free the Church from domination by lay princes and to make the Papacy supreme in all aspects of the life of Christendom, a struggle in which the great Popes of the Middle Ages had seemed to be succeeding. In some states the monarchs, supported by the rising tide of nationalism, curtailed the Papal revenues and judicial functions and limited the power of the Pontiffs to control the choice of the higher officers of the Church in their realms. Thus in 1438, as we have seen, the Pragmatic Sanction had reduced the Papal revenues from France. Not far from the same time, as we have also noted, similar actions were taken for England and Germany. Late in the fifteenth century Sixtus IV was constrained to concede to Ferdinand and Isabella the right to nominate to Spanish sees. In the fifteenth century the custom grew in France of taking appeals from the church courts to those of the king.

Decay in Monastic Life

The Christianity of Western Europe was suffering a decline in that feature of its life through which so much of the attainment of Christian perfection had been sought, the monasteries and religious orders. In the years around 1350 the Black Death took a heavy toll from them. While in some lands they recovered in numbers, the deterioration in discipline and morals which was one of their chronic threats seems to have been especially marked in the latter part of the fourteenth and in the fifteenth century. Conditions appear not to have been generally as bad as they had been before the reform movements of the eleventh, twelfth, and thirteenth centuries. Of this we cannot be sure, since data for accurate comparisons are lacking. However, it appears to be significant that in contrast with these centuries, in each of which major new orders arose, the only fresh monastic or semi-monastic movement that sprang up between 1350 and 1500 which attracted substantial numbers was that of the Brethren of the Common Life, of which we are to say more in a moment.

Along with this comparative dearth of fresh orders, we hear much of the sad condition of many of the existing houses. These reports may be an indication of a conscience which was becoming increasingly sensitive to contrasts between ideals and achievement. They may also seem to be more numerous because of the better state of our records for these decades. Yet they tell of widespread lethargy, luxury, laxity, and even stark immorality. In many monasteries poor financial management had brought evil days. Some others, heavily endowed, after years of earnest living, became vacant or all but vacant and their revenues went to the support of absentee and often worldly ecclesiastics. Nunneries were favorite places in which to domicile younger daughters of the aristocracy who were not provided with husbands. In them these scions of the nobility, having no inner call to the cloistered life, disregarded the rules, often went abroad, and had private incomes which made possible physical comforts. We read, too, of monasteries which were refuges for the sons of the nobility, of monks who were lazy, who spent much of their time in the chase, in frequenting taverns, and in frivolous and obscene talk, and who were avaricious. In Friesland monks and nuns mingled and are said often to have disposed of the results of their license by abortion or infanticide. We are told that in Spain some of the kings made their cast-off concubines abbesses.

THE STATE OF THE CLERGY

When conditions at the headquarters of the Church in Avignon and Rome are such as we have described, it is not surprising that in the rank and file of the bishops and priests there was widespread corruption. Clerical concubinage was prevalent, more so in some sections than in others. We hear repeatedly of bishops who behaved more like secular lords than fathers of their flocks, who were active in affairs of state to the neglect of their dioceses, and who went to war. In Spain it was said not to be uncommon for kings and other grandees to obtain support for their illegitimate sons by having them appointed bishops. We read of bishops with numerous illegitimate progeny for whom they provided. Reports were common of masses hurriedly and carelessly said, of colleges of chantry priests which were endowed for the purpose of prayers for the testators and the deceased of their families and where the stipulated services were neglected or grouped together. Absentee pluralists who drew the revenues from several, sometimes many benefices, and had the duties performed by poorly paid substitutes and lived elsewhere continued to be so numerous that attempts to end the scandal were futile.

THE SEEMINGLY IMPENDING DE-CHRISTIANIZATION OF WESTERN EUROPE

By 1500 it seemed that Western Europe, partially Christianized by the advances of the previous centuries, was being de-Christianized. The hardly won gains appeared to be in process of dissipation. Within the inner circle of the Church ill-concealed paganism was raising its head and in practice if not in word the Christian faith was denied by many of its official representatives. In much of the life of Western Europe there was a real though unavowed repudiation of Christian ideals. Much of what was being said would have shocked the high-minded even among pre-Christian pagans. This was true in literature. In his *Decameron* Boccaccio (1313–1375) mirrored the life of his day, and it was a life much of which clearly ignored Christian standards. Slightly more than a century later Machiavelli (1469–1527), a warm admirer of Cæsar Borgia and an active participant in Italian politics, in his treatises on political science, of which his *Prince* is the most famous, made expediency his rule in complete disregard of what the Christian must esteem as moral principles. His influence upon political theory, and he was a pioneer in later political thought, tended towards ruling out from the state and relations between states any attempt at regulation by Christian standards.

We scarcely need to say that in practice Western Europe had never been Christian. Yet it paid lip service to that faith, canonized some of its monarchs for what it deemed their approximation to the Christian ideal, and read with approval Augustine's *City of God*. Now it seemed to be throwing off even the pretense of honouring what great Christians had endeavoured to embody. It appeared to be in process of resolving the tension between the Christian demand on man and man's performance, so marked in the Middle Ages, by abandoning any attempt to live up to that demand.

Evidences of "The Exceeding Greatness of His Power"

Where, then, was "the exceeding greatness of his power"? The vessels were certainly earthen. The institutions which had been devised to conserve and further "his power"—the Papacy, general councils, monasteries, monastic orders, the bishops and clergy—were proving to be so much so that their earthiness seemed to have prevailed.

Yet "his power" was at work. It was welling up in many quarters, some of them quite unexpected. It was showing itself in thousands of lives, most of them humble, but some of them prominent. Here and there it was cleansing old vessels, such as existing monasteries and monastic orders. It was also giving rise to new movements. There were many more of these than in the dark centuries which followed the collapse of the Roman Empire. We must not take the space even to enumerate them all, much less to describe them fully. We will, however, say a little about some of the more outstanding individuals and movements in whom "the exceeding greatness of his power" was being manifested. While we shall mention them one by one and by certain classifications, we must remember that several of them were appearing simultaneously and that they were contemporary with the decay in the Papacy, the monasteries, and the clergy, and with the failure of the councils to effect thoroughgoing reform. Disease and health were both present in the Christianity of Western Europe. So "exceeding great" did "his power" prove to be that in the sixteenth and seventeenth centuries it rose to the challenge of mounting threats to the faith and broke out in a fresh forward surge in the Christian tide.

It is important to note that this forward surge was preceded by what might be described as a ground swell and to some degree issued from it. That ground swell was seen in several lands in Western Europe and had many different manifestations. While not apparent in the Papacy, only slightly making itself felt in the cardinalate, manifested in the general councils merely to be frustrated, absent from most of the monasteries, and seemingly negated by the majority of the bishops and parish clergy, it was potent. Moreover, to no small degree it arose from what had been accomplished through these institutions and agencies by devoted spirits of earlier years who had dreamed and laboured to make them instruments for cleansing the Church. Even if the moral and spiritual level of all Europe had not been lifted, a substantial proportion of the descendants of those who had come into the Christian faith through the mass conversions of the earlier centuries were growing in their intelligent commitment to it.

Two Outstanding Practical Women Mystics:
Catharine of Siena and Joan of Arc

Always one of the evidences of the working of "the exceeding greatness of his power" has been the type of life to which it has given rise in individuals. Some of these have been officially pronounced to be exemplars of the Christian faith and have been canonized. Many, presumably not a few of them equally worthy, have missed such recognition. While they were not proportionately as numerous as in the centuries between 950 and 1350, the century and a half between 1350 and 1500 saw many of them. Several combined, to an unusual degree, a life of activity in the world with that of the mystic. Two of the most prominent of these "practical mystics" were Catherine of Siena and Joan of Arc.

Catherine of Siena (1347–1380) was one of twins, the youngest and twenty-third child of a prosperous dyer, Giaccomo Benincasa, and his wife, Lapa di Piagenti di Puccio. Due chiefly to her father's influence, the home was deeply religious. From early childhood Catherine dedicated herself to Christ and the celibate life. At six she believed that she had had a vision of Jesus and at seven she is said to have vowed herself to him in virginity. At twelve her parents wished to arrange a marriage for her, but, at first to their annoyance, she refused, saying that she had promised to be the bride of Christ. They yielded and, since she did not wish to enter a monastery, they allowed her to have a room to herself in which for three years she lived in solitary meditation and physical austerity, with much inward struggle. She then took the vows of a member of the third order of Dominic. There followed three more years of solitary prayer and meditation in a room set apart for her under the parental roof. These were for her a time of peace and joy, for she was by nature of a sunny spirit.

Then came the conviction that she must reënter the world and begin a more active life. She gave herself to the service of the poor and the sick, including a year when an epidemic of the Black Death swept across Siena. Both she and her contemporaries believed that she had the gift of healing, and many were the cures attributed to her. She also served prisoners and had a notable conversion of one who was condemned to death.

Combining the visions of the mystic with deep interest in people and in the affairs of every day, Catherine of Siena wrote hundreds of letters, some of spiritual counsel to humble folk and some to those prominent in Church and state, including the Pope himself. In spite of many critics and one period in particular when calumnies were spread in an effort to besmirch her good name, even within her brief life time her fame spread through much of Western Europe. She reconciled enemies and warring factions. She concerned herself with politics and sought, in vain to her intense disappointment, to stimulate a crusade to bring Palestine again into Christian hands. She endeavoured to heal chronic feuds among prominent families in Siena. She urged upon Pope Gregory XI, then at Avignon and engaged in war with the Tuscan cities, to make peace, even if that cost him loss in worldly goods, to give himself to the cure of souls, and to come back to Rome. To resolve a struggle between Gregory XI and Florence in which the Pope had laid that city under an interdict, she first went to Florence, where the authorities hailed her coming, and then journeyed to Avignon and saw the Pope, who held her in reverential esteem. Although she failed in her effort to bring Gregory XI to the desired accord with Florence, she strengthened his wavering will to make his residence in Rome and had the joy of seeing that accomplished and peace made between his successor, Urban VI, and Florence.

Deeply grieved that the return of the Papacy to Rome was followed by what became the Great Schism, Catherine vigorously took the side of the Roman Pontiff, Urban VI, and wrote blistering letters to the French cardinals who, fleeing the Eternal City, had elected Clement VII. Summoned by Urban VI, she went to Rome and there exerted herself on his behalf. In the midst of that turbulent city she attempted, on at least two occasions with some success, to bring internal peace. It was in Rome that she died.

It is significant that in the second half of the fourteenth century one frail woman of humble birth, who died before she had reached her mid-thirties, should have had so profound an influence. Hers was a life of meditation, prayer, ecstatic vision, and of so great a devotion to Jesus, whose bride she believed herself to be, that she felt that she had received the stigmata of his wounds spiritually even though not physically. By nature joyous, she had a profound sense of her own sinfulness, attributed to it some of her failures to accomplish what she believed to be her divinely commissioned ends, and had periods of inward struggle and depression. Yet her life was also one of intense activity in personal ministrations and in the stormy and intricate complexities of Italian and Papal politics. The fickle crowd sometimes adored her and sometimes spurned her. However, in that century of growing corruption in high ecclesiastical quarters and in the Western Europe torn by wars, visited by the recurring scourge of the Black Death, with its fear of death and judgement, its stark depravity and callous cruelty set in contrast with the spiritual sensitivity and high aspirations of many of its sons and daughters, this humble young woman, although sometimes, as in her advocacy of a crusade, giving herself to a cause which from the perspective of a later day appeared fantastic, was a major figure. The fact that she could attain that position, without aspiring to it but only because she was driven by a sense of duty to undertake causes which she deemed laid upon her, was both a tribute to her character and evidence of the regard in which the Christian ideal when incorporated in an individual was held by thousands in the Europe of that day.

To be classed with Catherine of Siena as combining the visions of a mystic with practical activity was Joan of Arc or Jeanne d'Arc (1412–1431), often known as the Maid or the Maid of Orleans. The daughter of a prosperous peasant household, in her early teens she began to hear what she believed to be the voices of God and of some of the saints and angels. As a result she vowed to remain a virgin and gave herself increasingly to prayer. This was during the Hundred Years' War between France and England, and at a time when, after invasions by their King Henry V, the English were occupying much of France and were opposed by rising national sentiment in that unhappy land. However, the French were handicapped by the weak leadership of the Dauphin, the heir to their throne. Joan believed herself commissioned by God to raise the siege of Orleans, then beleaguered by the English, and to bring the Dauphin to Rheims and see him crowned as the lawful king, as against the child Henry VI of England, for whom the crown of France was claimed by his supporters. She made her way to the Dauphin, was accepted by him after some hesitation and an examination by theologians, donned armour, and went with the French force which set out for the relief of Orleans. The English were defeated, Orleans was saved for the French, and the Dauphin, the Maid beside him with her banner, was crowned at Rheims as Charles VII.

In the ensuing complexities of diplomacy and war Joan fell into the hands of the Burgundians, who were allies of the English, was sold to the English, was tried by an ecclesiastical court which was heavily weighted against her, and was condemned on twelve counts, the chief of which was that she held herself to be responsible directly to God and not to the Church. She was then turned over to the secular arm at Rouen and burned, and her ashes were thrown into the Seine. A quarter of a century later Charles VII's government obtained Papal permission for the review of the case by a church court which was as strongly biased in her favour as the earlier one had been against her.

As a result she was declared orthodox and the judgement against her was annulled. She had undoubtedly been sincere and single-minded, an instance of religious devotion which identified obedience to God with loyalty to the emerging French nationalism that centered itself around the king. That she, a peasant girl who was executed before she was twenty, had so great an influence was, as with Catherine of Siena, evidence of the fashion in which many in the Europe of the fourteenth century were moved by one whom they believed to be inspired by God and wholly committed to Him.

PRACTICAL MYSTICS AMONG THE MEN

Those who combined the way of the mystic and its prayer and contemplation with that of intense activity in the affairs of Church and state were not confined to one sex. They were also to be found among men. We have already met three of them, Peter d'Ailly, John Gerson, and Nicholas of Cusa, as leaders in the effort to unite and cleanse the Church through the conciliar movement.

In the midst of a life crowded with study, university administration, and prominent participation in the affairs of the Church, both in France and in Europe as a whole, Peter d'Ailly (1350–1420) took time for prayer, and to such good purpose that he wrote guides to contemplation, meditation, and prayer which were so obviously the fruit of profound experience, not only in his own life, but also as a spiritual guide to others, that they found a wide and continuing circulation.

Peter d'Ailly's pupil and close friend, John Gerson (1363–1429), as chancellor of the University of Paris was an active partisan in French politics and had a large share in the Council of Constance. When in his early fifties implacable political enemies forced him into retirement and semi-exile. Much of that time he gave himself to the care of neglected children. He wrote extensively on the life of the spirit, partly to describe and condemn what seemed to him false mysticism and partly to give positive advice to those who would follow the road of true mysticism. He held that reason as well as feeling should have a part in the mystic's experience. In some monastic circles there had been a reaction against scholasticism which went to the extreme of so great a distrust of reason as to hold that men could never really know God, whether as truth or goodness, but could only say what He was not. With this Gerson took sharp issue. He also denounced some of the writings of Ruysbroeck for what he regarded as pantheistic tendencies.

Nicholas of Cusa (1401–1464) led an extraordinarily active life as monastic reformer, a participant in the conciliar movement, bishop, and cardinal. He was a friend of some of the humanists and had himself studied Greek. Yet he, too, went far in the way of the mystic. He was profoundly influenced by

Augustine and Dionysius the Areopagite. He had his early education at the hands of the Brethren of the Common Life and was an ardent friend of them and of the Windesheim community, of whom we are to hear more in a moment. While not as extreme an anti-intellectualist as some of his contemporaries, he moved in that direction. He believed that what came to the mystic through his experience of God could never be expressed in words and rejoiced in the term *docta ignorantia*.

THE WAY OF THE MYSTIC HAS A CONTINUING AND GROWING ATTRACTION

We have seen (Chapter XXII) that the first half of the fourteenth century witnessed a luxurious flowering of mysticism in wide and not always interrelated circles in Western Europe. For this movement the year 1350 had no significance. It continued without interruption into the second half of the fourteenth century and had no diminution in the fifteenth century. It was not confined to those who, like Catherine of Siena, Joan of Arc, Peter d'Ailly, John Gerson, and Nicholas of Cusa, combined the way of the mystic with intense activity in the wider affairs of their nation, Europe, or the Church. It was also widespread among many whose lives were lived either in much narrower circles or entirely apart from the world. It seems not to have been affected by the corruption in the Papacy and the Papal curia or by the partial failure of the conciliar idea. It was an important phase of the ground swell which issued in the great awakenings of the sixteenth century.

In Germany the stimulus given by Eckhart, Tauler, Suso, and the Friends of God continued. The anonymous layman who was known as the Great Friend of God had his mature years in the second half of the fourteenth century. From the movement there came a number of works of devotion. Of these the most influential was the *Theologia Germanica,* probably written about the middle of the fourteenth century. It came to prominence in the sixteenth century through Luther. That great leader in the Protestant Reformation claimed that he had learned more from it of God, Christ, and man than in any other set of writings except the Bible and Augustine. He saw to it that it was circulated in printed form and through his endorsement it went through many editions.

THE BROTHERS AND SISTERS OF THE COMMON LIFE, WINDESHEIM, AND THE IMITATIO CHRISTI

In the Low Countries the long-lived John Ruysbroeck (1293–1381) did not die until well after 1350 and he and his writings made their effect felt throughout this period. For instance, the Franciscan Henry of Herp or Henry Harphius, Provincial of the Observants of Cologne and later attached to a monastery at Malines, was deeply impressed by them, especially in his work on *Mystical Theology.*

The influence of Ruysbroeck contributed to the rise and growth of what was known as the New Devotion. This found expression through the Brethren of the Common Life, the Sisters of the Common Life, and the Congregation of Windesheim, and had its crowning literary monument in *The Imitation of Christ.*

The chief moving spirits in the inauguration of the Brethren of the Common Life were Gerard Groote, or Gerard the Great (1340–1384) and Florentius Radewijns (Florence Radewin). Gerard was the son of a burgomaster of Deventer. Precocious as a student, he took a master's degree at the University of Paris, dabbled in magic, through family influence obtained the income of several benefices, and was living comfortably when the rebuke of a Carthusian whom he had known in the university led him radically to alter his life and to give himself to fasting, a hair shirt, and prayer. He began preaching, denounced current vices, including the concubinage of the clergy, stirred Utrecht and its environs, and then was silenced by the ecclesiastical authorities. He visited Ruysbroeck and, deeply impressed by him and his community, resolved to found others like it. In Deventer he began aiding school-boys, entertaining them at his table, and setting them to earning their living by transcribing books. His household grew, and presently, at the suggestion of his friend Florentius Radewijns, he formed it into a simple community in which all the earnings of the members were pooled. Characteristically Gerard Groote died of the plague caught from a sick friend whom he was endeavouring to help.

Out of this simple beginning, in spite of the opposition of the mendicant orders, houses of this kind multiplied, those for men under the name of the Brethren of the Common Life and those for women under that of the Sisters of the Common Life. They combined some of the principles of monasticism with the non-monastic life. They laboured with their hands and held in common the fruits of their toil. They had the practice of confessing their sins daily to one another. They prized books and aided in a revival of education which was already in progress. Their spread was chiefly in Germany and the Low Countries and it may well have been that the presence in these regions of houses of beguines and beghards served as a precedent and so furthered their popularity.

Florentius Radewijns, born near Utrecht, a graduate of the University of Prague, a convert of Gerard Groote, and to whose suggestion the action of the latter in founding the Brethren of the Common Life was in part due, took a further step, perhaps at the instance of Groote, and began a house at Windesheim near Zwolle which followed the rule of the Augustinian Canons. He was head both of Windesheim and of the Deventer Brethren of the Common Life, but in 1400, after his death, the two became distinct, and although for at least a time the movements kept in close touch with each other, Windesheim became the centre of what in 1419 was a congregation of twenty monasteries, some of them older than itself. It gave a marked stimulus to monastic reform in Germany and the Low Countries.

It is not strange that out of the awakening of which the Brethren of the Common Life and Windesheim were expressions there issued one of the most widely used aids to devotion, prayer, and meditation, *The Imitation of Christ*. Gerard Groote had prized the Bible and the great writers of the Church. He and his disciples made much of prayer, but, while they read Ruysbroeck and collected passages from books which would help them in it and their daily lives, they were not interested in speculative mysticism. It was among the Canons Regular of Windesheim that the literature of the New Devotion arose. Some of it was in German and some in Latin.

Of the writers of the New Devotion, Thomas à Kempis is the most famous, and of his works (if indeed he is the author of it) *The Imitation of Christ* is the best known. Born at Kempen, near Düsseldorf, in 1379 or 1380, Thomas à Kempis went to Deventer for his education and when he was in his late teens was admitted by Florentius Radewijns into his community of copyists. When he was nineteen or twenty he entered the monastery of Mount St. Agnes, a recently founded community of Augustinian Canons near Zwolle of which his brother was prior. There he spent the rest of his days, dying in 1471 as sub-prior. His life was one of quiet, a monastic routine of books, services, and writing. He was a calligrapher of note and was the author of tracts, sermons, biographies of Gerard Groote, Florentius Radewijns, others of their group, and a contemporary Dutch virgin, a mystic who was later canonized. His tracts and sermons dealt with prayer, contemplation, meditations on Christ and the Virgin Mary, the mystical union with Christ, and the ethical problems of members of a monastic community. Whether he was the author of *The Imitation of Christ* has been hotly debated. The book has been ascribed to several others, among them John Gerson. The majority opinion has settled on Thomas à Kempis. It may well be that the author was anonymous, but there seems to be no doubt that whoever he was he belonged to the Windesheim circle, either to the mother house or to some other monastery in that fellowship, and that the book distils much of the collective experience of the type of piety represented by the Brethren of the Common Life and Windesheim.

It must be added that as it went on, the New Devotion tended to regulate prayer by a precise methodology and so to become formal and sterile.

In the thirteenth and fourteenth centuries the mysticism of Germany and the Low Countries also found expression among the Carthusians. Ludolph of Saxony, also known as Ludolph the Carthusian (c.1300–1370), prior of a monastery of his order in Strassburg, wrote a *Life of Christ* which was translated into several languages and which had a wide vogue for two centuries or more. Its aim was to promote the love and imitation of Christ and it was meant to be read slowly, to promote meditation. Dionysius (1402–1471), a native of Ryckel in Limburg and a member of a Carthusian house near Liége, had frequent ecstasies and divided his days between study and prayer. He wrote voluminously, giving instruction in asceticism and contemplation.

This German and Low Country mysticism had a dark side. There were those, although not in any of the movements which we have mentioned, who professed to have a union with God which rendered yielding to the impulses of the flesh a matter of moral indifference. It led to the antinomianism which in various places and times has broken out under the Christian name.

ENGLISH MYSTICS

The flowering of mysticism in Germany and the Low Countries was paralleled by one in England. In the first half of the fourteenth century its chief figure was Richard Rolle, of whom we have already spoken (Chapter XXII). Rolle exerted a marked influence upon Walter Hilton, whose work lay in the second half of the century and who died in 1396. An Augustinian canon, Walter Hilton was an experienced spiritual director and his counsel was sought by monks, nuns, and men of importance in the secular world. Three books of his have come down to us. One, *The Scale of Perfection,* directing the soul in its progress to God, is said to have been more widely read in fifteenth and sixteenth century England than any other devotional guide. It had a continuing fruitage. *The Scale of Perfection* is characterized by what we now think of as typically English, a distrust of extravagance and extremes and a middle way between them. It is concerned as much with ethics as with contemplation. In it, as in Bernard of Clairvaux, contemplation is the communion of love. Like Bernard, it makes much of the human side of Jesus. In it are passages which remind one of the later English Protestant Evangelicalism.

Also belonging to the second half of the fourteenth century was Juliana or Lady Julian of Norwich. She was an anchoress who seems to have had her solitary dwelling in a house in the yard of the Church of St. Julian, near Norwich. The book which made her famous, her *Revelations of Divine Love,* is largely autobiographical. It is compiled of insights which came to her and which she believed had been showed her by God or by Christ. Some have to do with Christ, some with sin, forgiveness, and grace, some with God, and some with prayer.

Less well known was Margery Kempe, a younger contemporary of Walter Hilton and Juliana of Norwich. Born in 1373, she was the daughter of a mayor and alderman of Lynn and was married to a burgess of that city to whom she bore fourteen children. After her first youth there came a sudden revulsion against the vanities of life and the conviction that she should live as a virgin. To this resolution she won her husband's reluctant consent. She undertook pilgrimages, one of them to Palestine. Visions and revelations came to her, and had to do chiefly with how she should act on particular occasions. She met much criticism, but was also consulted by her neighbours as an oracle and was often called to pray over the dying. Her autobiography is interesting in its frankness and perhaps as one that might have been duplicated in its beliefs and its sense of direct guidance by God in numbers of others of her day and age.

ITALIAN MYSTICS

Catherine of Siena was an outstanding but by no means the only mystic of Italy in the century and a half between 1350 and 1500. In spite of the wide-spread corruption in morals of the laity, the priesthood, the monasteries, and the Papal court, there were those who were completely devoted to God and believed that they had direct experience of Him. One of these was Catherine of Bologna (1413–1463), abbess of the Poor Clares in her native city. Through prolonged struggles with temptation she became expert in the battles of the spirit and had visions, ecstasies, and revelations.

Catherine of Genoa (1447–1510) came from a family which had provided the Church with two Popes and several cardinals. One of her sisters, an Augustinian canoness, had joined in founding a convent. Well educated, at sixteen she was wedded by her family to one of the patrician youths of the city. The marriage proved unhappy, for the two were unsuited to each other and he was unfaithful and extravagant. After a decade, perhaps because of her attempt to find solace, she had a profound religious experience which she regarded as her conversion. In that change of heart her husband soon followed her. They then began to live simply in one of the humbler sections of the city and gave themselves to the care of the poor and the sick. She established the habit of taking the communion daily and inflicted on herself severe penances. She undertook prolonged fasts. Eventually she and her husband moved into a hospital the better to devote themselves to the orphans, the sick, and the dying. As matron of the hospital she showed remarkable administrative gifts and served heroically through a prolonged epidemic of the plague. In 1497 her husband died and not far from that time her health became so impaired that she resigned as matron and discontinued her practice of fasting. From her conversion Catherine had given herself to the love of God and, deeply conscious of her own sinfulness and her remoteness from the supreme Purity, felt that love cleansing her from all pride and filling her with a deep yearning to be transformed into that Purity. To her the love which she felt for God and the love of God for her were like the cleansing fires of purgatory.

THE INCREASING ROLE OF WOMEN

The thoughtful reader must have noted that one of the features of the century and a half between 1350 and 1500 was the increasing prominence of women in the Christian story. Throughout the preceding centuries women had had an important role. Paul had declared that in Christ there is neither male nor female. A woman, the mother of Jesus, had been revered across the generations and never more so than immediately preceding 1350. There had been many women saints. Now women appeared more strikingly as leaders and exemplars of the faith. It was still a man's world. The clergy were exclusively male. The great theologians and the founders of most of the monastic orders were men. However, more than previously, women were coming to the fore as mystics and saints. This was to continue, notably in the Roman Catholic Church.

THE EFFECTS OF PREACHING

Much preaching was heard in Western Europe in the fourteenth and fifteenth centuries. It may even have increased in this period. Some of it was by friars and some by the ordinary parish clergy and the bishops. Much of it was routine and quite uninspired, but some of it was profoundly stirring and moved multitudes. It contributed substantially to the ground swell which preceded and in part issued in the forward surge of the tide in the sixteenth century.

Among the most memorable of the preachers was the Spanish Dominican Vincent Ferrer (1350–1419). He travelled widely in Spain, Northern Italy, Switzerland, and France, preaching as he went. He was from an aristocratic family which presumably was deeply religious, for he had a brother who was general of the Carthusians. He had had a prolonged education in philosophy and theology, had taught, and had served the Avignon Papacy before beginning the career which brought him fame. Severely ascetic, he declined high ecclesiastical office, including that of cardinal. It was not until he was nearly fifty that the Pope started him on his preaching mission. His main themes were sin, impending judgement, and repentance, and were put in such fashion that thousands were smitten in conscience and by fear. Speaking only in his native tongue, he drew enormous crowds. Some of his followers were organized as flagellants who marched in processions, scourging themselves as they went. One of the young men whom he inspired, Bernardine of Siena, continued his work in Italy. From 1408 to 1416, he was almost continuously south of the Pyrenees. There he is said to have won thousands of Jews and Moslems. He also concerned himself with Spanish politics, part of the time as a trusted counsellor of kings. Yet he also gave himself to the lowly and tended sick children. In an epidemic of the plague in Genoa he fearlessly ministered to the stricken. Many miracles of healing were attributed to him. It is not strange that he was formally canonized in 1455, less than a generation after his death.

Vincent Ferrer is one of the more outstanding in a great throng. The friars travelled widely, not only preaching dogma but also attacking the amusements and frivolities of both the noble and the commoner and pillorying the oppression by the lords, the extortions of the merchants, the corruption of the law, and the exactions of the retainers of the mighty. Drunkenness, gluttony, and profanity were denounced, and the saints were praised. Some of the hermits preached, and several wandered about from place to place attracting casual audiences. To aid the preacher there were numerous manuals and treatises on his art.

Various Aids to Devotion

In the course of the fourteenth and fifteenth centuries various aids to devotion for both laity and clergy appeared or were further cultivated. It seems to have been in this period that the Way of the Cross, also known as the Stations of the Cross, began to be set up in churches. In Jerusalem the scenes of Christ's sufferings had long been a goal of pilgrims and among them had been the traditional route, later called the *via dolorosa,* which he traversed to his crucifixion. Obviously only a small minority of Christians of Western Europe could make the journey to that distant region. The device began slowly to be adopted of setting up in churches what would be a partial reproduction of this way with reminders at intervals, usually in the form of pictures, of incidents in that memorable and sad progress. By following it and pausing for prayer and meditation at each station the faithful would have their imaginations quickened and their devotion deepened.

Hymns were composed, many of them in the vernacular, both expressions of religious devotion and aids in its cultivation.

Religious dramas were continued and elaborated as a means of instruction. However, they tended to be secularized, to be taken from the churches to the churchyards, and to have so much buffoonery attached to them that purists in morals began to denounce them.

Art also contributed to nourishing the religious life. Painters arose whose works were expressions of prayer and profound meditation on Christian themes. Notable was he who is known as Fra Angelico (1387–1455), the Dominican who is best remembered for his deeply moving paintings in Florence, especially in the monastery of San Marco. Along with the earlier Giotto (c.1267–1337), he was a forerunner of the flowering of Christian art which mounted in the fifteenth century in such men as Donatello (c.1386–1466), Filippo Lippi (1406–1469), the latter's natural son Filippino Lippi (1457–1504), and Botticelli (1444–1510), and which, a generation later, in the fore part of the sixteenth century, was to have its highest expressions in Raphael (1483–1520) and Michelangelo (1475–1564). The main themes of these artists, whether in painting, sculpture, or architecture, were Christian. Some of the masters, like Botticelli, a warm admirer of Savonarola, and Michelangelo, a Christian Platonist and Dante devotee, were profoundly moved by deep personal Christian faith. In them was seen much of the ground swell and, in the greatest and latest of them, the full flood of new tide of the Christian awakening.

MONASTIC REFORM

Here and there were attempts to recall Europe to the ideals which had sought expression in monasticism. No new orders appeared which captured the imagination of such large numbers as had the Cistercians, the Franciscans, or the Dominicans. Yet there were movements which showed that the monastic way to the perfect Christian life had by no means lost its appeal. There were the Brethren of the Common Life and the family of monasteries which centered around Windesheim. The Jesuates (*Jesuati*) received Papal authorization in 1367. They gave themselves to the care of the sick, especially those stricken by the plague, to the burial of the dead, and to strict self-mortification, including scourging. They arose from the life and work of a patrician of Siena, John Colombini (c.1300–1367) who, after a sudden conversion, devoted himself to the indigent sick, to reconciling estranged friends, and to inducing those who had wrongfully taken property to restore it to its rightful owners. Late in the fourteenth century the Hieronymites, taking their name and inspiration from Jerome and the community which he gathered about him in Bethlehem in the fourth century, came into being. They were given the rule of Augustine. Their chief cradle was in Spain and in 1415 they are said to have had twenty-five houses in that land. The Hieronymite nuns were founded in Spain in 1426. In the sixteenth century the order was one of the channels through which the Catholic Reformation found expression. In Rome in the time of its depravity, Frances (1384–1440), a mystic from an aristocratic family, remembered by the name of that city and later canonized, founded the Oblates of St. Benedict, a community of women who followed the Benedictine rule and gave themselves to prayer and good works.

The mendicant orders, recovering from the tragic reduction of their staffs by the Black Death, continued to attract many and thousands enrolled in the ranks of their tertiates. Within the Franciscans the struggle, almost as old as the order itself, continued between those who held to a complete adherence to the ideals of the founder and those who would relax it. The strict party, the Observants, at times seemed to gain as against the others, the Conventuals. The Observants appeared in various countries in the fourteenth and fifteenth centuries. Prominent in furthering them in Italy were Bernardine of Siena and John Capistran. In 1517 a Papal decree gave the Observants a separate structure and declared them to be the true order of St. Francis. Late in the fifteenth century Francis of Paula founded in South Italy and Sicily what are usually known as the Minims, who sought to follow fully the exacting rule of Francis of Assisi. They spread rapidly to France, Germany, and Spain. There was conflict within the Order of Preachers, between those desiring a stern order of life and those who would ease it. While the Observants seem to have been in the minority as against the Conventuals, they were active. So, too, the Augustinian friars experienced a reform in several countries in the fourteenth and fifteenth centuries. In Germany the Observants dominated the order and their organization, officially recognized in 1493, comprised almost all the existing houses. They acquired special significance from the fact that when Martin Luther suddenly decided to become a monk it was an Observant house that he entered. A leader in the reform, Staupitz, had much to do with one stage of Luther's spiritual pilgrimage. A purification of the Carmelites was begun in Italy early in the fifteenth century. In several different places in Europe efforts were made to recall one or another of the Benedictine houses to their earlier ideals. Some of them achieved at least partial success.

MONASTIC REFORM MOVES INTO THE CHURCH IN SPAIN

By the end of the fifteenth century the ground swell was making itself felt in Spain which in the sixteenth century was to mount to a great forward surge. It was first markedly apparent in some sections of the monastic life and from there moved into the Church at large and did much to raise the general level of the quality of clergy and laity.

The closing years of the fifteenth century and the first quarter of the sixteenth century witnessed the political unification of Spain. By the last quarter of the fifteenth century the Christian kingdoms which emerged in the course of the reconquest of the Iberian Peninsula from the Moslems had loosely coalesced into four—Portugal, Castile, Aragon, and Navarre. Castile and Aragon were brought into a personal union by the marriage (1469) of Isabella (1451–1504), Queen of Castile and Leon, and Ferdinand (1452–1516), King of Aragon. In 1512 Ferdinand acquired the part of Navarre which lay south of the Pyrenees. In 1492 the last remaining Moslem stronghold, the Kingdom of Granada, was conquered by Ferdinand and Isabella. While deep internal differences remained in language, traditions, and administrative organization, Spain was more and more a unity under centralized rule.

Isabella was earnestly religious, worked a moral reform in the corrupt court of Castile, endeavoured to purify the convents in the realm, and promoted learning. Ferdinand was of a different stamp and while known as the Catholic was crafty and boasted of his success in deceit in diplomacy. Yet Isabella was too able and vigorous to be ignored.

Improvement was very much needed in the Spanish Church. Concubinage among the clergy was widespread and the level of general morality was low. The reform in the Franciscans through the Observants had spread to Spain. It found a friend in Isabella and a dauntless and extraordinarily able leader in Ximénes de Cisneros (1436–1517) whose long life gave him time to carry through many of his projects.

Ximénes de Cisneros was late in rising to prominence. He was well educated in civil and canon law, spent several years in Rome, and returned to Spain with a Papal appointment to a benefice in the Archbishopric of Toledo when one should fall vacant. The Archbishop was unwilling to recognize the Papal document. Ximénes would not yield his claim, and as a result was imprisoned by the Archbishop for six years. Released when in his early forties, he was given office by another bishop and at once displayed remarkable administrative gifts. Then he joined the Observant Franciscans and began a rigorously ascetic regimen. For three years he was a hermit and found deeply satisfying the life of austerity, solitude, prayer, and meditation. In 1492, over his protests, Isabella chose him as her confessor. Two years later he was elected provincial of his order in Castile. With the support of the Pope and Isabella, he carried through, against severe opposition, a reform designed to bring all Franciscans in that province under the Observant discipline. In 1495 Isabella had him appointed Archbishop of Toledo, the most influential ecclesiastical post in her kingdom. He at first refused and finally accepted only on the express command of the Pope. Once installed, he continued to live as a strict Franciscan and devoted the huge revenues of the see to such purposes as the relief of the poor and the ransom of captives. Indeed, Pope Alexander VI, his opposite in moral character, admonished him to live more in accord with the dignity of his high office. His vision, inflexible will, and administrative ability were directed towards the purification of the Church. He continued his measures to bring the Conventual Franciscans to Observant standards. He took action to purge the secular clergy, obtaining for this purpose a free hand from the Pope. In all this he had the support of Isabella.

Although active in affairs of state, twice regent of Castile, and a cardinal of the Roman Church, Ximénes never lost sight of his purpose of improving the quality of the Church. Late in life he founded the University of Alcalá, gave to it much time, thought, and money, and made it a centre of the teaching of religion. To further the study of the Scriptures he had compiled and prepared for printing the Complutensian (from Complutum, the Latin name of Alcalá) Polyglot Bible, in which Greek, Latin, Hebrew, and Aramaic were used. He employed that new medium, the printing press, to multiply for circulation other Christian literature. He revived the use of the ancient Spanish Mozarabic liturgy as against that of Rome.

THE INQUISITION IN SPAIN

A side of the religious life of Spain in this period which was intended to cleanse it was the extension and intensification of the Inquisition.

In the middle of the fourteenth century, with the possible exception of Lithuania, Spain had more self-confessed non-Christians than any other country in Western Europe. Jews were numerous and prominent, there were many Moslems, and Granada remained a frankly Moslem state. Late in the fourteenth century Lithuania became officially Christian, but in the fifteenth century the conversion of Jews and Moslems in Spain was still incomplete. Early in the fifteenth century, partly from fear of the widespread massacres which were being visited on their co-religionists and partly through the eloquence of Vincent Ferrer, thousands of Jews accepted baptism. Many of the converted and their descendants rose to prominence in the Church. Others married into highly placed Spanish families. In 1492 Ferdinand and Isabella ordered all Jews who held to their ancestral faith either to be baptized or leave the country. More baptisms followed. The monarchs acted with similar vigour to bring about the conversion of the Moslems. By the terms of the surrender of Granada (1492) the latter were guaranteed protection for themselves and their property. The first Archbishop of Granada after the capitulation respected the pledge and sought the conversion of the populace by persuasion and tact. As a result, thousands were baptized. However, Ximénes believed those methods to be too lenient and adopted more strenuous ones. These goaded the Moors to a rebellion which was put down by ruthless force. Partly in retaliation, Ferdinand and Isabella gave them the choice of emigration or baptism. In 1502 an edict forced a similarly unpleasant alternative on the Moslems who remained in Castile. Many thousands elected the easier course and were baptized.

Under these circumstances, for many baptized Jews (called *Marranos* or *Conversos*) and converted Moslems (called *Moriscos*) the change in religion was purely nominal. There was much popular feeling against them, especially against the Marranos. They were widely accused, probably justly in many instances, of maintaining their non-Christian rites in secret. Presumably envy for their economic prosperity contributed to the clamour. To ferret out the crypto-Jews and hidden Moslems, in 1478 Ferdinand and Isabella, partly through the urging of Thomas de Torquemada, prior of a Dominican house in Segovia, and of a Dominican prior in Seville, but apparently without any widespread demand from the Church in that kingdom and with reluctance on the part of Isabella, asked Rome for the extension of the Inquisition to Castile. The Pope, Sixtus IV, agreed, and in 1480, with his authority, the step was taken. In accord with the rising power of the monarch as against the Papacy, the Inquisition was to be directed by men appointed by the crown rather than by Rome. It was to have jurisdiction only over the baptized and not over non-Christians. Directed primarily against the *Conversos,* it soon brought numbers of these to the stake. However, the majority of the condemned were not burned but were heavily fined and were subjected to humiliating penance. Torquemada was named Inquisitor-general, with power in Castile, Aragon, Valencia, and Catalonia. Learned, sternly ascetic in his private life, observing strictly the vow of poverty, deeply pious, uncompromising, Torquemada extended the operation of the Inquisition. After his death (1498) it was continued.

The Inquisition was developed by men who had the zeal of reformers and made for a certain kind of unity in Spain, but it can scarcely be said to have contributed to the religious awakening of the sixteenth century. The conviction with which it was administered was perilously akin to fanaticism. It may have prevented Protestantism from gaining a firm foothold in the country, but the kind of devotion which it nourished was a caricature of that which is the fruit of the "exceeding greatness of his power" of which the New Testament speaks.

It may be significant that none of those who were most outstanding in the fifteenth century reform in Spain—Isabella, Ximénes, and Torquemada—was ever canonized. In spite of their devotion and labours, in the judgement of the Roman Catholic Church they were not assuredly exemplars of the Christian ideal.

These developments in Spain were of peculiar importance because of the prominence which that country was to have in the ensuing century. She was to become the mightiest military power in Western Europe and was to build an enormous overseas empire. Through her colonial possessions Christianity was to have an opportunity for wide geographical extension and the quality of the faith that was propagated reflected the temper of the Church within her borders.

"The Power" Infiltrates Humanism

Towards the end of the fifteenth century the ground swell which was preliminary to the flood tide of the sixteenth century began to make itself felt among the humanists. As we have reminded ourselves, in its earlier days humanism made little positive contribution to the religious life of Western Europe. Few if any humanists openly repudiated Christianity. They were Catholics and some of them drew their support from the Church. The value which they placed on man was in part of Christian origin. Yet the earlier leading humanists were largely negative in their attitude towards the Church and its faith. They were scornful of scholastic philosophy and theology and were contemptuous of monasticism. Laurentius Valla (1405–1457) was fairly typical of the prevailing attitude of humanists. He used his critical skill to reveal the spurious character of the Donation of Constantine. He took delight in showing that the Apostles' Creed was not framed by the Twelve Apostles, as legend declared it to have been, and by advocating the study of the original Greek and Hebrew texts began to shake confidence in the Vulgate as the authoritative version of the Scriptures. In the second half of the fifteenth century a change began to be seen. There were outstanding humanists who were also earnestly Christian. They might still be critical of some aspects of the Church but they were concerned more for positive than for negative measures.

One strain of Christian humanism issued from the Platonic Academy at Florence. Founded about 1442 by Cosimo de' Medici, the most powerful personage of the day in that city, it was designed to emulate the famous pagan Academy of Athens. One of its leading members, Marsilio Ficino (1433–1499), a protegee of Cosimo de' Medici, a translator and ardent student of Plato and Plotinus, was deeply enamoured of Dionysius the Areopagite, that inspirer of so much of Christian mysticism, held Augustine in reverence, in his personal morals remained uncontaminated by the fashionable vices of the Renaissance, was ordained to the priesthood, believed that religion in its purest form was revealed in Christ, and held that Platonism and Christianity could be harmonized. To that circle belonged Pico della Mirandola (1463–1494), the brilliant youngest son of the Prince of Mirandola. Learned in Greek, Latin, Hebrew, Arabic, and Chaldee, he sought to prove the truth of Christianity from Kabbalah, that Jewish school of thought which lent itself to mysticism and to theological and philosophical speculation and which had a strange similarity to the more ancient Gnosticism. A restless traveller, in the latter part of his brief years he was profoundly impressed by Savonarola, of whom we are to hear more a few pages below, and had dreams of going barefooted about the world preaching.

In France a distinguished Christian humanist, the teacher of several others, was Jacques Lefèvre d'Étaples (c.1455–1536). A priest, he studied in the University of Paris and in Florence, Rome, and Venice, made himself familiar with Greek, and was deeply impressed with Plato. Returning to Paris, he taught in the University and there profoundly influenced some of those who were to be pioneers in Protestantism. He devoted much of his time to Biblical studies, translated the Bible into French (although his was by no means the first French version), and pled for a return to primitive Christianity and for the Scriptures as the primary authority for Christians. He was the devout humanist who wished to go back to the primary sources and so to know the Christian faith as it came fresh from Christ and the apostles.

Eminent among the early German humanists was Roelof Huysmann (1443–1485), better known as Rudolf Agricola. A native of the Low Countries, as a youth he studied with the Brethren of the Common Life, then in Italy, and taught in the University of Heidelberg. Earnestly religious, he helped to give German humanism a Christian orientation. He was much admired by Erasmus, of whom we are to say more in a moment. More prominent and eventually an unwilling but quietly courageous centre of controversy between humanists and those within the Church who opposed them was Johann Reuchlin (1455–1522). A master of classical Latin and Greek, he was especially noted for his familiarity with Hebrew. In this he drew his inspiration in part from Pico della Mirandola. From the latter he also acquired an interest in Kabbalistic studies. With the humanist's concern for digging into first-hand sources, he went back of the Vulgate to the original texts and pointed out errors in that revered translation of the Bible. A stormy controversy which stirred Church and scholarly circles arose over Reuchlin's refusal to recommend the proposed destruction of all Jewish books except the Old Testament. This was being stoutly advocated by a converted Jew, Pfefferkorn, as a first step towards bringing over his former co-religionists to the Christian faith. Against Reuchlin were the universities, the Inquisition, and the friars, especially the Dominicans. For him were the humanists. Some of the latter came out anonymously with a series of satires, *Letters of Obscure Men,* which, directed against Reuchlin's antagonists, set the humanists of Europe to laughing. In an appeal to the Pope, Reuchlin won out, but somewhat inconclusively. He remained within the Catholic Church, but we shall meet his grand-nephew, Philip Melanchthon, whom he looked upon almost as a son, as one of Luther's staunchest supporters.

Prominent among the English Christian humanists were John Colet (c.1467–1519) and his younger friend and admirer, Thomas More (1478–1535). The sole surviving son of a Lord Mayor of London, Colet was born to wealth. After taking a degree at Oxford, he travelled in Italy and, returning to England, began lecturing on the Bible in a fresh way which commanded attention. A student of Plato, Plotinus, and Dionysius the Areopagite, there was in him something of the mystic. Eventually he became Dean of St. Paul's Cathedral in London. He was chiefly remembered for his Biblical studies, his preaching, his advocacy of reform, and his founding of St. Paul's School as a centre of humanistic studies. We are to see Thomas More at a later stage in our story, but here we meet him as a charming, witty humanist, a translator of the writings of Pico della Mirandola.

ERASMUS, PRINCE OF CHRISTIAN HUMANISTS

As the crowning glory of the Christian humanists we move naturally to Desiderius Erasmus (c.1466–1536). This is partly because of his fame among his contemporaries and partly because it was through him that the aspect of the ground swell represented by the combination of humanism with Christianity made a major contribution to the flood tide of the sixteenth century.

Desiderius Erasmus was born out of wedlock in Rotterdam. He was cared for by his mother, but he early lost her and his father in the plague. As a child he was put to school in Deventer and had part of his education through the Brethren of the Common Life. A student and an intense individualist by temperament, he reacted vigorously against well intentioned efforts by his guardian and other friends to induce him to take up the monastic life. Eventually he was ordained to the priesthood, but he had no taste for that profession. He studied at the University of Paris, and at various times was in Italy, England, the Low Countries, and Germany. He craved books and friends, but would never be too closely bound by the latter. Not a profound scholar, his great talent was the skill with which he handled Latin. He was a man of letters whose books commanded a wide audience, an audience which was multiplied by the increasing use of the printing press.

Erasmus was sincerely Christian and wished for the reformation of the Church. He had no use for monks or scholasticism and cared little for theology or the sacraments. He wished to see the Church purged of superstition through the use of intelligence and a return to the ethical teachings of Christ. He desired no break with the existing Catholic Church. He initiated no innovations in doctrine or worship. Rather he pled for ethical living, and in a politically divided Europe, racked by chronic wars, he argued for peace. His approach was rational. He appeared to cherish the conviction that through the appeal to man's reason both Church and society could be vastly improved.

Among the more widely read writings of Erasmus were his *Enchiridion*

Militis Christiani, or *Handbook of the Christian Soldier,* meant to be a guide to Christian living, deprecating formalism and ceremonies and emphasizing morals; *The Praise of Folly,* a satirical description of current life from the Pope and cardinals down through kings, nobles, monks, preachers, philosophers, and merchants, to the lower strata of society; *Querala Pacis* or *The Complaint of Peace,* in which he praised peace and pilloried war; and his *Familiar Colloquies,* in which he held up to ridicule what he deemed the corruptions in the Church and the monasteries. He got out an edition of the Greek Testament with a fresh translation into Latin. He stimulated editions of some of the early Christian writers. His moral earnestness and his attempt to stress the New Testament, combined with the wide vogue enjoyed by his writings did much to incite to reform and to turn humanism from its secularistic and pagan tendencies.

Wyclif and the Lollards

What, in the meantime, was happening to scholasticism? Could it survive the scorn which the humanists were pouring on it? Although the tide was running against it, it continued. From those nurtured in it there appeared men and movements which in their effort to give expression to "the exceeding greatness of the power" of the Christian Gospel advocated such drastic measures that they were condemned as heretical by the Catholic Church. They, too, were part of the ground swell which was to issue in the flood tide of the sixteenth and seventeenth centuries.

Outstanding and making a major contribution to later movements was John Wyclif. There is much uncertainty about the date of his birth, but it is clear that he was a native of Yorkshire. His student years were in Oxford and he became a master of scholastic philosophy and theology. In time he was the outstanding scholar among its teachers and his lectures were largely attended. In an age when nominalism seemed to be sweeping all before it, Wyclif was an unabashed realist. He was profoundly influenced by Augustine and through him by Plato. In this he reflected the revival of Augustinian studies in the England of his day which had as a leader Bradwardine, an Oxford theologian and later Archbishop of Canterbury. Wyclif stood with Thomas Aquinas rather than with Duns Scotus, but the latter, who had been at Oxford only a generation or so before him, seems to have had a profound influence upon him. Like Duns Scotus, he was critical of some existing beliefs and also held to the omnipotence of the arbitrary will of God. He was probably even more deeply indebted to Robert Grosseteste, who had been a powerful figure at Oxford only a few years earlier and who was outstanding as the reforming Bishop of Lincoln.

We must think of Wyclif as spending the major part of his career as student and teacher, chiefly within the confines of Oxford, stimulated by the debates among the school men, holding various ecclesiastical appointments outside the university which gave him a livelihood and the means to pursue his university course, and occasionally performing the duties attached to these offices. He was often an absentee recipient of income from parish sources. In 1374, through royal appointment, he became rector of the parish of Lutterworth. On one occasion he went on a political errand to the Continent for the crown and thus established a connexion with John of Gaunt, a younger and influential son of King Edward III, which later stood him in good stead.

It was not until the last eight or nine years of his life that Wyclif engaged in the writing and the activities for which he became famous. In treatises on divine and civil dominion, he put forth the theory that all ownership is God's, and that God grants the use of property on the condition that the holder render faithful service. If the trust is not fulfilled the use is forfeited. While the principle applied to property held by civil as well as ecclesiastical dignitaries, what gave it force in England was Wyclif's declaration that if an ecclesiastic habitually misused his holdings, he could be removed from them by the secular power. He also maintained that Popes might err and that they were not necessary for the administration of the Church. A worldly Pope was a heretic and should be removed from office. In an England which was smarting from exactions by the revenue-hungry Avignon Papacy, these assertions were welcomed by many. They were in accord with actions of the "Good Parliament" of 1376 in seeking to curtail the collection of Papal revenues in England and the enjoyment of English revenues by absentee Papal appointees. The powerful John of Gaunt, completely self-seeking, was prepared to champion Wyclif since the latter's advocacy of the intervention of the civil arm to remove unworthy clergy from their benefices gave him support in his ambition to replace ecclesiastics whom he could not control by men who were his creatures. The protection of John of Gaunt and other nobles shielded Wyclif from the action against him attempted by the Bishop of London and the Archbishop of Canterbury.

Wyclif progressively became more radical in his views, and in doing so lost the support of John of Gaunt and some others among the powerful of the realm. About the time that Europe was being scandalized by the outbreak of the Great Papal Schism, in a treatise on the Church, taking a strict Augustinian view of predestination, Wyclif argued that the true Church is made up only of those elected by God and is invisible, and that since it is God's choice which determines membership, no visible church or its officers can control entrance or can exclude from membership. Nor can Pope or bishop know who are true members. To his mind, salvation does not depend upon a connexion with the visible Church or upon the mediation of the priesthood, but solely upon election by God. He was critical of monks and friars. Later he held that every one of the elect is a priest and that the New Testament recognizes no distinction between priests and bishops. Priests and bishops, he maintained, should be honoured because of their character and should set an example to their flocks. Clergy who tried to enforce the collection of tithes by that very fact were revealed as unworthy of their office. He condemned the cult of the saints, relics, and pilgrimages. Soon, while holding to the real presence of Christ in the bread and wine of the mass, he attacked transubstantiation and taught that under some circumstances a layman might officiate in the Eucharist. While not rejecting the seven sacraments, he did not believe confirmation to be necessary. He repudiated indulgences and masses for the dead but retained a belief in purgatory. He declared that intelligent sincerity in worship was of more value than the form. Indeed, formalism and elaborate services might hinder true worship.

For a time at Oxford Wyclif was supported by the secular clergy, partly because in coming out against the monks and friars he had taken sides in the chronic conflict between the seculars and regulars in the university. Moreover, Oxford, as the leading university in England and for a time second only to the University of Paris in prestige in Northern Europe, was jealous of its independence of king and bishop. Before long, however, the episcopacy succeeded in expelling or winning the friends of Wyclif and the university passed into the hands of his enemies. In the meantime Wyclif had retired to Lutterworth and was making that the directing centre of his activities.

In furtherance of his convictions Wyclif had the Bible translated from the Vulgate. He insisted that the Scriptures are the supreme authority, that priests and bishops should be familiar with them, and that even unlettered and simple men can understand them and should study them. To make the Bible accessible to the rank and file he had it put into the English vernacular of his day. Before Wyclif undertook the translation, the Psalms had been given an English form either by Richard Rolle or some one inspired by him. There had been other translations of parts of the Bible. But it was due to Wyclif and those kindled by him that the entire Bible was made available in the English of the fourteenth century. The first attempt was in somewhat crabbed style, but later revisions were more idiomatic.

To give wide currency to the Gospel as he understood it Wyclif sent out travelling preachers. They had no uniform designation. He called them "poor priests," "poor priests that preach," "unlearned and simple" men, "faithful and poor priests," "true priests," or, simply, "itinerant preachers." They were to preach wherever they could gain a hearing—on the roads, in village greens and churchyards, or in churches. They were to be garbed in russet robes of undressed cloth reaching to their feet, and were to go, long staff in hand, without sandals or purse, taking such food and shelter as were offered them, and teaching in the vernacular the Lord's Prayer, the Ten Commandments, and the seven deadly sins. They might have with them a few portions of the translation of the Bible, especially the Gospels and some of the Epistles. For their guidance Wyclif wrote tracts and sermon outlines and prepared paraphrases of the Bible. In his own sermons, in contrast with much of the preaching of the day which dwelt upon miracles, fables, and the lives of the saints, he stressed the exposition of passages from the Bible. That was what he desired of his preachers. He wished them to continue the itinerant life and never to settle down. At the outset some of them were university graduates and from families of some social standing. As time passed they were drawn almost exclusively from the poor.

Wyclif's writings and the work of his itinerant preachers won a large number of adherents. They were known as Lollards. Some were attracted by the attacks on the abuses of the time, for Wyclif and his preachers were outspoken in their denunciation of the corruptions in the Church and of the clergy. Others were presumably drawn by the appeal of the Bible in the speech of every day. Among the Lollards or at least among those friendly to them, were members of the gentry who protected the preachers and enabled them to deliver their messages. Much of the popular poetry of the time reflected views which were in accord with those of Wyclif's preachers.

Persecution was inevitable, vigorous, and prolonged. The bishops could not ignore a widespread movement which cut at the roots of their power and denounced some of the accepted beliefs and practices of the Catholic Church. John of Gaunt, far from model in his morals, prided himself on his orthodoxy and was alienated by Wyclif's attack on transubstantiation. The itinerant preachers were accused of stirring up the Peasants Revolt of 1381. The charge was probably ill-founded. The insurrection was a protest against taxation and maladministration. It was a climax to unrest which had long been seething and which was symptomatic of the economic and social changes that were under way. To be sure, the unrest had religious aspects and in part religious sources. *Piers Plowman,* the contemporary allegory which pictured the evils of the day, voiced the current dissatisfaction and may have added to it. The "mad priest" John Ball had a more direct association with the revolt and preached that all goods should be held in common and the distinction erased between lord and serf. Wyclif's preachers seem not to have been among the social revolutionaries. However, many of the possessing classes, frightened by the revolt, held them responsible. Wyclif himself died in peace in 1384. The Lollard preachers had powerful friends. Yet in 1401 a strong act against heretics passed Parliament, in 1406 an anti-Lollard measure was enacted, and in 1407 the Archbishop of Canterbury gave vent to a series of blasts which were confirmed by a synod in London in 1409 and which condemned the doctrines of Wyclif and the unauthorized translation of the Bible and prohibited unlicensed preachers. There were some burnings of Lollards.

In the reign of Henry V (1413–1422) sweeping measures were taken. That king was vigorously anti-Lollard and a Lollard outbreak in which a knight, Sir John Oldcastle, was involved was ruthlessly suppressed. In 1415 the Council of Constance condemned Wyclif on 260 different counts, ordered his writings to be burned, and directed that his bones be exhumed and cast out of consecrated ground. In 1428, at Papal command, the remains of Wyclif were dug up and burned and the ashes were thrown into a nearby stream. Action against the Lollards continued, but Lollardy persisted and seems to have enjoyed something of a revival in the reign of Henry VII (1485–1509). Certainly there was continued persecution. Lollardy became one of the contributory sources of English Protestantism.

THE HUSSITE MOVEMENT

While measures against the Lollards were proceeding, in another land, Bohemia, the writings of Wyclif were reinforcing and helping to shape a revolt against the Catholic Church which was to be accompanied by far more bloodshed than was the attempted extirpation of their influence in England.

The second half of the fourteenth century witnessed a rising tide of reform in Bohemia. There many of the clergy were worldly and corrupt. There, too, preachers were denouncing the evils in the Church and society, were appealing to the Bible as the rule of life, and were demanding more frequent communion.

Of this reform movement John Hus (c.1373–1415) became the outstanding leader. He was of humble birth and death early deprived him of his father. He was reared by his mother and was encouraged by her in his struggles to obtain an education. He studied philosophy and theology at the University of Prague, then newly founded and one of the most famous in Europe. Not distinguished for brilliance and with only an average record as a student, he nevertheless took degrees, lectured on the Sentences of Peter Lombard, and by 1403, when he was at most in his early thirties and perhaps still younger, he was ordained to the priesthood. Eventually he was dean of the faculty of philosophy and rector of the University of Prague. He must have had charm and gifts of leadership so early to have risen to prominence. Moreover, not even his bitterest enemies seem to have been able to find anything amiss in his private life and one of his eminent critics spoke of his reputation for unblemished purity, a striking tribute in an age when that could not be said of many in high ecclesiastical position.

In 1402 Hus became rector and preacher in the chapel of the Holy Innocents of Bethlehem in Prague. In that post, by his eloquence and earnestness he attracted all classes, from the highest to the lowest, and speedily became one of the most influential men in the country. During Hus's boyhood the King of Bohemia, Charles IV, who also became Holy Roman Emperor, had made Prague a centre notable in architecture and letters. It was a time of national awakening and prosperity. Hus preached in both Latin and Czech and by his use of the latter stimulated a patriotism which was already growing. Yet he was not concerned so much with national feeling as he was to reach the populace in the speech of daily life. He denounced the evils in the Church, from parish priests to Pope, held that Christ and not Peter was the foundation on which God had founded the Church, and that, far from being inerrant, many Popes had been heretics. He was marked by high ethical purpose rather than radical theological speculation and wished moral reform rather than ecclesiastical revolution.

The reform movement of which Hus was the outstanding spokesman was given added stimulus by the writings of Wyclif. By the marriage of Richard II of England in 1382 to Anne of Luxemburg, sister of the King of Bohemia, a close connexion had been established between the two countries. Anne seems to have been a woman of high character and to have been interested in a purer religious life, for she is said to have brought with her to England copies of the Bible in Latin, German, and Czech, and so long as she lived to have exerted a moderating and wholesome influence upon her royal spouse who, only a few years after her restraining hand was removed by death, came to an inglorious end through his own folly. In Anne's day a number of Bohemians were students in Oxford. Since in 1383 the Archbishop of Canterbury, the high-born William Courtenay, great-grandson of Edward I, had succeeded in having vigorous action taken against the Lollards in that university, the controversy must have been prominent in student discussions. Whether through Oxford or other channels, the writings of Wyclif were being read in Prague at least as early as the fore part of the 1380's. Presumably Hus knew of them in his student days. Before he had attained fame as a preacher he had copied with his own hand some of Wyclif's writings. However, Hus was no blind reproducer of Wyclif. He differed from him on many points, generally in the direction of moderation and conservatism.

As was to be expected, opposition developed. Hus was popular with the masses and many of the aristocracy. The Queen made him her confessor and she and her ladies came to his preaching. Reform sentiments were embodied in popular songs. However, the clergy whose manner of life was being attacked were critical and the honest conservatives were disturbed. The situation was complicated by domestic political dissensions, divided loyalties in the Great Papal Schism, and the traditional Czech resentment against the Germans, prominent since the latter were in Bohemia and especially in Prague. In the German-Czech tension, in 1409 the Czechs were given control of the university and the German contingent, disgruntled, left the country. Hus was looked upon as a champion of the Czechs. His influence and that of Wyclif became dominant in the university. The Archbishop of Prague was antagonistic and obtained a decree from the first Pisan Pope ordering the surrender to the Archbishop of all Wyclif's writings for burning and what amounted to the silencing of Hus. Hus refused to comply, and that in spite of the burning (1410) of several scores of Wyclif's books, and on excommunication by the Archbishop he appealed to the new Pisan Pope, John XXIII. Yet he soon placed himself against that Pope by openly denouncing the crusade which the latter was invoking against the King of Naples and the indulgences which were being sold in Prague to raise funds for that venture. In taking this step Hus alienated the theological faculty of the university. John XXIII retaliated by putting Hus under stringent excommunication and issued an interdict against Prague. To relieve the situation, Hus left the city (1412). Yet he continued to preach from place to place and generally in the open air. Czech sentiment was with him.

Hus and the writings of Wyclif had by now attracted an attention which was not confined to Bohemia and England. They had become of European moment. Sigismund, who had a large part in making possible the Council of Constance, was much concerned, especially since he was a brother of the King of Bohemia. He urged Hus to present his case to that body. Hus complied and journeyed to Constance under letters of safe-conduct from Sigismund. There he was arrested and imprisoned, for he was under the ban of John XXIII. The Council of Constance formally condemned Wyclif and his writings, an action which made clear its attitude towards Hus. Hus was tried by the council on several counts, among them his alleged support of the teachings of Wyclif, and especially statements in his own works. One of these statements was the assertion that if a Pope, bishop, or prelate was in mortal sin he was not Pope, bishop, or prelate. To this Hus orally added kings. Hus declared that he was being accused of maintaining positions which he did not hold, that he was willing to be informed by the council of his errors, and that he was prepared to submit to its judgement, but only if by doing so he did not offend

God and his conscience. Here, it may be added, he took a position which was closely akin to that maintained by Luther a little over a century later and which was of the essence of Protestantism.

The issue was clearly joined. The council, insisting as a matter of principle on its supreme authority in the Church, could not dismiss Hus without compromising the basic convictions of its competence held by the leaders of the movement which had brought it into being. Hus was condemned. It may be added that both John Gerson and Peter d'Ailly were against him and that d'Ailly had a leading part in the proceedings. In a formal meeting of the council the charges against Hus were repeated, and the prisoner, wasted by prolonged imprisonment, illness, and sleeplessness, still protesting his innocence and refusing to abjure his alleged errors, was silenced, degraded from the priesthood, and turned over to the secular arm. He was thereupon (July 6, 1415) burned at the stake. His last audible words were said to have been: "Lord, into thy hands I commend my spirit."

The burning of Hus did not end the movement of which he had been the leader. Indeed, it furthered it. Hus became a national hero. While he was in prison in Constance some of his followers began giving the cup in the communion to the laity. Hus approved. In Bohemia those who held to Wyclif and Hus soon fell into two camps. One, aristocratic, known as the Utraquists because in the communion they gave both the bread and the wine to the laity, wished the free preaching of the Gospel and a moral clergy and stood against only those practices of the Catholic Church which they regarded as forbidden by the Bible. The other, the Taborites, who took their name from their chief fortress and who were led by a blind general, Ziska, were from the humbler ranks of society and went on the principle of rejecting everything for which they could not find express warrant in the "law of God" as set forth in the Bible. The Utraquists and the Taborites could not agree but for a time united against the crusading armies which were sent against them. The Utraquists administered an overwhelming defeat to the Taborites in the decisive battle of Lipan (1434). They won from the Council of Basel certain concessions (1436), among them the use of the cup for the laity, and in theory were restored to the communion of the Catholic Church. Although Pope Pius II declared that agreement to be illegal, the Bohemian Parliament gave them full equality with the Catholics.

Another group, the *Unitas Fratrum,* or the Bohemian Brethren, appeared about the middle of the fifteenth century and seem to have been made up of elements from the Utraquists, Taborites, and Waldensees. We are to meet them again, especially as spiritual ancestors of the Moravians.

Some Other Efforts at Reform

The movements which centered about Wyclif and Hus were not the only ones in Northern Europe which, in seeking for a purer expression of the Christian faith, were either cast out by the Catholic Church or were on the verge of heresy.

John Pupper of Goch (1400–1475), a native of the Low Countries, held that "only the Bible has irrefragable authority," and that the Church and even the fathers of the Church are subject to error and are of value only in so far as they are in conformity with the Scriptures. He had had a close connexion with the Brethren of the Common Life, was a priest, and for forty years was rector and confessor of a house of canonesses in Mechlin who followed the rule of Augustine. Deeply religious, he emphasized the love of God. Influenced by Augustine, he stressed grace in salvation. He opposed legalism and Pelagianism and emphasized the inner disposition of the soul and what seemed to him to be true Christian liberty. He appears never to have run afoul of the ecclesiastical authorities, perhaps because his quiet, contemplative manner of life kept him out of the public eye.

Far otherwise was the course of his friend, John of Wesel (c.1410–1481). A graduate of the University of Erfurt, a teacher in that institution, and later a distinguished preacher at Mainz and Worms, John of Wesel held as fundamental the conviction that he should not say or write anything contrary to what is contained in the Bible. He challenged the basis on which Papal indulgences were issued, declaring that while the Pope could absolve from the punishments imposed by man or positive law, he could not release any one from penalties inflicted by God for sin. He also challenged the accepted belief in the treasury of the Church and said that if the saints had acquired merit, it could be distributed only by God. He boldly asserted that no one has the authority to grant an indulgence. He held that the grace of God raises a sinner from his fall and that no reason exists for the mediation of the Church. Late in life he was haled before the Inquisition. He recanted, but was condemned to imprisonment in a monastery and to have his books burned.

A slightly younger contemporary of these two, John Wessel or Wessel Gansvoort (c.1420–1489), a native of Groningen, had part of his early training with the Brethren of the Common Life, was much impressed with *The Imitation of Christ,* and came to know Thomas à Kempis. Eager for learning, he travelled much in Western Europe, knew Paris and Rome, but seldom remained long in one place and did not tie himself by any continuing bonds. He was profoundly influenced by Plato and wrote extensively on theology. An earnest seeker for truth, in his mature years he was afflicted by doubts, but

eventually had them resolved and declared that he knew nothing but Jesus Christ and him crucified. He held that, being inspired by the Holy Spirit, the Bible is the final authority in matters of faith. To him the Church was the communion of saints. He denied that the sacraments are of themselves effectual means of grace, and declared that the infusion of love in the heart is true baptism and that the priest is only a minister of God and can contribute nothing to the power of the sacrament. He completely rejected indulgences. He held that all that Christ did and suffered was for the purpose of exciting and nourishing love and that in the Eucharist, although the physical eating is important, the spiritual eating is alone profitable.

A quite different manifestation of the ground swell which prepared the way for the great tide of the sixteenth century was the Flagellants. We have met them earlier in the Middle Ages. Shortly before 1350 they appeared again, probably first in Italy and as a result of the Black Death and of earthquakes. The uncertainty of life and the imminence of death, always marked in the Middle Ages and accentuated by disasters before which man seemed helpless, drove men and women to penitence. The Flagellants were characterized not only by scourgings but also by folk-songs on Christian themes and by brotherhoods which combined penance with works of mercy and care of the sick. They often demanded that their members be reconciled to their enemies. By 1349 Flagellants had spread, among other places, to the Low Countries, Bohemia, Poland, Denmark, and England. North of the Alps they developed into a kind of organization, sometimes called the Brotherhood of the Cross, with a distinctive white habit and a severe discipline which involved a public scourging twice a day. At least some of these northern Flagellants cast doubt on the necessity of the sacraments. They also are said to have taught that their penances would work the salvation of the world. In 1349 they were condemned by the Pope. Yet they broke out again from time to time in the fourteenth and fifteenth centuries. We hear of them in Provence in 1399 and in Germany as late as 1481.

Extremes Meet: Savonarola and Alexander VI

Near the close of the fifteenth century Florence was the scene of a contest in which the extremes met. The ground swell of surging life dashed itself against corrupt power entrenched in the Papacy and apparently was completely dissipated. The monastic ideal of the Middle Ages for a time captured one of the major cities of Europe, a chief centre of the Renaissance and humanism, but was soon frustrated by its impotence to transform society and succumbed to the utter worldliness of Rome. The outstanding figures in the unequal contest were Savonarola and Alexander VI.

Girolamo Savonarola (1452–1498) was born in Ferrara of a Paduan family. His father was quite undistinguished, but his mother was a woman of marked nobility of character and his paternal grandfather was a deeply religious and learned physician who was devoted to the poor. Girolamo was a bookish, serious lad who did not mix with his contemporaries and was early enamoured of religion and the writings of Thomas Aquinas. Although Ferrara was then, under the ducal family d'Este, a brilliant centre of the Renaissance, the young Savonarola was little affected by the new tide except to revolt against it. Disappointed in love, in his early twenties he fled to Bologna and joined the Dominicans. Sensitive and intense, he was deeply grieved by the corruption which he saw in the Church and in the monastery gave himself to fasting, prayer, and teaching the novices. Sent to Ferrara by his superiors to preach, he seems to have made little impression on his native city. A war drove him from Ferrara to Florence (1481) and he there entered the monastery of San Marco, a house of reformed Dominicans which had been rebuilt and equipped with a valuable library by Cosimo de' Medici the Elder, had been inspired by a remarkably saintly man, its founder, and had been decorated by Fra Angelico.

It was nearly ten years after he became a member of the San Marco community before Savonarola acquired fame as a preacher. He was heard in several cities where his superiors sent him and about 1491 he began to stir the multitudes in Florence. He had a burning conviction that God's judgement was soon to be visited on the earth and called his hearers to repentance before it should be too late. Crowds thronged to him and to accommodate them he began preaching in the cathedral. About 1493 he was chosen prior of San Marco and was appointed head of his province of the Dominicans. In these posts he furthered a stricter life which proved contagious in several houses of the order. Late in 1494, when grave losses in a war with France had thrown the Florentines into deep perplexity and had brought distrust of the leadership of the Medici, long dominant in the city, the voice of Savonarola pled for repentance in the face of what he declared to be divine punishment for the sins and frivolities of the citizens and may have prevented rioting and near-anarchy. After the Medici had been expelled from the city and after the French king had given up his occupation of the city and had departed with his cohorts, Savonarola was generally held to have been a true prophet, to have exerted some control of the king when he entered Florence, and to have induced him to depart. The king had a profound respect for him and heeded him at critical junctures. The friar, accordingly, was very popular. He had a large part in framing the form of government, a republic, which was adopted after the French left. He became the most influential personage in the city.

Although often voicing the conviction that he himself would come to a

violent death, Savonarola declared that the Church would be renovated after a period of scourging and that all unbelievers would be converted and the Gospel would triumph in the earth. He pled with the Florentines to accept Christ as their king. He urged Italy, Florence, the princes, and the prelates to repent and turn to Christ. He exhorted his hearers to give to the poor all beyond their barest needs. In a series of sermons during Lent in 1495 he called upon his fellow-citizens to live a godly life of union and concord and undertake a complete reformation of morals.

There followed a startling transformation of the life of the city. Women threw aside their finery and dressed plainly, bankers and tradesmen restored ill-gotten gains, there was much reading of the Bible and the works of Savonarola, churches were crowded, alms to the poor increased, and some scions of leading families and several mature men of outstanding ability entered San Marco as monks.

Savonarola inevitably made enemies. Some of them went to Rome and urged the Pope, Alexander VI, to act. In 1495 the latter courteously summoned the friar to the Holy See. Savonarola asked to be excused, pleading ill health and the urgent necessity of remaining in Florence if the reforms which had been begun were to be carried through. In October, 1495, the Pope commanded him to abstain from all preaching, whether in public or private. For a time the friar obeyed and gave himself to study. By personal persuasion he succeeded in 1496 in transforming the usually riotous carnival into a time of giving to the poor and of processions in which children marched through the streets singing hymns. In Lent, 1496, with Papal permission and at the invitation of the civic authorities, he returned to his pulpit. Later in the year Alexander VI attempted to curb him by putting the monastery of San Marco in a grouping of Dominican houses which would render it more directly subject to Rome. Savonarola defied the order.

Early in 1497 the influence of Savonarola in Florence was such that at the annual carnival season, indecent books and pictures and carnival masks and costumes were collected by bands of children and burned in a huge pyre in the main square to the sound of devotional hymns and denunciations of the carnival.

In Lent, 1497, the friar came out boldly against the evils in the Church and with thinly veiled allusions to the Pope. That Pontiff was all the more enraged because the republic in Florence which Savonarola was supporting was in alliance with France and against the league of Italian states of which the Pope was a member: the latter's enmity was as much on political as personal and religious grounds.

In May, 1497, Alexander VI launched a bull of excommunication against

Savonarola, on the ostensible ground of his disobedience of the Papal command to come to Rome and his blocking of the incorporation of San Marco in the new combination of Dominican houses ordered by the Pope. Savonarola again defied the Pope.

Savonarola was strong enough to make of the carnival season of 1498 another time of religious fervour with a public burning of "vanities."

However, the tide began to run against him. The Pope threatened Florence with an interdict and ordered the civic authorities either to silence the friar or send him to Rome for trial. Savonarola appealed to the sovereigns of Spain, France, England, Hungary, and Germany to call a general council of the Church and declared that Alexander VI was neither a true Pope nor a Christian. Yet, heeding the pleas of the civic authorities, he ceased preaching. Popular opinion began to swing away from him. A Franciscan publicly attacked Savonarola as a heretic, false prophet, and schismatic, and challenged him to prove his integrity by the ancient custom of ordeal by fire. In the discussions which followed, Savonarola finally agreed to the test. It was to be made by a representative Dominican and a Franciscan. But when a vast throng had assembled to witness it, the spectacle was delayed by a storm of rain and by disputes on procedure. The Franciscan ultimately slipped away and the disappointed crowd rioted against Savonarola and the Dominicans.

The city government, now in hostile hands, arrested Savonarola and tried him and two of his closest disciples, employing the familiar medieval device of torture. The trial was continued before two Papal commissioners who had their master's command to see that the friar died. Savonarola and the other two were condemned, hung, and their bodies burned (May 23, 1498) in the great piazza. Alexander VI had seemingly triumphed.

No large body of followers perpetuated the programme of Savonarola, as had the Lollards that of Wyclif and the Utraquists, Taborites, and the Bohemian Brethren that of Hus. The majority of Florentines returned to their old ways. Indeed, for a time there was a reaction and a distinct moral let down. Yet a faithful minority remembered and each year on the anniversary of the sorrowful event strewed flowers on the scene of the execution. Many individuals, moreover, were permanently changed. Among them were the painter Botticelli and the humanist Pico della Mirandola. Michaelangelo was a loyal admirer. While Florence did not heed the friar's exhortation permanently to accept Christ as king, and although his political activities quickly came to nought and a few years later the Medici were back in power, the memory of Savonarola's purposes, eloquence, and heroism did not die and he was honoured as one of Florence's great.

The Florence in which Savonarola rose to prominence illustrated, as in a kind of microcosm, the contrasts, contrasts which are so great as to constitute a paradox, between "the exceeding greatness of the power" of the Christian faith on the one hand and the palpably earthen vessels on the other. Here was one of the leading cities of the Europe of the fourteenth and fifteenth centuries. It was professedly Christian. In it were great wealth and extreme poverty. Its republican government had come under the control of the family of the Medici, and their expulsion and the attempts to restore republican methods were intimately associated with the career of Savonarola. Here had lived the great Christian poet of the Middle Ages, Dante. Here was the Platonic Academy, with its mixture of earnestly Christian and thinly veiled non-Christian humanism. Here were artists inspired by their Christian faith—Fra Angelico, Botticelli, and Michelangelo among them. In especially striking contrast were Savonarola and his younger Florentine contemporaries, Niccolò Machiavelli (1469–1527) and Francesco Guicciardini (1483–1540). Machiavelli, the hardheaded, experienced expert in government, a combination of crude immorality and obscenity, prodigious energy, and astute, almost cynical practicality, is often considered the father of modern political science and his name is synonymous with pure expediency. To be sure, he longed for the unification of weak and distracted Italy, did not ignore religion, and held private virtue to be essential to a healthy national life. Yet he would make religion ancillary to the purposes of the state and admired to the point of idolization Cæsar Borgia with his audacity, his skilful diplomacy quite unburdened with regard for the truth, and his resolute and ruthless use of cruelty and fraud. Guicciardini, who wrote what has been acclaimed the master history of Italy from 1494 to 1532, as a statesman sought to promote what he deemed his own interests with utter disregard for the principles and convictions to which he subscribed in theory.

This kind of contrast had been seen in earlier centuries and in later eras was to be marked and perhaps even accentuated. Indeed, one of the effects of Christianity appears to have been to heighten the contradictions in human society. By calling men to an ideal impossible of attainment within history and sensitizing men's consciences, it widens the gulf between those who give themselves to the ideal and those who either reject it outright or deny it in practice.

SUMMARY

In the century and a half between 1350 and 1500 all Western Europe was the scene of this contrast between the nominal acceptance but cynical and practical disregard of the Christian ideal on the one hand and on the other hand earnest efforts to bring men to it.

The nominal acceptance but actual denial of Christianity was striking in those institutions which the great dreamers of earlier ages had created and developed in the hope of bringing men to the Christian goal. With numerous exceptions, the hierarchy, from the parish clergy through the bishops and arch-bishops, and including the Papal curia and the Popes themselves, was corrupt. In much of Western Europe the structure which had been developed with the express purpose of serving the Christian community and lifting it towards the Christian standard had become a handicap rather than an aid. The Papacy especially, which many of the earlier reformers had strengthened in the hope that through it the entire Church would be purified and all society brought to conformity with the purpose of God in Christ, had become a scandal. For nearly two generations it retreated from its historic seat, and, in contrast with its claim to universality, fell under the control of one nation, the French. Then, in escaping from that thraldom, it was divided. When the schism was at last ended, the Papacy succumbed to the quite worldly side of the Renaissance and was mired down in the morass of Italian politics. The very machinery which the great dreamers had created to enable the Papacy to make their hopes for the Church a reality, by its weight and its temptation to an anti-Christian kind of power became a liability to the Christian cause. The general councils in which many believed they saw the remedy ended the Papal schism but failed to accomplish the cleansing of the Church.

Moreover, what to the far-seeing must have seemed fully as grave a menace, Western Europe was experiencing the rise of nation states under absolute monarchs, each of whom sought to control the Church and to make Chris-tianity subservient to his purposes. The battle between the Papacy and the Holy Roman Empire to prevent the secularization of the Church was now being waged on many fronts, some of them new. Not only was it going against the Church. It was also threatening the degree of Christian unity, limited though that was, which had been achieved through the Church of Rome.

The monastic movement which had come into being from the longing to lead the perfect Christian life had in most of its members become either list-less, humdrum, and comfortable routine or, among a minority, a handicap to morality and spiritual vision. Even the mendicant orders, which only four or five generations earlier had arisen from a great missionary passion to bring the masses of nominal Christians to a vital dedication to Christ and to win the non-Christian world, had almost ceased to reach out beyond the borders of Western Christendom and within that area had experienced a decline in morale.

It seemed that Western Europe, the scene of the most numerous and vigorous movements springing from the Christian faith in the great centuries between 950 and 1350, was being de-Christianized. The new forces of nationalism, a recrudescence of paganism through the Renaissance and humanism, and the obsession with wealth and secular power appeared to be stifling the manifestations of life which had been so encouraging to those who hoped that the Gospel was at last bringing order into the chaos which had followed the collapse of the Roman Empire and dreamed of it as moulding the emerging civilization of the region.

There was another side of the picture. Many movements were appearing, some of them revivals of earlier ones and others of them new, which were evidence of healthy vitality. Individuals were emerging, often in quite unexpected quarters, who were regarded as ideal exemplars of the Christian faith. In several regions the discipline of prayer and of devotion was taking new forms and was spreading. There were efforts to bring the monasteries and the mendicant orders back to their pristine purposes. Fresh forms of Christian communal living were emerging. Christianity was beginning to capture the new humanism. Here and there, notably in England and Bohemia, the new movements were unsubmissive to the existing ecclesiastical structure and were being expelled from it.

Two features of these expressions of vitality, of "the exceeding greatness of his power," are especially significant. One was that for the most part they were issuing from the grass-roots. Here and there, as in Spain, they were capturing the existing organization of the Church, but for the most part they did not begin with the upper levels of the hierarchy. As we have more than once remarked, they were a ground swell. They were an indication that Christianity had become, to no small degree, the conscious possession of the rank and file and not something imposed from above, as had been the fashion by which the nominal conversion of Western Europe had been accomplished.

A second feature, almost and perhaps quite as significant as the first, was one of geography. Within the areas which had been fully assimilated to Latin culture before the collapse of the Roman Empire and where conversion had taken place before the sixth century, the new movements tended to follow generally accepted patterns. That was true, for example, of Catherine of Siena, the reforms in which Ximénes led, the labours of Vincent Ferrer, and the Hieronymites. On the other hand, in regions which had not been so assimilated or where Latin culture had been erased, as in Britain, by the barbarian invasions, and among peoples where conversion had not come until after the sixth century, the movements tended to take on new forms. Some of these, among them the Friends of God, the Brethren of the Common Life, and such Christian humanists as Colet, Thomas More, and Erasmus, remained within the Roman Catholic Church. Others, notably the Lollards and those who had Hus as their outstanding figure, were so critical of that church and so refused submission to it that they were cast out by it.

Both of these facets were to take on special significance in the centuries which followed. The ground swell issuing from the rank and file of Christians was to come to flood tide. Within what had once been the Roman Empire that flood tide was for the most part to be contained within the Roman Catholic Church and was to purify it of some of its worst moral abuses. In great areas outside what had been the Roman Empire it was to break with the Roman Catholic Church and was to issue in one or another aspect of what is collectively known as Protestantism.

SELECTED BIBLIOGRAPHY

GENERAL WORKS

The Cambridge Modern History. Volume I, The Renaissance (Cambridge University Press, 1934, pp. xii, 724).

A. C. Flick, *The Decline of the Medieval Church* (New York, Alfred A. Knopf, 2 vols., 1930). It covers the fourteenth and fifteenth centuries. A large proportion of the space is devoted to the Avignon Papacy, the Great Schism, and the Conciliar Movement. It is good, but must be used with care.

P. Hughes, *A History of the Church. Volume Three, The Revolt against the Church: Aquinas to Luther* (New York, Sheed & Ward, 1947, pp. xvi, 556). By a Roman Catholic.

J. Huizinga, *The Waning of the Middle Ages. A Study of the Forms of Life, Thought and Art in France and the Netherlands in the XIVth and XVth Centuries* (London, Edward Arnold & Co., 1927, pp. viii, 328).

E. M. Hulme, *The Renaissance, the Protestant Revolution, and the Catholic Reformation in Continental Europe* (New York, Appleton-Century-Crofts, 1914, pp. 589). A useful summary.

J. Mackinnon, *The Origins of the Reformation* (New York, Longmans, Green and Co., 1939, pp. xi, 448). By an outstanding specialist.

THE GREAT SCHISM

G. J. Jordan, *The Inner History of the Great Western Schism. A Problem in Church Unity* (London, William & Norgate, 1930, pp. 216). Valuable for quotations from the sources.

C. Locke, *The Age of the Great Western Schism* (New York, Charles Scribner's Sons, 1900, pp. x, 314). A semi-popular treatment.

THE CONCILIAR MOVEMENT

E. F. Jacob, *Essays in the Conciliar Epoch* (Manchester University Press, 1943, pp. viii, 192). Carefully documented.

E. J. Kitts, *In the Days of the Councils. A Sketch of the Life and Times of Baldas-*

sare Cossa (*Afterward Pope John the Twenty-third*) (London, Constable & Co., 1908, pp. xxiv, 421). Carries the story through the Council of Pisa.

E. J. Kitts, *Pope John the Twenty-third and Master John Hus of Bohemia* (London, Constable & Co., 1910, pp. xxx, 446). Continues the story through the Council of Constance and the death of John XXIII.

THE DECLINE OF THE PAPACY

A. H. Mathew, *The Life and Times of Rodrigo Borgia Pope Alexander VI* (New York, Brentano's, 1912, pp. 413). Portrays the seamy side of the life of Alexander VI, but places that life in its setting.

L. Pastor, *The History of the Popes from the Close of the Middle Ages*, translated from the German by various scholars (St. Louis, B. Herder, and London, Kegan Paul, and Routledge and Kegan Paul, 36 vols., 1902–1950). The standard work by a Roman Catholic scholar, using the archives of the Vatican. Vols. I–VI deal with the period treated in this chapter.

P. de Roo, *Material for a History of Pope Alexander VI, His Relatives and His Time* (New York, The Universal Knowledge Foundation, 5 vols., 1924). Written with a strong bias in favour of Alexander VI.

MONASTIC LIFE

H. Bett, *Nicholas of Cusa* (London, Methuen & Co., 1932, pp. x, 210). A biography of one who was noted as monastic reformer, mystic, scholar, and cardinal.

G. G. Coulton, *Five Centuries of Religion. Volume IV. The Last Days of Medieval Monasticism* (Cambridge University Press, 1950, pp. xv, 833). By a distinguished specialist, based upon an extensive use of the sources.

THE STATE OF THE CLERGY

W. W. Capes, *The English Church in the Fourteenth and Fifteenth Centuries* (London, Macmillan & Co., 1900, pp. xi, 391). A useful handbook.

A. H. Thompson, *The English Clergy and Their Organization in the Later Middle Ages* (Oxford, The Clarendon Press, 1947, pp. xv, 327). With reference to the sources and extensive selections from them.

FOURTEENTH AND FIFTEENTH CENTURY MYSTICS IN GENERAL

P. Pourrat, *Christian Spirituality in the Middle Ages,* translated by S. P. Jacques (London, Burns, Oates & Washbourne, 1924, pp. xiii, 341). A standard survey, by a Roman Catholic.

CATHERINE OF SIENA

The Dialogue of the Seraphic Virgin Catherine of Siena Dictated by Her while in a State of Ecstasy, to Her Secretaries, and Completed in the Year of Our Lord 1370, translated . . . with an Introduction on the Study of Mysticism, by A. Thorold (London, Kegan Paul, Trench, Trübner & Co., 1896, pp. vi, 360).

Saint Catherine of Siena as Seen in Her Letters, translated and edited with an introduction by V. D. Scudder (London, J. M. Dent & Sons, 1927, pp. x, 352).

J. Jorgensen, *Saint Catherine of Siena,* translated from the Danish by I. Lund (New York, Longmans, Green & Co., 1938, pp. ix, 446). Well documented, with a Catholic imprimatur.

M. Roberts, *Saint Catherine of Siena and Her Times* (New York, G. P. Putnam's Sons, 1906, pp. viii, 300). A semi-popular account.

THE MYSTICISM OF THE LOW COUNTRIES AND GERMANY

E. F. Jacob, *Gerard Groote and the Beginnings of the "New Devotion" in the Low Countries (The Journal of Ecclesiastical History,* Vol. III, pp. 40–57).

R. M. Jones, *The Flowering of Mysticism. The Friends of God in the Fourteenth Century* (New York, The Macmillan Co., 1939, pp. 270). Carefully and sympathetically done.

S. Kettlewell, *Thomas à Kempis and the Brothers of the Common Life* (London, Kegan Paul, Trench, Trübner & Co., 2 vols., 1882). Carefully done. A standard work.

J. E. G. de Montmorency, *Thomas à Kempis, His Age and Book* (London, Methuen & Co., 1906, pp. xxiii, 312). Well done.

Nicholas of Cusa, *The Vision of God,* translated by E. G. Salter with an introduction by E. Underhill (London, J. M. Dent & Sons, 1928, pp. xxx, 130).

A. G. Seesholtz, *Friends of God. Practical Mystics of the Fourteenth Century* (Columbia University Press, pp. viii, 247). A careful, sympathetic study.

Theologia Germanica, translated from the German by S. Winkworth (London, Macmillan & Co., 1924, pp. lxxvii, 227).

Thomas à Kempis, *The New Devotion. Being the Lives of Gerard Groote, Florentius Radewin and Their Followers,* translated by J. P. Arthur (London, Kegan Paul, Trench, Trübner & Co., 1905, pp. xlvii, 266).

Thomas à Kempis, *The Imitation of Christ* (New York, E. P. Dutton & Co., 1910, pp. xx, 284). The *Everyman's Library* edition.

ENGLISH MYSTICS

T. W. Coleman, *English Mystics of the Fourteenth Century* (London, The Epworth Press, 1938, pp. 176). Semi-popular, with selections from the sources.

Walter Hilton, *The Scale of Perfection,* newly edited from manuscript sources, with an introduction by E. Underhill (London, John M. Watkins, 1923, pp. lxvi, 464).

Julian of Norwich, *Revelations of Divine Love,* edited by G. Warrack (London, Methuen & Co., 5th edition, 1914, pp. lxxviii, 208).

The Book of Margery Kempe, edited by S. B. Meech, prefatory note by H. E. Allen, notes and appendices by S. B. Meech and H. E. Allen (Oxford University Press, 1940, pp. lxviii, 441).

CATHERINE OF GENOA

F. von Hügel, *The Mystical Element of Religion as Studied in Saint Catherine of Genoa and Her Friends* (London, J. M. Dent & Sons, 2 vols., 1923). A thoughtful, scholarly study.

PREACHING

G. R. Owst, *Literature and Pulpit in Medieval England* (Cambridge University Press, 1933, pp. xxiv, 616). Based upon an extensive examination of the sources.

G. R. Owst, *Preaching in Medieval England. An Introduction to Sermon Manuscripts of the Period c.1350–1450* (Cambridge University Press, 1926, pp. xviii, 381). Extensive use of the sources and numerous quotations from them.

THE BEGINNINGS OF SPANISH REFORM AND THE SPANISH INQUISITION

von Hefele, *The Life of Cardinal Ximenez,* translated from the German by Dalton (London, Catholic Publishing & Bookselling Company, 1860, pp. lvi, 581). A standard older work by a Roman Catholic scholar.

T. Hope, *Torquemada, Scourge of the Jews, A Biography* (London, George Allen & Unwin, 1939, pp. 245). Popularly written.

H. C. Lea, *A History of the Inquisition of Spain* (New York, The Macmillan Co., 4 vols., 1906, 1907). A standard work of which the first volume is on this period.

R. Merton, *Cardinal Ximénes and the Making of Spain* (London, Kegan Paul, Trench, Trübner & Co., 1934, pp. xiv, 279). Carefully written with an attempt at objectivity.

R. Sabatini, *Torquemada and the Spanish Inquisition. A History* (London, Stanley Paul & Co., 6th edition, 1927, pp. 404). Vividly written.

CHRISTIAN HUMANISM

F. Seebohm, *The Oxford Reformers of 1498: Being a History of the Fellow-Work of John Colet, Erasmus, and Thomas More* (London, Longmans, Green & Co., 1867, pp. xii, 440). A standard older work.

ERASMUS

P. S. Allen, *The Age of Erasmus* (Oxford, The Clarendon Press, 1914, pp. 303). A series of lectures.

P. S. Allen, *Erasmus: Lectures and Wayfaring Sketches* (Oxford, The Clarendon Press, 1934, pp. xii, 216). For a general audience.

E. Emerton, *Desiderius Erasmus of Rotterdam* (New York, G. P. Putnam's Sons, 1900, pp. xxvi, 469). A standard account.

D. Erasmus, *The Education of a Christian Prince,* translated with an introduction by L. K. Born (Columbia University Press, 1936, pp. viii, 277).

D. Erasmus, *Enchiridion Militis Christiani . . . The Manual of the Christian Knight* (London, Methuen & Co., 1905, pp. 287).

D. Erasmus, *The Complaint of Peace, Translated from the Querela Pacis* (A.D. *1521*) (Chicago, Open Court Publishing Co., 1917, pp. 80).

D. Erasmus, *The Praise of Folly,* translated by L. F. Dean (Chicago, Packard and Co., preface, 1946, pp. 152).

F. M. Nichols, *The Epistles of Erasmus from His Earliest Letters to His Fifty-third Year.* English translation (London, Longmans, Green & Co., 3 vols., 1901–1918).

P. Smith, *Erasmus. A Study of His Life, Ideals, and Place in History* (New York, Harper & Brothers, 1923, pp. xiii, 479). A semi-popular study by a specialist on the period.

WYCLIF AND THE LOLLARDS

H. M. Smith, *Pre-Reformation England* (London, Macmillan & Co., 1938, pp. xiii, 556). An excellent survey of the situation at the beginning of the sixteenth century. It includes a sketch of the Lollards.

G. M. Trevelyan, *England in the Age of Wycliffe* (New York, Longmans, Green & Co., 1929—preface 1899—pp. xvi, 380). A well-written standard work.

H. B. Workman, *John Wyclif, a Study of the English Medieval Church* (Oxford, The Clarendon Press, 2 vols., 1926). A standard account, very well done.

HUS

The Letters of John Hus, with introduction and explanatory notes by H. B. Workman and R. M. Pope (London, Hodder & Stoughton, 1904, pp. xxxi, 286).

The Count Lützow, *The Life and Times of Master John Hus* (London, J. M. Dent & Co., 1919, pp. viii, 398). An excellent account based on the sources.

D. S. Schaff, *John Huss—His Life, Teachings and Death—after Five Hundred Years* (New York, Charles Scribner's Sons, 1915, pp. xv, 349). Carefully done, distinctly favourable to Hus.

M. Spinka, *John Hus and the Czech Reform* (The University of Chicago Press, 1941, pp. 81). An excellent study, stressing the ways in which Hus differed from Wyclif and his continuing, largely independently of Wyclif, an indigenous movement which wished the moral reform of the Church.

OTHER REFORMERS

C. Ullman, *Reformers before the Reformation, Principally in Germany and the Netherlands,* translated by R. Menzies (Edinburgh, T. & T. Clark, 2 vols., 1885). An excellent account.

SAVONAROLA AND MACHIAVELLI

P. Misciatelli, *Savonarola,* translated by M. Peter-Roberts (New York, Appleton-Century-Crofts, 1930, pp. xi, 274). A popular account by a warm admirer of Savonarola.

R. Roeder, *Savonarola. A Study in Conscience* (New York, Brentano's, 1930, pp. 307). A well-written account for the general reader.

P. Villari, *Life and Times of Girolamo Savonarola,* translated by L. Villari (New York, Charles Scribner's Sons, first edition 1888, many times reprinted, pp. xlvii, 792).

P. Villari, *The Life and Times of Niccolò Machiavelli,* translated by L. Villari (London, Ernest Benn, first published 1891, many times reprinted, pp. xxiv, 510, 547). A standard account.

Chapter XXIX

RETROSPECT AND PROSPECT

At the middle of the fifteenth century the civilized world and with it Christianity were being ushered into a new age. The Mongol Empire, which for nearly a century had been ruling the heart-land of Eurasia, was breaking up. With its disappearance the caravan routes across Asia became more insecure and China all but closed her doors to the outside world. Near the end of the century a Mongol, Timur (Tamerlane), was laying waste much of Central and Western Asia. The Ottoman Turks were building a huge realm, in 1453 overwhelmed the Byzantine Empire and established their capital at Constantinople, and threatened to engulf part or all of Western Europe. In Western Europe, where Christianity now had its main stronghold, the medieval structure of society and its associated culture were beginning to pass.

These changes brought heavy geographical losses to Christianity and confronted it with grave challenges. The Christian minorities which on the eve of 1350 had been found across Asia either shrank or disappeared. By 1500 Christianity was scarcely even a memory in China and Central Asia; in India it survived, but only in small, encysted minorities; and in Western Asia, including what had been an early major centre of the faith, Asia Minor, the Christian communities declined. The headquarters of Greek Orthodox Christianity, Constantinople, was in the hands of Moslem rulers and Saint Sophia, the main cathedral of that wing of the faith, had been converted into a mosque. The eastern shores of the Mediterranean, where once had been the chief scenes of Christian thought and activity, were ruled by Moslems. Of the five historic patriarchal sees of the Catholic Church, Jerusalem, Antioch, Alexandria, Constantinople, and Rome, all but the last were now under the Crescent.

Even in Western Europe, where those who professed the Christian faith remained politically in the ascendant, the threat was sobering. The institutions which had been erected as bulwarks of the faith—monasteries, the clergy, and especially the Papacy—were honeycombed with corruption. The populations remained nominally Christian, but in Italy, where was the administrative centre of the Western wing of the Catholic Church, Christian morality was widely flaunted and the intellectual currents, associated as they were with a revived admiration of pre-Christian art and literature, appeared to be setting in against the faith. The emerging nation-states were threatening even the imperfect unity in the Christian community which had been attained under the Holy Roman Empire and the Church of Rome. The Church had been associated with feudalism and a predominantly rural culture. Feudalism was passing and cities were growing. It was not at all clear that the Church could adjust itself to the new order and win it. It might slowly fade with the disappearance of the kind of society which it had earlier penetrated and with which it had become identified. Moreover, the tenuous bonds which held together the Western and Eastern branches of the Catholic Church had at last been severed. Christian unity, never all-inclusive, suffered further disruption.

Yet the losses were not as great nor was the prospect as grim as they had been during the great recession between the end of the fifth and the middle of the tenth century. Although over most of Asia the Christian communities died out, east of Mesopotamia they had never been more than small minorities. In contrast with that earlier period when about half of what might be called Christendom became subject to Moslems and the churches in it slowly withered, after 1350 the main body of Christendom remained. While the territorial gains were not as extensive nor ultimately as significant as had been those between 500 and 950, some advances were registered, notably in Russia, Lithuania, and against the Moslems in Spain.

Even more important was the vitality displayed within the churches. The vigorous monastic movements in Russia were evidence that in that land the Greek Orthodox form of the faith was not only firmly rooted but was sending out fresh shoots. Although in Western Europe no theological activity appeared which for depth and originality could compare with that of the Middle Ages and no new monastic orders came into being which for numbers and the impression made on the region equalled such earlier movements as the Benedictines, Cluniacs, Cistercians, Franciscans, and Dominicans, the period was by no means sterile. Christian mysticism was widespread and was probably more varied and perhaps richer than at any previous time. There were numerous attempts, some of them successful, at monastic reform. New communities, notably the Brethren of the Common Life and the Hieronymites, came into being. In Spain a wave of reform spread to much of the Church and Vincent Ferrer brought his fervour to thousands in that land, France, and Italy. In several countries preaching seems to have increased and to have reached more people than before. Humanism was being captured by the Christian faith. Wyclif and the Lollards, Hus and the Hussites were evidence that the faith was becoming the conscious property of thousands in England and Bohemia and was not being passively received from the South as had previously been the case. Catherine of Siena, Catherine of Genoa, and Savonarola were the most prominent among many who were proof that even in Italy, where Christian morality was widely flouted, the Christian faith was very much alive. In many places the Gospel was stirring the masses. A ground swell was appearing which in the sixteenth century was to become a flood tide. Under the impulse of that tide in the next two and a half centuries Christianity was to create new as well as to utilize old expressions and was to have a greater geographic expansion than it or any other religion had thus far displayed.

REFORM AND EXPANSION
A.D. 1500 — A.D. 1750

Chapter XXX

CHRISTIANITY FROM A.D. 1500 TO A.D. 1750: THE WORLD SETTING

Not far from 1500 Christianity found itself in a new and rapidly changing world which faced it with as great a challenge as it had thus far known. Challenge in the face of what seemed overwhelming odds was not a new experience. The most widely used symbol of the Christian faith was the cross and until Easter morn broke, the cross seemed to mean stark defeat and complete frustration. Even after Easter and Pentecost had nerved the disciples to go forward, they were a small and obscure minority confronted with hostile and powerful competitors. When the majority of the population of the Roman Empire had been won, though to a largely uncomprehending and superficial allegiance, that realm was disintegrating. The slow death of the culture and state with which it had come to be identified and the accompanying incursions of non-Christian peoples, some of them bearers of a new and aggressive faith, Islam, meant for Christianity the strong possibility of extinction. Christianity survived, and, winning some of the most unpromising of the invaders, those from Northern Europe, became a major factor in the emergence of a new civilization, that of Western Europe, and was carried clear across the largest of the continental land masses, Eurasia. Then, in the fourteenth and fifteenth centuries, political changes extinguished Christianity in most of Asia and confined it almost entirely to Europe. In South-eastern Europe a resurgent Islam brought Christian communities under Moslem rulers and menaced the independence of Western Europe. In Western Europe the stage of civilization with which Christianity had been interwoven, seemingly inextricably, was passing and the ecclesiastical structure which Christians had developed was shot through and through with dry rot and inefficiency and appeared to be an anachronism. Yet vigorous life was making itself felt and was mounting. Past experience gave ground for hope that, far from perishing, Christianity would rise to the challenge of the new age and go forward. However, partly because

689

the challenge differed substantially from the earlier ones, precedent was no infallible proof that it would be met.

In the sixteenth century the situation which confronted Christianity was compounded of several elements, some of them with parallels in the past, but others of them quite new. The chief old ones were the continuation of the Turkish invasion and the passing in Western Europe of what was known as the culture of the Middle Ages. For over a thousand years Christianity had been menaced by the invasions of non-Christian peoples and for over eight hundred years the most serious of these had been by peoples who held to Islam. Grave though it was, the advance of the Turks did not constitute a completely fresh problem. In the disintegration of a culture with which it had been closely associated Christianity was faced by what had become a familiar phenomenon. That had been seen in connexion with the decay of the Roman Empire and the Græco-Roman world. Moreover, the main features of the new order which was succeeding the medieval structure of Western Europe had begun to appear before the sixteenth century and had been among the causes of the recession of the fourteenth and fifteenth centuries.

Although in broad general terms the chief aspects of the new stage of Western civilization had become familiar by the beginning of the sixteenth century, some of the developments of these aspects were novel. Moreover, they were of prime importance for Europe and so for Christianity.

One group of developments came in connexion with the emergence of nationalism. We have seen that beginning at least as early as the fourteenth century nation states were beginning to threaten the partial unity which had been achieved in Western Europe under the Papacy and the Holy Roman Empire. In the sixteenth, seventeenth, and eighteenth centuries nationalism and nation states, the latter under absolute monarchs, became the prevailing pattern in the European political scene and affected other facets, including the religious, of the life of the area. National consciousness and particularism were augmented by the rise of literatures in the vernacular and the decline in the use of Latin as the language common to the educated.

In the sixteenth century outstanding among the nation states was Spain. Portugal, England, France, Sweden, and Russia were also prominent. Nationalism was present in Germany and Italy, but it was not sufficiently potent to bring about the political unification of these countries. Instead, each was divided into many units and remained so until the nineteenth century and was a prey to its more nearly consolidated neighbours. By the seventeenth century Spain and Portugal were waning and France was forging to the fore. Under Louis XIV, who came to the throne in 1643, assumed full charge in 1661, and reigned until his death in 1715, France was the strongest power in Western

Europe. Austria under the Hapsburgs was also prominent, partly as the heir of whatever prestige still clung to the fading ghost of the Holy Roman Empire. England was growing in importance, but chiefly on the seas and in colonial possessions. In the seventeenth century Russia recovered from her "Time of Trouble" and under the leadership of the Romanovs, one of whom, Michael, was elected Tsar in 1613, began to expand its territories. Late in the seventeenth century Peter the Great ascended the throne and not only enhanced the authority of the Tsar and continued the expansion of the realm, but also gave the land a Western European orientation. In the seventeenth and eighteenth centuries the Hohenzollerns made their possessions, under the name of Brandenburg and then of Prussia, a major Western European power.

In each of these states, and also in several of lesser might, the monarchs sought, with varying degrees of success, to control the Church. In some this entailed separation from Rome. In others communion with Rome was maintained but the administrative functions of the Papacy were markedly reduced. In all it meant an attempt to harness Christianity to the state and to render it ancillary to government and the purposes of the monarch. This, it is almost needless to say, was a major threat, for if successful it would pervert or stifle the true genius of the Gospel. Moreover, the nation states were chronically at war with one another and war was destructive not only of the unity among its adherents which was the essence of Christianity, but also of many of the other values for which the faith stood. Could the "power" overcome these handicaps and make itself effective in this new age?

Another group of developments which followed the passing of Western Europe from its Middle Ages into a fresh stage of culture was the striking enlargement of the world of the men of that area. In a very real sense this was an outgrowth of the Renaissance and humanism. It arose in connexion with that confidence of man in his powers which characterized these movements. Like them, it seems to have been in some degree an outgrowth of the trust in the orderliness and dependability of nature and the discipline given the spirit and mind of Western Europeans through the Christian faith.

The amazing development of scientific theory and method and through it the extension of knowledge, chiefly of the physical universe, can here be only high-lighted. Gradually there spread the realization, associated with the name of the Polish cathedral canon, canon lawyer, and physician, Koppernigk (1473–1543), better known by its Latinized form, Copernicus, that the earth is not the centre of the universe, but, with other planets, revolves around the sun. Kepler (1571–1630), trained for the Christian ministry, turned reluctantly to astronomy and, accepting the Copernican view of the solar system, did much to ascertain the orbits of the planets and contributed significantly to mathematics, including infinitesimal mathematics. Not far from the same time Galileo Galilei (1564–1642), educated at first in a monastery, eventually made major contributions to physical science in the discovery of the isochronism of the pendulum, the hydrostatic balance, the first principles of dynamics, and the fact that the path of a projectile is a parabola. He acquired notoriety by his pioneer use of the telescope in astronomy and his espousal of the Copernican theory. Francis Bacon (1561–1626), a contemporary of Kepler and Galileo, did much to shape the procedures of later natural science by stressing the importance of the observation of facts as the basis for conclusions.

A little later Thomas Hobbes (1588–1679), son of an Anglican clergyman, an Oxford graduate, a warm admirer of Galileo, and an amanuensis of Bacon, while outwardly conforming to the Church of England, revolted against scholastic philosophy. He was deeply interested in mathematics and physical science, but made no major contribution to them. Yet his philosophy tended to base knowledge upon what we learn through natural science. Popularly regarded as an atheist, he held that man can form no idea of God and that the state must decide religious issues. He stimulated thought on ethics and the study of society and government.

The somewhat younger Descartes (1596–1650), a devout Roman Catholic, in his intellectual processes methodically doubted everything. To him doubt entailed thought and thought implied a thinker. Accordingly he arrived at his basic conviction, *Cogito, ergo sum*—"I think, therefore I am." Beginning on that foundation, he argued for the existence of God as the supremely perfect Being. Contending that God would not deceive the beings whom He created, he held that our senses give us true insights into the world about us. His method and basic principles had a profound effect upon later Western philosophy. He was also a mathematician of note and was a pioneer in analytical and algebraic geometry. Slightly later than Descartes was John Locke (1632–1704). He regarded himself a Christian, but was the founder of English empiricism. His *Essay on the Human Understanding* was influential in stimulating thought and discussion on the certainty and adequacy of human knowledge and his *Treatises on Government* were important in political science.

Isaac Newton (1642–1727), deeply religious, made major contributions in mathematics, in his formulation of the "law" of gravitation, and in his "laws" of motion. Newton's contemporary, Leibnitz (1646–1716), philosopher and mathematician, elaborated differential calculus, a field in which Newton also claimed to have been an originator. Pascal (1623–1662), older than either Newton or Leibnitz but living on into their youth, will appear later in our pages because of his earnest Christian faith. A distinguished and original mathematician, he markedly furthered the development of calculus and, partly through novel experimentation, was one of the founders of hydrodynamics.

Through these and others man's horizons were enormously enlarged. The knowledge so acquired and the thought so formulated were spread by the growing use of the printing press. On many the effect was intoxicating and man seemed competent to achieve full understanding of the unimaginably vast universe in which he found himself and to bend that knowledge to his own use.

This growth of science and through it man's knowledge and mastery of his physical environment, then only in their incipient stages, were to attain colossal dimensions in the nineteenth and twentieth centuries. Although they were to no small degree the outgrowth of the Christian faith and were in large part the work of devout Christians, they brought a major threat to Christianity. The threat was that men might regard Christianity as untenable or irrelevant— untenable because it appeared to be contrary to reason or unsupported by it, and irrelevant because what men esteemed as the chief goods, namely, food, clothing, shelter, knowledge, and æsthetic enjoyment, were, so they thought, to be acquired through other channels.

Here was not only threat, but also challenge. Could Christians bring all of these new tools to the service of their faith? Could they, in seeking "first the kingdom of God and His righteousness," render the expanding knowledge and the material wealth which came through them ancillary to the "kingdom of God" and contributory to the welfare of man as the Gospel set it forth?

Closely connected with the expanding vistas into the universe which characterized the new age into which the major part of "Christendom" was entering were breath-taking geographic discoveries and conquests by peoples bearing the Christian name. The Americas were disclosed to Europeans and in part reduced to subjection. The coasts of Africa were traversed, the Philippines were conquered, and trading posts were established on the southern and eastern shores of Asia and in the East Indies. The Russians moved across northern Asia to the Pacific. Colonial empires were carved out by European peoples. The largest of these were held by Spain, Portugal, Russia, and, in the latter part of the period, by England, France, and the Netherlands. Never before had so much of the earth's surface been penetrated and controlled by any one group of mankind.

Here again a major contributory factor was the Christian faith. One of the declared motives of Columbus was the conversion of the peoples whom he might discover and he recorded that it was his faith in God which enabled him to persevere on his first trip across the Atlantic when his men would have turned back. Prince Henry the Navigator, who was the directing mind and will of expeditions which after his death carried the Portuguese around the

Cape of Good Hope to India, was an ardently religious man, Grand Master of the Order of Christ, who had a passion for the spread of the Christian faith as well as a desire for trade and allies against the hereditary foe, the Moslem. Magellan, who led the first expedition to circumnavigate the globe, had a marked zeal for propagating Christianity.

As in the growth of science, here were both threat and challenge. Here was threat because the professed Christians who carried through the explorations, commerce, and settlements were tempted to succumb to the lure of wealth and to exploit for their selfish ends the peoples with whom they came in contact. Indeed, most of them were obsessed with the passion for gain and brought in thrall many of the native peoples. The African slave trade was stimulated by the demand for cheap labour for the mines and plantations of the New World. It inflicted untold suffering upon millions, both in Africa and the Americas, and brutalized the masters. Yet Christians were challenged to bring their faith to the vast regions which were opened by them and to devise measures to eliminate the exploitation of non-Europeans and make the coming of the European a blessing and not a curse.

Due partly to the geographic discoveries, commerce, wealth, and cities continued to grow in Western Europe. The guilds by which industry and commerce had been organized declined, chartered joint stock companies came into being as a growing means for the conduct of business, and capitalism increased. Larger vessels were built and bulkier cargoes were carried. The growth of commerce and cities brought into prominence the *bourgeoisie,* a distinct and class-conscious group. The *bourgeoisie* often combined with the king to curb the power of the landed nobility. They were increasingly influential, and their distinctive mentality and customs modified the total social structure. Could Christianity permeate the economic life and the kind of society which were emerging?

Political changes in the largest bodies of population made more difficult the access of the Christian faith to the majority of mankind. The Ottoman Empire, dominant throughout this period in the Balkans, Greece, much of Southern Russia, all of Western Asia, and most of the north shore of Africa, effectively blocked efforts to win the peoples of these areas. China was under the rule of dynasties, first the Ming and then the Manchus under the official name of Ch'ing, which disdained or feared foreigners and made extensive Christian missionary effort all but impossible. In India the sixteenth century witnessed the founding of a regime by the Moslem Moguls which eventually extended over much of the country and which was not favourable to Christian missions. By the early part of the seventeenth century the rulers of Japan closed their country against Europeans with the express purpose of preventing the growth of the Christian communities which missionaries had brought into existence on the islands. Almost all the thickly populated portions of Asia were more nearly sealed against the spread of Christianity than they had been in the centuries before 1350 and some were more nearly barred than they had been before the sixteenth century.

In spite of all the threats and the obstacles, in the sixteenth and succeeding centuries Christians had the opportunity to influence with their faith a larger proportion of the earth's surface than at any previous time. The Americas and Siberia were relatively empty and in them were begun settlements which in succeeding generations were to grow until populations of European stock were to be dominant numerically and culturally. Here was the possibility of building new communities which would be Christian. Moreover, in the nineteenth and twentieth centuries Occidental civilization was to be carried to all quarters of the globe and all peoples were to seek to adopt the fruits and with them the methods of the science of the Occident. In other words, a civilization in the shaping of which Christianity had had a large part was now beginning to spread across the planet. Of that spread as well as of that civilization Christianity was in part the responsible cause. Would Christianity be sufficiently vigorous to continue to mould that civilization? Would it have the vitality to hold the allegiance and deepen the understanding commitment of those who went from "Christendom" to these new outposts of the Occident and to win the peoples who were now brought in contact with it, many of them for the first time? Could it convey the Gospel so persuasively that all men would respond? Or, if not all men, would minorities in every people and nation accept the Christian faith, begin to display evidences of the working of "the exceeding greatness of his power," and become effective centres of contagion among their fellows?

At the outset of the sixteenth century the prospects for the triumphant course of Christianity in face of this opportunity appeared to be far from encouraging. Christians were more divided than they had been for centuries and therefore less able to act in consort to meet the challenge. The churches in the East, the Christian communities nearest geographically to the vast aggregations of the civilized peoples of Asia who constituted the large majority of mankind, were subjects of the Moslems and were either dwindling or were on the defensive and only barely holding their own. In North-eastern Europe Russian Christianity had still to win many of the peoples and was only beginning to emerge from the Moslem Mongol yoke and to give evidence that it was possessed of a vigour which was not dependent upon the traditional connexion with Constantinople. In Western Europe the ecclesiastical structure of the Roman Catholic Church and the monasteries and orders from which heretofore had come most of the missionaries were, with striking exceptions, at a low spiritual and moral ebb.

The informed and thoughtful Christian might well be appalled and discouraged as he looked into the near and far future. The faith which he professed had never succeeded in bringing fully to its standards any people or, indeed, any individual. Even Paul had confessed that he had not yet attained and across the centuries even those who were regarded as saints, when measured by "the high calling of God in Christ Jesus," quite obviously were far from perfect. Great losses had been recently experienced in Asia where minorities scattered across the reaches of that continent, potential centres for the spread of the faith in that area of the most populous regions and seemingly highest civilizations of mankind, had either disappeared or had become encysted, effectively estopped from expanding. In Western Europe, where was to be found the largest body of Christians, the leadership of the Church was predominantly selfish and the attempt at reform through general councils had failed. Now Christianity, especially the Christianity of Western Europe, was confronted with a new age and problems which were complicated by fresh movements, some of them indifferent or even covertly hostile to the faith, and by the beginnings of a geographic expansion which challenged Christians with new vistas and ever more complex situations while they seemed to be losing out at home. Always on the south-eastern horizon, moreover, was the aggressive Turk, champion of the religion which had wrested more territory from Christianity than had any other, with an empire stronger than any of the diminutive kingdoms which supported the Christian cause, and against which a hopelessly divided and chronically warring Europe was unable to unite. The problems confronting Christians were more complex and had assumed larger dimensions than ever before. They seemed quite to dwarf the feeble men who had to face them.

However, there was ground for encouragement. Indications of vitality in Christianity were by no means lacking. These were numerous and widespread, especially in Western Europe, the area in which the most striking developments were taking place, and from which most of the geographic explorations were being made and the majority of the colonial empires were being constructed. We noted them earlier (Chapter XXVIII) and saw that they were a kind of ground swell.

From this ground swell, as we have hinted, was to issue a high tide in the course of Christianity. Great awakenings were to emerge from the vitality inherent in the Christian faith. They were to transform hundreds of thousands of individual lives, place their stamp on civilization, and inspire a geographic expansion of the faith which for extent was unequalled in the previous history of mankind. To these awakenings we now turn.

Chapter XXXI

THE GREAT AWAKENINGS OF THE SIXTEENTH AND SEVENTEENTH CENTURIES: INCLUSIVE GENERALIZATIONS

The next tide of the pulsing life in Christianity reached its height in the sixteenth and seventeenth centuries. The dates 1500 and 1750 are somewhat arbitrary. As we have seen, the ground swell which issued in it began well before 1500. In places the tide had passed its flood before 1750 and in at least one country, England, was moving forward again before that peak. Yet these round numbers approximately mark respectively the beginning of the onward surge and the time when its retreat became marked.

In the main the tide had three major aspects, two of them in Western Europe and one in Russia. The two in Western Europe were closely connected and, indeed, were related although seemingly contradictory forms of the same movement. They were the Protestant Reformation and the Catholic Reformation. That in Russia was almost entirely independent of the other two.

It is significant that all three phases were in areas under ostensibly Christian governments and politically independent of non-Christian rulers. They were in territories which had not been submerged by the Moslem wave which had reached a fresh crest in the fourteenth and fifteenth centuries.

Moreover, they were in the regions from which the discoveries, growth in commerce, and colonial empire-building were to come during the same era. With some striking exceptions, they were to be most marked in the lands which were to lead in this advance and roughly synchronized with the peak in other forms of creative vigour in those countries. Thus Spain was the earliest to feel the full impact of the Catholic Reformation, and the height of the Spanish reformation coincided with the period when that realm was the foremost European state in military might and in territorial expansion in the New World and had her chief painters, authors, and scholars. So, too, in France the

Catholic Reformation reached its crest about the time when French hegemony was attained in Western Europe, in England the Protestant Reformation roughly paralleled advances in commerce, the beginnings of overseas colonization, and unprecedented activity in thought and literature, and in Russia the most stirring religious movements were when that country was recovering from its Time of Trouble, was experiencing the rise of the monarchy which was to rule it until the second decade of the twentieth century, and was pressing across Siberia to the Pacific. How far the connexion was causal we cannot know. That the different aspects of national life partly stimulated one another is certain. But to what extent if at all one was the cause of the others or to what degree all are traceable to a common outburst of vitality whose source we can only conjecture we cannot be sure.

We will first describe the course of events in Western Europe and from there move on to Russia, adding brief comments on the other Eastern Churches. We will then summarize the story of the spread of Christianity beyond the borders of Europe and say something of the effect of Christianity on the world of that day.

Before we embark upon an account of the Protestant Reformation and the Catholic Reformation there are inclusive generalizations and contrasts which are of major importance and which might escape us were we to allow ourselves to be submerged in details.

One of these we have already mentioned, but it is of such importance that we must again call attention to it. The Protestant and the Catholic Reformation were two phases of one movement. Both sought to cleanse the Church and to bring it to a closer approximation to the Christian ideal.

A second generalization, closely related to the first, is that they differed as to the fashion in which this was to be accomplished. The Catholic Reformation insisted that it be done within the existing patterns of the Roman Catholic Church. It strove for the thorough and basic moral transformation of both clergy and laity. It endeavoured to bring all Christians to a more intelligent appreciation of the essential Christian teachings, to foster the life of prayer, to encourage service to others, and to carry the Gospel to all men. However, in doing this it would avoid any changes in doctrine, and would merely make more precise what Catholics believed that the Church had always taught. It saw in communion with the Church of Rome and its bishop, the Pope, the assurance of the maintenance of the faith as given by Christ and transmitted through his apostles. While the rising nationalism markedly curtailed the administrative control of the Pope over the Roman Catholic Church, there was no separation from him on matters of dogma. The historic hierarchy was preserved and strengthened. The sacraments were treasured as they had been defined and administered through the Catholic Church of the West. Monasticism was prized as a road to the Christian ideal. Old monastic orders were recalled to their pristine standards and new ones came into being. Some of the latter assumed novel forms, but they were clearly in the monastic tradition.

In contrast, in varying degrees Protestants broke with the Church of Rome. All rejected the authority of the Pope, although some would have been willing to accept him as *primus inter pares* among the bishops. Many preserved the hierarchy without the Pope. Even more held to the Apostles' and Nicene Creeds. All esteemed the Scriptures authoritative, but none would concede to the Pope the right to give interpretations to the Scriptures which would be binding on all Christians. Almost all observed baptism and the Lord's Supper, but few or none kept all the seven sacraments. Although in the nineteenth century it was to be revived in the Anglican Communion, at the outset all rejected monasticism.

A third generalization is that the geographic line of demarcation between those who adhered respectively to the Protestant and Catholic Reformation in part coincided with the boundaries of the Roman Empire. In the main, with important exceptions which we are to note in a moment, those lands which had been assimilated to Latin culture before the sixth century remained loyal to the Church of Rome. This was true of Italy, Spain, Portugal, and to a large degree, although not so overwhelmingly, of France and Austria. In regions which had been on the borders of the Roman Empire, as in the Low Countries, the Rhine Valley, Switzerland, and the upper reaches of the Danube, and where conformity to Latin culture had not proceeded as far as in these other lands, both Protestantism and Roman Catholicism were represented. It seems significant that in the Low Countries the southern sections, where Latin culture had penetrated, remained Roman Catholic, while in the northern portions, where the rule of the Roman Empire had sat lightly if at all, Protestantism prevailed.

The island of Great Britain might appear not to bear out this generalization, for England had been within the Roman Empire for more than four centuries. But the exception appears to prove the rule. The region had never been thoroughly assimilated to Latin culture and the barbarian invasions of the fifth and subsequent centuries had fairly well erased whatever there was of it.

Other lands which seem to invalidate this identification of the post-Reformation Roman Catholic Church with Latin Europe immediately come to mind. Ireland, Poland, and Lithuania had never been within the Roman boundaries. Bohemia had been only on the border, and whatever of Latin culture it may have had presumably had disappeared in the welter of the Slav occupation. Yet all these countries came through the era of the Protestant Reformation predominantly Roman Catholic. In each, special reasons accounted for that fact. In Ireland, since the English overlords were Protestant, their Irish subjects clung to the Roman Catholic Church as a faith and institution which was distinctly their own, a badge and tie of their national particularism. In Poland contributory factors seem to have been opposition to the Germans, who on the Polish borders were Protestant; the efforts of the king, who, in his attempt to make his power effective against the nobility, among whom Protestantism was strong, found it to his advantage to espouse the Roman Catholic Church; skilful Papal diplomacy which, among other moves, was willing to concede to the king the authority to nominate the bishops; the zeal of the Jesuits; and weakening divisions among the Protestants. Then, too, Protestantism was not indigenous but imported and had not made much headway among the peasantry before other adverse factors rendered it impotent. Lithuania had close Polish ties and had so recently been brought into the Christian fold that the faith had not been deeply enough rooted to develop a reform movement. In the fore part of the seventeenth century Bohemia was predominantly Protestant, but the political vicissitudes of the Thirty Years' War and an alien Roman Catholic ruler reinforced by the missionary zeal of the Jesuits almost entirely eliminated Protestantism.

However, in none of these non-Latin lands did the Roman Catholic form of the faith display the creativity that it did in the regions that had been assimilated to Roman culture. In no one of them did there emerge a major new monastic order or a theological thinker of the first water. They accepted what was given them from Latin Europe.

In a sense the emergence of Protestantism was the reaction of Teutonic peoples against religious control from the Latin South. It was a revolt directed against the attempt of Rome to dominate those who had been won to the Christian faith in North-western Europe after the seventh century. These folk had accepted uncritically what had come to them. Now they were becoming self-conscious and were restive under the efforts of a corrupt Papacy to exploit them to its selfish advantage. The causes leading to the rebellion of North-western Europe against the Papacy were multiform and complex, but here seems to have been one of them.

It may be further evidence of the close relation of the division of Western Europe between the Church of Rome and Protestantism and the degree of assimilation to Latin culture, that the Holy Roman Empire, which professed to continue the tradition of the political empire which was once ruled from Rome, and which in practice had embraced Germany and Italy, thus including Latinized and non-Latinized peoples and which was already sadly weakened, was dealt a fatal blow by the divisions between Protestants and

Roman Catholics in Germany. It seems also significant that the rulers who claimed the title of Holy Roman Emperor, as they did until early in the nineteenth century, all maintained their communion with the Church of Rome. What continued to insist that it was the Catholic Church had become more and more clearly the Roman Catholic Church and increasingly was narrowed to Latin Europe and the overseas colonies of Latin Europe. Before the sixteenth century, except for small minorities, mostly Uniates, the ties which had held it to the non-Latinized Christians of the East had been severed. Now, again with the exception of minorities, those by which it had bound to it the Christians of the non-Latinized North-western portions of Europe were also broken.

We must note that Protestants did not think of themselves as innovators. They regarded themselves as reformers, as seeking to purge the Church of the corruptions which they ascribed to the Church of Rome and its Bishop and to return to the pure Christian faith.

A fourth generalization and one which also carries with it a contrast between the Protestant and the Catholic Reformation is that the first sprang chiefly from the lower social strata and the latter from the aristocracy. As we are to see, most of the outstanding creators of Protestantism were of peasant or very humble birth. Luther and Zwingli were born and reared in peasant families, although families which were modestly prosperous and not disposed to rebel against the existing order. Calvin was reared in an aristocratic environment, but his maternal grandfather was a manual labourer. Melanchthon was of artisan ancestry. Cranmer, who left a profound stamp upon the Church of England, was of humble farming stock. John Knox, who more than any other one man shaped the Protestantism of Scotland, was of lowly birth. In contrast, almost all the leaders of the Catholic Reformation were from the nobility. Ignatius Loyola, the founder of the Society of Jesus, the most influential of the new orders which arose out of the Catholic Reformation, was of the aristocracy. So were the creators of two others of the new orders, the Barnabites and Theatines. As we proceed with our story we shall note that this was true of many others.

To be sure, the class lines between the two wings of the reform movement were not tightly drawn. Many princes espoused the Protestant cause and used it for their own ends. One of the new groups in the Roman Catholic fold, the Capuchins, a fresh offshoot of the Franciscans, had as a founder one of very humble birth. In both Protestant and Roman Catholic lands, except for minorities, all classes held to the official faith. Yet in the main the pioneers of Protestantism were of humble origin, while most of the leaders in the Catholic Reformation were from the aristocracy. This may be because the aristocracy is usually more conservative and with some rebellious exceptions holds to the order in which it has been reared and by which it has profited, while the revolutionaries are generally from the groups which do not have so strong a stake in the preservation of the existing structure of society.

As we move on to the story of the great awakening in Western Europe we will deal first with Protestantism. This is not because it began first, for, as we have seen, the initial waves of the Catholic reform had appeared in the fifteenth century. It is, rather, because the Catholic Reformation was in part the Counter Reformation, directed consciously against the Protestants. It can, therefore, be better understood if the emergence and shaping of Protestantism be treated first.

In describing the rise of Protestantism we will take up separately each of the chief branches of that movement. First we will sketch the origins of Lutheranism, then of the Reformed Churches, next of the Anabaptists, then of the Socinians, and finally tell of the Church of England and the English Protestant bodies which dissented from it. We must remember, however, that in actuality these were largely contemporary with one another and with the Catholic Reformation. They interacted upon one another. The separation in our narrative is in part arbitrary and for the purposes of a somewhat artificial clarity.

SELECTED BIBLIOGRAPHY

R. H. Bainton, *The Reformation of the Sixteenth Century* (Boston, The Beacon Press, 1952, pp. xi, 276). An admirable popular summary by an outstanding specialist.

The Cambridge Modern History. Volume II, The Reformation (Cambridge University Press, 1903). By various authors.

P. Janelle, *The Catholic Reformation* (Milwaukee, The Bruce Publishing Co., 1949, pp. xiv, 397). A Roman Catholic summary.

B. J. Kidd, editor, *Documents Illustrative of the Continental Reformation* (Oxford, The Clarendon Press, 1911, pp. xix, 742). A useful collection.

T. M. Lindsay, *A History of the Reformation* (New York, Charles Scribner's Sons, 2 vols., 1906). A standard work.

P. Smith, *The Age of the Reformation* (New York, Henry Holt and Co., 1920, pp. xii, 861). An excellent summary of the Protestant and Catholic Reformations and the general European setting.

W. Walker, *The Reformation* (New York, Charles Scribner's Sons, 1901, pp. vii, 478). A well-written summary by a specialist.

J. P. Whitney, *The History of the Reformation* (London, Society for Promoting Christian Knowledge, new edition, 1940, pp. xv, 527). A posthumous revised edition of a standard work.

Chapter XXXII

LUTHER AND THE RISE AND SPREAD OF
LUTHERANISM

Martin Luther is usually, and rightly, regarded as the chief pioneer of what we call Protestantism. Protestantism was and is multiform. It had several sources. It sprang up almost simultaneously in several countries. Some of its earliest formulators were contemporaries. To it contributions came from such diverse factors as Augustine, the Bible, including especially the New Testament and notably Paul, nationalism, humanism, the rise of the *bourgeoisie* or middle class, the zeal for moral reform, mystical disciplines, and such dissenting pre-Reformation movements as the Lollards, the Hussites, and the Waldensees. Yet Luther was the first outstanding leader. He became the dominant distinctive personality in the origin and shaping of Lutheranism, one of the numerically largest forms of Protestantism, and his influence was more or less potent in almost all other expressions of that movement.

Luther as Boy and Student

Martin Luther was the product of the Roman Catholic Christianity of the Middle Ages. He was born in Eisleben, November 10, 1483, the eldest of seven children. His parents were of free self-respecting peasant stock and were thrifty and hard-working. By the time Martin reached adolescence his father had become modestly prosperous through leasing several iron pits and furnaces. The atmosphere of the home was religious, but probably no more so than that of many peasant homes of the Germany of that day. Nor does it seem to have differed from the conventional views and practices of that class. The young Martin grew up to fear God, to believe in the reality of heaven, hell, angels, saints, the Devil, and demons. He stood in terror of Christ as judge, but he also believed in the efficacy of the intercession of the Virgin Mary, the apostles, and the saints. He was taught the Lord's Prayer, the Ten Commandments, and the Creed. He conformed unquestioningly to the Catholic Church as he knew it. He learned the popular hymns and could cry on occasion to St. Anne, the patron saint of the miners. His manners and speech were those of the peasant and throughout his life continued to bear the marks of that rearing.

In his seventh year Luther was sent to school and he continued, in various centres, through the university. During part of the time he had for teachers some of the Brethren of the Common Life. He was sturdy physically, quick of mind, diligent, and made an excellent record. The subjects in which he was drilled were the customary ones of the late Middle Ages. Apparently he had little or no introduction to humanism. He went to the most famous of the German universities of the time, Erfurt, and was trained in scholasticism of the Ockhamist kind that was then current as the "modern" philosophy. As we have seen (Chapter XXI), Ockham had taught that the truths of Christianity could not be demonstrated by reason but must be accepted by faith on the authority of the Church and the Bible. How much this had to do with the emphasis of Luther upon justification by faith is not clear. Since he later differed from Ockham in theology, the influence, if present, may have been in his sub-conscious mind. In his student days Luther was companionable and enjoyed singing and playing the lute, but seems not to have shared in the vices which were common in student circles. All of his education was in towns where ecclesiastical influences were strong, attendance at mass and other services of the Church was customary, and religious processions, festivals, pilgrimages, relics, and the other outward expressions of Catholic life were part of the accepted environment. After completing his Master of Arts, to his father's satisfaction in May, 1505, when he was twenty-one, Luther began the study of law and was presumably headed for a successful career in that profession.

Luther Becomes a Monk

Luther had scarcely embarked on that course when, suddenly, in July, 1505, he pledged himself to enter a monastery. While he was out walking, on a sultry summer day, a bolt of lightning felled him and, in terror of death, he called on St. Anne for help and made a vow to become a monk. Although the step appears to have been quite unpremeditated, it arose from the beliefs in which he had been nurtured and from his temperament. He had been reared in the fear of God and in the vivid certainty of judgement, heaven, and hell. In his student days at Erfurt he had known fits of deep depression, *Anfechtungen* he called them. What psychological or physiological basis they may have had we can only conjecture. It was inevitable that the threat of imminent death from the thunder clap brought terror of death and hell. It was natural that as the way of escape he bethought him at once of the monastic life, for it was by this road that the beliefs in which he had been reared held that hell could surely be avoided and heaven could be securely won. Luther had no liking for the way of the monk. Moreover, his father was bitterly disappointed and was made intensely indignant by the sudden step, for it robbed him of one of his dearest hopes, an eminent career for this able son and the security which that son could give to his sire's old age. Yet Luther had made his vow, believed himself to have been divinely summoned to the uncongenial road, and carried through with his plighted course. Within less than a month from that eventful hour he had entered in Erfurt one of those Observant Augustinian houses which, as we have seen (Chapter XXVIII), had arisen from a reform movement of the previous century. Having embarked on a monastic career, Luther was not content with easy-going compromise, but chose an order which would enforce rigorous discipline and so assure him the salvation which was his compelling goal.

THE INNER STRUGGLE FOR ASSURANCE

The monastery did not at once bring to Luther the assurance for which he longed. Indeed, for several years he was a disappointed, tortured soul. The time of his novitiate appears to have been one of inner peace. He was becoming accustomed to the routine of the monastic life. At the command of Staupitz, the Vicar-General of the Saxon province of his order, he studied theology. In 1507 he was ordained priest and on May second of that year celebrated his first mass. That initial mass brought him terror, terror at the thought that he, a sinner, was presuming to address himself to the living, eternal, and true God. So nearly overcome was he that he could scarcely finish the prescribed ritual. Now followed months of anguish. He sought by the means set forth by the Church and the monastic tradition to make himself acceptable to God and to earn the salvation of his soul. He mortified his body. He fasted, sometimes for days on end and without a morsel of food. He gave himself to prayers and vigils beyond those required by the rule of his order. He went to confession, often daily and for hours at a time. Yet assurance of God's favour and inward peace did not come and the periods of depression were acute. He visited Rome on business for his order and what he saw there of the carelessness and corruption of the clergy distressed him.

Only gradually did the light break. In obedience to his superiors Luther went further with the study of theology. Here he at first applied himself to such masters as Ockham and d'Ailly, and especially to Gabriel Biel. Biel was a fifteenth century nominalist of the Ockhamist tradition, who was a leader of the Brethren of the Common Life and a loyal Catholic whose works were widely influential in the Germany of the day. Luther read Augustine, Bernard of Clairvaux, and Thomas Aquinas, and next to Augustine valued Gerson. The doctrine of predestination brought him much distress. He accepted it, but to him it made God seem capricious. This view of the unpredictability and arbitrariness of God was heightened by the theology in which he was trained, for it held that God is not bound by law but may do what He pleases, even though from man's standpoint that may seem to be unjust. At times Luther almost hated God. At other times there would be a rebound of mystical exaltation. His condition was not helped by the burdens placed on him by his order. He was given heavy administrative duties. He also was assigned to teach theology in the University of Wittenberg, newly founded (1502) by the Elector Frederick III, "the Wise," of Saxony. It was from Wittenberg that he took his degree of Doctor of Theology. It was in the course of his lecturing at Wittenberg that assurance began to come. Staupitz, his confessor and spiritual director, had instructed him to study for his degree and undertake preaching and teaching. Presumably he hoped that thus, by seeking to help others, Luther would be delivered from his introspection and would find the way to peace. Moreover, Staupitz gave sage counsel born of his own struggles which helped Luther to growing insight.

THE LIGHT BREAKS

Although light began to dawn by slow degrees as the prelude to dawn, Luther later looked back to a particular occasion when, like the sudden appearance of the sun, it broke upon him. He had been lecturing on the Psalms in the summer of 1513. In the autumn of 1515 he lectured on Paul's *Letter to the Romans*. In 1516–1517 his subject was the *Letter to the Galatians*. Somewhere along the way, at what precise hour we cannot tell, the phrase in the *Letter to the Romans* (1:17), "the just shall live by faith," brought him the illumination by which he was thereafter to live. "Justification by faith" became, through him, a distinctive principle of Protestantism.

Luther had been taught in his boyhood to believe that Christ is judge. Yet by his cry on the cross, "My God, my God, why hast thou forsaken me," Christ had shown that he, too, had experienced the anguish which Luther knew of separation from God and so had suffered with those whom he condemns. In the cross, moreover, Luther saw God reconciling the world to Himself, and as not only a consuming fire but also as burning that He may purge and heal. This, so Luther felt, was beyond reason, but is to be accepted by faith. Through faith the sinner knows Christ as his Saviour and sees into the fatherly heart of God. God is judge and condemns, but He longs to save the sinner and in Christ has provided a means by which that can be accomplished.

To Luther faith was not primarily intellectual assent, as it had been for most of the school men. It was, rather, the grateful whole-hearted response of one's entire being to the love of God in Christ: it was full confidence in God.

Indeed, Luther believed that justification was by faith *alone* (*sola fide*). In emphasizing *alone,* he was conscious that he was adding a word which did not appear in the Scriptures. Yet he believed that it was in accord with the Scriptures and that Ambrose and Augustine had said it before him. Experience and study had led him to the conviction that man could never earn God's favour by good works of any kind, whether these were morality or fidelity in the sacraments. He did not discount good works, but to his mind they do not earn justification but are the fruits of faith, the response in gratitude and love to the love of God in Christ which is appropriated by faith, evidences of the new birth which follows faith as described in the Scriptures.

Reading Anselm, especially his *Cur Deus Homo,* deepened Luther's conviction. Bernard of Clairvaux helped him and he found added illumination in the *Theologia Germanica* and the sermons of Tauler. To the end of his days Luther was to be troubled with *Anfechtungen,* but he had been given a basic insight which kept him from being powerless before them and he gradually learned how to deal with them.

Such relief had the light brought and so compelling was it that Luther could not but seek to transmit it to others. This he did in his lectures to students in the University of Wittenberg and in his sermons in the parish church. Because of his experience he rejected the scholastic nominalistic philosophy in which he had been nurtured. He was incredibly busy with preaching, preparing a commentary on the Psalms, overseeing eleven monasteries, and writing letters, but the inner illumination had come in the light of which he was to walk to the end of the journey.

THE OUTER CONFLICT BEGINS

Without intending it and to his surprise, Luther's religious pilgrimage and his releasing experience of justification by faith soon made him a person of importance in Germany and then in all Western Europe. In preaching he urged the moral reform of the Church, as did many another priest of the day. This, however, was comparatively innocuous. It was over the issue of indulgences that the spot-light was focused on him and that he became a centre of controversy. Through the controversy he was led, by steps which were inherent in his experience and convictions but which he did not anticipate, far beyond the demand for moral reform to a complete break with the Roman Catholic Church and to an attack upon basic teachings of that church which, to his mind, were a betrayal of the Gospel.

We have seen (Chapter XXII) the rise of the issuance of indulgences in the eleventh and twelfth centuries and the belief that through them the Pope could draw on the treasury of the saints to remit the temporal penalties for sin not only for the living but also for the souls in purgatory. As time had gone on, the use of indulgences had increased and their sale had become an important source of revenue to the Pope and to those whom he favoured. The question was brought home to Luther by the granting of indulgences by the Pope to those who viewed on a specified day a famous collection of relics which the Elector Frederick had assembled at Wittenberg, provided they also made the required contributions. In sermons in 1516, to the uneasiness of the Elector, Luther questioned the efficacy of indulgences and declared that the Pope had no power to release souls from purgatory.

In 1517 indulgences were being hawked through parts of Germany by clever promotional methods by one Tetzel, a Dominican. Tetzel later defended his claim that as soon as the money fell into the coffer a soul was released from purgatory. It was announced that the proceeds were to aid the building of the new St. Peter's which the Popes were erecting at Rome. Actually half of them were to go to pay a debt which Albert of Brandenburg, of the aristocratic Hohenzollern family, had acquired in purchasing the Archbishopric of Mainz, a post which made him the ranking ecclesiastic of Germany.

This aroused Luther and on October 31, 1517, a date that is often called the birthday of the Protestant Reformation, he posted on the door of the castle church in Wittenberg, a kind of university bulletin board, ninety-five theses which he was prepared to debate. In academic circles this was a normal procedure for obtaining discussion. In crisp, vigorous language Luther challenged the indulgences. He protested against despoiling Germans to pay for the construction of St. Peter's, saying that few Germans could worship there, that the Pope was rich enough to do the building with his own money, and that he would do better to appoint one good pastor to a church than to give indulgences to them all. Luther said that indulgences did not remove guilt and that the Pope could remit only those penalties which he himself had imposed on earth and that he had no jurisdiction over purgatory. He denied that the saints had accumulated surplus credits. He held that indulgences bred a false sense of security and so were positively harmful.

To Luther's surprise, the ninety-five theses created an immense sensation. Within a few months they were printed in the Latin original and in a vernacular translation and were being read across Germany. That they had this effect was due in part to the skill and forthrightness with which Luther drafted them. It was even more because of an underlying restlessness which hailed them as saying what many were happy to have said. As a result, Luther was drawn into controversy. Although at the outset he had no thought of breaking with the Pope or the Church of Rome, he was not one to draw back, and prudence and guarded speech were alien to his nature. In the course of the debate he was led on step by step until he had declared that both Popes and general councils of the Church could err, that only the Scriptures are authoritative, and that he would concede that he was in error only if convinced that what he held was contrary to the Bible and to sound reason. In effect he was insisting upon the right and the duty of individual judgement which must not be surrendered, even to the Catholic Church.

Into the details of the stages by which Luther was driven to this position we must not take the space to go. We can only give them in rough outline. As was natural, Tetzel replied to Luther, but proved a somewhat stupid opponent whom Luther did not deign to refute. Luther had sent a copy of his theses to Archbishop Albert of Mainz and the latter sent it to the Pope. The then occupant of the Papal throne was that Giovanni de' Medici who through family pressure had been made a cardinal at the age of thirteen. Now, as Leo X, he was too deeply embroiled in Italian and European politics to take more than casual notice of what he regarded as a relatively unimportant debate among monks. He commanded the head of the Augustinians to quiet this member of his order, but instead the Augustinians tended to glory in him, perhaps because the leaders of the attack were their rivals, the Dominicans. At a chapter of the Augustinians Luther won followers, the most important of whom was Martin Bucer (or Butzer) (1491–1551) of whom we are to hear more.

In the summer of 1518 the Pope summoned Luther to Rome to answer to the charge of heresy and contumacy. Through the good offices of the Elector Frederick the hearing was transferred to Germany in connexion with a meeting of the imperial Diet (or Reichstag) at Augsburg. There the Pope was represented by Thomas Vio, better known, from his birthplace, as Cardinal Cajetan. The Diet was critical of the Church of Rome and of the fashion in which it took good German money beyond the Alps and through its absentee appointees left Germans without pastors. It declined to raise money for a crusade against the Turk. The atmosphere was not favourable to the Cardinal. To that dignitary's demand that he retract, Luther returned a refusal and appealed to the judgement of the universities and to the Pope "better informed." Fearing arrest, he appealed from the Pope to a general council.

Earlier that month a Papal bull clarified the position of Rome on indulgences, saying that they could only reduce the temporal penalties on earth and in purgatory, that they could not release a soul from hell, and that they could be applied only when guilt had been removed through the sacrament of penance. While affirming that the Pope could remit the penalties on earth it said that for those of purgatory he could only petition God, presenting the surplus merits of Christ and the saints.

Wishing the goodwill of the Elector Frederick in German politics, the Pope took a conciliatory attitude, for that prince was disposed not to deal with Luther in summary fashion. A Papal representative disowned Tetzel, who soon died of chagrin, and obtained from Luther a promise that he would refrain from debate if his opponents would do likewise.

THE CONFLICT DEEPENS

However, debate continued, for Luther's critics did not keep silent and outstanding members of the staff of the University of Wittenberg rallied to Luther's defence. One of these was Philip Melanchthon (1497–1560). Melanchthon, Luther's junior by nearly fifteen years, a grandnephew and protégé of the humanist Reuchlin, though unimpressive physically, was a competent scholar, especially in Greek, and had a facile pen which was later to be of outstanding service to Luther's cause. Newly installed as professor of Greek, he became convinced of the soundness of Luther's position and to some extent was an echo, although by no means merely an echo, of the older man.

The debate was joined at Leipzig, before a large and notable audience, between Luther and some of his colleagues on the one hand, and on the other hand Eck, a former friend, a humanist, and a professor at the University of Ingolstadt. Luther, affable, vivacious, and gay in company, but at times caustic in public speech, was led by the adroit Eck to admit that some of Hus's views were "Christian and evangelical," that general councils had erred and might err, that they had sometimes contradicted one another, and that articles of faith must come from Scripture and could not be established by Pope or Church. Soon Luther was to say that he and his supporters were "all Hussites without knowing it." He had broken with the authority of the Roman Catholic Church and against it had placed the Bible interpreted by the individual.

LUTHER ADVANCES TO THE ATTACK

The issue was now squarely joined. Luther was never one to hold back. In 1520 he boldly stated his position in five tracts which are often regarded as the primary expositions of his distinctive convictions. His *Sermon on Good Works* was completed in May, *The Papacy at Rome* in June, *The Address to the German Nobility* in August, *The Babylonian Captivity of the Church* in September, and *The Freedom of the Christian Man* in November. These were put in trenchant German vernacular and had a wide circulation.

In the first of the tracts Luther declared that the "noblest of all good works is to believe in Christ." He protested against limiting "good works" to praying in church, fasting, and giving alms, and held that they could also include "labouring at one's trade, coming and going, eating, drinking, and sleeping, and all the other acts that help nourish the body or are generally useful." He held that "the Christian who lives in confidence towards God knows what things he should do, and does all gladly and freely, not with a view to accumulating merit and good works, but because it is his great joy to please God and to serve Him without thought of reward." He held that seeking to amass good works by going on pilgrimages, fasting, confessing, and calling on the saints was evidence of a feeling of insecurity and of lack of oneness with God. Here, obviously, he was speaking out of his own bitter experience.

In the tract whose full title may be translated as *To the Christian Nobility of the German Nation Respecting the Reformation of the Christian Estate,* Luther held that the Roman Church had built up three walls in its defense from which Christendom had suffered. These he attacked. The first, the superiority of Popes, bishops, priests, and monks over the laity—princes, lords, artisans, and peasants—he declared invalid on the ground that all Christians are consecrated priests by baptism, and that the only difference among Christians is one of office. He held that the temporal power is ordained by God for the punishment of the bad and the protection of the good and should do its duty throughout the whole Christian body and without respect of persons, whether they be Popes, bishops, priests, monks, or nuns. He thus sought to sweep aside the principle which exempted the clergy from the jurisdiction of the civil authorities.

The second wall he described as the Papal claim to have the exclusive right to interpret the Scriptures. He proceeded to overthrow it by saying that many Popes had been in fact unbelievers and had therefore been incapable of understanding the Scriptures, but that every true believer, being by that fact a priest, was competent to discern what is right in matters of faith.

The third wall, Luther said, was the claim that only the Pope could summon a council and confirm its acts. He pointed out that the most famous of all the councils, that of Nicæa, had been called, not by the Pope but by the Emperor Constantine, and that after him "many other Emperors" had done the same. He held that when a Pope is a cause of offense to Christendom, temporal rulers should summon a council to deal with him. He attacked the pomp and luxury of the Pope and cardinals, and declared that Italy had been sucked dry to support it and that Germany was now going the same way. He challenged princes, nobles, and cities to forbid the payment of annates to the Pope, to abolish the practice of Papal reservations, commendam, and the like, and to show that the "drunken Germans," as the Italians derisively called them, were not to be mulcted forever but had also become Christians. He would have imperial law abolish the confirmation of any ecclesiastical appointment by Rome, the submission of temporal matters to Rome, the reservation of certain causes to the Papal curia, the appropriation of German benefices by the Pope, and the oaths of allegiance which bishops were required to swear to the Roman Pontiff. He would leave priests free to marry, and would have each town elect a "pious learned citizen from the congregation and charge him with the office of minister" and have him supported by the congregation and assisted by several priests and deacons. He advocated the abolishment, or at least the reduction, of the numbers of processions, annual festivals, and masses for the dead, the complete erasure of all saints' days, keeping only Sunday, the elimination of begging and the care by each town of its own poor, the expulsion of Papal legates from Germany, the reform of the universities, the exaltation of the teaching of the Bible in the schools, and advancing to thirty years the age at which one could enter a monastery.

Slightly longer was *The Babylonian Captivity of the Church*. In this Luther consciously went far beyond his earlier criticisms of the use of indulgences and freely acknowledged that his critics, whom he handled in caustic fashion, had assisted him to think more basically and to see more clearly the issues involved. To his mind the Papacy was the Kingdom of Babylon which had carried the Church into captivity. Here he dealt with the sacraments and in doing so emphatically departed from the teaching of the Roman Catholic Church.

One form of the captivity into which Rome had carried the Church, so Luther said, was the denial of the cup to the laity. From several passages of Scripture he argued against those who defended that practice and endeavoured to show that the weight of the Bible is on giving the communion to the laity in both the bread and the wine. He maintained that this sacrament belongs to all, not merely to the priests, and that the latter should give it in both kinds to those who sought it and as often as they sought it.

A second bondage Luther declared to be transubstantiation. He held that on the altar are real bread and real wine, not merely the "accidents," as the Pope had said, and that in them are the "real flesh and the real blood of Christ." Yet he would allow Christians to hold either for transubstantiation or with him. His own view is usually called, somewhat inaccurately, consubstantiation.

The third aspect of the captivity Luther described as teaching that the mass is a good work and a sacrifice. He maintained that the mass "is a promise of the remission of sins made to us by God and . . . has been confirmed by the death of the Son of God." Therefore it cannot be approached by works, strength, or merit, but by faith alone, and nothing is required for a worthy reception of the mass but faith, resting in confidence in the promise of Christ, and believing that Christ's body is given and his blood shed for the recipient. Luther maintained that although we are sinners and utterly unworthy of the gift of eternal life, God's incomprehensible mercy is such that we can cast ourselves upon Him in perfect trust and love Him above all things. The mass is not a sacrifice, an offering to God, and is therefore not a good work by which God's favour is earned, Luther said, but is a gift of God to be received with faith and thanksgiving.

Luther valued baptism and did not deny it to infants. He held that it is done, not by man, but by the Trinity through a man. But he also wrote that unless a man has faith, it profits him nothing. Baptism in itself, he declared, does not justify, but faith in the word of promise to which baptism is added. Baptism, in which the minister dips the child in the water, is a symbol of death and resurrection, and Luther therefore preferred total immersion. Through their entire lives, Luther held, Christians should carry out their baptism by dying to sin and living by faith in Christ. He maintained that the Popes caused Christians to forget their baptism and its meaning by requiring fastings, prayers, and almsgiving. Although when baptized the infants are not able to exercise faith, Luther said that they are aided by the faith of those who bring them to baptism and that through the prayers of the Church which brings the child in faith, the infant is changed, cleansed, and renewed by the faith infused in it. Here, as we are to see, Luther and those who were called Anabaptists parted company.

Luther insisted that no ground exists in the Scriptures for the other five of the seven sacraments. In some of these he found useful features, but he held that they had been corrupted by Rome. Thus in penance he believed that secret confession of sins is good and even necessary, but that it need not be to a specially ordained priest. Since Christ has bestowed the power of absolution upon every believer in him, it can be made to any brother Christian. He warned against regarding contrition for one's sins as a good work. He pointed out, probably with a vivid recollection of his own experience with confession, that "we can know only a small part of our sins," and said that it is enough to sorrow for those sins of which we are aware. He declared that while a contrite heart is of great moment, it can proceed only from a prior faith in the threats and promises of God. While he was prepared to acknowledge confirmation as a ceremony of the Church, Luther argued that the Scriptures give no ground for regarding it as a sacrament. He valued matrimony, abhorred divorce, and even preferred bigamy to it. But he inveighed against some of the regulations by which he believed the Pope had perverted matrimony and said that he could find no ground in the Bible for making it a sacrament.

Luther held that ordination had been invented by the Church of Rome. He admitted that as a rite practised for many ages it was not to be condemned, but he reiterated as one of his basic convictions that all Christians are priests, that what is called priesthood is merely a ministry entrusted to those who exercise it with the consent of other Christians, and that ordination is a ceremony for choosing preachers in the Church. As imposed by Rome, he said, the sacrament of ordination made for a separation of clergy and laity and the tyranny of the former over the latter which had wrought incredible injury to baptism and the communion. The Church, so he affirmed, can distinguish the word of God from the words of men and can do this—and here he seems to have reflected his Ockhamist training—by the illumination of the Spirit which she cannot demonstrate but which she holds as most sure. But he also said that the word of God is incomparably above the Church, and that she cannot ordain anything. Although not condemning extreme unction, Luther regarded its efficacy as depending upon the faith of the recipient and held that it is not warranted by the texts in *The Epistle of James* and *The Gospel according to Mark* to which the Church of Rome appealed as authority for it.

While not altogether sweeping aside or deprecating vows, Luther found no ground in Scripture for those of perpetual poverty, chastity, and obedience which are taken by monks and nuns, and advised growing youths and young men to keep aloof from them. This was partly because he could discover no precedent for them in the Bible and partly because they bred pride and contempt for the ordinary Christian life. He maintained that the works of priests and members of the religious orders are not a whit more sacred in the sight of God than those of a farmer in his fields or of a woman in her household duties.

The Freedom of the Christian Man, addressed to the Pope, contained the affirmation: "A Christian man is the most free lord of all, and subject to none; a Christian man is the most dutiful servant of all, and subject to everyone." By this Luther meant that, since justification is by faith alone and cannot be earned by good works, he who has this faith is freed from the bondage to the law and from seeking to earn his salvation by works. Here again are reflected the agony and seeming futility of Luther's struggle to win justification before God by the methods prescribed by the Roman Catholic Church and the monastic discipline. In the sense of release which had come to him Luther wrote: "One thing and one thing alone is necessary for life, justification, and Christian liberty; and that is the most holy word of God, the Gospel of Christ." Even here Luther was not bound by the literal word of Scripture, but declared that the word is "the Gospel of God, concerning His son, incarnate, suffering, risen, and glorified through the Spirit, the Sanctifier. To preach Christ is to feed the soul, to justify it, to set it free, and to save it, if it believes the preaching. For faith alone, and the efficacious use of the word of God bring salvation."

Yet, so Luther held, the Christian is the servant of all because he is bound by the faith which works through love to labour for the advantage of his neighbour. Faith does not permit immorality, for while good works do not make a good man, a good man does good works. "It is not from works that we are set free by the faith of Christ, but . . . from foolishly presuming to seek justification through works." A Christian man will fast, watch, and labour to keep down "the wantonness and concupiscence of the body," but with no thought of being justified by that discipline.

Through the rapidly multiplying printing presses, these and some of Luther's other writings were given a wide circulation. They were read not only in Germany but also in other countries. They created an enormous excitement, especially in Germany. Their burning conviction, obvious scholarship, and terse, bold expression quickly won them an extensive hearing. Thousands eagerly welcomed them, and for a wide variety of reasons. German patriots greeted them as giving leadership to the widespread resentment against what they considered the financial exploitation by aliens. Humanists heard in them a voice denouncing what they regarded as the superstitions and puerilities of much of the official religion. The cautious Erasmus was at best only moderately friendly, was soon to criticize Luther for the violence of his speech, and was later to break with him, but the fiery Ulrich von Hutten was outspokenly for him, largely on patriotic grounds. Many reformers saw here a heartening assurance of action against some of the abuses which had long been ineffectually decried.

In these tracts were set forth the convictions which became distinctive features of Protestantism—justification by faith alone, the priesthood of all believers, the authority of the word of God as contained in the Scriptures, and the right and duty of each Christian to interpret the Scriptures. Some of these convictions had been foreshadowed in groups which had been cast out of the Catholic Church in the centuries before Luther. Yet as compared with them the emphasis was new, especially the basic affirmation, justification by faith. Luther and his fellow-Protestants maintained that they were simply reasserting historic Christianity as it had been before its corruption by Rome.

As we are to see later, what is called Protestantism has been and is extraordinarily multiform. By no means all its manifestations have placed equal stress upon the principles which Luther enunciated. Some have given little weight to them. Others have made more of other convictions. Still others have carried them more nearly to their logical conclusions than did Luther. Yet among almost all the many kinds of Protestantism there is a family likeness. This, Protestants maintain, is due to their loyalty to the Gospel. They thought, and still think of themselves as Evangelicals, as holding to the Evangel, that is, the Gospel. However, to a greater or less degree, even when they were or are not aware of it, they were and are influenced by Luther. His basic views were set forth in these products of his pen thrown out at white heat in 1520.

For many the excitement caused by these publications was one not of approval but of outrage. They regarded them as heresy. In June, 1520, before the completion of some of the pamphlets, the Pope came out with the bull *Exsurge Domine,* which began "Arise, Lord, and judge Thy cause. A wild boar has invaded Thy vineyard." Forty-one alleged errors of Luther were condemned, the books containing them were ordered burned, and Luther himself was given sixty days to submit.

Efforts of two Papal nuncios and inquisitors commissioned to publish the bull in Germany met a varied reception. A few bishops found ways of evading or postponing formal publication. Luther issued a blast against the bull and on December 10, 1520, before an assembly of the students, teachers, and populace of Wittenberg, cast into the fire the bull, the works of his opponents, and some of the writings which traditionally had supported the Papal claims.

Since the sixty days had expired and Luther, far from recanting, had defied him, on January 3, 1521, the Pope issued the threatened bull of excommunication.

LUTHER BEFORE THE EMPEROR AND THE DIET

The Papal decrees made acute the question of what action would be taken by the Holy Roman Empire, the realm of which Luther was a subject. Would it harbour a heretic condemned by the Church, or would it extirpate him? In principle the Holy Roman Empire was the political aspect of the Christian community. Heresy was held to be a major peril to that community, for it might mislead Christians and bring them to hell instead of heaven. Now that the head of the Church had cut Luther off from its communion as a wild boar, would the state stand idly by or would it implement that action and burn the unrepentant offender?

At first thought there seemed to be only one answer. The newly elected Holy Roman Emperor was Charles V, the grandson of Ferdinand and Isabella, and not only shared his grandmother's desire for a moral reform of the Church but also her adherence to the doctrines of which the Pope was the guardian. He was under pressure from the Papal nuncio to rid the realm of this arch-enemy of the Roman Catholic faith.

However, the situation was by no means so simple. The Pope was not happy over the election of Charles to the imperial office for, with reason, he feared his influence in Italian politics. Moreover, German public opinion was largely with Luther, some of the German princes were for him, and his immediate superior, the Elector Frederick, while discreet in not as yet coming out firmly on his side, had taken no action against him and urged that he be given a fair trial. In Germany Charles was an alien, for he had been reared in the Low Countries. He had to rule as a constitutional monarch and it behooved him to walk warily.

Eventually, after much hesitation, the Elector agreed that Luther should answer to the Diet. In April, 1521, Luther appeared at Worms before that body and the Emperor. In his first hearing he admitted the books piled before the court to be his, but to the question whether he would stand by them all or would repudiate some of the views expressed in them, he asked time for reflection, saying that it affected the salvation of souls. At a hearing the next day he again acknowledged his authorship but refused to repudiate what he had said in them unless he were convinced of error from the prophets and the Gospel. On a further question he repeated that his conscience was captive to the word of God and that unless he were convicted by Scripture and plain reason, for he did not accept the authority of Popes and councils since they had contradicted one another, he would not recant anything. To do so would be neither right nor safe. He added, "God help me. Amen." Another version of his closing words, which may be accurate, has him say: "Here I stand. I cannot do otherwise." He spoke in German and, on being asked, repeated his statement in Latin.

It was a dramatic hour. A humble monk and university professor of peasant stock dared to set himself against the weight of constituted authority in Church and state. As at Augsburg, he did so at the risk of his life. Although the Emperor had guaranteed him safe conduct, the precedent of John Hus, who had come to his death in spite of a similar promise by an earlier Emperor, was by no means reassuring.

The scene was also highly significant. A single individual was pitting his reason and his integrity against established institutions which were the bulwark of society. To be sure, this was not new. Hus had taken a similar stand. Other less famous men who had been adjudged heretics had done the same. Yet the temper of the time was such that the deed stirred response in many hearts, some of ardent sympathy and some of uncompromising hostility. Here was what on the surface resembled the individualism of the contemporary humanists and that individualism which was to be a growing feature of Western civilization in the following centuries. However, unlike much of the latter, it was not selfish and irresponsible. It arose from a deep sense of divine compulsion. It was significant because it was characteristic of Protestantism. Yet it was also significant because the individualism which was not conscious of any such urge, which did not acknowledge responsibility, and which proved a disintegrating menace, probably arose in part from a distortion of the conception represented by Luther.

The scene was not only dramatic and significant. It was also tragic. It symbolized another breach in that unity among Christians which was part of the essence of their faith and which outwardly had been preserved among the majority in Western Europe. Now, from a variety of motives, but in part from profound and conscientiously held convictions on both sides, it was being broken and Western Christendom was being rent in twain. On the one hand were those who maintained that the individual must submit to the judgement of the collective Christian body. On the other were those who held that if he were true to God, the individual must pit his own judgement, when inspired as he believed by God, against that of the majority and the visible Church. Both positions were taken in the name of God and the Gospel. The result was disruption.

The Emperor Charles now frankly confessed his own Catholic faith, said that this monk in daring to set himself against the Christianity of a thousand years must be wrong, and declared his purpose to proceed against him. Shortly afterward, in May, 1521, with the consent of such members of the Diet as remained in Worms, Charles V adjudged Luther to be "a limb cut off from the Church of God, an obstinate schismatic and manifest heretic," and commanded all his subjects to refuse Luther hospitality, lodging, food, or drink, to take him prisoner and turn him over to the Emperor, and to deal similarly with all Luther's friends and adherents, confiscating their property. The decree also prohibited the printing, buying, or selling of Luther's works. To the end of his days Luther remained under the shadow of this edict.

THE WARTBURG AND THE BIBLE

The edict against Luther was never enforced. Before it had been issued many of the Diet had left, among them the powerful Electors Frederick of Saxony and Ludwig of the Palatinate. Luther had too many German sympathizers, among them his own prince, and the Emperor became too deeply engrossed in European politics to permit vigorous action against him.

Yet for a time the peril seemed great. Some days before the formal enactment of the edict Luther had left Worms. On his way home, at the command of the Elector Frederick, who thus sought to shield him, he was seized by friendly hands and taken to the nearly untenanted Wartburg castle. There, with the exception of a brief visit to Wittenberg in December, 1521, he remained, in the disguise of a knight and under an assumed name, until early in March, 1522.

For Luther the months were difficult. Living nearly in solitude, away from his friends, without the spur of action and battle to sustain him, he suffered from constipation, insomnia, and melancholia. To him the Devil was very real and his *Anfechtungen* returned in force. He was partially relieved by medical treatment and by rambles and rides.

Yet he was not idle. Indeed, unremitting intellectual toil probably contributed to his distress. In the nine months he wrote nearly a dozen books and translated the entire New Testament from Greek into German. In later years he also translated the Old Testament into his mother tongue and until his death he continued to revise what he had done to bring it more nearly to perfection.

Here was one of Luther's major achievements. His was by no means the first translation from the Bible into German. However, none other either before or later equalled it in dignity and felicity of expression. He endeavoured to make the apostles and prophets speak to the Germans as though they had been natives of the country. His version became the cherished possession of the nation and did much to standardize the literary language. It had an even more profound effect upon German than did the King James version of the Scriptures upon English. This emphasis upon the Bible and the influence of the book were typical of Protestants. To be sure, the Roman Catholic Church had cherished the Scriptures, but its fear of unauthorized interpretation had made it hesitant in circulating it widely among the laity. Luther, and with him other Protestants, stressed the primacy of the word of God as contained in the Scriptures and, holding to the priesthood of all believers, insisted not only that all Christians read the Bible but also on their competence, guided by the Holy Spirit, to understand it aright.

REVOLUTION GOES ON APACE

During the months that Luther was in laborious and suffering seclusion in the Wartburg the movement which he had spear-headed went on apace. As was to be expected, it centered at Wittenberg, but it was very widespread. It took radical forms. One of Luther's fellow-Augustinians denounced the mass and the use of images and urged the repudiation of clerical vows. In defiance of a command of the Elector Frederick, Carlstadt, a colleague of Luther on the faculty of the university, celebrated mass in abbreviated form without priestly garments or the elevation of the host, employed German in part of the service, and gave to the laity both the bread and the wine. Led by one of the reforming priests, some of the populace overturned altars and mutilated images and pictures of the saints. Carlstadt and others of the monks and clergy took wives. In his radical application of the principle of the priesthood of all believers, Carlstadt dressed like a peasant and wished to be addressed not as

Doctor but as Brother Andreas. There was denunciation of the use of music and musical instruments in church services. Auricular confession and fasts were falling into disuse. The town council took matters in hand, regulated public worship, and with provision for the sermon and words of consecration in German, permission to the communicants to take the bread and the cup in their own hands, and the gradual elimination of altars. Religious associations were abolished and their incomes together with other ecclesiastical revenues were placed in a common fund for the care of the unemployed and the orphans and the education of poor children. Begging and prostitution were forbidden and monks were required to earn their living by working. Radical preachers arrived from Zwickau, and, claiming direct divine inspiration, prophesied the early end of the world and denounced infant baptism.

Quite understandably the Elector Frederick was deeply disturbed by these measures and sought, not without some success, to restrain them.

LUTHER RETURNS AND OPENLY RESUMES LEADERSHIP

It was on March 6, 1522, that Luther finally returned to Wittenberg and openly resumed leadership of the movement which he had started. He did this at the invitation of the town council of Wittenberg and in part to hasten the publication of his writings and out of alarm at the radical measures of some of his followers. He did so at grave risk to himself, for the Elector Frederick had advised against it, the imperial edict condemning him still stood, and he could be by no means sure of Frederick's protection. The Elector's attitude towards the Reformation has been in debate. It is not agreed whether he acted more from political expediency or religious conviction. Perhaps he himself did not know. Certainly both factors seem to have been present.

Back in Wittenberg, Luther at once took charge of the situation. In a series of eight sermons he came out on the side of moderation, urging love and advocating freedom of choice on controversial issues. While not repudiating the monastic life or advocating the marriage of priests and nuns, he would leave that to the individual conscience. He would have the abolition of the mass carried through, but in orderly fashion, with the consent of the government, namely, the Elector.

LUTHER TURNS ORGANIZER

Luther felt constrained to exert a leadership far beyond the walls of Wittenberg. The Reformation spread rapidly and in many places congregations which sought to embody it were springing up. Not all of them yielded to Luther's authority, even when he might have been disposed to exert it. However, as the outstanding figure in the movement he felt in duty bound to offer guidance and to present a positive programme. He did this piecemeal as occasion seemed to demand and while continuing his duties in Wittenberg in the university and the town. Wittenberg became a centre to which eager students came to drink of the Reformation at its source. Many of them returned to their homes carrying with them what they had imbibed.

Luther was both radical and conservative. His basic principle was religious, justification by faith, and arose from his own experience. He gave primacy to the word of God and wished it to be presented in all its purity as he understood it. He held to the priesthood of all believers. He would have faith govern the entire conduct of all Christians and, since he contended that the distinction between sacred and secular was contrary to the Gospel, he wished them to carry on their occupations as vocations, callings of God. He would go back to the New Testament and the practice and faith of the early Christians, purging the Church of what he deemed the corrupting innovations of Rome. Yet he did not regard all the accretions of the centuries as evil. Holding that "what is not contrary to Scripture is for Scripture and Scripture for it," he preserved much from the post-apostolic past. He regarded confession before communion as desirable, but did not wish it to be obligatory. He favoured the use of candles, the crucifix, and pictures, although the latter were not to be specially revered.

For guidance to the clergy and congregations he prepared an *Ordering of Worship*, a *Formula Missae* ("Formula of the Mass"), and a booklet on baptism with a baptismal service in German. In the *Formula Missae* Luther omitted the portion of the liturgy called the canon of the mass, because it described the Eucharist as a sacrifice, and to him this smacked of earning something from God by good works, and so as contrary to justification by faith alone. In the Eucharist he stressed worship, fellowship, and thanksgiving to God. In 1526 he came out with a German mass.

Luther made much of music. One of the striking features of the Reformation, both Protestant and Catholic, was the fashion in which it found expression through hymns. Indeed, that seems to have been true of most and perhaps all of the great forward surges of the Christian tide. Luther seems to have been responsible for the musical settings of some of his hymns. Because of the high value that he placed on the Bible and its study by the ordinary believer, he was eager that the music in public worship should enable the words of Scripture to be clearly understood by the congregation. He prized and used polyphonic chorales, including those of Roman Catholic origin, and furthered the training of choirs. Congregational singing was one of his great joys and he took the initiative in encouraging it and giving it a large part in the liturgy and other services. Here was a corollary of his priesthood of all believers, and his own zest for singing, going back to his boyhood, reinforced it. He issued a hymnal and himself wrote some of the hymns. The most notable of the latter, *Ein feste Burg ist unser Gott* ("A Mighty Fortress is our God"), perhaps composed in 1527 or 1528 when Charles V was seeking to suppress the Reformation, was to inspire successive generations of Germans and in translation was to become a sturdy favourite in several other lands and branches of the Church.

To Luther the sermon was of first rate importance. He believed in it as the proclamation of the word of God. He himself preached regularly, often, and with great power. As with so much else, to no small degree although by no means entirely, Protestantism owed to him the prominence given to preaching.

Education was one of Luther's major concerns. This again was a logical outgrowth of his belief in the priesthood of all believers. He wished compulsory education under the direction of the state in which the Scriptures would be given prominence. He stimulated the production of religious literature for children. In doing so he blazed new trails. While Erasmus and the Bohemian Brethren had made a beginning in this direction, it was Luther who gave it a major creative impetus. He encouraged others to write and himself composed a Small Catechism for children. He also furthered adult education, for he wished the entire body of Christian believers to be intelligent in their faith. As one means towards this end he wrote his Large Catechism.

Luther emphasized the family. He helped arrange marriages for nuns who left the cloistered life and himself married one of them, Katherine von Bora. His was a happy home. Into it several children were born and at its table were numbers of his students who, admiringly, recorded his "Table Talk." Here was a precedent for the kind of parsonage which became characteristic of Protestantism.

The geographic spread of the Reformation confronted Luther with the problem of the structure and government of the Church. He declared that the true Church could never be identical with any visible institution, for it was comprised only of the redeemed and God alone knew who were and who were not of this number. Probably he would have preferred to assemble in groups those who had made the full commitment of faith. Yet he held to the territorial church into which all the inhabitants of a state are admitted by baptism. As we have seen, he advocated the retention of the baptism of infants. As the Reformation spread, great diversity was seen in practice and liturgy. Disorder appeared and chaos seemed threatened. Luther saw that some one must preserve order. Since the old ecclesiastical structure was dissolving before his eyes, he turned to the lay princes. In Saxony the Elector appointed visitors in 1527 and 1528 to report on the state of the parishes, much as bishops had formerly done. The Elector's domains were divided into districts and over each were superintendents responsible to the prince. They were to have administrative authority over the parish clergy with power to remove unworthy ministers and to bring some kind of uniformity into worship.

To Luther a repetition of the Inquisition with the execution of dissidents would have been abhorrent. From profound conviction he maintained that no compulsion should be used to induce individuals to believe as he did. Yet he desired orderliness in worship and held that in this the prince could help. He would not make the prince the head of the church in the latter's realms and he would not acquiesce in any attempt of the prince to constrain any one's conscience. But he believed that the convictions of the majority should determine the form of worship and religious instruction. Those who differed might go to a state where those of their beliefs outnumbered the others. Since Germany was divided into many states, large and small, this seemed a feasible method of dealing with differences.

Partly under the influence of Luther, *Landeskirchen,* or territorial churches, arose. Some parts of Germany remained Roman Catholic. In others the principles of the Reformation prevailed. Presumably this would have happened without the encouragement of Luther. As we have seen, nationalism and state consciousness were increasing in Western Europe. In Roman Catholic lands princes were insisting upon the administrative control of the Church within their borders. As Protestantism spread, whether of the Lutheran or some other form, each state where it became dominant gave preference to one or more kinds of it, putting the others under disabilities or suppressing them. In Germany great variety was seen among the *Landeskirchen* in ritual and organization.

LUTHER LOSES MANY HUMANISTS, PEASANTS, AND REFORMERS

Outstanding though he was as the first great leader of the Reformation, Luther did not long carry all those with him who wished change. Probably no one could have done so. So vital a movement inevitably had many expressions. Since they all had in common the repudiation of the authority of Rome, they were without an administrative centre to enforce outward unity. Luther would not have done so even had he possessed the power. Before many years numbers who at the outset were more or less sympathetic separated from him.

One of the early breaks was with the leading humanist, Erasmus. This was unavoidable. Humanism and Luther were incompatible. Humanism tended to take an optimistic view of human nature and to regard man as competent to work out his own salvation. His religious experience and the impress left upon him by his study of Augustine had been such that Luther completely rejected this view. He held man to be a sinner whose noblest deeds are corrupted by pride and selfishness. Man, therefore, can earn nothing from God and if he is to be saved it must be by the grace, the undeserved favour, of God. As we have seen, while in some ways sympathizing with Luther and for several years refusing to denounce him, Erasmus was early made uneasy by the former's outspoken and uncompromising denunciation of Rome. While the two were so much alike that there were those who attributed some of Luther's works to Erasmus, the latter was essentially a man of peace, a moderate, who wished the moral reform of the Church but dreaded violence and a breach in its outward unity.

As might have been expected, the issue between the two men was most sharply drawn over the question of predestination and the freedom of man's will. In 1524 Erasmus wrote a tract *On the Freedom of the Will* which he well knew would widen the breach. He held that God would be unjust and immoral if He were so to order the universe that man could not of himself fulfil the conditions which He had ordained for salvation and then were arbitrarily to choose some to be saved and by doing so condemn others to hell. Luther admitted that natural reason was offended by the doctrine of man's helplessness in sin and by a conception of God which, while holding Him to be good, taught that by His mere will He hardens and damns men whom He has not chosen to save. He confessed that at one time the apparent contradiction had so driven him to the abyss of despair that he wished that he had never been born. Luther stood in awe of the majesty and inscrutable justice of God. God, he maintained, is inaccessible to human reason. To Luther there was a paradox even in the self-revelation of God in Christ, that the Eternal and Omnipotent should be seen in a stable and on a cross. Man, so Luther held, does not have free will. Man's will is like a beast of burden. It is ridden either by God or by the Devil and does whatever the one who is in the saddle directs. In the heat of controversy Luther went beyond what he held in calmer moments, but his position was consistent with his basic conviction that none of a man's works avails.

Luther and Erasmus parted company. The latter never broke with the Roman Catholic Church and near the end of his life was wooed by the Pope with the tempting offer of an important post. Yet it was symbolic of his longing that the unity of the Church should not be broken that he died in Basel (July 11, 1536), by that time a Protestant city, and was buried in its cathedral.

Most but not all of the other humanists left Luther. Melanchthon remained loyal and some others of lesser note. Yet the breach with the majority was significant and important.

Luther also lost many of the class from which he had sprung, the peasants. In 1524 and 1525 there broke out the Peasants' War, the *Bundschuh*. The causes of the uprising were complex and were not primarily religious. Peasants' revolts had not been uncommon in medieval Europe and were against the economic and social disabilities under which that class suffered. The rebellion of 1524–1525 in Germany opposed rising taxes, deflation which made the taxes more burdensome, and curtailment of free access to woods, streams, and meadows. It was directed against the nobles, including the bishops and abbots, for they were, rightly, regarded as the exploiters. At the outset Luther looked with friendly eye upon the peasants' demands and some of the Roman Catholics charged him with the revolt. In Saxony a radical reformer, Thomas Müntzer, who had gone far beyond Luther, urged the peasants on and roused them to slaughter their oppressors. This was too much for Luther. He issued a fiery pamphlet *Against the Murderous and Thieving Hordes of Peasants* in which he urged the princes first to offer to come to terms with them and then, if they refused, to smite, slay, and stab them as rebels who were like mad dogs and were outside the law of God. Already the nobles were putting down the revolt and were butchering thousands. They needed no exhortation from Luther. Indeed, he issued another pamphlet in which he asked for mercy to captives. Yet the harm was done. The peasants in South Germany, where the uprising had centered, regarded him as a traitor. Here was one of the factors which lost much of the population of that region to Protestantism. Moreover, Luther was led to a deep distrust of the common man, to a fear of chaos, and to rely increasingly on the princes.

Luther also severed all connexion with the more radical reformers. They were increasing and held to diverse views. Some of them we are to meet again when we describe the Anabaptists. They rejected infant baptism and, repudiating the territorial church into which all in a given area were baptized, they would gather the true believers into congregations separated from the world. They wished, too, to return to the Christianity of the first century and thus free it from what they deemed the corruptions of later centuries. Luther had no use for those who advocated such measures and called them *Schwärmer*, fanatics. Luther had especially to deal with his former colleague, Andreas Carlstadt, and with Thomas Müntzer. Carlstadt denied the real presence of Christ in the mass and regarded the Lord's Supper simply as a memorial. He had no use for graven images or infant baptism and wished lay ministers who in no way would be distinguished from their fellow-believers. While holding to the priesthood of all believers, Luther insisted upon a specialized, trained ministry who would keep the rank and file from falling into ignorance of their faith. Wishing to be assured of the word of God, Müntzer believed that it continued to come, as it had to those who wrote the Bible, through prophets inspired by the Spirit. He sought to gather the elect into churches and to set them to slaughtering the ungodly and those who honoured images. Luther, appalled, urged the princes of Saxony to prevent such a use of the sword. He acquiesced in the banishment of both Carlstadt and Müntzer from Saxony.

Less radical, but still going beyond Luther were Zwingli and the reformers of Strassburg, whom we are to meet in the next chapter. Zwingli tended to regard the Lord's Supper simply as a memorial and the men of Strassburg took a position somewhat intermediate between that of Luther and that of Zwingli. In the interests of the common defense against the Roman Catholics, Philip, landgrave of Hesse, a leader among the princes who adhered to the Reformation, urged the outstanding representatives of the differing views to come together in an effort to reach agreement. This they did at Philip's castle at Marburg in October, 1529. Luther, Zwingli, Bucer, and Melanchthon were among those present. In a colloquy extending over several days, for a brief time it seemed that agreement might be reached. Zwingli was willing to concede that Christ is spiritually present in the Lord's Supper and Luther granted that no matter what the nature of Christ's presence only faith can make it of benefit to the Christian. Intercommunion might have been attained had not Melanchthon objected on the ground that for Luther to yield might make reconciliation with the Roman Catholics impossible. The differences between Luther and his followers on the one hand and those whom we are to call the Reformed on the other widened into a gulf.

THE APPEAL TO BATTLE

Armed conflict between the Roman Catholics and the reformers could scarcely be avoided. The imperial decree against Luther and his followers issued at Worms in 1521 still stood. The Emperor did not forget it, but until 1529 he was so occupied with wars against France and in Italy and the threat of the Turk had been so serious that no determined attempt had been made to enforce it. In the meantime the princes and cities of Germany had been ranging themselves on one or the other side. In the main the South remained loyal to Rome. In 1524 a Papal legate succeeded in bringing into a league the Roman Catholic princes in that area. The North was moving towards Luther. The princes of Brandenburg, Mecklenburg, and Mansfeld were sympathetic. City after city, including some in the South, came over, among them Magdeburg, Augsburg, Strassburg, Nuremberg, and Ulm. Albert, one of the Hohenzollerns, Grand Master of the Teutonic Knights, that crusading order which had ruled in Prussia, attached himself to Luther, married, and, although deposed from his office with the Knights, became Duke of East Prussia and carried that region with him. Livonia turned Lutheran.

Hostilities did not at once break out. When, in 1526, the Diet convened at

Speier, in spite of the demand of the Emperor that the edict of Worms be enforced, it decreed that pending a "council or a national assembly" each of the princes was "so to live, govern, and carry himself as he hopes and trusts to answer it to God and his imperial majesty." This was interpreted as giving the Lutheran princes and cities authority to regulate their religious affairs as they pleased. When, in 1529, the Diet again met at Speier, it had a Roman Catholic majority. It ordered that no further change in religion be made, that in Roman Catholic territories liberty of worship should not be granted to Lutherans but that in Lutheran territories toleration should be accorded to Roman Catholics. Against this the Lutherans in the Diet entered a formal protest. This was the origin of the term Protestant as applied to those who dissented from the Roman Catholic Church. At first limited to Lutherans, the designation was eventually applied to all those movements which broke with that Church in Western Europe in the sixteenth century.

In 1530, Charles V, returning from Rome from his coronation as Emperor, called a meeting of the Diet at Augsburg and sought by a conciliatory attitude to restore religious unity. He asked the Protestants to put forth their beliefs and point out wherein they differed from the Roman Catholic Church. Melanchthon was given the assignment and he carried it through after consultation with Luther (who, being under the imperial ban, was not at Augsburg) and with others. The result was the Augsburg Confession, a lengthy document which was henceforth to be regarded as an official statement of the Lutheran position. Melanchthon endeavoured to make it as irenic as possible, but this did not deter him from frankly presenting the Lutheran case. The first part of the document set forth the positive convictions of the Lutherans and attempted to show that these were in accord with those of the Universal Church, and even with those of the Church of Rome "so far as that church is known in the writings of the fathers." The second part enumerated what the Lutherans regarded as the abuses which had crept into the Church. Luther heartily approved it and it was endorsed by Lutheran princes and cities. The Swiss, largely following the Zwinglian tradition, and the Strassburgers refused to sign it and each presented their positions in a separate document. The Roman Catholic theologians replied, attempts by the Emperor to reach agreement through committee conferences failed, the Diet, dominated by its Roman Catholic majority, held that the Protestants had been refuted, and Charles gave the latter until April, 1531, to submit.

Unwilling to yield, the Protestant princes met in Schmalkalden and formed a defensive league which is usually called by the name of that town. Strassburg was induced to accede to the Augsburg Confession and join.

Pressed by the necessity of defense against a Turkish invasion, in July, 1532, the Emperor and the Schmalkaldic League agreed upon a truce. In the years which followed Protestantism continued to spread. Until 1541 the Emperor was out of Germany. Conferences of Protestants and Roman Catholics held at his instance in 1540 and 1541 failed to bring accord.

The Emperor now undertook to rid the realm of Protestantism. His grand strategy included the convening of a general council by the Pope as a gesture and possibly as a means of conciliation, fomenting dissensions among the Protestant forces, and a final appeal to war. As we are to see in a later chapter, the Pope called what is known as the Council of Trent, but far from effecting reconciliation it deepened the gulf between Roman Catholics and Protestants.

Charles V succeeded in dividing the Protestants. In this he was aided by what became a notorious affair in which Philip of Hesse, a leader in the Schmalkaldic League, and Luther were both unhappily involved. At the early age of nineteen Philip, for political reasons, had been married to the daughter of one of the German princes. Although he had seven children by her, he engaged in the promiscuity which was common to men of his rank and day, including Charles V himself. After his conversion to Lutheranism his conscience troubled him so badly that only once in thirteen years did he take of the communion, for he found himself powerless to desist from his adulteries. He felt that a second marriage might help him to continence. With the consent of his first wife and of the girl's mother and also of Bucer, Melanchthon, and Luther, he contracted a bigamous marriage with a seventeen-year-old maid. Luther opposed divorce and held monogamy to be the form of marriage endorsed by Christ, but cited the polygamy of the Old Testament patriarchs as a precedent. He advised that the second marriage be kept secret, for being bigamous it was against the law of the land. The marriage was performed by a court preacher, and when the news leaked out Luther advised "a good, strong lie." To this Philip would not agree, especially since the bride's mother would not consent to having her daughter regarded as a concubine. Both Roman Catholic and Protestant princes professed themselves shocked and Charles took the opportunity to exact promises from Philip which led to a rift in the Protestant ranks. Charles also bought off one of the other Protestant princes by an offer of territory.

Thus prepared, the Emperor declared under the ban two of the leading Protestant princes, Philip of Hesse and the Elector John Frederick of Saxony, nephew and successor of that Elector Frederick "the Wise" who had so long befriended Luther. In the ensuing war the two were defeated and imprisoned. Politically Protestantism seemed crushed. This was in 1547, thirty years after the fateful posting of the ninety-five theses on the church door at Wittenberg.

Yet Protestantism was far from being eradicated. In large areas the populace were for it and resisted a compromise creed, the *Augsburg Interim,* which Charles attempted to force on them. The war broke out afresh. This time the Protestant princes were aided by the King of France. In return he was to have the border cities of Metz, Toul, and Verdun, which more than once across the centuries were to have a tragic role in relations between France and Germany. The Emperor was defeated and almost captured (1552).

THE PEACE OF AUGSBURG DIVIDES GERMANY AND BRINGS A LONG TRUCE

By treaty, the settlement was referred to the Diet. This met at Augsburg three years later, in 1555. After months of debate what was known as the Peace of Augsburg was formulated (September 25, 1555). It was a compromise. By it those princes who adhered to the Augsburg Confession, namely, the Lutherans, were to be allowed to do so and those princes who held to the "old religion," namely, Roman Catholicism, were not to be disturbed. Neither group of princes was to molest the other. Each lay prince was, therefore, to determine the kind of religion which was to prevail in his territories. This principle, *cujus regio, ejus religio,* was henceforth to govern the religious geography of Germany. No forms of Protestantism other than Lutheranism were to be tolerated. If on religious grounds either Roman Catholics or Lutherans wished to migrate they were to be allowed to do so and were to be permitted to sell their property. Protestant princes were to retain ecclesiastical properties confiscated by them before 1552. If, however, any Roman Catholic bishop, archbishop, or prelate became a Lutheran, he was to give up the properties and incomes belonging to his office. In other words, a spiritual prince could not turn Protestant and retain as a secular lord the lands or revenues which he had by virtue of his ecclesiastical post. The Protestant princes declared that they would not be bound by this provision. In the imperial free cities both Lutheranism and Roman Catholicism were permitted. The Lutherans demanded toleration for those of their faith living in the territories of Roman Catholic princes, but, while the new Emperor-elect promised that this would be done, it was not written into the treaty.

THE DEATH OF LUTHER

In the meanwhile, on February 18, 1546, more than nine years before the Peace of Augsburg, Luther had died. Fittingly the end came at Eisleben, his birth-place, and while on his return journey from a successful effort to arbitrate a dispute between two counts of Mansfeld. His later years had been marked by a complication of various physical illnesses, presumably aggravated by the strains and labours of a tempestuous life. This may in part account for his frequent irascibility and occasional outbursts of wrath and coarse vituperation

Although earlier he had opposed the burning of Anabaptists by Lutherans, eventually he reluctantly approved the death penalty for them on the ground that they were guilty of sedition and blasphemy. They had, indeed, proved very irritating, and, as we are to see, in the 1530's fanatics among them had undertaken at the city of Münster a kind of society which shocked their contemporaries and which Roman Catholics and Protestants had joined in suppressing by the sword. He also came out with a blast against the Jews, not on racial grounds, but because of their refusal to accept Christ, and urged that either they be deported to Palestine, or their synagogues be burned, their books be taken away from them, and they be forbidden money-lending and be compelled to earn their livelihood by tilling the soil. He also railed against the Pope. Yet to the end he was preaching, teaching, and revising his translation of the Bible. Some of his best writing and most moving religious insights were in the closing period of his life.

LUTHERANISM IN GERMANY IN THE SECOND HALF OF THE SIXTEENTH CENTURY

The second half of the sixteenth century saw a partial ebbing of the Lutheran tide. This was both in territory and in spiritual dynamic.

Territorially Protestantism reached its greatest extent in Germany about the year 1566. It then began to lose ground. There were those among both Roman Catholics and Protestants who wished to find a middle way which would effect a reconciliation. Indeed, some Lutheran services were deliberately very much like those of the Roman Catholics and in one area a Lutheran breviary was long in use which resembled that of the old church. There were Roman Catholics who were willing to go far towards meeting Protestant convictions on justification, the mass, and clerical celibacy. However, these attempts, always by minorities, failed to bring accord. Revived by an inner reformation, the "old religion" began to regain areas which it had lost. In this it was aided by the Jesuits, of whom we are to hear much in later chapters.

Protestants suffered from inner divisions. These were partly between Lutherans and that wing which by the end of the sixteenth century began to be called the Reformed and among whom the influence of Zwingli and Calvin was strong. As we are to see in the next chapter, by the beginning of the seventeenth century the Reformed Churches had made striking advances, largely in South Germany and at the expense of Lutheranism.

Among the Lutherans themselves serious dissensions broke out. Human nature being what it is, these were to be expected. They arose partly from personal rivalries between princes and partly from differences among theologians. We must not take time to go into the weary details. In some of the disputes Philip Melanchthon, who lived until April 19, 1560, a little over four-teen years after the death of Luther, was deeply involved. Rather reluctantly he consented to the reintroduction by the Elector Maurice (Moritz) of Saxony of some Roman Catholic practices and forms of organization in an attempt to mollify Charles V. Melanchthon regarded them as *adiaphora* or indifferent and so tolerated them. Some Lutherans, however, looked upon them with horror, especially since they were in force in Wittenberg, where Luther had made his home. From this arose the Adiaphoristic Controversy. Melanchthon was also attacked for his view of the Lord's Supper, as too near to that of the Reformed, and so a "crypto-Calvinism," and for his teaching that good works, while not earning salvation, are essential evidence of it. Associated with the latter view was synergism, that man works together with God to effect his salvation. Those who sided with Melanchthon were known as the Philippists and his distinctive views as Philippism. To the distress both of Melanchthon and of some of the latter's critics, Osiander (1498–1552) held that justification is not by the imputed righteousness of Christ through his death but that in those who are justified a positive righteousness arises from the continual inpouring of Christ's divine nature. In the heat of debate, one of Melanchthon's opponents declared that, far from being essential proofs of justification, good works are an obstacle to the Christian life. There were those who, going far beyond Luther, who never maintained that God's image had been obliterated by sin, insisted that man had no more freedom of will than a stone or a corpse.

In an attempt to effect agreement among the Lutherans, there was prepared, through long negotiations and the efforts of some of the theologians, what was known as the Formula of Concord. This was published in 1580, half a century after the Augsburg Confession. Signed by princes, cities, and thousands of ministers, it represented the convictions of the large majority of German Lutherans. Yet some of the princes and cities would not subscribe to it. Then, as later, Lutheranism did not present a solid front to the world.

In Lutheran circles increasing emphasis was given to dogma. The trend was towards making faith consist in intellectual assent to creedal statements. The-ological discussion, a kind of Protestant scholasticism, tended to take the place of what faith meant to Luther, a commitment of the entire man, of which the intellect was a part but only a part. In the seventeenth century there came, as we shall see, a reaction in the form of Pietism. It stressed emotion, the commit-ment of the will, and conversion, and, while usually assenting to the historic confessions, made little of them.

Lutheran Hymns and Chorales

The absorption in dogma did not prevent a development, that in hymns and music, in which the Lutheran movement initiated and carried through a remarkable expression of religious faith. As we have seen, Luther himself wrote hymns and composed the music for some of them. Two of his contemporaries, John Walther (1496–1570) and Ludwig Senfl (1480–1555) did much to promote singing in which the entire congregation took part. Walther prepared a hymnbook which was published in 1524 and which took folk-songs or melodies after the manner of folk-songs and put them in forms in which all could join. Senfl developed chorales which prepared the way for the finished products of John Sebastian Bach (1685–1750). Late in the sixteenth century harmonies were simplified and popularized and in the seventeenth century additional chorales were composed.

The Northward Spread of Lutheranism: Scandinavia

From Germany Lutheranism spread northward into Scandinavia, Iceland, and Finland, and, in contrast with its homeland, became the religion of the entire region. Roman Catholics all but disappeared, and non-Lutheran forms of Protestantism made little or no headway.

The dominance of Lutheranism in Scandinavia is significant in view of the fact that Protestantism was not indigenous to that area. Catholic Christianity had also come in from the outside. As we have seen, it was introduced largely under royal auspices and at royal initiative, and at the outset was propagated chiefly by missionaries from England. German missionary effort had been discouraged, apparently because, coming from what was then a politically strong and expanding Holy Roman Empire, it had political implications and might be a precursor to incorporation in that realm. Again a change of religion was engineered by kings. It was accomplished more rapidly and encountered even less resistance than had the earlier one. This time the content of the religion adopted was from Germany. However, there was no danger that the reception of the new faith would be followed by political control from that land. Even had the Holy Roman Emperors been strong enough to attempt it, they were Roman Catholics and not Protestants, and would not have used Lutheranism to extend their authority northward.

Religiously, under Lutheranism as under Roman Catholicism, Scandinavia was long passive. It received what came to it from abroad without making major innovations. In its Roman Catholic centuries it had not produced a new monastic order which enlisted more than a minority of those of its sons and daughters who gave themselves to that way of life. To be sure, the Brigittines, of Swedish origin, spread widely, but compared with the Cistercians, Franciscans, or Dominicans, they were inconsiderable. Nor in its Roman Catholic days had Scandinavia given birth to a theologian of the first rank. Much the same was true after Scandinavia went over to Protestantism. There was marked vitality. We are to meet some men of great spiritual depth and zeal, such as Hauge, and of originality, such as Swedenborg and Kierkegaard, and of organizing vision, among them Söderblom, who were to have an influence which reached far beyond the borders of the North. However, they were late in appearing. It was long before Christianity had become sufficiently rooted in Scandinavia to stir any within that region to outstanding original creative thought and action.

At the beginning of the sixteenth century Denmark, Norway, and Sweden were ruled by the monarchs of Denmark under the Union of Calmar (or Kalmar), which had been formulated in 1397. However, while they had much in common, they differed in history and traditions and were really three nations. The tie between Norway and Denmark was much closer than that between these two lands and Sweden. In the second half of the fifteenth century the latter country was moving towards independence, and in a stormy fashion. German influence, especially through the merchants of the Hanseatic League, was strong in much of Scandinavia, but was resented, and was being weakened.

In the first half of the sixteenth century the Reformation came to the Scandinavian countries and was superficially accomplished in all of them.

LUTHERANISM TRIUMPHS IN DENMARK

In Denmark the Church was powerful and wealthy. It is said that on the eve of the Reformation in one or another way it owned a third of the land. The Pope claimed the right to make all ecclesiastical appointments, but the king made some of the nominations and the nobles, wishing to fill lucrative posts with their younger sons and resenting the diversion of Danish revenues to the creatures of Rome, demanded that bishops must be from their families and that other important church offices be filled either from their sons or by doctors of theology. Under these circumstances there was much corruption and worldliness.

Shortly before 1500 new life began to stir. In 1478 a university with a professor of theology was set up in Copenhagen. Early in the sixteenth century Paul Helgesen (or Eliae or Eliaeason) urged reform, especially in the sale of indulgences. In some circles the writings of Erasmus began to be read. From December, 1520, to March of the following year, Martin Reinhard, a German priest who had studied at Wittenberg, preached in Copenhagen as court chaplain and, to the distress of Helgesen, brought in some of Luther's views. King Christian II attempted a reform of discipline in the Church but was driven into exile (1523) before he could make it effective. Early in the 1520's Hans Tausen, who had been appointed professor of theology in Copenhagen and who had heard Luther preach in Wittenberg, began giving sermons which aroused popular enthusiasm. There were other preachers of the new views. Two Danish translations of the New Testament were circulated widely. Frederick I, who reigned from 1523 to 1533, moved in the direction of Lutheranism. A daughter and a son were married to German Lutherans. In spite of the opposition of the bishops, he permitted Tausen and others to teach Lutheranism and also declined to take action against priests and monks who were marrying Lutheranism won adherents among teachers and students in the University of Copenhagen.

In 1534 a son of Frederick, a convinced Lutheran, who seems to have been won by the impression made on him as a lad of eighteen by the great reformer at the Diet of Worms, came to the throne as Christian III and reigned until 1559. Under him Denmark became fully Lutheran. He had been elected king over the opposition of the bishops. Soon after he had defeated an attempt to restore Christian II, he had the bishops arrested and, with the approval of the lay members of the *Rigsraad* and of a national assembly (*Rigsdag* or *Thing*) confiscated the episcopal properties. Christian III asked Luther for help in carrying through the reorganization and the latter sent him John Bugenhagen, who had already performed a similar mission in Pomerania. Bugenhagen crowned the king and his queen. The king appointed seven superintendents who later were called bishops, and, although only a presbyter, Bugenhagen laid his hands on them in consecration. From the Catholic standpoint, therefore, they and those who followed them were not in the apostolic succession. An administrative structure for the Church was devised which had the approval of Luther. A liturgy was compiled, the Bible was translated into Danish, and eventually the Augsburg Confession, with modifications, was adopted. The translation of the Bible was the work of Christiern Pedersen, and was a literary masterpiece which by some has been deemed worthy of comparison with Luther's German version. Pedersen also translated various Lutheran works. He is said to have been the first writer of importance to use Danish and to have been the pioneer of a kind of Dane who wished his nation to combine Christian faith, popular education, and a knowledge of Danish history. The monasteries were not immediately abolished, but eventually they disappeared and their properties passed to the crown. Some Roman Catholic beliefs and practices persisted for a time, but the kingdom eventually became solidly Lutheran with a national church which had the monarch as its executive head.

In this adoption of Lutheranism Christian III seems to have been moved by genuinely religious motives. However, through it he greatly strengthened the power of the crown. The confiscation of church property gave the king large financial resources. His position as administrative head of the church in his realm enhanced his prestige and authority. Under him and his immediate successors Denmark entered upon an era of prosperity. Learning flourished as never before. Great care was taken to provide the kingdom with teachers, preachers, and schools.

LUTHERANISM IS IMPOSED ON NORWAY

In Norway the progress of the Reformation was not as happy as in Denmark. There appears to have been no popular demand for it. Under Frederick I, who was king in both countries, a Lutheran preacher arrived in the port of Bergen but seems to have had little influence outside the German community He was followed by two others who appear to have had letters of protection from Frederick. Before 1532, under the direction of royal officials, several churches in Bergen, including the cathedral, were destroyed. Lutherans came into possession of others of the churches. After the death of Frederick, the Archbishop of Trondhjem led the opposition to Christian III. However, as the country went over to the king the archbishop fled and remained a voluntary exile, thus depriving the Roman Catholics of their natural leader. Christian III made it his purpose to deprive Norway of its status as a separate kingdom united with Denmark by the personal tie of a common monarch, and to reduce it to a permanent dependency of the southern kingdom. All but two of the bishops were turned out. These two became Lutherans and retained their sees. However, religiously Norway was neglected. Only a few Lutheran pastors came, and some of them were embroiled in disputes over tithes and did not speak the Norse language which still prevailed in rural areas. The staffing of bishoprics was neglected. Many of the old priests remained until death and then there was delay in providing successors. At the outset some of these were of unworthy character. It was not until the beginning of the seventeenth century that conditions began markedly to improve.

LUTHERANISM WINS ICELAND

The early part of the fifteenth century had been one of hardship for Iceland and its church. The Black Death, arriving late, swept the island, severe winters added to the distress, population declined, and some of the bishops were foreigners who were far from worthy of their posts. The end of the century saw improvement. Native bishops of better character and education revived learning, and there was something of a religious awakening. By 1540 Lutheranism was penetrating Iceland through German merchants and youths who had travelled or studied in Norway, Denmark, or Germany. The New Testament was translated into Icelandic and published. Iceland was ruled from Denmark, and officials of Christian III, following the policy of that monarch, deposed the bishops and seized their property. In part of the island a native bishop resisted, using armed force, was supported by popular nationalistic resentment against the Danish innovations, was captured, and he and two of his sons were beheaded. Lutheranism made progress by more peaceable means, especially under Gudbrand Thorlaksson, the son of a priest, who, appointed by the king, was bishop from 1570 to his death in 1627, at the advanced age of eighty-three. He prepared a hymnal and published a translation of the Bible, both in Icelandic. Thanks in part to him, the old Norse tongue persisted and did not, as in Norway, give place to Danish. He had catechisms and other Lutheran literature produced and distributed, and it was in no small degree through him that Lutheranism prevailed. Yet many of the old customs persisted, among them auricular confession and reverence for the national saints.

LUTHERANISM PREVAILS IN SWEDEN

In Sweden Lutheranism was adopted in connexion with a political revolution. In 1520, in an effort to make himself supreme in Sweden, Christian II of Denmark had treacherously and dramatically executed some of the foremost men in the country in what was remembered as "the Stockholm blood bath." Executions were extended to other parts of Sweden and to Finland in an effort to root out all those of prominence who might resist his rule. The banner of revolt was raised by a young nobleman, Gustavus Ericksson, usually known as Gustavus Vasa, from the *vasa*, or sheaf, which was on his coat of arms. He was already among the opposition, for having as a hostage been carried captive to Denmark he had, before his escape, conceived a lasting distrust and hatred of Danish power. The deaths of his father and brother-in-law in the Stockholm massacre and of his mother and two sisters in prison in Denmark confirmed his hostility. He recruited his forces from the peasants, was elected king in 1523, drove the Danes out of Sweden, and was crowned in 1528. He then had the even more difficult task of consolidating his authority and bringing internal order in his realm.

As did monarchs elsewhere in Europe in that century, whether Roman Catholic or Protestant, Gustavus Vasa sought to bring the Church in his realms under the control of the crown. The Church had been both powerful and wealthy. Yet at the time that he fought his way to the crown it had been weakened by a loss of leadership. Two of its bishops had been victims of the "blood bath" and the primate, Gustav Trolle, Archbishop of Uppsala, a partisan of Christian II and from a family that was in chronic rivalry and enmity with the Sture, from which Gustavus Vasa sprang, had been deposed and had fled the country. Only one regularly consecrated bishop remained, and he went abroad when the ecclesiastical changes were well under way. The king was in desperate need of additional financial resources. These he found, as did Christian III of Denmark, in the appropriation of the possessions and revenues of the Church.

Ecclesiastical alterations went hand in hand with a great surge of national vigour which expressed itself creatively in several ways, and the Church of Sweden became the religious facet of that life. In it the Swedish people were bound together in a self-conscious community. State and Church were two aspects of one whole.

The Reformation had begun to penetrate Sweden only about the time that Gustavus Vasa was fighting his way to the throne. Its chief preacher was Olavus (or Olaus) Petri (Olaf Petersson) (1493–1552). The son of a smith, he studied at the recently founded University of Uppsala and then in several other places on the Continent. He took a master's degree at Wittenberg in 1518. He was, therefore, in that first home of the Reformation when Luther nailed his ninety-five theses on the church door. However, he had left Wittenberg before the movement there had reached its more radical stages and while Luther had as yet no thought of breaking with the Roman Catholic Church. Returning to Sweden, Olavus Petri began teaching in the cathedral school at Strängnäs. While his views reflected what he had heard at Wittenberg, they were for moderate reform and not for thoroughgoing changes. The archdeacon, Laurentius Andreas, was friendly. In 1523 Gustavus Vasa met these two men at Strängnäs. Impressed by them, the next year he asked Olavus Petri to Stockholm to serve as preacher. He also made Laurentius Andreae (Lars Andersson) (1480–1552) his chancellor. Thus the Reformation was given his endorsement.

A break soon came with Rome, but over Papal administrative authority rather than doctrine. The Pope supported the deposed Archbishop Gustav Trolle and appointed one of his own creatures, an Italian, to a Swedish bishopric. This angered the king. Recently he had written to the Pope asking authority for the Archbishop-elect of Uppsala to reform the Church, requesting confirmation of four bishops-elect, and saying that because of the poverty of the land the customary annates would not be paid to Rome. Now he said that if confirmation of the bishops was denied, he would have that given them by "Christ the only and highest pontiff." With this (November, 1523) the tie with Rome was severed, for neither king nor Pope would yield. Eventually consecration of the new bishops was obtained through two bishops who protested their loyalty to Rome and one of whom had been ordained at Rome. Thus the post-

Reformation Swedish episcopate was regarded as being in the apostolic succession. While the Church of Sweden put little emphasis upon this fact, at least some Roman Catholic opinion accepted it as probable, but deplored the variance of the ceremonies of ordination of priests from those of Rome and the emphasis in Sweden upon the preaching functions rather than the sacramental powers of the priests. In 1527 the Västerås Recess and the *Västerås Ordinantie* confiscated the bulk of the property of the Church, gave the king large powers over the Church, abolished compulsory confession, and made other innovations.

Changes in the Church of Sweden proceeded apace but did not lead to as wide a departure from those of the Roman Catholic Church as in much of Lutheran Germany. The incomes and powers of the bishops were greatly reduced. Marriage of priests, monks, and nuns was permitted. Preaching of the word of God was enjoined on the clergy. The Bible was translated into Swedish. In all this Laurentius Andreae, Olavus Petri, and the latter's brother, Laurentius Petri (Lars Petersson) (1499–1573), as Archbishop of Uppsala, had a large part. Olavus Petri especially had an important place in the creation of literature. He shared in the translation of the Bible, wrote voluminously, prepared hymnals in Swedish for the use of congregations, and brought out a Swedish mass. This last, with modifications, was long to remain standard in the Church of Sweden. It owed much to the *Canon Missae* of the Roman Catholic Church, but was not a slavish translation. Olavus Petri held that the words of institution were unalterable and that at each celebration the Gospel must be proclaimed, but that with these exceptions variations in the service were permissible. Olavus Petri attacked monasticism and clerical celibacy. Both disappeared, although not necessarily or primarily because of his onslaughts.

In these changes Olavus Petri and his associates were strongly influenced by Luther and were his warm admirers, but they did not follow him in every detail. Nor were the disputes between the various factions in German Lutheranism reproduced. Echoes of them were heard, but only faintly. In Sweden the Reformation took a course peculiar to that land. In some respects it held more closely to the old ways than it did in most of the Lutheran sections of Germany. The *kyrkoordning* ("church manual") prepared by Laurentius Petri and given official sanction in 1571 was distinctly Swedish and also retained some of the old customs, such as confession, excommunication, and public penance. Many of the parish priests continued in their posts and married their housekeepers or concubines to legitimatize their children.

Gustavus Vasa wished fully to subordinate the Church to royal authority and was irritated by what he deemed the independence of the bishops and some of the other clergy. Moreover, he differed from them on the course which reform should take, and, quite understandably, wanted his own way. He repudiated prayers for the dead and confession. On his deathbed he turned a deaf ear to the clergy who urged him to confess his sins and seek absolution. He moved much further from the old church towards an extreme Protestant position than did most of the clergy. He broke with Olavus Petri and Laurentius Andreae and markedly reduced the power of the bishops. Indeed, at the time of his death (1560) episcopacy seemed on the way out. Yet Laurentius Petri survived him, through him the episcopal succession was continued, and the Church regained partial autonomy.

Efforts of Eric XIV, son and successor of Gustavus Vasa, to introduce Calvinism were thwarted. The attempts of Johan (John) III, another son of Gustavus Vasa and the second king after him, to effect a *rapprochement* with Rome came to nought. When in 1592 the crown passed to Sigismund, a devoted Roman Catholic, a meeting of the Church at Uppsala in 1593 decided to hold to the unmodified Augsburg Confession. Charles IX, still another son of Gustavus, followed Sigismund on the throne. He had Calvinist leanings, was deeply interested in theology, and wrote hymns and prayers. His attempts to promote Calvinism met with determined and successful opposition, especially by professors in the University of Uppsala and the Archbishop of Uppsala. Sweden remained staunchly Lutheran.

LUTHERANISM ON THE EAST COASTS OF THE BALTIC

For centuries much of Finland had been subject to Sweden. It was to be expected that the Reformation would be carried there by Swedes. Gustavus Vasa was chiefly responsible for introducing and furthering it. About a hundred years later Isaac Rothovius, Bishop of Åbo from 1627 to 1652, did much to raise the level of the Christianity of the land. Through him church attendance was enforced, the quality of the clergy was improved, education was advanced, a university founded, and a Finnish translation of the Bible was printed.

Here and there along the east shore of the Baltic south of Finland, Lutheran enclaves arose, largely among the German and Scandinavian elements of the population.

LUTHERANISM SPREADS TO CENTRAL EUROPE

Lutheranism spread eastward as well as northward. It enjoyed no great vogue in Poland. It won some adherents, but the Protestantism of the land was chiefly Calvinism and Socianianism.

In Bohemia and Moravia the movements of which Hus had been the outstanding figure persisted into the sixteenth century. Luther made sympathetic contacts with them. On some points, notably the fashion in which Christ is present in the Lord's Supper, he was at variance with them. However, Bohemian students came to Wittenberg and in time those groups who looked back to Hus as their great hero were more and more permeated by Lutheran views. They grew in numbers and it is said that by the end of the sixteenth century nine-tenths of the population of Bohemia was Protestant. In general, the German elements were Lutheran and the Slavic elements tended towards the Swiss type of Protestantism in which Calvin's thought became dominant. In face of a common danger from an aggressive Roman Catholic attempt to rewin the country under a ruler of that faith and spear-headed by the Jesuits, Lutherans and Calvinists drew together for defense and in 1575 formulated a common confession of faith.

In Hungary and Transylvania several factors facilitated the spread of Protestantism. Here as in so much of Europe, in the fifteenth century the Catholic Church was suffering from corruption in both clergy and laity. The Hussite movement found sympathizers, a Hungarian translation of the Bible was made by two priests who adhered to it, and there may have been traces of the Waldensees. Humanism found a following in aristocratic circles, and while some of it undercut Christian faith, from it also came demands for reform. In the overwhelming defeat of the Hungarians by the Turks at the battle of Mohács in 1526, five bishops, two archbishops, and the king lost their lives, thus depriving the Catholic Church of much of its leadership. A large part of the country was occupied by the Turks and they tended to favour Protestants as against Roman Catholics, presumably because the former were less likely to support attempts by princes of the West, Roman Catholics, to reconquer the region. Possibly, too, many in the population subject to the Turks sought a deeper religious faith to support them in their trials and believed that they found it in Protestantism.

Protestantism first came in the form of Lutheranism. It spread through the Germans who were numerous in the area, especially in Transylvania. Hungarians studied at Wittenberg and brought back with them the teachings of Luther and Melanchthon. Among them were Matthias Biró of Déva, also known as Devay, who, a great preacher, came to be known as the Hungarian Luther, and Stephen Kis of Szeged, a doctor of theology from that university, whose theological works went through many editions and who trained many of the Protestant ministers. Both these men later swung towards the Swiss form of the Reformation. Anabaptists and anti-Trinitarians also won followings. By the end of the sixteenth century Protestants were probably in the majority in Hungary and Transylvania. Then began the partial reconversion of the population to Roman Catholicism through the Jesuits.

In Hungary and Transylvania Protestants were divided, largely along racial lines. In general, Lutheranism was recruited from Germans and Slavs, while most Magyar Protestants were of the Reformed faith. West of the Danube, where Magyars had tended to mingle with Germans and Slavs, the Protestants among them were mainly Lutheran. In Transylvania in 1568 the prince granted equal rights to Catholics, Lutherans, Reformed, and Unitarians. In 1571 this was confirmed by the Transylvanian Diet.

THE WIDE DISSEMINATION OF LUTHER'S WRITINGS

It was not only in lands where his views stimulated the formation of continuing churches which embodied his teachings that Luther was influential. His writings spread widely in other countries in Western Europe and with more or less pronounced effects. In the Low Countries Lutheran communities came into being but, as we are to see, the Reformed Churches were much more prominent. Luther's writings were circulated in Great Britain. In several sections of Italy, notably Venice, they were read, although in limited circles. They were known in Spain, but there humanism and especially Erasmus and his type of reform were more popular.

SUMMARY

In the early years of the sixteenth century the tide of new life which had been preceded by the ground swell of the fifteenth century came to its flood in the Protestant and Catholic Reformations. The Protestant phase of that tide first appeared almost simultaneously in several lands. However, its earliest manifestation was in Germany in Martin Luther. Moulded by a profound religious experience issuing from soul-shaking struggles to satisfy the demands of a righteous and holy God, this peasant-born monk, priest, and university professor unexpectedly found that a courageous attempt to protest against abuses connected with the sale of indulgences made him a European figure. By his insistence, the fruit of his spiritual pilgrimage, on the sufficiency of the Scriptures as the record of the word of God, justification by faith alone, and the priesthood of all believers, he was led first to challenge and then to break with the Roman Catholic Church. It was a kind of individualism which was to characterize Protestantism, that of the naked soul face to face with God, redeemed by Him, and, responsible to Him, convinced that without disloyalty to Him it cannot submit to other authority unless convinced by reason and the Scriptures. Luther knew that he was not yet perfect and that within this life he would always be a sinner. He continued to be visited by periods of depression and inner conflict which he called *Anfectungen*. He had come to the conviction that he could never earn God's favour, whether by moral acts, deeds of mercy, or the ceremonies of the Church. Yet he believed that God's grace in Christ is sufficient and, received in faith, makes the sinner acceptable with God.

Quite without planning or intending it, Luther became a catalyst, to use a chemical analogy. Elements of many kinds, nationalistic and religious, found in him something which brought them to a fresh and partially unified reaction. Or, to use another chemical term, he set off a chain reaction which issued in an explosion that tore away much of Western Europe from the Roman Catholic Church. He was not alone responsible. The ingredients for the explosion were already there. Had he not given the decisive impulse some one else would soon have done so. However, he contributed distinctive features to what followed. In most of Northern Germany, in all of Scandinavia, and among minorities in adjacent lands on the Baltic and in Central Europe, Christianity took on a form which has rightly been called Lutheranism. By the middle of the twentieth century, through missions and migrations of peoples, Lutheranism was to be carried to all the other continents and to scores of countries.

Luther and his convictions were to have repercussions of greater or less intensity upon other forms of Christianity. Justification by faith alone was found in many more strains of Protestantism than those which bore the Lutheran name. Indeed, it was so widespread as to be the most distinctive feature common to Protestantism. Even among Roman Catholics there were those who went far towards accepting it and in some other respects were not unfriendly to Luther. He undoubtedly quickened the reform movement which remained within the Roman Catholic Church. This was in part in heartening some who were painfully aware of the moral evils in that church. It was also in part in stimulating many to work for reform to counteract the appeal of Luther and thus to prevent more from going over fully to Lutheranism and, if possible, to win back those who had followed him out of the Roman fold. It is to the wing of Protestantism which owed much to Luther and yet differed enough from him to constitute another ecclesiastical family, that of the Reformed Churches, that we must next turn.

Selected Bibliography

GENERAL WORKS ON PROTESTANTISM WHICH HAVE MUCH ON LUTHERANISM

R. H. Bainton, *The Reformation of the Sixteenth Century* (Boston, The Beacon Press, 1952, pp. xi, 276). An admirable popular brief summary by an outstanding specialist.

B. J. Kidd, *Documents Illustrative of the Continental Reformation* (Oxford, The

Clarendon Press, 1911, pp. xix, 742). A very useful collection of texts, about half on Lutheranism, with introductory notes.

T. M. Lindsay, *A History of the Reformation* (New York, Charles Scribner's Sons, 2 vols., 1906). A standard work, but not without mistakes.

E. de Moreau, P. Jourdan, P. Janelle, *Le Crise Religieuse du XVI*e *Siècle* (Paris, Bloud & Gay, 1950, pp. 461). Vol. 16 of A. Fliche and E. Jarry, *Histoire de l'Église depuis les Origines jusqu'a Nos Jours*). A Roman Catholic treatment attempting, not unsuccessfully, to be objective.

P. Schaff, *The Creeds of Christendom. Volume III, The Evangelical Protestant Creeds, with Translations* (New York, Harper & Brothers, 1877, pp. vii, 920). A standard compilation.

P. Smith, *The Age of the Reformation* (New York, Henry Holt and Co., 1920, pp. xii, 861). An excellent summary of the Protestant and Catholic Reformations in their general European setting.

W. Walker, *The Reformation* (New York, Charles Scribner's Sons, 1901, pp. vii, 478). A well-written summary by a reliable specialist.

MARTIN LUTHER

R. H. Bainton, *Here I Stand. A Life of Martin Luther* (New York and Nashville, Abingdon-Cokesbury Press, 1950, pp. 422). A superb combination of accurate scholarship based upon a thorough knowledge of the sources and secondary works with insight, vivid, readable literary style, and reproductions of contemporary illustrations. It also contains so valuable a bibliography as to render needless an extended one in this chapter.

H. Boehmer, *Road to Reformation. Martin Luther to the Year 1521.* Translated from the German by J. W. Doberstein and T. G. Tappert (Philadelphia, The Muhlenberg Press, 1946, pp. xiii, 449). Well written, semi-popular, by an outstanding German specialist.

E. M. Carlson, *The Reinterpretation of Luther* (Philadelphia, The Westminster Press, 1948, pp. 256). A useful summary of recent Swedish studies of Luther.

H. Grisar, *Luther,* translated from the German by E. M. Lamond, edited by L. Cappadelta (St. Louis, B. Herder; London, Kegan Paul, Trench, Trübner & Co., 6 vols., 1913–1917). By a Jesuit, very critical of Luther. There is a later edition, adapted from the 2d German ed. by F. J. Eble, edited by A. Preuss (Westminster, Md., The Newman Bookshop, 1950, pp. x, 609).

D. Martin Luther's Werke. Kritische Gesammtausgabe (Weimar, H. Bohlau, 82 vols. in 93, 1883–1948). The standard edition.

Luther's Correspondence and Other Contemporary Letters, translated and edited by P. Smith (Philadelphia, The Lutheran Publication Society, 2 vols., 1913).

Luther's Primary Works together with His Shorter and Larger Catechisms, translated into English, edited, with theological and historical essays, by H. Wace and C. A. Buchheim (London, Hodder & Stoughton, 1896, pp. xvi, 492).

M. Luther, *Three Treatises* (Philadelphia, The Muhlenberg Press, 1947, pp. 290).

Contains his *Open Letter to the Christian Nobility of the German Nation, The Babylonian Captivity,* and *The Treatise on Christian Liberty.*

Works of Martin Luther, translated and edited by H. E. Jacobs *et al.* (Philadelphia, A. J. Holman Co., and the Castle Press, 1915–1932).

A. C. McGiffert, *Martin Luther, the Man and His Work* (New York, Appleton-Century-Crofts, 1911, pp. xi, 397). Semi-popular, by a distinguished American church historian.

J. Mackinnon, *Luther and the Reformation* (London, Longmans, Green & Co., 4 vols., 1925–1930). Carefully done, by a Scottish Presbyterian historian.

M. Reu, *Luther's German Bible. An Historical Presentation together with a Collection of Sources* (Columbus, Ohio, The Lutheran Book Concern, 1934, pp. xiv, 364, 226). A careful study with extensive notes. About one-third is source material.

E. G. Schwiebert, *Luther and His Times: The Reformation from a New Perspective* (St. Louis, Concordia Publishing House, 1950, pp. xxii, 892). Competent, the most comprehensive account in English, by a Lutheran.

MELANCHTHON

J. W. Richard, *Philip Melanchthon, the Protestant Preceptor of Germany 1497–1560* (New York, G. P. Putnam's Sons, 1898, pp. xv, 399). Semi-popular.

LUTHERANISM OUTSIDE OF GERMANY

C. Bergendoff, *Olavus Petri and the Ecclesiastical Transformation in Sweden (1521–1552). A Study in the Swedish Reformation* (New York, The Macmillan Co., 1928, pp. 264). Based upon extensive research.

G. K. Brown, *Italy and the Reformation to 1550* (Oxford, Basil Blackwell, 1933, pp. 324). Based upon both the sources and secondary studies.

C. M. Butler, *The Reformation in Sweden. Its Rise, Progress, and Crisis; and Its Triumph under Charles IX* (New York, Anson D. F. Randolph & Co., 1883, pp. iv, 259). A useful summary.

E. H. Dunkley, *The Reformation in Denmark* (London, Society for Promoting Christian Knowledge, 1948, pp. 188). A good summary, based largely on secondary studies in Danish.

J. C. F. Hood, *Icelandic Church Saga* (London, Society for Promoting Christian Knowledge, 1946, pp. 241). A survey of the church history of Iceland from the beginning through the nineteenth century.

E. Révész, J. S. Kováts, L. Ravasz, *Hungarian Protestantism. Its Past, Present, and Future* (Budapest, Bethlen Gabor Literary and Printing House Co., 1927, pp. xiv, 222).

W. Toth, *Highlights of the Hungarian Reformation* (*Church History,* Vol. IX, pp. 141–156).

T. B. Willson, *History of the Church and State in Norway from the Tenth to the Sixteenth Century* (London, Constable & Co., 1903, pp. xii, 382). Semi-popular.

J. Wordsworth, *The National Church of Sweden* (London, A. R. Mowbray & Co., 1911, pp. xix, 459). By an Anglican bishop.

Chapter XXXIII

THE RISE AND SPREAD OF THE REFORMED
AND PRESBYTERIAN CHURCHES

Parallel with Lutheranism another kind of Protestantism was emerging and developing. It usually goes by the name of Reformed. In it were varieties, including Presbyterianism in its several manifestations. Yet, like Lutheranism, it constituted a family of churches which in the nineteenth and twentieth centuries was to be drawn together in a loose, world-wide association. Luther had an effect upon it, but in its origin humanism was more influential than it was in Luther. No single leader placed so profound a stamp upon it as did Luther upon the churches which are often known by his name. John Calvin more nearly shaped it than did any other man, but some, notably Zwingli, Farel, and Bucer (or Butzer), were earlier connected with it than was he. In the sixteenth and seventeenth centuries its chief geographic spread was on the borders between the lands in the north-west of Europe which became fairly solidly Lutheran and the countries in the south-west of Europe which remained either predominantly or overwhelmingly Roman Catholic. Most of such Protestantism as survived in Latin Europe was Reformed. That, however, was in France, Switzerland, and the mountain valleys in North Italy. No Protestantism succeeded in maintaining itself in the deep south of Latin Europe. The Reformed Churches stretched in a somewhat interrupted belt from Transylvania and Hungary on the east, through Switzerland, down the Rhine Valley into Holland, and across the North Sea into Scotland and North Ireland. Eventually, through migrations and missions the Reformed Churches were to have a much wider extension. In the twentieth century they were to be found on all the continents and in many of the islands of the sea.

The significance of the original geographic distribution of the Reformed Churches and especially the underlying reasons for it are obscure. It may be more than a coincidence that the area is on the border between those regions which had been fully assimilated to Latin culture and those into which that culture had not penetrated until after their conversion to Christianity and then chiefly through the Church. As we have noted, the lands in which Latin culture had been well established before their conversion remained within the Roman Catholic fold and there in general the renewed currents of life which produced reform fitted into religious patterns which were already developed and fairly well fixed. In the lands of the North the awakening profoundly stirred individuals, especially Luther, for whom the existing patterns proved an intolerable strait jacket. Even when these were in part retained, the effort was made to subordinate them to the life which issued from a fresh experience of the faith as seen in the Scriptures. The Reformed Churches more nearly rejected the inheritance from the Roman Catholic Church than did those churches that arose through Luther.

At first sight this is contrary to what might have been expected from the fact that the Reformed Churches were on the borders of the Latin lands. It arose at least partly from the share which Christian humanism had in the emergence of these churches. The two chief early figures, Zwingli and Calvin, were much more influenced by humanism than was Luther. As we have seen, humanism arose in Latin lands which had long been under Christian influence from a revival of the pre-Christian Græco-Roman tradition which had entered so strongly into Latin culture. It had the effect of driving men back to the original sources—in Christianity to the earliest documents, namely, the Scriptures. It did not necessarily imply the rejection of all subsequent developments in the Church, but it insisted that these be subjected to the test of whether they could be supported from the Scriptures.

To be sure, in Lutheranism humanism was strongly represented, notably through Melanchthon. Yet the experience of Luther, which was so largely apart from humanism, was controlling. However, stronger though humanism was in the creation of the Reformed than of the Lutheran wing of Protestantism, it was not as potent as it was in a much more radical Protestantism whose chief exponents came from Italy and Spain, deep in the Latin South.

In another way the Reformed Churches may have reflected the Roman tradition, possibly from unconscious contagion from the Latin culture on the fringes of which they emerged. Luther and those who were moulded by his views tended to be pessimistic about the possibility of bringing human society or any of its segments into conformity with the will of God. The kingdom of God would not be realized on this earth. Man is a sinner and even when an individual has been justified by faith he continues to sin. God's grace in saving man through Christ is an unfathomable mystery, for man can do nothing to deserve it. God's gift in Christ is to be accepted in amazed, glad, humble gratitude. But although Christians, especially Christian princes, can do much to restrain evil, the kingdom of God can never be realized within history. So said

Luther and those who thought with him. In contrast, the Reformed Churches, while recognizing as keenly as the Lutherans the depravity of man and the wonder of God's grace, were more hopeful that through the labours of those who in faith had accepted the salvation offered by that grace God would effect within history an approximation to His kingdom. This was more nearly akin to the Roman imperial tradition of striving through good laws, morals, and government to create civilized society and resembled what the great Popes of the Middle Ages had dreamed of realizing through the Roman Catholic Church.

The Beginnings of the Reformed Churches: Zwingli

The movements which produced the Reformed Churches arose almost simultaneously with those which had come through Luther. While they quickly became aware of Luther, they largely went their own way.

The earliest outstanding leader was Huldreich Zwingli (1484–1531). Zwingli was born in Switzerland. That in itself was important. Although nominally a part of the Holy Roman Empire, in practice Switzerland was substantially autonomus. It was divided into several cantons, some of them predominantly rural in their Alpine valleys, and some with small cities, such as Basel, Zürich, and Bern, which had a well-to-do citizenry and where the Renaissance had been welcomed and humanism flourished. Swiss mercenaries were in high repute and fought in many of the battles of Europe. The independent spirit made revolt from Rome more natural than in some other regions. Here, too, was a trend towards democracy which had an effect upon the thought and organization of the Reformed Churches.

Zwingli was born January 1, 1484, and so was only a few weeks younger than Luther. Like the latter, he was from a prosperous peasant home. His father was the village bailiff and an uncle the village priest. Another uncle was an abbot. A bright lad, the family determined to give him an education and prepare him for the priesthood. In his student days he acquired Latin and Greek and read in the Latin and Greek Fathers. Like Luther and so many others in Western Europe, he was much impressed by Augustine. The writings of Christian humanists appealed to him, among them those of Pico della Mirandola and especially Erasmus. He found congenial the latter's passion for reform and the Greek New Testament of that master so enthralled him that he memorized much of its text.

Zwingli seems never to have had the kind of soul-shaking religious experience which moulded Luther. His had been a happy boyhood and he grew up with no great sense of sin. Indeed, like so many priests of his day and quite unlike Luther, he did not observe the clerical obligation of chastity. However, most of his contemporaries regarded that as a peccadillo and it did not keep him from having a genuine moral earnestness. Serving for a time as a chaplain with Swiss mercenaries in Italy, he returned with a deep dislike for the practice which led Swiss sons to sell their bodies and prostitute their souls in the service of alien princes. He opposed it and thereby so won the dislike of the French that he was forced to leave his parish of Glarus. He then became people's priest at the famous pilgrimage centre, Einsiedeln, in 1516, the year before Luther came forward with his ninety-five theses. There his fame as a preacher increased and in 1519 he became people's priest in the Great Minster at Zürich, a small city of perhaps 7,000, but wealthy and with political influence.

It was at Zürich that Zwingli became prominent as a reformer. Although he had received a Papal pension, when he reached that town he was already advocating some reforms. Independent, in good Swiss fashion, with little regard for ecclesiastical authority, he thought of his rôle as that of a preacher, not unlike that of an Old Testament prophet. He greeted Luther's early writings with joy and did much to further their circulation. Yet he later belittled their influence upon him. At first his preaching seems to have been directed partly to an exposition of *The Gospel according to Matthew* and against the practice of providing mercenary soldiers and receiving pensions. He himself surrendered his Papal pension in 1520.

Zwingli stressed the authority of the Scriptures and soon began denouncing whatever in the old faith was not expressly warranted in them. Under his leadership and in accord with this principle Zürich moved by rapid steps away from the Roman Catholic Church. In December, 1520, the civil rulers decreed that priests should preach in freedom conformably with what they received from the Scriptures. In 1522 the issue of Lenten fasting arose, and while Zwingli supported the practice, the civil authorities, by taking the initiative in ruling for them on the ground of good order, virtually rejected the jurisdiction of the Bishop of Constance, in whose diocese Zürich lay. In 1523 Zwingli came out against monastic vows, clerical celibacy, the intercession of the saints, the existence of purgatory, the sacrificial character of the mass, and the teaching that salvation can be earned by good works. He proclaimed the doctrine of salvation by faith. The civil government supported him. Priests and nuns married, and in 1524 Zwingli himself was formally wedded to a widow with whom he had had an irregular connexion. By Easter, 1525, images, relics, and organs had been eliminated from the churches, monastic establishments had been confiscated and their properties largely devoted to schools, and the mass had been discontinued. A simple church service in German was developed in which the sermon was central. In all of this Zwingli acted in close coöperation with the civil government and an even closer union of Church and state was achieved than in Luther's Saxony.

Zwingli broke with Luther. He differed from the latter in temperament and in his religious experience. His was largely the intellectual and, eventually, the moral approach. Luther was mentally fully as able and was more many-sided, but his tempestuous struggles for an assurance of justification before God had made on him an emotional and religious mark much deeper than any which Zwingli knew. Zwingli stressed conformity with the sovereign will of God as revealed in the Scriptures. Luther could never cease to marvel at the forgiving grace of God in Christ and to rejoice in the release and freedom which it brought. Open separation between Luther and Zwingli came over the significance of the Lord's Supper. To Luther the declaration of Christ as he broke the bread, "This is my body," was to be taken at its face value. To him, through the eye of faith, Christ was actually present in the consecrated elements, even though the manner of that presence defied a fully rational explanation. In the communion, he held, the believer partakes of Christ. To Zwingli, in the Lord's Supper the command, "Do this in memory of me," was controlling. Although he believed Christ to be present and to be discerned by faith, he regarded the rite primarily as a memorial through which the worshippers were bound together in an expression of loyalty to their Lord. It was the Eucharist, the common rejoicing of those who declare the death of Christ. To him Christ's words, "The flesh profiteth nothing," were determinative. Luther's view seemed to him to be an irrational persistence of Roman Catholic superstition.

Yet Luther and Zwingli both taught that salvation is by faith alone. Zwingli said that one is only free from sin when his "mind trusts itself unwaveringly to the death of Christ and finds rest there," that faith is born "only when a man begins to despair of himself and to see that he must trust in God alone," and that "it is perfected when a man wholly casts himself off and prostrates himself before the mercy of God alone, but in such fashion as to have entire trust in it because of Christ who was given for us."

Zwingli perished (October 11, 1531) in an inter-cantonal war which arose from the attempt of Zürich to force Protestant preaching upon neighbouring Roman Catholic cantons.

The Spread of the Reformed Churches

Before death removed Zwingli from the scene, the Reformation was spreading to other Swiss centres and in it the views of Zwingli loomed large. Basel, Bern, and several other cities came over to the movement. At Basel, John Hussgen, Heusgen, or Hausshein, better known as Oecolampadius (1482–

1531), was outstanding. Some of the cities of South Germany tended to side with the Zwinglian views. They were led to this partly by their affinity with the Swiss and partly by their distrust and fear of the princes who were supporting Luther. Among them Strassburg, on the French side of the Rhine, was prominent.

Zwingli wished to draw together in a league the Protestant cities, and Philip of Hesse hoped to have a comprehensive alliance of Protestant princes and cities which would include those who held to Luther as well as those moulded by Zwingli. In spite of the conciliatory efforts of Bucer, now influential in Strassburg, Luther and Zwingli could not agree and the dream of Philip of Hesse was frustrated. Bucer tried to make peace. He had led in the triumph of the Reformation in Strassburg and through his writings and the preachers whom he sent out he was potent in much of Central Europe. In the moot question of the Lord's Supper he took a middle ground between Luther and Zwingli. However, although some of the cities of South Germany accepted his view, it failed to heal the breach between Zwingli and Luther. The First Helvetic Confession, drafted at Basel in 1536, while conciliatory, also did not succeed in winning the Lutherans. The Lutheran and the Reformed wings of Protestantism were parting company. The Reformed Churches presented a variety of views and were by no means fully agreed among themselves. However, most of Protestant Switzerland except Basel, while by no means uniform, was drawn together by the Second Helvetic Confession (1562–1566) and to this Basel gave its adherence eighty years later.

In Zürich the work of Zwingli was continued and consolidated by his pupil and friend, Henry Bullinger (1504–1575). Conciliatory, Bullinger came nearer to the Lutheran view of the Lord's Supper than had Zwingli and gave refuge to persecuted Lutherans. Yet he remained true to the Reformed tradition. His enormous correspondence and his writings had a profound effect in England.

In French-speaking Switzerland Guillaume Farel (1489–1565) was a fiery preacher of the Reformation. Scion of an aristocratic family in Dauphiné, as a student he came under the influence of Jacques Le Fèvre (c.1455–1536). Modest, scholarly, deeply religious, Le Fèvre was a humanist who wrote commentaries on the Scriptures and wished to reform the Catholic Church from within. He had as a friend Guillaume Briçonnet (1470–1534), who was abbot of the monastery in Paris where Le Fèvre resided and who later, as its bishop, made Meaux a rallying point of Catholic reformers. Although he was under suspicion and for a time took refuge in Strassburg, Le Fèvre was later tutor to the children of Francis I of France and died without formally separating from the Roman Catholic Church.

Farel, however, was too impetuous to remain within that communion. His outspoken utterances made it necessary for him to leave France. He went to Basel, but his attack on Roman Catholic doctrines brought down on him the wrath of Erasmus and he was temporarily in Strassburg. He passed like a whirlwind through several cantons and cities in French-speaking Switzerland, and, visiting the Waldensees in their Alpine valleys, won some of them to the Reformation. He inspired and trained young men as preachers, sending them out to spread the Gospel. Fearless, singularly free from self-seeking, chivalrous, devotedly nursing the sick, he is one of the most attractive figures of an heroic era.

In 1532 Farel was for a time in Geneva, where the Council of Two Hundred had ordered the "pure Gospel" preached in every church and cloister, but the bishop's vicar soon brought about his expulsion. In 1533, after pressure from Bern had obtained freedom of worship for the Protestants, he returned to Geneva and in 1535 the mass was suppressed and the monks and nuns were driven out of the city. The Genevan movement towards the Reformation seems to have been as much from political as from religious motives. A commercial centre, Geneva was attempting to achieve its independence of both its bishop and the Duke of Savoy. Its adoption of Protestantism aided it in the struggle.

At this juncture John Calvin appeared on the scene. Urged by Farel to remain and help in the reorganization of the religious life, he began the connexion with Geneva which, with one interruption, continued until his death and was to make that city the main centre of the kind of Protestantism which bore the designation Reformed. Indeed, so potent was his influence that eventually he had more to do with giving the Reformed Churches their distinctive characteristics than did any other individual. Calvin was by no means dominant in all the Reformed Churches, for, like the Lutheran bodies, they displayed variety. Yet to a greater or less degree they were all indebted to him.

The Contribution of John Calvin to the Reformation: His Early Life

Although of humble ancestry (his forefathers had been barge men on the Oise), John Calvin was reared in aristocratic society and had the manners of that class. He was born on July 10, 1509, at Noyon in Picardy, about sixty miles north-east of Paris. His father was in comfortable circumstances. Although he was never ordained, the young John was designed by his father for the Church and was educated, as was the custom in those lax days, by the income from ecclesiastical benefices the duties of which he did not perform. As a lad of fourteen he went to the University of Paris. There he seems to have escaped the vices which corrupted many of the youths who came to that stormy seat of learning. Indeed, from boyhood he was deeply religious and critical of any laxity in morals. He won and kept friends among some of the more serious of the students. By a strange coincidence he was in the university when Francis Xavier and Ignatius Loyola matriculated, men who were to be outstanding in the Catholic Reformation, but he may not have met them. When nineteen, he left Paris to study law. His interests were those of the current humanism. He wrote in lucid, almost elegant Latin, he acquired a knowledge of Greek and Hebrew, and, in accord with these interests, his first book, published when he was twenty-three, was a commentary on Seneca's *De Clementia*.

Not far from this time Calvin had what he regarded as a sudden conversion, but we have no knowledge of its details. It is clear that he had come under the influence of an earnestly religious group in Paris from which issued several Protestants, and it is probable that he had become acquainted, directly or indirectly, with some of the writings of Erasmus and Luther and that they had impressed him. In 1534, when he was about twenty-five, he left Paris, surrendered his ecclesiastical revenues, was imprisoned, freed, and found a haven in Basel, then recently become a strong Protestant centre.

CALVIN'S INSTITUTES

It was at Basel, at the age of twenty-six, that Calvin finished and had published what was probably the most influential single book of the Protestant Reformation, his *Institutio Christianæ Religionis* (early translated as *The Institution of the Christian Religion,* but more usually later as *The Institutes of the Christian Religion*). He addressed it to Francis I, who, unstable and inconstant, had for a time shown favour to the reformers. Written in Latin, he soon put it into French. Indeed, he is said to have done more than any other one man to make that language a vehicle for philosophical and theological discussion. Worked over again and again and enlarged, Calvin gave it the fourth and final revision in 1559, only a few years before his death.

The *Institutes* did not owe their prominence to the originality of the ideas which they contained, for Calvin was intent upon demonstrating that the Christianity which he set forth was not novel, but was simply what had been taught in the Church before what he regarded as the changes—to his mind the innovating corruptions—made by the Roman Catholic Church. They won their way because of their clarity, the orderly arrangement of their thought, and their comprehensiveness. They were the most inclusive and systematic presentation of the Christian faith as held by Protestants which had thus far appeared. They set forth the entire cosmic drama of creation, sin, and redemption under the sovereign will of God as Calvin believed that it was taught in the Scriptures. He prized the Scriptures as the authoritative record of God's dealings with the universe and man.

In the final edition of the *Institutes* there were four books. They were intended to conform to the order in the Apostles' Creed, for Calvin was intent upon holding to that early and generally accepted summary of the Christian faith. The first dealt with God the Father as creator, preserver, and governor of the universe, for God was primary in Calvin's thought. The second outlined the redemption wrought by God in Christ, the third had to do with the Holy Spirit, and the fourth with the Church and the relation to it of civil governments. Calvin showed himself familiar with much of the literature of pre-Christian Græco-Roman antiquity and with many of the outstanding Christian thinkers across the centuries, but he laid especial stress upon the Scriptures and Augustine. He was not so much concerned with refuting what he believed to be the errors of the Roman Catholic Church and of Protestants with whom he was in disagreement as he was in stating positively and giving the reasons for what he maintained was true Christianity. Here was a comprehensive statement of what Calvin believed about God, Christ, the nature of man, immortality, sin, redemption, the manner in which God's grace works in the lives of men, the Church, and the relations of Church and state. Calvin stressed the sovereignty of God and submission to His will.

Calvin held that although the essence of God transcends all human thought, something of a knowledge of God is to be had on the one hand through observation and study of the orderliness of the universe which He has created, both the stars and the symmetry, beauty, and use of the human body, and on the other hand through the Scriptures. He came out boldly for the Trinitarian understanding of God, using Augustinian language. He held God to be the creator and sustainer of the universe and to be sovereign in it. He declared God to be omnipotent and that "governing heaven and earth by His providence, He so overrules all things that nothing happens in it without His counsel." By God's providence Calvin meant not an idle Deity Who sits by and watches what takes place under the operation of the general laws which He has ordained, but One Who concerns Himself with every individual, Who holds the helm and overrules all events, so that not even a sparrow falls to the ground apart from His will. Calvin boldly faced the problem of whether, if nothing occurs without the direct will of God, God is responsible for evil and why, if wicked men do evil by the decree of God, as the Scriptures in many instances maintain, even in the crucifixion of Christ, God should hold them responsible. Here, as in so many places, he cited Augustine. He held that God is completely free from any taint of injustice or wrong and that, while He has ordained the evil deeds which men do, the latter are fully to blame. Calvin does not resolve the mystery of the paradox but exhorts to a meek acceptance of what is taught in the Bible.

Calvin dealt with the creation of man. He declared that of all of the works of God man is the noblest, most admirable specimen of His justice, wisdom, and goodness. He held that man is both body and soul, that he was created in the image of God, that the image is in the soul, that the soul is endowed by God with intellect, the power to discern good from evil, justice from injustice, and that it is immortal. Calvin described the sin of the first man, Adam, and said that its essence was revolt against the authority of God, and that this entailed pride, ambition, and ingratitude. Through that offense of the primal man corruption, "original sin," warped all his descendants. By it the image of God was not effaced but was distorted, and with results which in some respects were worse than if it had been completely erased. The pride which sprang from the likeness to God and the distortion of that likeness which is inseparable from sin penetrated to the inmost soul of man. Total depravity followed. Man's will was so impaired that he could do no good works unless he was assisted by grace, the special grace which God has given to the elect, those whom He has chosen and received through regeneration. Apart from grace every man is under the deserved wrath of God. Man's salvation is entirely from the initiative of God.

To effect man's redemption, Calvin went on to say, God of His great love and mercy gave the law to keep alive the hope of salvation until Christ should come. From the beginning of the world this had been in the plan of God. Although God hated the sin in man, He found in man that which claimed His love. To be the redeemer and the mediator it was necessary that Christ should be fully God and fully man. Here Calvin was clearly on the side of what had been expressed by the Catholic Church at Chalcedon and as in so much else he was in positive accord with what had been held by the majority of Christians in both East and West. Christ, so he said, fulfilled the expectation recorded in the Old Testament and was prophet, priest, and king. By freely giving himself in sacrifice, and by suffering not merely physical death, but also the torments of one irretrievably lost, the horror of spiritual death, the descent into hell, which, so Calvin held, had been appropriately added to the Apostles' Creed, Christ as man had fully satisfied the righteous judgement of God, had removed the curse laid on man for his sin, and had destroyed the spiritual death which is the punishment for sin. By his resurrection, so Calvin taught, Christ appeared as the conqueror of death. Therefore it is upon his resurrection that our faith chiefly rests. Christ's ascent into heaven marked the beginning of his kingly reign. At the last day he will appear as judge of all and as redeemer of the elect.

The Holy Spirit, so Calvin proceeded to say, moves the sinner to the faith which accepts what has been done for him in Christ. To Calvin, as to Luther, justification, or salvation, is by faith. Faith can come only as the result of the work of the Holy Spirit. It is more than intellectual assent to truth. It is "a knowledge of the divine benevolence towards us" and if it is to be valid that which the mind has grasped must "be transfused into the heart." Faith and repentance are indissolubly connected, as Calvin saw them, but repentance is a consequence of faith. By repentance is meant forsaking ourselves and turning to God and laying aside our mind and assuming a new one. It is "a true conversion of our life to God, proceeding from a sincere and serious fear of God, and consisting in the mortification of our flesh and of the old man, and in the vivification of the Spirit." The fruits of repentance are love towards God and charity towards men, with sanctity and purity in our whole life.

The evidence that one has entered into the new life of faith is that he does works pleasing to God. "We are justified not without, and yet not by works." Calvin placed great emphasis upon character. We are not saved by character, but salvation issues in character. We never become perfect in this life, but we are always to strive to advance "in the way of the Lord." We are not to "despair on account of the smallness of our success," but are "to press forward to the goal." We are to present our bodies "a living sacrifice, holy, acceptable unto God," "depart from ourselves that we may apply all the vigour of our faculties to the service of the Lord," and resign ourselves "wholly to the direction of the Divine Spirit."

With Luther, Calvin believed in the divine calling. He held that God had appointed "to all their particular duties in different spheres of life," and that the Christian is not "to attempt more than is compatible with his calling," whether that be obscure or prominent, seemingly sordid or respectable.

Like Luther, Calvin affirmed the liberty of the Christian. That liberty is seen in being reminded by the law of one's duty, yet being lifted above the law, yielding a voluntary obedience to the will of God, and being freed from an obligation before God in external things, for these can sometimes be used and at other times omitted.

Calvin stressed prayer and described it as entering into conversation with God. He wrote that since no one of us is worthy to present himself before God, the heavenly Father has given us Christ as our advocate and mediator with him.

Calvin came out plumply for election. He held it to be a "comfortable doctrine," for to him it meant that nothing can be out of the control of God. He asserted what is often called double predestination. By that is meant that God has chosen some to be saved and some to be lost—election and reprobation. The reconciliation of God's love with His choosing some for eternal damnation does not seem to have caused Calvin the anguish that it did Luther. He held it to be a mystery and, agreeing with Augustine, declared that we must not "set up the standard of human justice as the standard by which to measure the justice of God." Nor would he have a man constantly anxious whether he is among the elect. While, if we were absolutely sure in this life that we are among the chosen of God for salvation, we would be tempted to complacency and pride, there are marks which are evidence that we are presumably of the elect. If we have them, we are to stop our worrying. The tests are a profession of faith, an upright life, and participation in the sacraments. Men were not to make their salvation the major aim, but are to put first the glory and honour of God.

Finally, Calvin's *Institutes* dealt with the Church. The Church, so he maintained, is not identical with any visible institution, but includes all the elect, the dead as well as the living. As the creed declares, the Church is Catholic, that is, universal. It cannot be divided, for this would mean that Christ is divided, and that is impossible. Its head is Christ, and through him all the elect grow up together as one body. The Catholic Church is invisible and is known only to God. Calvin also believed that there is a visible Church, which, though composed of particular churches in different towns and villages, yet embraces all the living throughout the world "who consent to the same truth of divine doctrine and are united by the bond of the same religion." In it are many hypocrites who have nothing of Christ but the name, yet it exists "wherever we find the word of God purely preached and heard, and the sacraments administered according to the institution of Christ," and we should acknowledge as its members "all those who by a confession of faith, an exemplary life, and a participation of the sacraments profess the same God and Christ as ourselves." All Christians should associate themselves with the external communion of the Church, even though the Church be imperfect. Moreover, so Calvin confidently and hopefully declared, while the Church has not yet arrived at perfection, it is daily improving. None of the elect is perfect, and they stand daily in need of the forgiving grace of God, but in the creed there is the affirmation of faith not only in the communion of saints but also in the forgiveness of sins. Calvin recognized two sacraments, baptism and the Lord's Supper.

As to the structure of the visible Church, Calvin held that it should ensure that everything be done decorously and in order. It should have judiciaries appointed to censure vice and to excommunicate. For officers of the Church, Calvin, quoting Paul, held that they were originally apostles, prophets, evangelists, pastors, and teachers. The first three, he declared, are raised up only for special occasions, while the pastors and teachers are constant. He held that the terms bishop, elder, pastor, and minister have the same meaning. There are also deacons, who administer the alms and care for the poor. Ministers have the inner call of God and are to be chosen with the consent and approbation of the people at elections over which other ministers preside. Here is democracy, although not equalitarianism, with orderly procedure. Calvin recommended ordination by the laying on of hands.

To Calvin the holy community should have in it both Church and state. The state, so he said, should help to obtain food and drink for its citizens. It should also prevent sacrilege against God and other offenses against religion, preserve the public peace, protect the property of the individual, enable business to be transacted without fraud or injustice, ensure a public form of religion among Christians, and maintain a civilized society. He favoured an elective aristocracy and shrank from anything that savoured of revolution. He sanctioned capital punishment by the magistrate in executing the judgement of God and said that some wars are lawful. Nations need not be bound by the law given to Moses, but are to be free to enact such legislation as seems to them expedient, provided that it is in accordance with the law of love.

CALVIN MAKES GENEVA AN EXAMPLE AND CENTRE OF THE REFORMED RELIGION

It was this Calvin, then in his late twenties, the youthful author of the *Institutes*, who was induced by Farel to help him with the Reformation in Geneva. The two worked closely together and sought to make of the little city a model community, organized in such fashion that Church and state worked together in harmony. After a little less than two years, in April, 1538, they were banished for refusing compliance with what they regarded as improper interference of the civil authorities in the Church's sphere. Their dream seemed to have come to naught.

Calvin found refuge in Strassburg and there was befriended by Bucer. Now followed a little over three years which were happier and more peaceful than any which he was again to know. He became pastor to the French refugees and built up a congregation organized and disciplined in accordance with his principles and with a liturgy which, an adaptation of one already in use in German churches and with later modifications made after his return to Geneva, became a model for public worship in Reformed Churches elsewhere. At Strassburg he also showed his skill as a teacher. In spite of chronic ill health, he added literary labours to his other duties and brought out an enlarged revision of the *Institutes*. It was at Strassburg that he married. In spite of the early death of their only child and his wife's invalidism, the union was happy. From Strassburg, too, he went to conferences with other reformers, among them Germans, and formed a warm friendship with Melanchthon.

Meanwhile, a shift in the political situation in Geneva brought into power the party friendly to Calvin. Its leaders besought him to return. Pressed by Farel and from a deep sense of duty he reluctantly complied. From his arrival in September, 1541, until his death nearly a quarter of a century later, May 27, 1564, he was the dominant figure in the city. This was in spite of the fact that he often faced opposition, held no other office than that of one of the ministers, and in the earlier years was not even formally a citizen. Under his leadership, close coöperation between Church and state was carried through. A form of church organization was set up through the *Ordonnances,* a catechism was prepared, and a liturgy was introduced based on that which he had developed at Strassburg. He had the discipline of community morals and the sumptuary legislation enforced which in theory had long been advocated by the Roman Catholic Church. He did much to develop commerce and the weaving indus- try. This made for a prosperous community. He encouraged the lending of money, but only at what he believed to be a fair interest. He thus contributed to a new industrial and commercial economy. Here he was in contrast with Luther, for the latter held to medieval concepts which condemned interest and advocated a just price, and would have welcomed a return to a rural economy. Calvin encouraged education and founded what eventually became the Uni- versity of Geneva. Indeed, he emphasized schools, for he believed in the neces- sity of learned ministers who could set forth the true faith, and of an educated laity who could understand them. He maintained that religious education is especially important. He preached, taught, wrote, carried on an enormous cor- respondence, and advised in matters of legislation, law enforcement, and ad- ministration. His commentaries covered most of the Bible.

Under Calvin Geneva became a haven for oppressed Protestants from many lands. In it men were trained who went back to their native countries to fur- ther the Reformation. While they did not always slavishly reproduce what they had seen there, through them and his writings Calvin became the most power- ful single factor in shaping the distinctive features of the Reformed Churches.

In the early years after his return, Calvin's position was by no means unchal- lenged. Some were restive under the strictness of the discipline for which he stood. Many of the native stock resented the influx of strangers and sought to prevent them from having a voice in the city's affairs. There were those who vigorously and volubly dissented from Calvin on matters of doctrine. Among the latter was Sebastien Castellio (1515–1563), of Savoy, a humanist scholar who had become a Protestant, and for a time was a protégé of Calvin. Castellio aspired to the pastorate, but Calvin blocked him, largely on questions of doc- trine, for Castellio questioned the inspiration of the Song of Songs and Calvin's interpretation of the phrase in the Apostles' Creed about Christ's "descent into hell." He failed of appointment, was dismissed from his teaching post, and, embittered against Calvin, went to Basel. He continued to engage in controversy, in part directed against Calvin, but he was now out of Geneva.

More serious was the test given by Michael Servetus (1511–1553). Servetus was a Spaniard, a scholar, a physician and scientist of originality and note, who by the time he was twenty had become a radical reformer. Deeply religious and devoted to Christ, wishing to restore what he believed to be true Christianity, he would not conform with the accepted doctrine of the Trinity. He also denounced predestination and infant baptism and believed that the millennial reign of Christ was about to begin. Temperamentally a controversialist, his was a stormy career. He and Calvin had already violently disagreed when, in 1553, fleeing from condemnation for heresy in Roman Catholic Vienne and passing through Geneva, he was recognized and arrested, certainly at Calvin's instance. In his trial for heresy Calvin's enemies rallied to his support. Had he been acquitted, Calvin's power in Geneva would have been threatened. Indeed, Servetus demanded that Calvin be arrested as a false accuser and a heretic, be driven out of the city, and his goods be given to him, Servetus. Servetus was condemned by the civil authorities on the charge that he had denied the Trinity and rejected baptism, offenses punishable by death under the Justinian Code. In spite of Calvin's plea for a more merciful form of execution, Servetus was burned at the stake (October 27, 1553), crying through the flames: "O Jesus, thou Son of the eternal God, have pity on me."

The condemnation of Servetus was a major defeat for Calvin's opponents. Henceforward his position in Geneva was not to be seriously contested. Abstemiousness in food, drink, and sleep, prodigious labours, the stress of controversies, and distressing moral delinquencies in his immediate family undermined an already frail health. Calvin died May 27, 1564, in the arms of Theodore Beza. His last letter had been to Farel. Reserved, except among his intimates, he was loyal to his friends. Few were close to him, but these few had for him an unshakable affection.

Like Luther, through his writings Calvin had an influence which extended over much of Western Europe. The two men were very different. Luther, deeply emotional, was moulded by his soul-shaking experience. He gave little or no thought or effort towards achieving an ideal social order here and now. Calvin, intellectual, clear, logical, seemed to put a minimum of emotion in his preaching and writing. He sought to bring to actuality ideal Christian communities. Although recognizing the imperfections in the Church and among Christians, he believed that progress could be made towards this goal. Efforts for social improvement arose within both the Lutheran and Reformed Churches, but they were more characteristic of the latter. However, the similarities between Luther and Calvin were fully as marked as their differences. Both were impressed with the majesty and sovereignty of God, both held to the historic creeds of the Catholic Church, both revered the Scriptures as authoritative, and both believed in predestination and salvation by faith. Although they did not fully agree as to the nature of the presence of Christ in the Lord's Supper, Calvin was nearer to Luther than was Zwingli.

After the death of Calvin Geneva was still a major centre towards which the Reformed Churches continued to look. Calvin's mantle fell on the shoulders of Theodore Beza (1519–1605). Ten years younger than Calvin, Beza was born in Vézelay, in Burgundy, about 150 miles south-east of Paris. He was of aristocratic stock and was reared with the nobility. A precocious lad, he was put to school in the household of Melchior Wolmar, who was also a teacher of Calvin. There he was given a thorough grounding in the humanistic studies of the day and acquired facility in the use of Greek and especially of Latin. Wolmar was deeply religious and became so committed to the views of Luther that he had to flee to Germany. Beza was designed by his family for the law. When he was twenty he went to Paris, wishing to be a poet, and there, supported by the income from benefices, was following a life of literary leisure when, in his late twenties, illness struck him low. He rose from his sick bed a changed man, cast in his lot with the Reformers, and went to Geneva. Soon he was established as a professor in the academy at Lausanne. There he became famous as a scholar and teacher and from there he went on trips into Germany to seek aid for the persecuted Waldensees and to attempt to draw Lutherans and Reformed together. In 1559 he was appointed rector of the School of Theology of the newly founded Academy in Geneva, the precursor of the later University of Geneva. He had a leading part in the constitution of the Reformed Church in France. Elected as Calvin's successor, he continued to make Geneva a refuge centre for Protestants. He wrote prodigiously and was the leading Reformed theologian in the generation after Calvin.

One of the developments in which Beza was of great assistance was in Reformed psalmody. Zwingli had opposed music in public worship and it was a century or so after his death before the Reformed Churches in which his influence was strong departed from that precedent. Calvin did not go as far as Zwingli, but confined the use of music to congregational singing in unison of metrical versions of the Psalms and Canticles. In 1539 at Strassburg and in 1542 and 1551 a Psalter was issued and in 1562 this was followed by what became the definitive edition of what was known as the *Geneva Psalter*. The musical portions were largely the work of Louis Bourgeois, master of the choristers in Geneva. Although the precise origin of that tune is debated, it is to him that the familiar *Old Hundred* (or *Old Hundredth*) is ascribed. A metrical version in French of about a third of the Psalms had been made by

Clement Marot, who died in 1544. It was Beza who completed the task of putting the Psalter into French poetic form. Marot and Beza's Psalter speedily achieved popularity and passed through many editions. Put to music, much of it popular ballad tunes, its Psalms were sung on the streets and in services of public worship. With alterations, Marot and Beza's Psalter long remained standard for French Protestantism. For use in the Reformed Churches, there were several versions of the Psalms in German and Dutch. As we are to see a little later, paraphrases of the Psalms in English were to be widely sung in the English-speaking churches of the Reformed tradition.

SWISS REFORMED CHURCHES DRAWN TOGETHER

During Calvin's lifetime the Reformed Churches of Switzerland began drawing together. The process was not automatic. In addition to cantonal and civic particularism and to linguistic and cultural differences between French and Germans, those who followed Zwingli tended to look askance at Calvin's views of the Lord's Supper. Basel was not inclined to favour Calvin's convictions on predestination, and Bern disliked the independence of the Church from domination by the state which was part of his programme. However, in 1549 Calvin and Bullinger reached an accord on the sacraments which eventually was adopted in other Swiss centres. While the Germans did not approve of the rigid discipline of Geneva and variations remained, French and German Reformed Churches increasingly recognized their kinship.

THE WALDENSEES JOIN THE REFORM MOVEMENT

The Waldensian remnants became associated with the Reformed Churches. This was natural. They had taken refuge in valleys of Piedmont and so were adjacent to the Swiss. The ideas of the Swiss reforms were carried to them in the 1530's, partly by Farel, and partly by a deputation of their pastors which visited Strassburg, Basel, and Bern. They seem to have greeted the new movement with enthusiasm and through it to have experienced a revival. Their Confession of 1655 was Calvinistic. They suffered severe persecution from Roman Catholic princes but a sturdy nucleus survived.

THE REFORMED CHURCHES IN CENTRAL EUROPE

We have already seen (Chapter XXXII) something of the rise of Reformed Churches to the east of Switzerland. We have noted that in Bohemia Slavonic Protestantism and in Hungary Magyar Protestantism tended to find expression through them, while German Protestants held to Lutheranism. In the sixteenth century Bohemia and Hungary seemed about to be swept fully into Protestantism, but in the seventeenth century reverses left only a minority of that faith. In Transylvania, on the extreme eastern fringe of Hungary, the German communities which had been there since the Middle Ages adopted Lutheranism, the Magyars constituted the main constituency of the Reformed Churches, the Socinians, of whom we are to hear later (Chapter XXXV), won a following among the Szeklers (a racial group which was probably closely related to the Magyars), some of the upper classes remained Roman Catholic, and much of the peasantry was Orthodox. Before the end of the sixteenth century the first four forms of Christianity were accorded official status by the state and were given an equal legal basis. Lutherans, Reformed, Anabaptists and Socinians all won adherents in Poland. Indeed, as we are to see (Chapter XXXVIII), the divisions among Protestants were a major cause of the triumphant resurgence of the Roman Catholic Church in that country. Many of the Bohemian Brethren, expelled from Bohemia in 1548, sought refuge in Poland. In 1555 they and the Reformed Churches in that land united in a permanent union.

THE REFORMED CHURCHES IN GERMANY

The Reformed Churches multiplied in Germany. Through Bucer and the temporary residence of Calvin, Strassburg was early inclined in that direction. The mediating influence of Melanchthon also made for that trend. In the controversies which arose after the death of the great reformer, those who held to a stiff Lutheranism, especially on the nature of the presence of Christ in the Lord's Supper, alienated many who were not prepared to go to such extremes. Accordingly, the latter moved in the direction of the Reformed Churches. Even before his death, the views of Calvin had begun to gain ground on German soil. Frederick III, the "Pious" (1515–1576), who became Elector Palatine in 1559, came out stoutly on the side of Calvinism, made it the established faith in the Palatinate, and persecuted both Roman Catholics and Lutherans. In 1563 the Heidelberg Catechism was issued. Written by younger friends of Calvin and Bullinger, one of whom had also been a student and friend of Melanchthon, it was less polemic and more based on Christian experience than were some of the other documents of the Reformation. It was widely adopted among the Reformed Churches, was used in Scotland, and became standard in the Netherlands and in the Dutch and German Reformed Churches in America. In the latter half of the sixteenth century the Reformed Churches also gained headway in Nassau, Bremen, Hesse, and Brandenburg.

THE REFORMED CHURCHES IN THE NETHERLANDS

The Reformation made great strides in the Netherlands and was intimately associated with a notable struggle for political independence. When Luther began the Reformation, Charles V was consolidating his rule in the Low Countries. The region had been more a geographic expression, the lowlands at the mouths of great rivers, than a political entity. It contained important and thriving commercial cities and prosperous farms, but it was divided linguistically and racially. Its chief elements were Dutch in the north, Flemings in the centre, and French-speaking Walloons in the south. Charles V, who had received the region by inheritance and had been reared there, attempted to weld the country together and build in it an absolute and unified monarchy after the manner of other states which were then emerging in Western Europe. Part of his programme was the creation of territorial episcopal sees which would make for more efficient discipline.

The writings of Luther early found an eager response in the Netherlands. The way for them had been prepared by movements in the previous century which we have already recorded, among them the Brethren of the Common Life, Christian mysticism, and Christian humanism. Here *The Imitation of Christ* had been composed and here Erasmus had been born and reared. Between 1513 and 1531 more than a score of translations of the Bible or the New Testament were produced in Dutch, Flemish, or French. Charles V undertook strenuous measures to stamp out Lutheranism, but in spite of them it prospered. Anabaptists were numerous and were severely dealt with. However, although there were martyrs among both Lutherans and Anabaptists, the successive regents who ruled for Charles, his aunt and his sister, were much more tolerant than he.

By the fourth quarter of the sixteenth century Calvinism was largely supplanting Lutheranism, especially among the Dutch, and in 1561 a Walloon who had studied at Geneva, Guy de Bray, prepared the Belgic Confession, a strongly Calvinistic document, which with some modifications long remained standard in the Dutch Reformed Church. The first general synod of that church was held in 1571.

In 1555, on the abdication of Charles V, his son Philip II took over the reins of government. Philip attempted to complete the work begun by his father of consolidating the region under royal rule. Part of the plan was carrying through the project for dividing much of the land among new dioceses. In 1559 Philip left the Netherlands, never to return, but he continued to govern it from a distance through his illegitimate half-sister Margaret and a Council of State. Local opposition soon arose, directed against the presence of Spanish troops, the stringent measures for the repression of heresy, the new bishoprics, and the disregard for the local charters and privileges which Philip had sworn to maintain.

In 1566 several scores of young nobles led by a Lutheran, a Roman Catholic, and a Calvinist demanded a change of policy and the suppression of the Inquisition. They called themselves "beggars," a name at first given them contemptuously. Their emblem, a beggar's sack, was adopted by thousands, both high and low. The numbers of the Reformed grew apace through services conducted by excommunicated ministers. Some of the more fanatical demolished images, pictures, and shrines in churches, chapels, and at least one cathedral. Philip II responded by sending additional Spanish troops under the Duke of Alva and set up a tribunal to stamp out opposition. Thereupon armed revolt broke out. It was led by William, Prince of Orange, also known as William the Silent. Although born of Protestant parents, he was a Roman Catholic. It was upon his arm that Charles V had leaned at the ceremony of abdication.

Into the details of the war which followed we need not go. Resistance to the Spanish forces was most effective by sailors and fishermen. Famous was the siege of Leiden which was relieved when, the dykes having been cut, the Sea Beggars, as the patriotic naval forces were called, sailed across the flooded fields to the aid of the beleaguered city. The University of Leiden, founded as a reward for the resisting townsmen, became a leading centre of the Reformed faith. Further fighting followed, the Duke of Parma proving an able general for Philip. Attempts to bring together permanently the Protestant North and the Roman Catholic South in an effective league against the Spaniards did not succeed. The Protestant North formed itself into the United Provinces, led by William of Orange, who in 1573 from deep conviction joined the Reformed Church. In 1581 the United Provinces renounced allegiance to Philip and declared themselves an independent republic. Religiously tolerant in an age and region where passions rose high, William failed to hold Protestants and Catholics together, but with patience, resourcefulness, and courage he led in what for years seemed a hopeless struggle for the achievement of the autonomy so boldly claimed. Assassinated in 1584 at the age of fifty-one, for Philip had placed a price upon his life, William did not see full independence. Not until 1609 did hostilities stop. The United Netherlands (as the United Provinces came to be called) had won their freedom.

While the struggle was still in progress, the Dutch Reformed Church was taking shape. Successive synods, some of them held at Dort (Dordrecht), helped to give it form. It adopted a Presbyterian government, the Heidelberg Catechism, and the Belgic Confession. The closeness of the tie with the state varied from province to province. In the exigencies of the struggle against Philip II and Spain, only in part religious as it was, to present a common front the United Provinces found it necessary to grant a degree of freedom to others than Calvinists. Anabaptists were protected and Roman Catholics were conceded the right of residence and employment, although not of public worship or office-holding.

After the political fighting had ended, a momentous struggle over doctrine broke out within the Dutch Reformed Church. Theologians were divided between supralapsarians and infralapsarians, namely between those who held that before He created the world God had decreed who should be saved and who should be damned, and those who maintained that in view of man's fall in Adam's sin, but not until after that catastrophe, God had decreed that certain men should be lost and others saved. Against both these views some, who came to be known as Remonstrants, protested. The chief figure among them was Jacob Arminius, a pupil of Beza and professor of theology in the University of Leiden, who, setting out to refute them, became convinced by them. Accordingly the Remonstrant position has been known as Arminianism. Rejecting supralapsarianism and infralapsarianism, limited atonement (namely, the teaching that Christ died only for the elect), irresistible grace, and the perseverance of the elect, it held that Christ died for all men, that salvation is by faith alone, that those who believe are saved, that those who reject God's grace are lost, and that God does not elect particular individuals for either outcome. Feeling ran high. Remonstrants were chiefly from the wealthy and favoured states rights. Their opponents were nationalists who wished a general synod to deal with the issue. At a synod held at Dort in 1618 and 1619 delegates came from Switzerland, Bremen, Hesse, the Palatinate, and England. In other words, it was widely representative of the Reformed Churches. It condemned Arminianism in strongly Calvinistic canons, and reaffirmed the Heidelberg Confession and the Belgic Confession. One of the leading Remonstrants was beheaded a few days after the synod adjourned. Another, Hugo Grotius, to become famous from his treatise *De Jure Belli et Pacis,* was imprisoned but escaped. Arminianism was by no means crushed. The Remonstrants continued in Holland as a distinct church and again and again where Calvinism was taught Arminianism raised its head.

THE REFORMED CHURCHES IN FRANCE: THE HUGUENOTS AND THEIR FATE

As in the Netherlands, so in France, Protestantism had a stormy history. In both lands, compounded with other factors, it contributed to protracted wars. In contrast with the Netherlands, however, in France no permanent territorial division ensued. Here, rather, Protestants constituted a minority which won a special, tolerated status in the midst of a predominantly Roman Catholic population. Eventually, partly for the purpose of extending the monolithic power of the absolute monarchy and partly under the guise of stamping out heresy and

obtaining religious uniformity, that status was abrogated, persecution was instituted, and a notable exodus followed.

In France the Protestant Reformation came from several sources. It had
strong humanistic roots. We have already met Jacques Le Fèvre and Guillaume
Briçonnet. As Bishop of Meaux the latter made his episcopal family a centre
of reform. He was the spiritual director of Margaret (1492–1549), sister of
King Francis I and by her second marriage Queen of Navarre and the grandmother of Henry of Navarre who, as we shall see in a moment, a fighting
champion of Protestantism, eventually brought a semblance of unity to France
by adopting Roman Catholicism and reigning as Henry IV. Margaret was
intensely interested in humanistic studies, was deeply religious, was strongly
impressed by Luther and Calvin, was a mystic of the Christian Platonist type,
but, while dissenting from much in the Roman Catholic Church, never became
a Protestant. The attitude of Francis I towards Protestants varied with his
shifting international policy. At times he found it expedient to persecute them
and there were executions. When he wished the friendship of the Protestant
princes of Germany he smiled upon them.

A chief centre of vigorous opposition to the Reformers was the Sorbonne.
Founded in the thirteenth century by Robert de Sorbon as a college within the
University of Paris, it had become a faculty of theology and was regarded by
the Roman Catholic world as an outstanding authority on questions concerning the Christian faith. The Sorbonne came out with a statement of the doctrines of the Catholic Church in refutation of Calvin's *Institutes* and compiled
a list of prohibited books on which were the works of Luther, Calvin, Melanchthon, and Marot. Parlement issued proscriptions of Protestantism, the majority
of the villages of the Waldensees were destroyed, and numbers of the Meaux
group were burned at the stake.

Henry II, the son and successor of Francis I, was unrelenting in his attempts
to extirpate the Reformation. However, the movement continued to spread.
Monks and priests were converted to it. Schools and colleges became hotbeds.
It was natural that it should follow the patterns of the Reformed Churches
already in existence in the adjacent French-speaking parts of Switzerland.
French youths, trained as missionaries in Geneva, Lausanne, and Strassburg,
traversed the country, selling literature and meeting groups of converts. The
writings of Calvin, a Frenchman, made an appeal to his fellow-countrymen.
In 1559, five years before the death of Calvin, a national synod was convened
in Paris. It framed a confession of faith based upon one drawn up by him. It
also adopted a form of organization which was to have a marked effect upon
churches of the Reformed family in Holland, Scotland, and America. French
Protestants came to be known as Huguenots. They were strongest in the cities.

They had their chief spread among artisans, tradesmen, and farmers, but they also won converts from the aristocracy. Among the latter were Gaspard de Coligny, Admiral of France, the titular King of Navarre, and his brother, the Prince of Condé.

Henry II died in 1559 and was followed by his fifteen-year-old son, the feeble Francis II, son of Catherine de' Medici and husband of Mary "Queen of Scots." Francis died the following year. During his brief reign he was under the control of his uncles, the Cardinal of Lorraine and the Duke of Guise. These two were for extirpating Protestantism. Sprung from Lorraine, the Guises were regarded as foreigners and upstarts by such nobles as the Prince of Condé, descended as he was from Louis IX, the Saint, and their dominance was resented.

Francis II was succeeded by his younger brother, the ten-year-old Charles IX, and his mother, Catherine de' Medici, became Regent. An attempt at reconciliation between Catholics and Huguenots was made by the government in a colloquy in which Beza was among the representatives of the Protestants. No agreement was reached, but the Protestants were accorded a limited toleration.

In 1562 what were known as the Wars of Religion broke out. They were waged intermittently until 1594. Into the complicated and wearisome details we need not go. The most famous incident was what was remembered as the Massacre of St. Bartholomew, in August, 1572. Huguenot leaders had gathered in Paris for the marriage of Henry of Navarre, a Protestant, to Marguerite, daughter of Catherine de' Medici. By orders from Catherine, many among the Huguenots were killed. The massacre spread to other parts of France. War was resumed. As in its earlier stages, although the ostensible cause, religion was by no means the only factor. Personal and family rivalries and ambitions entered. On the Catholic side the Guises were prominent. In the later phases of the struggle the leader of the Protestants was Henry of Navarre. Since Henry III, the brother and successor of Charles IX, had no son, by right of descent from St. Louis Henry of Navarre was the heir presumptive. At first he declined to give up his faith and the war went on, even after the death of Henry III. The Protestants were a minority. As a means of uniting the realm Henry of Navarre, now legitimately Henry IV of France, decided to become a Roman Catholic. With characteristic wit he is said to have remarked: "Paris was well worth a mass." His conversion and coronation (1594) and his promise of protection to the Huguenots brought peace.

The Huguenots required more than this royal promise from one whom they regarded as an apostate. As a result, in 1598 the Edict of Nantes was promulgated. It guaranteed them freedom of public worship in several scores of specified towns, in two places in each of certain kinds of administrative divisions of the kingdom, and in more than three thousand castles. Although Paris was not among the cities where public Huguenot worship was permitted, private services might be held there in the apartments of high officials. Protestants were assured full civic rights and the privilege of admission to all public offices and to universities, schools, and hospitals. Protestant clergy were granted the same exemptions from military service and other charges as the Catholic clergy enjoyed. Huguenots could freely hold their church assemblies. As a safeguard, until 1607, later extended five years, they were to have complete control of two hundred towns, including La Rochelle and Montpellier, and the state was to pay the garrisons and governors of these strongholds.

The Edict of Nantes did not bring permanent peace. Causes of friction remained, partly religious and partly political. Roman Catholics and Protestants found it difficult to live amicably side by side in the same town. The Jesuits, of whom we are to hear more in later chapters, were active in seeking to win Protestants and to establish themselves in Protestant centres. In a realm where the king and his ministers, notably the great Richelieu, were endeavouring to extend the authority of the crown, the semi-independent status of the Huguenots was an irritant, especially since, in seeking to maintain themselves, the latter allied themselves with some of the nobility who were challenging the growing centralization of power under the king and sought foreign aid. Under Henry IV's son, Louis XIII, three domestic wars were fought in which the Huguenots and their cause were major factors. They culminated in the siege of their stronghold, La Rochelle, and its capitulation (October 29, 1628).

There then ensued three decades of comparative peace and prosperity. The Peace of Alais (June 27, 1629), which followed the fall of La Rochelle, while specifying the destruction of the fortifications of the towns held by the Huguenots, promised the restoration of most of the privileges which had been granted by the Edict of Nantes. So long as this was observed the Huguenots flourished. They seem never to have been more than a ninth of the total population, but they were especially strong in the South and South-west, possibly in part because of a tradition of revolt against the Catholic Church from the days of the Cathari. In some towns and cities they were in the majority. They stressed schools for their youth and were much better educated than the rank and file of their Catholic neighbours. Thrifty, prominent in the professions and business, they were more influential in national and community life than their numbers would have led one to expect.

Then, in the reign of Louis XIV, the "Grand Monarch" who followed Louis XIII, progressively severe restrictions were imposed. They culminated in the destruction of churches, the compulsory removal (1681) of Protestant children from their parents to be reared as Catholics, and, in 1685, the formal revocation of the Edict of Nantes. Louis was moved to these steps by his heightened devotion to the Catholic faith which came in middle age under the influence of his wife, Madame de Maintenon, and by his settled purpose to be supreme in his realm. This latter desire had been hampered by what remained of the privileged position of the Huguenot community.

To escape the persecutions which preceded, accompanied, and followed the abrogation of the edict, tens of thousands of Huguenots left the country and found refuge in other lands—in Prussia, Holland, England, Ireland, the English colonies in America, and even in remote South Africa. Some who remained conformed to the Catholic Church. Protestantism in France declined in numbers but did not disappear. It persisted and was to have a notable record in the nineteenth and twentieth centuries.

THE REFORMED FAITH BECOMES THAT OF THE CHURCH OF SCOTLAND

In the sixteenth century Protestantism made its way into Scotland. There it was to become the faith of the overwhelming majority of the population and the official religion of the state and the community. The form of Protestantism which prevailed was Presbyterianism, a Presbyterianism which owed a profound debt to Geneva and Calvin but which did not fully conform to either. This development was to have a wide influence on the future history of Christianity. Although Scotland is a small country and in the sixteenth and seventeenth centuries it was sparsely settled and economically poor, in later centuries its Presbyterianism was to have an expansion which carried it into many lands. This was partly through its effect on English Puritanism, partly through extensive migrations to Ireland, North America, Australia, New Zealand, and South Africa, and partly through far-flung missions. To the story of the winning of Scotland we must now turn. As usual, we must content ourselves with the briefest possible summary.

At the dawn of the sixteenth century the Catholic Church in Scotland was in dire need of reform. Lawlessness was rife, the nobility were turbulent, unwilling to submit to royal authority, and divided into warring factions, some episcopal sees were vacant, where they were filled their incumbents were embroiled in the political strife of the realm, and many ecclesiastical posts were given to sons of the nobles who enjoyed the revenues but, absentees, did not perform the associated duties. The country was torn between those who wished closer relations with the hereditary foe, the English, and those who stood for the traditional anti-English tie with France.

Precursors of the later religious revolution were beginning to be seen. Through contact with England, Lollardy had some influence. Several of

Luther's writings were being read. Here and there preachers were boldly advocating the new views. In 1528 Patrick Hamilton was burned at the stake in St. Andrews, the ecclesiastical capital of the country. Of gentle birth, he had taken a degree at the University of Paris, had studied at Wittenberg, and, returning, before his arrest and condemnation had been allowed to present his views in the University of St. Andrews. In the next few years edicts against heresy were issued and several other advocates of the Reformation were put to death. One of these, George Wishart, was sent to the stake in 1546. Cardinal Beaton, Archbishop of St. Andrews, who had brought about his death, was murdered a few weeks later, partly in revenge and partly from opposition to his pro-French policy. The assassins fortified themselves in a castle on the coast, expecting aid from England, but were overwhelmed by forces sent on a French fleet.

The outstanding leader in the Scottish Reformation was John Knox. Born between 1505 and 1515 in or near Haddington, east of Edinburgh, of humble parentage, Knox studied in one of the Scottish universities and was ordained to the priesthood. He himself tells how he attended upon Wishart when the latter preached in Haddington and would have followed him had Wishart not dissuaded him. After Wishart's death and Cardinal Beaton's murder he and some of his "bairns" (presumably his students) joined the group in the St. Andrews castle and there preached Protestant views. He was captured, taken to France, for nineteenth months was a galley prisoner, and then, released (early in 1549), went to England, where the Reformation was at full tide under Edward VI. He was one of the chaplains of the king, refused a bishopric, fled to the Continent when the Catholic reaction came under Edward VI's sister and successor, Mary, and was in a number of places, including Frankfort and especially Geneva. In Geneva he became an ardent disciple of Calvin. He married Margaret Bowes, from Northumberland, to whom he had been betrothed while in England.

While Knox was abroad, the Reformation was making progress in Scotland. In it national loyalty and religious fervour were combining. The child monarch, Mary "Queen of Scots" (1542–1587), born a few days before the death of her father, James V, was affianced to the Dauphin and was sent to France at the age of five. In 1558 she was married to the Dauphin, who was soon to be Francis II. In Scotland her mother, Mary of Lorraine, served as regent in her place. The regent was unpopular, partly because she was French and the Scots feared, with good reason, that this and the marriage of their Queen to a French king would lead to an attempt to annex their country. A possible English tie through the earlier proposed marriage of Mary to the future Edward VI was fully as abhorrent.

During several months in Scotland in 1555 and 1556 Knox gave a marked impetus to the Reformation. He preached extensively in the south of the country and had an attentive hearing. Partly as a result, on December 3, 1557, some of the nobility who were anti-French entered into a covenant to "establish the most blessed word of God and his Congregation." They were, accordingly, called the Lords of the Congregation.

It was in 1560 and 1561 that Scotland officially went over to the Reformation. In 1559 the regent forbade Reformed preaching. Civil war followed, with French troops supporting the regent, and English forces, sent by Queen Elizabeth of that country, aiding the Protestant party. The regent died and the French troops sailed for home. In August, 1560, the Scottish Parliament adopted a confession of faith which had been drafted by Knox and some others. It was more Calvinistic than Lutheran or Zwinglian. That month the same body declared that the Pope no longer had jurisdiction in Scotland and forbade the mass. Like Luther, Calvin, and many others of the reformers, Knox had turned to the civil authorities to effect the changes which he desired.

No detailed provision was made by Parliament for the organization and administration of the Church. Knox and his associates accordingly drew up what was known as the *First Book of Discipline*. It provided for the dedication of the wealth of the Church, including the continuation of the tithes, to the support of the ministry, education, and the relief of the poor. Parish ministers were to be nominated by the people, examined by the learned, and publicly admitted to their offices. There were to be superintendents who roughly corresponded to the old bishops, but they were to be of no higher rank than parish ministers and their functions were to be purely administrative, such as planting churches and placing clergy. A comprehensive system of schools was projected, culminating in universities, an expression of an emphasis on education which was already present in Scotland and which the Reformation was greatly to accentuate.

Not all the nobles assented to the document. This was partly because some had appropriated ecclesiastical lands and revenues. Although enough subscribed to it to give it standing, the failure of official approval by Parliament was an indication of the partial independence of Church from state which, in contrast with England, was to characterize the course of the Reformed faith in Scotland. Moreover, in the completed ecclesiastical structure which was here given its preliminary and partial formulation, the laity and the people were accorded a voice which monarchs were rightly to regard as a threat to their claims to absolute power. Provision was made on the parish level for the lay elder, and in the General Assembly which acted for the entire Church of Scotland the rank and file had a much larger voice than in Parliament. By declaring that "before God there is no respect of persons," *The Book of Discipline* furthered in the Scots a sturdy independence and democratic spirit.

The Book of Common Order, often known as *Knox's Liturgy,* adopted by the General Assembly in 1564, governed public worship. It showed the influence of the form employed in the English congregation in Frankfort, of Calvin, Farel, Strassburg, and Geneva. It was to be standard until 1645.

In August, 1560, a few months after the actions of Parliament in abolishing the mass and adopting a Reformed confession of faith, the weak Francis II of France breathed his last and in August, 1561, Mary, widowed, returned to Scotland. Reared a loyal Roman Catholic, she had mass said in her chapel in Holyrood Palace. Charming, determined, and intelligent, she could prove a formidable foe to the religious innovations. Although she made no immediate effort to upset them, she certainly was not their friend. Knox, a formidable preacher and now in the pulpit of St. Giles, the cathedral of Edinburgh up the street from Holyrood, thundered against this revival of the mass. He inveighed against the frivolities at the court and his audiences with Mary did not relieve the tension.

For a time, the tide seemed to be running against the Reformation. Knox temporarily lost the support of some of the more powerful of the Lords of the Congregation. Mary married her cousin, Darnley, a Roman Catholic. In complex politics which involved relations with England and Mary's ambition to win the succession to the English throne after the childless Elizabeth, a succession to which her Tudor blood gave her claim as the next of kin, the Protestant nobles were temporarily worsted.

However, Mary badly misplayed her hand. Her unwise matrimonial ventures and the intrigues, murders, and civil strife which were associated with them eventually drove her to seek refuge in England (1568). After years of detention in that land she was executed (1587) on the charge of complicity in a plot to assassinate Elizabeth. Her son, James VI (1566–1625, to become James I of England after the death of Elizabeth, in 1603), who came to the throne after the compulsory abdication of his mother (1567), was reared in the Reformed faith and Knox preached at the infant's coronation. Knox lived to see his cause apparently triumphant. A war horse to the end, he died November 24, 1572, after having earlier in the month inducted his successor to the pulpit of St. Giles.

Knox's work was carried forward by others. Outstanding among them was Andrew Melville (1545–1622), distinguished scholar, friend of Beza, teacher, reorganizer of the Universities of Glasgow and Aberdeen, and Rector of the University of St. Andrews. He led in giving to the Church of Scotland a thorough-going Presbyterian organization. This was embodied in the *Second*

Book of Discipline, adopted by the General Assembly in 1577, which was authoritative whenever the Church was left free by the state to follow it. In it, the terms pastor, bishop, and minister were employed to designate the same office. A few years later (1580–1581) the administrative powers which the *First Book of Discipline* had conferred on superintendents were transferred to presbyteries, ecclesiastical courts which were to exercise many of the functions of bishops.

For hymns the Scottish Presbyterians used versifications of the Psalms. In 1564, with the authorization of the General Assembly, a Psalter was issued. In 1635 the Great Scottish Psalter appeared, with tunes of various origins, some of them native and most of the others French and German. The Westminister Assembly of 1643 supervised the preparation of a drastic revision. As a result, in 1650 the Scottish Psalter was published which long remained standard.

The Presbyterian system and the Reformed faith continued to have a stormy course. James VI (James I of England) sought to foist episcopacy on the Church of Scotland, for to him it was essential to the royal prerogative. "No bishop, no king," was his conviction. Because of his firm Presbyterianism, Melville was forced into exile. Yet James left the presbyteries largely undisturbed. Moreover, he sent representatives to the Synod of Dort, and although none of these could speak officially for the Church of Scotland, the latter accepted the decrees of that gathering. James VI's son Charles I attempted not only to make the Church of Scotland episcopal but also to bring its services into conformity with the Book of Common Prayer of the Church of England. It was Scottish abhorrence of these measures which led to the resistance of the great body of Scots through the National Covenant (1638) and paved the way for the civil war which cost Charles the English and Scottish thrones and which culminated in his execution. In the course of the civil war, the Scots entered into the Solemn League and Covenant with the English Parliament which brought a Scottish army to the aid of that body against Charles and which was responsible for convening the Westminster Assembly of English churchmen and Scottish commissioners (the latter without vote) that drew up a system of Presbyterian church government, the Westminster Confession, and the Westminster Directory of Public Worship. In an effort to achieve religious uniformity in the two realms, the Scottish General Assembly and Parliament adopted the latter two documents.

When, with Charles II, the Stuarts were restored to power, that monarch reimposed bishops on the Church of Scotland and lay appointment to the parish pastorates was revived. Vigorous resistance greeted these acts, many ministers were ejected from their churches, and the disaffected met in secret conventicles.

Extreme Covenanters resorted to armed rebellion, a step of which moderate Presbyterians disapproved and which the government met with force and penal laws. In his effort for toleration of his fellow Roman Catholics, the successor of Charles II, James VII (James II of England), took measures similar to the ones which he adopted in England, and gave toleration to dissenters from the state church.

When James was forced to leave Britain, Scotland joined England in accepting William and Mary (1689). In 1690 an act was passed which established the Church of Scotland as it was to remain for generations, the laws favouring episcopacy were repealed, and the Westminster Confession was recognized. That year the General Assembly met for the first time since 1653. Queen Anne, who succeeded William and Mary, took oath to preserve the Presbyterian form of church government and the confession of faith.

Dissenters from the established church remained. Some were Episcopalians who had their own bishops. For many years Episcopalianism was especially strong in the North-east and centered in Aberdeen. There the combination of episcopalianism with the presbytery and synod long persisted and few representatives were sent to the General Assembly. Some, notably in the Highlands, were Roman Catholics. Numbers were Presbyterians who for one reason or another had broken with the Church of Scotland. However, the Church of Scotland embraced a larger proportion of the population of the country than did the Church of England in England. Like the latter and several of the Lutheran state churches, it was a continuation of the church of pre-Reformation days. Like them it had broken with Rome and had freed itself from what it deemed the corruptions that it associated with the Papacy. Yet it was in unbroken succession with the Christianity which had been planted by Columba and other early missionaries. Its leaders thought of it as being an integral part of the Catholic Church.

SUMMARY

On the Reformed Churches the impress of no one man was as marked as was that of Luther on the family of churches which are usually known by his name. Indeed, in the Reformed Churches the contributions made by Luther shared in importance with those features which were more specifically identified with them. In important ways, such as their conception of the manner in which Christ is present in the Lord's Supper, the relation of Church and state, and the degree of departure from what had come through the Catholic Church of previous centuries, they differed from Luther. They were more inclined to the independence of Church from state, more hopeful of realizing a Christian society, and less intent on perpetuating what had been inherited in ritual and organization. Yet they held to Luther's central distinctive affirmation, salvation by faith. They were clearly Protestants. Their outstanding figure, John Calvin, was to have an influence in Protestantism second only to that of Luther. Like the latter, it was to be felt far beyond the borders of the churches with which his system was most closely associated.

Selected Bibliography

GENERAL WORKS ON PROTESTANTISM WHICH HAVE TO DO WITH THE REFORMED CHURCHES

R. H. Bainton, *The Reformation of the Sixteenth Century* (Boston, The Beacon Press, 1952, pp. xi, 276). An admirable popular brief summary by an outstanding specialist.

The Cambridge Modern History. Volume III, The Reformation (Cambridge University Press, 1903).

B. J. Kidd, *Documents Illustrative of the Continental Reformation* (Oxford, The Clarendon Press, 1911, pp. xix, 742). A very useful collection, about half on the Reformed Churches.

T. M. Lindsay, *A History of the Reformation* (New York, Charles Scribner's Sons, 2 vols., 1906). A standard work.

E. de Moreau, P. Jourda, and P. Janelle, *La Crise Religieuse du XVIe Siècle* (Paris, Bloud & Gay, 1950, pp. 461. Vol. 16 of A. Fliche and E. Jarry, *Histoire de l'Église depuis les Origines jusqu'a Nos Jours*). A Roman Catholic treatment, which attempts to be objective.

P. Schaff, *The Creeds of Christendom. Volume III, The Evangelical Protestant Creeds, with Translations* (New York, Harper & Brothers, 1877, pp. vii, 920).

P. Schaff, *History of the Christian Church. Volume VII. The Swiss Reformation* (2d ed., revised, New York, Charles Scribner's Sons, 1894, pp. xvii, 890). A standard work, sympathetic with the Reformed tradition.

P. Smith, *The Age of the Reformation* (New York, Henry Holt and Co., 1920, pp. xii, 861). An excellent summary of the Protestant and Catholic Reformations in their general European setting.

HULDREICH ZWINGLI

S. Simpson, *Life of Ulrich Zwingli, the Swiss Patriot and Reformer* (New York, The Baker & Taylor Co., 1902, pp. 297). Semi-popular, based on extensive research, contains an excellent bibliography.

U. Zwingli, *Sämtliche Werke* in *Corpus Reformatorum*, II Ser., Vol. 88–100 (Berlin, C. A. Schwetschke und Sohn, and Leipzig, M. Heinsius Nachfolger, 1905–1944).

The Latin Works and Correspondence of Huldreich Zwingli Together with Selections from His German Works, translated by various scholars, inaugurated by W. J. Hinke (3 vols., 1912–1929. Vol. I published by G. P. Putnam's Sons, New York; Vols. 2, 3 by the Heidelberg Press, Philadelphia).

JOHN CALVIN

T. Beza, *The Life of John Calvin,* translated by H. Beveridge (Philadelphia, The Westminster Press, 1909, pp. 115). By an admiring, intimate friend.

Q. Breen, *John Calvin: a Study in French Humanism* (Grand Rapids, Mich., Wm. B. Eerdmann Publishing Co., 1931, pp. ix, 174). A doctoral dissertation of the University of Chicago.

J. Calvin, *Institutes of the Christian Religion,* translated from the Latin and collated with the author's last edition in French by J. Allen. Seventh American edition, by B. B. Warfield (Philadelphia, Presbyterian Board of Christian Education, 2 vols., no date).

Calvin, *Opera supersunt omnia* in *Corpus Reformatorum,* II Ser., Vols. 29-85 (Brunswick, C. A. Schwetschke et filium, 1863-1897).

H. G. Reyburn, *John Calvin, His Life, Letters and Work* (London, Hodder & Stoughton, 1914, pp. viii, 376). Carefully based on the sources.

W. Walker, *John Calvin, the Organizer of Reformed Protestantism 1509-1564* (New York, G. P. Putnam's Sons, 1906, pp. xviii, 456). A standard biography by a specialist.

MARTIN BUCER

H. Eells, *Martin Bucer* (Yale University Press, 1931, pp. xii, 539). Carefully done with extensive references to the sources and secondary works.

THEODORE BEZA

H. M. Baird, *Theodore Beza, the Counsellor of the French Reformation* (New York, G. P. Putnam's Sons, 1899, pp. xxi, 376). Semi-popular.

THE REFORMED CHURCHES IN THE NETHERLANDS

J. L. Motley, *The Rise of the Dutch Republic* (New York, E. P. Dutton & Co., 3 vols., 1906). The *Everyman's Library* edition of a standard work, warmly sympathetic with William of Orange, first published in 1855.

THE HUGUENOTS

H. M. Baird, *History of the Rise of the Huguenots of France* (New York, Charles Scribner's Sons, 2 vols., 1879). Warmly sympathetic with the Huguenots.

H. M. Baird, *The Huguenots and Henry of Navarre* (London, Kegan Paul, Trench, Trübner & Co., 2 vols., 1886). Well written, based upon extensive research.

H. M. Baird, *The Huguenots and the Revocation of the Edict of Nantes* (New York, Charles Scribner's Sons, 2 vols., 1895). Like the other two works by Baird, well written, sympathetic with the Huguenots, and based upon extensive research.

THE CHURCH OF SCOTLAND

J. Cunningham, *The Church History of Scotland* (Edinburgh, James Thin, 2d ed., 2 vols., 1882). A solid piece of work.

G. D. Henderson, *Religious Life in Seventeenth-Century Scotland* (Cambridge University Press, 1937, pp. 311). Based upon a careful study of the sources.

The Works of John Knox, collected and edited by D. Laing (Edinburgh, The Wodrow Society, 6 vols., Johnstone and Hunter, Thomas George Stevenson, 1846–1864).

John Knox's History of the Reformation in Scotland, edited by W. G. Dickenson (London, Thomas Nelson & Sons, 2 vols., 1949). Contains a valuable introduction, a useful bibliography, and excellent notes.

A. Lang, *John Knox and the Reformation* (London, Longmans, Green & Co., 1905, pp. xiv, 281). Carefully done.

H. M. Luckock, *The Church in Scotland* (London, Well Gardner, Darton & Co., 1893). A useful historical survey.

A. R. Macewen, *A History of the Church of Scotland* (New York, Hodder & Stoughton, 2 vols., 1913, 1918). A careful study from the beginning to 1560, terminated by the author's death.

T. M'Crie, *Life of Andrew Melville* (Edinburgh, William Blackwood, 2 vols., 2d ed., 1824).

M. Patrick, *Four Centuries of Scottish Psalmody* (Oxford University Press, 1950, pp. xxiii, 234).

Lord Eustace Percy, *John Knox* (London, Hodder & Stoughton, 1937, pp. 438). Very well done.

H. Watt, *John Knox in Controversy* (New York, Philosophical Library, 1950, pp. ix, 109). By an outstanding expert.

Chapter XXXIV

THE RADICAL REFORMERS:
THE ANABAPTISTS

Thus far in recounting the Protestant Reformation we have dealt with two of its more conservative wings, Lutheranism and the Reformed and Presbyterian Churches. Both were in many ways a continuation of the Catholic Church in their respective lands. In principle Lutheranism rejected only those features of the Catholic Church which seemed to it expressly forbidden in the Scriptures. The Reformed Churches went further and retained from the Catholic Church only what they believed to have warrant in the Scriptures. Each sought to be the church of the entire community. In this they succeeded in several lands. Both continued infant baptism and by it endeavoured to bring into the visible church all who were born in the community. To be sure, Luther was not entirely happy over this procedure, for it did not fully accord with his basic principle of salvation by faith. Calvin taught that many so baptized were not among the elect and did not belong to that invisible church whose membership was known to God alone. Yet each wished the visible church to include all in a given area. Although they recognized it as imperfect and sinful, both maintained close relations with the state, believing it to be ordained of God. Calvin and the Reformed in general went further in standing for the independence of the Church from the state than did Luther. Yet both coöperated with it.

Contemporaneously with Lutheranism and Calvinism there was another kind of Protestantism, much more radical than either. It took many forms and was more remote from a common definition of the Christian faith than were these others. Yet those who adhered to it had much in common. In general they looked to the Scriptures and especially the New Testament as their authority and tended to discard all that they could not find expressly stated in that basic collection of sources. They wished to return to the primitive Christianity of the first century. They thus rejected much more which had come through the Catholic Church than did Lutherans and the Reformed. They believed in "gathered" churches, not identical with the community at large, but composed of those who had had the experience of the new birth. Rejecting infant baptism as contrary to the Scriptures, they regarded only that baptism valid which was administered to conscious believers. They were therefore nick-named Anabaptists, those who baptized a second time, but to them that designation was false, for they held infant baptism not to be baptism. The form of baptism seems in their eyes to have been of secondary importance. For many, perhaps for most, it was not by immersion but by what is known as affusion.

Many Anabaptists had as little as possible to do with the state. Some entirely refused coöperation with it. Large numbers were convinced that the Christian should never participate in war. They tended to withdraw from society and constitute communities of their own which would be uncontaminated by the world about them. Their forms of worship were marked by simplicity. In its heyday the movement gave rise to many hymns. Some looked for the early end of history and the imminent visible return of Christ to set up his millennial reign. Many believed that in them prophecy had been revived and that the Holy Spirit continued to guide and to speak. Some denied the divinity of Christ and regarded him simply as a leader and example. Many were ardently missionary, seeking to win not only professed Christians to their views but also dreaming of carrying the Gospel to all mankind. They tended to austerity in morals and simplicity in food, dress, and speech.

Anabaptists maintained a high standard of morality. Indeed, theirs was an ethical as well as a religious urge. They did not believe in salvation by works, but they taught that if salvation were genuine it would issue in good works. They expelled from their fellowship those who slipped from their standards. Even among their severe critics were those who admitted that they were honest, peaceable, temperate in eating and drinking, eschewed profanity and harsh language, and were upright, meek, and free from covetousness and pride. Many were total abstainers from all alcoholic beverages. They endeavoured fully to live up to the ethical demands of the Sermon on the Mount. The Catholic way of striving for Christian perfection was that of the monastery, communities of celibates apart from the world. The Anabaptists were akin to the monks in seeking perfection in communities separate from the world, but, unlike the monks, they married.

Usually Anabaptists were bitterly persecuted by other Protestants and Roman Catholics, for to both they seemed to be dangerous revolutionaries, upsetting the established order. Some may have had a continuity from groups which had been regarded as heretics in pre-Reformation centuries. Violence all but stamped them out on the Continent. Yet some survived. Moreover, they contributed to the emergence or development of movements in Britain, chiefly the Independents, Baptists, and Quakers. Through these, especially the first two, they were to have a profound and growing influence on the Christianity of the eighteenth and notably of the nineteenth and twentieth centuries.

EARLY ANABAPTISTS

Precisely when the Anabaptists began we do not know. As we have suggested, some of their communities may have sprung from heretical pre-sixteenth century movements. There have been those, indeed, who have asserted for them unbroken continuity from the Christians of the first century, a kind of apostolic succession different from that claimed by the Catholics. This, however, has not been incontestably proved. If continuity existed there was great diversity in its manifestations.

We would expect that in a time of religious ferment and of rebellion against the Roman Catholic Church such as was seen in the sixteenth century, when the Bible was being widely read in the vernacular and salvation by faith and the priesthood of all believers were being preached, Anabaptists would emerge independently and without collusion in several places and would display marked variety. This, indeed, was what happened. Some groups interacted on one another.

One early centre of the Anabaptists was Zürich. Here, in the city where Zwingli contributed so largely to the Reformed Churches, Conrad Grebel (c.1498–1526) and Felix Manz, young scions of prominent families, led in a radical movement which went far beyond Zwingli. In his student days Grebel was in Basel, Vienna, and Paris, and there imbibed the humanism which was popular in that day. Back in Zürich, he came in contact with Zwingli. His conversion occurred in 1522–1523, but of the details we know little or nothing. At the outset he was a warm friend and earnest follower of the reformer. In the autumn of 1523 he began to part from Zwingli. The latter would move no faster in abolishing the mass and the use of images than the city council, while Grebel believed that the civil authorities should not control the Church. Around Grebel there gathered what were known as the Swiss Brethren. They wished a more thoroughgoing reformation of the Church than Zwingli was prepared to advocate. They made contact with Carlstadt, who, it will be recalled, was one of the radicals who moved beyond Luther. They sought, apparently in vain, to get in touch with the much more violent Thomas Müntzer. Grebel wrote Luther, urging him to apply the Scriptures with less compromise than he was doing. In many places in Switzerland and South-west Germany the Scriptural basis for the baptism of infants was being questioned. By the autumn of 1524 Grebel and his associates had rejected infant baptism and, although they were also opposed to tithes being collected by the state for the support of ministers and to "usury," it was over baptism that they came into conflict with the

Zürich authorities. In January, 1525, the city council decided to stand by infant baptism and ordered Grebel and the Brethren to discontinue their movement. In spite of the city council, Grebel and his associates gave baptism to those believers who wished it. The Brethren also observed the Lord's Supper with very simple rites.

With missionary zeal, Grebel moved on to other cities. At Schaffhausen, a few miles north of Zürich, he met at first with favour. At the nearby Waldshut Balthasar Hübmaier was of kindred mind. In other centres, notably in St. Gall, Grebel and his colleagues had an enthusiastic popular reception. However, Grebel, Manz, and others were arrested, tried by the civil authorities in Zürich, and condemned to life imprisonment for not abiding by the city council's commands. After some months they escaped. Manz, recaptured, was executed by drowning (January 25, 1527), apparently the first martyr to the Anabaptist cause. Grebel had died a few months earlier.

Balthasar Hübmaier, a university graduate, a priest, a former pupil of that Eck whom we have met in his Leipzig debate with Luther, and a distinguished preacher, by 1523 had become a convert to the Reformation. He carried with him many of his parish in Waldshut. At first friendly with Zwingli and his colleagues, by 1525 he had rejected infant baptism. In that year he was baptized and at Easter in that year he baptized about three hundred and followed this with other baptisms, the Lord's Supper, and foot-washing. For a time he was in Zürich and there was imprisoned and tortured. Released, he went to Nikolsburg in Moravia and preached with such effect that thousands were baptized. He was arrested by order of the Archduke Ferdinand of Austria, was taken to Vienna, tried, condemned, and burned (March 10, 1528).

In the 1520's Anabaptist views spread rapidly and widely in much of German-speaking Switzerland, Austria, and South-east Germany. Strassburg was early an important centre and in the North-west Anabaptist views made rapid headway in the Low Countries. In places the way was prepared for Anabaptist convictions by the Friends of God and other fifteenth century mystics, and possibly by such communities as those of the beghards and beguines.

The missionaries of the movement were numerous. Melchior Hoffmann (c.1498–c.1543), a Swabian-born furrier of Livonia, wandered widely along the Baltic, in Scandinavia, the Low Countries, and Strassburg, preaching as he went and in some places winning converts and gathering communities. Even the fairly tolerant Strassburg found him impossible and he died in prison in that city. Hans Denck (1495–1527), a humanist scholar, a graduate of the University of Ingolstadt, for a time one of the Erasmian circle in Basel, influenced by Tauler, proficient in Greek and Hebrew, wishing an inner reformation by heeding the voice of the Spirit within us, the indwelling Christ, and the Scripture, and eschewing violence, was in several cities, among them Nuremberg, St. Gall, Strassburg, Worms, and Augsburg, and in his early thirties died of the plague in Basel. Denck's friend, for a time also a friend of Zwingli, the Swiss Ludwig Hetzer (1500–1529), who had been educated in humanist studies and who had drunk deeply from such mystical writings as the *Theologia Germanica,* was banished from Zürich for his Anabaptist teachings. For a few months in 1525 he headed the radicals in Augsburg, was for a time in Basel in the home of Oecolampadius, then was in Strassburg as a guest of Wolfgang Capito, a Zwinglian with Anabaptist leanings, joined with Denck in translating into German the prophetical books of the Old Testament, with Denck was forced to flee from Worms, and early in 1529 was tried and executed in Constance on the charge, probably false, of adultery. These were only some of the better known among those who propagated Anabaptist convictions.

As we have suggested, the Anabaptists presented a great variety. They were recruited mainly from the lowlier elements of the population, but they also included some men of learning. They were chiefly in the towns and cities, but were not grouped around any one centre or leader. Some advocated community of goods among the faithful. For many the rejection of infant baptism and insistence on the baptism of believers was only incidental. Some opposed all use of force, even in resistance to persecution. Others wished to employ force. Several, among them Hans Hetz, who disturbed Hübmaier in Nickelsburg, proclaimed that the day of the Lord was near and that the saints were the chosen people who, as had the children of Israel in conquering Palestine, were to root out the wicked before the visible reign of Christ was set up on the earth. Michael Sattler, a former monk who, after having been flayed and having his tongue torn out, was burned in May, 1527, had led, in February of that year, in drawing up articles of faith for Anabaptists. These regarded the Church as made up of local units of those who had been baptized as believers. Each of the local units was to choose its own officers and to be bound together through the Lord's Supper. The articles of faith rejected the Roman, Lutheran, and Zwinglian worship as "servitude of the flesh."

However, by no means all Anabaptists conformed to that statement.

ANABAPTISTS ARE PERSECUTED BY ROMAN CATHOLICS, LUTHERANS, AND REFORMED

As we have seen, Roman Catholics, Lutherans, and Zwinglians regarded Anabaptists as dangerous radicals, threatening to bring in anarchy in Church and state. Among all three there were those who sought to stamp them out by force. Late in the 1520's and early in the 1530's hundreds of Anabaptists were killed, some by drowning, some by beheading, and others by burning.

Persecution of the Anabaptists was intensified by the belief that they shared in responsibility for the peasant uprising of 1524–1525. Indeed, there was plausible ground for the accusation. Thomas Müntzer was the major fomenter of the revolt in Saxony. He is usually classed with the Anabaptists, and, while he did not make as much of it as did most of them, he rejected infant baptism and therefore, if the term were sufficiently inclusive, could be grouped with them. Certainly those concerned for the maintenance of public order were the more savage against the Anabaptists because of the fear that, coming as most of them did from the underprivileged classes, they would breed rebellion.

The Münster Episode Confirms the Fears of the Opponents of the Anabaptists

The worst fears of the critics of the Anabaptists were reinforced by events in Münster in 1533–1535. Münster, a city in Westphalia, not far from the Dutch border, in the Middle Ages a prominent member of the Hanseatic League, was the seat of a bishop. There about 1529 a young humanist chaplain, Bernhard Rothmann, began preaching justification by faith. He attracted many among the masses who were already restless under the exploitation of ecclesiastical rulers. In spite of the opposition of successive bishops and neighbouring nobles, the city was declared to be Protestant and was enrolled in the Schmalkaldic League. Yet Rothmann seems never to have been a Lutheran but to have been closer to the Anabaptists. By 1533 he had become convinced that infant baptism was wrong. Since he refused to baptize infants, some of the leading citizens, Lutherans, attempted to depose him from his pulpit, but were estopped because of his popularity with the masses. In a public disputation with a Lutheran and a Roman Catholic, the populace deemed Rothmann to have been the victor.

The news spread that Münster had become Anabaptist and to it flocked many of the followers of Melchior Hoffmann. Hoffmann had predicted that after his imprisonment and death he would return, in 1533, with Christ in the clouds of heaven, that the wicked would be judged, and the New Jerusalem be set up in Strassburg. The year 1533 passed, Hoffmann was still in prison, and the end of the age had not come. Outstanding among the immigrant Anabaptists was Jan Matthys, a baker from Haarlem, in Holland, who believed himself a prophet and who was convinced that Münster, not Strassburg, was to be the site of the New Jerusalem where the saints would reign. Another was Jan Beukelssen, a tailor of Leiden. The Anabaptists obtained control of Münster and there attempted to organize what they believed to be a Christian society. The Bishop laid siege. Aided by Lutherans and Catholics he took the city (June 24, 1535). Matthys had already perished in a sortie. The surviving leaders, including Jan of Leiden, were tortured and killed, and the authority of the bishop was reëstablished.

The effect of the Münster episode was to confirm the bad odour attached to the name of Anabaptist. Reports circulated of the extremes to which Anabaptist fanaticism had gone during the months of stress in community of property, polygamy, and the ruthless suppression of opposition. As is the manner of such reports, they grew as they were told and retold and departed further and further from the facts. Actually private property had not been abolished and, while some of the leaders had contracted polygamous marriages, severe laws were enacted against adultery and fornication. Although only a minority of the Anabaptists were involved, and these chiefly from one strain of the movement, that associated with Hoffmann, it was popularly believed, especially among the governing and respectable classes, that all Anabaptists made for chaos in government, society, morals, and religion.

MENNO SIMONS AND THE MENNONITES

The largest body of Anabaptists which survived the persecutions on the Continent was the Mennonites. They took their name from Menno Simons (1496–1561). Menno Simons was born in the Low Countries, was educated for the priesthood, along the way acquired an excellent knowledge of Latin and some acquaintance with Greek, and was consecrated priest in 1524. At first he seems to have been the worldly type of cleric so common in that age. Yet reform was in the air, and before he had been ordained Luther had become a familiar name. Within a year of his ordination Menno Simons had doubts about the efficacy of the mass. He had begun a careful study of the Bible when the execution of an Anabaptist in his native West Friesland deeply shocked him. Although still serving as a priest in the Roman Catholic Church, he came to the conclusion that that church and Luther, Zwingli, and Calvin were wrong in practising infant baptism and that only believer's baptism had Scriptural authority. Yet he disapproved of the Anabaptists of Münster and believed that they and the followers of Hoffmann were in error in appealing to the sword in self-defense. However, their heroism under persecution smote his conscience for his acceptance of ease and security in his priestly post. January 30, 1536, he publicly renounced his Roman Catholic connexion and not long afterwards was baptized by Obbe Phillips, an Anabaptist who had been influenced by Hoffmann but who had no lot with the Münsterites, was deeply disturbed by the claim of Matthys and others among them of the gift of prophecy, and held closely to the Scriptures. Menno Simons knew that this step, with its separation from the world, would entail persecution.

Menno Simons' expectation of persecution was amply fulfilled. He was ordained as an Anabaptist minister, became an itinerant missionary of the cause, and for years lived in the Netherlands as a fugitive and an outlaw under condemnation of death. Yet he married and had children. In 1543 he extended his missionary labours into Germany, almost always with persecution facing him from Roman Catholics and Lutherans. Eventually he found a refuge on the estates of a nobleman in Holstein, in Denmark, who, impressed by the courage of Anabaptists whom he had seen martyred, believed them to be harmless and protected them. There Menno Simons made his home for the remainder of his days, but still continued to venture forth on travels in the Netherlands and Germany. By the time of his death, through his extensive writings, his preaching, his organizing of congregations, and his journeys, he had become the outstanding leader of the Anabaptists in the Netherlands and North Germany.

Mennonites were very numerous in the Netherlands. Indeed, before the spread of the Reformed Churches, they probably there constituted the majority of Protestants. They also multiplied in various parts of Germany. They found it difficult to agree in doctrine, and various confessions of faith were drawn up. We hear of ones dating from 1577, 1579, 1582, 1591, 1600, and 1627. The Dortrecht Confession, 1632, was an attempt to bring about a union of the various bodies and was widely used in Flemish, Friesian, and Alsatian congregations. The differences were chiefly over the degree to which members should shun those who had been excommunicated. Mennonites were deeply concerned to maintain a high level of Christian living and to that end employed excommunication of those who were guilty of offenses.

CONTINUING VARIETIES OF ANABAPTISTS

Anabaptists continued to be divided. The Mennonites were the most numerous, but even they were not bound together in a single fellowship and differed among themselves. One branch, the Amish, taking their name from Jacob Ammann, of the latter part of the seventeenth century, endeavoured to return to a stricter discipline. The Hutterites, or Hutterian Brethren, from Jacob Hutter, who was tortured and burned in 1536, for several generations practised community of goods. Especially strong in Moravia, they suffered severely in the Thirty Years' War (1618–1648). Remnants took refuge in Hungary. Late in the eighteenth century many of them settled in South Russia, where they were welcomed because of their industry and thrift.

Driven by persecution and refusing to resist by force of arms, the Mennonites scattered widely. In the seventeenth century many of the Swiss Mennonites, constrained by persecution, especially in Bern and Zürich, found homes in the

Palatinate. Late in the eighteenth century under the religiously sceptical Catherine the Great many of them moved to South Russia, attracted by the promise of free land and exemption from taxation for a period of years. Numbers were also to make their homes in North and South America, especially in the United States.

A group having Anabaptist principles but with a distinct and relatively late origin was the Church of the Brethren or Taufers. Their founder was Alexander Mack and their inception may be dated in 1708 when eight men and women, stirred by the Pietist movement, of which we are to hear more later, and wishing to take the New Testament as their only rule and guide, were immersed in the River Eder. Their early centres were Schwarzenau, the Palatinate, and Marienborn. By 1750 several groups, moved by persecution, had taken refuge in religiously tolerant Pennsylvania.

In the course of their history the Mennonites and other descendants of the Anabaptists became ingrowing. Originally vigorously missionary, persecution caused them largely to withdraw within themselves and to perpetuate themselves by birth rather than conversion. In some places, especially the Netherlands, they became prosperous and gave up pacifism. In some other lands they held tenaciously to their historic convictions and practices.

SUMMARY

Anabaptists were manifestations of a continuing strain in Christianity which had been present from the very beginning and which before and since the Reformation has expressed itself in many forms. It was seen in the Christians of the first century who, impressed by the wickedness of the world, sought so far as possible to withdraw from it and live in it as distinct communities but not to be of it. Montanists, Marcionites, and Novatians were in the tradition. Monasticism in its myriad forms arose from similar convictions. The Paulicians seem to have been originally from a corresponding impulse. The Waldensees, the Lollards, and many another movement of the thirteenth, fourteenth, and fifteenth centuries both inside and outside the Catholic Church were of that kin. We shall meet Christians of similar convictions again and again in the eighteenth, nineteenth, and twentieth centuries. There is that in the Christian Gospel which stirs the consciences of men to be ill content with anything short of full conformity with the ethical standards set forth in the teachings of Jesus and which awakens the hope and the faith that, seemingly impossible of attainment though they are, progress towards them can be made and that they must be sought in communities of those who have committed themselves fully to the Christian ideal.

SELECTED BIBLIOGRAPHY

R. H. Bainton, *The Travail of Religious Liberty. Nine Biographical Studies* (Philadelphia, The Westminster Press, 1951, pp. 272). Well written, by an outstanding specialist.

E. B. Bax, *Rise and Fall of the Anabaptists* (New York, The Macmillan Co., 1903, pp. 407). Chiefly an account of the Münster episode.

H. S. Bender, *Conrad Grebel, c.1498–1526, the Founder of the Swiss Brethren Sometimes Called Anabaptists* (Goshen, Ind., The Mennonite Historical Society, 1950, pp. xvi, 326). Thoroughly scholarly.

H. S. Bender, *Menno Simon's Life and Writings. A Quadricentennial Tribute 1536–1936* (Scottdale, Pa., Mennonite Publishing House, 1936, pp. viii, 110). A semi-popular biography by an expert.

A. Coutts, *Hans Denck, 1495–1527, Humanist and Heretic* (Edinburgh, Macniven & Wallace, 1927, pp. 262). Carefully done.

H. E. Dosker, *The Dutch Anabaptists* (Philadelphia, The Westminster Press, 1921, pp. 310). Carefully done.

R. Friedmann, *Mennonite Piety Through the Centuries, Its Genius and Literature* (Goshen, Ind., The Mennonite Historical Society, 1949, pp. xv, 287). Based upon extensive research.

J. Horsch, *Menno Simons, His Life, Labors, and Teachings* (Scottdale, Pa., Mennonite Publishing House, 1916, pp. 324). The fruit of careful research.

J. Horsch, *Mennonites in Europe* (Scottdale, Pa., Mennonite Publishing House, 1942, pp. xiii, 425). Embodying extensive research.

R. J. Smithson, *The Anabaptists: Their Contribution to Our Protestant Heritage* (London, James Clarke & Co., foreword, 1935, pp. 228). A competent popular survey incorporating wide reading.

H. C. Vedder, *Balthazar Hübmaier, The Leader of the Anabaptists* (New York, G. P. Putnam's Sons, 1905, pp. xxiv, 333). A semi-popular account by a careful scholar.

F. L. Weis, *The Life and Teachings of Ludwig Hetzer, a Leader and Martyr of the Anabaptists, 1500–1529* (Dorchester, Mass., Underhill Press, 1930, pp. 239). A doctoral dissertation.

J. C. Wenger, *Glimpses of Mennonite History and Doctrine* (Scottdale, Pa., Herald Press, 2d ed., 1947, pp. 258). Especially valuable for its bibliographies and translations from the sources.

Chapter XXXV

THE RADICAL REFORMERS: MEN OF THE INNER LIGHT AND RATIONALISTIC HUMANISTS

The vast and sweeping religious movement which was the Reformation had a multitude of manifestations. It stirred countless individuals to their depths and made of them quite unusual men and women. Many of these, as we are to see, remained within the Roman Catholic Church, working for moral and spiritual improvement, joining old religious orders, or organizing new ones. Others fitted in with what became standard forms of Protestantism—the Lutheran, Reformed, Presbyterian, and Anglican bodies. Even the Anabaptists, diverse as they were, conformed in the main to one or another of the patterns developed by their outstanding leaders. However, many individuals found any large community difficult. Some of them gathered small groups about them. Their number was legion. They remind one of the hermits and small communities which arose in connexion with monasticism, especially in its early days. But, unlike these, they owned no allegiance, even as tenuous as was that of many of the monks, to any ecclesiastical authority. Because they broke away from the Roman Catholic Church, they are usually regarded as Protestants. Yet many of them were not accepted by other Protestants. In general, they fell into two categories. One was made up of those who were either mystics or close kin to mystics and believed themselves to be guided by the Spirit through inward illumination, an illumination possibly aided and interpreted by Scripture. The other, for the most part arising from humanism, stressed the use of reason. The line of division between the two categories was by no means sharp. Many individuals could be classified under either or both. Some, especially among the mystics, tended towards pantheism. Others, usually humanists, made much of the rational approach to Christianity, emphasized the ethical aspect of New Testament teaching, and were inclined to be anti-Trinitarian and to regard Christ as an example and a leader to be followed rather than the divine-human redeemer.

Here is not the place for a detailed account or even a full catalogue of the individuals and the movements stemming from them which might be dealt with in this chapter. We must content ourselves with brief mention of a very few of the more outstanding. Some were popularly supposed to be Anabaptists and so may follow in close succession our treatment of that multiform expression of the Reformation.

Mystics of the Inner Light

One of the more prominent of these individuals, a contemporary of Luther, was Sebastian Franck (1499–c.1542). A German, educated under strong humanist influences, for a time a Roman Catholic priest, about 1525 he left the old church, became a preacher of the reformed faith, and was accused of Anabaptist tendencies. Although himself a prolific author, he rebelled against what he deemed excessive emphasis upon the written word. He also denounced external observances, machinery, and organization. He was convinced that there is in each man a divine element which is the source of all spiritual life. The spirit of Christ, he held, makes men religious and all who have received the grace of God are members of the Church. He believed in the eternal Christ, the ever-living, ever-present self-revelation of God, but he was not limited to Jesus. He gloried in the heretics throughout the ages, and included among them all great souls "who had dared to strike out for the Church herself new paths to truth," naming among them Jesus, Paul, and Augustine. He was a pacifist and regarded persecution as a crime.

A friend of Franck was Caspar Schwenkfeld (1487–1541). Of noble blood and rearing, he was awakened by Luther and for a time was a zealous supporter of the Wittenberg reformer. However, he differed from the latter on the Lord's Supper and wished the Church to enforce a stricter discipline on its members than was customary in Lutheran circles. A mystic, he was unhappy over the attempt to confine the Christian faith by precise dogmas and stressed the inner experience of the grace of God. That grace needs neither sacrament nor formal institutions. The fact of its presence, so he held, would be demonstrated by its fruits in righteousness of life. He was looked at askance by Catholics, Lutherans, and Reformed. Opposed to coercion of conscience, because of his religious convictions he was perforce a wanderer. His followers formed societies in Silesia of the "Confessors of the Glory of Christ," but were usually known as Schwenkfelders. In the eighteenth century persecution forced some of them to seek refuge in the religiously free air of Pennsylvania.

Some of those attracted by Schwenkfeld found spiritual kinship with the devotees of the writings of Jacob Boehme (1575–1624). Boehme, the son of a peasant, reared in a Lutheran environment, was a mystic of the first water.

What to him were visions and revelations and the illumination which came with them led him to views of God, Christ, and man which differed radically from Lutheran orthodoxy and brought persecution. Yet his works long continued to be cherished.

INDIVIDUALISTS AND PILGRIMS

In Spain and Italy the new tides of life led, as we have more than once hinted and are to see at more length a little later (Chapter XXXVIII), to a cleansing of the Roman Catholic Church but were contained in it. They also created reformers who, while they remained within the Roman Catholic Church, had strong spiritual kinship with the Protestants. In addition they gave rise to striking individuals who, repudiating the Roman Catholic Church, were never comfortable within any of the existing patterns of Protestantism but were pilgrims and strangers. Most of them bore the humanistic stamp and directly or indirectly were indebted to that great Christian humanist and individualist, Erasmus.

For a time in the sixteenth century the influence of Erasmus was strong in Spain. That was partly because of the connexion between Spain and the Low Countries which resulted from the fact that Charles V, reared in the latter, also became King of Spain. In his train were scholars who were enamoured of their fellow-Netherlander, the great humanist. It was from this vintage that Servetus drank the heady wine which led to his rejection by the Catholics and to the stake in Calvin's Geneva.

From Spain, too, came Juan de Valdés (c.1500–1541). Of noble blood, he was shaped by a combination of the Catholic heritage, Erasmus, and the mystics of the North. Seeking reform in the Church in his native land, he fell under the suspicion of the Inquisition and took refuge in Naples, then with the same rulers as Spain. Here in his villa on an island in the Bay of Naples he gave himself to Biblical studies and the way of the mystic and became the centre of a coterie of devout souls. Some of these, like himself, died in the communion of the Church of Rome. Others broke with it.

One of the circle of Valdés who left the Roman Catholic Church was Pietro Martire Vermigli (1500–1562), often known as Peter Martyr. A native of Florence, son of a warm admirer of Savonarola, he was highly educated and for a time was abbot of an Augustinian monastery and a friend of Reginald Pole, whom we are to meet in the next chapter. As prior of a house of his order in Naples, he came under the spell of Valdés and his group. He also became acquainted with some of the writings of Bucer and Zwingli. Falling under the suspicion of the ecclesiastical authorities both outside and within his order, he fled to Zürich, went on to Basel and Strassburg, and in Strassburg, befriended by Bucer, married and became professor of theology. On invitation from Cranmer, then working the reformation of the Church of England, he went to that country and became regius professor of divinity at Oxford. On the accession of Mary and the restoration by her of the Roman Catholic faith, he again fled, and died as professor of Hebrew in Zürich.

Even more spectacular was the career of Bernardino Ochino (1487–1564). A native of Siena, Ochino early joined the Franciscans of the Observance. Even the strictness of that branch of the Brothers Minor did not satisfy his zeal and he became a member of the Capuchins, a still more austere scion of the spiritual family of the Poverello of Assisi which had newly sprung from the Catholic Reformation. There he rose to be the head of that branch of the Order of Brothers Minor and was one of the outstanding preachers of the day. His fire, eloquence, and sincerity attracted thousands. He, too, came within the circle of Valdés. Given a dispensation by the Pope to read and refute the Protestant works which were filtering into Italy, instead of shattering their arguments he was convinced by them. At the age of fifty-six he fled from Italy. First he went to Geneva, where he seemed fully to subscribe to Calvin's system. There he married. He next moved to Basel, where Castellio and he formed a friendship. Then he made his home in Augsburg where, coming in touch with the Schwenkfelders, he found spiritual kinship with them and began to doubt Calvinism. The advance of Charles V's forces compelled him again to flight, first to Basel and then to England, where he helped in the reformation of the church of that kingdom. The advent of Mary sent him once more on his travels, eventually to Zürich. Differences in doctrine developed between him and the authorities in that heir of Zwingli, and, at the age of seventy-six, he resumed his pilgrimage, this time to Poland. Forced out of that realm, he found a refuge with the Hutterian Anabaptists in Moravia and there died.

Celio Secundo Curione (1503–1569), a native of Piedmont, a humanist and a university professor, at the age of twenty was already reading the books of Luther. He heard lectures by Vermigli. Leaving Italy to escape the heresy-hunters, he was in Zürich, Lausanne, Basel, and Poland, and died in Basel. He never fitted fully into any of the forms of Protestantism, and was a champion of religious toleration.

Pierpaolo Vergerio, a contemporary of Vermigli and Curione, Papal nuncio, was for a time bishop of his native city, Capodistria, not far from Trieste in North Italy. Longing for the purification of the Church, he became convinced of the truth of the Protestant position and began to preach it throughout his diocese and to strive for a reform not only of doctrine but also of morals. Summoned to Rome, he resisted, was deposed by the Inquisition, and fled across the Alps. He, too, never conformed completely with the northern Protestantism, was a wanderer and something of an enigmatic figure, and his death (1565) must have been a relief to many in the Reformed ranks.

ANTI-TRINITARIANS

The books of the Protestant reformers which were read south of the Alps contributed to the thinking of numbers of individuals and groups, especially in North Italy. Many were those who, in peril from the Roman Catholic authorities, took refuge north of the Alps. Protestant tendencies were especially strong in Venetian territories, for the writings of the reformers entered through the extensive commercial contacts with Germany and Switzerland, and the Venetian authorities, jealous for their independence, resisted attempts of Rome to extend its inquisitorial activities to their domains. Anabaptist as well as Lutheran views gained headway in Venetian lands, and some of the Italian Anabaptists began to develop anti-Trinitarian convictions. These seem to have been traceable to writings of Servetus. The anti-Trinitarian Anabaptists multiplied and had congregations and pastors. In 1550 they held a council in Venice which formulated a statement of belief. Among other points, it declared that Christ is not God, but man, born of Joseph and Mary, but filled with all the powers of God, and that the elect are justified, not by the merits, the blood, or the death of Christ, but by the eternal love of God, and that Christ died to show forth the sum of all the mercy and the goodness of God. Persecutions soon scattered the congregations and numbers sought refuge in Moravia or in the lands ruled by the Turks.

Another centre of anti-Trinitarian views was in the Grisons, at that time an independent and democratic republic between Italy and Switzerland. Zwinglian doctrines early found rootage and in 1526 the state granted liberty to both Catholics and Reformed. Here many Italians found refuge in their flight from the Inquisition. With them came anti-Trinitarian views. These made for dissensions and the churches which followed the Swiss Reformation attempted to impose a Trinitarian faith. In 1553 the Synod of the Grisons adopted the Rhaetian confession which incorporated the Apostles', Nicene, and Athanasian Creeds and required subscription by all pastors. By 1575 anti-Trinitarian ministers had been largely rooted out.

Some of the Italian humanists who found refuge at Geneva sympathized with Servetus and, to the distress of Calvin, tended towards anti-Trinitarianism. Similar trends disturbed the Reformed Churches in Bern and Zürich.

THE SOCINIANS

Anti-Trinitarianism had a marked development in Poland. There it became associated with the names of the Sozini, uncle and nephew, Italians, and was given the appellation of Socinianism. Laelius Socinus (Lelio Sozini), the elder of the two, was born in 1525 at Siena of a distinguished family of jurists. While studying law at the University of Padua he became engrossed in the reading of the Scriptures, gave himself to the reform movement, and sought refuge first in the more liberal Venice and then in the Grisons. He travelled widely among Protestant churches and leaders north of the Alps and in England, and had friendly contacts with Calvin. Courtly in manner, modest, deeply religious, a reverent sceptic, and of irreproachable morals, his spiritual pilgrimage never led him to a formal break with the Swiss and Genevan reformers. However, he deplored the burning of Servetus and some suspected him of unsound doctrines. Yet he had the confidence of Bullinger and, after journeys in Poland and Italy, died in Zürich in 1562, still in his thirties. In the humanist tradition, he brought reason to bear on questions of faith and valued it as well as the Scriptures.

More famous than Lelio Sozini was his nephew, Faustus Socinus (Fausto Sozini). Born in 1539, he was educated more in letters than the law. From boyhood he had been inclined towards Protestantism, but outwardly conformed to the Roman Catholic Church and from 1563 to 1574 was a secretary in the court of the Medici in Florence. Eventually he left Italy for Basel. While there he wrote a treatise, *De Jesu Christo Salvatore,* in which he said that Christ did not appease the wrath of a righteous God by suffering the penalty that we deserve because of our sin, but that he becomes our saviour by making known the way of eternal salvation and that we may reach that goal by imitating him. For a time he was in Transylvania, where an anti-Trinitarian form of Protestantism was making rapid progress. He then spent a quarter of a century in Poland, dying in 1604. There he was the outstanding figure in a branch of the Reformed Churches which was anti-Trinitarian.

The Reformation early penetrated Poland. Dissatisfaction with the wealth and corruption of the Catholic Church facilitated its spread. It entered in several forms. Lutherans, Anabaptists, Bohemian Brethren, and Reformed all made their appearance and flourished. At first strong in the towns and cities, it won many of the nobility and progressed among the peasants. It had an able leader in Jan Laski, also known as John à Lasco (1499–1560), of a distinguished Polish family, nephew of a primate of the Polish Church. A priest and with the prospect of rapid advancement in the Church, Laski became a friend of Erasmus, laboured for reform in Poland, then spent a number of years abroad furthering the Reformation in several countries, and during the last four years of his life was in his native land, preaching, holding synods, stimulating the translation of the Bible into Polish, and seeking to bring the varieties of Protestantism into one ecclesiastical structure. There was a brief period when it seemed that Protestantism would sweep the country. Divisions in the

Protestant ranks, a Catholic monarch, and especially the missionary zeal of the Jesuits, brought the downfall of Reformation and issued in the reconversion of most of those who had left the Catholic Church.

Before that reconversion, anti-Trinitarian views developed in the Reformed Churches in Poland and led to a division in which the minority held to them. To this minority Faustus Socinus gave leadership. The standard formulation of the beliefs of these churches was the Racovian Catechism, bearing the name of Rakow, the headquarters of the Socinians and where it was first published. It was the work of Faustus Socinus and some of his friends and disciples. Although it became an object of attack by Lutheran and Reformed theologians, it was not as radical a departure from the main stream of historic Christianity as were the convictions of some of the other anti-Trinitarians. It sought to base its positions solidly on the Scriptures as the divine revelation of the way to eternal life. It held that the authenticity of the Christian religion was established by the miracles and the resurrection of Christ. The way to eternal life, it maintained, is through the knowledge of God and Christ. Christ was a real but not an ordinary man and showed us how to return to God. He is prophet, priest, and king. Baptism was regarded as not appropriate for infants, but as an outward act by which converts acknowledge Christ as their master. The Lord's Supper was celebrated, but purely as commemorative of the death of Christ. The Holy Spirit is a divine power in the hearts of men. The Church is the company of those who hold to saving doctrine. The Christian life is characterized by prayer, thanksgiving, joy, the renunciation of the world, and patient endurance. Christians are to obey lawful magistrates, are not to lay up wealth beyond what is required for the ordinary needs of life, are to use any surplus for the relief of the poor, and are not to ask more than a reasonable interest on loans.

The Polish Socinians were actively missionary. For a time they seemed to have an opportunity in Russia and gained a footing in Volkynia, in what was later known as the Ukraine. They established contacts with many of similar views, including the Remonstrants and some of the Mennonites in Holland. Complete accord was not reached with these others nor did they fully agree among themselves. Some were pacifists, forswearing all war, while others maintained that armed resistance to injustice is permissible. In general they did not regard the Racovian catechism as a permanently binding statement of Christian belief, and subsequent editions of that document contained substantial modifications of the original. The Socinians tended to make an increasing appeal to reason in support of the convictions which they set forth. They stood for religious liberty, asking to be allowed to hold to such views as seemed to them sound and not seeking to constrain others, whether of their own number or of other religious bodies, to conform to any one pattern of belief.

Persecution wrought ruin in Poland for the Socinians as to Protestantism in general. Late in the sixteenth century and early in the seventeenth century it became acute during the forty-five year reign of Sigismund III. Of the house of Vasa, but a devout Roman Catholic, Sigismund was strongly under the influence of the Jesuits. During the rule of Sigismund and his immediate successors wars with Sweden, Moscow, and Turkey, and rebellion spear-headed by the Cossacks added to the distresses of those who survived the persecutions. In 1658 and 1659 in the stormy reign of John Casimir, formerly a Jesuit, a priest, and a cardinal, the Socinians were banished from Poland by decree of the Diet. Some of them found refuge in Transylvania. Here anti-Trinitarians were already strong, especially among one of the racial groups, the Szeklers. Indeed, the name "Unitarian," a general later designation, seems to have been first officially applied to them in 1600 in a decree of the Transylvanian Diet. Here, in the second half of the sixteenth century, Lutherans, Reformed, Unitarians, and Roman Catholics were accorded equal recognition before the law and were in effect state churches. A few others of the Polish Socinians found a precarious asylum in East Prussia and the Rhenish Palatinate. More went to Holland where they had an influence among the Remonstrants and the Mennonites.

It seems to be more than a coincidence that anti-Trinitarianism, or Unitarianism, was chiefly of humanist origin and that it found its most congenial soil among churches of the Reformed tradition. Its chief gains on the Continent were not among the Lutherans but among the Reformed. In England it was Presbyterians from whom most of the Unitarians were drawn. In the United States Unitarianism developed from the Puritanism around Boston. This may have been because humanism, with its emphasis upon the competence of human reason, tended to rule out all that seemed to it irrational and because the chief shapers of the Reformed theology came to Protestantism through humanism and made much of the use of reason. This does not mean that Calvinism and other strains within the Reformed tradition necessarily led to Unitarianism. It indicates, however, that the rational approach so congenial to humanism could easily exalt the competence of the intellect, stress the human side of Christ, regard Jesus as simply the best of men, emphasize the ethical aspects of the Biblical teachings, and believe that man is able to attain to them with the aid of God but without the basic new birth of which the New Testament speaks and which the majority of Protestants, along with Augustine, contend comes only through grace, the quite unmerited favour of God which no man can earn.

Selected Bibliography

R. H. Bainton, *The Travail of Religious Liberty* (Philadelphia, The Westminster Press, 1951). Sketches of individuals, popularly written, by a thorough scholar and expert.

J. Böhme, *The Incarnation of Jesus Christ,* translated from the German by J. R. Earle (London, Constable & Co., 1934, pp. viii, 284). One of the more significant works of Boehme.

G. K. Brown, *Italy and the Reformation to 1550* (Oxford, Basil Blackwell, 1933, pp. 324). Carefully done.

Concerning Heretics . . . an Anonymous Work Attributed to Sebastian Castellio Now first done into English together with excerpts from other works of Sebastian Castellio and David Joris on religious liberty, by R. H. Bainton (Columbia University Press, 1935, pp. xiv, 342). Extremely well done.

F. C. Church, *The Italian Reformers 1534–1564* (Columbia University Press, 1932, pp. xii, 428). Well documented.

R. M. Jones, *Spiritual Reformers in the 16th & 17th Centuries* (London, Macmillan & Co., 1928, pp. li, 362). Based upon careful research into Continental and English precursors of Quakerism, with special emphasis upon Jacob Böhme, by a distinguished American Quaker.

C. Schultz, *A Vindication of Caspar Schwenckfeld von Ossig. An Elucidation of his Doctrine and the Vicissitudes of his Followers,* translated from the German and edited E. S. Gerhard (Allentown, Pa., Edward Schlechter, 1942, pp. 347). The first German edition was in 1771.

E. M. Wilbur, *A History of Unitarianism: Socinianism and its Antecedents* (Harvard University Press, 1945, pp. xiii, 617). A sympathetic account, based upon extensive research, by an American Unitarian.

Chapter XXXVI

THE ENGLISH REFORMATION

In our treatment of the Protestant Reformation we have saved to the last an account of its course in England and the English dependencies, Wales and Ireland. That is not because in England the Reformation was less important than on the Continent. It was fully as significant. Indeed, through the global spread of English-speaking peoples and their culture in the seventeenth, eighteenth, and especially the nineteenth and twentieth centuries, and the missions which emanated from the English churches, it was world-wide in its influence. If we are to understand the Christianity of later years and particularly of the era after 1815 we must know the developments in English Christianity in the sixteenth and seventeenth centuries. Nor was the Reformation in England later than that on the Continent. It was almost simultaneous with it. As we are to see in a moment, its roots go back before the sixteenth century. However, while it was largely indigenous, the English Reformation was profoundly influenced by what was taking place on the Continent. Into it eventually entered to a greater or less extent all the main strains which we have thus far described. Luther, Zwingli, Calvin, the Reformed Churches of the Rhine Valley and Holland, Anabaptists, some of the men of the inner light, and the Socinians all made contributions. Yet in taking them over, the English worked them into a texture which was essentially and characteristically English.

PREPARATION FOR THE REFORMATION IN ENGLAND

The ground in England was made fallow for the Reformation by developments which reached back into the fifteenth century and earlier. As in most of Western Europe, fifteenth century English Christianity had in it much of corruption and decay. Many of the devout were saying that the monasteries had outlived their usefulness and that the monks were idle and ignorant. Hundreds of the clergy had concubines. Pluralism and absentee enjoyment of the revenues of benefices were common. Scholasticism and scholastic theology were

797

beginning to be out of fashion in intellectual circles. Yet the revival of Augustinian studies with which Wyclif was associated and the influence of the late scholastics, both natives of British soil, John Duns Scotus and William of Ockham, must have helped positively to prepare the way for the subsequent movements.

The old social, political, and economic order with which the Church was associated was passing. Beginning with the first of the line, Henry VII, and followed more emphatically by his son, Henry VIII, the Tudor monarchs were insisting on being full masters in the realm and were building an English variation of the absolute royal power which was growing on the Continent. Cities and their thrifty, industrious middle classes were increasing in importance.

Most of the bishops, although many were engrossed in affairs of state to the frequent neglect of their dioceses, were upright and able, and the rank and file of the populace were so devout that visitors from the Continent remarked upon it. Lollardy had never completely died out. It persisted, chiefly among the poor and often in outward conformity with the Church. Translations of the Bible existed in English and were read, although not by any means as widely as after the invention of printing. The writings of the mystics whom we have met in earlier chapters were circulated. We have also noted the presence of earnestly religious humanists who desired the reform and renewal of the Church, among them Colet, who eventually occupied the post of Dean of St. Paul's in London, the witty, learned, and deeply devoted Thomas More, and Erasmus himself. Preachers, some of them wandering friars, were denouncing vices. The morality plays, given in churchyards and churches and drawing appreciative audiences, pilloried vice and exalted virtue. Satirists were arraigning current sins. Didactic literature was issuing from some of the earliest printing presses. Then, too, a sturdy nationalism was restive under interference in ecclesiastical affairs by a foreign Pope and hotly resented the fashion in which Papal appointees battened on English revenues in luxury-loving circles in Avignon and Rome. This patriotism could readily be invoked by monarchs who sought to identify themselves with it and use it for their own ends.

First Moves towards Reformation

In this fallow ground the writings of Luther would certainly find fruitage. They were not long in reaching Oxford and Cambridge. In Cambridge, especially, they awakened interest. Here was a circle whose members, aided by the Greek New Testament of Erasmus with its Latin translation, were earnestly studying the Scriptures. The leader, Thomas Bilney, after an inner struggle of soul had come to inward peace. He had also become acquainted with some of the writings of Luther. In 1531 he was burned in Norwich as a heretic, but before his death he had a profound influence upon a young priest and graduate of Cambridge, Hugh Latimer, who was later to loom prominently in the Reformation and was also to seal his witness at the stake.

Even more influential as a pioneer was William Tyndale (c.1494–1536). Born of a prosperous yeoman family not far from Gloucester, he took a degree at Oxford and then went to Cambridge. He was ordained, but when and where we do not know. Soon after leaving Cambridge, he formed the purpose of putting the New Testament into English, to make it accessible to those who could not easily read Latin. This he did, apparently without taking advantage of the Wyclif translation, but using the Greek text and the Latin translation of Erasmus, the Vulgate, and Luther's translation into German. Eventually he added to it a large part of the Old Testament, utilizing the Hebrew text, the Vulgate, the Septuagint, and Luther's Bible. He also revised his translation of the New Testament. Most of his work was done on the Continent, but in spite of efforts to suppress them, his translations, printed, circulated in England. They were of substantial assistance to the translators of that later, seventeenth century Authorized or King James' Version, which became standard in English-speaking lands and which did almost as much to give form to English literary style as did Luther's translation to German.

While on the Continent Tyndale moved further over to the Protestant position. In 1528 he issued *The Parable of the Wicked Mammon* in which he came out flatly for justification by faith, and took over most of the text of a sermon by Luther on the unjust steward. That same year another book by him appeared which denied that he preached rebellion against secular rulers and declared that civil authorities should be obeyed, and all rulers, whether parents, husbands, masters, or landlords. Arrested for heresy in the Low Countries, he was tried, condemned, degraded from the priesthood, and strangled, and his body was burned (1536).

HENRY VIII LEADS IN A BREACH WITH ROME

What course the Reformation would have taken in England had it not been for Henry VIII we cannot know. It was that monarch who broke with Rome, set the Church of England on its independent course, and helped to give it some of its distinctive features.

Henry VIII (1491–1547), younger son of Henry VII, was being prepared for ecclesiastical office when the death of his older brother, Arthur, in 1502, made him heir to the throne. Handsome, athletic, able, well educated, musical, having more than a cursory knowledge of theology, masterful, he was not quite eighteen when (1509) his father's death made him king.

It was over the question of marriage that the strain between Henry and Rome arose. In 1501 Arthur, aged fourteen, had been wedded to Catherine, aged sixteen, daughter of Ferdinand and Isabella of Spain. It was purely an affair of statecraft whereby Henry VII, the hold of his family on the throne still shaky, sought to ally himself with a powerful neighbour, and whereby that neighbour was glad of a tie with a kingdom which, while far inferior to Spain in power, might prove useful in the chronic struggle among the monarchs of Europe. Catherine's dowry, too, proved attractive to the avaricious and parsimonious Henry VII. When, less than six months later, Arthur died, the father-in-law, loath to be deprived of the financial and other advantages of the match, arranged to have Catherine betrothed to the future Henry VIII. Since it was against the law of the Church for a man to marry his deceased brother's widow, a Papal dispensation was needed. Doubt existed as to whether the Pope had the right to remove so serious an obstacle, but after some delay the permission was granted. This was in 1504, when the young Henry was only thirteen. It was not until 1509, a few weeks after the death of his father, that Henry VIII was willing to proceed to marriage. Although he had doubts about the validity of the union, Warham, the Archbishop of Canterbury, officiated at the ceremony. After the manner of the princes of his day, Henry was not faithful to his marriage vows, but at the outset he and Catherine seem to have been happy and in the course of the years she bore him several children. Of these only one survived infancy, and she was a daughter, Mary. Henry passionately longed for a male heir, for only through a son could he be confidently assured of the succession of his family on the throne. Only once, and that in the twelfth century, had a woman sought to reign in England, and then the realm had been thrown into civil strife. Henry, therefore, began to wonder whether he was not being visited with divine displeasure for having married his brother's wife. After a time his doubts were sharpened by the attractions of Anne Boleyn. Anne had a strange fascination for him and would accept none of his favours except as his queen.

Now began efforts on the part of Henry and his compliant ministers to obtain a divorce from Catherine. Into the tortuous intricacies of the prolonged proceedings we must not take the time to go. Thomas Wolsey, cardinal, Archbishop of York, and long the king's first minister, failed, was dismissed, and died of chagrin (1530). The Popes could scarcely comply with Henry's urgent desire, for by doing so they would offend Catherine's nephew, the Emperor Charles V, who was more powerful than the English monarch and a much more serious menace.

Shortly before Wolsey's death a fresh figure, Thomas Cranmer (1489–1556), emerged, who was speedily to become prominent and was to have a major part in carrying out the Reformation in the Church of England. A younger son of a farmer, Cranmer was designed for the priesthood. He went to Cambridge, graduated, was made a fellow of his college, before he could be ordained was married, then, his wife dying in child-birth, he again became a fellow (for marriage had deprived him of that position), and c.1523, a few years after the posting of Luther's ninety-five theses, was ordained. Studious, learned, modest, dignified, courteous, deeply religious, by nature conservative, he did not become a member of the group led by Bilney. In 1529, in a casual conversation Cranmer suggested that the question of the legality of the marriage of Catherine to Henry could be put to the universities. The universities, it will be recalled, were regarded with respect when they spoke on matters of theology. The suggestion having come to his ears, Henry took Cranmer into his service and had him appointed a chaplain in the Boleyn household.

By successive steps Henry VIII reduced the clergy of the realm to submission and broke with Rome. In accordance with Cranmer's proposal, the question of the marriage was referred to the universities, and the majority of the replies, thanks in part to more or less adroit pressure from the king, were in accordance with his wishes. He had the clergy indicted for a breach of the statute of *Praemunire* on the ground that they had accepted Wolsey as Papal legate. That law, it will be remembered, had first been enacted in 1353 to prevent suits being carried outside the realm to Papal tribunals. In January, 1530, Convocation, representing the clergy of the archdiocese of Canterbury, was constrained to vote a large financial grant to the king *in lieu* of a fine and to declare Henry to be "the singular protector, the only and supreme lord, and as far as is permitted by the law of Christ, even the supreme head" of the Church in England. In 1532, under constraint, Convocation also undertook not to enact any canon affecting the laity without royal approval. That same year, at royal initiative, Parliament abolished the payment to the Pope of annates. The year 1532 also saw the death of Warham, Archbishop of Canterbury, who had been unhappy because of the course of events, and the appointment of Cranmer to succeed him. The approval of the Pope was obtained and Cranmer was consecrated. In January, 1533, Henry and Anne were secretly married, for she was pregnant (with the future Elizabeth) and Henry wished legitimacy for the child. In March an obedient Parliament passed an act in restraint of appeals, which affirmed that the Church of England was competent to decide its own cases, that Papal dispensations were unnecessary, and that no Papal interference in the appointment of bishops would be tolerated. The case of the marriage of Henry to Catherine was thereupon brought into the court of Cranmer as archbishop and the decision desired by the king was obtained, although with the stipulation that Mary was legitimate, and the union of Henry and

Anne Boleyn was declared valid. Catherine, who had carried herself with dignity through the difficult years, refused to acknowledge the competence of the court. The Pope reaffirmed the validity of her marriage to Henry and excommunicated the king. In 1534 Parliament forbade the payment of Peter's Pence to Rome. Late in 1534 Parliament declared that the king "is and ought to be the supreme head of the Church." The following year Henry announced himself as *"in terra supremum caput Anglicanæ ecclesiæ"* ("supreme head on earth of the English Church") and a royal proclamation erased the Pope's name from all the service books. The breach with Rome was complete.

There were those in England who protested or refused to acknowledge the royal supremacy over the Church and paid for their temerity with their lives. These included several Carthusians, the devout and upright John Fisher, cardinal, Bishop of Rochester, former chancellor of Cambridge University, friend of Erasmus, and confessor to Catherine, and Thomas More, whom we have already met, humanist, scholar, earnest Christian, and a former chancellor of the realm and intimate of Henry. These executions, especially of Fisher and More, sent a thrill of horror through Western Europe, but Henry was not to be deterred from making himself autocrat in both Church and state. In the chronic struggle between the Church and the monarch which in England as elsewhere in Europe had been going on for centuries, Henry had won. To a degree which would have been the envy and admiration of even his strongest predecessors, he had made himself master of both state and Church.

Changes in the Church of England under Henry's Headship

The separation of the Church of England from Rome did not necessarily mean that Protestantism was to prevail. Indeed, Henry was proud of his orthodoxy and was punctilious in his daily attendance at mass and his use of a confessor. He was careful to give the guise of legality to his many acts. Earlier he had affixed his name to a book which professed to refute Luther and had received from a flattering Pope the designation of Defender of the Faith, a title which he and his successors were to continue to bear. The question was still unanswered as to whether the currents in England and on the Continent which were making for reform would work significant changes in the Church of England, either in the direction of Protestantism or of the kind which were occurring within the Roman Catholic Church.

By the time that death removed Henry from the scene, significant innovations had been introduced, all with his consent and some on his initiative. Autocrat though he was, Henry was careful not to move until he was fairly confident of carrying the bulk of public opinion with him. Much of his strength lay in his popularity with the majority of his subjects and in his ability to sense the temper of the nation.

To act as his agent as head of the English Church, Henry appointed Thomas Cromwell as his vicar-general and vicegerent. Cromwell, of lowly parentage, had been in the service of Wolsey. He had Protestant leanings, although how sincere they were has been a matter of debate. Thoroughly committed to the royal supremacy, he presided at Convocation, taking precedence over the Archbishop of Canterbury. Under his direction a systematic visitation of the monasteries was begun. This was followed by the dissolution of the monasteries. First the smaller ones were disbanded and then the friars were suppressed. The larger monasteries held out slightly longer, but by 1540 they had gone the way of the smaller ones. Some voluntarily surrendered their property to the king. The heads of three prominent houses were executed. The chief shrines of the saints, famous goals of pilgrimages, including that of Cuthbert at Durham, and especially that of Thomas Becket at Canterbury, for whom Henry had a marked antipathy, presumably because of his resistance to royal authority, were dismantled and despoiled of their treasures. The Pope retaliated for the treatment of Becket's tomb by placing England under the interdict, but the time had passed when that act by a Roman Pontiff could bring a king of England to his knees. The proceeds of the confiscated properties were used in part to endow new dioceses, schools, professorships in the universities, and Trinity College in Cambridge, for pensions for dispossessed monks and nuns, and for coastal defenses. However, as in Denmark and Sweden, the larger part went into the royal coffers, for Henry was chronically short of funds, and to royal favorites. Many of the populace availed themselves of the opportunity for plunder, and some of the monks were not above disposing of the movables of their houses.

Various results followed. Those given monastic properties were bound to the king and could be counted on for support against a renewal of the tie with Rome. The power of the clergy in Parliament was curtailed, for in the House of Lords there were no longer abbots and priors, and of the Lords Spiritual only the bishops remained. The poor who had formerly been cared for by the monasteries were thrown on the public and beginnings were made of the later system whereby they became the charge of the parishes.

Apart from the separation from Rome, the suppression of the monasteries was the most drastic change made under Henry VIII in the religious life of England, for the monks, their houses, and the friars had long been a prominent and accepted part of the social, economic, and religious structure of the realm. However, the monasteries were already waning. It is said that in the fifteenth century only eight new houses had been founded. Some had earlier been dissolved. Only slight resistance was offered to the step. The most notable was the uprising in the North known as the Pilgrimage of Grace, and this had the changes in religion as only one of its causes and was speedily put down. Except for the brief and partial revival under Mary and a few feeble remnants, monasticism disappeared from England and was not again to appear until the nineteenth century.

Successive statements of doctrine for the Church of England were issued. In 1536, two years or so after the final break with Rome, Ten Articles, drafted by Henry with the help of Cranmer, were promulgated. They mentioned three sacraments, baptism, penance, and the Eucharist, stressed the importance of teaching the people the Bible and the Apostles', Nicene, and Athanasian Creeds, declared that justification is by faith and by confession, absolution, and good works, that Christ is physically present in the Eucharist, and that masses for the dead, the invocation of the saints, and the use of images are desirable. In 1537 the *Institution of a Christian Man,* popularly known as the Bishops' Book, came out, a manual on Christian doctrine for the rank and file. In 1543 a thorough revision, greatly altered, of this treatise was published over the king's name, *A Necessary Doctrine and Erudition for Any Christian Man,* generally called the King's Book. In 1539 what were known as the Six Articles were passed by Parliament in the presence and under the authority of Henry, and over the opposition of Cranmer. They were much closer to the Catholic position than were the Ten Articles, for they came out flatly for transubstantiation, against the necessity of communion in both kinds, for the celibacy of the clergy, for the observance of vows of chastity taken by men or women, for private masses, and for auricular confession.

In accordance with this zeal for doctrinal orthodoxy as defined in the Catholic tradition, a few Zwinglians and Lutherans were condemned and burned, and several others were burned for denying transubstantiation.

Yet steps which might look in a Protestant direction were taken. In 1536 Cromwell, as the king's vicar-general, ordered a Latin and an English Bible placed in every church to encourage its reading by the laity. Later in the 1530's priests were commanded to set up a large English Bible in such a manner that it might be read by all who wished. The circulation of Tyndale's Bible, especially the edition with his glosses, for they were regarded as heretical, stimulated the authorities to essay a translation of which they could approve. Miles Coverdale, a former Augustinian friar, a graduate of Cambridge and a member of the reforming circle of which the martyred Bilney had been a leader, had made a full translation of the entire Bible into English, not from the original Greek and Hebrew, but probably from the Vulgate, another Latin version, Luther's translation, and a Zürich version, and possibly utilizing Tyndale. As a work of scholarship it was of dubious value, but it possessed marked literary merit, and some of its phrases were later taken over by the King James Version. What was called the Great Bible, had the approval of Cranmer, and had been assisted by Cromwell, was to be placed in the churches. It was a revision, by Coverdale, of Matthew's Bible. This took its name from Thomas Matthew, probably an alias for John Rogers. Matthew's Bible was made up of Tyndale's Pentateuch and New Testament, most of Coverdale's Old Testament, and a translation of the Apocrypha by Rogers. The Great Bible went into several editions, some of them with a preface by Cranmer and accordingly called Cranmer's Bible.

While Henry was still alive, Cranmer had begun the preparation of forms of worship, including a litany. By the king's order the litany was to be sung in English in the churches.

Henry was gathered to his fathers in 1547. Cranmer was with the dying king. Although he had dared to oppose more than one of his royal master's acts and to intercede with him for some of the latter's victims, Henry had trusted him and had supported him against his enemies.

THE REFORMATION UNDER EDWARD VI

Henry VIII was succeeded by the son, Edward VI, whom his third wife, Jane Seymour, had borne to him. He had married her after the execution of Anne Boleyn for infidelity and her failure to present him the desperately desired male heir. Edward was only nine years of age when he came to the throne and, always frail of body, died in 1553, when he was not yet sixteen. He was highly intelligent, was given a strenuous education of a humanist, Renaissance kind, had a mind of his own, and was deeply religious and strongly Protestant. But policies during his reign were largely determined by his seniors. First to rule was his mother's brother, Edward Seymour, Earl of Hertford and then Duke of Somerset, who was given the title of Lord Protector. Then, after about two-and-a-half years, he was followed by John Dudley, Earl of Warwick and then Duke of Northumberland.

In the six-and-a-half years of Edward's reign England was carried towards Protestantism. Somerset was Protestant in his sympathies, probably sincerely so. Northumberland moved even further in that direction, although presumably more from expediency than from religious conviction, for just prior to his execution under Mary he professed reconversion to Roman Catholicism.

The main steps towards Protestantism can be quickly summarized. Early in the reign a step which Henry had planned and initiated was taken: chantries, hospitals, and free chapels were dissolved and the capital thus released went largely to the depleted royal exchequer. The first Parliament of the new reign repealed the Six Articles, all restrictions on the printing and circulation of the

Scriptures, and the laws under which heretics had been tried. The reign was not many weeks old when the removal of images from the churches was ordered. In some places violent iconoclasm followed. Indeed, in many quarters enthusiasts were moving faster than the government and the latter took measures to restrain them. In 1548 an Order of Communion was printed for use in connexion with giving the communion to the laity. In it appeared a general confession, taking the place of private confession to the priest. Yet the Latin mass was continued. Leading Continental reformers were welcomed. Among them were Peter Martyr, Ochino, and Bucer, each of whom was given an important post. Disputes over the Eucharist and whether mass should be said waxed hot and in places led to fighting and riots. The marriage of priests was legalized. The influences from the Continent which helped to shape the English Reformation were more from humanism and the Reformed Churches than from Luther and Lutheranism.

Partly to restore and preserve order, in 1549 an Act of Uniformity was passed by Parliament which required the clergy to use a Book of Common Prayer which was drawn up by a commission headed by Cranmer. Cranmer wished to move much further in the direction of Zwingli than many in Parliament were prepared to go, and to reject not only transubstantiation but the real presence in the Eucharist, the elevation and adoration of the host, and the use of the word "oblation." However, conservatives in Parliament led him to modify the Book of Common Prayer in the direction of the Catholic tradition. Cranmer had a deep religious conviction, a sensitivity to the things of the spirit, a wide familiarity with liturgies both Catholic and Protestant, Roman and Greek, and a command of dignified and felicitous English. In the Book of Common Prayer he combined what had previously been in the missal, the breviary, and the pontifical, and levied toll from forms of worship which had been developed in various branches and ages of the Church. Advantage was taken of uses employed in England, especially the Sarum missal, breviary, and pontifical, but these were by no means slavishly followed. For instance, from the breviary the eight daily offices were reduced to two, matins and evensong, with the hope that they would be of aid to the laity as well as to the clergy.

The First Prayer Book of Edward VI was of major importance. With modifications it has endured and has been a bond which has held together the diverse elements in the Church of England and the several branches of the Anglican Communion which arose in subsequent centuries in other countries. It has also had a profound influence upon the devotional life of individuals and on other communions which employ the English language. Its collects eventually became the common property of almost all English-speaking Protestants.

Yet the Book of Common Prayer did not immediately win its way. Those with Catholic leanings believed that it went too far towards Protestantism and many Protestants held that it retained too much from the hated Roman tradition. The swing towards Protestantism contributed to uprisings in various parts of the realm. Some of the bishops with Catholic convictions opposed the Act of Uniformity, were deposed, and were replaced by appointees in sympathy with the Reformed Churches.

In 1552 a new Act of Uniformity was enacted and Parliament gave its sanction to a revised edition of the Book of Common Prayer, the Second Prayer Book of Edward VI. This moved much further in the direction of Protestantism. It was the work of Cranmer and Ridley with some help from Bucer and Peter Martyr. In it, among other changes, the "altar" was called a "table," and the "priest" a "minister," the minister's vestments were limited to the surplice, and exorcism and anointing were omitted. The new Act of Uniformity was more stringent than was the earlier one. The laity were enjoined to attend service on Sundays and holidays and severe penalties were specified for failure to comply. The use of the revised Book of Common Prayer was made compulsory.

It will be noted that Parliament, an organ of state, rather than Convocation, the body through which the Church spoke, took responsibility for the Book of Common Prayer and imposed it on the nation. This, together with the supremacy of the crown over the Church, was in accord with the trend in both Western and Eastern Europe, and in Protestant, Roman Catholic, and Orthodox circles.

In 1553 the Forty-two Articles of Religion, giving the doctrinal position of the Church of England, were issued under the authority of the king. Their formulation was largely the work of Cranmer.

It was during the reign of Edward VI that English paraphrases of the Psalms began to have wide currency. The chief pioneer was Thomas Sternhold, a groom of the robes to Henry VIII and Edward VI. He seems to have drawn his inspiration in large part from what was being done in Geneva.

Marked though its progress was, by no means all the English were committed to the Reformation. It had a much larger following in London and the South-east, areas in close commercial contact with the Continent, than in the North and West. In the latter areas the majority were probably still attached to the old forms, although not necessarily to Rome.

THE CATHOLIC REACTION UNDER MARY

From the movement towards Protestantism which was being pushed in the name of the crown during the reign of Edward VI a reaction was to be expected. The Catholic elements were still strong and the majority of the population were either indifferent or attached to the old ways. Reform had not sprung widely from the rank and file of the nation and with the exception of minorities had not really penetrated to them. However, the reaction was greatly intensified by the accession to the throne of Mary, daughter of Henry VIII and Catherine.

Mary reigned for a little over five years, from the summer of 1553 to her death, November 17, 1558. It was a foregone conclusion that she would attempt to bring England back into the Roman Catholic fold. The daughter of Henry VIII and Catherine, she was intensely loyal to her mother's memory. During much of her life she had suffered indignities because of her birth, and by the nullification of the marriage between her mother and her father serious doubt had been cast on her legitimacy. Although her father's will had declared her and Elizabeth to be bastards, it had provided that in case Edward VI died without issue they should succeed to the throne in the order of their birth. The attempt of the Duke of Northumberland to have Lady Jane Grey, a grand-niece of Henry VIII, succeed Edward VI quickly failed, but while Mary was magnanimous, it did not serve to make her less opposed to Protestantism. Physically unprepossessing, thirty-seven years of age, and far from well, Mary had courage and intelligence of a high order and an indomitable will, and was very well educated. She could be counted on to give vigorous leadership to the realm.

With all her determination and ability, not for some months was Mary able to restore the Papal authority in England. Yet the trend was quickly in that direction. Many Protestants, including foreigners who had been prominent under Edward, seeing the writing on the wall, sought refuge on the Continent. A few went to France, but most of them found haven in cities where the Reformed Churches were strong—Zürich, Basel, Geneva, Strassburg, Heidelberg, and Frankfort. Important results from contacts in these places of refuge were to follow in the next reign. Mary had mass said in her private chapel. Catholic bishops, notably Stephen Gardiner of Winchester, who had been dispossessed under Edward, were restored to their sees. Although refusing to renew the tie with Rome or to restore the alienated ecclesiastical properties, in October, 1553, Parliament repealed all the laws enacted under Edward which affected religion, thus banishing the Book of Common Prayer, removing the permission for clerical marriage, and withdrawing communion in both kinds. Church services were back where they were in the last years of Henry VIII.

However, in 1554 Mary had her way. By her own choice she was married, not to an English nobleman, as Parliament had wished, but to her cousin, Philip, soon (January, 1556) by the abdication of his father, Charles V, to become King Philip II of Spain. Possessors of church lands were given assurances that they would not be disturbed in their holdings. In November, 1554,

Reginald Pole, Cardinal and Papal legate, formally absolved the realm from its schism and disobedience and received it back into communion with the Church of Rome. Closely related to Henry VIII and so to Mary, as a younger son Pole had from childhood been trained for an ecclesiastical career. Sincerely religious, impeccable in his private life, a friend of Thomas More, he had refused to approve of Henry's efforts to be separated from Catherine, had frowned on his move to make himself head of the Church of England, and had lived abroad for years. There he had been made a cardinal and had been a member of a circle of Catholic ecclesiastics and laywomen who desired the reform of the Church. Indeed, he had been denounced to the Inquisition for harbouring heretical views. Yet he narrowly missed being elected Pope. He now (1556) became Archbishop of Canterbury. In that office he sought to reform the Church of England, to revive monasticism, to raise up good priests, and, as chancellor of both Oxford and Cambridge, to make those universities serve the revived Roman Catholicism.

The reign of Mary witnessed a number of beheadings and burnings, so much so, indeed, that her critics remembered her as "Bloody Mary." That was not because she, Pole, or her chancellor, Gardiner, were cruel or vindictive. Indeed, all were kindly in their personal relations and Pole by temperament and conviction preferred reason and lenience to harshness. Yet the brief reign was punctuated with rebellions and the spirit of the times regarded as normal the execution of the leaders. Moreover, to the Catholic, heresy was a major crime against God and society. The laws against heresy were revived and under them about three hundred went to the stake. About a third were clergymen and about a fifth women. Two-thirds were in the stronghold of Protestantism, London and the South-east. By Continental standards the number was small, but it was much greater than the burnings of Lollards in a century and a quarter before 1529 or than the number of Catholics who suffered the death penalty in the long reign of Elizabeth. The most famous of the victims were Bishops Latimer, Ridley, and Cranmer, all of them burned at Oxford. The first two suffered together. Latimer is said to have encouraged his comrade at the stake with the words: "Be of good comfort, Master Ridley, we shall this day light such a candle by God's grace in England as, I trust, shall never be put out." Cranmer was in a hard dilemma. He had a profound conviction, on which he had acted under Henry and Edward, that the monarch was by right master of the religion of his realm and that his subjects must bow to his will in this as in other matters. Now the monarch was a Roman Catholic and demanded that England return to that faith. By disposition and long habit, Cranmer's mind moved slowly to new conclusions. It seems to have been at least in part for this reason that at first he submitted and made seven recantations. At the end, however, on the very day that he was given to the flames, he publicly, in St. Mary's, before a great throng, repudiated his recantations. At the stake he held in the flames the hand which had signed the documents he now bitterly regretted, that it might first be reduced to cinders.

THE ELIZABETHAN SETTLEMENT

Mary died an unhappy woman, for Philip was with her infrequently, she remained childless, and she had alienated the affections of many of her subjects. She was succeeded by her half-sister, Elizabeth, daughter of Henry VIII and Anne Boleyn.

Elizabeth reigned for nearly half a century, from 1558 to 1603. Her name is associated with one of the most glorious eras in English history, remembered for its literature, its commerce and growth in wealth, and its exploits on the seas, especially the defeat of the formidable armada by which Philip II of Spain thought to prepare the way for the invasion and conquest of the country. Disciplined by the adversities of a difficult youth in which a misstep might have meant her death, Elizabeth was astute in gaining and keeping power and popularity. Identifying the welfare of England with her own, she sought to bring unity to a divided nation and so far as possible to keep it out of weakening embroilment in foreign wars. She knew much about Christianity, but probably had little religious conviction. She loved pomp and ceremony and approved of them in church services. Although, for an adequate return, the Pope might have found a way to alter her status, from the Roman Catholic standpoint she was illegitimate and therefore was prejudiced against the recently reëstablished tie with Rome. Presumably, too, she wished, like her father and many another strong monarch, to have full control of the Church within her borders. She was not above despoiling it of some of its wealth. She kept some of the bishoprics unfilled for years and appropriated their revenues. Several ecclesiastical posts were paid for by their appointees by alienating portions of their endowments. Yet she wished such an ordering of the Church of England as would satisfy as many of her subjects as possible. Therefore she sought to make it include both Catholic and Protestant elements. She could not hope to please both Roman Catholics and extreme Protestants, but she could and did achieve a settlement which proved acceptable to the vast majority of the Englishmen of her day and which, without basic alterations, was to characterize the Church of England from then onward.

The main features of the Elizabethan settlement of the ecclesiastical issues were shaped in the early months of her reign. In April, 1559, by what was generally known as the Act of Supremacy, the authority of the Pope and all payments and appeals to him were forbidden. In it she was called not the

"Supreme Head," but the "Supreme Governor of this realm, and of all other her highness's dominions and countries, as well in all spiritual or ecclesiastical things or causes as temporal," and members of the clergy and civil officials were required to acknowledge her as such and to renounce the jurisdiction of any foreign prince or prelate within the kingdom. Parliament also passed an Act of Uniformity restoring, with some alterations, the Second Prayer Book of Edward VI, and commanding it to be used in all cathedrals and parish churches for matins, evensong, and the administration of the sacraments. All inhabitants of the queen's dominions were to endeavour to be present at service on every Sunday and holyday or else be fined. To enforce the Act of Uniformity, royal visitors were commissioned and for their guidance what were known as injunctions were issued, modifications of those under the name of Edward VI, which regulated the clergy, public worship, and the care of the poor through the parishes. They permitted the marriage of the clergy but ordered that in each instance it should be by consent of the bishop, two justices of the peace, and the bride's parents. They commanded the destruction of shrines and all "monuments of feigned miracles, pilgrimages, idolatry, and superstition," in pictures, paintings, and glass windows. They provided for a censorship of books and for a holy table for the Lord's Supper in churches from which the altars had been removed. Simony was forbidden.

  Most of the parish clergy subscribed to the Act of Supremacy. Many of them had continued from Henry through the reigns of Edward and Mary and were willing to conform to the monarch's wishes. Only about two hundred lost their posts. However, the episcopacy was sadly depleted, for Mary's bishops had died or would not accept the Act of Supremacy. Those who refused were deprived of their sees. Pole, mortally ill, had died twelve hours after Mary breathed her weary last and a new Archbishop of Canterbury was required. For this office Matthew Parker, the queen's instructor, was appointed. He was consecrated by four who had been bishops under Henry VIII and Edward VI but had been ousted under Mary. In due course other bishops were chosen and consecrated. Customarily, as in all subsequent reigns, the crown appointed the bishops but used the legal device of permitting the dean and chapter of the cathedral of the diocese formally to elect the person named. The spokesmen for the Church of England have insisted that, in spite of the separation from Rome and the deposition of the Marian bishops, the apostolic succession of the episcopate was preserved. This many Roman Catholics denied, partly because the forms used did not clearly state the conception of the priesthood held by their church. However, it was not until 1896 that the Pope, after careful investigation, formally declared the orders of the Church of England invalid.

  Further to define the faith held by the Church of England, the Thirty-nine

Articles of Religion were issued. They were a modification of the Forty-two Articles of the reign of Edward. They were finally promulgated in 1571. That same year subscription to them was made compulsory for all priests and ministers.

Scholars were not wanting to give a reasoned defense for the Church of England as constituted under the Elizabethan settlement. John Jewel (1522–1571), a pupil of Peter Martyr who died as Bishop of Salisbury, wrote *Apologia Ecclesiæ Anglicanæ* (1562) in which he maintained the position of the Church of England against that of the Church of Rome. More notable was Richard Hooker's *Laws of Ecclesiastical Polity,* a massive work left uncompleted by the author's death (1600). This was a positive argument for Anglicanism against the attacks of the Puritan Presbyterians on the one hand and against the Roman Catholics on the other. Directly or by implication it included much more than the structure of the Church and the sacraments. In the midst of bitterly contending bodies of Christians, Hooker tried to make for peace by seeking a common ground in the rational principles which permeate the universe, which man, being rational, can apprehend, and which accord with the teachings of Scripture. The rational principles are seen, so Hooker said, in the eternal law by which God governs the universe. Human laws by which states and the Church are ordered should be in accord with this law of reason. They should be adapted to meet the needs of particular historical situations. With that as a basis, Hooker argued that the episcopal form of government was best for the Church of England, and that Church and state were two aspects of the same commonwealth, a commonwealth in which both were rightly under the monarch.

Although Elizabeth and her counsellors arrived at a structure, a form of worship, and a statement of belief of the Church which satisfied the large majority of Englishmen and which guarded the realm against the kind of civil strife complicated by religion which was so violent in France and Germany and which in the next century was to distress England, it was by no means acceptable to all. On the one extreme were those who held to Rome. On the other were those who were convinced that the Reformation should go much further. They were made up of various kinds of Puritans and, near the far extreme, of Independents and Separatists.

THE ROMAN CATHOLIC REVIVAL

During the reign of Elizabeth, in spite of persecution, Roman Catholicism had something of a revival in England. Through the reigns of Henry VIII, Edward VI, and, of course, Mary, there were those who held to Rome. The death of Mary and Pole and the popularity of Elizabeth and the Elizabethan settlement made impossible for the majority the renewal of the tie with Rome. However, not far from 1568, after Elizabeth had been on the throne for a decade, a marked renewal of Roman Catholic activity began. It arose in part from the rising tide of the Catholic Reformation on the Continent. The outstanding leader was William Allen (1532–1594), eventually cardinal. A graduate of Oxford and principal of one of its halls, he refused to take the oath of supremacy under Elizabeth, after a few years went to Rome, and was chiefly responsible for the founding (1568) of a Seminary in Douai, in Spanish Flanders, easily accessible to England and under Roman Catholic rulers, for the training of English missionaries to their mother country. In 1578, because of political troubles, the seminary was moved to Rheims. It was there that a translation of the Bible into English was made which is usually called the Douai Version. At Rome, partly at the suggestion of Allen, the hospice formerly used by the English was transformed into a college for the training of English priests. Jesuits and men prepared in these centres made their way into England, ministering to the faithful, strengthening the doubtful, and seeking to win converts. They dreamed of the time when England would again come into the Roman fold. To that end there was also a network of political intrigue, much of it pinning its hopes on Mary Stuart, "Queen of Scots," who by right of blood had a claim to the throne. It was this which led to the execution of Mary. Yet the intrigues and the fear of foreign intervention tended to augment the loyalty of the majority of the population to Elizabeth and the national church.

Slightly later, but part of the Catholic revival, was the work of Mary Ward (1585–1645). Of a Roman Catholic Yorkshire family, Mary Ward began in 1609 a religious community of women at St. Omer for the active, not the cloistered life. She met opposition, was dubbed the Jesuitess, and in 1630 the community was suppressed, for the Papacy looked askance at the suggestion of non-cloistered nuns. However, a few of her circle persisted and in 1703 their rule obtained Papal approval. The community was known as the Institute of Mary and more informally as the English Ladies and the Loretto Nuns. It spread widely.

THE GROWTH OF PURITANISM

Much more numerous and influential than the Roman Catholics were those who were known as Puritans. They wished to "purify" the Church of England from all traces of what they held to be the remains of the corruption which survived from the Roman connexion. Many of them had been refugees on the Continent during the reign of Mary and there had had intimate contacts with Protestants. These were much more with Basel, Strassburg, and various other cities in the Rhine Valley than with Geneva. Moreover, Puritanism antedated the Marian interlude and, largely indigenous, was deeply rooted in England's own past.

Puritans differed among themselves as to the extent to which they would depart from the Elizabethan settlement. Some focused their attack on the vestments prescribed for the clergy, holding that they tended to perpetuate the conception that, contrary to the priesthood of all believers, the clergy are distinct from the laity and with special powers. This led to the Vestiarian Controversy. Some opposed kneeling to receive the bread and wine at the Lord's Supper as adoration of the bodily presence of the Christ. They emphasized the memorial aspects of the Lord's Supper, but in neither the Lutheran nor the Zwinglian sense. Some wished a Presbyterian form of church government, with the election of pastors by their people, and placing bishops, presbyters, and pastors on an equality.

In general, Puritans held to a covenant or federalist theology. This maintained that God had made promises to man but that they were conditioned upon man's obedience to His laws. God's laws, so this conception had it, are seen in the Scriptures. It was to enable men to read the Bible and to know these laws that Tyndale undertook his vast labour of translation. The covenant theory had a long history and went back to the Middle Ages and even earlier. By this theology there were eventually meant two covenants of a somewhat different nature—a covenant of grace between God and His elect and a covenant of works between God and Adam as the representative of all mankind. As developed in the Rhineland the covenant of works stressed man's obligation to God.

The covenant of works laid a theological foundation for an obligation binding on all men, elect and non-elect, and gave support to the political theory which held that the state and all society came into being as a contract, an expression of natural law. While this had been talked of at Heidelberg, its political applications were more extensively worked out in England. It was used to limit the power of the monarch and in an extreme form held both state and Church to be associations or contracts entered into voluntarily by those who constituted these units and therefore subject to modification or even revolution as the members of these units might agree.

Prominent among the exponents of Presbyterian Puritanism under Elizabeth was Thomas Cartwright, appointed in 1569 Lady Margaret Professor of Divinity at Cambridge. John Whitgift, as vice-chancellor of the university, deprived him of his chair (1570) and as master of Trinity College had him dismissed (1571) from his fellowship. Thereafter Cartwright led a persecuted and wandering life, much of it on the Continent. In several places some of the Puritans organized a classis or presbytery, but still within the Church of England. In 1572 and 1573 they issued two Admonitions to Parliament, the second by Cartwright, denouncing government by bishops and demanding that it be by presbyters. Some Puritan ministers ceased to use the Book of Common Prayer either entirely or in part.

To all this Whitgift was opposed, and as Archbishop of Canterbury from 1583 to his death in 1604 he stood for the sturdy enforcement of Elizabeth's policy of uniformity. To accomplish this he had created a Commission for Causes Ecclesiastical, popularly known as the High Commission. It became an agency for repressing the Puritans. In protest there came out under the pseudonym of Martin Marprelate a succession of tracts denouncing Whitgift and the bishops with witty and coarse epithets. Under pressure from Elizabeth and Whitgift Parliament passed (1593) acts directed at the Puritans under the guise of "seditious sectaries and disloyal persons" and ordering all those who would not conform to the laws by "coming to church to hear divine service" to leave the realm.

THE SEPARATISTS OR INDEPENDENTS

Even more radical were the Separatists or Independents. The Puritans wished to remain within the Church of England and to have it, cleansed according to their patterns, as the religious wing of the nation's life to which all the queen's subjects would belong. In contrast, the Separatists or Independents, like the Anabaptists on the Continent, believed in "gathered" churches, not made up of all the inhabitants of a particular area, but only of those who were consciously Christian. They were to be united with one another and with Christ in a covenant. Each congregation so united, with Christ as its head, was a self-governing church which elected its own pastor and other officers after what was believed to be the pattern discernible in the New Testament. No church was to have authority over any other and in each church every member was responsible for the welfare of the whole and of his fellow-members. In theory and to a large extent in practice, such churches were pure democracies. They were the spiritual ancestors of the later Congregationalists. They were Separatists in that they withdrew from the Church of England and were Independents in that they believed in the full autonomy of each local church. They were not Anabaptists.

An outstanding pioneer was Robert Browne (died 1633), a graduate of Cambridge and originally a Puritan. Indeed, he may never have given over the idea of a church embracing all the nation. Politically, he wished magistrates to hold office only by the choice of the people. He had a varied and stormy career, part of it in prison for his views and part in exile. Then at last he submitted to the Archbishop of Canterbury. Although at times the early Independents were called Brownists, it has been questioned whether he ever really was one of them.

RELIGION IN ENGLAND UNDER THE FIRST OF THE STUARTS

With the death of Elizabeth (1603), the fears of Henry VIII were realized, and none of his descendants was left to claim the throne. The crown passed to James, the son of Mary Stuart "Queen of Scots," and greatgrandson of Margaret, daughter of Henry VII.

As we have seen (Chapter XXXIII), James, reared a Presbyterian but favouring episcopacy on the principle of "no bishop no king," was King of Scotland as well as of England. The tie was purely personal and involved no union of the two realms. James was on the throne of England from 1603 to 1625, or for a little over two decades. The years were marked by growing prosperity, partly because James managed to keep the realm from being deeply embroiled in foreign wars, and by a rising tension between king and Parliament. James was determined to rule as an autocrat by divine right and the trend of national sentiment made that much more difficult than under the Tudors.

In the religious life of the nation, Roman Catholicism was being discredited and Puritanism was growing. The extreme Protestants outside the Church of England, although still a small minority, were increasing in numbers. Dissent from the state church, it may be noted, was expressing itself quite differently in England than in the neighbouring Scotland. While influenced by Continental movements, it took on peculiarly English forms.

At the outset of his reign, James seemed to be veering towards the Roman Catholics. However, he soon changed his attitude. In February, 1604, he ordered priests banished, and soon Parliament confirmed the Elizabethan laws against them. This led to what was known as the Gunpowder Plot associated with the name of Guy Fawkes. Its purpose was to store a cellar under the Parliament buildings with barrels of gunpowder and blow up both houses, along with James and his eldest son. The plot was discovered and the chief conspirators were shot or executed. This aroused much anti-Roman Catholic feeling and led Parliament to enact even more stringent acts against those of that faith.

On his way to London in 1603 Puritans presented James with what was known as the Millenary Petition, so called because it was supposed to bear a thousand signatures. It set forth some of their desires, on the whole fairly moderate, for changes in the Church of England. There followed, in January, 1604, a conference of bishops and Puritans at Hampton Court. The one tangible result of consequence, and that of first-class importance, was the initiation of a fresh translation of the Bible.

This was needed. Two new versions had been issued during the preceding reign. One, known as the Bishops' Bible, had followed in general Tyndale's translation, was of large size, and was used chiefly in the churches. The other, the Geneva Bible, had Tyndale's New Testament as its basis but contained a new translation of the Old Testament and was later than the Bishops' Bible. Especially in its marginal notes it had a strong Calvinist and Puritan tinge. Embodying thorough scholarship, it also had an English style which delighted the rank and file of readers, was printed in Roman rather than black letters and in convenient style, and enjoyed a wide circulation. A version was called for which would embody the best in the existing versions and which could be read both in the public services of the Church and in homes and by private individuals.

To produce the translation James appointed fifty-four scholars (of whom we have the names of forty-seven), presumably after consultation. They were divided into six companies of seven or eight men each, who worked individually and in conference. Then the whole text was gone over by a committee of twelve and two prepared the product for the press. They utilized the original languages in the best texts available, but also took advantage of previous translations. Indeed, the end product was essentially a revision of the earlier versions. Work was begun about 1607 and the Bible was published in 1611. Although it was called the "Authorized Version," no record exists to prove that it was ever submitted to the Privy Council or that it had the formal approval of the king. It did not bear the stamp of the genius of any one man as distinctively as did the German translation by Luther. It was, rather, the product of many hands and minds. Although other versions appeared, especially late in the nineteenth and in the twentieth century, it remained standard in the English-speaking world.

During the reign of James I Puritans were increasingly active. In many parishes they were establishing "lectureships" for Sunday afternoon preaching of a kind which favoured their convictions. They stressed the observance of Sunday and made much use of the metrical versions of the Psalms and of the music to which they were set. They emphasized Bible reading, had services in their homes, and, in the midst of an age of loose living and looser speech, endeavoured to be uncorrupted in morals by the world about them. They repeatedly clashed with James, partly on political issues, for they were a growing force in Parliament, partly over the royal encouragement of sports on Sundays, such as dancing, May games, athletics, and May poles, on which the king had made a formal declaration in 1618, and partly over forms of worship. James sought (1622) to restrict preachers to topics which seemed to him non-controversial and forbade them to deal with predestination or matters of state or to rail at "either Papists or Puritans," an obvious attempt to curb both Puritans and their opponents.

Separatists and Independents continued and grew, although still small minorities. Persecuted, some sought refuge on the Continent, especially in Protestant Holland, but many remained in England. They displayed a great variety of views. That was true even of those who were later called Congregationalists. There were the Seekers, who held that Antichrist had ruled so long that no true churches or valid office-holders existed and could not until God sent apostles to establish and ordain new ones. Baptists now appeared and spread. They differed from the Congregationalists chiefly in their repudiation of infant baptism and their insistence that the rite be given only to believers. The first English Baptist church arose in Amsterdam from among the Separatists and centred about John Smyth (died 1612, of tuberculosis, before he was forty-five), a graduate of Cambridge. It held what are usually termed Arminian views and was the spiritual ancestor of the General Baptists of Britain. Some of Smyth's followers united with the Mennonites. Thomas Helwys, one of Smyth's intimates who later broke with him but remained "Arminian," founded (1612) what seems to have been the first Baptist church on English soil, outside the walls of London, and took pains to disassociate himself from the Mennonites. A few years later, in the next reign, what were known as Particular Baptists arose, so designated because they held to a restricted or particular atonement which was only for the elect. They began as a secession from the (Congregational) Separatists. The two strains of Baptist churches, General and Particular, Arminian and Calvinist, continued apart until late in the nineteenth century.

Warm religious life was not confined to Puritans and Independents. It was also present among those in the Church of England who held to the Catholic tradition. Such a one was Lancelot Andrewes (1555–1626), a graduate of Cambridge, successively Bishop of Chichester, Ely, and Winchester, a trusted counsellor under Elizabeth, James I, and Charles I, and one of those who prepared the King James Version of the Bible. Scholarly, a noted and erudite preacher, presenting reasoned arguments against Roman Catholic views but not a Puritan, he may be longest remembered for his *Devotions,* composed in Greek for his private use, but published after his death.

CHARLES I AND THE PURITAN REVOLUTION

James I was succeeded in 1625 by his son, Charles I. Although he was handsome, dignified, athletic, pure in his private life in the midst of a corrupt court, courageous, a lover of beauty, and deeply religious, Charles increasingly alienated a large proportion of his subjects, both in England and Scotland. He held sincerely to the conviction that as king he ruled by divine right and that while seeking their welfare he must not in any way be controlled by his subjects. Nor did he believe that he need keep his promises, even when solemnly given, if they curbed his prerogatives. Increasing tension developed which culminated in civil war and the defeat and execution of Charles (1649). On the one side were the king, most of the nobility, and those who held to the established order and Catholic tradition in the Church of England. On the other side were Parliament, the growing urban middle classes, many of the lesser country gentry, the great body of Puritans, and the extreme Protestants, including the Independents and Separatists. Charles attempted to see as little of Parliament as possible, for each time that it met it was critical. Yet he was compelled to call it to obtain financial grants. From 1629 to 1640 he managed to rule without it. However, his attempt to force episcopacy and the English Book of Common Prayer upon Scotland led, as we have seen (Chapter XXXIII), to an uprising in that country which brought added expense and forced him to summon Parliament to seek more taxes. First came a short and stormy session in the spring of 1640 and then what was called the Long Parliament which assembled in November, 1640, and with which Charles was eventually in open war.

Into the intricacies of the prolonged and complicated struggle we must not go. In it religion was only one factor. However, religion was prominent. Both the king and many of his opponents professed, quite honestly, to be acting from what they deemed Christian motives. The triumph of the king's enemies brought with it the rule of the Puritans and the extreme Protestants. While reaction eventually swept them out of power, these children of Protestantism left an indelible mark upon the political and religious life and structure of England.

In the earlier years of the reign, before the Puritans gained control, the Catholic element was in the ascendant in the Church of England. Charles was a loyal Anglican. To him as to his father the royal power was associated with the episcopacy and he appreciated the form and pageantry of elaborate church services. His queen, Henrietta Maria, daughter of Henry IV of France, was a Roman Catholic, but in spite of accusations to the contrary, he had no intention of carrying the Church of England back to Rome. Yet he favoured those who stood staunchly for episcopacy and against the Puritans.

In his ecclesiastical policies, Charles found an able ally in William Laud (1573–1645). A graduate of Oxford, as chancellor of the university Laud did much to improve its intellectual and moral discipline, enriched it with benefactions, and made it a stronghold of Anglican, anti-Puritan orthodoxy. Succes-

sively Bishop of St. David's, Bath and Wells, and the strongly Puritan London
(1628–1633), and then Archbishop of Canterbury (1633–1645), he was a firm
supporter of what later was known as the Anglo-Catholic tradition. He believed that the Roman Catholic Church was a true church and not as apostate
as Puritans viewed it. However, he held that the Church of England, much
more than Rome, preserved the Catholic faith and tradition in its purity. He
transformed communion tables into altars, moving them back to the east end
of the churches. He opposed Calvinistic theology and stood for "Arminianism."
Wherever possible he suppressed Puritan lectureships. He discouraged the
Puritan observance of Sunday and moved Charles to renew the encouragement
to Sunday sports and amusements that had been given by James. A prodigiously
hard worker, courageous, conscientious, he laboured to root out evils in the
Church, fought corruption and irreverence, restored church fabrics, cleared
tradesmen and lawyers out of St. Paul's in London, and sought to enforce
uniformity against the Roman Catholics on the one hand and the Puritans on
the other. While he had none of his opponents burned, he sponsored harsh
penalties. He was very unpopular with the Puritans and became to them a
kind of symbol of all that they hated in the ecclesiastical policies of Charles.
The Long Parliament impeached him for high treason and imprisoned him in
the Tower of London (March, 1641). After a delay he was tried, but was not
found guilty. Thereupon a bill of attainder was passed and under it he was
decapitated (January 10, 1645).

The Long Parliament took advantage of its power to work revolutionary
changes in the Church of England. For months it intermittently debated
various proposals which were urged on it. There was general conviction that
the Catholic features introduced by Laud must go, such as making the communion tables into altars, the use of images and candles, and communion rails.
On other points sharp differences of opinion developed. It was necessary to
have the help of the Scots in the struggle with the king. Parliament accordingly
agreed (1643) to accept the Solemn League and Covenant. In February, 1644,
it was imposed upon all Englishmen over eighteen years of age. It stood for the
preservation of the Reformed religion in the Church of Scotland, sought to
make uniform with it religion in England and Ireland, and agreed to extirpate
"popery" and "prelacy," meaning by the latter church government by archbishops, bishops, archdeacons, deans, and chapters. In accordance with this
undertaking Parliament abolished the use of the Book of Common Prayer,
substituted for it a directory for worship framed by the Westminster Assembly
and without set forms of prayer, and ordered (June, 1646) the establishment
of the Presbyterian form of church government. This last was never fully
enforced.

The Westminster Assembly, called to advise Parliament on religious questions and composed of clergy and laity, mostly Puritans with a sprinkling of Episcopalians and Independents, and with Scottish commissioners without vote, convened in July, 1643. In addition to the *Directory for the Public Worship of God* it drew up what is usually called the Westminster Confession of Faith. This required several months and was completed in November, 1646. It was methodically considered and debated in Parliament, was ordered printed, but was never formally authorized by that body. To it the Westminster Assembly added a longer and a shorter catechism, the former for exposition in the pulpit and the latter for the instruction of children. All three had extensive use in Presbyterian churches both in Great Britain and America. They were formally adopted by the Church of Scotland. Setting forth the Reformed system of theology and church government, they were shaped much less by Calvin than by the Augustinian and federalist or covenant theology. They were influenced by earlier similar statements framed on the Continent but especially by the Irish Articles of 1615 which are usually supposed to have been the work of Archbishop James Usher (1581–1656), of the Church of Ireland, who is best remembered for compiling a long accepted Biblical chronology and who had refused to come to the Westminster Assembly.

THE PROTESTANT RADICALS IN THE SADDLE: CROMWELLIAN ENGLAND (1649–1660)

The civil war ended in the triumph of the Parliamentary armies. These were under the command of Oliver Cromwell. Quite without premeditation but through the inexorable course of events, by the defeat and execution of the king Cromwell found himself the ruler of the British Isles. The discrediting and death of Charles had created a political vacuum. Parliament and the army would not tolerate the continuation of the Stuart monarchy, Parliament was incompetent as an administrative body, and there were radicals who combined religious zeal with sweeping programmes for social and political reorganization and who, although minorities, wished to bring the country to their mind.

Chief among the extremists were the Levellers, the Diggers, the Fifth Monarchy Men, and the Quakers. The Levellers, with John Lilburne as their outstanding leader, were recruited in part from discontented London tradesmen. Lilburne had been won by the Baptists and was an ardent student of the Bible and of various works on law and political theory. Vain, quarrelsome, stubborn, he yet attracted followers. He held that there is a natural law to which all laws of man and the structure of state and society should conform, that it is written in the hearts and consciences of men, that sovereignty resides in the nation at large, that Parliaments should be elected by universal manhood suffrage, that they should have only limited administrative and police powers, and that no one should sit in two successive Parliaments. The Diggers protested against private ownership of land. The Fifth Monarchy Men maintained that according to Biblical prophecy Christ was soon to return to establish on earth the "Fifth Monarchy" in succession to the Assyrian, Persian, Greek, and Roman empires, and that he would reign, with his saints, for a thousand years. They differed greatly among themselves. Some wished to use force to establish the Fifth Monarchy, while others would await quietly the coming of Christ.

The Quakers, to use the nickname given them, or Society of Friends, to give them the title which they preferred, were to have a much longer existence than these others and were to play a more prominent role. Their founder was George Fox (1624–1691). Of humble birth, from boyhood he had heard Puritan preaching and had acquired an intimate familiarity with the text of the English Bible. At the age of nineteen, shocked by the contrast between the profession and practice of nominal Christians, he left home and entered upon a religious quest which led him to consult clergymen of the Church of England and of the dissenting groups. For four years he suffered severe spiritual depression induced by the spectacle of human suffering, especially in the civil war which was then raging, and by the doctrine of predestination which he heard expounded from Puritan pulpits. By temperament a mystic, he was eager for direct and unhindered access to God. None of the many priests and preachers from whom he sought help brought him relief and he came to have an impatient disdain for them. Eventually (1647) the light broke. He came to feel that Christ could speak to "his condition," his heart leaped for joy, and to him "the whole earth had a new smell." He believed that God is love and truth and that it is possible for all men so to open their lives to Him as to live victoriously in that power "that is a-top" of all evil and "that is over all." He would follow and have others follow the Inner Light. He renounced oaths, insisted on honesty and truth-speaking, practised simplicity in dress, food, and speech, opposed any participation in war, protested against all shams and formalism in religion and worship, pioneered in the care of the insane, demanded just treatment for the American Indians, held that governments exist for the benefit of the people as a whole and are bound by the moral law, advocated an extreme democracy which would put men and women on an equality, permitted women to preach, refused to doff his hat to any man, used the singular pronoun in addressing members of all classes, thus seeking to denounce special class privilege, came out for universal religious toleration, and wished to bring the Gospel to all. Completely fearless, he was often imprisoned for proclaiming his convictions.

Fox's appeal found a response in many hearts, for he was proclaiming what in one way or another many believed. He travelled widely in England, Ireland, Wales, the Continent, and America. Large numbers of the Seekers became his followers. Societies of Friends sprang up and hundreds of missionaries became "publishers of Truth." The Quakers provoked much opposition and met persecution, but during the remainder of the century their numbers multiplied.

Faced with these many radical movements, Cromwell strove to prevent chaos, to maintain order, and to help to make of England a genuinely Christian nation. He had not sought to rule the country, but as head of the Parliamentary army he found himself forced step by step to the headship of the government and to what in effect was a dictatorship. Yet he refused the suggestion that he become king and took instead the title of Lord Protector. The government was called the Commonwealth and was a kind of republic.

Himself deeply religious, inclined towards the Independents, and wishing to act always according to the will of God, in the midst of the strife of tongues Cromwell desired and in part obtained a large degree of religious toleration. He stood for a national church, endowed and supported by the state. It was not to have bishops and the Book of Common Prayer was not to be used in its services. Yet the Word must be preached and to this end the clergy must be carefully chosen and must be supported by tithes and by a central fund to supplement the income of the poorer parishes. All Protestants except Quakers were to be tolerated. The clergy might be Presbyterian, Independent, or Baptist, dissenters might form "gathered churches" of their own, Episcopalians might meet for worship if they did so quietly, and even Roman Catholics were left alone if they did not disturb the public peace. Episcopalians, Roman Catholics, Levellers, Fifth Monarchy Men, and Quakers were unfriendly or even hostile to him, but Cromwell gave to England a nearer approach to religious liberty than it had thus far known. He also laboured for the reform of morals, sunk to a low ebb during the civil wars, and worked for the improvement of education.

THE RESTORATION OF THE STUART MONARCHY AND THE REVIVAL OF EPISCOPACY

The Commonwealth could not last. It was rule by a minority and when once death had removed the strong hand of the Lord Protector it speedily came to an end. Oliver Cromwell died in 1658 and was succeeded by his son Richard. Although of pure life and popular as a man, Richard did not have the force of character, the experience, or the control of the army which were needed in the emergency. George Monck, the strongest of the generals, marched to London, and the son of the executed Charles I returned from exile as Charles II (1660).

Witty, charming, utterly unscrupulous, completely selfish, immoral in his private life, committed to the divine right of kings, Charles II did not wish to go again on his travels and was sufficiently clever to maintain himself on the throne. Parliament was restored much as it had been before the civil war, but was far from being inclined to servile compliance with the royal wishes. Privately preferring Roman Catholicism as the "religion for gentlemen," Charles hated the Presbyterians and extreme Protestants but outwardly conformed to the Church of England of which he was nominally the head.

Episcopacy was restored and through bishops dispossessed under the Commonwealth was enabled to continue the apostolic succession. The Book of Common Prayer, revised in a manner peculiarly distasteful to Puritans, was accepted by Parliament and through an Act of Uniformity was ordered read in all the churches. Non-episcopally ordained clergy were removed from their benefices. By the Conventicle Act, 1664, passed over the opposition of the king, meetings for worship of more than five persons were forbidden unless they used the Prayer Book. The Five Mile Act, enacted in 1665, ordered that no non-conforming minister come within five miles of a city or incorporated town or teach in any school unless he promised that he would not "at any time endeavour the alteration of government in Church and state." Since Puritans and other dissenting Protestants were strongest in the towns, the Five Mile Act bore especially heavily upon them. A second Conventicle Act was passed in 1670. When, in 1672, Charles II, with the purpose of aiding Roman Catholics and winning the goodwill of Protestant dissenters, issued the Declaration of Indulgence permitting public worship to both, Parliament forced its withdrawal (1673) and passed the Test Act which provided that all civil or military officers must take the oath of supremacy and allegiance and receive the Lord's Supper according to the usages of the Church of England.

In spite of these stringent measures and the laxity of morals of much of the population, dissenting congregations persisted and men and women of outstanding Christian character appeared in both the Church of England and non-conforming Protestantism. In the state church Jeremy Taylor (1613–1667), after the Restoration a bishop in Ireland, wrote extensively, but is best remembered for *The Rule and Exercises of Holy Living* (1650) and *The Rule and Exercises of Holy Dying* (1651), both composed during the Commonwealth. The Puritan Richard Baxter (1615–1691) had a noted record as a pastor during the Commonwealth in reforming morals and religion within his parish, refused a bishopric under the Restoration, was forbidden to preach, and was fined and imprisoned. He was a voluminous author, but it is significant that with him, as with Taylor, his best remembered work was one on Christian life and prayer, *Saints' Everlasting Rest*. Even more famous was John Bunyan

(1628–1688), Baptist preacher of Bedford. He had come into a warm Christian faith after a prolonged struggle and deep depression of which he later told in a moving spiritual autobiography, *Grace Abounding to the Chief of Sinners.* Imprisoned for years for preaching in violation of the Conventicle Act, while in jail he began to write *The Pilgrim's Progress,* an allegory of conversion and the Christian life which was to become one of the most widely read books in the English language and was to be translated into many other tongues. We do well also to remember that the Puritan, John Milton, closely identified with the Commonwealth and Latin secretary to Oliver Cromwell, escaped the scaffold at the Restoration and completed *Paradise Lost,* presenting the human drama as conceived by Christians.

It was during the Commonwealth and especially during the Stuart Restoration that there flourished the Cambridge Platonists, so-called because most of them were Cambridge graduates. They were against the views represented by Laud on the one hand, some of the extreme Protestant sects on the other, and extreme scepticism on still another front, and sought to reconcile science and religion. Chief among them was Ralph Cudworth (1617–1688), fellow of Emmanuel College and master of Christ's College, Cambridge. They stressed Plotinus rather than Plato and thought of love as the chief manifestation of God in human life.

These men were mountain peaks. There were many of lesser stature and fame who were evidence of the richness of the life which issued from the Reformation.

Charles II died in 1685, in his last hours was received into the Roman Catholic Church, and was succeeded by his brother, James II, an avowed member of that communion. James II favoured those of his faith and by a Declaration of Indulgence sought toleration for both Roman Catholics and those Protestants who dissented from the Church of England. It was widespread resentment against this policy, culminating in the popular support of seven bishops who were tried for refusing to read the Declaration from the pulpit and alarm at the birth of a son which seemed to mean a Roman Catholic successor that led to the "Glorious Revolution" of 1688. James was driven from the country and his Protestant daughter, Mary, and her consort, William of Orange, came to the throne.

THE HALF CENTURY AFTER THE "GLORIOUS REVOLUTION" OF 1688

The flight of James II and the coming of William and Mary were followed by the final victory of Protestantism and the permanence of many of the fruits of the Puritan revolution. The Bill of Rights, enacted in 1689, declared illegal many of the measures of James II and stipulated that no Roman Catholic should ever wear the crown. That same year, thanks largely to William who, although reared a Calvinist, was broad in his sympathies, the Toleration Act was passed. It suspended the laws against Protestant dissenters who did not attend services in the Church of England on condition that they took the oath of allegiance and supremacy and subscribed to a statement against transubstantiation. Roman Catholics and those who did not believe in the Trinity were excluded from the benefits of the measure. Dissenters were still under some disabilities and were taxed to support the Church of England. Yet such persecution as had been known under Laud and Charles II was a thing of the past. Two political parties developed, the Tories, reinforced by squires and country parsons and opposed to toleration of dissenters, and the Whigs, composed largely of the town clergy, most of the bishops, dissenters, merchants, and the Protestant elements in the Church of England. Under a Tory ministry, in 1711, it was made more difficult for dissenters to evade the Test Act, and in 1714 the Schism Act was passed which provided that no one could teach in a school unless he was a communicant of the Church of England. This latter would have made it impossible for dissenters to educate their children. However, four years later the Schism Act was repealed. Nonconformity and the Church of England went on side by side and in the latter there were still those who held to the Catholic tradition and those who leaned towards Protestantism. Henceforth no monarch dared seriously to challenge the supremacy of the voice of the nation expressed through Parliament or to attempt to rule without that body.

John Locke (1632–1704), reared in a staunchly Puritan home, would probably have gone into the ministry but for the intolerant attitude in the Church of England after the Restoration and continued to be interested in theology. Famous for his *Essay Concerning Human Understanding* (1690), in which he pointed out the limits to human knowledge, and condemned by some of the strictly orthodox for not subscribing to all that they deemed basic in the Christian faith, he would exclude atheists and Roman Catholics from the religious toleration which he advocated. His *Treatises on Government* reflected the political principles of popular sovereignty which had arisen largely through the Puritans and had found expression in the Puritan revolution and the Commonwealth, and were to go far toward shaping the democracy of the later England and the United States.

The Reformation had by no means completely purified the religious life of the country or the Church. Many of the clergy had little intellectual or spiritual interest and carried on the services of the Church in routine fashion. Some were viewed contemptuously by the upper classes and some were younger sons of the aristocracy for whom the Church was a way to a secure and easy living.

There was still pluralism and numbers of the higher ecclesiastics drew the revenues from more than one post. As we are to see, the rationalism which found expression in the Deism and religious scepticism that came to a climax in those years had begun to appear and to be formulated late in the seventeenth and in the fore part of the eighteenth century.

However, while the intense religious ferment which had marked the sixteenth century and which had boiled over in the seventeenth century seemed to have subsided, there was much of vigorous life, both within the Church of England and among the Protestant dissenters. As we are to see again later, George Berkeley (1685–1753), Bishop of Cloyne, formulated a philosophical defense of Christianity, criticizing the "natural religion" of the opponents of revealed religion and holding that the whole of the natural order is a conversation between God and man. Joseph Butler (1692–1752), whom we are to meet again, in his *Analogy of Religion, Natural and Revealed, to the Course and Constitution of Nature,* produced another apology for the Christian faith which was to be widely read in the eighteenth and nineteenth centuries. William Law (1686–1761), a mystic, profoundly influenced by Jacob Boehme, with high church convictions, in addition to controversial works, wrote much on the devotional life and, among others, produced two books, *A Treatise on Christian Perfection* (1726) and *A Serious Call to a Holy and Devout Life* (1728), which were to make important contributions to the Evangelical Revival which began in the second quarter of the eighteenth century and of which we are to hear much after 1750.

The earnest and buoyant religious life of the time was finding expression in hymns, especially among the Protestant dissenters. Notable were Isaac Watts (1674–1748) and Philip Doddridge (1702–1751), both nonconformists. Watts gave many hymns to the Church, among them "Oh God our help in ages past," "Joy to the world, the Lord has come," "When I survey the wondrous cross on which the prince of glory died," and "Jesus shall reign where'er the sun doth his successive journeys run." In addition to hymns which had prolonged and wide usage, such as "O God of Bethel by whose hand thy people still are led," "Awake my soul, stretch every nerve and press with vigour on," and "How gentle God's commands," Doddridge also wrote the extensively read devotional work *The Rise and Progress of Religion in the Soul.* It was late in this period, in 1738, that John Wesley had the stirring experience which is generally regarded as the beginning of the Evangelical Revival. In the 1720's and 1730's, moreover, there began the Great Awakening in the English colonies in America which was the precursor of the mass movements which revitalized the Protestant churches and brought into them an increasing proportion of the partially de-Christianized population. In the first half of the eighteenth century

England presented a striking contrast between much practical paganism and religious illiteracy on the one hand, with low moral conditions, and on the other a vital religious life which was to have world-wide repercussions in the nineteenth and twentieth centuries.

THE WELSH VARIETY OF THE REFORMATION

Of the mountainous principality of Wales we can take time in this comprehensive survey for only three short paragraphs.

Under Henry VIII a formal act of union (1536) and a further act of 1542 incorporated Wales with England and sought to bring its people into administrative and political equality with the English. Welsh members sat in the Parliament at Westminster and English was made the language of all legal proceedings. Welshmen were to be found at court and in the universities. Among them were some who laboured for the reform of the Church and religion. Separation from Rome and the dissolution of the monasteries came by the same steps which accomplished them in England. This was followed by a decline in the quality and numbers of clergy and deterioration in the Church buildings. Richard Davies, Bishop of St. Davids, and a colleague put into Welsh the New Testament and the liturgy from the Book of Common Prayer. In 1588 the complete Bible in Welsh was published, the work of William Morgan, vicar and eventually bishop. Later this was supplanted by a Welsh translation of the King James Version done by a Welsh bishop. These translations did much to fix the form of literary Welsh. Late in the sixteenth and in the fore part of the seventeenth century marked improvement took place in the religious life of Wales. Many of the clergy were educated in Oxford and Cambridge, notably in Jesus College, Oxford, founded for the Welsh.

Puritanism was slow in penetrating Wales, but began to do so before the coming of the Commonwealth. By then, moreover, at least one Independent congregation had been formed. Wales was loyal to Charles I. After his execution, Parliament ejected most of the clergy of the established church and sought to replace them by preachers acceptable to the new regime, and that in spite of the protest by high churchmen and moderate Puritans. This brought new confusion. After the Stuart Restoration most of such of the old clergy as survived were reinstated and Puritan incumbents who refused to comply with the Act of Uniformity were dismissed. Thereafter the bishops were largely of the Catholic wing of the established church and sympathized with the Stuarts. The state church ceased to attract the masses and the latter knew little or no English and had few books in their own tongue. There was much pluralism, most of the clergy were of poor quality, and many parsonages were falling into ruin.

In the first half of the eighteenth century Griffith Jones, a clergyman, began what were known as "circulating charity schools" which taught thousands to read the Bible in their own tongue and raised the level of the religious life and education. The Society for Promoting Christian Knowledge, founded in 1699 by members of the Church of England, although having Wales as only one of its fields of effort, aided in the improvement of religious conditions. The way was being prepared for the great revivals of the latter part of the eighteenth and the nineteenth century.

THE LONG AGONY OF IRELAND

Much more complex was the course of the Reformation in Ireland. Centuries before, that island, it will be recalled, had been the centre of a vigorous religious life when, relatively free from the incursions of the barbarians who were dealing serious blows to civilization and Christianity on the Continent and Britain, it was the scene of a distinctive monasticism which enriched both Britain and much of Western Europe.

Then came wave after wave of invasion and settlement, first by pagan Scandinavians and later by the Anglo-Normans. In the twelfth and thirteenth centuries the latter conquered most of the island and sought to bring it into conformity with English law and institutions. The Church, moreover, was drawn into a closer relationship with that of England and with Rome. Yet the Gaelic Irish were restless. In the fourteenth century they threw off the English yoke in much of the island and the conquerors were partly assimilated in language, law, and blood. In the fifteenth century the Gaelic Irish and the descendants of the older English settlers were almost independent of England.

The first Tudors, Henry VII and Henry VIII, attempted, with partial success, to revive the authority of the English crown in Ireland. In accordance with the procedure in England, Henry VIII was declared the head of the Church of Ireland and the dissolution of the monasteries was ordered. However, there was little or no indigenous movement for reform, the bishops were slow to accept the royal supremacy, and many monasteries persisted into the seventeenth century. Great resentment was felt against the attempted imposition of Protestantism under Edward VI. Although Elizabeth insisted upon the Acts of Supremacy and Uniformity, the established church which was loyal to her had few adherents outside of Dublin, the capital. Both the Gaelic population and the older English stock held to the Roman Catholic faith, partly from conservatism and partly in opposition to rule from England. While only a minority could be called practicing Catholics, so far as the majority had a religious allegiance it was to Rome. The Roman Catholic Church was becoming a symbol and a bond of Irish nationalism. Especially was that true of the Gaelic stock. During Elizabeth's time rebellions broke out, provoked partly by the grant of Irish lands to English adventurers.

During the reign of James I an extensive English and Scottish colonization of Ulster in the north of the island was begun, largely at the instance of the royal government. The immigrants were Protestant—Anglicans and Presbyterians. The Scottish Presbyterians were especially strong. Similar Protestant colonies were planted in some other sections. Rebellion broke out in 1641 and in Ulster thousands of the colonists were killed. The uprising was soon complicated by the civil war in England.

The Irish had no use for the Puritans and after the execution of Charles I the supporters of his son, Charles II, controlled most of the island. To meet the crisis, Parliament sent Cromwell as commander-in-chief of its armies. Within a few months he had subdued the east of the island, partly through the terror which he inspired by the slaughter of the garrison after his capture of Drogheda. By the end of 1652 the rest of the island had been overrun, but with a fearful toll of life. Fighting, famine, and pestilence are said to have reduced the population by a third. The Roman Catholic religion was ordered suppressed and extensive land grants were made to members of the conquering army and to those who had supported the Commonwealth forces by contributions of money. In theory the dispossessed Irish proprietors were given compensation in the form of lands in the western part of the island, but these were of poorer quality. As in England, the state church was in the hands of the extreme Protestants.

The Stuart restoration (1660) brought only partial relief to the Roman Catholics. Charles II was not disposed to jeopardize his rule by throwing the Protestants overboard. While about a third of the lands which had been given to the Cromwellians were returned to the Roman Catholics, the government was almost entirely in the hands of Protestants, and of Episcopalians rather than Presbyterians. The Presbyterians were at a decided disadvantage. During his brief reign James II favoured his co-religionists and after his flight from England (1688) he sought (1689) to regain the throne by way of Ireland. During the fifteen or sixteen months that he was in the island he set up a predominantly Roman Catholic government. In the ensuing war James and his forces were defeated by the "Orange men," the supporters of William of Orange.

While William stood for moderation, the Protestants in Ireland would have none of it. By the extension of the Test Act of 1691 to Ireland, Roman Catholics were excluded from the Irish Parliament. Roman Catholics were debarred from the legal profession, were kept out of the trades and from juries, could not vote, and were forbidden to teach publicly or to bear arms. Only a small proportion of the land was owned by them. The overwhelming majority of the Roman Catholics were tenants of Protestant landlords. Drastic penal laws made the lot of the Roman Catholics even harder and Roman Catholic prelates were banished. The outstanding leaders of the Irish either perished or fled the country. The Church of Ireland, sister to the Church of England and established by law, was in the ascendant and in close association with the state. Presbyterians as well as Roman Catholics were discriminated against. Laws restraining the commerce of the island added to the distress. Many of the poorer Presbyterians, the "Scotch-Irish," sought relief by migration to the American colonies, thereby laying the foundations of much of the Presbyterianism of the future United States.

While after the coming of the Hanoverian dynasty to England (1714) freedom of worship was granted Roman Catholics and the right to hold minor offices, and some relief was given the Presbyterians, tithes continued to be exacted for the support of the Church of Ireland, the English and Anglican minority were in control, and the poverty and distress of the masses were acute. The majority of the population were Roman Catholics and even more than before their church was for them the tie and symbol of Gaelic Ireland. The fear of Irish revolt hardened the attitude of the English. A legacy of bitterness augmented by religious differences was transmitted to later generations.

SELECTED BIBLIOGRAPHY

GENERAL

L. Elliott Binns, *The Reformation in England* (London, Duckworth, pp. 224). A useful introduction carrying the story through the Elizabethan settlement.

J. Gairdner, *The English Church in the Sixteenth Century from the Accession of Henry VIII to the Death of Mary* (London, Macmillan & Co., 1902, pp. vii, 430). A standard work.

H. Gee and W. J. Hardy, *Documents Illustrative of English Church History compiled from Original Sources* (London, Macmillan & Co., 1896, pp. xii, 670). Very useful.

P. Hughes, *The Reformation in England* (London, Hollis & Carter, Vol. I, 1952, pp. xxi, 404). Very well written. Based on careful research.

PREPARATION FOR THE REFORMATION

J. Gairdner, *Lollardy and the Reformation in England. An Historical Survey* (London, Macmillan & Co., 3 vols., 1908–1911). Chiefly an account of the English Reformation through the reign of Edward VI, stressing the indigenous character of the movement. Based upon careful research.

H. M. Smith, *Pre-Reformation England* (London, Macmillan & Co., 1938, pp. xv, 556). Begins with the accession of Henry VII. Very well done, with extensive excerpts from the sources.

THE REIGN OF HENRY VIII

G. Baskerville, *English Monks and the Suppression of the Monasteries* (Yale University Press, 1937, pp. 312). Based upon extensive research.

G. Constant, *The Reformation in England. I. The English Schism: Henry VIII (1509–1547)*, translated by R. E. Scantlebury (New York, Sheed & Ward, 1934, pp. xxi, 531). An able, fairly objective Roman Catholic work.

The King's Book or a Necessary Doctrine and Erudition for any Christian Man, 1543, with an introduction by T. A. Lacey (London, Society for Promoting Christian Knowledge, 1932, pp. xx, 165).

H. E. Jacobs, *The Lutheran Movement in England during the Reigns of Henry VIII and Edward VI, and Its Literary Monuments* (Philadelphia, General Council Publication House, rev. ed., 1916, pp. xv, 376). Carefully done, by a Lutheran.

H. M. Smith, *Henry VIII and the Reformation* (London, Macmillan & Co., 1948, pp. xv, 480). Very well done.

THOMAS CRANMER

A. F. Pollard, *Thomas Cranmer and the English Reformation 1489–1556* (London, G. P. Putnam's Sons, 1905, pp. xv, 384). A standard account, favourable to Cranmer.

WILLIAM TYNDALE

S. L. Greenslade, *The Work of William Tindale* (London, Blackie & Son, 1938, pp. vi, 222). Important chiefly for selections from Tyndale's works.

J. P. Mozley, *William Tyndale* (New York, The Macmillan Co., 1937, pp. ix, 364). Contains extensive excerpts from Tyndale's writings.

EDWARD VI

G. Constant, *The Reformation in England. II. Introduction of the Reformation into England: Edward VI (1547–1553)*, translated by E. I. Watkin (New York, Sheed & Ward, 1942, pp. ix, 370). Based on extensive research, fairly objective, by a Roman Catholic.

C. H. Smyth, *Cranmer & the Reformation under Edward VI* (Cambridge University Press, 1926, pp. x, 315).

MARY

R. Demaus, *Hugh Latimer, a Biography* (London, Dalls, Lamar & Barton, no date. First published in 1869 by the Religious Tract Society, pp. 568).

C. H. Hallowell, *The Marian Exiles. A Study in the Origins of Elizabethan Puritanism* (Cambridge University Press, 1938, pp. ix, 388). Especially valuable for brief biographies of nearly five hundred exiles.

J. F. Mozley, *John Foxe and His Book* (London, Society for Promoting Christian Knowledge, 1940, pp. xi, 254). An account of Foxe's life and of his famous *Book of Martyrs*. That book went through many editions, supplemented by many hands. It is warmly sympathetic with the martyrs. In its original form it is chiefly valuable for its accounts of those who were killed under Mary.

J. A. Muller, *Stephen Gardiner and the Tudor Reaction* (New York, The Macmillan Co., 1926, pp. xiv, 429). Carefully and sympathetically done.

W. Schenk, *Reginald Pole, Cardinal of England* (New York, Longmans, Green & Co., 1950, pp. xvi, 176). Sympathetic, judicious, based upon careful research.

ELIZABETH

H. W. Clark, *History of English Nonconformity from Wyclif to the Close of the Nineteenth Century. Vol. I, From Wyclif to the Restoration* (London, Chapman & Hall, 1911, pp. xvii, 439). Well documented.

W. H. Frere and C. E. Douglas, editors, *Puritan Manifestoes, a Study in the Origin of the Puritan Revolt. With a Reprint of the Admonition to Parliament and Kindred Documents, 1572* (London, Society for Promoting Christian Knowledge, 1907, pp. xxxi, 155).

M. M. Knappen, *Tudor Puritanism. A Chapter in the History of Idealism* (University of Chicago Press, 1939, pp. xii, 555). Admirably done.

D. J. McGinn, *The Admonition Controversy* (Rutgers University Press, 1949, pp. xii, 589). Contains extensive excerpts from the sources.

W. Pierce, *An Historical Introduction to the Marprelate Tracts* (London, Constable & Co., 1908, pp. xvii, 350).

J. H. Pollen, *The English Catholics in the Reign of Queen Elizabeth: A Study of Their Politics Civil Life and Government* (London, Longmans, Green & Co., 1920). Sympathetic, based upon careful research, by a Jesuit.

JAMES I AND CHARLES I

C. Burrage, *The Early English Dissenters in the Light of Recent Research (1550–1641)* (Cambridge University Press, 2 vols., 1912). More than half is made up of original documents.

C. C. Butterworth, *The Literary Lineage of the King James Bible 1340–1611* (University of Pennsylvania Press, 1941, pp. xi, 394). Carefully done.

H. R. Trevor-Roper, *Archbishop Laud 1573–1645* (London, Macmillan & Co., 1940, pp. ix, 464). Soberly written, based solidly on careful research.

A. C. Underwood, *A History of the English Baptists* (London, The Baptist Union Publication Dept., 1947, pp. 286). Sympathetic, but objective.

B. F. Westcott, *A General View of the History of the English Bible*. Third edition, revised by W. A. Wright (New York, The Macmillan Co., 1927, pp. xx, 356). By a distinguished scholar.

THE COMMONWEALTH

W. C. Braithwaite, *The Beginnings of Quakerism* (London, Macmillan & Co., 1923, pp. xliv, 542). Based upon extensive research.

J. Buchan, *Oliver Cromwell* (Boston, Houghton Mifflin Co., 1934, pp. xi, 458). A standard life, very well written.

W. Haller and G. Davies, editors, *The Leveller Tracts 1647–1653* (Columbia University Press, 1944, pp. vi, 481).

H. Davies, *The Worship of the English Puritans* (Westminster, Dacre Press, 1948, pp. xi, 304). Represents careful work in the sources.

E. Russell, *The History of Quakerism* (New York, The Macmillan Co., 1942, pp. xxv, 586). A standard work, by a Quaker.

W. A. Shaw, *A History of the English Church during the Civil Wars and under the Commonwealth 1640–1660* (London, Longmans, Green & Co., 2 vols., 1900). Contains extensive excerpts from the sources.

FROM THE RESTORATION TO 1750

H. W. Clark, *History of English Nonconformity. Vol. II, From the Restoration to the Close of the Nineteenth Century* (London, Chapman & Hall, 1913, pp. xx, 458).

S. Hobhouse, *Selected Mystical Writings of William Law, Edited with Notes and Twenty-four Studies in the Mystical Theology of William Law and Jacob Boehme* (London, C. W. Daniel Co., 1938, pp. xv, 395). By a warm admirer.

N. Sykes, *Church and State in England in the XVIIIth Century* (Cambridge University Press, 1934, pp. xi, 455). A thorough and highly competent description of some phases of the Church of England, especially the clergy, in the eighteenth century. Gives a more favourable view than is sometimes done.

C. E. Whiting, *Studies in English Puritanism from the Restoration to the Revolution 1660–1688* (London, Society for Promoting Christian Knowledge, 1931, pp. xvi, 584). Comprehensive, scholarly.

B. Willey, *The Seventeenth Century Background. Studies in the Thought of the Age in Relation to Poetry and Religion* (London, Chatto & Windus, 1934, pp. vii, 315). Covers a wide range.

B. Willey, *The Eighteenth Century Background. Studies on the Idea of Nature in the Thought of the Period* (London, Chatto & Windus, 1940, pp. viii, 302). A semi-popular survey of religious and philosophical thought in the British Isles in the eighteenth century, especially of rationalism.

T. Wright, *Isaac Watts and Contemporary Hymn-Writers* (London, C. J. Farncombe & Sons, 1914, pp. xii, 280). Popularly written, but with research back of it.

WALES

A. G. Edwards, *Landmarks in the History of the Welsh Church* (London, John Murray, 1912, pp. vi, 317). By a Bishop of St. Asaph, friendly to the established church.

W. Hughes, *A History of the Church of the Cymry from the Earliest Period to the Present Time* (London, Elliot Stock, 1916, pp. xv, 412). By a clergyman of the established church. Contains a large assemblage of information.

IRELAND

J. C. Beckett, *Protestant Dissent in Ireland 1687–1780* (London, Faber & Faber, 1948, pp. 161). Well documented.

R. D. Edwards, *Church and State in Tudor Ireland. A History of Penal Laws against Irish Catholics 1534–1603* (New York, Longmans, Green & Co., 1935, pp. xliii, 352). Based upon an extensive use of the sources.

W. A. Phillips, editor, *History of the Church of Ireland from the Earliest Times* (Oxford University Press, 3 vols., 1933). A standard work, by several authors, from the introduction of Christianity through the nineteenth century.

Chapter XXXVII

PROTESTANTISM: A PAUSE FOR PERSPECTIVE

Before we move on to describe the reform within the Roman Catholic Church and to trace the somewhat parallel but quite distinct course of events in the Russian Orthodox Church, we will do well to pause for a moment to look at the emergence of Protestantism as a whole. Here was a vast movement which issued in churches which were to continue. Unlike the groups of the Middle Ages in Western Europe which dissented from the Roman Catholic Church, they did not disappear. Indeed, not only did they persist, but they also grew, and in the nineteenth and twentieth centuries displayed a far greater proportionate and numerical geographic expansion than did the rapidly spreading Roman Catholic Church. From them, moreover, came a succession of quite novel organizational and functional expressions of the Christian faith. Although seemingly the most divided of all the forms of Christianity, in the nineteenth and twentieth centuries Protestants increasingly found new ways of coming together which eventually drew in not only the majority of their own ranks, but also many from the Roman Catholic and Orthodox Churches. In several ways the Protestant era was not the sixteenth and seventeenth but the nineteenth and twentieth centuries. In the middle of the twentieth century Protestantism was still expanding, giving rise to fresh movements, and finding ways of drawing Christians together across ecclesiastical barriers. It was proving to be extremely flexible without surrendering the basic beliefs about God and the purpose, nature, and meaning of His revelation in Christ which the majority of Christians had formulated in the first five centuries of Christian history.

At first sight Protestantism seemed a confused medley of sects which warred with one another and the Roman Catholic Church. Moreover, its sources were not purely religious. They included political, national, social, and personal factors. Peoples and monarchs shared, somewhat confusedly, a common desire to be freed from the administrative control of the Papacy and from the diversion of their revenues to the support of the Holy See and of those who, basking in its favour, as absentees battened off benefices to the exclusion of native sons. In some of the cities many from the growing middle class found Protestantism congenial. Extreme forms, such as Anabaptism, flourished among the proletariat.

Yet the core of Protestantism was a strong religious impulse expressing itself in convictions which were common and central in all the varied forms. Protestantism sprang up in many different places and countries, seemingly almost independently, and had numerous creative leaders. However, common to all its forms, but not always equally stressed, was what had been emphasized by Luther, salvation by faith. As a corollary, even when not acknowledged in practice, was a principle, also formulated by Luther, the priesthood of all believers. Since salvation by faith meant the faith of the individual, by implication Protestantism entailed the right and the duty of the individual to judge for himself on religious issues. This was vividly demonstrated in Luther's dramatic refusal at the Diet of Worms to regard Pope or general council as infallible. Yet, so Luther and other Protestants held, this did not mean ungoverned, rampant individualism. To them the Christian was bound by his allegiance to God. Protestants acknowledged authority, the authority of the word of God as recorded in the Scriptures. The Scriptures must be interpreted by reason, the reason of the individual. On that memorable occasion Luther had declared, and in this he was enunciating a basic characteristic of Protestantism, that he would not renounce any of his beliefs unless "convicted by Scripture and plain reason." He had said: "My conscience is captive to the Word of God. I cannot and I will not recant anything, for to go against conscience is neither right nor safe." In this, whether they knew or did not know of Luther and his words, Protestants of otherwise diverse views were to share. This was true of Cranmer, the ranking bishop in the Church of England, who, holding to much of the Catholic tradition, slowly worked his way to clarity of insight and in his last hours repudiated the authority of the crown which he had regarded as set over him by God and went to the stake. At the other extreme was George Fox, who rejected all sacraments and inherited ecclesiastical traditions and forms.

Their distinctive convictions, Protestants declared, were of the essence of the Gospel and therefore were not new. They insisted that theirs was the primitive and therefore the true Christianity and that it was not they, but the Roman Catholics who were innovators and heretics. They had much in common with some of the pre-Reformation movements which the Catholic Church had denounced. Hus, as we have seen, had been burned because he was convinced that to bow to Pope or council was to be disloyal to Christ, and the remnants of the Waldensees had found the Reformed Churches sufficiently congenial to associate themselves with them. Yet in its emphasis upon salvation by faith alone, *sola fide,* Protestantism was distinct from other movements which had been cast out of the Catholic Church.

Salvation by faith alone and the attendant insistence of the individual that his conscience must not be surrendered to the authority of state or Church seemed to violate the sense of community so prominent in the Scriptures which the Protestants professed to revere and appeared to lead to anarchy. It is true that here was a sharp contrast between Protestants and Catholics and especially between Protestants and Roman Catholics. In principle Catholics submitted their consciences to the authority of the Church. They were not yet agreed on where that authority was finally lodged, whether in general councils or the Bishop of Rome, but "holy obedience" to ecclesiastical superiors was demanded of monks and clergy and in questions spiritual and moral the laity were under the direction of the clergy. Were salvation by faith alone and the priesthood of all believers to be carried to what seemed their logical conclusion, endless division and eventual rejection of beliefs inherited from previous generations of Christians would seem to follow. This, indeed, Roman Catholics have declared to be inevitable. At times their prediction has appeared to be proved by the event. Organizationally Protestantism, especially among those who sought to carry out its principles in thoroughgoing fashion, became more and more divided. Minorities went over to a rationalistic Unitarianism and, moving still further, ceased to believe in God, at least in any such sense as most Christians had conceived Him.

However, the vast majority of Protestants retained a sense of community. Their individualism was not irresponsible but submitted itself to the divine sovereignty. Luther, Zwingli, and Calvin and those who followed them were profoundly impressed with the majesty of God. It was that which was to a large degree the sustaining element in their individualism. They held themselves to be accountable to God and believed that to submit their conscience to Pope or council was to put another authority above Him. They remembered that Christ had made love to one's neighbour a corollary to the primary command of love to God. Luther had expressed it in the seeming paradox: "A Christian man is the most free lord of all, and subject to none; a Christian man is the most dutiful servant of all, and subject to everyone." The fashion in which, in increasing measure, in the nineteenth and twentieth centuries Protestants devised fresh ways of giving organizational forms to a sense of community reaching out to all who called themselves Christians was evidence that they were not atomistic.

It was no accident, moreover, that out of Protestantism arose democratic movements in Church and state. Such extreme Protestant groups as the Independents and Baptists were in theory pure democracies, with each member of the local church on an equality with every other. Luther, conservative in many ways, had stopped short of pushing the priesthood of all believers to its extreme implications. However, Calvin and others in the Reformed Churches moved in that direction. Puritans, Independents, and others on the far edge of Protestantism reinforced the principle that there is a body of law which the king must obey, and used as an instrument Parliament, inherited from the pre-Protestant Middle Ages, to curb the power of the monarch and to give a major impetus to the kind of democracy which was seen in the United States and in the nineteenth and twentieth century Britain.

In Protestantism the "exceeding greatness of the power" found fresh expression. Although mixed with alien and even contradictory elements, it gave rise to currents of life which were increasingly to mould human culture in art, literature, thought, government, economics, morals, and religion.

Chapter XXXVIII

THE CATHOLIC REFORMATION

The burst of life in Christianity which expressed itself through the various phases of the Protestant Reformation also issued in a reform movement which was contained within the Roman Catholic Church. As we have already noted (Chapter XXXI), this had begun before Luther and was proceeding simultaneously with the emergence of several varieties of Protestantism. It had its heart in Latin Europe, notably at the outset in Spain and Italy. However, eventually it made itself felt as well in most of Western and Central Europe, and through the extensive missions to which it gave rise it won back to the Roman Catholic Church large portions of Europe which had been lost to Protestantism and helped to plant the faith in wide territories in Asia, Africa, North and South America, and the islands which fringed the south and east coasts of Asia.

The Catholic Reformation is sometimes called the Counter-Reformation, but that designation can be misleading. It is accurate if by it is meant that it was in part a reaction against Protestant criticisms and secessions and that through it the Roman Catholic Church regained some of the ground which it had lost to Protestantism. It is inaccurate if it is intended to convey the impression that but for Protestantism the Catholic Reformation would not have come.

One effect of Protestantism was that the Roman Catholic Church became less inclusive. Heretofore it had permitted diversity of views on some of the issues raised by Protestants. Now it felt itself constrained to state its convictions more precisely. The definitions of dogma framed by the Council of Trent, to which we are to come a little later, were consciously directed against Protestant teachings. They ruled out opinions held by some who had remained within the Roman Communion. Those who cherished these opinions had either to surrender them and conform or to leave the fellowship of the Church of Rome. The inclusiveness for which many had hoped and which might have held thousands within the Roman Catholic fold was rejected. In this the Roman

Catholic Church was consistent. It could not have retained all or even the majority of Protestants without disavowing its genius and departing in drastic fashion from a course which it had been pursuing for centuries, perhaps from its very beginning. Yet if by sect it meant a division in the Christian Church, the Roman Communion had ceased to be catholic in the sense of embracing all Christians, if, indeed, it had ever been that, and had become a sect. Within a hundred and fifty years it had finally and irrevocably lost on the one hand the vast majority of what had once been the Eastern wing of the Catholic Church and on the other about half of Western Europe. It had clearly ceased to be universal and, although it was to achieve a wider geographic extension than it had yet known, it was to be more obviously centered in Latin Europe and especially in Italy. This was made vivid by the fact that after 1500, with one exception, all the Popes were Italians. Previously, while the large majority had been from that land, some had been drawn from beyond the Alps.

It is more than a coincidence that the Protestant and the Catholic Reformation ran concurrently. They were different expressions of a common fresh burst of life in Christianity. It is significant, moreover, that they paralleled the amazing vigour in other aspects of the culture of Western Europe—in geographic explorations, commerce, colonization, art, literature, political theory, and education. These movements interacted on one another, but, as we must again and again remind ourselves, we cannot be clear that they all arose from common causes, nor can we know precisely to what extent if at all the "exceeding greatness of the power" inherent in Christianity was the underlying factor.

In outlining the course of the Catholic Reformation we will follow the procedure of tracing it by major regions and countries. First we will describe it in Spain, then in Italy, and finally in France. We will also recount the efforts to win back Protestant Europe. We must not forget, however, that movements were taking place concurrently in several lands and that the geographic treatment is in part artificial. In the next chapter we will sketch the titanic series of struggles which is known collectively, but somewhat inaccurately, as the Thirty Years' War and the stabilization of the geographic boundaries in Europe between the Protestant Churches on the one hand and the Roman Catholic Church on the other.

THE CATHOLIC REFORMATION IN SPAIN

We turn, then, to Spain. We do this because here the Catholic Reformation early had extensive developments. We have already seen (Chapter XXVIII) how with the encouragement of Isabella, Ximénes de Cisneros had carried through measures for the improvement of monastic life and the better education of the clergy. Incidentally, he died at an advanced age in the very year in which Luther posted his epoch-making theses on the church door in Witten-berg. We have noted, too, the establishment of the Inquisition with its purpose of rooting out heresy, and the expulsion of all Jews and Moslems who refused to accept baptism.

In the sixteenth century the course of Christianity in Spain was one of a zealous orthodoxy which gave rise to strange contrasts. In accordance with the prevailing practice in Europe, the Spanish monarchs curtailed the administra-tive power of the Popes within the country and insisted upon dominating the Church, yet they encouraged the Inquisition to root out all dissent from the Roman Catholic faith. Charles V, who ruled during most of the first half of the century, laboured to restore religious unity in Western Europe and bled Spain to support his wars. His son, Philip II, who reigned from 1556 to 1598, was enormously hard-working, conscientious, hated heresy with a bitter hatred, and sought to use the strength of Spain to extirpate Protestantism in Europe, but in doing so brought great misery on the land. The Inquisition was better organized and more ruthless than anywhere else, but in spite of it thousands of professed Christians of Jewish and Moslem ancestry continued some of the religious observances of their pre-Christian forefathers, and many of the higher and lower clergy were morally corrupt. Zeal for a faith whose primary com-mandment is love contributed to extreme cruelty, through the Inquisition, in the chronic treatment of the Marranos, nominally Christian converts from Judaism, and in harshness towards the Moriscos, proselytes from Islam. An uprising of Moriscos provoked by drastic measures against them was sup-pressed with revolting barbarity and in 1609 the unhappy people were ordered expelled from the country. The hostility towards Marranos and Moriscos was aggravated by racial antipathy and jealousy of their economic prosperity, but far from allaying it devotion to the Catholic faith intensified it. From this Spanish Christianity there also arose in the sixteenth century the Society of Jesus, the largest and most powerful new religious order since the birth of the Franciscans and Dominicans, and as great mystics as the Church has ever seen. From this Spanish Christianity there also emerged as noteworthy champions of exploited peoples as the world has ever known, Bartolomé de Las Casas and Pedro Claver, and one of the pioneers in the struggle to place the rela-tions between nations on the basis of law rather than brute force, Francisco de Vitoria.

This Spanish Christianity, given added vitality by the reform movement, and with such stark inner contrasts, had a more extensive geographic spread than the Christianity of any other country in the period between 1500 and 1750. It was to prevail in large sections of the Western Hemisphere and the Philip-pines and, through the Society of Jesus, became the chief driving force in countering Protestantism in Europe and winning back to the Roman Catholic Church thousands who had departed from that form of the faith.

Ignatius Loyola and the Society of Jesus

The Spaniard who was to have a wider and more enduring influence than any other of his fellow-countrymen of the sixteenth century was Ignatius Loyola (c.1491–1556). He can scarcely be called a product of the Catholic Reformation, for the decisive stages of his spiritual pilgrimage were little influenced by the new currents of life which were already running strong in his native land. However, no one else contributed as potently to that movement. A younger contemporary of Martin Luther, in his youth he experienced an intense spiritual conflict which reminds one of the agony through which the great German passed on his way to inward assurance. The soul struggles had similar yet strikingly different outcomes. Through them there came the two outstanding leaders of the Reformation. For Luther the path led to revolt from Rome and to the Protestant Reformation. For Loyola there came an enhanced devotion to the Papacy and a discipline and an organization which were the major new force in effecting and shaping the Catholic Reformation.

Ignatius Loyola was a younger son of a noble family of some antiquity in Guipuzcoa, one of the mountainous Basque provinces only slightly south of the Bay of Biscay on the Spanish side of what is now the French border. The family was conventionally and loyally Catholic and an older brother of Ignatius was a priest. The precise date of the birth of Ignatius is debated, but it was probably no earlier than 1491 and no later than 1495. He was baptized under the name of Iñigo López, but eventually he took the more familiar name Ignacio, or in its Latin form Ignatius. Although in his early youth he may have been given the tonsure, he grew up to a military career and may have shared in some of the vices common to men in that way of life.

The great change in the young aristocrat, what he rightly looked back on as his conversion, came in his late twenties as an outcome of what at first looked like disaster. In 1521, while engaged in the unsuccessful defense of the citadel of Pamplona against a French invasion, he was severely wounded. A cannon ball broke his leg and long weeks of suffering followed. They were prolonged because the leg had to be rebroken and reset. Then, since his pride balked at a protuberance which remained, he insisted on a fresh operation to remove the lump and had the leg stretched by means of a weight to keep it from being shorter than the other. The surgery was only partly effective, for always thereafter he walked with a limp. During the tedious convalescence, Loyola relieved the monotony by reading. Since none of the books on chivalry in which he delighted were at hand, he turned to the only literature available, a life of Christ by a Saxon Carthusian and a volume of the lives of the saints. These and his meditations led him to give himself fully to the way of the saint. He went to a Benedictine monastery on Montserrat, west of Barcelona, there made a comprehensive confession of his past life, gave away his fine clothes to a beggar, took the vows of chastity and poverty, and, hanging up his arms in a chapel of the Virgin Mary, kept a night's vigil before them. Thus, after the manner of the knight, he dedicated himself as a soldier of Christ.

From Montserrat the newly committed devotee of Christ set off on foot to the nearby town of Manresa. There he undertook the way of the ascetic which he believed to be entailed by his self-dedication. He fasted, prayed, begged his food from door to door, tended the sick, went to services in the Dominican priory where he made his home, and read works of devotion, among them *The Imitation of Christ,* a book which had a profound effect upon him. Like Luther, after the first joy and release of self-surrender, he went through grievous struggles of the soul and found the Devil a very present enemy. As did Luther, he followed assiduously the way commended by the "athletes of God," of confession, subduing the body by rigorous austerities, and prayer, but for a time found only anguish. Often he was tempted to commit suicide. Peace came, but not as to Luther by the way of salvation by faith which took the Saxon monk out of the Roman Catholic Church. It arrived, rather, through visions, trances, and ecstasies which kept within the confines of the church of his nativity and confined his ardent loyalty to it. In some of these visions Ignatius believed that he saw the "Trinity under the form of three keys to an organ" and was shown "how God created the world."

At Manresa, from his own experience Ignatius worked out the earliest form of the *Spiritual Exercises* which were to be one of his major contributions to the world. These were for the examination of conscience and to serve as a guide for meditation, contemplation, and prayer. Normally they were to require about four weeks and were to be taken under the supervision of a spiritual director. They were to enable the one who used them to conquer himself, to regulate life, and to avoid coming to a decision from any inordinate affection.

After about a year at Manresa, Ignatius went on a pilgrimage to Palestine. He planned to spend his life in Jerusalem, seeking to convert the Moslems. He reached the holy city and visited the sacred places, but the Franciscans in charge forbade him to carry out his missionary purpose. An obedient son of the Church, he acquiesced and returned to Europe, but not before he had had a vision of Christ on his way back from the Mount of Olives. Moreover, his sense of vocation to be a missionary did not die, but eventually matured, greatly broadened in its geographic horizons.

Once more in Spain, Ignatius spent some time in Barcelona in seeking the education with which his soldier youth had not equipped him. Although then about thirty years of age, he attended school with young boys and acquired Latin. He became acquainted with one of the writings of Erasmus, but was repelled by it. From Barcelona he went to the University of Alcalá, that institution which had recently been founded by Ximénes de Cisneros as a centre for Catholic reform. As had become his custom, he helped others in the religious life and put them through the regimen of his developing *Spiritual Exercises*. He preached informally in homes and hospitals, catechized children, talked with devout women, gathered about him a little group of like-minded young men, and sought to reach artisans and peasants with the Gospel. But he fell under suspicion from the dreaded Inquisition, he and his companions were commanded not to wear a common garb, for a time he was in jail, and he was released with the command not to teach or to hold meetings for three years and even then not without express permission from the proper diocesan authority. He and his companions went from Alcalá to the University of Salamanca, but he was there only two months, was clapped into prison, and, while he was soon released, restrictions were placed on what he could teach until he had studied four years more. The Church was taking no chances with a zealous free lance who might, in his ignorance, mislead souls.

From Salamanca Ignatius went to the University of Paris, to continue his studies in the most famous centre of Christian theological learning of the day. If the ecclesiastical authorities required further education, he would not be content with limiting himself to the mere letter of the law. It was a momentous step. Ignatius was in Paris for seven years, from 1528 to 1535, studied theology, and took a Master of Arts degree. More important still, he gathered about him the nucleus of what was to become the Society of Jesus. He refrained from the street preaching which he had done in Spain, but he formed intimate friendships with students and younger teachers, sought to win them to complete dedication to Christ, and gave to a few his *Spiritual Exercises*. One of the men with whom he roomed, Francis Xavier (1506–1552), was slow to yield, but proved to be a prize worth the effort. An aristocrat from Spanish Navarre and so, like Ignatius, of the Basque region, but several years younger, he was charming, able, and ambitious. He was, as we are to see, to become one of the greatest missionaries of all time. On August 15, 1534, Ignatius and six others took the customary three-fold monastic vows of poverty, chastity, and obedience, and were given the communion by the only one of their number who was a priest. This was the humble beginning of the Society of Jesus, which was to be the most potent expression and instrument of the Catholic Reformation.

A few months before, in November, 1533, Cop, the rector of the University of Paris, had delivered an inaugural address in which, advocating reform in language taken in part from Erasmus and Luther, he had given rise to great excitement. Moreover, it was only recently that another in that university circle, John Calvin, had had the sudden conversion which made him a leader in the Protestant Reformation. It was in the very year in which, stimulated by Ignatius, the immortal seven took their vows that Calvin renounced his benefices and fled to Protestant Basel, there to begin the composition of his *Institutes,* a book which was to have as wide and deep an effect as the *Spiritual Exercises.*

It may be unfair to both to contrast the two, for one was frankly a work in theology and the other a guide to private prayer and devotion. Different though they were, a basic assumption in each was the sovereignty of God, the redemption wrought by Him through Christ, and the conviction that human beings find the meaning and the fullness of life only through Christ and through dedicating themselves to the will and glory of God. Both saw in the beatific vision and enjoyment of God the goal of human life and of God's purpose for man. To both the Protestant and the Catholic Reformation the University of Paris, founded for the study of Christian theology—man's knowledge of God through Christ—made major contributions. Although emphatically opposed to each other, Calvin and Loyola were much alike in their deepest convictions.

In spite of the fact that many of its students and teachers were disgustingly corrupt morally, from the University of Paris issued springs which did much to swell that religious revival which had two such different forms as the Protestant and Catholic Reformations. In conflict though they were, the two had a great deal in common. In the University of Paris was seen in miniature something of the manner of the operation of Christianity in human history and of the interaction of the Gospel and human nature.

In 1535 Ignatius left the little band, for a digestive trouble which had long plagued him and which was aggravated by his austerities led his physicians to advise him to return to Spain. He spent a few months in his native province, teaching, catechizing, and preaching. He also visited the families of the Spanish members of his group to bring them news of the absent. Thence he made his way to Venice and a year or so later was joined by the other members of the company, now augmented by a few recruits. There he met Giovanni Pietro Caraffa, the future Pope Paul IV, a zealous, ardent, haughty reformer, one of the founders of the Theatines, an order of which we are to hear more a little later. While at Venice several of the group gave themselves to the care of the sick.

On Palm Sunday, 1537, the band arrived at Rome, there to seek of the Pope permission to make a pilgrimage to Jerusalem and license for ordination for such as were not yet priests. They obtained their wish and returned to Venice to wait for a ship to the Holy Land. It was in Venice that Ignatius and several of the others were ordained. Since, after a year, no opportunity developed to go to Palestine, Ignatius and two others went to Rome to place the services of the nascent order at the disposal of the Pope.

When nearing Rome, Ignatius, who, that he might better prepare for it, had allowed a year and a half to lapse between his ordination and the celebration of his first mass, had a vision of God the Father and God the Son, the latter carrying the heavy cross, in which Christ, at the request of the Father, accepted him as his servant.

It was in Rome that the companions took a step which they had not previously contemplated. After much prayer and consultation they came to the conclusion that they should seek permission to constitute themselves into an order. After some delay, due chiefly to the opposition of a cardinal who was against the multiplication of such organizations, in 1539 the Pope gave his oral approval and followed this, in September, 1540, with a formal bull of authorization. The new order was to be known as the Society (originally the Company) of Jesus. The name may have been suggested by the vision which had come to Ignatius as he was about to enter Rome.

The Society of Jesus was to be in the nature of an army whose members were soldiers of God. They were to fight under the direction of the Pope and to this end, to the perfect mortification of their wills, they took a special vow to do whatever the Pope commanded "for the good of souls, and the propagation of the faith in whatever countries he" might wish to send them, "whether to the Turks, or other infidels, or to the regions called India, or to the lands of heretics, schismatics, or of faithful Christians." All were to take a vow to obey the head, or General, of the society "in all things that appertain to keeping this rule," and were to "acknowledge and reverence him, as is befitting, as they would Christ, if He were present in person." Particularly were they to give themselves to "the instruction of children and the uneducated in Christian doctrine, teaching the Ten Commandments and the principles of faith." But they were also "to advance souls on the way of Christian life and doctrine, to propagate the faith by public preaching and expounding Holy Scripture, to give the *Spiritual Exercises,* to do works of charity . . . and, finally, to try to bring spiritual consolation to the faithful by hearing confession." They were to take the vows of chastity and poverty, and were not to own permanent property collectively, except for the colleges and universities which they might possess. Ignatius was unanimously chosen the first General. He protested and acquiesced only after prolonged prayer and the express command of his confessor, a Franciscan of the Observance. Having accepted, he lived up to the demands of the office. Small physically, slightly less than five feet two inches tall, he was every inch the commander. Resourceful, calm, confident, considerate of the welfare of each member, he would brook no disobedience.

Here was the Catholic faith giving birth to a new order, like yet unlike its monastic predecessors. It was like them in its three vows of chastity, poverty, and obedience, and in its practice of austerity and prayer. It resembled the mendicants in its emphasis upon preaching, teaching, and humble personal service to others. It was unlike all that went before it in its military-like organization, its intense discipline through the *Spiritual Exercises,* and its stress on obedience to the Pope and the General. Its members wore no special garb, but adapted their dress to circumstances. While given much to prayer, they were activists, seeking to influence the work-a-day world. Since the original group were university men, trained in theology, the Jesuits made much of education and insisted upon a prolonged training in philosophy and theology for their priests. They produced many notable scholars.

The Society of Jesus had a phenomenal growth. By the time of his death, only sixteen years after the Papal bull authorizing its formation, Ignatius had seen the Society grow to about a thousand members. They were in Italy, Portugal, Spain, and France, labouring for spiritual and moral reform in the nominally Roman Catholic populations. They were in Germany, combatting Protestantism, and in Ireland, seeking to strengthen the Roman Catholic Church. They stiffened the backbone of the reforming Council of Trent in its intransigence towards Protestants and its bowing to Papal direction. Francis Xavier had planted it in India, Malacca, the East Indies, and Japan, and had died seeking entrance into China.

Singularly adapted to the mission of the Roman Catholic Church of these centuries, the Society of Jesus continued its phenomenal growth after death had removed its founder. It attracted some of the ablest youth of the day and became the chief spearhead of the Catholic Reformation. Among its early members was Peter Canisius (1521–1597), a native of Holland, who was the great apostle of the Catholic Reformation to Germany. He became a Jesuit in 1543, was trained in Rome under the personal direction of Ignatius, was an eloquent preacher, taught in universities, established Jesuit colleges in Cologne, Ingolstadt, and Prague, composed catechisms which were used extensively in giving instruction in the Roman Catholic form of the Christian faith, and had marked influence at the Council of Trent. Robert Bellarmine (1542–1621), later cardinal, the nephew of a Pope, was from a noble Tuscan family, studied in a Jesuit college, joined the Society in his late twenties, became a scholar of extraordinary and varied erudition, aided in a revival of the study of Thomas

Aquinas which had begun at the University of Salamanca, for years taught controversial theology at Rome, and wrote what was probably the ablest literary defense of the Roman Catholic faith against Protestants to be composed during the sixteenth and seventeenth centuries. Aloysius Gonzaga (1568–1591), of a princely Italian family, created a sensation through much of Latin Europe by joining the Society. Before he could be ordained priest he died of the plague while nursing sufferers from an epidemic. Eventually he was made the patron saint of youth. Spectacular evidence of the changes being wrought by the Catholic Reformation and the Society of Jesus was the career of Francis Borgia (1510–1572), Duke of Gandia and great-grandson of the notorious Pope Alexander VI. Deeply religious from his boyhood, Francis Borgia early encouraged the Society and after the death of his wife joined it, was ordained priest, and at the command of Ignatius became an itinerant preacher in Spain. Elected the third General of the Society, he brought to the post marked administrative genius and is often spoken of as its second founder. He revised its rule, encouraged mental prayer, edited the *Spritual Exercises,* strengthened the training of the novices, and furthered the Society's missions, especially on the expanding frontiers of the Spanish empire in the Americas.

The Jesuits addressed themselves to youth. They developed a system of education under what was known as the *Ratio Studiorum,* first drafted in 1585 and given its definitive form in 1599. They sought to produce strong moral character and to train their pupils to think for themselves. For a time they were among the most progressive schoolmasters in Europe.

The Society of Jesus vied with the spiritual sons of Francis of Assisi in producing more missionaries than any other order of the Roman Catholic Church. Its members were the chief agents in pressing back the Protestant tide and rewinning some areas, notably Bohemia, Moravia, and Poland, to the Roman Catholic Church. They ranged over much of North and South America, had enterprises in Africa, and were the outstanding sixteenth and seventeenth century pioneers of the faith in India, Annam, China, and Japan.

So widespread and active an organization could not fail to arouse opposition. Indeed, it faced this from the first. It was distrusted and feared by both Roman Catholics and Protestants. Some critics objected to its appropriation of the name of Jesus. Others denounced what they believed to be the attempts of its members to attain its purposes through political intrigue and asserted that the vow of obedience to the General took precedence over the individual's own judgement of right and wrong and so made the members skilful and ruthless tools of their superiors. Some asserted that through their casuistry the Jesuits confused truth with falsehood. A Grand Inquisitor clapped several of their superiors into prison. Bishops disliked their independence of episcopal control.

Many from other religious orders were antagonistic, partly out of jealousy. Numbers of Jesuits, including Bellarmine, were adherents of a theology called Molinism, from one of their sixteenth century members, Luis de Molina (1535–1600). Molinism wrestled with the problem, which also concerned Protestants, of how to reconcile grace and the unchangeable decree of pre-destination with free will. Here they differed sharply from the solution offered by Thomas Aquinas and held to by a large proportion of non-Jesuits. As we shall see, after 1750 the Jesuits were expelled from the French and Spanish domains and then, for about a generation, were suppressed by the Pope.

GREAT SPANISH MYSTICS

The Society of Jesus was the most influential but not the only new movement which arose from the Catholic Reformation in Spain. The sixteenth and seven-teenth centuries were marked by many evidences of Spanish vitality. Spaniards were building a vast empire in the Americas and the Philippines. For part of the time their armies were regarded as the mightiest in Western Europe. Mountain peaks in art and literature appeared—notably Velasquez, Murillo, Cervantes, Lopez de Vega, and Calderon. Simultaneously religious geniuses appeared, some of them, like many in other ages, combining mysticism with practical achievement. To what extent these varied expressions of vitality had a common cause and to what degree Christianity was responsible for each we do not know. Presumably, as in so many other periods of marked creativity, here was more than a coincidence. Whatever else may be said, it is clear that Christianity was by no means the only contributory common factor. It is also certain that to Christianity must be ascribed a major share in the impulse which shaped the mystics.

Mysticism characterized thousands of Spaniards and gave rise to scores of writers and a vast literature. It was not confined to any one religious group but was found in several of the existing orders and now and again produced a new one. Like the Spanish phase of the Catholic Reformation it became noticeable late in the fifteenth century, reached a climax in the sixteenth cen-tury, began to decline in the seventeenth century, and by the middle of the eighteenth century had largely faded out. Its course paralleled the rise and decline in other aspects of Spanish greatness, some of them apparently only slightly related to Christianity. The Spanish mystics were not, as a rule, philo-sophical or even speculative. They were, rather, intent on the practical means of nourishing the life of the spirit and had uncanny insight into what would now be called psychology, with an analysis of the state of the soul.

Fittingly, the first outstanding pioneer of the classic era of Spanish mysticism was Francisco García Ximénes de Cisneros (1455–1510), cousin of the Ximénes de Cisneros who led in the reform of the Spanish church. Moreover, he it was who, only a few years before Ignatius Loyola came there for guidance in the early stages of his spiritual quest, had purified and reinvigorated the Benedictine monastery on Montserrat. How far if at all his *Book of Exercises for the Spiritual Life,* which appeared in 1500, influenced the more famous *Spiritual Exercises* of Ignatius has been hotly debated, but without clear proof of any conscious copying.

Ignatius Loyola must be given a place in the list, although we need not repeat what we have already said about him, but only point out that he is easily among the first three or four in eminence and probably first in wide-ranging influence.

It is usually and rightly said that the leading Spanish mystic was Teresa (or Theresa) of Avila (1515–1582). She is sometimes regarded as the outstanding woman of all Spanish history. We are fortunate in having a singularly candid autobiography, devoting especial attention to her spiritual development. Like the *Confessions* of Augustine, it ranks with the more important documents of the Christian faith.

Of aristocratic birth, one of a large family of children, six of whose seven sons became soldiers, Teresa was reared in an earnestly religious home. From infancy she had a deep strain of piety. When still a child, she and her favourite brother, inspired by reading the lives of the saints, set out, as she later recorded, for "the country of the Moors," begging their way "for the love of God," "and to be beheaded there." They had scarcely crossed the bridge outside the city gate of Avila when an uncle overtook them and brought them back to their mother.

Against home opposition, in 1536, when twenty-one years of age Teresa entered a Carmelite convent in Avila as a novice. For many years she remained an obscure nun. Troubled by chronic ill health, at one time in her twenties she fell into a kind of trance which left her helpless and seemingly paralyzed for more than eight months. For years the paralysis recurred intermittently. In her early forties she began to hear interior voices, see visions, and experience what to her were revelations. As she looked back upon her life she believed that during the first nearly twenty years of her monastic career she had almost constant inner conflict and knew "neither any joy in God nor any pleasure in the world." She thought of herself as a great sinner. Yet usually she spent many hours a day in prayer. Then came improvement, but in no single hour. She was helped by the sight of an image of Christ, "sorely wounded," and by the *Confessions* of Augustine. She began to find deep satisfaction in long and uninterrupted periods of communion with God and knew the "prayer of quiet." There came also union and rapture. To her these were gifts for which to be profoundly grateful.

When in her mid-forties Teresa came to believe that a stricter way of life was demanded than that practised in her convent. The older rule had been mitigated. Instead of having perpetual solitude, nuns were allowed visitors and might even go out into the town. The Lenten fasts were not kept as at first enjoined. In the face of opposition, but with her bishop's reluctant permission, in 1562 she founded in Avila what proved to be the initial convent of Reformed (or Discalced) Carmelite nuns. She began in a small way, with only four novices, but in the early years of the new community she had the most peaceful days of her life. Then, in 1567, with the consent of the general of her order, she began to travel up and down the land, inaugurating new houses of the reform. She enlisted two monks, one of them best remembered as John of the Cross, and through them established reformed Carmelite houses for men. The journeys entailed physical hardships of heat, springless carts, bad roads, worse inns, and unbridged rivers. As was to be expected, her successful efforts at reform aroused opposition within the order. After a few years, in 1580–1581, the Discalced Carmelites were allowed to form a distinct province and elect their own superior. Stricken with paralysis about the time that this was accomplished, Teresa was a sufferer the rest of her days. Yet she continued to be an itinerant and died while on a trip to start a new house. In her own person she had founded thirty-two houses.

Within her lifetime Teresa was revered as a saint. Her official canonization came only forty years after her death, simultaneously with that of Ignatius Loyola and Francis Xavier, both of whom had to wait longer than she for that recognition. Organizer, efficient administrator, careful of details as well as concerned with the wider sweep of her plans, repeatedly ill with fever, ague, quinsy, abscesses and tumours, in addition to paralysis and disorders which might be classified as primarily nervous, at times despondent, keenly aware of her sinfulness, she was first of all and always a mystic, given to prayer and with a growing faith, increasing inward calm, and a sense of the marvellous and quite unmerited mercy and love of God. None other of their saints has quite so gripped and held the affection of the Spanish people. Here is evidence both of the quality of her life and of a strain in the Spanish soul which responded to it.

Only slightly less famous than Teresa of Avila was her close friend, John of the Cross (1542–1605). Younger than she by a quarter of a century, he was profoundly influenced by her. Born and christened as Juan de Yepes, he was the son of an aristocrat who had been disinherited for marrying below his station. Reared in poverty by his early-widowed mother, he obtained his education partly in return for serving in a hospital and partly in a school established by the Jesuits. Before he was twenty he felt the call to the monastic life. Early in his twenties he entered the ranks of the Carmelites and for several years was a student in Salamanca. Frail and short of stature, he subjected his diminutive body to severe austerities. When he was twenty-five he attracted the attention of Teresa and became to her almost a spiritual son. As we have seen, she chose him to help initiate men's houses of her reform movement. Imprisoned for some months by fellow-Carmelites who opposed the reform, he wrote some of his choicest poetry and had some of his most vivid visions while in a noisome cell. Escaping, he went from monastery to monastery, strengthening his brethren, founding houses, serving as a prior of one and for a time as vicar-provincial. In his last months, internal dissensions among the Discalced Carmelites stripped him of his offices but freed him for intense and uninterrupted communion with God.

John of the Cross believed profoundly that to be filled with God the soul must empty itself. He treated of this and the road to this goal in his exquisite lyrics and in his three chief prose works, the *Ascent of Mount Carmel, The Dark Night,* and the *Living Flame of Love.* The road was difficult, and, with keen insight into human nature, he forewarned those who would undertake it of the perils along the way. Only the few could attain the higher reaches of which he wrote. Yet he had a profound influence, was canonized in 1726, and two hundred years later was proclaimed a doctor of the Church.

Space fails even to name all the other Spanish mystics, lesser peaks below these higher ones. There was Francisco de Osuna (c.1497–c.1542), the Franciscan whose *Third Spiritual Alphabet* aided Teresa of Avila in one stage of her pilgrimage. Luis de Granada (1504–1588), a Dominican, prior, provincial of his order for Portugal, famous as a preacher, wrote voluminously, but is best remembered for his *Sinners' Guide,* of use to the ordinary Christian in his prayers and devotions. The Franciscan Juan de los Angeles (c.1536–1609), in spite of his duties as provincial of his order, found time to write guides to the mystic life, among them *Triumphs of the Love of God, Spiritual Strife, Dialogues of the Conquest of the Spiritual and Secret Kingdom of God,* and a continuation of this last, *Manual of the Perfect Life.* Peter of Alcántara, eventually canonized, was counsellor to Teresa of Avila both in things material and things spiritual.

Much later and of a quite different kind was Miguel de Molinos (1640–1697). A mystic, he taught interior annihilation as the means to purity of soul, perfect contemplation, and inner peace. Here was a form of quietism. Yet it contained features which sanctioned gross immorality, for it held impure carnal acts to be excusable since only the lower, sensual man was concerned in them and they need not taint the soul. He had a wide influence in several countries, but in 1687, while in Rome, was condemned as a heretic and sentenced to life imprisonment in the garb of a penitent.

Reform in Portugal

In Portugal there were no indigenous movements for reform at all comparable in vigour and magnitude with those in Spain. Portugal gave birth to no new order which approached the influence of the Jesuits or the Discalced Carmelites. It knew no such flowering of mysticism as did its larger neighbour. This does not mean that the Catholic Reformation did not touch it. The Jesuits early extended their operations to Portugal and it was through the Portuguese that Francis Xavier carried out his amazing mission in India, the East Indies, and the Far East. Portugal had zealous monks and eloquent preaching. Yet most of the reinvigoration of Portuguese Christianity came by contagion from other lands.

This lack of a major native reform movement in Portugal had significance for wide areas of the globe. In the sixteenth century Portugal built a colonial empire which was second in extent only to that of Spain. Portuguese established themselves in Brazil, along the coasts of Africa, in India, Ceylon, Southeast Asia, the East Indies, Japan, and China. Everywhere they went Catholic missions arose under their ægis. Yet in general these never had the vitality of the Spanish enterprises. The difference was reflected in the future course of Christianity in Brazil and much of Africa and Asia.

The Catholic Reformation in Italy

While the Catholic Reformation was proceeding in Spain, what was taking place in Italy? Here was the centre of the Roman Catholic Church. From Italy had come some of the greatest theologians, notably Anselm and Thomas Aquinas. Here had arisen several of the largest orders, especially the Franciscans. Here, more recently, had been such saints as Catherine of Siena, and here Savonarola had only recently perished in his attempt to make Florence fully Christian. In Italy, too, some of the most notorious corruption in the Church was found. Here was the home of the Renaissance, with its paganizing tendencies. Here, in spite of notable attempts to effect a viable reconciliation with Christianity, humanism was displaying de-Christianizing trends. The Papacy and the Papal curia had succumbed to the evils which we have earlier described (Chapter XXVIII) and attempts to cleanse the Augean stables had thus far proved unsuccessful. How effective was the fresh pulsation of life?

As in Spain, so in Italy, the era was one of creativity in culture. Although divided and weak politically, Italy, as the original centre of the Renaissance and humanism, was producing magnificent art and exquisite literature. The flowering came somewhat earlier than in Spain and before 1600 had passed its peak. Leonardo da Vinci died in 1519, Raphael in 1520, the Titanic and long-lived Michelangelo in 1564, and Titian in 1576. Palestrina (1526–1594), who set a new standard for the music of the Church, was a sixteenth century figure, in part the product of the Catholic Reformation, as was the unhappy, mad Tasso (1544–1595), with his master epic, *Jerusalem Delivered*. Machiavelli died in 1527 and Ariosto in 1533. The Catholic Reformation was slightly later in getting well under way, but, as in Spain, it reached its peak before the close of the sixteenth century.

A major precursor and instrument of the Catholic Reformation in Italy was the Oratory of Divine Love. A confraternity, a type of fellowship which had long been common in the Catholic Church, it may go back to a group which came into being as early as 1497. The centre of the Oratory of Divine Love was in Rome and it counted among its members men of deep devotion and outstanding ability who wished the moral reform of the Church. Prominent among them was Giovanni Pietro Caraffa (1476–1559), later, as we have seen, to be Pope Paul IV. Its members, highly placed though they were, showed their zeal by visiting hospitals and prisons. Branches arose in several Italian cities.

Partly in association with the Oratory of Divine Love, there came into being the Theatines, the earliest of a new kind of monastic order. Their purpose was the reform of the secular clergy, the rank and file of the priests who ministered to the nominally Christian population. The founders of the Theatines were aristocrats. The chief mover was Gaetano dei Conti di Tiene (also known as Cajetan, but not to be confused with his contemporary, Cardinal Cajetan, whom we met in connexion with Luther). He was one of the Oratory of Divine Love and consecrated the order to the cross of Christ. He was eventually canonized. The first head of the Theatines was Caraffa, who, with Papal permission, divested himself of his various benefices to assume the post. Since he had been Bishop of Chieti (in Latin Theate), the popular designation of the order, Theatines, was from that see. Papal approval of the Theatines was given in 1524. They multiplied rapidly, soon spread to Spain and France, and also conducted foreign missions.

Somewhat similar to the Theatines were the Regular Clerics of St. Paul, better known as the Barnabites, from the Church of St. Barnabas in Milan, with which they were closely associated in their early days. They were founded in 1530 by three Italians of noble family. In addition to the customary vows of poverty, chastity, and obedience, their members solemnly promised not to seek any office. They catechized, heard confessions, and conducted missions, but as means to their chief end, the revival among the clergy of a zeal for souls.

The Somaschi, so-called from the site of their mother house, were begun (1532) by Jerome Emiliani (1481–1537), who gave himself so devotedly to the founding of hospitals, orphanages, and a home for fallen women, and to personal ministrations to the physically wretched that he was later canonized. The chief work of the Somaschi, like that of the founder, was the care of the sick and the poor.

Resembling the Somaschi, but eventually having a much wider extension, were the Brothers Hospitallers of St. John of God. Their founder, John of God (1495–1550), was Portuguese by birth but was reared in Spain and spent most of his life there. His was a striking spiritual pilgrimage which at one stage led him to go through the streets of Granada, scourging himself in such fashion that many thought him mad. John of God was a designation which he believed had been given him in a vision by the infant Jesus. In Granada he began devoting himself to the sick. Eventually an order arose which was accorded Papal approval in 1572 and which was to follow the rule of Augustine. The order spread to Rome in 1584 and there what was regarded as its mother house was established. Other hospitals were soon inaugurated in Italy and France.

A movement, that of the Oratory, which was to be the means of deepening the Christian faith and life of many thousands was begun in Rome by Philip Neri (1515–1595). Philip Neri was a native of Florence and had some of his early instruction from the Dominicans of San Marco, the house intimately connected with Savonarola. When he was eighteen he went to Rome and there laboured for the sick and the poor and through informal conversations sought to lead chance acquaintances in many different walks of life to more earnest Christian living. He founded a confraternity to minister to the pilgrims who thronged the city. In 1556 he began an institute, the Oratory, for religious meetings of a novel kind. They were held in the evening and consisted of prayers, readings from the Scriptures and the fathers, and lectures or sermons of an informal and unconventional kind calculated to reach those not usually moved by the formal services of the Church. Hymns and music were prominent in the meetings, and Palestrina did much of the composing for them. Musical settings for scenes from sacred history were written. Known as the oratorio, this novel use of music gained wide circulation. For a time Philip Neri met bitter opposition, but in 1575, when he was sixty years of age, Papal permission was given for a community of secular priests known as the Congregation of the Oratory. Its members were bound by obedience but by no vows. Each house was independent of the others. The movement spread in

Italy, Spain, and France, and with modifications the various units followed the rule of the founder. The successor of Neri as superior of the Roman Oratory, Cæsar Baronius (1538–1607), was especially distinguished as the author of a voluminous church history, *Annales Ecclesiastici,* which carried the story down to 1198 and was in part an answer to the Protestant *Centuriæ.*

What was to become the most extensive of the sixteenth century religious orders of Italian origin was the Capuchins. Like the Jesuits, they were evidence of the new tides of life which were beginning to run strong and were a stimulus to them. They were also proof of the attraction of the ideals of Francis of Assisi in times when men were seeking to follow Christ without compromise or reservation. They arose from the Observants, the branch of the order of Brothers Minor who in principle more nearly held to the rule of Francis than did the Conventuals. Yet the Observants had also become lax. One of their number, Matteo di Bassi (or da Bascio), believed that he had heard a voice which repeatedly commanded him to observe the rule "to the letter." He obeyed and in such meticulous fashion that he insisted on wearing what he believed to be the primitive Franciscan habit. Part of this was a pointed hood, a *cappa* or *capuche,* which became a kind of symbol of the reform. Hence came the designation Capuchin. Matteo di Bassi did not at first intend to separate from the Observants but sought, rather, to win them to a return to what tradition declared was the pristine way of the *Poverello.* As he might have expected, he encountered opposition. In 1526 a Papal brief permitted the Capuchins to separate in part from the Observants and to follow, as they wished, the way of the hermit. In 1528 they were made a distinct family within the Franciscans. Much emphasis was placed, as it had been by Francis of Assisi, on preaching. Similar movements sprang up elsewhere among the Observants and swelled the ranks of the Capuchins.

For a time the Capuchins were under the suspicion of heresy. These fears seemed to be confirmed when one of their early heads, Ochino, whom we have earlier met, became a Protestant. The Pope gave serious consideration to suppressing them and for two years forbade them to preach.

Other counsels prevailed, partly because some of the new recruits proved to be staunchly orthodox and zealous. In 1619 the Capuchins became a separate order with their own minister general. They multiplied rapidly and were effective preachers of the Catholic Reformation in both Roman Catholic and Protestant areas. This was partly because they mingled with the ordinary life of the masses, serving the sick and the poor and giving themselves with noteworthy devotion to the sufferers from epidemics. While they did not do as Matteo di Bassi had wished, observe the primitive rule of Francis "to the letter," but relaxed some of its austerities, they were a revival of the zeal of the early Brothers Minor and were missionaries to much of Europe and on the new geographic frontiers opened by the explorations of the sixteenth and seventeenth centuries.

The creative vitality in the Catholic Reformation is also shown in the coming into being of the Ursulines, an order of women of a quite new kind. They were begun by Angela de Merici (1474–1540). From childhood deeply religious, at about the age of twenty she believed that a great need of her time was the better instruction of girls in the rudiments of the Christian faith. She turned her home, in Desenzano, into a school and later moved it to Brescia. She chose other virgins to multiply her work. They lived with their families and met at stated intervals for conference and prayer. In 1535 twelve of them formed a community named for St. Ursula. The idea caught fire and similar groups quickly arose in Italy, Germany, and France. A constitution was adopted in 1540 and in 1544 Papal approval was received. The rule was that of Augustine. The functions of the order were primarily teaching. Several congregations sprang up, each calling itself Ursuline, and with varying garbs and customs. The foundress was canonized in 1807.

Among the furtherers of the Catholic Reformation in Italy were some of the bishops. A pioneer was Giberti, who in his personal and public life was an example of the progress of the reform and did much to encourage it in his diocese, Verona. His beginnings were quite unpromising. The illegitimate son of a Genoese admiral, he owed his rapid advancement in the Church to the Medici who was later Pope Clement VII. Although naturally religious and in his youth wishing to become a monk, he allowed himself to be drawn into administrative duties, made his home in Rome a hospitable centre of the humanists, and accepted appointment as non-resident Bishop of Verona. However, he was brought into the circle of the Oratory of Divine Love, was a friend of Caraffa, aided in the formation of the Theatines, and about 1528, when in his mid-thirties, he took up his residence in his see, resigned all his other benefices to which the cure of souls was attached, began a strictly ascetic way of life, and devoted himself to the diocese. He went from village to village, examining the priests, reconciling enemies, caring for the poor, and insisting that the clergy perform their duties and maintain a worthy way of life. He improved the services in the parish churches, enjoined on his priests weekly confession, had a bell rung at the elevation of the host, and had the sacrament reserved in a tabernacle on the high altar. He reformed both the secular and the regular clergy, encouraged confraternities for the care of the poor, and had prepared and published a catechism and a manual for preachers. Several other prelates followed Giberti's example.

Outstanding among the reforming bishops was Charles Borromeo (1538–

1584). Of aristocratic birth in a deeply religious family, he was a nephew of Pope Pius IV. His uncle gave him rapid ecclesiastical promotion and when he was twenty-two made him a cardinal and entrusted him with important administrative duties. To these responsibilities was soon added the Archbishopric of Milan, one of the most important sees in the Church. For some years Borromeo seemed to be one of the prelates who were unhappily very common even after the Catholic Reformation was well under way, drawing the incomes from many benefices, pushed forward by influential relatives, living in splendour, and a handicap rather than an aid to the professed purpose of the Church. Yet he was never guilty of the gross vices which were widespread in Rome and his religious life deepened. The death of a beloved brother is said to have done much to promote his spiritual growth. After the death of Pius IV and the election of a worthy successor, partly with his support, Borromeo took up his residence in Milan and gave himself unsparingly to carry through a thorough transformation of the archdiocese. He founded seminaries to train priests, reformed monasteries, inaugurated schools for the nobility, furthered elementary education for the masses, encouraged the Ursulines, sought to relieve the poor, provided advocates to help them in their lawsuits, set himself against usury, established homes for beggars, worked for conciliation in labour disputes, and in a **great epidemic reduced his own table, sold his** plate to aid in the relief of the sufferers, and had his tapestries made into clothing for the destitute. He emphasized frequent communion and set the example in fasting and pilgrimages. It is not surprising that he wore himself out and died in his middle forties. It speaks for the new temper of the Roman Catholic Church that he was canonized in 1610, less than a generation after his death.

The Reformation Captures the Papacy

A time lag existed between the forward surge of the wave of reform in the Roman Catholic Church and the permanent commitment of the Papacy to it. Reform was already well under way in Spain when the Spaniard, Alexander VI, was bringing the Papacy to the lowest point of moral degradation since the tenth century. It had made substantial progress in Italy before it was securely entrenched in Rome. In this the record was not unlike that in the earlier and more serious recession, from A.D. 500 to A.D. 950. Then, it will be recalled, the reform associated with the name of Cluny had made substantial progress elsewhere before it seated its advocates on the throne of Peter.

A brief review of the Popes of the sixteenth century may illustrate this generalization and will also shed light on some of the other problems faced by the Holy See.

As we enter upon this survey we do well to recall something of the complexity and magnitude of the problems with which the Popes had to deal. There was the tradition, reinforced by the dreams and actions of the reforming Pontiffs of the Middle Ages, that the Papacy should be not only the exponent and guardian of doctrinal orthodoxy but also, for the achievement of a fully Christian society, the administrative head of Christendom. This entailed both authority over the entire ecclesiastical structure and active participation and even dictatorial powers in all aspects, including especially the political, of the life of Christendom. To implement these claims, the Popes had built up a centralized bureaucracy and to support it had been driven to financial expedients which had aroused much opposition, especially in distant countries, and which had furthered corruption in the curia. The corruption was of sufficient magnitude to tax the ability and resolution of any Pope who would seek to curb it. In addition, the Popes of the sixteenth century were confronted by the chronic menace of the Ottoman Turks who might at any time engulf Western Europe. As the traditional leaders of Christendom against the Moslems they strove desperately, but in vain, to unite against them a hopelessly divided Europe. They were faced with a rising tide of nationalism headed by monarchs who were building for total control in their respective realms. This nationalism and these monarchs, even when emphatically Catholic in doctrine, were intent upon limiting the administrative and taxing functions of the Papacy within their borders. Catholic monarchs insisted upon controlling appointment to bishoprics and other important ecclesiastical posts in their realms. The more prominent sought to dominate the Papacy and to use it as a pawn in the unremitting struggle of power politics. Spanish, French, and Italian cliques among the cardinals had to be reckoned with in Papal elections. Militarily weak, the Popes attempted to play off one monarch against another. On one memorable occasion, in 1527, the unruly troops of the Emperor Charles V, orthodox Catholic though he was, seized Rome, forced the Pope to take refuge in the castle of St. Angelo, and for months held and pillaged the city. Charles was presumably not unwilling to see the Pope thus dealt with, for the latter had been siding with France. To many the emotional shock was even greater than the physical destruction. Some careless devotees of the Renaissance believed the disaster to be divine retribution for the wickedness of the city and the curia and were led to repentance. Even more serious for the Papacy was the defection of the major part of North-western Europe and Great Britain to Protestantism. Distracted by other pressing crises, Rome was never entirely free to deal with that movement.

It is not surprising that under these circumstances the Papacy was slow in being fully committed to reform or that reforming Popes, when elected, found the obstacles to improvement mountainous.

The succession of Popes reveals much of the story. Alexander VI was followed (1503) by Pius III, a man of ability and blameless life, who reigned for only a few months. Next came Giuliano della Rovere who as Julius II held the post from 1503 to 1513. Sixty years of age when elected and troubled by gout, he nevertheless proved himself a man of energy and determination. Impetuous, he was more like an emperor than a bishop and much of his ten years in office was devoted to restoring, consolidating, and extending the territorial domains of the Papacy and rendering the Holy See independent of any temporal prince by its possession of a strong state under its direct rule. Yet he wished reform, repudiated the nepotism which characterized so many of his fifteenth century predecessors, condemned simony in Papal elections, laid the foundation stone of the new St. Peter's, was a patron of art, and encouraged missions in America, India, and Africa.

Next on the Papal throne was Giovanni de' Medici (1475–1521), son of Lorenzo the Magnificent, whom we have already met (Chapter XXVIII) as having been loaded with benefices since childhood and as having been named cardinal-deacon in his early teens. When elected he was not yet a priest. As Leo X he was Pope from 1513 to 1521. Although he was punctilious in his religious observances, promoted art, and, elegant in his manners, made Rome a growing centre of culture, he was a lover of luxury and the chase, was intent upon the aggrandizement of his family, and, engrossed in the political and diplomatic intrigues of the time, employed in them the kind of deceit and shrewdness associated with the name of Machiavelli. No reform could be hoped for from him, and under him corruption increased. Something of the moral condition of the Papacy and its entourage can be visualized from a plot in 1517 (the year of the ninety-five theses of Luther) to rid the post of Leo by poisoning him. In retaliation Leo had the leader, a twenty-two-year-old, dissolute cardinal, tortured and executed, imposed heavy fines upon other cardinals who had been implicated, and then ensured his control of the sacred college by creating thirty-one new members. Leo sought to replenish his coffers and obtain funds to build St. Peter's by the promotion of the sale of indulgences. He was not the man to sense the significance of Luther or of the movement which the great German spear-headed.

After death had removed Leo X, for a brief time, 1522–1523, reform seemed to have come to its rightful own. To break a deadlock in the college of cardinals over the election, a native of Utrecht of lowly birth, a boyhood tutor and trusted official of the Emperor Charles V, was elected and took the title of Adrian VI. Scholarly, ascetic, deeply religious, an experienced administrator, he set himself to the herculean task of reform. But he aroused bitter opposition, especially by his attempts at urgently needed financial retrenchment, was confronted by the advancing Turks, rising Protestantism, and feuds among the Christian princes, and died after less than two years in office. Incidentally, he was the last non-Italian Pope.

Following Adrian VI came another of the Medici, who under the title of Clement VII wore the tiara from 1523 to 1534. They were crucial years in the rise of Protestantism, in the relations of Henry VIII of England with Rome, and in the growth of the reform movement in the Catholic Church. Of illegitimate birth, the future Clement VII had been declared legitimate by his cousin, Leo X, and had been raised by him to the purple. Although neither extravagant nor pleasure-loving as had been Leo X, hard-working, upright in his private life, and a patron of the arts, he was given to procrastination, indecision, timidity, and inconstancy of purpose. He made some steps towards reform, but his interests were predominantly political and he was caught in the Maelstrom of Italian and European intrigue and diplomacy. His appointments to high ecclesiastical office were largely from political or personal considerations and few of the cardinals created by him had at heart the real interests of the Church. One of them was his nephew, a Medici who at the time of his elevation had only entered his eighteenth year. It was during his reign that the sack of Rome occurred to which we have already referred. Yet around him, even in groups in Rome, although still minorities, the reform wave was rising. It was he who gave the needed Papal approval to the Theatines, and the Oratory of Divine Love had its headquarters in the city.

With the coming to the chair of Peter of Alessandro Farnese (as Paul III, Pope from 1534 to 1549), the Catholic Reformation may be said to have made significant strides towards capturing the Papacy. The early life of the later future Paul III gave no hint that here would be an active furtherer of reform. Of an ancient and noble lineage, Alessandro Farnese had been reared in the circle of the Medici and owed his cardinal's hat to Alexander VI who, before he became Pope, had had a liaison with his sister. He himself had sired illegitimate children. In common with many ecclesiastics of his age he accumulated benefices. A skilful diplomat, able, and prudent, he had succeeded in winning the favour of successive Pontiffs, but by instinct and experience he was more a secular prince than a priest and bishop. However, after he was ordained priest (1519) his private life seems to have been above reproach. As Pope, although he used the post to advance members of his family, including his grandsons, he turned his great abilities to the physical improvement and adornment of Rome and to the reform of the Church. He curbed some of the worst abuses connected with the sale of indulgences, ordered absentee bishops to go

e to bestow favours on members of his family. He was intensely unpopular
.h the Roman populace and on his death they rioted, mutilated his statue,
·ed the prisoners of the Inquisition, and destroyed its records.

Pius IV, the next to wear the tiara (1559–1565), continued the reform, re-
·onvened the Council of Trent, had it complete its work, and confirmed its
decrees. He had two Caraffa cardinals, nephews of his predecessor, accused
of high crimes, and caused one of them to be convicted and executed, thus
showing his power as against the Sacred College. He was a patron of the arts
and in his later months scandalized some of the reformers by his pleasures.

Pius V (1566–1572) was outstanding. The fact that he was the latest of the
Popes to be canonized (although in 1951 Pius X, reigned 1903–1914, was
beatified) and the first to be accorded that recognition since Gregory X, who
reigned in the latter half of the thirteenth century, is indication of the esteem
with which he was regarded. A Dominican, a teacher of theology and philosophy, an inquisitor, humble, keeping the rule of poverty, he was the candidate
of the reformers. He continued in the Vatican his ascetic way of life, made
the Papal court a model in morals, sought to enforce the observance of Sunday,
and discouraged profanity, animal baiting, and prostitution. He set his face
against nepotism, disciplined some members of his own family, refused to
show special favour to his order, and stiffened the Inquisition. Under him a
new catechism and a revised breviary and missal were issued. He laboured for
the improvement of the secular and regular clergy. Pius V was evidence that
the Catholic Reform was now in full charge of the Papacy. It was not again
really to lose control.

In his youth he had had an illegitimate child, but in his maturity he who
was to be Gregory XIII (1572–1585) had led a blameless life. Best remembered for the reform of the calendar accomplished during his pontificate, he
encouraged the Jesuits and sought to win back some of the ground lost to
Protestants. A gifted organizer, he enforced the decrees of the Council of
Trent and refused to confirm the nominations by secular princes to bishoprics
until he was convinced of the worthy character of the candidates. He struggled to curb the control of the Spanish monarchs over the Church in their
domains, not hesitating to challenge even the mighty Philip II.

Although he reigned for only five years, 1585–1590, Sixtus V, a Franciscan, a
former inquisitor-general in Venice, a noted preacher, ardent in his devotions,
proved to be one of the ablest of the Popes, carried through extensive building
enterprises in Rome, reorganized the Papal curia, and furthered the Catholic
Reformation in Germany, Poland, Switzerland, and the Netherlands. Yet in
his effort to put Papal finances on a sound basis he sold offices right and left
and increased the taxation in the Papal states.

to their sees and attend to their episcopal duties, a
formers to the cardinalate, among them Pole and C
Inquisition with headquarters in Rome, appointed a co.
lined a notable programme for reform, gave Papal approv.
Jesus, forbade the enslavement of the Indians in the New W
brought about the assembling of the Council of Trent, of w.
hear more in a moment.

It was during the reign of Paul III that Luther died. The ris.
Catholic reform was about to surge against the Protestant tide which.
evoked.

Julius III, Pope from 1550 to 1555, came to the post with an excellent rec
for he had been a member of the commission on reform appointed by Pau
III, had served as Papal representative at the Council of Trent, had apparently
been zealous for the improvement of the Church, and had conscientiously performed his part in religious ceremonies. In supreme authority he was a disappointment. Lacking in steadfastness and firmness, easily dispirited, coarse
in his jokes, a lover of pomp, worldly, popular in Rome because he encouraged
the amusements connected with the carnival, fond of the chase, gambling with
his intimates for large sums, enjoying jesters and unseemly theatrical perform-
ances, given to nepotism, elevating a quite unworthy seventeen-year-old
favourite to the cardinalate, he was a belated and unhappy relapse into the
pre-reform days. Yet the Catholic Reformation had gathered such momentum
that Julius III could not have stopped it even had he wished to do so. Indeed,
officially he took measures to further it. He commanded bishops to reside in
their sees, encouraged the reform commission, and at the time of his death
was preparing a bull to further comprehensive changes for the improvement
of the secular and regular clergy.

After the three weeks' reign of Marcellus III, the reform party won a complete victory and put in the Papacy one of its most zealous members, Caraffa,
a member of the Oratory of Divine Love and the first head of the Theatines.
Although nearly seventy-nine years of age when elected, his physical energy
was unabated and during the four years of his pontificate (as Paul IV, 1555–
1559) he gave vigorous leadership. Learned, incorruptible, deeply religious,
ascetic, uncompromising, forthright, often hasty of speech and temper, he had
ideals for the Papacy such as Hildebrand and Innocent III cherished and held
that as vicar of Christ he should have all princes at his feet. He carried through
reforms with a high hand, stiffened the Inquisition, had the index of forbidden
books revised, was implacable towards those suspected of heresy, and had one
of the most eminent of the cardinals, Morone, a zealous reformer, thrown into
prison and tried before the Inquisition. Yet he was guilty of using his high

In spite of the fact that he was given to nepotism, Clement VIII (1592–1605) promoted some excellent men to the cardinalate. He granted absolution to Henry IV of France, and so helped to end the wars of religion and to ensure the triumph of the Roman Catholic faith in that troubled land. He obtained the readmission of the Jesuits to France. Aspiring to restore Papal sovereignty over the rulers of Europe, he helped to make peace in the chronic feud between Spain and France. He saw to a revision of the breviary, missal, and pontifical and the completion of the revision of the Vulgate which had been begun under Sixtus V.

Paul V (1605–1621), a canon lawyer, cherished exalted conceptions of the prerogatives of his office, sternly sought to enforce what he believed to be the rights of the Church in several of the Italian states, opposed Gallicanism, the attempt to render the Church in France administratively independent of Rome, and encouraged missions. Like so many of his predecessors, he used his authority to further the interests of the members of his family.

Urban VIII (1623–1644), holding office as he did during more than half of the Thirty Years' War (1618–1648), wished to make the Papacy the arbiter in the international scenes, but without success.

And so we might continue through the list of the Popes of the seventeenth and eighteenth centuries. Some aided their relatives to acquire wealth, but for the most part they were virtuous in their private lives, several laboured at the perennial problem of improving the morals of the clergy, and not a few of them encouraged the missions which, as we are to see, were planting the Catholic faith among many peoples in both hemispheres.

None of the Popes of the sixteenth, seventeenth, and eighteenth centuries ranked with such predecessors as Leo the Great, Gregory the Great, Gregory VII, or Innocent III. They seem not to have had the ability of these men. Nor were the times propitious for the exercise of such gifts. After 1648 the Roman Catholic Church made very few counter advances against Protestantism. In that respect the Catholic Reformation had spent its force. The more powerful Catholic states insisted upon controlling the Church within their borders: the struggle between Church and state which had punctuated so much of the course of Christianity in Western Europe during the Middle Ages had been resolved in favour of the state. Now and again the Popes had an important part in negotiations between Catholic monarchs and they were chronically involved in Italian politics. Some contributed to victories against the Ottoman Turks. Yet none exerted as much power as had many of the pre-fourteenth century Pontiffs. The fact that the Church canonized only one after the thirteenth century is apparently an indication that none of the others attained to the spiritual and moral stature of their sainted predecessors of earlier ages.

THE COUNCIL OF TRENT FURTHERS REFORM AND
DEEPENS THE BREACH WITH PROTESTANTISM

Again and again in the troubled years when the Roman Catholic Church was palpably suffering from moral corruption and large segments of Europe were leaving it and becoming Protestant, the cry went up for a general council. In spite of the failure of the councils of the fifteenth century to effect substantial reform, many continued to look longingly towards that device as a means of curing the Church's ills. Charles V urged it and on several occasions the cardinals sought to exact from candidates for the Papacy the promise to convoke one. That was probably in part because of the tradition begun at Nicæa in 325 for seeking the common mind of the Church through a general or ecumenical council, and partly because the Popes had thus far not reformed even their immediate entourage, the Roman curia.

It was Paul III who at long last brought a general council together. It held its first session in Trent in December, 1545. In 1547 the Italian members obtained its transfer to Bologna, farther from the North. In May, 1551, it was once more at Trent. Less than a year later, in May, 1552, it adjourned, and did not again convene for nearly a decade, in January, 1562. It finally completed its work in December, 1563. The Roman Catholics count it as the nineteenth ecumenical council.

The council was called by the Pope and not, as had been that of Nicæa and several of its successors, by the Emperor. Powerful though he was and Holy Roman Emperor, Charles V did not presume to convene it. Moreover, the Popes dominated it. Many, including Charles V, had hoped that the council would heal the breach between the Lutherans and other Protestants on the one hand and the Church of Rome on the other. In this, however, they were to be disappointed.

In the council itself there were many elements and numbers of currents and cross currents. Some members, including eminent Spanish prelates, resented any effort by the Pope to control the gathering and stood for the independence of the bishops within the framework of the Catholic Church. The Spanish and northern bishops, especially the French, were particularly emphatic that while they were prepared to admit that the Bishop of Rome was *primus,* he was only *primus inter pares* and that, as Cyprian had long ago insisted, each bishop drew his authority directly from Christ through apostolic succession and not through Rome. Some, and in general this was the viewpoint of Charles V, wished the moral reform of the Church but feared discussions of debatable doctrinal issues as jeopardizing efforts to win the Protestants. They held that if the Church were morally what she should be, Protestants and those who differed from them might come together and discuss amicably the issues which divided them. Charles V and the German Roman Catholics wished permission to give the cup to the laity, the marriage of priests, the singing of vernacular hymns in public worship, the use of some of the ecclesiastical revenues for schools for the poor, and the reduction of the power of the Pope. Reginald Pole, one of the earlier delegates, was from a group of Catholic reformers of whom Gasparo Contarini (1483–1542) was the leader. A Venetian, and, like Pole, of distinguished aristocratic lineage, Contarini was inclined to find common ground with Protestants on the issue of justification by faith. Marcello Cervini represented reformers of whom Caraffa, the later Paul IV, was the outstanding spokesman. While zealous for moral cleansing, they distrusted Pole and Contarini as verging on heresy and stood for a stiff formulation of dogma which would make it emphatic that the Church of Rome could have no part or lot with Protestants. There were those who opposed any meddling with the existing state of affairs and were suspicious of those who in the name of moral reform would disturb the perquisites of the hierarchy and of members of the Papal curia. Some, perpetuating the conciliar ideal of the preceding century, were fearful of Papal interference with the work of the gathering. Others, notably the Jesuits, stood for the authority of the Pope.

Into the complicated details of the history of the Council we need not go. Much of the work was done in committees. The physical surroundings were uncomfortable and proved trying to elderly prelates accustomed to luxury. Because of the long life of the council, more protracted than any other in the series that claimed the title ecumenical, and the interruptions, one of them for many years, the personnel was far from continuous. Yet in its achievements the Council of Trent proved to be one of the most important and significant in the history of the Church. It gave definitive formulation to the principles of the Catholic Reformation, cut off all possibility of reconciliation with the Protestants, and reinforced the forward surge of the Roman Catholic Church, revived and in part cleansed, into territories lost to Protestantism and into lands opened to the faith by the explorations, conquests, and commerce of the fifteenth and sixteenth centuries.

In general it was the views represented by the Jesuits and the group centering around Caraffa which triumphed. Roman Catholic dogma was explicitly stated on the distinctive convictions of Protestantism and in such fashion as to make it clear that the latter were regarded as no longer debatable but were heresies. So far as legislation could accomplish it, thoroughgoing moral reform was enacted and concrete measures devised and enjoined for enforcing it. Moreover, the council in part rebuilt the hierarchical structure, making provision for the better training and support of the parish clergy, extending the powers of the bishops within their dioceses, untangling conflicting jurisdictions, and enhancing the authority of the Pope.

Among the decisions on dogma reached by the Council of Trent the following stand out. The council declared the Old Testament (which was made to include what Protestants call the Apocrypha), the New Testament, and the unwritten traditions believed to have been received by the apostles from the mouth of Christ and preserved in the Catholic Church to have been dictated by the Holy Spirit and to have God as their author. It held that of all the Latin editions of the Scriptures, the Old Vulgate was to be regarded as authentic. It ordered that no one should presume to interpret the Bible contrary to the sense authorized by the Church. It affirmed the transmission of Adam's sin to all his poserity, that this original sin is taken away only by the merit of one mediator, Jesus Christ, that this merit is applied both to adults and infants by the sacrament of baptism administered in the form used by the Church, and that infants are baptized for the remission of original sin. Although, so the council declared, Christ died for all, only those receive the benefit of his death to whom the merit of Christ's passion is communicated. Justification can be given only through the new birth which is wrought through baptism or the desire for it, for "unless a man be born again of water and the Spirit he cannot enter into the kingdom of God." Reaffirming the modified Augustinianism substantially as expressed by the Council of Orange in 529, the Council of Trent held that while by his grace God moves men to turn to Him and that one cannot of his own free will, without God's grace, take the initiative towards being just in God's sight, men are free to reject God's grace and are also free to coöperate with it. Thus, by implication, the council rejected irresistible grace. While stating that we are justified by faith and grace and not by works, the Council declared that it could not be asserted that anyone is justified by faith alone, since heretics and schismatics boast in "vain confidence" that they are thus justified, and "no one can know with certainty of faith, which cannot be subject of error, that he has obtained the grace of God." The council held that Christians can advance and be still further justified by observing the commandments of God and of the Church, "faith coöperating with good works," and that it is possible for one who is justified to keep the commandments of God.

Striking at Protestants, the council anathematized those who taught that since Adam's sin the free-will of man is extinguished, that all works done before justification are sins and merit the hatred of God, that justification is by faith alone, by confidence in the divine mercy which remits sins for Christ's sake, that justification is only attained by those who are predestined to life and that all others are predestined to evil, and that the just ought not for their good works done in God to expect an eternal reward from God. The council came out plumply for purgatory and for merits earned by good works.

Again with Protestants in mind, the council put itself on record for the seven sacraments, declared that they are necessary for salvation, and that through them grace is conferred by the act performed (*ex opere operato*). The council denounced the beliefs held by some Protestants about the sacraments, such as the power of all Christians to administer the word and all the sacraments, in other words, the priesthood of all believers, and the denial of the validity of infant baptism. The council reaffirmed transubstantiation, came out for the reservation of the sacrament, denied "consubstantiation," and held that the whole Christ is in both the bread and the wine, thus making it unnecessary to give the cup to the laity. It declared that only bishops and priests have the power to pronounce the forgiveness or the retention of sins. It came out emphatically for the invocation of the saints, for the veneration of the relics of the saints, for sacred images and paintings, and for indulgences.

To aid pastors in teaching the Catholic faith the council entrusted to a commission the preparation of a catechism. This, bearing the name of the council, was compiled and accorded Papal approval.

Measures for the reform of the Church and of the laity were numerous and were closely associated with those for an improved preparation of the clergy and a better ordered hierarchical structure. Duelling was forbidden on pain of excommunication. The celebration of the mass was closely regulated to ensure that it should be done with reverence. In it only such music was permitted as would contribute to dignity and true worship. The sale of indulgences was controlled and some of the worst abuses were eliminated. Magical properties popularly ascribed to images were disavowed. Earlier decrees against non-residence of bishops in their sees were renewed. Similarly, the absence from their charges of those having the care of souls (*cura animarum*), while not proscribed, was carefully restricted. The holding of several cathedral churches by any one incumbent was forbidden and the guilty were required to resign all but one of them. Those who, contrary to earlier canon law, enjoyed the incomes of several benefices were to be deprived of them. Provision was made for the repair of church buildings and the adequate supervision and management of hospitals. As to ordination, no one was to be promoted to the diaconate before his twenty-third year or to the priesthood before his twenty-fifth year. Much attention was paid to education in preparation for the priesthood. This was not new, but was now extended and provided for more adequately. Every cathedral and metropolitan church was to have near it a college or seminary for training boys for the clergy and specific measures were taken to ensure adequate financial support. All in holy orders were to be appointed to definite posts, so that the wandering, impoverished cleric might disappear. The ancient custom of provincial synods was reinforced, and it was directed that they be held at least every third year. Similarly, the traditional visitation, by travel, of his entire diocese by the bishop or those delegated by him to the task, was reaffirmed and was commanded to be made completely at least once in two years. Bishops and parish priests were to preach and were to explain the sacraments to their congregations in the vernacular. Private confession to priests was continued, but, unless commuted by the bishop, in the case of public sin the rebuke was to be public. Bishops were admonished to live frugally and not to use the property of the Church to enrich their relatives. The prohibition of clerical concubinage was renewed.

The authority of bishops within their dioceses was strengthened and some of the limitations which had gradually weakened it were annulled. None, whether regular or secular, could preach in a diocese without the bishop's license, a decree directed especially against the friars, who had wandered about, preaching as they wished, often without even nominal regard for episcopal jurisdiction. Similarly, within his diocese only the bishop had the right to confer ordinations. Candidates for benefices within the dioceses, even if presented by a Papal nuncio, were not to be admitted unless they were examined by the bishop and found worthy. To correct the trend which had made cathedral chapters largely independent of the bishops with what amounted to episcopal powers, the bishops were now clearly supreme.

The custom which had grown across the centuries of placing monasteries under the immediate protection of the Pope had made for a lamentable lack of discipline and was sharply curtailed. All monasteries were now either to be under the jurisdiction of the bishop or were to be organized into diocesan or provincial orders with their own visitors or general chapters. The heads of orders were commanded to visit their monasteries.

Thus the administrative machinery of the Roman Catholic Church was overhauled and tightened. Territorially, as of old, the area ruled by the Church was governed through dioceses. Now the effective power of each bishop within his diocese was augmented. The system of taxation and administration which had been developed in the Middle Ages by the reformers to enable the Popes to purify the Church and which, beginning with Avignon Popes, had become a source of corruption and scandal was curtailed. The demands of the bishops were so far met as to restore much of the authority that had been taken from them by the Papal curia.

Yet, in principle, and this also, at least in theory, made for administrative efficiency, the authority of the Papacy was stressed. The Pope was expressly declared to be the vicar upon earth of God and Jesus Christ, and all patriarchs, primates, archbishops, and bishops were to promise obedience to him. To the Pope the council left the confirmation of its decrees. In carrying out this mandate, the Pope made clear his position that the council had acted only with his permission, and reaffirmed his authority by commanding all prelates to observe the decrees, by admonishing the Emperor-elect and all Christian kings and princes to assist in their enforcement, and by reserving to his See all right of interpretation.

The Council of Trent marks an epoch in the history of the Roman Catholic Church. The centuries since it met are rightly called post-Tridentine. Through it, as far as any ecclesiastical assembly could bring that about, the Roman Catholic Church put its house in order and girded itself for combat with the Protestants and for the pursuance of its world mission. It so defined its dogmas that no room was left for such distinctive Protestant convictions as salvation by faith alone and the priesthood of all believers. It cleared the ground for dealing with the moral corruption of which its own sons as well as Protestants had complained. It made its structure more effective. In doing so it scrapped much of the machinery that had mushroomed from the measures of the reforming Popes of the Middle Ages. It so far yielded to the demands of the episcopate of Spain, France, and Germany that it revived and augmented the authority of the bishops in their dioceses. While, by a close vote, the council seemed to come out against the claim that each bishop rules directly by divine right and not by authority delegated by the Pope, the Pope did not press the point. Yet on paper the authority which the Popes had long claimed was recognized. While not expressly disavowed, the theory urged in the preceding century which would have subordinated the Popes to ecumenical councils was in practice repudiated. No recognition was given to the claims of secular princes, including the kings of Spain, Portugal, and France, to control the Church and its hierarchy within their domains.

The way was cleared to put the Roman Catholic Church in fighting trim. While still containing a majority of those who bore the Christian name, it embraced only a small minority of the peoples of the earth. As the centuries passed, it was even more tightly integrated under the Pope. It continued to be a minority, but a minority whose leaders were intent upon the spiritual conquest of mankind. However, it had become more emphatically the Roman Catholic Church and its heart-land was more clearly Latin Europe, that region which had been assimilated to imperial Rome.

THE FURTHER PROGRESS OF THE CATHOLIC REFORMATION

The reforming decrees of the Council of Trent were not permitted to become empty words. The leaders of the Catholic Reformation who were responsible for them regarded them as mandatory. Given direction and added momentum by them, to no small degree the Catholic Reformation put them into effect and swept on into lands which thus far had been but little affected by it. Many of the old evils were chronic, as they had been for centuries, and were never completely eliminated. Successive Popes found it necessary to inveigh against them. Moreover, Papal administrative control of the Church was largely blocked by the crown and national particularism in Spain, Portugal, France, and their colonial possessions, as well as in some lesser states. Philip II published the decrees, but with the reservation that he was doing so "without prejudice to his royal rights". There were long delays in gaining acceptance of them in France, and in Germany only the Catholic princes acceded to them. In the course of the seventeenth century the reforming impulse began to wane in Spain and Portugal. Yet, viewing Europe as a whole, the Catholic Reformation continued, made itself felt in new territories, and in some countries, notably France, did not reach its peak until late in the seventeenth and early in the eighteenth century. While in the eighteenth century the Roman Catholic Church was faced by a mounting series of new threats, never again did it suffer so severely as it had before the sixteenth century from the kind of corruption against which the Catholic Reformation had been a reaction.

Some of the ways in which the decrees of the Council of Trent were carried out we have already noted. The index of books prohibited to Catholics was modified. A catechism was compiled, partly on the model of the one drawn up by Peter Canisius, and was translated into several vernaculars. The missal and breviary were reworked. The latter was given a drastic revision. Many of the lives of the saints formerly in it were excised and more readings from the Scriptures were added. A corrected edition of the Vulgate was prepared and published. All these had Papal authority. Worship in the churches was improved. Substantial progress was achieved in the education of the secular clergy. Notable was the founding in Rome of colleges for the training of priests from a number of countries and special groups. The last quarter of the sixteenth century saw the inauguration in that city of a German college, a Hungarian college, an English college, and a Greek college. There were also a college for the Armenians, one for the Maronites, and one for converts from Judaism and Islam. All these were largely under the direction of the Jesuits. For them a central teaching institution, the Roman College, later the Gregorian University, was founded, and in it Bellarmine and other distinguished Jesuits lectured.

FURTHER VITALITY IN ITALY

In Italy the Roman Catholic Church continued to give evidence of vigour in the emergence of additional religious orders. In 1732 Alphonsus Maria Liguori founded the Redemptorists (officially the Congregation of the Most Holy Redeemer). This was at Amalfi. The purpose was "to preach the word of God to the poor." The order conducted missions and retreats and eventually had a wide spread. In 1720 Paul Francis Danei, better known as Paul of the Cross (1694–1775), a native of the Genoese Republic, drew the rule for the Passionists, an order which received Papal approval in 1741. It was especially devoted to the passion of Christ, and combined the contemplative life of the Carthusians with the active missionary life of the Jesuits.

The Catholic Reformation in Germany, Switzerland, Poland, and Hungary

As we have suggested, the Catholic Reformation was given a marked impulse in Germany by one of the early Jesuits, Peter Canisius. His work was reinforced and continued by other members of his Society. They established colleges and residences in several centres. Clergy trained by them in Germany and Rome spread through the Empire, bringing improvement in morals and enhancing zeal. In 1564 Duke Albert V of Bavaria (1550–1579) and several prelates decided to observe the decrees of the Council of Trent. Fresh schools were begun and entrusted to Jesuits and youths were forbidden to attend Protestant universities. Although from a Protestant family, Balthazar von Dernbach, the prince-abbot of the territory which included the ancient foundation of Fulda, associated with the name of the great English missionary to the Germans, Boniface, aided by Jesuits and those trained by him and in spite of opposition which fought him for three decades, largely purged his domains of Protestantism and enforced discipline in the various monastic houses. Assisted by the Abbot of Fulda, and encouraged by the Trentine decrees, numbers of the Benedictine abbeys in Germany came together in a union for the better observance of discipline. A similar movement centered around the Benedictine abbey of Melk or Melek in the diocese of Passau. In Austria Peter Canisius was a pioneer in reinvigourating the Roman Catholic Church and combatting Protestantism. The movement was aided by the Hapsburg Emperors, Ferdinand I, Maximilian II, and Rudolf II.

In Switzerland the Jesuits and Capuchins headed the Catholic Reformation and held large sections to the Roman Catholic Church. On the Italian side of the Alps Borromeo, while Archbishop of Milan, made extensive and arduous journeys into the mountain valleys, combatted Protestantism, and improved the quality of Catholic life.

In Poland, Stanislas Hosius, who had studied in Italy with the future Gregory XIII and in 1549 became Bishop of Chelmno, was a pioneer in the Catholic Reformation. The king, Sigismund II, promptly enforced the Trentine decrees. They were confirmed by a synod in 1574. The Jesuits were in the fore front of the Catholic revival. Peter Canisius was there for a time in 1558. The first Polish Jesuit college was founded in 1565 and this was followed rapidly by the inauguration of others. The rising tide of Protestantism which had threatened to overwhelm the land was swept back and Poland became one of the bulwarks of the Roman Catholic Church.

For a time it had seemed that Hungary might go over to Protestantism. In part because of the Jesuits, Protestants were reduced to minorities and the Roman Catholic Church was purified and strengthened.

THE CATHOLIC REFORMATION IN FRANCE

The Catholic revival was slower to gain substantial headway in France than in Spain or Italy. As we have seen, early in the sixteenth century there were stirrings of reform, some of them in high ecclesiastical and aristocratic circles and in the University of Paris. Moreover, it was at the University of Paris that the nucleus of the Society of Jesus came into being, although not through Frenchmen. However, what are usually known as the wars of religion racked the land. They did not end until the 1590's. While the kingdom was in such turmoil, Catholic Reform was retarded.

Yet in France the Catholic Reformation had a luxuriant even if somewhat belated fruitage. It began in the sixteenth century and came to a climax in France's heyday as the dominant power in Western Europe, during the reign of the *Grand Monarque*, Louis XIV (1643–1715). As in Spain, the peak of vigour in the Church roughly paralleled that in literature, art, and prominence in the international scene.

The Society of Jesus spread rapidly. About 1550 Jesuits among the students in the University of Paris were gathered into the Paris residence of the Bishops of Clermont and there began what was known as the Collège de Clermont, which soon developed into a school. They met bitter opposition from the faculty of theology of the university, the Sorbonne, for the latter were champions of Gallicanism and the conciliar tradition and were critical of the support given by the Jesuits to Papal authority. The Sorbonne also deemed the immaculate conception of the Virgin Mary to be a matter of faith, a dogma to which the Jesuits were not yet prepared to agree. Moreover, the Sorbonne denounced the teaching of a leading Jesuit that the pains of purgatory might not be of more than ten years' duration. In spite of opposition, before the end of the seventeenth century numbers of Jesuit colleges had been established in France, a Jesuit university had been begun, and Jesuit preachers were attracting large congregations. The attempted assassination (1594) of Henry IV by a former student in the Collège de Clermont precipitated an anti-Jesuit storm and led to the expulsion of the Society from Paris and several other cities. Yet in 1603 they were restored by an edict of Henry IV, and a Jesuit became the confessor of that king and tutor of his successor, Louis XIII. Between 1606 and 1640 forty-seven new Jesuit colleges were begun in France.

The Catholic Reformation was early stimulated by other new monastic movements, some of them from abroad and some of them indigenous. In the 1570's Italian Capuchins came, established houses, and quickly gained popularity and recruits. Early among the latter was one of the highly placed men of the court. Before 1600 the Cistercians were brought back to their primitive rule and the Benedictines complied with the decree of the Council of Trent which called for the grouping of their houses in assemblies that could help enforce discipline. Not far from 1593 the Congregation of Christian Doctrine was founded at Avignon. It was composed of secular priests who were to give themselves to teaching the catechism to the rank and file of Catholics, thus raising the level of intelligent Christian living. One branch of the new movement eventually became an order of regulars and another modelled itself on the Roman Oratory of Pierre de Bérulle.

Pierre de Bérulle (1575–1629), in later life a cardinal, was the pioneer of what was known as the French School of mysticism. Reacting against the current humanism with its optimism about man and strongly influenced by Augustine, he stressed the sovereignty of God, the depravity of fallen human nature, the complete dependence of man on God, and the wonder of the incarnation. Indeed, when he was only seventeen years of age, while assisting at Christmas matins and mass, he had a vision which brought him vivid insight into the significance of the birth of Christ. This was repeated after his ordination as priest, when he was making a retreat with the Jesuits. A diligent student of Paul's epistles and *The Gospel according to John,* he sought to subject himself fully to the Word made flesh and to the Virgin Mary, "the Mother of God."

Following Bérulle, the French School stressed devotion to the Word made flesh, the Augustinian conception of grace, dedication to Jesus Christ both in his humanity and in his divinity, and to the Virgin Mary. To have no other being or life but in Jesus, the French School said, the Christian must be rid of all that is of himself and of the fallen Adam within him.

A warm admirer of Augustine and Thomas Aquinas, Bérulle found especial spiritual kinship with his older contemporaries, Teresa of Avila and Philip Neri, and introduced to France both the Discalced Carmelites and the Oratory. He was also active in political affairs.

Bérulle had a widespread and expanding influence. Many Jesuits were partly shaped by him. Even more striking was his contribution through his disciple, the second Superior of the French Oratory, Charles de Condren (1588–1641).

Attracted at an early age to the priesthood, Condren studied at the Sorbonne and in 1614 was ordained priest. He wrote little or nothing, abstaining, so he said, "from the love of Jesus Christ," but gave himself to the mission of "illuminating souls." He stressed the necessity of annihilating within us our evil inclinations and even ourselves that we may acknowledge our nothingness before God. One outcome of his teaching and that of Bérulle was devotion to the Child Jesus and to the Sacred Heart of Jesus, a devotion which was to have a growing popular clientele.

One of Condren's followers and a member of the Oratory was Jean-Jacques Olier (1608–1657). In his student days Olier had shared in the dissipations in Paris common to that class. However, he was converted and was ordained priest (1633). He taught that the Christian should unite himself to Jesus by clinging to him. Olier also learned much from Francis de Sales and Vincent de Paul, of whom we are to hear more in a moment.

Intimately associated with the French Oratory were efforts to provide better training for the priesthood: obviously, it would be through priests, especially the seculars who served in the parishes, that the rank and file of the population would be reached by the awakening. These efforts were reinforced by the Council of Trent, for that body, as we have seen, stressed the foundation of seminaries. The French Oratory founded numbers of colleges in which philosophy and theology were taught and which were to rival the schools of the Jesuits. Olier was one of a group of Oratorians who began a seminary near Paris. He himself founded a seminary in the parish of St. Sulpice in Paris of which he was the priest, and laboured for the conversion of one of the worst quarters of that city. He inaugurated seminaries in the provinces and to serve them created the Society of St. Sulpice.

Even more famous than Olier was Vincent de Paul (1576 or 1580–1660). He not only founded seminaries but was also the initiator of other enterprises, including the Congregation of the Priests of the Mission. Unlike most of the leaders of the Catholic Reformation, for generally they were of aristocratic stock, Vincent de Paul was the son of peasants. Spiritually he was deeply indebted to Bérulle and Condren and must be counted among their disciples. Ordained in 1600, five years later he was captured by Turkish pirates and sold as a slave. However, he converted his master, an apostate from the Christian faith, and in 1607 escaped with him. Ever after he had a compassionate heart for galley slaves and for Christians who, captured by Barbary corsairs, were in servitude in North Africa. He did what he could to relieve the physical and spiritual sufferings of the former and to ransom the latter.

Deeply concerned for the spiritual nurture of the Catholic masses and the conversion of Protestants, Vincent de Paul founded (1625) the Congregation of Priests of the Mission. It was an association of seculars, but eventually took on some of the aspects of an order. Beginning in a small way with the approval of the Archbishop of Paris (1626), within the more than thirty years that Vincent de Paul led it, it grew to large dimensions. Before long its headquarters were established at the house of St. Lazare on the outskirts of Paris, and its members were, accordingly, often called Lazarists. Commonly, too, they were alternately known as Vincentians. Not only did the Lazarists carry on missions among the masses. They also conducted retreats for candidates for holy orders and conferences for clergymen, better to equip them for the cure of souls. From this arose seminaries for the preparation of priests, and when in 1789 the storm of the Revolution broke over France, about a third of the seminaries in the kingdom were conducted by the spiritual sons of Vincent de Paul. Within the lifetime of their founder, Lazarists were going as missionaries to other lands.

Not content with these wide-ranging and arduous labours, Vincent de Paul founded (1633) the Sisters (or Daughters) of Charity, also known as Servants of the Sick. As the latter designation indicates, they dedicated themselves to nursing. He called into being the Ladies of Charity, recruited from the nobility, for the care of the ill. He founded in Paris a home for the aged and a general hospital. He organized relief for sufferers from the Thirty Years' War (1618–1648) and from the civil war known as the Fronde (1648–1652). He stimulated reform movements in several of the older religious orders of France. He also mingled in international politics.

Like many other mystics, of abounding energy and superb organizing and administrative gifts, Vincent de Paul was inspired and sustained in his colossal labours by the love of God, devotion to Christ, and unhurried meditation and prayer. His great passion was the "illumination of souls."

Vincent de Paul was indebted not only to Bérulle and Condren but also to his older contemporary, Francis de Sales (1567–1622). Of the aristocracy of Savoy, Francis de Sales had the title of Bishop of Geneva. By the time he was given the post, Geneva was in the hands of the Reformed, for he was also contemporary with Beza, Calvin's successor in that city. Although he visited Geneva and attempted to win Beza to the Roman Catholic Church, Francis de Sales had to make his headquarters elsewhere. Within such of his diocese as was accessible to him, he inspired priests and laboured personally to raise the level of Christian living and to convert Protestants. He founded the Institute of the Visitation, made up of women. However, he is best remembered for his discourses and writings on the life of the spirit. Here he blazed a trail which was distinctly his own. He stressed the love of God and loving fidelity to His will. Issuing from a heart overflowing with the love of God and men, his writings have nurtured both Catholics and Protestants. He has been classed among the devout humanists.

Of the Berullian school of mysticism and devotion and for a time a member of the Oratory was John Eudes (1601–1680). At fourteen he took the vow of chastity. In his youth he was distressed by the indifference of the clergy, the neglect of church structures, and the slovenliness of church services. In 1623, in his early twenties, he joined the Oratory, and hoped to improve conditions by founding seminaries and so furthering the training of a better corps of clergy. An eloquent preacher, he held missions for the masses, sometimes out of doors, conducted religious services with pomp and dignity, organized leagues to fight blasphemy and duelling, and presided at the burning of immoral books and pictures. He was the creator of the Congregation of the Good Shepherd for the care of fallen women. When its superior general refused to permit him to found seminaries, he left the Oratory and (1643) initiated what were popularly known as the Eudists. The Eudists were made up of secular priests, postulants, and lay brothers, who did not take the stringent vows of most religious orders, but were organized into a society under the joint names of Jesus and Mary. They began and conducted seminaries for the preparation for the priesthood and, like the founder, conducted missions. True to the tradition of Bérulle and Condren, to whom he owed much, John Eudes furthered the mystical life by interior devotion to Jesus and Mary. He is credited with having inaugurated the liturgical worship of the Sacred Hearts of Jesus and Mary which was to spread widely in succeeding generations.

The devotion to the Sacred Heart of Jesus was especially connected with the name of Margaret Mary Alacoque (1647–1690). To her came what she profoundly believed to be visions of Christ, especially in 1675, in which he allowed her to rest her head on his heart and commanded her to propagate that devotion, a recognition of his incarnate love by gratitude, penitence, and frequent communion.

In 1713 Louis-Marie Grignion de Montfort founded the Missionaries of the Company of Mary. Recruited from secular priests, they promoted the recital of the rosary and held missions and retreats under the protection of the Virgin Mary.

The list of those who were at once the products and the stimulators and shapers of the Catholic Reformation in France could be greatly lengthened. It would include a number of Benedictine abbesses who revived the religious life for women. High on it would be the name of John Baptist de la Salle (1651–1719) who, impressed with the paucity of schools and the need of teachers, resigned his comfortable post as canon in the Cathedral of Rheims, begged funds to found schools, opened (1684) a normal school, developed an educational method which earned him the title of "father of modern pedagogy," a designation, incidentally, which could be accorded to several men who were inspired by either the Protestant or the Catholic Reformation, and founded the Institute of the Brothers of the Christian Schools. On the list would also go the name of the nobleman Francis le Clerc du Tremblay (1577–1638), known by his name in religion as Father Joseph. A brilliant scholar, in his early twenties he joined the Capuchins, thus committing himself to humility, asceticism, and the life of the spirit. He shared in the reform of the Benedictines, assisted the Bernardines, a reformed branch of the Cistercians, established numerous houses of the Capuchins, was a zealous spiritual director, and wrote an *Introduction to the Spiritual Life by an Easy Method of Prayer* which was an adaptation of Loyola's *Spiritual Exercises*. He is also remembered for his activity in politics. He helped to put an end to a civil war in 1616 and laboured long though without success to unite Western Europe in a crusade against the Turks. As a trusted counsellor of Richelieu (1585–1642), who was dominant in the state during much of the reign of Louis XIII, he strengthened the chief minister's resolution to curb the Huguenots and persevere in the Thirty Years' War.

A development from the Catholic Reformation in France which was to culminate in bitter controversy and schism was associated with the name of Cornelius Jansen (1585–1638), Bishop of Ypres. As a student Jansen had been in the University of Louvain, where a dispute was raging between the Jesuits and those who held to a strict Augustinianism. Through life he continued to be at verbal sword's points with the sons of Loyola. Eventually he was professor of theology at Louvain, where the Society of Jesus had a rival theological faculty. Towards the end of his life he produced a book, *Augustinus,* intended to be a digest of Augustine's teaching and setting forth his own views. It was only two years before his death that he was made Bishop of Ypres.

In important respects Jansen seemed to be a Calvinist, for he stressed the divine predestination of those who were to be saved, but he insisted that he was no Protestant. He was against a moralism more akin to Stoicism than Christianity which he believed that he saw about him. He emphasized personal religious experience, the direct relation of the individual soul to its Maker which might come by a sudden conversion. Yet he rejected justification by faith as the Protestants understood it and held that the full Christian life was possible only through the Roman Catholic Church.

Jansen's views won an extensive following. One of his disciples, Antoine Arnauld, wrote a book on *Frequent Communion* which evoked a storm of criticism. Another leader of the school, Pasquier Quesnel, wrote *Réflexions morales sur le Nouveau Testament,* which had a wide circulation as an aid to devotion but which was also denounced. A convent at Port Royal became a Jansenist centre. Notable among the Jansenists was Blaise Pascal (1623–1662), a mathematical genius who had a sudden conversion through contact with them and especially through a sister who became a member of the Port Royal community. In his *Provincial Letters* Pascal came out with a brilliant defense of Arnauld against the Jesuits.

Eventually Jansen was condemned by the Roman Catholic Church. In 1653 Pope Innocent X declared heretical several propositions from the *Augustinus*. In 1661 the general assembly of the clergy endorsed an anti-Jansenist formula which all the clergy were required to sign. Four years later a similar formula was issued by the Pope. Under it four bishops were tried, but since several other bishops rallied to their support a compromise was reached under which Jansenism continued. Under pressure from the Jesuits Louis XIV asked the Pope to leave no doubt about the status of Jansenism. In 1713 the Pope responded in the bull *Unigenitus,* which ruled out Jansenist teachings. The quarrel continued, for many regarded Papal intervention as a violation of the liberty of the Church in France. Even the Cardinal Archbishop of Paris protested and appealed to a general council. Some of the Jansenists found refuge in the Netherlands where many Roman Catholics had long been in sympathy with their views. There, early in the eighteenth century, partly because of Jansenist convictions and partly out of antagonism to the Jesuits, several thousand of the laity and clergy broke with Rome and formed what is known as an Old Catholic Church with its Archbishop of Utrecht as its ranking ecclesiastic.

Famous also was a controversy arising from the mysticism of a remarkable woman and an equally remarkable man. Madame Guyon (1648–1717), a highly neurotic woman of great energy and charm, had an unhappy married life from which she was released by her husband's death before she was thirty. Partly under a Barnabite spiritual director she developed a type of mysticism which attracted many, among them the high-born Fénelon (1651–1715), Archbishop of Cambrai and tutor to the heir apparent. Fénelon modified Madame Guyon's ideas after his own pattern. In it Neoplatonism mingled with the Christian faith. He became a spiritual counsellor to many. The famous preacher, Bossuet (1627–1704), one of whose main dreams, incidentally, was the conversion of Protestants, vigorously criticized both Madame Guyon and Fénelon. The former was imprisoned and then was released on the condition that she would henceforth live on her son's estate under careful episcopal supervision. Bossuet declared dangerous some features of Fénelon's writings. Fénelon appealed to Rome. Feeling ran high in France, for both Bossuet and Fénelon had their ardent partisans. Louis XIV urged the Pope to act. The result was the Papal condemnation of several of Fénelon's views. Fénelon at once submitted, was exiled by the king to his diocese, and there lived until his death, faithfully performing his episcopal duties.

SUMMARY AND PROSPECT

Through the great reformation which swept across it in the two and a half centuries between the latter part of the fifteenth century and the second quarter of the eighteenth century, the Roman Catholic Church was reinvigorated and was cleansed of some of the worst of the evils which had threatened its existence. Moral abuses remained to challenge the zeal of earnest spirits and in many places much of formalism and lassitude persisted. By the end of the seventeenth century the fresh burst of energy began to show signs of having passed its peak. Yet the sixteenth and seventeenth centuries were ones of extraordinary vitality. Out of it came the prodigious geographic expansion of which we are to hear more in a later chapter.

What would happen as this revived and expanding Roman Catholic Church met an aggressive and expanding Protestantism? We have already seen that, largely through the Society of Jesus, the Roman Catholic Church won the victory in some lands which were wavering, but where Protestants were still in the minority. This was especially true in Bavaria, some other sections of Germany, and Poland. In the first half of the seventeenth century the struggle between the Roman Catholic Church and Protestantism contributed to one of the most exhausting armed conflicts in the history of Europe. Waged intermittently between 1618 and 1648, it is known as the Thirty Years' War. Through it the Roman Catholic Church achieved some gains, but after it the territorial boundaries in Europe between that church and Protestantism remained substantially unchanged. The western part of the continent was permanently divided between these two wings of the Christianity of the Occident.

It is a strange and tragic fact that the greatest revival which had thus far been experienced in the religion which has at its very heart the kind of sacrificial and self-giving love seen in the humility of the incarnation and the non-resistant suffering on the cross and whose primary commands are love for God and neighbour, was a major factor in bringing on an exhausting war and intensified the resolution, the bitterness, and the hatred with which the war was waged. Here is high-lighted one of the paradoxes with which the course of Christianity has been marked. Men fired with what they believe to be devotion to the will of God as seen in Christ have been nerved to prolonged and mortal combat, not only with non-Christians, but also with one another. In the Thirty Years' War other factors, of palpably un-Christian and even anti-Christian origin, were mixed and became more prominent as the struggle dragged out its weary length to an only partially decisive conclusion.

Yet out of the tragedy of these years there emerged, largely from regions which had been most badly laid waste and from minorities of passive sufferers, movements which were to prepare the way for even greater awakenings than the Reformation and which were to issue in enterprises world-wide in ambition and eventually in extent for the alleviation or elimination of many of the chronic ills of mankind.

To that story we now turn. Only the Thirty Years' War and its early aftermath to about the year 1750 will be covered in the succeeding chapter. To the far outreach in the two centuries which followed that year reference will be made from time to time in later stages of our narrative.

SELECTED BIBLIOGRAPHY

THE ROMAN CATHOLIC REFORMATION IN GENERAL

P. Janelle, *The Catholic Reformation* (Milwaukee, The Bruce Publishing Co., 1941, pp. xiv, 397). An excellent comprehensive account from a Roman Catholic viewpoint, slanted favourably towards the Jesuits.

IGNATIUS LOYOLA AND THE SOCIETY OF JESUS

P. Dudon, *St. Ignatius of Loyola,* translated by W. J. Young (Milwaukee, The Bruce Publishing Co., 1949, pp. xiv, 484). By a Jesuit, based upon extensive and prolonged research.

M. P. Harney, *The Jesuits in History. The Society of Jesus through Four Centuries* (New York, The America Press, 1941, pp. xvi, 513). A useful, but somewhat uncritical review by a Jesuit.

H. D. Sedgwick, *Ignatius Loyola* (New York, The Macmillan Co., 1923, pp. xiii, 399). Well written, based on extensive research, sympathetically objective, by a non-Roman Catholic.

THE SPANISH MYSTICS

Saint John of the Cross, Doctor of the Church. The Complete Works, translated and edited by E. A. Peers from the critical edition of P. Silverio de Santa Teresa (London, Burns, Oates & Washbourne, 3 vols., 1947).

E. A. Peers, *Spanish Mysticism, a Preliminary Survey* (London, Methuen & Co., 1924, pp. xi, 277). By the outstanding English specialist: contains extensive excerpts from the works of the mystics.

E. A. Peers, *Studies of the Spanish Mystics* (London, The Sheldon Press, 2 vols., 1927, 1930). The best survey in English.

The Complete Works of Saint Teresa of Jesus, translated from the critical edition of P. Silverio de Santa Teresa and edited by E. A. Peers (New York, Sheed & Ward, 3 vols., 1946).

THE ROMAN CATHOLIC REFORMATION IN ITALY

C. Orsenigo, *Life of St. Charles Borromeo,* translated by R. Kraw (St. Louis, B. Herder & Co., 1943, pp. lx, 390). A semi-popular, laudatory biography.

L. Pastor, *The History of the Popes from the Close of the Middle Ages,* Vols. VI–XXXV (St. Louis, B. Herder & Co., 1902, and London, Kegan Paul, Trench, Trübner & Co., 1902–1949). These volumes, by an eminent Roman Catholic scholar, cover the years embraced in this chapter.

THE COUNCIL OF TRENT

H. J. Schroeder, *Canons and Decrees of the Council of Trent: Original Text with English Translation* (St. Louis, B. Herder & Co., 1941, pp. xxxiii, 608). A useful reference volume.

THE ROMAN CATHOLIC REFORMATION IN GERMANY

J. Brodrick, *Saint Peter Canisius, S.J., 1521–1597* (London, Sheed & Ward, 1939, pp. xiii, 859). Sympathetically written by a Jesuit.

THE ROMAN CATHOLIC REFORMATION IN FRANCE

H. Bremond, *A Literary History of Religious Thought in France,* translated by K. L. Montgomery (London, Society for Promoting Christian Knowledge, 3 vols., 1928–1936). Confined almost entirely to the seventeenth century, based on extensive research and with copious quotations from the sources.

P. Pourrat, *Christian Spirituality. Later Developments. Part I. From the Renaissance to Jansenism,* translated by W. H. Mitchell (Vol. III of the larger work. New York, P. J. Kenedy and Sons, 1927, pp. xii, 405). A standard work by a Roman Catholic; well documented.

L. Rea, *The Enthusiasts of Port-Royal* (New York, Charles Scribner's Sons, 1912, pp. xiv, 354). Sympathetic, scholarly.

E. K. Sanders, *S. François de Sales 1567–1622* (New York, The Macmillan Co., 1928, pp. x, 304). A sympathetic biographical account, based on the sources.

W. J. Sparrow Simpson, *A Study of Bossuet* (London, Society for Promoting Christian Knowledge, 1937, pp. viii, 222). Thoughtful and vigorous.

Chapter **XXXIX**

THE CONFUSED ARBITRAMENT OF ARMS
AND THE AFTERMATH

The Roman Catholic Church, reformed and resurgent, pressed forward to reclaim the territories which it had lost to Protestantism. One result was the Thirty Years' War. In this confused and titanic struggle, as we have just now suggested, the religious conflict was only one factor. Rivalries between ambitious monarchs, generals, and adventurers, reinforced by burgeoning national loyalties, entered and may have been more important. Had the religious element not been present, they alone might have produced the war. Yet the contest between Roman Catholics and Protestants was prominent. In general the Roman Catholics won. They regained some ground which was either about to turn Protestant or already had become such. However, they did not succeed in erasing Protestantism. Unlike the movements of the Middle Ages which the Roman Catholic Church branded as heretical, Protestant Christianity persisted. Indeed, from areas and groups which suffered most from the war and the Roman Catholic advance, tides of life issued which in the eighteenth, nineteenth, and twentieth centuries were to be of major importance in the world-wide extension of Protestantism.

THE SETTING OF THE THIRTY YEARS' WAR

As we saw in the previous chapter, Luther had been dead only about twenty years and Calvin's body was scarcely cold in its grave when the Roman Catholics began to rewin much of the debatable ground which they had lost in Germany and its dependent regions. In Bavaria, in the territories ruled by the Abbot of Fulda, the Archbishop of Mainz, and the Archbishop of Trier, the Catholic princes were eliminating the Protestants. The principle of *cujus regio, ejus religio* embodied in the Peace of Augsburg (1555) gave legality to their measures, for by it each prince was to determine the faith of his subjects. An aggressive Roman Catholic regime was also bringing distress to Protestants in

Austria. The princes were aided by the Jesuits and the progress of the Catholic Reformation in renewing the vigour of the old church. In the territory under the Archbishop of Cologne, in 1582 the incumbent, Gebhard von Truchsess, adopted the Reformed faith, wished to marry, and proposed to continue to rule and to take his subjects with him. One of the seven electors of the Holy Roman Empire, he was an important personage. Had he succeeded, the Roman Catholic cause would have been given a serious blow. However, he was acting in defiance of the Peace of Augsburg, he was placed under the ban of the Empire, a rebellion broke out in his domains, aid came to it from Bavaria, most of the Protestant princes stood idly by, partly because they were Lutheran and he was Reformed, and he was defeated and driven from his see. In 1608, at the imperial Diet Catholics demanded that the terms of the Peace of Augsburg be strictly observed and that ecclesiastical properties which had become Protestant after 1552 be restored to the old faith. Enforcement would mean heavy losses to Protestantism. In 1607 Maximilian, Duke of Bavaria, was given an imperial mandate to deal with the free city, Donauwörth. Overwhelmingly Protestant, it contained Catholic monasteries and smouldering antagonism had broken into flames when in 1606 a Catholic religious procession had been stoned. Maximilian kept Donauwörth under his rule and, in violation of the Peace of Augsburg, suppressed Protestant worship.

The Roman Catholic gains had been chiefly in South Germany and in the Rhine Valley. Here, in contrast with the nearly solidly Lutheran North, the Reformed Churches were strong. The Peace of Augsburg had given no recognition to the latter, but only to Roman Catholics and Lutherans. The division between Reformed and Lutherans weakened the Protestant forces.

The Donauwörth episode helped to draw together several of the Protestant princes. In 1608, headed by the Elector Palatine, Frederick IV, who was of the Reformed wing, they organized themselves into the Evangelical Union. Roman Catholics, led by Maximilian, aligned themselves in what was eventually known as the Catholic League.

The situation was complicated by economic distress, by heightened sensitiveness among both Catholics and Protestants which vented itself on supposed witches, and by the intrigues of the French rulers, who were quite willing to take advantage of the divisions among the German princes to extend their borders into what was still the Holy Roman Empire.

The Outbreak and Course of the Thirty Years' War

Hostility broke out into open war in Bohemia in 1618. There Protestantism was strong and was resentful of the rule of the Catholic Hapsburgs. In May, 1618, a group of Protestant nobles flung two Hapsburg regents from a high window in Prague and began open rebellion. In 1619, after the death of his cousin, Ferdinand, Archduke of Styria, became head of the Hapsburgs, Holy Roman Emperor-elect, and King of Bohemia. He had been educated by the Jesuits, was an ardent Roman Catholic, and on dynastic and religious grounds was determined to make himself master of Bohemia and eliminate Protestantism. The revolting Bohemians chose as their king the Elector Palatine, Frederick V, son of Frederick IV and of the daughter of William of Orange, "the Silent," son-in-law of James I of England, and an adherent of the Reformed faith. The Lutheran princes were not minded to come to the support of the Reformed Elector Palatine. James I wished not to become embroiled and did not go further than permit English "volunteers" to participate. Ferdinand was aided by Maximilian of Bavaria and Spanish troops under the Walloon General, Tilly. The hapless Frederick was driven from Bohemia, Protestant properties were confiscated, and the vigorous and ruthless eradication of Protestantism was begun. Spanish troops overran Frederick's hereditary possession, the Palatinate, the title of elector and much of the territory were given to the staunchly Catholic Maximilian, and Catholicism was restored and enforced. Concurrently, the eradication of Protestantism was proceeding in Austria. One stage of the war was ended (late in 1622 and early in 1623) and the Roman Catholic cause was in the ascendant.

The next stage of the conflict involved North-west Germany and Denmark. In North-west Germany, in violation of a provision of the Peace of Augsburg to which many Protestant princes had declined to assent, much ecclesiastical property had become Protestant, including several bishoprics and many monasteries. Some of the Protestant princes drew together in defense against anticipated attack. The year 1623 saw the defeat of a leading Protestant prince by Tilly. In 1625 King Christian IV of Denmark and Norway entered the fray. This was after prolonged and complicated diplomatic negotiations in which, among others, England and France were involved. The Emperor Ferdinand called to his aid a remarkable adventurer, Wallenstein. Born a Protestant, Wallenstein had nominally become a Catholic and had profited by the acquisition of confiscated Protestant estates in Bohemia. Utterly upscrupulous, he had no deep religious convictions. In 1626 Christian IV was defeated by Tilly and in the following two years, partly through Wallenstein, Catholic forces overran much of Protestant North Germany.

Now, in March, 1629, the triumphant Catholics, insisting upon the enforcement of the Peace of Augsburg, obtained an imperial "Edict of Restitution" which ordered that all ecclesiastical property which had been alienated by Protestants since 1552 once more become Catholic. This led to the return to Catholics of several bishoprics, scores of monasteries, and hundreds of parish churches. The Edict of Restitution also approved of the exclusion of Protestants from the territories of Catholic rulers and gave no countenance to Protestants who did not adhere to the Augsburg Confession. Thus the Reformed as well as other non-Lutheran Protestants were denied toleration.

This triumph of the anti-Protestant forces was frustrated by two developments. The victorious Catholics were divided by internal dissensions which resulted, among other things, in the dismissal of Wallenstein, and Gustavus Adolphus intervened. Gustavus Adolphus, grandson of Gustavus Vasa, staunchly Lutheran, highly educated, and ambitious, was intent upon making the Baltic a Swedish lake and saw in the Hapsburg advance in the North a threat to this dream. In June, 1630, he landed with an army and drove the Hapsburgs out of Pomerania. In his German enterprise he was aided by the chief minister of France, Richelieu. Catholic though he was, Richelieu was more intent upon the aggrandizement of France than upon the defeat of Protestantism and mixed in the troubled sea of German affairs to gain, if possible, territory and prestige for his king. The leading German Protestant princes did not at first support the Swedish monarch. However, skilful diplomacy and the fear inspired by the capture by Tilly of Protestant Magdeburg (1631) and its sack through horrible atrocities brought the powerful Brandenburg and Saxony to his side. The tide of battle now turned. Gustavus Adolphus defeated Tilly and marched to the Rhine. The Saxons captured Prague. Terrified, the Emperor recalled Wallenstein and that doughty warrior soon defeated the Saxons. Wallenstein, in turn, was soundly beaten by Gustavus Adolphus at Lützen, near Leipzig (November 16, 1632), but in that battle the latter lost his life.

The war, already long, now bogged down into a kind of stalemate. The death of Gustavus Adolphus was a staggering blow to the Protestant cause. The Swedes continued the war, but were overcome by a combination of Spanish and imperial armies (September, 1634). In the meantime (February, 1634) Wallenstein had been removed by assassination by some of his own officers. It had become clear that the Roman Catholics could not regain the overwhelmingly Protestant North Germany and that the Protestants could not hope to become dominant in the prevailing Roman Catholic South Germany. In 1635 peace was made between the Emperor and Saxony. Most of Germany assented to it.

It was Richelieu who further dragged out the war. Eager for French gains at the expense of the Hapsburgs who, ruling in Spain and Austria, menaced French ambitions from both south and north, he sought to take advantage of the divisions in Germany to gain territory. Spain and Sweden also continued to be embroiled. Sweden wished to assure her position on the Baltic. More and more the religious issue faded. Roman Catholic France was in association with Lutheran Sweden. The struggle was a sordid one for power. Germany, divided, was the battle ground. Armies ranged across it devastating large areas of a land that had already been wasted by years of fighting.

THE PEACE OF WESTPHALIA AND THE FIXING OF RELIGIOUS BOUNDARIES

The Peace of Westphalia, October 27, 1648, eventually marked the terminus of the seemingly interminable struggle. Negotiations had long been in progress and a congress of representatives of the interested powers had been at work since 1645. It is significant that the Papacy, while represented, played no such important part in the negotiations as it had in the Middle Ages or even in the preceding century. The time had passed when it could dictate to Western Christendom.

With the territorial aspects of the Peace of Westphalia we are not greatly concerned except as they affected religious boundaries. France was confirmed in her possession of the bishoprics of Metz, Toul, and Verdun, and, at the expense of the Hapsburgs, was given much of Alsace. In Alsace, divided religiously, France was placed under obligation to maintain Catholic worship wherever it had been carried on under the Hapsburgs and was to restore it wherever it had been interrupted by the war. Sweden was given a continuing slice of German territory and a voice in the affairs of the Holy Roman Empire. This, however, did not seriously affect the religious aspects of German life. The branch of the Hohenzollern family which ruled in Brandenburg was awarded additional territory, notably the Bishoprics of Minden and Halberstadt and the Archbishopric of Magdeburg. Since Brandenburg was Protestant, its growth strengthened the Protestant cause. What remained of the Holy Roman Empire of the German Nation was substantially weakened, for its princes were permitted to make alliances with foreign powers and not only Sweden but also France now had a voice in it. However, the prestige of the Hapsburgs who ruled in Austria was such that the title of Holy Roman Emperor in effect became hereditary in that house. Since the Hapsburgs were resolutely Roman Catholic, the office never passed into the possession of Protestants. In connexion with the general European settlement, Spain formally recognized (1648) the independence of Holland, and the Protestant cause was thus reinforced. The Peace of Westphalia gave formal legality to what also had long been tacitly accepted fact, the independence of Switzerland.

What most interests us are the specifically religious phases of the Peace of Westphalia. A settlement was effected which fixed the boundaries between Catholics and Protestants as, with slight modifications, they were to remain. While the terms had to do only with Germany, they were an indication that through Europe the two forms of the faith had reached comparatively stable boundaries. Henceforward in that continent neither made substantial gains at the expense of the other.

In general, the Peace of Westphalia was more favourable to the Protestants than conditions a few years earlier would have warranted. The Catholic counter-advance had reached its height and had slightly retreated. The Reformed were now officially tolerated along with the Lutherans. The Edict of Restitution was in effect annulled, with its attempt to restore to Catholics the ecclesiastical properties which had become Protestant. January 1, 1624, not 1552, was fixed as the date beyond which no ecclesiastical property was to be alienated to Protestants. This left many former Catholic bishoprics, monasteries, and churches in Protestant hands. Yet further Protestant advance was also halted and the debatable West and South-west remained largely Roman Catholic.

While the principle of *cujus regio ejus religio* still had some validity, Catholic princes were required to permit Protestant worship in their realms where it had existed in 1624, and Protestant princes were to do likewise with Catholic worship in their domains. Subjects who were of another faith than that of their ruler were to be permitted to conduct private worship and to educate their children in the religion of the parents. The same provision for reciprocal toleration applied as between Lutherans and Reformed in territories where the ruler was of the opposite form of Protestantism. In a few places Catholics and Protestants worshipped in the same church building, but at different hours.

The major exception to this toleration was in the regions ruled by the Austrian Hapsburgs. Save for the prevailingly Protestant duchies in Silesia, the city of Breslau, and the nobility of Lower Austria, in the domains of the Hapsburgs no Protestants enjoyed the free exercise of their religion.

The year 1624 was also set as determinative for the status of religion in the free cities of the Empire. Those that were then Catholic were to remain so, and those Protestant were to hold to that form of the faith. Cities where Protestantism and Catholicism were about equal in that year were to continue to be mixed religiously.

A curb was placed on Roman Catholic missions among Protestants by the provision that no religious order founded since the Reformation was to be introduced. Obviously, although not by name, directed against the Jesuits, it proved a brake on the activity of the Society to which much of the counter-gains of the Roman Catholic Church had been due.

The religious settlement was not completely satisfactory to either Protestants or Roman Catholics. The Pope condemned it. Yet it proved to be a viable compromise.

Could the Christians of Western Europe achieve unity under these new conditions? To many it seemed that whatever of unity had existed had been irretrievably shattered by the Protestant revolt. As we have earlier noted, the true unity among Christians, that of love, had never been realized. Behind the façade of the visible structural unity achieved through the Catholic Church bitter dissensions had been chronic. However, even that façade had now been broken. Not only were Protestants separated from Roman Catholics, but among themselves Protestants were deeply divided. Could inclusive fellowship be achieved, perhaps in some new way, and if not between Roman Catholics and Protestants, at least among the many varieties of Protestantism?

Efforts were not wanting to attain that goal. Roman Catholics continued, but largely in vain, to seek to win Protestants. Some Protestants were adventuring, mainly in new directions, for unity among themselves and a few dreamed and laboured for a reunion of Protestants and Roman Catholics which would be without the sacrifice by either of cherished central convictions.

The outstanding leaders of the Protestant Reformation did not surrender the hope of comprehensive Christian fellowship. Luther and Calvin longed for it. Luther held to the Apostles', Nicene, and Athanasian Creeds as *tria symbola catholica sive ecumenica,* "three catholic or ecumenical symbols," thus stressing a universal church inclusive of all Christians. He affirmed the "communion of saints."

While maintaining that councils of the universal church might err, Luther did not abandon the hope that general councils might be assembled, later ones correcting earlier ones if and when necessary. Calvin believed in both a visible and an invisible Church, the latter made up of all whom God had predestined to eternal life and the former found wherever the Word was purely preached and reverently heard and the sacraments "administered according to the institution of Christ." The Augsburg Confession, the formulation of the faith to which more Lutherans adhered than to any other, declared "that one Holy Church is to continue for ever. Moreover, the Church is the congregation of saints in which the Gospel is rightly taught and the sacraments are rightly administered. And unto the true unity of the Church, it is sufficient to agree concerning the doctrine of the Gospel and the administration of the Sacraments." Similarly among the Reformed Churches, the First Helvetic Confession declared that there is "one holy universal Church, the society and assembly of all the saints, the spotless bride of Christ," and the Second Helvetic Confession said "that there is but one Church which we call Catholic for the reason that it is universal and is spread out through all parts of the world and extends to all times."

We have noted that before the Council of Trent stiffened the official Roman Catholic attitude and made impossible the healing of the breach, there were those among both Roman Catholics and Protestants who laboured to close it. Among them were humanists, including Erasmus, and some of the German rulers, notably the Emperors Charles V, Ferdinand I, and Maximilian II.

In the first generation of Protestant Reformers there were several who worked for solidarity among those who broke with Rome. Discussions were held between the Bohemian Brethren and Luther. Bucer endeavoured to bring Zwingli and the Lutherans together. For a time it looked as if Bullinger and Luther might agree. The large majority of the Waldensees were drawn into fellowship with the Reformed. Although differing on the sacraments and especially upon the fashion in which Christ is present in the Lord's Supper, Calvin and Bullinger reached accord and with them most of the Reformed Churches in Switzerland. Calvin, Farel, and Beza hoped and strove for coöperation with the Lutherans, especially in behalf of the persecuted Protestants in France. Cranmer attempted to induce Melanchthon to come to England, and, as we have seen, several of the Continental reformers of varying views found haven in that realm when, under Edward VI, important changes were being made in the Church of England. Jan Laski (John à Lasco), influential in shaping Protestantism in Poland, was an irenic soul who exerted himself in behalf of accord among Protestants.

Late in the sixteenth and early in the seventeeth century there were efforts for the union of Protestants. The national synods of the French Reformed Church sent emissaries to England, Switzerland, Germany, Denmark, and the Netherlands to see whether steps could be taken towards accomplishing it. In the Netherlands Jacob Arminius suggested a general council as a way of bringing Christians together. David Pareus (1548–1622), a Reformed theologian of Heidelberg, in his *Irenicum* proposed that Protestants seek union against the Roman Catholics through "a regular and free council." Pressure in that direction was often exerted by princes, but more from political expediency than deep religious conviction. Most of it had as its object religious uniformity within their respective realms, but sometimes monarchs and their ministers strove through diplomacy to unite some or all of their fellow-Protestant rulers in a common front against the Roman Catholic menace.

During and after the Thirty Years' War numbers of Protestants sought to bring together their fellow-Protestants and some even dreamed of the union of Protestants and Roman Catholics. Thus John Valentine Andreae (1586–1654) in his picture of an ideal society in his *Christianopolis* maintained that unity in learning and in society could be given by Christianity which "unites men together" and made his confession of faith accord with the creeds on which Roman Catholics and most Protestants were agreed. The Lutheran George Calixtus (1586–1656) whose father had studied under Melanchthon and who himself taught theology at Helmstadt for nearly a third of a century, wished union, even with a reformed Roman Catholic Church, on the basis of the formula put forward by Vincent of Lerins in the fifth century, *"quod semper, quod ubique, quod ab omnibus creditum sum"* ("what has been believed always, everywhere, and by all"). He advocated councils as a means of reaching agreement. We must note, however, that he was far from carrying all of his fellow-Lutherans with him, and that his views provoked a controversy which continued after his death. John Amos Comenius (1592–1670), bishop of the Bohemian Brethren (*Unitas Fratrum*), an exile and refugee from the terrors of the Thirty Years' War which all but extinguished his church, uncrushed by the seeming disaster, a friend of Pareus and Andreae, hoped for the union of all Christians and the integration of all civilization under the leadership of religion. To this end he urged that Christian missions be supported. Hugo Grotius (1583–1645), an Arminian, best remembered for his pioneer treatise on international law, *De Jure Belli et Pacis,* wished the elimination of divisions among Christians and brought out a book on *The Way of Ecclesiastical Peace,* and that in spite of the fact that he was embroiled in theological controversy. The Scot John Durie (Dury) (1596–1680) spent more than half a century of his long life working for the union of Protestants. He accepted reordination from Archbishop Laud, was a member of the Westminster Assembly, wrote pamphlets, carried on an extensive correspondence, travelled widely on the Continent, had the support of Gustavus Adolphus, and was the agent of Oliver Cromwell in seeking to bring together the Protestants on the Continent. In his last work he wished union to embrace the Roman Catholics.

In the closing quarter of the seventeenth century a Spanish Franciscan, Spinola, Bishop of Neustadt, for part of the time with Papal consent, negotiated with Protestants for reunion through a council to which Protestants would be admitted as "visible members of the Catholic Church." He had conferences with Lutherans, especially with G. W. Molanus (1633–1722), a pupil of Calixtus, who prepared an irenic proposal which was viewed with some favour in Rome. G. W. Leibnitz (1646–1716), Protestant by rearing, son of a professor of moral philosophy at Leipzig, wide-ranging in his intellectual interests, and distinguished as scientist, mathematician, and philosopher, as a youth had read extensively in theological literature of the Roman Catholic and several Protestant churches. He worked for the union of the Lutherans and Reformed of Prussia and carried on an amicable correspondence with the great

French Roman Catholic preacher, Bossuet, on the possibility of the union of all Christians. He looked to general councils as a means towards this end, but would not regard their decisions as final.

Similarly in the fore part of the eighteenth century there were those in Western Europe who dreamed of unity and worked for it, at least among Protestants. The Lutheran Christoph Mathew Pfaff (1686–1760) of Tübingen, in his *Pacific Address* to the Protestants (1720), held that all the Protestant communions are basically one. Count Nicolaus Ludwig von Zinzendorf, of whom we are to hear more in a moment, saw the Catholic Church in all the churches and carried on a friendly correspondence with a French cardinal. Three Swiss whose major work was in the first half of the eighteenth century sought to make the Reformed Churches of their native land more appreciative of other Protestants and laboured for union among Protestants.

Seventeenth and eighteenth century Great Britain and Ireland also had those who strove for unity both among the Christians of the British Isles and with those, especially Protestants, on the Continent. Archbishop James Usher (or Ussher) (1581–1656), Anglican primate of Ireland, noted as a scholar, held that bishop and presbyter differed merely in rank and not in order, advocated union with the Presbyterians, and regarded the latters' ordinations as valid. Oliver Cromwell seems to have favoured a central council for all Protestants. Richard Baxter, a Presbyterian, whom we have already met, was an ardent proponent of Christian unity, wrote extensively on it, and with others proposed to Charles II a plan of union like that of Usher. Edward Stillingfleet (1635–1699), an Anglican, in his *Irenicum* (1661), held that while they might be useful, neither the episcopal nor the presbyterian form of church government rested upon divine right, that neither was unalterable, and that from the Anglican standpoint presbyterian ordination was not invalid. William III, brought to power by the "glorious revolution" of 1688, reared in the Reformed tradition and now an Anglican by virtue of his office, wished all his Protestant subjects to be united and a bill to bring this about failed of passage in the House of Commons only by a narrow margin. John Robert Tillotson, Archbishop of Canterbury from 1691 to his death in 1694, sought, unsuccessfully, to persuade his fellow bishops to agree to concessions to the Protestant Nonconformists. Archbishop William Wake carried on a friendly correspondence with a French Catholic who stressed the rights of the Church of France as against the Church of Rome and also with several leaders of the Reformed churches.

How much of these efforts for unity carried over into the nineteenth and twentieth centuries and contributed to what eventually came to be called the Ecumenical Movement we cannot certainly know. That some connexion existed is clear.

AWAKENING OUT OF TRAGEDY

The Thirty Years' War was a major tragedy. By it much of Germany was laid waste. Prosperous cities and villages were decimated or destroyed and even greater damage was suffered in the coarsening and lowering of morals. As the chief victim, Germany would have seemed to be the last place in Western Europe to which to look for fresh stirrings of Christian life. Yet here, in part from the tragedy itself, came vital currents which, swelling from small beginnings to significant proportions, persisted into the nineteenth and twentieth centuries and even in the eighteenth century contributed powerfully to the awakenings elsewhere in Protestantism that after 1750 made that form of the faith the most vigorous and rapidly growing branch of Christianity.

Why this was true of Protestantism rather than of the Roman Catholic Church we cannot say. Both Protestant and Catholic portions of Germany shared in the devastation. While in the later stages of the conflict some of its earlier gains were lost, territorially the Roman Catholic Church came out of the war better off than when it entered it, and at the expense of Protestantism. Yet it was within Protestantism, and notably from one of its churches, the Bohemian Brethren or *Unitas Fratrum* which had been the major victim, that the new tides of life chiefly issued.

Even during the long agony of the war there were evidences of vigour. It was in 1612, on the eve of its outbreak, that the first book appeared of Jakob Böhme (1575–1624), whom we have already met. Shoemaker and mystic of Upper Lusatia, across the mountains from that Bohemia which was soon to be the scene of the first stages of the struggle, he lived to see the initial years of the disaster. His thought, which scarcely belongs in what may be called orthodox Christianity, had wide repercussions in Germany, the Netherlands, Russia, and England, and among others influenced Isaac Newton and the much read Anglican, William Law, whose *Serious Call to a Devout and Holy Life* made a profound impression on John Wesley. Paul Gerhardt (1607–1676), whose youth and early manhood spanned the years of the war, was one of the greatest of Lutheran hymn-writers. Some of his hymns were translated into English by John Wesley, among them "Jesus, thy boundless love to me" and "Give to the winds thy fears, trust and be not dismayed," and were used widely.

The most striking phase of the religious awakening which followed the Thirty Years' War was Pietism. It had its roots far in the pre-war past. To it contributions came from the mysticism which we met in pre-Reformation Germany, from Luther, from English Puritanism, and possibly from the Anabaptists. Profoundly influential was the *Wahres Christenthum* ("True Christianity") of the Lutheran John Arndt (1555–1621), a work which appeared in the first decade of the seventeenth century, was translated into several European languages, and carried far the *unio mystica* side of Luther's teachings. It was a chief means of awakening Philip Jacob Spener (1635–1705), who is regarded as the immediate source of Pietism.

A Lutheran, as a student in Strassburg and Geneva Spener had become familiar with practices of the Reformed Churches which seemed to him admirable. In 1663 he became a pastor in Strassburg and then (1666) in Frankfort. While in Frankfort, a commercial city which had been dealt severe blows by the war but which was making a rapid recovery, he sought to nourish a deeper Christian life in his flock. Perhaps because of what he had seen at Strassburg, he took seriously catechetical instruction. More important, he gathered in his own home a group for the cultivation of the Christian life through the discussion of the Sunday sermons, prayer, and the study of the Bible. The movement spread and the groups became known as *collegia pietatis,* from which came the designation Pietism which clung to the movement.

Spener was intent upon a moral and spiritual reformation. He was grieved by controversy over doctrine, sometimes bitter as it was and often arid and having little direct bearing upon everyday living. Much of the contemporary preaching was of that kind. The lives of many of the clergy were unworthy and among the laity, partly as an aftermath of the long war, there were drunkenness and immorality. Church services tended to be formal and sterile. The state, he felt, interfered overmuch in the affairs of the Church. What he stressed was genuine conversion and the cultivation of the Christian life. To this end he discounted doctrinal sermons, preached the necessity of the new birth, a personal, warm, Christian experience, and the cultivation of Christian virtues. He gathered the serious-minded into small groups, *ecclesiolæ in ecclesia*—"little churches in the Church"—he called them, for the reading of the Scriptures and for mutual assistance in spiritual growth. As did the Catholic Church in the Middle Ages and many of the Calvinist and Puritan traditions, he inculcated a self discipline which included abstinence from cards, dancing, and the theatre and moderation in food, drink, and dress. Much of this he set forth in his *Pia Desideria,* published in 1675.

Almost inevitably, Spener and his methods aroused a storm of criticism. He was accused of being untrue to Lutheran doctrines. In this his opponents were not altogether incorrect. While he did not attack Lutheran orthodoxy, Spener held that if one had been really converted and had a right heart, doctrinal differences were relatively unimportant. In Frankfort opposition developed among the civil authorities, partly because some of those who came to his groups did not attend public worship and absented themselves from the Lord's Supper. In 1686 he went to Dresden as court preacher, but there met with hostility from the Saxon universities, Leipzig and Wittenberg, and eventually from the prince, whom he reproved for his drunkenness. In 1691 he accepted the invitation of the Elector of Brandenburg, later to become the King of Prussia, to Berlin. There, with growing influence, he remained until his death.

Prominent in the Pietist movement was a younger contemporary of Spener, August Hermann Francke (1663–1727). While teaching in the University of Leipzig, Francke and some of his friends inaugurated what they called a *collegium philobiblicum* for the study of the Scriptures. A few months later, when in his mid-twenties, Francke experienced what he believed to be the new birth. Then followed some weeks with Spener and the hearty acceptance of Pietism. As might have been expected, opposition developed at Leipzig. Francke was forced out of the university, especially because his meetings aroused much excitement among the students, and then out of a post in Erfurt. Through Spener's influence he was appointed to the University of Halle, at that time being founded by the Elector of Brandenburg, and to a pastorate in a neighbouring village.

Largely through Francke Halle became a chief centre of Pietism. Of prodigious energy, enthusiasm, and organizing ability, he was the dominant figure on the theological faculty and in the training of young men for the ministry. A faithful pastor in his own parish, he brought to his lecture room not only theory but also practical experience. At Halle he founded schools which became popular because of new educational programmes carried on in an atmosphere saturated with Pietism. He inaugurated an orphanage. The maintenance of these institutions was made possible by gifts which Francke profoundly believed came in response to prayer. From Halle missionaries went forth, some of them to India, some, from an institute founded for that purpose, to the Jews, and at least one, Muhlenberg, to the German colonists in America. Incidentally, but by no means of slight importance, the Halle schools had a part in shaping the future educational system of Prussia.

Pietism proved contagious. It had numerous and varied expressions. While many, perhaps the majority, were indifferent or even hostile, it spread rapidly through the Lutheran Churches. For example, it had a following in the Scandinavian countries. Arndt's works were widely read. In Norway, where, as we have seen, the Reformation had been largely imposed from without, Pietism stirred the masses. There Erik Pontoppidan, a Pietiest, drew up an explanation of Luther's catechism which with the Bible and hymnbook became a part of almost every Norwegian's library and was called "the dogmatics of the common people of Norway." Hans Adolph Bronson (1694–1764) wrote hymns which sang the Pietist awakening into the hearts of the rank and file. In 1736, largely as a result of the Pietist movement, confirmation was made compulsory in Norway. Pietism became especially vigorous and widespread in Württemberg. Here it became part of the warp and woof of parish life. This was due largely to Johann Albrecht Bengel (1687–1752), scholar and notable Bible commentator, who was high in the ecclesiastical structure of that state.

Closely linked with Pietism and combining it with the heritage of Hus and the *Unitas Fratrum* was the Moravian movement. Beginning in 1722, a few refugees from the persecutions of Protestants in Bohemia and Moravia settled on the estates of Nicolaus Ludwig, Count of Zinzendorf (1700–1760), near Berthelsdorf, about seventy miles from Dresden. Sensitive, able, with a global, encompassing imagination, this young nobleman had been reared in a strongly Pietist atmosphere and had been educated at Halle. His Pietism took the form of an ardent devotion to Jesus, so that he said of him: "I have one passion, 'tis he." He also had an intense desire to spread the Christian faith throughout the world. In the handful of persecuted refugees he saw the means of fulfilling that vision. They founded the village of Herrnhut on his property, he identified himself with them and became a bishop of their church, and through him missionaries from among them went out to various parts of the world. Zinzendorf wished them to become members of the state church of Saxony, but in 1745, while being a section of that church, they were formally organized with their own bishops, in the succession of those of the *Unitas Fratrum,* and with their distinct services, liturgy, and hymnology. As we are to see in a later chapter, contact with the Moravians contributed significantly to the profound experience of John Wesley which made him the outstanding leader of the Evangelical Awakening and the founder of Methodism. From Zinzendorf and other Pietists, as usual from awakenings in Christianity, many fresh hymns issued.

SUMMARY

The Roman Catholic Church did not succeed in eliminating Protestantism as, except for a few remnants, it had the earlier movements in Western Europe which it deemed heretical. That was probably partly because Protestantism proved to have much greater inner vitality than did these others. It was also, and quite certainly, in large measure because of the political situation and emergent nationalism. The peoples of North-western Europe and Great Britain were restive under Roman domination and their princes, many of them joining in the resentment and seeing in it means of augmenting their authority, acquiesced in it and sometimes gave it leadership. Confronted by nationalism and absolute monarchs in its historic stronghold, South-western Europe, embroiled in Italian politics, and at first weakened by internal corruption and inefficiency, Rome could not enforce its will as it had at the height of the Middle

Ages. Although internal reform and reorganization eventually enabled it to win back some of the lost ground, that was chiefly on the border between Latin and non-Latin Europe. Most of North-western Europe and Great Britain became and remained overwhelmingly Protestant.

Arising in part from the efforts of Roman Catholics to regain Bohemia, Moravia, and Germany but complicated by other non-religious factors, the Thirty Years' War drew in most of Western Europe. After its end few changes were made in the boundaries between Protestants and Roman Catholics. What had been the Catholic Church of Western Europe now became unmistakably the Roman Catholic Church, with its heart-land henceforward clearly Latin Europe. Most of the Christianity of the non-Latin North had torn away and, displaying great inner vitality, was to have an amazing growth, both in territory covered and in new movements. Indeed, the precursors of that expansion and of some of those movements were to become apparent within two generations after the war which laid waste much of the orginal home of Protestantism. Protestants were badly divided, but efforts were not wanting to bring them together. In the following centuries the fresh currents which began to be apparent in Pietism were to go far towards a basic and visible unity. However, in spite of efforts on both sides, the gulf which separated Protestants and Roman Catholics remained and seemed permanent.

SELECTED BIBLIOGRAPHY

The Cambridge Modern History. Volume IV, The Thirty Years' War (Cambridge University Press, 1906).

H. E. F. Guerike, *The Life of Augustus Herman Franke,* translated from the German by S. Jackson (London, R. B. Seeley and W. Burnside, 1837, pp. viii, 296).

J. T. McNeill, *Unitive Protestantism. A Study in Our Religious Resources* (New York and Nashville, Abingdon-Cokesbury Press, 1930, pp. 264). A study of Protestant efforts at union, chiefly in the sixteenth, seventeenth, and eighteenth centuries. Admirably done.

H. Römer, *Nicolaus Ludwig Graf von Zinzendorf* (2d ed., Gnadau, Unitäts-Buchhandlung, 1900, pp. 193).

Chapter XL

STAGNATION AND ADVANCE: THE
EASTERN CHURCHES, A.D. 1500 - A.D. 1750

While the great burst of life was making itself felt in the Christianity of Western Europe through the Protestant and Catholic Reformations, what was happening in the Christianity of the East? Did the adversities which had overtaken it between 1350 and 1500 continue, or did they ease their impact?

The story is a mixture of stagnation and advance. The older churches centering around the historic patriarchal sees of Jerusalem, Antioch, Alexandria, and Constantinople, whether Monophysite or Orthodox, continued to suffer from the political dominance of Moslem masters. The same was true of the Nestorians and, for the most part, of the Armenians. The Roman Catholic Church still reached out to the East, seeking to bring its Christians under the control of the Papacy, largely through Uniate bodies, and its fresh access of life augmented those efforts. In one region, Russia, the Christianity of the East exhibited great vitality. This had little connexion with the awakenings in Western Europe and expressed itself in forms peculiar to its genius. Yet in its own way it was as remarkable as the larger and more varied movements in Western Christianity. Moreover, as we are to see in the next chapter, the Christianity of the West, predominantly Roman Catholicism, was carried to the South and East of Asia and to the islands which there fringed that continent and gave rise to continuing Christian communities which were more numerous and spread over a larger area than any which that part of the world had yet known.

THE OLDER EASTERN PATRIARCHATES

The stagnation of the Christianity connected with the historic patriarchates of the East was to be expected. The capture of Constantinople in 1453 was not the highwater-mark of the advance of the Crescent under the Ottoman Turks. In the sixteenth century those doughty empire-builders enlarged their conquests. Syria and Egypt came under their rule, their borders were extended northward not only to include almost all the Balkan Peninsula, but also into Hungary, and such Christian outposts in the Mediterranean fell to them as Rhodes (the stronghold of the Knights [Hospitallers] of St. John), Crete, and Cyprus. Since the Turks were sturdy Moslems and under them conversions from Islam to Christianity were all but impossible, the Christian communities could at best hold their own, reproducing themselves by birth but losing by leakage to Islam.

As before 1500, the Turkish rulers treated the Christian churches as social and legal entities, governing them through their clergy and especially their patriarchs. The Orthodox Patriarch of Constantinople was particularly important because of the prominence of his see in the past and the size of the Christian community over which he was the titular head. The Turkish authorities were careful that those who held the post were subservient to them. The office was usually bought from them, for the approval of the sultan was required. Changes in it were frequent, intrigues were chronic, and some of the occupants came to violent ends. The character of the Patriarchs was reflected in that of the bishops. Like the former, according to the tradition of the Eastern Churches, they were monks. They, too, often, perhaps usually, held their offices through purchase. The Phanariots, inhabitants of the Phanar quarter in Constantinople, largely controlled appointments to the higher posts in the Greek Orthodox Church. The Orthodox Patriarchates of Antioch and Alexandria, ruling as they did over small minorities, seem not to have been deemed sufficiently important by the Turkish rulers to warrant much attention. They appear, therefore, to have been filled through the customary forms of election without interference by the civil authorities.

An outstanding exception to the dubious character of the higher clergy of the Greek Orthodox Church was Cyril Lucar (1572–1637). Born in Crete while that island was under Venetian rule, he was reared in the Orthodox Church. Part of his education was in Italy, but he seems early to have acquired a strong dislike for the Roman Catholic Church, although later for a brief time he may have leaned in its direction. He travelled in Western Europe and came in touch with the Protestant Reformation, especially with the Reformed Churches. For a period he was in Poland as a representative of the Patriarch of Constantinople among the Orthodox. In 1602 he was elected Patriarch of Alexandria and in 1621 he became Patriarch of Constantinople. In these high offices he worked for the moral and spiritual improvement of the Orthodox Church. To this end he sent young men to study in the Protestant churches in Europe. He entered into correspondence with church leaders in non-Roman Catholic Western Europe, among them Archbishop Laud. His tenure of the Patriarchate of Constantinople was stormy, and he was several times deposed and as many times reinstated, not without the payment of money. He had implacable foes among the Jesuits, for they were seeking to bring about the submission of the Orthodox Church to the Pope and he was known to be intimate with the Dutch and English ambassadors and to have Protestant leanings. Indeed, a confession of faith which is attributed to him (and which he seems at least to have endorsed) but the authorship of which has been hotly debated has in it Protestant elements, including salvation by faith and predestination. Eventually he was strangled by order of the Sultan. In 1638 a synod of the Orthodox Church anathematized both Cyril and the confession attributed to him. In 1642 another synod condemned the confession and Calvinism, but without mentioning Cyril.

Many conversions from Christianity to Islam occurred, especially during the years of the forward surge of the Ottoman Turks. Some of the clergy went over, and throngs from the lower and middle classes. In 1620 a sultan ordered all churches turned into mosques and all Christians to become Moslems. Only with difficulty did a Patriarch dissuade him. Later two other sultans nearly carried out a similar project. In Crete after the Turkish conquest several thousand children of Christians were forcibly taken from their parents, circumcized, and reared as Moslems. In the seventeenth century many Serbs became Moslems and in Bosnia numbers of Bogomils took the same step. In that same century a ruler in Georgia, reared a Moslem in Persia, attempted to force Islam on his realm. Early in the preceding century a Moslem conqueror compelled many Christians in Abyssinia to apostatize—although several years later, when Moslem rule was overthrown, hundreds of the unwilling converts returned to their ancestral faith.

In Armenia, in spite of adverse political conditions, something of an awakening was seen. That mountainous country lying between powerful neighbours was, as earlier, debatable ground and was a chronic battle field. In these centuries Persians and Ottoman Turks were the antagonists. This meant that civilization and the Church suffered severely. However, in the seventeenth century an awakening began. Zealous monks, inspired partly by what they had seen in Jerusalem, set about the renewal of monasticism. Using the ancient foundation of the monastery of Datev as a centre, they began the Order of Siunik. As was customery in fresh monastic movements, whether in the East or the West, a strict discipline was adopted. Here it included renunciation of all private property, complete obedience to the abbot, stringent fasting, confession of sins each morning and evening, and meditation with the use of helpful books.

The revival was not confined to the monasteries. Some of the monks who had caught the contagion went out among the rank and file of the population preaching, founding schools, and seeking to improve morals, reconcile enemies, and discourage superstition. Outstanding among them was Moses of Datev. He began his work as an itinerant preacher about 1618. Later he was consecrated bishop and eventually (1629) Catholicos or Patriarch, thus bringing the reform movement into the supreme leadership of the Church of Armenia. Another centre of the revival of religion and learning was a monastery in Bitlis.

Among the Armenian churches of the dispersion these centuries also saw life, some of it in Constantinople and some in Persia. At New Julfa in Persia there was an Armenian community from which merchants went out into many parts of Europe and Asia. It was a centre of religious devotion and learning, but in 1721 an Afghan invasion wrought great damage. In 1652 a synod was held in Jerusalem which passed decrees designed to promote reform and to allay friction. In the seventeenth century the printing press made possible the wider distribution of religious literature, including an Armenian version of the Bible.

A constant feature in the history of the Eastern Churches, especially after reform had begun to take effect in the Roman Catholic Church, was the effort of zealous missionaries to bring all the Christians of the East to submit to the Pope and to enter into communion with the Church of Rome. As we have seen, Uniate Churches, namely those from the Eastern bodies who acknowledged the Pope and brought their creeds into conformity with Rome but who preserved their ecclesiastical languages and many of their peculiar rites and customs, had come into being before 1500. After 1500 Jesuits, Capuchins, Discalced Carmelites, and Theatines, products of the Catholic Reformation, as well as Dominicans and Franciscans, orders much longer in the area, ranged through much of the East, seeking to strengthen the Uniate bodies and eventually to bring about the full reunion of the several branches of the Catholic Church under the leadership of the Pope.

We must not take the time or the space to tell of all these Uniate bodies and their growth. We may, however, pause to notice a few of them. They included the Ruthenians, largely of Russian stock, formerly Orthodox. One was in domains under Polish and therefore Roman Catholic political control and came formally into being from a congress at Brest in 1596. In 1652 large groups of White and Little Russians living south of the Carpathians entered into communion with Rome and were known as the Podcarpathian Ruthenians. In 1701 about two hundred thousand Rumanians submitted to Rome, along with some of their clergy. There were Uniates in Egypt under a Patriarch of Alexandria. In Syria, Palestine, and Egypt those of the Byzantine rite who were in fellowship with Rome were known as Melchites, a term which had also been used to designate the Greek Orthodox in these areas. They had their own Patriarchs distinct from those who ruled the Greek Orthodox who kept aloof from Rome. In the sixteenth century, supported by Portuguese who came in to help the Ethiopians against the Turks, Jesuits brought numbers of the Abyssinians into communion with Rome. In 1555 Pope Julius III appointed a Jesuit as Patriarch of the Church in that country. Early in the seventeenth century another Jesuit was named for the post and for a time a ruler sympathetic with the Jesuits seemed to bring most if not all of the Ethiopian Church into accord with Rome. However, a nationalistic reaction drove out the missionaries and severed the Roman connexion. Roman Catholic missionaries were active in Constantinople, seeking to draw both the Greek Orthodox and the Armenians into fellowship with Rome. The ensuing friction looms large in the annals of these bodies. Numbers of the Jacobites, in Syria, were won to fellowship with Rome and in time had a Patriarch of their own. In the sixteenth century an aspirant for the headship of the Nestorians made his submission to Rome and carried many with him. Thus came into being the Chaldean Christians, Nestorian Uniates, and a continuing division in that ancient church. In that same century Jesuit missionaries succeeded in bringing over to Rome the Syrian Christians of India, who had been closely associated with the Nestorians in Mesopotamia. Indeed, in 1599 the Synod of Diamper seemed to have accomplished that union. However, in the following century unrest arose and the majority, led by their clergy, severed the Roman tie, leaving only a minority in communion with the Pope. Zealous though Roman Catholic missionaries were, they were unable to win more than a minority of the Eastern Christians to fellowship with Rome. Only the Maronites, largely in the Lebanon, remnants of the Monothelite controversy, came over fully to the Pope. The connexion had been made during the Crusades, and after 1516 became uninterrupted.

THE CHURCH IN RUSSIA

In Russia one of the Eastern Churches, the Orthodox, had a striking territorial expansion and in it and from it issued fresh movements of remarkable power. This vitality was closely associated with the development of the monarchy, the beginning of which we have noted in the preceding period, and which had Moscow as its capital. The rulers were professedly Christian and identified themselves and their authority with the Orthodox Church. It was that fact which favoured the spread of the faith in and near the territories governed from Moscow and which did much to shape the course of Christianity in Russia.

The Strange Story of Ivan "The Terrible"

In an earlier chapter (XXVII) we have noted that on the north-eastern frontier, around Moscow, there was arising a state which, achieving its independence of the Mongols, took over something of the autocratic idea which it had seen in them. Its rulers were descendants of that Vladimir through whom Kiev had been converted late in the tenth century and who is usually regarded as the founder of Christianity in Russia. In the sixteenth century this state was greatly expanded under one of the most remarkable men in Russian history, Ivan (John) IV, "the Terrible" (1530–1584), grandson of Ivan III. He was little more than an infant when, in 1533, his father's death brought him nominally to power, so that his reign extended over more than half a century.

At the time of his accession the state over which Ivan IV ruled occupied an area much smaller than the later Russia. The Mongols still had territory in Europe. The Cossacks, sturdy frontiersmen who in the fifteenth century had arisen in the southern part of Russia, largely between the Mongol and the Muscovite domains, were organized in a democratic fashion and were formidable warriors. To the west the Poles and Lithuanians held lands which were chiefly peopled by Russians, members of the Orthodox Church.

Ivan IV extended his domains over Kazan towards the east (1552) and southward to the Caspian, and exercised some authority east of the Urals. On the west he fought, not always successfully, with the Poles, Lithuanians, and Swedes. The menace of his arms helped to force the Poles and Lithuanians together under Polish leadership and made the two peoples an even greater menace to Moscow.

Ivan IV augmented his office. He reduced the power of the ancient nobility and created a new court nobility, largely dependent on himself. He also did much to curtail the freedom of the peasants by fixing them to the soil in the condition of serfdom in which they were to remain until the nineteenth century. When he was seventeen (1547) and assumed full charge of the government, Ivan IV had himself crowned as Tsar (Cæsar) and thus professed himself to be Emperor in the succession of the Christian Emperors of Constantinople, since that city was now in the hands of the Moslem Ottoman Turks.

In character Ivan IV was a combination of contradictions. He was highly sensitive and after a fashion deeply religious. Yet his childhood rearing had accustomed him to licentiousness and to impulsive lack of control. He was undoubtedly able, as the record of his achievements shows. But, especially in his later years, his contradictions seem to have developed into insanity. Extravagant orgies would be followed by periods of equally extravagant remorse and penance. He would destroy monasteries and then found new ones. Murders multiplied at his command, and he would send the list of his victims to monasteries commanding prayers for their souls.

Moscow "The Third Rome"

During the reign of Ivan IV important developments took place in Russian Christianity. In the Russian Orthodox Church the Josephites (Chapter XXVII) were dominant. Early in the sixteenth century, as we have seen, the Non-possessors had been decisively defeated. The Josephites, it will be recalled, believed in the possession of property by the monasteries and the Church. They were ascetic, approved works of charity, and stressed ritual, with elaborate services, large choirs, and ornate churches and vestments. Intensely patriotic, they held Moscow to be the third Rome, the successor of the first Rome, which had succumbed to the heresies of the Latins, and of Constantinople, the second Rome, which had fallen victim of the Moslems. Moscow, therefore, they regarded as the guardian of the Gospel in all its purity. The Josephites believed in the maintenance of a close tie between Church and state.

A leader of the Josephites was Makary, Metropolitan of Moscow during the early years when Ivan IV assumed full control of the state. A high-minded and able churchman, Makary had much influence with the young monarch. In 1551 he called a council, known as the Stoglav, or "Hundred Chapters," because of its resolutions which came to that total, which endeavoured to correct many of the evils in the Church. Its decisions had mainly to do with the liturgy and public worship, but it also sought reforms in ecclesiastical government, in clerical life, in the monasteries, and in the life of the laity.

Since Ivan IV had raised his office to that of tsar, Makary held that the head of the Church in Russia should have the title of Patriarch, thus placing crown and altar on an equal footing and giving visible recognition to Moscow's claim to be the third Rome. Long negotiations were required to gain formal consent to this step by the other members of the family of Orthodox Churches. These were not completed until after the death of Makary, but in 1589 the Patriarch of Constantinople agreed to the creation of a Russian Patriarchate and in 1590 a council of the other Orthodox Patriarchs in Constantinople confirmed the decision. The Patriarchate of Moscow was formally admitted to the list which included Constantinople, Alexandria, Antioch, and Jerusalem. Presumably it was to take the place of the Patriarchate which Rome was deemed to have forfeited. After Moscow became the seat of a Patriarch, four Russian sees were raised to the rank of metropolitan, several bishoprics became archbishoprics, and a number of new dioceses were created, partly by the subdivision of old ones, and partly by the extension of the Church into areas newly conquered by Moscow.

INTERNAL DISSENSIONS

Shortly before Ivan IV there began an interesting stage of an important controversy which lasted not only into his lifetime but which in the following century was to lead to a major disruption in the Church in Russia. It had to do with what to many outsiders seemed absurdities, matters of form in the services of the Church and the correctness of the translations of the texts which were used in them. As early as the fifteenth century a dispute had arisen as to whether in the public use of the Psalms the *Alleluia* should be recited twice before the *Gloria* as was the Greek custom, or thrice, as had been the Russian manner. The contender for the Greek form was deemed to have denied the Trinity and was branded as a heretic. In 1551, the Stoglav decided in favour of the double rather than the triple repetition.

In 1518 Maxim, a monk, an Albanian who had studied in Italy, had been a member of a monastery on Mt. Athos, and was learned in Greek and Latin, was invited to Moscow by one of the princes and was asked by the Metropolitan to revise the translations of some of the service books. In these many variations and errors were found, partly because of the mistakes of the original translators, partly because of the several sources through which they had come to Russia, and partly through the errors of copyists. Some changes had been made by the Judaizers (Chapter XXVII) who had regarded Christ as merely a created man and said of him that he had died an eternal death. So great a storm was aroused among the conservatives by the corrections made by Maxim (and he was also guilty of mistakes of his own) that the luckless foreigner was clapped into a monastic prison, was kept there for several years, was transferred to another monastery for confinement, and only after a long interval, perhaps at the instance of Makary, was released. His tragedy was complicated and the enmity against him intensified by his endorsement of the stand of the Non-possessors as against the dominant Josephites.

TERRITORIAL EXPANSION OF THE RUSSIAN CHURCH

While these developments were taking place within the church which centered around Moscow, the area occupied by that church was also expanding. This was partly in connexion with territorial conquests by the state and partly through the northward advance of the monks and the population of which we have earlier spoken (Chapter XXVII). Thus in the sixteenth century, after the annexation by Ivan IV of Kazan and the region around it, Kazan was made the seat of an archbishop. The first incumbent, Gurius, a man of noble birth, laboured indefatigably for the conversion of the non-Christians, especially the Cheremis (also called Tcheremis and Marii), a people speaking a Finnish tongue. On the middle reaches of the Volga the Mordvs, with a Finnish-Ugrian language, were subdued by Ivan IV. Ivan charged the nobles among whom he divided the land to prepare the inhabitants for baptism and monks were active in seeking to make the conversion effective. As late as the eighteenth century, as among the Cheremis, conversion was still far from being fully accomplished and special exemption from taxation, forced labour, and military service was offered by the state to those who accepted baptism. In 1602 a bishopric was erected at Astrakhan, a short distance above the mouth of the Volga. In the opposite direction, in the extreme North the borders of Christianity were being pushed forward. During the reign of Ivan IV and partly through his encouragement, zealous monks were founding monasteries and winning converts among the Lapps. By the end of the sixteenth century what we may now call the Russian Orthodox Church had extended its borders southward to the Caspian Sea, northward to the White Sea and the coasts of the Arctic, and eastward to and even beyond the Urals.

The Uniate Secession

While these territorial gains were being made in Eastern and Northern Europe, the Orthodox Church was losing ground on its western borders to the Roman Catholic Church. This was because of a combination of Polish rule and the missionary activity arising from the Catholic Reformation, chiefly through the Jesuits. We have seen that the Poles and the Lithuanians had long been extending their rule over Russians who held to the Orthodox Church. Since the Poles and the Lithuanians were Roman Catholics, this quite naturally tended to bring the Orthodox under the control of Rome. The impact of the Catholic Reformation roughly coincided with the reigns of Stephen Batory (1575–1586), who as one of Poland's ablest kings markedly strengthened Polish rule eastward, and of Sigismund III (1586–1632) who, although a descendant of that Gustavus Vasa who had been largely responsible for the transfer of Sweden to Lutheranism, was ardently Roman Catholic. Both monarchs supported the Jesuits.

Under these circumstances the sections of the Orthodox Church which looked for leadership to Kiev, the historic centre of early Russian Christianity, were hard pressed. A Jesuit college which had been opened at Vilna in 1570 attracted the sons of the Orthodox nobility. The Polish kings took a hand in the choice of bishops for their Orthodox subjects and favoured men who would cooperate with them. Many of these bishops were scions of the nobility who regarded their posts as opportunities for comfortable living, some were married and quite secular and had little either of education or character. Numbers of the nobles who had remained Orthodox and of the Orthodox laity in the middle classes in the cities rallied to the support of their faith and formed brotherhoods on its behalf. Among other activities they subsidized the printing of Orthodox books. In 1588 the Patriarch of Constantinople visited the region, sought to stem the tide towards Rome, deposed the Metropolitan of Kiev, and replaced him with another man. Several of the Orthodox bishops had their Rome-ward proclivities strengthened by irritation at the activity of the laity. Some of them met at Brest in 1591 and complained to the king and by the end of 1594 several bishops expressed their desire for union with Rome.

The decisive step was taken in 1596. Sigismund III had issued a manifesto announcing the union of the Orthodox with Rome and called a council at Brest. When the gathering assembled, it was found to be divided. The Orthodox party included Cyril Lucar, then in his mid-twenties and representing the Patriarch of Alexandria, and also a spokesman for the Patriarch of Constantinople. It broke away from the council, met separately, and adhered to its traditional faith. The elements favouring union with Rome passed resolutions endorsing it. Sigismund and the Polish and Lithuanian governments regarded these as authoritative and sought to enforce them. A large proportion of the Orthodox acceded and became Uniates. Pressure was brought by Jesuits to bring the Uniates into closer conformity with Roman customs, but the Uniates resisted and, while in communion with Rome, maintained much of their distinctive rites and procedures. Among them arose (1604), with its mother house at Vilna, partly on the model of Roman Catholic monasticism, what was known as the Basilian Order, a name which suggested an Eastern precedent. It spread rapidly and did much for the intellectual and moral advancement of the Uniates. It also entered actively into the controversy with the Orthodox.

The Orthodox did not all become Uniates. The lay brotherhoods which had been loyal continued. They engaged in controversy with the Uniates and a substantial output of books and pamphlets followed. They carried on schools which, in contrast with those of the Jesuits, were Orthodox and often had Greek teachers. Some Orthodox monasteries survived and new ones were organized, and that in spite of the confiscation by the government of many of their properties for the benefit of the Uniate Basilians. Indeed, something of a religious awakening occurred.

The persistence of the Orthodox branch of the Church was not on purely religious grounds. Much of it was from nobles who resisted the extension of the authority of the king. Part of it was racial and an incipient nationalism which looked upon the Uniate movement as a surrender to the hated Poles and Lithuanians. The Cossacks who were spreading in the region held to the

Orthodox Church as a badge of independence from the foreigner. On one occasion a mob, resenting his efforts to suppress Orthodox worship, fell upon a Uniate bishop, beat him to death, and flung his body in the river.

The Orthodox eventually scored signal victories. Their Patriarch of Jerusalem visited the region in 1620 and consecrated a metropolitan and six bishops. After the death (1632) of the ardently Roman Catholic Sigismund III, the Diet which elected to the throne his son and successor, Vladislav (Ladislaus) IV, also granted the Orthodox the right to have a hierarchy consisting of a metropolitan (at Kiev) and four suffragan sees. As metropolitan it appointed Peter Mogila. Mogila, of noble stock, had been well educated in the schools of the Orthodox brotherhoods and abroad. At Kiev he made important innovations, largely in the field of education. He inaugurated schools which took over much of the newer methods that were appearing in Western Europe, made Latin a medium of instruction, raised standards, and founded an academy which he wished to equal the best of the education that was being given by the Jesuits. He wrote voluminously. He attacked Lucar's confession of faith and partly as a rejoinder compiled a catechism in which he set forth what he believed to be the Orthodox faith. Although he was looked upon with suspicion by conservatives as bringing in Latin influence, he made Kiev an outstanding centre of Orthodox theological activity which was to have marked fruits in wider ranges of the Russian Orthodox Church. He did much to put Kiev in touch with the thought of the Roman Catholic Church and one of his many writings, his *Orthodox Confession of Faith*, was eventually accepted as an authoritative statement of the beliefs of Russian Orthodoxy.

THE RUSSIAN ORTHODOX CHURCH A STABILIZING CENTRE IN THE "TIME OF TROUBLE"

For a few years at the end of the sixteenth and the beginning of the seventeenth century Russia went through a period of disorder which is technically known as the "Time of Trouble." In 1598, with the death of Tsar Fedor (Theodore), the childless son of Ivan IV, the dynasty which had had Vladimir as one of its distinguished early monarchs came to an end. There were uprisings due to social unrest. A disputed succession augmented the civil strife. Dmitri who believed, mistakenly, that he was the youngest son of Ivan IV had the support of the Poles and the Jesuits. With Polish aid he organized an army which took Moscow and for the moment it looked as though the Jesuit dream might be fulfilled and the Russian Church submit to Rome. Dmitri was killed, but other aspirants for the throne were put forward, among them a second false Dmitri, and the land fell into a sad state of anarchy. The Poles occupied Moscow and Smolensk and the Swedes held Novgorod.

Under these trying circumstances the Orthodox Church provided leadership and a rallying centre for the Russian spirit against the foreigner and Rome. The Patriarch Hermogen headed the resistance and was supported by the monasteries. He was cast into prison by the Poles and died there, presumably of starvation. A combination of patriotic forces took Moscow, expelled the Poles, and called a representative assembly to put the country in order. This assembly, or *Zemsky Sobor,* elected (1613) as tsar a sixteen-year-old noble, Michael Romanov, of a family related by marriage to the former imperial house, thus founding a dynasty which was to last until 1917. The "Time of Trouble" was at an end and Orthodoxy and nationalism, aiding each other, had triumphed. Philaret, the father of Michael Romanov, who earlier had been forced by a political enemy to enter a monastery and his wife to become a nun, became Patriarch of Moscow. For twenty-four years father and son as Patriarch and tsar coöperated in restoring order and strengthening the power of the Romanovs.

After the disorders of the preceding years morality and religion were at a low ebb. The Christianity of Russia had sufficient vigour to produce men who sought to reform the Church and raise the level of Christian living. Reform took at least two roads. One was conservative, partly of the Josephite tradition, endeavouring to revive the Church by a stricter observance of the old Russian ways. The other welcomed contact with the outside world, especially with the Greeks, and strove to bring improvement by adopting the usages of the mother church, the Greek Orthodox, from which the Russian Church had sprung.

The Patriarch Nikon and the Great Division in the Orthodox Church of Russia

We now come to one of the most momentous series of events in the history of Christianity in Russia. It resulted in a secession from the state church which for persistence, although not for magnitude, can be compared with the emergence of Protestantism from the Roman Catholic Church in Western Europe more than a century earlier. There was no connexion between the two movements. Each was purely indigenous and had features peculiar to itself. Both had social aspects. The rise of Protestantism was aided by nationalism and in some places, as in England, by the growth of the urban middle class. In Russia the secession was associated with the unrest of the common people and the parish clergy against the wealth and dictation of the higher clergy. Each had profoundly religious aspects. Protestantism was an effort at the moral reform of the Church and to go back of the changes associated with Rome to the original Christian faith. In Russia the revolt was in part a desire to reform the monasteries and adherence to the liturgical books through which the masses received their faith against an effort at the thoroughgoing correction of those books to make them conform more nearly to the Greek originals. That effort at correction was led by the Patriarch, so that in a sense the Russian dissent was akin to Protestantism in that it was a reaction against innovations by the administrative centre of the Church.

Yet Protestantism and seventeenth century Russian dissent, although having much which seemed in common, were quite different. In the latter there was nothing akin to salvation by faith and the priesthood of all believers. While Protestantism was eventually to be strikingly missionary and was to have a phenomenal growth, Russian dissent had few if any converts from non-Christians. However, as Protestantism was the source of much of the later democracy in Western Europe, the Russian seventeenth century dissent is said to have laid the foundations for liberty and revolution in that land.

This attempt at a parallelism with Protestantism is not altogether happy. There was more resemblance between the Russian dissent and that of Western Europe of the Middle Ages. Yet here, too, the differences were greater than the similarities.

The great seventeenth century secession from the Russian Orthodox Church was closely connected with one of the most remarkable men in Russian history, the Patriarch Nikon. Nikon (1605–1681) was of peasant, possibly Finnish stock, and was earlier known as Nicetas or Nikita Minin. As a lad he was noted both for his asceticism and for his rapid progress in learning. He wished to be a monk and, indeed, undertook a monastic novitiate. However, his relatives urged him to marry and become a parish priest. He yielded, was ordained, and served in Moscow. Before he was thirty his children died. Perhaps seeing in this divine judgement or direction, he persuaded his wife to take the veil (she eventually became an abbess) and he became a monk and went north. Before many years he was prior of a monastery on the western shore of the White Sea. In connexion with the duties of that office he journeyed to Moscow to attend a council. There the Tsar Alexis noticed him, was impressed by him, put him in a position of prominence in a monastery near the capital, gave him public duties, and frequently consulted him. It speaks well for Nikon that he used his influence with Alexis to intercede for widows and orphans who had not been able to obtain their rights in the courts. Soon (1649) he was made Metropolitan of Novgorod. In that post he showed initiative, marked ability, and reforming zeal, and helped to put down a revolt. Then, in 1652, he was appointed Patriarch. He was very reluctant to take the post, but the tsar insisted, and he finally consented, but only on his own terms, and with the approval of the synod, clergy, and people. He stipulated that his convictions of the high place of the Patriarchate should be observed, and that the tsar and the Church *Sobor,* or assembly, obey him in everything as "shepherd and father." He took the title of Great Sovereign.

As Patriarch, Nikon inherited many problems. Not many years earlier, some of the laity and nobles, desiring to regulate the monasteries, many of which were rich and badly managed, and the Church, enormously wealthy and with privileges which hampered civil administration, had a code enacted for the regulation of the civil side of the Church and set up a civil department, the "Monastic Office" (*Monastyrskii Prikaz*). As a result many privileges of the clergy and monasteries were curtailed. The bureau also reached out into highly debatable ground and dealt with the spiritual functions of the Church. Many of the clergy were bitterly opposed to it and sharp dissensions arose. After the great tradition established for the Patriarchate by Hermogen and Philaret, in which that office had overshadowed the tsar, recent Patriarchs had been weak. Nikon had a lofty conception of the Patriarchate and was determined to make it a reality. That way lay trouble. Moreover, he inherited the thorny problem of the revision of the translations of the sacred books, to bring them more nearly in accord with the Greek originals.

The issue of the service books and ritual had not been finally settled by the decision of the *Stoglav* and the death of the luckless Maxim. It arose from time to time and early in the seventeenth century became acute over the section in the Epiphany rite of the benediction of the waters, where in copies long in use the prayer was offered that the water might be sanctified "by the Holy Spirit and by fire." In seeking a correct text for this passage Archimandrite Dionysius of the influential Trinity-Sergius Monastery, together with his collaborators, could find the phrase "and by fire" in only two old Slav copies and in no Greek copy. Accordingly he omitted it. This aroused intense opposition, for it was held to be a denial that the Holy Spirit is composed of fire, an ancient and widely held belief. Dionysius and his associates were haled before the Patriarchal court, tortured, and imprisoned. However, after his accession, the Patriarch Philaret pardoned them and in 1625, following opinions of the Patriarchs of Alexandria and Jerusalem, had the debated words "and by fire" excised from the ritual. The work of editing the texts of the books used by the Church was carried on under the direction of Philaret and of the Patriarchs who immediately preceded Nikon. This was done in connexion with the preparation of editions for the press, for printing was being increasingly employed. Much of the scholarship was faulty and the confusion became worse confounded. Yet some of the revisers were competent. Among them were Greek scholars imported for that purpose. Here was a knotty problem to which a prelate of Nikon's vigour would be fairly certain to address himself.

In making innovations any Patriarch would find himself confronted by the conservatism associated with large elements of the Josephite tradition and also by the nationalistic and anti-Roman Catholic sentiment which had been aggravated by the unhappy events of the "Time of Trouble." As an example of this attitude, a synod declared that since Roman Catholics were guilty of many heresies, their baptism was not valid and that any of them seeking membership in the Russian Orthodox Church must be rebaptized. The synod also declared that the only valid baptism was by immersion, and that Orthodox coming from the Kievan jurisdiction or elsewhere who had had the rite through sprinkling must be rebaptized through the correct form.

Nikon was not one to hesitate before difficulties. During his first few years as Patriarch he had the unqualified support of Alexis. The tsar consulted him on matters of state and while he was away on his wars Nikon was dominant in the civil as well as the ecclesiastical phase of the empire's administration. Nikon addressed himself vigorously to Church affairs. He insisted upon rigid discipline for the clergy, a policy much needed in an age which had not yet recovered from the license of the last years of Ivan IV and the "Time of Trouble." He encouraged preaching. He made it clear that he believed that the Church should not be subject to the state and curbed the activities of the Monastic Office. He held that the tsar should not control synods, the appointment of bishops, ordinations, or ecclesiastical courts.

Nikon continued the revision of the books in use in the Church. To that end he established contacts with Kiev, where, as we have seen, marked advances had been made in education and scholarship. He sought to discover Greek usage and in part to adopt it, and to help him brought in Greek scholars. Some of this may have been out of a desire to bring the Russian Church into close contact and full fellowship with other units of the Orthodox Church. Nikon's purpose, too, seems to have been to induce the Orthodox in the South-west who looked to Kiev, including Kiev itself, to accept the jurisdiction of Moscow. He insisted upon the use of three fingers instead of two in crossing oneself or giving the blessing. He had a synod (1656) condemn the rebaptism of Roman Catholics and gave recognition to the baptism and orders of the Roman Catholics and Orthodox in South Russia. He made official the revised copies of the service books and required their use throughout his jurisdiction.

Nikon sought to crush opposition, especially to his service books. He suppressed most of it and had one of its leaders, Avvakum (Habbakuk), exiled to Siberia. Avvakum belonged to a group of priests in the circle of the Archpriest Stephen Vonifatievich, the spiritual father of the Tsar Alexis. They were seeking reform by the older Russian ways of observance of the ecclesiastical rules of prayer, fasting, and strict morals. They stressed preaching and confession.

Much of the resistance arose not only from conservatism but also from the conviction that the section of the Orthodox Church headed by Moscow, the third Rome, could not be in error and from the suspicion of influences stemming from the first Rome, now become heretical, and from the Greeks who after the fall of the second Rome, Constantinople, so it was believed, had fallen into errors. Criticism also arose from what was interpreted as the Patriarch's oppression of the parish clergy and their flocks. Nikon enforced the tithes on cities and towns and on the deacons and priests. He was accused of strengthening the grip of the higher grades of the hierarchy on the lower grades and on the masses. He widened the gulf between the parish priests, married as they were, and the bishops who by the Eastern tradition were monks and celibate. In seeking to make the Church independent of the civil authorities, Nikon withdrew the parish priests from the jurisdiction of the village elders and placed them more directly under the bishops and the archpriests. Resistance from the lower clergy was, accordingly, especially marked.

Here was leadership such as the Russian Orthodox Church had not previously known. More nearly than any other figure in the history of Russia Nikon resembled the great Popes of Rome. His was the dream of making the Russian Church, led by the Patriarch, dominant in the life of the nation. Yet it ended in tragedy for Nikon personally and for the Church.

Nikon's power lasted only about six years. Then came his downfall. He had alienated a large proportion of the nobles, the clergy, and the monks, but so long as the tsar backed him he was relatively secure. In 1658 it became clear that he was out of favour with the tsar. Alexis seems to have resented the fashion in which Nikon dominated him and determined to break the spell which the Patriarch had exerted over him. Finally, when the tsar purposely absented himself from services where Nikon was officiating, the latter withdrew from Moscow in protest and ceased to perform his patriarchal duties. He retired to a monastery, first one near by and then one on the White Sea. Yet he still regarded himself as Patriarch.

Nikon's absence was followed by confusion, for his post was not filled and the removal of his strong hand gave the seething discontent opportunity for expression. Those who opposed his changes won the ear of the tsar. Avvakum was recalled from his Siberian exile and Alexis went out of his way to ask his blessing. Some among the Moscow populace besought the tsar to restore the old ways and hailed Avvakum as a hero. Numbers of the clergy returned to the use of the unrevised service books and the ways of singing in the services which Nikon had proscribed. As the year 1666 approached, many connected it with 666, the number of the beast in *The Revelation of John,* and charged

Nikon with being associated with it, if not actually being that monster itself, and with the prophesied apostasy through the worship of the beast.

Efforts were made to force Nikon out of office. In 1660 a synod met at imperial command, with the purpose of deposing him. The Patriarch was charged with arrogance, ambition, maladministration, and encroaching on the civil authority. Yet objectors declared that a Patriarch could be deposed only with the concurrence of the other Patriarchs and the administration of the office was entrusted to a *locum tenens*. The other Patriarchs were approached. Pressure was put on Nikon to resign or to come before a civil court, but he declined to do either. In December, 1664, Nikon returned to Moscow. He appeared dramatically in patriarchal state at a service in the cathedral and, according to custom, called on the tsar to attend. This the tsar declined to do and ordered Nikon back to a monastery to await the verdict of the other Patriarchs.

Eventually Nikon's enemies prevailed. In November, 1666, a synod assembled in Moscow which was attended by the Patriarchs of Alexandria and Antioch and a throng of bishops and other prelates. It gave Nikon a formal trial, condemned him, deposed him, and sent him into exile. The chief grounds urged for the action were that he had cursed bishops without trial, that he had deserted his throne and left the Church defenseless, that he had slandered the tsar and the Church, that he had used improper language against his opponents, that he had not treated his judges with proper respect, and that his administration had been cruel and arbitrary. The synod avoided what was to Nikon, in addition to his personal grievances, the central issue, the control of the Church by the state, and the interference of the tsar with functions properly reserved to the Church, such as ordinations, the decisions of ecclesiastical courts, the appointment of bishops, and synods.

Nikon was never rehabilitated. For a time he and Alexis resumed contact by letter, but on the coming of the next tsar, Nikon's enemies, implacable, had him sent into deeper obscurity and he died while on the way (August 17, 1681).

Nikon's work was not completely undone. Before his death the Monastic Office to which he had objected was abolished. Synods enacted discipline and monastic reforms in the direction which he had envisaged, and some restraint was placed on lay interference with ecclesiastical jurisdiction. Even more significant was the action of the synod (1666–1667) which deposed Nikon in accepting much that he had accomplished in the revision of the service books. The books as corrected under his direction were approved and also the use of the three fingers in giving the blessing. The recalcitrants who held to the old ways were ordered to repent. Some did so. Others refused and for their obstinacy numbers among them were excommunicated and sent to prison.

The action of the synod of 1666–1667 hardened the resistance. Those who refused to conform were known as the Old Ritualists, the Old Believers, or Raskolniks. The last designation, from *Raskol,* or division, schism, is a general term which may be applied to all who had withdrawn from the Russian Orthodox Church. The Old Believers held that the official church had become apostate by following the errors of the Greeks. The first Rome, they contended, had become heretical, the second Rome, Constantinople, had also departed from the true faith, and now the third Rome, Moscow, by adopting the errors of the later Greeks, had followed in the way of the first two. Many of the Old Believers were convinced that the end of the world was at hand and lived in expectation of it.

The Old Believers were in part rebels against the upper ranks of the hierarchy. No bishops joined them and while some among the higher classes held to them they were chiefly recruited from the monks, the parish priests, and the common people. In at least one monastery the abbot refused to join in the use of the old books and the body of the monks persisted in spite of him. The movement was, then, in large measure a revolt of the underprivileged. In that respect it was not unlike several of the dissident movements in Western Europe during the Middle Ages and some aspects of Protestantism.

The state viewed the Old Believers as seditious and took vigorous action. In 1685 an imperial decree was issued against them. If they did not give up their Raskol ways they were to be tortured and if obdurate they were to be burned alive. Those who repented were to be sent to an ecclesiastical prison for reëducation. Death was the penalty for Raskol rebaptism, both for him who administered it and for the unrepentant recipient.

While the edict was seemingly concerned with the religious aspects of the movement, the government may have been quite as much alarmed by the social and political implications. Thus in 1682 there broke out an uprising among the *Streltzy,* the Moscow garrison of infantry, the organization of which went back to Ivan IV. The *Streltzy* had the sympathy of many of the populace of the capital. One of their officers succeeded in injecting the religious issue into the movement and induced the *Streltzy* to champion the cause of the Old Believers and to demand the restoration of the old service books. It was Sophia, elder sister of Ivan, co-tsar with Peter, of whom we are to hear as the Great, who was responsible for the edict of 1685. A woman of marked force of character, she was regent, for Ivan was weak and Peter was in his early teens. Obviously she wished to suppress a movement which was closely tied with what she deemed insubordination and a dangerous threat to the authority of the tsar.

The authorities were not content with words but engaged in active persecution. The Old Believers were hounded down. For example, Avvakum was confined to a subterranean prison and in 1682, in the year following the death of

Nikon, to whom he was the great opponent, he was burned at the stake. Both men had been rejected by the official church and the state. Thousands of Old Believers were put to death, some by hanging and others by burning. To escape death at the hands of their persecutors or from despair at the state of the world, many of the Old Believers burned themselves alive. Thousands are said to have perished in this fashion. Others starved themselves to death.

Yet the Old Believers persisted. Some hid themselves. Others fled from the vicinity of Moscow, where the central authorities could reach them, to regions where the power of tsar and Patriarch was weak. Numbers found this refuge in the northern forests. Some went south, some to Poland, and others into Swedish territory.

The Old Believers had no one central organization and varied greatly among themselves. Since no bishops had come out with them from the state church, they had no episcopacy and did not ordain priests. They would not accept the ministrations of the state church, because from their standpoint it was apostate. Among them were former priests of the state church. The latter's services were, accordingly, acceptable. In the course of time the Old Believers divided into those who had priests, the *Popovsty,* and those who did not have them, the priestless, *Bezpopovsty.*

Those who had priests at first depended upon the clergy who had seceded with them. Later they accepted priests who had been ordained in the state church but who for one reason or another threw in their lot with them. These priests were required by their flocks to use the service books which were free from the changes brought in by Nikon. At first they were rebaptized, some of them fully garbed in their clerical vestments. Lay converts coming over from the state church were also rebaptized. Eventually some of the *Popovsty* dropped the requirement of rebaptism. Usually, however, they at least anointed with oil the priests who joined them. In the first half of the eighteenth century a bishop of the state church joined them, but died after a few months. Some priests were obtained with the consent of the bishops of the state church. Others were accepted from the Uniates. In the nineteenth century a branch obtained a bishop from the Greek Orthodox Church and through him had bishops in the apostolic succession and who could ordain clergy.

The priestless among the Old Believers divided into many groups. They agreed that the true priesthood had ended with the death of those who had been ordained before the time of Nikon. On many other issues they were not in accord. Some of them held that for baptism, confession, and burial a priest was not necessary and a layman or an unordained monk could officiate. None had the Eucharist. Many held that, since marriage required a priest, they would live strictly as celibates. Some others tolerated concubinage without marriage.

Others were for marriage by the priests of the state church. Some declined to pray for the tsar since, from their standpoint, he was unbaptized. Others offered prayers for him. Many held that Antichrist had appeared or was about to appear and some identified Peter the Great with him. Numbers entirely repudiated baptism, contending that no layman could administer it. Some practised communal living. Others were wanderers. The varieties of the priestless multiplied with the years.

Some of the Old Believers sought to win converts from the Orthodox. Others lived in what were in effect closed communities, refusing to marry outside their group and having as little as possible to do with those not of their particular sect.

Here, then, in the Old Believers was a movement, or, rather, a number of movements, peculiarly Russian, evidences of vitality in Orthodox Christianity. They attracted many of the more independently minded and those searching for a way of satisfying their religious hunger. The majority were peasants. A minority were merchants with a sturdiness of character which won them success in business.

Other Dissident Movements

The Old Believers were not the only Russians who departed from the state religion. There were also the Khlysty, who called themselves the People of God. Their origin is obscure. We do not know the date of their origin or whether here was a purely indigenous movement or one which sprang from foreign contacts, possibly with the Bogomils. They themselves dated their beginnings from the seventeenth century, but they may have been much older. They regarded their founder as a peasant, Daniel Filippov, who is said to have been one of the priestless Old Believers. Khlysty tradition had it that the God Sabaoth descended from the clouds and took possession of Daniel, who thus became the living God. It is said that Daniel began preaching, saying that he had come to save men's souls and that none other teaching than his was true. His followers were to abstain from intoxicating liquors and marriage. If married, husbands and wives were to separate. Stealing and foul words were to be shunned, hospitality and charity were to be practised, with prayer, and keeping the commandments of God. Daniel had a spiritual son, Suslov, who was declared to be a Christ. The Khlysty held that there were many incarnations, or Christs, of whom Jesus Christ was merely one, and that all could be saved by their own good works. They kept their membership secret and outwardly conformed to the state church. Their secret meetings included dances which induced ecstasy and speaking with tongues. Discovered, they were persecuted. They were not exterminated but merely driven underground.

It may be that the Dukhobors and Molokans, of whom we are to hear more later (Chapter XLIII), were in existence at this time.

The Russian Orthodox Church Is Influenced by the Roman Catholic Church but Rejects It

While the Old Believers were hiving off from the state church, influences from the Roman Catholic Church were being felt in that body. They entered largely through Kiev but partly through the Jesuits in the regions under Polish influence and in the Austrian embassy in Moscow. The innovations at Kiev which were mainly the work of Peter Mogila had admirers in Moscow. In the 1680's an academy for theological study was begun in that city. It was inspired by the one in Kiev. A struggle ensued for the control of the institution between those sympathetic with Rome and those of the Orthodox tradition. The latter won, and the assignment of inaugurating the Moscow Academy was given to two brothers, Greek monks who had studied in Venice and Padua but who had kept their Orthodox convictions. A controversy also arose over the Eucharist, whether, according to the Roman Catholic view, the consecration of the bread and wine was through the words of Christ recited by the priest or, as the Orthodox maintained, by the invocation of the Holy Spirit at a later point in the prayer of consecration. In 1690 a council condemned the Roman Catholic position. The reaction against any influence from the West became so strong that the academy, even though it was safely in Orthodox hands, was allowed to fall into a sad state of neglect.

While it was rejecting anything that smacked of Rome, the Russian Orthodox Church was expanding westward into territory which was threatened by the Roman Catholic Church. In the middle of the sixteenth century the Cossacks of the Ukraine broke away from Poland and became incorporated with Russia. In 1685 a further shrinkage of Polish political influence was accompanied by the extension over Kiev of the ecclesiastical authority of Moscow.

The Striking Changes under Peter the Great

The defeat of Nikon in his efforts to free the Church from the domination of the state and to make the Patriarch more important than the tsar was not merely the frustration of one individual. The great Patriarch's body was scarcely cold in its grave when there came to power a tsar who brought the Church into more extensive subjection to the throne than it had yet been and who caused the Patriarchate to lapse for about two centuries. Nikon died, banished, in 1681. Eight years later, in 1689, at the age of seventeen, Peter, who had come to the throne as a child in 1682, the year after the death of Nikon, dismissed his sister Sophia, the regent, and took full charge. The most vigorous

tsar since Ivan IV, he was the dominant figure in Russia for nearly a generation, until his death (1725).

Into the dramatic and often repeated story of those three and a half decades
we need not go, except in the briefest summary. It included the subjugation of
the rebellious *Streltzy*, Peter's sojourn in Western Europe, his Westward
orientation of Russia, symbolized by the founding of St. Petersburg and the
transfer of the capital from Moscow to that city with its Baltic and Western
confrontation, his reorganization of the state on the models of Western administration and absolute monarchies—for he was a contemporary of Louis
XIV of France—and his wars and extensive conquests.

We are here concerned with what Peter did to the Russian Orthodox Church
and through it to the Christianity of Russia. Peter was not irreligious, but
while outwardly he conformed, his faith was not by any means in full accord
with that of the Orthodox Church. As he was bringing all the state and society
under the control of the throne and disregarding old traditions and precedents,
so he insisted that the Church be subordinate to the crown. He had seen
Protestantism in Western Europe with its principle of *cujus regio ejus religio*
and the domination of territorial and national churches by the princes. It may
be, too, that Peter was influenced by the experience of his father, Alexis, in his
conflict with Nikon and had been convinced by it that as tsar he must not be
embarassed by the rival power of the Church.

Peter made the Church distinctly subordinate to the state. When, in 1700, the
Patriarch died no one was appointed to succeed him. The office was not formally
discontinued, but it was not filled. Since the Patriarch's court was in abeyance,
many cases were taken from the tribunals of the Church to those of the state.
Questions of doctrine and ecclesiastical discipline were left to the Church, for
the experiment of putting the clergy under the civil courts was soon abandoned.
The Monastic Office was reëstablished and to it was given the management of
the huge properties of the Church and the monasteries. Some of the revenues
from them were diverted to education, charity, and purely secular objects. In
1721 a substitute for the Patriarchate was inaugurated. Instead of an individual,
a body, a Spiritual College, later called the Holy Synod, was put in charge of
the Church. This body was entrusted with the reform of superstitious customs,
the direction of education, both secular and religious, for the two were combined in the same schools, the supervision of the religious duties of the laity,
the censorship of writings, the investigation of miracles and of charges of
heresy, the examination of those proposed for the episcopate, the trial of
bishops, and the supervision of the finances of the Church. The duties of the
collegium, then, were to be administrative, legislative, and judicial.

Peter took other actions which affected the Russian Orthodox Church. He restricted the number of the clergy, regulated the interior life of the monasteries, and commanded the laity to make at least an annual confession and to attend church every Sunday and feast day. At first Peter was inclined to be lenient towards the Old Believers. Later, however, he enforced the existing legislation against them and treated them with great harshness. He tended to make the parish clergy an hereditary class. He stressed the education of the priesthood and of the sons of the clergy. By his insistence that the Church keep out of civil affairs he strengthened a trend which was already present, that of emphasis upon worship and the liturgy as the chief concern of the Church.

With his desire to give Russia a Western outlook, Peter favoured those among the clergy who had been trained with that viewpoint. Some of them he called from Kiev, where, as we have seen, Western influence was stronger than in Moscow. Some, while Orthodox, had a Roman Catholic orientation. Others were inclined towards Protestantism, especially since through his residence in the West Peter had imbibed sympathy for that form of the faith. Numbers of Russians became acquainted with Western theologians, including Augustine, others of the Roman Catholics, and several of the Protestants.

After Peter a partial reaction occurred. His changes aroused opposition among the conservatives. Under the brief reign of Peter II (1727–1730) it was marked. Then came a decade of German influence under Ann of Courland (1730–1740) a niece of Peter the Great and Ivan VI (1740–1742), grandnephew of Ann. Under Peter the Great's daughter Elizabeth (1742–1762) reaction was again in full swing, with the unpopularity of things Western and the attempt to restore what was purely Russian. Yet many of the changes of Peter persisted.

SUMMARY

In contrast with Western Europe it was a fairly sombre picture that the East presented in the two hundred and fifty years after 1500. In contrast with the abounding vitality in the West which expressed itself in the Protestant and Catholic Reformations, in most places in Western Asia and South-eastern Europe the churches which represented Christianity either only barely held their own or lost ground. The one exception was Russia. Here was geographic expansion and here were currents of life which cut themselves channels which were peculiar to that country. One would like to know more of the Christianity of the masses, especially in Russia. Monasticism continued and in Russia, although we hear little of it, the kenotic tradition persisted.

Although not making striking gains or breaking out in new ways as did the Christianity of the West, the Eastern Churches believed themselves to be preserving the Christian faith in its purity as it had come from the apostles. That was true of all of them, but it was especially the conviction of the Orthodox

Churches, both Greek and Russian. They knew that they were on the defensive as against the politically dominant Islam, but they believed themselves to be the guardians of a sacred treasure.

SELECTED BIBLIOGRAPHY

W. F. Adeney, *The Greek and Eastern Churches* (New York, Charles Scribner's Sons, 1908, pp. xiv, 634). A useful summary.

L. Arpee, *A History of Armenian Christianity* (New York, The Armenian Missionary Association of America, 1946, pp. xii, 386). Warmly sympathetic, by an Armenian Protestant.

S. Bolshakoff, *Russian Nonconformity* (Philadelphia, The Westminster Press, 1950, pp. 192). A useful, comprehensive summary.

F. C. Conybeare, *Russian Dissenters* (Harvard University Press, 1921, pp. x, 370). A useful collection of material from Russian accounts.

G. P. Fedotov, *A Treasury of Russian Spirituality* (New York, Sheed & Ward, 1948, pp. xvi, 501). Valuable for this chapter for its autobiography of Avvakum, pp. 137–181.

A. Fortescue, *The Orthodox Eastern Church* (London, Catholic Truth Society, 1929, pp. xxxiii, 451). By a Roman Catholic, based upon wide reading.

A. Fortescue, *The Uniate Eastern Churches. The Byzantine Rite in Italy, Sicily, Syria, and Egypt* (London, Burns, Oates & Washbourne, 1923, pp. xiii, 244). A posthumous work, by a Roman Catholic.

W. H. Frere, *Some Links in the Chain of Russian Church History* (London, Faith Press, 1918, pp. xvi, 200). A comprehensive survey by an eminent Anglo-Catholic scholar, making extensive use of Russian materials.

A. H. Hore, *Eighteen Centuries of the Greek Orthodox Church* (London, James Parker & Co., 1899, pp. vi, 706). Semi-popular, not always critical.

G. Vernadsky, *A History of Russia* (Yale University Press, rev. ed., 1930, pp. xix, 413). A comprehensive survey by a distinguished specialist.

NORTH AND CENTRAL A

AND THE WEST INDIES

SOUTH AMERICA
1500-1815

AFRICA
1500–1815

Scale of Miles
0   300   600   900

INDIAN OCEAN

ATLANTIC OCEAN

MEDITERRANEAN SEA

Strait of Gibraltar

MADEIRA
CANARY IS.
C. Bojador

CAPE VERDE IS.

MAURETANIA

SAHARA

SENEGAMBIA

SIERRA LEONE

Niger R.

SUDAN

GUINEA COAST

Cape Coast Castle

SÃO THOME

Benue R.

Loango

São Paulo de Loanda   LOANDA

ANGOLA

UoBaji (San Salvador)

Congo R.

SOUTH AFRICA

Cape Town
Cape of Good Hope

Zambesi R.

MOZAMBIQUE

Inhambane

Mombasa

Melinde

ABYSSINIA

Nile Valley

RED SEA

ARABIA

SOCOTRA

ASIA

MADAGASCAR

Mozambique Channel

MAURITIUS
(ILE DE FRANCE)

REUNION
(BOURBON)

ASIA AND ADJACENT ISLANDS

Chapter XLI

CHRISTIANITY RESUMES ITS WORLD-WIDE SPREAD

One of the most striking features of the two hundred and fifty years between 1500 and 1750 was the resumption of the world-wide spread of Christianity. As we have seen, the century and a half between 1350 and 1500 saw a marked loss of territory. During the preceding four centuries the faith had been carried across Eurasia, even to Greenland, and probably to North America. It was also found as far south as the Sudan, Ethiopia, and South India. Yet by the end of the fifteenth century its outer boundaries had shrunk. It had died out in China and in most of Central Asia, in Western Asia it was slowly losing ground, it was retreating in Egypt and the Sudan, with the extinction of the feeble Scandinavian settlements it had vanished from Greenland, and any footing in North America had been ephemeral. Beginning with the closing years of the fifteenth century Christianity renewed its geographic expansion. By the middle of the eighteenth century Christian communities were on all five continents and on many of the islands that fringed these continents. It had been replanted in China and had a larger following there than ever before. It had been introduced to Japan, had won the majority of the population of the Philippine Islands, had been carried across Siberia to the north-eastern shores of Eurasia, had taken root in South-eastern Asia and the East Indies, had established a substantial foothold in Ceylon, and had become more widely extended in India. It was represented by scattered communities along the coast of Africa south of the Sahara. It had been reintroduced to Greenland and had become the prevailing religion in the West Indies and the more thickly settled portions of North and South America. With a pause and slight recessions for a generation or more after 1750, its forward march continued in the nineteenth and twentieth centuries. By 1750 it was more widely spread than it or any other religion had ever been. Three other faiths, Hinduism, Buddhism, and Confucianism, although within narrower geographic boundaries, may have outnumbered its professed adherents and Islam was still a formidable rival with a constituency not far from its size. Two centuries later, in the 1950's, in spite of serious recent losses, Christianity was still spreading and had clearly outstripped every other religion, not only in the area covered but also in numbers of professed adherents and in influence upon mankind.

This phenomenal spread of Christianity accompanied an equally remarkable expansion of European peoples and culture. Both were chiefly from Western Europe. Viewed superficially, the spread of Christianity in the four and a half centuries after 1500 was an integral, secondary, and inevitable phase of the world-wide extension of Europeans and their influence. That extension was partly by exploration, partly by conquest, partly by vast migrations, and partly by commerce. Since Christianity was the professed faith of Western Europeans and the Russians, it was to be expected that they would carry it with them.

Yet the spread of the Christian faith was not an inevitable accompaniment of the expansion of Europe. In important respects the latter hampered it. A large proportion, probably a majority of the Europeans through whom it was accomplished, although nominally Christian, denied it by their conduct. There were cruel exploitation and here and there extermination of non-Europeans. Withdrawn from the environment in which they had been reared, which, though by no means fully Christian, gave at least lip service to Christian standards, many Europeans deteriorated morally. Coming from societies where baptism and confirmation were practically universal and attendance at Christian instruction and public worship a social convention, in migrating to another region thousands and eventually millions tended to drift away from the Church and their children and grandchildren to lose what little of Christian tradition remained and to become quite de-Christianized.

The spread of Christianity in connexion with the expansion of Europe was chiefly through minorities, sometimes small minorities, who, committing themselves fully to it, became expressions of the abounding vitality inherent in the Gospel. That commitment was largely through awakenings in Christianity. In the years between 1500 and 1750 these were what we have described as the Protestant Reformation, the Catholic Reformation, and the movements, much less powerful, in Russia. It was these minorities, especially from the first two, who laboured to make the coming of the European a blessing and not a curse to non-Europeans, who strove to hold to the faith the migrating Europeans and their descendants, and to see that Christianity became an effective leaven in the new nations that arose from the migrations.

ROMAN CATHOLIC PREPONDERANCE

Between 1500 and 1750 the geographic spread of Christianity was mainly through Roman Catholics. This was for three reasons. It was first and chiefly because in the fore part of that period the expansion of Europe was predomi-nantly by Spain and Portugal, countries which were almost solidly Roman Catholic. The majority of the first voyages of exploration were through them and it was they who established the largest colonial empires. Spain ruled most of the West Indies, the southern coasts of North America, Mexico, most of Central America, the western and much of the southern and northern coasts of South America, and the Philippines. Portugal held Brazil, established posts along the shores of Africa, obtained footholds in India, conquered much of Ceylon, and had outposts on the Malay Peninsula and in the East Indies and China. Somewhat tardily Roman Catholic France entered into the race for colonies and at one time staked out a claim to the heart of North America, the region of the Great Lakes and the Mississippi Valley. Protestant powers were late in entering the race for commerce and colonies. In the seventeenth century Great Britain and Holland became active, but until after 1750 their colonial possessions, while far-flung, had only a small fraction of the population and the territorial extent of those of the Roman Catholic powers. In contrast with the Roman Catholics, the areas which contained the majority of the Protestants, Germany, Scandinavia, and Switzerland, before the nineteenth century had very little share in the expansion of Europe. While spreading over a huge area which stretched across all the northern reaches of Asia and after 1750 extended down the west coast of North America, Russian expansion was in regions which were thinly populated and did not count as much in the world scene as did those occupied by Western Europeans.

In the second place, the fact that the Roman Catholics had the leading place in the spread of Christianity between 1500 and 1750 was because the Catholic Reformation coincided with the explorations, conquests, commerce, and settle-ments of the Roman Catholic powers. The Catholic Reformation began in Spain on the eve of the discoveries of Columbus and the daring achievements of the *conquistadores*. It was an order begun by a Spaniard, the Society of Jesus, which carried on the most extensive missions of the era. The great days of the French colonial empire in North America followed soon after the height of the Catholic Reformation in France. Most of the Roman Catholic missions, whether by Spaniards, French, Portuguese, Italians, or from areas under the control of Spain in Italy and the Low Countries, were through orders which either came out of the Catholic Reformation, such as the Jesuits, Capuchins, Theatines, and Lazarists, or had been reinvigorated by that awakening, notably the Franciscans, Dominicans, and Augustinians.

A third but less important reason for the predominant role of Roman Catho-lics in the spread of Christianity during this period was that in the great monastic orders they had both the tradition and the instruments for spreading the faith, while at the outset the Protestants had neither. There had been a long standing precedent for the support and even the inauguration of missions by Roman Catholic princes. The missionaries had generally been monks, and such orders as the Franciscans, Dominicans, and Jesuits had missions as a major objective, whether among nominal Christians or non-Christians. Moreover, in the seventeenth century Rome devised a new instrument for the furthering and supervision of missions. This was the *Sacra Congregatio de Propaganda Fide,* usually known as the Propaganda. Begun in 1622, under it was placed a college, founded in 1627, for the training of missionaries. Eventually it was to become the major Papal agency for the coordination and direction of missions in non-Christian and non-Roman Catholic lands.

In contrast, by abandoning monasticism Protestants had deprived themselves of that instrument and most of their princes were so intent upon gaining the control of the Church in their domains by promoting Protestantism and were so engrossed in the struggles which engaged Protestantism in its early years that they could give little attention to missions, even had they desired to do so. Some of the Protestant reformers were frankly not interested in missions to non-Christians. It is significant, however, that as soon as explorations, commerce, and migrations put Protestants in close touch with non-Christians, among Protestants there were those who saw in the contacts both an opportunity and a duty and quickly devised means for propagating their faith.

As we recount the expansion of Christianity in the two and a half centuries after 1500, we can do it with less confusion if we trace its course region by region. We will begin with Africa south of the Sahara, then move to India, South-east Asia, the East Indies, the Philippines, Japan, China, and Siberia, and from there journey to the Western Hemisphere, ending our survey with the Thirteen Colonies which were soon to become the United States and, in point of numbers and influence, eventually to be the most important region in which Christianity was freshly planted in this period.

AFRICA SOUTH OF THE SAHARA

The planting of Christianity on the islands which fringe the west and east coasts of Africa and on the shores of Africa itself was mainly by Portuguese and so by Roman Catholics under their auspices. It was the Portuguese who led Europe in the discovery of the route to the East by way of the Cape of Good Hope. It was chiefly they who spotted the shores of Africa with trading posts. The pioneer in the undertaking, Prince Henry the Navigator, was, as we have more than once reminded ourselves, Grand Master of the Order of Christ, a military monastic body which in Portugal succeeded to the property of the Knights Templars. In his direction of the enterprise he seems to have been moved in part, or at least so a Papal bull declared, by the desire to unite with the Christians of India against the Moslems and pagans of that land and to spread the Christian faith.

The chief commodity derived from Africa was Negro slaves for the plantations of the New World. Here, as we have suggested, was a major exploitation of one race by another, an exploitation with a record of untold suffering and brutality. It is thought-provoking for those who would enquire into the effect of Christianity that explorations commenced partly for the purpose of propagating the Christian faith and carried through by those who bore the Christian name had as one of their effects a traffic brutalizing both to those who constituted its wares and to those who conducted it. As we are to see later, those fully committed to Christ did much to mitigate it and eventually it was those moved by the Christian faith who brought to an end both the traffic and the slavery which fed on it. Yet here is a sobering paradox.

Beginning in the fifteenth century Portuguese colonized the Azores, the Madeiras, and the Cape Verde Islands. Under Portuguese auspices and in part by missionaries from Portugal, the colonists were given spiritual care and churches were built.

At several points on the African coast Christian communities arose from the conversion of the Negroes. In the area just south of the Congo in what was known as the Kingdom of the Congo a native chief was baptized near the end of the fifteenth century. His son who succeeded him seems to have been earnestly Christian and under him a large proportion of his subjects were baptized. A son of this second generation Christian was consecrated bishop. So far as we know he was the first Negro to be raised to that dignity. Several other Negroes were ordained to the priesthood. Schools were begun, and what gave promise of becoming a permanent and thriving African Christian community came into being. Jesuits from Portugal were there through much of the sixteenth century and near the end of that century Franciscans arrived. There were also Capuchins and Discalced Carmelites. Yet in time Christianity died out, leaving only a few physical relics and possibly some traces in folklore. There were also important missions farther south, in Angola, and on the east coast at Mombasa and Mozambique.

In the sixteenth and seventeenth centuries several efforts were made by Portuguese to propagate Christianity in the island of Madagascar, but without continuing success.

Protestant Christianity came late to Africa. Its chief centre was on the southern tip of the continent. Here, in 1652, the Dutch began a continuing settlement as a way station to their trading posts in India, Ceylon, Malacca, and the East Indies, and a community arose made up of the Dutch and their descendants, of Huguenot refugees, of Malays and others brought from the East, and of local Hottentots. Within a few years a resident clergyman arrived and services and religious instruction were carried on according to the faith of the Reformed Church. In 1737 a Moravian missionary came who for six years laboured among the Hottentots. The Dutch ministers also baptized some of the non-Christians and a church was built in Capetown for the converts. In this fashion began what in the nineteenth and twentieth centuries was to be a major stronghold of Protestant Christianity.

FRANCIS XAVIER, THE GREAT PIONEER IN SOUTH AND EAST ASIA

In the half century after the first of their number rounded the Cape of Good Hope and arrived in India, the Portuguese established commerce and trading posts from the west coast of that land to Japan. In several of these centres there were priests, and efforts were made to hold the Portuguese to the faith, to baptize the children which sprang from their unions with the women of the region, and to win the non-Christians.

The great pioneer in the missions in South and East Asia and the fringing islands was one of the children of the Catholic Reformation and an initial member of the Society of Jesus, Francis Xavier. Xavier had only a decade in the East, from 1542 to 1552, but in that brief time he laboured in several lands, introduced the faith to Japan, and died while trying to make his way into China. A flaming spirit, few missionaries of any religion have made so notable a record.

Francis Xavier was born in 1506, of Basque stock and of a noble family in the Spanish part of Navarre, not far from the Pyrenees. Although lithe and athletic, he was fond of books, had no desire for a military career, and, the youngest son, chose to prepare for service in the Church. When less than twenty he went to the University of Paris to obtain the necessary training and was there eleven years. He seems to have been uncontaminated by the vices which were common among the student body and younger teachers, but for a time in that early flush of the Reformation before lines were tightly drawn he was on the fringes of a group with Protestant tendencies. However, as we have noted, he came in touch with Ignatius Loyola. Loyola, a fellow-countryman and about fifteen years his senior, set out to win the charming, brilliant Basque, and with success. Xavier was one of the Paris group who made their dedication with Loyola and journeyed to Italy.

While in Rome, Loyola received a request from King John III of Portugal for four missionaries for that monarch's possessions in the Indies. Loyola felt that he could not spare so many from his small company, for his vision was even farther-ranging than all the East. However, he agreed to send two. One of the two fell ill and, giving him only a day's notice, Loyola commanded Xavier to fill the vacancy. Xavier unhesitatingly obeyed, the more readily since he had already dreamed of going to India. He and his companion went to Lisbon and while waiting for passage were missionaries among the nominal Christians in that capital. The other was detained in Portugal to continue that mission, and Xavier sailed (1541) for India without him. On the long, tedious voyage he gave himself unstintedly to his fellow-passengers, surrendering to the sick his own privileged quarters.

Landing in India, Xavier was not content to remain long in any one spot. His was the vision of the pioneer and he ranged over most of the vast area covered by Portuguese commerce, blazing new trails for the faith and for the Society of Jesus. A devoted friend, intensely interested in individuals, seeking by love, gayety, and a timely word to win them to the Christian faith or to a deeper Christian life, Xavier also had an imagination which covered whole countries and peoples. He sought to raise the level of Christian living of the Portuguese adventurers and their nominally Christian mixed-blooded children. He recruited members for his Society, asked for more missionaries from Europe, and made provision for training for the service of the Church converts from among the peoples of the East.

The geographic range of Xavier's travels was prodigious. In Goa, the head-quarters of the Portuguese in India and the Far East, Xavier cared for the sick and the prisoners, preached, heard confessions, taught the children, and founded a college to prepare youth of several races and nations as possible missionaries. After a few months he went to South-east India to the Paravas, a low-caste pearl-fishing folk about twenty thousand of whom, to obtain Portuguese help against their hereditary enemies, the Moslem Arabs, had recently accepted baptism. Without priests, the sacraments, or Christian instruction, they attracted Xavier. He was with them about two years and learned enough of their language to impart to them in their vernacular the Apostles' Creed, the Ten Commandments, and some of the prayers, including the Lord's Prayer. He concentrated his attention on the children, encouraging them to teach their elders and to destroy idols and other symbols of their former religions. He baptized whole villages and trained and appointed catechists. It is interesting to record that the Paravas remained Christians, rose in economic status, and in the twentieth century were still bulwarks of the Roman Catholic Church. From the Paravas Xavier went to Travancore where, aided by Indian priests, he won several thousand converts from fishermen of a still lower social level. He was in Ceylon, then at Malacca, and then in the Moluccas. Back in India he strengthened the Goa college, observed that the Parava mission was advancing, and founded a college in Cochin, on the west coast south of Goa. In 1549 he went to Japan, where the Portuguese had begun commerce a few years earlier. There he inaugurated what was to be one of the most successful and tragic missions of the period. Having seen that enterprise begun and in responsible hands, his imagination was fired with the hope of starting a mission among the Chinese, the most numerous and most highly civilized people in the Far East. Before making that attempt and in part to prepare for it, he was once more in Goa. Then he went to an island off the coast of South China, where the Portuguese had a commercial rendezvous, hoping to gain access to the mainland. Failing but still hoping, he remained after all the Portuguese ships except his own had left. There he fell ill and died, late in 1552. As we are to see in a moment, his fellow Jesuits followed his lead and in several areas, notably India, Japan, and China, partly fulfilled his dream.

The Spread of Christianity in India

It will be remembered that the Portuguese were not the first to bring Christianity to India. Legend, unfortunately not fully dependable, has it that the faith was introduced by Thomas, one of the original apostles. There were almost certainly Christians in India before the fourth century. When the Portuguese arrived they found a large body of Christians on the south coast having Syriac as their ecclesiastical language and with ties with the Nestorians in Mesopotamia.

Partly under Portuguese auspices and partly independently of them, in the sixteenth, seventeenth, and eighteenth centuries Roman Catholic missions were widely spread in India. Early in the eighteenth century Protestant missions were begun.

In the course of time the overwhelming majority of the population of the areas in India under Portuguese political control adopted the Christian name. These areas were not large and had ports, chiefly Goa, as their nuclei. Not far from 1700 the number of Christians in the Portuguese possessions is said to have been half a million. Later the French established themselves in India, with their main centre at Pondicherry, on the south-east coast. There, too, a Christian community arose. However, French territories were much less extensive than those of the Portuguese.

Roman Catholic missions were by no means confined to the Portuguese and French enclaves. They were scattered over much of India. They were begun and maintained by the Franciscans, Dominicans, Carmelites, and Augustinians, and the orders which arose out of the Catholic Reformation, such as the Jesuits, Capuchins, and Theatines.

The Jesuits long maintained a mission in the centres of Mogul power in the North. The Moguls were descendants of the Mongols. They established themselves in the North in the first half of the sixteenth century and built an empire which eventually stretched over much of India. They were Moslems, but one of the line, Akbar, who reigned from 1556 to 1605, conceived the idea of devising one religion for his subjects which would combine the qualities of several and would thus help to unify his realm, divided as that was by deep cleavages between various religious communities. In his attempt to work out such a religion he asked Jesuits to his court and questioned them about their faith. With interruptions, the Jesuit enterprise continued under Akbar's successors into the latter part of the seventeenth century. Not many converts were made, but a few were gathered in Agra, Lahore, and Delhi.

More fruitful and in some ways more interesting was a Jesuit mission with headquarters at Madura, in the South, inaugurated by Robert de Nobili (1577–1656). Nobili was of a distinguished Italian family, nephew of Bellarmine, Jesuit theologian and cardinal, and related to Pope Julius III. On reaching India he found that Catholics were from the lowest social levels and were regarded as Portuguese. The term *prangui* was given to both. He was assigned to Madura to care for Paravas who resided there. Noting the contempt in which they were held by the majority of Indians, he realized that if Christianity were to have a wider appeal, a fresh approach must be devised. He found that the Brahmins were the highest caste and believed that by winning leaders from among them much of the rest of the population would be attracted. He therefore announced that he was not a *prangui,* built a hut in the Brahmin quarter of the city, declared himself to be a Roman rajah and ascetic, adopted a manner of life and dress much like that of the Brahmin teachers, made himself familiar with the local vernaculars and the Sanskrit in which the sacred classics of Hinduism were written, and prepared an extensive Christian literature in Indian languages. He excluded Parava Christians from the church which he built and permitted his Brahmin converts to dress in a manner not unlike their pre-Christian garb. His methods soon aroused a storm of criticism among some of his fellow-missionaries, for they charged him with compromising the Christian faith. However, his archbishop supported him and in 1623 Rome pronounced in his favour. In the course of time an extensive enterprise arose in Madura and the vicinity which followed his procedure and amplified it. Only a minority of the converts were from among the Brahmins, but by 1703 the total Christian community was said to number two hundred thousand. In that year a Capuchin complained to Rome that in several ways the Jesuits were allowing their flocks to retain pagan customs. Controversy followed which disturbed the missions in South India and in 1744 was ended by a Papal bull which specifically condemned the questionable practices—the Malabar rites as they were called.

An Indian clergy was recruited and trained and we hear of bishops of Brahmin stock. Not a few of the clergy were said to be of inferior moral quality, but some of them were zealous and courageous missionaries.

The Portuguese connexion proved both an asset and a liability to Catholic missions in India. It was an asset, for Portuguese protection, especially in Goa and other Portuguese possessions, assisted in the process of conversion and in other ways the civilian authorities aided the Church. It was a handicap, partly because of the scandalous lives of many Portuguese who were far from ideal exemplars of the Christian faith. It also proved an obstacle because the Portuguese claimed the right to control missions throughout the country, as, indeed, they did in much of South Asia and the Far East. Papal decrees had given the King of Portugal what was called the *padroado,* or patronage, over ecclesiastical affairs. This included the naming by the crown of bishops and other forms of control. It was a phase of the domination of the Church by the crown which was, as we have seen, widely prevalent in Roman Catholic as well as Protestant lands. In India, Rome insisted that the *padroado* applied only to territory actually under Portuguese rule, while the Portuguese held that it covered all the land. Rome sought to dodge the issue and ease the friction by appointing to supervise the Church in non-Portuguese areas not bishops, but vicars apostolic. Since Portugal claimed the right to name the bishops, and this Rome conceded, vicars apostolic were given the titles of bishops of extinct sees, usually in Western Asia, and exercised their episcopal powers not in their own names but as direct representatives of the Pope. However, this device only slightly eased the tension. The Portuguese often placed obstacles in the way of missionaries sent out under the authority of Rome in disregard of the *padroado.* The issue troubled Catholic missions in India well down into the twentieth century.

We have already noted the attempt, in part successful, to bring into submission to Rome the Syrian Christians, and have seen that later the majority severed their Roman connexion. The Syrian Christians had in effect become a closed community, like an Indian caste, and made no effort to spread their faith among non-Christians.

Protestantism was late in coming to India. In the seventeenth century it arrived in the persons of Dutch, British, and Danish traders. Each of these groups had chaplains who ministered to the Europeans and their servants. However, while here and there were those who proposed to seize the opportunity to spread the Protestant faith among the Indians, nothing of consequence was done until early in the eighteenth century. The mission then begun sprang from Pietism. The first two missionaries, Ziegenbalg and Plütschau, had been students at the Pietist centre, Halle, and in 1706 arrived at Tranquebar, a Danish trading post on the south-east coast. They came at the instance of the Danish king. They were not welcomed by the local Danish authorities, but persevered, learned Tamil, and won converts from Hinduism and Roman Catholicism. Recruits came from Pietist circles in Germany, financial aid was given by Anglicans and Danes, and a Lutheran community arose which grew and persisted into the twentieth century.

CEYLON

On Ceylon, predominantly Buddhist in religion, a substantial Roman Catholic community arose in connexion with the Portuguese conquest of part of the island. That conquest began early in the sixteenth century. The missions were chiefly by the Franciscans. Some of the conversions were by force. Others were of native chiefs or kings and their followers from the hope of obtaining Portuguese support. Some groups accepted baptism in the expectation of Portuguese protection and of freedom from galling social, legal, and financial restrictions and exactions. In a few sections early in the seventeenth century Christians were in the majority.

In the seventeenth century the Dutch drove the Portuguese out of Ceylon. In 1658 they captured the last of the Portuguese strongholds. They sought to eliminate Roman Catholicism and substitute for it the Reformed faith. Roman Catholic clergy were expelled and in 1658 the death penalty was decreed for any who harboured a Roman Catholic priest. Many Roman Catholic church buildings were converted to Protestant uses and public and private meetings of Roman Catholics were forbidden. Non-Protestants, both Roman Catholics and non-Christians, were declared ineligible for office or employment under the Dutch and we hear in one temple of the suppression of Buddhist worship. We also read of the imposition of fines for non-attendance at church services and of the confiscation of a third of the property of some who refused to be baptized. Dutch clergy were sent out from Holland and an ecclesiastical structure was set up. In 1722 the number of Protestant Christians in Ceylon was said to be 424,392. However, the faith of most must have been very superficial, both because of the manner in which conversions were effected and of the lack of clergy. In 1747 it was reported that in all the island there were only five ministers and that of these only one understood the language.

In spite of the Dutch prohibition, thousands of Roman Catholics held to their faith. Indian priests, chiefly from Goa, ministered to them, often working in secret. They not only instructed Christians and gave the sacraments to them. They also won some non-Christians.

SOUTH-EAST ASIA

In the sixteenth, seventeenth, and eighteenth centuries Roman Catholic Christianity was planted in Burma, the Malay Peninsula, Siam, Cambodia, Cochinchina, Annam, and Tonkin.

In Burma no extensive Christian communities were gathered, but Jesuits, Dominicans, and Barnabites, especially the last, were active and made converts.

The Malay Peninsula was fairly solidly Moslem. From 1511 to 1641 the Portuguese were in possession of Malacca and there had churches and clergy. In 1641 they were driven out by the Dutch and the latter either turned the church buildings into Protestant houses of worship or diverted them to secular uses.

Roman Catholic missionaries came to Siam in connexion with the Portuguese and their commerce. As in Ceylon and Burma, the population was predominantly Buddhist. Unlike Ceylon, but like Burma, Christianity made little appeal, possibly because Europeans did not rule any of the land, and only a small Christian community was gathered.

In the region later known as Indochina, composed of Cambodia, Cochinchina, Annam, Tonkin, and the thinly settled Laos, extensive missions were carried on, chiefly by Jesuits, Dominicans, Franciscans, and the Paris Society of Foreign Missions. This last organization arose out of the appeal of a Jesuit who had laboured in Cochinchina and had become convinced that among the missionaries there should be secular priests who would not only seek to win non-Christians but also raise up and train a secular native clergy to care for the converts. In Paris he found a group of young men, fruits of the Catholic Reformation, who gave him an eager response. The result was the organization of the Society of Foreign Missions, formally founded in 1663. Eventually it had missions in much of South-east and East Asia. By the middle of the eighteenth century Indochina had Christian communities which totaled several tens of thousands.

THE EAST INDIES

South and east of Asia there stretches a vast congeries of islands which Europeans have known as the East Indies or the Malay Archipelago. It presents a mixture of races, languages, and religions. The Malay stock in its various divisions predominates racially and linguistically. Animism, Hinduism, Buddhism, and Islam had been present before the coming of Christianity and all these except Buddhism had followings when the first Christian missionaries landed. Islam was the most recent arrival and by the beginning of the sixteenth century had won the large majority of the population and was still spreading.

Christianity was introduced by the Portuguese, Spaniards, and Dutch. The first two brought the Roman Catholic form of the faith and the third propagated the Reformed variety of Protestantism. All three, but especially the Portuguese and the Dutch, were attracted by the spices of the islands, for these were much in demand in Europe. The Portuguese were the first to appear. Members of several religious orders took advantage of their trading posts to begin missions. In 1569 the Jesuits were said to be in charge of eighty thousand Christians. As we are to see in a moment, the Spanish strength was in the northernmost extension of the archipelago, the Philippines, but some of their missionaries reached southward, and an Italian Theatine from Palermo, then under Spanish rule, was called the apostle to Borneo and became the first vicar apostolic on that island.

The Dutch arrived late in the sixteenth century. Before many years they drove the Portuguese out of most of the archipelago and established their headquarters at Batavia, on the island of Java. The Roman Catholic communities dwindled or disappeared in the areas under Dutch control and persisted mainly on what remained to the Portuguese, chiefly part of the island of Timor. Dutch interests were in the hands of their East India Company. The Company supported pastors of the Reformed Church and in some of the islands gave active assistance to efforts at conversion. Many of the Malays accepted baptism, probably usually from the desire to stand well with the Dutch. Translations of the Bible were made into Malay and the New Testament in Malay was the main textbook in the schools. The Christianity of the majority was largely formal, but a state Protestant church came into being which continued into the twentieth century and then, disestablished, proved to have sufficient vitality to survive the adverse vicissitudes of World War II and its aftermath.

THE PHILIPPINE ISLANDS

As we have suggested, the Philippine Islands are actually the northernmost of the East Indies. They owe their name and their distinctive culture to the Spanish conquest which began in the sixteenth century. Their inhabitants are predominantly of Malay stock. At the dawn of the sixteenth century they were mostly animists in religion and in the primitive stages of culture. Islam was entering and had won some of the peoples in the South, Moros, as they were called by the Spaniards, not because of any racial difference but because of the Moslem faith and culture.

Sailing under commission from the Emperor Charles V, Magellan was the first European to reveal the islands to Western Europeans. He there lost his life (1521), and it was not until the third quarter of the sixteenth century that the effective Spanish conquest was begun. The Spaniards came by way of Mexico, a vast distance. Their occupation had little commercial significance, for only a limited trade was carried on by way of Manila and Mexico. It was primarily missionary and was accompanied and followed by the conversion to the Roman Catholic faith of the large majority of the population. The Philippines became the first nation in the Far East in which the majority bore the Christian name and into the twentieth century continued to be the only one to have that distinction.

Conversion and religious instruction were encouraged by the Spanish rulers and were through the members of religious orders, first the Augustinians, then the Franciscans, the Dominicans, the Jesuits, and a reformed branch of the Augustinians, the Augustinian Recollects. A few seculars came and some members of the hospital order of St. John of God. To avoid friction and duplication of effort, the civil authorities forbade more than one order to labour in any one province. Expenses were met chiefly from the royal purse, from tithes collected from the Filipinos, and by the Spanish landowners. By the end of the sixteenth century more than four hundred and fifty regulars had embarked for the islands. Very little armed force was employed. The Filipinos, docile and with neither a high culture nor an advanced religion to offer resistance, quickly conformed to the wishes of their masters. It is said that by 1586 four hundred thousand had been baptized. In 1612 there were reported to be 322,400 Christians on the one island of Luzon alone and in 1735 a total of 837,182 Christians was given for all the islands. In 1750 there were said to be over a million Christians if children were included.

The islands were divided into dioceses and a native clergy was recruited and trained. However, the control of the Church continued in the hands of the Spaniards, for from them came the bishops and they made up the membership of the religious orders. Friction was chronic between the civil and ecclesiastical authorities, between the regulars and the seculars, and between the bishops and the regulars, for the latter resisted episcopal supervision.

Much of the Christianity was superficial and was mixed with remnants of pre-Christian beliefs. Yet the missionaries strove to purify the morals of their flocks, did much to improve agriculture, cultivated a love of music, maintained hospitals, and founded schools, including two universities.

THE STRANGE AND THRILLING STORY OF JAPAN

When in 1549 Francis Xavier introduced Christianity to Japan, that land was emerging from a long period of disunion and civil strife. Union was being accomplished by Oda Nobunaga, Toyotomi Hideyoshi, and Tokugawa Ieyasu. Nobunaga was then in power. The country had received most of its civilization from China, including Buddhism, its leading religion. Upon that culture as it was imported the Japanese had placed their own stamp and to it had made additions of their own. In spite of the efforts of Nobunaga, the land was still divided into a number of feudal states, each of which was governed by an hereditary lord known as a *daimyo*. The Portuguese had reached Japan about 1542 and their commerce was proving profitable to them and to those *daimyo* with whose domains they traded. These were chiefly on the island of Kyushu, and the port which eventually enjoyed more of the Portuguese trade than any other was Nagasaki.

Xavier was in Japan only about two years, but he found the country so promising a mission field that other Jesuits quickly followed him. They had immediate and startling success. In 1582 churches were said to number about two hundred and Christians about 150,000. The growth seems to have been due to a number of factors. Nobunaga was friendly, partly because he was being opposed by some of the powerful Buddhist monasteries and hoped in the Christians to have a counter-poise to them. The *daimyo* who found the Portuguese commerce lucrative favoured the missionaries, for they saw that the latter were honoured by their fellow-countrymen and thought in this wise to obtain a greater share of the trade. Having learned eagerly from the Chinese, the Japanese were predisposed to be taught by another foreign people. The head of the Jesuits in the Far East deemed the Japanese the ablest of those whom he had known in that region and made efforts to raise up a clergy among them and to admit some of them to the Society of Jesus.

The death of Nobunaga (1582) and the advent of Hideyoshi to power did not immediately alter the situation. To be sure, in 1587 Hideyoshi issued an edict against Christianity, but a nephew of his wife became a Christian and one of the two commanders in the invasion which he launched against China by way of Korea was also of that faith. In 1588 Rome made Japan a bishopric. Although in 1585 Rome had specifically reserved Japan to the Society of Jesus, in the 1580's and especially the 1590's, to the great annoyance of the latter, Franciscans and Dominicans made their way to that country and won converts, but from lower social strata than those touched by the Jesuits.

In 1596 Hideyoshi began active persecution, but for specifically what reason is not entirely clear. Several missionaries and Japanese Christians were crucified, *daimyo* were forbidden to become Christians, numbers of churches were destroyed, and missionaries were ordered assembled at Nagasaki preparatory to deportation. The early death of Hideyoshi (1598) brought a pause to these measures.

Ieyasu, who soon became the effective power in Japan, eliminated Hideyoshi's son and placed his own family, the Tokugawa, so firmly in control that as

Shoguns they gave Japan its real rulers, although in the name of the *faineant* Emperors, until the 1860's. At first he was friendly to the missionaries. That seems to have been because he wished to develop foreign commerce. Missionaries flocked to Japan, not only Jesuits, Franciscans, and Dominicans, but also Augustinians. Ieyasu received the bishop with honour and gave financial aid to the Church. Christians rapidly increased. How many there were we do not know. Soon after 1600 they are variously estimated as between two hundred thousand and seven hundred and fifty thousand. Certainly they were a larger proportion of the population than they were to be in the nineteenth or the first half of the twentieth century. They were especially numerous in the South. In Nagasaki the majority seem to have been of that faith.

Then came the renewal of persecution, first under Ieyasu and even more drastically under his successors. The reason seems to have been primarily political. Ieyasu and the other Tokugawa Shoguns feared Christianity as a threat to the unity and the dominance of their family which they had so painfully established. It might be, so they thought, a precursor to Portuguese or Spanish invasion or the occasion for rebellion. The fears of those who followed Ieyasu were heightened by the pertinacity of missionaries in seeking entrance to the country, by the contumacy of the Japanese Christians in holding to their faith in the face of anti-Christian edicts, and, in 1637 and 1638, by a rebellion in which many Christians joined. Christians were visited with excruciating tortures and many of those who held to their faith were killed. To keep out missionaries, commerce was cut off with the Portuguese and Spaniards, and Japanese were forbidden to leave the country. At first English and Dutch traders were permitted in the ports, for they showed no disposition to spread their faith and were Protestants, not Roman Catholics. However, when for a time the English discontinued their trade they were not allowed to resume it. Only the Dutch were admitted and they were confined to an island in the harbour of Nagasaki and required to submit to other galling restrictions. Edict boards were posted throughout the realm proscribing Christianity.

Yet Christianity persisted. Several thousand Christians, most of them in the hills back of Nagasaki, held to their faith. Outwardly they were Buddhists, but they kept up baptism and Christian prayers, transmitting them to their children and the latter in turn to theirs. It was not until the second half of the nineteenth century that they were revealed to a startled Europe and to hostile Japanese political authorities.

THE REPLANTING OF CHRISTIANITY IN CHINA

Twice, in the seventh and then in the thirteenth century, Christianity had been introduced to China. Both times its constituency seems to have been prevailingly foreign and neither time does it appear to have won many converts from among the Chinese themselves. Twice it had died out, and so completely that we do not know precisely when or how.

Now, in the sixteenth century Christianity was brought again to China. It was through Roman Catholics and was planted so firmly that in spite of persecution it persisted and grew.

The reintroduction of Christianity was in connexion with Portuguese trade. As we have seen, Xavier had attempted it and had perished (1552) while seeking to enter the empire. Within less than a generation after his death the Portuguese acquired a permanent foothold at Macao, not far from Canton. In 1576 Macao was made the seat of a bishop and the King of Portugal agreed to provide financial aid for him and his cathedral staff. It was largely through Macao, as a small key hole, that Christianity reëntered China.

The situation was not propitious. Under the ruling dynasty, the Ming, the Chinese did not care for intimate contacts with the outside world. They considered themselves as givers not recipients of culture. Confucianism was dominant. Officialdom was made up of those who had been recruited through a highly competitive system of civil service examinations which were based on the Confucian classics. The state, the family, and ethics were governed by Confucian ideals and precepts. Every *hsien,* or local administrative unit, had a temple to Confucius and the other worthies of his school in which ceremonies were periodically held which all scholars were supposed to attend. Unless in some way Christianity could make its peace with Confucianism, it would find the going very hard.

Although it was through Macao that many of the missionaries came, it was chiefly by those from other countries than Portugal that the planting of Christianity was achieved. The Jesuits led, but several other orders and groups were active.

After Xavier the leading pioneer was Matteo (Matthew) Ricci (1552–1610). Born in the very year that Xavier died, apparently frustrated, Ricci, a Jesuit and well educated in mathematics and astronomy, arrived in Macao in 1582. By his knowledge of geography, mathematics, and astronomy, he won the somewhat grudging respect of a number of Chinese scholars and officials. He set himself to the diligent study of Chinese and the Confucian classics and became expert in them. He believed that Christianity could so be presented to the scholars and the masses as to win them without requiring them to make a complete break with Confucianism. For translating the word God he employed terms which he found in the Confucian classics, *Shang Ti* and especially *T'ien,* thus seeking to present Christianity as something not entirely new and to say, as Paul had long before said at Athens: "Whom ye ignorantly worship, him declare I unto you." He believed that the ceremonies in honour of ancestors which constituted an integral part of family life and those celebrated in the Confucian temples did not possess a religious significance in the sense that would make participation in them compromising for Christians. Thus a Chinese might become a Christian while still remaining a loyal member of his family, an official, and a Confucian scholar. Thanks to his friendship with scholars and officials, Ricci succeeded in establishing a residence for himself and his fellow-Jesuits in the capital, Peking. Before his death he had seen the conversion of a number of important persons, including an imperial prince.

The mission inaugurated in Peking by Ricci had a long but chequered history. Soon after his death the Jesuits were given charge of a revision of the Chinese calendar and of the bureau of astronomy which was closely connected with it. They thus had official position and status. From time to time they faced persecution, largely instigated by those who accused them of plotting for the overthrow of the dynasty or by jealous rivals for their position in the astronomical bureau. Yet the change of dynasty from the Ming brought by the Manchu conquest in the middle of the seventeenth century did not displace them. Under the greatest of the Manchu rulers, best known under the designation K'ang Hsi, who reigned from 1661 to 1722, and who was therefore a contemporary of Louis XIV of France and Peter the Great of Russia, they long enjoyed imperial favour. In 1692 what was in effect an edict of toleration was issued.

Reinforcements came. Some of these were to the Jesuits, among them a contingent from France, men who by their scholarly attainments won the friendship of K'ang Hsi, for that Emperor had an eager and inquiring mind. Other orders and societies also established themselves in China. They included Dominicans, Franciscans, and Augustinians from Spain by way of the Philippines, Italian Franciscans sent by the Propaganda, and members of the Paris Society of Foreign Missions.

By the beginning of the eighteenth century Christianity was making marked progress. Christians were found in almost all the provinces, perhaps in them all. They numbered between two hundred thousand and three hundred thousand. To give the nascent Church a structure, bishops and vicars apostolic were appointed, one of them a Chinese. Chinese were recruited and trained for the priesthood. In spite of occasional persecutions the prospects were encouraging.

Shortly after the beginning of the eighteenth century misfortunes began to beset the course of Christianity. They arose from a number of causes. The Portuguese insistence upon extending the *padroado* over all China proved a handicap. The waning of Spain and Portugal reduced the support of missions from those lands. More serious was a prolonged and bitter division among the missionaries known as the rites controversy. It centred about the methods which had been adopted by Ricci. Even some of the Jesuits were not at first convinced that these were not compromising the faith. Members of other missionary bodies, especially Dominicans and the Society of Foreign Missions of Paris, perhaps not uncontaminated by jealousy of the Jesuits, were emphatic that to follow the course pursued by Ricci would denature Christianity. They appealed to Rome. The struggle lasted for almost a century, from the first appeal to Rome, in 1643, to the final Papal bull, in 1742. The Jesuits insisted that nothing in the rites in honour of the ancestors and of Confucius as they permitted them were idolatrous and that to forbid them would convince the Chinese, already suspicious, that Christianity was subversive to Chinese morals and culture. The opponents of the Jesuits insisted that the rites were idolatrous. In an effort to adjust the difficulty two Papal embassies were sent to China. The first angered K'ang Hsi and fell afoul of the Portuguese *padroado* by seeking to by-pass it. Much of scholarly Europe became interested and a flood of argument poured from the presses. K'ang Hsi became involved and eventually insisted that if they were to remain in China missionaries must have official permits and that these would be given only to those who agreed to the attitude of Ricci. Since the Pope had come out against the methods of Ricci, the missionaries were posed with the unhappy choice of either leaving China or disobeying Rome. Some of them left. Others remained, hoping that on further representations Rome would alter its opinion. Rome was adamant and required all missionaries going to China to promise obedience to its decree against the rites. Yet that decree was provisional and contained the saving words: "Until it is decided otherwise." In the twentieth century the attitude of Rome towards the rites in honour of ancestors was reversed. Further disasters overtook missions in China in the second half of the eighteenth century, but of these we are to speak in a later chapter. In 1750 Christians still numbered about two hundred thousand.

THE SPREAD ACROSS NORTHERN ASIA

Christianity was carried across Northern Asia by the Russians. Russian trans-Asian expansion commenced shortly before 1500, but it was not until the sixteenth century that the region began to be politically subject to Moscow. By the middle of the seventeenth century Russian adventurers—Cossacks, fur-traders, and trappers—had made their way across the continent to Bering Strait. Russian Orthodox Christianity accompanied or followed that expansion. It was supported by the state, notably by Peter the Great and more for political than religious purposes. The missionaries were priests and monks. The population was sparse. Some of it was made up of Russians from west of the

Urals. For obvious reasons these were most numerous in the areas nearest Europe. They were held to a nominal allegiance to the faith. Much of the population was indigenous. Among them missions were conducted. They reached as far east as Kamchatka and by 1750 most of the peoples of that distant peninsula were reported to be Christian. There were also many conversions nearer Europe. A Russian mission was established in Peking, but it was more diplomatic than religious and confined its religious efforts chiefly to caring for a small contingent who had been taken captive by the Manchus in a border war and brought permanently to Peking.

In Asia, then, by 1750 Christianity was more widely spread than it had ever been. It had not recovered the ground lost in the central and western parts of the continent, but on the southern, eastern, and northern shores it was more widely represented than ever before.

THE SPREAD OF CHRISTIANITY IN THE WESTERN HEMISPHERE

It was not in Africa or Asia but in the Western Hemisphere that Christianity was to have its major spread between 1500 and 1750. In the first two continents and their fringing islands, except the Philippines, only minorities were won. In the major centres of civilization, Western Asia, India, Japan, and China, the minorities were only small fractions of the population and with some exceptions were under constant threat of persecution. Save for some of the islands, the thinly peopled northern reaches of Asia, and small enclaves in Africa, India, Malaya, and China, Europeans had no political control and effected no continuing settlements. In contrast, in the Western hemisphere by 1750 Europeans had made themselves masters of the more thickly peopled and civilized areas, had extended their control over almost all the coasts of South America and Central America, over the southern and eastern shores and much of the eastern interior of North America, and over most of the fringing islands. They had won to the Christian faith the majority of the pre-Columbian populations, including those highest in the scale of civilization, and had formed extensive settlements which in wide reaches, notably in the West Indies and the east coast of North America, by the middle of the eighteenth century constituted the overwhelming majority of the population. So far as they had religious loyalties, these settlements were professedly Christian. However, that faith sat more lightly upon some of them than it did on the countries from which they came. Here lay one of the challenges to Christianity. That faith was also challenged by the thousands of Negroes, most of them non-Christians, who were brought as slaves from Africa to work on the farms and plantations of the white men.

A major reason for the contrast between the course of Christianity in Africa and Asia on the one hand and the Western Hemisphere on the other was that the Eastern Hemisphere was well peopled and the home of high civilizations while in the Western Hemisphere man was relatively a new comer, for the most part had only sparsely occupied the wide reaches, and in only a few places, on the uplands of Mexico, Central America, and the northern cordillera of South America, had developed civilizations. These civilizations could not offer effective resistance to those of Europe. The more nearly primitive cultures of the other pre-Columbian peoples were even more yielding when once close contact was had with the white man.

Before 1750 European conquests, settlements, and the spread of Christianity were chiefly through the Spaniards, the Portuguese, the French, and the British, with lesser contributions from the Dutch, the Swedes, the Danes, and the Germans. It is convenient, therefore, to tell of the planting of Christianity by national categories and the areas occupied by each.

The Planting of Christianity in Spanish America

It was under Spanish auspices that Columbus made his momentous voyages of discovery. It was the Spaniards who occupied more territory than did any other European people before the middle of the eighteenth century. It was through them that the earliest major spread of Christianity was accomplished in the New World.

Spanish America included most of the major islands of the West Indies, Mexico, almost all Central America, Florida, part of the northern and southeastern, and nearly all the western coast of South America. The Spaniards were also reaching north from Mexico into what was later much of the southern border of the United States. In the West Indies the native populations died out within a few years after the advent of the Europeans. The cruelty, the exploitation, and the diseases of the white man accomplished their destruction before the Christian conscience could stir the home authorities to effective action. The populations which replaced them were white or Negro or a mixture of the two. In most of the mainland of Spanish America the white men were in the minority. They were the ruling minority. Under them were the Indians, generally the large majority, with here and there enclaves of Negroes. Wherever the white men could do it, they compelled the Indians to labour for them in mines and on plantations. The main centres of Spanish power and the largest populations were in Mexico and Peru. Here had been the most numerous peoples and the highest civilizations at the time of the Spanish conquest and from here most of the wealth, especially in the precious metals, was obtained for export.

We can take time for only the briefest summary of the spread of Christianity in Spanish America and must content ourselves with a few broad generalizations, some of them illustrated by concrete examples.

First of all we must note that the Church and the spread of Christianity were under the direction of the crown. This was exercised from Spain but was carried out by officials appointed from Spain who were mostly Spanish-born rather than American-born whites. This minute and absolute control by the crown was part of the general colonial policy and was seen in all aspects of Spanish American life, whether economic, political, or religious.

A second generalization is closely associated with the first. Most of the missions to the Indians were staffed from the Old World and not from the whites in the New World.

A third generalization follows almost inevitably from the first two. The Christianity of Spanish America was largely parasitic and passive. Depending as it was constrained to do by royal colonial policy upon the Old World for its missionaries and bishops, it showed little inclination to be missionary or to act for itself. Increasingly priests and monks were recruited from the American-born whites and here and there from Indians and mestizos. By the end of the eighteenth century the majority of the bishops were natives of America. However, the tradition had been established that leadership must come from Europe. Here in time arose one of the largest bodies of professing Roman Catholics in the world. Yet even in the nineteenth and twentieth centuries it did not produce enough clergy to fill its own needs and contributed very little in personnel and money to the spread of the faith beyond its borders. Roman Catholics of Europe and later of the United States sent clergy to care for the nominally Christian population as well as to reach out to the non-Christian Indians.

A fourth generalization is that the Papacy had practically no voice in Spanish America. The crown appointed the bishops and no Papal decree could be published in the Spanish colonial possessions without royal consent. Doctrinally the Spanish American church conformed to Rome. No serious schisms or heretical groups arose. The Inquisition and royal authority would have crushed them even had the Christianity of the region possessed sufficient vitality to produce them. Yet administratively Rome had almost no authority.

A fifth generalization is that in the main centres of pre-Columbian population and civilization, Mexico and Peru, accession to the Christian faith was by mass conversions. In Mexico in 1523 a royal letter to Cortés, the leader in the conquest, declared that the conversion of the Indians was the king's chief interest in that enterprise. In 1523 Cortés ordered that those who had been given *repartimientos,* or bodies of Indians to work on their lands, must see that idols were done away and that provision be made for the instruction of their charges in the Christian faith. Scores of Franciscans, mostly of the strict branch called the Observants, arrived to carry through the work of conversion. Dominicans and Augustinians soon followed. Then came Jesuits, Discalced Carmelites, and a member of the order of St. John of God. Benedictines and a few seculars also entered. The Indians, accustomed to docility under their former rulers, were quite willing to follow the wishes of their new masters. It was said that in 1531, only twelve years after the first landing of Cortés, the Franciscans alone had baptized more than a million persons. In 1536 a missionary estimated the number of baptized at between four and nine millions. One of the most famous of the early missionaries was a Franciscan, Peter of Ghent. A relative of Charles V, while a courtier he had been won to the religious life by two confessors of the Emperor and had declined a bishopric to remain a humble lay brother. In 1529 he wrote that he and a colleague often baptized fourteen thousand in one day and that together they had administered the rite to more than two hundred thousand. Instruction was given to the neophytes much more slowly, but various devices were employed to impart it, so that the change of faith would be more than purely formal. By the end of the sixteenth century the pre-Christian pagan cults had disappeared in the more thickly settled portions of Mexico.

After the initial enthusiasm of the converts passed and when the first generation of missionaries was followed by new arrivals, complaints began to be heard. The clergy were too few, the dioceses were too large, and many of the priests were accused by even the first Archbishop of Mexico of being ignorant, immoral, and corrupt. The old faiths were said to persist in attitudes and in rites in connexion with supposedly Christian worship.

In Peru the story was very similar. The second Archbishop of Lima, Toribio Alfonso de Mogrovejo y Robles, later canonized, of a noble family, highly educated, came to the New World in his late forties, acquired an Indian language, and is said to have administered confirmation to about eight hundred thousand. He built roads, schools, chapels, and hospitals, introduced the reforming decrees of the Council of Trent, and stood up for the rights of the Indians and the Negroes. Francis Solanus (1549–1610), also canonized, a Franciscan of the Observance, acquired a command of several Indian tongues, journeyed widely, barefoot, crucifix in hand, preaching, and teaching his hearers to join with him in chanting Psalms to the accompaniment of his violin.

A sixth generalization is that in Spanish America after the first wave of conquest the mission was the characteristic pioneer institution. It was through missionaries that the frontier was usually pushed forward into territories hitherto unoccupied by the whites. As a rule little or no force was employed. An armed guard might be sent with the missionaries to afford them protection, but it was by other means that the missionaries persuaded the Indians to receive instruction. Offers of food and clothing were employed to induce the Indians to settle around the mission. In time the Indians were drawn into a community of which the church was the centre and where they were taught agriculture and simple industries and had their entire lives supervised by the missionaries.

These frontier missions were broadly scattered. Eventually they were found in places as widely separated as California, Texas, Florida, Central America, Venezuela, the upper reaches of the Amazon and its tributaries, and Paraguay.

One of the most famous of the frontier missions was that of Jesuits in Paraguay. Various attempts to establish continuing stations had been made in the sixteenth century, but not until the first decade of the seventeenth century was the enterprise really inaugurated. Its purpose was the conversion of the Indians and their protection against the vices and exploitation of the colonists. The Indians were gathered into villages under the supervision of the missionaries. Here they were given Christian instruction, were taught to work, and were organized into a closely regulated communal pattern. Each village had a church on which wealth and devotion were lavished and where much was made of music, choirs, and religious dances. Cattle-raising and agriculture were nurtured and the Indians were trained in various handicrafts. Armed forces were organized to guard against raids by slave-traders. At one time about one hundred and fifty thousand Indians are said to have been under the Jesuits and in more than two score villages in much of the vast interior of the later Patagonia, Paraguay, Uruguay, and Southern Brazil.

A seventh and final generalization is that Christianity made for the softening of the impact of the Spaniards on the Indians. In its first few years the Spanish occupation was marked by extreme cruelty. Nor did exploitation ever cease. The Spaniards were a minority and most of them had come to America to improve their fortunes. If they were to do this, they must have labour for their mines and plantations. They were unwilling to undertake the kind of work demanded and could not obtain enough labourers from Europe. They partly made up the deficiency with Negroes, but it was chiefly to the Indians that they had recourse. Yet, moved by the Christian conscience, there were Spaniards who appealed to the monarchs and obtained legislation on behalf of the Indians.

Queen Isabella charged Bobadilla, who followed Columbus in the governorship of the Indies, to respect the liberty of the Indians. Allotments (*repartimientos*) of Indians were made to grantees (*encomenderos*) to enable them to work plantations and mines, but Isabella stipulated that the *encomendero* was to see that his Indians entered voluntarily into the relationship, were treated as free, were paid for their labour with wages adequate to support themselves and their families, that the work was non-hazardous and in proportion to the strength of the labourer, and that Christian instruction was given to all. These provisions were so frequently ignored in practice that the system became one of the chief targets of the reformers.

As conquest and colonization progressed, additions were made to what were called the *Laws of the Indies* which had the protection and the temporal and spiritual welfare of the Indians at heart. Officials were appointed to see that they were observed. Selfishness and economic considerations tended to make the code a dead letter, but from time to time men arose who sought to have it enlarged and obeyed. Some of these were in Spain. Francisco de Vitoria, a Dominican, a leading theologian of the sixteenth century and a pioneer in international law, championed the rights of the Indians, to his personal hurt, and there were many others.

Outstanding among those who laboured for the Indians was Bartolomé de Las Casas (1474–1566). It is symbolic of the effect of Christianity that he seems to have been the first in the New World to be ordained a Christian priest. His father was one of the companions of Columbus on the latter's second voyage to America. Bartolomé came as a youth after having received the conventional education of his time. He was slow to awake to his mission. On the island of Hispaniola where he first made his home he shared in the raids on the Indians and had some of the captives assigned to him for his plantation. In his middle thirties he was ordained to the priesthood and not far from that time had his conscience troubled by the preaching of a Dominican. He did not at once break with the system and shared in the conquest of Cuba. Before long, however, in a sermon before the governor and leading settlers he denounced the cruelties that he saw about him. Since the crown exercised a minute direction over the colonies, Las Casas went to Spain, for it was from there that effective action must begin. After vexatious delays he won the ear and the good will of the powerful Cardinal Ximénes. He was appointed Protector-general of the Indians and in 1516 returned to the New World in that capacity. He found himself blocked and went again to Spain to renew his suit. Faced with the argument that to adopt his method would deprive the settlements of labour and so work their ruin, he attempted a colony to prove that the Indians could be won by kindly treatment and without force and brought with him whites to be labourers. That experiment, made west of one of the mouths of the Orinoco, proved a failure. Baffled, he retired for some years to Hispaniola and joined the Dominicans.

Eventually Las Casas was again on his travels. Once more he voyaged to Spain to seek royal decrees on behalf of the Indians in Peru, for that region was then being conquered. He was soon back in America with the desired orders and went to Peru to obtain their publication. In Nicaragua he had a part in a mission which seemed to him to demonstrate his contention that Indians could be won to the Christian faith through friendship and to assent to Spanish authority without the use of armed force. He was ordered to Hispaniola to deal with an Indian revolt and induced a chief who had long terrorized the colonists to lay down his arms and persuaded his followers to accept baptism. For several years he was a missionary among the Indians of Guatemala, seeking further to prove the truth of his theory that force should not be used against the Indians and that coercion was quite powerless to effect the changes demanded by true Christian conversion.

In the 1530's he was again in Spain and probably had large influence on the New Laws which were framed in 1542. He was offered the see of Cuzco, in some respects the most important in the New World, but instead chose that of Chiapa, in Mexico, one of the poorest. He was consecrated and at the age of seventy again set out for America. There he met bitter opposition, for the colonists held him responsible for the New Laws, legislation which they believed meant their ruin. In 1547 he returned for the last time to Spain and there, until an advanced old age, continued to argue the case for the Indians.

Las Casas was by no means alone. Many, some of them laymen and others clergy, took a similar position. Several missionaries lost their lives in the attempt to win warlike tribes without asking for the protection of armed forces. Others persisted and proved successful. It was an heroic record. It seems almost invidious to single out one among many. Fairly typical, however, was Domingo de Salazar (1513–1594), a Dominican, a student of Vitoria and a follower of Las Casas, who, over twenty-five years in Mexico, made himself fluent in Indian languages to preach in them, and as the first Bishop of Manila championed the cause of the Filipinos.

There were also those who gave themselves to serving the Negroes who had been so cruelly wrenched from Africa into slavery in the Americas. Famous among them was the Jesuit, Pedro Claver (1581–1654). A Catalonian and of noble lineage, like many of the high born youth of his day he was early caught up into the devotion and enthusiasm of the Society of Jesus. He was sent to Cartagena, long the chief port of entry of the slave ships from Africa. There for nearly forty years he spent himself in behalf of the poor wretches whom greed had torn from their homes in Africa. On their arrival he visited the slave-ships, foul with the stench of crowded and ill-tended humanity, and carried food, fruit, wine, and tobacco to their black cargoes. He baptized the infants, cared for the ill, gave instruction in religion and morals, and trained catechists to supplement his labours. He made long journeys to visit the blacks in the mines and plantations. He braved the enmity of slave-dealers and slave-owners. Against vigorous opposition he insisted that Negroes be admitted to the church where he served on full equality with the whites. He is said to have baptized more than three hundred thousand. That he became the patron saint of missions to the Negroes is proof that there were those who appreciated him and followed his example.

As a result of the labours of many, lay and clerical, the overwhelming proportion of the population in Spanish America were nominally Christian. It is true that this Christianity was to a large degree passive, parasitically dependent upon continued fresh blood from Europe in the form of clergy and missionaries. It is also true that in 1750 and later millions of pagan Indians remained untouched on the fringes of the Spanish settlements. Yet an ecclesiastical structure covered most of the vast area, with parishes, dioceses, and archdioceses. Education was fostered, universities were founded and maintained, and gradually, even though in insufficient numbers and often of inferior quality, clergy were recruited and trained from the Indians, mestizos, and American-born whites.

The Planting of Christianity in Portuguese America

In some ways the course of Christianity in Portuguese America was like that in Spanish America. Here, in Brazil, which embraced the Portuguese possessions, was an area, not as populous as that of Spanish America and with no high pre-Columbian civilizations, but still enormous in extent. Here, too, were the problems of holding the European immigrants to the Christian faith and of winning the Indians and the imported Negro slaves. As in Spanish America, the crown directed the Church, the state, and the economic life. As elsewhere in these years, the missionaries were largely from those orders which were the fruits of the Catholic Reformation—among them Jesuits, Capuchins, and Observant Franciscans. Here, too, heroic individuals were stirred and emboldened by the Christian faith to plead the cause of the exploited, to obtain legislation on their behalf, and to strive to see that it was enforced.

Among the latter was Mem de Sá, a governor who came out in 1558, who forbade any Indian from one of the Christian communities being sold as a slave, and prohibited, except on explicit authorization by himself, the restoration to their masters of slaves who had taken refuge with missionaries. Another was the Jesuit, Antonio Vieira. Having served as a youth among the Indians and Negroes of Brazil, he returned to Portugal and became one of the most famous preachers of the day. But he insisted on going again to Brazil. Once there, he was appalled by the neglect of the sacraments and Christian morals by the Portuguese settlers, by the low quality of many of the clergy, by the enslavement and progressive extermination of the Indians, and by the inadequacy of episcopal ministrations. Sailing for Portugal to press reform measures on the king, he obtained a decree (1655) which was designed to remedy the worst of the abuses. He then went to Brazil to aid in the enforcement of the edict and to resume his labours as a missionary. The decree aroused great resentment among the colonists and Vieira and several of his fellow-Jesuits were deported. Yet the law wrought some improvement. Eventually Vieira made his way back to Brazil and died there at an extreme old age.

In spite of the efforts of Vieira and men like him, Christianity in Brazil remained distinctly behind that in Spanish America, far from ideal as was the latter. Educationally the colony was backward. Apart from the missions maintained by the regulars, the religious care of the whites, the mixed population, and the Christian Indians was woefully inadequate. Stipends for the seculars were niggardly, few from the better classes entered the priesthood, and outside the main cities there were not many resident pastors. The low state of the Roman Catholic Church in Brazil in the nineteenth and twentieth centuries had its roots in the early days of the colony.

ROMAN CATHOLIC CHRISTIANITY IN FRENCH AMERICA

For more than a century the French seemed to be building a colonial empire in the Americas which in geographic extent rivalled those of Spain and Portugal. In the West Indies, on the northern coast of South America, along the Atlantic seaboard of North America north of the British possessions, in the vast valleys of the St. Lawrence River, the Great Lakes, and the Mississippi and its tributaries the French staked out and partly occupied a region which might have made them dominant in much of the Western Hemisphere. In the eighteenth century they lost nearly all of it, largely in conjunction with European wars and notably in the course of the Seven Years' War (1756–1763).

Before they were driven off of North America the French made lasting contributions to the Christianity of that continent. Most of it was through colonists. Few at first, the latter multiplied by a wide margin between births and deaths and laid the basis of a French-speaking element in the white population which under English rule identified its faith with its French nationality and remained conservatively and loyally Roman Catholic. Eventually it spread over much of Canada and southward into the New England portion of the United States.

There were also wide-flung missions to the Indians. However, the aboriginal population was small, scattered, and lived largely by hunting, trapping, and an unthrifty agriculture. Numerical success was slight.

As in so much of the rest of the world, the missions in French America were by the orders which sprang from the Catholic Reformation—Jesuits, Recollects (Franciscans), Capuchins, Sulpicians, and Ursulines. Montreal, in the nineteenth and twentieth centuries the second city in size in Canada, was founded as an idealistic Christian community from which secular priests would go out as missionaries to the Indians and to the colonists. Famous was the Jesuit mission to the Hurons, cut short by attacks from other Indian tribes. Missionaries of various orders ranged over most of the area claimed by France and here and there made converts.

THE PLANTING OF PROTESTANT CHRISTIANITY OUTSIDE THE THIRTEEN COLONIES OF THE BRITISH

Compared with Roman Catholicism, Protestantism was late in establishing a continuing foothold in the Americas. However, long before 1750 it had been planted by white settlements and by missions among Eskimos, Negroes, and Indians. In 1721 there went to Greenland Hans Egede, a Norwegian Lutheran pastor who wished to make contact with the Scandinavian population which he believed might have survived on that island from the colonies of earlier centuries but which had not been heard from within the memory of living man. He found that all the Europeans had long since perished, but he remained, learned the Eskimo tongue, and began a mission which after several generations won most of that people to the Christian faith. The Danish-Norwegian mission was supplemented by Moravians who arrived in 1733. Shortly after 1750 the Moravians extended their operations to Labrador. Through the initiative of Zinzendorf, in 1732 Moravians began a mission to the Negroes in the Danish West Indies and in 1735 in the Dutch possessions on the north coast of South America.

Numerically more impressive was Protestantism in the British West Indies. Here, until after 1750, it was introduced and nourished chiefly by the Church of England. In Bermuda, Barbados, the Leeward Islands, the Bahamas, and especially in the largest of the British West Indies, Jamaica, churches were erected for the white settlers and missions were carried on among the African slaves. In 1680 Barbados had eleven churches. In 1701 the Society for the Propagation of the Gospel in Foreign Parts was begun with the British colonies as its original scope. It had representatives among both the white population and the Negroes. The settlers from the British Isles also included Presbyterians, Independents, Baptists, and Quakers.

CHRISTIANITY IN THE THIRTEEN COLONIES

Far more important for the future course of Christianity than the Protestantism in Greenland, Labrador, and the West Indies was what was taking place in the Thirteen Colonies which soon after 1750 became the United States of America. In the nineteenth and especially in the twentieth century, the

Christianity of the United States had a much larger share in the total life and world outreach of that faith than did that in Spanish, Portuguese, or French America, or, indeed, than all the rest of the Christian communities in the Western Hemisphere taken together. This was not so much in numbers, although in this respect the Christianity of the United States was impressive, as it was in vitality as seen in new movements, in the fashion in which it initiated and maintained missions in the United States and in much of the rest of the world, and in its effect upon the United States and mankind as a whole. Because of the significance of Christianity in the Thirteen Colonies for later history we must give more space to it than we would if we were considering only its numerical strength before 1750 or if we were confining our attention to the world scene between 1500 and 1750. Judged from the situation the world around in those two and a half centuries what was taking place in the Thirteen Colonies was of minor moment. Like the other phases of their life, the Christianity of the Thirteen Colonies was merely a projection of Western Europe and chiefly of portions of the British Isles among a few hundred thousand people scattered along a part of the eastern seaboard of North America.

In our brief summary of the history of Christianity in the Thirteen Colonies we must speak first and chiefly of the white population and then, much more quickly, of the Indians and Negroes.

For the white population we must content ourselves with brief but important generalizations, here and there amplified by specific incidents, individuals, and movements.

The white population of the Thirteen Colonies was predominantly from the British Isles. That British element was mostly from England, but before 1750 a large contingent had entered of what were known as Scotch-Irish, namely, those of Scotch descent who had their homes in Ireland and who came to the New World because of adverse conditions in that island. They were distributed quite widely from north to south and were Presbyterians by heredity. In addition there were many Germans, mostly in Pennsylvania, some Swedes from a short-lived Swedish colonial enterprise on the Delaware, a substantial contingent of Dutch who survived from the Dutch enterprise in New Amsterdam, after its transfer to the English known as New York, Huguenot refugees, found at intervals all the way from South Carolina to Massachusetts, and a few Roman Catholic Irish.

So far as the white inhabitants of the Thirteen Colonies had a church connexion, it was overwhelmingly Protestant. Roman Catholics constituted only a very small fraction of the population. One of the Thirteen Colonies, Maryland, was founded by English Roman Catholics, George and Cecil Calvert, successively Lords Baltimore, but it was upon the basis of religious liberty, the large majority of the settlers were Protestants, and within a generation the Church of England was established by law.

Religion was very important in the inauguration of some of the colonies. That was especially true in New England and Pennsylvania, but was by no means confined to these areas. It was Separatists who, coming on the *Mayflower*, in 1620 founded Plymouth. In the 1620's and 1630's Puritans, seeking to escape Charles I and Archbishop Laud, made extensive settlements around Massachusetts Bay. A group from Massachusetts Bay guided by their pastor, Thomas Hooker, founded Hartford (1636) and Connecticut. In 1638 another band of Puritans, led by Theophilus Eaton and John Davenport, began New Haven, later to be united with Connecticut. The Puritans and the Separatists merged and formed churches of a Congregational pattern. In principle New England was made up of Christian commonwealths where Christians controlled both the Church and the state and where all society was governed by Christian standards. Although in New England they were supported by public taxation and were intimately tied with the state, the churches were "gathered." Their membership was not composed of all the inhabitants, as was the theory in the state churches in Europe, but only of those who could narrate a conscious Christian experience. They were bound together by a covenant with one another and with Christ, as the head of the Church.

At first the Congregationalists in Massachusetts sought to force conformity with their conceptions of the Church. Quakers especially fared badly at their hands. For a time pastor at Salem, but banished from Massachusetts as an irritating non-conformist, Roger Williams founded Providence as "a shelter for persons distressed in conscience." Later this united with other settlements as the colony of Rhode Island on the basis of complete religious liberty and full civic democracy. With the counsel of George Fox and William Penn, Quakers founded West Jersey and East Jersey. William Penn himself, a leading Quaker, inaugurated Pennsylvania as a "holy experiment" with Philadelphia, the City of Brotherly Love, as its capital, and operating under a *Frame of Government* which, like Massachusetts and Connecticut, sought to lay the foundations of a society built on Christian principles and governed by Christian ideals. The *Frame of Government* granted religious liberty, but limited the franchise and office-holding to "such as profess faith in Jesus Christ."

It must also be noted that it was radical Protestantism which was prominent in these beginnings in the Thirteen Colonies. While in several of the colonies, notably the oldest, Virginia, the Church of England was established, in the majority it was not. Everywhere in the Thirteen Colonies it suffered from having no resident bishop. The colonies were under the Bishop of London, and he was represented by ecclesiastical officials called "commissaries," but without a bishop confirmation was not administered and aspirants for ordination had to make the long, expensive, and sometimes dangerous journey to England for that rite. The Anglican churches were chiefly dependent for clergymen upon those who came from England.

Radical Protestantism was relatively more prominent than in the British Isles or anywhere on the Continent of Europe. In 1750 the most compact and the most numerous and influential group of churches was not the Church of England but New England Congregationalism.

In general, the radical Protestants were of the Reformed tradition. Whether Puritans, Independents, Separatists, Baptists, or Quakers, they were either distinctly of it or had been profoundly influenced by it, even when, like the Quakers, they had rebelled against it. New Englanders had a large share in founding Presbyterianism in the Thirteen Colonies. They were closely allied in spirit and in some instances in personnel with the more widely spread Presbyterianism. The New England churches held to the Westminster Confession as standard. Usually those who moved away from New England to other colonies organized themselves into Presbyterian churches. The Reformed strain from England was reinforced by Reformed from Holland and Germany and by Scotch-Irish Presbyterians.

In the Thirteen Colonies Christianity presented a much greater variety than in any country east of the Atlantic. In addition to the several kinds of Protestantism from the British Isles, it had German and Swedish Lutherans, German Reformed, Dutch Reformed, and, as we have said, a few Roman Catholics. In this it foreshadowed the even richer variety which was to characterize the United States.

In spite of the part which Christianity had in initiating and shaping the Thirteen Colonies, in 1750 the large majority of the white population were without a formal church connexion. It has been estimated, although this may be excessively low, that in 1750 only about five out of a hundred were members of churches. The overwhelming proportion of the settlers came to the colonies for economic or social rather than religious motives. They were mostly from the underprivileged and by migrating to the New World sought to better their financial or their social standing. They were from countries where baptism and confirmation or its equivalent were social conventions which in some places were required not only by custom but also by law and where attendance at church was expected or made a legal obligation. In the Thirteen Colonies these rules, if they existed at all, usually were not rigidly enforced. In the absence of a bishop, those affiliated with the Church of England could be baptized, but were not confirmed, and many did not partake of the communion. In consequence, away from the patterns of the Old World, most of the population were in danger of being largely de-Christianized. From heredity and to some degree, particularly in New England, by local custom, remnants of Christianity survived among the unchurched in ethical standards and religious ideas. However, there was a decided trend towards allowing them to fade out. That was especially the case in the newer settlements away from the coast, on the westward-moving frontier. Here the traditional institutions and habits of Europe were even less in evidence than on the seaboard and in the fluid society of these newer regions tended not to be reproduced.

In New England the situation was partly remedied by what was known as the Half-Way Covenant, a designation given it by its critics. Even before the first generation of immigrants had died, complaints began to be heard of waning zeal. In the initial contingents there were many who were not in full sympathy with the high purposes of those who wished to build an ideal Christian society. In at least one of the New England colonies at the outset only a minority were church members. As time passed, those who could qualify for church membership by offering evidence of a spiritual rebirth were few. In consequence, the custom gradually spread of permitting those who as children of church members had been baptized and were regarded as sharing in the covenant to present their children for baptism. Usually only full church members could partake of the communion, but eventually in some churches all the baptized were allowed to do so. The Half-Way Covenant was the occasion for much controversy. Its opponents regarded it as an ungodly compromise, but in 1662 a synod sanctioned it and its use spread rapidly. Yet it tended to make baptism a mere form.

Efforts were not lacking to win the unchurched. These were partly from the other side of the Atlantic but were chiefly from the inherent vitality of the Christianity of the Colonies.

From the other side of the Atlantic the concern for the religious welfare of the colonists was mainly in the Church of England. As we have seen, the Bishop of London, as head of the Church of England in the chief seaport, was given ecclesiastical jurisdiction over the English colonies and was represented in the Thirteen Colonies by commissaries. One of the latter, Thomas Bray (1656–1730), although only a few months in America, made two outstanding contributions, the organization of the Society for Promoting Christian Knowledge (1699—1698 old style) and of the Society for the Propagation of the Gospel in Foreign Parts (1701). Bray was eager that clergymen going to America have books. Accordingly he founded libraries in the chief ports in England from which they sailed and in a number of colonial parishes. The Society for Promoting Christian Knowledge was created by him to perpetuate this activity. With the purpose of publishing and distributing books, it eventually extended its operations to many countries. The Society for the Propagation of the Gospel in Foreign Parts, for which Bray obtained a charter, was primarily for sending to the colonies and supporting clergymen and school-masters of the Church of England. It is said that when it was founded, in all the Thirteen Colonies there were only fifty clergymen of the Church of England and that most of these were in Virginia and Maryland, and that seventy-five years later, when the colonies declared their independence, the churches numbered about three hundred and the clergymen about two hun-dred and fifty. Most of the increase was due to the Society for the Propaga-tion of the Gospel in Foreign Parts. Its missionaries were mainly among the whites, but some spent their years among the Indians and a few gave atten-tion to the Negroes.

Missionaries were sent not only from England but also from the Continent. A few of them were Roman Catholics, and went chiefly to Maryland. In that colony, founded by men of their faith, there were both Jesuits and seculars and Jesuits went from there to the neighbouring Delaware, New Jersey, and Pennsylvania, to care for their co-religionists. They did not have a resident bishop until after the formation of the United States of America. A Swedish colony was founded on the Delaware in 1638, largely at the instance of Gus-tavus Adolphus, who had in mind not only commerce but also the conversion of the Indians and the dominance of Protestantism in the New World. Al-though in 1655 the Dutch eliminated Swedish rule, a Swedish population remained and to it until 1791 the Church of Sweden continued to send clergy-men and financial aid. The Swedish Lutheran churches, some of them prosper-ous, eventually became Episcopalian. Because of the strength of the common Catholic tradition, the transition was easy.

The Germans were much more numerous than the Swedes. Thousands of them, mostly Protestants, came to the Thirteen Colonies. Some fled from the Palatinate when it was being ravaged by the armies of Louis XIV and settled in New York, the Carolinas, and Pennsylvania. Others were from the Arch-diocese of Salzburg, which the archbishop who came to the post in 1728 was attempting to purge of all Protestants. William Penn had travelled in Germany and had induced some Germans to come to his colony. With its religious liberty, Pennsylvania proved peculiarly attractive to small, persecuted groups, such as the Mennonites and the Church of the Brethren (Dunkers). The Moravians inaugurated a colony which had headquarters at Bethlehem, Pennsylvania, with Spangenberg as its chief leader, and were visited by Zinzendorf. Zinzendorf found the Germans more than half of the population of Pennsylvania, but largely without clergy and schools. They were of varying forms of Protestantism, but mostly Lutheran and Reformed. He wished to bring them all together in one Protestant Church.

Moved partly by apprehension that the Germans would go over to Zinzendorf's plan of union, but chiefly by the fear that they would drift entirely away from Christianity, the Pietists of Halle sent money and missionaries. Of the latter the chief was Henry Melchior Muhlenberg (1711–1787). He arrived in Philadelphia in 1742. With the motto *Ecclesia plantanda,* "the Church must be planted," he became a pastor of Lutheran churches in Philadelphia, travelled widely, in 1748 brought together the first Lutheran synod in the colonies, and became the outstanding organizer and overseer of Lutheranism. The Germans were not confined to Pennsylvania but were found in others of the colonies, especially in the South. To them also came ministers and missionaries, some of them from Halle.

For the Germans of the Reformed church, Michael Schlatter (1716–1790) was the outstanding missionary and organizer. A native of Switzerland, he was sent to America by the Dutch synods. There he organized a *coetus* or synod, helped to bring order into the congregations, and induced ministers to come from Europe. He also stimulated the formation in England of a society to maintain schools among Germans of all denominations.

Even more far-reaching in effect than the missionaries from the other side of the Atlantic were movements from within the churches in the colonies themselves. The chief of these was what was known as the Great Awakening. It arose in New England and in Presbyterian circles closely associated with New England and swept through most of the Thirteen Colonies.

Revivals or awakenings were not new in those of the Separatist tradition in the colonies. The conception of the "gathered" church which was integral in New England Congregationalism contributed to them, especially since so large a proportion of the population were not members of churches. A "gathered" church meant that each of the members, as a prerequisite for admission, must be able to narrate an experience of the new birth without which no one could enter the kingdom of God. The alternative to the eternal life begun by the new birth was being eternally lost. In communities where, as in the Thirteen Colonies, the large majority of the population were unregenerate, the regenerate, especially among the clergy, were deeply concerned. Among many of the unregenerate they would find those prepared to listen to them, for such knowledge of Christian belief as had been spread abroad bred convictions or at least an uneasiness which would respond to the preacher who pled with the unconverted and urged them to repent and turn in faith to God. The doctrine of election, out of the Augustinian heritage which was dominant in the churches of the Reformed tradition and which except for those influenced by Arminianism was generally accepted in New England and the Presbyterian churches, would seem to have discouraged any appeal to the unregenerate. If one were among the elect, so the belief ran, God's grace would prove irresistible and would reach all those whom He had chosen for salvation. If, on the other hand, one were not among the elect no amount of preaching could change his status. Yet it was mainly in the circles of British ancestry which were most committed to what was usually called Calvinism and its doctrine of election that the Great Awakening began and made its chief appeal.

Part of the appeal was due to an alteration in traditional Calvinism which prevailed in New England as an early importation from England. Calvin had held that the evidences that an individual was among the elect were adherence to correct doctrine, a worthy life, and faithful attendance on the sacraments. In New England it was maintained that the evidences were adherence to correct doctrine, a worthy life, and an experience of salvation. This last was akin to Pietism. Since experience was essential, and that experience had in it much of emotion, seasons were to be expected when a community was aroused and tides swept through it changing many individuals. There were those, especially among the clergy, who prayed for such seasons and sought to encourage them.

The Great Awakening was an early stage in a mass conversion of the partially de-Christianized population which characterized the religious history of the Thirteen Colonies on the eve of independence and then of the United States. That mass conversion, in part by "revivals" and "evangelistic" preaching for reaching the "unconverted" or "unsaved," was one of the distinguishing features of the Christianity of the United States, and especially of those elements of the population of Protestant, particularly Anglo-Saxon heredity.

The beginnings of the Great Awakening were in New Jersey. Frelinghuysen, a German, educated under Pietist influence, pastor of Dutch Reformed churches in the Raritan Valley, in the 1720's began proclaiming with impassioned conviction the necessity of a deep inward transformation rather than the mere outward performance of religious ceremonies. He also introduced private prayer meetings. His preaching provoked criticism from other ministers of the Dutch churches, but won a wide following. Freylinghuysen contributed to the shaping of Gilbert Tennent, minister of a Presbyterian church in New Brunswick, also in the Raritan Valley. Gilbert Tennent was the son of William Tennent, an Irish minister who had come to America in 1716, had become a Presbyterian, and had trained for the ministry his sons and other young men in what was somewhat scornfully called the "log college," a building which he erected opposite his manse in Neshaminy, Pennsylvania. Through Gilbert Tennent and others prepared in the "log college" the revival spread among the Scotch-Irish. Graduates of the "log college" founded other "log colleges," largely for the education of ministers, and from them young men went out to preach the urgency of conversion.

In 1734–1735 the Great Awakening broke out in Northampton, Massachusetts, under the preaching of Jonathan Edwards. Jonathan Edwards (1703–1758) was one of the outstanding figures in the history of the Thirteen Colonies. The son of a Congregational pastor and through his mother a grandson of Solomon Stoddard, the dominant personality in the Connecticut Valley, Edwards combined a precocious and brilliant mind with a deep Christian devotion. A graduate of the infant Yale, after brief pastorates he taught there for a time and then, in 1727, succeeded Solomon Stoddard as minister of the Congregational church in Northampton. Edwards was acquainted with the writings of Locke, Newton, and the Cambridge Platonists, especially Cudworth (Chapter XXXVI). He had a keen, penetrating intellect, there was something of the mystic in his temperament, and he responded to both these predispositions. He combined Calvinism with Neoplatonism. At Northampton he denounced the tendency towards Arminianism by which many in New England were in actuality departing from the Westminster Confession while they still adhered to it in theory. Speaking slowly, distinctly, and with great solemnity, he made vivid the loathsomeness of sin. In the winter and spring of 1734–1735 a wave of conviction swept over the community and hundreds professed conversion.

The Great Awakening was powerfully reinforced by George Whitefield (1714–1770). Born at Gloucester, England, the son of an inn-keeper and reared in poverty, Whitefield had entered Oxford in 1733, was closely associated with the Wesleys, and had gone through a religious crisis from which he emerged with great joy in the love of God. Of him as of the Wesleys we are to hear more later (Chapter XLIV). Having a voice which could reach thousands in the open air, expressive, dramatic, and with intense feeling, he could sway audiences as few men have ever done. He moved even so practical and religiously unorthodox a man as Benjamin Franklin. He came to Georgia in 1738 at the suggestion of John Wesley and made six other visits to America. In 1739–1741, then in his mid-twenties, he had his first preaching tour of the Colonies. He landed in Delaware and spoke in many centres. In Boston it is said that thirty thousand heard him at one time on the common. He found congenial those who were already preaching the revival and had more of a following among the Presbyterians and Congregationalists than among his fellow-Anglicans.

The Great Awakening spread through the Colonies, mostly through Presbyterians and Congregationalists. After 1750 it was to give rise to many Baptist preachers who, mostly men of little education, could speak the language of the lowliest and won an increasing following among the humblest of the unchurched.

Much excitement and many emotional disturbances accompanied the revival. Although the expressions were different, one is reminded of the Flagellants whom we have met in Roman Catholic circles. There were screaming, laughing, trances, visions, and convulsions. Some of the preachers and lay exhorters deliberately stimulated these phenomena.

Divisions in the churches accompanied and followed the Great Awakening. The more ardent preachers of the revival had sharp words for those ministers whom they deemed unconverted. Whitefield occasionally spoke caustically of those who did not follow him. Others were even more vehement. On the other side were many, both clergy and laity, who were alienated by the emotional excesses, were angered by the denunciations of the more ardent itinerant preachers, and held to the cold, rational approach to religion which was becoming characteristic of what was dubbed the Age of Reason. "New Lights" and "Old Lights" in Presbyterian and Congregational churches often separated into distinct units. The "Old Lights" were critical of what they deemed the lack of education of the "New Light" clergy, trained as many of the latter were in the "log colleges." Jonathan Edwards was forced out of his parish in Northampton (1750).

The Baptists began the rapid growth which was later to be so marked. Holding that infant baptism was not true baptism and stressing a regenerate church membership to which entrance was had through the baptism of conscious believers, usually by immersion, they attracted many.

The Great Awakening was evidence of vigour inherent in the Protestantism of the Thirteen Colonies. Here was a vitality which through succeeding decades was to reach a growing proportion of the partially de-Christianized population, was fairly steadily to augment the percentage of church members, and was to continue the mass conversion of which the Great Awakening was the beginning. Out of the Great Awakening came a large increase in churches, of young men entering the ministry, of earnestness among the rank and file of professing Christians, and of missions. The Great Awakening emphasized the importance of individual decision, tended to nurture the belief that the Christian should be able to tell the day and the hour of his conversion, and to encourage each Christian to seek to win his non-Christian or only nominally Christian fellows. It also fostered education and gave rise not only to "log colleges" but also to some institutions of a more permanent character, including, before 1750, the College of New Jersey, the later Princeton University, and the University of Pennsylvania. Others were to emerge after 1750.

Partly stimulated by the Great Awakening there were currents in theology which were increasingly prominent after the Thirteen Colonies became the United States of America. Jonathan Edwards was the first great formative figure in what has often been called New England Theology. His powerful mind expressing itself through widely read writings stimulated and helped to shape a modification of the Reformed faith which, while not denying the doctrine of the sovereignty of God, and, indeed, stressing it, or of election to salvation by divine decree, made more room for the action of the sinner in accepting the divine forgiveness. It was at once the outgrowth of, and helped to encourage the preaching central in the Great Awakening and the subsequent revivals which urged the hearers to repent. There were still the "Old Calvinists," holding to pre-Edwardsian views, but in New England they tended to give way to Edwards and his successors. Partly as a reaction against the revivals, an already existing tendency was strengthened which soon was to reject Calvinism with its doctrine of the total depravity of man and the arbitrary choice by God of some for salvation. It was strongest in and around Boston, where in the comfortable and well-to-do merchant and professional groups a more optimistic view of man was congenial. It was reinforced by contacts with similar movements in England and late in the eighteenth and early in the nineteenth century was frankly to become Unitarian.

It was later said of the Pilgrim fathers that they fell first on their knees and then on the aborigines. This had enough truth in it to give it sting, but it was so far from the whole truth that it was not even a caricature. In every one of the Thirteen Colonies there were missions to the Indians. In New England they were very extensive. Especially outstanding was John Eliot who, a graduate of that nursery of Puritans, Cambridge, came to America in 1631 and became pastor of a church on the outskirts of Boston. Through a long life he preached to the Indians in the neighbourhood of Boston, gathered them into churches, and translated the entire Bible into their tongue. Roger Williams and the Quakers established friendly relations with the Indians and insisted that lands be not taken from them by violence but be acquired through voluntary sale. For nearly two generations, or so long as they were in control of the colony, the Quakers kept peace with the Indians in Pennsylvania. From the earliest settlements in Virginia, clergy of the Church of England sought to win the Indians to the Christian faith. After its organization the Society for the Propagation of the Gospel in Foreign Parts took over most of the Anglican effort for the Indians and numbers of its missionaries specialized on them, notably on the borders of British influence in upper New York. Famous among the missionaries to the Indians were Moravians. The Great Awakening stimulated many missions to the Indians. Prominent among them was a prospective son-in-law of Jonathan Edwards, David Brainerd, who died before his marriage and whose journals marked by deep and sensitive devotion were widely read and had a profound influence on many youths both in America and in Britain. The Indian population was sparse, found adaptation to the agricultural economy of the white man difficult, and suffered from the diseases and the strong liquors introduced by the whites. However, in most of the Colonies Indian churches were gathered and through them adjustment to the new cultural environment was aided.

Nor were the Negroes entirely neglected. During the colonial period the mass conversion which we are to follow after 1750 had scarcely begun. Yet there were those who were seeking to win the Negro slaves who were increasingly providing the labour for the plantations of the South and who, some of them free, were in cities in the North. The Great Awakening spread among the Negroes. Before 1750 agitation for emancipation had scarcely commenced. However, among both Mennonites and Quakers there were those who believed slavery and the slave trade to be wrong and were beginning to protest against them.

As a result of the factors which we have briefly mentioned, there was arising in the Thirteen Colonies a distinctive Christianity. Predominantly Protestant and having its roots in the Old World, in the New World it was being modified. In it the extreme forms of Protestantism were relatively more prominent than anywhere on the other side of the Atlantic. Because of the varied sources from which the immigrants came—English, Scotch-Irish, German, Dutch, French, and Swedish—Christianity presented a greater variety than in any one country in Europe. Partly for this reason and partly out of profound conviction, especially in Pennsylvania and Rhode Island, there was more religious liberty than in Europe. It was by no means complete. In more than half of the Thirteen Colonies one or another church was either fully established or given special preference, but even in them enforcement of that status was more difficult than in most countries in Europe and by 1750 was weakening. The separation of Church and state was foreshadowed. This also meant the principle of voluntarism, the support of the Church not by public taxation levied on all, as was the practice in Europe, but by free will offerings by the membership. In several of the colonies the European procedure was followed, but in them it was beginning to break down. This Protestant Christianity was much less passive and less dependent on the Old World than was the Roman Catholicism of Spanish, Portuguese, and French America. Some help, mostly in the form of clerical personnel, continued to come from the other side of the Atlantic. Yet increasingly the churches were producing their own leadership. Confronted with a majority in the white population which, uprooted from its

European environment where affiliation with the Church was required, was drifting towards pure secularism, they rose to the emergency. Through the Great Awakening they were reaching out to the unchurched. Here and there, notably in Jonathan Edwards, independence of thought was appearing in the American-born whites. In general, perhaps because of its predominantly Reformed rootage, American Protestantism was activistic. Especially in New England and in the Quaker colonies, it was seeking to build here and now an ideal Christian society.

This extreme Protestantism with its strong Reformed strain was helping to shape the nascent nation. Even though those with a formal church membership constituted only a small fraction of the population, ideals and institutions were being moulded by their faith. Moral standards were set by it. It was resisting sexual irregularities, profanity, faithlessness to promises, drunkenness, quarreling, and gambling. It was easing the impact of the whites upon the Indians and the Negroes. It was responsible for most of such formal education as existed. All the colleges founded before 1750 had their beginnings in the zeal of earnest Christians and most of them were closely connected with the churches. The Protestantism of the Thirteen Colonies was laying the foundations for the democracy which found expression in the American Revolution and the United States. For example, in New England the clergy were preaching the rights which come from nature and nature's God, the theory that all men are born free, the duty of resistance to encroachments on those rights, and the popular element in government. While many of the clergy looked askance at pure democracy, the radical Protestantism which predominated in the churches in the Thirteen Colonies, seeking as it was to carry through the distinctive principles of the Reformation, salvation by the faith of the individual and the priesthood of all believers, underlay and permeated the democracy which characterized the United States.

SUMMARY

The two and a half centuries which followed 1500 witnessed a phenomenal spread of Christianity. This accompanied the equally phenomenal expansion of European peoples which marked these years. For that expansion of European peoples Christianity was to some degree responsible. The exact measure of that responsibility we do not know, for other factors entered. Yet the Christian faith did not automatically accompany that expansion. Indeed, some features of the expansion were flagrantly contrary to it and hampered it. The lives of many, probably most of the nominal Christians who represented the impact of Europe upon the rest of mankind were a denial of the faith. The greed, the sexual irregularities, the violence, the exploitation of subject peoples, the arrogance, and the truculence of the large majority of Europeans were accentuated in the contacts of exploration, conquest, and settlement. However, the great access of vigour in Christianity which was seen in the Catholic and Protestant Reformations produced a missionary activity which for geographic extent had never been equalled by any other religion. While surpassed by Christianity itself in the nineteenth and twentieth centuries, it was greater than anything which that faith had displayed up to that time. Christianity was now planted along the fringes of Africa south of the Sahara, in India and China attracted a larger constituency than before, and was introduced for the first time to much of South-east Asia, the East Indies, the Philippines, Japan, and the northern reaches of Asia. In the Western Hemisphere it won the majority of the Indian population and was firmly established among the settlements made by Europeans.

In this spread of Christianity Roman Catholics had the chief part, and the heroic lives and achievements of its great missionaries are among the most stirring in the history of mankind. But it was through Protestantism that the most vigorous churches were planted, those in the British colonies on the Atlantic seaboard of North America which were soon to become the United States.

SELECTED BIBLIOGRAPHY

GENERAL SURVEY

K. S. Latourette, *A History of the Expansion of Christianity. Volume III, Three Centuries of Advance* (New York, Harper & Brothers, 1939, pp. ix, 503).

FRANCIS XAVIER

A. Brou, *Saint François Xavier 1506–1548* (Paris, Gabriel Beauchesne & Cie, 2 vols., 1912). A standard life, containing footnote references to the pertinent sources and literature.

H. J. Coleridge, *The Life and Letters of St. Francis Xavier* (London, Burns, Oates & Washbourne, 2 vols., 1872). Fairly good, by a Jesuit.

E. A. Robertson, *Francis Xavier* (London, Student Christian Movement Press, 1930, pp. 207). Brief, popularly written.

INDIA

A. Jann, *Die katholischen Missionen in Indien, China und Japan. Ihre Organization und das portugiesische Patronat vom 15 bis ins 18 Jahrhundert* (Paderborn, Ferdinand Schöningh, 1915, pp. xxviii, 540). Scholarly, by a Capuchin.

E. Maclagan, *The Jesuits and the Great Mogul* (London, Burns, Oates & Washbourne, 1932, pp. xxxi, 434). A scholarly study based on the sources.

J. Richter, *Indische Missionsgeschichte* (Gütersloh, C. Bertelsmann, 2d ed., 1930, pp. 294). The standard history of Protestant missions in India. It also contains a brief sketch of the Roman Catholic missions of the sixteenth, seventeenth, and eighteenth centuries. There is an English translation of an earlier edition.

CEYLON

S. G. Prakasar, *A History of the Catholic Church in Ceylon. I. Period of Beginnings, 1505-1602* (Colombo, Literature Committee for the Catholic Union of Ceylon, 1924, pp. xiv, 283). In general objective, based upon wide reading, by an Oblate.

Fernão de Queroz, *The Temporal and Spiritual Conquest of Ceylon,* translated by S. G. Perara (Colombo, A. C. Richards, Acting Government Printer, 1930, pp. 28, xxviii, 1274). Written 1671-1686, by a Jesuit, and based in part upon original sources. Seeks to animate Portugal to recover Ceylon.

J. E. Tennent, *Christianity in Ceylon: Its Introduction and Progress under the Portuguese, the Dutch, the British, and American Missions; with an Historical Sketch of the Brahmanical and Buddhist Superstitions* (London, John Murray, 1850, pp. xv, 345).

THE EAST INDIES

C. W. T. van Boetzelaer van Dubbeldam, *De Gereformeerde Kerken in Nederland en de Zending in Oost-Indië in de dagen der Oost-Indische Compagnie* (Utrecht, P. Den Boer, 1906, pp. viii, 358). A doctoral dissertation.

THE PHILIPPINES

E. A. Blair and J. A. Robertson, *The Philippine Islands 1493-1803. Explorations of Early Navigators, Descriptions of the Islands and their Peoples, Their History and Records of the Catholic Missions, as Related in Contemporary Books and Manuscripts, Showing the Political, Economic, Commercial and Religious Conditions of Those Islands from their Earliest Relations with European Nations to the Beginning of the Nineteenth Century* (Cleveland, The Arthur H. Clark Co., 55 vols., 1903-1907). A standard collection.

JAPAN

C. R. Boxer, *The Christian Century in Japan 1549-1650* (University of California Press, 1951, pp. xv, 535). Scholarly, readable, the best survey of the subject.

CHINA

K. S. Latourette, *A History of Christian Missions in China* (New York, The Macmillan Co., 1929, pp. xii, 930).

A. H. Rowbotham, *Missionary and Mandarin* (University of California Press, 1942, pp. xi, 374). A careful, scholarly survey.

SPANISH AMERICA

C. S. Braden, *Religious Aspects of the Conquest of Mexico* (Duke University

Press, 1930, pp. xi, 344). By a Protestant, objective, in large part from printed first-hand sources.

M. Brion, *Bartholomé de las Casas, "Father of the Indians,"* translated from the French by C. B. Taylor (New York, E. P. Dutton & Co., 1929, pp. xvii, 314). Popularly written, favourable to Las Casas, based partly upon Las Casas's writings.

L. Hanke, *The Spanish Struggle for Justice in the Conquest of America* (University of Pennsylvania Press, 1949, pp. xi, 217). Scholarly. Deals chiefly but by no means entirely with Las Casas. Carries the story down to 1600.

J. M. van der Kroef, *Francisco de Vitoria and the Nature of Colonial Policy* (*The Catholic Historical Review,* July, 1949, Vol. XXXV, pp. 129–162).

J. F. Rippy and J. T. Nelson, *Crusaders of the Jungle* (The University of North Carolina Press, 1936, pp. x, 401). The story of missions in tropical South America during the colonial period. Scholarly, semi-popular in style.

E. Ryan, *The Church in the South American Republics* (New York, The Bruce Publishing Co., 1932, pp. viii, 119). By a Roman Catholic priest; popular in style, scholarly.

FRENCH AMERICA

F. Parkman, *The Jesuits in North America in the Seventeenth Century* (Boston, Little, Brown & Co., 1903, pp. xvii, 586). Based chiefly on the *Jesuit Relations.*

R. G. Thwaites, *The Jesuit Relations and Allied Documents: Travels and Explorations of the Jesuit Missionaries in New France 1610–1791. The Original French, Latin, and Italian Texts, with English Translations and Notes; Illustrated by Portraits, Maps, and Facsimiles* (Cleveland, The Burrows Brothers, 73 vols., 1896–1901).

THE THIRTEEN COLONIES

P. Miller, *Jonathan Edwards* (New York, William Sloane Associates, 1949, pp. xv, 348). Well written, based upon careful research.

W. W. Sweet, *Religion in Colonial America* (New York, Charles Scribner's Sons, 1942, pp. xiii, 367). A standard survey.

L. J. Trinterud, *The Forming of an American Tradition. A Re-examination of Colonial Presbyterianism* (Philadelphia, The Westminster Press, 1949, pp. 352). Very well done. Especially valuable for the Great Awakening.

L. A. Weigle, *American Idealism* (Yale University Press, 1928, pp. 356). About a third of this highly competent survey of the religious history of the United States is on the colonial period.

Chapter XLII

THE EXPANDING EFFECT OF CHRISTIANITY

In the two and a half centuries between 1500 and 1750 Christianity was having effects over more of the surface of the globe than in any earlier era. It continued to be the professed faith of the majority of the population of Europe and of minorities in Western Asia and North-eastern Africa. As we have seen in the preceding two chapters, through the Russians it was making itself felt in parts of Eastern Europe which previously had known it only slightly if at all and for the first time it was being represented, even though by little minorities, across the northern reaches of Asia. It was now, also for the first time, touching the coastal fringes of Africa south of the Sahara, was making its initial penetration of South-east Asia, of the islands which fringed that area, and of Japan. Although still excluded by Islam from Central Asia where it had once been, it was probably touching more of the peoples of India and of China than at any former time. The majority of the population of the Americas had given it their nominal allegiance.

Did this wider geographic spread mean an enhanced influence upon mankind as a whole? If so, what was the quality of that influence? Judged by the standards of the New Testament, was it for good or for ill?

It may seem surprising and even impertinent to suggest that it may have been for ill. Yet there is much in the records of these years which could be adduced to support that thesis. The geographic explorations and conquests which marked the period were by professedly Christian peoples, most of whom had been under the influence of Christianity for many generations. Some of the explorers and conquerors avowed themselves to be moved by the Christian faith. But, as we have seen, grievous exploitation of non-European peoples followed, including the African slave trade, Negro slavery in the Americas, and the near enslavement and even the extermination of a large proportion of the American Indians. In Europe itself, as we have also noted, especially in Western Europe, where Christianity had done much to shape civilization, forces were at work which were actual or practical denials of the faith. Some of them were accentuated by Christianity and others had their roots partly in Christianity. Wars were not new in Europe. For several of them, notably the Crusades, loyalty to Christianity had been the declared motive. Crusades were dying out, although successive Popes sought in vain by invoking them to unite Western Europe against the Turks. Now, however, the division of Western Europe between Roman Catholics and Protestants was either causing wars or making them more bitter. Such were the wars of religion in France and the Thirty Years' War. In England and Germany civil strife was either brought on or heightened by the appeal to rival conceptions of the Christian faith. What seemed like a secularization of Europe was in progress and this was in part from forces set in motion by Christianity. The Renaissance and some aspects of the humanism which was associated with it and followed it were in part, as we have said, fruits of Christianity. Yet they made for pride and attempts at human self-sufficiency which tended to rule out the Christian faith. The Papacy had less and less influence in the relation between states and with occasional exceptions, such as Richelieu and Mazarin, members of the clergy had a much smaller part in the affairs of their respective governments than a few centuries earlier. The intellectual life centered less around the Christian faith than in the Middle Ages. Theology was no longer regarded as the "queen of the sciences" in the sense of being the central subject of study. Some thinkers were challenging the truth of Christianity, a trend which was to assume larger proportions after 1750. Literature and art were more concerned with secular subjects and less devoted to specifically Christian themes. If these aspects of the story were all, the impartial observer might be pardoned if he came to the conclusion that Western Europe was outgrowing the faith which had done much to guide and shape its infancy and that what survived of that faith was being perverted to man's hurt and was destroying such remnants of itself as persisted.

However, this is only one side of the picture. Christianity was also producing the positive fruits which were to be expected from it, and these were more widely evident than in the centuries which had gone before. It is at least an arguable explanation of the seeming contrast that as the Gospel is longer in the world and makes its way more widely across the earth, God entrusts men with more knowledge and more mastery of their environment. He does this fully aware of the risk that He is taking, realizing that some will pervert His gifts, but also confident that others will be so gripped by the Gospel that they will be stirred and empowered not only to counteract the evil but also to produce fruits far greater than if the possibilities for the abuse of God's gifts had not been present. It is conceivable that this is God's way of dealing with men, that He is seeking to produce men of character, not automatons, and that this can be done only by giving men freedom of choice either to their infinite hurt or to their infinite good, but that He is also sovereign and will not permit evil to get completely out of hand, but will overrule it for His own purposes of love. It may be that something of this is hinted at in such passages of Scripture as "where sin abounded, grace did much more abound," "God is faithful, who will not suffer you to be tempted above that ye are able," and "My thoughts are not your thoughts, neither are your ways my ways, saith the Lord. . . . My word . . . shall not return unto me void, but it shall accomplish that which I please. . . . Ye shall go out with joy and be led forth with peace. . . . Instead of the thorn shall come up the fir tree and instead of the brier shall come up the myrtle tree, and it shall be to the Lord . . . for an everlasting sign that shall not be cut off."

The Effect Outside of Europe

In the preceding chapter we have seen many instances of the fashion in which Christianity not only stirred men to counteract the evils brought by the impact of Europeans upon non-Europeans but also to make of that impact a positive blessing. Thus Las Casas and less famous advocates of the cause of the Indians brought about legislation to protect the aborigines and then laboured as missionaries to bring the Gospel to them and through it to open to them a larger life. Protestants seized the opportunity given by the discovery of America to plant settlements through which the Gospel could be more nearly realized in human society than in the Old World. In doing so they laid the foundations for a new nation many of whose ideals were to be shaped by Christianity, especially by Protestantism of the Reformed tradition. In later chapters we shall see, as we sketch the course of Christianity in the United States, how profoundly that country was moulded by Christianity and how that faith was the source of many movements for social and moral reform and for the embodiment of the teachings of the New Testament.

The Effect on Europe

We must now seek to enquire how far and in what ways Europe, especially Western Europe, was affected by Christianity during these two hundred and fifty years. Here the faith had longer enjoyed a nearer approach to free course than anywhere else. Unlike the Eastern Churches, while threatened, except recently and in limited areas, it was not engulfed by the aggressive Islam. Here Christianity was the official religion of the several states and of the community. In South-western Europe it had occupied that position for a thousand years or more and in most of North-western and Central Europe by 1500 it had held it for at least five centuries. In much of Eastern Europe its adoption was much more recent and there were still unassimilated pagans and Moslems in its midst or on its fringes.

THE EFFECT ON RELIGION

First of all, we turn, as is natural, to the area of life which we call religious. In a very real sense this is a narrowing of the scope of religion which is contrary to fact, for religious convictions permeate all phases of life. However, there is a degree of validity in focusing attention on the ecclesiastical structures, the formal acceptance of beliefs, the worship, public and private, and the movements, new and old, which are clearly religious. When we define religion in this fashion, it is demonstrable that Christianity was shaping this aspect of the life of Europe more profoundly than at any earlier time. This was seen in a variety of ways.

To a greater degree than ever before, unless it may have been in the first two or three centuries, in the years between 1500 and 1750 Christianity gave rise to new and potent religious movements. This was seen in both the Protestant and the Catholic Reformation. The emergence of Protestantism came from a powerful thrust of the vigour inherent in Christianity. Although, as we have seen, factors extraneous and even hostile to Christianity, such as nationalism, the ambitions of monarchs, and the growth of an urban middle class, must be counted among the causes of the Protestant Reformation, they were distinctly secondary. They helped to make possible the survival of Protestantism as against the Catholic Church and did much to shape the forms which Protestantism assumed, but in themselves, either singly or collectively, they could not have produced Protestantism. Without them, although it might not have flourished and survived, Protestantism would have come into being. It was to the dynamic which is of the essence of Christianity that Protestantism owed its origin. It was that dynamic which chiefly accounted for the variety exhibited by Protestantism. The "denominations," "confessions," and "communions" of Protestantism roughly corresponded to the monastic orders in the Catholic Church. Like the latter, they arose basically from a fresh surge of conviction and devotion. They owed their forms partly to the political and social environment in which they emerged, but they were primarily the creation of individuals who had been gripped by the Christian Gospel. These individuals would have remained individuals were it not for the fact that there were others, sometimes only a few scores or hundreds, at other times thousands, similarly moved, to whom they gave leadership.

In the Roman Catholic Church, as we have seen, the fresh access of life in Christianity made for the revivification of old monastic orders and brought about the rise of new ones. Several of these, like the Society of Jesus, seeking to meet the needs of the times, took forms somewhat different from those of their predecessors. In the main they were more missionary and activistic.

In the Russian Orthodox Church the new burst of life was not as marked as in Western Europe, but it was largely indigenous, and although somewhat affected by what was taking place in the Christianity of Western Europe had expressions which were quite native to Russia.

The religious awakenings of the age touched every class. In this they were in partial contrast to their predecessors in the Middle Ages and were evidence that Christianity was penetrating all levels of society and becoming their conscious property. It will be recalled that in the tenth, eleventh, and twelfth centuries the new monastic movements had their creators and leaders chiefly from the aristocracy. In the thirteenth century some of the new movements, notably the Franciscans and several of those which the Catholic Church branded as heretical, were strongest in the growing urban population. Now all classes were stirred. Loyola and most of the founders of new monastic orders in the Roman Catholic Church were from the nobility. Luther, Zwingli, and a number of other Protestant pioneers were of peasant stock. Cranmer was of sturdy but humble farming parentage. Not many generations back, Calvin's paternal ancestors had been boatmen. George Fox was the son of a weaver. Many of the Anabaptists were in the towns and cities. Numbers of intellectuals were prominent in both the Protestant and the Catholic Reformation. Christianity was less and less passively accepted from social convention, as had been the case in the conversion of Europe, and was increasingly moving all classes of society.

Even the conscious departure from Christianity which was being fore-shadowed in this period and was to assume much larger proportions in succeeding centuries was evidence that men were no longer willing to conform to the faith uncritically, but were insisting upon investigating it for themselves. This very freedom was in part the fruit of Christianity.

The new life was accompanied by an improvement in the education and morals of the clergy. In the Middle Ages the majority of the clergy, whether in Western Europe or Russia, had little education. In Europe, both Western and Eastern, with notable exceptions, the parish clergy, those who set the level for the masses, were badly tarnished exemplars of Christian living. As the recurring efforts of reformers show, they were notorious for their avarice, sexual laxity, and ignorance. The higher clergy were little better. On the average they had an education which was superior to the rank and file of those who served the parishes, and among them were some of worthy character, even saints, but in involvement in secular affairs and in lust for power and wealth many set a corrupting example for their subordinates.

Perfection did not come with the Reformation, whether in Protestantism or in the Roman Catholic Church. Not all the clergy, either Protestant or Roman Catholic, were well educated or were of high moral character. Pluralism, that is, holding more than one office in the Church and drawing the revenues without performing the functions, continued. For example, it was notorious in the Church of England.

Yet the Reformation wrought distinct improvement, both in the areas served by Protestants and in the Roman Catholic fold. In general, the clergy of both wings of the Church in Western Europe exhibited a higher level of morality and better educational preparation than had been characteristic of the Church in that area during the Middle Ages.

For the rank and file of the laity the level of intelligent comprehension of the Christian faith was lifted by both the Protestant and the Catholic Reformation. The widespread discussion of religious issues was promoted by the controversies which accompanied the rise of Protestantism and its separation from the Roman Catholic Church. Printing made books and pamphlets accessible to a larger proportion of the population and much that issued from the presses dealt with religion. For the instruction of church members catechisms for their respective constituencies were prepared by both Protestants and Roman Catholics. Among Protestants the circulation of the Bible in vernacular translations markedly increased. Among Roman Catholics education in the tenets of the faith was promoted by such organizations as the Congregation of the Priests of the Mission. The emphasis upon preaching made for a similar advance among Protestant constituencies.

Whether equivalent gains were made in approximation to Christian moral standards would be difficult either to prove or to disprove. It is clear that both Protestant and Roman Catholic leaders sought to inculcate morality among the membership of their churches. In Protestantism the "gathered" churches, such as the Independents and the Anabaptists, especially stressed a high standard of morals among all their members. The Reformed tradition, notably in Puritanism, operated in the same direction. So also did Pietism in the Lutheran Churches.

Most and perhaps all awakenings within Christianity have given rise to hymns and singing. The Reformation was no exception. We have noted them in Protestantism. In that branch of Protestantism which is designated by his name, Luther was only the first in a long succession. The Reformed Churches favoured paraphrases of the Psalms, and of these there were many. German Pietism and English dissent gave birth to hundreds of hymns. With its emphasis upon the active participation of those assembled in public worship, Protestantism was particularly productive of hymns and metrical versions of the Psalms and Canticles which could be sung by congregations, but hymns for less formal use as well as great music for the mass emerged from the Roman Catholic Reformation.

Whether Protestant or Roman Catholic, the Reformation stimulated the life of the spirit and issued in a fresh surge of mysticism. By mysticism is meant, as it has throughout our narrative, the sense of the presence of God. In some degree, although for the majority very slight, this is common to most of those for whom the Christian faith is more than a nominal acquiescence in beliefs and customs shared by the community. From time to time there emerge from the mediocre level of the rank and file those who can be called great mystics, by whom the sense of the immediacy of the Divine presence is sought with intense desire and in whom it is realized. Their numbers are an indication of the temperature of the Church. In times of quickening, when devotion is warm, they multiply. We would expect that they would be numerous in this period. In this, as we have seen, we are not disappointed. They were found among both Protestants and Roman Catholics. Some were retiring contemplatives. Others were activists, their deeds in organization and leadership intensified and multiplied through the vision and strength which came from prayer and meditation. Among the common run of Christians there may have been more of private and group prayer than in the preceding periods. Certainly printing was utilized to give wide circulation to books of devotion. We read that in Scotland early in the eighteenth century most country houses and even flats in Edinburgh had closets for private prayer to which members of the family were supposed to retire daily. For respectable Scottish families Sundays were marked by abstinence from work and play and were given to family prayers and attendance at church services. Presumably there were other areas than Scotland in which the equivalents of these customs were maintained.

Whether religious liberty is evidence of the growing influence of the Gospel can be and has been hotly debated. It is certain that during this period there were Protestants who stood for religious liberty and did so on grounds which they believed were rooted in the Gospel. They constituted a minority and were mostly in or near the radical wing of Protestantism. Some were in the Reformed tradition. Only rarely and then chiefly in a few of the Thirteen Colonies, was there within Christendom a near approach to religious liberty. In some countries in Europe, notably the Netherlands and England, a limited religious toleration existed, but toleration differs from freedom. Toleration was usually more from political expediency or necessity than from religious conviction.

EXTRA-RELIGIOUS AREAS IN GENERAL

In other areas of life than the strictly religious the effect of Christianity continued to be marked. Indeed, it had fresh manifestations, evidence that it was not a dwindling survival of what are often, but mistakenly, called the Ages of Faith.

At first sight this statement will be surprising and may provoke dissent. The traditional Christendom, the *corpus Christianum,* appeared to be in process of secularization. The dream of a Christian society cherished by many in the Middle Ages seemed to be shattered. Not only Popes and lesser ecclesiastics, but also some among the laity had pictured the ideal society as one in which the Church would be regnant. Pope and Holy Roman Emperor were to be the joint rulers, the one of the spiritual and the other of the temporal aspect of the human community. Many had asserted that the Pope must be superior to the Emperor. The struggle between Church and state had been chronic, and some of the outstanding saints, among them Anselm, Becket, and Hildebrand, were famous for resistance to what they deemed the encroachments of the state. After 1500 the state had seemingly triumphed. On the eve of the sixteenth century the breach between the Eastern and Western wings of the Catholic Church had become final. In the sixteenth century what the Catholics called the Protestant revolt shattered what remained of Catholic unity in Western Europe. In the course of the fifteenth, sixteenth, and seventeenth centuries the severed fragments of the Church became subject to monarchs who sought absolute power over their subjects. In much of the East that power was not even nominally Christian, but was exercised by Moslem rulers, chiefly the Ottoman Turks. Where the rulers were professedly Christian, whether Protestant, Roman Catholic, or Orthodox, they were dominant. In Lutheran lands and England this was supported by many of the leaders of the Church on grounds of principle. The principle was called Erastianism, from Thomas Erastus (1524–1583), a German-Swiss physician, a Zwinglian, accused of Socinianism, who held that the sins of Christians should be punished by civil, not ecclesiastical authorities. The doctrine which wrongly goes by his name maintains that the Church is of right dependent on the state and is to be controlled by it. In the more powerful Roman Catholic states, as we have seen, the monarchs, while professing to be orthodox in belief, some of them zealously and even militantly so, insisted upon administrative direction of the Church in their realms. In Russia efforts of Nikon to make the Patriarchate preëminent failed and within a generation after his death Peter the Great allowed the office to remain unfilled and substituted for it the Holy Synod, completely a creature of the tsar. What is called Cæsaropapism was a fact.

CHRISTIANITY AND POLITICAL LIFE AND STRUCTURE

In spite of the control of the Church by the state, the influence of Christianity on the political life of Europe was striking and was exhibited in both old and new ways. With the exception of the Turks, the monarchs professed to be Christian. Claiming absolute power, they did so on the theory of divine right. Hence in principle they held themselves accountable to God. This was old.

Here and there after 1500 ecclesiastics held high political office and exerted a striking influence over governments. As in the Middle Ages when the chief ministers of monarchs were often bishops, this did not necessarily mean that Christianity was potent in determining their actions. Indeed, as in earlier centuries, in political office clergy were usually as un-Christian in their advice and action as though they had been frankly pagans. Outstanding in this period were Wolsey in England, Richelieu, Mazarin, and Fleury in France, and Alberoni in Spain. All cardinals of the Roman Catholic Church, they were as avid for power and as little governed by Christian principles in their policies of state as though they had not borne the Christian name. It is doubtful whether even Nikon in the days when he controlled the tsar was an exception to this generalization.

Some of the lay rulers were as intent upon exercising their power as Christians as had been any of the monarchs of the Middle Ages. Examples can be found among both Roman Catholics and Protestants. To mention only a few, they include Philip II of Spain, Mary of England, Gustavus Vasa and Gustavus Adolphus of Sweden, William the Silent of the Netherlands, and Oliver Cromwell of England.

Partly old and partly new were the efforts to bring order into what threatened to be destructive chaos in the relations between the nation-states ruled by absolute monarchs into which Europe was divided. War among them was chronic. The power of the Papacy over their relations had been declining since the thirteenth century and, except for Italy, had virtually disappeared.

The Christian faith and conscience inspired and constrained Christians to formulate principles for regulating the relations between states. What came to be known as international law was developed. Some of its basic ideas went back to pre-Christian philosophy, but the courage to give them actuality came chiefly from the Christian Gospel. The family of nations envisaged by international law was at the outset made up of professedly Christian states.

This is not the place for a full account of the rise and growth of international law. We must, however, pause to note a few outstanding figures. Francisco de Vitoria, a Basque by birth, a Dominican, Professor of Theology at the

University of Salamanca, whom we have already met as a champion of the cause of the American Indians, in the first half of the sixteenth century in *De Indis Noviter Inventis* and *De Jure Belli* set forth a conception of a community of nations which was broader than Christendom and coextensive with the human race. He declared that no attempt to right a wrong to a particular state should be undertaken if it involved a greater injury to the entire world community. He maintained that differences in religion, the glory of a prince, and the extension of an empire were not just causes for war and that if the subjects of a prince were convinced that a war was unjust they should not serve in it. Both Emperor and Pope were offended by his plain speaking. In the next generation a Jesuit, Francisco Suarez (1548–1617), who had been educated at Salamanca, helped further to develop the theory of international law. A contemporary of Suarez, Alberico Gentili (1552–1608), who for his Protestant convictions left his native Italy and became Professor of Civil Law at Oxford, gave to the world a book, *De Jure Belli,* which was another landmark in the growth of international law. Most famous of all the pioneers was the Dutch Protestant, Hugo Grotius or Huig van Groot (1583–1645). From his youth he had been deeply interested in theological issues. He was an Arminian and suffered persecution for espousing the cause of the Remonstrants. A layman and a lawyer, the spectacle of professedly Christian nations disregarding divine and human law in their conduct of war led him to write *De Jure Belli et Pacis,* a treatise which was long a classic for its formulation of principles. Significantly, it was published in 1625, while the Thirty Years' War was being waged. Although treating with respect what was called the law of nature, Grotius maintained that the New Testament is more authoritative and gave it preëminence.

A small minority of Christians were impelled by their faith to denounce all war and some went further and declined to participate in it in any fashion. Erasmus declared that all war is un-Christian. Dean Colet of St. Paul's Cathedral in London aroused the displeasure of Henry VIII by asserting in a sermon preached in his presence that wars are seldom undertaken except from hatred and that a Christian prince would do well to seek to imitate, not Cæsar or Alexander, but Christ. Several of the radical Protestant groups kept aloof from any active share in war. These included the early Mennonites, others of the Anabaptists, and the Friends. Something of the same attitude had been taken by most Christians in the first two centuries and in the Middle Ages by several of the groups adjudged heretical by the Catholic Church. Now as then it had little if any effect upon the policies of governments. Those who held it were not as influential as had been those who had laboured for the Peace of God and the Truce of God or as were those who sought to place the relations between states on the basis of law, whether in peace or war. Yet their witness was evidence that there were those whom the Christian faith impelled to be unreconciled to what to them were compromise and half-way measures.

The Christian faith inspired a few to suggest structures which would obviate war and ensure peace. In 1623, a monk, Émeric Crucé, put forward a plan for establishing perpetual peace and freedom of commerce throughout the world. This entailed an assembly of representatives of the monarchs of the world to adjust differences which might lead to war. William Penn, the Quaker, in his *Essay toward the Present and Future Peace of Europe* suggested a European diet or parliament in which disputes could be settled by vote. In 1710 a devout Quaker and a friend of Penn, John Bellers, proposed an organization for Europe which would curtail armaments and ensure peace. Soon after the close of the War of the Spanish Succession (1713), Charles Irénée de Saint-Pierre, a French priest who had been a secretary in the negotiations which ended that costly struggle, developed a plan for permanent peace which included non-Christian as well as Christian states.

In these projects and in the development of international law, Christian faith was inspiring thoughtful men to meet constructively a changed situation. In the Middle Ages Christian idealists built their hopes for world order on the achievement of a universal state with two heads, the Pope and the Holy Roman Emperor. The attainment of that dream had clearly become impossible. Europe was now divided among numbers of nation-states, each of which was seeking to be sovereign and fully independent. Undiscouraged, Christians were now daring to propose and make actual a society of nations which would be governed by law.

Christianity also had important effects upon the political theories which governed individual states. As we have suggested, it was called upon to reinforce the absolute monarchies which characterized the period. Generally monarchs were believed to hold their office by divine appointment. They were usually crowned with a ceremony which was a religious service designed to symbolize their dedication to their high office as Christians responsible to God.

When carried to its logical conclusion, Protestantism made for democracy. Its basic principles, salvation by faith and the priesthood of all believers, issued in governments in which each citizen had a voice and possessed rights and responsibilities equal with those of all his fellows. The majority of Protestants did not go as far as this. Most Lutheran states were monarchies. The Reformed Churches moved further towards democracy. Calvin disliked monarchies, but held that if God ordains governments we must obey them. He was not an egalitarian or a leveller. He taught liberty and fraternity but not equality. He shrank from revolution and desired an elective aristocracy. Yet under his leadership Geneva became a firmly established republic. The organization of the Reformed Churches had in it much of democracy. That was especially true of the Presbyterians. Still more democratic were the "gathered" churches, including the Independents, the Baptists, and the Quakers. The seventeenth century struggle in England in which Puritanism and the Independents were prominent and even more radical groups had a voice, contributed immeasurably to the democratic trend in the government of that country.

In the Thirteen Colonies the aristocratic patterns of the mother country were weakened and the radical groups—Puritans, Congregationalists, and Quakers—were much stronger than in England. Because of that fact, democracy flourished earlier and more vigorously in the Thirteen Colonies than in the British Isles. Sometimes the democracy of the United States is attributed to the westward-moving frontier, for it is said that conditions on it made for individual initiative and for the belief that one man is as good as another and that any one, regardless of birth, is competent to occupy any post. Yet the frontier was a constant factor in the Spanish, Portuguese, and French possessions in America and in none of them did democracy and the democratic dream develop in the form prized in the United States. The difference seems in large part to have been due to contrasts in religion. In the Spanish, Portuguese, and French colonies Roman Catholicism was the only religion permitted. In the Thirteen Colonies, so far as the population adhered to any religion, it was to one form or another of Protestantism, and in that Protestantism the Reformed and radical wings were in the majority. In the Thirteen Colonies John Locke (1632–1704) had more immediate influence than in England. From a Puritan home and educated in a Puritan atmosphere, Locke was widely read and quoted by those who, after 1750, shaped the nascent United States. In Locke, for example, was the assertion that men are "by nature, all free, equal, and independent. No man can be put out of his estate without his full consent." This was to be echoed, partly in the identical words, in the Declaration of Independence of the Thirteen Colonies.

In contrast, the Roman Catholic Church did not make for democracy as the Anglo-Saxon world understood that term. In France, reinforced by that church in his effort to make the crown supreme, Louis XIV sought to crush out the Protestant minority. That minority, it will be recalled, was of the family of Reformed Churches, from which issued much of Anglo-Saxon democracy. Bossuet, the most famous preacher of France in the age of Louis XIV, supported with his eloquence the power of the crown and inveighed against the theory propounded by such Protestants as Hugo Grotius that there is a law higher than the state and which the king must obey. As we are to see (Chapter XLIV), those who created French democracy drew their inspiration partly from Christian sources, but in doing so denounced the Christian faith, identified as that was for them with the Roman Catholic Church.

THE EFFECT ON ECONOMIC THEORY AND PRACTICE

What effect, if any, did Christianity have upon the economic life of Europe? That the economic aspects of Western Europe were passing through a revolution is one of the commonplaces of history. The surviving traces of feudalism were fading. Commerce was mounting. The guilds through which industry and trade had been conducted in the Middle Ages were disappearing. There was more of individual initiative, foreshadowing the *laissez faire* which was to characterize much of the eighteenth and nineteenth centuries. *Laissez faire* was in large part a reaction against the close control of all commerce by states dominated by absolute monarchs. Stock companies were being organized and capitalism was developing. In what fashion, if at all, was Christianity connected with the economic changes, whether as cause, deterrent, or regulator?

It has been argued brilliantly and with much erudition that Protestantism and especially Calvinism were a major source of capitalism. The thesis is propounded in the following manner. The Reformed faith made incumbent upon all its adherents a kind of asceticism. It taught that every Christian, and not alone clergymen, should regard his occupation a vocation which he should pursue in response to the "call" of God. In it he should work conscientiously as in the sight of God. He was to seek to produce what would be useful for the community. He was not to be idle nor was he to spend in selfish or luxurious fashion the fruits of his labours. He was to make all he could, spend only what was necessary, and save the surplus, although giving part of it for worthy causes. This led to the accumulation of private wealth and so made capitalism possible. Moreover, while Luther followed the precedent of the Church of the Middle Ages and forbade the taking of interest, Calvin permitted it. This also furthered capitalism. The acquisition and use of capital could be a virtue. Thus Protestantism encouraged the growth of the *bourgeoisie,* the urban middle class, which thrived on capitalism. In support of this generalization it is pointed out that the Netherlands, committed to the Reformed faith, became a great commercial power and that in England Puritanism had its chief strongholds in the middle class in the cities which were thriving on the expanding industry and trade of the realm.

This thesis has been vigorously attacked. In criticism it is said that the hypothesis quite misunderstands the Protestant teaching of "calling." The Puritans used it to rebuke covetousness and ambition, both qualities associated with capitalism. More cogently, it is pointed out that capitalism has its roots far back in the Middle Ages, long before the emergence of Protestantism, that the earliest European bankers were not Protestants but Catholics, that the urban middle class is a phenomenon of both Roman Catholic and Protestant countries, that in some countries Protestantism is quite as much rural as urban, and that this is true of the Reformed phase of Protestantism (as in Scotland, Switzerland, the Netherlands, and France), the phase which has been charged with primary responsibility for capitalism. In light of these considerations, so it is said, it cannot even be proved that Calvinism gave a decisive impulse to the development of capitalism, much less that it was the primary cause of it.

The Effect on Various Aspects of Social Life

On wide ranges of social life Christianity was having effects. Some of these were a continuation of what we have noted in earlier centuries. Others were new. They were more marked in Western Europe than in the East. What is often called activism, the attempt to better social conditions, was far more prominent in the Christianity of Western Europe, whether Roman Catholic or Protestant, than in the Christianity of the East. This seems to have arisen from several causes. One was the fact that in the West the practical spirit had been inherited from the pre-Christian Roman tradition. Another was the collapse of the Roman Empire in most of the West in the dark period after the fifth century and the assumption by the Church of some of the functions previously performed by the state, especially in the protection of the weak. In the East, in contrast, the Roman Empire persisted, gradually becoming the Byzantine Empire, and the populace could look to it for the social services which the Church undertook in the West. After the seventh century, the control by Moslem states of an increasing proportion of the area of the Eastern Churches worked against the undertaking by the latter of extensive care for the poor, the helpless, and the sick. Whatever the reasons, in the West the power inherent in the Christian faith gave rise to many efforts on behalf of the underprivileged and for social reform.

Among the social services traditional with Christians in the West was care for the sick and the poor. In the Roman Catholic Church this was continued, partly in the accustomed ways and partly through new organizations, some of them formed specifically for that purpose. The latter included bodies which we have already noted, such as the Brothers Hospitallers of St. John of God and the Sisters (or Daughters) of Charity, also known as Servants of the Sick. Only partially new, but greatly expanded, was the ransoming of those taken captive by Moslems, especially by the corsairs from North Africa who infested the Mediterranean. Also both old and new was the provision for the reclaiming of prostitutes.

Protestants were slow to do as much for the poor, the sick, and the orphans as were the Roman Catholics. This was partly because, stressing salvation by faith alone, they decried efforts to win merit by doing good works. It was chiefly because, from conviction, they had no monastic orders, and these were the chief instruments through which Roman Catholics cared for those members of society. Yet eventually Protestants developed means of performing these functions. They did it partly through the parish, as in England and Scotland, and partly through new types of institutions, such as the orphanage which the Pietists created at Halle.

From both Roman Catholics and Protestants there were the beginnings of prison reform which in the nineteenth century was to assume major proportions. Thus a leader of the Reformation in Sweden, Olavus Petri, denounced the use of torture as a means of compelling criminals to confess. James Oglethorpe, the Anglican, had as one of his motives in furthering the settlement of Georgia enabling convicts to make a new start and urged in Parliament projects for prison reform. Almost at its very beginning the Society for Promoting Christian Knowledge was discussing plans for bettering conditions in prisons in London. Late in the seventeenth century the Benedictine Mabillon advocated more humane treatment of prisoners.

Both Roman Catholics and Protestants did much for women. Societies and orders made up of women now became more prominent in the Roman Catholic Church. In extreme forms of Protestantism, notably the Quakers, women were placed either on a near equality or a complete equality with men.

The married clergy of the Protestants marked a distinct change in family life in the West and gave new honour to the wife. No longer was marriage unlawful for the clergy and concubinage of the clergy condoned as a lesser evil than clerical promiscuity. Nor, even as in the East, where the lower clergy were married and the bishops were required to be monks, was celibacy esteemed the higher way for the Christian. So far from regarding the unmarried state as nearer to the Christian ideal, Protestants repudiated monasticism and the overwhelming majority of their clergy, including bishops, were married. This added dignity to marriage, to the home, and to the wife.

Before 1750 there were to appear convictions of the perfectibility of man and of human society which were to be widely influential in the eighteenth and nineteenth centuries. Some of them were cherished in earnestly Christian circles. They were found in England in several of the churches and religious movements. For instance, George Fox and other Quakers insisted that every man who comes into the world is illumined by an inner light which is Christ. Many, and not alone the Friends, believed that a better age was dawning. This conviction led to active efforts to improve mankind. There was much of optimism. A familiar expression of it was in the hymn of Isaac Watts:

Jesus shall reign where'er the sun
Does his successive journeys run.
His kingdom spread from shore to shore
Till moons shall wax and wane no more.

THE EFFECTS ON INTELLECTUAL LIFE

At first sight, a survey of the intellectual life of Christendom between 1500 and 1750 would seem to indicate progressive de-Christianization. To be sure, the acute paganism of early stages of the Renaissance and its attendant humanism was partly dulled. The humanism of the North had more nearly held to Christian faith and morals than had that of the South. Both the Protestantism of the North and the Catholic Reformation in the South to some degree counteracted the paganizing tendency. The vast majority of intellectuals continued to pay at least lip service to the Church and Christianity and many, perhaps most, were sincere in their profession.

Yet some of the new learning, especially in the realm of natural science, was in seeming conflict with what many Christians had held to be essential in their faith. This was notable in the Copernican theory which taught that the earth revolves around the sun and not the sun around the earth. As popularized by Galileo Galilei (1564–1642) it was opposed by elements in the Roman Catholic Church. But others who accepted it and developed it were devout Christians.

Moreover, principles developed by convinced Christians were later to undercut the Christian faith of many. Thus, as we have seen, a younger contemporary of Galileo, René Descartes (1596–1650), often hailed as the father of modern philosophy, as a basic instrument of enquiry doubted everything. He believed that after all had been questioned one irrefragable truth remained, his own existence as a thinker. This was stated in the famous proposition, *cogito ergo sum* ("I think, therefore I am"). With that as a starting point, he was persuaded that he could believe in God as absolutely perfect being and continue to be a Roman Catholic.

Others, however, using the method of Descartes, did not reach that conclusion. The insistence of Descartes that all must be doubted until proved and that proof must be as logical as mathematical demonstration, led many away from the Christian faith. Nicolas Malebranche (1638–1715), born in Paris, trained in theology at the Sorbonne, and at one time a member of the Oratory, devoted to patristics and church history, had the course of his life changed by reading Descartes. He elaborated a system of philosophy which, while having a place for God, brought on him attacks from orthodox Catholics. Spinoza (1632–1677), of Jewish parentage, a native of Amsterdam, beginning with the *cogito ergo sum* of Descartes, departed from the latter's sharp distinction between matter and spirit and became a pantheist. He believed in God, but God as he conceived Him was not God as Christians believed Him to be. To Spinoza, God and nature are identical. All is determined and no room is left for creation, divine purpose, or miracle. Yet he regarded Jesus as the greatest of the prophets, in whom the wisdom of God assumed human nature.

Gottfried Wilhelm Leibnitz (1646–1716), for forty years a librarian at Hanover, was a man of enormous erudition in many fields. As we have noted, he sought ways of achieving unity among Christians—between Roman Catholics and Protestants, and between Lutherans and Reformed. He was a Lutheran. Yet whether his view of God can be called Christian is questionable. He held that the essential to all substance is active force. Substances are individual. Each is an atom or monad, an indivisible centre of force. Monads differ qualitatively, but all proceed as "fulgurations" or radiations from God, Who is the perfect, primary, and supreme monad.

John Locke (1632–1704), of Puritan rearing, trained at Oxford, we have already met more than once. He regarded himself as a Christian. Throughout his life he was deeply interested in religion and in his last years gave much of his time to the study of the Scriptures. In his *Reasonableness of Christianity* (1695), while holding that the Bible contains truths which unaided human reason could not discover and which are there attested by miracles, he maintained that nothing in the central message of the Scriptures is contrary to reason and that miracles are not unreasonable. He acknowledged Jesus as the Messiah and regarded as binding his moral teachings. These he held are in accord with reason. By stressing the ethics of Jesus and the consonance of Christianity with reason, Locke hoped to by-pass theological disputes, and by emphasizing what he believed to be essential Christianity to bring Christians together and to allay the strife of tongues among the many divisions of the Church. He was an advocate of religious toleration. Yet the most famous and widely read of his works, translated as it was into several languages, his *Essay Concerning Human Understanding,* while not intended to do so, led some of its readers to a complete scepticism.

A pupil of Locke, the third Earl of Shaftesbury (1671–1713), grandson of Locke's great friend and patron, wrote extensively. While himself believing in God, instead of basing morality, as had Locke, upon the command of God, he held that it is dependent upon an inner "moral sense" and so made possible ethical systems which have no place for God.

Isaac Newton (1642–1727), born the year in which Galileo died, did much more for astronomy and natural science than had the latter. While he himself was deeply interested in theology, his scientific findings were used by some as a means of disregarding or even denying Christianity.

Further from Christianity than these was Thomas Hobbes (1588–1679). Vigorous to an extreme old age, he wrote extensively. In philosophy a materialist, believing only in the existence of matter, he was violently attacked by some of the churchmen of his day. In political theory he upheld absolute monarchy as the way of preventing chaos in society.

A contemporary and friend of Hobbes, Edward Herbert, Baron Herbert of Cherbury (1583–1648), laid foundations for Deism, a view which was to be popular in the eighteenth century. While many who continued to call themselves Christians were profoundly influenced by it, some of its advocates openly repudiated Christianity. Herbert held that there is a natural religion which was that of primitive man. Its main tenets are that God exists and is to be worshipped, that He is served by virtuous lives, that man must and can repent of his sins, and after death there are reward for the virtuous and punishment for the wrong-doer.

Before the middle of the eighteenth century several had further developed Deism. Among them was John Toland (1670–1722) who, reared a Roman Catholic, in adolescence became a Protestant. In 1696 there appeared his *Christianity not Mysterious* in which he held that anything in the Bible which seems beyond the reach of reason will, on further investigation, prove to be quite understandable by the mind of man. He held that God never acts in a supra-rational manner, but always in such fashion that man can comprehend. God is not aloof, so Toland held in his later years, but is universally present. Some Deists attacked the reliability of the Bible and in general denied miracles.

Most of the early Deists were English. This may have been in part because of the multiplicity of the forms of Christianity in England. Underneath them all men were looking for the common denominator. That led some to seek not only for what all Christians believed but for what was universal in all religion. In the eighteenth century, especially after 1750, Deism was to have a wide vogue not only in the British Isles, but also on the Continent.

Deism had many variations, but in general it held that there is a universal religion which is in accord with reason. All that is best in Christianity, so the Deists were prone to say, is older than Christianity and is completely in accord with reason. This universal, rational religion includes belief in God as the great Architect of the universe. He created the world, planted reason in man, gave him the moral law, and governs the universe by laws which are in accord with reason. God is to be revered and is to be honoured by a life which observes the moral law. Religious beliefs and practices which cannot be justified by reason, so the Deists went on to say, are superstitious and, being irrational, are to be rejected. Irrational superstitions have been imposed by priests of various religions. These include what Deists deemed irrational elements in the

Christian relevation. The law of nature, God's law, can be discerned by reason and is to be obeyed. To follow reason is to be loosed from the shackles of superstition. Therefore man must be a "free thinker," namely, he must insist on his right to bring all beliefs to the bar of reason, and must be liberated from inhibitions which would curb the use of his intellect. Obviously consistent Deists had no place for such central Christian convictions as the incarnation and grace. Deism tended to be optimistic. Man, so its adherents held, was on the eve of full emancipation from the superstitions which had hampered him in the past and was now moving into a better, grander age in which he was to govern himself by pure reason.

In view of these trends it might easily be believed that Christianity was fading out of the intellectual life of Western Europe.

However, here, as in so many other aspects of the course of history in Europe, is only one side of the picture. The truth is far more complex. In this phase of European culture, as in others, there was striking evidence of the "exceeding greatness of the power."

We must remind ourselves first of all of the large place which Christianity had in stimulating fresh approaches to education and with them in broadening the base and scope of learning and devising new methods to quicken and train the human mind and spirit. We have already noted something of the fashion in which both the Protestant and the Catholic Reformation and the later awakenings in Protestantism gave rise to novel movements in education and thought. Indeed, this seems to be characteristic of Christianity. We have seen that in the first five centuries, in a culture which was thinking and saying little that was new, Christianity was inspiring the creation of great systems of theology. In Western Europe in the twelfth, thirteenth, and fourteenth centuries, it was the chief impetus which gave rise to scholastic philosophy and theology, to the cathedral and monastic schools, and then to the universities. Now, in the sixteenth, seventeenth, and eighteenth centuries, Lutheranism worked a marked improvement in educational methods in Germany. Melanchthon and another friend of Luther, John Hugenhagen, brought the *volksschule* into existence and reconstructed the university curriculum. It was Hecker, a pupil of the Pietist Francke, who created the prototype of the *realschule* which had a large part in later German education. John Amos Comenius (1592–1670), a bishop of the *Unitas Fratrum,* made a refugee by the Thirty Years' War, was a pioneer in an educational theory which was to exert a wide influence, especially in its understanding handling of the child as a child. In Scotland John Knox had high ideals for a comprehensive system of education for the entire country. Although this was not fully carried out, it was not forgotten and contributed to the characteristic Scottish hunger for learning.

Out of the Catholic Reformation came many new movements for education. We have noted the *Ratio Studiorum* of the Jesuits and the extensive development of schools by the Society under its pattern. In the sixteenth, seventeenth, and eighteenth centuries several congregations of women arose with the education of the masses as their aim. Some of these we have met, among them one of the earliest, the Ursulines. In the latter part of the seventeenth century John Baptist de la Salle founded the Brothers of Christian Schools largely for the purpose of instructing the children in the rural districts. In the seventeenth and the fore part of the eighteenth century several teaching brotherhoods came into being with the education of the children as their objective. In Ireland the "hedge schools," with lay teachers and encouraged by the priests, were a major agency in giving what education was had by the poverty-stricken Roman Catholic peasantry. The Jansenist Gentlemen of Port Royal began a number of schools which stressed the use of the vernacular, paid considerable attention to science, and emphasized love for the child and close personal contacts between pupils and teachers.

Moreover, from Christianity came impulses to creative thought which did not issue in departure from the faith but, rather, sought to reinforce it. Such were the theological systems of the Protestant reformers, including Calvin's *Institutes.* Joseph Butler (1692–1752), whom we have already mentioned, was reared a Nonconformist but in his youth joined the Church of England and died as Bishop of Durham. He intended his *Analogy of Religion Natural and Revealed, to the Constitution and Course of Nature* (1736) as an answer to the Deist criticism of the Christian revelation. The result of prolonged and profound reflection but written in an English style which was quite lacking in grace, it was widely read and in some circles was long considered the standard intellectual support of the Christian faith. It maintained that since the objections raised to the Christian revelation can also be directed against the structure of the universe and the course of nature, the probabilities are that both Christianity and the universe have God as their author. So, too, the resemblances of the Christian revelation and the course of nature warrant the same conviction. We know too little of nature to deny the probability of revelation, and the truth of revelation is confirmed by miracles and the fulfilment of prophecy.

A contemporary of Butler was George Berkeley (1685–1753), whom we have also already named. A native of Ireland and educated in Trinity College, Dublin, an Anglican institution, in his later years Berkeley was Bishop of Cloyne, of the established church of that island. A man who won the respect of many who knew him for a singularly pure and unselfish character, and persuaded, to use his own words, that "westward the star of empire takes its way, the four first acts already past, a fifth shall close the drama with the day,' time's noblest offspring is the last," he dreamed of founding in Bermuda an institution for training clergy for the care of the colonists and missionaries to the Indians. To that end he spent some time in Rhode Island, but the funds promised to carry through the enterprise were not provided and he returned to England. He is best remembered for his philosophy. To him, only mind and ideas have real existence. What we call matter is not outside the mind but within it and is imposed on the mind by the power of God. We must believe in God, for ideas are universal and constant and must arise from an eternally active mind, which is God. Since, from this viewpoint, matter does not exist, the materialist conception of the universe must be false. It would then follow that the Deist philosophy is untenable, for it maintains that the universe is a vast mechanism set running once for all by God and governed by His immutable laws.

Berkeley's philosophy had a profound influence on many minds in several countries, both in the eighteenth century and later. However, numbers of those who agreed with some of its premises about the primacy of mind did not accept his conclusions about the existence and operation of God. They were either sceptical about the truth of Christianity or completely abandoned the Christian faith.

We must remind ourselves that many of the scientific discoveries and much of the closely related developments in mathematics were by men of Christian faith. At once there come to mind such names as Kepler, Isaac Newton, and Pascal. Others less widely known could be added. Among them was John Flamsteed (1646–1719), a clergyman of the Church of England, founder of the royal observatory at Greenwich, compiler of an early catalogue of the fixed stars, and famous in his day for his observations of the moon.

There was that in Christianity which stimulated minds to activity. Many of them dissented from Christianity but others, among them some of the finest which Europe knew, were sincerely committed to it. Not all of the latter were fully orthodox, either from the standpoint of the Roman Catholic Church or of any of the major Protestant communions. Yet they regarded themselves as Christians and were deeply interested in the problems which that faith presented to the human intellect.

Not only in philosophy but also in literature in general the effects of Christianity were mixed. Some literature was pagan. Some, even when the work of those who were professionally committed to Christianity and drew their support from the Church, was of dubious Christian content. In this group belonged Rabelais, for a time a Franciscan and then a Benedictine, and Jonathan Swift, priest and dean in the established church in Ireland. Several, notably the many-sided Shakespeare, while having spots which could not be made to square with Christian morals, had passages which revealed profound insight into the Christian faith and warm sympathy with it. Some of the most notable literature of the time, as we have suggested, was devoted to Christian themes and was clearly inspired by the Christian faith. Such were Milton's *Paradise Lost* and Tasso's *Jerusalem Delivered*. There were also many lesser poets who were deeply gripped by the Christian faith. Among them were, in Italy, Luigi Tansillo (1510–1565) and Erasmo de Valvasone, pioneers in poems of remorse, centering largely on the tears of Peter and of Mary Magdalen, which enjoyed a wide vogue in circles affected by the Catholic Reformation. Writing in English were the Anglicans George Herbert (1593–1633), younger brother of Lord Herbert of Cherbury, deeply religious, by choice a clergyman, who put his dream of what that calling should mean in *The Country Parson,* and Henry Vaughan (1622–1695), much influenced by Herbert. Richard Crashaw (c.1613–1649), son of an Anglican clergyman and a convert to Roman Catholicism, wrote lyrics on the raptures of the saints and martyrs.

EFFECTS UPON ART AND MUSIC

As in scholarship and literature, so in art and music, a contrast was seen. No longer were Christian themes as dominant as in the Middle Ages. Yet Christianity had a marked influence. It inspired some of the greatest painting, sculpture, architecture, and music ever produced.

In painting some of the most treasured examples of art with Christian themes are from this period. It was in 1498, on the eve of the Catholic Reformation, that the extraordinarily versatile Leonardo da Vinci completed his memorable mural of the Last Supper in the refectory of a monastery in Milan. As we have reminded ourselves, Raphael and Michelangelo made their contributions in the sixteenth century. Spending most of his life in the opulent surroundings of commercial and worldly Venice, from which, significantly, came no great religious movement, Titian devoted much of his genius to quite secular and even pagan subjects. Yet Christian themes also appealed to his genius. Velásquez (1599–1660) gave most of his attention to other than religious subjects, but the crucifixion moved him to one of his most notable pictures. His younger contemporary, Murillo, was a member of an austere brotherhood whose members devoted themselves to the burial of the bodies of the drowned and the murdered and to the spiritual care of the last hours of those condemned to death. Murillo's themes were Christian, especially memorable being his treatment of the immaculate conception.

The construction of Christian churches continued to call forth the genius of architects. Notable was St. Peter's in Rome, in part the creation of Michelangelo. In their early days the Jesuits did much to produce a new style of church building. While, like St. Peter's, making pre-Christian classical style serve Christian purposes, they designed their churches so that the worshipping congregation could see the celebration of the mass, thus more appreciatively participating in it, and removed the screen which in many earlier churches had separated the altar from the nave. With the increased emphasis on preaching as a result of the Catholic Reformation, more prominence was given to the pulpit and greater care was devoted to so building the churches that the sermon could be heard.

If this was true in Roman Catholic church architecture, even more were Protestant churches so planned that the sermon might be easily heard. Reacting against what they deemed the idolatry in the use of images, sculptures, paintings, and stained glass windows in Roman Catholic churches, many Protestants made their churches severely plain. Yet among them, too, the Christian impulse inspired architecture which adapted pre-Christian classical forms to Christian worship. Outstanding were the structures which Christopher Wren (1632–1723), son of an Anglican clergyman, designed for the Church of England and those built, often by unremembered architects, in the Thirteen Colonies.

The Reformation, both Catholic and Protestant, called forth superb music. Giovanni Pierluigi (1524–1594), better known as Palestrina from his birthplace, successively choir master in three of Rome's largest churches, wrote more than ninety masses as well as scores of other musical settings for public worship. As we have seen, the Oratory gave rise to a new form, centering about Christian themes. Some of the greatest music ever written was by Johann Sebastian Bach (1685–1750), a Lutheran, who devoted most of his genius to the service of the Church. George Frederick Handel (1685–1759), born the same year as Bach but surviving him by nearly a decade, had his earliest musical training in Pietist Halle. He wrote much secular music, including operas, but he is best remembered for his oratorios and anthems, above all for his *Messiah*.

THE EFFECT ON INDIVIDUAL LIVES

It is not only by its impress upon various aspects of civilization and the collective life of mankind that the effect of Christianity is to be appraised. It is also, and primarily, by what it does to individuals. While Jesus had much to say of the kingdom of God and taught men in masses, he gave himself to men and women one by one. Some of his most moving parables had to do with single persons—the man who fell among thieves and the Samaritan who rescued him, the prodigal younger son and his older brother—and he warned his disciples not to despise even a single child. Obviously individuals are profoundly moulded by others and the society and culture in which they are immersed. They also leave their impress on their social environment, some of them so markedly that great masses of men are different because they have lived.

That Christianity placed its stamp on individuals in the two and a half centuries which followed the year 1500 must be apparent. This is one of the most obvious conclusions from the preceding chapters. It is clear that it affected individuals over a larger proportion of the earth's surface than at any earlier time.

A moment's reflection will bring the conclusion that the impact of Christianity was followed by more kinds of responses by individuals than in any previous period. This was partly because Christianity had more different expressions than in any preceding age, not even excepting the first three centuries when it proliferated into the many kinds of Gnosticism, the Ebionites, the Marcionites, the Montanists, and the Novatians—to mention only the best remembered. After 1500 there were not only the several Eastern Churches, the Roman Catholics, and the Protestants, but in most of these there were varieties. We have seen them in the Russian Orthodox Church, in the new expressions of the monastic tradition in the Roman Catholic Church, and in the many kinds of Protestantism. Moreover, as Christianity moved beyond Europe and Western Asia into East and South-east Asia, Africa south of the Sahara, and the Americas, individuals and groups from many different cultures were brought within the scope of the Christian impact and reacted to it far from uniformly.

Even from as cursory a summary as we have made in the preceding chapters, there can be no doubt that within all of its many variations in many individuals Christianity was producing distinctive and characteristic fruits—love, joy, peace, longsuffering, gentleness, goodness, faith, meekness, and self-control. We can be certain that for each of those individuals whom we have named in which these qualities were being displayed there were thousands in whom they were seen.

It is equally indubitable that in none of the men and women whom we have described were these fruits perfectly realized. All displayed qualities which contradicted them. At the very outset of Christianity this had been obvious. It was seen in the original apostles. Paul spoke of the Christians whom he knew as "being saved," implying that they were not yet fully saved, and frankly said of himself that he was not perfect and had not attained, but was pressing on to the "high calling of God in Christ Jesus." So in the period from 1500 to 1750 in some who called themselves Christians traits contrary to the Christian virtues were accentuated. For instance, out of what they believed to be zeal for the Christian faith many became bigoted, hard, unloving, and tortured or killed others, among them those who also regarded themselves as followers of Christ.

Whether the individuals who were being brought into conformation to the Christian ideal were fewer or more numerous than in the preceding eras we cannot know. Probably, in view of the wider geographic spread of the faith and the dynamic shown in the Protestant and Catholic Reformations, there were more of them, more who in the New Testament use of that term could be called saints, than in any other previous period of equal length.

SUMMARY

How shall we summarize the effect of Christianity in the two and a half centuries which we have just now surveyed? If, as we must, we seek to answer that question from the standpoint of mankind as a whole, it is clear that more of the earth's surface and a larger proportion of mankind had been touched than at any earlier time. With the advance of the Ottoman Turks in the East, the main centre of Christianity was more and more in Western Europe, with a secondary major centre in Russia. Western European peoples were rapidly extending their domains and their commerce, especially in the Americas. Roughly parallel with the growth of the colonial and commercial empires of European peoples went the spread of Christianity. Each aided the other, but the association was not inevitable. The missionaries were from the fresh burst of life within Christianity. Sometimes they preceded and sometimes they followed their non-missionary fellow-countrymen. The latter never went where the missionaries did not eventually come, but the missionaries went to many areas where merchants, conquerors, and settlers did not make their way until after 1750. How far the non-missionary expansion of Europeans was due to Christianity we cannot determine. That it was often accompanied and followed by ruthless and quite un-Christian exploitation is obvious. It is also clear that the Christian conscience softened the impact and at times made it of advantage to individuals and groups.

In "Christian" Europe itself contradictory movements were seen. On the one hand there was much tacit and a little patent denial of the faith. Although taking some new forms, the ruthless competition for power and prestige among monarchs, usually masked by the profession of righteous motives, but issuing in chronic war, was no more marked than in earlier centuries. Yet it was contrary to Christian precepts. So, too, was the struggle for wealth by individuals and groups. Much more of art and literature was secular than in the Middle Ages. Rather more of the philosophy which engaged the intellectuals denied or would seek to make unnecessary distinctive Christian tenets than did that of the Middle Ages. However, before we declare that a progressive de-Christianization of thought was setting in, we must recall the popularity of Averroes and Maimonides in the high Middle Ages, the persistent reverence for Plato, and the vogue enjoyed by Aristotle, all with non-Christian implications.

As against these features of Western Europe which seemed to argue the waning of Christianity, we must remember the profound effect on religion, probably making that phase of life a closer approximation to Christian standards than ever. We must also remind ourselves of the fashion in which Christian faith and conscience dealt with the relations between states and with political theory, of the Christian family aided by the Protestant Reformation, of the results in new educational systems and principles, and of the literature, art, and music which were inspired by Christianity. We must remember that much of the science which by many was deemed destructive to the Christian faith was the achievement of men committed to that faith and at least to some degree inspired by it to courageous search. Even the philosophy that denied or ignored central Christian convictions was to no small degree stimulated by the vigour of the Christian position.

In view of these facts, we must not lightly say that the world was becoming more Christian, or, on the other hand, bewail the departure of the Ages of Faith and declare that Christianity was a declining force. The picture is far too complex to permit sweeping generalizations. The geographic impact of Christianity had undoubtedly widened and a larger proportion of mankind was affected than ever before. But whether the world was more or less conforming to Christian standards it would be hard to determine.

Selected Bibliography

E. D. Bebb, *Nonconformity and Social and Economic Life 1660–1800. Some Problems of the Present as They Appeared in the Past* (London, The Epworth Press, 1935, pp. 198). Carefully done.

C. C. Conrad, *The Papacy and World-Affairs as Reflected in the Secularization of Politics* (University of Chicago Press, 1937, pp. xiv, 310).

C. Dawson, *Progress and Religion: An Historical Inquiry* (London, Longmans, Green & Co., 1929, pp. xvii, 254). A thoughtful study by a Roman Catholic layman.

P. J. Dowling, *The Hedge Schools of Ireland* (London, Longmans, Green & Co., 1935, pp. xvii, 182).

J. N. Figgis, *Studies in Political Thought from Gerson to Grotius 1414–1625* (Cambridge University Press, 2d ed., 1931, pp. vii, 224). A standard survey.

G. P. Gooch, *English Democratic Ideas in the Seventeenth Century. Second Edition, with Supplementary Notes and Appendices,* by H. J. Laski (Cambridge University Press, 1927, pp. x, 315). A standard work.

H. G. Graham, *The Social Life of Scotland in the Eighteenth Century* (London, A. & C. Black, 1937, pp. xi, 545). Well documented; full of detailed information.

P. Janelle, *The Catholic Reformation* (Milwaukee, The Bruce Publishing Co., 1948, pp. xiv, 397). Sympathetic, by a Jesuit.

C. M. Kennedy, *The Influence of Christianity on International Law* (London, Macmillan & Co., 1856, pp. xvi, 158). A Hulsean prize essay in the University of Cambridge.

W. S. M. Knight, *The Life and Times of Hugo Grotius* (London, Sweet & Maxwell, 1925, pp. xiv, 304). Carefully done and well documented.

L. Lallemand, *Histoire de la Charité* (Paris, Alphonse Picard et Fils, 4 vols., 1902–1912). Well documented, favourable to the Church.

K. S. Latourette, *A History of the Expansion of Christianity. Volume III, Three Centuries of Advance* (New York, Harper & Brothers, 1939, pp. ix, 503). Chapter XVI deals with the subject of this chapter.

A. Lincoln, *Some Political and Social Ideas of English Dissent 1763–1800* (Cambridge University Press, 1938, pp. 292). Well documented.

A. C. McGiffert, *Protestant Thought before Kant* (New York, Charles Scribner's Sons, 1911, pp. 261).

J. T. McNeill, *Christian Hope for World Society* (New York, Harper & Brothers, 1937, pp. vii, 278). A thoughtful series of lectures by a church historian.

J. ter Meulen, *Der Gedanke der Internationalen Organization in seiner Entwicklung* (Haag, Martinus Nijhoff, 2 vols., 1917–1929). Well documented.

P. Monroe, *A Text-book in the History of Education* (New York, The Macmillan Co., 1914, pp. xxiii, 772). By an outstanding expert.

H. R. Niebuhr, *The Kingdom of God in America* (New York, Harper & Brothers, 1937, pp. xvii, 215). A brilliant interpretation of the religious history of the United States.

H. M. Robertson, *Aspects of the Rise of Economic Individualism: A Criticism of Max Weber and his School* (Cambridge University Press, 1933, pp. xvi, 223).

J. B. Scott, *The Spanish Origin of International Law. Francisco de Vitoria and His Law of Nations* (Oxford, The Clarendon Press, 1934, pp. 19a, 288, clviii). Scholarly.

W. R. Sorley, *A History of English Philosophy* (New York, G. P. Putnam's Sons, 1921, pp. xv, 371). By an outstanding specialist.

F. H. Stead, *The Story of Social Christianity* (London, James Clarke & Co., 2 vols., no date). Laudatory of the social changes wrought by Christianity throughout the course of its history.

L. Stephen, *History of English Thought in the Eighteenth Century* (New York, G. P. Putnam's Sons, 2 vols., 1876).

R. H. Tawney, *Religion and the Rise of Capitalism* (London, John Murray, 1926, pp. xiii, 339).

E. Troeltsch, *The Social Teachings of the Christian Churches,* translated by Olive Wyon (New York, The Macmillan Co., 1931, pp. 1019). A standard work.

M. Weber, *The Protestant Ethic and the Spirit of Capitalism,* translated from the German by T. Parsons (London, George Allen & Unwin, 1930, pp. xi, 292). A study which provoked a warm discussion.

B. Willey, *The Seventeenth Century Background. Studies in the Thought of the Age in Relation to Poetry and Religion* (London, Chatto & Windus, 1934, pp. viii, 315). A competent survey.

B. Willey, *The Eighteenth Century Background. Studies on the Idea of Nature in the Thought of the Period* (London, Chatto & Windus, 1940, pp. viii, 302).

Chapter XLIII

RETROSPECT AND PROSPECT

At the dawn of the sixteenth century the outlook for Christianity was decidedly grim. The old order with which Christianity had been associated was passing. In the East the once flourishing minorities in Central Asia either had disappeared or were disappearing. Constantinople, long a bulwark against Islam, had fallen to the Turk. All the historic patriarchates except Rome were under Moslem rule. In Russia a professedly Christian state was emerging from Mongol domination, but its church, while vital, appeared to give little hope for the future now that the Greeks, to whom it had traditionally looked, were mostly Turkish subjects. Western Europe, although politically independent of non-Christian princes and nominally holding to Christianity, appeared to be outgrowing that faith. The Renaissance and humanism had brought a thinly veiled recrudescence of paganism. The Papacy was morally decadent and emerging nation states under absolute monarchs were extending their control over the Church in their realms and were seeking to make it ancillary to their purposes. As time passed, the expanding intellectual horizons, with the growth of natural science and the attendant enlargement of knowledge of astronomy, physics, and mathematics, although due in no small degree to Christianity, shook the confidence of many in the Christian faith. Geographic explorations and conquests led to an exploitation of non-European peoples in ways which were a negation of Christian ethics. Christianity appeared impotent to deal with the new age which it had helped to call into being.

Yet within the Church movements and individuals witnessed to continued vitality, to a ground swell which issued in a fresh tide of life. There followed the greatest forward surge which Christianity had known since its first centuries. Here and there this showed itself in the Eastern Churches, notably in Russia, largely but not entirely independently of what was taking place in Western Europe.

The forward surge was most prominent in Western Europe. This was partly because Western Europe was more nearly free from the Moslems and the invasions which from time to time had poured into the East from the heartland of Eurasia and partly because, beginning with Augustine and Benedict of Nursia in the fifth and sixth centuries, the Christianity of the West had given rise to more creative movements than had that of the East.

In Western Europe the forward surge of the tide took two main forms. One was a complete separation from the Church of Rome which came to be known collectively, although with dubious accuracy, as Protestantism. The numerically largest expressions of Protestantism were Lutheranism, the Reformed Churches, and the Church of England, but there were several others. Varied though Protestantism was, and more varied still though it later became, it had common characteristics. Negatively, it repudiated the jurisdiction of the Pope and what it deemed the corruptions for which the Pope stood. Among the latter were the invocation of the saints, the cult of the Virgin Mary, the treasury of the Church, and indulgences. It also would have none of monasticism or of the obligatory celibacy of the clergy. Positively it made much of the Bible as the authoritative record of God's revelation of Himself and His redemption of man through Christ, it declared that salvation is by faith alone in the quite unmerited love of God in Christ and not by works that men do in an attempt to acquire merit, and it maintained the priesthood of all believers. Protestants had a specialized ministry. Insisting as they did upon God's call, or vocation, to various specialized occupations, all of them made sacred by God, they held that the ministry was one of these callings. Yet it was not dominant as was the hierarchy in the Roman Catholic Church, but shared with the laity the control of the churches. The large majority adhered to the formulations of the faith which the Catholic Church, both East and West, regarded as standard, especially what were known as the Apostles' and Nicene Creeds. However, a minority either rejected these or, endeavoring to go back to the primitive church and its beliefs and practices as pictured in the New Testament, declined to be bound by creeds. They deemed them later developments, even though they might assent to much or all of what was expressed in them. Protestantism was not a purely religious movement. It was associated with nationalism, the aspirations of absolute monarchs to control all phases of the life of their realms, including the churches, and here and there with the growing urban middle class. Yet it was primarily religious.

The other form taken by the forward surge in the Christianity of Western Europe was in the Roman Catholic Church. It purified old monastic orders, called new ones into being, brought about an improvement in the morals of laity and clergy, revised the organization in such fashion as to make for better discipline, and so defined the beliefs of that branch of the Church that they became more explicit as against Protestantism. In practice the Pope had slighter influence in the politics of Europe and less administrative control over the Roman Catholic Church than in the Middle Ages. Moreover, while maintaining even more emphatically than ever that it was the guardian of the Christian faith and the Catholic Church, the one founded by Christ and the apostles, in fact the Roman Catholic Church was only one of a number of churches, several of which made similar claims. The ties which had bound it with the Orthodox Church of the East had been finally severed and most of Great Britain and North-western Europe had been lost to it.

Although it had become a sect in the Catholic Church, to use that term to designate the Church Universal, the "blessed company of all faithful people," "all who profess and call themselves Christians," the Roman Catholic Church was making territorial gains which appeared to justify its claim to be *the* Catholic Church. By the middle of the seventeenth century it had won back some of the territory which it had lost to Protestants. By the middle of the eighteenth century it had gained the allegiance of minorities within all the Eastern Churches. Taking advantage of the colonial expansion of Spain, Portugal, and France, sturdy adherents to the faith of Rome although jealously limiting its administrative power, it was the chief channel for a phenomenal geographic spread of the Christian faith. By 1750 the Roman Catholic Church had adherents on all five continents and in many of the islands which fringed them. The same was true of Protestantism, but it had not nearly as large a share in the spread of Christianity as had the Roman Catholic Church. The only one of the Eastern Churches which was winning fresh converts was that of Russia, and these were limited to Eastern and North-eastern Europe and to the northern, sparsely settled reaches of Asia. In light of these facts, Roman Catholics might well view Protestantism as a congeries of heresies, doomed to disappear as the once numerous Gnostics, Marcionites, Novatians, Donatists, and Arians had done, and to look forward to the time when the severed Eastern Churches would be reunited under the Pope.

In the latter part of the eighteenth century great changes were to gain headway which were to go far towards altering this picture. A combination of movements and events was to deal severe blows to Christianity and to usher in another recession in the Christian tide. This recession was not to last as long or to be as severe as its two great predecessors, those from A.D. 500 to A.D. 950 and from A.D 1350 to A.D. 1500. As we are to see, it differed from both in presenting a paradox. On the one hand there was a growing and what looked like a permanent de-Christianization of large elements in the traditionally Christian peoples of Europe and, at the same time, on the other hand, there were marked renewals of life in the Christianity of these very peoples and what was to become a geographic expansion of the faith of unprecedented proportions. At the outset these blows affected the Roman Catholic Church much more than Protestantism and the renewal of life began in Protestantism much earlier than in the Roman Catholic Church. It was not until after 1815 that revival became marked in the latter. Throughout the eighteenth century and nineteenth centuries, and through as much of the twentieth century as has thus far elapsed, the tides of life ran more vigorously through Protestantism than through any of the other branches of Christianity, not even excepting the Roman Catholic Church, and proportionately the geographic expansion of Christianity was more through Protestantism than through any of the others. It is to an early stage of that story, from 1750 to 1815, that we must now turn.

REPUDIATION AND REVIVAL
A.D. 1750 — A.D. 1815

Chapter XLIV

REPUDIATION AND REVIVAL,
A.D. 1750 - A.D. 1815

Not far from 1750 there came another recession in that pulsation of advance, retreat, and advance which has characterized the history of Christianity. The initial date, like the others, is only a round number. An earlier or a later year might be given. Some of the movements and events which made the period a recession and which also marked it as one of revival began before that year. Others began after it. The year 1815 is a more precise date, for it registered the end of the Napoleonic Wars and the beginning of a century of relative peace and was quickly followed by another forward surge of the Christian tide.

This particular recession was not as prolonged or as severe as its predecessors. However, as we suggested at the close of the last chapter, it differed strikingly from the others in what were possibly highly significant ways. The others had been marked by the decay or collapse of cultures with which Christianity had become intimately associated, by extensive losses of territory due largely to invasions of non-Christian peoples, mainly Moslems, and by a decline of morale in the churches. This recession was due to a more complex set of factors, it saw no major losses of territory, nor was it accompanied by any such corruption of morals within the Church as had been the case in the earlier recessions. It was, rather, characterized by the open or tacit repudiation of Christianity by growing elements within what had been known as Christendom, a repudiation which was to continue, especially in Europe, after 1815. But it was paralleled by a remarkable revival, primarily in Protestantism, which was also to continue and to swell to large proportions after 1815, which was largely to reshape that branch of Christianity and which, joined with other factors, was to lift it from the position of a narrowly regional faith and make it world-wide.

FACTORS ADVERSE TO CHRISTIANITY

The factors adverse to Christianity were varied, but, as we have suggested, bore most severely on the Roman Catholic Church. They permit of no logical order, but must be arranged in almost haphazard fashion.

A major movement militating against Christianity was the decline of Spain and Portugal, especially of Spain. It was in Spain that the Catholic Reformation had had its rise. It was from Spain that the Society of Jesus had sprung, that chief organized agency of the Catholic Reformation and the major instrument in rewinning territories lost to Protestants and in pushing forward the frontiers of Christianity into previously non-Christian territories. Through Spain and Portugal most of the territorial expansion of Christianity between 1500 and 1750 had been effected. By 1750 both countries were palpably in decline. The reasons for that decline are in part conjectural and we must not take the space to go into a discussion or even an enumeration of those which have been suggested. The decline had been apparent as early as the seventeenth century and continued in the eighteenth century at an accelerated pace. Although nominally it was not terminated until after 1815, actually control by Spain of most of its possessions in the New World came to an end between 1750 and 1815 as a result of the occupation of the mother country by the Napoleonic armies. Slight territorial advances were made by Spanish missions after 1750. For example, some new ones were opened in Texas, partly to hold that area against the French, for until 1762, when they transferred Louisiana to Spain, the former had been extending their control in the valley of the Mississippi. Another expansion was accomplished in California. There the Spanish authorities were occupying the country to counter the advance of Russia southward from Alaska. Between 1750 and 1800 at least eighteen missions were begun in that region by the Franciscans. Yet these were efforts of a waning power which was soon to be expelled from the mainland of the Americas.

Another blow to Christianity, with particularly grave repercussions on its geographic frontiers, was the dissolution of the Society of Jesus. The Jesuits had long been viewed with suspicion and rising antagonism, not only in Protestant but also in Roman Catholic quarters. For this, as we have suggested, there were several reasons. Their tight organization combined with their numerical strength led many to fear them. Members of other religious orders and of the secular clergy were jealous of them. They were accused of mixing in politics and of being untruthful if that served the purposes of their superiors. They engaged extensively in commerce. Statesmen who were committed to the rationalism of the day regarded them as bulwarks of obscurantism. In 1759 they were expelled from the Portuguese domains, both in Europe and overseas. In 1764 they were suppressed in France and French colonies. In 1767 Spain and Naples took similar action, effective throughout all the vast Spanish colonial possessions. In 1773, under pressure, the Pope dissolved the Society. On the plea that the Papal brief could not be published in Russia, the Jesuits continued a precarious existence in that realm. They also persisted in Protestant Prussia, and, partially disguised under other names, in Belgium, Italy, and France. In 1801 their reconstitution in Russia received Papal approval, in 1804 they were restored in Naples, and in 1814 the Pope authorized their full legal existence throughout the world. However, the lapse, lasting as it did for a generation or more and in a period when the Roman Catholic Church was suffering from an accumulation of other reverses, brought severe losses, from some of which there was no recovery. The extensive missions which the Jesuits had initiated in Asia, the Americas, and Africa were entrusted to other orders, in China to the Lazarists, in parts of India to the Society of Foreign Missions of Paris, and in much of the Americas to the Franciscans. Yet in the transition there was inevitable loss of headway, and in few if any of the missions did those who substituted send enough experienced personnel to compensate for what the Jesuits had supplied.

We must also note some quite unrelated circumstances which in these years combined to hamper the spread of Christianity on its geographic frontiers. Japan was all but hermetically sealed against the outside world, a step, it will be recalled, which had been taken in an effort to stamp out Christianity. Christians still were in that country, but only in secret. In China severe persecutions were directed against Christians, in striking contrast with the toleration of the 1690's and the early 1700's. In the 1780's Christianity was introduced to Korea but after a brief period of prosperity was visited with resolute efforts at extermination.

While by no means anti-Christian, Freemasonry, which flourished in this period, tended to adopt Deist views. It spread from Great Britain to the Continent and there for many became a centre of opposition to the Roman Catholic Church.

A set of movements which militated against Christianity was in the climate of opinion. Intellectual currents, some of which antedated 1750, were circulating which were adverse to the faith. They reached a climax in these years. They affected the Russian Orthodox Church and Protestantism, but they proved especially embarrassing to the Roman Catholic Church.

One of these currents we have already noted (Chapter XLII). The eighteenth century is often called the age of reason. What seemed to be the prevailing belief in Western Europe was confidence in man's mind. Man, so it was held, had heretofore been bound by ignorance and superstition. Now, by the use of reason he was achieving emancipation and there was nothing that, with this tool, he could not hope to accomplish. In view of the advances in the natural sciences and mathematics, this attitude is quite understandable. It gave rise to what in German was known as the *Aufklärung* and in English as the Enlightenment. Religiously it found its chief expression in Deism. As we have seen (Chapter XLII), Deism held to what was called natural religion. This was said to be universal, discernible by all men everywhere through their reason, quite apart from special revelation. It believed in God and revered Him as the great Architect of the universe. God was to be worshipped. Virtue was his true service. After death virtue was to be rewarded and sin punished. But Deism held that God governed all through immutable law which He had created. It left no room for miracle, the incarnation, or the Trinity. In the new age in which they were living, so it was maintained, men were being enlightened by the use of their reason and were moving away from superstition.

Those affected by this view were legion. One of its most popular advocates was he who chose to call himself Voltaire (1694–1778). His voluminous writings, clever and daring in style, had a wide reading. Much as Erasmus had been the outstanding popularizer of sixteenth century humanism, Voltaire was the most widely known and read author of the Enlightenment. It is significant, however, that in contrast with Erasmus, who was earnestly Christian, Voltaire openly attacked that faith. Here seemed to be evidence to support the thesis that in the movement which began with the Renaissance, Christendom was moving away from Christianity.

Some thinkers went beyond Deism in their departure from Christianity. Thus in Scotland David Hume (1711–1776), whose first significant book, *Treatise of Human Nature,* appeared in 1739, followed in 1748 by *Philosophical Essays,* in 1751 by *Inquiry into the Principles of Morals,* and in 1757 by the *Natural History of Religion,* was a thoroughgoing sceptic. Starting from Locke, he went far beyond that thinker in challenging accepted beliefs. Declaring that cause and effect are figments of our mental processes, arising from our noting the association of our experiences, he believed the argument for the existence of God as the primal cause to be invalid. He thus undercut not only Christianity but also Deism. He challenged the Deist contention that the primitive universal religion of mankind was monotheism and maintained that polytheism preceded monotheism. He also attacked the belief in miracles, in his day put forward as one of the chief evidences for the truth of Christianity. Pure in his own conduct, he held to a frankly utilitarian ethics. He had a wide influence, both in staunchly Presbyterian Scotland, where the Church looked on him with disfavour, and far beyond the borders of his native land. Edward Gibbon (1737–1794), reared in a deeply religious home in England and for a brief time a convert to Roman Catholicism, in his famous *Decline and Fall of the Roman Empire* described that event as the triumph of barbarism and religion—and by religion he meant Christianity.

Rationalism and Deism had repercussions on the several churches. In Russia a large proportion of the upper classes, while keeping a formal connexion with the state church, were committed to the rationalism which was the vogue in Western Europe, for since the days of Peter the Great it had been fashionable to look towards the West.

Most branches of Protestantism were also affected. Many, even among the clergy, sought to present that faith as rational and to decry emotion. The trend was vividly seen in Halle, that major centre of Pietism. Here taught Christian Wolff (1679–1754), a rationalist, akin to the Deists in his religious beliefs. Here rationalism cooled the missionary zeal of many and undercut the enterprises which had drawn recruits from it. Hermann Samuel Reimarus (1694–1768), professor of Oriental languages at Hamburg, who acquired Deist views while in England in early life, in posthumously published writings expressed belief in a wise Creator, morality, and immortality, but decried special revelation and miracle and declared that the authors of the various books of the Bible were selfish and dishonest. The critic and dramatist Gotthold Ephraim Lessing (1729–1781), who saw to the publication of the works of Reimarus, spread the impression that Christianity belonged to a stage in civilization which the human race, in its advance, was now leaving. In England anti-Trinitarian views attracted a following among some of the intellectuals. The Presbyterian churches in that country, small in numbers, largely became Unitarian. Some of the General Baptists also moved in that direction. Prominent among the Unitarians was Joseph Priestley (1733–1804), originally a minister of dissenting congregations, and the discoverer of oxygen. A few of the Anglican clergy were inclined towards anti-Trinitarianism or actually moved out of the Church of England. Theophilus Lindsey (1723–1808) was one of these and organized a Unitarian congregation. Some of the bishops in England and Ireland were close to Unitarianism. Even the defenders of Christianity were affected. William Paley (1743–1805), whose *View of the Evidences of Christianity,* published in 1794, and *Natural Theology,* issued in 1802, while widely acclaimed by Christians, showed the effect of Deism and of rationalism.

The Roman Catholic Church particularly suffered, for rebellion against Christianity was especially marked in its constituency. Voltaire had his early education in a Jesuit school and, as we are to see in a moment, it was in strongly Roman Catholic France that a revolution broke out which largely incorporated the rationalism that had been one of its complex sources.

Another intellectual current which in some of its aspects undercut Christianity was romanticism. Romanticism is a term which is used to cover an attitude in feeling and thought which has been found in many peoples and ages. In the eighteenth century it was in large part a reaction against rationalism and the closely associated conventional classicism. It was not necessarily anti-Christian. Indeed, some of its leading exponents were earnestly Christian. Several, however, could not be put in that category. Prominent among the latter was Jean Jacques Rousseau (1712–1778), whose writings enjoyed wide popularity. Also to be classed here was the more profound Goethe (1749–1832). While in much of romanticism there was a warm and even deep religious feeling, for many it could not be contained within historic Christian patterns but took forms at variance with it, at times a pantheistic mysticism.

These intellectual currents contributed to movements which attempted to bring in reforms and in doing so treated the Church cavalierly, whether Russian Orthodox, Protestant, or Roman Catholic. The second half of the eighteenth century has been called the age of enlightened despots. Monarchs, endeavouring to follow the dictates of reason, sought to improve conditions in their realms. Among them were Frederick II of Prussia, a Deist, and Catherine II of Russia, who made presents to Voltaire and discussed the possibility of emancipating the serfs. In Spain Charles III (1759–1788) encouraged manufactures and agriculture, curbed the Inquisition, and suppressed the Jesuits. Joseph II of Austria (1765–1790), although a Roman Catholic, was much influenced by Rousseau, confiscated many church lands, abolished some religious orders, put the training of priests under state control, altered religious ceremonies, nominated the bishops, and forbade the publication of Papal bulls in his domains without his permission. His ecclesiastical policy was known as Josephism. In Tuscany a brother of Joseph attempted to restrict the power of the Pope. What was known as Febronianism, from its author, a bishop who wrote under the pen name of Febronius, had much influence. It advocated that the secular rulers control the Church in their domains and that general councils be superior to the Pope.

These intellectual currents came to a flood in revolutions which swept away much of the old order. The first was in the Thirteen Colonies and gave birth to the United States of America. The American Revolution was by no means anti-Christian. Some of its basic ideals were from John Locke and the way for it had been prepared by the Reformed faith and the sermons of the clergy, especially in New England. As we have suggested (Chapters XLI, XLII), the democracy of the United States was largely from Christian rootage. However, the American Revolution brought a pause in the Great Awakening, for the absorption of the population in agitation for and against independence and in war, and the moral disintegration attendant on war worked against serious attention to the Christian message. Some of the outstanding builders of the new nation, while not antagonistic to Christianity, were more Deist than Christian. Prominent among them were Thomas Jefferson, the framer of the Declaration of Independence, the third President of the United States, and the chief creator of what is known, from him, as Jeffersonian Democracy. Here, too, must be classed Benjamin Franklin. In some intellectual circles, with a strong appeal to youth, there were much more outspoken critics of Christianity than these two men. For instance, Thomas Paine (1737–1809), a warm advocate of American independence and whose pamphlets *Common Sense* and *Crisis* gave impetus to that movement, was an ardent Deist and in his *The Age of Reason* was as much opposed to Christianity as he was to atheism. In the latter part of the eighteenth century a militant rationalism and Deism had something of a vogue in the United States.

Much more serious from the standpoint of Christianity were the French Revolution, the repercussions of that revolution in Western Europe, and the wars which issued from it, culminating in Napoleon Bonaparte. The French Revolution broke out in 1789. It arose from criticism of an incompetent government which had brought the state to the verge of bankruptcy, from seething discontent with basic social and economic conditions to which objection came from the rising middle classes in the cities and the humble folk, including especially the peasants, and from ideas which had been given form by such men as Locke, Voltaire, Rousseau, Montesquieu, and others of lesser fame.

Some of these ideas were of Christian origin. They could be traced to both Roman Catholics and Protestants. Centuries earlier, Augustine had declared that man should not have dominion over man, for man is a rational creature, made in God's image. The Jesuit cardinal, Bellarmine, had said that it depended on the consent of the people whether kings, consuls, or other magistrates were to be established in authority over them, and that if there was legitimate cause the people should change a kingdom into an aristocracy, or an aristocracy into a democracy. In England, largely through the efforts of radical Protestants, more effective control of the nation over the king had been established. In the newly constituted United States, mainly through ideas formulated and propagated by Protestants, progress had recently been achieved towards a democracy. Out of a desire to weaken her ancient foe, Great Britain, France aided the Thirteen Colonies to obtain their independence, and the ideals expressed in their Declaration of Independence had a marked effect on the French. Most of the recent French thinkers and pamphleteers who had laid the ideological foundations for the revolution in their land were children of the Enlightenment, rationalists or romanticists, more Deist than Christian. Yet many of their convictions were from Christian sources and their hope of creating an ideal human society had more than an accidental likeness to the hope which had inspired the *De Civitate Dei* of Augustine and the dreams of Christians of Western Europe across the centuries to create a society embodying Christian principles. The French Revolution was to a large extent a secularized version of the heavenly city as conceived by Christians.

The French Revolution was of major importance for the world. That was partly because it quickly had repercussions throughout most of Christendom, both in Europe and America. Paris, where the Revolution centered, was the most populous city of Western Europe and for a century or more France had been the most powerful realm in that region. So sweeping a series of changes could not fail to have effects of primary importance in the rest of Western civilization. Of even more consequence was the fact that the French Revolution was an early and potent stage in a succession of similar movements which were to spread across the earth and which by the middle of the twentieth century were to alter profoundly the life of all mankind. The series began with the English Civil War, the Commonwealth and "Glorious Revolution" of the seventeenth century, continued in the American Revolution of the 1770's and 1780's, came to an even more explosive phase in the French Revolution, went on with ever expanding geographic scope in Europe and the Americas in the nineteenth century, in the latter half of the nineteenth and in the twentieth century swept into Japan, China, and India, and through the Russian Revolution and its aftermath profoundly moulded much of mankind.

It is highly significant that this series of revolutions had its beginning and its early course in Christendom and that the ideas which inspired and shaped them had their birth and initial formulations in lands and among peoples which for centuries had been under the influence of Christianity. Many of the revolutionary programmes repudiated that faith, but most and perhaps all of them embodied ideals and conceptions which had come through it. They took only part of what had been given by Christianity and to a lesser or greater extent distorted what they took, but even when they did not recognize or acknowledge their source, they were deeply indebted to it.

We must hasten to say that this generalization is not framed as an attempt to claim for Christianity whatever of good may be in these movements. If Christianity is to any degree the source of what, from its standpoint, is admirable, it may also be charged with at least some responsibility for what, by its criteria, is evil.

Here, rather, we are seeking to point out what we have more than once had occasion to note and what we must remark even more frequently as our narrative proceeds. This is the part which Christianity has had in shaping the most dynamic civilization which mankind has thus far known, that of Western European peoples. The precise extent of that part we may not be able to determine. We know, however, that it was present and that Western civilization reached and changed all mankind. Much in that civilization and its effects bore a family likeness to Christianity and was in the direction of what is intrinsic in that faith. Much, on the other hand, was in tacit or open contradiction of Christianity. The contrast between these two aspects of Western civilization and its fruits in mankind as a whole became increasingly striking as the nineteenth and twentieth centuries progressed. To the possible meaning of the contrast we must recur again and again.

The purpose of our story does not require even an outline of the course of the French Revolution. We need only point out the immediate effects upon Christianity. These effects were especially serious for the Roman Catholic Church. They dealt it severe blows. As we are to see in later chapters, the blows were not to end with 1815 but were to continue through the nineteenth and into the twentieth century.

Some of the earliest stages of the French Revolution brought actions which struck at the privileges and status of the Roman Catholic Church. To meet the grave financial situation which confronted his government, Louis XVI called the Estates General. This met in May, 1789. Late in the following month it resolved itself into the National Assembly and began drastic changes in the life and structure of the nation. Among them were some which were momentous for the Roman Catholic Church. On August 4, 1789, tithes were abolished, thus at once relieving the peasants of a burden which had taken about a twentieth of their produce and depriving the Church of one of its chief sources of revenue. That same year all the land of the Church, which then comprised about a fifth of the area of France, was confiscated and became the property of the state. In 1790 the monasteries were ordered dissolved. In July, 1790, what was called the Civil Constitution of the Clergy was enacted by the National Assembly. By it parish priests and bishops were to be chosen by elections in which all citizens, Protestants and Jews as well as Roman Catholics, were to vote and were to have their salaries paid by the government. The Pope might still define its doctrines, but he could no longer have any administrative control of the Church in France. The old diocesan boundaries were erased and each civil division, or "department," was to be a diocese. Most of the clergy refused to accept the new arrangement and the Pope strengthened their resolution by forbidding them to assent to it. The National Assembly retaliated by requiring the bishops and clergy to swear to abide by it. About a third of the parish priests and seven of the bishops complied, but the large majority did not and thus set themselves against the Revolution. The constitution of 1791 gave complete religious freedom to all citizens, thus fulfilling the dreams of such men as Voltaire, but cutting further into the privileges of the Roman Catholic

Church. From then into the twentieth century many Roman Catholics, laity and clergy, were opposed to the principles of the Revolution.

From 1792 to 1795 the Revolution mounted. Neighbouring governments took alarm at it as a threat to their own positions. Urged on by emigré nobles and clergy, they attempted to suppress it by armed force. Revolutionary France resisted, and the wars began which were to culminate in Napoleon Bonaparte and his empire. The threat from abroad threw the Revolution into the hands of the radicals. In 1792 a new assembly was elected, known as the National Convention. The National Convention successfully defended the country against the foreign invaders, conquered Belgium and Holland, and declared that the French armies would come to the relief of any people who wished liberation from the tyranny of kings and nobles. It also transformed France into a republic with "liberty, equality, and fraternity" as its slogan, and executed Louis XVI and his queen, Marie Antoinette. The threat of foreign invasion and domestic insurrection stimulated the "Reign of Terror," in 1793 and 1794. Hundreds were executed on the charge of being "partisans of tyranny . . . or enemies of liberty."

On June 8, 1794, on the eve of the height of the Terror, a new religion was formally inaugurated. In Deist fashion, the National Convention decreed that the people of France recognized the existence of a Supreme Being and the immortality of the soul. Atheism, vice, and folly were decried and the triumph of wisdom celebrated. Christianity was denounced as superstition, a new calendar was adopted to begin its reckoning with the establishment of the republic, and instead of the seven day week each month was divided into three periods of ten days each. The worship of the new religion would be festivals in honour of the great events of the Revolution.

After the Terror came a conservative reaction and in 1795 a new constitution placed the state under the government of a Directory. Religious freedom was proclaimed, but the Directory and its regime were anti-Christian. In 1798 the armies of the Directory created a republic in Rome and the Pope (Pius VI, reigned 1775–1799), who had been hostile to the Revolution, was carried to France, a prisoner, and within a few months was dead.

It was under the Directory that Napoleon Bonaparte (1769–1821) came to power. The most successful general that revolutionary France had known, in 1799 he did away with the Directory, by this time proved to be incompetent and corrupt, and had himself chosen as the first of three consuls to govern the state. In 1802 he had himself made consul for life and in 1804, with the outward consent of the overwhelming majority of the French people, he terminated the republic and turned France into an empire with himself as the first of a line of supposedly hereditary emperors. He held this position until his enforced abdication in 1814 and then again briefly in 1815 until, defeated at Waterloo, he was exiled to the island of St. Helena.

The attitude of Napoleon towards the Church was masterful. He was himself a nominal Roman Catholic, but had very little religious faith. Yet he saw that a large proportion of his subjects were loyal Roman Catholics and he regarded that Church as an institution which must be recognized and used for his purposes. At his orders, the vacancy in the Papacy left by the death of Pius VI was not immediately filled. However, in 1800 a conclave was held in Venice which elected a Benedictine monk, Chiaramonti, who took the title of Pius VII and reigned through striking vicissitudes until 1823. Napoleon restored Rome to the Pope, but by no means all the Papal States. After long negotiations, in 1801 a concordat for France was concluded between the Pope and Napoleon. Such of its confiscated lands as were in the possession of the state were to be restored to the Church, bishops were to be appointed by the Pope on nomination by the state, and while the lower clergy were appointed by the bishops, the government could veto the episcopal choices. The clergy were to be paid by the state. To this concordat Napoleon added (1802) the Organic Articles, but against the protest of the Pope. By them no Papal decrees were to be published or synods held in France without the permission of the state. At the same time Protestants were given religious freedom and their ministers were to be paid by the government.

When he assumed the title of emperor, harking back to the precedent of Charlemagne, Napoleon had the Pope share in the coronation (1804). However, he treated that dignitary far more cavalierly than Charlemagne had the Pontiffs of his day. Napoleon brought Pius VII to Paris for the ceremony, was anointed by him, and then placed the crowns on his own head and the head of his empress.

Pius VII and Napoleon had a complete break. The latter attempted to induce the Pontiff to abandon his neutrality in the life and death struggle with England and to join in the blockade against that power. The Pope refused. In 1808 Napoleon's troops occupied Rome and in 1809 the Papal States were merged in the French Empire. Napoleon contemplated making Rome his second capital. Pius VII retaliated by excommunicating Napoleon as "robber of the patrimony of Peter." Napoleon countered by having him imprisoned, eventually at Fontainebleau. In 1813 Napoleon published the Concordat of Fontainebleau. The Pope at first assented to the document but later repudiated it. In Rome Napoleon drastically suppressed monasteries.

After the fall of Napoleon Pius VII returned to Rome (1814) amid great popular acclaim. However, he fled during the hundred days of Napoleon's brief return to power. When Napoleon was finally defeated (1815) and the Congress of Vienna met to undo what had been accomplished by the French Revolution and the emperor, all the Papal territories were restored to the Pontiff except Avignon, another bit of land in France, and a section on the left bank of the Po.

Elsewhere in Europe the Napoleonic storm shook the Roman Catholic Church. For instance, in Germany, in 1801, the ecclesiastical states, some of them dating back to the tenth century and the policy of Otto I, were divided among secular princes. In Spain a reform cortes which met in 1810 suppressed the Inquisition and reduced the privileges of the clergy.

The French Revolution and Napoleon also brought grave embarrassment to Roman Catholic missions. Added to the other factors which we have mentioned, especially the decline of Portugal and Spain and the dissolution of the Society of Jesus, they led to sharp decline on some of the geographic frontiers of the faith. From 1789 to 1815 few new missionaries were sent from Europe and it was difficult to give financial aid to those already abroad. For a time the Society of Foreign Missions of Paris was forced to seek headquarters outside of France. Later Napoleon wished to combine it with two other missionary bodies and make it a tool of his imperialism. Even more serious were the vicissitudes of the Congregation for the Propagation of the Faith, the bureau through which the Papacy supervised missions abroad. In 1798 it was driven out of Rome and from 1810 to 1814 Napoleon sought to reduce it to an instrument of his ambition. In consequence there was a marked falling off in numbers and morale of the Roman Catholic community in India. In China adverse domestic conditions added to the handicaps in Europe and threatened the extinction of the Church in that land. Missions in Latin America suffered, especially after the occupation of Spain by Napoleonic armies and the attack on Portugal.

As we have hinted, conditions in Russia were also adverse. From 1762 to 1796 that country was ruled by Catherine II, sometimes called the Great. A German, owing her position to the fact that she had been the consort of the feeble Tsar Peter III, who reigned for only a few months, she was a woman of great force and ability, and intellectually a child of the Enlightenment. Under her the vast holdings of the monasteries in lands and serfs were expropriated by the state and support of these institutions came from grants from the government. In consequence the numbers of monks markedly fell off. In court and aristocratic circles religious scepticism was common. The masses, but little affected by currents from the West, held to the historic Church or were members of the non-conforming sects which had flourished since the days of the revolt against the changes made by Nikon or even earlier and of which we are to say more. The state regarded the Church as an instrument for the moral education of the masses. Catherine's successor, Paul, declared that "the tsar is the head of the Church." It was under Paul that, in 1797, by imperial ukase, the parishes lost the right of electing their clergy, a function which they had held even under Peter the Great. Appointments to parishes were made by the state. This meant that the parish priests were government quite as much as Church officials.

BEGINNINGS OF REVIVAL

Grievous as were the losses suffered by Christianity in the latter part of the eighteenth century and in the first fifteen years of the nineteenth century, there was ample evidence that the faith was by no means moribund. Indications of vitality, some of them old, others of them new, were seen. After 1815 they were to swell to major proportions. They were found among Roman Catholics, in some of the Eastern Churches, and in Protestantism. To them we now turn.

THE BEGINNINGS OF REVIVAL IN THE ROMAN CATHOLIC CHURCH

During the storm of the Napoleonic Wars a revival began in the Roman Catholic Church. As we have seen, although he dealt rudely with the Roman Catholic Church, Napoleon did not treat it as drastically as had his precursors of the high tide of the Revolution. Nor was he, as had been some of them, openly anti-Christian. This was a gain, even though cold comfort. Some aspects of the romantic movement were distinctly friendly to the Roman Catholic Church. Many caught up in it conceived a warm admiration for the Middle Ages and for that Church as an integral part of medieval culture. In 1802 there appeared *Génie du Christianisme, ou Beautés de la Religion Chrétienne,* by Chateaubriand. It helped to make Roman Catholicism intellectually respectable and emotionally attractive. Although his first work was placed on the index of books denounced by that Church, Louis Claude de Saint-Martin (1743–1803) always remained attached to the Roman Catholic faith. A mystic, he was much influenced by Jacob Boehme.

Here and there new monastic orders, congregations, and societies began to appear, always a sign of life. In 1800 Madeleine-Sophie Barat founded the Society of the Sacred Heart of Jesus, a congregation of women devoted to education. In that same year Coudrin, a priest who had laboured in secret in France during some of the most anti-Christian years of the Revolution, took monastic vows and began what was known as the Congregation of Picpus, officially called the Congregation of the Sacred Hearts of Jesus and Mary and of the Perpetual Adoration of the Blessed Sacrament. It grew and obtained formal Papal approval in 1817. Its members gave themselves to missions and to prayer. In 1802 Edmund Ignatius Rice founded the Christian Brothers of Ireland.

In Germany the conversion to Roman Catholicism of two men of Protestant rearing, the poet Friedrich Leopold Stolberg (1800) and Friedrich von Schlegel (1808), a poet and a critic of the romantic school, was an indication of a trend to the Roman Catholic Church, still limited, but which might become important.

In the United States before 1815 the Roman Catholic Church began the policies and the growth which were to give it prominence in that country and in the world-wide life of that communion. In 1789 Roman Catholics in the United States numbered only about thirty-five thousand, because of the founding of that colony by a peer of that faith fully half of them in Maryland and about a fourth in religiously tolerant Philadelphia. They had been under the ecclesiastical jurisdiction of the Vicar Apostolic of London. In 1784 John Carroll (1735–1815) of a prominent Maryland Roman Catholic family, a former Jesuit, was made Prefect Apostolic and in 1789, at the request of the American clergy, was appointed Bishop of Baltimore. He proved an able and devoted leader, travelled extensively in his huge diocese, and strove to weld into one church the various nationalities, resisting the attempts, especially of the Germans, to have separate national bodies. He also successfully fought "trusteeism," an effort of the lay trustees of the property of various parishes to choose and dismiss their pastors without reference to the bishop. For the training of an American clergy he founded a college at Georgetown (1789) adjoining the national capital. In 1808 he was made archbishop with four suffragan sees. One of these was in Kentucky, on the westward moving frontier. The others were strategically located in the chief cities, Philadelphia, New York, and Boston. In 1809 Elizabeth Ann Seton, a convert, inaugurated a religious community which took the name Sisters of Charity. In spite of strong prejudices against Roman Catholics and provisions in some of the state constitutions excluding men of that faith from some or all offices, in its first amendment the Constitution of the United States assured religious liberty. By 1815 the Roman Catholic Church was prepared to take advantage of its opportunity in the new republic.

SIGNS OF LIFE IN THE EASTERN CHURCHES

Here and there were indications of vigour in the Christianity of Western Asia and Eastern Europe. Some of these arose from changes in the political situation, but the latter would have had no effect had there not been sufficient life in Christianity to take advantage of them.

In these years the Russian Empire advanced southward at the expense of Moslem rulers. The Turkish Empire was waning and its Christian subjects were beginning to hope that the Cross might not always be ruled by the Crescent. Russia, officially Christian, enlarged its holdings on the Black Sea. For a brief time the Russians occupied the predominantly Christian Wallachia and Moldavia, the later Rumania, and while by the treaty which ended the war (1774) these provinces were restored to Turkey, by that document Russia was accorded a protectorate over the Orthodox Christians in the Turkish domains.

Armenian Christianity seemed to be making advances. In the Armenian community in Constantinople numbers of church buildings were erected and several parochial schools were begun. In Armenia itself gains in education were achieved and the training of the clergy was improved.

In Russia, in spite of the deadening effects of the Enlightenment, especially among the upper classes, and the blows dealt monasticism by Catherine the Great, in several ways Christianity was showing signs of life and was making territorial gains.

Influences were entering from the West and were stimulating the native faith. Freemasonry had been introduced and now, partly in Russian guise, was having a positive religious effect of a mystical kind. A press in Halle was set up especially for the purpose of preparing Pietist literature in Russian. Arndt's *On the True Christianity* passed through several Russian editions. Works of the mystics Jacob Boehme and Saint-Simon were translated into Russian. In some circles the Latin fathers, including Augustine, were being read. In the theological seminaries which existed in most dioceses for the training of priests, text-books by Roman Catholics and Protestants adapted to the Russian Orthodox Church were widely used and much of the teaching was in Latin. Typical of these influences was Tikhon of Zadonsky (1724–1783), originally known as Timofey Sokolov, who was to became a favorite saint of nineteenth century Russia. For six and a half years a zealous and effective diocesan bishop, by his own choice he retired to a monastery and there spent the rest of his life. His spiritual counsel was sought by many. He knew deep inner conflict, depression, and ecstasy. He combined the traditional Russian kenoticism with meditations on the sufferings of the crucified Christ, a devotional practice derived from the West, some of it from Roman Catholicism and some probably from Pietism. He also fused theological conviction and adherence to dogma with study of the Bible, especially the New Testament, and a living faith in Jesus Christ.

In this period, too, was formed the spiritual life of Seraphim of Sarov (1759–1833) who after 1815 was to become a religious guide to many laymen. The son of a building contractor, from boyhood he was deeply religious and at the age of eighteen decided to become a monk. He spent years alone in austerities and prayer, seeking self-mastery. It is said that for a thousand days and nights he stood on a stone in the woods, repeating in essence the prayer of the publican, "God be merciful to me a sinner." For years he maintained the rule of silence. When he finally emerged from it, many miracles of healing were attributed to him. He became spiritual adviser to a convent of nuns.

In some monasteries there was a revival of the methods of the hesychasts.

There were also notable ecclesiastics. Prominent among them was he who was known as Platon (1732–1812), successively head of the famous Trinity monastery near Moscow, a member of the Holy Synod, Bishop of Tver, tutor to the future Tsar Paul, and Archbishop and then Metropolitan of Moscow. He was famous as a preacher, wrote what became standard text-books on the doctrine of the Russian Orthodox Church in the form of manuals of instruction, and promoted the study of the history of the Russian Church. It was he who drew up rules which (1800) sought to formulate a compromise by which the Old Believers and some other dissenters would be admitted to the communion of the state church while being permitted to retain their distinctive rites.

Soon after 1800 a revival in the state church gained momentum. Plans were set on foot for the development of church schools. Through Pietist contacts Golitsyn, Procurator (head) of the Holy Synod, had been converted from indifference to a warm religious interest and became the first president of a newly organized (1813) Russian Bible Society. The Napoleonic invasion led to a revulsion against rationalistic French influence and to something of a religious awakening. Philaret, a protegee of Platon, became head of the Academy of St. Petersburg and encouraged the circulation of the Bible in translations into the vernacular. The tsar himself, Alexander I, had a profound experience through several channels, among them the writings of Swedenborg, of whom we are to hear more later in this chapter, and contact with Madame Krüdener of the Livonian nobility, who had been converted under Moravian and Pietist influence. He became earnestly Christian, with results which were to be even more apparent after 1815. Swedenborg helped to shape not only Alexander I but also some who eventually held high office in the Russian Orthodox Church.

As Russia expanded its territories, larger areas were brought within the sphere of the Orthodox Church. When, through the partition of Poland in the 1790's, a large slice of that country was assigned to the tsar, Ruthenians who had become Uniates under Polish Roman Catholic rule returned to the Orthodox faith of their fathers. It is said that by 1796 over two million had taken that step. At the other geographic extreme of the empire, in the second half of the eighteenth century Russian authority was extended over the Aleutians and Alaska. Missionaries accompanied or followed this advance and baptized many of the aborigines.

Dissent from the Russian Orthodox Church continued to flourish, and that in spite of persecution by the state. The Old Believers persisted and in the

North had a following which in some places may have numbered as much as half the population. The Khlysty went on. From them came the Skopsty. The Skopsty had as their chief originator Selivanov, whose real name was Andrei Ivanov. He found that some of the Khlysty failed in their efforts to maintain their principles of strict sexual abstinence. To make that effective, he emasculated himself and induced others to do likewise. Exiled to Siberia, Selivanov professed to be the Tsar Peter III, who had been assassinated. Brought back to the capital, he attracted a wide following, among whom were some of the army and the clergy. In 1820 he was confined to a monastery, but even after his death a decade or more later the Skopsty persisted and spread, largely among artisans and merchants.

The Dukhobors emerged to prominence in the second half of the eighteenth century and gained adherents over wide reaches of the empire. They appealed especially to the humble, the peasants and the labourers. Their origin is obscure and they may have begun long before the eighteenth century. They repudiated the Russian Orthodox Church, but were noted for their excellent moral lives, temperance, and industry. Among their tenets was the belief that God dwells in all men, but especially in some, and that each generation possesses its Christ. In their meetings they sang Psalms and commented on a collection of extracts from the Bible. They had no priests. One of their main precepts was mutual love and in following it they practised community of goods. They were hospitable to travellers and refrained so far as possible from killing animals. In formulating their creed they were aided by Gregory Skovoroda (1722–1794), a Ukrainian mystic and philosopher who had travelled widely in Western Europe. They regarded Jesus as a man who was inspired by the word of God much as were the saints and taught that the Father, Son, and Holy Spirit are merely aspects of the one God. They held that in the Old Testament the Son of God revealed himself as divine wisdom and that the New Testament inaugurated the age of the Holy Spirit. They believed that souls who fell with the angels enter human bodies when these reach years of discretion and that each is saved by his own efforts. They insisted that there is one church of God, invisible, transcending all races and religions, and that they, the visible Church, were the core of the invisible Church. They rejected baptism by water. Like some other dissenting groups, they divided into several sects.

Molokan was a nickname given to a movement the members of which thought of themselves as Spiritual Christians. Molokan is from the Russian word for milk and was applied to the sect because, contrary to the custom of the Russian Orthodox Church, its adherents drank milk during Lent. The beginnings of the Molokans, like that of the Dukhobors, are not clear. Some trace them to a leader who was martyred under Ivan the Terrible. Others assign them to Simeon Uklein, of the latter part of the eighteenth century, who broke from the Dukhobors. It is certain that the Molokans were in existence before 1815. They made more of the Bible than did the Dukhobors. They refused to take human life and therefore would not do military service. Icons were repugnant to them, they had no buildings especially consecrated for worship, and they did not have the historic sacraments. Their religious services generally consisted of the recital of passages from the Scriptures and of prayers. They had love feasts and on the anniversary of the institution of the Last Supper they met and broke bread in memory of Christ but did not regard that act as a sacrament. They were industrious, thrifty, and cleanly, and abstained from luxuries and condemned gambling and drink. Eventually, like the Dukhobors, they split into sects.

Into Russia in the latter part of the eighteenth century there came colonies of Mennonites. They were attracted by special concessions offered them by Catherine the Great, for she saw in their industry and thrift a means of promoting the economic progress of her realms.

The Revival among Protestants: General Features

It was in Protestantism rather than the Roman Catholic Church or the Eastern Churches that after 1750 awakening was most marked. Here, by 1815 movements were under way which in the nineteenth century were to swell to major proportions. In connexion with them and largely as a result of them Protestantism was to exhibit a rapid expansion. By the middle of the twentieth century it was to be spread far more widely than were the Eastern Churches. While, so far as statistics went, it still was not as strong numerically as was the Roman Catholic Church, it was in as many countries as the latter and in proportion to its adherents in 1750 it had grown far more rapidly.

The awakening was not confined to any one branch of Protestantism. It cut across existing denominational and confessional lines. It began with the Pietist movement in Germany in the seventeenth century and at first was most marked in Lutheranism. Mainly because of the leadership of Zinzendorf, it had a striking manifestation in the rise of the Moravians and their spread from Herrnhut. Almost simultaneously it was seen in the Great Awakening in the Thirteen Colonies and in Great Britain in the Evangelical Awakening in which the Wesleys and Whitefield were outstanding. In the Thirteen Colonies its chief channels were the churches of the Reformed tradition. In Great Britain it was initially most prominent in the Church of England, but it was also manifest in the Church of Scotland and in bodies which dissented from both, mostly Methodists, Congregationalists, and Baptists. Later it spread to the Reformed Churches on the Continent of Europe.

In whatever country or branch of Protestantism it appeared, the awakening had distinctive features. It was characteristically Protestant and stressed the authority of the Scriptures, salvation by faith alone, and the priesthood of all believers. It made much of a personal religious experience, of a new birth through trust in Christ, commitment to him, and faith in what God had done through him in the incarnation, the cross, and the resurrection. Indeed, some beliefs were so widely held by most of those touched by the awakening that the faith held by all came to be known technically as "Evangelical." The awakening was intensely missionary. To employ technical terms, it was "evangelistic" and emphasized "evangelism." It sought to win to an acceptance of the Gospel the nominal Christians and the de-Christianized in Christendom and non-Christians throughout the world. It endeavoured hopefully, in the words of the New Testament command, to "preach the Gospel to every creature." A youth organization which sprang from it late in the nineteenth century, the Student Volunteer Movement for Foreign Missions, took as its "watchword": "The evangelization of the world in this generation."

The awakening gave rise to efforts to relieve suffering and to remedy collective evils. Many of those touched by it, while believing that it was not in accord with the Scriptures to work and hope for the transformation of society as a whole, were active in promoting such institutions as orphanages and hospitals and in such enterprises as nursing the sick and relieving famine. Others, taking seriously a form of the "great commission" more sweeping than "preach the Gospel to every creature," namely, "make disciples of all the nations, baptizing them in the name of the Father, and of the Son, and of the Holy Ghost: teaching them to observe all things whatsoever I have commanded you," laboured to bring all mankind to obedience to Christ in all aspects of its life.

The fact that the awakening spread across denominational and national boundaries and had common characteristics and beliefs tended to draw together all who were committed to it. It brought them into coöperation for common objectives, such as religious education in Sunday Schools, efforts for youth and for students, and movements for the abolition of slavery, for international peace, for temperance in the use of alcoholic beverages or the complete prohibition of the manufacture and sale of such beverages, and for giving the Gospel to particular countries or classes or to the entire world. In the nineteenth century the numbers of these enterprises multiplied. In the nineteenth century, too, there arose what was eventually known as the Ecumenical Movement. While beginning with Evangelicals, namely those who were the products of the awakenings, in the twentieth century it reached out far beyond them and in one or another of its expressions drew in the majority of Protestants, some of the Eastern and other non-Protestant bodies, and even individuals who retained their membership in the Roman Catholic Church.

Although the awakening drew Christians together regardless of their denominational affiliations, it also either gave rise to new denominations or greatly strengthened existing ones. Among these were the several branches of Methodists, Baptists, Congregationalists, fellowships known as Christians and Disciples of Christ, and scores of smaller bodies. They were not territorial, as were most of the Lutheran and Reformed Churches, and as was the Church of England. Seldom did they win the allegiance of all or even the majority of the inhabitants of a particular geographic area. They were more nearly akin to the many religious orders within the Roman Catholic Church. Like them they were consciously within one branch of Christianity, in this case Protestantism. As were the Roman Catholic orders, each was bound together in a common organization. Like that of the Benedictines, this might be very loose, giving much autonomy to the local congregation. Or, like the Jesuits, it might be closely knit. Increasingly, moreover, branches of Protestantism which were at the outset territorial tended to conform to this denominational pattern. As Lutherans, Reformed, Presbyterians, and Anglicans migrated to the Americas or Australasia, or as they founded missions among non-Western peoples, they ceased to be dominant in a particular country and became minorities, one of several branches of Protestantism.

The awakening greatly strengthened what might be called the extreme fringe of Protestantism. It brought new vigour to Lutheran, Reformed, and Anglican bodies. But it especially stimulated the growth of denominations further removed from the Catholic tradition, such as Congregationalists, Baptists, and Methodists. Within those churches which had retained more that had been developed in the Catholic form of the faith it brought into being groups which tended to discard much of the Catholic heritage. The trend was to go back to Christianity as described in the New Testament, regarding as at best dubious what had been added by the Catholic Church, whether Roman or Orthodox.

Akin to this last modification of Protestantism by the awakening was another. The lay element became prominent. This was to be expected from the Protestant principle of the priesthood of all believers, but what had been held in theory now became more of a reality in practice. In some of the major new movements, such as the societies for distributing the Bible and the Sunday Schools, the laymen were outstanding. In the nineteenth and twentieth centuries the laity were increasingly to the fore. Women had a growing place and laymen had more and more initiative and participation. This was in striking contrast with the Roman Catholic Church, where the clergy were emphatically in control. The Orthodox Churches accorded a larger place to laymen than did the Roman Catholic Church, but the Protestantism which arose from the revivals of the eighteenth and nineteenth centuries had far more of lay leadership than did they.

While the impact of the awakening was felt in all lands where there were Protestants, it was especially potent in the British Isles, the United States, and the newer countries of English speech, Canada, Australia, and New Zealand. This is significant because in the nineteenth and the fore part of the twentieth century it was these lands which had the largest growth in territory and wealth and, proportionately, in population. As Spain and Portugal, Roman Catholic lands, had led in the expansion of Europe between 1500 and 1750, after 1750 it was through peoples that are often called Anglo-Saxon that this expansion was chiefly accomplished. Here again, as so often, the question arises of the connexion between marked vitality in a particular form of Christianity and creativity in other aspects of life. The two were contemporary. Was this pure coincidence or was the relationship causal? If causal, was Christianity the source of the other features of the cultural activity? Or were the causes in neither but common to them both? We do not know. However, we are certain that each acted on the other. Anglo-Saxon Christianity in part reflected the abounding vigour in other ranges of British and North American achievement, and its forms were to some extent determined and its expansion made possible by them. In turn, the other phases of Anglo-American civilization were moulded, several of them profoundly, by the revived Christianity.

While Anglo-Saxon peoples were exhibiting a phenomenal growth which was being accompanied by striking vitality in the Protestantism within their ranks, significant movements were afoot in the Protestantism of the Continent of Europe, chiefly in Germany and Scandinavia. Some of them were in the Pietist tradition, some a reaction from rationalism towards conservative Lutheranism, and others, following up the rationalist tradition but not entirely dominated by it, gave rise to currents of thought and scholarship which put Germany in the forefront of Biblical and theological study in the nineteenth and the early part of the twentieth century.

From what we have outlined it may be gathered that through the revival Protestantism was exhibiting striking modifications. It was still true to the main principles of the Protestant Reformation. Indeed, the developments which were taking place were largely the outgrowth of these principles. Here was more and more emerging a form of Christianity which was not sectional, chiefly confined to North-western Europe and the British Isles, as Protestantism had been down to 1750, but which, under the impulse of the awakening, in the nineteenth and twentieth centuries was to have a world-wide spread and from which was to issue a new kind of inclusive fellowship embracing Christians from all divisions of Christianity. From it were to spring many movements, numbers of them quite without precedent, and in it were to take place fresh developments in thought and institutions. If the vitality of a religion is measured by its ability to give rise to new expressions, then the Protestantism which emerged from the revival was one of the most potent forms of religion that mankind has known. Although in the nineteenth century the Roman Catholic Church and Russian Christianity displayed a somewhat similar vigour, in neither did it have as manifold and novel manifestations as in Protestantism. To this the developments between 1750 and 1815 were preliminary.

REVIVAL AMONG PROTESTANTS IN THE BRITISH ISLES

It was in the British Isles and especially in England that between 1750 and 1815 the awakening in Protestantism was particularly marked. It commenced before 1750 and was to swell to much larger proportions after 1815. However, in the years between 1750 and 1815 it began to develop forms which were to characterize it in the nineteenth and twentieth centuries.

The revival was by no means all from one source nor did it centre about any single individual. The Great Awakening in the Thirteen Colonies had repercussions in the British Isles, notably in Scotland and England. The writings of Jonathan Edwards describing that revival had a wide circulation in Great Britain. New England Congregationalism and Scottish Presbyterianism were closely akin. Both, for example, regarded the Westminster Confession as a standard statement of the Christian faith. It was natural, therefore, that the Great Awakening, largely channelled as it was through Congregationalism and the Reformed Churches, should be followed with peculiar interest in Scotland and that Edwards should be in frequent correspondence with Scottish friends. After he was ousted from his church in Northampton he was invited to come to Scotland. Although he declined, the tie with Scotland continued to be close. There were also men in England and Scotland who were little influenced by Edwards or that more prominent leader of the revival, John Wesley, who contributed to the Evangelical movement. Prominent among them were the Haldane brothers, Robert and James Alexander, who had a profound effect in Scotland and on the Continent of Europe, and, through Thomas and Alexander Campbell, in the United States. Moreover, late in the seventeenth century and early in the eighteenth century a large number of informal societies had sprung into being, mainly but not entirely among members of the Church of England. They were for reading the Bible, prayer, frequent communion, and service to prisoners, the poor, soldiers, and sailors.

The Revival in the British Isles: The Birth of Methodism

The most famous leader and creator of the Evangelical movement was John Wesley (1703–1791). Prominent with him were his brother Charles (1707–1788) and their friend George Whitefield (1714–1770). John and Charles had for father Samuel Wesley (1662–1735) who, the son of a Nonconforming clergyman, had become a priest of the Church of England and was long in charge of the rural parish of Epworth. The wife of Samuel Wesley was Susanna, whose father, Samuel Annesley, was a nephew of the first Earl of Anglesea and, a clergyman, had also been among the Nonconformists. Samuel and Susanna Wesley had nineteen children, of whom eight died in infancy. John and Charles owed much to both parents. Their father, hard-working, had organized one of the religious societies then in vogue. Their mother, a woman of great force of character, exercised a methodical discipline over her large brood, setting the elder to care for the younger children and exacting regularity and obedience. In 1709, when both John and Charles were still very young, the parental home was burned and they so narrowly escaped perishing with it that John came to regard himself as "a brand snatched from the burning." John went to the Charterhouse School in London and thence to Christ Church, Oxford. Although not profoundly philosophical, he was a diligent and able student. Throughout his life he read widely. Eventually he became adept in several languages, ancient and modern. He loved riding and walking and was an expert swimmer. Deeply religious, he early treasured Thomas à Kempis and Jeremy Taylor. He was ordained deacon (1725) and priest (1728) in the Church of England. He was a fellow of Lincoln College, Oxford. At intervals for a few years after he was given the appointment he had leave from its duties to help his father in the latter's parish.

While John was away, Charles came to Oxford, also as a member of Christ Church, and formed with two others (1729) a little club to aid one another in their studies, to read helpful books, and to participate in frequent communion. When, in November, 1729, he returned to Oxford, John became the leader of the group. They attracted other students, but probably not more than twenty-five. John later considered this as the first rise of Methodism. The group was called the Holy Club and for its disciplined ways was given the nickname of Methodist, a term which had been in use in the seventeenth century. It was that name which stuck and became the official designation of what was eventually a world-wide movement. The members tended to be Catholic and were influenced by the ideals of an older Cambridge contemporary, William Law, who in turn had been much impressed with Jacob Boehme and whose *Serious Call to a Holy and Devout Life* was published in the very year in which the group was formed.

In this stage of his Oxford career, John Wesley gave himself to an intensive reading of the Greek New Testament, fasted on Wednesdays and Fridays, received the communion weekly, which, according to the practice of the time was deemed frequent, and laboured among the prisoners in the local jail. It was in 1735, while still at Oxford that he preached a sermon on "the circumcision of the heart" which he later declared to have contained all the principles which he taught in after years, among them salvation from all sin and loving God with an undivided heart. However, these had not yet become emotionally his possession.

It was in 1735 that George Whitefield, then only twenty years of age, joined the group. He had entered Oxford in 1733 and a severe illness in the spring of 1735 brought a depth that was reflected in his amazing career as a preacher on which he launched soon after his ordination, in 1736.

In 1735 there began another important stage in the career of John and Charles Wesley. They sailed for Georgia as missionaries of the Society for the Propagation of the Gospel in Foreign Parts. Georgia had been founded two years before by the philanthropist James Oglethorpe as a refuge for debtors and for persecuted Protestants from Germany. On the voyage to Georgia the Wesleys made the acquaintance of Moravians who were on the same ship and John was impressed and humiliated to find that in the midst of storm and the imminence of death they had a quiet fearlessness which his religion had not given him. Arriving in Savannah, he met the Moravian leader Spangenberg. The latter pointedly asked him: "Do you know Jesus Christ?" John could only reply: "I know he is the saviour of the world." Whereupon Spangenberg countered: "True, but do you know that he has saved *you?*" In spite of their lack of the inner assurance of which the Moravian had spoken, the Wesleys laboured earnestly in the young colony. They had intended to be missionaries to the Indians but confined their efforts chiefly to the whites. Ill, Charles returned to England in 1736. John remained and in 1736 gathered a small society of serious Christians, on which he later looked back as the second rise of Methodism. Yet he felt himself frustrated. A stiff high-churchman, he irritated some of the colonists by his requirements. He had an unfortunate love affair and, refusing to give the communion to the young lady involved who, after he had not pursued his courtship, had married another man, he aroused further resentment. Suits were started against him. Disheartened, he returned to England.

It was soon after he arrived in London that John Wesley had the profound experience which sent him out as preacher and organizer of the Methodist movement. Impressed as they had been by the Moravians while on the Georgia mission, he and Charles sought counsel with one of that church who was in London on his way to Georgia. He spoke to them of self-surrender, instantaneous conversion, and joy in conscious salvation. On May 21, 1738, quiet confidence and inner peace came to Charles. Three days later, on May 24, 1738, they found John. After attending evening prayer in St. Paul's Cathedral, John went to a meeting of an informal Anglican society on Aldersgate, not far away. While Luther's preface to the *Commentary on Romans* was being read, there suddenly broke upon him something similar to what that epistle had brought to the tortured soul of the great German. As Wesley recorded it in his journal: "About a quarter before nine, while he [Luther] was describing the change which God works in the heart through faith in Christ, I felt my heart strangely warmed. I felt I did trust in Christ, Christ alone, for salvation; and an assurance was given me that he had taken away my sins, even mine, and saved me from the law of sin and death." Thus did the experience so central in Protestantism, of salvation by faith alone, grip the seeking high Anglican. It sent him out to start what was to be in all its various branches one of the largest of the Protestant denominations, Methodism. But that did not come at once.

After that Aldersgate night, John Wesley not unnaturally sought to learn more from the Moravians, for it was they who had been decisive in his quest. He was an original member of the Fetter Lane Society which a Moravian had gathered in London, but that was not enough. He went to Germany, met Zinzendorf, and had several days at Herrnhut. Although he was critical of some features of what he saw there, he adopted and adapted more than one of the Moravian methods.

Back in England, John Wesley preached extensively, as did his brother Charles. At first this was only in religious societies and churches. In many of the latter his message provoked such opposition that he would record in his journal that he was not to preach there again. His main themes were conscious acceptance with God and daily growth in holiness. He held that a Christian could have as his dominant motives the love of God and of his neighbour and that these could free him from sin. However, he recognized that perfection was seldom attained in this life.

In 1739 Whitefield, whose sermons in Bristol were arousing great excitement, began preaching in the open air to the miners and saw the tears make channels down their coal-begrimed faces. He urged John Wesley to try that method. John went to Bristol, his high-churchly prejudices were melted by what he saw, and he himself began proclaiming his message in the fields. He travelled widely, speaking wherever he could gain a hearing, in churches or out of doors. According to the regulations of the Church of England he was not to preach within the boundaries of a parish until the clergyman in charge gave his consent. When a clergyman refused permission, Wesley preached without it, declaring: "The world is my parish." This phrase was to become a Methodist slogan.

In the initial years of his itinerary Wesley faced persecution. The emotion which his message aroused brought criticism, not only in church circles and among the upper classes where, under the influence of the current vogue of reason, any enthusiasm was looked at askance, but also among the masses. Sometimes Wesley was met by mobs and violence. Yet he never quailed nor was he deterred from his mission.

The preaching of John Wesley, like that of Whitefield, attracted chiefly the lower and middle classes. In spite of widespread vulgarity, drunkenness, obscenity, and calloused cruelty in eighteenth century Britain, and a large degree of religious illiteracy and scepticism, there was a general, even if super-ficial knowledge of the main tenets of Christian teaching about morals and faith. In many, although a minority, there was a hunger left unsatisfied by the formal services in most of the churches. Among them the preaching of Wes-ley, Whitefield, and others of similar stripe awakened a response. Wesley did not have the kind of eloquence for which Whitefield was noted. Nor did he have a commanding physical presence. In cold print his sermons seem doc-trinal, practical, and even prosaic. Yet, as with those of Whitefield and as in the Great Awakening in the Thirteen Colonies and some of the later revivals in the United States, they often released striking emotions. Men and women screamed, were physically convulsed, or fell insensible.

Although John Wesley believed the physical accompaniments of his preach-ing were due either to the resistance of the Devil or to the Holy Spirit, he did not allow himself to be diverted by them. He was intensely practical, an ex-traordinarily able organizer and administrator, and had an unusual capacity to accept suggestions and to adopt and adapt methods from various quarters. He himself realized that this gift for organization was his "peculiar talent." He gathered his converts into "societies," in part after the pattern of the ones in which he had shared in Oxford, organized in Georgia, and had had his heart-warming experience, and of that which the Moravian had brought to-gether in Fetter Lane. One of the earliest of the Methodist societies was in Bristol and another in an old foundry in London. After the Moravian pattern, the societies were at first divided into "bands" to aid their members in the nourishment of the Christian life. Early, in addition, they were divided into "classes," each with its "class leader." Originally mainly a device for raising money, for each member was to give a penny a week and the leader was to collect it, the classes became primarily a means of intimate fellowship for spiritual and moral growth under the direction of a mature Christian. "Love feasts" were early introduced, again a Moravian custom. Members of the societies were at first received on trial and, after testing, were issued tickets to show that they were in full standing. When some laymen began preaching, Wesley demurred. However, his mother admonished him that in doing so he might be thwarting the Holy Spirit. He yielded and lay preachers became an outstanding feature of Methodism. Other devices which Wesley learned from others were watch-night services, covenant services, and stewards to care for the property of the societies.

Within John Wesley's long lifetime the societies multiplied and were knit into an inclusive organization. In 1790, on the eve of his death, they were said to have 71,668 members in Great Britain. For a time Wesley himself visited each of the societies to supervise them and enforce discipline. As they increased this became impossible and he assembled his preachers in "annual conferences." As societies and preachers further grew in numbers, he established "circuits" with travelling preachers and soon, as an assistant to himself, a "superintendent" was placed in charge of each circuit. He himself kept an autocratic control of the whole.

Wesley travelled almost incessantly. In spite of the physical difficulties of poor roads, he averaged about five thousand miles a year, much of them on horseback, and fifteen sermons a week. He not only covered England but also visited Ireland and Scotland again and again. In his later years he was greeted with acclaim and his journeys became triumphal progresses. The short, slight figure, with its clean-shaven ruddy face, its bright eyes, and its snowy locks, evoked something akin to veneration.

Wesley was distinctively an activist. Not only was he an organizer and administrator. Himself an inveterate reader, he encouraged the taste for literature and to this end saw to the publication and sale of inexpensive editions of good books. He also wrote extensively. From a substantial income from the sale of his books he aided what he deemed good causes. He furthered the care of deserving poor and the creation of lending funds to assist struggling business men.

John Wesley devoted himself to his mission with singleness of purpose. He did not marry until he was in his late forties. Then it was to a widow, the marriage proved unhappy, and he and his wife parted.

In common with many of the fresh outbursts of the Christian faith, from the outset Methodism gave rise to song. John Wesley contributed notable translations of German hymns. His brother Charles composed hundreds of hymns. Many of the hymns of the Wesleys gained wide circulation far outside the boundaries of Methodism. Among the more famous of Charles Wesley's hymns were "Jesus lover of my soul," "Love divine, all loves excelling," "O for a thousand tongues to sing," "Christ the Lord is risen today," "Rejoice the Lord is King," and "Ye servants of God your master proclaim."

By degrees Methodists separated from the Church of England. John Wesley thought of himself as remaining within the church of his birth. He tried to bind his societies to the Church of England and to encourage their members to receive the sacraments through it. Doctrinally he did not wish to be an innovator, but desired simply "to spread Scriptural holiness over the land." However, the Methodist movement had not been many years under way when he became convinced that in the New Testament presbyters and bishops were the same order. He believed that, as a presbyter, he had as much right to administer ordination as had any bishop. Moreover, the problem arose of finding enough priests of the Church of England to give the sacraments to the members of his societies. This first became acute in the United States. There, as we are to see in a moment, Methodism spread rapidly. Yet there the Church of England was weak numerically and the number of priests of that communion in the country declined sharply as a result of the rift with the mother country. Moreover, not until late in the 1780's were bishops consecrated for the remnant and a national organization achieved by the Anglicans. Accordingly, in 1784, the year after the formal recognition by Great Britain of the independence of the United States, John Wesley and Thomas Coke, the latter also a priest (presbyter) of the Church of England, ordained two as presbyters ("elders") for the United States and, assisted by other ministers, Wesley set apart Coke as "superintendent" for America and appointed Francis Asbury, already in the United States, to a similar office. Later he ordained other presbyters for Scotland, where the Anglican communion was weak, and eventually ordained some for England. His brother Charles, it may be added, disapproved of this procedure.

It was in 1784 that by a Deed of Declaration John Wesley, now in his eighties, provided for the continuation of the organization after his death by naming a "conference" of one hundred ministers to hold the property and to assume the direction of the movement. Upon his death, in 1791, the Wesleyan Methodist Church was formally constituted. Before the decade was out the Methodist New Connexion hived off in protest against what it called the priestcraft of the other body.

As we are to note, Methodism, thus inaugurated by John Wesley, had a growth which made it the largest group of Nonconforming Protestants in England, next to the Baptists the largest body of Protestants in the United States, along with the Church of England and the Presbyterians one of the three largest Protestant denominations in the British overseas dominions of Canada, Australia, and New Zealand, and through its missions prominent on the Continent of Europe, and in Asia, Africa, Latin America, and many of the islands of the sea. It divided into several churches, partly by nations. Yet everywhere it preserved common characteristics which went back to John Wesley—zeal in preaching, especially to the middle and lower classes, tightly knit organization, and emphasis upon education and social service.

THE REVIVAL IN THE BRITISH ISLES: OUTSIDE OF WESLEYAN METHODISM

The eighteenth century awakening in Christianity in the British Isles was by no means confined to the societies which were associated in the Wesleyan Methodist Church and the Methodist New Connexion. As we have suggested, it was also in the Church of Scotland and among Presbyterians in Scotland who dissented from that body. It was seen as well among the Congregationalists and Baptists in England. It spread to Wales and Ireland. It made itself felt in circles in the Church of England which did not follow Wesley or Whitefield.

Whitefield and the Wesleys drew apart. The cause was doctrinal. John Wesley was Arminian. Whitefield believed in predestination. At first the break was with bitterness. Although reconciliation was effected and friendship was restored, the difference in theology persisted and the paths remained distinct. Whitefield was supported by Selina, Countess of Huntingdon (1707–1791). Wealthy, widowed in her late thirties (1746), and a woman of forceful character, before her husband's death the Countess of Huntingdon had been an early member of the Methodist society of Fetter Lane. Too independent to be happy under the autocratic control of John Wesley, and a Calvinist rather than an Arminian, she formed what came to be known first as the Countess of Huntingdon's Connexion and later as the Calvinistic Methodists. She built chapels and appointed to them men whom she designated as her chaplains. Whitefield was one of them. In 1779 she and those associated with her separated from the Church of England. Until her death she dominated the movement. Unlike Wesley, Whitefield did not have the gift of organization and administration. Yet from him arose a distinct body, the Welsh Calvinistic Methodists.

Strong for the doctrine of election was Augustus Montague Toplady (1740–1778). A clergyman of the Church of England, he vigorously attacked John Wesley for the latter's Arminianism. However, he is best remembered for his hymn, "Rock of Ages."

The attacks by the predestinarians tended to confirm Wesley and his followers in their Arminianism. A stout defender of Wesley was the Swiss Jean

Guillaume de la Fléchère, better known as Fletcher of Maddeley (1729–1785), who, having come to England, had a parish in the established church.

Within the Church of England the revival strengthened the Protestant element that had been there since the Reformation. Those who were committed to it were known as Evangelicals. In general they were Calvinistic in theology. They stressed conversion, strict morals, a life of active service to others, and simplicity in worship. Prominent among them was John Newton (1725–1807) who, self-educated, after an adventurous life at sea, part of the time as captain of a ship engaged in the African slave trade, was ordained, served in Olney, in Buckinghamshire, and then as rector of a church in London. A friend of Wesley and Whitefield, he was a notable preacher and was the author of widely popular hymns, among them "How sweet the name of Jesus sounds" and "One there is above all others." Newton was a close friend of William Cowper (1731–1800), whose life was saddened by periods of melancholic insanity, but who in long lucid intervals wrote verse and hymns, some of them notable. The Milner brothers, Joseph (1744–1797) and Isaac (1751–1820), both graduates of Cambridge, the latter senior wrangler and later professor of experimental philosophy and master of Queen's College in that university, were strong Evangelicals. Isaac Milner was a close friend of William Wilberforce (1759–1833), was instrumental in the conversion of that charming scion of a wealthy home, and did much to make Cambridge a centre of Evangelicalism. The tradition was reinforced and continued by Charles Simeon (1759–1836) who, born in the same year as Wilberforce, was a member of King's College, Cambridge, and for more than fifty years was in Trinity Church in that city and as preacher and pastor had a profound influence in the university. A notable succession was Henry Venn (1725–1797), a graduate of Cambridge and a distinguished Evangelical clergyman, a son, John Venn (1759–1813), one of the founders of the Church Missionary Society, and a grandson, Henry Venn (1796–1873) for nearly a third of a century honorary secretary of that society. Hannah More (1745–1833) moved in the literary and artistic circles of the England of her day, had a warm Evangelical piety, and was a prolific author whose writings, largely of a religious and moral nature, enjoyed an enormous circulation. The list of prominent Evangelicals might be greatly lengthened. Evangelicals were a minority in the Church of England, but their influence was striking.

Although they were loyal to the Church of England, Evangelicals in general were willing to coöperate with Nonconformists of Evangelical views. Indeed, they often encouraged the latter. Since new parishes could be created only by act of Parliament, to provide better facilities for the masses Evangelicals built numbers of chapels in existing parishes, placed in them Nonconforming ministers, and supported a school to train incumbents.

THE OUTREACH OF THE BRITISH REVIVAL

The eighteenth century revival in British Protestant Christianity had repercussions which touched life at many angles, both in the British Isles and in many other parts of the world. They did not attain their largest proportions until after 1815, but by that year some of their characteristic manifestations were seen. The emphasis of the revivals was upon the transformation of the individual through faith in Christ and his sacrifice on the cross, through complete dedication to God, and through the work of the Holy Spirit. Those so committed were ardently missionary and sought to win others to a similar experience. They also strove to alleviate or abolish social conditions which warped or destroyed human lives. The movement begat radiant hope and inspired many to intense and unremitting activity.

It was a time when Britain was growing in wealth and empire. The loss of the Thirteen Colonies proved an asset, for Britain was relieved of the cost of their defense and after a period of adjustment the United States continued to be a major outlet for British manufactures and capital. Britain engaged in a life and death struggle with Napoleon, but won, and in so doing achieved and confirmed a mastery of the seas. The industrial revolution was beginning, with its early home primarily in Great Britain, and a sense of boundless opportunity was in the air. In this many of those touched by the religious awakening shared. They dreamed and laboured to take advantage of the new day to reduce the evils inherited from the past or brought by the new conditions and to make of British trade and empire a blessing and not a curse. Their efforts were legion. For them the year 1815 is an artificial date, for the end of the Napoleonic Wars did not bring them to a pause but, if anything, gave them an added impetus. We can take the space merely to mention a few of the more outstanding.

Some of the efforts at improvement at the outset were primarily for the British Isles but ultimately were not confined to meeting domestic problems. In 1780 an Evangelical layman of the Church of England, Robert Raikes (1735–1811), began a Sunday School in his home city, Gloucester. A lover of children, he designed it to give moral and religious instruction to the very poor on the day of the week when most of them were not working. This involved teaching many of the pupils to read. The idea was not new. Somewhat similar procedures had been known at least as early as the seventeenth century. However, through Raikes it was given a decisive impetus, partly through the *Gloucester Journal* which his father and then he owned. In 1785 there was formed in London the Sunday School Society for extending the movement throughout the British Empire. Among her other activities, Hannah More organized schools among the neglected miners and colliers of the Mendip Hills. Joseph Lancaster (1778–1838), a Quaker, inaugurated a method of teaching the underprivileged which for some years enjoyed a wide vogue.

John Howard (1726–1790), a warm friend and admirer of John Wesley, a worshipper in Nonconformist congregations, used the leisure made possible by inherited wealth to labour indefatigably for the reform of the appalling conditions in the prisons. He did this first as high-sheriff of Bedfordshire, then as the inspirer of acts of Parliament to improve prison conditions throughout the realm, and later by prolonged journeys to study prison conditions in Great Britain, Ireland, and Europe. Characteristically, he lost his life while in Russia, travelling to find ways of preventing the spread of the plague. Evangelicals were active in promoting a stricter observance of Sunday and in seeking to curb the gambling, duelling, and cruel sports which were then prevalent. They also strove to regulate child labour in the newly emerging factories and to protect the boys employed as chimney sweeps. They promoted the education of the masses. They objected to the immoral character of current eighteenth century fiction.

At Clapham, a suburb of London, several wealthy Evangelicals made their home. Known derisively as the Clapham Sect, they worked, sometimes together and at other times individually, for a wide variety of religious and philanthropic projects. One of their number, Granville Sharp, was chiefly responsible for the founding, in 1787, of Sierra Leone, for freed Negroes. Another, Zachary Macaulay, father of Lord Macaulay, the historian, was also active in fighting slavery. Even more famous for his prolonged and successful struggle against Negro slavery, another resident of Clapham, William Wilberforce, led in Parliament the campaign which in 1807 put on the statute books an act abolishing the slave trade in the British Empire and lived to see the assurance of the abolishment of slavery (1833) in the British domains. For this end also laboured Thomas Clarkson (1760–1846), son of a clergyman of the Church of England, who gave up his plans to follow his father's profession to devote himself to the anti-slavery cause.

It was in these years that the revival brought about the formation of a number of missionary societies. Although the seventeenth and the opening years of the eighteenth century had witnessed the founding of several such bodies, including some Dutch undertakings, the Society for the Propagation of the Gospel in New England, the Society for Promoting Christian Knowledge, the Society for the Propagation of the Gospel in Foreign Parts, the (Scottish) Society for Propagating Christian Knowledge, and the Moravian efforts, the

1790's and the opening years of the nineteenth century have generally been counted as seeing the beginning of the Protestant foreign missionary enterprise. We shall find this issuing both from the United States and from the Continent of Europe. However, it was in Great Britain, mainly England, and from impulses given by the awakening, that most of the societies of this period were begun. In 1792 the Baptist Missionary Society was organized, primarily as the result of the efforts of William Carey (1761–1834), self-educated, teacher, shoemaker, and pastor. Three years later, in 1795, what was at first called the Missionary Society, later the London Missionary Society, was inaugurated. It was intended to enlist the support of those of "Evangelical" sentiments, regardless of denomination, but it drew its funds and personnel chiefly from the Congregationalists. In 1796 the Scottish Missionary Society and the Glasgow Missionary Society were begun. In 1799 Evangelicals within the Church of England, prominent among them some from the Clapham group, started what was eventually called the Church Missionary Society. That same year the Religious Tract Society was organized, to enlist both Anglicans and Nonconformists in the spread of Christian literature. In 1804, partly through the efforts of Thomas Charles, a Calvinistic Methodist pastor in Wales, and with the endorsement of several of the Clapham circle, the British and Foreign Bible Society was founded for the purpose, as its name indicates, of printing and distributing the Bible at home and abroad. It was not until 1817–1818 that the Wesleyan Methodist Missionary Society was organized, but long before then Methodists had been active in proclaiming the Gospel outside the British Isles. For that purpose Thomas Coke travelled extensively in the United States and the West Indies and died (1814) on a journey to establish a mission in the East. Beginning in 1790 the Wesleyan Conference made organizational provision to assist him, and in 1813 auxiliary societies were formed.

By 1815 these various societies and efforts independent of them were spreading Christianity in several parts of the rapidly growing British Empire and were reaching beyond into vast areas hitherto untouched by Protestant Christianity. In 1793 William Carey and a colleague sailed for India, there to initiate the first undertaking of the Baptist Missionary Society. Since the East India Company, which then enjoyed a monopoly of British territory and trade in India, was hostile to missions, Carey eventually settled in Serampore, a Danish possession near Calcutta. There he, Marshman, and Ward, the "Serampore Trio," translated and printed part or all of the Bible into several of the languages of India and the East of Asia, including Chinese, and founded a school for the training of Indian Christians. David Brown, a protégé of Charles Simeon of Cambridge, conducted an orphanage in Calcutta. Another protégé of Simeon, Henry Martyn (1781–1812), senior wrangler at Cambridge and fellow of St. John's College, arrived in India in 1806 as a chaplain of the East India Company, exclaiming in his diary: "Now let me burn out for God." He did just that, adding to the faithful performance of his duties to the troops of the Company schools for Indians, preaching to Hindus and Moslems, and translations of the New Testament into three different languages. When in his early thirties he died in Asia Minor on his way to England. By 1815 the London Missionary Society had begun enterprises in several parts of India. In 1813, due largely to efforts of Evangelicals, among them Wilberforce, the charter of the East India Company was so altered by Parliament that missions became possible within the Company's territories and an episcopal establishment of a bishop and three archdeacons was set up in India for the Anglican Communion.

East of India, before 1815 English Baptists had begun, through Carey's sons, missions in Burma and the East Indies. By 1815 the London Missionary Society, the English Baptists, and the English Methodists had inaugurated missions on Ceylon, for during the years of the French Revolution and Napoleon the Dutch had been driven from that island by the English. In 1807 the first Protestant missionary to China, Robert Morrison, sent by the London Missionary Society, reached Canton.

The pioneer undertaking of the London Missionary Society was not in Asia, but in the South Pacific. In 1796 a party sent by that society sailed on *The Duff* and landed its missionaries on three widely separated island groups. The majority were placed on Tahiti and, after a few discouraging years, shortly after 1815 most of the population of that island and a smaller neighbour had become at least nominally Christian.

The earliest continuing white settlement on Australia was by convicts transported by the British Government. In 1787, with the first contingent, went a chaplain of the Church of England, an Evangelical. He was soon (1793) given a colleague, Samuel Marsden, also an Evangelical, who served until his death (1838) and did much to plant Christianity not only in Australia but also in New Zealand and some of the other islands of the Pacific. It was he who persuaded the Church Missionary Society to appoint men to the Maoris of New Zealand. The first contingent landed in New Zealand in 1814. In 1795 during the wars of the period the British took over the Dutch possessions in South Africa. The London Missionary Society sent representatives, most of whom gave themselves to the Africans, but at least one of whom served the Dutch churches.

In the British West Indies Anglicans, Methodists, and Baptists spread the Christian faith among the Negroes who formed the larger part of the population of most of the islands. Except for a few small islands off the coast, in 1763 France lost to England all of such territory as remained to her in what in the next century became the Dominion of Canada. English and Scottish settlers and some New Englanders, all predominantly Protestant by ancestry, moved into what were later the Maritime Provinces and the provinces of Quebec and Ontario. Numbers of those who were loyal to Britain when the Thirteen Colonies revolted migrated into these regions. Here, with some help from the British Isles, and, in the case of the Methodists, from the United States, the largest Protestant communions became the Church of England, the Presbyterians, the Methodists, and the Baptists. By 1815 all these were strongly represented.

THE REVIVAL IN THE UNITED STATES

As we have suggested, the immediate effect of the war for independence was adverse to Christianity in the United States. The political agitation and the fighting distracted attention from religion and in some quarters led to a decline in morals. Independence had barely been attained (1783), a constitution for the United States adopted, and a government under it set up (1789) when the French Revolution broke out. That upheaval and the rationalism and Deism associated with it had ardent sympathizers, especially among youth.

However, well before 1815 recovery was more than achieved, the mass conversion of the partially de-Christianized population which had been furthered by the Great Awakening was resumed, and the faith continued to make progress among Indians and Negroes.

Soon after independence some of the churches set up national organizations. In 1789 the Presbyterians formed a General Assembly as the capstone of their judicial and administrative structure and as a country-wide cohesive agency. In 1792 the (Dutch) Reformed Church and the following year the (German) Reformed Church ceased their dependence on the Continent of Europe and became fully self-governing.

In the 1780's the Anglicans drew together in what became the Protestant Episcopal Church. As we have said, the Church of England suffered greatly from the Revolution and independence. Many of the clergy, loyal to the king, left, never to return. Nearly all the missionaries of the Society for the Propagation of the Gospel in Foreign Parts were forced to retire and the society itself, formed as it had been for work in the British Empire, withdrew. There was no bishop and with independence such episcopal supervision as had been given by the Bishop of London and his commissaries ceased. Disestablishment came in such states, notably Virginia, as had given the Church of England the support of the government. Moreover, not all the Anglicans were of one mind.

In the North, and especially in New England where they were a dissenting minority from the "Standing Order," the dominant Congregationalism, they tended to be high church, stressing the Catholic features of their inheritance. In the South, where they had been socially and politically in control, they were usually low church, emphasizing the Protestant tradition. There was much objection to bringing all into a national church. Yet there was vitality in what had been the Church of England. Some of its more prominent clergy had supported the Colonies in their struggle for independence and many of those who led in creating the new United States of America were among its members.

Largely due to the tireless efforts of the irenic William White, rector of Christ Church, Philadelphia, in 1789 all parties met in a General Convention and formed the Protestant Episcopal Church. As early as 1780 a conference of clergy and laity in Maryland had suggested the name Protestant Episcopal, for the designation "Church of England" would scarcely be acceptable in a country which had so recently become independent of the mother country. In 1782 White sketched a plan for a national organization, in 1784 a gathering representing eight states assembled in New York, and in 1785 a General Convention adopted a constitution which was largely the work of White and asked the English bishops to ordain bishops for the United States. Samuel Seabury, chosen by the Connecticut constituency, was consecrated by bishops of the Scottish Episcopal Church in 1784. An act of Parliament was obtained authorizing the consecration of bishops through the Church of England, and in 1787 two, one of them White, were given that rite. At the General Convention of 1789, therefore, the Protestant Episcopal Church could be formally constituted. Both laity and clergy were represented and the Book of Common Prayer, modified to meet American needs, was adopted.

The Protestant Episcopal Church early received additions from the Swedish and German Lutherans. In 1791 the tie of the Delaware Swedish Lutherans with the mother country was severed, thus enabling them to move towards the Episcopal Church. Some of the English-speaking Lutherans of German descent were repelled by an effort to maintain the German language in the Lutheran congregations and went over to that church.

The revivals first represented by the Great Awakening broke out afresh with augmented fervour and swept various parts of the country.

In the South they had never really ceased. Preaching largely to those with low incomes and scanty or no education, the Baptists grew rapidly, notably in North Carolina, Virginia, and Kentucky. In Virginia they were at first persecuted, for the Church of England was established by law. In 1776 the principle of religious liberty was put into the Virginia bill of rights, and in 1785 it was made effective by appropriate legislation. This facilitated the further growth of the Baptists. In 1785 a revival began in Virginia which added thousands to the Baptist churches and many to other denominations.

In the 1790's what was known as the Second Awakening stirred the Congregational and some other churches in New England. Less marked by intense emotional manifestations than the movement earlier in the century, it stimulated the rise of missionary societies and the founding of academies, colleges, and theological seminaries.

Late in the 1790's and early in the 1800's a revival swept across Kentucky, then on the frontier. It seems to have begun in 1797 through the preaching of a Presbyterian clergyman. It broke out afresh in 1799. In 1800 came what was sometimes regarded as the first of the "camp-meetings." In preparation for the Lord's Supper hundreds gathered from miles around to listen to preaching. Several clergymen solemnly exhorted to searchings of conscience before coming to the communion table. Intense excitement followed. The custom of camp-meetings spread and persisted. Hundreds, sometimes thousands, flocked to a camp ground, many from curiosity or as a social gathering in a new country where opportunities for large concourses of people were rare. The meetings lasted for days and several preachers might be exhorting the hearers simultaneously in various parts of the grounds. The emotional and physical accompaniments were often extreme and bizarre. Yet some of the preachers sought to restrain them.

Several denominations shared in the revivals, but those which made the largest numerical gains were the Baptists, the Methodists, and new movements variously called Christians or Disciples of Christ. All emphasized the importance of conscious conversion.

The Baptists had a peculiar appeal to the masses. Their preachers, usually with very slight education, knew their audiences and how to address them in language which would hold their attention and bring conviction. They tended to be highly emotional. Their churches, simple democracies, fitted into the temper of the rural communities and isolated farmsteads in which most of the population lived. The informality of the services and of the singing and the simple language and music of the hymns were congenial to the rank and file. Baptists multiplied in many parts of the country, but especially in the South. In the nineteenth and twentieth centuries they constituted the large majority of all the Baptists in the world.

There were several different kinds of Baptists. Some were strict predestinarians, Particular Baptists, believing that Christ died only for the elect. Others were Arminian, like the General Baptists of England, holding that Christ died for all. A group of the latter, organized as a separate denomination and known as the Free Will Baptists, owed their origin to Benjamin Randall. A New

Englander by birth and rearing, Randall was converted through Whitefield—although after the latter's death. He preached widely, had marked gifts of organization, and at his own death (1808) the churches which he had called into existence numbered one hundred and thirty, with about six thousand members.

Methodists were not far behind the Baptists in their nation-wide spread. They far outnumbered the Methodists in any other country and next to the Baptists became the single largest Protestant denominational family in the United States.

Methodism seems not to have reached the Thirteen Colonies until after 1750. Some Methodists arrived in New York in 1760 and what appears to have been the first Methodist society in the Colonies was organized in that city in 1766. Other societies were soon formed in Maryland. In 1769 John Wesley sent two missionaries, one to New York and the other to Philadelphia. In the 1770's in Virginia a revival followed the preaching of an Anglican clergyman, Devereux Jarratt, and it was aided by one of Wesley's missionaries. By 1777 there were six Methodist circuits in Virginia and one in North Carolina with a membership of over four thousand, nearly two-thirds of the entire Methodist enrollment in the Colonies at that time. Jarratt gave the sacraments to these Virginia and North Carolina Methodists.

At first the Revolution seemed to be dealing Methodism a mortal blow. John Wesley issued a public appeal to the Colonies urging submission to the king. All but one of the missionaries whom Wesley had sent left, and for a time native-born Methodist preachers were persecuted. However, Methodists continued to increase. They are said to have multiplied from five hundred in 1771 to fifteen thousand in 1784.

Because of this growth, the opportunity in the new land, and the lack of Anglican priests to give the communion, drastic measures were necessary. Wesley and the Methodists of the United States had the courage to take them. As we have seen, in 1784 Wesley appointed Coke as "superintendent" of the Methodist societies in the United States and named Asbury to be his colleague in that office. Knowing the temper of the new country, Asbury refused to accept the post unless he was freely elected to it by his fellow preachers. In 1784 a conference of these preachers met in Baltimore, approved Wesley's plan of organization, formed the Methodist Episcopal Church, and chose Asbury and Coke as superintendents, a title soon to be changed to bishop. The autocratic Wesley was not happy over this refusal to continue under his direction, but, while respectful to him, the American preachers were firm.

Francis Asbury (1745–1816) was the organizer, the dominant figure, and the driving power in the formation and early growth of the Methodist

Episcopal Church. Born in England of humble and devout parents, himself deeply religious from boyhood, he was early caught up in the Methodist movement, became a lay preacher, and offered and was accepted by Wesley for service in America. Arriving in the Colonies in 1771, he went through the difficult days of the Revolution and eventually won the confidence of the country by braving Wesley's possible displeasure and coming out boldly for independence. At the Baltimore conference he was unanimously chosen as superintendent and was ordained deacon, elder, and superintendent on successive days. Since Coke was not content to remain in one country but travelled across much of the face of the world furthering Methodism, the burden of leadership fell on Asbury. Deliberately remaining unmarried the better to give himself to his mission, Asbury was incessantly on the road. Frail and often ill, from Maine to Georgia and from the Atlantic seaboard to the newest settlements on the far frontier in Kentucky, Tennessee, and Ohio he ranged. Dauntless, the crude accommodations and the cruder roads and trails and even the pathless wilderness did not deter him. Like Wesley, but under much more difficult physical conditions and over a much wider area, he was almost always on the road. Although, unlike Wesley, he was not a university graduate, like him he was well read and believed in education. As did Wesley, he went both preaching and organizing. By the time of his death the Methodists of the United States had grown from the fifteen thousand who greeted him on his election as superintendent to about two hundred thousand.

The growth of Methodism in the United States, even more striking than that in England, was due to a variety of factors. Here was a largely de-Christianized population, but with remnants of Christian belief to which appeal could be made. The country was new, virile, and hopeful, and the western frontier was being rapidly settled. It was predominantly rural. Like the Baptists, the Methodist preachers were usually men from the people, with slight education, and, speaking the language of ordinary folk, were able to reach them. Moreover, Arminian in theology and not holding to the doctrine of election as did Presbyterians, Congregationalists, and many Baptists, the Methodists proclaimed the love of God for all and that all might repent and be saved.

Methodist growth was predominantly in the rural sections and on the frontier, both North and South. This was in part because of the Methodist organization. The circuit plan which Wesley had devised for England proved singularly adapted to the rural and frontier areas of the United States. Under Asbury and the bishops who were later given him as colleagues were district superintendents. Under the district superintendents were circuit riders. As the name indicates, the latter were assigned areas to cover. Over some of these the route might be as much as five hundred miles. It had to be traversed by whatever conveyance was possible—on horseback, by canoe, or, where these failed, on foot. The circuit riders spoke wherever they could gain a hearing—in log cabins, court houses, school houses, taverns, or in the open air. Asbury wished them, like himself, to remain celibate, and while they took no vows, and some married, for the most part in effect theirs were the three obligations of the Roman Catholic monastic orders, poverty, chastity, and obedience. There was that about them which strongly resembled the Franciscans in the initial days of that movement. Like the latter they preached and sang the love of God in Christ. Even more than the latter they desired above all things conversions. In addition to the circuit riders there were local preachers, exhorters, quarterly meetings which gathered the members from farms and villages for fellowship, and camp-meetings. The system of classes and class leaders provided the pastoral function.

Methodists, like Baptists, were found all over the United States, but in general Baptists became more numerous in the South and Methodists in the North. The reason for this distinction is by no means clear.

From Methodism issued other bodies in addition to the Methodist Episcopal Church. The latter had only barely been launched when what was called the Republican Methodist Church arose in protest against the extensive powers granted to Asbury. The United Brethren in Christ had as their chief creator Philip William Otterbein (1726–1813). Born in Germany of a family of clergymen and coming to America in 1753 as a minister of the Reformed Church, in Pennsylvania Otterbein had a profound religious experience which made him an earnest and compelling preacher of the new life. As an associate he had Martin Boehm (1725–1812), of Pennsylvania Mennonite stock who, after a marked conversion, also began preaching in a heart-stirring manner. From the labours of these two men and of lay preachers of their fellowship there arose a new denomination which at the outset preached only in German and which was consciously modelled after the Methodist Episcopal Church, both in spirit and organization. Its constitution was adopted in 1799 and its first annual conference was held in 1800. Smaller than the United Brethren but, like it, patterned after the Methodist Episcopal Church and ministering to the German-speaking population, was the Evangelical Association. Its founder was Jacob Albright (1759–1808), a Pennsylvania German Lutheran who, out of the anguish which followed the death of several of his children, came into a joyous faith and joined the Methodists. A layman of little formal education, he began preaching among his fellow-German-Americans with marked success. In 1803 a council of his followers ordained him and in 1807 an annual conference assembled which elected him bishop.

Quite new movements arose from the revivals and after 1815 the majority of them coalesced into new denominations. In the freedom of the New World with the sense of emancipation from the confining institutions of the Old World across the Atlantic and of adventuring as pioneers in building a new and better order which characterized the United States in its youth, many, especially converts and preachers of the revivals, became dissatisfied with inherited denominational divisions. They sought to transcend them by simply calling themselves Christians or Disciples of Christ and going back to the New Testament to find the initial Gospel in its purity and the organization, forms, worship, and ceremonies of the pristine churches, which they idealized, before what they deemed corruptions and divisions had been added by later generations. Independently of one another, these groups sprang up in several different parts of the country, but chiefly on the frontier. What became the two main movements, movements which fused in 1832, were led by Barton W. Stone and Thomas and Alexander Campbell.

Barton W. Stone (1772–1844) was born in Maryland and was reared in the backwoods of Virginia. Hungry for education, in a pioneer academy he had as good training as the frontier could offer. After a heart-searching struggle he came into a Christian faith which had as its central tenet the conviction that God is love. With reservations openly expressed, he was ordained a Presbyterian clergyman, became a pastor in Kentucky, and was caught up in the revivals and camp-meetings which were then in their early heyday in that frontier state. Becoming increasingly dissatisfied with the doctrines of total depravity and unconditional election which he found in the Westminster Confession, he and a few others of like mind began preaching that God loved the whole world and had sent His Son to save all men if they would but believe, and that sinners were capable of fulfilling that condition. They urged sinners to believe immediately. This led to the expulsion from their synod of Stone and his friends. Accordingly they formed themselves into an independent presbytery. In 1804, distressed by the controversy produced by this action, they dissolved their presbytery, desiring it, so they said, to "sink into union with the Body of Christ at large." They called themselves simply Christians, foreswore the right of ordination, passing it back to "the Church of Christ," asked that the Bible be taken "as the only sure guide to heaven," and pled "that preachers and people cultivate a spirit of mutual forbearance, pray more, and dispute less." They also came to the conviction that the baptism of infants was wrong and baptized one another by immersion.

Thomas Campbell, of Scottish lineage and education, had been a Presbyterian pastor in Ireland. He had contact with one of the Haldanes. In 1807, in search of health, he came to Western Pennsylvania. Long disturbed by the sectarian strife among Christians, he admitted Presbyterians of various beliefs to the Lord's Supper. Censured for this by his presbytery, he withdrew. He and his followers formed "The Christian Association of Washington" (Pennsylvania), adopting as a slogan "where the Scriptures speak, we speak; where the Scriptures are silent, we are silent," and declared that "division among the Christians is a horrid evil. . . . It is anti-Christian." In 1809 Thomas Campbell was joined by his son, Alexander Campbell (1788–1866). The latter had remained in the British Isles after his father had come to America. There he had had a deep religious experience induced by a shipwreck and had come in touch with the ideas of the Haldanes and with the Sandemanians, a small group founded by John Glas (1695–1773), originally a Scottish Presbyterian clergyman. It took its name from Glas's son-in-law, Robert Sandeman, and had reached some of the conclusions arrived at by the "Christians" in the United States. On joining his father, Alexander found himself in accord with the latter's views. The more forceful, and a willing and able debater, he soon took over the leadership. In 1812 infant baptism was repudiated and the baptism by immersion of believers was adopted. For a time, beginning in 1813, fellowship was found with the Baptists, but after a few years (1827–1830) separation came over differences in doctrine and practice. The following of the Campbells grew rapidly, under the name of Reformers or Disciples.

Stone and Alexander Campbell met, found their views to be very much alike, and adjusted such differences as they discovered. Eventually about half those associated with Stone joined with the followers of Campbell.

The revivals produced a further rupture in Presbyterianism, the Cumberland Presbyterian Church. In the Cumberland region of Tennessee, partly as a result of the rapid growth which issued from the revivals, a presbytery was formed in 1802. Its members came to believe that the high educational standards required by the Presbyterian Church for training for the ministry were unsuited to the frontier and also dissented from the doctrine of predestination as held by that church. This led the Synod of Kentucky to order the presbytery dissolved. Appeal was taken to the General Assembly, but in vain, and in 1810 three members of the Cumberland Presbytery constituted themselves an independent body. Numbers grew rapidly and methods were adopted, including that of circuit riders, suited to the needs of the frontier.

The revivals combined with other movements to bring changes in Congregationalism. As we have seen, Congregationalism was the prevailing form of Christianity in New England. Confined almost entirely to that region, with some overflow into Presbyterianism in New York and New Jersey, in 1776 it had more than a third of all the ministers and congregations of the nascent nation, far outdistancing any of the others. By long tradition believing in gathered churches made up of members who could relate an experience of conversion, Congregationalists were deeply stirred by the Great Awakening and the renewal of that awakening which began in the 1790's. They stressed an educated clergy and some of the clergy as well as the laity were affected by the Arminianism, Socinianism, and rationalism which enjoyed a vogue across the Atlantic. Subscribing officially as they did to the Westminster Confession and to doctrines contained in it, including that of predestination and election, Congregationalists committed to the revivals were forced to seek to reconcile their doctrines with the preaching which urged men to repent. These currents and counter-currents led to divisions and changes in theology.

In and around Boston, partly in opposition to the theory and methods of the revivals, partly from contacts with movements in England, there was a trend towards Arminianism and Socinianism. Charles Chauncy (1705–1787), pastor of the influential and staid First Church of Boston, and Jonathan Mayhew (1720–1766) were among its leaders. In the 1780's King's Chapel, Boston, the oldest congregation of the Church of England in New England, officially abandoned belief in the Trinity. In 1800 a schism over "liberalism" took place in the church in Plymouth. In 1805 a man of known anti-Trinitarian views was chosen to the professorship of divinity in Harvard. In protest, those who held to Trinitarian convictions founded (1808) Andover Theological Seminary for the training of ministers. In his pulpit in Boston and in his writings, William Ellery Channing (1780–1842), out of deep, painful struggle of soul, became a saintly, persuasive exponent of Arian or Socinian views. In 1815 he accepted the name Unitarian for the movement. It was in 1818 that the main division began in the Congregational churches. In most cases the Unitarians won possession of the church property and the Trinitarians withdrew and formed new churches. In 1825 the American Unitarian Association was organized. Unitarians never constituted more than a minority of the population, but because of their ability, wealth, and education they exercised an influence far out of proportion to their numbers.

In the second half of the eighteenth century those who repudiated the doctrine of election and believed that God would find a way ultimately to save all began to raise their voices, especially in New England and in part as a result of the revivals. The most influential leader was Hosea Ballou (1771–1852), long a pastor in Boston and of Arian views. In 1790 the Universalists, as he and those of like mind were called, held a convention in Philadelphia and in 1793 organized a convention in New England which in 1803 adopted a creed that long remained the basis of the Universalist churches of the United States.

As we have suggested, those committed to the revivals were constrained to seek so to rethink their inherited belief in predestination as to make room for their preaching. Jonathan Edwards, to whom we have already referred, led the way. Others followed. Among them were Joseph Bellamy (1719–1790), Samuel Hopkins (1721–1803), Jonathan Edwards the younger (1745–1801), and a nephew of the latter and a grandson of the elder Jonathan Edwards, Timothy Dwight (1752–1817), President of Yale. Especially influential were Timothy Dwight, who by his force of character and preaching moulded several student generations at Yale and made that institution a centre from which issued clergymen who carried the views for which he stood to many parts of the country and of the world, and his older contemporary, Samuel Hopkins, whose writings set the standard for what was known as Hopkinsianism. Hopkinsianism was particularly potent in the Second Awakening. These men did not completely agree among themselves. Yet they all believed in conversion. In general they taught that this side of the grave no one could be sure that he was among the elect. They declared that all should submit unconditionally to the will of God, even to the extent of being reconciled to being among those whom God had not chosen for salvation. Hopkins made much of the phrase "disinterested benevolence," by which was meant living and labouring for the love of God and men with no thought of reward, no concern as to whether this would bring happiness to oneself in this world or the world to come. Indeed, one was to be willing to be damned, should that in His inscrutable wisdom be held by God to make for His glory. Under the influence of this theology, candidates for the Congregational ministry were often asked as a test of their fitness: "Are you willing to be damned for the glory of God?" Common to many was also what was known as the "governmental" theory of the atonement, that Christ's death was a satisfaction of "general justice" rather than of the specific sins of a particular individual. In general they agreed with the elder Jonathan Edwards that while all men have the natural ability to repent and turn to God in faith, they do not have the moral ability to do so. Some reacted vigorously against these views. For instance, William Ellery Channing was reared under the preaching of Hopkins and Universalism had its main stronghold in New England.

We must pause to note that the Friends, who had had a large share in the settlement of Pennsylvania, New Jersey, and Rhode Island, continued. Always a minority, they remained so. Out of them came notable contributions. Famous as a work of devotion, valued not only among the Quakers, was the *Journal* of John Woolman (1720–1772), begun in 1756 and interrupted only by his death.

THE ACCENTUATION OF THE DISTINCTIVE CHARACTER OF THE CHRISTIANITY OF THE UNITED STATES

The developments between 1750 and 1815 helped to strengthen features present in the colonial period and to add others which made the Christianity of the United States different from that of the Old World of Europe and from anything which had thus far appeared elsewhere, even in the Americas. It was clearly continuous with historic Christianity, but it was also distinctive. It was of major importance because of the increasing place which it was to have in the total Christianity of the world, both in its numerical strength and in its growing part in the spread of Christianity.

In 1815 the Christianity of the United States, like that of the Thirteen Colonies, was still overwhelmingly Protestant. The great Roman Catholic immigration of the nineteenth century had not yet begun. Even more than in the Thirteen Colonies, it was showing a marked variety. To the denominations brought from Europe, several were being added. Some were divisions from the old and others were quite new. Still more than in colonial days, the Christianity of the United States represented the extreme wing of Protestantism. To the Congregationalists, the largest body in 1750, and the Quakers were added the rapid growth of the Baptists, a body only feebly represented in that year, the Methodists, now fully separated from the Church of England, and the several kinds of Christians or Disciples of Christ.

The trend, already present in a few of the Colonies, towards placing all churches in a position of legal equality and not giving financial support to any through taxation, was continued. The first amendment to the Constitution of the United States, adopted in 1791, forbade Congress to make any "law respecting an establishment of religion or prohibiting the free exercise thereof." There was no prohibition of such action by individual states, but the traces of that privileged position which existed in 1750 disappeared fairly rapidly. This did not mean that the government, either of the nation or of individual states, was anti-Christian or purely secular. The armed forces and both houses of Congress had chaplains. In many of the schools maintained by the state the reading of Scripture and the Lord's Prayer were required. Presidents took the oath of office on the Bible. Although feeling against Roman Catholics was strong, no one church was given a favoured position. This was quite different from the situation in any country in Europe in 1750. By 1815, under the influence of the French Revolution, a somewhat similar situation was beginning to appear across the Atlantic, but due far more to a religiously sceptical spirit than in the United States. In the nineteenth and twentieth centuries, as we are to see, the pattern was to spread to much of the world.

Another feature, present before 1750 but now accentuated, was upon "evangelism," the seeking to win every individual to allegiance to Christ. From the standpoint of the churches this was especially important in view of the fact that there was no legal requirement of membership and that a large majority of the population were not formally connected with any church and were in danger of being de-Christianized. In such bodies as the Congregationalists, Baptists, Methodists, and most Presbyterians, in other words those comprising the large majority of the church members of the country, personal conversion was stressed. This was not so general among Episcopalians and Lutherans, but except in some communities these churches were in the small minority.

The emphasis on individual decision and conversion led to a modification of the Augustinian, Reformed theology which usually went by the name of Calvinism and which was the heritage of most of the churches and was contained in the official statements of the faith of several of them. Some churches quite abandoned as much of that theology as taught the divine election of specific individuals to salvation. In practice, most but not all of the others tended to ignore it.

There was also a trend in some denominations, in part the heritage from the Quakers and the founders of New England, to seek to make all society conform to Christian standards. After 1815 this was to issue in many reform movements. Some of these, indeed, notably against Negro slavery and for temperance in the use of alcoholic beverages, began before that year.

In several denominations modifications were made in what had been inherited from Europe. Thus in the Protestant Episcopal Church the name itself was significant, stressing the Protestant element and ignoring the national character of the Church of England: the lay element was given prominence and there were no archbishops, only a presiding bishop. In the Lutheran bodies, under the influence of Muhlenberg, who lived on well into this period (he reached Philadelphia in 1742 and died in 1787), a congregational form of government was adopted in which officers were chosen by the local congregation and the ministers were organized into synods.

The Beginning of the World Outreach of the Protestantism of the United States

By 1815 the Protestantism of the United States was reaching outside the borders of the country and propagating its faith in other lands. This began slightly later than in the British Isles and did not soon reach the dimensions that it attained in the mother country. Late in the nineteenth and in the twentieth century, however, it was to supply the majority of the funds and the personnel of Protestant foreign missions.

The revivals of the eighteenth century stimulated a marked accentuation of missionary activity. This showed itself in increased efforts to win the Indians to the Christian faith. In a few states missionary societies were formed, partly for missions among the Indians. In 1801 the Congregationalists of Connecticut began a plan of union with the Presbyterian General Assembly which spread to other Congregational churches for joint effort in planting Christianity on the westward-moving frontier. In some circles there was much interest in what was being done in Britain through the Baptist Missionary Society and the London Missionary Society. The Moravians were active in missions to the Indians and in 1787 reorganized their Society for Propagating the Gospel among the Heathen.

The most notable pioneer undertaking was the American Board of Commissioners for Foreign Missions. It was organized in 1810 by the Congregationalists of New England in response to an appeal by students of the recently founded Andover Theological Seminary. The leader of the student group was Samuel John Mills (1783–1818), spiritually a child of the Second Awakening. While an undergraduate in Williams College he had taken the initiative in the formation of the Society of the Brethren, whose purpose it was "to effect in the persons of its members a mission or missions to the heathen." The American Board of Commissioners for Foreign Missions long attracted the support not only of Congregationalists but also of Christians of other denominations, especially the Presbyterians. In 1812 it appointed its first contingent of missionaries, with Asia as their goal. After they left the United States three of the appointees, Adoniram Judson and his wife and Luther Rice, felt constrained by their consciences to become Baptists, resigned from the society which sent them, and asked support of the American Baptists. The latter rose to the occasion and so began their enterprise abroad. The Judsons inaugurated a continuing mission in Burma and those who remained with the parent society obtained access to India. Rice returned to the United States to arouse the Baptist churches to rally to the Judsons and to missions. This he did with marked success.

THE PROTESTANT REVIVAL ON THE CONTINENT OF EUROPE

The awakening in Protestantism was chiefly in the British Isles and the United States but it was by no means confined to these countries. It was also marked on the Continent of Europe. There it was a continuation of Pietism and the Moravians and was reinforced with repercussions from the awakenings in Great Britain. It was in large part a reaction against the cold rationalism of the Enlightenment which had gripped a large proportion of the pulpits. As in the British Isles and the United States, it gave rise to undertakings to bring about the conversion of nominal Christians within Christendom and to spread the Gospel throughout the world. We can take the time to point out only a few of its outstanding examples.

In 1797 there was organized in the Netherlands, partly on the model of the London Missionary Society, the Netherlands Missionary Society (Nederlandsche Zendelinggenootschap). It had its immediate rise through John Theodore Vanderkemp who by a devious and tragic route had come from the life of a dissolute army officer to a warm Christian experience. In 1800 Johann Jänicke, a pastor in Berlin of Moravian descent and with Moravian and Pietist contacts, founded a school to train youths for service as missionaries. He received financial aid from England and like-minded circles in Germany. Most of those whom he prepared were German Pietists and served under the London Missionary Society, the Church Missionary Society, and the Netherlands Missionary Society. In the second half of the eighteenth century several groups arose in Germany and Switzerland largely from Pietist sources to pray and labour for a revival. One of their fruits was the founding of a school at Basel (1815) which trained missionaries. As with the products of Jänicke's institution, most of the early Basel graduates served under British societies. Not until 1822 did Basel develop an organization to send out and support its men. In Germany a mounting tide of Pietism profoundly affected that and other countries and after 1815 gave rise to several movements and societies to win other Germans and to carry the Gospel to other lands.

In a poverty-stricken community in the Vosges Mountains John Frederic Oberlin (1740–1826) devoted himself through a long ministry to the spiritual, moral, and material transformation of his parish. He built roads, founded what are said to have been the first of the "infant schools," and pioneered in the application of scientific agriculture. He became famous for that combination of individual and group transformation which is found along much of the course of the history of Christianity.

Norway was the scene of the beginning of a notable awakening which had as its initial leader Hans Nielsen Hauge (1771–1824). From a deeply religious family, Hauge was led by a serious accident when a boy and by much reading of the Bible to undertake preaching. Although unordained, in six years he travelled about ten thousand miles, preaching nearly every day, proclaiming the need and the possibility of a warm personal Christian experience. This was in contrast with the cold rationalism which prevailed among most of the clergy, for here as elsewhere in Scandinavia the Lutheran state church, from which there was almost no dissent, was strongly impregnated with currents from the Germany of the *Aufklärung*. He denounced the dead orthodoxy and inconsistent lives of the pastors, wrote hundreds of books and tracts, and taught his followers to be preachers and to build mills and factories to help them to a better economic status. In 1804, after less than a decade, Hauge was arrested for preaching as a layman. For about ten years, until 1814, he was incarcerated. When at last, through the importunities of his friends, he was released, he was a broken man. However, the movement which he had encouraged continued in groups and individuals called by his name. They did not break with the state church, but they had lay preachers, stressed conversion, and were known as *Leser* because of their diligence in teaching and reading the Scriptures. They were mostly from the farmers and represented a revolt against the aristocracy, a class which included the pastors.

A figure which emerged in Scandinavia from Protestantism but which was much further removed than Hauge from the usual forms of Christianity was Emanuel Swedenborg (1688–1772). The son of a professor of theology and bishop in the Church of Sweden who had been suspected of heresy for stressing faith, love, and communion with God above dogma, he travelled widely in Western Europe and had a broad range of learning and a mind of marked originality, especially in the natural sciences and engineering. He wrote voluminously. Late in middle life he gave himself fully to religion and to an intensive study of the Scriptures. He had visions and dreams through which he was convinced that fresh revelations had come to him from Christ. Although he did not attempt to organize a religious body, he believed himself commissioned to teach of the New Church and from his writings there arose a widely spread but numerically small body, the Church of the New Jerusalem. His writings had an influence on such diverse men as Kant, Goethe, and Russian churchmen.

INTELLECTUAL CURRENTS IN PROTESTANTISM IN GERMANY

While these awakenings, largely Evangelical and of what in the broad sense of the term could be called Pietistic were occurring among minorities across the length and breadth of Protestantism, another set of movements was in progress. They were present in several countries but were most marked in Germany. They were largely intellectual. They were not confined to religion but were seen in a wide range of cultural activity, in Germany notably in philosophy, literature, and music. Becoming entrenched in the universities of Germany and growing in the nineteenth century, they were to make of these institutions centres to which students were to flock from much of the Occident, especially from Scandinavia, Great Britain, and the United States.

By 1815 these movements were only in their beginnings, but already they were showing the direction which they were to take in their heyday. They were to have a profound effect upon Christianity, particularly upon Protestantism, and in every land where Protestantism was found. In general Evangelicals and Pietists were to regard them and their effect upon Christianity with suspicion and even hostility, but like the Evangelical movement they were to overpass existing denominational and ecclesiastical boundaries and were to have wide repercussions which were not confined to Protestantism but which were to have a greater or less effect upon most of the other branches of the faith. In the end they were to be rejected by the Roman Catholic Church and did not make major inroads on it or on the Eastern Churches. Yet they constituted one of the most potent combinations of movements which Christianity had thus far known. They embodied what was called the scientific and rationalistic approach to the study of the Scriptures and the history of Christianity and applied to theology the results both of these studies and of current philosophy. Arising largely from the currents out of which issued Deism and the Enlightenment, they were not confined to them.

We can here do little more than list the names of a few of the outstanding scholars who shared in these movements before 1815, with some slight indication of the contributions of each. Johann Lorentz von Mosheim (1694–1755), successively professor at Helmstädt and Göttingen, in his *Institutiones Historiæ Ecclesiasticæ* (1726, revised edition 1755) wrote a comprehensive history of the Christian Church in which he attempted to be purely objective and factual rather than controversial. He thus inaugurated a new era in the study of the history of Christianity. Jean Astruc (1684–1766), professor of medicine at Paris, and Johann Gottfried Eichhorn (1752–1827), professor of Oriental languages at Jena and Göttingen, who wrote extensively on the Old and New Testaments and has been called the founder of Old Testament criticism, held that there are distinct documents in Genesis, a view which was later accepted as axiomatic by scholars who applied to the Bible the methods of historical criticism. Jean le Clerc (1657–1736), reared in Geneva, later an Arminian in Amsterdam, endeavoured to find the actual meaning of the words and passages of the Bible rather than to seek in the Scriptures texts to prove preconceived doctrines. Somewhat similarly Johann Albrecht Bengel (1687–1752), a Pietist of Württemberg whose commentary, *Gnomon Novi Testamenti* (1742), was used by John Wesley in preparing his *Notes on the New Testament* (1755), worked on the conviction that in attempts to understand the Bible nothing should either be omitted from or read into the Biblical text, but that the meaning should be sought through the strict application of grammatical principles. His contemporary, Johann Jakob Wettstein (1693–1754), out of a lifetime of study produced a work giving the various readings of the text of the New Testament, thus furthering the effort to establish the original forms of the writings of that fundamental document of the Christian faith. Johann August Ernesti (1707–1781) of Leipzig, eventually professor of theology in that university, vigorously anti-Roman Catholic, a distinguished student of the Greek and Latin classics, approached the New Testament with the same criteria that he applied to non-Christian writings. Reimarus, whom we have already met, brought to the New Testament records of the life of Christ the principles which he would employ in the study of the biography of any historical figure. In doing so he ruled out the supernatural and miraculous, for, like all historians, he could not achieve complete objectivity but came to his task with either conscious or unconscious presuppositions, but he stimulated further studies of Jesus. Johann Salomo Semler (1725–1791), educated in Halle and for nearly forty years professor of theology there, was a leader in the rationalistic trend which cooled the ardour of that centre of Pietism. He believed in revelation and held that it is to be found in the Bible, but that not everything in the Bible is revelation, that not all parts of the Scriptures are of equal value, and that while the Bible contains permanent truths, they are conditioned by the circumstances in which the various books were written. He declared that a difference existed between the Pauline and Jewish types of Christianity and prepared the way for the kind of study of the Scriptures and theology which in the nineteenth century had a major development at Tübingen. Johann Gottfried von Herder (1744–1803), preacher, writer, child and stimulator of the romantic movement, and friend of Goethe, maintained that the various books of the Bible can be understood only in the light of the views and feelings of the environment and times in which they were written.

Why rationalism and romanticism should have acquired these particular religious aspects in the Protestant areas of Germany is not entirely clear. It may have been for reasons akin to those which about three centuries earlier had directed humanism in Germany into religious channels. It is clear that the German soul and mind had been ploughed deep by the Reformation and that when confronted by the new movements of the mind and the spirit represented by rationalism and romanticism, many Germans sought to relate them to their inherited religious faith. By no means all German Protestants, then or later, accepted the methods or the conclusions of these new trends. Yet the latter were strong in the universities in which the intellectuals, including many of the clergy, were trained.

A figure who must have two or three paragraphs to himself is Immanuel Kant (1724–1804). While he was a philosopher rather than a theologian, Kant had so profound an influence on theology as well as philosophy, and especially on Protestant theology, that he must be given special attention. He was born and spent his life in Königsberg, a strong Pietist centre in East Prussia. At first he seemed designed for the ministry and is said to have preached a few times. But it was to philosophy and to teaching and writing that he gave his life. Refusing offers to go elsewhere, he remained in his native city and eventually, when he was in his middle fifties, a professorship in the local university was given him. He had a wide range of intellectual interests. Early he majored in the Greek and Roman classics, then in mathematics and physics, and his chair was one of logic and metaphysics. With some areas of knowledge he was not particularly concerned, but he read widely, keeping abreast of new books. In philosophy he was not much impressed by Descartes and those who followed him, but Locke and Leibnitz influenced him and he knew and was critical of the work of his older contemporary, Wolff. Frail, short of stature, slight, with a concave chest and a deformed right shoulder, he held to a rigid physical discipline and until his later years did not know serious illness. He never married. He matured slowly and it was not until 1781, when he was in his later fifties, that the first work which brought him fame was published, *The Critique of Pure Reason,* and its second and enlarged edition did not appear until 1787, when he was in his early sixties. The book quickly attracted excited attention in the German universities and eventually won a wide hearing in other countries. Dealing drastically as it did with the scope and limitations of reason, in which the intellectuals of eighteenth century Western Europe placed their confidence, it was very timely. Kant's other important works were his *Critique of Practical Reason* and his *Critique of Judgement.*

Kant's views aroused a storm of criticism in conservative Protestant circles. They, and the fear that he might be on the side of the French Revolution, led the government of Prussia to exact a promise from him, in the 1790's, that he would not lecture or write on religion. With this he complied, but regarded the death of King Frederick William II (1797) as releasing him from that obligation. By that time his mental and physical powers were beginning to show symptoms of the decay that enfeebled his later years. Although of high moral character, exemplifying the exacting standards which he set forth in his treatment of ethics, he disturbed the orthodox by his religious convictions and their implications.

Yet Kant was by no means anti-Christian. To be sure, his *Critique of Pure Reason* undercut the grounds which Deists, notably the then popular Wolff, gave for a belief in the existence of God. Kant maintained that the knowledge which comes to us through our minds and reason is compounded of two elements, what enters from without, through our senses, and the interpretation given by our minds. That interpretation is governed by the laws of our intellect. This means that we cannot know things in themselves, but only what our minds transmit to us from without. If this is true, through reason alone, or "pure reason," we can never, as Wolff and other Deists who depended on it claimed, demonstrate the exact nature of the universe or of God as they actually are. Kant dealt ruthlessly with the traditional arguments for the existence of God.

However, in his *Critique of the Practical Reason* Kant declared that in addition to his reason man is aware of a feeling of moral obligation and is confronted by the "categorical imperative," an unconditional and unqualified command. This awareness of moral obligation, so Kant maintained, is the highest quality of man. If he obeys the categorical imperative, Kant said, each man will live in such fashion that the principles on which he acts can become those on which all men should act. It followed, Kant was convinced, that man can obey the categorical imperative and is, therefore, free; that man must be immortal, for only thus can he live long enough fully to respond to the categorical imperative; and that God must exist, for only He can make happiness the outcome of virtue. In his *Religion within the Limits of Unaided Reason*, which appeared in 1793, six years after his *Critique of Pure Reason*, Kant went on to say that any man governed by obedience to the categorical imperative is pleasing to God and is a son of God. He believed Jesus Christ to have been the highest example of that obedience and therefore of that sonship, that the visible Church should be a fellowship for mutual stimulus to that obedience, and that there is an invisible Church made up of all the obedient.

While his effect was great during his lifetime, since he was late in maturing and died in 1804 it was not until after 1815 that Kant had his greatest influence upon Christian thought.

SUMMARY

In the brief but important period between 1750 and 1815 the situation in respect to Christianity became increasingly complex and more patently paradoxical.

Always the course of Christianity had been marked by seeming contradictions. At the very outset there had been the apparent impotence of a Nazarene carpenter-preacher-healer pitted against the established order in the Jewish combination of Pharisees and Sadducees and in the Roman state, to the casual observer a powerlessness confirmed by what looked like its end in futility on a cross. The proclamation by Jesus of the kingdom of God and of the impossibly high standards of members of that kingdom seemed to be the most fantastic of dreams. Yet within five centuries the overwhelming majority of the population of the Roman Empire had given at least nominal allegiance to that Nazarene as the unique Son of God. For the majority that professed adherence was contradicted by lives at variance with the ideals set forth by Jesus. But, on the other hand, at least a minority were haunted by those ideals and were giving evidence of the new life of which Jesus had spoken. In a civilization which had ceased to do or to say much that was new they had created the Christian Church, Christian worship, and Christian theology, the latter daring and universe-embracing in its affirmations.

There followed almost five centuries in which it seemed that Christianity was dying. Christianity failed to save the Roman Empire and about half of what had been Christendom was overrun by the followers of a later, more warlike, and seemingly more practical prophet. Then Christianity surged forward, having held about half the area which had been the Roman Empire, won the avowed loyalty of the pagan barbarians who from the North and East had seized upon that part of the Empire, and pressed out into Central and Eastern Asia.

The life of the Christendom of what we call the Middle Ages, sometimes in retrospect viewed nostalgically by later generations as the age of faith, also presented striking contrasts. All but a very few in that Christendom called themselves Christians. But the perfidy and self-seeking of the Byzantines, the chronic wars of the Byzantine realm and of Western Europeans, the pride, the sexual irregularities, the lust for power, and the callous cruelty, even in the Church, practical denials of the faith, were all the more starkly set forth because of the continuing challenge of Christ and the fashion in which a minority responded to it in monastic and other movements, in art, literature, and thought, and in attempts to lift society to "the high calling of God in Christ Jesus."

There followed, after 1350, a thinly veiled recrudescence of paganism, partly stimulated by the very success of Christianity and paying lip-service to it. This was paralleled by fresh advances of the followers of the Arab prophet and corruption in the strongest of the churches which posed as the guardian of the Christian heritage.

When the night was at its blackest streaks of a coming dawn were visible which heralded a new day in what was called the Reformation. Yet in the centuries of the Reformation there was much which contradicted the Christian faith in the individual and group performance of its professed adherents and by 1750 the revived paganism of the Renaissance had been followed by what was a more nearly open repudiation of the faith by intellectuals and the ruling classes than had yet been seen in lands which bore the Christian name.

In the second half of the eighteenth century a culmination of movements appeared to be sounding the death knell of the faith. The Spaniards and Portuguese, recently the most active in the geographic propagation of the faith, were declining, the climate of opinion favoured Deism, which ruled out as irrational some of the distinctive convictions of Christianity, a scarcely less Christ-denying romanticism was making headway, and the revolutions spearheaded by that of France, committed to Deism and on its extreme front blatantly anti-Christian, seemed to be the wave of the future. Naked power in the form of Napoleon sought to tie the Church to its chariot wheels. There were intelligent and apparently well informed men who seriously believed that Christianity would not outlast another century. Yet in the very years of what looked like the triumph of these forces, life was breaking out again in Christianity. It was still among minorities, but these were in peoples who in the following century were to show the most spectacular growth and were to shape much of mankind.

After 1815 contradictions were to be intensified. On the one hand were movements which appeared to make certain the demise of Christianity. On the other were pulsing tides of life which planted Christian communities over practically all the inhabited globe and which made themselves felt in all cultures. From one angle, never had the prospect for Christianity seemed so grim. From another, never had the faith been so widely spread or exerted such extensive effects on mankind.

SELECTED BIBLIOGRAPHY

GENERAL SURVEY

H. Hermelink, *Das Christentum in der Menschheitsgeschichte von der französischen Revolution bis zur Gegenwart.* Vol. I, 1789–1835 (Tübingen and Stuttgart, J. B. Metztersche Verlagsbuchhandlung and Hermann Leins, 1951, pp. xix, 528). Chiefly on Germany and France.

MOVEMENTS ADVERSE TO CHRISTIANITY

A. Aulard, *Christianity and the French Revolution,* translated by Lady Frazer (London, Ernest Benn, 1927, pp. 164). Carries the story through 1802.

C. L. Becker, *The Heavenly City of the Eighteenth-Century Philosophers* (Yale University Press, 1932, pp. 168). By a thorough-going sceptic, but showing the contribution of Christianity to the conceptions of the intellectuals whose ideas shaped the French Revolution.

H. N. Brailsford, *Voltaire* (New York, Henry Holt and Co., 1935, pp. 256). In the *Home University Library.*

The Cambridge Modern History, Vol. VIII, *The French Revolution,* Vol. IX, *Napoleon* (Cambridge University Press, 1904, 1906). A standard work by various authors.

J. Y. T. Greig, *David Hume* (Oxford University Press, preface 1931, pp. 436). By an expert.

W. H. Jervis, *The Gallican Church and the Revolution* (London, Kegan Paul, Trench, Trübner & Co., 1882, pp. xxiii, 524). Carefully done, by an Anglican; carries the story through Napoleon; favourable to the Pope.

J. Leflom, *La Crise Révolutionnaire, 1789–1846* (Paris, Bloud & Gay, 1949, pp. 524). By a Roman Catholic scholar.

H. M. Morais, *Deism in Eighteenth Century America* (Columbia University Press, 1934, pp. 203). A competent survey.

John Viscount Morley, *Rousseau and His Era* (London, Macmillan & Co., 2 vols., 1923. First published 1873, revised by the author 1921).

John Viscount Morley, *Voltaire* (London, Macmillan & Co., 1923, pp. xiii, 365. First published 1872, revised 1921).

J. W. Oman, *The Problem of Faith and Freedom in the Last Two Centuries* (New York, A. C. Armstrong and Son, 1906, pp. xxiv, 443). Less than half on the pre-nineteenth century period.

J. Orr, *English Deism, Its Roots and Its Fruits* (Grand Rapids, Wm. B. Eerdmans Publishing Co., 1934, pp. 289). A comprehensive survey.

The Confessions of Jean Jacques Rousseau (New York, Random House, 1945, pp. xviii, 683).

L. Stephen, *History of English Thought in the Eighteenth Century* (New York, J. P. Putnam's Sons, 2 vols., 1876). Long a standard work.

N. Sykes, *Church and State in England in the XVIIIth Century* (Cambridge University Press, 1934, pp. xi, 455). Thorough and competent. Gives a more favourable view of the Church of England than is sometimes done.

N. L. Torrey, *Voltaire and the English Deists* (Yale University Press, 1930, pp. x, 224).

B. Willey, *The Eighteenth Century Background. Studies in the Idea of Nature in the Thought of the Period* (London, Chatto & Windus, 1940, pp. viii, 302). An excellent survey, confined to British thought.

THE BEGINNINGS OF REVIVAL IN THE ROMAN CATHOLIC CHURCH

P. Guilday, *The Life and Times of John Carroll Archbishop of Baltimore (1735–1815)* (New York, The Encyclopedia Press, 1922, pp. xiv, 864). A standard biography.

T. Maynard, *The Story of American Catholicism* (New York, The Macmillan Co., 1941, pp. xv, 694). Sympathetic, readable, by a Roman Catholic.

C. S. Phillips, *The Church in France, 1789–1848: A Study in Revival* (London, A. R. Mowbray & Co., 1929, pp. viii, 315). Sympathetic.

SIGNS OF LIFE IN THE EASTERN CHURCHES

S. Bolshakoff, *Russian Nonconformity* (Philadelphia, The Westminster Press, 1950, pp. 192). A comprehensive survey.

F. C. Conybeare, *Russian Dissenters* (Harvard University Press, 1921, pp. x, 370). Based on standard Russian secondary accounts.

W. H. Frere, *Some Links in the Chain of Russian Church History* (London, Faith Press, 1918, pp. xvii, 200). By a competent scholar, a high Anglican.

N. Gorodetzky, *Saint Tikhon Zadonsky, Inspirer of Dostoevsky* (London, Society for Promoting Christian Knowledge, 1951, pp. xii, 249). Based upon extensive research. Well done.

E. J. Knapton, *The Lady of the Holy Alliance. The Life of Julie de Krüdener* (Columbia University Press, 1939, pp. xiii, 262). Well written, based on extensive research.

THE RISE OF METHODISM

A. D. Belden, *George Whitefield—the Awakener. A Modern Study of the Evangelical Revival* (New York and Nashville, Abingdon-Cokesbury Press, 1930, pp. xvii, 302). Warmly sympathetic, based on earlier biographies.

J. W. Bready, *England: Before and After Wesley: The Evangelical Revival and Social Reform* (London, Hodder & Stoughton, 1938, pp. 463). Based on solid research, stressing the change wrought by Wesley.

W. A. Candler, *Life of Thomas Coke* (New York and Nashville, Abingdon-Cokesbury Press, 1923, pp. vi, 408). Very favourable to Coke.

L. F. Church, *The Early Methodist People* (London, The Epworth Press, 1948, pp, viii, 286). Sympathetic, based on careful research.

L. F. Church, *More about the Early Methodist People* (London, The Epworth Press, 1949, pp. xviii, 324).

The Journal of the Rev. John Wesley, A.M., edited by N. Curnock (London, The Epworth Press, 8 vols., 1938). The standard edition.

The Letters of the Rev. John Wesley, A.M., edited by J. Telford (London, The Epworth Press, 8 vols., 1931). The standard edition.

F. J. McConnell, *John Wesley* (New York and Nashville, Abingdon-Cokesbury Press, 1939, pp. 355). A brilliant and remarkably objective appraisal by a distinguished Methodist bishop.

THE BRITISH REVIVAL OUTSIDE OF METHODISM

Memoirs of the Life of the Rev. Charles Simeon, M.A., . . . with a Selection from His Writings and Correspondence, edited by W. Carus (London, J. Hatchard & Son, 2d ed., 1847, pp. xxx, 848).

THE OUTREACH OF THE BRITISH REVIVAL

W. Canton, *A History of the British and Foreign Bible Society* (London, John Murray, 5 vols., 1904–1910). An official history.

S. P. Carey, *William Carey, D.D., Fellow of Linnæan Society* (New York, George H. Doran Co., preface 1923, pp. xvi, 428). By a great-grandson; a standard biography.

R. Coupland, *Wilberforce, A Narrative* (Oxford, The Clarendon Press, 1923, pp. vi, 528).

J. Field, *The Life of John Howard* (London, Longmans, Green & Co., 1850, pp. xvi, 495).

R. Lovett, *The History of the London Missionary Society, 1795–1895* (London, Henry Frowde, 2 vols., 1899).

E. Stock, *The History of the Church Missionary Society* (London, Church Missionary Society, 4 vols., 1899–1916). An official history.

THE REVIVAL IN THE UNITED STATES

J. H. Allen and R. Eddy, *A History of the Unitarians and the Universalists* (New York, The Christian Literature Co., 1894, pp. ix, 506). One of the *American Church History Series*.

The Heart of Asbury's Journal, edited by E. S. Tipple (New York, Eaton and Mains, 1904, pp. xii, 712).

G. N. Boardman, *A History of New England Theology* (New York, A. D. F. Randolph Co., 1899, pp. 314). A comprehensive survey.

J. M. Buckley, *A History of Methodists in the United States* (New York, Charles Scribner's Sons, 1903, pp. xix, 714).

J. W. Chadwick, *William Ellery Channing, Minister of Religion* (Boston, Houghton Mifflin Co., 1903, pp. xiv, 463). A sympathetic biography.

C. C. Cleveland, *The Great Revival in the West, 1797–1805* (The University of Chicago Press, 1916, pp. xii, 215). Carefully done.

F. H. Foster, *A Genetic History of New England Theology* (The University of Chicago Press, 1907, pp. xv, 568). Critical, but in places sympathetic.

R. V. Foster, *A Sketch of the History of the Cumberland Presbyterian Church* (New York, The Christian Literature Co., 1894, pp. 258–509). In *The American Church History Series*.

W. E. Garrison, *Religion Follows the Frontier. A History of the Disciples of Christ* (New York, Harper & Brothers, 1931, pp. xvi, 317). Readable, scholarly.

W. M. Gewehr, *The Great Awakening in Virginia, 1740–1790* (Duke University Press, 1930, pp. viii, 292). Scholarly, well documented.

E. F. Humphrey, *Nationalism and Religion in America, 1774–1789* (Boston, Chipman Law Publishing Co., 1924, pp. viii, 536). Competent, comprehensive.

C. R. Keller, *The Second Great Awakening in Connecticut* (Yale University Press, 1942, pp. ix, 275). Scholarly.

W. W. Manross, *A History of the American Episcopal Church* (New York, Morehouse-Gorham, Inc., 1935, pp. xvi, 404). A competent comprehensive survey.

B. W. Stone, *The Biography of Eld. Barton Warren Stone, Written by Himself: with Additions and Reflections by Elder John Rogers* (Cincinnati, J. A. and U. P. James, 1847, pp. ix, 404).

L. J. Trinterud, *The Forming of an American Tradition. A Re-examination of Colonial Presbyterianism* (Philadelphia, The Westminster Press, 1949, pp. 352). About half of this excellent book is on the post-1750 years.

R. G. Torbet, *A History of the Baptists* (Philadelphia, The Judson Press, 1950, pp. 538). A comprehensive, competent survey, with valuable footnotes and bibliographical references to the literature and the sources.

C. W. Ware, *Barton Warren Stone, Pathfinder of Christian Union. A Story of*

His Life and Times (St. Louis, The Bethany Press, 1932, pp. xiv, 357). Based largely upon printed sources.

L. A. Weigle, *American Idealism* (Yale University Press, 1928, pp. 356). A competent survey, with running commentaries on pertinent illustrations, of the religious history of the United States.

THE BEGINNING OF THE WORLD OUTREACH OF THE PROTESTANTISM
OF THE UNITED STATES

T. C. Richards, *Samuel J. Mills* (Boston, The Pilgrim Press, 1906, pp. 275).

S. Warburton, *Eastward! The Story of Adoniram Judson* (New York, Round Table Press, 1937, pp. xi, 240). Very carefully done.

THE PROTESTANT REVIVAL ON THE CONTINENT OF EUROPE

M. Dawson, *Oberlin. A Protestant Saint* (New York, Harper & Brothers, 1934, pp. ix, 166).

W. Schlatter, *Geschichte der Basler Mission, 1815–1915* (Basel, Basler Missionsbuchhandlung, 3 vols., 1916). Based especially on unpublished sources.

Swedenborg's Works, Rutch edition (Boston, Houghton Mifflin Co., 32 vols., no date).

G. Warneck, *Abriss einer Geschichte den protestantischen Missionen von den Reformation bis auf die Gegenwart mit einem Anhang über die katholischen Missionen* (Berlin, Martin Warneck, 10th ed., 1913, pp. x, 624). A standard survey.

INTELLECTUAL CURRENTS IN PROTESTANTISM IN GERMANY

E. Caird, *The Critical Philosophy of Immanuel Kant* (Glasgow, James Maclehose and Sons, 2d ed., 2 vols., 1909). A comprehensive treatment of Kant by an eminent British philosopher.

Immanuel Kant's Critique of Pure Reason, translated by F. M. Müller (New York, The Macmillan Co., 2d ed., 1907, pp. lxxix, 808).

Immanuel Kant, *Critique of Practical Reason and Other Writings on Moral Philosophy,* translated by L. W. Beck (The University of Chicago Press, 1949, pp. xv, 370).

Kant's *Critique of Judgment,* translated by J. H. Bernard (London, Macmillan & Co., 1931, pp. xlviii, 429).

THE GREAT CENTURY:
GROWING REPUDIATION PARALLELED
BY ABOUNDING VITALITY
AND UNPRECEDENTED EXPANSION
A.D. 1815 — A.D. 1914

THE GREAT CENTURY:
GROWING REPUDIATION PARALLELED
BY ABOUNDING VITALITY
AND UNPRECEDENTED EXPANSION
A.D. 1815—A.D. 1914

Chapter XLV

GENERAL CONDITIONS WHICH CONFRONTED CHRISTIANITY: THE CHALLENGE OF DISAFFECTION, REPUDIATION, AND OPPORTUNITY, A.D. 1815 - A.D. 1914

The ninety-nine years from 1815 to 1914 formed a distinct period in the history of mankind and of Christianity. They, rather than the conventional 1800 to 1900, were the nineteenth century. Because of a combination of geographic expansion, inner vitality, and the effect upon mankind as a whole, they constituted the greatest century which Christianity had thus far known. This achievement of Christianity was associated with a prodigious burst of creativity in Western European peoples, the traditional Christendom. It was paralleled by movements which seemed to threaten the very existence of the faith and by challenges which called forth all its inner resources.

MOVEMENTS WHICH CONSTITUTED THE SETTING FOR CHRISTIANITY

Following the final defeat and exile of Napoleon in 1815, the Western world entered nearly a century of relative peace and mounting prosperity which persisted until the outbreak of a succession of world wars in 1914. Never over so prolonged a period had Christendom been as nearly free from war. Wars there were, notably that centering about Crimea, in 1854–1856, in which Turkey, Russia, Great Britain, France, and Sardinia were engaged, the Franco-German War of 1870–1871, and, most destructive and prolonged of all, the Civil War in the United States, 1861–1865. Wars were waged on the widening fringes of the expansion of European peoples—with the Indians in the United States, in India, in Burma, in Indochina, in China, with the Maoris in New Zealand, between the British and the Boers in South Africa, and between the Russians and Japanese. None of these, however, were of major dimensions in the number of lives lost. In China an uprising, that with the name of T'ai P'ing, which was due partly to ideas derived from contacts with Christianity, cost hundreds of thousands of lives. Yet contrasted with the eighteenth and the twentieth centuries there was no war which involved all of Christendom or which approached the dimensions of a world conflict. Seldom if ever had mankind been so nearly free from the scourge of war for so long a period. It is not surprising that many were hopeful that the human race was outgrowing war and that beginnings of international organization were made and still more extensive plans proposed for putting the intercourse between peoples on the basis of law.

The century was also marked by the rapidly mounting exploration by man of his physical environment. Through the scientific approach and at an exhilarating pace men pushed out the boundaries of their knowledge of the world about them and within them. Through daring hypothesis, observation, and experiment they delved into the constitution of matter, became more and more aware of electricity, peered into the stellar spaces, and began to unravel the story of the geologic past of the planet which was their habitation. By conjectures associated with the name of Charles Darwin scientists sought to understand the course of life on the planet. By methods to which the name "psychology" was given they endeavoured to disclose the workings of their own and others' minds. Anthropology and sociology were labels placed on efforts to comprehend men as animals and the manner in which the societies in which they associated operated. Through what was called economics scholars probed into the fashion in which wealth was produced and distributed.

This increasing knowledge was utilized to effect progress in the mastery by men of their environment. Steam was harnessed, at first in manufactures and then in transportation by boats and railways. Through the telegraph, the telephone, and the trolley men made electricity their servant in speeding up communication. They constrained electricity to light their homes and their streets. Through antisepsis and anesthesia surgery was robbed of some of its terrors. By the discovery of germs and of ways to control or eliminate them disease and the death rate were reduced and the span of life was prolonged. Men found new ways of fighting the pests which assailed their crops and domestic animals and of supplying more nourishment to their plants. By better seed selection and by improved methods of breeding they augmented their supply of food.

The additions to the knowledge and mastery of the physical environment contributed to great and transforming changes in the life of mankind. They made possible the industrial revolution. This began in the eighteenth century but mounted in the nineteenth century. Wealth grew by leaps and bounds. As throughout history, great extremes existed in the possession or absence of wealth. Huge fortunes were accumulated by the few, moderate comfort was achieved by a large minority, but for another minority, in some places a majority, the new industrial processes meant grinding toil, sordid poverty, and moral and physical degradation. Populations multiplied. Cities mushroomed. The largest of them attained unprecedented dimensions. A new kind of urban life arose. It was the age of the urban middle class, the *bourgeoisie*. Capitalism, private enterprise, open competition, *laissez-faire,* the reduction of control by the state to a minimum, were the vogue and were believed by many to be indispensable to the rising prosperity.

These developments had their origin and were most marked among Western European peoples, whether in the Old World or the New. They were accompanied by a general atmosphere of optimism. To be sure, there were many who were sensitive to the evils of the new order and were pessimistic. However, the prevailing temper was hopeful and expectant. Belief in progress, apparent in the eighteenth century and even earlier, became widespread among peoples of Western European stock. Man was held to be moving upward and onward towards the conquest of the evils, collective and individual, which had historically beset him, to an inconceivably happy future. He was to do this by the use of his reason and his will. The eighteenth century is often thought of as the age of reason. Yet the coming of the nineteenth century did not mean that Western man had lost confidence in his intellect. He still trusted it as a tool to ever greater achievements.

The nineteenth century also witnessed either the development or the initial appearance of revolutionary theories for the social organization of mankind and the extensive application of some of them. We have seen that beginning at least as early as the Middle Ages schemes had been propounded for the organization of society. They had multiplied in the sixteenth, seventeenth, and eighteenth centuries. They were largely, perhaps chiefly, the effects, direct or indirect, of Christianity. The ideals which had triumphed in the French Revolution were in part divorced from Christianity and were even antagonistic to it. Yet to no small degree they had their roots in it. In the nineteenth century the hopes which had shaped the Revolution continued to operate in France and in most of the rest of Europe. For a time after 1815 the old order was in part restored. The Bourbon monarchy was renewed in France with the ancient union of crown and altar, and there and elsewhere what was known as the age of Metternich, from the statesman who controlled Austria, appeared to prevail. However, the revolutionary tide ebbed only temporarily. It surged forward afresh in the 1830's and especially in 1848. In the latter year Metternich was swept out of office and into exile and the tide was once more at the flood. Democracy pulsed forward on the Continent of Europe, in the British

Isles, in the Americas, and in the British colonial territories in Canada, Australia, New Zealand, and South Africa. Under the word "democracy" several conceptions were gathered. Some of them were compatible with the prevailing *laissez-faire,* but others were antagonistic to it.

Most of the theories which reacted against *laissez-faire* were known as socialism. Socialism was varied. In general it stood for equality of economic opportunity as well as for the political egalitarianism which was associated with democracy. Some socialists, prominent among them Robert Owen (1771–1858), sought to establish communities in which there would be no poverty, vice, intemperance, or strife. In France Fourier (1772–1837) proposed the organization of industrial communities of eighteen hundred persons each in which there would be a distribution of the earnings among capitalists, workmen, and talent according to a fixed proportion. Comte Henri de Saint-Simon (1760–1825) advocated a form of socialism in which men of science rather than the Church would be the spiritual directors and in which the organization would be by productive labour. It was in France that the journalist Louis Blanc urged that the state establish "social workshops" in which the workmen would elect the managers and divide the profits.

Outstanding among the socialists was Karl Marx (1818–1883). The son of a middle class Jew who for prudential reasons had formally accepted the Christian faith for himself and his family, Karl Marx, baptized as a child, had been reared as a Christian. He attended German universities, and in Berlin came under the influence of Hegel, of whom we are to hear more later. Although he eventually repudiated the latter's philosophy of history, Marx was profoundly shaped by it. Caught up in the politically liberal movements of his youth, his enthusiastic advocacy brought him under the suspicion of the authorities and so kept him from fulfilling his ambition to become a university professor. He became more and more radical, formed an enduring friendship with Friedrich Engels (1820–1895), the son and heir of a German Jew who was a cotton manufacturer in Manchester, England, and from 1849 to his death lived in London, eking out a precarious livelihood by writing. In 1848 he and Engels issued the *Communist Manifesto,* a pamphlet which, almost ignored for the moment, was later regarded as the birth-cry of modern socialism. Marx's major work, *Das Kapital,* the first volume of which appeared in 1867 and the second, third, and fourth volumes of which, edited by Engels, were published posthumously, became the standard for the kind of socialism which was to be known by his name. In the twentieth century, as we are to see, that form of socialism was to sweep across much of the world.

Stirred by the squalor of the urban proletariat in the mines and the new manufacturing and commercial cities and the contrast with the comfort of the dominant middle classes, Marx was filled with burning indignation and hate for the institutions and the classes, especially the "capitalists," which seemed to him to be battening off the misery of the majority. He denounced the Church and believed that the course of history would eliminate the *bourgeoisie* and religion and bring the proletariat to power. He held that history was controlled by economic factors, that the society of his day had developed out of class struggles in the past, and that capitalistic society would inevitably give way to another structure. The process could be accelerated, so he contended, by political measures. He climaxed the *Manifesto* with the challenge: "The proletarians have nothing to lose but their chains. They have the world to win. Workingmen of the world, unite."

For the attainment of his aims, in the 1860's Marx led in forming the International Working Men's Association, known as the "International" or the "First International," with units in various lands. It came to an end in the 1870's. It was followed, in 1889, by the "Second International," a loosely knit assembly of workers' organizations of many shades of opinion. This in turn disintegrated, but not until after 1914.

In the meantime socialist parties were formed. In the second half of the nineteenth century they became prominent in the politics of several European countries. That in Germany which had the name of Social Democratic was especially strong.

Socialists by no means agreed among themselves. They held some principles in common, but they differed sharply, particularly as to method—whether their goals should be achieved by revolutionary tactics, with resort to war, or by slower, peaceful steps. The advocates of the latter were often known as the "reformists," "revisionists," or "possibilists."

Other social programmes were put forward. One of them was anarchism. A pioneer in formulating and advocating it was William Godwin (1756–1836), an Englishman who had been educated for the Nonconformist ministry. More prominent, and the one who coined the word "anarchist," was Pierre Joseph Proudhon (1809–1865), a Frenchman. Reacting against the growing wealth of the owners of factories through what seemed to him the exploitation of the labourers, Proudhon declared that "property is theft," rejected it and all forms of government, and held that if they lived together by compacts entered into voluntarily and not under the compulsion of the state, the innate goodness of human nature would lead men to observe their contractual obligations. He decried violence and believed that by gradual education men could make progress towards perfection. It was a Russian, Bakunin (1814–1876), who advocated "direct action" through terrorism and "general strikes" of workingmen as the means of annihilating the state and existing classes and traditions.

Bakunin's form of anarchism found a congenial home in Russia as a protest against the repressive autocracy of that realm and was known as nihilism.

These programmes for the reorganization of society were not merely doctrinaire, nor were they entirely the product of visionaries who had completely lost touch with reality. They were symptomatic of a vast restlessness, a passionate desire, especially among the urban proletariat of the industrial and commercial cities, for more of the good things of life. The majority of their formulators were not from the proletariat, but from the middle class. They attracted an extensive following because they offered a rationale and proposed concrete action for the largely inarticulate and imperfectly formulated longings and demands of the masses.

Not necessarily espousing any of these programmes, labour unions sprang up and multiplied. They sought through collective action to better the lot of their members. In many places the state attempted to suppress them or control them, but they became increasingly prominent and influential.

Another movement which was widespread in the Occident was nationalism. Nationalism was not entirely new. From at least the fourteenth century it had contributed to the growth of nation states. However, in the nineteenth century it attained such dimensions that it seemed a new phenomenon. It was a major factor in the achievement of the independence from the Turkish yoke of Greece, Bulgaria, Rumania, and Serbia. It brought about the unification of Germany and Italy. It held the United States together against threatened disruption by sectionalism. There were no European countries in which it did not make itself felt.

The nineteenth century was also marked by the acceleration of the expansion of European peoples. This was partly by migration. On a scale hitherto unmatched by any segment of mankind, Europeans thronged across the Atlantic to the Americas, especially to the United States, but also to Canada and the southern sections of Latin America. Lesser numbers, but still totalling hundreds of thousands, founded new nations in Australia and New Zealand. The expansion was in part commercial. In search of raw materials for their factories and of markets for the output of industries augmented by the new machines, Europeans penetrated to all but the remotest corners of the globe. Much of the expansion was political. Several states built colonial empires, some large and some small.

In mechanical inventions, in the industrial revolution, in commercial and political expansion, and in the growth of wealth, the lead was taken by Great Britain and the United States. The British navy controlled the seas. Great Britain had the largest commercial fleet and the dominant share in overseas commerce. It became a cliché that hers was an empire on which the sun never set. It was found in all the continents and in islands in all the major oceans.

As the pioneer in the industrial revolution Great Britain for a time held a near monopoly of its processes and of the commerce which arose from it. London became the largest city and the banking centre of the world. The United States was not far behind, although in a somewhat different way. The new republic rapidly reached across North America, annexing vast sparsely peopled areas fabulously rich in soil, forests, and minerals. Its population increased by leaps and bounds, partly by an immigration from Europe which immediately before 1914 was more than a million a year and partly by a birth rate far in excess of the death rate. That population swelled the cities, manned the multiplying factories, and poured westward, before 1914 eliminating the frontier. In both Great Britain and the United States wealth mounted at a dizzying pace and fortunes, large and small, multiplied.

Several other nations shared in the expansion of European peoples, although not as markedly as Great Britain and the United States. France built a new colonial empire in Africa and Asia. Emerging late as a united nation, Germany acquired colonial territories in areas not occupied by the British and the French. By 1914 it was more and more industrialized and in shipping and commerce was threatening British supremacy. Italy, also tardily united, picked up African territories of dubious value. Russia strengthened her hold on the northern reaches of Asia and encroached on the Chinese Empire. Portugal expanded its footholds in Africa. The Netherlands annexed more land in the East Indies, and its neighbour, Belgium, acquired possession of a huge slice of Equatorial Africa.

The Spanish Empire broke up and by 1914 had almost entirely disappeared, but from its fragments new nations of European culture emerged and increased in wealth and population. Portugal lost her major overseas possession, Brazil, but this meant the appearance of another new and growing nation of the cultural family of Europe.

The impact of Europeans and their cultures brought the beginnings of vast revolutions among non-European peoples. After 1914 these were to assume gigantic proportions, but even before that year they were spreading. The so-called primitive cultures were the first to disintegrate, notably those of the American Indians and of the peoples of the islands of the Pacific. But even so advanced a civilization as that of China was crumbling, and, without sacrificing the essentials of their inherited culture, outwardly the Japanese were becoming Westernized.

THE CHALLENGE OF THREAT

Much in the new situation threatened the very existence of Christianity. As more than once in the past, Europe was moving into a new age. In contrast with its earlier periods of rapid change, the entire human race was now involved. Until now cultural revolutions had been localized. Even the tremendous transition between 1500 and 1750 and the drastic movements which from 1750 to 1815 radiated from the United States and France did not reach all mankind. They had repercussions far outside of Europe, but the majority of the world's population, embraced as it was in China, Japan, and India, was either completely untouched or was as yet but slightly affected. After 1815, however, the currents which were ushering European peoples into a fresh era increasingly, through the expansion of Europe, produced cultural and political revolutions the world around.

By its very success Christianity might seem to have prepared the way for its own downfall. That faith had been woven into the warp and woof of the civilization of Europe: most of that continent had become Christendom. As the old order with which it had appeared to have become identified faded away or was violently swept aside, the casual and even the thoughtful observer might well expect Christianity to wane and, if it survived, to do so only in areas, largely rural, as yet unpenetrated or but little altered by the new currents. Thus weakened, presumably Christianity would be in no condition to move effectively into the areas opened by the expansion of Europe and to enter into the new cultures which would emerge from the revolutions induced by the impact of the Occident. Unless he were biased by identification with them, in the fore part of the nineteenth century the student of the contemporary scene would scarcely believe that the awakenings in Protestantism and the Roman Catholic Church, confined as they were as yet to small minorities, would prove sufficiently potent to offset the adverse forces. Throughout the nineteenth century even the convinced Christian, if he were really aware of the forces which were shaping European peoples and through them the rest of the world, could not but question whether he and his fellow-believers would rise to the challenge. He would reluctantly harbour the sobering fear that he and they were fighting a rear guard and delaying action in a losing campaign.

The forces arrayed against Christianity were undeniably potent. To many, both among the intellectuals and the masses, science, in its multiplying ramifications and amazing discoveries, appeared to be making Christianity untenable to the honest and informed mind. The evolutionary hypothesis associated with the name of Charles Robert Darwin (1809–1882) seemed to render obsolete the story of the creation of living things, including man, in the first chapters of Genesis and thus to cast doubt upon the reliability of the Bible. Stretching out as they did the history of the universe and of the earth to time dimensions which numbed the imagination, astronomy and geology discredited the chronology which the learned Archbishop Usher (1581–1656) had worked out in the middle of the seventeenth century on the basis of what he believed that he found in the Bible and which placed the creation of the world at 4004 B.C. Since this had been printed in the margin of the King James or Authorized Version of the English Bible, it seemed to many readers to be part of the Scriptures and in the minds of some of them the latter suffered in credibility. While the roll of distinguished scientists included the names of devout Christians, many others on that roster either repudiated the faith or held it to be irrelevant.

Even to list the names of all the widely read thinkers of the nineteenth century who either denounced Christianity or were lukewarm to it would prolong this chapter unduly. We can take the space to mention only a few outstanding examples. In Germany Arthur Schopenhauer (1788–1860), distinguished as a philosopher, was outspoken in his criticism of theism and Christianity, denied the priority of reason, sought to show the limitations of science, and accorded primary place to the will. Another German philosopher, Ludwig Andreas Feuerbach (1804–1872), declared belief in personal immortality to be untenable, held that Christianity had in actuality long since "vanished from the life of mankind," maintained that God did not have a separate existence, and made of Him simply a projection of men's conscience or unconscious inner needs.

Both the father and the grandfather of Friedrich Wilhelm Nietzsche (1844–1900) were Protestant clergymen and his mother and his father's mother were daughters of clergymen. Nietzsche entered the university as a student of theology but, persuaded by Schopenhauer and to the great grief of his family, abandoned his inherited faith. For a time he was under the influence of Wilhelm Richard Wagner (1813–1883), the famous writer of opera, but he later broke with him and with Schopenhauer. Through painful inner struggle he worked his way to his own philosophy. That philosophy rejected as illusory and as a handicap to life what he deemed the ruling values in Western civilization—the good, the true, and the beautiful—and stressed the will to power. The will to power through which each individual seeks to affirm and promote his own life should use, so he held, the true, the good, and the beautiful, but merely as means to that end. He declared that it was from the Jews, a chronically subject people, that there had arisen the moral standards which through religion and ethics had shaped the modern world. The Jews, so he said, possessed the will to live, but their mentality and moral ideals were those of slaves, for they exalted humility, cleverness, pacifism, mendacity, and adaptability and decried as evil self-respect, strength, hardness, energy, and exuberance. Through Jesus of Nazareth, so Nietzsche went on to maintain, the Jews had bequeathed this slave morality to Christianity. Christianity had accentuated it, proclaiming salvation to the sick, the sinful, and the poor. From it had come the movements which were dominant in the nineteenth century—pacifism, the emancipation of women, democracy, socialism, and the casting off of the yoke of the ruling classes. Nietzsche looked forward to the time when Europe would be rid of what he deemed the handicaps of the Jewish-Christian heritage and when through wars and revolutions a new ruling caste would emerge and from it would come Superman.

Ernst Heinrich Haeckel (1834–1919), an eminent German biologist who gave the weight of his great name to promoting in Germany the acceptance of Darwinian evolution, applied his findings to religion, held to a materialist determinism, and denied the freedom of the will, the immortality of the soul, and the existence of a personal God.

In France Auguste Comte (1798–1857) was the creator of Positivism, which for many intellectuals, especially in Latin Europe and Latin America, became a substitute for Christianity. He wished to apply scientific principles to the study of society and to bring all the sciences to serve the welfare of mankind. Deeply religious after his own fashion and with the *Imitatio Christi* and Dante as close companions, he elaborated a cult in which humanity conceived as the Great Being took the place of God, which had as its object the progressive welfare of mankind, and which was to possess a priesthood and forms of worship.

In Great Britain there were distinguished and influential intellectuals who either repudiated Christianity or promulgated views which shook the faith of many. Thomas Carlyle (1795–1881) began preparing for the ministry of the Church of Scotland. However, while still a young man he felt himself constrained to give up Christianity, and while he believed profoundly in God as inspiring human effort and revealed by all nature, he emphatically rejected the accepted Christian dogmas. Charles Darwin's *On the Origin of Species* (published in 1859), setting forth the evolutionary hypothesis, aroused a storm of criticism from many Christians and seemed to others to make their faith untenable. Although he did not accept all of Darwin's views, Thomas Henry Huxley (1825–1895), distinguished as a scientist, especially in biology, insisted upon observed fact as the basis of knowledge and discarded Christianity on the ground that "the exact nature of the teachings and the convictions of Jesus is extremely uncertain" and that there is no proof for the existence of the God of the theologians. Yet he was not an atheist, but rather an agnostic, declaring the evidence to be insufficient for either the affirmation or the denial of the central Christian convictions. Moreover, he advocated the teaching of the Bible in the London schools both for its literary qualities and for its usefulness in inculcating morality. Darwin himself, who had been designed by his father for the clergy and who studied in Cambridge with that purpose, was eventually an agnostic religiously. John Stuart Mill (1806–1873), in childhood and youth subjected to a severe mental discipline by his able father, James Mill (1773–1836), a thinker of distinction, helped to give vogue to a utilitarian ethics which seemed to leave little room for Christianity. However, in an essay on theism written late in life he declared that the balance of evidence favoured creation by intelligence, said that science does not refute immortality, and applauded Christ as the ideal guide of humanity.

Herbert Spencer (1820–1903), who in his extensive writings had a wide influence, believed profoundly in progress and in evolution and coined the phrase "survival of the fittest." He held that religion began with the worship of the ghosts of ancestors—ghost fear—and that it dealt with the realms of the mysterious which transcend the kind of knowledge acquired by the scientific method. In the United States William Graham Sumner of Yale, in his youth an Episcopalian pastor, followed Spencer and did much to shape the early forms of sociological thinking in that country.

Leslie Stephen (1832–1904), of Evangelical stock, on his mother's side with the background of the Clapham circle and in his early manhood a clergyman of the Church of England, became an agnostic. He declared that most men of intellect had really ceased to be Christians, even though some still called themselves such and either did not have the courage to deny the central affirmation of that religion, the divinity of Christ, treated it and other Christian dogmas as irrelevant, or hesitated to think through their faith and to part with what still seemed to them the good which it contained. He believed theology to deal with realms which are beyond human intelligence, and that Christ, far from being an incarnation of God, was merely a man and that attainment of character such as Christ's was within the range of the possible for other men.

The widely read Matthew Arnold (1822–1888), son of a distinguished clergyman of the Church of England who had attempted to fuse the new knowledge with Christianity, regretted the waning of the beliefs which he had held in boyhood. Yet to him religion was all that mattered. While he could not hold to orthodoxy, he wished England to remain religious and hoped that Christianity would be rethought in terms of the new knowledge.

The popular and respected novelist who wrote under the pen name of George Eliot, Mary Ann Evans, later Mrs. J. W. Cross (1819–1880), reared in a devout home of the Evangelical type, in her early twenties departed from orthodox Christianity and rejected a belief in God and immortality. But she kept a high moral sense and a deep and not unsympathetic understanding of Evangelical convictions and experience.

In lowlier social circles there were those who pointed out what seemed to them inconsistencies in the Bible and declared that they could not believe in God. Many of them propagated their views through public lectures and the press. They met determined opposition and some of them were haled before the courts for violations of laws which sought to protect religion. In the course of time changes in legislation permitted freedom of speech and of publication, including attacks on the Christian faith. Among the many who struggled for that freedom through repeated lawsuits and much obloquy was Charles Bradlaugh (1833–1891). It must also be said that some of these religious radicals were originally earnestly Christian in belief and had been driven to a repudiation of their early faith by those who in the name of Christianity denounced honest doubts as wicked or presented lives which were palpably contrary to Christian standards. Often the revolt against Christianity was associated with indignation against the injustices of the existing order and the connexion of the Church and the clergy with it.

In the United States, as in Britain, Thomas Paine's *Age of Reason* had a continuing and wide reading. Robert Green Ingersoll (1833–1899), son of a Congregational clergyman, a lawyer and politician of some distinction, was best known for his lectures directed against the Bible and Christianity and was heard by audiences in many parts of the country. On a quite different level was Ralph Waldo Emerson (1803–1882), from a long line of New England ministers, himself a Unitarian minister and for a time a pastor. Without attacking the historic Christian faith he departed from some of its central affirmations. Famous as a lecturer and an essayist, regarded as a spokesman for Transcendentalism, a rôle which he disclaimed, but a movement, also remote from historic Christianity, which owed much to him, he had an influence which was nation-wide and which expressed and shaped much of the self-reliant, optimistic idealism of the youthful United States. Near the end of the century and carrying over beyond 1914 in mounting effect was the non-Christian instrumentalist philosophy of which John Dewey (1859–1952) was the chief formulator and spokesman. While he distinctly disavowed atheism, Dewey gave a meaning to the word God which was far from having a Christian content. His views became the more menacing to Christianity because, issuing from his professorial chair in the University of Chicago and then in Columbia University, both institutions begun on Christian foundations, they dominated the field of education from the primary schools through the universities and thus touched most of the population.

As may be gathered from what was said of them a few pages above, many of the most popular movements for the reorganization of society were either tacitly or frankly anti-Christian. That was notably true of the kind of socialism which was associated with the name of Marx. Marx held that the proletariat needed courage, self-confidence, pride, and a sense of personal dignity and independence, but that Christianity inculcated self-contempt, abasement, submission, and humility, and thus was an enemy. By no means all socialists were anti-Christian. Some were frankly Christian. Yet in the main, even when it did not attack Christianity, socialism tended either to ignore it or to drift away from any Christian moorings which it once had. This last was especially seen in the labour movement and the later Labour Party in Great Britain. Largely socialist in its trend, in its early stages some of its outstanding organizers were earnest Christians, men who owed their skill in public speech to their training and experience as Methodist lay preachers. Yet as the years passed that element became less prominent.

Also threatening to the persistence of Christianity were the vast movements of population which were one of the features of the nineteenth century and the conditions to which the industrial revolution subjected great masses of mankind. Millions left Europe for the Americas, Australia, and New Zealand. For the most part they came from lands where churches were established by law and drew much or all of their support from public taxation and where baptism, confirmation, and church attendance had been part of the pattern of life. They went to lands where the establishment was non-existent or fading, where society was in flux, and where the Old World habits of life were not binding. In the United States they found themselves in a country where church members were in the minority. Other millions moved from rural sections where the Church was firmly integrated with the life of the community to rapidly growing cities where the erection of churches lagged behind the growth of population and where the routine and conditions of life, especially for those in the factories and in transportation, made parish life in its traditional forms difficult or impossible. The Church found the going less arduous in the middle classes, but the urban proletariat often regarded it with indifference or hostility as part of the order which was exploiting them.

Nationalism and the growing power and expanding functions of the nation state added to the threat. In the long struggle between Church and state which was as old as Christianity the Church seemed to be losing. Education, for centuries under the auspices and control of the Church, now was being made a function of the state. That meant that youth was being trained primarily for the service of the state and was being indoctrinated with the ideology to which the state was committed rather than reared in the Christian faith. To be sure, in some lands, both in the Old and the New World, the Church still controlled education and in several others, where the state was in full charge of education, religious instruction was given. Increasingly, however, the schools tended to be purely secular, not necessarily combatting Christianity but indifferent to it or ignoring it. This trend was early marked in the United States, where the absence of a state church and the inability of the several churches to agree on the form and content prevented any religious instruction from being given, except that in some places the reading of the Bible without comment and the formal repetition of the Lord's Prayer were maintained. In several countries, notably in France, the elements in control of the state looked upon the Church as an enemy and sought to debar members of religious orders from teaching. The mounting trend was to render marriage a civil ceremony, thus ushering the Church out from another important stage in life which had long been under its control. The tendency was towards making the state supreme and harnessing Christianity and the Church to its purposes rather than subordinating the state to the Christian conscience.

Moreover, Church and state were being separated. The trend was against the traditional relationship which had regarded them as coördinate expressions of the faith of an officially Christian nation. This was due to two quite different movements. The one arose from conviction within the churches themselves, partly from a desire for religious liberty for all branches of organized Christianity and partly from the belief that the Church should be freed from control by the state. The other was a symptom of de-Christianization. It was moved by enmity against the Church and its faith and was often called anticlericalism. The former was strongest in predominantly Protestant countries and the latter was most prevalent in traditionally Roman Catholic lands. Whatever the cause, the effect was towards cancelling the position which Christianity had long held of being the faith professed by all members of a particular people. Christendom could no longer be described by that name. In what had once been avowedly Christian nations convinced Christians were becoming a minority.

That these movements menaced the very existence of Christianity is clear. They also constituted a challenge. Did Christianity possess sufficient vitality to rise to them? Would it be stirred by them to fresh creative manifestations of vigour? In earlier ages some of the challenges had proved too great. That had been notably true of the one posed by Islam. Only in the Iberian Peninsula and Sicily had Christianity regained ground lost to that religion. Some other threats had been the occasion for fresh advances. That was the case in Western Europe after the break-up of the Roman Empire and the barbarian invasions from the North. It was seen again after the low ebb which followed the disintegration of the Carolingians. It had been vividly displayed in the response through the Protestant and Catholic Reformations to the menace presented by the passing of the medieval order, by the Renaissance, and by the fifteenth, sixteenth, and seventeenth century expansion of Europe. Yet in some respects the danger was now greater than at any time since the great recession between the close of the fifth and the middle of the tenth century.

Fully as sobering was the fact that to no small degree the threats to Christianity arose from Christianity itself. Nietzsche was hitting close to the truth when he declared that democracy and the various forms of socialism were sprung from the Christian faith. As we have more than once indicated, science owed its origin and development to Christianity, albeit to an undetermined degree. Man's increased knowledge and mastery of his physical environment must, therefore, in part be attributed to Christianity. In many instances the professed repudiation of the faith was to some extent due to impulses which issued from Christianity, such as an honesty which refused to hold to accepted views without careful investigation, and moral indignation against social injustices which were ignored or condoned by those who bore the Christian name, including spokesmen for the churches. Even in the abbreviated list of those who led the procession away from Christianity which we gave a few moments ago, it is evident that numbers of those who repudiated the faith had been reared as Christians and were not led to their stand by ignorance of it. Was Christianity to be the source of its own dissolution?

Here, then, was a combination of threats which constituted a test of the viability of Christianity. Would Christianity fade out of the human scene or did it possess the power of self-renewal which would prove equal to the occasion?

The Challenge of Opportunity

Christianity was challenged not only by the threats to its continuing existence. It was also challenged by an unprecedented opportunity. Western civilization was in rapid flux and if Christianity were sufficiently dynamic to enter creatively into its reshaping it could be more profoundly influenced by that faith than at any earlier stage in its history. The impact of the Occident was producing revolutions in all the other cultures under which men lived. Here was an opportunity to help mould the future of non-Occidental mankind. Coming as it did in association with the culture which was producing the revolutions which were disturbing the human race, Christianity met an opposition which arose from resentment against Occidentals as its supposed adherents. But it also was accorded a wider hearing than if it had not derived prestige from that association. The dominance by Occidental peoples broke down political and cultural barriers which had stood in the way of the spread of Christianity. The reduction of time-distances and the improved methods of transportation and communication made possible the development and maintenance of a world-wide missionary enterprise. The growing wealth of European peoples supplied Christians with the material means for the support of that enterprise on an unprecedented scale. Here was an opportunity greater than Christianity had ever faced to carry its message to all mankind and to make itself felt by every human being.

PREVIEW OF THE RESPONSE

In an amazing fashion Christianity rose to the challenge of threat and opportunity. It did not fully meet it. The de-Christianization of much of Christendom continued. As we have hinted and shall see again and again, Christians were becoming a minority in what had once been called Christendom. Even in the United States, where the mass conversion of a partially de-Christianized population was in progress, in 1914 the members of churches were less than half the whole. Christianity did not fully keep pace with the expansion of Europe. A major effect of that expansion and of the accompanying revolutions in non-Occidental cultures was the progressive secularization of mankind. Other religions suffered from the impact of the Occident and the currents of the new age, most of them much more than did Christianity. An outstanding Chinese intellectual declared shortly after 1914 that mankind was outgrowing religion and that the Chinese were to be the first to complete that process. Yet all the major branches of Christianity experienced revivals. These were seen in the Orthodox Churches, notably the largest, that of Russia, in the Roman Catholic Church, and in Protestantism. They were much more marked in the Roman Catholic Church than in the Orthodox Churches and they were even more striking in Protestantism. That was all the more significant in view of the fact that the abounding life in Protestantism was especially prominent in Great Britain and the United States, lands which led in the industrial revolution, in the rapid growth in wealth, and in the increase in territory and population. For the first time in its history Christianity made actual its inherent genius and became world-wide. In this it surpassed the achievement of every other religion. Mankind was far from conforming fully to Christian standards. In most lands not only were professed Christians merely a minority: in the major population masses in Asia and Africa even by the year 1914 after a century of growth they were still but a small fraction of the population. Yet by 1914 nearly every culture felt to a greater or less extent the influence of Christianity.

This growth of Christianity in spite of the adverse conditions in the lands of its historic strength is the more remarkable when it is contrasted with the course of other religions. The latter were suffering from the impact of movements which had their origin in the historic home of Christianity and which were strongest in the traditional Christendom. Presumably, Christianity would have been more nearly shattered by them than were these others, for more than they it bore the full brunt of the onslaught. Yet far more than any of the others it rose to the challenge, put forth fresh life, and spread. It is to this story that we now turn.

Selected Bibliography

In a field so extensive as that covered in this brief chapter it is almost impossible to give a bibliography which will at once be not too long and at the same time cover the field with something approaching satisfaction. The following list by no means achieves this ideal. For instance, only two of the works of the many writers cited are given. Yet it may prove of some assistance.

J. Baillie, *The Belief in Progress* (Oxford University Press, 1950, pp. viii, 240). A history of the belief and some affirmations by a competent Christian theologian.

J. B. Bury, *The Idea of Progress. An Inquiry into Its Origin and Growth*. Introduction by C. A. Beard (New York, The Macmillan Co., 1932, pp. xl, 357). An American edition of a well-known work by a distinguished historian.

The Cambridge Modern History (Vols. X, XI, XII, XIII, Cambridge University Press, 1909–1911). A standard survey, primarily political, by several authors.

J. E. Courtney, *Freethinkers of the Nineteenth Century* (London, Chapman & Hall, 1920, pp. 260). A sympathetic, well-written account of several English intellectuals.

J. Dewey, *A Common Faith* (Yale University Press, 1934, pp. 87). The religious position of Dewey comprehensively stated by himself.

F. J. C. Hearnshaw, *The Social & Political Ideas of Some Representative Thinkers of the Age of Reaction and Reconstruction 1815–1865* (London, George G. Harrap & Co., 1932, pp. 220). Essays by several writers.

F. J. C. Hearnshaw, editor, *The Social & Political Ideas of Some Representative Thinkers of the Victorian Age* (New York, Barnes & Noble, 1930, pp. 271). A series of lectures by several authors.

R. N. Carew Hunt, *The Theory and Practice of Communism. An Introduction* (New York, The Macmillan Co., 1951, pp. 231). An excellent, penetrating survey, both historical and critical.

Karl Marx, *Capital. A Critique of Political Economy*. Translated from the third German edition by S. Moore and E. Aveling, edited by Frederick Engels, revised and amplified according to the fourth German edition by E. Untermann (New York, The Modern Library, 1906, pp. 869).

J. M. Robertson, *A History of Freethought in the Nineteenth Century* (New York, G. P. Putnam's Sons, 2 vols., 1930). Warmly sympathetic.

H. C. Sheldon, *Unbelief in the Nineteenth Century. A Critical Survey* (New York, Eaton & Mains, 1907, pp. vii, 399). From the viewpoint of a Christian scholar.

B. Willey, *Nineteenth Century Studies: Coleridge to Matthew Arnold* (London, Chatto & Windus, 1949, pp. v, 287). A very important survey and interpretation of religious thought.

ARCTIC

ICELAND

ATLANTIC OCEAN

NORWAY

Christiania

Stavanger

SMÅLW

Stockh

SCOTLAND
Aberdeen

NORTH

St. Andrews
Edinburgh

Glasgow

York

SEA

DENMARK

Lund

Copenhagen

IRELAND

ULSTER
Belfast

Lancashire
Manchester

Dublin

Liverpool

ENGLAND

Nottingham
Leicester
Birmingham
WALES
Coventry
NORTHAMPTONSHIRE
Oxford
Kettering
Cambridge

Amsterdam
NETHERLANDS
Utrecht

Hamburg
Bremen

Berlin
PRUS

Hanover

GERMAN

Bristol

London

Brighton
Canterbury
Plymouth

JERSEY

Rotterdam
Bornheim
Louvain
Brussels
BELGIUM
Steyl

Barmen

Halle

Leipzig

Kaiserswerth

Dresden
Herr

Eichstatt

LUXEM-
BURG

Tubingen
Nuremberg

Paris

Nancy

WURTTEM-
BERG

BAVARIA

M

Strasburg

Munich

AUST

Issoudun

Basel
Lucerne
Lausanne
Engelberg
SWITZERLAND
Münster

Einsiedeln

CARN

FRANCE

Lyons

Rhine R.

Turin
PIEDMONT
Milan

AUST

Nimes

Piacenza

ADRIATIC

B

GALICIA

Valladolid

Lourdes

Pisa

IBERIAN PENINSULA

PORTUGAL

Lisbon

Madrid

CORSICA

Rome

ITALY

SPAIN

Naples

SARDINIA

Gibraltar

MEDITER

AFRICA

SICILY

MALTA

RRAN

OCEAN

FINLAND

L. Ladoga

Helsinki
Kronstadt
St. Petersburg

Vyatka R.

Volga R.

Kazan

URAL MOUNTAINS

SIBERIA

Moscow

Kaluga

R U S S I A

SAMARA

Volga R.

LAND

Dnieper

Don R.

Kiev

U K R A I N E

R.

THIAN BUKOWINA

Czernowitz

GARY

MTS.

TRANSYLVANIA

ALPS

Blaj

Belgrade

Bucharest

ROUMANIA

(WALLACHIA)

R.

ENINSULA

Sofia

BULGARIA

GREECE

Salonica

MEDONIA

AEGEAN SEA

Athens

CRETE

CASPIAN SEA

C A U C A S U S   M T S.

Tiflis

GEORGIA

Echmiadzin

ARMENIA

B L A C K   S E A

Constantinople

T U R K E Y

CYPRUS

SEA

**EUROPE IN THE
NINETEENTH CENTURY**
(Political Boundaries of 1914)

Scale of Miles

0   100   200   300   400   500

Chapter XLVI

THE ROMAN CATHOLIC CHURCH ON
THE CONTINENT OF EUROPE,
A.D. 1815 - A.D. 1914

The Roman Catholic Church suffered more from the inroads of the adverse conditions of the nineteenth century than did Protestantism. It was more intransigent than was the latter. It found itself less flexible, less able to adapt itself to the age. Yet it also displayed remarkable vigour. It put forth many new movements. Although it lost ground in Europe and Latin America, lands where it had had its chief strength, it achieved an amazing geographic spread in Asia, Africa, the islands of the Pacific, Australia, Canada, and the United States. More than at any time since the conversion of Constantine, it was a self-conscious minority. Much more than ever before it was tightly knit, under the increasingly close direction of a central authority, the Papacy.

THE ROMAN CATHOLIC REVIVAL

After the fall of Napoleon the Roman Catholic Church experienced a striking revival. As we have seen (Chapter XLIV), it had suffered severely from the upheaval of the French Revolution, the accompanying movements elsewhere in Europe, and the Napoleonic measures. Much of its property had been confiscated, many of its monasteries had disappeared, and its clergy had declined in numbers. However, by 1815 the tide had begun to turn and in the ensuing century a marked revival was seen.

The revival was due to a number of factors. It was partly because of the reaction against the Revolution, the desire to restore conditions as nearly as possible to what they had been before 1789. The Bourbons returned to the thrones of France, Spain, and Naples, and the King of Portugal from his refuge in Brazil. Metternich, the symbol and leader of the effort to revive the *status quo,* was all powerful in Austria and in much of Central Europe. Austria controlled large portions of Italy. All of these lands were predominantly Roman Catholic and the attempted return to "legitimacy," the pre-revolutionary order, included the renewal, so far as feasible, of the former privileges and institutions of the Church. Rome and the larger part of the Papal states were restored to the Pope. In 1814 the Pope formally revived the Society of Jesus, but without censuring the action of his predecessor in dissolving it or clearing it of the charges which had been given as the grounds for that action. The Jesuits were readmitted to France and Spain. In Spain the Inquisition was reëstablished. In France penalties against sacrilege and blasphemy were strengthened.

However, we must note that while for the moment political and emotional reaction seemed to favour the Roman Catholic Church, all was not well. That Church by no means fully regained its former position. The Congress of Vienna which effected the post-Napoleonic settlement of Europe did not return to it all its former properties. Some of the Papal lands were left in the hands of secular princes. In Germany the confiscated ecclesiastical territories were not restored. In Austria Josephism continued. More serious was the association of the Church with reaction. The revolutionary movements had merely paused. They soon again swept forward. Not unnaturally, their leaders looked upon the Roman Catholic Church as an enemy.

Another cause of the revival was the desire for security in a rapidly changing world. To many the Roman Catholic Church seemed to stand for a timeless stability, the one solid institution in an age of storm.

Still another factor was romanticism. Although among many it weakened the authority of the Church, it led others back to it. As we have suggested, some phases of the romantic movement were accompanied by a nostalgic admiration for the Middle Ages. Since the Roman Catholic Church had been an integral and prominent part of medieval life, it profited by this enthusiasm.

A much more potent cause of the Roman Catholic revival was the vitality inherent in the Church. Without it the other factors would have been ineffective.

The Roman Catholic Church was a minority, but probably more than at any time since the mass conversions which began in the third century a substantial portion of that minority made their faith and the Church a major concern.

To this there were striking exceptions. For reasons which we shall describe at the appropriate place, in Latin America, nominally Roman Catholic, the overwhelming majority were even more spiritually parasitic than they had been before the nineteenth century, dependent on Europe for many of their clergy and leaving missionaries from Europe to bear the main burden of missions to the non-Christian Indians on the fringes of white settlement. Yet in most countries which by tradition were predominantly Roman Catholic the challenge of adverse conditions, while bringing many defections, tended to make those who remained loyal more active in the expression, the support, and the propagation of their faith.

THE RENEWAL OF MONASTIC LIFE AND THE MULTIPLICATION OF ORDERS AND CONGREGATIONS OF MEN AND WOMEN

One manifestation of the Roman Catholic revival was the strengthening of the monastic life. As we have repeatedly seen, an invariable expression of a forward surge of the Roman Catholic Church had been a revitalization of monasticism. It had been through this channel that Roman Catholics had normally sought to give themselves fully to the call of Christ. This had meant the reinvigoration of older orders and congregations and the emergence of new ones. Between 1815 and 1914 this experience was repeated. Numbers of the monastic houses, orders, and congregations that had suffered from the lethargy of the eighteenth century and the onslaught of the Revolution were restored or renewed. Many new ones came into being. None of the latter attained the dimensions of the Franciscans, Dominicans, or Jesuits. However, more of them appeared than in any other single century. Here was evidence of abounding vitality.

Even to list all the new bodies of a monastic character which sprang up in the course of the century would unduly prolong this chapter. Here we can merely mention and briefly describe a few of them. It appears to be significant that most of them continued a trend which had been evident in the Roman Catholic Church for several centuries. They were concerned primarily not for the salvation of their own souls but for service to others. Some were for teaching, some for ministering to the poor and the sick, and many were for missions, either at home or abroad or both. Even the contemplatives who devoted themselves to prayer gave a large place to intercession for others and for the spread of the faith. The many orders and congregations and the numerous societies, less tightly knit than the former and making fewer demands on their members, constituted a kind of spiritual army and increasingly made of the Roman Catholic Church a force for world-wide extension.

In 1815 three priests founded the Society of the Missionaries of France, with the purpose of reviving the religious life in the parishes. In that same year William de Chaminade inaugurated the Marianists, who directed schools, workshops, and boarding schools in the south of France. In 1816 Charles Joseph Eugene de Mazenod (1782–1861) began the Oblates of the Immaculate Virgin Mary. Mazenod was of the French nobility. A priest, he deplored the fashion in which the Revolution had drawn so many thousands away from the faith. The Oblates had their rise in Provence, and Mazenod designed them to be missionaries among the de-Christianized population. They received Papal approval in 1826. Their founder died as head of the See of Marseilles.

The year that saw the beginning of the Oblates of the Immaculate Virgin Mary was also that of the birth, likewise in France, of the Society of Mary (the Marist Brothers, or Little Brothers of Mary). The Society of Mary was begun by a group of students in a theological seminary of whom the retiring and modest Jean Claude Marie Colin (1790–1875) was the leader. It adopted a simple rule, like the long familiar one of Augustine. Its members carried on missions among the de-Christianized or partially de-Christianized masses. Their bishop wished to confine it to his diocese, but Colin had wider dreams, obtained for it Papal approval (1836), and as its first superior general expanded its operations not only in France but also to the islands of the Pacific. Like Mazenod, he reacted against the traditional Gallicanism of the French Church and emphasized obedience to the Holy See.

The Congregation of the Most Precious Blood, inaugurated in 1815, owed its existence in part to the desire of Pope Pius VII to revive the quality of Christian living in the Papal States. Returning to Rome after the fall of Napoleon, he was distressed by the deterioration of the faith in his domains. The actual founder was Gaspare del Bufalo (1786–1837). A native of Rome and of humble birth, deeply religious from childhood, while yet in his teens as a catechetical instructor he was called "the little apostle of Rome." He inaugurated the congregation, made up of secular priests, to conduct missions and to spread devotion to the Most Precious Blood. He himself was a convincing itinerant preacher. Pius VII saw in the congregation a means of improving the religious life of his subjects and gave it his official recognition and encouragement. The congregation spread in Italy and North America. With it were associated the Sisters of the Precious Blood, who undertook the instruction of youth and works of charity.

It was in the Rome of the restoration of Papal power that there lived Vincent Mary Pallotti (1798–1850), the founder of what was officially known as the Pious Society of Missions, but whose members were usually called Pallottines. Pallotti, of a noble Roman family and educated in the Eternal City, was ordained priest in 1820. Although possessing high academic degrees, he gave himself with selfless devotion to the physical and spiritual care of the poor and the sick. He won the respect of aristocrats, bishops, and the Pope. In 1835 he began what he at first called the Catholic Apostolate, a name soon changed to the Pious Society of Missions. Its members included laymen, priests, and sisters. Its purpose was to preserve and nurture the faith of Catholics, especially emigrants. Strictly speaking, it was not an order, for its priests were seculars. It spread through Italy and into England, Germany, the Americas, and Africa.

The Society of the Holy Ghost had its origin early in the eighteenth century, but it was reconstituted, in Paris, in 1816. Its rules obtained Papal approval in 1824. It was to find its chief fields in the French colonies. Eventually (1848) there was merged with it the Congregation of the Immaculate Heart of Mary. The latter's founder was a Jew, Jacob Libermann. The son of a rabbi and himself preparing for that profession, Libermann became a Christian while trying to win back to Judaism a brother who had been converted by reading the New Testament. Baptized as Franz Maria Paul (1826), he studied theology in the seminary of St. Sulpice, was ordained priest, and in 1841 inaugurated the Congregation of the Immaculate Heart of Mary with missions among the Negroes of Africa and America as its objective.

Two other converts from Judaism, Maria Theodore Ratisbonne (1802–1884) and his brother, Maria Alphonse Ratisbonne (1814–1884), had an important part in the beginnings of new congregations. The former inaugurated the Sisterhood of Our Lady of Sion, which had as its purpose the Christian education of Jewish youth. The latter, won to the faith while on a visit to Rome by what he believed to have been a vision of the Virgin Mary, shared in the founding of the Fathers of Sion, whose aim was the conversion of Jews and Moslems.

John Bosco (1815–1888) was responsible for the formation of what were called the Salesians of Don Bosco. The name Salesian was from Francis de Sales, for whom Bosco had great admiration. A priest, Bosco gave himself to the underprivileged boys in the rapidly growing industrial city of Turin. The society which he founded was intended to extend and continue his work. It spread widely on both sides of the Atlantic. In coöperation with Bosco, Domenica Mazzarello (1837–1881) inaugurated the Sisters of Maria Conciliatrix.

THE REVIVAL AND ENLARGEMENT OF FOREIGN MISSIONS

Several orders and congregations were founded for the spread of the faith outside Christendom. They multiplied as the century wore on. What were known as the White Fathers, officially the Society of Missionaries of Our Lady of Africa, were begun in 1868 by Charles Martial Allemand Lavigerie (1825–1892). Lavigerie, Archbishop of Carthage and primate of Africa and eventually cardinal, was a leader in the renewal of the Roman Catholic Church in North Africa. The White Fathers had their popular designation from their garb, designed to resemble that of the Moslems of North Africa whom they were at first intended to serve. However, they early extended their operations south of the Sahara into Equatorial Africa.

In the 1860's Theophile Verbist founded in Belgium the Congregation of the Immaculate Heart of Mary, with headquarters at Scheutveld, near Brussels. Its first mission was in Inner Mongolia. Verbist went with the initial contingent and died before the enterprise was well established. However, the Congregation persisted, and in time had extensive missions in Inner Mongolia, the Belgian Congo, and other parts of the world.

The Society of the Divine Word was a German order, inaugurated in 1875 by Arnold Janssen. It had its headquarters at Steyl, in Holland, not far from the German border. Its purpose was to create an institution for training and sending Germans to non-Christians. Its first mission was in China, but it later spread to other lands. It also recruited and trained missionaries, largely of German ancestry, in the United States.

In England, out of the nineteenth century revival of the Roman Catholic Church, came St. Joseph's Society of Mill Hill, founded by Herbert Vaughan, later head of the British hierarchy and cardinal. It drew its students chiefly from Holland.

Several institutions for the preparation and support of secular priests as missionaries were begun somewhat on the pattern of the Society of Foreign Missions of Paris which, as we have seen, dated from the seventeenth century and had had a large part in missions in the Far East. One, at Milan, dated from 1850. Another was in Rome.

Scores of communities of women were instituted for foreign missions. The largest was the Franciscan Missionaries of Mary, founded by Helene Marie Philippine de Chappotin (1839–1904), better known by her religious name, Mary of the Passion. In 1866 Mary of the Passion went to India under the newly inaugurated Society of Marie-Réparatrice and rose to become head of three houses of that congregation. Differences developed between her and her superiors in Europe and with some of the sisters. She withdrew from the society and, with Papal permission, began a fresh organization. After a period of intense opposition, it flourished prodigiously, and its houses multiplied in several countries.

Numbers of brotherhoods and sisterhoods were created with the primary purpose of teaching. Among them were the Brothers of Christian Instruction, begun in France in 1817 by Jean Marie de Lammenais, whom we are to meet again a little later.

Societies were formed to enlist lay activity for the care of the sick and the poor. Famous was the Society of St. Vincent de Paul. This was organized in 1833 in France by Antoine Frédéric Ozanam (1813–1853). Stung by the taunt of the socialist critics of the faith that Christianity had lost the power to stir its adherents to service of the underprivileged, Ozanam instituted a society to recruit laymen for that purpose. It spread rapidly and widely, not only in France but also in other lands.

Novel kinds of bodies sprang up to mobilize the prayers and the financial support of the laity for Roman Catholic missions. Before the nineteenth century, missions to non-Christians had very little active assistance from the rank and file of Christians. They were aided by the state, and the personnel and the financial undergirding were mostly from monastic orders. In the nineteenth century vigorous and successful efforts were made to widen the base of missions and to enroll in their behalf men and women in the ordinary occupations of life. That they were marked by growing success was evidence of mounting loyalty among the Roman Catholic constituency. That constituency might be dwindling percentage-wise in historic Christendom, but it was increasingly and actively committed to the Church.

What became the most widespread of the movements on behalf of missions was the Society for the Propagation of the Faith. It arose out of the revival of the Roman Catholic Church in France. It had its origin in 1822 in Lyons, a growing industrial centre, and in part from the efforts of Pauline-Marie Jaricot (1799–1862). In her early twenties Mademoiselle Jaricot began collecting from a circle of her friends weekly contributions of a centime a week. As the society developed, it adopted the principle of recruiting members who would pray daily for missions and give at least a centime weekly. It sent out no missionaries, but subsidized orders, societies, and congregations which did so. Its growth was little short of spectacular. Until after 1914 it had its headquarters in France, but by then it had spread to several other lands.

A sister organization was the Association of the Holy Infancy. Pauline-Marie Jaricot is said to have aided its inauguration, but its main founder was Charles de Forbin-Janson, Bishop of Nancy, and its first council was assembled in 1843. It sought to enlist children to pray daily for missions and to give a centime a week to aid work for infants and children. Like the older society, it did not send out missionaries but gave subventions to organizations that were doing so. Also like that society, it was long French in its leadership but gained support from other countries as well.

Similar to these in purpose and methods were the Leopoldinen-Stiftung, or Leopold Association, begun in 1829 and with its seat in Austria, and the Ludwig-Missionsverein, of Bavaria, dating from 1828 but not formally organized until 1838. Both arose originally from an appeal of Frederic Rese, Vicar General of the see of Cincinnati, for assistance in holding the German immigrants to their hereditary faith.

THE REVIVAL OF EDUCATION AND SCHOLARSHIP

The Roman Catholic revival also found expression in the creation of schools, including universities, which would be frankly of that faith. Instead of succumbing to the drift towards secularism, as had many of the older universities, including that historic citadel of theological orthodoxy, the University of Paris, they were intended to be radiating centres of sound scholarship under the control of the Church and under the inspiration of the Christian faith. After their restoration, the Jesuits, following their tradition, multiplied their schools under a revised *Ratio Studiorum,* issued in 1832. The many teaching brotherhoods and sisterhoods inaugurated and conducted schools. A notable university was begun at Louvain, in Belgium, in 1834. After 1875 five Roman Catholic universities were founded in France. As we are to see in a later chapter, in the United States the Roman Catholic Church developed an extensive system of schools from the primary grades through several universities.

Roman Catholic scholarship again became vigorous. The century was not one of creative theological activity. Roman Catholic savants gave themselves, rather, to apologetics, some of the sciences, and historical studies. Numerous learned journals were published, notable books were written, and enormous collections of sources were compiled in a diversity of fields, including philosophy, archeology, history, and several of the natural sciences. Scholastic philosophy and theology were stressed. In 1879 Pope Leo XIII came out with an emphatic endorsement of Aquinas, declared him standard for theology, and thus gave marked impetus to the study of his works. Congresses drawing together theologians from many countries helped to make theology international rather than provincial or national.

THE DEEPENING OF THE RELIGIOUS LIFE OF THE RANK AND FILE

The religious life of laity and clergy displayed a growing earnestness. There was a rising tide of devotion to the Virgin Mary. A vision of Mary which Catherine Labouré, a Parisian Sister of Charity, believed that she had in 1830, emphasizing the immaculate conception of the Virgin, led to the striking of the Miraculous Medal and the spread of that medal to many lands. The increase of devotion to Mary was encouraged by successive Popes and in 1854 Pope Pius IX formally declared the immaculate conception to be a dogma of the Church. By this was meant that from the first moment of her existence Mary was "immune from all taint of original sin." This gave added impetus to the cult of the Virgin. It seems to have been in this atmosphere that in 1858 a peasant girl, Bernadette Subirous, believed that the Virgin appeared to her eighteen times in a grotto near Lourdes, in France, and that at the Feast of the Annunciation she had heard her say: "I am the immaculate conception." Pilgrims thronged to the place, miracles of healing were reported, and within half a century the shrine of Our Lady of Lourdes is said to have attracted more than five million visitors. Devotion to the Heart of Mary also became widespread.

It may have been because of the devotion to Mary that added honours were paid to her consort, Joseph. Pope Pius IX proclaimed him patron of the entire Church and in 1889 Pope Leo XIII issued an encyclical enumerating the virtues of Joseph and emphasizing his position as patron.

Parallel with added reverence for the Virgin Mary went increased devotion to the Sacred Heart of Jesus. We have seen this in France in the seventeenth century in connexion with the Catholic Reformation and a fresh stage of mysticism. It was much older than the seventeenth century, but it was then given especial emphasis, partly through John Eudes and partly through the visions of Margaret Mary Alacoque. In the nineteenth century it spread through the entire Roman Catholic Church. It emphasized the sacrificial love of Christ in his incarnation and his suffering. The physical heart of Jesus was its sacramental symbol. It stressed consecration to Christ, reparation for his sufferings, and frequent communion. In the course of the nineteenth century groups, societies, and congregations, especially of women, dedicated themselves to the Sacred Heart of Jesus. Several of them bore that designation. Pictures and scapulars of the Sacred Heart multiplied. There were also such movements as the Apostleship of Prayer, the Month of the Sacred Heart, confraternities of the Sacred Heart, and the Confraternity of Prayer and Penance.

In numbers of orders and congregations perpetual adoration of the Blessed Sacrament was practised. It was by no means a new custom. It seems to have developed first in the Middle Ages, but then it was not common. It became much more frequent in the sixteenth and seventeenth centuries, in association with the Catholic Reformation. In the nineteenth century it spread very widely. Not only monastic congregations and orders, but also confraternities of lay folk observed it. Its purpose was in part to seek to make reparation for the lack of regard by the majority of mankind for the incarnation and the sufferings of Christ. Its popularity in the nineteenth century may have been furthered by the realization that multitudes whose ancestors had professed to be Christians were drifting away from the faith. It was certainly one aspect of the intensification of the faith of what was becoming the self-conscious Roman Catholic minority.

The popularity of devotion to the Sacred Heart of Jesus was by progressive stages. In 1856 the Pope extended to the entire Roman Catholic Church the feast of the Sacred Heart. In the next few decades the adoration spread and at least one state, Ecuador, was formally dedicated to the Sacred Heart. In the 1870's over five hundred bishops petitioned the Pope to consecrate the entire Roman Catholic Church to the Sacred Heart. Late in the 1890's the Pope formally consecrated all of mankind to the Sacred Heart.

Partly associated with the adoration of the Sacred Heart of Jesus was added emphasis upon the Eucharist and frequent communion. In 1905 Pope Pius X invited all Roman Catholics to daily communion. To combat the drift away from the Church in France, beginning in 1881 Roman Catholics of that country from time to time held Eucharistic congresses. These spread to other lands and eventually were convened on a world-wide scale. The custom of paying visits to the reserved sacrament for prayer and adoration increased.

In the nineteenth century there arose what was known as the liturgical movement. It is said to have received its first major impetus from Guéranger, Abbot of Solesmes, who died in 1875. One aspect of it was the discontinuation of the Gallican and local German rites and the substitution for them of the Roman rite. This phase was part of ultramontanism, the enhancement of the power of the Pope, of which we are to say more in a moment. Another and quite as significant feature was the promotion of intelligent and earnest worship, especially by the laity, and thus the nurture of the spiritual life of the rank and file of Roman Catholics, both clergy and laity. It was to swell to much larger proportions after 1914.

Associated with the liturgical movement was more attention to the music of the Church. In 1903 Pope Pius X issued *motu proprio* on church music. In it, in the interest of public worship, he set forth what he believed to be the characteristics of sacred music and commanded that these should be observed throughout the Church but with variations to suit conditions in particular countries. He declared that the Gregorian form, going back traditionally to Pope Gregory the Great, although not necessarily his creation, should be standard. He ordered that so far as possible the Gregorian chant be restored.

The Enlistment of the Laity Through Catholic Action

In the second half of the nineteenth century stress began to be placed on what was called Catholic Action. Catholic Action seems to have had its origin in Bologna in 1868 in an effort to band youth together for the defense of the Church through the *Gioventù Cattolica Italiana,* under the motto, "Prayer, action, sacrifice." Beginning in 1874 national congresses of the Catholics of Italy were held annually. Under the leadership of a Venetian lawyer, Count Giambattista Paganuzzi, Catholic Action became very influential in Italy.

Like the liturgical movement, Catholic Action was to assume larger proportions after 1914. Subsequent to that year it was to receive the Papal definition of "the participation of the laity in the hierarchic apostolate of the Church." It was under the direction of the bishops and its expressions varied from diocese to diocese. In general it was by groups of the laity in the service of the bishop and trained to extend Catholic life. It was to seek the development of the spiritual life of the individual, the family, and society. It was an attempt to bring the rank and file of Roman Catholics to a higher plane of Christian living and to make Christian principles effective in society. Catholic Action might express itself in endeavouring to win individuals to the Roman Catholic faith, in promoting Roman Catholic schools, in political activity, or in one of several other channels. It was another facet of the movement which tended to make Roman Catholics an intelligent, loyal, disciplined community under the direction of a tightly knit hierarchy headed by the Pope, striving to win the world.

The Appearance of Saints

The nineteenth century witnessed the appearance of several who were adjudged by the Roman Catholic Church to be ideal Christians and who, even before the 1950's, had been officially so recognized by solemn beatification or canonization. Two of them were John Bosco and Bernadette Soubirous, whom we have already mentioned. Among the others was Jean Baptiste Marie Vianney (1786–1859), better known as the Curé of Ars. He spent most of his life as a priest in charge of the parish of Ars, a village near Lyons. There he established what he called "The Providence" for the care of girls, and with such success that it served as a model for similar institutions in other parts of France. He became especially famous for his skill and power in the direction of souls. High and low, bishops, priests, and laity, poor and rich, flocked to him. In the last ten years of his life he is said to have spent from sixteen to eighteen hours a day in the confessional. Strictly ascetic in his eating and drinking, humble, cheerful, patient, radiating faith and the love of God, he had a singular ability to read character and to see the sins and weaknesses of those who came to him in the confessional even when the penitent would not or could not fully disclose them to him. His good judgement and his spiritual insight and faith brought to him thousands of the sick of soul or body and of those bewildered by the rapidly moving times in which they lived. We shall find parallels to him in both the Protestant and the Russian Orthodox branches of the Church.

It seems to have been significant that the age produced the only Pope for many generations who was deemed to have a character and quality of life which deserved formal beatification. This was Giuseppe Sarto (1835–1914), who as Pius X reigned from 1903 to 1914. Born of humble parents, he rose to high office after years as a parish priest, and was known as the "peasant Pope." He was declared blessed in 1951.

NUMERICAL GAINS

Although the Roman Catholic Church lost substantial numbers to a non-religious secularism, in at least three countries of Europe, predominantly Protestant, as we are to see slightly more at length later, it registered gains. These were the Netherlands, Scotland, and England. In the Netherlands the increase was due to the excess of births over deaths. Protestants did not have so high a birth rate and watched with some trepidation the growth of the Roman Catholic minority. In Scotland, overwhelmingly Presbyterian by long allegiance, immigration from Ireland, mainly of labourers, to the manufacturing city of Glasgow, produced a substantial Roman Catholic element. England saw a few conversions to the Roman Catholic Church, chiefly through the Oxford or Tractarian movement of which we are to hear in a subsequent chapter. However, here as in Scotland the increase was mostly by the influx of Irish labourers to industrial and commercial centres.

THE INCREASING AUTHORITY OF THE POPE

The nineteenth century witnessed the growing administrative authority of the Pope and with it the tightening of the hierarchical structure of the Roman Catholic Church under his direction. More than at any earlier time in its long history the Roman Catholic Church became a world-wide organization under one administrative centre operating through the territorial episcopate. Minority though it was, embattled against the new and old forces which were sweeping the world and especially Europe, suffering numerical losses in lands where it had once held the nominal allegiance of almost all the population, losses which were to mount as the century wore on, the Roman Catholic Church was more and more knit into a global community guided by a single head working through loyal subordinates, bishops, priests, monastic orders and congregations, and a devoted laity.

Perfection in this structure was by no means achieved. Hundreds of thousands of professed Roman Catholics were still only nominally of the faith and over them the hierarchy had little control. In some lands the clergy were too few, notably in Latin America, and their quality in morals and intelligence left much to be desired. With the Church in several countries, strikingly in Spain, Portugal, and Latin America, the Pope had to walk warily. The tradition of independence of Papal administrative control did not quickly die. Yet in the main the movement was in the direction which we have indicated.

The reasons for the growth of Papal power were several. One was the persistence of the spirit and actions of the Council of Trent. That gathering, it will be recalled, had been marked by the enhanced power of the Papacy and by administrative changes which enlarged the effective power of the bishops within their dioceses. Another cause was the movement towards the separation of Church and state. In predominantly Roman Catholic countries this came from anti-clericalism, namely, hostility to the Church and its influence in the government. It was especially marked in France, as we are to see in a moment, but to a lesser degree was found in other Latin lands and was also vigorous in Germany. One effect of anti-clericalism was to curtail or end the control of the state over the Church within its borders, including the appointment of bishops, and to render the bishops more dependent upon the Pope. Roman Catholics, with the tide setting against them, were inclined to ultramontanism, to look "beyond the mountains," the Alps, for support from Rome. Thus the Gallicanism which had long been characteristic of the Church in France was decidedly weakened. Still another cause was the geographic expansion of the Church. The Vatican exercised more direct control over the Roman Catholic Church in lands where it was weak or newly planted than in countries where it was better established. The Congregation for the Propagation of the Faith had suffered severely at the hands of Napoleon and in 1808 had been discontinued. However, in 1814 it was revived and much of its property was restored. It was the instrument through which the Papacy supervised and directed missions in lands where the Roman Catholic Church was non-existent or in the minority. Some of the nineteenth century Popes made much of it. Through it they exercised greater authority over the ecclesiastical structure in those lands than they could in Europe where traditions of semi-autonomy, even though weakened, persisted. This was the situation in most of Asia and Africa, in the Pacific, and in the rapidly expanding Roman Catholic Church in the United States.

The administrative authority of the Pope was augmented by increased acquiescence in his claim to have the right to define dogma. Thus, without seeking the concurrence of an ecumenical council, Pius IX pronounced that the immaculate conception of the Virgin Mary was to be held by all the faithful as true. There had long been division of opinion as to the validity of that doctrine. Now the Pope removed it from the category of the debatable and in doing so encountered no serious opposition.

More important was the action of the Vatican Council, counted by Roman Catholics as the twentieth in the ecumenical succession, in coming out flatly for Papal supreme administrative power and doctrinal infallibility. No general council of the Roman Catholic Church had been held since the adjournment of that of Trent, in 1563. Thus a period of slightly over three hundred years had elapsed without such a gathering, the longest gap in the series since the first had been convened at Nicæa in 325. In summoning it the Pope took the initiative. This in itself was an assertion of authority. He invited not only all Roman Catholic bishops, abbots having episcopal jurisdiction, and heads of orders, but also Orthodox bishops and Protestants. It was made clear that if the Orthodox and Protestants accepted, they would by that act be acknowledging the supremacy of the Pope. Obviously none of them came. In contrast with earlier councils, no secular princes were asked. This was at least partly because some of them had broken their concordats with Rome. The council assembled late in 1869 and continued into 1870.

The chief issue before the council was Papal infallibility. There were some who wished the formal approval of the dogma of the bodily assumption of the Virgin, but this was not to be given until 1950, and then by Papal, not by conciliar action. The bishops were by no means unanimous. Some held what was often called the Gallican position, namely, that only the body of bishops, and no particular bishop, not even the Bishop of Rome, could make infallible judgements on matters of dogma. With this, in one or another form, stood some of the French, Austrian, and German episcopate. On the other extreme were those who wished the enactment of the complete authority of the Pope over the bishops.

The council approved a "dogmatic constitution on the Catholic faith" to be proclaimed by the Pope. In this, because of the many departures from that faith through, so it said, Protestantism, rationalism, and nationalism, the main tenets of the Catholic faith were reaffirmed, including the relation of reason and faith in ascertaining and accepting truth. In the same fashion, the "first constitution on the Church of Christ" known, by its opening words, as *Pastor æternus,* was promulgated by the Pope "with the approval" of the council. It affirmed that "the primacy of jurisdiction over the universal Church of God was immediately and directly promised and given to Blessed Peter the Apostle by Christ the Lord"; that Peter's successors are "the Bishops of the Holy See of Rome"; that they therefore "by the institution of Christ himself obtain the primacy of Peter over the whole Church"; and that "it has at all times been necessary that every Church—that is to say, the faithful throughout the world—should agree with the Roman Church." The *Pastor æternus* went on to declare that to the "jurisdiction of the Roman Pontiff . . . . all, of whatever right and dignity, both pastors and faithful, both individually and collectively, are bound . . . . to submit, not only in matters which belong to faith and morals, but also in those which appertain to the discipline and government of the Church throughout the world." This, however, was said not to weaken the power of the bishops, but to strengthen and protect it. Hitting directly at the fashion in which some Catholic monarchs had insisted that all communications between the Pope and the Church in their realms be permitted only with the consent of the crown, the *Pastor æternus* held that free communication between the Pope on the one hand and the bishops and their flocks on the other could not lawfully be impeded and that it should not be subject to the will of the secular power. It also expressly declared that no appeal could be taken from the Roman Pontiffs to an ecumenical council, thus asserting the superiority of the Pope over the latter. The Pope was emphatically pronounced to have the office not "merely of inspection and direction" but also "full and supreme power of jurisdiction over the Universal Church." This power was to be exercised not indirectly, but directly and without an intermediate authority.

The climax of the *Pastor æternus* was the solemn declaration that "it is a dogma divinely revealed that the Roman Pontiff, when he speaks *ex cathedra,* that is, when in the discharge of the office of pastor and doctor of all Christians, by virtue of his supreme apostolic authority he defines a doctrine regarding faith or morals to be held by the universal Church, by the divine assistance promised to him in blessed Peter, is possessed of that infallibility with which the divine Redeemer willed that His Church should be endowed for defining doctrine regarding faith or morals: and that therefore such definitions of the Roman Pontiff are irreformable of themselves, and not from the consent of the Church." This authority was held not that the Popes might make known new doctrine, but that by the aid of the Holy Spirit "they might inviolably keep and faithfully expound the revelation or deposit of faith delivered through the apostles" and "that the whole flock of Christ, kept away by them from the poisonous food of error, might be nourished with the pasture of heavenly doctrine; that the occasion of schism being removed, the whole Church might be kept one, and, resting on its foundation, might stand firm against the gates of hell."

By this action the council, professing to speak for the entire Church, came out plumply for the supreme authority of the Pope, both as the administrative head of the Church and as the custodian of the Christian faith. This was asserted against the state, other bishops, and ecumenical councils.

PAPAL INTRANSIGENCE WIDENS THE GULF BETWEEN THE ROMAN CATHOLIC CHURCH AND OTHER CHURCHES AND THE STATE, BUT EXCEPT FOR A SMALL MINORITY WINS GENERAL ACQUIESCENCE IN THE ROMAN CATHOLIC CHURCH

The action of the Vatican Council widened the gulf, already great, between the Roman Catholic Church and other Christian churches. The claims set forth for that church were not new, but their reiteration in clear and emphatic form accentuated the impossibility of reconciliation with the Eastern Churches and the Protestant bodies except through acceptance of the authority of the Papacy both in administration and in doctrine.

Pastor æternus also placed the Roman Catholic Church unequivocably against the kind of control exercised in the past by several governments which were professedly loyal to the Catholic faith. It made more acute the historic conflict between Church and state, a conflict already sharpened by the trends of the nineteenth century.

Within the Roman Catholic Church there had by no means been unanimity. While in the final formal vote the council's approval was by an overwhelming majority, only a little over two-thirds of the bishops of the church were there at the time. When the vote was taken, four-fifths of those present were Italian bishops, cardinals, officials of the church, and vicars apostolic, the last named being bishops who were the direct agents of the Papacy. Even then, one of the dissenting votes was by an Italian bishop. Several of the bishops who were opposed left before the final action. Some felt that having voted in the negative at an earlier session they had fulfilled their duty. Most of the dissidents submitted.

However, some prominent Roman Catholics refused to conform, and from them came what were known as the Old Catholics. The Old Catholics had their centre in Germany, Austria, Bohemia, and the German portions of Switzerland. Their leaders were scholars, mostly members of the teaching staffs of universities. Outstanding was Johann Joseph Ignaz von Döllinger (1799–1890), of Bavaria, who had been a vocal and determined critic of Papal infallibility. For a time the governments of Bavaria and Prussia were sympathetic and the tradition of national churches in communion with Rome but largely independent of its administrative control, known variously as Gallicanism and Febronianism, favoured the movement. Febronionism had its origin on the border between France and Germany and was especially influential in the Roman Catholic part of Germany. It took its name from Justinus Febronius, the pseudonym of Johann Nikolaus von Hontheim, auxiliary bishop of Trier. In a book, *De Statu Ecclesiæ Præsenti et de Legitima Potestate Romani Pontificis,* published in 1763, with the professed purpose of facilitating the union of the churches, he had attacked the more extreme claims of the Papacy. He held that while the Pope was necessary to unity, his legitimate place was only that of *primus inter pares* among the bishops and that he should be subordinate to the Church as a whole. The book won a wide hearing. Some of the Old Catholic leaders were hopeful that union could be achieved with the Eastern Churches and the Church of England on the basis of the historic episcopate and creeds freed from Papal domination. In the 1870's the Old Catholic Church was organized. Although he had been excommunicated by his archbishop and gave it counsel, Döllinger refused to join it. No Roman

Catholic bishop adhered to it. Episcopal succession was obtained through the small church which had left the Roman Catholic fold partly over the issue of Jansenism and which had its headquarters at Utrecht. Only a few thousand adherents were attracted, but the Old Catholic Church persisted as a distinct body.

The net result of the Vatican Council and of the development of which it was a major stage was, as we have suggested, to render the Roman Catholic Church a still more tightly coördinated body under the direction of one man exercising absolute administrative and religious authority. In principle this had long been the ideal of the Papacy. That ideal was now made an actuality. More than before, although that had long been the trend, especially after the Council of Trent, the Roman Catholic Church had become a sect, that is, a hard and fast division within the total body of organized Christianity. It was the largest of the sects. It was probably represented in more countries than was any other of them. Like several of them it claimed to be the only one which had held firmly to what had been taught by the original apostles and regarded the other churches as having wandered from that faith. Its attitude precluded compromise on what it deemed the essentials of the Christian faith and made impossible in the foreseeable future an inclusive unity of all who bore the Christian name. Because of the rapid growth of Protestantism in the nineteenth and twentieth centuries, both in numbers and geographic outreach, a growth which made that branch of Christianity as world-wide as the Roman Catholic Church, in 1914 and even more a generation later, the Roman Catholic Church embraced a smaller proportion of Christians than it had in 1500, 1750, or 1815. Moreover, there was much less prospect of its attracting what was fast becoming the majority of Christians, those who were not in communion with it, than there had been in 1500 or even in 1815. Although it made some gains from the Eastern Churches, and a few slight ones from Protestantism, by 1914 it was losing heavily to Protestantism in Latin America and the Philippines, lands in which it had had its major territorial gains between 1500 and 1750.

In the meantime, as we are to see, there was emerging from Protestantism a fresh approach to Christian unity. In one way or another by the middle of the twentieth century it drew in not only the majority of Protestants but also several of the Eastern Churches and even many individuals of Roman Catholic allegiance.

THE ROMAN CATHOLIC CHURCH SETS ITSELF FIRMLY
AGAINST THE TREND OF THE AGE

The Roman Catholic Church, increasingly closely knit, set itself consciously against some of the dominant trends of the age. Probably it would have done this no matter who the individuals were who occupied the chair of Peter. However, the attitude was made more emphatic because of the convictions and policies of the Popes who reigned during the larger part of the century. Leo XII, Pope from 1823 to 1829, frail, stern, hard-working, openly opposed some of the movements of his day. He denounced liberty of faith and conscience, condemned the Bible societies for circulating the Scriptures in the vernacular tongues as furthering interpretations deemed erroneous by the Roman Catholic Church, restored the Inquisition, struggled against the Freemasons and the revolutionary *Carbonari* in the Papal states, and supported monarchs against efforts of liberals. Skilful diplomacy, largely due to the policies of the able Consalvi in the preceding reign, obtained favourable concordats with several states. The brief rule of Pius VIII (1829–1830) was marked by efforts to restrict mixed marriages between Protestants and Roman Catholics in the Rhineland. Pius VIII was followed by Bartolommeo Alberto Cappellari (1765–1846) who reigned from 1831 to 1846 under the title of Gregory XVI. A Camaldulese monk, a scholar, head of the Propaganda, and a cardinal, he was in his middle sixties at the time of his election. Conservative by temperament and conviction, he opposed the revolutions which were sweeping through Italy and did nothing to reform the inept and unpopular administration of the Papal states.

When in his mid-fifties and at the height of his powers, Giovanni Maria Mastai-Ferretti (1792–1878), a scion of a noble family, came to the Papal throne (1846) as Pius IX. He ruled the Church for almost a third of a century. Those decades witnessed momentous changes in Italy and Europe. They saw a triumph of nationalism in the political unification of Germany and Italy. They covered the period of revolt against the age of Metternich and the victories of the resurgent Revolution in the constitutional monarchy in Italy, the coming of the Second and Third Republics in France, and liberal movements in much of the rest of Europe, with emphasis upon the secular state. They spanned the appearance of Darwin's *On the Origin of Species* and *Descent of Man* and the spread of the evolutionary theory with its challenge to the conception of creation held by the majority of Christians.

At the outset Pius IX was hailed as a liberal. In the first few months of his reign he instituted reform measures, including a constitution for Rome, greater freedom of the press, permission to build railways in his domains, and the appointment of laymen to office in the Papal states. In protesting against the Austrian occupation of Ferrara he seemed to be placing himself at the head of the movement for a united Italy freed from foreign intervention.

However, the apparently liberal phase of the reign was of short duration. Pius IX was essentially a conservative. Alarmed by what he deemed the excesses of the revolutions which broke out in 1848 and which swept across Western Europe, including Italy, he set his face against the new forces. It was during his pontificate that the Papal states were incorporated into the new Kingdom of Italy and that Rome was made the capital of that state. Unreconciled, he refused to acquiesce, declined the proffered financial compensation for the confiscated territories, and became the protesting "prisoner of the Vatican." Moreover, he issued momentous decrees in which he strengthened the power of his office over the Roman Catholic Church and blasted at the prevailing trends of the age.

It was Pius IX who proclaimed as dogma the immaculate conception of the Virgin Mary, who called the Vatican Council, and who affirmed, with the manipulated consent of that body, the supremacy of the Pope over the Roman Catholic Church and Papal infallibility.

The most famous of the pronouncements of Pius IX on the movements of the times was contained in what is usually known as the *Syllabus of Errors*. Issued in December, 1864, as a supplement to the encyclical, *Quanta cura,* it was addressed to the bishops of the Roman Catholic Church. It had been in preparation for some time and its subjects had been discussed with theologians and bishops. The *Syllabus* listed under eighty headings what the Pope deemed the errors of the day. Its denunciations were collected from his "allocutions, encyclicals, and other apostolical letters."

Among what were labelled as errors were the belief that God is not distinct from the universe, but is nature; that human reason, without regard for God, is the sole judge of truth and falsehood; that all the truths of religion are derived from human reason; that divine revelation is imperfect and is therefore subject to continual and indefinite progress; that Christian faith contradicts human reason; that the prophecies and miracles recorded in the Scriptures are the fictions of poets; that Jesus Christ is a mythical invention; that theology is to be treated by reason in the same manner as philosophy; that the dogmas of the Christian religion are of such a nature that human reason, by its own strength, can arrive at a true knowledge of them; and that the Church ought never to stand in judgement on philosophy.

The *Syllabus* went on to condemn the current belief that the decrees of Rome fettered the progress of science; that the principles and methods of the school men were not congruous with the needs of the age or the progress of science; that every man is free to adopt whatever religion he deems in accord with the light of reason; that in any religion men may find the way to eternal life; that there is a well-founded hope for the eternal salvation of those who are not in the true Church of Christ; and that Protestantism is another form of the Christian religion in which it is as possible to be pleasing to God as in the Roman Catholic Church.

The *Syllabus* also strongly dissented from the views that socialism, communism, secret societies, Bible societies, and clerico-liberal societies were to be permitted rather than regarded as pests condemned by repeated Papal pronouncements; that the civil power might define the rights and limits within which the Church could exercise authority; and that the obligation which binds Catholic teachers and writers extends only to such matters as are set forth for universal belief as dogmas of the faith by the infallible judgement of the Church.

The *Syllabus* dealt with the relations of Church and state and in so doing rejected as error the assertions that Roman Pontiffs and ecumenical councils had usurped the rights of princes and had committed errors in defining matters of faith and morals; that the Church might not use force or direct or indirect temporal power; that ministers of the Church and the Roman Pontiff should be excluded from all charge and control over temporal affairs; that bishops could not promulgate their own apostolic letters without the consent of the state; that ecclesiastical courts should be abolished; that the immunity of the clergy from military service should be discontinued; that the teaching of theological subjects is not exclusively a prerogative of the Church; that national churches could be separated from the authority of the Pope; that definitions made by national councils are final and not subject to further discussion; that the state is the source of all rights and that its right is unlimited; that the civil power, even when exercised by an unbelieving ruler, has a veto in spiritual affairs; that the civil power may interfere in matters which pertain to religion, morals, and spiritual rule; that the civil power should have full control of the public schools for the education of youth in Christian states; that public schools should be freed from all ecclesiastical authority; that the secular authority can present bishops and require of them that they take office before having been formally confirmed by the Holy See; that the secular power can depose bishops; that the state can suppress religious orders, churches, and benefices, and make what disposition it pleases of their properties and revenues; that in disputed questions of jurisdiction kings and princes are not under the jurisdiction of the Church but are superior to it; that Church and state should be separated; that philosophy and morals and civil laws should be freed from divine and ecclesiastical authority; that authority is nothing but the sum of numerical superiority and material strength; that it is permissible to refuse obedience to legitimate princes and to rise in rebellion against them; that the violation of a solemn oath is not only permissible but praiseworthy when done for the love of country; that divorce may be pronounced by the civil authority; that marriage is not a sacrament and that civil contract constitutes true marriage among Christians; that the state has jurisdiction over marriage; that the abolition of the temporal power of the Holy See would contribute to the freedom and prosperity of the Church; that it is no longer expedient that the Catholic religion should be the only religion of the state to the exclusion of other forms of worship; and that the Pope should become reconciled to progress, liberalism, and modern civilization.

From this long list of what he deemed errors, it is clear that Pius IX was holding to the position which the Roman Catholic Church had been taking for centuries in its conflict with the state, in its claim to be the sole custodian of saving truth, in its struggle against what it regarded as heresies, and in its efforts to shape youth and to direct the lives of Christians. The area of conflict had broadened. The state was now entering into areas which in Western Europe since the disintegration of the Roman Empire had been the domain of the Church, the education of youth and the control of marriage. Here the Roman Catholic Church found itself fighting what was largely a delaying battle in a slow retreat. Similarly, in its efforts to hold men to the faith the Roman Catholic Church was setting itself against the kind of use of reason which was increasingly becoming the accepted, almost the axiomatic mode of thought among the majority of intellectuals in the Occident.

THE ROMAN CATHOLIC CHURCH PARTIALLY ACCOMMODATES ITSELF TO SOME OF THE CURRENTS OF THE DAY

Under Leo XIII, the successor of Pius IX, the Roman Catholic Church sought to accommodate itself to some of the currents of the day and to control and direct them into channels which it regarded as in accord with Christian principles. This it did primarily in the new conditions of labour and politics. That accommodation was by no means complete. Basically Leo XIII did not depart from the principles of his predecessor. Indeed, he reinforced some of the latter's policies. However, he was more diplomatic, less negative, and instead of merely setting himself against the tide sought to guide some of its manifestations.

Gioacchino Pecci (1810–1903), who as Leo XIII was Pope from 1878 to 1903, was of a Sienese family and was educated by the Jesuits. He early displayed skill in diplomacy, and for thirty-two years was Archbishop in Perugia. In that see he built many churches, laboured to raise the intellectual and spiritual level the clergy, and was zealous for social reform and learning. Although he was lukewarm towards the *Syllabus of Errors,* he was made a cardinal by Pius IX. He openly opposed the termination of the temporal power of the Pope, would not welcome the King of Italy to his diocese, protested against the confiscation by the state of the property of the religious orders, and denounced the enactment of the Italian law of civil marriage.

During his quarter of a century on the Papal throne Leo XIII issued many encyclicals. In general these did not surrender the ground claimed by his predecessor. In stressing the education of the clergy, notably in the encyclical *Æterni patris* (1879), he based it largely upon the theology of Thomas Aquinas, thus being in accord with the loyalty of Pius IX to the school men. His emphasis upon the right of private property, his condemnation of socialism and of the control of marriage and the permission of divorce by civil law, his criticism of the theory of the sovereignty of the people and of the assertion that society arises from a social contract arrived at by the consent of its members, his opposition to the attitude of the state which placed all religions on an equality, regarding them as equally good, his denunciation of the belief that public education is a duty of the state and of the freedom of the press, and his insistence that the state recognize its duty to God and religion and to protect the Church were in the same direction as the pronouncements of Pius IX. He held to the decree *Non expedit* of the preceding reign which forbade Roman Catholics to vote or hold office under the Kingdom of Italy, thus showing his adament displeasure at the absorption of the Papal states by that realm. He maintained unflinchingly that the features in the political and intellectual life of Europe which he deplored were the fruitage of the Protestant Reformation.

However, in other ways Leo XIII was more positive and conciliatory. While holding it to be unlawful to place various forms of Divine worship on the same level, he said that under some circumstances religious toleration by the state was permissible. He declared that the Roman Catholic Church did not repudiate the discoveries of modern scientific research and he himself added to the equipment of the Vatican observatory.

Leo XIII might have adduced as evidence for the friendliness of the Roman Catholic faith to science the fact that what became generally accepted as laws of heredity were worked out by an Augustinian monk, Gregor Johann Mendel (1822–1884), later abbot, in his monastic garden, and that Louis Pasteur (1822–1895), whose investigations greatly promoted the knowledge of germs, antisepsis in surgery, and the protection of men and animals against bacilli, was a devout believer.

In the encyclical *Libertas præstantissimum* (1888), Leo XIII held that the Church is not hostile to liberty and that Catholic governments are not bound to crusade against liberals. In the encyclical *Sapientiae Christianæ* (1890), while insisting that all Catholic political organizations give full obedience to the Church and the Pope, he said that Catholics might participate in politics, even in states not based on Catholic principles, although looking forward to the time when these governments would be thus organized. He sought to induce French Catholics to support the Third Republic, a regime which regarded the Roman

Catholic Church as a major enemy. While coming out (1896) against the validity of the orders of the Church of England, he took kindly notice of the jubilee of Queen Victoria's accession to the throne. He established friendly relations with Russia, Switzerland, and the German Empire, and so won the confidence of Bismarck after the latter's war against the Roman Catholic Church, of which we are to hear a little later, that the Iron Chancellor asked him to arbitrate a dispute between Germany and Spain over the Caroline Islands.

Abstemious in his private life almost to the point of asceticism, Leo XIII was generous in his charities. By his character and his deeds he greatly enhanced the prestige of the Holy See.

One of the most memorable pronouncements of Leo XIII, and which gained for him the popular designation of "the workingman's Pope," was his encyclical *Rerum novarum* (1891). In this he distinctly put himself on the side of labour in the mounting industrialism. Condemning socialism as a false remedy for the evil conditions under which workingmen suffered, supporting private property, rejecting the theory of the inevitability of class warfare which was postulated by Marxian socialism, and declaring that religion enjoined workingmen to fulfill contractual obligations freely assumed and to refrain from violence in pressing their claims, he also insisted that religion taught that the employer must not tax his employees beyond their strength, must not assign to them work unsuited to their age and strength, nor deprive them of their wages. The employer was commanded to see that his workmen received just wages, had time for the duties of piety, were encouraged in their family life, and were guarded against corrupting influences. Leo XIII came out for the right of both employers and workmen to organize, and therefore for labour unions. He held that it was the duty of the state to see that labour was properly housed, clothed, and fed. He said that laws should be enacted to prevent strikes by removing the causes of conflict between employers and employees. He declared that work should cease on Sundays and certain festival days, and that these days were not to be used for idleness or dissipation, but for the observances of religion. He maintained that hours of labour should be regulated, that proper provision should be made for rest, and that the labour of women and children should be so safeguarded that conditions under which it was carried on would not injure the health or the morals of either. Associations of labouring men, so he insisted, must look first and foremost to God, must provide for the religious instruction of their members, and must encourage the latter to reverence and love the Church and frequent its sacraments.

Even before Leo XIII, some leaders in the Roman Catholic Church had inaugurated measures which looked in this direction. Thus Wilhelm Emmanuel von Ketteler (1811–1877), Archbishop of Mainz, had encouraged the formation of labour unions and had advocated laws for the regulation or the prohibition of the labour of women and children, the limitation of working hours, and the provision in factories of satisfactory sanitary and moral conditions. In 1868, at the instance of a priest, Joseph Schlimps, the Roman Catholic social organizations in Germany banded together and in 1878 published a programme for social reform.

Leo XIII established in Italy what was known as the Work of the Conferences which brought together on a national scale Roman Catholic associations, including the press, popular conferences, circles, and parochial committees. In some other countries Catholic labour organizations came into being.

The Stiffening of the Attitude of the Papacy under Pius X

The "peasant Pope," Pius X (1903–1914), held in high honour and eventually beatified, was more pronounced in his opposition to current trends than had been his predecessor. Positively he set himself to reform some of the abuses which had crept in during the later years of Leo XIII, for that Pontiff had lived to be past ninety years of age and during his last days did not have the vigour which had once characterized his reign. Pius X tightened the discipline of the clergy, suppressed numbers of inefficient schools and seminaries, and, as we have seen, encouraged frequent communion of Catholics the world around.

However, Pius X refused to be reconciled to some of the trends in France and probably made conditions more difficult for the Church in that land.

Most notably of all, he took emphatic measures against what was known as "modernism." There had arisen in the Roman Catholic Church a minority, small to be sure, but including some very able priests and laymen, who sought to accommodate Christian scholarship and methods to the age. To the movement had contributed the widely read *Life of Jesus* (1863) by Ernest Renan (1823–1892), once a theological student but who had left the Church and who painted Jesus in glowing colours as a man, but not as God. The "modernists" applied current methods of historical criticism to the study of the Scriptures and the history of the Church. Among them were Hermann Schell in Germany, Alfred Loisy in France, the Jesuit, George Tyrrell, a convert to Roman Catholicism, in England, and the devout and learned layman, Baron von Hügel, who spent much of his life in Britain. In 1907 Pius X issued the decree, *Lamentabili,* and the encyclical, *Pascendi,* in which he commanded the bishops to "purge their clergy of modernistic infection." A number of books were banned as departing from orthodoxy, some priests were excommunicated, and several teachers were dismissed. The kind of critical scholarship which was being increasingly applied by Protestant scholars to the Bible and church history was condemned. In 1910 Pius X required all clergy having the cure of souls or engaged in teaching to take a drastic anti-modernist oath.

In 1910 Pius X issued an encyclical proscribing a kind of "social modernism," especially the programme advocated by the periodical *Le Sillon,* which advocated social action in coöperation with Protestants or those of any or no faith. In 1912 he followed this with restrictions on a practice found in Germany of admitting to Catholic syndicates all men of good will, regardless of their religion. He said that this should be done only with modifications and held (1911) that all Catholic organizations must be subject to the control of the bishops.

THE STRUGGLE IN VARIOUS COUNTRIES BETWEEN THE ROMAN CATHOLIC CHURCH AND THE NEWER TRENDS

The struggle between the Roman Catholic Church and the major currents in Western civilization of the nineteenth century was not confined to the Papacy. It was to be found in every country in Western Europe. In some it was more severe than in others. The outcome varied, but in most lands the Church suffered confiscation of much of its property, was placed under restrictions, and lost some of its former control of education and marriage.

The conflict bore most heavily on the Roman Catholic Church in France. The Revolution which had begun in 1789 continued, with varying success, throughout the nineteenth century. It seemed to be thwarted by the restoration of the Bourbons after the fall of Napoleon I, but it broke out afresh again and again, notably in 1830, in 1848, and, after the fall of the Second Empire and Napoleon III, in 1870 in the Third Republic. In general the conviction prevailed that the Roman Catholic Church and the Revolution were incompatible and that each was the enemy of the other. Thus after the return of the Bourbons Count Joseph Marie de Maistre (1754–1821) contemplated with horror the sovereignty of the people, believed that the greatest crime of the Revolution was that it sought to make men free, maintained that king and Pope were both ordained by God with absolute authority, and held that the Pope is above kings. Another of the prophets of the Restoration, Vicomte Louis Gabriel Ambroise de Bonald (1754–1840), regarded the spirit of the Revolution as "satanic," taught that the king could not be deposed under any circumstances, and was convinced that Roman Catholicism meant order and Protestantism disorder.

There were, to be sure, outstanding Roman Catholics who believed that their faith and political democracy were not reciprocally contradictory, but they were frowned upon by the Papacy. Prominent among them were Lamennais, Lacordaire, and Montalembert. Hugues Félicité Robert de Lamennais (1782–1854), a priest, sensitive and subject to periods of deep gloom, early acquired fame by his *Essai sur l'indifférence en matière de religion* in which he argued that the right of private judgement ended in atheism and that Europe could be regenerated only by accepting ecclesiastical authority. He was ultramontane and against the Gallican liberties of the Church in France. Later he came out against monarchy and advocated a theocratic democracy. He wished the Church to be freed from all civil domination. He began the periodical *L'Avenir* with the motto "God and liberty." But Rome condemned his programme and he broke with the Church and became an ardent advocate of the principles of the Revolution. Jean Baptiste Henri Locordaire (1802–1861), led to enter the priesthood by the *Essai* of Lamennais, sought to show that Roman Catholicism was consistent with the slogans of the Revolution—liberty, equality, and fraternity—and that popular sovereignty in civil government could be reconciled with Papal supremacy in religion. He became a Dominican, hoping to rewin France to Christianity by the preaching and teaching of that order. He openly declared himself a republican. Charles Forbes René de Montalembert (1810–1870), a layman, a friend of Lamennais and Lacordaire, a political liberal, while emphatically opposed to the *Syllabus of Errors,* did not break with the Church. The ultramontanes were his enemies and some of his teachings were condemned by the Pope.

In the Revolution of 1848 which ended the July Monarchy and sent Louis Philippe into exile, the old antagonism between the Roman Catholic Church and the French Revolution seemed to have died. Partly because of the influence of Lamennais and his disciples, democracy and the Catholic faith were held to be interdependent. The bishops praised the Revolution and the Second Republic which it inaugurated. The initial National Assembly included in its membership several priests and three bishops. Under Louis Napoleon the Second Republic and the Second Empire maintained the Pope in Rome by the support of French arms as against the recently inaugurated Kingdom of Italy.

When, after 1870, the Second Empire was followed by the Third Republic, most leading Roman Catholics, both clergy and laity, were opposed to the latter and wished the restoration of the monarchy. This made the government anticlerical, and clericalism was declared to be its enemy. Restrictions on Roman Catholic influence and teaching in the schools were enacted. Priests were forbidden to share in asylums and charitable institutions, all chaplaincies in the army and the normal schools were suppressed, divorce was legalized, and Sunday labour was authorized.

Thanks in part to the conciliatory tactics of Leo XIII and in part to the desire of the leaders of the government for peace, for a time the tension between the Church and the French state was eased. In 1879 the Papal legate advised Roman Catholics to accept the fact that the monarchy would not be restored and in 1892 in a Papal encyclical urged that the faithful accept the republic.

Then, in the 1890's, in the famous Dreyfus case which shook all France for years, Roman Catholic opinion in general was against Dreyfus and the eventual exoneration of that unhappy victim of the miscarriage of justice tended to discredit the Church. In 1901 the Associations Act was passed which forbade any religious order to exist in France without governmental authorization. Authorization proved difficult to obtain and hundreds of members of orders were driven out of the country. In 1902 and 1903 several thousand Catholic schools were closed. This was followed, in 1905, by the abrogation by the French Government of the Concordat of 1801 which since that year had been the basis of the relations of Church and state. This meant the disestablishment of the Roman Catholic Church and giving it no more favoured place than other cults. Pope Pius X condemned the act and forbade Catholics to form the associations which the law required for the use of buildings for public worship. In 1907 a new law eased the situation, but did not restore the establishment of the Church.

The antagonism of the Roman Catholic Church and the Third Republic accelerated the progressive de-Christianization of France. In general the Church remained strong in the rural districts, where pre-nineteenth century conditions more nearly persisted, and was weakest in the cities, where the new currents were potent.

In striking contrast with the drift away from Christianity was the vitality in the Roman Catholic Church in France. Among other manifestations, this showed itself in new foreign missionary movements, such as the creation and rapid growth of the Society for the Propagation of the Faith, and in the leadership which French Catholics took in the overseas missions of their Church in the nineteenth century. Here the Catholics of France out-distanced those of every other country.

In Germany the Roman Catholic Church was more successful than in France in its struggle with the state. In South Germany Febronianism persisted into the nineteenth century, but then faded. In the 1830's and 1840's a contest between Prussia and Rome in the Rhine provinces over the question of mixed marriages issued in concessions by the state.

The major conflict in Germany is usually known as the *Kulturkampf* ("struggle for civilization"). It began in South Germany in the support accorded by the governments in that area to the Old Catholics in their protest against the doctrine of Papal infallibility. Those loyal to Rome found a rallying point in the Centre Party, but it was not until 1890 that they were sufficiently strong in Bavaria to obtain the repeal of the concessions granted to the Old Catholics.

In the *Kulturkampf* the main opponent of the Roman Catholic Church was Bismarck. It was largely by Bismarck that German nationalism was utilized to bring unity to that long divided country. This was accomplished by making the prevailingly Protestant Kingdom of Prussia the dominant nucleus, first in the North German Confederation, formed in 1867, and then in the German Empire, the constitution of which was adopted in 1871. Since Austria was not in the Empire, the latter had a Protestant majority, but with a strong Roman Catholic minority. For several reasons, Bismarck was antagonistic to the Roman Catholic Church. He was a Protestant. Ultramontanism culminating in the recent promulgation of Papal infallibility appeared to him to threaten with the interference of a foreign power the German unity which had been so painfully achieved. The Centre Party stood for the rights of the South German states as against Prussia and so tended to perpetuate the weakening divisions which Bismarck was determined to overcome. Bismarck was irritated by the pressure from German Roman Catholics to intervene to restore the temporal power of the Pope, for it was disturbing the friendly relations between Germany and Italy.

In 1872 Bismarck embarked on measures designed to weaken the power of the Roman Catholic Church in Germany and especially in Prussia. Diplomatic relations between the Vatican and Germany were severed. The Jesuits, the Redemptorists, and some other religious orders were expelled. In Prussia laws were passed requiring all who held office in the Roman Catholic Church to be Germans who had received the larger part of their education in German institutions and placing theological seminaries under the control of the state. When some of the bishops refused to comply, governmental financial aid to the Church was discontinued in their dioceses and additional punitive measures were taken.

The opposition proved so great that Bismarck found it wise to retreat. In 1880 diplomatic relations with the Vatican were resumed and in 1886 most of the laws against which Roman Catholics had complained were repealed.

The net result was that the Centre Party, led by Ludwig Windthorst, the former Hanoverian minister, was greatly strengthened. It championed the cause of religious liberty, won the votes of Roman Catholic workingmen by promises to support social legislation in their favour, and flirted with the Socialists. The Roman Catholic cause, far from being weakened by the *Kulturkampf*, was enhanced.

In Austria the Papacy registered gains, but gains which were partly offset by reverses. Through the concordat of 1855 between Austria and the Holy See the last remnants of Josephism were removed. Among other concessions to Rome were the freedom of communication between the bishops and the Vatican, the control of the elementary schools, the education of the clergy by the Jesuits, the surrender by the state of all share in the administration of ecclesiastical property, and the increase of clerical authority in questions connected with marriage. Yet in 1861 an edict of toleration was issued which eased the restrictions on those who were not in the Roman Catholic Church. Moreover, in Hungary, a partner in the dual Hapsburg monarchy, in 1894, against the opposition of Roman Catholics, civil marriage was made compulsory. Late in the nineteenth century Bohemia, then also under Hapsburg rule, was the scene of a movement away from Rome.

In Belgium and the Netherlands the Roman Catholic Church made advances. In 1830, Belgium, united to the Netherlands by the Congress of Vienna which had made the post-Napoleonic settlement, declared its independence and succeeded in maintaining it. It was overwhelmingly Roman Catholic by religion. It also became highly industrialized, and the supposition would have been that, in common with industrialized areas elsewhere, it would drift towards de-Christianization. As in other Roman Catholic countries a struggle between clericals and anti-clericals ensued. With some modifications, the former won. From 1847 to 1884, the Liberals, anti-clerical, were generally in control and abolished religious instruction in the public schools. This aroused intense opposition among the more ardent Roman Catholics and for a time the Belgian ambassador was recalled from the Vatican. However, in 1884 the elections gave the government to the clericals and from then until after 1914 the Catholic party was in power. Partly to undercut the Liberals and the Socialists, it enacted legislation which promoted democracy, brought in a factory code to protect labour, recognized trade unions, began a system of old-age pensions, and promoted better housing. Education was fostered to such good effect that literacy was markedly advanced. Religious instruction was restored in most of the schools. Strong Roman Catholic labour organizations were formed which had a large part in the political, industrial, and social life of the land. In the predominantly Protestant Netherlands Roman Catholics mounted in numbers, chiefly, as we have said, because of the excess of births over deaths, and in 1853 the Vatican created a hierarchy for the country.

In Scandinavia, nearly solidly Lutheran since the sixteenth century, religious toleration gave opportunity for the growth of Roman Catholics. In Norway toleration was enacted in 1845, in 1892 a bishop was consecrated, and in 1897 most of the remaining legal disabilities of Roman Catholics were removed. In Denmark religious freedom was granted in 1849 and the first vicar apostolic was appointed in 1892. It was not until 1873 that a Swedish law permitted departure from the state church, and then only for those over eighteen years of age.

The Roman Catholic Church faced official opposition in Russia, committed as was that realm to the Orthodox Church. Especially stringent measures were taken in those portions of Poland which were under Russian rule, for there the

Roman Catholic Church, historically very strong, was regarded with suspicion as a possible rallying centre of Polish nationalism. Revolts in 1831 and 1863 accentuated Russian apprehensions. After the rebellion of 1863, in which some of the clergy were active, religious orders were suppressed and diplomatic relations between Russia and the Vatican were discontinued. In 1839 what is said to have been a total of about two million Uniates who had been constrained by the Polish authorities to assume that status after the merger formally effected at Brest in 1596, resumed their connexion with the Orthodox Church. More followed in 1875. In connexion with the varied revolutionary movements in the Russian Empire which took advantage of the Russo-Japanese War to come to a head in 1905, a group of Poles who combined "modernistic" views with the veneration of Mary broke from the Roman Catholic Church and found fellowship with the Old Catholics.

In linguistically and religiously diverse Switzerland friction developed which in 1847 led to civil war. The Catholic *Sonderbund* was defeated. However, under the constitution of 1848, while religious orders, including the Jesuits, were not permitted in any canton, religious liberty was accorded all Christians, and many Roman Catholics and Protestants moved into cantons which had hitherto been restricted to the opposite form of the faith. The constitution of 1874 was deemed by Roman Catholics to have placed them at a serious disadvantage and relations between the Swiss Government and the Vatican became strained.

In Spain, Portugal, and Italy, where, with the exception of the small Waldensian minority in the last named country, the Roman Catholic faith had long been the only religion, the nineteenth century was peculiarly stormy for that Church. The liberalism which was the child of the movement that had produced the French Revolution often found the Roman Catholic Church a major opponent and through various organizations, including the Freemasons, had anti-clerical manifestations.

In Spain the record was especially violent and marked by sharp extremes. As we have seen, Ferdinand VII, the returning Bourbon who was restored by the British in 1814, revived the old order, including the Inquisition and the Jesuits. In 1820 opposition exploded in an insurrection. This led (1823) to the intervention of a French army in support of the king. Back in full control, Ferdinand VII was even more fanatical in his suppression of liberalism. Following his death (1833) civil war broke out between contenders for the throne. The liberals gave their support to Christina, the mother and regent of the youthful Isabella II, daughter of Ferdinand, while in general the clericals rallied to the support of Don Carlos, the brother of Ferdinand. The Pope endeavoured to remain neutral. The forces of Isabella were victorious and her government banished the Jesuits, suppressed almost all the monasteries, confiscated their property, and refused to appoint bishops acceptable to the Vatican. In 1841 the number of bishops in Spain had been reduced to six. Isabella's rule satisfied neither the liberals nor the Roman Catholics. In 1868 an insurrection sent the incompetent and immoral Isabella into a French exile and was the prelude to seven years of civil strife with vain attempts at union, first under an Italian prince and then, even more briefly, under a republic. During these chaotic years anti-clericalism was rampant. In 1875 the Bourbons were restored in the person of Alphonso XII, son of Isabella II, and on his death (1885) the throne passed to his posthumous son, Alphonso XIII. Under Alphonso XII anti-clericalism was checked and the Jesuits and other religious orders returned, flourished, and had charge of the schools in which more than half of such of the youth as were educated were enrolled. The Queen-mother, Maria Christina, who served as regent during the minority of Alphonso XIII, was loyal to the Church, but did not hesitate to call a liberal to be her premier. For a time in 1909–1910, after Alphonse XIII came of age (1902), anti-clericals were sufficiently strong to have Protestant worship legalized and to prohibit the founding of new religious houses without government consent. Diplomatic relations with the Vatican were temporarily broken off, but were renewed in 1912.

The majority of Spaniards remained Roman Catholics. Their Roman Catholicism was singularly rigid, true to the tradition which both had given rise to the Inquisition and had been enforced by it. Spanish foreign missions were continued, but they were pale and attenuated when compared with their predecessors in the sixteenth and seventeenth century heyday of Spanish power. Moreover, there were those who either broke with the Church or remained only loosely attached to it. Some thought vigorously and independently. Notable among them was Miguel de Unamuno y Jugo (1864–1936), a university professor, whose writings were widely read and were known far beyond the borders of Spain.

In Portugal the nineteenth century was marked, as in Spain, by political struggles in which anti-clericalism was a marked feature. The House of Braganza occupied the throne until 1910, when it was overthrown and a republic established. As in Spain, the population was overwhelmingly Roman Catholic, but, also as in Spain, Freemasonry became a rallying centre of anti-clericals and there were liberals, socialists, and republicans. Elective, representative institutions made headway. From 1831 to 1840 anti-clericalism held sway. The Jesuits were expelled, religious orders were dissolved and their properties confiscated, the clergy were not allowed to administer the sacraments without the permission of the civil authorities, the crown exercised the power to appoint to all ecclesiastical offices from the bishops to the parish priests, and some of the episcopate were consecrated without so much as notifying the Pope. While, after 1840, confiscated religious properties were returned and uneasy relations were renewed with the Vatican, the state continued to control theological education. In several dioceses the populace refused to accept the bishops appointed by the crown. The Concordat of 1886 permitted the Pope to appoint the bishops on the nomination of the crown. Some years later religious orders were allowed under certain restrictions. The republic was strongly anti-clerical. In 1911 the religious orders were expelled, their properties were taken over by the government, and the formal separation of Church and state was carried through. In 1913 relations with the Holy See were severed. Yet, as in Spain, so far as the masses had a religion it was Roman Catholicism. Secularism made headway, especially among the intellectuals and the upper classes, but Protestantism had few adherents. Overseas missions were continued, but feebly, and were confined almost entirely to the Portuguese colonial possessions.

In the first decades after 1815 many of the leaders of the nationalism which was sweeping across Italy advocated the political unification of that long-divided country under the presidency of the Pope. Indeed, in 1847 the colourful and popular patriot, Garibaldi, offered his services to the Pope. However, after his initial brief liberal period, Pius IX became an opponent of Italian unity and the effective leadership passed to the Kingdom of Sardinia and its ruling family, the House of Savoy (which had its chief territories in Piedmont), engineered by the extremely able premier, Cavour. Cavour (1810–1861), a liberal, was strongly anti-clerical. Under the slogan, "A free Church in a free state," he expelled the Jesuits and suppressed many of the monasteries. In 1860 much of North Italy came over to the House of Savoy and a revolution in the Kingdom of the Two Sicilies (Sicily and South Sicily, with the capital at Naples), led by Garibaldi, drove out the decrepit Bourbons and brought their realm into the Kingdom of Italy, formed under the House of Savoy. In 1866 Venetia was annexed. Supported by French bayonets, until 1870 the Pope precariously held on to Rome and a small area about it. Then the Franco-Prussian War led to the withdrawal of the troops of Napoleon III and in September an Italian army entered the city. In 1871 the Italian Government sought to mollify the Pope by the "law of Papal guarantees." It offered the Pope the status of a reigning sovereign with full authority over the two chief Papal properties in Rome, the Vatican and the Lateran, and the Papal summer resort, the villa of Castel Gandolfo, and, as an indemnity for the loss of the Papal states, a substantial annual pension. To this Pius IX refused to accede, holding that it was unilateral action by the Kingdom of Italy and had not been arrived at by a concordat as between equals. He appealed to Catholic princes to restore his temporal power and in 1868 (through the decree *non expedit*) forbade Roman Catholics to vote or hold office under the new regime. Yet, although it confiscated much of the property of the Church, reduced by several thousands the number of monasteries, made it difficult for some bishops to assume office, and put all works of charity under the state, the Italian Government continued to pay the salaries of the clergy, permitted religious instruction in the schools, did not require a civil ceremony before the religious ceremony of marriage, and did not offend Papal convictions by sanctioning divorce. However, although the large majority ignored the Papal prohibition, the abstention of the more loyal Roman Catholics from the government left the state in the hands of those lukewarm to the Church or hostile to it and thus heightened the division between Church and state, weakening them both.

The tension was gradually relaxed. King Victor Emmanuel, under whom Italian unification was achieved, on his death bed (1878) was reconciled to the Church. His successor and Leo XIII exchanged courtesies on the latter's accession (1878) and that same year the government deleted clauses which were offensive to the bishops in the documents which they were required to fill out when drawing their salaries from the state. From time to time Leo XIII permitted Catholics to vote in local elections. In 1905 Pius X made it possible for the faithful to vote in national elections. Almost all Italians remained nominally Roman Catholic and there were flourishing Italian foreign missions. Yet much of religious indifference existed.

SUMMARY

In Western Europe, the home and traditional centre of the Roman Catholic Church, the nineteenth century record was one of contrasts.

On the one hand, the currents which had been flowing strongly against the faith of that Church in the eighteenth century continued and were augmented by others which issued from the new political, economic, social, and intellectual movements of the day. Many liberals regarded the Church as an enemy. In countries which had been the main strongholds of the Roman Catholic faith thousands of monastic houses were dissolved and their properties confiscated, and the education of youth was in part taken out of the hands of the Church. In several marriage was put under the control of the state, and in France Church and state were formally separated. The Popes were deprived of the territories upon which they had depended to make them politically independent. The Popes set themselves resolutely against these currents, and, condemning them, sought to stem them. Thus the distinction between the Church and the world was made sharper than at any time since the conversion of Constantine. In some respects the Roman Catholic Church lost ground. The de-Christianization of large elements of the population proceeded apace.

On the other hand, after the storm of the French Revolution and the cavalier treatment by Napoleon Bonaparte, the Roman Catholic Church made a striking recovery. Religious orders which had suffered severely were revived in part or in whole. New religious orders arose. Between 1815 and 1914 more seem to have come into being than in any previous hundred years. In general the devotion of the rank and file of the laity who remained faithful was increased. Fresh agencies for Catholic action by the laity began to be developed. Notably in Germany and Belgium, Catholic labour unions were organized, partly offsetting the secular labour organizations, and Catholic political parties appeared. A larger proportion of the laity were stirred to give financial support to the world-wide extension of the faith than ever before. Roman Catholic missions attained a geographic and numerical extent never before equalled. Papal administrative authority in the Roman Catholic Church was greatly augmented, and Papal infallibility in questions of faith and morals was formally affirmed. The Roman Catholic Church more and more took on the aspect of a militant minority, represented in more and more lands, and knit together and directed by the central authority in Rome. None of the Popes of the century was corrupt. The earlier ones were rigidly intransigent and of only moderate ability. The two later ones were of outstanding character. The next to the last, Leo XIII, was a man of first-class ability and brought the prestige of the office to a higher point than it had reached since the Reformation. The last, Pius X, was the first in several hundred years to be deemed worthy of beatification with the prospect of canonization.

Selected Bibliography

J. B. Bury, *History of the Papacy in the 19th Century (1864–1878)* (London, Macmillan & Co., 1930, pp. lx, 175). By a distinguished historian, covering the *Syllabus of Errors* and the Vatican Council.

C. Butler, *The Vatican Council. The Story Told from the Inside in Bishop Ullathorne's Letters* (New York, Longmans, Green & Co., 2 vols., 1930). By a Roman Catholic monk.

C. C. Eckhart, *The Papacy and World-Affairs as Reflected in the Secularization of Politics* (The University of Chicago Press, 1937, pp. xiv, 309). Mostly on the pre-nineteenth centuries.

M. Heimbucher, *Die Orden und Congregationen der katholischen Kirche* (Paderborn, Ferdinand Schöningh, 2 vols., 1897). A useful compendium.

H. Hermelink, *Das Christentum in der Menschheitsgeschichte von der Französischen Revolution bis zur Gegenwart, Vol. I, 1789–1835* (Stuttgart and Tübingen, J. B. Metzlersche Buchhandlung and Herman Leins, pp. xix, 528).

F. R. Hoare, *The Papacy and the Modern State. An Essay on the Political History of the Catholic Church* (London, Burns, Oates & Washbourne, 1940, pp. xiv, 413). By a Roman Catholic, mainly on the nineteenth century.

E. Hoçedez, *Histoire de la Théologie au XIX Siècle* (Paris, Desclée de Brouwer, 3 vols., 1947, 1948). The standard survey of Roman Catholic theology in the nineteenth century, by a Jesuit.

H. L. Hughes, *The Catholic Revival in Italy (1815–1915)* (London, Burns, Oates & Washbourne, 1935, pp. xii, 177). Sympathetic with the Roman Catholic Church.

P. Hughes, *The Popes' New Order. A Systematic Summary of the Social Encyclicals and Addresses from Leo XIII to Pius XII* (London, Burns, Oates & Washbourne, 1943, pp. viii, 232). Useful as a summary, but usually not giving the precise texts.

J. Husslein, *Social Wellsprings. Fourteen Documents by Pope Leo XIII* (Milwaukee, The Bruce Publishing Co., 1940). A useful compilation, by a Jesuit.

J. Husslein, *The Christian Manifesto. An Interpretative Study of the Encyclicals Rerum Novarum and Quadragesimo Anno of Pope Leo XIII and Pope Pius XI* (Milwaukee, The Bruce Publishing Co., 1931, pp. xxiv, 329). By a Jesuit.

C. K. Murphy, *The Spirit of Catholic Action* (London, Longmans, Green & Co., 1943, pp. xi, 197). Describes Catholic Action in simple terms, chiefly for Catholics.

J. H. Nichols, *Democracy and the Churches* (Philadelphia, The Westminster Press, 1951, pp. 298). By a Protestant scholar, dealing with both Protestantism and Roman Catholicism, chiefly in the nineteenth and twentieth centuries, critical of the Roman Catholic Church.

F. Nielsen, *The History of the Papacy in the XIXth Century,* translated under the direction of A. J. Mason (London, John Murray, 2 vols., 1906). Objective, through the reign of Pius IX.

F. Nippold, *The Papacy in the 19th Century,* translated by L. H. Schwab (New York, G. P. Putnam's Sons, 1900, pp. iv, 372). Critical of the Papacy.

C. S. Phillips, *The Church in France 1789–1848: A Study in Revival* (London, A. R. Mowbray & Co., 1929, pp. viii, 315). Scholarly.

C. S. Phillips, *The Church in France 1848–1907* (London, Society for Promoting Christian Knowledge, 1936, pp. 341). Carefully done.

C. Poulet, *A History of the Catholic Church,* translated and adapted by S. A. Raemers (St. Louis, B. Herder Book Co., Vol. II, 1948, pp. xxi, 735). A useful handbook, by a Roman Catholic.

P. Schaff, *The Creeds of Christendom, with a History and Critical Notes* (New York, Harper & Brothers, Vol. II, 1877, pp. vii, 607). Valuable for the Latin text and English translation of the *Syllabus of Errors* of Pius IX and the encyclical *Immortale Dei* of Leo XIII.

J. Schmidlin, *Papstgeschicte der neuesten Zeit* (Munich, Josef Kosel & Friedrich Pustet, 3 vols., 1933–1936). Covers the period from 1800 to 1922. A continuation of the famous work of Pastor, by a competent Roman Catholic scholar. Based largely upon the archives.

W. J. S. Simpson, *Roman Catholic Opposition to Papal Infallibility* (London, John Murray, 1909, pp. xv, 374). Sympathetic with the opposition.

E. Soderino, *Leo XIII Italy and France* (London, Burns, Oates & Washbourne, 1935, pp. viii, 280). Sympathetic with Leo XIII, based upon careful research.

Miguel de Unamuno y Jugo, *The Tragic Sense of Life,* translated by J. E. C. Flitch (London, Macmillan & Co., 1921, pp. xxxv, 332).

Chapter XLVII

PROTESTANTISM ON THE CONTINENT OF
EUROPE, A.D. 1815 - A.D. 1914

As we have suggested, the Protestant wing of Christianity was not as adversely affected by the dominant currents in the Occident of the nineteenth century as was the Roman Catholic wing. In proportion to its geographical distribution and its numerical strength at the outset of the century, it had a much greater expansion than did the Roman Catholic Church. It displayed much more creativity than did the latter. From it issued far more novel movements, both in visible organizations and in thought. The Roman Catholic Church, as we saw in the last chapter, exhibited amazing vitality. In it there arose many expressions of a pulsing vigour. Yet most of these, whether monastic congregations or forms and objects of worship, largely fitted into existing patterns. Here and there were quite fresh creations, among them Catholic Action, Catholic labour unions, Catholic political parties, and new ways of enlisting the support of the laity for missions. By and large, however, the vitality of the Roman Catholic Church found vent in familiar stereotypes inherited from earlier ages. Led by the Popes, the Roman Catholic Church expressly disavowed an evolutionary growth in doctrines. In contrast, Protestantism, while in general holding to the historic convictions which it shared with the Roman Catholic Church and the Orthodox Churches, gave birth to an astonishing number of fresh movements, many of which we shall see as we pursue our narrative. Among them were new denominations, the Young Men's and Young Women's Christian Associations, scores of missionary societies, a rich and varied outpouring of hymns, original methods of presenting the Christian faith to non-Christians, a mounting number of organizations and associations for coöperation across confessional and denominational boundaries, and new approaches to the study of the Bible, theology, and the history of Christianity.

To be sure, many of the trends in Western civilization worked adversely to Protestantism, as they did to other forms of the faith. Some of the programmes for the reorganization of society, such as anarchism and Marxist socialism, were frankly anti-Christian. The drift of intellectuals away from the faith was seen in traditionally Protestant peoples as well as those of Roman Catholic and Orthodox background. The forms of community life which arose from the industrial revolution, such as factories and the manufacturing and mining towns and cities, and the passing of the older, agricultural order, presented problems to Protestantism as well as to the Roman Catholic Church. In Protestant as in Roman Catholic and Orthodox lands the de-Christianization of some elements of the population was occurring. Yet Protestantism did not suffer as striking or as extensive losses as did the Roman Catholic Church.

The reasons for the greater success of Protestantism in the nineteenth century were complex. Some of them are in part conjectural or at least debatable. One of them obviously was the fact, to which we have already called attention, that it was the predominantly Protestant Great Britain and United States which had the largest increase in wealth, population, and territory. Probably another was that Protestantism was more congenial than Roman Catholicism to the kind of liberal democracy which was having the widest spread of any of the political and social programmes of the age. That form of democracy had its main origin and chief expression in Great Britain and the United States, was intimately associated with Protestantism, and was to no small degree the fruit of the more radical wing of that branch of Christianity. Closely related to this last was still another. As Pius IX rightly discerned, an historic connexion existed between Protestantism and the rationalistic humanism which was potent in the intellectual and social movements of the day. The two were by no means identical, but more convinced Protestants than devout Roman Catholics were willing to bring to the tenets and documents of their faith the assumptions, findings, and procedures of the science and philosophy of the age. This led to the greatest ferment in theology that had been seen since the thirteenth and sixteenth centuries. It was possibly more daring and creative than anything in theology since the fourth century. A factor, and one which is so palpable as not to be debatable, was the vitality inherent in Protestantism and which was already apparent in the surge of life that before 1815 was beginning to find expression in Pietism, the Evangelical Awakening in the British Isles, and the revivals in the United States. Increasing in the nineteenth century, that surge of life cut across denominational and confessional lines and in one or another form was seen in all the main and many of the minor branches of Protestantism.

In this chapter we will describe Protestantism on the Continent of Europe. In the next chapter we shall see it in the British Isles. Later chapters will trace its course, along with that of Roman Catholicism, in the United States and other countries.

On the Continent of Europe, as elsewhere, any attempt at a comprehensive, accurate picture must face a complex action and interaction of movements. Individually, in groups, and in churches, Christians were played upon by diverse and often contradictory forces. Some were from the general environment and some from within the several Christian bodies. In addition to the factors external to the churches which we have mentioned, there were many currents within these organizations. Much of the rationalism associated with the eighteenth century and the "Enlightenment" continued. Numbers of Christian intellectuals, repelled by this rationalism, moved towards romanticism. Others repudiated both. Kant was a pervasive influence. Theologies were formulated which showed the effects of several preceding systems but went on to partially fresh approaches and conclusions. The older orthodoxy, holding to the historic confessions and creeds, had a striking revival, rejecting both the rationalism of the *Aufklärung* and some of the newer philosophical and theological speculations and methods of Biblical study. Pietism persisted and spread, reinforced and paralleled by somewhat similar movements in the British Isles and the United States. Many new efforts for welfare issued from men and women of Christian faith. Here was a prolific ferment which was evidence of abounding vitality.

Here was also great peril. The very flexibility and diversity of Protestantism might mean the abandonment by that branch of Christianity of historic and distinctive Christian convictions. Many Roman Catholics believed that this was taking place. In some of the extreme expressions of Protestantism it was undoubtedly occurring. It was the risk which Protestants took, whether consciously or unconsciously. Yet the "exceeding greatness of the power" inherent in Christianity was very much in evidence, probably more so than in any other branch of the faith.

PROTESTANTISM IN GERMANY

On the Continent it is fitting that we should first address ourselves to Germany, for it was in that country that Protestantism had its rise, it was there that the oldest form of Protestantism, Lutheranism, had its chief stronghold, and there the Reformed Churches, while a minority, were vigorous. In the German universities in the nineteenth century theological thought and a kind of study of the Bible and of the history of Christianity flourished which gained wide circulation in the Protestant world. In Germany, indeed, most of the trends and currents which we noted in the last paragraphs had expressions, many of them with repercussions far beyond that land.

The religious developments of nineteenth century Germany were intertwined with other aspects of that country's life. Germany experienced a remarkable awakening and showed a creativity which had many facets. Politically, as we saw in the last chapter, a wave of nationalism which was in part a reaction against the conquests and drastic measures of Napoleon and also in part a fruit of the French Revolution brought the large majority of Germans into a new empire. In this unification Prussia, predominantly Protestant, took the lead. A strong liberal movement came to a climax in the revolutionary year of 1848, but it suffered defeat and it was through the conservatives, led by Bismarck, and through "blood and iron" that the consolidation of Germany was achieved. In that consolidation Austria, prevailingly Roman Catholic, was left out. It was through Protestant, largely conservative Protestant Prussia, that it was attained. Literature and music had a flowering which was the admiration of the Occident. The universities became centres of intellectual activity in philosophy, the natural sciences, and historical, literary, and social study which attracted students from most of the Western world, and particularly from those lands in which Protestantism was strong—Scandinavia, the Netherlands, Switzerland, Great Britain, and the United States. Towards the end of the century industry mounted. Germany became highly industrialized and won a rapidly growing share in the world's commerce. Rather late, in the 1880's, it began to build a colonial empire and entered into competition with Great Britain and France, the major colonial powers of the century.

This abounding and varied vitality was paralleled by religious awakenings. These were seen, as we have hinted, in the Roman Catholic Church. They were even more prominent in Protestantism. The deadening influence of eighteenth century rationalism was passing. In a variety of ways German Protestantism was blossoming forth in what promised a rich harvest.

Fully as much as in any other country there was diversity. Rationalism, romanticism, the newer philosophies, including notably those of Kant and Hegel, the older creedal or confessional orthodoxy, Pietism, and new currents from British and American Protestantism, all had their effect. Also of importance were the official churches, the *Landeskirchen,* by which German Protestantism was organized. The division of Germany into many states and cities, large and small, in 1815 largely independent of one another, combined with the principle of *cuius regio, eius religio* inherited from the Reformation and post-Reformation struggles, made for variety. The political unification of Germany in the third quarter of the nineteenth century did not completely erase it. It was to be reckoned with even beyond 1914.

PROTESTANT SCHOLARSHIP IN NINETEENTH CENTURY GERMANY

It was most strikingly in Germany that the challenge was daringly accepted by Protestants: could the intellectual forces first released by the Renaissance, themselves in part the product of Christianity, be reconciled with the faith and be used to enrich its insights into the meaning of what Christians believed had been revealed and wrought by God in Jesus Christ? To this question the Roman Catholic Church had given an emphatic no. Some Protestants were to do the same, and, like the Roman Catholic Church, to hold tenaciously to inherited beliefs. In wrestling with the issue some other Protestants felt constrained to give up the faith. Still others were convinced that they had met the challenge and that in doing so had come to a deeper understanding of the Gospel. However, it is significant that in general those Protestants who were most active in propagating the faith were the least reconciled to the interpretations given by the German theologians and Biblical scholars of the "modern" schools. The labours of the latter, honest and earnest though they were, took from those Christians who followed them something of conviction and urge to share the faith with others. This might be an indication that they had not met the challenge with entire success.

Even to sketch the entire outline of German Protestant theology and Biblical and historical scholarship in the nineteenth century would extend these pages far beyond their proper length. We must content ourselves with singling out only the main figures, and them only briefly. We turn first of all to theology.

In theology the outstanding thinker of the first part of the century was Friedrich Daniel Ernst Schleiermacher (1768–1834). He exerted a prolonged and wide influence both in Germany and in several other countries. His father was an army chaplain and his mother, earnestly religious, was from a family high in the Reformed Church. His father had been profoundly moved by the Moravians. It was to them that he entrusted the education of his son and to them and their Pietism the latter was indebted to the end of his days. In later years he declared himself to be still one of them, "only of a higher order," and his theology was based upon what he called *Gefühl*, roughly but not with entire accuracy translated as "feeling," perhaps better, but somewhat paraphrased, as "religious experience." In the Moravian school in which his father had placed him the discipline was supposed to induce the experience of the risen Christ. This did not come to him. While emotionally he remained a Moravian, he had a marked critical faculty. It was first stirred by Kant. In the Moravian school in which young Schleiermacher was enrolled, Kant's writings, then in their first heyday, were forbidden. He obtained a copy, read it with his roommate behind drawn curtains, and was thrilled. He went to the University of Halle, where Kant was being studied, there to gain more familiarity with him. While still in his youth he became acquainted with other philosophers, ancient and modern, among them Plato, Spinoza, Leibnitz, Fichte, and Schelling, but Kant remained a profoundly moulding influence.

Ordained, in his late twenties and early thirties Schleiermacher was chaplain in a hospital in Berlin and there became a member of a fashionable circle of young intellectuals, some of them rationalists and some of them romanticists who had reacted against both orthodox theology and the rationalism and moralism of the Enlightenment. It was primarily to them that he addressed his first work, *Reden über die Religion, an die Gebildeten unter ihren Verächtern* ("Discourses on Religion to the Cultured among Its Despisers"). In it he argued that what his friends believed that they were rejecting was not really religion, for religion is not primarily a set of dogmas to be accepted by the reason nor a system of ethics, but arises from *Gefühl* and is based upon it. The book made a profound impression.

For a time Schleiermacher was a pastor in Pomerania and next was professor of theology and philosophy at the University of Halle. For the last twenty-seven years of his life he lived in Berlin, where he was minister in Holy Trinity Church and professor of theology in the newly organized University of Berlin. While holding his professorial post he continued to preach and to carry on his duties as pastor. As a preacher he was not emotional but was clear, forceful, and attracted large congregations. Patriotic, he worked earnestly for the recovery of independence from Napoleon, reinforced the national spirit, shared in the reorganization of the Prussian church, and, although he did not wish it to be imposed by the state, laboured for the union of the Lutheran and Reformed. He lectured on a wide variety of subjects, philosophical, ethical, and theological. His major work, *Der christliche Glaube nach den Grundsätzen der evangelische Kirche in Zusammenhange dargestellt* ("The Christian Faith According to the Fundamentals of the Evangelical Church Systematically Set Forth"), first appeared in 1821–1822 and then, in a thoroughly revised edition, early in the 1830's. By some it was hailed as the most important formulation of Protestant theology since Calvin's *Institutes*. Others regarded it as a major threat to Christianity. Among their criticisms was that to them its view of God was pantheistic. Singularly pure, high-minded, with a deep love for people, Schleiermacher made a profound impression, and his death was regarded as a public calamity.

To Schleiermacher religion was "the feeling of absolute dependence." As he conceived it, true Christianity is not primarily a set of intellectual propositions, a system of dogma to which the would-be believer must give assent. It is, rather, an inner experience, the experience not merely of the individual, but also of the Christian community, of the Church as he believed that term should be used. Out of that experience, he maintained, verbal formulations of the faith had and would come, but they were secondary and derivative. They had changed and would change again. His death bed remark was characteristic:

"I feel constrained to think the profoundest speculative thoughts and they are to me identical with the deepest religious feelings." He believed that the feeling of dependence is common to all religions and that the object of the latter is to bring men into harmony with God. Religions, he maintained, vary in the degree to which they attain this end, and of all religions Christianity is, so he declared, the highest.

Schleiermacher held that we have no objective knowledge of God, but that we know Him in relation to ourselves, in our feeling of absolute dependence on Him, and in His relation to the universe. God is eternal, omnipresent, almighty, in the sense that He can do whatever He wills, is the Creator, and is all-knowing. The world and man as created by God were originally good, so Schleiermacher maintained. He believed that sin is man's claim to self-sufficiency and is in seeking to find satisfaction elsewhere than in God. Sin, he taught, is original in that it is not simply the act of an individual but is an inescapable trend in all men. The world about man has so far lost its pristine perfection that from it continually come promptings to sin. Were men rightly related to God these promptings would not prove temptations, but, because of sinful tendencies in man, they induce men to sin. Through sin men are alienated from God and therefore fear Him as judge, knowing that they deserve His wrath.

There comes, however, the experience of redemption. This, so Schleiermacher said, had been the purpose of God as an integral part of His plan of creation. In redemption are seen both the love and the wisdom of God, love in seeking to bring men into union with Himself, and wisdom in the skill with which God makes all things serve His loving purpose. He maintained that redemption is by grace through Christ and that in Jesus Christ human nature reached perfection. Jesus Christ was a man, but a man who was entirely unique in that he was dominated by the consciousness of God as no man had been before him and no man has since been. Here was a miracle, quite unpredictable. Christ's perfection could be only because of the presence of God in him. Jesus Christ, therefore, was both human and divine. Redemption works through a dynamic without which men could not attain the goal which God has for them, but through which, because Jesus Christ is perfect man, men are enabled to have fellowship with Him and sin in them is overcome by the consciousness of God working in them. The experience of redemption by the individual involves a response in faith and love which is regeneration, justification, and sanctification. This means the birth and the growth in believers of the experience of God which comes through Jesus Christ. What Christians have called the Holy Spirit, so Schleiermacher explained, was the consciousness of God in Jesus Christ operating through the community of believers which is the Christian Church. That Church is made up of all those in whom the consciousness of God is dominant. It is also visible institutions, institutions which are shaped by being involved in history. Within them true believers constitute the invisible core. The Church is the custodian of the means of grace and of the Scriptures. The Scriptures are the record of those who had the word of God. They are reports of experience. Schleiermacher recognized that the world in which the Church is set is hostile, but he hoped that it would ultimately be completely transformed and that the whole created world would be saved.

Much of this, it will be seen, was historic Christianity as Protestants had understood it. The novelty in Schleiermacher was his method of approach. He began, not with the Bible, a creed, or revelation, but with personal experience, with what happens to the individual and to the community.

The earnestness and the freshness which which Schleiermacher presented Christianity had a profound and eventually a wide influence. He contributed powerfully to the religious awakening in German Protestantism in the nineteenth century and aided it in other lands. To many he seemed to make the Christian faith compatible with the thought forms of the day and therefore acceptable to honest minds. Many theologians, both in Germany and in other lands, owed him a great debt. In Germany some followed philosophical and psychological paths, others reinforced loyalty to existing confessions, and some tried to find common ground for Lutherans and Reformed by minimizing creeds and stressing the identity of the religious experience which was found in both.

Contemporary with Schleiermacher both in years and as a professor in the University of Berlin and far more famous and influential in the general history of thought than he was Georg Wilhelm Friedrich Hegel (1770–1831). In his late teens Hegel entered the University of Tübingen as a student of theology and five years later received a theological certificate from that institution. After leaving the university, for several years he was a private tutor in Switzerland and then in Germany. In his leisure he gave much time and thought to the study of Christianity, and especially of Jesus. He wrote a life of Jesus, regarding him as the son of Joseph and Mary, and seeking to discover what it was in his teachings and conduct that had given him so unique a place in history. Hegel developed slowly. He taught at Jena, Nüremberg, Heidelberg, and eventually (1818–1831) in the University of Berlin. There fame came to him and hundreds of students flocked to his lectures. Hegel thought that he saw in the universe, as a clue to understanding it, a dialectical process. The dialectical process consists of a thesis interlocking with an antithesis, followed by a transition to a synthesis. The synthesis incorporates everything both in the thesis and the antithesis. The synthesis immediately becomes a new thesis. This involves an antithesis and the process is repeated.

Hegel held that religion arose in the tension between the individual and his world. He believed religions to advance from natural religion to moral religion and then to spiritual religion. He maintained that Christianity is the highest of all religions, the only one which can be called absolute. He declared that through myths Christianity had already presented truths which philosophy could fully define. Among these myths were the incarnation, the atonement, and the Trinity. He was convinced that the meanings which he gave to these terms were those intended by the Early Church Fathers. In some ways his understanding of Christianity resembled that of the Gnostics. Like them he conceived Christianity to be a philosophy stated in the form of myths. With them he made history subordinate to what he deemed universal and eternal truths.

While not primarily a theologian, Hegel influenced theologians, both those who regarded him as shedding fresh light on Christian truths and thus reinforcing them, and those who radically disagreed with him.

After Schleiermacher, the most prominent German Protestant theologian of the nineteenth century was Albrecht Ritschl (1822–1889). The son of a Lutheran bishop, he studied in several universities, and at Halle came under the influence of Hegelianism. He reacted against the Pietism which he had known, with its assurance based exclusively upon an inner experience. He had no use for mysticism. Eventually he repudiated Hegelianism. For a while he was won to the Tübingen school of Biblical studies of which we are to read in a moment, and by one of its outstanding representatives, Baur, but in time he rejected it. He was successively professor of theology at Bonn and Göttingen. His major work was *Die christliche Lehre von der Rechtfertigung und Versöhnung* ("The Christian Doctrine of Justification and Reconciliation"). Ritschl professed to believe that metaphysics and philosophy are a hindrance rather than a help to theology and must be excluded from it. He rejected ecclesiastical dogma. Yet he was not always consistent. He took much from the theory of knowledge of a contemporary German philosopher, Rudolf Hermann Lotze (1817–1881), who, while agreeing with Kant that things cannot be known in themselves, maintained that they could be known in their attributes or activities. Ritschl held that we pass "value judgements" on these attributes and activities as they affect us, namely, as they give us pleasure or pain, and that religious knowledge is from these value judgements. He maintained that we can know God not through philosophy or "natural religion," but only through Christ, and only if we belong to the company of believers. God revealed through Christ is love.

Christianity, as Ritschl saw it, is not a circle described from a single centre, but an ellipse around two foci, the one the relation of the individual to God as a son of God and the other the kingdom of God. Christianity, he declared, "is the monotheistic, completely spiritual, and ethical religion, which, based on the life of its Author as Redeemer and as Founder of the kingdom of God, consists in the freedom of the children of God, involves the impulse to conduct from the motive of love, aims at the moral organization of mankind, and grounds blessedness on the relation of sonship to God, as well as on the kingdom of God." Ritschl held that Christ is central in Christianity and is unique because he first realized in himself and then reproduced in others the perfect religion and revelation. This uniqueness is expressed in the value judgement which appraises him as divine. The Christian life is seen in the Church, the worshipping community, and the kingdom of God, or the moral community. The Church and the kingdom of God are interdependent. The one cannot really exist without the other.

Ritschl influenced many. Some of them emphasized one phase of his teaching and some another. In general, he made for a joyous faith, based on the Gospel of Jesus Christ and stressing the ethical and the practical. Himself deeply religious, humorous, wholesome, unafraid of controversy, he radiated confidence and brought light and hope to many a perplexed soul. Men were moved to trust in God's love and to labour to make all human society the kingdom of God, where God's will as seen in Christ would be perfectly done. Much that Ritschl taught was congenial to the activistic, optimistic temper which was prevalent in the Western world in the nineteenth century, and especially in the second half of that century. Young men from Great Britain and the United States, coming in touch with Ritschlianism in their student days in German universities carried it back with them. In the United States it contributed to what we are later to see described as the "social gospel."

One of the outstanding Ritschlian theologians was Wilhelm Herrmann (1846–1922). The son of a clergyman, at Halle in his student days he was urged to make philosophy his life work. However, from deep conviction he chose theology and from 1879 to his death taught it in Marburg. Like Ritschl's, his was a warm religious faith. Also like Ritschl, he exerted an influence, although not as wide as that of his master, in Great Britian and the United States.

In Biblical and historical studies of Christianity nineteenth century German universities were also the scene of a ferment of daring thought and conflicting convictions. Indeed, theological, Biblical, and historical studies interacted, each stimulating and modifying the others. This Biblical and historical scholarship was a flowering of what had been begun in the eighteenth century. It applied to the Bible and to the history of Christianity the methods of research and analysis which were being developed by historians, especially German historians, to determine the dates, authorship, and reliability of the documents upon which they depended in their efforts to understand and reconstruct the past. It was also moulded by the current philosophies and theologies.

No other documents were subjected to as prolonged and minute study by as many inquiring minds as were those which constituted the Bible. Uniformity in findings was far from being completely attained and substantial agreement appeared to be reached only to be challenged. The methods and the results spread through much of Protestantism and, although eventually condemned, as we have seen, by the Pope, through small minorities in the Roman Catholic Church.

Here again, as in theology, we can take the space to mention only some of the more prominent figures.

It was inevitable that scholars who combined a religious interest with confidence in reason as expressed in eighteenth century rationalism should address themselves to the Bible and especially to the Gospels. Thus H. E. G. Paulus (1761–1851), after 1811 professor in Heidelberg, sought to rule out the miraculous from the Gospels and to offer explanations which would make such events accord with human experience. For example, he suggested that when Jesus was reported to be walking on the sea he was actually walking on the shore by the sea, and that the feeding of the five thousand was made possible by the generosity with which Jesus shared his meagre store and which stirred others to follow his example. He held that Jesus had only swooned on the cross and that his seeming resurrection was due to an earthquake which revived him and released him from his tomb.

Much more epoch-making was the work of what was known as the Tübingen school. Its pioneer was Ferdinand Christian Baur (1792–1860). Educated in Tübingen, in 1826 he became professor of theology in that university. Captivated by the philosophy of Hegel, he applied it to the New Testament and the history of Christianity, particularly of early Christianity. He maintained that Christianity as taught by the original intimates of Jesus, especially Peter, was a messianic Judaism. In this he saw the Hegelian thesis. The antithesis he believed to be in Paul, who, he maintained, first made Christianity a universal religion. The synthesis he found in the combination of the two in the Catholic Church which emerged in the second century. He attempted to date the books of the New Testament by the fashion in which they gave evidence of the struggle and believed that most of them were written in the second century. He later began a five-volume survey of Church history which, finished by other hands, carried the story from the beginning into his own day.

More sensational was the *Leben Jesu* ("Life of Jesus"), by one of Baur's students, David Friedrich Strauss (1808–1874). Educated in a Protestant seminary and in Tübingen and Berlin, Strauss became familiar with the thought of both Hegel and Schleiermacher. To his *Leben Jesu* he devoted years of study and writing. In his preface he said that the Christian faith was quite independent of any criticism that he might make, that "the supernatural birth of Christ, his miracles, his resurrection, and ascension, remain eternal truths, whatever doubts may be cast on their reality as historical facts," and that "the dogmatic significance of the life of Jesus remains inviolate." Yet he held that while not all the history of Jesus as given in the New Testament is mythical, in it there is an admixture of the mythical. He cast doubt on the historicity of much in the Gospels, including the virgin birth of Jesus, the details of the accounts of the crucifixion, the resurrection, and the post-resurrection appearances of Jesus, and questioned the accuracy of the reports of the sayings and deeds of Jesus. In spite of his initial avowal, he also doubted the basic Christian dogmas built upon the New Testament accounts of the life of Jesus. He summed up the queries which had thus far been raised about the historicity of the picture given by the Gospels, introduced some of his own, and left the impression of a lack of dependable knowledge of Jesus as an historical character. He attacked the positions of both the rationalists and the orthodox. The book created an enormous stir and awakened a mixture of hearty agreement, partial endorsement, and vigorous and often emotional rebuttal. Its repercussions continued to be felt at least as late as the middle of the twentieth century. In his *Christliche Glaubenslehre,* published in 1841 and 1842, Strauss undermined confidence in Christian doctrines by tracing their history in such fashion as to cast doubt on their validity. At the outset a Christian, Strauss, unable to find employment as teacher in a theological faculty and embittered by the intense criticism directed against him, eventually broke completely with his early faith and died a materialist and a pessimist.

Strauss added stimulus to the application to the New Testament of nineteenth century historical methodology with its attempt to determine "what actually happened," as Ranke, one of the greatest of the German historians of the period, put it. Scores of names of distinguished scholars were added to the list of those who devoted themselves to the problem, and a voluminous literature poured from the presses.

Much the same intensive study was devoted to the Old Testament and here also the names of earnest students were legion. Prominent and provocative was Julius Wellhausen (1844–1918). Beginning in theology and for a time professor of that subject, before he was forty his conscience compelled him to resign from a position where he could no longer teach what was expected, and, devoting himself to oriental languages, he spent most of his professional life at Göttingen. Although he wrote on the New Testament, it was to the Old Testament that he gave his chief attention. Here his conclusion both brought on him attacks from those holding the older accepted views and spurred others to go further along the trails which he had broken.

In the history of religions and of Christianity one of the most stimulating scholars was Ernest Troeltsch (1865–1923). Indeed, Troeltsch was the outstanding representative of a distinctive approach to the study of Christianity as a phase of the history of religion. A teacher of theology and philosophy, first in Heidelberg and then in Berlin, he was deeply concerned with the philosophy of history and especially of the history of religion. In a sense he was in the succession of Schleiermacher. To him religion was the direct sense of the presence of God. Enormously learned and familiar with much of the thought of his time, he sought to work out the kind of theology which was required by the age. Yet he believed that religion could never be really reconciled with culture and held that a tension must always exist between Christianity and the thought world in which it is set. He was familiar with Hegel but did not fully follow him. He was also influenced by Ritschl, so much so that with the latter he maintained that religion is not philosophy, but is quite different from it. Yet he could not fully subscribe to Ritschl's sharp distinction between faith and reason. In philosophy an idealist, he believed that the cosmic process is the effect in space and time of a Reality which cannot be grasped by our senses.

History, Troeltsch held, is permeated by the self revelation of God. Yet he was not willing to say that in Christ mankind has the conclusive revelation of God. He viewed Christianity as one of many religions. To him religions, including Christianity, are the outgrowth of religious feeling. Even though not reconcilable with culture, they are affected and their distinctive forms are in part determined by the cultures of which they are a part. Holding that the Christian Gospel "is the loftiest and most spiritual revelation we know," he described it as "a profound inner experience." That experience is "the criterion of validity, but . . . only of its validity *for us*. It is God's countenance revealed to us; it is the way in which, being what we are, we receive and react to the revelation of God." Christianity, as Troeltsch viewed it, is not necessarily final. Like other religions, it is relative, associated with a particular culture. Being inseparably linked to a civilization which may, like other civilizations, pass away, it too may eventually be left behind in the stream of time. In a later stage of history, so his view would lead him to say, men might become conscious of needs which the Christian Gospel does not meet. In that event, presumably, the Divine Reason, the Divine Life (and there was something akin to pantheism in Troeltsch's view of God), would manifest itself afresh in a new way, which, valid for the men of that age and culture, would in turn pass and be superseded by another manifestation.

A historian of Christianity who was very much in the Ritschlian tradition was Adolf von Harnack (1851–1930). The son of a professor of pastoral theology, most of his mature years were spent as professor in the University of Berlin. His writings had a wide circulation, both in German and in translation. Especially famous was his account of the history of Christian doctrine. In general his thesis was that Christian beliefs were early so moulded by the Greek thought in which they took shape as to introduce permanently into the teachings of the Church much that was not of the true essence of the faith. He would, accordingly, have Protestants reëxamine what had come from the past and seek to recover the original Gospel. He connected the Gospel inseparably with Jesus and described it as "the knowledge and recognition of God as the Father, the certainty of redemption, humility and joy in God, energy, and brotherly love." He believed that in spite of the fashion in which it had been compromised and obscured by the churches and by the cultural environments and heritages through which it had been transmitted, it had persisted, "still traceable, like a red thread in the centre of the web," and was sure to "emerge afresh and free itself from its entangling connexions."

Most of the scholars whom we have thus far mentioned in this extraordinary ferment of thought centering around theology and the Bible departed more or less widely from what had been inherited from the Christian past, including the beliefs cherished by the Lutheran and Reformed churches which constituted the prevailing forms of German Protestantism. Varied and often reciprocally contradictory as their views were, not all of them could be accepted by any one person or group. No one of the men whom we have listed was followed unquestionably by more than a small minority. The effect, rather, was to stimulate further thought which often issued in conclusions which differed, sometimes widely, from those which had provoked them.

Among the responses to the radical departures from accepted views were vigorous reassertions of the historic doctrines contained in the confessions of the Lutheran and Reformed churches. In Lutheranism confessional conservatism was often closely associated with political conservatism and, like the latter, was strengthened by a reaction against the liberalism that had been prominent in the revolutionary year of 1848. As were those of radical tendencies, the conservatives by no means fully agreed with one another. Much of this confessional orthodoxy was opposed not only to rationalism but also to Pietism.

Sometimes called "New Lutheranism," much of the confessional orthodoxy tended to emphasize the sacraments, including the sacrament of ordination, and to make of the ministry of the Church a distinct clerical priesthood. Here again we can take the time to do no more than note a few of the outstanding figures.

Prominent among the staunch "New Lutherans" was Friedrich Julius Stahl (1802–1861). Of Jewish parentage, in his late teens he joined the Lutheran Church under the influence of Schelling, the brilliant romanticist and philosopher. For years he was in Berlin. There he departed from the philosophy which he had imbibed from Schelling and became a vigorous exponent of Lutheran confessionalism. Denouncing revolution and rationalism as the great menaces of the day, leading to revolt against the authority of the state and the Church and to the attempted rejection by man of his creatureliness and obedience to God, he stoutly maintained that kings rule by divine right, insisted that the policies of the state must be governed by Christian principles, held to the close union of Church and state, and believed episcopacy to be the ideal form of Church government. Eloquent and persuasive, he became the leader and the spokesman of the conservatives in Prussian politics, especially of the landed gentry and aristocracy and the Lutheran pastors who made common cause with them.

Others of this "New Lutheran" school of thought held that purity of doctrine is the sign of the true Church, that there can be only one true Church, and that the Lutheran Church has in its confessions of faith the full truth and therefore is that Church. Like Stahl, they tended to identify the kingdom of God with the Church. For example, Theodor Kliefoth (1810–1895), for nearly a generation the leader of the *Landeskirche* of Mecklenburg, in conscious opposition to Pietism held that the object of salvation is not so much the individual as all humanity, and that the saving grace of God is not transmitted through individuals to the world, but rather through peoples and their institutions to individuals. In the sacramental emphasis of the "New Lutherans," one writer placed the sacraments above the word of God, holding that since the latter, transmitted through the mouth of man, is subject to alteration, the sacraments, requiring passivity on the part of him who ministers and of them who receive them, are much more an act of God.

The "New Lutherans" were not all of one mind. For example, Johann Christian Konrad von Hoffmann (1810–1877) put forward a view of the atonement which he believed was that of the Bible but which brought down on him the charge of heresy from others of that school.

In some of the *Landeskirchen* the "New Lutherans" with their strong confessionalism were in control and in several others they were very influential. In Prussia, for instance, in the reaction after the revolution of 1848 they had much power in the schools and universities, saw to it that the head body of the church was given an influential role in the appointment of professors of theology, and weakened the union of the Lutheran and Reformed of which we are to hear more in a moment.

Parallel with the "New Lutheranism," but distinct from it, was an orthodoxy, some of it in the Reformed but much of it in the Lutheran churches, which had a strong Pietist strain. There was, indeed, a revival of Pietism which had similarities to the evangelical awakenings in the British Isles and the United States. Some of it made common cause with the latter in foreign missions and other enterprises. True to the Pietist tradition, it stressed personal commitment. This orthodoxy, some of it called "Old Lutheranism," like the "New Lutheranism," varied, and, also like it, denounced the rationalism inherited from the eighteenth century, rejected the methods and the conclusions of the current radical historical study of the Scriptures, held to the inerrancy of the Bible, and looked askance or with open hostility at the radical theologians. Pietism had especially strong centres in Württemberg and Basel, but was to be found as well in other places.

One of the leaders in the revival of orthodoxy was Klaus Harms (1778–1855). A native of Holstein and of peasant stock, he early passed from rationalism to Schleiermacher and then to Lutheran orthodoxy. He supported absolute monarchy. As pastor and writer he exerted a marked influence.

Another prominent figure in sturdy orthodoxy, but for a time with a much stronger Pietist strain, was Ernst Wilhelm Hengstenberg (1802–1869). At the outset inclined to rationalism, in his early twenties he entered the missionary training school at Basel, a stronghold of Pietism, and became thoroughly committed to that religious movement. In 1824 he became the head of the Pietist group in Berlin. As such, beginning with 1826, he was a professor in the University of Berlin. He stood stoutly for the infallibility of the Bible and gave to its passages allegorical interpretations. He believed that the millennial reign of Christ had begun with Charlemagne in 800 and had been concluded in 1800 and that the end of the world and the final judgement were at hand. As the founder and editor of the *Evangelische Kirchenzeitung* he denounced rationalism, democracy, and France, and, in late youth (1840) breaking with Pietism, he became a champion of the Lutheranism of the sixteenth century confessions and the orthodoxy of the seventeenth century and denounced as heretics all who departed from it.

In all this theological strife there were not wanting those who sought to mediate, to combine the best from each of the major views, and to make for peace and Christian unity. They were in part the products of the religious awakenings of the day. Among them was he who is best known as Johann August Wilhelm Neander (1789–1850). Of Jewish parentage and in his boyhood known as David Mendel, he was led to the Christian faith by reading

Schleiermacher and at seventeen was baptized and took the name of Neander to signify that he had become a new man in Christ. A pupil and warm friend of Schleiermacher and beginning with 1812 his colleague on the faculty of the University of Berlin, he was by no means a slavish imitator of the older man. He disliked theological polemics and for that reason severed his connexion with Hengstenberg's *Evangelische Kirchenzeitung* when it attacked two rationalistic professors of Halle. Warmly and deeply religious, with a childlike Christian trust, he won the affection of hundreds of students and sought to lead them into an earnest and joyous Christian experience. In scholarship his great contribution was his *Allgemeine Geschichte der christlichen Religion und Kirche* ("History of the Christian Religion and Church") which he did not live to complete. Based upon an exhaustive examination of the sources, it saw the history of Christianity as the permeation of human life by the divine life and stressed the place of individuals rather than the community or institutions.

Another who is usually said to belong to the conciliators was Friedrich August Gottreu Tholuck (1799–1877). While a student in Berlin he came under the influence of Pietism and Neander. In 1826, when in his late twenties, he was appointed professor of theology at Halle with the hope that he would combat the rationalism which had captured that earlier radiating centre of Pietism. He sought to combine the Pietist heritage with what seemed to him best in the methods and findings of rationalism. Full of vigour, transparently good, an eloquent preacher, insisting upon a personal religious experience, holding that to love Christ is preferable to scholarship, warm in his personal friendships with students, a prolific writer, the author of many books, including several collections of sermons and works of devotion, he did much to shape the Pietism of the nineteenth century.

Similarly of the mediating school was Isaac August Dorner (1809–1884). Moved in his youth by the controversy aroused by Strauss's *Leben Jesu,* he deplored the bitterness of the attack on that book and, while not accepting its conclusions, sought to use it as a stimulus to a further understanding of Christ. This he attempted in his *Entwicklungsgeschichte der Lehre von der Person Christi* ("History of the Development of the Doctrine of the Person of Christ"). He added other books, chief among them *System der christlichen Glaubenslehre* ("System of Christian Doctine") and *System der christlichen Ethik* ("System of Christian Ethics"). He believed that much in the modern views could be accepted without discarding the historic doctrines and attempted to demonstrate how this could be accomplished. He held that to the enlightened Christian mind its faith and experience are in harmony with what is seen in the Scriptures and in the historic faith of the Church. He believed that the core of Christianity is the revelation in Christ of what God is and what man may become. To his mind the Son, the perfect image of God, is also the ideal man. Translated into English, his books had a wide influence in the British Isles and the United States.

ATTEMPTS AT UNION

A movement which entered largely into the life of German Protestantism and which, seeking harmony, both produced it and provoked strife was the union of the Lutheran and Reformed churches. As we have seen (Chapters XXXII, XXXIII), unsuccessful efforts at union had been made near the outset of Protestantism. It had since been attempted more than once, but had fallen short of the goal. Eighteenth century rationalism, dulling the sharpness of historic convictions which had separated the two main forms of German Protestantism, had prepared the way. Actual union came in part as a result of the weakening of the old patterns by the Napoleonic conquests. Between 1815 and 1830, after the defeat of Napoleon and the opportunity for a new beginning, unions of the two confessions were achieved in several German states.

The chief union, that in Prussia, which did much by example to bring the others into being, was mainly the work of Friedrich Wilhelm III, who reigned from 1797 to 1840. Although not a particularly strong monarch, Friedrich Wilhelm III was deeply religious and took an active interest in the Church. His purpose in seeking to accomplish the union was in part the desire to have religious uniformity in his domains, so that with one state there would be one church. In 1817, the tercentenary of the Protestant Reformation, the union was declared. The royal attempts to enforce the use of a uniform liturgy met with stubborn opposition. For years the king persisted and by dint of force seemed to have some success. However, numbers of the Lutheran pastors and their flocks, denominated "Old Lutherans," continued to resist. When, under the next reign, that of Friedrich Wilhelm IV (1840–1861), constraint was relaxed, many of the Lutheran congregations drew together (1841) and in a general synod constituted the Evangelical Lutheran Church in Prussia. In 1845 this was accorded loyal recognition.

Resistance to the union developed in several other *Landeskirchen* in the 1850's and 1860's. This arose in part from the conservative reaction after the revolutionary year of 1848. It also sprang from hostility to the growing political strength of Prussia.

PARTY STRIFE

To the strife over the attempt to bring about the union of the Lutherans and the Reformed was added that among the adherents of the several main strains of theology. The contestants grouped themselves by organized parties.

For a time in the 1830's and 1840's some of the minority among the pastors who held to rationalism, irked by the rising tide of orthodoxy and its power in the *Landeskirchen,* formed separate congregations. They drew together in what were known as the *Lichtfreunde* ("Friends of Light") or the *protestantischen Freunde* ("the Protestant Friends"), but in the conservative reaction after 1848 the movement lost ground.

In 1849 the Prussian Lutherans formed an association. In 1868 the Lutherans in Prussia and in the territories newly annexed by Prussia organized the *Allgemeine lutherische Konferens* ("The General Lutheran Conference") and began publishing a periodical.

In 1857 the more conservative friends of the Lutheran-Reformed Union associated themselves with the Evangelical Alliance.

In the 1860's theological liberals formed the *Protestantenverein* ("the Protestant Union"). It stood for the reconciliation of religion and modern culture, resistance to compulsory conformity with doctrine, and Lutheran-Reformed Union.

Between these various groups there was distrust which often broke out into open and bitter conflict.

It is sobering to observe that while the leaders of the churches had much of their energy absorbed in internecine strife, a large proportion of the laity were drifting away from the faith. They were still bringing their children to be baptized and confirmed, religious instruction was given in the schools, and taxes were collected for the support of the churches. However, many of the intellectuals were reading Strauss, Feuerbach, Renan, and Schopenhauer and were having their faith shaken by them, thousands of the labourers in the new industries were moving away from contacts with the churches, and the revival of orthodoxy and its alignment with political conservatism were alienating numbers of political and social liberals. Especially in the cities the churches were losing ground. Their strength was chiefly in the rural districts where the old social and economic order more nearly persisted.

ORGANIZED EFFORTS TO PREVENT DE-CHRISTIANIZATION AND TO REACH THE DE-CHRISTIANIZED

Party strife and the progressive de-Christianization of large elements in the population were only one side of the picture. Protestants were reaching out in fresh ways to serve the needy and to win back those who were rejecting the faith or were drifting away from it.

The examples of this vitality in Protestantism were numerous. Bible and tract societies were formed, partly stimulated by similar earlier organizations in England. They had been begun even as early as 1811 and 1814. In the second decade of the century several individuals, moved by Christian charity, took steps to care for the children orphaned by the Napoleonic Wars. In 1833 Johann Hinrich Wichern (1808–1881), who had been nourished in Pietism, founded a home for underprivileged and delinquent children near the rapidly growing Hamburg. In 1849, the year after the far-reaching revolutionary disturbances, and partly stimulated by them, Wichern instituted what was known as the Inner Mission. It sought, partly through sisterhoods and lay brotherhoods, to reach the masses, and to serve seamen, the unemployed, prisoners, and needy children. Its programme included Sunday Schools, city missions, colporteurs to distribute Christian literature, and Christian lodging houses. Local units were formed to further the Inner Mission and a national organization for it was instituted. It was associated with the *Kirchentag* which drew throngs and met annually in some large city and which had for its purpose the spiritual rebirth of the German nation. In 1849 Konrad Wilhelm Loehe (1808–1872), a pastor in Neuendettelsau in Bavaria, founded a Lutheran society for the Inner Mission and four years later inaugurated a union of deaconesses.

Efforts were made towards improved pastoral care for the masses in the growing cities. The larger parishes were sub-divided, new church structures were erected, and more clergy were provided. Reforms in liturgy and the wider use of hymn books helped to enrich the services and make them more attractive. Discussion evenings were held for labourers to give them more contact with the Church and the faith. Better methods of preparing for confirmation were devised, with an improvement in the confirmation vows. Women were accorded a larger place in the churches. The Young Men's Christian Association movement, which had been begun in England, found kinship in similar groups in Germany and brought into its fellowship Christian young men, largely in the cities.

The use of deaconesses had a marked spread. In 1833 Theodore Fliedner, a pastor at Kaiserswerth, a destitute parish, began the use of deaconesses to assist him. He founded a training school for them. They nursed the sick as well as cared for the spiritually destitute. Partly stimulated by this precedent, in 1894 in Germany nearly eight thousand deaconesses were serving in hospitals, poor-houses, orphanages, and schools, and as parish-helpers. Partly through contact with Elizabeth Fry, Fliedner also, and earlier, organized (1826) the Prisoners Society of Germany and he and his wife inaugurated a home for discharged women convicts.

In general, the quality of the Protestant clergy improved in the nineteenth century. At the outset it was low and a marked difference existed between those in the cities and those in the rural districts. The former were much better educated and better paid than were the latter. Gradually the gap was narrowed as the preparation and status of the rural clergy rose.

INCREASING AUTONOMY IN THE LANDESKIRCHEN OF GERMANY

Parallel with the political unification of Germany and in part as a sequel to it, the *Landeskirchen* developed forms of government which promoted their autonomy as against the state. Characteristic, but with variations from state to state, was an ascending structure beginning with a representative body in each congregation, going on to regional synods, and culminating in a general synod for the entire state. The members in each higher body were chosen by the bodies below it. The synodical organization facilitated legislation by the churches. The tie with the state was maintained and included support through taxation. However, the churches had more control over their own affairs than formerly.

The progress towards ecclesiastical autonomy, while by no means entirely ascribable to it, was facilitated by the reduction of the powers of the states as they were drawn into the newly formed North German Confederation (1867) and its successor the German Empire (1871). Some of the states lost their separate existence through annexation by Prussia, but even in these the *Landeskirchen* persisted and maintained their identity. Presumably under the new order the states and their princes were in a less favourable position to control the churches in their realms. It may well have been, moreover, that something of the spirit of local particularism which had flourished in the days before the union when each German state was practically independent of every other found refuge in reinforcing the autonomy of the churches, continuing as they did the earlier territorial divisions.

In general the *Landeskirchen* were controlled by the conservatives. The liberals and radicals were usually small minorities in the synods by which the churches were governed.

THE GROWTH OF FREE CHURCHES

Not all Protestants were in the state churches. As the nineteenth century wore on, "free churches" appeared and grew, independent of the established ones.

Several of these were of purely German origin. As we have seen, some were constituted by the liberals. Others were by conservatives who were of the strict confessional Lutheranism. Those in Prussia was aided by a law of 1908 which made it easier for members of the *Landeskirche* to join them. The Evangelical Free Church of Hanover was formed (1878) by Theodor Harms in connexion with the Hermannsburg training school for missionaries which had been founded in 1849 by his brother, Ludwig Harms.

Others of the free churches arose from contacts with other countries. Methodism entered from Great Britain and the United States, chiefly through missionaries from the latter country. Baptist churches came through a German who had been in touch with the revival movement in Scotland and through assistance from the United States. It was from the United States that Seventh Day Adventists were represented. In 1914 none of these churches numbered more than 50,000 members.

THE OUTREACH OF GERMAN PROTESTANTISM TO OTHER LANDS

If British and American forms of Protestantism found footholds in Germany, even more did German Protestantism make itself felt in other lands. This was partly, as we have suggested, through the writings of German Protestant scholars. It was also through the extensive emigration of Germans, chiefly to the Americas. We will say something of it when, in our geographic pilgrimage, we come to these regions and will note how missionaries from the Fatherland helped to hold the settlers to their ancestral faith and to shape the forms which it took.

Much of the overseas expansion of German Protestantism was through missions to non-Christian peoples. The vitality of nineteenth century German Protestantism was vividly seen in the number and extent of the societies which were created as a means of stimulating and carrying on these missions. Unlike most of the missionary societies in the United States, the majority had no organic connexion with the official ecclesiastical bodies: few churches as such conducted missions. The missionary societies were, rather, the creation of individuals and groups and depended for their support not on the general funds of a church but upon the gifts of friends. In 1914 there were at least thirty-two societies which sent missionaries, all but two of them organized after 1815, six societies exclusively for the collection of funds, twenty-three missionary conferences (provincial unions composed principally of clergymen and for the purpose of cultivating interest in missions), and more than a dozen organizations for the support of medical missions. German missionaries were in all the continents and some of the islands of the Pacific. They were predominantly from Pietist and confessionally conservative constituencies. A partial list of the major societies will give some indication of the extent and nature of the movements.

The pioneers in German foreign missions were the Moravians. Early and continuously prominent was the Basel Evangelical Missionary Society. Although officially Swiss, it drew much of its financial support and many of its missionaries from Germany. Organized in 1815 as an institution for training missionaries, until 1822 its graduates went out under British societies, but in that year it began sending them under its own auspices. Also prominent were the Berlin Missionary Society, begun in 1824, the Rhenish Missionary Society, founded in 1828, the Leipzig Evangelical Lutheran Mission, stemming from the Basel Mission and dating from 1836, the North German Missionary Society, formed in 1836 by the union of several societies which had been affiliated with Basel, and the Bethel Mission, inaugurated in 1886, with headquarters at Bielefeld, where it also had an extensive institution for the care of unfortunates.

CREATIVE DANISH PROTESTANTISM

From Germany we turn naturally northward to Scandinavia, for that region was overwhelmingly Lutheran by faith and many of the religious movements in German Lutheranism had repercussions in it. As in Germany, Pietism was strong, although only among minorities, and the years which followed 1815 saw marked awakenings and a revulsion against the rationalism of the Enlightenment. We come first to Denmark, as the only one of the Scandinavian lands with a common boundary with Germany.

Denmark emerged from the Napoleonic Wars in a parlous condition. It had lost its fleet, Norway, long joined to it, had become independent, it was deeply in debt, and bankruptcies were common. In the 1860's Denmark had a disastrous war with Prussia and Austria which cost it the partly German provinces of Schleswig and Holstein. Yet following 1815 the country became prosperous, and there were significant achievements in literature and education.

Religiously, the years after 1815 saw a remarkable revival. The nineteenth century was the most creative in the history of the Church in Denmark. Not only was Danish Christianity vigorous. It also took on distinctive forms within the general framework of Lutheranism and in one of its sons, Søren Aaby Kierkegaard, made a contribution which in the twentieth century had wide and deep effects, far beyond the borders of the country.

In Denmark the religious awakening took a number of forms. One feature of the revival was the strengthening of Pietism. In Denmark in the nineteenth century, instead of being opposed by the official church, as it was in the Hauge movement in Norway, it was given hospitality by that church, permeated it, and had a marked effect upon its life.

Closely connected with Pietism was the Inner Mission. Distinctively Danish and not a copy of the German Inner Mission, it had as its purpose the deepening and enrichment of the religious life of the nation. It stressed personal conversion and drew together those who had experienced it into circles for the cultivation of the spiritual life. It was utterly opposed to the kind of critical study of the Bible that flourished in German universities and contributed little to hymnody, but it made much of preaching. It grew in the course of the century and eventually had several hundred mission houses and nearly a thousand lay preachers. About a third of the pastors of the country were intimately connected with it.

In Denmark, as in much of Protestantism, there was a strong reaction against eighteenth century rationalism. One of its chief exponents was J. P. Mynster (1775–1854). A university graduate, in his early days as a pastor he was profoundly influenced by Kant and showed a strong pantheistic trend. Before he was thirty he had a heart-warming and transforming Christian experience. Later as court preacher, teacher in a theological seminary closely connected with the university, bishop, and primate of the Church of Denmark, he had an effect upon the entire nation. Although he was frankly opposed to rationalism, he sought to be positive rather than negative and to emphasize the heart of the Gospel and the work of Christ for man and in man as interpreted by historic Lutheranism.

Even more distinctive and influential was Nicolai Frederick Severin Grundtvig (1783–1872). The son of a clergyman, himself also a clergyman, late in life Grundtvig was made a bishop of the Church of Denmark. He believed in an indissoluble connexion between the Christian life and the national life and wished the latter to be permeated and transformed by Christian faith and action. Stressing baptism and the Lord's Supper as means to a living faith, he fought both rationalism and an arid and dogmatic adherence to the historic Lutheran dogmas. He sought to promote a singing church. He wrote more than fourteen hundred hymns, of which about two hundred found their way into the hymnal of the Church of Denmark. His was a joyous faith and he wished Christians always to be joyful for God's grace and to God's honour in the name of Jesus Christ. In politics he was a liberal. He inaugurated "folk schools" which stressed training in practical subjects and which became widely popular not only in Denmark but also in the other Scandinavian lands. He encouraged the coöperative movement in agriculture. Through what he did for education and through coöperatives he contributed notably to the prosperity of the country. "Grundtvigism" became a potent and characteristic strain in Danish life. It and the Inner Mission were sharply opposed to each other and the conflict issued in party strife in the Church.

As we have suggested, it was Søren Aaby Kierkegaard (1813–1855) who was eventually the most widely known and read of Danish Protestants. Said to have been the most original thinker in Danish history, Kierkegaard was a tortured soul who after prolonged struggle progressed from dread to faith. He was reared by a profoundly gloomy father who made him an intimate. When a poor peasant lad his father had at one time in bitterness at his hard lot deliberately cursed God. Later, although he became prosperous, he believed that by this act he had committed the unpardonable sin. To this he had added a secret sin which he later confided to his son, thus intensifying the latter's sense of guilt. Yet the father was also deeply religious and, placing great dependence upon Mynster and his sermons, reared his son on them. For a time in his student days Søren was dissipated and idle. Brilliant in conversation he could also be caustic and cynical. In his mid-twenties there came an emotional shock which made him believe that the entire family had the curse of God resting on it and was to disappear, wiped out by the hand of God. He studied theology and took a degree in philosophy. He became affianced to a girl whom he never ceased to love, but broke off the engagement because he felt that he must not burden her with his melancholy, the secret sin of his father, and the sins of his own youth. In his thirties and early forties, with one interruption of about two years, he wrote prodigiously. In his last months there came a measure of peace and he died at the age of forty-two.

Kierkegaard's works dealt with both philosophy and religion. He denounced the trend in thought represented by Hegel, with its serene confidence in human reason, its calm objectivity, detached from struggle, and its optimism. He held it to be quite irreconcilable with the Gospel. Idealist philosophers such as Hegel, he maintained, assumed the attitude of spectators of the drama of life, refusing to take sides. They reduced the Gospel to ideas and were blind to the gulf between the Creator and the creature. To such men the incarnation was unnecessary and the cross a scandal. Kierkegaard insisted that true Christianity demands decision and action, a commitment which abandons the rôle of the spectator. He looked upon Christianity as entailing a dialectic, but, unlike that of Hegel, which was one of thesis and antithesis resolved in a synthesis, it was composed of opposites which could not be reconciled and which negated each other, such as time and eternity, holiness and love, grace and responsibility. He saw in Christianity what for men are paradoxes, but paradoxes which for God are transcended. Christianity, so he believed, confronts man with God and the necessity of decision. Before God man is always a sinner and his best as well as his worst stands under the judgement of God and needs divine pardon. We are born as sinners and by our deeds add to our sins. Between God, Who is sinless, and sinful man a vast abyss yawns. Yet what to human reason is impossible is done by God. The Son of God becomes incarnate. He appears incognito, in weakness and obscurity. In himself Christ unites two elements which repel each other, man and God, and the Eternal enters time. Here is at once an affront to human reason and an object of saving faith. The cross of Christ offends man's reason and his moral sense. In the leap of faith we sacrifice our intellects and accept what is to us the great paradox, that God and man are opposites and yet in Christ have become one. To Kierkegaard to follow Christ entails suffering, suffering which must be borne without the benefit of human companionship. One must stand solitary before God in pure pain, with his soul naked under the divine eye which knows our every sin and its infinite guilt. In being reconciled to God we must absorb the agony and humiliation of Christ as our own.

In all this can be discerned the significance of a term which is closely associated with Kierkegaard, "existential." By it "existence" is contrasted with mere "life." "Existence" is reached by the inner decisions of the individual. To think "existentially" is to abandon the pose of a spectator on the ultimate issues and to act.

Even from this brief summary it can be seen that Kierkegaard was driven to adopt an attitude which became prominent in the last years of his brief life, the condemnation of what he saw about him which was called Christianity and which was accepted as such by the masses. To him it was exemplified by one who had been his father's spiritual guide and his own friend, Mynster. In an address preceding his funeral Mynster was acclaimed as one of the genuine witnesses to the truth. This provoked Kierkegaard to pronounce as false to the Christianity of the New Testament what Mynster had preached. Kierkegaard's denunciation included the established church as "an impudent indecency," with its paid ministers, half-Christian, half-worldly civil servants, who on Sundays proclaimed what they contradicted by their actions on Mondays. He declared that official Christianity resembled the Christianity of the New Testament no more than enjoyment resembles suffering, or being at home in the world resembles being a pilgrim and a stranger. Consistently, on his death bed Kierkegaard refused to accept the sacrament from the "king's officials."

In his life time Kierkegaard was little noticed. This was because he wrote in Danish, a language known by few outside that country and Norway. It was only later that his works were translated into more generally read languages. It was also because he ran counter to the prevailing temper of his time.

After 1914 Kierkegaard had a profound influence in widening and varied circles. This was in large part because he spoke to the condition of an age which knew two world wars and was sobered by what it believed to be the fatal illness of Western civilization. In his denunciation of the confidence in reason which characterized the Occident he seemed to have laid bare a basic weakness of Occidental culture. His emphasis upon human sinfulness appealed to many who were impressed with the tragedy which mankind was bringing on itself. His stress on the utter contrast between the holiness of God and the sinfulness of man and on the un-Christian character of the official churches struck a responsive note in the hearts of many disillusioned Christians who had been nurtured on the theological liberalism of the nineteenth century, a liberalism which with its optimism and its confidence in reason had now seemed to end in futility. "Existentialism" became a pass-word in many intellectual circles. It was adopted by Christian theologians and by non-theistic, even atheistic philosophers. Protestant theology was deeply affected and some Roman Catholics were interested. Long almost unknown, Kierkegaard was acclaimed by some as the "greatest Christian thinker of the nineteenth century."

Denmark continued to be overwhelmingly Lutheran. However, in the course of the nineteenth century a few other churches constituted growing although small minorities. They were aided by the grant of religious liberty in 1849. In 1907 Roman Catholics numbered about 12,000. There were also Methodists, Baptists, Disciples of Christ, and the Church of the Brethren, all of them springing chiefly from contacts, mainly through missionaries, with the United States.

Danish Lutheranism spread far beyond the confines of Denmark. This was partly through emigration, mainly to the United States. It was also by missions to non-Christian peoples. Here was evidence of the mounting life in Danish Christianity. The eighteenth century Danish missions in India had been staffed by Germans and latterly had been aided financially from England. Between 1815 and 1914 several missionary societies came into being in Denmark, chief among them the Danish Missionary Society, formed in 1821, and eventually operating in Greenland, India, and Manchuria. They were manned and supported from Denmark.

Christianity did not have its full way in Denmark. Here, as elsewhere, scepticism and secularism were at work. A symbol and a furtherer of a non-Christian naturalism was the eminent critic and literary historian, Georg Morris Cohen Brandes (1842–1927). Born in Copenhagen, the son of a Jewish merchant, widely travelled in Europe, he was a radical whose extensive and influential writings were contrary to the religious strains which had been dominant in Danish life.

CHRISTIANITY IN NORWAY IN THE NINETEENTH CENTURY

The course of Christianity in Norway in the nineteenth century was far from being a pale reproduction of that in Denmark, the land with which there had been a close political bond. By the post-Napoleonic settlement at Vienna in 1815 Norway was transferred from Denmark to Sweden. However, the tie with Sweden was purely through the crown. The two realms had one monarch and under him foreign affairs were conducted and military matters managed, but Norway was declared to be "a free, independent, and indivisible kingdom." It preserved its own constitution and in domestic affairs was autonomous. Predominantly agricultural and commercial, with a large merchant marine, it was a nation of sturdy farmers and sailors. The Norwegian constitution, adopted in 1814, was strongly democratic and placed the supreme authority in a parliament elected indirectly by male tax-payers.

In the nineteenth century Norway developed a vigorous national and cultural life. Out of it came at least two writers of European fame, Bjornstjerne Björnson (1832–1910), poet, dramatist, and novelist, and Henrik Johan Ibsen (1826–1906), poet and dramatist. Both men were critical of the Church, but both bore to no small degree the impress of Christianity, even when they reacted against it. Björnson was the son of a pastor. Ibsen was widely read in theology, and while he waged war on the conventional religion about him, he did so in behalf of a more intense Christianity and was a mystic to whom the final wrong was the denial of love.

Nineteenth century Norwegian Christianity had in it many elements, several of them from without, some of them indigenous, and all of them having in the Norwegian environment a distinctive vitality.

That Christianity was inherited from a long past. It could not forget Olaf Haraldsson who, as patron saint, represented the era of conversion and what had survived from the Middle Ages. It bore deeply the impress of the Reformation. It was prevailingly Lutheran and the state church was of that confession.

The severing of the political tie with Denmark brought to the Church a sense of freedom. However, influences continued to flow in from Denmark and other countries. Eighteenth century rationalism survived for a time. Grundtvig's ideas had their followers. Pietism was strong. The Moravians were active. The revival of Lutheran orthodoxy in Germany and Denmark found congenial soil and Hengstenberg was potent. The example of the Inner Mission movement in these two lands helped to stimulate a similar one in Norway. Ideas entered from Sweden. The repeal in 1842 of the conventicle act of 1741 made easier the lot of dissenters from the state church. In 1845 legal restrictions on dissent were further relaxed. This helped to make possible the growth of Methodists and Baptists, stimulated by missionaries from the United States, and of the Plymouth Brethren through contacts with England. In the latter part of the century the radical theologies and Biblical study which flourished in Germany won something of a following.

At the same time there were Norwegians who were in the forefront of religious awakenings and in shaping the religious life of the nation. Although he did not die until 1824, Hans Nielsen Hauge had done his main work before 1815. Yet what he had begun grew. As a lay movement it was potent in a land where democratic tendencies were strong and where there was a large element of sturdy farmers who owned the soil that they tilled. It was in part nationalistic, directed against the half-Danish clergy. It gained momentum after the repeal of the conventicle act. Gisle Johnson (1822–1894), lecturer beginning in 1849 and from 1860 to his death (1894) professor of theology in the University of Christiana (Oslo), attempted to domesticate the lay revival in the state church. In 1868 he inaugurated a society named after Luther to send out Bible colporteurs and to prepare and distribute literature to educate the masses in Lutheran beliefs. Johnson had a close friend and colleague in C. P. Caspari (1814–1892), of German origin and training. The movement stimulated by Johnson and Caspari was in part due to the resurgence of Lutheran confessionalism in Germany and one of its effects was to lessen the influence of Grundtvigianism. It had affinities with Pietism and attracted some of the Haugeans. A revival in Western Norway, not content with the clergy-controlled movement of Johnson, gave rise to a lay organization which, without leaving the state church, built its own "prayer houses," and called its units Inner Mission Unions. Increasingly laymen won a voice in the Church's affairs. Beginning with 1888 they could speak in the Church. Pastors possessed less and less exclusive authority. The declining proportion of clergy to the population and their insufficient number contributed to a greater dependence upon lay preachers. Those reached by the religious awakening were largely contained in the official Church through voluntary organizations within it. A synodical organization developed. The conservative reaction after the revolutionary year of 1848 strengthened the Pietist and theologically conservative trend. The hymnal and the liturgy were revised to give expression to the new life. G. A. Lammers (1802–1878), a pastor in the state church, was profoundly changed by contact with the Moravians, preached repentance and conversion, for a time left the establishment, and led in a free church movement.

The vigorous life in Norwegian Christianity stimulated the formation of numbers of missionary societies, some for special enterprises for Norwegians, such as the large seafaring class, and others for non-Christian peoples. Norwegian Lutheranism was also carried overseas by the large emigration, notably to the United States.

CHRISTIANITY IN SWEDEN IN THE NINETEENTH CENTURY

In Sweden, as in so many other countries after 1815, there came a revival of historic Christianity and a reaction in the Church against the rationalism of the eighteenth century. As in some of the others, the reaction may have been furthered by the sufferings and humiliations of the Napoleonic Wars. Sweden had lost Finland to its hereditary foe, Russia, and was also forced to surrender

Pomerania to Denmark, although the injury to its pride had been partly assuaged by having the close tie established with Norway. The dynasty founded by Gustavus Vasa and associated with the days of the country's military glory had proved incompetent and had died out, and an alien, Bernadotte, one of Napoleon's marshals, had been elected monarch. Sobered by these changes, many felt the rationalism of the *Aufklärung* to be shallow and unable to meet the needs of the day. The reaction in part took the form of romanticism, but romanticism united with deep religious feeling. The influence of Pietism and the Moravians persisted and had fresh expressions.

Here, as elsewhere, the revival had a variety of aspects. It was seen in a new church hymnal, completed in 1819, largely the work of J. O. Wallin, who, a poet and a preacher, died as Archbishop of Uppsala (1839). It had an early leader in Henrik Schartau (1757–1825), pastor in the university town of Lund, who was strong as a preacher but was particularly earnest and skilled in spiritual counsel to individuals. He was critical of the sentimentality often associated with Pietism and stressed the sacraments of the Church. Eric Gustaf Geijer (1783–1847), a layman, a distinguished historian and professor at Uppsala, regarded history as a continuous manifestation of God and exerted a profound influence on a whole generation of intellectuals in leading them to a deeper religious life. Within the state church two theological trends, both in the nature of a strengthening of Christianity, issued from the universities, Uppsala and Lund. Uppsala stressed subjective experience and a philosophic view of Christianity and made little of the Church. Lund exalted the Church, was influenced by Kliefoth, whom we have already met in Germany, and became the radiating centre of a high-church tendency.

There were movements which either maintained only a loose connexion with the state church or completely broke with it. In the eighteenth century the North had been the scene of a revival, due in part to contact with Pietism and the Moravians. It stressed free grace through the blood of Christ, the conversion of the individual, lay preaching, and informal conventicles outside the churches. Its adherents were called "readers," because of their use of the Bible and other Christian literature. Some of the "readers" administered the sacraments. The "reader" movement found kinship with one which had as its chief stimulus George Scott, an English Methodist, who came to Stockholm in 1830 as chaplain to a group of English labourers employed by an English manufacturer. Scott's preaching attracted crowds of Swedes and did much to further the distribution of Bibles and tracts, foreign missions, Sunday Schools, and total abstinence from alcoholic beverages. Scott was joined by two young students from the North, C. O. Rosenius and Anders Wiberg. When, in 1842, Scott was forced out of the country by the authorities, Rosenius took over the leadership and, although the tie became tenuous, kept most of the former's followers within the communion of the state church. Rosenius was followed by Paul Peter Waldenström (1838–1917). Waldenström eventually severed fellowship with the disciples of Rosenius over the question of the atonement, putting forward a subjective view in contrast with the one which spoke of the expiatory death of Christ being "for all," for he held that the latter was being made an excuse for immorality. In 1878 he brought together most of the free church movement into what was called the Swedish Mission Covenant. The strain with the state church was heightened by the refusal of the authorities to permit Waldenström and those associated with him to have a free celebration of the Lord's Supper and liberty to preach. Although the Swedish Mission Covenant technically remained within the state church, it built scores of chapels throughout the kingdom and maintained its own foreign mission society.

To the Swedish Mission Covenant were added other dissenting groups. Among them were the Baptists, who arose from contacts with the United States and had Anders Wiberg, who had resigned from his pastorate in the state church, as an outstanding leader. There were also Methodists, although they were only about a third as numerous as Baptists. The Mormons attracted several thousand to Utah but a few hundred of their converts remained in Sweden. By 1914 Seventh Day Adventists, also of American origin, had nearly a hundred churches. The way was made easier for dissenters by the removal (1858) of the act against conventicles and further legislation in 1860 and 1873 in the direction of religious liberty.

The rising tide of life within Swedish Christianity expressed itself in many other ways. The Church of Sweden acquired a larger voice in the control of its own affairs. Although the king was still the highest earthly ruler of the church and the Riksdag, or Parliament, passed, repealed, or altered church laws, the monarch exercised his power only on the counsel of a minister of church affairs and of the Council of State. Moreover, a national ecclesiastical council, the Kyrko-möte, authorized in 1863, holding its first meeting in 1868, made up equally of laymen and clergy, representative of each of the dioceses and of the two universities and in part elected, had an important voice in crucial decisions. Deaconesses were trained. More lay initiative and lay organizations were seen in the congregations of the Church of Sweden. As Stockholm grew, additional church buildings were erected, partly by voluntary contributions. Christian youth movements came into being, some of them among students, and the latter were brought into touch with similar movements outside of Sweden through the World's Student Christian Federation, which was organized in 1895 in Sweden and partly by Swedes. More than a dozen missionary societies were created to spread the Gospel overseas. They represented either various theological convictions in the Church of Sweden or the different free churches. Among them was the *Evangeliska Fosterlands-stiftelse* ("Evangelical National Institute"), founded in 1856, and originally for work in Sweden by lay evangelists in connexion with the state church, but later extending its operation to seamen and to other lands. The large Swedish emigration, notably to the United States, was in general held to distinctively Swedish churches, some of them springing from the establishment and others, notably the Swedish Mission Covenant and the Baptists, from dissenting bodies. As in several other countries, out of Protestantism arose a vigorous movement to combat the use of alcoholic beverages. It was provoked in Sweden by a widespread addiction to brandy and other liquors of heavy alcoholic content. Outstanding as an advocate of total abstinence was Peter Wieselgren (1800–1877), scholar and clergyman. Efforts were made to reach the labourers, especially the youth in the growing factories. A Christian social settlement arose in Stockholm. Some pastors were active in the social democratic movement and at least two represented it in the Riksdag.

Swedish Christianity could not hope to remain unaffected by the multiform movements which were shaping the Occident of the nineteenth century. In the more strictly religious realm the currents, such as Ritschlianism, the critical study of the Bible, and the historical approach to religions which were potent in Germany quickly reached Sweden, for many Swedes studied in German universities. Here, as elsewhere, they provoked controversy. In general, the University of Uppsala was hospitable to them. Waldenström and others of similar convictions viewed them with suspicion or hostility. Frankly anti-Christian ideologies and philosophies also entered, among them Marxist materialism. Many of the labourers in the growing industries tended to drift away from the faith. Numbers of the educated, while retaining their formal connexion with the Church, were indifferent or sceptical.

As a whole, however, in Sweden, as in Germany, Denmark, and Norway, Protestantism was much more vigorous in 1914 than it had been in 1815.

PROTESTANTISM IN FINLAND

Separated from Sweden and placed under Russia by the outcome of the Napoleonic Wars, Finland was permitted to preserve its constitution and its distinctive institutions and culture. The attempt of the tsar in 1899 to assimilate Finland to Russia and to "Russify" the country broke down within a few years. Because of the long connexion with Sweden, the Finns were overwhelmingly Protestant and Lutheran. The Lutheran Church was the established Church of Finland. Less than 2 per cent. of the population were Russian Orthodox and even by 1914 a still smaller per cent. were Methodists, Baptists, and Roman Catholics.

Nineteenth century developments in the religious life of Finland must be sketched only in summary fashion. In the eighteenth century both Pietism and the rationalism of the *Aufklärung* made themselves felt. As in Scandinavia, after 1815 Pietism continued, but, unlike most of Scandinavia, the reaction against rationalism was late in coming. The rationalism of the Enlightenment remained dominant in the Church until the middle of the nineteenth century. During the first years of Russian overlordship the Church of Finland was fortunate in having extraordinarily able leadership in its primate, Jacob Tengström, Archbishop of Åbo (Turku) from 1803 to 1832. He aided in the formation of a Bible society and a tract society and encouraged the formation of voluntary organizations to reinforce the official church. Yet he and his successor represented the spirit of the *Aufklärung*. Ostensibly the traditional orthodoxy remained, but it was largely sterile. Partly influenced by the Russian pattern, the clergy tended to be a bureaucracy emphasizing the administrative side of their functions.

Late in the eighteenth century a religious awakening began, chiefly among the laity, especially the farmers. It developed lay preachers. It spread to the students and the younger clergy and had its major centre in the new capital, Helsinki. Although opposed by the leadership of the state church, the revival reached a peak in the 1840's. It was closely associated with a rising tide of nationalism. The state church became the religious bond and symbol of Finnish patriotism. Mainly as a result of the revival, it acquired, through legislation in 1869, a large degree of independence from the state and was brought together and given a central organization under a national synod. In the second half of the nineteenth century a revision was made in the liturgy, a revised catechism was issued, and a new hymnal was compiled. All reflected the fresh life brought by the revivals. While in the 1880's many of the educated, affected by the secularism and the anti-Christian or agnostic strains in Western thought, were alienated from the Church, new revivals broke forth, partly under Finnish leadership and partly through contacts with Britain and the United States. As a result, some dissenting bodies arose. Sunday Schools, the Young Men's and Young Women's Christian Associations, and the Student Christian Movement entered and flourished. Missionary societies were founded and were concerned with both Finland and other countries. They sent representatives to China, Africa, Palestine, Japan, and the Finnish tribes in Russia.

PROTESTANTISM IN THE NETHERLANDS

What was the state of Protestantism in the nineteenth century in the Netherlands, the country where the struggle for independence had been so inextricably associated with that form of the faith?

Here, even after the separation of the predominantly Roman Catholic Belgium (1830) from the unnatural union which had been forced on the two countries by the Congress of Vienna (1815), a large Roman Catholic minority remained. By 1914, due chiefly to its birth rate, higher than that of Protestants, it constituted slightly more than a third of the population. A significant movement away from all formal connexion with any religion began and in 1909 those in that classification numbered nearly 5 per cent. of all the inhabitants, a proportion which trebled in the next two decades. In 1914 Protestants constituted about three-fifths of the population.

The Netherlands Reformed Church (*De Nederlandsch Hervormde Kerk*), long closely associated with the state, remained the largest of the Protestant bodies. When, during the Revolution, the French "liberators" had set up the Batavian Republic, the tie between the Reformed Church and the state was severed (1798) and was never again fully restored. For a time the effect upon the Reformed Church was serious and loosened the bond which held it together. After the downfall of Napoleon the House of Orange returned and one of the early acts of King William I (January 7, 1816) was to promulgate an order which gave to the Reformed Church a structure which it was to keep until after 1914. This was almost entirely administrative and accorded a degree of self-government through local and synodical bodies. Yet it also curbed the full independence of the local congregation and in 1819 church property was put under the control of the crown. Subsidies from the state continued in lieu of expropriated ecclesiastical lands. In 1852 and 1866 the crown returned to the church the control of the latter's finances.

Partly as a result of its loose organization and partly because of the complexity of the forces which played upon most churches in the nineteenth century, many parties, groups, and tendencies developed in the Netherlands Reformed Church. There was an early awakening, a repudiation both of eighteenth century rationalism and the orthodoxy of Dort. Its leaders were the poet W. Bilderdijk (died 1831) and Isaac de Costa (died 1860), a converted Jew. The main alignment was between orthodox and liberals, but there were many sub-divisions. Some of the liberals were much influenced by Hegel, had a pantheistic trend, and made little of sin, grace, and Christ. Others stressed the Jesus of the Gospels, regarded him as divine but hesitated to call him God, viewed as secondary the epistles and their theology, and had no use for the vicarious atonement. German theology had marked repercussions, especially in the universities, and some of the professors of theology were more radical than were the Germans who shaped their thinking. The Tübingen school of Biblical criticism won acceptance from many. The trend which regarded Christianity as a phase of the general development of religion was represented. There was also a movement which, stressing the ethical side of Christianity, rejected the conclusions of the critical study of the Gospels and emphasized the authority of the Bible, especially the New Testament. Some from most of these groups coöperated in missions, the care of orphans, and social efforts with those, of whom there were many, who held to the older orthodoxy. In general, liberal views prevailed among those who taught Biblical and theological subjects in the universities.

Liberalism became dominant in the Netherlands Reformed Church. Under its influence the tie with the state was made more and more tenuous, the teaching of the Reformed confession in the state schools was discontinued (1856), and the doctrinal subscription of candidates for ordination was relaxed, until, in 1883, all that was required was a promise to "further the interests of God's Kingdom."

The nineteenth century saw two major secessions from the Netherlands Reformed Church. One was in 1834 by those who in 1869 took the name of the Christian Reformed Church (De Christelijke Gereformeerde Kerk). Its original leader was Hendrik de Cock. It was a protest against the prevailing rationalism in the Netherlands Reformed Church and held strictly to the findings of the famous Synod of Dort of 1619. The majority united in 1892 with the Reformed Churches in the Netherlands, the other of the chief secessions, but a minority maintained its separate existence, holding to infralapsarianism rather than supralapsarianism as did the other.

The Reformed Churches in the Netherlands (De Gereformeerde Kerken in Nederland), the largest of the Protestant bodies outside the Netherlands Reformed Church, in 1909 had attained about a fifth the size of the former body. Its chief early figure was Abraham Kuyper (died 1920) and the major break with the Netherlands Reformed Church occurred in December, 1886. The movement was a protest against the liberalism of the Netherlands Reformed Church. It crystallized a discontent which had long been simmering, a discontent which had given rise to private schools in which the historic confessions of the Reformed Churches were made the basis of religious instruction and to the founding, by Kuyper, of the Free University of Amsterdam. Beginning with 1887 the dissenting congregations began the development of a national ecclesiastical structure. Kuyper was a vigorous leader, carried his principles into politics, and from 1901 to 1905 as premier was the real executive head of the state.

Other Protestant bodies were represented in the Netherlands. The most prominent among them were Lutherans, Mennonites, and a small remnant of the Remonstrants, a church going back to the Arminian controversy in the seventeenth century.

We must also note that towards the end of the century movements for reaching youth through voluntary organizations mounted. Through contacts with Great Britain, in 1896 the Netherlands Student Christian Union was formed. In addition there were Christian youth organizations which by 1914 enrolled several scores of thousands. In the Netherlands, as in Protestant circles in neighbouring lands, an Inner Mission was active.

In spite of these many divisions and the drift towards secularism of a large part of the population, Dutch Protestantism gave birth to a varied and growing missionary enterprise. Indeed, the divisions were evidence of vitality, of conviction which was not content with standing on the defensive but which sought to propagate the faith in other lands. Most of the missionary effort was directed towards the Netherlands East Indies, that vast area with its teeming and growing population where the Dutch were building a colonial empire and which absorbed much of the energy and provided a large proportion of the livelihood of the Dutch people.

Christian principles had a large part in Dutch politics, for there were many who sought to make them effective in the affairs of state and in the nation's colonial policies. Not only was there a Roman Catholic party, but there was also a Christian national party which was Protestant and interconfessional which drew chiefly from the farmers and the middle classes.

PROTESTANTISM IN SWITZERLAND

In Switzerland, as in Western Europe in general, rationalism pervaded the Protestant churches in the decades which immediately preceded 1815. Not far from that year a revival began which was either directly from Pietism or was closely akin to it. It stressed individual conversion. To it contributed several foreign visitors and residents, prominent among them being Robert Haldane from Scotland and Madame Krüdener. The awakenings took many forms and issued in several quite different expressions. Prominent were the Basel Evangelical Missionary Society which, as we have seen, was begun in 1815, depending largely on a Pietist constituency, and the Pilgrim Mission of St. Chrischona, on the outskirts of Basel, begun in 1840, for the training of evangelists for work at home and abroad.

The awakening met with resistance in the state churches—for it will be remembered that each of the cantons into which Switzerland was divided had an established church. In several cantons this led to the formation of free churches. Prominent among them was one in Lausanne, where the step was taken in 1845, led by Alexander Vinet (1797–1847), sometimes called the Schleiermacher of French Protestantism, and who had long been advocating on religious grounds the separation of Church and state.

The relations of Church and state were long a vital issue. They became such in the revolutionary period of 1830 and 1831, when, as in much of Western Europe, there was a swing towards democracy from the aristocratic post-1815 reaction. The constitution of 1848 which transformed Switzerland from a league of states into a federal republic permitted public worship of any recognized Christian confession in all the cantons. Amendments to the constitution in the 1870's strengthened the control of the Church by the state, forbade the creation of new Roman Catholic bishoprics without the consent of the state, made civil marriage compulsory, guaranteed liberty of belief and conscience, forbade the restriction of civil or political rights on the grounds of religious belief, and said that no one need pay taxes for the support of a religious body to which he did not belong. For the most part the loosening of the ties between Church and state, especially in predominantly Protestant cantons, did not arise from anti-clericalism. The situation varied from canton to canton, but in general each of the state churches was left free to manage its affairs and only a financial connexion remained. The chief authority in church administration was in the individual congregations and in some of these women as well as men were given a voice.

Protestants outnumbered Roman Catholics. They constituted about three-fifths of the population, but a slightly smaller percentage in 1914 than in 1815. Before the end of the century both branches of Christianity were found in each canton, but the proportionate strength varied greatly, some cantons being overwhelmingly Protestant and others predominantly Roman Catholic.

The free churches included the Baptists and Methodists. They arose through contacts with Great Britain and the United States.

PROTESTANTISM IN CENTRAL EUROPE

In the Central European countries—Poland, Bohemia, Slovakia, Austria, and Hungary—Protestants were minorities. The nineteenth century witnessed the loosening of the restrictions placed on them by governments in which Roman Catholic influence had been potent.

Throughout the century Poland remained divided between Russia, Prussia, and Austria. Thousands of Germans, among them many Protestants, moved into the zones controlled by Prussia and Austria and thus greatly strengthened the Protestant minority which since the Catholic Reformation had been subject to persecution. There were also Protestants in the Russian zone. The Protestants were divided among Lutherans, Reformed, Moravians, and the church which represented the union of Lutherans and Reformed. There were smaller groups of Baptists and of what was known as the Christian communion.

In Bohemia and Slovakia where under Hapsburg rule and the Catholic

Reformation Protestantism had suffered chronic persecution and had been reduced to small minorities, an edict of toleration of 1781 brought some relief. In the course of the nineteenth century, especially after the revolutionary year of 1848, further progress was made towards religious liberty and relaxing control by the Roman Catholic Church.

Similarly in predominantly Roman Catholic Austria the century witnessed increasing freedom for Protestants. An imperial edict of 1861 gave them full civil rights and legal equality with Roman Catholics and permitted them to choose their own clergy. Within the next few years both Lutherans and Reformed achieved national organizations. Beginning with 1898 a movement away from Rome brought several thousand converts from the Roman Catholic Church.

In Hungary the position of Protestantism became less unfavourable. Lutheran, Reformed, and Unitarians had been present since the Reformation. Here as elsewhere in the Hapsburg domains the edict of 1781 eased earlier restrictions. In the first half of the nineteenth century Protestants were accorded equal civil rights with Roman Catholics. In the latter half of the century the awakenings which were stirring Protestantism in Western Europe, Great Britain, and the United States began to be felt and to infuse new life into churches which had been largely formal and rationalistic.

Protestantism in Latin Europe

In Latin Europe, predominantly Roman Catholic, the nineteenth century brought the Protestant minorities varying degrees of relaxation of adverse pressure.

In Spain and Portugal Protestantism in 1815 was non-existent. In the course of the nineteenth century missionaries entered, chiefly from Great Britain and the United States. Through their efforts small Protestant bodies came into being.

Italy had an indigenous Protestantism, the Waldensees. In the nineteenth century some of the Waldensees moved from their ancestral Alpine valleys into the cities. They were aided by financial grants from fellow-Protestants in Great Britain and the United States and by measures looking towards religious liberty taken under the Kingdom of Italy. Missionaries also came from several British and American denominations.

Belgium had a few small Protestant congregations in the midst of an overwhelmingly Roman Catholic population. In the 1830's, after the achievement of Belgian independence, these drew together in two national unions.

France contained more Protestants than did any other Latin country. They were partly Lutheran, chiefly in the border province of Alsace, and partly Reformed, the descendants of the Huguenots who had suffered severe persecution across the years. Napoleon I had granted them toleration and the position of state churches. This status was respected by the successive regimes which controlled the state in the nineteenth century. For Protestants as for Roman Catholics, the separation of Church and state came in 1905 and for a time brought financial embarrassment.

As with Protestantism elsewhere, so in France, the nineteenth century witnessed a revival of a Pietist nature (due in part to the efforts of Haldane) and a liberalism which arose from the attempt to accommodate the faith to the intellectual temper of the age. In the French Reformed Church these contrasting currents brought on a conflict which led to division (1849). The orthodox, with a warm personal faith, had the Monods, Adolphe and Frédéric, as leaders, left the Reformed Synod, thus renouncing all endowments, and depended on voluntary gifts for support. They constituted themselves as the Union of Evangelical Free Churches.

The annexation (1871) of Alsace and Lorraine by Germany led to a sharp diminution of the numbers of Protestants, especially Lutherans, under the French flag. In place of the theological faculty of Strassburg, lost by the cession, a Protestant theological school was founded in Paris in which both Reformed and Lutherans joined. The Reformed also had missions to the Roman Catholics and the unchurched. The McCall Mission, begun in 1872 and supported from Great Britain and the United States, endeavoured, with the cordial concurrence of French Protestants, to reach the labourers in the cities who were being de-Christianized by the forces of the age. Missionaries, mostly Methodists and Baptists from the British Isles and the United States, gathered converts, but these never exceeded more than a few thousand.

Summary

From what has unavoidably been a somewhat bewildering array of details several generalizations emerge which characterize the Protestantism of Continental Europe in the nineteenth century.

First of all is extreme complexity. In spite of an attempt to reduce the narrative to a minimum and the omission of many important names and movements which would have to be given a place in a complete story, the perusal of this chapter must leave even the most courageous and painstaking reader somewhat bewildered.

As a second generalization there is an impression of abounding vitality. The multiplicity of details may arise in part from our nearness to the period and a consequent lack of perspective which would enable us to sort out the more significant. However, it is primarily due to the extraordinary vigour of nineteenth century Protestantism. Although it was faced by hostile forces which threatened the existence of Christianity and which were progressively de-Christianizing large elements of the population, Protestantism was experiencing a marked revival, was inspiring many of the intellectuals to re-think their faith in terms of the new methods and knowledge of the age, was moving others to seek to bring their faith to bear upon the social and political forces of the day, was working in millions a transforming experience, and was giving birth to societies which were spreading the Gospel in all the continents and in many of the islands of the sea. That vitality was mounting. Continental European Protestantism came to 1914 more vigorous than in 1815 and, by immigration and missions, more widely spread than at any earlier time.

A third generalization is that there was in progress a separation of Church and state. Unlike the similar dissociation which was affecting the Roman Catholic Church, it had in it little of hostility to the Church. It arose partly from the democratic secular liberalism which was prominent in politics and partly from the desire of the churches for freedom from control by the state. It was accompanied by growing autonomy in the churches, an autonomy which was at once an evidence and a contributory cause of enhanced vigour.

A fourth generalization is the rise of fresh tensions and divisions in Protestantism. They cut across denominational, confessional, and national boundaries. In general they fell into three classifications. One was the emphasis upon historic creeds, confessions, and forms of worship. Another stressed a personal religious experience and tended to exalt the Bible as the inspired word of God to men. The third endeavoured to accommodate the faith to current philosophies and the scientific approach. The three interacted on one another, but the conflicts were often sharp.

A fifth generalization is the leading place held by Germany in Continental Protestantism. Through Pietism in its varied forms, through its historic confessions, and through its new formulations of theology and its Biblical studies German Protestantism, especially German Lutheranism, was dominant. The reasons are not entirely clear. They are to be found partly in the fact that Germany was the original home of Protestantism, partly in the size of the country, and partly in the surge of nationalism which was uniting the country politically. Yet these seem not to have been all. There may be other reasons which defy the methods and the insights of the historian.

A sixth generalization which can be only dimly discerned from what has been said in the preceding pages was the growing unity of Protestantism, a unity which after 1914 was to mount by leaps and bounds. In spite of the many frictions and the new divisions added to the old, Protestantism was not a congeries of relatively isolated movements. The multiform aspects of Protestantism were affecting one another, often profoundly. Currents in one land or branch of Protestantism were flowing into other lands and into other branches of that wing of the faith. The Protestantism of the Continent was influencing that of the British Isles and America. In turn, British and American Protestantism was making itself felt on the Continent. As we are to see in later chapters, as never before Protestants were beginning to find ways of coöperating interconfessionally on a world-wide scale. Here was a new kind of Christian unity, as yet very imperfect, but growing.

SELECTED BIBLIOGRAPHY

R. B. Brandt, *The Philosophy of Schleiermacher. The Development of His Theory of Scientific and Religious Knowledge* (New York, Harper & Brothers, 1941, pp. viii, 350). Useful.

T. K. Cheyne, *Founders of Old Testament Criticism. Biographical, Descriptive, and Critical Studies* (New York, Charles Scribner's Sons, 1893, pp. ix, 372). Judiciously sympathetic.

G. Cross, *The Theology of Schleiermacher. A Condensed Presentation of His Chief Work "The Christian Faith"* (The University of Chicago Press, 1911, pp. lx, 344). Sympathetic.

A. L. Drummond, *German Protestantism since Luther* (London, The Epworth Press, 1951, pp. x, 282). Contains much useful material. Especially valuable for the nineteenth and twentieth centuries.

A. E. Garvie, *The Ritschlian Theology, Critical and Constructive. An Exposition and an Estimate* (Edinburgh, T. & T. Clark, 1899, pp. xxvii, 400). A useful and sympathetic summary by a competent Scottish theologian.

M. Gerhardt, *Ein Jahrhundert Innere Mission. Die Geschichte des Central-Ausschuss für die Innere Mission der Deutschen Evangelische Kirche* (Gütersloh, C. Bertelsmann Verlag, 2 vols., 1948). Excellent not only for the Inner Mission but also on the German Church in general and on the relations of Church and state.

J. I. Good, *History of the Swiss Reformed Church Since the Reformation* (Philadelphia, Publication and Sunday School Board of the Reformed Church in the United States, 1913, pp. xii, 504). Sympathetic, especially with the free churches.

W. Herrmann, *Systematic Theology (Dogmatik)*, translated by N. Micklem and K. A. Saunders (New York, The Macmillan Co., 1927, pp. 152). A brief posthumous summary of his views.

F. Kattenbusch, *Die deutsche evangelische Theologie seit Schleiermacher. Ihre Leistungen and ihre Schäden* (Giessen, Alfred Topelmann, 5th ed., 1926, pp. vi, 160).

Kierkegaard's Attack upon "Christendom" 1854–1855, translated with an introduction by W. Lowrie (Princeton University Press, 1944, pp. xviii, 303).

S. Kierkegaard, *The Gospel of Suffering and the Lilies of the Field,* translated by D. F. Swenson and L. M. Swenson (Minneapolis, Augsburg Publishing Co., 1948, pp. 239).

[S. Kierkegaard] Johannes Climacus, *Philosophical Fragments or A Fragment of Philosophy,* translated by D. F. Swenson (Princeton University Press, 1936, pp. xxx, 105).

H. Koch, *Grundtvig,* translated by L. Jones (Yellow Springs, Ohio, Antioch Press, 1952). A standard work.

F. Lichtenberger, *History of German Theology in the Nineteenth Century,* translated by W. Hastie (Edinburgh, T. & T. Clark, 1889, pp. xxxix, 629). A comprehensive sketch.

H. R. Mackintosh, *Types of Modern Theology Schleiermacher to Barth* (New York, Charles Scribner's Sons, 1937, pp. vii, 333). By a competent Scottish theologian.

K. D. Macmillan, *Protestantism in Germany* (Princeton University Press, 1917, pp. viii, 282). A semi-popular and sketchy historical survey.

E. C. Moore, *An Outline of the History of Christian Thought Since Kant* (New York, Charles Scribner's Sons, 1912, pp. x, 249). A useful, popular, critical summary survey of Protestant thought in Europe and America.

J. W. Oman, *The Problem of Faith and Freedom in the Last Two Centuries* (New York, A. C. Armstrong and Son, 1906, pp. xxiv, 443). Mainly on Continental Protestant thought in the nineteenth century. By a competent scholar.

J. Orr, *Ritschlianism. Expository and Critical Essays* (London, Hodder & Stoughton, 1903, pp. xii, 283). The author believes Ritschlian theology to be basically unsound.

O. Pfleiderer, *The Development of Theology in Germany since Kant, and Its Progress in Great Britain since 1825,* translated by J. F. Smith (London, Swan Sonnenschein & Co., 1890, pp. xii, 403).

E. Révész, J. S. Kováts, L. Ravasz, *Hungarian Protestantism, Its Past, Present and Future* (Budapest, Bethlen Gábor Literary and Printing House, 1927, pp. xiv, 222).

A. Ritschl, *A Critical History of the Christian Doctrine of Justification and Reconciliation,* translated by J. S. Black (Edinburgh, Edmonston and Douglas, 1872, pp. xvi, 605).

A. Ritschl, *The Christian Doctrine of Justification and Reconciliation. The Positive Development of the Doctrine.* English translation edited by H. R. Mackintosh and A. B. Macaulay (New York, Charles Scribner's Sons, 1900, pp. xii, 673).

F. E. D. Schleiermacher, *Schleiermacher's Werke* (Leipzig, Felix Meiner, 3 vols., 1927).

F. Schleiermacher, *The Christian Faith,* translated from the second German edition by H. R. Mackintosh and J. S. Stewart (Edinburgh, T. & T. Clark, 1928, pp. xii, 760).

W. B. Selbie, *Schleiermacher, A Critical and Historical Study* (New York, E. P. Dutton & Co., 1913, pp. ix, 272). By a competent British theologian.

The Life of Schleiermacher as Unfolded in His Autobiography and Letters, translated by F. Rowan (London, Smith, Elder & Co., 2 vols., 1860).

F. Siegmund-Schultze, editor, *Ekklesia. Eine Sammlung von Selbstdarstellungen der Christlichen Kirchen:*

II. *Die Skandinavischen Länder. Die Kirche in Schweden* (Gotha, Leopold Klotz, 1935, pp. 180).

II. *Die Skandinavischen Länder. Die Kirche von Norwegen* (Gotha, Leopold Klotz, 1936, pp. 207).

II. *Die Skandinavischen Länder. Die Kirche in Dänemark. Die Kirche in Island* (Leipzig, Leopold Klotz, 1937, pp. 195, 35).

II. *Die Skandinavischen Länder. Die Kirche in Finnland* (Leipzig, Leopold Klotz, 1938, pp. 203).

III. *Die Mitteleuropäischen Länder. 9. Die Evangelischen Kirchen der Niederlande* (Gotha, Leopold Klotz, 1934, pp. 176).

III. *Die Mitteleuropäischen Länder. 10. Die Evangelischen Kirchen der Schweitz* (Gotha, Leopold Klotz, 1935, pp. 254).

V. *Die Osteuropäischen Länder. Die Kirchen der Tschechoslowakei* (Leipzig, Leopold Klotz, 1937, pp. 250).

V. *Die Osteuropäischen Länder. Die Evangelischen Kirchen in Polen* (Leipzig, Leopold Klotz, 1938, pp. 274).

This very useful series is composed of carefully written articles, historical and descriptive, but chiefly historical, by specialists in the respective countries.

P. Stiansen, *History of the Baptists in Norway* (Chicago, The Blessing Press, pp. xi, 175). Carefully and sympathetically done.

D. F. Strauss, *The Life of Jesus Critically Examined,* translated from the fourth German edition by M. Evans (New York, Calvin Blanchard, 2 vols., 1860).

A. T. Swing, *The Theology of Albrecht Ritschl, Together with Introduction in the Christian Religion by A. Ritschl,* translated by A. T. Swing (New York, Longmans, Green & Co., 1901, pp. xiv, 296).

J. Wordsworth, *The National Church of Sweden* (London, A. R. Mowbray & Co., 1911, pp. xix, 459). An historical survey by an Anglican bishop.

Agnes von Zahn-Harnack, *Adolf von Harnack* (Berlin, Walter de Gruyter & Co., 1951, pp. xiii, 453).

Chapter XLVIII

CHRISTIANITY IN THE BRITISH ISLES,
A.D. 1815 - A.D. 1914

In the history of Christianity in the nineteenth century the British Isles were peculiarly important. They were dominant in the commerce and banking of the world of that day. They led in the phenomenal expansion of Western European power and culture that was bringing the world-wide revolutions which, affecting all mankind, were mounting, especially in the latter part of the century, and which after 1914 were to display ever-increasing acceleration. They built an empire on which, so it was proudly said, the sun never set. Largely through emigration from them new nations arose in Canada, Australia, and New Zealand. That emigration also contributed notably to the growth and character of the United States and South Africa. Near to the Continent of Europe and intimately related to its life and problems, and yet partially detached by the North Sea and the English Channel, the British Isles influenced the Continent and were influenced by it, and also had a distinct development. In this rôle of the British Isles in the nineteenth century course of mankind the Christianity of the islands had a very important part. As we pursue our geographic survey of the globe of these days we shall find it again and again. For this reason as well as for its place in the islands themselves, we must seek to understand it.

GENERAL FACTORS AFFECTING THE NINETEENTH CENTURY COURSE OF CHRISTIANITY IN THE BRITISH ISLES

At the outset of our attempt to trace the history of the Christianity of the British Isles in the nineteenth century we must note a number of factors which to a greater or less degree had a part in shaping it. They were very diverse and not all of them were interrelated, but we must bear them in mind, even when, absorbed in the details of our narrative, we do not specifically call attention to them. They do not fall into any logically arranged order. We can simply mention them one by one.

Prominent both in the general life of the islands and in its challenge to Christianity was rapid and progressive industrialization. Great Britain was the pioneer in the industrial revolution. During much of the nineteenth century it held what was almost a natural monopoly of the new industrial processes. This entailed vast changes in the life of Great Britain and, to a less extent, of its sister island, Ireland. It contributed to a striking increase in population which challenged the resources of the churches. Even more significantly, it led to enormous shifts of population and the phenomenal growth of cities. The churches' structure had been adapted to a rural economy and small cities. Now proportionately farming was declining, new cities were springing up, and existing cities, such as London and Glasgow, were becoming larger than any one would have once believed possible. Could the churches build enough physical plants to care for the expanding urban populations?

Still more challenging and perplexing were the altered social conditions produced by the industrial revolution. Not only were the majority of the people now in cities. In the towns and cities the environment which shaped the lives of their inhabitants was changing. Mining, especially coal mining on which industry and commerce depended, gave rise to communities in which life was drab and working conditions grim. Factories brought larger and smaller aggregations of labour, usually in overcrowded tenements. At the outset they were characterized by long hours, no protection to women and children, a lack of safeguards against disease and accident, and insecurity of employment. The port cities were no better. Poverty and squalor were not strangers in the British Isles. However, in the slums of mining, industrial, and commercial towns and cities they now attained unprecedented dimensions. They were the frightful price that Britain paid for her collective power and wealth. Could Christianity win and retain and hold a place in such a society? Still more, could it ameliorate the lot of those who were caught in its toils?

A concomitant of industrialization was the rising power of the middle classes and the declining place of the landed gentry and aristocracy. This was to contribute to a change in the religious complexion of the country. Especially did it make for the growth of Nonconformity in England, for it was among the middle classes that the "free" churches had their chief strength.

Intimately connected with the mounting industrialization were movements, some of them revolutionary, in politics and social organization. Democracy gained headway. The Reform Bill of 1832 gave a larger voice in the House of Commons to the towns and cities, especially the newer ones, and to the middle class. The year 1848 which witnessed sweeping changes on the Continent was paralleled in England by the culmination of the Chartist movement. Chartism gained rapid headway among the industrial workers and made demands which were eventually granted. The Reform Act of 1867 accorded additional seats in the House of Commons to the cities and broadened the franchise, largely among the urban working classes. The adoption of the secret ballot (1872) furthered democracy, and in 1884 and 1885 the privilege of voting was extended to almost all adult males. In 1911 the power of the House of Lords as against the House of Commons was drastically restricted. Labour organized into unions. In 1800 these had been forbidden, but in 1824 that action was repealed, and in 1825 legislation was enacted which permitted workmen to organize "to determine the scale of wages and the hours of labour." Unions increased in numbers and power. A Labour Party was organized and in 1914 it controlled forty seats in the House of Commons. There was also an Independent Labour Party which was frankly socialist. In the course of the century much humanitarian legislation was put on the statute books for mitigating the criminal laws and regulating the hours and conditions of labour.

Here again was a challenge. Could Christianity shape these movements towards Christian ends? Many of those who pioneered in the march towards democracy, for the organization of trade unions and the Labour Party, and for laws to improve the conditions of the masses were earnest Christians, products of religious awakenings and acting from Christian motives. However, some of the leadership was agnostic or even anti-Christian. Much of labour was hostile to the Church, and especially to the Church of England, for the latter was regarded as a bulwark of entrenched privilege and the exploiting classes. Moreover, it was in London that Marx did much of the formulation of the socialism which is associated with his name and he was bitter against the Church and its faith.

Closely related to the industrialization of the British Isles was a vast and multiform emigration. As we have hinted, most of it went to North America, Australasia, and South Africa. Much of it was from England, Scotland, and Wales. Much, too, was from the Roman Catholic elements of the population of Ireland. In the first half of the nineteenth century an increase in population, the evils of landlordism, and, in the 1840's, a blight that ruined the potato crop which was a main source of food and which was followed by famine, brought about a vast migration from Ireland. This was especially to the United States and the British colonies, but it was also to the manufacturing towns and cities of Great Britain. It did much to shape the Christianity of the lands to which it went.

The intellectual currents which were noted in Chapter XLV and which challenged Christianity operated in the British Isles as well as on the Continent. Here, as on the Continent, many believed that science and its findings had made Christian faith impossible for an intelligent, honest mind and turned either atheist or agnostic. The task of reconciling science and Christianity became one of the major concerns of Christian scholars.

Not only did the Christianity of the British Isles influence that in many other portions of the world. It was also in part shaped by what came to it from current movements in several other lands. In theology and Biblical studies it showed the effect of what was taking place on the Continent, especially in Germany. There was little or no slavish acceptance of Continental thought. Much of the latter was rejected outright, much was taken over in modified form, and much proved a stimulus to fresh approaches and conclusions. The Christianity of the United States was potent. That was partly because of the common heritage in language and religious life. The effect of the United States was seen chiefly in a reinforcement of the continuation of the Evangelical Awakening and of the movements which issued from it. Numbers of American "evangelists," itinerant preachers who sought the conversion of non-Christians and the deeper commitment of Christians, toured the British Isles. Prominent among them in the first half of the century was Charles G. Finney (1792–1875), who had two preaching missions to the British Isles and whose writings, notably his *Lectures on Revivals of Religion,* had an extensive sale. In the second part of the century Dwight Lyman Moody (1837–1899) and the singer who accompanied him, Ira David Sankey (1840–1908), made three extended visits to the British Isles, in 1873–1875, 1881–1884, and 1891–1892, with effects comparable with those of Wesley and Whitefield in the eighteenth century. No new denomination arose as a result of their meetings. Rather, most of the existing denominations were stirred to deeper life. Their *Gospel Hymns,* with simple and moving melodies and words, became the common property of thousands. Partly from the Moody movement came two other Americans, John Raleigh Mott (1865——) and Robert Parmelee Wilder (1863–1938), of both of whom, especially the former, we are to hear more later, and who addressed themselves primarily to students. Mott held evangelistic meetings in universities. Wilder introduced the Student Volunteer Movement for Foreign Missions, which had begun at a summer student conference under Moody's leadership in 1886 and had swept with great power through the colleges, universities, and theological seminaries of the United States. Out of the Student Volunteer Movement sprang the Student Christian Movement of Great Britain and Ireland, soon to be the major agency for volunteer student Christian activity in the colleges and universities of the British Isles.

We have designedly named this chapter "Christianity in the British Isles A.D. 1815–A.D. 1914," for we must seek to cover both of the main branches of the faith that were represented there, namely Protestant and Roman Catholic. As we are to see shortly, the Roman Catholic Church was important, especially in Ireland. However, it was Protestantism that predominated. There was a memorable revival of the Catholic tradition in the Church of England, but it was Protestantism which was chiefly notable for abounding vitality.

British Protestantism continued to be invigorated by the Evangelical movement. This movement persisted through the century. To a greater or less extent it affected all the churches except the Roman Catholic. From time to time it reached a crescendo. Especially striking was a revival in the late 1850's which stirred Anglo-Saxon Protestantism on both sides of the Atlantic.

Most of the nineteenth century was embraced by the reign of Queen Victoria (1837–1901). While, because of the declining power of the British monarchs before the growing authority of Parliament, Victoria did not leave as deep an impress on the country as had Elizabeth, it was no accident which named the latter half of the century the Victorian era. The queen both symbolized and reinforced much that characterized the period. Especially was that true of religion. She was genuinely devout and took an active interest in the Church of England. In her personal and family life she was in striking contrast with the monarchs who immediately preceded her and was an indication of the improvement which the mounting momentum of the religious awakening was making in the faith and morals of large elements in the population.

Although under one rule, the British Isles contained four nations, England, Wales, Scotland, and Ireland, each with a somewhat distinct culture and religious life. We must, therefore, pursue our way through them one by one rather than attempt to treat them as a unit. Yet they interacted on one another and clearly belong together. We first turn to England as the largest, richest, and most populous of the four lands.

England: The Established Church

In England we naturally begin with the Church of England, for of the several Christian communions it was the largest, the only one established by law, and in theory represented the religious facet of the nation, paralleled by the government which stood for the political phase of the people's life.

Taken as a whole, in 1815 the Church of England was far from healthy. It was rich in its endowments and its revenues, but it was closely bound to the existing order and its leaders were fearful of any change that would jeopardize their position. In a manner reminiscent of pre-Reformation abuses, pluralism, non-residence, and carelessness in the observance of the services and sacraments abounded. Even some of the higher ecclesiastics drew the revenues from more than one post and entrusted the performance of their duties to substitutes. In 1831 it was said, apparently on the basis of official statistics, that more than half the clergy did not reside in their benefices. Among the bishops were those who were distrustful of enthusiasm, worldly, indolent, luxurious, and attached to the perquisites of their office. Confirmation was often administered in a slovenly manner and with notable exceptions services were performed carelessly and in a routine fashion or were even neglected. Many cathedrals were in disrepair and were far from being centres of orderly worship and spiritual life. The bulk of the parish clergy, especially in the rural districts, were decent men who were interested in the physical welfare of their flocks, but they shared in the manner of life and the prejudices of the country gentry. They were better educated and probably more moral than their predecessors of fifteenth century, pre-Reformation days, but they left much to be desired. The prevailing system of pew rents tended to shut out the poor and to identify the Church of England with a class.

There was a happier side of the picture. The Evangelicals, although a small minority, were active. Outside their ranks worthy bishops and clergy were also found. However, in general the Church of England entered the nineteenth century in poor condition to meet the threats and the challenges which that age presented to Christianity. The bulwark and refuge of privilege, it is not strange that it was viewed with dislike and even hostility by many who longed and worked for the betterment of the conditions of the masses and by multitudes of those on whom the new industrialization bore heavily.

The nineteenth century witnessed a striking awakening and transformation within the Church of England. In a sense the real reformation of that church was then rather than in the sixteenth and seventeenth centuries. This came both from without and from within.

The forces which, working from without, made for improvement in the Church of England were in part those which brought modernization in the political structure of the state, were a phase of the onward march of democracy, and operated through the government. Aided by some churchmen, they found expression in acts of Parliament in the 1830's, after the Reform Bill of 1832 which based the House of Commons on a wider and more representative electorate. They were designed to correct the more flagrant abuses and to enable the Church of England better to meet the conditions of the new day. A permanent body was set up called the Ecclesiastical Commissioners for England, which was to see that the new laws were carried out and was to manage the property entrusted to it. Several of the larger sees were reduced to a more manageable size and new sees were created. The revenues of the archbishoprics and of some of the wealthier bishoprics were so managed that the incomes of the incumbents were reduced and the savings used to augment the stipends of the poorer sees. Several sinecure benefices were suppressed and the number of resident canons attached to cathedrals was curtailed and the sums thus freed were assigned to needy livings. Pluralism was all but abolished and non-residency was proscribed. Parish boundaries were altered to make them more nearly coincide with current needs. The tithe, a form of revenue for the Church which had come down from the Middle Ages and which had largely been paid in the produce of the soil, was increasingly irritating and was commuted to a rental to be paid in cash. In 1868 as a result of agitation which began at least as far back as the 1830's and which was pushed by Dissenters, the compulsory payment of local parish rates for the maintenance of the church fabric was abolished and was made purely voluntary.

Many movements worked from within the Church of England. One of these was for the erection of new church buildings to care for the growing urban population and for the repair and restoration of older church fabrics. Several societies were formed for this purpose. To them came gifts from private individuals. In 1818 and 1828 they were augmented by substantial grants by the government. In 1836 the Pastoral Aid Society was organized to increase the number of clergy.

Another movement was the continuation of the Evangelical strain within the Church of England. At the outset of the nineteenth century the Evangelicals, although a minority, were the most active and zealous in that church. They preached the necessity of conversion, stressed family prayers and the observance of Sunday, endeavoured to live their lives "in the great Taskmaster's eye," were ardent students of the Bible, produced a religious literature which was widely read, brought more of the singing of hymns into the church services, elevated marriage, were self-sacrificing in their gifts to charity, and were zealous in promoting social reform. Although often derided, even by clergymen of the Church of England, they contributed in large measure to the improvement in the language and morals of the land which became noticeable in the fore part of the nineteenth century. They were not especially active in speculative theological thought. Indeed, they had little interest in the philosophy of religion or of history, nor did they stress scholarship. Distrustful of the nineteenth century critical study of the Bible, they were content to regard the Scriptures as the authoritative word of God. They believed firmly in the incarnation, in the substitutionary death of Christ, in justification by faith, in the salvation of the individual, and in the present operation of the Holy Spirit. They were willing to coöperate with those of like views in other communions and were active in home and foreign missions.

From the Evangelicals and those sympathetic with them issued a wealth of hymns. The tradition in the Church of England, supported by the weight of Cranmer, had been to employ only the metrical versions of the Psalms in public worship. Now, thanks in part to the Evangelicals but also to other influences, hymns of "human" composition came into use. Among Evangelical hymn writers were Henry Alford (1810–1871), eventually Dean of Canterbury Cathedral, whose best remembered productions were "Come ye thankful people, come" (1844), "Ten thousand times ten thousand" (1867), and "Forward be our watchword" (1871); Anna Laetitia Waring (1820–1910), whose "In heavenly love abiding" (1850) had a long and wide use; George Croly (1780–1860), Irish by birth and rearing, a magnetic preacher in London, and the author of "Spirit of God, descend upon my heart"; Edward Henry Bickersteth (1825–1906), in later life Bishop of Exeter, compiler of the hymnal *Christian Psalmody,* and author of "Oh God the Rock of Ages" (1860); Arabella Katherine Hankey (1834–1889), whose father was a member of the "Clapham sect" and who wrote "I love to tell the story" (1866); and especially Francis Ridley Havergal (1836–1878), daughter of an Anglican clergyman who did much to improve church music, herself highly educated, a talented musician, an earnest and happy evangelist, the writer of many hymns, among them "Lord, speak to me that I may speak" (1872) and "Take my life and let it be consecrated, Lord, to Thee" (1874).

It is said that in the first half of the century the Evangelicals began to be popular, especially among the well-to-do, and to have become conventional. However, Evangelicalism was revitalized by the revivals in the latter part of the century, especially those which accompanied the visits of Moody and Sankey. Conferences were held for the deepening of the spiritual life at which not only Anglicans but also Nonconformists were welcome. A famous centre for them was at Mildmay, where William Pennefather was vicar, and where in 1870 a hall to seat 2,500 was built. It was Pennefather who first asked Moody to England. Another centre, begun in 1875 at Keswick, in the Lake District, in Cumberland, by T. D. Harford-Battersby, a clergyman of the Church of England, persisted annually into the twentieth century. At first looked upon with suspicion by some Evangelicals of the old school, eventually it became a radiating focus of spiritual power among Evangelicals and those among dissenters who held kindred convictions. Evangelicals also began schools for the training of deaconesses, among them one founded at Mildmay by Pennefather, partly suggested by the one at Kaiserswerth, in Germany.

Another current making for revival in the Church of England was what is sometimes known as the Tractarian movement but more often as the Oxford movement. It contributed powerfully to the Anglo-Catholic movement. Like the Evangelical Awakening, it was from within the Church, but in several respects the contrast between the two was striking. While loyal to the Book of Common Prayer and to the ecclesiastical structure, the Evangelicals, stressing, as we have seen, individual conversion, holy living, missions, and moral and social reform and improvement, had little sense of the historic Church and the Catholic tradition, willingly coöperated with Christians of similar convictions outside their communion, and, as we have said, had few profound scholars and were not much interested in speculative theology. On the other hand, the Oxford movement was deeply concerned for the historic Church, looked back nostalgically to the Catholic Church as it was in the early centuries before it had been torn apart through the stresses of regionalism, nationalism, and conflicting dogmas, and longed for what it called "reunion." It saw in the apostolic succession of the episcopate an essential characteristic of the Catholic Church, prized the sacraments, holding them to be valid only when administered by clergy ordained by bishops in the apostolic succession, valued the writings of the Early Church Fathers, made much of theological scholarship, and distrusted or completely rejected the contemporary intellectual currents which undermined Christian faith as expressed in the creeds of the Catholic Church. It stressed worship, both private and public, and, insisting that the latter be conducted with dignity and beauty, brought back from the Catholic practice such appurtenances as vestments, candles, and incense. While tolerating the connexion between Church and state and holding that the Church was the instrument appointed by God to guide the nation in the path of truth, the Oxford movement wished the Church to be free from the state in issues which concerned its inner life, such as creeds and forms of worship.

The Oxford movement had affinities with several other trends, both past and contemporary, yet it was not identical with any of them. It was in part a fresh expression of one which had been present in the Church of England ever since the breach with Rome, namely, that which cherished the Catholic heritage rather than the Protestant changes. It found in the Church of England a high church wing which emphasized the connexion with the state and had kinship with an orthodox wing which gave much weight to the historic creeds and the theology inherited from the Catholic tradition. Romanticism, strong in England in the first half of the century as on the Continent, with its nostalgic admiration for the Middle Ages, contributed to a climate of opinion and feeling congenial to the movement. There were similarities to the reaction against the French Revolution which on the Continent contributed to the revival of the Roman Catholic Church and to orthodox Protestant confessionalism and kinship with the loosening of the control of the Church by the state and the return to much in Catholic practice which was seen in some Lutheran circles in Germany and Scandinavia. Yet affinities and similarities did not mean identity. Here was a vital movement, based upon profound thought, deep conviction, and intense religious feeling and commitment which was the channel for a fresh burst of life in the Church of England.

The Oxford movement is usually dated from a sermon, "National Apostasy," preached in the university pulpit at Oxford on July 14, 1833. The sermon was a protest against the act of Parliament which had reduced the number of bishoprics of the (Anglican) Church of Ireland. To the preacher this seemed an infringement of civil authority on prerogatives which by divine appointment belonged solely to the Church. The preacher, John Keble (1792–1866), the son of a clergyman, had had an extraordinarily brilliant student career at Oxford. Inflexible in his conservatism, antagonistic to liberalism, he was moved by a profound conviction of the divine origin and authority of the Church. His *Christian Year* had already been published (1827). It was a devotional book made up of poems fitted to each Sunday and festival and saint's day observed by the Church of England. It had an enormous circulation and in less than fifty years went into over 150 editions. Early associated with Keble were Richard Hurrell Froude (1803–1836) and John Henry Newman (1801–1890). Froude, brother of the more famous and ultimately sceptical historian, James Anthony Froude (1818–1894), died young, leaving behind him a spiritual diary, his *Remains,* which revealed an unusually, almost morbidly sensitive conscience. With this he combined fierceness of attack on those who differed from his convictions. Newman had been reared an Evangelical and from this background derived assurance of personal salvation, a deep direct awareness of God, and a conviction of personal guidance by God. Possessed of a subtle and powerful intellect he was for some time the chief figure in the movement.

The Oxford movement was spear-headed by *Tracts for the Times.* Of these ninety were published between 1833 and 1841, when they were abruptly terminated. Newman reinforced them by his sermons from the pulpit of St. Mary's, the university church in Oxford, of which he was the vicar.

The group early had a powerful recruit in Edward Bouverie Pusey (1800–1882) who, with Keble and Newman, was a fellow of Oriel College. In 1828 he was made regius professor of Hebrew and canon of Christ Church, Oxford, but it was not until 1835 and 1836 that he became fully associated with the movement. Deeply religious, implacable in controversy, humble and generous in his charities, he was later regarded as the outstanding leader. Indeed, the movement was often called Puseyism.

The *Tracts for the Times* and the other writings and the preaching of those associated with the Oxford movement provoked excited opposition. In England Protestantism was strong and the antagonism to Rome pronounced. The latter had been accentuated by the removal, in 1829, of the restrictions which had debarred Roman Catholics from public office and membership in Parliament. Criticism reached a high pitch when, in 1841, the ninetieth *Tract,* which had Newman as its author, was published. In this Newman declared that the

Thirty-nine Articles which officially stated the position of the Church of England were not contrary to Catholic doctrine and practice but simply condemned some of the abuses which had arisen in connexion with them. He recognized other sacraments than baptism and the Lord's Supper, came out for the real presence of Christ in the Eucharist, made room for purgatory and the invocation of the saints, qualified the Protestant doctrine of salvation by faith alone, and in other respects attempted to show how those who held to the faith of the Catholic Church could subscribe to the Thirty-nine Articles. The *Tract* caused such a commotion that the Bishop of Oxford commanded the termination of the series.

The fears of the critics were confirmed and their opposition heightened when numbers affected by the Oxford movement, mostly from the clergy and largely younger men, left the Church of England and were admitted to the Roman Catholic Church. Of these the most notable were Newman himself, who made his submission to Rome in 1845, and Henry Edward Manning (1808–1892), an ascetic, devoted, able Oxford graduate and priest. Manning was received into the Roman Catholic Church in 1851, in 1865 was made Archbishop of Westminster and head of the English hierarchy, was strongly ultramontane, worked zealously for the acceptance of the dogma of Papal infallibility, was indefatigable in labours to better the conditions of the poor, and died a cardinal. Newman was created a cardinal late in life, but was regarded with suspicion in stricter Roman Catholic circles. He had intellectual kinship with some of the modernism which was officially condemned a few years after his death, for he believed that the doctrine of the Church had developed. Yet, distrusting reason, he held that an infallible authority was required to control the course of that development and he regarded Rome as that authority. He joined the Oratory, founded, it will be remembered, by Philip Neri during the Catholic Reformation, and inaugurated a community of the order in Birmingham. There he henceforth made his home.

The large majority of those committed to the Anglo-Catholic movement remained within the Church of England. Through them many changes were introduced in the practices of that church. More elaborate ritual was developed, with eucharistic vestments, genuflexions, and incense. Private confession to the priest was revived. Monasticism reappeared, with communities and orders of men and women living by rule. Frequent communion was encouraged.

Much of this continued to be met with criticism which at times and in a few places became riotous. Not only were the Anglican Evangelicals among the opponents. Nonconformists were also critical and the adoption of Catholic practices drove them further from the Church of England. Here was one of the sources of the formation of the Evangelical Alliance. Inaugurated in 1846, its purpose was partly negative, but was also and primarily positive. It sought to draw together the great body of Evangelicals of all denominations for fellowship and prayer.

The Anglo-Catholic movement was not simply intent upon strengthening the sense of the corporate Church and the Catholic tradition in doctrine, sacraments, and worship. It was a revival of Christian devotion which showed itself in many other ways. Its clergy and sisterhoods often gave themselves unstintedly to the service of the poor who abounded in the cities of industrialized England. There was a fresh outburst of hymn writing. Newman's "Lead kindly Light" dated from his Anglican days. Especially prominent was John Mason Neale (1818–1866), noted for putting some of the hymns of the Latin and Greek Catholic past into exquisite and compelling English verse. Numbers of hymns written by former Anglicans after they made their peace with Rome won their way into Anglican and Protestant hymnals. Among them were Frederick William Faber's "Faith of our fathers, living still," "Hark, hark my soul, angelic songs are swelling," and "There's a wideness in God's mercy"; Matthew Bridges' "Crown him with many crowns"; and Adelaide Anne Proctor's "My God I thank Thee Who hast made the earth so fair."

The Anglo-Catholic movement had effects beyond the circles that were committed to it. It contributed to the growing improvement in worship which generally characterized the Church of England in the nineteenth century. It gave an impetus to a corporate sense in the Church of England which encouraged the renewal or inauguration of institutions and devices through which that body could express its voice and not be as completely subservient to the state as in the past. Thus in the 1850's the convocations of the two provinces of Canterbury and York, which had held only brief and formal meetings since 1717, began to be more active. Eventually they were enlarged by the addition of laymen. Diocesan synods were also revived. Here was a parallel to what was taking place on the Continent, where the Protestant state churches acquired organs for a nearer approach to independent action and for a consciousness of a corporate life.

How far could the Church of England make its peace with the new currents of thought and the programmes for the organization of the state and society which were sweeping across Europe and the British Isles? We have seen (Chapter XLV) that numbers of men and women rejected Christianity, some gladly, others reluctantly. Some held to Christian ethics while surrendering the religious convictions upon which they rested. There were others, among them men of prominence and influence in the Church, who held that reconciliation was impossible and regarded any peace as a compromise of essential Christian truth. At the most they would consent only to a truce. Still others were prepared to adopt at least some of the conclusions of the contemporary critical historical study of the Bible and the methods, findings, and even the hypotheses of the scientists of their day, including Darwin, and to seek to find a way at the same time to hold without contradiction to the historic beliefs of the Church. Many were vividly aware of the social evils for which the several varieties of socialism offered remedies and strove to remove them, some through legislation, others through personal ministry and private initiative through voluntary societies, and still others through a socialism which endeavoured to embody Christian hopes and principles. Some who sought one or another of these solutions were Evangelicals, others were Anglo-Catholics, and still others belonged with neither. Many of these last were classified as Broad churchmen. Indeed, as the nineteenth century wore on, there were said to be three parties in the Church of England, Evangelical, Anglo-Catholic, and Broad. The lines which separated them were not sharp and there were numbers who could not rightly be placed plumply in any of the three.

To list even the more important names of those who in one way or another attempted to adjust the Church of England to the currents and demands of the day would issue in what to the uninitiated would be a dreary catalogue. We must select a few men and groups and say something about each, but at the same time be painfully aware that others of equal or nearly equal importance have been omitted. It is evidence of the abounding life of the nineteenth century Church of England that in it were so many able and devoted men and women who displayed such a variety of convictions and activity.

One of the men who must be mentioned was Samuel Taylor Coleridge (1772–1834). He had a spiritual pilgrimage which began in a vicarage under a father whose memory he revered and which included an uncompleted course at Cambridge, a brief period in the army, enthusiasm for the French Revolution, friendships with Southey and Wordsworth, a few years when he planned to become a Unitarian minister, a residence in Germany, pantheism, disillusion as to the Revolution and Napoleon, a long and tragic struggle with addiction to opium, and a return to the Church of England, so that for the last twenty years of his life he was a practising churchman. Brilliant and charming in conversation, poet, and writer of prose, Coleridge exerted a profound influence upon a younger generation. The religious convictions of his Christian maturity are seen in his *Aids to Reflection* and his *Confessions of an Inquiring Spirit*. In them he maintained that "Christian faith is the perfection of human intelligence" and that "the scheme of Christianity, though not discoverable by reason, is yet in accordance with it—that link follows link by necessary consequence—that religion passes out of the ken of reason only where the eye of reason has reached its own horizon, and that faith is then but its continuation."

He did not believe in what is usually called the verbal inspiration of the Scriptures, but he declared that "whatever finds me bears witness to itself that it has proceeded from the Holy Ghost. In the Bible there is more that finds me than in all other books which I have read."

Coleridge gave his own definition to "reason," distinguishing it from "understanding." Reason he believed to be the organ of the supersensuous, an "inward beholding," the eye of the spirit by which we directly perceive religious truths, the knowledge of the law of the whole considered as one. To him understanding was the faculty by which we generalize and arrange the phenomena of perception. It is not strange that he is sometimes called the English Schleiermacher. Yet it was from different backgrounds that the two developed the quality which gave them similarity. Both showed the effects of the current romanticism, but romanticism was by no means the sole cause of the resemblance.

One of the younger men who felt the influence of Coleridge was Thomas Arnold (1795–1842). A graduate of Oxford and a clergyman of the Church of England, deeply religious with a life "rooted in God," and of noble moral character, he was chiefly remembered for the fashion in which, as headmaster of Rugby, he set a standard which largely made over, for the good, the public schools of England. He was neither an Evangelical nor an Anglo-Catholic, but frankly differed from both schools. He deeply desired to realize a fully Christian society in which the entire life would conform to Christian ideals and wished to make Rugby such a society in microcosm. He aroused opposition among several of the conservatives by his view of the Bible. Aware of some of the contemporary German critical study of the Scriptures and partly approving it, he held that the Bible must be viewed in the light of the times in which it was written. Yet, with Coleridge, he maintained that it had in it divine truth which finds us.

Another of the younger men who owed a debt to Coleridge but one who was by no means solely the product of his influence was John Frederick Denison Maurice (1805–1872). The son of a politically liberal Unitarian clergyman and school teacher who came out of a long line of English Presbyterian dissent, Maurice had been designed by his father for the Unitarian ministry. In the course of the years, which included Cambridge and Oxford, from profound conviction he entered the Church of England and was ordained. For many years he was in London, part of the time holding professorships in King's College from which he was removed (1853) for alleged departure from orthodoxy. Yet he continued as chaplain of Lincoln's Inn and as priest in a parish church. In 1866 he was made professor of moral philosophy at Cambridge. A man of singularly pure life, integrity of mind, sensitive spirit, and high purpose, he attracted some and repelled others. The controversies in which he was engaged arose partly but not entirely from the fresh way in which in his efforts to make them accord with current knowledge he stated the historic Christian convictions and from the misunderstandings to which it gave rise. He also rejoiced in paradoxical language which proved provocative. He held that God is love, that Christ is the head of all humanity, and that man is not only depraved but also has a natural righteousness because of the indwelling of Christ, the Son of God. To him revelation is the unveiling of the knowledge of God and aids the intuitive knowledge of God which may exist in every human soul. The atonement is not the offering of a vicarious sacrifice of the innocent for the guilty to satisfy the requirements of a just God, but the fulfilment of the law of righteousness by sharing the sufferings of mankind, of which Christ is the head, and by the perfect obedience of the Son of God whose will is one with the Father's. Eternal death has nothing to do with time, but is alienation from God because of unrepented sin. All that men need do to be reconciled is to recognize their sonship, repent, and give God the love which is the natural relation of a son to the Father. Presumably God's love will ultimately triumph and all men be led to repent and turn to God in trust and love.

Maurice has sometimes been classified with the Broad wing of the Church of England. He himself would have repudiated that identification, for he was grieved by party strife, his longing for the unity of all Christians was one of the reasons why he left what he regarded as a sect, and by his attitude towards the Scriptures he antagonized some of those who could with a nearer approach to accuracy be placed with that group.

Partly because of his boyhood background, for his father was a social liberal and took him to anti-slavery meetings, and partly because of his theological convictions, Maurice laboured indefatigably to improve the lot of the under-privileged. In a day when higher education for women was a generally distrusted novelty he founded Queen's College for them (1848). The revolutionary year of 1848 and the Chartist movement spurred some Christians to seek to bring Christianity to bear upon the construction of a better order. What was known as Christian Socialism arose. Maurice was the spiritual leader of the group and incurred added opprobrium from those to whom the word "socialism" stood for destructive revolution. While the movement accomplished little immediately beyond the passage of an act of Parliament giving legal status to coöperatives, the ideal which inspired it did not die. Moreover, the better to prepare the masses for intelligent participation in the new age brought by the industrial revolution, Maurice headed the Workingmen's College in

London, furthered similar projects in other cities, and thus was a pioneer in the adult education which later attained substantial proportions.

A younger contemporary of Maurice was Frederick William Robertson (1816–1853). Highly sensitive, reared in a strongly Evangelical environment, intense, somewhat lacking in the sense of humour which might have softened some of his inner suffering, by deep conviction he turned aside from a career in the army to become a clergyman. Honest, unwilling to accept traditional views without examining them for himself, by the hard road of agonizing struggle he came to a clear faith, but it was not one which fitted him into any of the existing groups in the Church of England. For six years, 1847–1853, he filled the pulpit in Trinity Chapel, Brighton. One of the greatest preachers in English history, he attracted throngs from all classes. Speaking to revolutionary years, and believing that Christianity has a message for daily living, for the nations, and for the world, he aroused fear and criticism among the conservative, but attracted ardent support from many of the thoughtful. Through lectures in a workingmen's centre which he helped to establish he won a hearing among the servants and labourers. He burnt himself out physically at the early age of thirty-seven, but his published sermons had a wide circulation in the English-speaking world and profoundly influenced more than one generation of preachers.

Along with Maurice and Robertson there should be mentioned Charles Kingsley (1819–1875). A graduate of Cambridge, a clergyman classed theologically with the Broad churchmen, he is best remembered as a novelist. To his contemporaries he was also known as a Christian socialist and as one whose sympathies were with the Chartists. Yet in many ways he was conservative and orthodox, more so as the years passed.

Biblical studies akin in method to those in vogue in German universities, but usually less drastic in their conclusions, made headway among scholars of the Church of England. Famous were the three friends, Brooke Foss Westcott (1825–1901), Joseph Barber Lightfoot (1828–1889), and Fenton John Anthony Hort (1828–1892). All three were graduates of Cambridge and at one time and another all occupied professorships in that university. All were experts in the critical study of ancient texts, especially of the New Testament, and were skilled in methods of discovering the original reading and meaning. Lightfoot and Westcott occupied successively the ancient and influential see of Durham. Both wrote commentaries on books of the Bible and were theologians of distinction. Westcott and Hort's reconstructed text of the New Testament became a standard. Oxford had Thomas Kelly Cheyne (1841–1915), William Sanday (1843–1920), and Samuel Rolles Driver (1846–1914). Cheyne and Driver were especially noted for their work on the Old Testament, and Sanday for his studies in the life of Christ.

The newer views did not immediately gain assent. While by 1914 most of the clergy and numbers of the laity had accepted many of the more moderate findings of nineteenth century Protestant Biblical scholarship and of those theologians who were attempting to think through inherited beliefs in light of current scientific and philosophical views, acquiescence in them was by no means universal. So far as it had been reached, it had come only through debate, much of it acrimonious.

A few of the landmarks of that struggle centered about a volume entitled *Essays and Reviews,* another book, *Ecce Homo,* a work on the Pentateuch by Colenso, and a volume of essays called *Lux Mundi.*

Essays and Reviews, published in 1860, the year following the appearance of *The Origin of Species,* was made up of contributions from seven liberals, lay and clerical, mostly from Oxford, who included Frederick Temple (1821–1902), later Archbishop of Canterbury, and the redoubtable Benjamin Jowett (1817–1893), professor of Greek and later master of Balliol College, Oxford. Most if not all of the views put forward would not have been considered especially radical or dangerous fifty years later, but at the time they provoked a storm of protest.

Ecce Homo, issued anonymously in 1866 and with John Robert Seeley (1834–1895), later professor of modern history at Cambridge, as author, while marked by religious fervour and portraying Christ as king of the spiritual realm, stressed the human side of Christ, contained the phrase "enthusiasm for humanity," and was regarded in some quarters as highly dangerous.

John William Colenso (1814–1883) was the object of violent attack. A graduate of Cambridge, a mathematician, and the first Bishop of Natal, he had already been accused of laxity in dealing with polygamy among his African flock, when, in 1862–1863, a work by him, *The Pentateuch and Book of Joshua Critically Examined,* was published. Among other startling statements it declared that little if any of the Pentateuch was written in the Mosaic age, that Moses may never have lived, that Joshua is a purely mythical figure, that the Books of Chronicles are fictitious, and that Christ's knowledge of history in speaking of Moses was not more than that of any educated Jew of his day and might be faulty. Forty-one bishops advised Colenso to resign. He did not do so and was deposed by the Bishop of Cape Town, who claimed jurisdiction as metropolitan in South Africa. An unhappy, involved, and prolonged struggle followed, in which the original issues faded into the background and Colenso stood by his claim to hold office under patent from the crown and the Bishop of Cape Town denied the authority of the crown in purely ecclesiastical matters.

The question became one of the degree to which the Church was subject to the state. Not until after the death of Colenso was it resolved.

Lux Mundi, published in 1889, was the work of a group of Oxford Anglo-Catholics and one Cambridge man, and was edited by Charles Gore (1853–1932), later successively Bishop of Worcester, Birmingham, and Oxford. It sought to put "the Catholic faith in its right relation to modern intellectual and moral problems" and thus to commend "the faith to the acceptance of others." Some of the older Anglo-Catholics believed that it went too far towards liberal views, especially in its attitude on the critical study of the Bible. It nearly caused a split in that wing of the Church of England.

The controversies did not stop the growth in vigour of the Church of England. Indeed, they were evidence of life. As the century advanced that church displayed increasing vitality. While still controlled by the state, subject to Parliament, its bishops and other leading officers appointed by the crown, it was more nearly autonomous than it had ever been. An unofficial series of gatherings, the Church Congress, which first met in 1861 and which afforded an opportunity for hearing and discussing papers, but which passed no resolutions, became a flourishing institution. The parish clergy and the bishops showed decided improvement. Among them were so many devoted and extraordinarily able men that simply to list them would require a small volume. From time to time new dioceses were created the better to meet the growth of population and its city-ward shift. In the cities hundreds of new churches were erected. Increasingly the clergy interested themselves in the social problems posed by industrialization and urbanization. Movements were initiated for furthering better housing. Christian social settlements were founded. In 1889 the Christian Social Union was formed. Confined to members of the Church of England and with Westcott as its first president, it sought "to claim for the Christian law the ultimate authority to rule social practice," "to apply the moral truths of Christianity to the social and economic difficulties" of the age, and "to present Christ in practical life as the Living Master and King."

The Church of England also spread widely overseas. As we have suggested, this was partly by migration and partly by missions among non-Christian peoples. The missionary societies organized before 1815, notably the Society for the Propagation of the Gospel in Foreign Parts and the Church Missionary Society, greatly expanded their staffs and the areas covered. To them were added others, among them the Colonial and Continental Church Society, begun in 1823, especially, as its name implied, for English settlers and merchants in other lands. The family of autonomous Anglican Churches markedly increased in numbers, membership, and geographic extent. To tie it together the Lambeth Conferences were begun, so called because they convened in the London residence of the Archbishop of Canterbury. To the Lambeth Conferences all bishops of the Anglican Communion were invited. The first assembled in 1867. They were held approximately every ten years thereafter. They met on the invitation of the Archbishop of Canterbury, for while he had no authority outside England and some of the colonies, he was looked up to as the ranking ecclesiastic, *primus inter pares*. The Lambeth Conferences could not legislate for their respective churches. However, they gave opportunity for something more important, the knitting together of the bishops of a world-wide communion in fellowship and in prayer, the discussion of common problems, and the formation, where possible, of a common mind.

In the latter part of the nineteenth century the Church of England was more vigorous than in any earlier period of its history and it came to 1914 on a mounting tide. To be sure, the bishops were less prominent in the House of Lords and in civil administration than they had been in the eighteenth century. The lay element in that body had been augmented while the number of bishops in it had not increased. The proportion of the population who attended the services of the church seems to have declined in the second half of the century, especially in the large cities. Yet the average quality of the clergy in learning and devotion was higher than at any previous time. The Church of England was more nearly in control of its own life than in any period since the separation from Rome. It had in large part made its adjustment to the new learning. It displayed marked variety, from extreme Evangelicalism to a Catholicism which held a high view of the Church, its ministry, and its sacraments. It had given rise to a revival of monasticism. For the first time the Anglican communion had become world-wide. It still constituted only a small minority of the total number of Christians, but the ability of its leadership combined with the prestige of the British Empire to accord it a large voice in the Church universal.

THE GROWING VIGOUR OF ENGLISH PROTESTANT NONCONFORMITY

The nineteenth century witnessed a growth of English Protestant Nonconformity which was fully as striking as that of the Anglican Communion. Even in 1815 organized Christian dissent from the established church was stronger than in any other country on the Continent of Europe or the British Isles, with the exception of Ireland, where Roman Catholics were a majority, Wales, where Protestant dissent was strong, and possibly Russia, where the Old Believers and some of the other movements which we noted in Chapter XLIV were potent. On Sunday, March 30, 1851, a census was taken of those attending church. About 40 per cent. of the population were in church on that day. Of them about 52 per cent. were of the Church of England, about 44.3 per cent. of Protestant Nonconforming churches, and about 3.5 per cent. Roman Catholics.

In proportion to its situation in 1815, in the nineteenth century in its growth in England and in its world-wide spread English Protestant Nonconformity outstripped any other congeries of religious movements in Europe.

To this phenomenal record several factors contributed. One was the position of Nonconformity at the outset of the century. Ever since the prodigious vitality, the civil war, and the Commonwealth of the seventeenth century it had had a larger place in the life of the country than had Protestant dissent anywhere else east of the Atlantic. It had been reinforced by the revivals of the eighteenth century and especially by the emergence of Methodism from the established church. It came to 1815 on a rising tide. In the nineteenth century it was further augmented by the continuation of what in its broadest sense may be called the Evangelical movement. It experienced an almost continuous awakening, an awakening which was largely indigenous but which was repeatedly aided by visitors from the United States, particularly Moody. Moreover, Nonconformity had its strength chiefly in the classes which were prospering and multiplying in the nineteenth century. It numbered relatively few from the landed aristocracy and gentry, an element in the population which was losing its dominance in government and in economic life. It drew chiefly from the lower and the upper middle classes, the thrifty and self-respecting among the farmers and the labourers in the cities, the artisans, the clerks, the small shopkeepers, and the manufacturers and merchants. It was these classes which were coming to the fore in England. As they became wealthy, many from them moved out of Nonconformity into the Church of England, but the majority remained true to the religious groups in which they had been nurtured. Then, too, Nonconformity was favoured by the progressive removal of the legal disabilities from which it had suffered. That emancipation was due in large part to the liberalism which marked the nineteenth century Occident and which had somewhat similar effects in several countries in Europe and in lands outside that continent dominated by peoples of European descent and culture. Finally, and chiefly, the cause must be found in the vitality inherent in the Nonconforming churches and the faith of which they were an expression.

It was by a series of measures scattered over many years that Protestant Nonconformists were accorded legal equality with members of the Church of England. The year 1813 saw the removal of the statutes enacting penalties for those denying the Trinity and thus brought relief to Unitarians. In 1828 the Test and Corporation Acts were repealed which had made as a prerequisite for office-holding taking the communion in the Church of England. These had long been circumvented by annual Acts of Indemnity which safeguarded Dissenters, but the laws themselves, a chronic irritant, were now removed. Beginning with 1836 marriages were permitted in Nonconformist places of worship and a generation later, in 1880, burial services by dissenters were allowed in churchyards. In 1868 the payment of church rates for the maintenance of the fabrics of the parish churches was made voluntary. The religious tests for degrees in Oxford, Cambridge, and Durham which had debarred Nonconformists were abolished by acts of Parliament in 1871, except for theology.

Some Nonconformists laboured for still more drastic measures. In 1844, led by a Congregational pastor, Edward Miall, they formed the British Anti-State-Church Association, after 1853 called the Society for the Liberation of Religion from State Patronage and Control. Nonconformists fought vigorously and long against state financial aid to denominational schools, holding that it would work against them and for the Church of England. They did not win, and the education acts of 1870 left religious instruction in the schools and in 1902 legislation assisted denominational schools by public taxation.

At the outset of the century the largest Nonconforming Protestant bodies were the Congregationalists, Baptists, and Methodists. Much smaller but influential were the Friends (Quakers) and the Unitarians. The Unitarians were chiefly the descendants, physically or spiritually, of the Presbyterians, for the latter, thrown out of the Church of England by the Stuart Restoration in the seventeenth century, had objected to creedal or confessional tests and under the influence of the rationalism of the eighteenth century had moved increasingly towards a non-Trinitarian faith. In general the Unitarians were from the upper income classes and highly educated. In economic level and education the Congregationalists ranked next to them. The General Baptists were on the whole from a higher level of culture than the Particular Baptists. The latter were largely humble folk.

In the course of the nineteenth century Congregationalists, Baptists, and Methodists increased greatly, but the Methodists had the largest growth. Quakers and Unitarians persisted, still small minorities. Presbyterianism of the Scottish type reappeared, by migration from Scotland. Some other denominations and movements were added. In general, it was what in the Church of England was known as Evangelicalism which prevailed. Among the Nonconformists there was, naturally, almost nothing corresponding to the Oxford movement. The liberalism in theology and Biblical studies which was current in the Church of England, in Scotland, and on the Continent made itself felt and here and there produced controversy. Enough community of conviction existed to make possible a degree of coöperation. This showed itself in many ways, including the formation of a Free Church Council, and in 1892 it took a further step in the meeting of the Free Church Congress out of which came the National Free Church Council (the National Council of the Evangelical Free Churches). With it the majority of the Nonconformists were associated. We must say something about each of the major denominations, both old and new, but it must be tantalizingly brief.

Congregationalism entered the nineteenth century on the rising tide brought by the Evangelical revival. The Congregationalists were the spiritual descendants of the Independents of the seventeenth and eighteenth centuries. In the middle of the eighteenth century they suffered somewhat from the spiritual lethargy of the age. However, they preserved the sobriety, the deep interest in theology and politics, the loyalty to the Westminster Confession, the austerity in morals, the delight in intellectual pursuits, and the Sunday observance which had long characterized the movement. The Evangelical Awakening wrought marked changes. Many former Presbyterians, distressed by the drift towards unitarianism in their own churches, became Congregationalists. Thousands, stirred by Congregational revival preaching, flocked in from the Church of England or from the religiously indifferent multitudes. Under the revival preaching the inherited Calvinism was weakened, with its doctrine that only the elect could repent. Mid-week prayer meetings became common. Lay preaching increased. New academies and colleges came into being to prepare men for the pastorates of the rapidly multiplying churches. In 1832 a national organization was formed. It was eventually known as the Congregational Union of England and Wales and was a federation of Congregational churches. In 1833 that body adopted a Declaration of Faith and Order which, in contrast with the Savoy Declaration of 1658, long a standard for the Independents, was only mildly and vaguely Calvinistic. In addition to the London Missionary Society which, it will be recalled, was formed in 1795 and depended chiefly upon Congregational churches for its support and personnel, various societies were organized to aid Congregationalism in Great Britain and Ireland and the colonies. While in Britain hundreds of new chapels were built, especially in the growing cities, in the colonies Congregationalism was weak as compared with its strength in England and Wales. Congregationalism produced outstanding ministers and laymen. Prominent among the former was Robert William Dale (1829–1895), for more than forty years minister in Carr's Lane Church in the rapidly growing industrial city of Birmingham. There he was not only a great preacher, but he also took an active part, on the progressive side, in municipal and national politics.

The Baptists entered the nineteenth century far from united. The division persisted between Particular and General Baptists, the one holding what are usually called Calvinist views and the latter what is generally termed Arminianism. It went back to the separate origins in the seventeenth century.

Other divisions had entered, one in the General Baptists late in the eighteenth century in protest against a trend towards unitarianism and universalism which resulted in the New Connexion General Baptists, and others over the question of the standards for admission to the Lord's Supper. There were some Seventh-Day Baptists, partly descended from the Fifth Monarchists of the seventeenth century, observing Saturday rather than Sunday. No national or even local organization bridged the gulf. General Baptist churches were more inclined to draw together in regional associations and a national union than were the Particular Baptists. Both General and Particular Baptists felt the invigorating impact of the Evangelical Awakening. It was among Particular Baptists of moderate Calvinistic convictions that the Baptist Missionary Society was organized in response to the appeal of William Carey. Although they were slow to meet the challenge of the shift of population to the cities, Particular Baptists formed various societies for specific purposes, some of them home missionary. They grew in numbers and eventually organized new churches in the cities.

The most famous English Baptist preacher of the nineteenth century was Charles Haddon Spurgeon (1834–1892). Reared a Congregationalist, in his teens he joined the Baptists. At nineteen he became pastor of an old church in London and before he was thirty his preaching had attracted such throngs that (1861) the Metropolitan Tabernacle was erected, seating over five thousand. A moderate Calvinist, warmly evangelistic, a Liberal in politics and a friend of Gladstone, he was an indefatigable worker, the founder of orphanages and of a school for training ministers, the editor of a monthly magazine, and the author of many books.

Formed in the 1890's, the Baptist Union of Great Britain and Ireland drew together both Particular and General Baptists and embraced the majority of the Baptists of the British Isles. A leader in that merger, John Clifford (1836–1923), a General Baptist London pastor, was also prominent in the founding of the Baptist World Alliance (1905) and in the National Free Church Council.

Of the Nonconforming bodies it was the Methodists who attained the largest dimensions. The zeal, long life, and organizing ability of John Wesley had inspired Methodism, had given it a structure, and had attracted to it and channeled through it much of the Evangelical Awakening. After Wesley's death the first outstanding leader was Thomas Coke (1747–1814) whom we have already met and who had a major share in the spread of the movement overseas as well as in the British Isles. In the nearly half a century following Coke the most influential man in British Methodism was Jabez Bunting (1779–1858). An organizer, administrator, and forceful and persuasive preacher, he held many offices and for years to an unusual degree displayed the ability to embody, express, and put into effect the will of the majority of the Methodist constituency.

As was inevitable, Bunting was accused of being autocratic. Restlessness developed and after his strong hand was removed open division came. Even before he had become well established in power, and not as an opposition movement to him, the Bible Christians (1815) arose under the leadership of William O'Bryan, who, a flaming evangelist, rebelled against control by the tightly knit Methodist organization. Between 1827 and 1857 the United Methodist Free Churches were formed out of a union which attracted successive secessions from the main body of Wesleyan Methodists. First were the Methodist Protestants (1827), then the Wesleyan Methodist Association (1835), then the Wesleyan Reformers (beginning in 1849), and finally the formation (1857) of the United Methodist Free Churches. In 1907 the Bible Christians, the Methodist New Connexion, founded in 1797 by Alexander Kilham (1762–1798) and those who sympathized with him, and the United Methodist Free Churches came together in the United Methodist Church.

The majority of Methodists remained within the Wesleyan Methodist Church. In the latter part of the nineteenth century its outstanding figure, called by some the most notable Methodist since Wesley, was John Scott Lidgett (1854——). Inspired by a great predecessor, Hugh Price Hughes, he was outstanding as a theologian, a preacher, a social reformer, and a leader in the Liberal party.

Taken together in all its various branches Methodism had outstanding characteristics. It was warmly evangelistic and grew rapidly and fairly steadily. It drew largely from the middle classes and the sturdier, more reliable labourers. It developed great preachers. Many of these were ordained. Many were laymen. Lay preaching, indeed, was very prominent. Women were recruited and trained as deaconesses: Methodism as well as the Church of England and some of the Continental Protestant churches was finding a way to utilize the full-time service of women which roughly paralleled the sisterhoods of the Roman Catholic Church. Methodism proved adaptable to the rising cities. In addition to its familiar chapels, it instituted mission centers in the low income areas and great "central halls" in strategic locations for preaching and social work. It stressed education. From Methodism came leaders in the early stages of the trades union movement and in inaugurating coöperatives. Methodist chapels were friendly social centres for colliers and other labouring folk. Methodism was ardently missionary. It spread rapidly in the colonies among the settlers and their children and there attained larger dimensions than any other denomination except the Church of England, the Presbyterians, and the Roman Catholics. It multiplied missions in Asia, Africa, and the islands of the sea. As we are to see, it had an even more phenomenal growth in the United States.

In spite of its divisions, Methodism maintained and developed a sense of community throughout the world. In 1881 it held the first of the conferences which took the name ecumenical. There followed at fairly regular intervals similar gatherings which drew together for fellowship Methodists from many lands.

On the smaller pre-nineteenth century Protestant denominations in England we can pause for only fragmentary notice. The Unitarians had as an outstanding figure James Martineau (1805–1900). Of Huguenot ancestry, a man of noble and independent character, as preacher, author, and teacher he exerted a wide influence. The Friends (Quakers) had an effect far greater than their numbers would have given ground for anticipating. Thus Stephen Grellet (1773–1855) and Elizabeth Fry (1780–1845), the latter in spite of her responsibilities as the mother of a large family of children, had a share in the initiation of the urgently needed prison reform in Britain and the Continent second only to that of Howard. On the outskirts of Birmingham the Cadbury family, which made a fortune in the manufacture of chocolate, developed around their factories a community which was a model in housing, education, and parks, and encouraged the Selly Oak Colleges for the training of religious workers and teachers of several denominations. The Sandemanians, really springing from John Glas of Scotland, but taking their name from Robert Sandeman, had their beginning in the middle of the eighteenth century and contributed to the rise of the Christian denomination in America and Britain. From another small group, the Moravians, came one of the greatest hymn writers of the nineteenth century, James Montgomery (1771–1854). Montgomery, who never married, was the son of a Moravian clergyman and in middle life made a public profession of faith, returning to the church of his boyhood. He wrote about four hundred hymns, of which many made their way into the use of numbers of Protestant denominations. Among them were "Angels from the realms of glory, wing your flight o'er all the earth"; "Hail to the Lord's anointed, great David's greater Son"; "Prayer is the soul's sincere desire, uttered or unexpressed"; and "In the hour of trial, Jesus pray for me."

The swelling tide of life gave birth to new denominations and groups which were akin to denominations. Of these we can take the space for brief mention of only three. One was the Catholic Apostolic Church, sometimes known as the Irvingites, because of the part which Edward Irving (1792–1834) had in its inception. Irving, a Scot, a Presbyterian clergyman, was profoundly influenced by Coleridge. A compelling preacher in a Presbyterian church in London, he came to believe that the second coming of Christ was near at hand and held that the early apostolic gifts of prophesying, speaking with tongues, and healing by faith were being revived. He was ejected from the Presbyterian Church for heresy, but his views found expression in the Catholic Apostolic Church (begun in 1832) which had an elaborate organization of apostles, prophets, evangelists, and pastors, and a liturgy based upon Eastern rites.

More numerous were what were popularly known as the Darbyites, or Plymouth Brethren, but who called themselves simply the Brethren, Christians, or Christian Brethren. The outstanding early leader was John Nelson Darby (1800–1882), a clergyman of the (Anglican) Church of Ireland. They began in Dublin but soon had a second centre at Plymouth. At first they were largely an upper class movement, recruited from those who were dissatisfied with what seemed to them the worldliness and spiritual dryness of the existing churches, especially the Church of England. Eventually they drew chiefly from middle class and humble folk. They endeavoured to take the Bible literally and to gather themselves together on the model of the New Testament. Students of the Biblical prophecies, many of them believed the second coming of Christ to be imminent. They held that in preparation for Christ's coming they were to live separate from the world in righteousness and holiness, eschewing the amusements and whatever else in the world might be contaminating. They looked with distrust upon the existing churches, for they believed them to have compromised with the world. They gathered in meetings but had no central organization. They rejected creeds and maintained that the Holy Spirit guides true Christians and binds them together in faith and worship. They believed in conversion. Holding that social reform is useless, they taught that the mission of Christians is saving men and women out of the world. They had believer's baptism by immersion, and the breaking of bread (the Lord's Supper) every Sunday. They did not have ordination, but had lay evangelists. They early were divided, partly on the issue of the degree to which it was permissible to mix with other Christians. Prominent among them was George Müller (1805–1898). A native of Prussia, at about the age of twenty he was converted in a Pietist circle in Halle. In 1829 he went to England as a missionary to the Jews. Influenced by the example of A. H. Francke and the latter's orphanage at Halle, he began and maintained orphanages at Bristol, relying entirely on faith and prayer for the necessary material means. The Brethren were zealous missionaries and developed what they called Christian Missions in Many Lands, and eventually were on all the continents.

More conspicuous than the Brethren and devoted to serving and saving the dregs of the industrial urban civilization was the Salvation Army. The Salvation Army was the creation of William Booth (1829–1912). Born in humble circumstances, at fifteen Booth was converted and became a preacher. For about nine years he was with the Methodist New Connexion, but he broke with it and became an independent evangelist. Hating the dirt, squalor, and vice of the cities and believing profoundly in the power of the Gospel to transform even the most degraded lives, in 1864 Booth went to London, where the most extensive slums were found, and there, in one of the worst districts, began the Christian Mission. In 1878 this became the Salvation Army. The latter was organized in military fashion, with uniforms, military titles for its officers, and with Booth as its general. It sought to enlist its converts in efforts to win others to the Christian life and to minister physically as well as spiritually to the lowest of the underprivileged. Its methods were unconventional, with open-air meetings on the streets and with drums and other musical instruments. At first the Salvation Army aroused ridicule and violent opposition, and its members were even arrested as disturbers of the peace. After a few years criticism either diminished or entirely ceased. Booth's *In Darkest England and the Way Out* (1890) described the desperate economic, social, and moral conditions in the slums and proposed concrete measures for relief and cure, among them a farm colony, emigration overseas, rescue homes for prostitutes, preventive homes for girls, a poor man's bank, and model suburban villages. He and his subordinates laboured to make at least some features of the programme a reality. In all this Booth was helped by his wife, especially in reaching and caring for women. The Salvation Army spread rapidly, chiefly in the United States, the British colonies, and India. In its tightly knit organization, its selfless devotion, its zeal for the spiritual and physical care of the unfortunate, and its internal dissensions, it had much in common with some of the orders of the Roman Catholic Church, notably the Franciscans in their early days.

MOVEMENTS WHICH CROSSED DENOMINATIONAL BORDERS

Nineteenth century England saw either the origin or the extensive development of numbers of societies and movements which transcended denominational lines. They were recruited chiefly from those who shared the convictions and the experience of the Evangelical Awakening and who sought and found fellowship with those of similar mind on the Continent, in other countries of the British Isles, and in the United States and the British colonies. They were very numerous, and from them only three can here be singled out for specific mention.

Sunday Schools, as we have seen (Chapter XLIV), had their rise late in the eighteenth century. Originally intended to give religious and moral instruction to the very poor and including teaching the illiterate to read and write, they proved adaptable to the children of other classes and spread to various denominations as a means of religious education. At least one of their early

London promoters dreamed of them as an instrument for teaching every one in the world to read the Bible. They flourished especially among Protestants in the English-speaking world and of British tradition, and most notably in the United States. They were used by missionaries in Asia, Africa, and the Americas. In 1889 the first of a series of World's Sunday School Conventions assembled in London, and at the seventh of these, in Rome in 1907, the World's Sunday School Association was constituted. Although having strong support from the clergy, the Sunday School movement was largely a lay enterprise, depending chiefly on laymen and women for its teachers, a voluntary un-salaried service.

Another movement, somewhat different, was the Young Men's Christian Association. The first Young Men's Christian Association was begun by George Williams (1821–1905). George Williams was of yeoman ancestry. Born and reared on a farm in Somerset County, in his early teens he sought his fortune as an apprentice in a draper's shop in the nearby town of Bridgwater. In Bridgwater he committed himself as a Christian and joined a Congregational Church. He was profoundly influenced by the books of Charles G. Finney, the American evangelist. At nineteen he finished his apprenticeship and then went to London and at the age of twenty was a clerk in a large draper's house. There he was both faithful in business and active in religious work. He sought to win his fellow-clerks to the Christian life and began a prayer meeting. In June, 1844, twelve young men, all but one of them fellow-employees in the same firm with himself, met in his room and formed a society to win other young men to the Christian faith. The idea of a Young Men's Christian Asso-ciation, as the group called itself, was contagious, for it came on a rising tide of the Evangelical movement. Other similar groups quickly sprang up in the British Isles. Within less than a decade they had begun to be seen in the United States and Canada. Similar societies, some of them older, were appearing on the Continent. In 1855, only eleven years after the first Association had been formed in Williams' room, the World's Alliance of the Young Men's Christian Associations was constituted in Paris by representatives from both sides of the Atlantic. George Williams lived to see the Young Men's Christian Associations spread to many other lands. He himself became wealthy and was knighted. To the end of his days he was active in his support of missions and in his devotion to various religious and philanthropic enterprises, mainly those of Evangelical origin and connexions.

The Young Men's Christian Association appealed chiefly to those of the lower income levels of the white collar class, not unlike those among whom it had its origin. Born in evangelism, prayer meetings, and Bible study, it added educational, social, and athletic facilities to promote the wholesome life of young men and boys. In the United States and Canada in the latter part of the century it was the chief channel and promoter of voluntary religious activities among students. It had its greatest growth in the United States and there in time built many physical plants, some of them large. Primarily a lay movement, it reminds one of some of the Roman Catholic confraternities, except that, unlike them, it was not under the control of the hierarchy and drew members from many denominations. In its origin Protestant and always predominantly such, it attracted many who continued their affiliation with the Roman Catholic and Eastern Churches. At least one of its national movements was predominantly Roman Catholic and another Greek Orthodox in membership. It far overspread confessional boundaries.

The sister organization, slightly younger, the Young Women's Christian Association, first arose in the 1850's in Germany and Great Britain, and, like the Young Men's Christian Association, had its largest development in the United States. In 1894 the World's Young Women's Christian Association was organized.

The Roman Catholic Revival

It was in the nineteenth century that the Roman Catholic Church again raised its head in England, began to gain in numbers, and revived its hierarchy and its monastic orders. In 1815 Roman Catholics were under serious political disabilities. To be sure, in 1778 and 1791 some of the most severe of the penal laws against them had been repealed, but they still could not hold public office. Yet Roman Catholics were to be found, mostly in Lancashire and Yorkshire, and had the support of some of the landed gentry who had clung to their ancestral faith. The number of Roman Catholics had been augmented by refugees from the French Revolution. In 1829, largely as a result of agitation in Ireland, what was known as the Roman Catholic Emancipation Act was passed and took effect throughout the United Kingdom of Great Britain and Ireland. Roman Catholics might now hold office and sit in Parliament, but all who occupied these posts, whether Protestant or Roman Catholic, were required to disavow the temporal sovereignty of the Pope within the kingdom and to promise support to the Protestant settlement of Church and state. Roman Catholics were still debarred from the throne, from the Lord Chancellorship of England and Ireland, and from the Lord Lieutenancy in Ireland.

In 1850, by a step which because of the historic fear of Roman Catholicism provoked a great furor in England, the Pope reëstablished the English hierarchy. Nicholas Patrick Stephen Wiseman (1802–1865), of Anglo-Irish ancestry, was created cardinal and Archbishop of Westminster, thus, from the Roman Catholic standpoint, renewing the succession of the Archbishops of

Canterbury which had been broken in the reign of Henry VIII and, revived briefly under Mary, had again been interrupted under Elizabeth.

Not far from 1850 the numbers of Roman Catholics rapidly mounted through the immigration of Irish who were fleeing from the famine brought by the blight on the potato crop, their chief source of food. The Irish, poverty stricken, sought employment as unskilled labourers, chiefly in the rapidly growing industrial, commercial, and mining towns and cities. Henceforward they and their descendants constituted the major element in the Roman Catholic Church in England, Wales, and Scotland. There were added immigrants from Italy. As we have seen, some, a large proportion of them clergymen, came over from the Church of England as a result of the Oxford movement. Difficulty was experienced in bridging the gulfs which separated the various new elements from one another and from the old native Roman Catholic communities. The contrast was enhanced by the fact that the former were predominantly urban and the latter mainly rural.

In spite of the initial extreme poverty of the immigrants, striking progress was made by the Roman Catholic Church. As in the United States at the same time, this was not by conversions, for, except through marriage, these were relatively few, but by creating and developing the physical and institutional expressions and facilities of Roman Catholic life. Churches were erected, hundreds of parochial schools were built and maintained, some higher schools were founded, provision was made for the care of the poor, a priesthood was recruited and trained, and religious communities of men and women were brought into being. This last was chiefly by renewing or introducing the familiar monastic orders, but was also through the inauguration of new ones.

THE ADVANCE OF CHRISTIANITY IN NINETEENTH CENTURY WALES

At the outset of the nineteenth century the religious life in Wales had only begun to recover from the sad state into which it had fallen after the Stuart Restoration in the second half of the seventeenth century. The Evangelical Awakening was making itself felt and improvements in education had been initiated by earnest Christians. However, the established church was in poor condition. Its bishops were political appointees, Englishmen most of whom did not know or take the trouble to learn the Welsh tongue, its clergy were too few and most of them were desperately poor, and it was viewed by some of the English as a means of assimilating the Welsh to the English language and culture and was, accordingly, separated from the rank and file.

In the nineteenth century awakenings came which brought the religious life of the country to the highest level that it had ever known. These were in large part through revivals which swelled the Nonconformist Churches. In the revivals and Nonconformist Churches the preaching and the services were mainly in the Welsh language and thus reached the masses, many of whom knew no English and the majority of whom knew Welsh and English but with English as a second tongue. The revivals were enriched and furthered by vernacular hymns: Welsh Christians became famous for their deeply moving congregational singing. The revivals continued at intervals through the century. The denominations which had the major growth through them were the Calvinistic Methodists, the Independents (Congregationalists), the Wesleyan Methodists, and the Baptists.

The (Anglican) Church of Wales shared in the religious awakening and helped to further it. The organization of the church was modified and improved. In 1835 clergy serving Welsh-using parishes were commanded by act of Parliament to have an adequate knowledge of the language. Residential canons were added to the cathedrals. Increasingly Welshmen were appointed to the episcopal sees. Scores of new churches were built, and better provision was made for preparing the clergy. In contrast with any of the other bodies the established church had a diocesan and parochial organization which covered the entire country and in some parishes possessed the only facilities for public worship. In 1915 an act of Parliament was passed which disestablished the Church of Wales. Because of World War I it was not put into force immediately, but in 1920 it came into effect.

REVIVAL, DIVISION, AND ADVANCE IN SCOTLAND

Scotland shared with England in the processes and fruits of the industrial revolution. Coal mines were developed. Manufacturing communities arose. Commerce flourished. Glasgow became the second city in size on the island of Great Britain, ranking immediately after London. Rural populations tended to be depleted by the drift to the towns. The nineteenth century currents of thought made themselves felt. All this worked vast changes in the setting in which the Church operated. In face of the changing conditions, as in England, Christianity, far from waning, displayed a striking revival. Partly as a result of that revival, a major division split the Church of Scotland. Following the division even greater vigour was seen in Scottish Christianity. This vitality showed itself in part in measures to meet the altered situation in Scotland and partly in phenomenal geographic expansion. Some of the expansion was by missions among non-Christian peoples. More of it was through migration. Scots vied with the English and the Irish in the rapid settlement of the British colonies, especially in Canada, Australia, New Zealand, and South Africa. Presbyterianism, their inherited faith, was sufficiently vital to inspire them to build strong Presbyterian Churches in these regions and to make that branch of the faith, along with the Church of England, Methodism, and the Roman Catholic Church, characteristic of the life of these emerging nations.

Presbyterianism was even more dominant in the Christianity of Scotland than was the Anglican Communion in that of England. It is, therefore, on that form of the faith that in this rapid survey we must centre our attention. At the outset of the nineteenth century the overwhelming majority of the Presbyterians were in the state church, the Church of Scotland. There were Presbyterian minorities who had broken away from that church, not primarily on matters of doctrine but because of what they believed to be a compromise of Christian standards and of too great subservience of the Church to the state.

The religious awakening which had begun in Scotland before 1815 continued to mount after that year. As we have seen (Chapter XLIV), it had come partly from indigenous vitality, partly from contact with the Great Awakening in America, especially through the writings of Jonathan Edwards, and partly through Wesley and other leaders of the Evangelical movement in England. As elsewhere, its exponents were unhappy over the fashion in which eighteenth century rationalism had penetrated the Church and had weakened conviction and warmth.

Outstanding in the awakening in the years which immediately followed 1815 was Thomas Chalmers (1780–1847). Coming from a large family of children, with enormous physical vitality, merry, lively, impetuous, quick-tempered, and with a wide range of intellectual interests and an extensive knowledge of mathematics and science, he was early ordained into the ministry of the Church of Scotland. He was already winning fame as a preacher and a scholar when, at about the age of thirty, partly through family sorrows and problems and aided by reading Wilberforce, he had a religious experience which made him a leader in the Evangelical revivals. From 1815 to 1823 he was minister successively in two parishes in Glasgow. There he distinguished himself not only as a preacher but also for his work among the poor of that growing metropolis. Through a system of organized visitation, care of the poor, and education he wrought a striking improvement in the physical, moral, and spiritual condition of his parishioners. In his forties he occupied chairs first in St. Andrews and then in Edinburgh. In his teachings and writings he did much to reconcile the newly emerging science with the Christian faith. At Edinburgh especially he became a national figure, deferred to and consulted by the more influential in Church and state. He was outstanding in a movement which added scores of church buildings and ministers to enable the Church of Scotland to keep pace with the growth and shifts in population. In the year 1831–1832 as Moderator he held the highest office in his church. He believed profoundly in the principle of a national, established church as the best way of covering comprehensively the entire population of a country, but he maintained that such a church should not be subservient to the state but should have Christ as its one and only head and should be unfettered by king, magistrate, or legislature in her "sacred and spiritual jurisdiction." This conviction of the necessity of the autonomy of the Church made Chalmers an outstanding leader in a major event in the religious history of Scotland, the Disruption, which in 1843 rent the Church of Scotland and led to the formation of the Free Church of Scotland.

Although, when it came, the Disruption seemed sudden, it was the climax of a long movement. Repeatedly since the Reformation there had been those who were conscientiously opposed to any subordination of the Church to the secular arm. Indeed, from the Reformation onward the Church of Scotland had been far less acquiescent in the attempts at control by the state than had the Church of England. Much as in the Middle Ages in many places in Western Europe there were those who believed that appointment to ecclesiastical office by lay lords and princes corrupted the Church and was an unholy compromise of the latter's divine commission, so in Scotland the issue had been chiefly although not solely joined over the power of the lay proprietors to determine the choice of ministers for the parishes. In the eighteenth century there had been several secessions from the established church. There were the Cameronians, largely a lay movement, who refused adherence to the settlement after the Revolution of 1688 which brought in William and Mary, on the ground that, being uncovenanted, the regime was not a lawful government. In 1743 it constituted itself into a Reformed Presbytery. In 1733 Ebenezer Erksine led what was known as the Secession, which, believing that the union of 1707 which made the Parliament at Westminster the only one for Great Britain and the ensuing Act of Patronage of 1712 were infringements on pledges given at the time of the Revolution and had been followed by the inroads of rationalism in the ministry, broke with the established church. The Seceders divided between what were known as the Burghers and the anti-Burghers over the issue of whether a Christian could take the oath of the burgess, but in 1820 the two wings came together in the United Secession Church. In 1761 Thomas Gillespie founded the Relief body, from a protest against forcing on unwilling congregations patrons' nominees of moderate, namely, rationalistic views.

As the Evangelicals, products of the rising tide of spiritual life, grew in numbers, they became increasingly restive over any hint of subservience to the state and the lay proprietors. In 1820 they carried through the General Assembly an action refusing to recognize as binding the orders of the Privy Council commanding prayers for the new king, George IV. They did this on the ground that they were an infringement on the right of the Church of Scotland to determine its own modes of worship. In 1834, by what was known as the Veto Act, the General Assembly declared "that no pastor shall be intruded on any congregation contrary to the will of the people." A test case soon arose in which, against the wish of the overwhelming majority of the congregation, the Earl of Kinnoull made an appointment to a parish. The question, carried to the highest court, the House of Lords, was decided against the Church, thus saying in effect that the Church was a creature of the state and subordinate to it. In the next few years the issue came up in several more appointments in which a presbytery either refused to ordain and install a candidate appointed in contradiction to the Veto Act, or, in violation of that Act, complied.

The final breach came in 1843. The Church of Scotland and with it most of Scotland were deeply stirred. On the one hand were those who insisted that the Church must not be under the state. For the most part they were Evangelicals, committed to the new tides of revival. On the other were those, largely moderates not moved by the revival, who believed in submission to the state. The decision was precipitated by the action of the House of Lords in 1842 in requiring a presbytery to ordain a candidate presented by a patron to an unwilling congregation and imposing a fine on the presbytery for recalcitrance. The controversy was brought to the House of Commons through the presentation of what was called the Claim of Rights. Predominantly English as it was, and not really comprehending why Scotland should be so excited, the House decided against the Evangelicals. Seeing that protest was of no avail, in a dramatic scene those standing for the full independence of the Church walked out of the General Assembly, formed themselves into the Free Church of Scotland, and elected Chalmers as their first Moderator. More than a third of the ministers of the Church of Scotland went with them.

The action was heroic, for it meant that the ministers of the Free Church had surrendered all claim to support by the ancient endowments and that the congregations had lost the buildings in which they and their ancestors had worshipped. The foreign missions of the Church of Scotland were also lost. With great enthusiasm and much sacrifice the laity of the Free Church erected new buildings, supported their ministers, and organized for the initiation and support of foreign missions. The way had been prepared by the generosity of the voluntary gifts which had aided the earlier remarkable building of new churches that had been promoted by Chalmers.

The formation of the Free Church of Scotland was not an isolated movement. It grew out of the Evangelical revival which was strong in much of Protestantism in Europe and America. It was reinforced by the contemporary swing towards democracy in Europe, the British Isles, and America. It had similarities with the Oxford movement, for, while by no means, as did the latter, seeing the life of the Church in the historic Catholic ecclesiastical structure and sacraments, like it the Free Church of Scotland stressed the Church as a distinct community with its own life. Indeed, it was partly because of the similarity and the unpopularity of the Tractarian movement that the House of Commons rejected the Claim of Rights. Here, too, was one phase of the trend towards the separation of Church and state which, for several and often conflicting reasons, was fairly general in the contemporary Roman Catholic and Protestant world. Fully accomplished in only a few lands in Europe, it prevailed in the United States and the British colonies.

In Scotland the majority of the Presbyterians outside the Church of Scotland gradually drew together. In 1847 the Secession and Relief churches became one in the United Presbyterian Church. In 1852 those known as the Original Seceders joined the Free Church. In 1900 the Free Church and the United Presbyterian Church formed the United Free Church of Scotland. Fresh sacrifice seemed to be entailed by the refusal of a minority of the Free Church, the "Wee Frees" as they were derisively called, to go into the merger and the action of the courts in awarding them as the legal Free Church the properties of that body. However, an act of Parliament removed that menace.

The established church survived the shock of the withdrawal of the Free Church and displayed marked vigour. It endowed new parishes and constructed additional church buildings. It inaugurated young men's and young women's guilds and recruited and trained deaconesses.

The established church drew progressively nearer to the Free Church and its successor, the United Free Church. At the Disruption it had retained the majority of the clergy and the laity. In 1874 Parliament abolished lay patronage, thus giving to the congregations the right to choose their own ministers which had been the crux of the original dissension. A movement for disestablishment made some headway. In 1898 the churches adopted a common hymnal, *The Church Hymnary*. But not until after 1914, namely, in 1929, was reunion consummated.

These controversies by no means constituted the entire history of Christianity or even of Presbyterianism in Scotland. Indeed, only from time to time did they come to the fore. The churches were channels and expressions of a pulsing life which showed itself in many ways. Some of this was in preaching, for much emphasis was placed on it in the Scotch churches. Several very great preachers appeared. Even to list them would unduly lengthen this section. Here, as in so many other places in nineteenth century Protestantism, hymn writers emerged and their contributions were used to vary the metrical versions of the Psalms which until the nineteenth century had prevailed in public worship. Outstanding among them was Horatio Bonar (1808–1889), a pupil of Thomas Chalmers who went with the Free Church at the Disruption and who for nearly a quarter of a century was pastor of the Chalmers Memorial Church in Edinburgh. A prolific author of evangelistic tracts and devotional books, he also wrote hundreds of hymns. Among them were "Go, labour on: spend and be spent, thy joy to do thy Father's will" and "I heard the voice of Jesus say." Elizabeth Cecilia Douglas Celephane (1830–1869), who in spite of physical frailty ministered to the sick and poor near her home, wrote at least two hymns which came into wide use, "Beneath the cross of Jesus I fain would take my stand" and "There were ninety and nine that safely lay in the shelter of the fold." The latter gained currency through Moody and Sankey. The brilliant blind preacher and pastor, George Matheson (1842–1906), both scholar and mystic, contributed, among other hymns, "O love that will not let me go."

The interest in scholarship, philosophy, and theology which was a strong strain in the Scotch mind flowered in notable literature. Some of this was highly provocative. William Robertson Smith (1846–1894) was a pioneer in introducing the type of Biblical criticism which was flourishing in Germany. As professor of Oriental Languages and Old Testament in the Free Church college in Aberdeen and as the author of articles on Biblical subjects in the ninth edition of the *Encyclopædia Britannica,* he distressed some of the conservatives. In the 1870's he was tried for heresy by the General Assembly of the Free Church, and while the indictment was dropped, a vote of lack of confidence was passed and he was deprived of his chair. Yet he was soon appointed to a professorship at Cambridge. In general the Scottish scholars were moderate, open-minded to new views, willing to accept those which seemed to them sound, but not inclined to go to extremes. Thus George Adam Smith (1856–1942), who, as a specialist on the Old Testament, combined deep religious insight with a knowledge of German scholarship acquired at Tübingen and Leipzig and through continuing studies, commanded the confidence of both scholars and the popular evangelist, Dwight L. Moody, and in his later years had a term as Moderator of the United Free Church. A slightly older contemporary, whose biography he wrote, Henry Drummond (1851–1897), was notable for aiding many to fit the findings of modern science, especially the belief in evolution, then a relatively fresh challenge, into a rational scheme with the Christian faith. Through lectures and writing, especially *Natural Law in the Spiritual World* and *The Ascent of Man,* two works which enjoyed an enormous circulation, Drummond answered the questions of thousands. As an evangelist to students and other intellectuals and as a friend of Moody he had a wide hearing in the British Isles, Germany, America, and Australia and gave a great impetus to growing student Christian movements. In the New Testament, Marcus Dods (1834–1909), of the Free Church, professor and principal of that church's theological school in Edinburgh, New College, and the author of books which had an extensive circulation, was exonerated of the charge of heresy by the General Assembly. J. McLeod Campbell's *Atonement* (1856) presented the reconciling work of Christ as purely through love and was regarded by some friendly critics as the greatest work in theology in English in the first six decades of the century.

Developments in public worship were seen, with the introduction of organs and the use of liturgical forms, some of them drawn from the ancient and modern practices of other churches. A prolific devotional literature appeared. Action was taken through the Church to further various social reforms, among them better housing, the reduction of drunkenness, and the simplification of the transfer of land.

The minority of Christians in Scotland outside the several Presbyterian churches were divided among several bodies. There was the Episcopal Church, a member of the Anglican Communion. It knew some of the controversies which were troubling its larger neighbour south of the border and in general tended to move in a high churchly direction. The Independents or Congregationalists and the somewhat similar body, the Evangelical Union, merged in 1897. In 1869, Baptists, long lacking cohesion and presenting a wide variety, came together in a union. The Methodists were not numerous and were chiefly in the cities. A few thousand Roman Catholics, mostly in the Highlands and islands, had preserved their faith uninterruptedly since pre-Reformation times. In the nineteenth century they were augmented and swamped by a huge Roman Catholic immigration from Ireland, predominantly in the cities, especially Glasgow, and by 1914 the total membership of that church was approximately a half million. Religious orders reappeared and in 1878 the Pope restored the hierarchy, with two archbishops and two suffragan bishops.

THE IRISH STORY: ROMAN CATHOLIC EMANCIPATION AND THE DISESTABLISHMENT OF THE (ANGLICAN) CHURCH OF IRELAND

While these developments, with their marked increase in the vigour of the churches, were taking place in Great Britain, what was happening on that island, Ireland, which across the centuries had suffered so much from its large neighbour, England?

The problem which the past had bequeathed to the nineteenth century was grim. The Anglo-Irish minority, largely identified with the Church of Ireland, sister to the Church of England, had long been in control. They were the landlords, the officials, the well-to-do farmers, the clergy of the Church of Ireland, and the elements associated with them. The Scotch-Irish, in Ulster in the North and predominantly Presbyterian, business men and farmers, had suffered from discrimination and had often been disaffected. The large majority of the population was Roman Catholic and most of it, peasants and labourers, was poverty-stricken and ignorant. To Protestant England, Roman Catholic Ireland had been a threat, for it might rise in support of the Roman Catholic claimants to the throne of England of the House of Stuart. During the wars of the French Revolution and Napoleon, for England a life and death struggle, there was the chronic danger that Ireland might go over to the enemy, and at times open rebellion broke out. In 1800 a parliamentary union was effected and the Irish Parliament was abolished. Henceforward representatives from the island were to sit in the Parliament at Westminster. However, the majority of the Irish, Roman Catholics, were under legal disabilities. In the years immediately succeeding 1815 the fiscal union of the governments of the two islands was completed.

The nineteenth century story was one of mingled tragedy and achievement. As we have more than once noted, the blight which destroyed the potato crop in 1846 and 1847 precipitated famine. This was aggravated by a striking increase in population, from about 1,250,000 in 1700 to about 4,500,000 in 1800, and to 8,175,124 in 1841. Famine relief by the government and the emigration of more than 1,500,000 in the ten years after 1847 partly mitigated the misery. In 1861 the census showed a population of about 5,800,000, a substantial decline in two decades. A combination of necessity, agitation in Ireland, prudential self-interest, and conscience led Parliament to improve conditions. In 1829 what was known as Catholic emancipation removed most of the legal disabilities under which those of that faith had laboured. In the 1880's and the 1890's land reform measures first gave relief to tenants, then assisted tenants in the purchase of their holdings, and later reduced the rentals of such lands as were still tilled by tenants. In 1869 the (Anglican) Church of Ireland was disestablished. The local government act of 1898 transferred the control from the landlords to elected county councils and in these the rising Roman Catholic middle class was strong. It was in this setting that developments in the Christianity of Ireland took place.

Improvement in the condition of the Roman Catholic majority was achieved. In addition to the removal of legal disabilities, in 1831 a system of primary schools was inaugurated which worked especially for the benefit of the previously underprivileged Roman Catholics. In 1879 an act which subsidized intermediate education aided them. The national university begun in 1908 was predominantly Roman Catholic. The economic condition of Roman Catholics was mitigated. Better provision was made for the preparation of Irish clergy. Until the French Revolution many of the priests had been educated in France.

The hostility of the Revolution to the Church made that impossible and in 1795 by act of the Protestant government a college for the training of priests was authorized. The institution was placed at Maynooth and was assisted by a grant of funds for the erection of buildings and by annual subsidies. In the first half of the century, due in part to active missions and in part to the economic and social benefits which accrued from the step, several thousand Roman Catholics became Protestants. Rome took alarm, a prelate of ultramontane convictions was appointed to one of the archiepiscopal sees, in 1850 a national synod was convened, the first in many years, and discipline was tightened on clergy and laity. To hold the children to the faith, Roman Catholic schools were emphasized and the work of the Christian Brothers in teaching them was stressed.

The Protestant Churches flourished. In mid-century Protestants constituted a little less than a fourth of the population. Slightly more than half of them were in the Church of Ireland and most of the remainder were Presbyterians, mainly in Ulster. The awakenings which characterized the churches in Great Britain also extended to Ireland. In the first half of the century the Evangelical movement brought a marked increase in vitality to the Church of Ireland. Voluntary societies arose for various purposes, at least two for missions among the Roman Catholics which were followed by many conversions. In the course of time bishops were appointed who concerned themselves more with the spiritual welfare of their flocks than had their predecessors. The Oxford movement had repercussions which brought new life. More churches were built, largely by private gifts, some of them proprietary chapels and many in the rapidly growing cities, especially Belfast. More facilities were provided for the preparation of the clergy. Disestablishment required readjustments, but the constituency rose to the challenge. The Presbyterians also were quickened. Revivals, notably that of 1859, felt on both sides of the Atlantic, brought an access of vigour. In 1840 the General Assembly of the Presbyterian Church of Ireland was formed, uniting the Synod of Ulster and the Secession Synod, and thus added strength. Better provision was made for the education of the priesthood. Foreign missions were undertaken. Next to the Church of Ireland and the Presbyterians the Methodists were the largest Protestant body. They grew rapidly, but were only a small minority of the whole.

The Christianity of Ireland entered the twentieth century much stronger than it had been a hundred years earlier.

THE PART OF CHRISTIANITY IN SHAPING THE LIFE OF THE BRITISH ISLES IN THE NINETEENTH CENTURY

What did Christianity do to shape the life of the British Isles in the nineteenth century? In that age of abounding vitality and of rapid change, when the British built the most extensive and populous empire that the world had ever seen and were the leaders in industry, commerce, and banking, in that period when the land presented the contrast between great wealth on the one hand, with a prosperous middle class, and abject squalor on the other, when it was stirred by urgent movements to better the lot of the underprivileged, what part did Christianity have? From the preceding pages it is obvious that the churches were more vigorous at the close than at the outset of the century. To what extent and in what ways did the Christianity of which they were the partial expression and the vehicle modify or mould the scene about them? No brief or simple answer can be given. Only a few facts can be summarized which would have to be given prominence in any fully-rounded picture.

From what has been said, it must be clear that in spite of the perplexities presented by the broadening horizons of human knowledge and widespread agnosticism and scepticism, among a larger proportion of the population in 1914 than in 1815 Christianity was a force in shaping the outlook and the purposes of life. In nominal allegiance there had been little change. In actuality, on the one hand, probably both among the workingmen and among the intellectuals, more were pronouncedly sceptical or antagonistic, and on the other hand more were zealously committed. Probably, too, in morals a larger number more nearly approximated to Christian standards in 1914 than in 1815.

A striking example of improvement was in the agitation to reduce drunkenness. Christians led the way in it, sometimes backed but sometimes unsupported by their churches. Protestants were notable in their leadership, but some Roman Catholics had a share. Outstanding was the Capuchin, Theobald Mathew (1790–1856), an Irish priest who first came to the public notice through his untiring devotion to the sufferers from a cholera epidemic in 1832 and who was won to the temperance cause by a Quaker. In Ireland it was he who is said to have been chiefly responsible for a striking reduction in the consumption of spirits. He extended his campaign to Britain and America.

In addition to the efforts of the Salvation Army, there were many other enterprises springing from Christian motives to better the lot of the underprivileged. Among them were the orphanages of George Müller, which we have already mentioned; Toynbee Hall, the precursor of many "settlements," named for one who made much of the *Imitation of Christ;* the homes begun by Thomas John Barnardo (1845–1905), who while in London preparing to be a medical missionary to China became interested in the waifs of the metropolis and founded institutions with the rule "no destitute child ever refused admission"; and various city mission societies.

Impelled by a Christian motive, Florence Nightingale (1820–1910), who went to Pastor Fliedner's school at Kaiserswerth in Germany for training, rose to fame for her organization of the nursing service to the fighting men in the

Crimean War, and was outstanding in promoting the development of the nursing profession.

Many names spring to mind of those who, inspired by their Christian faith, led in efforts for various aspects of social reform, some by legislation and others through private philanthropy. Thomas Fowell Buxton (1786–1845), reared a Quaker and married to a sister of Elizabeth Fry, succeeded the Evangelical William Wilberforce in the leadership of the anti-slavery movement which culminated in the act of Parliament (1833) that ended Negro slavery within the British Empire (1838). Anthony Ashley Cooper (1801–1885), heir to a great title, eventually the seventh Earl of Shaftesbury, who owed his sturdy Evangelical faith to a boyhood nurse, was for many years a champion in Parliament of legislative measures to improve the lot of the labourers in mines and factories. He was also president of numerous philanthropic and missionary societies, among them the Ragged School Union and the National Society for the Prevention of Cruelty to Children, and aided the Young Men's Christian Associations and workingmen's institutes. J. K. Hardie, socialist and pioneer in the formation of the Independent Labour Party, began his public career as a lay preacher in the Evangelical Union. Methodist local preachers led in the formation of several of the early labour unions.

That literature felt the effects of Christianity is obvious, especially when such poets as Alfred Tennyson and Robert Browning are recalled.

Some of the statesmen who moulded British domestic and foreign policy, particularly in the latter half of the century, sought to make Christian principles effective in the actions of the government. Outstanding was William Ewart Gladstone (1809–1898), who would have preferred to become a clergyman but, urged by his father, entered politics. Many years in Parliament and on the cabinet, and four times prime minister, he endeavoured always to act as a Christian. The high sense of public duty which characterized a large proportion of British civil servants and colonial administrators in the nineteenth century, which was in striking contrast to the prevalence of corruption and selfishness in the eighteenth century, must be in part ascribed to the mounting influence of Christianity.

SUMMARY

One of the most striking parallels in history is the fact that a flood tide in the Christianity of the British Isles, and especially of the dominant partners, England and Scotland, went *pari passu* with enormous growth in wealth, power, population, and empire. This was in spite of intellectual and social currents which were running strongly against the faith. In this there seems to be something akin to the coincidence of the high peak of creative life in the

Middle Ages of Western Europe with the revivals in Christianity represented by the mendicant orders, great formulations of theology, and such "heretical" movements as the Waldensees and Cathari. Resembling it was likewise the fashion in which the Protestant and Catholic Reformations were contemporary with the many other vigorous movements in the sixteenth century. We have also remarked that the Catholic Reformation in Spain came at approximately the same time with the era of Spanish colonial empire building and the most notable contributions of Spanish artists.

That here is more than coincidence seems probable. As we have said before, it would be difficult to know which are causes and which are effects. We can be sure, however, that, whether cause or effect, in each of these periods the forward surge of Christianity profoundly influenced the other phases of the life and culture in the midst of which it occurred.

SELECTED BIBLIOGRAPHY

J. Barr, *The United Free Church of Scotland* (London, Allenson & Co., 1934, pp. 302). A useful historical survey.

G. A. Beck, editor, *The English Catholics 1850–1950* (London, Burns, Oates & Washbourne, 1950, pp. xix, 640). By various authors, all friendly, and in general designed to show the advance of the Roman Catholic Church in the century after the reëstablishment of the hierarchy. Contains some very useful data.

K. Bliss, *The Service and Status of Women in the Churches* (London, Student Christian Movement Press, 1952, pp. 208).

W. Booth, *In Darkest England and the Way Out* (London, International Headquarters of the Salvation Army, preface 1890, pp. 285, xxxi). The famous programme of General Booth.

[S. Brooks], *Life, Letters, Lectures, and Addresses of Fred'k W. Robertson* (New York, Harper & Brothers, no date, pp. xxiii, 840).

S. C. Carpenter, *Church and People, 1798–1889. A History of the Church of England from William Wilberforce to "Lux Mundi"* (London, Society for Promoting Christian Knowledge, 1933, pp. 598). In general, objective, comprehensive, and carefully done.

H. Cnattingius, *Bishops and Societies. A Study of Anglican Colonial and Missionary Expansion 1698–1850* (London, Society for Promoting Christian Knowledge, 1952, pp. viii, 248). Carefully done.

T. K. Cheyne, *Founders of Old Testament Criticism. Biographical, Descriptive, and Critical Studies* (New York, Charles Scribner's Sons, 1893, pp. ix, 372). By an expert.

H. W. Clark, *History of English Nonconformity. Vol. II. From the Restoration to the Close of the Nineteenth Century* (London, Chapman & Hall, 1913, pp. xx, 458). Sympathetic. Carefully done.

S. T. Coleridge, *Aids to Reflection with a Preliminary Essay by J. Marsh.* From the fourth London edition, edited by H. N. Coleridge (New York, Gould, Newman and Saxton, 1840, pp. 357).

F. W. Cornish, *The English Church in the Nineteenth Century* (London, Macmillan & Co., 2 Parts, 1910). A valuable survey by an Anglican.

A. W. Dale, *The Life of R. W. Dale of Birmingham* (London, Hodder & Stoughton, 1902, pp. x, 771). By his son.

R. W. Dale, *History of English Congregationalism* (London, Hodder & Stoughton, 1907, pp. xii, 787). Left unfinished by the death of its author, a distinguished Congregational clergyman.

J. E. de Hirsch-Davies, *A Popular History of the Church in Wales from the Beginning to the Present Day* (London, Sir Isaac Pitman & Sons, 1912, pp. xii, 356). By an Anglican.

L. L. Doggett, *History of the Young Men's Christian Association* (New York, Association Press, 1922, pp. 405). A competent survey.

L. E. Elliott-Binns, *Religion in the Victorian Era* (London, The Lutterworth Press, 1936, pp. 525). A standard survey, covering the entire range of Christianity in England during that period.

L. E. Elliott-Binns, *The Development of English Theology in the Later Nineteenth Century* (London, Longmans, Green & Co., 1952, pp. ix, 137). Brief, but comprehensive.

St. John Ervine, *God's Soldier. General William Booth* (London, William Heinemann, 2 vols., 1934). A full-length, sympathetic biography.

J. R. Fleming, *The Story of Church Union in Scotland, Its Origins and Progress, 1560–1929* (London, James Clarke & Co., pp. 176). A popular, sympathetic survey, by an expert.

J. R. Fleming, *A History of the Church in Scotland 1843–1874* (Edinburgh, T. & T. Clark, 1927, pp. x, 276). A standard survey.

J. R. Fleming, *A History of the Church in Scotland 1875–1929* (Edinburgh, T. & T. Clark, 1933). A continuation of the preceding book.

W. Y. Fullerton, *C. H. Spurgeon, A Biography* (London, Williams & Norgate, 1920, pp. xii, 358). Sympathetic, based upon careful research, well written, by a fellow Baptist.

D. Gwynn, *Cardinal Wiseman* (Dublin, Browne & Nolan, 1950, pp. x, 197). Admiring.

W. Hanna, *Memoirs of the Life and Writings of Thomas Chalmers, D.D., LL.D.* (New York, Harper & Brothers, 4 vols., 1851, 1852). By a son-in-law, valuable for its extensive inclusion of portions of Chalmers' journals and letters.

G. D. Henderson, *The Claims of the Church of Scotland* (London, Hodder & Stoughton, 1951, pp. vii, 251). An excellent survey, largely of history, from the Reformation. Especially good on the nineteenth century.

J. W. James, *A Church History of Wales* (London, Arthur H. Stockwell, 1945, pp. 190). A good summary with an Anglican emphasis.

W. D. Killen, *The Ecclesiastical History of Ireland from the Earliest Period to the Present Times* (London, Macmillan & Co., Vol. II, 1875, pp. xix, 592). By a Presbyterian, with an inclusive coverage, but stressing the Presbyterian phases of the story and with a strong Protestant bias.

W. F. Knapp, editor, *The History of the Brethren* (Denver, W. F. Knapp, 2 vols., 1936). Detailed, sympathetic, with many excerpts from the sources.

E. A. Knox, *The Tractarian Movement 1833–1845* (London, Putnam, 1933, pp. xix, 410). By a former Bishop of Manchester, frankly critical of the Oxford movement, yet attempting to be fair, and placing it in the general contemporary setting of the religious revival.

J. Scott Lidgett, *My Guided Life* (London, Methuen & Co., 1936, pp. 279). The autobiography of an outstanding British Methodist.

H. B. Marks, *The Rise and Growth of English Hymnody* (New York, Fleming H. Revell Co., 1937, pp. 288). By a long time student of the subject.

The Life of Frederick Denison Maurice, Chiefly Told by His Own Letters, edited by his son, F. Maurice (London, Macmillan & Co., 2 vols., 1884).

Autobiography of George Müller, compiled by G. F. Bergin (London, J. Nisbet and Co., 1905, pp. xiv, 735).

J. H. Newman, *Apologia pro Vita Sua, Being a History of His Religious Opinions* (New York, The Macmillan Co., 1931, pp. xxi, 380). Frankly in answer to criticism: one of the most famous of spiritual autobiographies.

W. A. Phillips, editor, *History of the Church of Ireland from the Earliest Times to the Present Day, Volume III, The Modern Church* (Oxford University Press, 1933, pp. 499). From an Anglican point of view.

C. E. Raven, *Christian Socialism, 1848–1854* (London, Macmillan & Co., 1920, pp. xii, 396).

T. Rees, *History of Protestant Nonconformity in Wales from Its Rise to the Present Time* (London, John Snow, 1861, pp. vii, 512). Sympathetic, based upon extensive use of the sources.

P. Rogers, *Father Theobald Mathew Apostle of Temperance* (Dublin, Browne and Nolan, 1943, pp. xxiii, 166). Sympathetic, based upon careful research.

G. A. Smith, *The Life of Henry Drummond* (New York, Doubleday & Company, 1898, pp. xiii, 541). Sympathetic, by a friend and distinguished scholar.

V. F. Storr, *The Development of English Theology in the Nineteenth Century 1800–1860* (London, Longmans, Green & Co., pp. viii, 486). A competent survey. The best on the years which it covers.

J. Stoughton, *Religion in England from 1800 to 1850. A History, with a Postscript of Subsequent Events* (London, Hodder & Stoughton, 2 vols., 1884). Comprehensive, temperate in spirit, with major emphasis upon Nonconformity.

W. J. Townsend, H. B. Workman, and G. Eayrs, editors, *A New History of Methodism* (London, Hodder & Stoughton, Vol. I, 1919, pp. xx, 598). By distinguished Methodist scholars, this volume deals with the history of Methodism in the British Isles.

J. Tulloch, *Movements of Religious Thought in Britain during the Nineteenth Century* (New York, Charles Scribner's Sons, 1886, pp. xi, 338).

D. O. Wagner, *The Church of England and Social Reform since 1854* (Columbia University Press, 1930, pp. 341). Sympathetic, a doctoral dissertation.

W. Ward, *The Life of John Henry Cardinal Newman Based on His Private Journals and Correspondence* (London, Longmans, Green & Co., 2 vols., 1912). Written with insight, with a combination of objectivity and sympathy.

R. F. Wearmouth, *Methodism and the Working-class Movement of England 1800-1850* (London, The Epworth Press, 1937, pp. 289). Based upon careful research.

C. C. J. Webb, *A Study of Religious Thought in England from 1850* (Oxford, The Clarendon Press, 1933, pp. viii, 192). A competent brief survey.

B. Willey, *Nineteenth Century Studies: Coleridge to Matthew Arnold* (London, Chatto & Windus, 1949, pp. v, 287). A very important survey and interpretation of religious thought.

W. T. Whitley, *A History of British Baptists* (London, The Kingsgate Press, 2d ed., 1932, pp. xii, 384). A comprehensive survey.

J. Whitney, *Elizabeth Fry Quaker Heroine* (Boston, Little, Brown & Co., 1937, pp. 337). Charmingly written, with many excerpts from the sources.

Chapter XLIX

THE CHRISTIANITY OF NORTH AFRICA, WESTERN ASIA, AND EASTERN EUROPE: REEMERGENCE, SUFFERINGS, COMPLEXITIES AND VITALITY, A.D. 1815 - A.D. 1914

The Eastern Churches, continuations of regional branches of the Catholic Church of the first three centuries, had a chequered course in the nineteenth century. As the Turkish tide retreated, some of them reëmerged and became autocephalous national bodies and rallying centres of nationalism. Others, remaining encircled, suffered further from the attrition which had been their lot since the Moslem-Arab conquest. The largest, the Russian Orthodox Church, displayed vitality in a variety of ways. Upon them all and upon all the regions which they occupied, the Christianity of the West, Roman Catholic and Protestant, impelled and empowered by the awakenings of the nineteenth century, had greater or less effect. To give some indication of what took place we will make a geographic pilgrimage, beginning on the southern shore of the Mediterranean, journeying eastward and northward, and ending with what because of their magnitude and their importance for the world as a whole were the most significant, the developments in Russia.

THE NORTHERN SHORES OF AFRICA AND THE NEAR EAST

On the north shore of Africa west of Egypt the Christian churches which had flourished in the early centuries had gradually disappeared under Moslem rule. At the dawn of the nineteenth century Christianity was represented only by Spanish footholds in Morocco, European merchants, and the captives of the corsairs.

Between 1815 and 1914 most of the north shore west of Egypt was occupied by Western European powers and this led to a striking increase in the numbers of Christians. Almost all the growth was by immigration from north of the Mediterranean. There were also missions, both Roman Catholic and Protestant, among the Moslems and Jews, although with very few converts. Most of the Christians were in Algeria, conquered by the French in the 1830's and 1840's, and in Tunisia, occupied by France in 1881. By the end of the century Algeria contained about half a million who were registered as Roman Catholics. The majority were French but there were substantial numbers of Italians, Spaniards, and Maltese. There were also several thousand in Tunisia. A Roman Catholic hierarchy was developed and in 1884 the Archbishopric of Carthage, made famous in the early centuries by a distinguished succession of prelates, chief among them Cyprian, was revived. The first to hold the renewed see and the outstanding nineteenth century bishop in North Africa was Charles Martial Allemand Lavigerie (1825–1892). Lavigerie was also cardinal and primate of Africa. Lavigerie was a man of sweeping vision, who wished the French holdings in North Africa to be the vantage from which the Roman Catholic faith would spread throughout the continent. As we have seen (Chapter XLVI), he was the founder of what were known as the White Fathers (1868), who extended their activities south of the Sahara. In spite of the coolness or outright hostility of French officials, due partly to fear that the revived Christianity would arouse resentment among the Moslems and partly to the anticlericalism of the Third Republic, other religious orders entered and dioceses and parishes multiplied. There were also some Protestant immigrants, mostly from France. Libya, occupied by Italy in 1911, contained a few thousand Roman Catholic immigrants of the nineteenth century.

In Egypt the story was somewhat different. Here were ancient churches which had never died out. The largest was Monophysite in faith, and, although the vernacular of its members was Arabic, it continued its services in the Coptic language which had been the speech of the most of the population before the Moslem-Arab conquest. Its numbers are said to have grown in the second half of the nineteenth century, but from an excess of births over deaths and not by conversions. The chief strength of the Coptic Church was in the cities and Upper Egypt. The Greek Orthodox Church had been present before the Arab occupation and had existed continuously ever since. It was under its own Patriarch of Alexandria. In the latter part of the nineteenth century its numbers were augmented by the immigration of Syrians and Greeks, and schools, hospitals, and other charitable institutions were carried on. Armenians and Syrian Monophysites were also in Egypt, but in smaller numbers. Roman Catholics had been present since the seventeenth century, but at the outset of the nineteenth century were very few. Like the other churches, they increased in the second half of the century. This was partly by immigration from Europe. It was chiefly by accessions from the Copts, the fruits of missions by several religious orders. These converts and their descendants were gathered into a

Coptic Uniate body which in 1895 was given a Patriarch of Alexandria and in 1904 was said to have 22,000 members. Protestantism was represented by several denominations. Among them were the Church Missionary Society which gathered a few converts from the Moslems and the Copts and the United Presbyterian Church of North America, which built up a community of several thousand, almost entirely from the Copts and chiefly in Upper Egypt.

Christianity reëntered the Sudan, in the upper part of the Nile Valley, south of Egypt. There, it will be recalled, it had been introduced in the sixth century and had been strong for many years, only to succumb to slow extinction by Islam. Shortly before the middle of the nineteenth century Roman Catholic missionaries gained a footing and in the second half of the century the British and Foreign Bible Society, the Church Missionary Society, and the United Presbyterians made their way into the region.

South-east of the Sudan, in the mountain fastnesses of Ethiopia (Abyssinia), an ancient church, the official faith of the realm, held out against the encroachments of Islam. It drew its head from one or another of the Coptic monasteries of Egypt and was Monophysite in creed. The country also contained pagans, Jews, and Moslems. In the nineteenth century Roman Catholics renewed the efforts to win the Ethiopian Church which had enjoyed a fleeting success in the sixteenth and seventeenth centuries. They gathered several thousand into a Uniate Ethiopian Church. Protestants, largely Germans, Swiss, and Swedes, entered. For a brief time in the 1880's there was an attempt to bring the Church of Ethiopia into union with the Russian Orthodox Church, but as much in an effort to offset the encroachments of French, British, and Italian imperialism as from religious motives.

Palestine, the "Holy Land," with Jerusalem as its chief city, presented a varied religious complexion which was enhanced in the nineteenth century. Jerusalem was regarded by Jews, Christians, and Moslems as especially hallowed. Although, as was most of the Near East, ruled by the Ottoman Turks, Moslems, during the larger part of the nineteenth century, it contained many Christians. In 1815 several ancient branches of the Catholic Church were represented, among them Orthodox, Armenians, and Roman Catholics. During the course of the century the Roman Catholics were reinforced and several kinds of Protestantism entered. To the Franciscans who had been the traditional representatives of the Roman Catholic Church were added other orders. In the latter part of the century much was made of the several Uniate Churches. An interesting phase of Protestantism was a bishopric in Jerusalem which was a joint enterprise of the Church of England and the Evangelical Church of Prussia. The incumbents were named alternately by the crowns of England

and Prussia. It was begun in 1840, but the Prussian Government withdrew in 1886.

Syria, to the north of Palestine, had a larger proportion of Christians than did Palestine. In it at the outset of the century the Christians were mostly Jacobites, Greek Orthodox, and Roman Catholics. The Roman Catholics were chiefly Maronites. Massacres of Maronites by the Druzes in 1860 were the occasion for French intervention. As a result, Syria became an autonomous province within the Turkish Empire and with a Christian governor. Under these conditions Roman Catholic missionaries increased. The two chief Uniate bodies, Maronite and Syrian, flourished. The latter was from the Jacobites and had its origin late in the eighteenth century. It was augmented from time to time by the accession of Jacobite bishops. Protestantism was introduced, chiefly by American missionaries.

Cyprus, administered by the British after 1878 but until 1914 nominally under Turkish suzerainty, was predominantly Greek Orthodox in religion and continued to be such. Here the Orthodox Church had been autocephalous since the fifth century, independent of any of the historic patriarchates.

To the Armenians the nineteenth century brought additional suffering. Russia moved southward across the Caucasus. In 1828, after a long war with Persia, she established her control over a considerable section of Armenia, including Echmiadzin, the seat of the Catholicos, and in 1878, after a war with Turkey, obtained from that power a large slice of Armenia on the west of the portion acquired in 1828. In 1836 Russia reorganized the Armenian Church in her domains, according the tsar authority over it through his representatives. In Turkey the chief Armenian official was the Patriarch who resided in Constantinople. Following the Crimean War, in the 1860's the Armenians in Turkey were given a constitution which governed both their civil and ecclesiastical affairs, for by the Ottoman regime each major religious body was regarded as a distinct *millet,* or nation. Under this arrangement the quality of the clergy and the life of the Church seem to have improved.

But the Armenians were caught in the intrigues of the great powers, especially Russia and Great Britain. By the Russo-Turkish Treaty of San Stefano, in 1878, Russia was awarded a kind of protectorate over the Armenians in Turkish territory. The British Government was disturbed by this and other provisions of the treaty and a congress of European powers at Berlin (1878), among other measures, substituted the joint guardianship of the powers for that of Russia. A secret convention between Great Britain and Turkey placed the Christians of Asia Minor under British protection. Partly from fear that Armenian nationalism, centering around the Church, might become a British tool, the Russians tightened their control, prohibited the use of the Armenian language in the schools, and in 1903 confiscated the properties of the Church. In the meantime, in the mid-1890's the Turks, from alarm at Armenian nationalist agitation and because of chronic animosity, launched massacres which took a toll of several thousand lives. By 1914, however, the Armenians were effecting a recovery.

The Armenian religious scene was complicated by other factors. There was a revival of an indigenous religious movement which was apparently either a continuation of the ancient Paulicianism or akin to it and which was labelled by the Armenian Church as heretical. The Roman Catholics augmented their missionary activity and won numbers to the Uniate body drawn from the Armenian Church. The Armenian Uniates were under the protection of France, for that power saw in this a means of extending its political influence in Western Asia. Thanks to French pressure, in 1830 the Turkish Government recognized the Uniates as a separate *millet*. The laity were restive under the restrictions by Rome of their participation in the affairs of their church and the course of the Uniates was troubled by their insistence on a larger voice. Protestants, mainly missionaries of the American Board of Commissioners for Foreign Missions, addressed themselves to the Armenians. At first they sought to stimulate fresh life in the Armenian Church rather than bring into being Protestant churches. To this end they translated the Bible into the vernacular and opened schools and theological seminaries. However, conservatives took alarm and in 1846 the Armenian Patriarch in Constantinople formally excommunicated those who followed the missionaries. As a result what were known as Evangelical churches were formed. Later friendly relations between Evangelicals and the old church were to some degree restored.

It may be noted that early in the nineteenth century the Georgian Church, in the Caucasus, Orthodox by long tradition, was subjected by the Russian conquerors to the Holy Synod of the Russian Orthodox Church and was forcibly assimilated to that body.

In the nineteenth century the Nestorians had their chief centre around Lake Urmia, in the mountainous north-west of Persia. They had sadly dwindled since the days, centuries earlier, when communities of them were to be found from Mesopotamia to the China Sea. They were sometimes known, not quite correctly, as Assyrian Christians, and also were called the Church of the East. Again and again, notably in the 1830's and 1840's, their numbers were reduced by massacres by their fierce neighbours, the Kurds. As early as the sixteenth century some of the Nestorians had become Uniates. Known as Chaldeans they persisted, and in the nineteenth century, thanks in part to Roman Catholic missionaries from Europe, their numbers increased. In the nineteenth century Protestants, chiefly Anglicans and Americans (the latter at first under the

American Board of Commissioners for Foreign Missions and then Presbyterians), established missions among them. They sought to infuse new life in them rather than produce separate communities, but, as among the Armenians, distinct churches came into being, in this instance Anglican and Presbyterian.

It must be added that while in the nineteenth century Roman Catholic and Protestant missions multiplied on the northern shores of Africa and in the Near East, they won very few except from the existing Christian bodies. Now and then a Jew was converted and occasionally a Moslem. However, Moslem law and custom made accessions from Islam almost impossible. Through personal contacts, literature, schools, and hospitals thousands of Moslems were brought under the influence of Christianity and here and there a Christian leaven penetrated some elements of Moslem society. But very few declared themselves Christians by receiving baptism.

THE REËMERGENCE OF ORTHODOX CHURCHES IN SOUTH-EASTERN EUROPE

The nineteenth century witnessed the rapid decline of the once mighty Ottoman Empire. Indeed, it became known as "the sick man of Europe." By 1914 it had surrendered all its possessions in Europe except Constantinople and a small area north and west of that city. It had also lost Crete and most of the islands in the Ægean. The retreat of the Turks was accomplished partly with the help of Russia but chiefly through the surging nationalism of the peoples of the Balkan Peninsula. Nationalism was closely associated with the Orthodox Churches. Indeed, they were the symbol and the rallying centres of the reëmerging nations. As a result, there came into being national, autocephalous churches which were independent of one another and of the Patriarch of Constantinople. That ecclesiastic, while enjoying the title of Ecumenical and having a priority of dignity, ceased to have the administrative control in the Balkan Peninsula which he had exercised under the Turks. His effective authority was limited to the Orthodox within the Turkish realm. In 1914 these were mainly the Greeks in Constantinople and in the coastal cities of Asia Minor.

The story of the achievement of the independence of the Balkan nations and with it the autonomy of the several Orthodox Churches is fairly complicated. Here we can take the space to give it only in the barest outline. As we have seen, the Ecumenical Patriarchs were under the control of the Turkish rulers. The latter gave them the administration of the Orthodox Church in their realms. In some areas this meant the appointment of Greek bishops and clergy who did not know the language of their flocks, who sought to exploit them for their own profit, and who were hated as aliens. Political independence was, accordingly, accompanied and at times preceded by the throwing off of the Patriarchal yoke and the achievement of ecclesiastical independence.

Before the year 1815 the Orthodox Church in Montenegro had been auto-cephalous. For most practical purposes its mountain people, Serbs, had long been independent, governed by a succession of prince bishops. In 1766 their archbishop was recognized as autonomous, but with a formal dependence on the Holy Synod of the Russian Orthodox Church.

In 1804 revolt against the Turk broke out among the Serbs. In 1817 what amounted to political autonomy was gained, although still under the nominal suzerainty of the Sultan of Turkey. As a result of the Russian invasion of Turkey in 1828–1829 and as one of the provisions of the Treaty of Adrianople (1829), this position was accorded international recognition. A national Ortho-dox Church was organized under a metropolitan with his seat at Belgrade. As a result of the defeat by Russia in 1877–1878 Turkey recognized the full in-dependence of Montenegro and Serbia. In consequence, in 1879 the Serbian Orthodox Church became completely free from the Ecumenical Patriarch. But from time to time it was in conflict with that prelate over the appointment of Greek bishops in Macedonia, where both claimed jurisdiction. The Congress of Berlin (1878) gave to Austria-Hungary the right to occupy and administer the adjacent Bosnia and Herzegovina and in that year the Austria-Hungarian Government entered into an agreement with the Ecumenical Patriarch by which the latter recognized the autonomy of the Orthodox Church in those provinces but retained a nominal oversight.

There were other Orthodox in the Austria-Hungarian realms. Late in the seventeenth and early in the eighteenth century several thousand Serbs took refuge from the Turks in the south of Hungary and there formed an auto-cephalous church which had its primate at Karlowitz. In 1848 the Austrian Emperor Francis Joseph gave to that ecclesiastic the title of Patriarch. In 1873 the Austria-Hungarian Government took from the See of Karlowitz two dioceses of Serbs and some Orthodox in Bukowina and grouped them under another autocephalous church with headquarters at Czernowitz in Bukowina.

In Greece in 1821 a movement for political independence broke out into an uprising. The war was fought with great ferocity and dragged on to 1829. Russian intervention (1828–1829) led to the virtual recognition of what soon became the Kingdom of Greece. In the struggle most of the clergy supported the insurgents. In 1833 the national assembly passed a resolution, signed by thirty bishops, which declared that the Church of Greece owned no head but Christ, and the king gave a charter to the autocephalous national Church of Greece. This was done without consultation with the Ecumenical Patriarch, presumably because the latter was still under the Turk. Not until 1850 did that prelate formally accede to the step and then only with reservations. These were designed to keep the Church of Greece in the same faith as the other Orthodox

Churches, with the Church in Constantinople as the centre to which all questions of dogma were to be referred and the Patriarch of Constantinople as the source of the holy oil which he consecrated for all the Orthodox Churches. As Greece extended its territories the Church of Greece brought more areas under its jurisdiction, thus restricting further the territory directly under the Ecumenical Patriarch.

In 1829, because of the defeat of Turkey by Russia, Wallachia and Moldavia had their autonomy confirmed under a Russian protectorate. In 1862 nationalism fused the two principalities into the state of Rumania. Under Turkish rule the Orthodox Church had been subjected to the administration of Greeks from the Phanar district in Constantinople. Greek was substituted for the traditional Slavonic as the liturgical language. However, by the end of the eighteenth century the use of the vernacular Rumanian had become general in church services. Under the first prince of the unified Rumania the Church was declared autonomous. The Ecumenical Patriarch protested, but in 1885 formally recognized the autocephalous status of the Church of Rumania. It is said that the quality of the parish clergy, poorly trained, poorly paid, and overworked though they were, tended to improve in the latter part of the century. In Transylvania, which in 1918 was to become part of Rumania, the Orthodox Church became autonomous in 1864.

Bulgarian nationalism led to ecclesiastical as well as political independence. When, in 1856, as a result of the Crimean War, the Turkish Government decreed the freedom and equality of the Christians in its realms, Bulgarians demanded reforms in the Orthodox Church in their midst. The Ecumenical Patriarch in part complied and appointed some bishops of Bulgar blood. However, in 1860 the Bulgarians were insisting upon full antonomy for their Church and in 1870 the Ottoman Government formally conceded it. The Ecumenical Patriarch was indignant, excommunicated the clergy and members of that Church, and in this was sustained by a synod (1872) in which more than a score of bishops, four ex-Patriarchs, and the Patriarchs of Alexandria and Antioch participated. They declared heretical the nationalism ("phyletism") which, from their standpoint, was dividing the Church of Christ. Not until 1945 was the Bulgarian Church received back into the communion of the Ecumenical Patriarch. In Macedonia the Greeks and Bulgars competed for control. Rival bishoprics were set up and the Greeks supported the Turks in the forcible suppression of the Bulgars.

In much of the Balkan Peninsula the ecclesiastical picture was further complicated by Roman Catholics and in some places by Protestants. On the eastern shores of the Adriatic there were, as had been true for centuries, Roman Catholics of the Latin rite. In the Balkans there were Uniates, mostly of the

Byzantine and, in Constantinople, also of the Armenian rite. These were augmented in the nineteenth century, partly as the result of missions among the Greeks and partly by Bulgarian restlessness under the Greek yoke of the Ecumenical Patriarch. Protestant missionaries, chiefly from the United States, were in Greece and Bulgaria, but they had only slight numerical success.

THE INCREASING COMPLEXITY OF THE RUSSIAN SCENE

In Russia, even more than in Western Europe, in the nineteenth century the religious life was marked by stark contrasts and increasing complexity. The domain of the tsars was expanding, partly to the southward at the expense of the decadent Turkish Empire but chiefly east of the Caspian and on the northeastern shores of Asia. This vast area, in square miles the largest continuous empire on the globe, contained a variety of peoples and religions. Even in Europe, in addition to the Christian majority, there were pagans, Moslems, and Jews, and in Asia there were pagans of many stripes, Buddhists, and Moslems. As we are to see, the government put forth strenuous efforts to weld together the diverse conglomeration through a programme of Russification which had as one of its features the incorporation of as much of the population as possible into the Orthodox Church. Yet this did not prevent a mounting diversity. On the one hand, as in Western Europe, there was an extensive de-Christianization of traditionally Christian elements, especially among the intellectuals. On the other hand, also as in Western Europe, but in somewhat different fashion, there was fresh access of vigour in the churches. Much, both of the de-Christianization and of the religious awakening, was through currents from Western Europe. There was also an indigenous and emphatically anti-Western trend. Russian Christianity did not show as great vitality as Protestantism or Roman Catholicism, but it displayed more variety than at any previous time and, far from being moribund, registered decided advances.

Important though they were, we cannot devote any considerable amount of space to the de-Christianizing and anti-Christian movements. We must, however, note several general facts about them. First is what we mentioned a moment ago: they were largely through contagion from the Occident. The science and philosophy of the new age were penetrating Russia and here as in Western Europe they furthered religious scepticism among many who were touched by them. Among others, Hegel and Comte were influential. The social theories of the West also entered. Liberal democracy had its advocates. Socialism, including that of Marx, won followers, and anarchism and nihilism had their devotees. Much of the social radicalism was anti-religious.

At the beginning of the century the Tsar Alexander I (reigned 1801–1825) moved towards liberalism, but in his later years he became fearful of it. His successor, Nicholas I (reigned 1825–1855) was staunchly conservative. In the first decade of the next reign, that of Alexander II (1855–1881), a number of liberal measures were put through, including the emancipation of the serfs (1861) and the institution of zemstvos (1864) to further local self government. For the last fifteen years of his reign Alexander II reversed his early policy and supported repressive measures. He met his death through the bombs of terrorists who had resorted to violence to sweep aside the old order. It is not surprising that the next tsar, Alexander III (reigned 1881–1894), was even more intent on curbing the political and social theories from Western Europe. Under his son and successor, the amiable but weak Nicholas II (reigned 1894–1917), and after the defeat of Russia in a disastrous war with Japan (1904–1905) had enfeebled the existing regime, the most potent revolution which modern Russia had thus far known broke out (1905) and wrought what at the time seemed to be drastic changes in the direction of a liberal government.

Under these circumstances, when through much of the century stern measures were being taken to suppress the political and social theories issuing from the Occident, the advocates of these programmes, driven underground, resorted to plots and counter-violence and, after the complete discrediting of the tsarist regime in World War I (1914–1918), they staged an explosive revolution (1917) which was captured by the extremists.

In this setting the Russian Orthodox Church had its life. It continued to be controlled by the state through the Holy Synod instituted by Peter the Great. It was played upon by various currents, some of them from the West and some from within Russia. From abroad came influences from Protestantism and Roman Catholicism. From within issued contributions from the past and from great souls nurtured in the Orthodox Church. Closely tied to the state as it was, the Russian Orthodox Church also reflected in part the shifts of attitude of the tsars towards the forces emanating from the West.

As we sketch the course of the Russian Orthodox Church in the nineteenth century we will first follow in rough chronological outline the successive stages. Then we will speak of some of the more notable men and movements in the Church.

We have seen (Chapter XLIV) that the Russian Orthodox Church came to the year 1815 on a rising tide. The Tsar Alexander I had experienced what was akin to a conversion. The Procurator of the Holy Synod, Golitsyn, had undergone a similar change and had given the support of his high position to the Russian Bible Society, formed (1813) under the inspiration of the British and Foreign Bible Society. Translations of the Bible into the vernaculars were prepared and distributed. They enjoyed a wide reading and created a religious ferment. In 1817 the Ministry of Religious Affairs and Public Education was created, Golitsyn was appointed to head it, and under it were placed the Holy Synod and the supervision of all forms of religion. Golitsyn laboured to promote education.

In the exaltation of his religious enthusiasm and partly under the influence of a Roman Catholic theologian who believed the salvation of Europe would be as a community ruled by a universal church, in 1815, the year which saw the end of the Napoleonic Wars, Alexander I, hoping that the world was being ushered into a new day, called on his fellow-monarchs to rule as Christians. At his instance the majority of the sovereigns of Europe subscribed to what was called the Holy Alliance, by which the signers undertook to base their reciprocal relations "on the sublime truths which the Holy Religion of our Saviour teaches" and declared that "the precepts of justice, Christian charity and peace . . . must have an immediate influence on the councils of princes and guide their steps."

As the zeal of Alexander I cooled, reaction set in. It was marked under the next tsar, Nicholas I. Attacks were made on the Bible Society, partly by the conservatives and partly through pressure from the Jesuits, for the latter were in favour with some in high places. Golitsyn fell (1824) and in 1826 the Russian Bible Society was suppressed. Earlier, in 1815, alarmed by the inroads which they were making among the nobility to the detriment of the Orthodox Church, Alexander I had banished the Jesuits from the capital and in 1819 had expelled them from the empire. The Holy Synod was removed from the jurisdiction of the Ministry of Religious Affairs, its Procurator was given the status of minister, and through him the control of the Church by the state was tightened. The formula Orthodoxy, autocracy, nationalism became the tsar's policy and entailed the reciprocal support of Church and state. To enable the clergy better to inculcate their flocks with greater loyalty to the tsar additional provision was made for their education. More theological seminaries were founded and from them the kind of training was banned which had been based on what had been learned from the Jesuits. The state paid the salaries of the clergy, thus giving them better financial support and tying them more closely to the government.

What were known as the Slavophiles became vocal. In opposition to those who admired the West, including those who looked with friendly eyes upon the Roman Catholic Church or Protestantism, they held that the Slavs had been divinely commissioned to preserve the Christian faith in its purity and that the Russian Orthodox Church and the Russian state were the guardians of true Christianity and the ideal society. They maintained that, in contrast, the West was marked by class conflict and that in it the Christian faith either had been corrupted and distorted by Papal tyranny and Protestant individualism or had been weakened by the misuse of reason. They believed, therefore, that Russia should free all Slavs from alien rule and induce all Christians to come into the Orthodox fold. Obviously they reinforced the belief that Moscow was the third Rome, the centre of true Christianity, and that Russia was Holy Russia. They did not win all Russians to their side, but from time to time their views prevailed in the policies of the state and the Holy Synod and were in part reëchoed by spokesmen of the Russian Orthodox Church under the Communist regime in the next century.

In the liberal period of Alexander II, some of the clergy hoped for a less iron-clad control of the Church by the state. Indeed, they asked the tsar that the Church might have a degree of self-government. The tsar put them off and before action was taken reaction set in.

In the latter part of the century the dominant figure in the administration of the Russian Orthodox Church was C. P. Pobiedonostsev, Procurator of the Holy Synod from 1880 to 1905. A layman, a lawyer, extraordinarily able, he was profoundly and sincerely committed to the Russian Orthodox Church and to the monarchy. He distrusted all that came from the West and was resolved to use his office to keep Russia so far as possible uncontaminated by the ideas from that region which, as he believed, would undermine the existing order in Church and state and weaken Christian civilization. He was against trial by jury, parliaments, newspapers, and secular schools. To safeguard Russia he furthered a strict censorship of the press. He wished to assimilate the diverse peoples of the empire to Russian culture. To this end he encouraged missions of the Orthodox Church among non-Christians, supported the repression of social radicals and revolutionaries, was sympathetic with the Slavophiles, and was against the Jews and Judaism. So far as he could, he put the Orthodox Church solidly on the side of the existing order with its secret police and its use of Siberia and Siberian prisons as places of exile for those convicted or suspected of endangering that order.

The Revolution of 1905 seemed to give promise of the emancipation of the Church from its servitude to the state. For some time there had been those who had been agitating for more self-government in the local parishes, for a council (*sobor*) which would be a voice for the Church and reform it, and for the restoration of the Patriarchate. However, while a few minor reforms were made and a council was promised, the latter was not called. A minority among the priests were active in the revolution, but the majority were on the side of the conservatives.

Under these circumstances it is not surprising that the quality of the clergy left much to be desired. Parish priests and diocesan bishops were state functionaries. A large proportion of the priests were regarded by their flocks with contempt or dislike. They tended to become an hereditary caste with no sense of vocation. Many of them had difficulty in making a living, some of them were regarded as grasping, not a few of them were drunkards, and numbers of the sons of priests were unemployed and discontented. Church periodicals which constituted much of their limited reading matter helped to make them supporters of autocracy.

In spite of the many adverse factors the Russian Orthodox Church gave evidence of internal vigour and in the course of the nineteenth century its vitality seems to have mounted. The evidence is in part notable personalities. One of these was Philaret Drozdov (1783–1867). The son of a priest, in his student days he displayed marked ability as a scholar. In 1808 he became a monk and in 1812 he was put at the head of the ecclesiastical academy in St. Petersburg. In 1819 he was made a member of the Holy Synod and in 1821 he was appointed Archbishop of Moscow. He was active in promoting the translation of the Scriptures into the vernacular. At the request of the Holy Synod he compiled a catechism in Russian rather than the ancient Slavonic. In spite of criticisms it became a standard. Although for a time his opponents had him put out of office, Nicholas I restored him to the Holy Synod and made him Metropolitan of Moscow. In 1842 his enemies finally forced him into retirement, but although the last ten years of his life were spent in strict monastic seclusion, for the quarter of a century between 1842 and his death (1867) Philaret exerted great influence. His counsel was sought by many of the outstanding leaders in Church and state and he is said to have drafted the proclamation of 1861 by which Alexander II emancipated the serfs. Well read in the mystical literature of several churches, he believed in prayer and practised it. Reticent about his inner life, he was intense in it. He had a marked effect upon theological thought and study, probably more than any other bishop of the nineteenth century.

Prominent in the religious life of nineteenth century Russia were *startzi* (elders), monks who through spiritual discipline developed characters which commanded reverential respect. To them many came for counsel. Especially famous as a nursery of the *startzi* was Optina Pustyn, a monastery in the province of Kaluga, south of Moscow. Typical of the *startzi* was one whom we have already mentioned (Chapter XLIV), Seraphim of Sarov (1759–1833), who was canonized in 1903.

The *startzi* represented a tradition which was remote from the nineteenth century Western world and perpetuated the monastic discipline and the mystical experience which went back to the early Christian centuries, to the solitaries and monastic communities of Egypt and Syria. In it was much of the Hesychast movement and of the kenoticism which we have repeatedly met in

Russia. The *startzi* were in part the fruits of a revival which began late in the eighteenth century through Païsius Velochkovsky. Païsius was a Russian monk who had been in monasteries in Rumania and on Mt. Athos and who had put into Slavonic a compilation of Greek mystical ascetic writings called the *Philocalia*.

Among the *startzi* who were outstanding in the nineteenth century was Bishop Feofan of Vysha (1815–1894). He rearranged the *Philocalia*, adding to it from other writings. He carried on a prodigious correspondence with those who wrote him for counsel in the life of the spirit, and his letters, posthumously published, were extensively read.

A philosopher who is classed as a Slavophil was Ivan Kireyevsky (1806–1856). Of noble birth, widely travelled, and familiar with the thought of the Western Europe of his day, he was a frequent visitor at Optina Pustyn and established close friendships with its *startzi*, especially with Makary (1758–1842), to whom another "elder," Philaret, a hermit of the Novospassky monastery, entrusted him and who was marked by humility and love for men. In his youth tending to drift from the Orthodox Church, Kireyevsky soon returned to it. While not rejecting Western philosophy, he believed that Russian Christianity and the Eastern fathers had a depth of spiritual life which was in contrast with the abstract rationalism which he regarded as characterizing Western theology.

Outstanding as a Slavophile philosopher was A. S. Khomiakov (1804–1860). Of the aristocracy, deeply religious from boyhood, and never swerving from his loyalty to the Russian Orthodox Church, he believed that the latter ideally displayed *sobornost*, or community. He regarded *sobornost* as combining unity and freedom derived from the love of God and as shown in the mutual love of those who love God. This he held was in contrast with the Roman Catholic Church which, so he maintained, had unity without freedom, and with Protestantism which he viewed as possessing freedom but not unity.

Here and there a parish priest stood out as a spiritual guide. This was rare. It is said that no secular priest of the Russian Orthodox Church has been canonized. In general, parish priests were not held in high esteem. However, a few exceptions made their appearance in the nineteenth century. Prominent among them was John Sergiev of Cronstadt (1829–1908). The son of a deacon, he was given as thorough an education for the priesthood as Russia could provide. For more than fifty years he was in charge of the parish of Cronstadt near St. Petersburg and never aspired to rise in the ecclesiastical hierarchy. Like other seculars, he was married. He was not an ascetic or a mystic of the contemplative kind. Apparently his growth in religious faith and experience was without intense struggle with doubt or a striking crisis. He believed profoundly in prayer, especially in prayer for others. For him officiating at the Holy Communion was a stirring emotional experience. He encouraged frequent communion and, since the Russian Orthodox Church required confession before communion and he could not hear individually all who came, he encouraged each to confess orally, publicly, and simultaneously with others in the congregation. Thousands, and from many ranks in society, asked for his prayers and many miracles of healing were believed to have been wrought through them. He was steeped in the Bible, preached many sermons, and his spiritual diary revealed the quality of his inner life. Large sums passed through his hands for the relief of the sick and the poor. He made journeys, some of them extensive, to assist those who sought his aid. He was called to the death bed of Alexander III to administer the last rites. A staunch supporter of the crown and the Church, in the revolutionary years that came in his old age he was denounced by liberals as an arch reactionary.

By no means all the earnest Christians in communion with the Russian Orthodox Church were Slavophiles, believing pure Christianity to be confined to that body. Famous as an outstanding intellectual and deeply religious soul who sought the unity of all Christians was Vladimir S. Soloviev (1853–1900). He has been described (although this is not a unanimous judgement) as the greatest of Russian systematic religious thinkers, at once a mystic, a philosopher, a theologian, a prophet, and a moral teacher. The grandson of a priest and the son of a distinguished historian and university professor, from childhood he was deeply religious and, an ardent student, acquired great erudition. Through most of his life he had visions, some of them of a mystical character. Disappointed in love, he never married, but lived a wandering life. He thought of becoming a monk, but was unwilling to undergo the loss of liberty which that would have entailed. For a somewhat similar reason he would not undertake the duties of a university professorship, but made a precarious living through writing. Generous to a fault, gay and charming in conversation, he had many friends among the lowly, the intelligentsia, and the highborn. After a period of doubt and inner struggle in his teens during much of which he was an atheist, a socialist, and a communist and read several of the Western contemporary philosophers, he came to a deep religious faith, holding that rational philosophy is darkness and that "God is everything." He made much of Sophia, God's Wisdom, which he conceived to be the eternal and perfect feminine. In him the Platonist, the gnostic, the theosophist, and the orthodox Christian were mixed. A member of the Russian Orthodox Church, he longed to see all Christians, Orthodox, Roman Catholics, and Protestants, brought together. It was said that he became a Roman Catholic, but this appears to be at least highly doubtful. The report seems to have arisen from his effort to achieve Christian unity in his own person by taking the communion, after a manner which left his own position ambiguous, in both the Orthodox and the Roman Catholic Church.

Soloviev sought to give the Christian faith a philosophical and theological basis for his day in such fashion that it would again become relevant to those who had discarded it and that thus the truth of Christ might regenerate humanity and reform the world. True knowledge, he maintained, comes through the right inter-connexion of the empirical, rational, and mystical ways. He held God to be the Absolute, Nothing, the Super-personal, transcending all form and content, but existing as three persons, bearers of the love which renounces self-assertion and which form a perfect unity through perfect love. He declared that God is love. As love He pervades the cosmos. God's love reveals itself through the Logos in the rationality of the universe. Through the incarnation the Logos descends into the stream of events in Jesus Christ and "from being the centre of eternity becomes the centre of history." Through the life, death, and resurrection of Jesus Christ, the God-man who combines the Logos and Sophia, what should be the relation between the divine and the human and has been disturbed by man's sin is restored and the redemption from evil is accomplished. Soloviev accepted evolution from lower to higher forms of life, but taught that evolution is not through materialistic means but through creative spirit. He maintained that nations should regulate their relations with one another on the basis of Christian principles. In his youthful hopefulness he believed in the possibility of all mankind becoming a redeemed society ruled by a theocracy through love. For a time he seemed to side with the Slavophiles, for he hoped that the Slavs and especially the Russians, because of what he deemed to be their proved ability to combine Western and Eastern principles, would lead mankind in the formation of a universal free theocracy.

In Soloviev's later years came disillusionment and despair, both for the Slavophiles and for the realization within history of the theocracy of which he had dreamed. He was made unhappy by the policy of forcible russification which was being pursued by the tsarist regime and regarded the Slavophiles as having succumbed to nationalist egoism. He maintained that the course of mankind on the planet would culminate in a world empire governed by an ascetic, philanthropic reformer, an intellectual genius, who would in reality be Antichrist, for he would be ruled by vanity rather than love and would tempt mankind with the promise of a social order which would ensure to every one "bread and circuses," the satisfaction of their material cravings. He believed that a small minority, remaining really Christian, would retire to a desert, achieve the union of the churches, and prepare for the second coming of Christ. The second advent would then bring the millennial reign of Christ.

Partly through the impact of the thought and writings of Soloviev, early in the twentieth century some intellectuals passed through a youthful Marxist stage and worked out, either independently or in collaboration, a Christian understanding of the universe and history. They were a minority and after the revolution of 1917 and the triumph of the Bolsheviks lived in exile. Their writings, especially those of N. A. Berdyaev (1874-1948) were to have an influence far wider than Russia and Russian communities. We are to meet them again in a later chapter.

Among the creative developments connected with the Russian Orthodox Church we must note music. A striking feature of public worship was the male choirs, singing without instrumental accompaniment. For them deeply moving music was written, much of it in the nineteenth century.

The Christian stream in nineteenth century Russia was by no means confined to the channels of the Russian Orthodox Church. Several of the nonconforming bodies which had existed before 1815 continued. At times they were persecuted, but in 1905 as a result of the revolution in that year, religious liberty was promised and they flourished. Among them were the Old Believers. These, it will be recalled, were divided between those who had priests, the *Popovsty,* and those who did not have priests, the *Bezpopovsty.* Both branches persisted. The *Popovsty* had difficulty in attracting priests from the state church, especially under the strict rule of Nicholas I, and they possessed no bishops who could ordain them. However, in the 1840's they obtained permission from the Austrian Government to import a foreign bishop into the Austrian domains and persuaded a Greek bishop to accept the post. Through him apostolic succession was acquired, eventually dioceses were set up in Russia, and the *Popovsty* ceased to be dependent upon the state church for priests. In the 1880's they were said to number three millions. The *Bezpopovsty* were divided into several sects and to them at least one was added in the nineteenth century. Some sects which held property in common were classed with the *Bezpopovsty.* The Khlysty, the Skoptsy, the Dukhobors, and the Molokans also perpetuated themselves.

During the religious ferment in the reign of Alexander I several movements arose, some of them remaining technically within the Orthodox Church and most of them ephemeral. Thus, in 1817, after a conversion which came partly through the Khlysty and the Skoptsy and partly through German Pietist writings and which led her into the Orthodox Church, Catherine Tatarinov, a widow in high social circles, began prayer meetings in her home which attracted some of the aristocracy and which gave rise to the Spiritual Union.

Still other sects were added in the nineteenth century. Several of them were proliferations of the *Bezpopovsty.* Some were from the Molokans. Others were of independent origin. Several were inspired by contacts with the Protestantism of Western Europe. One of the largest, itself of diverse origins and not fully united, was that of the Stundists and the Baptists. It arose partly through the influence of the Mennonites from Western Europe who had settled in Russia, partly from other German immigrants, and partly among the aristocracy through Lord Radstock of the Plymouth Brethren. The movement made many of its early accessions from the Molokans. In the 1870's and 1880's one of the converts of Lord Radstock, V. A. Pashkov, was an ardent missionary, especially through literature, and sought to unite the Stundists, Baptists, and Molokans. He did not succeed in his effort to bring these various groups together. The government dealt severely with them. Pashkov was banished and died in exile, and many of their leaders were deported to Siberia. Pobiedonostsev, as Procurator of the Holy Synod, was especially vigorous in his attempts at suppression. However, they continued. In general they fell into two camps, the Evangelicals and the Baptists, but they had many similar views.

Another movement, not so much a sect as a social and economic project which sought to build ideal communities on Christian principles, was the Religious Working Brotherhoods, founded in the latter part of the nineteenth century by N. Neplieuv, a man of wealth who set up as a basis for them factories and estates owned and operated communally by the workers.

One who did not form a new sect but who, while not fitting into the pattern of the Orthodox Church, exerted a profound religious influence both in Russia and in other countries, was Count Leo Nikolayevich Tolstoy (1828–1910). Tolstoy had already achieved fame as an author, had lived a varied life, and, happily married to a wife much younger than he, was prosperous as a farmer and from the sale of his books when, in middle life, profound religious disquiet seized him. For a time he sought an answer in science, but could not find it. Then he looked to the lives of those of his own class but returned disillusioned. He felt that the common folk were nearer to the truth and for a time he turned to the Orthodox Church and complied with its worship and its rites. Here, too, what he craved seemed to be lacking. Then, through a reading of the Gospels an answer came which satisfied him and instead of despair he knew happiness which no fear of death could obscure. He had been converted.

But Tolstoy's conversion was to his own variant of Christianity. It rejected the dogmas of the Church and the approval by the Church of persecutions, executions, and wars. It took as central Christ's teachings and found the key to them in the injunction: "Resist not him that is evil." He stressed the light that is in the human conscience. He believed that the Christian must abstain not only from war but also from all forms of violence. To Tolstoy property was the chief source of violence. He held that love must embrace all living things and will lead the Christian to abstain from eating the flesh of slaughtered animals. He eschewed the use of alcohol and tobacco. Only a relatively few of his fellow-countrymen followed Tolstoy's teachings. Yet his writings had a circulation which was almost world-wide.

The Russian Orthodox Church had missions, but these were not nearly as extensive as were those of Roman Catholics and Protestants and were mostly within the Russian Empire. The chief exception was one in Japan. There was also some slight missionary activity in China and Korea. Missions were maintained in Alaska, but they were begun while that region was in the empire. Migrations were the source of Russian Orthodox Churches in the United States and South America. For political purposes the Russian Government gave aid to the Orthodox in the Balkans and Western Asia. However, none of these enterprises outside the Russian Empire could compare in size with what was being done by Roman Catholics and Protestants. Within Russian territories the missions were endorsed and partly supported by the state and were closely related to the efforts at assimilating the non-Russian elements of the diverse population to Russian culture. Yet many missionaries seem to have been moved primarily not by nationalism but by their faith.

The main outlines of the chief missions in the Russian Empire can be quickly given. In 1870 the Orthodox Missionary Society was organized to raise funds for the support of missions. Endorsed by the Holy Synod it eventually had branches in fifty-five dioceses. A mission Sunday, with sermon and collection, was made obligatory on all parishes. Long before the Orthodox Missionary Society was formed, the Holy Synod was sending missionaries to Moslems between the Urals and the Volga and translations of the Bible were being made in the languages of non-Christian peoples. Outstanding in this effort was Nicolai Ivanovitch Ilminski (1822–1891). With his centre at Kazan and eventually with the hearty support of Pobiedonostsev, he led in translating the Bible and the liturgy into various tongues and in the utilization of the vernaculars by missionaries. Missions to non-Christian peoples under Russian rule in Asia and its fringing islands were carried on. They had existed before 1815. They were now increased. They were found not only in regions adjacent to European Russia, but also in the Altai region on the borders of Mongolia and in Kamchatka, the Aleutians, and the Kuriles. They were also in Alaska, for that region was under Russia during the first half of the century.

SUMMARY

The Eastern Churches experienced no awakenings in the nineteenth century comparable in vigour and extent to those in the Roman Catholic Church and

Protestantism. Both these forms of the faith had repercussions on them. In Egypt and Western Asia they gathered communities from them. In Russia Protestantism stimulated the emergence of groups who separated from the Orthodox Church. Russian Christianity was by no means entirely dependent upon Roman Catholicism and Protestantism for its vitality. The Orthodox Church displayed movements which rose from its own past and the majority of Christians who dissented from that Church were in sects of purely Russian origin. In the nineteenth century Russian Christianity showed greater variety than at any previous time. Here was evidence of vitality, even though the Orthodox Church itself was tied hand and foot to the state.

SELECTED BIBLIOGRAPHY

W. F. Adeney, *The Greek and Eastern Churches* (New York, Charles Scribner's Sons, 1908, pp. xiv, 634). An excellent historical survey, but with only small sections on the nineteenth century.

L. Arpee, *The Armenian Awakening. A History of the Armenian Church, 1820–1860* (The University of Chicago Press, 1909, pp. xi, 235). By an Armenian Protestant.

L. Arpee, *A History of Armenian Christianity from the Beginning to Our Own Time* (New York, The Armenian Missionary Association, 1946, pp. xii, 386).

N. Arseniev, *Holy Moscow. Chapters in the Religious and Spiritual Life of Russia in the Nineteenth Century* (London, Society for Promoting Christian Knowledge, 1940, pp. vii, 184). A warmly sympathetic description of the religious life of the Russian Orthodox Church, especially in Moscow.

D. Attwater, *The Christian Churches of the East* (Milwaukee, The Bruce Publishing Co., rev. ed., 2 vols., 1947, 1948). By a Roman Catholic. The first volume is on the churches in communion with Rome and the second volume on the churches not in communion with Rome.

S. Bolshakoff, *Russian Nonconformity* (Philadelphia, The Westminster Press, 1950, pp. 192). A comprehensive historical survey.

F. C. Conybeare, *Russian Dissenters* (Harvard University Press, 1921, pp. x, 370). Contains much useful information from Russian secondary accounts.

J. S. Curtiss, *Church and State in Russia. The Last Years of the Empire 1900–1917* (Columbia University Press, 1940, pp. ix, 442). Based on careful research.

G. P. Fedotov, compiler and editor, *Treasury of Russian Spirituality* (New York, Sheed & Ward, 1948, pp. xvi, 501). Especially useful for its translations from the sources and its historical introductions to the translations.

A. Fortescue, *The Orthodox Eastern Church* (London, Catholic Truth Society, preface 1911, pp. xxxiii, 451). A careful historical survey with a description of current beliefs and practices, by a Roman Catholic.

A. Fortescue, *The Lesser Eastern Churches* (London, Catholic Truth Society, preface 1913, pp. xv, 468). A useful historical survey by a Roman Catholic.

W. H. Frere, *Some Links in the Chain of Russian Church History* (London, Faith Press, 1918, pp. xvi, 200). Only briefly deals with the nineteenth century.

N. O. Lossky, *History of Russian Philosophy* (New York, International Universities Press, 1951, pp. 416). By a Russian Christian philosopher. Deals mostly with the nineteenth and twentieth centuries. The best survey of that period in English. Stresses the religious aspects of philosophy.

H. Y. Reyburn, *The Story of the Russian Church* (London, Andrew Melrose, 1924, pp. vii, 323). About a third of the book is on the nineteenth and twentieth centuries.

E. Smirnoff, *A Short Account of the Historical Development and Present Position of Russian Orthodox Missions* (London, Rivingtons, 1903, pp. xii, 83). By the chaplain of the Russian Embassy in London, based on the reports of the Procurator of the Holy Synod and of the various missions.

A Solovyov Anthology, arranged by S. L. Frank, translated from the Russian by N. Duddington (New York, Charles Scribner's Sons, 1950, pp. 256).

L. Tolstoy, *A Confession and What I Believe,* translated, with an introduction, by A. Maude (Oxford University Press, 1921, pp. xii, 390).

L. N. Tolstoï, *What Is Religion and Other Articles and Letters,* translated by V. Tchertkoff and A. C. Fifield (New York, Thomas Y. Crowell & Co., 1902, pp. 177).

THE UNITED STATES
IN THE
NINETEENTH AND TWENTIETH CENTURIES

Scale of Miles
0   100   200   300   400   500

Chapter L

THE NINETEENTH CENTURY COURSE OF CHRISTIANITY IN THE UNITED STATES

It was in the United States that in the nineteenth century Christianity had its greatest numerical growth and its most striking changes.

Superficially the Christianity of the United States seemed at most a mild variant of that of the Old World. It stemmed from that of Europe and the majority of those who had a formal connexion with the faith were in denominations which had had their origin on the other side of the Atlantic and which remained in communion with their respective mother churches. Moreover, many of the forces and movements which affected Christianity in Europe were also found in the United States. The United States was a part of the Occident and much more nearly than Russia its life was an extension of Western civilization. Here science had some of its most daring achievements, both in expanding the boundaries of man's knowledge and in extending man's mastery of his physical environment. Here the machine and the industrial processes eventually displayed their greatest growth. Here wealth mounted to dizzying heights. Here cities multiplied in numbers and in size to a greater degree than elsewhere on the planet. Here private enterprise and capitalism attained their largest dimensions. While most of the social theories which characterized Western culture in the nineteenth century had their formulation in Europe, they also found followers in the United States and that country became the chief representative and champion of the kind of democracy which had arisen in the British Isles. In the United States the threat and challenge of these movements to Christianity were fully as great as in Western Europe. In some respects the Christianity of Western Europe appeared to be in better condition to meet the threat and rise to the challenge than did that of the United States. At the dawn of the nineteenth century a much larger proportion of the population of Western Europe were members of churches than in the United States and, to a much greater degree than in that country, the faith had the official support of the state.

Yet, similar though the Christianity of the United States and
which confronted it were to those of Europe, there were also s
ences. In many respects the Christianity of the United States wa
proved bewildering and at times irritating to the Christians to tl
Atlantic. Moreover, while in Western Europe a progressive de-
tion of large elements in the population was taking place, and that in spite of
the abounding and rising vitality in the churches, in the United States a mass
conversion of large non-Christian elements and the re-conversion of partially
de-Christianized elements was in progress. The Christianity of the United
States and that of Europe interacted on each other. However, as time passed,
movements indigenous to the United States added to the differences. Because
of the rapidly mounting population and wealth of the United States and the
vigour and missionary outreach of its churches, the Christianity of that land
had a growing share in world-wide Christianity and the life of mankind. To
that story we must now turn.

Conditions Confronting Christianity in the United States of the Nineteenth Century

We have already hinted at some of the conditions which confronted Christianity in the United States in the nineteenth century. If we are to have the
entire picture before us we need again to summarize them and to add to them
the others with which Christianity had to deal.

One of the conditions was the rapid and enormous growth in area. In 1783,
when Great Britain formally recognized the independence of the United States,
the Western boundary was the Mississippi River. Before 1815 the Louisiana
Purchase had carried that boundary far beyond the Mississippi. In 1818 joint
occupancy with Great Britain of the Oregon Country brought the United
States to the Pacific. In 1819 Florida was purchased. In the 1840's Texas was
brought in, the ensuing war with Mexico added a huge region in the South-
west, including California, New Mexico, and Arizona, and the end of joint
occupancy gave the United States undivided possession of the territory later
carved into the states of Oregon, Washington, and Idaho, and a part of Montana. The purchase of Alaska in 1867 substantially lengthened the Pacific lit-
toral. Late in the 1890's Puerto Rico, Hawaii, and the Philippines were annexed.

Along with the growth in territory went an even greater one in population.
In 1800 the census showed the total population to be 5,305,937. In 1820 it was
9,638,191; in 1840, 17,069,453; in 1860, 31,443,322; in 1880, 50,155,783; in 1900,
75,994,575; and in 1910, 91,972,266. From 1800 to 1900 the increase percentage-
wise was eight times as great as that in the British Isles and nearly seven
times that in Belgium, the country which held the record in Europe. Much of

this growth, especially in the first part of the century, was due to the high birth rate of the native-born stock. Beginning in the 1830's, it was even more because of a vast flood of immigration, mostly from Europe, and the birth rate of the foreign-born elements.

The increase in territory and population was partly the cause and partly the result of an even more striking multiplication of wealth. The enormous natural resources of the new country in soil, forests, and minerals were tapped. The inventiveness of the American became proverbial in devising machines, in building factories and transportation systems, and in organizing and managing companies small and large to take full advantage of them. The fact that the wide expanse of the country was under one central government and without internal tariff barriers contributed to the utilization of these assets.

Industrialization was made possible by developments in mathematics and the scientific method. It was accompanied and facilitated by the wide extension of education. Primary education became almost universal and secondary and higher education, instead of being an aristocratic privilege, as in the rest of the world, was increasingly placed within the reach of all and with a growing emphasis in the curriculum upon science and the application of science to man's livelihood.

A concomitant of the rapidly mounting industrialization was the growth of cities and the decreasing proportion of the population engaged directly in agriculture. It is estimated that at the dawn of the century less than a twentieth were in cities of more than three thousand and that 90 per cent. lived on farms. In 1860 only two out of five engaged in gainful occupations were in agriculture and about a sixth of the population were in cities of eight thousand and over. In 1910 about two-fifths of the population was classified as urban and if towns and cities of twenty-five hundred and over be put in that category, in 1914 less than half of the population could be counted as rural.

United though it was, the nation was not without sectionalism and inter-sectional rivalries. The most distinct section was what was called the South. Embracing all the states south of the northern border of Maryland and of the Ohio River, and Missouri, Arkansas, and Texas, it was almost a separate nation with its own culture. The difference was largely due to the presence of the Negro and, until the 1860's, Negro slavery. To a large extent the South was rural and had a plantation economy, until the 1860's based upon slavery. After emancipation, the presence of the Negro and of agriculture which to a considerable extent depended on Negro labour continued to keep it apart. The attempt to withdraw from the rest of the country by forming the Confederate States of America was frustrated by the North in what, along with the roughly contemporary T'ai P'ing Rebellion in China, was the most costly war of the century in life and treasure. For the most part nineteenth century immigration avoided the South and the latter's white population remained more nearly representative of the older, pre-nineteenth century stock than was that of any other part of the United States.

Each of these factors brought a threat and a challenge to the Christian faith. Could Christianity keep pace with the rapidly westward moving population as it poured into the territories on the frontier, heretofore only sparsely occupied by Indian tribes? Could it hold to the faith the immigrants from Europe? Could it protect the Indians against exploitation by the whites and bring them into the fold of the Church? Could it win the Negroes, all of them non-Christian when brought to America, and the sprinkling of Chinese and Japanese who settled on the West coast? Could it counter the materialism encouraged by the pursuit and enjoyment of wealth? Would it follow successfully the movements of population from the farms to the cities and, after having adapted itself to a rural society, devise methods for dealing effectively with urban conditions and problems? Would it be able to demonstrate that it was not disproved by science but that its insights and imperatives were necessary to the fullest life?

In several respects Christianity seemed ill-prepared to meet the threat and the challenge. It has been estimated that in 1800 only 6.9 per cent. of the population had a church membership. Removed from Europe where Church and state, while often in conflict, were in close association, where the churches were generally supported by public taxation, and where baptism and confirmation or its equivalent were either required by law or were an established social convention, and in a country where churches were supported only by voluntary contributions and church membership was the exception rather than the rule, white elements in the population were in danger of complete de-Christianization. Moreover, the Church did not present a united front. Even in 1815 Christianity displayed a greater variety and was represented by more different ecclesiastical bodies than in any other country in its history. As the century advanced this was augmented, chiefly by the addition of more denominations from the Old World but also by some of indigenous creation. Instead of working unitedly, the churches were in competition which was often unseemly. Even small towns had several churches, most of them too feeble to be really effective and only slowly and imperfectly developing coöperation with one another. It was chiefly because the denominations could not agree on what form of the faith should be taught that in the public schools, namely, those supported and controlled by the state, either no religious instruction was given or only a bare minimum was to be had.

Not only did much religious indifference and scepticism exist. There was also some militant atheism. We have already noted (Chapter XLV) the vogue of Thomas Paine's *Age of Reason* and the lectures of Robert G. Ingersoll. Probably more dangerous was the less obviously hostile humanism represented by such men as John Dewey. Possessing points of sympathetic similarity and to no small degree with historical roots in Christianity, it was basically a denial of the Christian faith. Capturing many intellectuals in positions of influence in education, it filtered into large elements of the population.

In spite of these adverse conditions, in an amazing fashion Christianity rose to the challenges and made progress towards solving the problems which confronted it. We have earlier seen (Chapter XLIV) that in the United States Christianity entered the nineteenth century on a rising tide. A mass conversion of the non-Christian and partially de-Christianized elements of population was under way. It was to continue through the nineteenth century and into the twentieth century. In 1910, as contrasted with the 6.9 per cent. in 1800, the percentage of the population having formal membership in some religious body was 43.5. This mass conversion was primarily through Protestantism, for at the outset such Christianity as existed was predominantly of that wing of the Church and it continued to spread. Roman Catholicism also displayed a remarkable growth and the Eastern Churches, although small minorities, were represented.

We will now turn to the several aspects of this mass conversion. Although they were proceeding simultaneously and in places and at times interacted on one another, for the sake of clarity we will take them up one by one.

Advance of the Frontier

One aspect of the progressive mass conversion of the partially de-Christianized elements of the population was the spread of the faith in the new communities which sprang into being on the rapidly moving frontier. Frontier society was fluid. Many of the minority who had had a church connexion before coming West made no effort to reëstablish one in their new homes. There was a tendency to ignore Christian moral standards. Yet it was on the frontier that Christianity made some of its most striking advances.

The advances were by a variety of channels and agencies. Some were in existence before 1815. Others came into being after that year. In the variety may have been one of the reasons for the success.

We have already seen the channels and agencies that ante-dated 1815. Here and there a group organized a church before leaving their home in the older states and, settling together, already possessed a Christian nucleus. Much more numerous were laymen and women who took the initiative in the new communities in gathering others together in Sunday Schools and prayer meetings which grew into churches. Many clergymen moved West and, without support from the East, took up farms, worked on them six days a week for a livelihood for themselves and their families, and preached on Sundays. Eventually voluntary gifts from those to whom they ministered made it possible for numbers of these clergymen to give a larger proportion of their time to the Church. "Revivals" continued. They had been a feature of much of Protestantism in the new country even before political independence and had broken out spectacularly in the Great Awakening, the Second Awakening, and the camp-meetings. The "evangelism" which was already characteristic of American Protestantism and which had as its aim winning all the population to the Christian faith stressed revivals as a normal way of attaining this goal. Baptists, Methodists, and the Disciples of Christ, the last also known as Christians, who had demonstrated their appeal to the new communities, maintained their spectacular growth. State missionary societies were organized, chiefly by Congregationalists but also by some other bodies, partly with the frontier in mind.

After 1815 more agencies and channels were added. Churches in the older centres began missionary societies on a national basis. In 1826 the American Home Missionary Society was formed. Having as its foundation the United Domestic Missionary Society which had been organized four years earlier by Presbyterians and (Dutch) Reformed, it drew its chief support from Presbyterians and Congregationalists. As we have seen, at the outset of the century Congregationalism was the strongest of the denominations of the United States. Compact in its New England setting, where it was dominant, with able leaders, many of them highly trained, and earnestly evangelistic, with it were connected the three outstanding figures in the movements for mass conversion in the eighteenth and nineteenth centuries, namely Jonathan Edwards, Charles G. Finney, and Dwight L. Moody. Congregationalism was long in intimate coöperation with Presbyterianism. Theologically the two were akin. Beginning in the 1790's the state organizations of Congregationalists in New England exchanged delegates with the Presbyterian General Assembly. By the Plan of Union inaugurated in 1801 Congregationalists and Presbyterians joined in planting churches in the West. They worked together not only in the American Home Missionary Society but also in other organizations, among them the American Bible Society, begun in 1816 to unite the various local and state Bible Societies, the American Tract Society, inaugurated in 1825, and the American Sunday School Union, founded in 1824. As what was known as the New England theology moved further and further from the traditional Presbyterian theology, the majority of the Presbyterians, especially those of Scottish and Scotch-Irish antecedents, known as the "Old School men," and with their main centre of ministerial training at Princeton, repudiated the Plan of Union

(1837), severed their ties with the American Home Missionary Society and some of the other interdenominational bodies, and cut off from their fellowship four synods in which the New England theology prevailed. The expelled synods formed their own General Assembly and, known as the New School Presbyterians, continued their collaboration with the Congregationalists until 1861. In 1852 a national gathering of the Congregational churches abrogated the Plan of Union. In 1893, to recognize what had been fact since 1861, the American Home Missionary Society was renamed the Congregational Home Missionary Society. After 1815 several other denominations organized societies, either purely for home missions or for both home and foreign missions.

Out of thousands who served devotedly under these societies it seems almost invidious to choose any for special mention. Yet two can be mentioned as showing in an outstanding way what was done, although usually in lesser measure, by many others. George H. Atkinson (1819–1889) established Congregational churches in Oregon and Washington, had a major share in founding a college and in inaugurating the public school system of Oregon, and contributed to the development of wheat-growing in the Pacific North-west. Sheldon Jackson (1834–1909), from ancestry which had been prominent in the political life of the state of New York and dedicated from childhood by his parents to the Christian ministry, served as a Presbyterian missionary to the Indians in what was later Oklahoma and then helped to begin Presbyterian churches in Minnesota. For many years he was Presbyterian "Superintendent of Missions for Western Iowa, Nebraska, Dakota, Montana, Wyoming, and Utah." He travelled throughout that vast area planting churches, enlisted in the East young men to serve as their pastors, and extended his labours to Colorado, New Mexico, Arizona, and Nevada. He spent the last period of his life in Alaska, especially serving the Indians and introducing reindeer from Siberia to provide food for the Eskimos.

Three of the interdenominational societies which we have mentioned, the American Bible Society, the American Tract Society, and the American Sunday School Union, drew their support from others in addition to Congregationalists and Presbyterians. They covered both the frontier and the older sections of the country. Several times during the century, first in 1829, the American Bible Society attempted to put a copy of the Scriptures in every family in the United States, including both the cities and the frontier. In 1830 the American Sunday School Union framed a programme for organizing a Sunday School in every community west of the Alleghenies where one was needed, and doing it within two years. In 1832 the American Tract Society adopted a plan to place some of its literature in every religiously destitute family in the United States. In 1847 most of its 267 colporteurs were in the

Mississippi Valley, in much of which frontier conditions still prevailed.

Another channel through which Christianity spread on the frontier was educational institutions planted under the auspices of the several denominations. In time each of the major and some of the minor denominations had a chain of academies, colleges, and universities stretching across the country, most of them founded when frontier conditions existed in their respective regions. In them in their pioneer days men and women taught at great personal sacrifice to give an education to the laity and prospective clergy of churches in the new communities and to train under Christian auspices leaders for the future commonwealths.

To the denominations that rose or flourished on the frontier one more large one was added after 1815, the Church of Jesus Christ of Latter Day Saints, more generally known as the Mormons. Eventually, although not until after 1914, it had a membership of over a million. Its founder, Joseph Smith (1805–1844), was born in Vermont of old New England stock. He was from a family of the floating, semi-illiterate, poverty-stricken type which was frequently found on or near the frontier. As a boy he went with his parents to Western New York, then not far removed from pioneer conditions. The region had been swept by revivals preached by itinerant or semi-itinerant Baptists and Methodists and Smith was touched by them. Impatient with existing denominational differences and eager to know which was right, he believed that he had visions which told him that no existing ecclesiastical body represented the divine will and that God had chosen him to restore the true Church. He maintained that at the behest of the visions he dug in a hill, found a book written in strange characters, and translated it through miraculous assistance. This translation was published in 1830 as the *Book of Mormon.* It contained extensive excerpts from both the Old and New Testaments along with what purported to be a history of peoples descended from a family which, fleeing from Jerusalem before its fall to the Babylonians, had made its way to America. To the *Book of Mormon* was later added a *Book of Commandments,* soon called *Doctrine and Covenants,* which came out of the sermons and revelations of Smith.

The Church of Jesus Christ of Latter Day Saints was founded by Smith in 1830 in Seneca County, New York. Self-confident, tall, athletic, witty, of distinguished appearance, Smith attracted followers. They made their centre first in Ohio, then in Missouri, and eventually in Illinois. They were persecuted and in Illinois Smith was killed. The majority then followed one of Smith's early converts, Brigham Young (1801–1877), to Utah. There, beyond what was at that time the frontier, Young led them in forming an idealistic community. Young was an extraordinarily able organizer and administrator. Under him a closely knit economic-social-ecclesiastical community grew up. It increased rapidly, partly through a high birth rate to polygamous marriages which Young set the example of contracting and partly through converts who were won from the underprivileged partly in the United States but mostly in Europe by extensive and zealous missions. Polygamy was later discontinued, but the Church of Jesus Christ of Latter Day Saints continued to mount in numbers. A minority of Smith's disciples did not follow Bringham Young to Utah but, under Joseph Smith, Junior (1832–1914), moved to Iowa and then to Missouri. It did not practise polygamy and did not become nearly as large as the other wing.

The chief growth of Christianity on the frontier was not by the Mormons, numerous though they became, but, as we have suggested, by Baptists, Methodists, and the Disciples of Christ or Christians. They spoke the language of the common frontiersman and knew how to win him. Congregationalists, Presbyterians, and Episcopalians, with their highly educated ministry, as a rule could not effectively reach the rank and file but attracted mainly the better educated minority.

HOLDING OR WINNING THE IMMIGRANTS: THE PHENOMENAL GROWTH OF THE ROMAN CATHOLIC CHURCH

What of the nineteenth century immigration from abroad? How well was it held to its inherited forms of the faith or won by other branches of the Church? The flood that poured in was prodigious. Down to the 1880's it was mostly from the British Isles and North-western Europe. Between 1820 and 1865 nearly two million came from Ireland, most of them poverty-stricken, seeking escape from intolerable economic conditions rendered acute by the famine of the 1840's which followed the blight that killed the potatoes upon which much of the population depended for food. In that same period about a million and a half Germans entered and about three-quarters of a million from England. Hundreds of thousands also came from Scandinavia. In the last decades of the century the majority of the immigrants were from Italy, Central Europe, Russia, Greece, the Balkans, and the Near East. Several hundred thousand French Canadians moved south, principally into New England. Into the South-west filtered Mexicans, by 1914 about a quarter of a million. Except for Jews, the overwhelming majority of the immigrants were from Christian backgrounds. A few tens of thousands of Chinese and Japanese entered, almost all of them non-Christians, but legislation prevented either group from totalling more than 100,000. Numbers of the immigrants became farmers, many of them on the frontier in the Middle and Far West. However, the majority made their homes in the manufacturing and mining towns and cities of the North-east. There the first generation, usually poor, eked out a living as unskilled labourers in mines and factories or in building railroads.

We have hinted at the problem which the immigrants presented. Coming to a land where churches depended upon voluntary offerings, would they contribute out of their poverty to erect churches and parochial schools and to train and support teachers and clergy? Whether Roman Catholics, Protestants, or Orthodox, they did so to an amazing degree.

This was not always or even predominantly from religious motives. The Church formed the main tie with the old home. Its worship was familiar, its sermons were in the mother tongue, and in Protestant churches the services were in the old country vernacular. The churches were social centres where the immigrant could find those of his native speech and cultural background. Denominations tended to arrange themselves according to national origins. Although, as we shall see in a moment, the Roman Catholic Church brought all its adherents together under one hierarchical structure, individual parishes were often predominantly or entirely of one nation.

Whether Roman Catholic or Protestant, the success of the Church in holding the immigrants was not due entirely or even chiefly to sociological factors. Had there not been in it inner vitality, greater than that of any social institution which came out of the immigrants' background except the family, the Church would not have existed. The immigrants were attracted not merely because the Church provided social centres. They were drawn by the religious imperative.

To the Roman Catholic Church the immigrants were both a problem and an opportunity. At the outset of the nineteenth century Roman Catholics were only a small minority in the United States. So far as they had any religious attachment, the overwhelming majority of the population was Protestant. In contrast, in 1910 about seven and a half millions of the foreign born, approximately 60 per cent. of those in that category, were Roman Catholics in background. It was no easy task to make provision for the religious education and spiritual care of these millions. They were in danger either of drifting entirely away from the faith or of being assimilated to the prevailing Protestantism. Moreover, the Roman Catholic Church operated in the face of chronic Protestant opposition which from time to time broke out into active and even violent anti-Roman Catholic movements. In the 1830's and 1840's the Native American Association opposed the easy naturalization of foreigners, most of whom were Irish and Germans, and was anti-Roman Catholic. It was followed in the 1850's by the Know Nothing Party and in the latter part of the century by the American Protective Association.

To help meet the challenge personnel and money were contributed from

Roman Catholics of Canada and the Old World. From Canada came clergy and nuns to serve their fellow-countrymen. Some priests and sisters were sent from France, but since very few immigrants were from that country and other nationalities found them difficult, theirs was a minor role. Numbers of priests, especially regulars, were from Belgium. In 1857 there was founded at Louvain, in Belgium, an American College in which in the course of seventy-five years over a thousand young Americans were prepared for the priesthood. Many priests, lay brothers, and nuns were from Ireland, Germany, and Switzerland. Some money came from Europe. It was partly with the purpose of collecting it for the United States that the Society for the Propagation of the Faith was organized (1822). For years the United States was the chief beneficiary of the Ludwig-Missionsverein which was founded in Bavaria to raise money for missions. In 1871 the Raphaelsverein was begun under the leadership of Cahensly, a merchant, for the purpose of aiding German immigrants.

The Raphaelsverein was the chief source of what is usually known as the Cahensly movement. That movement declared that by ignoring their national origins the Roman Catholic Church was losing thousands of the immigrants. As a remedy it urged that separate parishes and missions be set up for the several nationalities, that each of them be entrusted to priests of the appropriate nation, that in the parochial schools instruction be given entirely in the language of the parents, that church societies be grouped by nationalities, and that in each diocese the bishop be appointed from whichever group was in the numerical ascendancy. This would have made for a church organized by trans-Atlantic national patterns. It was viewed with alarm by non-Roman Catholics as preventing assimilation to American life and as threatening disloyalty to the United States. The American hierarchy were opposed to the plan, for it was a menace to the unity of the Church and gave ground for the charge that the Roman Catholic Church was promoting un-American enclaves. Rome sided with the hierarchy and the movement died.

Extensive as was the aid which came from abroad to help the Roman Catholic Church hold its hereditary constituency to the faith, even more was from Roman Catholics in the United States. Theological seminaries for training youths for the priesthood were begun. By 1900 they numbered thirty-seven and in 1915 preparatory seminaries totaled thirty-four. An American College in Rome, founded in 1859, was supported by funds from many dioceses. In addition to the orders and congregations of Old World origin which more and more recruited their ranks from native-born youths, new ones sprang up in the United States. Especially was this true of sisterhoods, most of them with teaching as their purpose.

Most of the funds for the construction and maintenance of Roman Catholic churches and schools and for the support of clergy, monks, and nuns came, not from Europe but from the immigrants and their children. In 1910, for instance, nearly a million and a quarter pupils were in parochial schools. This achievement becomes all the more remarkable when we recall the poverty of the vast majority of the immigrants.

Roman Catholic priests, monks, and nuns were recruited chiefly from those of Irish and German birth or descent. This seems to have been partly because until past the middle of the century these two nationalities constituted the bulk of the Roman Catholic immigration and partly because in the mother country they were the more actively loyal. As we have seen, for the Irish the Roman Catholic Church had been the tie and the symbol of Irish nationalism as against the English overlords.

Several of the Uniate Churches were represented among the immigrants. Some provision was made to supply them with clergy of their own rites and thus to keep them from being lost to the Church. The Ruthenians constituted the largest of these bodies. They were mainly concentrated in the coal mining communities in Pennsylvania. By 1909 they had a bishop and more than a hundred churches and priests. From time to time groups of Ruthenians, dissatisfied with attempts to alter their traditions and bring them more nearly into conformity with the Roman pattern, went over to the Russian Orthodox Church.

Efforts were put forth by Protestants of the older American stock to win Roman Catholics. This was partly through interdenominational agencies but chiefly through denominational societies. Numerically these attempts had only slight success. Foreign language churches composed of former Roman Catholics were few and usually small. As time passed, especially after 1914, and the immigrants were more and more assimilated into the patterns of life of the United States, an increasing number of Roman Catholics joined Protestant churches. However, in doing so they went, not into churches which were especially designed for them, but into congregations which were prevailingly of the traditionally Protestant elements of the population. Some of this was by marriage to Protestants, some was because of residence in predominantly Protestant communities, some from the desire to be accepted socially, and some from profound religious conviction. Although accurate statistics are lacking, it seems probable that most of such Roman Catholics as abandoned their hereditary faith did not become Protestants but drifted away from all religion.

Roman Catholics also endeavoured to win Protestants. There were notable converts. One of them founded the Sisters of Charity of Emmitsburg, Maryland. Another, Isaac Thomas Hecker (1819–1888), a scion of German immigrant stock, was the chief mover in the formation of the Missionary Society of St. Paul the Apostle, whose members were better known as the Paulists. At first made up mostly of converts, it sought to adapt Roman Catholicism to the American environment and thus to attract Protestants. However, accessions through these direct methods were not numerous. They came mainly through marriages with Roman Catholics.

By the year 1914 the Roman Catholic Church, while having only a minority of the total church membership, was the largest of the Christian denominations in the United States. It counted between fifteen and seventeen millions as being in its fold. Its hierarchical structure covered the entire nation. Chiefly dependent as it was on the nineteenth century immigration, it was strongest in the places where this had settled—in the urban centres of the North-east, in many of the cities of the Middle West and West, and in some rural sections in the Middle West. Through the French and Spanish background of these areas, it had pockets of strength in Louisiana and the South-west. Because of the comparative absence of the nineteenth century immigration, with the exception of Louisiana it was weak in the Southern states east of the Mississippi.

The Roman Catholic Church in the United States was knit together as one ecclesiastical body loyal to Rome. In 1829 what was called the First Provincial Council was held in Baltimore and directly or by association was representative of all the hierarchy of the nation. Six other provincial councils of Baltimore followed. In 1852 the First Plenary Council met. It was a demonstration of the growth of the Roman Catholic Church and its hierarchy and sought to give unity to it in the United States. Other such gatherings convened. In the Roman Catholic Church in the United States there were many differences due partly to the diverse national sources from which it was drawn and partly to contrasts between outstanding members of the episcopate. Yet, with the exception of a few small minorities, the faithful had no thought of rebelling against Rome. Until 1908 the Holy See exercised control through the Congregation for the Propagation of the Faith. In that year the United States was removed from the jurisdiction of the Propaganda. The act was a formal recognition that the Roman Catholic Church in that country had come of age.

Before that step was taken it had become clear that the Roman Catholic Church in the United States could be trusted to hold to the faith and not to succumb to the predominantly Protestant environment by which it was encompassed or to the diverse national origins of its constituency. It had successfully overcome what at the time seemed major dangers. One was trusteeism, the effort of local congregations represented by trustees who were the legal owners of the property of a parish to choose and dismiss pastors without reference to the ecclesiastical superiors. This procedure had seemed to be in accord with American democratic principles, but it limited the authority of the bishop. Eventually a series of court decisions recognized the bishop as in control of the property of each congregation. A plan approved by the Holy See (1911) vested the property in a board of trustees composed of the bishop, the vicar general, the parish priest, and two laymen approved by the bishop. Another danger was one which we have already mentioned, that rivalries among the several national groups would tear the Church apart. Thus early in the century the appointment of French priests to predominantly Irish parishes and of French bishops to sees in which the Irish were numerous aroused deep resentment among the latter. In Charleston and Philadelphia open rebellion was followed by schisms and in New York there were quarrels over the issue. We have noted the Cahensly movement, a feature of the chronic friction between the Irish and the Germans.

Late in the century came agitation over what was known as Americanism. The storm centered around Hecker and especially around his methods as described in a French translation of his biography and in an enthusiastic introduction by the translator commending him as worthy of imitation by the French clergy. The founder of the Paulists, Hecker had been prominent and persuasive in presenting the Roman Catholic faith to non-Roman Catholics. To meet the widespread criticism that the Roman Catholic Church was from another culture and alien to the American tradition and way of life, he had insisted that as the Church divinely appointed for all mankind it was adaptable to the religious needs of every people and culture, including the United States. Many, especially in Europe, believed that by this Hecker meant that to gain converts missionaries should pass over or modify doctrines which gave offense and allow each individual in terms of American freedom, to follow his own judgement without reference to the Church and its hierarchy. A tempest arose in the Roman Catholic press, and in some circles in Europe the Roman Catholic Church in the United States was looked at askance as at least verging on heresy and perhaps as actually guilty of it. In 1899 the Pope sent a kind but firm formal letter, *Testem benevolentiæ*, to Cardinal Gibbons, the outstanding member of the hierarchy in the United States, condemning views which the critics had said characterized "Americanism" and setting forth the proper stand on the issues under discussion. The American bishops hastened to say that they were completely in accord with the letter and declared that the errors which it condemned were by no means widespread.

Although it did so without compromising its inherited faith, in important ways the Roman Catholic Church in the United States reflected its environment. This arose from the problems forced on it by the vast influx of immigrants who were of its fold. As we have seen, it had to give itself to an almost impossible programme of recruiting and training clergy, nuns, and lay brothers, of erecting thousands of churches, and of developing a system of schools from the elementary grades through theological seminaries and universities. In this it did what only a few Protestant denominations attempted. The majority of Protestant churches did not have elementary schools on the parish level. They maintained secondary schools, theological schools, colleges, and universities, but for the primary grades they depended on the schools financed and managed by the state, and for the religious instruction of their children they relied upon the home, the Sunday School, a large number of youth organizations closely or loosely related to the churches, catechetical classes, and the regular services of the Church. The Roman Catholic Church was not content to trust its children to the public schools. It had long insisted that training the child was its obligation. It held that religion must be fully integrated with the rest of education. As we have seen (Chapter XLVI), in the *Syllabus of Errors* Pius IX expressed the official attitude of Rome in condemning the growing practice of freeing schools from all ecclesiastical authority and of putting the civil power in full control of the public schools. Although in a country in which it was a minority the Roman Catholic Church might perforce acquiesce in something less than its ideal, it could do so only as a temporary expedient until such time as it was in the clear majority. In the meantime it must, where possible, set up schools of its own. The First Provincial Council (1829), representing the hierarchy of the country, decreed that wherever possible each parish should have a school. This was reiterated by the First Plenary Council. In 1875 the Third Plenary Council ordered the erection of a school near each church within two years, declared it to be the obligation of Roman Catholic parents to send their children to these schools unless they were otherwise adequately instructed, and recommended that pastors who were negligent in carrying out the programme be removed.

Leading Roman Catholic bishops advocated state aid to religious schools, but this aroused controversy and reduced the likelihood of its being given. An attempt was made at compromise, the so-called Faribault plan from the city in Minnesota where it was tried, by which the state leased the parish school buildings during school hours and paid nuns who taught in them. On this, however, the bishops were not united. In general the Church erected and maintained its own schools and staffed them with members of its sisterhoods, teaching brotherhoods, or monastic orders. The Catholic University of America was opened in the national capital in 1889 under the control of the hierarchy. It tended to be Irish, and, drawn into some of the controversies which were agitating the Church, including that between the Irish and the Germans, it grew slowly.

Numbers of religious orders and congregations, both of men and of women, entered the country, and for them physical plants had to be provided. Many hospitals and orphanages were founded and equipped.

All this building of churches, schools, monasteries, seminaries, colleges, universities, hospitals, and orphanages entailed raising money from a constituency most of whom were of the poor of the land. This meant that the clergy and especially the bishops were of necessity promoters, organizers, and administrators. They tended to be activists. Periodicals of various kinds were numerous, but scholarship was slow in developing. No great theologians emerged. Sanctity of the traditional kind was rare: by the middle of the twentieth century only one citizen of the United States had been canonized, and she was not native born, but was an Italian immigrant nun. Outstanding representatives of the life of prayer and mystics of the first water were either few or entirely lacking. The energies of the Church were too absorbed in caring for the immigrants to permit much share in the missions outside the United States.

With the dwindling of immigration to a trickle after 1914 these qualities distinctive of the Roman Catholic Church in the United States began to change, but not rapidly.

A Roman Catholic organization which was distinctly American was the Knights of Columbus. Organized in New Haven, Connecticut, in 1882, it eventually spread throughout the country. It was similar to the many fraternal bodies which flourished in the United States, such as the Masons and the Oddfellows, and had as one of its outstanding features a plan of life insurance for its members. It also engaged in various charitable undertakings and in attempts to present the Roman Catholic faith to non-Roman Catholics.

Moreover, in part reflecting the predominantly Protestant environment, the Roman Catholic Church in the United States did not display some of the features which marked it in prevailingly Roman Catholic lands. Public religious processions were less in evidence. Shrines of healing, such as that at Lourdes, were not as prominent. Much of the popular Roman Catholicism which to the Protestant appeared superstition was either absent or inconspicuous.

It was not strange that out of the struggle to care for the immigrant and build the Church some extraordinarily able Roman Catholic bishops emerged, with something of the breadth of vision which is often termed statesmanship. Even to enumerate them would unduly prolong these pages. The most eminent was James Gibbons (1834–1921). A native of Baltimore, he was ordained priest in 1861, rose rapidly, was the youngest bishop at the Vatican Council, in 1877 became Archbishop of Baltimore, and in 1886 was created cardinal, the second from the United States to attain that **dignity**. He wrote extensively but not profoundly. He was ardently American, approved the separation of Church and state, threw the weight of his position and skill on the side of giving the Roman Catholic Church in the United States a unified structure rather than letting it divide on national lines inherited from Europe, worked for the founding of the Catholic University of America as a national institution, and in the controversy over the Knights of Labour in the 1880's came out flatly for the right of labour to organize.

HOLDING THE IMMIGRANTS: THE EASTERN CHURCHES

Some thousands of the immigrants were members of one or another branch of the Orthodox Church. Before 1815 the Russian Orthodox Church had missions in Alaska. When, in 1867, Alaska was bought by the United States the Church continued, although without the financial support of the Russian Government. In 1872 the bishop transferred his residence to San Francisco. In 1904 the see was raised to an archiepiscopate, and in 1905 its headquarters were moved to New York City. Until after 1914 it had jurisdiction over all the Orthodox in the United States. The numbers of the Orthodox mounted rapidly in the latter part of the century. Greeks, Roumanians, Bulgars, Serbs, Syrians, and Albanians were among them. Armenians arrived, especially after the massacres of the 1890's in their home land. Jacobites and Nestorians were also among the immigrants. For all of these congregations were organized and clergy obtained.

HOLDING AND WINNING THE IMMIGRANTS: THE PROTESTANTS

The Protestant immigrants were partly from the British Isles and partly from the Continent of Europe. If they sought a church connexion, those from the British Isles, a minority of the whole, had little difficulty in fitting into the churches of the older American stock. Most of these churches were offshoots of British denominations, orders of service and hymns tended to be the same as in their British counterparts, and Americans were often familiar with current developments in theology and religious life in the British Isles. Communicants of the Church of England were easily at home in the Protestant Episcopal Church with its familiar Book of Common Prayer, vestments, and architecture. Presbyterians from Scotland and the North of Ireland did not feel the Presbyterianism of the United States entirely alien. Congregationalists, Baptists, and Methodists often found congenial the corresponding churches in the United States. Welsh Calvinistic Methodists and Welsh Congregationalists for a time formed distinct churches in which the Welsh language was used, but as the younger generation grew to maturity with English as their tongue the former merged with the Presbyterians (although not until 1920) and the latter went into the wider Congregational fellowship.

In somewhat similar fashion the majority of the immigrants of the Reformed faith from the Netherlands, large numbers of whom settled in Michigan, were absorbed into the Dutch Reformed Church, later called the Reformed Church in America. A minority, ultra-conservative, withdrew (1857) and formed what eventually (1904) was known as the Christian Reformed Church. So, too, from immigrants from Hungary of that faith there was organized (1904), with assistance from the homeland, the Hungarian Reformed Church in America.

A very large proportion of the Protestant immigration was German. Many had been largely de-Christianized by the rationalistic and politically radical movements of the day. Numbers of others were glad to be freed from the obligations to support the Landeskirchen of the homeland. Yet others were earnestly Christian and took the initiative in welcoming and even seeking pastors.

A small minority of the Germans were Mennonites, many of whom were from Russia. They had earlier sought haven in that empire and when conditions became adverse came to the United States, hoping for the religious liberty and freedom to abide by their pacifist principles the promise of which had lured them to the tsar's domains. They divided into several groups.

A considerable minority of the Germans were of the Reformed faith and were eventually served either by missionaries of that confession from Germany or by pastors from the German Reformed Church which had its stronghold in Pennsylvania. Others, also a minority, were from the Evangelical churches which had arisen in Prussia and some other German states from the union of Lutheran and Reformed.

The majority of the German Protestants were Lutheran by heredity. Indeed, that was true of Protestants in general from the Continent of Europe. In contrast with the Roman Catholics, no centre of administrative or doctrinal control existed for Lutherans, whether German or Scandinavian, either in Europe or in America. As we have seen, in Europe Lutheranism was divided, partly by territorial, partly by national, and partly by theological groupings. Pietism was also a pervasive influence and sometimes was a source of controversy. In the United States all these factors entered and were complicated by others of American origin. By 1914, next to the Roman Catholics, Baptists, and Methodists, the Lutherans constituted the largest family of churches in the United States. However, they were not an integrated family, but, as we shall see, were badly severed. For a variety of reasons, some linguistic, for they were slow to use English in their services, some doctrinal, and some from the fact that, being state churches in Europe they were inclined to look with disfavour and even contempt on other denominations, they tended to hold aloof from non-Lutheran

Protestants and were tardy in moving into the main stream of American religious life.

In general the Lutheran bodies in the United States were conservative. The Biblical scholarship and the theological ferment which were marked in German universities in the nineteenth century and which profoundly affected Continental European and British Protestantism and much of the Protestantism of the older American stock were, with a few exceptions, rejected. That kind of Christianity seemed not to have enough dynamic to inspire and sustain those who held to it to undertake the hard labour required to gather and nurture churches in the rough and often raw environment of a new country. It was Pietists and those who held staunchly to unmodified older Lutheranism who were mainly responsible for the founding and growth of Lutheran Churches in the United States. We have seen (Chapter XLVII) that in Germany these strains had enjoyed a revival in the fore part of the nineteenth century, partly as a reaction against the rationalism of the Enlightenment and the French Revolution.

It was the American Lutheranism of the eighteenth century which had been organized by Henry M. Muhlenberg (Chapter XLI) which constituted the nucleus of what by the formation of the United Lutheran Church (1918) out of three other bodies, the General Synod, the General Council, and the United Synod, South, became the largest of the Lutheran bodies of the United States. The General Synod, the first Lutheran organization which aspired to be nation-wide, was constituted in 1820. Its early years were stormy but it was saved from dissolution by Samuel Simon Schmucker (1799–1873). Reared in a Pietist minister's family, the best educated clergyman of his church in his day, Schmucker became the initial professor in its first theological seminary, at Gettysburg. A leading advocate of Christian unity and of fraternal relations among the denominations, he also endeavoured to nourish in his own fellowship an intelligent loyalty to Lutheranism. Missionaries, many of them graduates of Gettysburg, went to the West and the General Synod extended its boundaries far beyond the older states. In Schmucker's later years, partly under the influence of the newer immigration, Lutheranism became more emphatically confessional and he was rejected as too liberal, too willing to conform to the American environment, and even as heretical. For a time the General Synod languished because of withdrawals. During the Civil War the Lutherans in the Southern states separated and formed what was eventually the United Synod of the South. In 1867 the General Council was constituted, partly by groups from the General Synod with additions of other synods and with Charles Porterfield Krauth (1823–1883) as its leading spirit. It was not until 1918, as we have said, that the three were fused in the United Lutheran Church.

In the West still more conservative Lutheranism arose. Its conservatism was accentuated by the desire to hold to the German language, dislike for the use of English which was creeping into the General Synod, and distrust of the tendencies in that body to depart from staunch Lutheranism. It was also in part a phase of the reaction against rationalism which was seen in some Lutheran circles in Germany and against the union of Lutherans and Reformed.

The largest of the conservative Lutheran bodies and one which eventually vied with the United Lutheran Church as the most numerous Lutheran group in the United States was officially called the German Evangelical Lutheran Synod of Missouri, Ohio, and other States, but was usually known as the Missouri Synod. It was constituted in 1847. The leader in its creation was Carl Ferdinand Wilhelm Walther (1811–1887). The son of a Saxon parsonage, a great lover of music, under pressure from his father Walther had enrolled in Leipzig, as a student of theology. There, poverty-stricken and troubled by doubts, he came in touch with a Pietist circle and rebelled against the prevailing rationalism of the university. He came to the United States in a company of about seven hundred led by a pastor, Martin Stephan, for whom he had a great admiration. They formed a colony near St. Louis. Stephan proved to be a libertine and a rascal and was deposed. This disillusioning experience might well have been followed by the disintegration of the colony. Walther rose to the emergency. Characterized by an extraordinary combination of organizing ability, a genius for friendship, magnetic charm with audiences large and small, generous hospitality, an enormous capacity for work, a mastery of the Lutheran theology of the sixteenth and seventeenth centuries and its literature, a skill in vigorous polemics, and a self denial which was content with frugal living and which turned the income from the sale of his writings into synodical channels, he enabled the Missouri Synod to achieve phenomenal dimensions. Through the periodicals which he founded and edited, a weekly, *Der Lutheraner,* and a monthly, *Lehre und Wehre,* he exerted a continuous and pervasive influence. In Concordia Seminary in St. Louis and its branches in other cities a growing leadership was raised up, shaped by the strict Lutheranism of the pre-rationalistic period. A network of parochial schools undergirded the whole. Lutheran pastors from Germany, also conservative theologically, were attracted, with their congregations. A system of inspection by district presidents helped to knit the synod together and to prevent departure from strict adherence to its doctrinal standards. Before his death Walther saw the Synod expand to fifteen hundred congregations and nearly a thousand pastors. He also became the first President of the Lutheran Synodical Conference of North America. Organized in 1872, it drew into association with the Missouri Synod several other synods on a plan which emphasized the autonomy of the congregation. After Walther's death the Missouri Synod continued to expand. It reached from the Pacific to the Atlantic and had strong foreign missions.

Other Lutheran synods arose out of the nineteenth century immigration of Germans. We must not take the space even to name all of them. One, centering in Buffalo, was in some ways even more conservative than the Missouri Synod and was charged by Walther with continuing too much of the Roman Catholic tradition. Another, the Evangelical Synod of Iowa and Other States, was largely the creation of missionaries sent from the Missions Institute of Neuendettelsau by Konrad Wilhelm Loehe, a leader in the Inner Mission who had become interested in the needs of the Germans in America. For a time the Neuendettelsau men worked with the Missouri Synod, but Walther and Loehe had differences as to the nature of the Church and its ministry which were not removed by a trip that Walther made to Germany for a conference with Loehe. The Synod of Iowa and Other States established churches in every state west of the Mississippi except Arizona and New Mexico. Into it eventually went the Lutheran Evangelical Synod of Texas which was the outgrowth of the labours of men from the Pilgrim Mission of St. Chrischona.

Missionaries who helped in more than one synod came from the missionary training institution at Basel, from a missionary society founded by Pastor Goss-ner of Berlin, from the Rhenish Missionary Society, and from Barmen.

Out of the German immigration there sprang what was at first known as the *Kirchenverein des Westens* and then as the Evangelical Synod of the West. In it Lutherans and Reformed united. Congregations of Germans in which Lutherans and Reformed combined early came into being in several centres in the West. When Germans of Lutheran and Reformed background first moved into a community in the West the bond of language and nationality often drew them together. This was facilitated by clergymen in whom Pietist convictions and a theology which embraced features common to both were stronger than the differences which separated the Lutherans and the Reformed. Moreover, many of the immigrants were from German states in which Lutherans and Reformed had fused into one Evangelical Church. While in the freedom of the New World some immigrants took the opportunity vigorously to repudiate that union and joined outspokenly Lutheran synods, others held to it. In its early years the *Kirchenverein des Westens* owed much to missionaries from Bremen, Strassburg, and the Rhenish Missionary Society. It was especially in-debted to the men from Basel, for the latter, Pietists trained in a school which held both Lutherans and Reformed, found the union natural. The *Kirchen-verein des Westens* spread widely in Missouri, Indiana, Illinois, Ohio, Iowa, and Wisconsin, and in 1877 its successor, the Evangelical Synod of the West, drew in other similar bodies to form the Evangelical Synod of North America.

In 1910 about a million and a quarter in the United States were of Scandinavian birth, the outcome of a vast movement in the latter part of the nineteenth century. A small sprinkling came from Iceland, about a sixth were from Denmark, about a third from Norway, and slightly more than a half from Sweden. Here also, because of geography and their Lutheran-Scandinavian culture, may be classed the Finns. In the United States the Scandinavians were widely scattered, but the majority settled in the block of territory made up of Northern Illinois, Iowa, Wisconsin, Minnesota, and the Dakotas. Since Lutheranism was the state religion in the Scandinavian countries and embraced the overwhelming majority of the population, almost all the immigrants were technically of that faith. While in the new environment some of them left it, either to drift entirely away from Christianity or to be enrolled in some non-Lutheran body, such as the Baptists or the Methodists, most of them were held to the Lutheran fold. The Scandinavian Lutherans grouped themselves ecclesiastically by languages and according to national origins.

The smaller groups can be quickly summarized. In 1885 those from Iceland formed themselves into a synod. The Danish Lutherans were of various ecclesiastical traditions. They were chiefly of the high church wing, of the Grundtvig tradition, or of the Inner Mission, with kinship to Pietism. Separate churches arose, but in 1906 the two largest united to form the United Danish Evangelical Lutheran Church in America, from which the word Danish was later deleted. By 1914 the Finns were in three distinct Lutheran churches.

In the Norwegian immigration several Lutheran traditions were represented which issued in distinct bodies. Among them were Haugeans, Grundtvigians with a high church background, and some who were opposed to coöperation with the Missouri Synod. In 1917 the majority came together to form the Norwegian Lutheran Church of America. Eventually the word Norwegian was omitted and the name became the Evangelical Lutheran Church of America.

Several thousand Swedes were gathered into the Augustana Synod. The Augustana Synod was clearly Lutheran and obviously had the Church of Sweden for its mother. However, it had in it so strong a Pietist strain, and under the influence of the American environment was so modified in the direction of Presbyterianism and Congregationalism, that its parent looked at it askance and did not formally recognize it until 1903. Only a minority of the Swedes were gathered into the Augustana Synod. Many were drawn into two synods and some independent congregations, fruits of revivals and in part inspired by the Swedish Mission Covenant Church of the mother country (Chapter XLVII) which in 1885 united to form the Swedish Evangelical Mission Covenant.

The Protestant denominations of the older American stock attracted a greater number from the immigrants of Protestant background than they did from the Roman Catholics and Orthodox. Much of this was a phase of the assimilation, so natural as to be almost unnoticed, of individuals and families to the dominant culture. Some was into churches which maintained the language of the mother country. Of these the largest were the Methodists and the Baptists. The Methodists had several German conferences, a Danish-Norwegian Conference, and Swedish churches. Partly with the assistance of the American Baptist Home Mission Society and Baptist state conventions, Danish Baptist churches, Norwegian Baptist churches, Swedish Baptist churches, and German Baptist churches came into being and grouped themselves into associations and conferences. The American Home Missionary Society gave assistance to German pastors without asking them to change their denomination, but in the 1880's German Congregational churches became sufficiently numerous to constitute themselves into a distinct conference.

Of the large Jewish immigration only a small minority became Christians. Some of the latter were Protestant and some Roman Catholic. Few were in purely Jewish-Christian congregations. Most converts joined predominantly non-Jewish congregations. It is said that many became Christian Scientists, but accurate statistics could not be had. Most of the Jews who either drifted away from the synagogue or openly repudiated it did not become Christian but abandoned all religion.

Christianity, mainly Protestantism, made headway among the Chinese and Japanese. These peoples were restricted by discriminatory measures to small minorities in the continental United States and were mainly on the West Coast. They constituted the largest element of the population of Hawaii.

THE RAPID SPREAD OF CHRISTIANITY AMONG THE INDIANS

The Indians were a challenge to the Christian churches. They constituted only a small minority, for they seem never to have totalled as many as half a million. Yet they were found in every state. In 1815, in spite of missions among those nearest to the white settlements, the vast majority were non-Christian. In an utterly different stage of culture than the white man, their lands coveted by him, they were in constant danger of exploitation. The chronic friction broke out from time to time into open war, the inherited patterns of life disintegrated, and both morals and morale tended to deteriorate. Conscience prodded Christians to action. Some of this was by bringing pressure on the government to see that the Indians had fair treatment and an opportunity for the kind of education that would enable them to adjust successfully to the white man's world. Much was through missions which sought to win the Indians to the Christian faith.

A full account of Christian missions to the Indians would require several volumes. Since the Indians were divided into many tribes and languages and there were missions in almost every tribe, each with its own history and with varying degrees of success, the complete story has never been told. It would be a record of heroism, of mistakes and achievements, and of failures and successes spelled out in thousands of individual lives. Both Protestants and Roman Catholics would be included, for the two wings of Christianity won about equal numbers. There were also the much more restricted efforts of the Russian Orthodox in Alaska.

Extensive financial aid came from the United States Government, not with the purpose of furthering conversion but to schools conducted by missions, for these were a major means of education. As government schools increased the aid to mission schools was reduced. For some years after 1869, presumably to lift the Indian Service from the morass of incompetence and corruption into which it had fallen through political appointments, the nomination of government Indian agents was delegated to the several religious bodies.

A few of the more famous missions can be singled out for brief notice, not because they are typical, but as indications of the variety which characterized the record. One was among the Cherokees, a semi-civilized tribe which dwelt in the piedmont and mountains of the southern states from Virginia southward to Georgia and which in the fore part of the nineteenth century was imbibing much of the white man's culture. To them several Protestant bodies, especially the American Board of Commissioners for Foreign Missions, sent missionaries. Schools were started, churches were gathered, and able Cherokee youths were trained to lead the Christian community. Then the white peoples of the neighbouring regions, coveting their fertile lands, induced the United States Government to compel the Cherokees, along with other tribes, to move west of the Mississippi River, into what was eventually administered as Indian Territory, the later state of Oklahoma. Two of the missionaries of the American Board went to prison to test the legality of a law of Georgia which deprived the Indians of their lands and in other ways the American Board strove to prevent the deportation. When, mainly in the 1820's and 1830's in spite of protests, the Cherokees were forced to go West, missionaries went with them and sought to mitigate the hardships entailed and to aid the Indians in adjusting to their new homes.

Several missions arose out of an incident in the early part of the 1830's. In 1831 four Indians from beyond the Rocky Mountains came to St. Louis, then on the frontier of white settlement, seeking information about the pale-face's religion. Two of the four died while in St. Louis and while ill were baptized by Roman Catholics. The other two returned to their own people, but without the desired knowledge. The news of the Indians' quest made its way into the religious press. Both the Methodists and the American Board of Commissioners for Foreign Missions responded. The former soon began several missions in the Pacific North-west under the leadership of Jason Lee (1803–1845). Within the same decade the American Board inaugurated an enterprise in the Pacific North-west but farther inland. Its most famous figure was Marcus Whitman who, with his wife, was killed by the Indians in 1847. In the 1840's, partly under the stimulus of the Indian delegation to St. Louis and to a large degree through the initiative of a Jesuit, Pierre-Jean DeSmet (1801–1873), the Roman Catholics moved into a number of tribes in the Far West, including the Pacific North-west.

As a result of the efforts of Roman Catholics and Protestants, in 1914 about 120,000, approximately 45 per cent. of all the Indians, had a church connexion, slightly more than half of them as Protestants. This was a little larger than the percentage of church members in the white population. Beyond these bare statistics is a record of helping the Indians in various ways to make the painful adjustment to the engulfing culture of the white man. The adjustment was by no means fully successful, but that it was not less so was due in no small degree to the missionaries.

Winning, Freeing, and Advancing the Negroes

A challenge to Christianity of much larger dimensions than that presented by the Indians was that of the Negroes. In 1815 the Negroes constituted slightly less than a fifth of the total population. In 1910 they numbered 9,827,763, or a little over a tenth of the whole. In 1815 the vast majority were slaves in the Southern states and were pagans. Torn from their homes in Africa, scattered among the whites, and without their hereditary tribal organization, their ancestral culture and language quickly dropped from them. They acquired English and in additional ways began to adopt the ways of their masters. With this they tended to conform to the religion of their masters, especially since that was then spreading, chiefly by revivals and camp-meetings, among the partly de-Christianized white population. By the middle of the century emancipation had been achieved in the North. In the 1860's, largely under the pressure of the Christian conscience and through the tragic arbitrament of arms in the Civil War, emancipation was forced upon the South and so far as the Constitution of the United States could do it the Negroes were given civil rights and the franchise. This brought sudden and drastic changes to the Negroes and posed them and the nation with the problem of helping them and the white men to adjust themselves to the new status.

Before the Civil War considerable progress had been made in the conversion of the Negroes. In the South in 1859 Negro church members were said to number 468,000, of whom 215,000 were reported to be Methodists and 175,000 Baptists. The gain was partly through the efforts of white masters and mistresses, partly through white missionaries, especially Methodists, partly through the efforts of white pastors, and partly through Negro preachers. Some of the Negroes were members of white churches. More were in purely Negro churches. Two denominations, the African Methodist Church, later the African Methodist Episcopal Church, organized in 1816 in Philadelphia, and the African Methodist Episcopal Zion Church, which grew out of a congregation begun in 1800 in New York City and which in 1821 was formally organized, sprang up in the North. Some beginnings were made towards schools for the Negroes. By 1860 about 11.7 per cent. of the Negroes were church members, or about half the proportion of the whites who were then in churches. It is significant that most of the Negro Christians were of those denominations, the Methodists and Baptists, which flourished among the whites of lower income and educational levels. Moreover, few were Roman Catholics.

After emancipation the growth of Negro membership was rapid. In 1916 the total was reported as 4,602,805. This was about 44.2 per cent. of the total Negro population, a proportion which was almost exactly the same as that of whites in churches in that year. The overwhelming majority of the Negro membership was in denominations and congregations entirely under Negro control. Although with some encouragement by the whites, this was primarily by the choice of the Negroes themselves. Their churches were almost the only institutions in which they were fully independent of the white men. They were the Negroes' own. They were not only expressions of his religious life but were also social centres. Often insurance companies, burial societies, and banks were closely connected with them. The overwhelming majority of the Negro church members were still Baptists and Methodists. Whereas before emancipation Methodists had been more numerous than Baptists, by 1914 the reverse was the case. This seems significant, for in the South white Baptists outnumbered white Methodists and were on the average from a lower economic and educational level than were the latter. To this pattern the Negroes tended to conform. The Methodists and especially the Baptists ministered to the proletariat of the older American stock, white and black. There were Negro minorities in other churches. Some were in the Methodist Episcopal Church, the main Methodist organization of the North. A few were in the Protestant Episcopal Church. Others were Presbyterians. After emancipation several tens of thousands withdrew from the Roman Catholic Church in Louisiana, presumably to assert their independence. Roman Catholics had missions among them which multiplied in the latter part of the century, but without large numerical results.

In 1916 about nine-tenths of Negro church members were in five Baptist and Methodist bodies entirely controlled by them.

After emancipation, the assistance of white churches to the Negroes was chiefly in the realm of education. For years after the Civil War the white churches of the South, impoverished by that struggle, even when they had the desire did not have the financial resources to do much for the freedmen. In contrast the churches of the North felt an obligation to help and had the financial means to do so. They believed that they could be of most use by furthering the preparation of leaders. Several denominations were active, but the most extensive programme was that of the American Missionary Association. Founded in 1846, from its inception it had been unequivocally against slavery. In principle it was undenominational and members of several churches contributed funds and personnel. However, it depended primarily on the Congregationalists. At the outset it sought to establish schools of all grades, from the elementary level through college and university. It also maintained theological schools to provide an educated ministry. However, by 1872 the governments of the Southern states had made such strides in opening and conducting elementary schools that the American Missionary Association confined its attention to secondary and higher education. Some of this was in handicrafts and agriculture and some of the kind offered in liberal arts colleges for the whites. Outstanding among the institutions inaugurated by the American Missionary Association were Hampton Institute, Atlanta University, and Fisk University. Several private foundations, initiated from avowedly Christian motives, also substantially aided Negro education. Especially notable were the gifts of John D. Rockefeller, partly through Baptist home mission societies and partly through the General Education Board which, an outgrowth of the Baptist Education Society, was incorporated in 1903.

The Negroes did much for themselves in education, in no small degree through their churches. Thus Booker T. Washington, who received most of his training at Hampton, was the chief creator of an institution at Tuskegee, Alabama, which was one of the most progressive in fitting the Negro to share and improve the life of the community.

In general, the Christianity of the Negroes was a modification and adaptation of the patterns of the white churches, especially of the Baptists and Methodists. There were prayer meetings, Sunday Schools, "revivals," and "protracted meetings." The Negro "spirituals" which were a distinct contribution to the hymnody of the United States had white prototypes. Yet the Negro added something of his own. His religious gatherings often had a heightened emotionalism beyond what was seen among the whites. Even if as a class the "spirituals" were originally inspired by white originals, the majority were entirely original both in words and music.

The advance made by Negroes in the first half century after emancipation was phenomenal. It left much to be achieved, but when it is remembered from what a low level it began and what had been accomplished in a little over a generation for a body of people who by 1914 numbered about ten millions, the record is amazing. To no small degree it was due to the fact that the Negroes were immersed in the white man's culture and because many whites gave themselves unselfishly to the freedmen and their children. Much must be ascribed to the native ability of the Negroes themselves. Not a little, however, was because of the impulse which came through Christianity.

The Effort to Win the Cities

Rapid though the growth of cities was in the Old World under the impetus and facilities of the industrial revolution, it was even greater in the United States. Millions flooded in from the rural districts and the majority of the immigrants from Europe chose for their homes not the country but the city, and this in spite of the fact that on the other side of the Atlantic most of them had been peasants. Could Christianity so adjust itself to the new urban conditions that it could not only hold those who before coming to the cities had had a church connexion but also win those who in their pre-urban days were among the de-Christianized elements of the population?

The Roman Catholic Church had remarkable success in meeting the challenge. For it the problem was probably less difficult than that presented by the cities on the Continent of Europe and was more nearly akin to that which it faced in the Irish in England and Scotland. As we have seen, the bulk of the nineteenth century Roman Catholic immigration went as unskilled labourers to the industrial, commercial, and mining towns and cities. There, because of its vitality and initiative, the Roman Catholic Church provided what were both religious and social centres which were the chief places where the immigrants, nostalgic and seeking fellowship with their own kind, found familiar ceremonies, an institution, the use of their native speech, and peoples which gave them a sense of being at home. They therefore rallied to them, much as did the Irish in a somewhat similar situation in the cities of Great Britain. In contrast, on the Continent of Europe, the urban industrial proletariat tended to be anti-clerical and to regard the Roman Catholic Church as a tool of exploiters. In the United States, however, the main strength of the Roman Catholic Church was in the hearts of the great cities.

Protestantism was not as successful in the centres of the cities as was the Roman Catholic Church. Its constituency was chiefly from the older American stock. This tended to move "uptown" and to the suburbs, for it prospered through the toil of the newer arrivals and found the physical and cultural environment more pleasant away from the older sections. In the latter the Protestants were usually either the very poor without much sense of community or cohesion, or, in their town houses, the very wealthy. In general the churches followed their constituencies. Protestant churches, some of them very strong, were numerous in the suburbs. Thus in time, so far as they retained a religious complexion, Boston and Manhattan Island were predominantly Roman Catholic, but Protestantism was vigorous on the fringing outskirts.

To this generalization there were many exceptions, some of them striking. Protestantism by no means abandoned the cities, not even the hearts of the largest of them. Nor did it entirely fail. In the cities of the United States the Young Men's and Young Women's Christian Associations had their greatest growth. Often erecting large buildings, they developed a varied programme, mainly for those in the lower income brackets of the middle class. In time the more strictly religious phases of their activities declined and stress was placed on the educational, social, and athletic aspects of their life. For the lowest income groups there were the Salvation Army and many "rescue missions."

As the years passed, itinerant "evangelists," those who gave themselves as missionaries to winning non-Christians and the de-Christianized, utilizing preaching, "personal work," and "revivals," devoted themselves increasingly to the cities. Their number was legion, but among them two stood out preëminently, Charles Grandison Finney (1792–1875) in the middle of the century and Dwight Lyman Moody (1837–1899) in the latter part of the century.

Born in New England, as a child Finney was taken to what was then the frontier in the west central part of New York. Handsome, musical, exuding energy, he was a leader among the youth, dissented from much of the preaching which he heard, and entered the legal profession. Then, still young, after intense struggle, he was converted and became a travelling preacher-missionary. He was the outstanding figure in the religious awakenings which swept across much of the North in the second quarter of the century. At the outset a Presbyterian, he eventually left that denomination, largely because, contrary to strict Calvinism, he taught that every individual had the ability to repent and in his preaching urged that all do so. At the height of his career as an evangelist he made New York City his headquarters, first as pastor of a Presbyterian Church and later in Broadway Tabernacle, erected especially for him, in which there grew up about him an independent Congregational church. He also had preaching tours in cities in the British Isles. From middle life until extreme old age he taught theology at Oberlin, an idealistic institution in Ohio which pioneered in the co-education of the sexes and in enrolling both Negroes and whites. There he was also pastor of the First Congregational Church and for fifteen years was president of the college.

In contrast with Finney, Moody was never ordained. He was born in Northfield, Massachusetts. His father died when he was a child and his formal education ended when he was thirteen. Baptized a Unitarian in the only church in his native town, when in his later teens he sought his fortune in Boston he came in contact with a Congregational church, was converted, and became active in its life. Then, still under twenty, he went to Chicago and quickly proved himself a successful salesman of shoes. However, he devoted an increasing proportion of his abounding vitality to voluntary religious work, organizing a Sunday School, prayer meetings, home visitation, and welfare activities, and promoting preaching and efforts to win individuals one by one. In 1860, in his early twenties, he gave up business and became an independent city missionary. He gathered an undenominational church and was a secretary and then president of the Young Men's Christian Association of Chicago. For about two years, 1873 to 1875, as we have seen, he held evangelistic meetings in the British Isles. There and through much of the rest of his life he had as an associate Ira David Sankey (1840–1908). Sankey was a singer who usually played his own accompaniments on a reed organ. With deep conviction and with emotional feeling he made popular "Gospel hymns" a means of stirring audiences, large and small. The Moody and Sankey tour of the British Isles culminated in meetings in London which attracted wide attention. Returning to the United States, Moody, often with Sankey, conducted similar meetings in many cities and with great effect. In 1881–1884 and 1891–1892 he made other prolonged tours in the British Isles. Although equipped with only an elementary education, he was increasingly acceptable among students, had missions in American and British universities, and, beginning in 1886, chaired student conferences at or near his home in Northfield. The profits from the sales of the *Gospel Hymns* went largely into a school for girls at Northfield and one for boys in the adjacent Mt. Hermon, both for those of limited means. Making no pretense of being a profound theologian, believing unquestioningly in the Bible as the word of God, Moody, stressing the love of God for all men, wished all men everywhere to know of that love and, repenting, to accept it. Irenic, possessed of excellent judgement, he worked happily with men of quite different religious convictions, enlisted the help of such scholars as George Adam Smith and Henry Drummond, and commanded the confidence of many different elements, including business men of large means. He had a wide and profound influence through the length and breadth of Protestantism in the English-speaking world, especially that of the Evangelical tradition, and through it upon much of mankind.

It was through the preaching not only of itinerant "evangelists" but also of resident pastors that Protestantism made its impression on the burgeoning cities of the United States. There were many ministers of urban churches who had a wide hearing, not only by huge audiences reached by the voice but also by much larger constituencies, often nation wide, who read their sermons and books. Two of the most outstanding were Henry Ward Beecher (1813–1887) and Phillips Brooks (1835–1893).

Henry Ward Beecher was one of a remarkable family of children which included Harriet Beecher Stowe whose novels, especially *Uncle Tom's Cabin,* had an enormous circulation. His father, Lyman Beecher (1775–1863), was one of the most distinguished preachers of "revivals" of the first half of the century. Lyman Beecher was himself an example of the effort to reach the cities, for beginning as pastor in rural communities, he later served churches in Boston and the rapidly growing Cincinnati. Henry Ward Beecher first attracted attention as pastor in the youthful Indianapolis but achieved fame during his forty years (1847–1887) as pastor of Plymouth (Congregational) Church on Brooklyn Heights, overlooking lower New York City. Not original or profound, hating theological controversy and reacting against the Calvinism in which he had been reared, he had a deep sense of the love of God, thought of Christ as ever near him to help and sustain him, sought to effect moral change in his hearers, and had great power over the heart.

Phillips Brooks, like Beecher, was of old New England stock. His maternal relatives had endowed two academies which bore the Phillips name and had been a main stay financially of Andover Theological Seminary. He was first an Episcopal rector in Philadelphia, then became widely known as rector and inspiring preacher of Trinity Church in Boston, and died as Bishop of Massachusetts. Strikingly handsome and impressive physically, of singular nobility and purity of character, influenced by Coleridge, Maurice, Robertson, and Bushnell (the American Congregationalist of whom we are to hear more in a moment), he was an interpreter of the theological trends represented by these men rather than a pioneer. He brought to his calling high vision, poetic insight, and deep earnestness.

Influential in helping Protestants to meet the problems of the cities were various movements directed towards youth. Outstanding were Sunday Schools and the Young People's Society of Christian Endeavour. The latter, initiated by a young New England Congregational pastor, Francis E. Clark, was followed by denominational organizations such as the Epworth League, the Luther League, and the Baptist Young People's Union. There were also the Daily Vacation Bible schools, begun in 1899 in New York City.

In one important phase of urban life Protestantism made little headway. It did not successfully reach many of the element in the population which was usually known as "labour," namely, that employed in the factories, mines, and forms of transportation which were multiplying as the century progressed. This, as we have seen, was true of Christianity, both Protestant and Roman Catholic, on the other side of the Atlantic. In the United States the record of the Roman Catholic Church was somewhat better than that of Protestantism, but nearly everywhere, whether in America or Europe, industrialization made for the de-Christianization of the masses of workers who were caught up in it.

THE INTELLECTUAL CHALLENGE

As in Europe, so in the United States, the intellectual currents of the nineteenth century constituted both a threat and a challenge. Many believed that science was outmoding Christianity. In the rapidly growing colleges and universities, including those begun through the churches and officially Christian, the trend, especially in the later years of the century, was away from Christianity. Yet Christians were far from abject surrender. Books, some of them notable and many for popular consumption, appeared in defense of the faith or to demonstrate, by restatement, that the faith and the new knowledge and methods were not incompatible. On the campuses voluntary student Christian movements sprang up and flourished. In the latter part of the century these were chiefly Young Men's and Young Women's Christian Associations. Through the Student Volunteer Movement for Foreign Missions, a Protestant organization which, as we have suggested, had its birth in 1886 at a student Christian conference under Dwight L. Moody at Mt. Hermon, Massachusetts, and which spread rapidly, thousands from the colleges, universities, and theological seminaries went to other lands to spread the faith and to plant and nourish churches.

It was through the Student Young Men's Christian Association and the Student Volunteer Movement for Foreign Missions, and largely through contacts, direct and indirect, with Moody, that there emerged John R. Mott (1865——). Coming from Iowa to Cornell, it was at that university that Mott was enlisted, largely through J. K. Studd, a Cambridge athlete who was one of the converts of the Moody movement. Soon after graduation Mott became a travelling secretary of the student department of the Young Men's Christian Associations. He was one of the original members of the Student Volunteer Movement and was long the chairman of its executive committee. A layman, he travelled widely across the world, first as an evangelist and an organizer among students and later as an outstanding leader in Protestant missions and what came to be known as the Ecumenical Movement. We shall meet him again more than once, especially after 1914. Combining a simple faith issuing from a complete commitment to Christ with a commanding platform presence, world-wide vision, skill in discerning and enlisting young men of ability, and the capacity to win the confidence of men of affairs, and reaching out across ecclesiastical barriers in the effort to unite Christians of many traditions in the endeavour to win all mankind to the faith, Mott became one of the outstanding leaders in the entire history of Christianity.

The Changing Character of the Christianity of the United States

At the outset of this chapter we noted that the Christianity of the United States was in many respects unique and different from that of Europe. That was true at the beginning of the century and was still true in 1914. Some of the developments of the century heightened the contrast. Changes came in the Christianity of the United States. Some of them accentuated characteristics which had been present in 1815. Others introduced new elements.

It will be remembered that we pointed out (Chapter XLIV) the distinctive marks of the Christianity of the United States at the dawn of the nineteenth century. These were that it was prevailingly Protestant and with the more radical Protestant denominations in the majority, that it showed great variety, that all churches tended to be legally equal with no one accorded a privileged position, that "evangelism" was stressed, the effort to win all to an allegiance to the Christian faith, that the attendant emphasis upon conversion was modifying the Augustinian, Reformed theology, usually called Calvinism, which was the common heritage of the denominations which enrolled the majority of the church members, and that there was among many Christians the ambitious purpose to bring all society into conformity with Christian standards. All of these features continued, even though modified.

In 1914, in spite of the phenomenal growth of the Roman Catholic Church through the immigrant flood of the preceding century, the United States was still prevailingly Protestant. The total membership of Protestant churches was larger than that of the Roman Catholic Church. The ideals of the country were those which the radical Protestantism of the older American stock had done much to shape. That radical Protestantism continued to be numerically in the ascendant. Baptists far outnumbered any other type of Protestants and the Methodists were second. Protestants of the denominations which went back to colonial days or those with that kind of background predominated in the national and most of the state governments, business, and the professions. In some of the cities Roman Catholics were in control, but no Roman Catholic had been elected President. Although the violence with which the opposition to the Roman Catholic Church was sometimes expressed was deplored by most Protestants, there was widespread recognition of the fact that the Roman Catholic

Church was alien to much that was basic in the principles on which the United States and its life were built and that if Roman Catholics were ever to be in control and were true to what had again and again been enunciated by the Popes, including those of the nineteenth century, they would work fundamental alterations in the life of the nation.

The variety presented by the Christianity of the United States was markedly increased. We have noted (Chapter XLIV) that in the interval between 1750 and 1815 the multiplicity of denominations resulting from immigration had been augmented by others of American origin. Methodists and Baptists, although owing their inception to impulses from abroad, were spreading rapidly. Denominations sharing Methodist convictions and having a Methodist ecclesiastical structure but not included in the Methodist Episcopal Church had sprung up, notably the United Brethren and the Evangelical Association. Groups calling themselves Christians or Disciples of Christ had come into being, centering chiefly around Barton W. Stone and Alexander Campbell. In New England the Unitarians and the Universalists were becoming distinct denominations. As we have seen in the present chapter, between 1815 and 1914 the number of denominations was swelled through the nineteenth century immigration. Roman Catholics multiplied. The Orthodox Churches were represented. Lutheranism rose to prominence and the number of Lutheran synods mounted, some of them so distinct from one another as to constitute separate churches. We have also noted the appearance of new Protestant churches on the frontier, notably the Church of Jesus Christ of Latter Day Saints.

From the fertile religious soil of the United States sprang additional Protestant denominations. Several of them either began in New England or had for founders men of New England stock. One was the Seventh Day Adventists. The Seventh Day Adventists arose from William Miller (1782–1849). Born in Western Massachusetts and coming to manhood in New York, a farmer, at first a Deist, after prolonged struggle with doubts and a painstaking study of the Bible, Miller was converted and joined a Baptist church. Meditation on the Bible prophecies convinced him that Christ was to return in 1843. Earnest disciples spread his views and a movement arose which attracted wide attention. When the first date passed without the expected Second Advent, a rechecking of the data set the day in 1844. Although this, too, came and the world still stood, Miller's followers, persecuted in the existing religious bodies, formed themselves into Adventist churches. Through contact with the Seventh Day Baptists the larger proportion of the Adventists adopted the seventh instead of the first day of the week for worship and abstention from labour. Although numbering only about 80,000 in 1916, they were well organized, actively missionary, and propagated their views through much of the world.

Of more strictly New England birth was the Church of Christ, Scientist, teaching what was called Christian Science. The founder was Mary Morse Baker Eddy (1821–1910). Reared in a devout home, a member of a Congregational church, as a young woman she was frail and suffered much from what appear to have been nervous disorders and hysteria. What seemed to her to be health came through a faith-healer, also a New Englander, a man of complete sincerity and beauty of character who believed in Christ but not in an orthodox way. From him and at least one other she acquired convictions which she elaborated in her own way and set forth in a volume, *Science and Health,* first published in 1875 and to which she subsequently gave many revisions. In 1879 the Church of Christ, Scientist, was chartered in Massachusetts and headquarters were eventually set up in Boston. Mrs. Eddy proved to be an able organizer and devised a structure for the movement which placed a large amount of authority at the centre. Although in her later years officially retired, she was long the directing spirit. The Christian Science churches had a rapid growth. They were chiefly urban and their appeal was mainly their assurance of physical healing.

A movement, not of New England origin, which began before 1914 and was to be widely spread after that year was what was known variously as Jehovah's Witnesses, the International Bible Students' Association, the Watch Tower, and the Russellites. It came into being through the teachings of Charles Taze Russell (1852–1916). On the basis of his study of the Bible Russell believed that Christ had come in invisible form in 1874 and that the millennium had begun. He denounced all existing churches as rejected by God. He travelled and preached widely and hundreds of congregations sprang up which theoretically had him as pastor.

A number of small denominations arose, some of them offshoots of Methodism and regarding the Methodist Episcopal Church as too lax. Several of them believed that freedom from sin is attainable. Some taught faith healing. There were also similar groups which in one combination or another had the word Holiness in their title and spoke of a "second blessing" beyond conversion and an ensuing perfection of life. There were various Pentecostal churches, believing in the outpouring of the Holy Spirit as at Pentecost with a resulting "speaking with tongues." The Church of the Nazarene spread fairly widely. The Christian and Missionary Alliance, at first undenominational, later a distinct ecclesiastical body, warmly evangelistic, sent missionaries to several parts of the world. The roster of these denominations was long and included both white and Negro bodies, but the total membership was but a small fraction of that of the larger, what might be called the "standard" churches.

A feature of the variegated denominational picture of the Christianity of the

United States was sectional division. Because of the strains brought by the issue of slavery and the Civil War, a cleavage took place in some of the larger Protestant denominations. Thus in 1845 the Southern Baptist Convention was organized by delegates from eight slave-holding states. That same year saw the coming into being of the Methodist Episcopal Church, South, precipitated by an action of the General Conference of the Methodist Episcopal Church in 1844 which asked a Southern bishop to suspend his episcopal duties until he had divested himself of some slaves which he had acquired through a second marriage. In 1861 the Old School Presbyterians in the South formed the Presbyterian Church in the Confederate States of America which after the defeat of the South became the Presbyterian Church in the United States. The body from which it withdrew retained the name the Presbyterian Church in the United States of America. The Lutherans also divided. During the Civil War the southern dioceses of the Protestant Episcopal Church organized a separate Confederate church, but the parent body did not officially acquiesce in the action and at the end of hostilities the Southern bishops were welcomed back into the General Convention. In contrast, the breach in the Baptist, Presbyterian, Methodist, and Lutheran ranks persisted. In the case of the last two it was healed after 1914.

In the social stratification of the churches still another element entered to multiply the variety. We have noticed it in the groupings according to the national and racial origins of the population. It also reflected the economic and educational status of the members. Thus Unitarians, Episcopalians, Presbyterians, and Congregationalists tended to be in the upper income brackets. Of the larger bodies the Methodists and Baptists were drawn predominantly from those of the older American stock who were of the lower income and educational levels. In general this was more true of Baptists than of Methodists.

As the years passed the theological complexion of the Christianity of the United States changed. Obviously it was rendered much more varied by the growth of the Roman Catholic Church, the coming of the Orthodox Churches, and the multiplication of the shades of Lutheranism which we have noted.

Alterations took place in the theologies of the Protestant churches which were drawn largely from the older American stock. As we have seen (Chapter XLIV), these had begun before 1815. Augustinian or Calvinistic theology had been that of the Congregational, Presbyterian, Reformed, and many of the Baptist churches. Before 1815 this had begun to be abandoned by the Unitarian wing of New England Congregationalism. On the extreme left of that movement, going far beyond his older contemporary, William Ellery Channing (1780–1842), the outstanding earlier formulator of Unitarianism, was the intellectually eager and extraordinarily learned Theodore Parker (1810–1860) who presented religion in terms of inner experience, "the felt and perceived presence of Absolute Being infusing itself" in the soul. Reared in Unitarianism, but eventually moving beyond it away from historic Christianity, was Ralph Waldo Emerson (1803–1882), whom we have already met and who by his lectures and writings exerted a widespread and enormous influence.

In the orthodox Congregational churches the inherited theology was being modified by the stream which issued from Jonathan Edwards. In the nineteenth century what was called New England theology departed further and further from the Augustinian tradition with its doctrines of original sin and divine election or predestination. Much of this, as we have noted, was from the purpose of making room for the preaching which urged men to repent and was a necessary accompaniment of the revivals which were then a feature of Congregationalism. It was also in part through influences from contemporary European Protestant thought. Some of it came from Nathaniel William Taylor (1786–1858) of Yale. Some was through Andover Theological Seminary.

These trends were countered by adherents to Augustinianism as represented in Calvin, the Westminster Confession, and the historic faith of the Reformed Churches. Outstanding was Charles Hodge (1797–1878) who, a graduate of Princeton, both the college and the theological seminary, through a long life taught in the latter institution and by his influence in the class room and his extensive writings in journals and books was a bulwark of the older orthodoxy both in Presbyterian circles and in the country at large. Hodge's voluminous *Systematic Theology* was at once a history of Christian doctrine and an orderly presentation of the standard Reformed faith, giving what was to Hodge the logical basis for that faith, answering objections to it, and pointing out the weaknesses in the rival positions. A man of deep emotional piety with the love of God in Christ at its heart, through his writings Hodge gave the impression of a massive intellectual structure erected on the foundation of the infallible Bible by means of uncompromising logic. Somewhat similar was the slightly later *Systematic Theology* by Augustus Hopkins Strong (1836–1921), a Baptist, professor and president in the Rochester Theological Seminary. It, too, had wide use both in and beyond the denomination of the author.

Radical in his departure from Augustinianism as traditionally represented in the Reformed Churches was Horace Bushnell (1802–1876). Reared in Connecticut, early joining a Congregational church, educated at Yale, he was familiar with the modified Calvinism of that environment. He rebelled against what seemed to him to be the hair-splitting logic of the vigorous and often acrimonious theological debate about him and the kind of revivalism which prevailed. Yet it was a revival at Yale while he was a young tutor there which took him out of the study of law and sent him to the Yale Divinity School.

Coleridge, and especially the latter's *Aids to Reflection,* had, so he said, a greater influence upon him than any writings outside the Bible. As a pastor in Hartford, Connecticut, from 1833 to 1858 and especially through his writings then and later he helped to shape the thought of many, particularly among the clergy and thoughtful laymen. A mystic, he believed that truth is apprehended by intuition. Reacting against revivalism with its insistence upon the conversion of the adolescent or adult as the only entrance to the Christian life, in his *Christian Nurture* he maintained that "the child is to grow up as a Christian and never know himself as being otherwise." He believed in miracles, but not as a suspension of natural law. To him nature and the supernatural were a single universe created and governed by God. He was a Trinitarian, but sought to rescue the doctrine from the danger of tritheism. He exalted Christ, but appreciated his humanity as well as his divinity. He was convinced of the efficacy of the death of Christ, but through what is often called its "moral influence." He was denounced by many of his fellow-clergymen in the Congregational churches, but for his singular nobility of character and the force of his thought he was held in honour by thousands.

In the latter part of the century there arose other formulators of what came to be called "liberal" theology. Among them were the Baptist, William Newton Clarke (1841–1912) whose *Outline of Christian Theology* (1898) had a wide circulation, and Henry Churchill King (1858–1934), a Congregationalist, for many years teacher and president at Oberlin. Borden Parker Bowne (1847–1910), earnestly religious, intensely critical of Herbert Spencer, long a teacher at Boston University, a Methodist institution, attacked mechanistic determinism, emphasized the freedom of the self and its relation to the Unseen, was near to the conservative position in his estimate of Christ, and formulated a philosophy known as Personalism which helped to shape much of contemporary Methodist theology.

Also in the latter half of the century there came into prominence in wide reaches of the Protestantism of the United States what was known as the "Social Gospel." It sought to inspire Christians to strive to bring all society as well as the individual into conformity with the teachings of Jesus. To no small degree it was an outgrowth of the dream which had brought the Independents, Puritans, Quakers, and many another Christian minority across the Atlantic, that of building in the New World an ideal Christian society. It was favoured by the optimism of the era, was given impetus by a poignant appreciation of the evils which attended the growing industrialization, and was encouraged by the Ritschlian theology which was entering from Germany and by the writings of Thomas Chalmers and Frederick Denison Maurice. Bushnell and some of the Unitarians helped to prepare the way for it.

The Social Gospel had many expressions and spokesmen. Among the more prominent was Washington Gladden (1836–1918), for thirty-six years a Congregational pastor in Columbus, Ohio. A champion of what he called "applied Christianity," he attacked *laissez faire* on the ground that it often meant "let ill enough alone," served on the city council, advocated municipal ownership of public-service utilities, and sought to ease the tension between employers and labour unions. The outstanding prophet of the Social Gospel was Walter Rauschenbusch (1861–1918). Of German ancestry, the seventh in an unbroken succession of clergymen in his family, he was born in the United States of parents who had taken refuge in that country after the defeat of liberalism in Germany in the outcome of the revolutionary year of 1848. A graduate of the University of Rochester and of Rochester Theological Seminary, Baptist institutions, after a period as a pastor in New York City in which he came to know the people and problems of a great city he returned to Rochester Theological Seminary as a teacher. His *Christianity and the Social Crisis,* published in 1907, brought him nation-wide recognition and was followed in quick succession by additional volumes of a similar tenor. Dynamic, gracious, winsome, and vividly humorous, he was much sought after as a speaker and lecturer.

The trends of which Bushnell and Rauschenbusch were outstanding expressions and spokesmen aroused alarmed opposition in much of the Protestantism of the United States. It was heightened by the efforts of scholars to reconcile science and religion and by the application to the Scriptures of the kind of historical method which was known as the "higher criticism." "Evolution" became to thousands a symbol of all in the scientific approach that seemed to them destructive of the Christian faith. The tension was aggravated by radical departures, in the name of Christianity, from many historic Christian convictions, notably by scholars connected with the Divinity School of the University of Chicago. That institution, under Baptist auspices, built on earlier beginnings, dated its founding from 1892 when through the first of a succession of princely gifts by John D. Rockefeller and the daring vision of its young President, William Rainey Harper (1856–1906) it entered upon a spectacular rise to prominence in the world of education. Here and there heresy trials punctuated the course of the struggle of conservatives against the new views. Not long before 1914 the opposition began to call themselves and to be called Fundamentalists, from their adherence to what they deemed the fundamentals of the Christian faith. After 1914 the contest was to be intensified.

A feature of the Christianity of the United States which became increasingly prominent in the Protestantism of the country as the century progressed was the share of laymen. As we have seen, the hierarchy of the Roman Catholic Church early defeated the efforts of the laity to take control of its parishes. In

Protestant circles laymen and women more and more came to the fore. They did this partly through their financial gifts to the churches and various religious organizations and institutions. Laymen's organizations sprang up, first in connexion with local churches, and then as denomination-wide fellowships. Many women's societies appeared, both in the individual parishes and on a national scale. By deliberate policy the American Bible Society was under lay control. The Young Men's and Young Women's Christian Associations were primarily lay institutions. The laity were prominent in the Sunday Schools. Some of the outstanding evangelists, notably Moody and Mott, were not ordained. This made for a kind of lay Christianity. For the most part it had little patience with what it regarded as theological subtleties. Largely from the Evangelical background of the revivals, it respected, studied, and taught the Bible, sought to win individuals to a personal Christian commitment, was activist, and was generous in giving time and money.

The lay element and the emphasis upon evangelism and revivalism with the consequent mass conversion were phases of a kind of popular Christianity. Among other expressions were hymns which had about them the quality of folk songs. Prominent among them were those which were born from the camp-meetings of the early part of the century. They were followed by what were often called Gospel hymns. We have already met them in connexion with Moody and Sankey, but they were by no means confined to these two men. Appealing by words and simple tunes they sang their way into the hearts of millions. They were numbered by the thousands and were published in inexpensive hymnals which together attained circulations of hundreds of thousands. Here was a singing faith which voiced and helped to shape the aspirations, prayers, and actions of multitudes. Probably nothing of this kind of similar dimensions had previously appeared in the history of Christianity or of any other religion. Prominent among the writers was Fanny Jane Crosby (1820–1915) who, blind from birth, is said to have composed at least eight thousand songs. Among them were "Jesus keep me near the cross," "Blessed assurance, Jesus is mine," and "Rescue the perishing, care for the dying."

The abounding religious life of the Protestantism of the United States gave rise to still other hymns, many of them of a more dignified kind, but also having a wide appeal. When taken together with the religious folk songs of the masses they constituted most impressive evidence of the vitality of the Protestantism of the country.

Some came from the Unitarians and Quakers, who, although small minorities, penned hymns which were in use in much larger denominations and on both sides of the Atlantic. Among the Unitarians were Samuel Johnson (1822–1882), memorable for "City of God, how broad and far outspread thy walls sublime" and "Life of ages, richly poured," and Samuel Longfellow (1819–1892), younger brother of the more famous Henry Wadsworth Longfellow and author of "I look to Thee in every need and never look in vain." The Quaker whose poems were most used as hymns was John Greenleaf Whittier (1807–1892). Among others he gave to the world "O brother man, fold to thy heart thy brother" and "Immortal love, forever full, forever flowing free."

Still more of the hymns issued from the larger denominations. A Congregational layman, Lowell Mason (1792–1872), promoted the multiplication of singing schools and the introduction of music in the public schools. Alone or in collaboration with others he compiled hymnals, some of which went through several editions. He himself composed many hymn tunes, some original and others adaptations of what he had acquired elsewhere. Mason's most important collaborator was likewise a layman, a Presbyterian, Thomas Hastings (1784–1872), who with him sought to raise the level of church music in the United States. Hastings also worked independently, did much for the church music of New York City, issued several hymn books, and composed many tunes and numbers of hymns, among the latter "Hail to the brightness of Zion's glad morning." Samuel Francis Smith (1808–1895), a Baptist clergyman, wrote hymns for Mason, among them "America," the most widely used of the patriotic songs of the United States. He was the author of "The morning light is breaking." Ray Palmer (1808–1887), a Congregational clergyman, contributed "My faith looks up to thee, thou lamb of Calvary," "Jesus, these eyes have never seen that radiant form of thine," and English paraphrases of Latin hymns, among them "Jesus, thou joy of loving hearts." Phillips Brooks gave to the world "O little town of Bethlehem, how still we see thee lie," written for the children of his Philadelphia parish for their Christmas service and set to music by his organist. George Washington Doane (1799–1859), from the age of thirty-three until his death bishop of the Protestant Episcopal Church in New Jersey, among other hymns composed "Softly now the light of day," "Thou art the way; to thee alone," and "Fling out the banner, let it float." Washington Gladden was best remembered not so much for his advocacy of the Social Gospel as for his hymn, "O Master, let me walk with thee in lowly paths of service free." The list might be greatly lengthened. Hundreds of hymnals were compiled, some for use in dignified services, others for meetings of a more informal character, and many for both kinds of services. American Protestantism was a singing religion.

The Protestant Christianity of the United States made much of assemblies in the open air and in camp grounds. In the fore part of the nineteenth century these were predominantly the camp-meetings of which we have spoken. In the latter part of the century sites with more enduring buildings were developed.

Some were by the ocean, some by the lake-side, some in mountains, and others by rivers. To them groups came for shorter or longer periods for recreation, fellowship, study, worship, and hearing lectures and sermons. Notable was the summer assembly begun on Lake Chautauqua, in New York, in 1874, by John H. Vincent (1832–1920), the first chairman of the International Sunday School Lesson Committee, for the training of Sunday School teachers. It grew into an institution for adult education, encouraged and aided home reading and study, and was copied in many places across the country. Numbers of other summer assemblies were restricted to specifically religious programmes.

Still another feature of the Christianity of the United States was a trend towards common patterns. This was most marked among the Protestant bodies which had been longest in the country, but it gradually became apparent in ones more recently arrived. It included forms of worship, hymns, and orders of service. Sunday Schools became characteristic of most Protestant churches, and through the International Sunday School Lessons, prepared by an interdenominational committee, the same passages of Scripture and often the same materials for teachers and pupils were used simultaneously by several different denominations. Youth organizations multiplied, mid-week meetings for all members, usually under the name of prayer-meetings, were common, and missionary societies became normal. This meant that a stranger going from church to church would find striking similarities, regardless of the denomination. In general, Roman Catholics and Eastern Orthodox stood outside the trend.

A closely associated feature of the Christianity of the United States, especially of the Protestantism of the older American stock, was a growing co-operation across denominational lines. It was furthered by the fact that no denomination was accorded preference by the state and that all were on the basis of legal equality. Coöperation took many forms. It was seen in organizations in which Christians of several denominations joined as individuals and not as official representatives of their respective churches. Such were the American Bible Society, the Young Men's and Young Women's Christian Associations, and the Young People's Societies of Christian Endeavour. In others more than one denomination coöperated, as in the Plan of Union of the Presbyterians and Congregationalists, the American Board of Commissioners for Foreign Missions, and the American Home Missionary Society. In 1838 S. S. Schmucker, whom we have already met as a creative figure in American Lutheranism, issued a *Fraternal Appeal to the American Churches, with a Plan for Catholic Union on Apostolic Principles*. In it he suggested a federation which would not abolish existing denominations or do violence to doctrines held by any one and believed by him to be true, but which would be based upon the Apostles' Creed and a *United Protestant Confession* stating the faith common to all orthodox Protestant bodies and among whose members there should be "free sacramental, ecclesiastical, and ministerial communion." In part in response to the *Appeal* a society for promoting Christian union was launched. In 1846, to some extent because of this movement, the Evangelical Alliance was begun in England. It brought together not churches but individuals and was international in its scope. A branch of the Alliance was organized in New York in 1867. In 1873 a notable meeting of the general conference of the Alliance with representatives from a number of countries was held in New York.

Prominent in the Alliance was Philip Schaff (1819–1893). Born in Switzerland, educated in Germany, at the sacrifice of a promising scholarly career in the latter country he came to the United States as a young man to teach in the theological seminary of the German Reformed Church in Mercersburg, Pennsylvania. In his later years he was professor in Union Theological Seminary in New York City. An outstanding church historian, author or editor of a prodigious number of volumes, he directed his energies, including those which found outlet in his prolific pen, to furthering unity among Christians.

In the 1890's and the opening years of the twentieth century several bodies for coöperation in which churches or denominational missionary societies officially coöperated came into being. Among them were state federations of churches, the Foreign Missions Conference of North America (1893), the Home Missions Council (1908), and the Federal Council of the Churches of Christ in America (1908). In a later chapter we are to see the amazing fashion in which after 1914 these organizations grew and similar organizations multiplied.

THE EFFECTS OF CHRISTIANITY IN THE UNITED STATES

It is hazardous, indeed almost preposterous, to attempt to estimate and still more so to attempt to summarize in a few paragraphs the effects of Christianity in the United States. Some of the most important elude statistics or concrete statements which can be compressed on the printed page. Who can accurately record the results in millions of individual lives, some slight, others transforming and issuing in radiant but usually obscure men and women who were noted and remembered only by their families and local communities? Yet, as in other countries and ages, it was such fruits which were the most significant.

However, it is possible to give some hint, even in a few pages, of what a fuller and more discerning account would include and from it to gain an inkling of the fashion in which Christianity entered into the shaping of the life of the United States in the nineteenth century.

We have already seen that the percentage of church members in the population increased more than six-fold. Whether this meant a decline or an increase in the average quality of the faith and life of church members we do not know. No statistics are available for church attendance, on the comprehension of the Christian faith, or on the degree of approximation to Christian ethical standards which would make possible an accurate comparison.

That Christianity had an important part in moulding the ideals of the country is certain. The American dream of realizing in the New World a better social order than that of the Old World was largely from Christian sources, predominantly from the extreme wing of Protestantism, especially since the latter attained much larger prominence in the United States than in Europe.

The hope of creating a model society expressed itself in many ways. The kind of democracy which was the purpose of the United States, although far from perfectly achieved, was predominantly from radical Protestantism. The same was true of the many reform movements which characterized the United States in the nineteenth century.

The Christian conscience and resolution were a factor, probably the major factor, in bringing about the abolition of Negro slavery. This was seen in many ways, notably in the great increase in the anti-slavery movement which issued from the Finney revivals. We have noted the manner in which those moved by the Christian faith aided the former slaves and their descendants to adjust themselves to emancipation and take a worthy and growing part in the life of the country, sharing its opportunities and its obligations.

Another outstanding effort for moral improvement was that directed against alcoholic beverages. In the fore part of the century liquors of high alcoholic content were in wide use. Whiskey was characteristic of the frontier and in the eighteenth century rum had popularity through the extensive trade with the West Indies. Before 1815 some churches, notably the Methodists, began to protest against the customs which made drunkenness common. Throughout the century the revivals had as one of their fruits temperance movements and campaigns to prohibit the sale of alcoholic drinks. In 1826 the American Temperance Society was organized, largely by clergymen. In the 1850's thirteen states, led by Maine and all but one in the North, forbade the manufacture and sale of intoxicating liquors except for industrial and medicinal purposes. A reaction followed, heightened by the lowering of morals which accompanied and followed the Civil War. However, the temperance movement revived. In 1869 a National Prohibition party was formed, with a clergyman as the first chairman of its executive committee. The Woman's Christian Temperance Union came into being in 1873 and soon became nation-wide. In 1895 the National Anti-Saloon League was organized, growing out of local movements.

Drawing its support largely from Protestant churches, mainly those of the radical wing and of the older American stock, it sought to enlist voters of all denominations. By 1900 more than thirty states allowed voters in a given area to decide by "local option" whether they would permit the sale of liquor. By 1916 nineteen states had entirely forbidden the sale of liquor, and in 1919 an amendment was ratified which wrote prohibition into the Constitution of the United States.

Organizations for the achievement of world peace flourished, mainly through the initiative and leadership of earnest Christians. In 1815 David Low Dodge, a New York merchant of New England birth and ancestry, the progenitor of a long line of Christian philanthropists, along with his father-in-law, a clergyman and convert of Whitefield, formed the New York Peace Society. That same year two clergymen led in constituting the Massachusetts Peace Society. In 1828, largely through the leadership of William Ladd, an earnest Congregationalist, the American Peace Society was created. The Mexican and Civil Wars dealt blows to the peace movement, but it revived. In 1914, shortly before the outbreak of World War I, the Church Peace Union came into being.

Other reforms which owed much to Christianity were that which opposed secret societies, the attempt, ultimately successful, to place women on an equality with men in legal status and in social, intellectual, and economic opportunity, the improved care of the insane, more enlightened treatment of criminals, and efforts to clean out the political corruption in the great cities. As an example of this last, it was a Presbyterian clergyman, Charles H. Parkhurst (1842–1933), who in the 1890's by his fearless preaching contributed to the defeat of the noisome Tammany Hall and the placing of a reform government in control in New York City.

Another of the results of Christianity was seen in the vast extent of private philanthropy. By the end of the century the voluntary gifts by both rich and poor totalled hundreds of millions of dollars annually. Hundreds of hospitals, large and small, were founded by Roman Catholics and Protestants. Many orphanages and homes for the aged were maintained under church auspices. Christians pioneered in care for the blind and the deaf. Numbers of the wealthy gave lavishly and often, perhaps usually, from Christian motives. In the first half of the century Arthur and Lewis Tappan, devout Christians, were well known for their generosity. Through more than a century members of the Dodge family, avowed Christians, were devoted in giving both time and money. John Davison Rockefeller (1839–1937), a Baptist layman, who accumulated the nucleus of his vast fortune through pioneering in developing and marketing the petroleum resources of the country, sought counsel in the initial stages of his philanthropies from friends among the Baptist clergy, and largely channelled his enormous giving through organizations which he either chose or set up on their advice. His son, John Davison Rockefeller, Jr., for years the teacher of a men's Bible class, continued in the paths marked out by his father, although without as much counsel from the clergy.

Literature felt the influence of Christianity. By no means all the outstanding authors were committed to it. Some were critical and even hostile. However, several of the most prominent writers were consciously and deeply indebted to it. Among them were Henry Wadsworth Longfellow, John G. Whittier, Harriet Beecher Stowe, James Russell Lowell, Ralph Waldo Emerson, Oliver Wendell Holmes, and Nathaniel Hawthorne.

Education was markedly furthered by Christianity. All the older colleges and universities owed their existence to it. The same was true of several of the newer universities and of a majority of the colleges which were begun in the nineteenth century. As we have seen, some denominations, notably the Roman Catholics, conducted elementary and secondary schools. Protestants pioneered in higher education for women and, as we have said, in primary, secondary, and higher education for Negroes. Acting from frankly Christian motives, in several states Protestant clergymen and laymen were chiefly responsible for the beginnings of the system of state public schools.

THE SHARE OF THE CHRISTIANS OF THE UNITED STATES IN THE WORLD-WIDE SPREAD OF THE FAITH

We have already seen (Chapter XLIV) the fashion in which the Protestants of the United States, not content with confining their energies to winning the Indians, Negroes, and de-Christianized whites about them, shared with their fellow-Christians on the other side of the Atlantic in spreading the faith to other lands. As the nineteenth century progressed American Protestant foreign missions were augmented. This is not the place for a detailed account of what was done. However, we must pause to note that by 1914 foreign as well as home missions became part of the normal programme of all Protestant denominations. Although usually only a minority of the membership were actively interested, almost every denomination made foreign missions a part of its commitment. Protestant denominations new to the American scene for the most part conformed, even though slowly, as they did to Sunday Schools and other features of the religious life about them.

A great forward surge came to the Protestant missionary movement through the Student Volunteer Movement for Foreign Missions which, as we saw a moment ago, was born in 1886 at a summer conference held at Mt. Hermon, Massachusetts, under the direction of Moody. From it in subsequent years thousands went abroad, or, remaining at home, led mission boards or formed a convinced and sacrificial constituency for the support of the enterprise.

By 1914 more missionaries served from the United States in the overseas extension of Protestant Christianity and more money was given than from any other country. Americans served in every continent and in scores of lands and formed the large majority of the Protestant missionaries in Latin America, Japan, the Philippines, and Korea.

Roman Catholics of the United States, as we have said, were slower than Protestants in undertaking foreign missions. They were so absorbed in taking care of the vast immigration of those who by heredity were of their faith and in building churches and schools that they had little energy to spare for enterprises abroad. It was not until after 1914, when immigration dwindled to a trickle, that they began to take a substantial share in the missions of their church in other lands.

SUMMARY

The nineteenth century course of Christianity in the United States was like and yet unlike that in Europe. Here was a new nation, fired by the spirit of hopeful adventure, essaying in what it called the New World to make a fresh beginning and, as its great seal declared, to build, under the eye of God and with His benevolent approval, an enduring structure in a new order of the ages. Its territory grew by leaps and bounds. Its population mounted even more rapidly. An immigration of unprecedented magnitude, drawn from all the countries of Europe and to some extent from Asia, added to one which was already diverse because of a composite of aboriginal Indian tribes, settlers from several nations in Western Europe, and slaves from Africa. The majority of the immigration was from Christendom and was Christian by heritage. It brought with it almost all the existing varieties of Christianity and made for a scene of greater ecclesiastical complexity than the world had ever known.

Yet, coming to a land where, except for a few remnants which early disappeared, no church enjoyed a privileged status given it by law, where only a small minority were members of churches, and where it was easy to drop Old World patterns of life, the immigrant population was in grave danger of de-Christianization. The peril was accentuated by the threats to Christianity in both Europe and America brought by the temper and currents of the new age which, arising in part from the distortion of impulses emanating from Christianity, seemed to threaten the very existence of the faith.

Under these apparently untoward conditions, Christianity achieved phenomenal gains. It won an increasing proportion of the older, partially de-Christianized white stock, both on the westward moving frontier and on the Atlantic seaboard. It held a majority of the nineteenth century nominally Christian immigration. It made striking advances among those of non-Christian ancestry—the Indians, the Negroes, the Chinese, and the Japanese—but not, significantly, among the Jews, and that in spite of the fact that this people was being rapidly secularized. Christianity was confronted by the mounting urbanization and industrialization of the nation's society. While not completely solving the problem, it was not defeated by it.

In the course of the century the Christianity of the United States became increasingly distinctive. It continued to be predominantly Protestant and the churches which embodied radical Protestantism enjoyed a striking growth. In endeavouring to bring about the mass conversion of the de-Christianized and non-Christian elements of the population the older Protestantism, especially of the radical wing, moved forward through revivalism. Out of the Protestantism of the older American stock there came new denominations, some of them far removed from traditional Christianity. The variety presented by Christianity was even more diversified by the addition of Protestant denominations of the newly arrived immigration grouping themselves according to national origins, by contingents from the Eastern Churches, and, even more prominently, by the rapid growth, through immigration, of the Roman Catholic Church. From being one of the smaller denominations in 1815, by 1914 the Roman Catholic Church was the largest. In the United States the Roman Catholic form of Christianity departed in no way from the accepted dogmas of its church or from obedience to the Pope: it was neither heretical nor schismatic. Yet it was inclined to be more activistic than in Europe. Much of the Protestantism of the older American stock tended to move away from the Augustinian theology which it had inherited from Europe through what is often called, with only partial accuracy, the Puritan strain. Through its revivalism and mass conversion it sought hopefully to win all men, disregarding in practice the doctrine of predestination which regarded some as elected by God to salvation and others left, irremediably, to the consequences of original sin. Impelled by what was termed the Social Gospel, many within it laboured for the transformation of society with the avowed goal of complete accord with Christian standards.

While the dream of the advocates of the Social Gospel was by no means fully realized, Christianity had a profound effect on many aspects of the life of the United States. It was responsible for some of the basic and most compelling ideals of the nation. It brought about the end of Negro slavery and aided the freedmen in their progress towards social, educational, and economic equality with their former masters. It fought the excessive use of alcoholic beverages and inspired better care of the sick, the insane, the criminals, the blind, the orphaned, and the aged. It contributed strikingly to education and intellectual advance.

Moreover, the Christianity of the United States took an increasing part in the world-wide extension of the faith and began to make significant contributions to coöperation among Christians of different denominations and towards new approaches to Christian unity.

SELECTED BIBLIOGRAPHY

L. Abbott, *Henry Ward Beecher* (Boston, Houghton Mifflin Co., 1904, pp. xxviii, 457). By a friend and admirer.

J. T. Addison, *The Episcopal Church in the United States, 1789–1931* (New York, Charles Scribner's Sons, 1951, pp. xii, 500). Well done.

A. V. G. Allen, *Life and Letters of Phillips Brooks* (New York, E. P. Dutton and Co., 2 vols., 1900). The standard biography.

O. F. Ander, *T. N. Hasselquist. The Career and Influence of a Swedish-American Clergyman, Journalist, and Educator* (Rock Island, Ill., The Augustana Library Publications, 1931, pp. 260). Based in large part on manuscript sources and contemporary periodicals.

G. G. Atkins and F. L. Fagley, *History of American Congregationalism* (Boston, The Pilgrim Press, 1942, pp. ix, 432). A sympathetic, comprehensive account.

N. B. Atkinson, *Biography of Rev. G. H. Atkinson, D.D.* (Portland, Ore., F. W. Baltes and Co., 1893, pp. 508).

W. C. Barclay, *History of Methodist Missions. Part One. Early American Methodism 1769–1844* (New York, The Board of Missions and Church Extension of the Methodist Church, 2 parts, 1949, 1950). An official history based upon extensive research. To be further extended.

G. H. Barnes, *The Antislavery Impulse, 1830–1844* (New York, Appleton-Century-Crofts, 1933, pp. ix, 298). Based upon careful research.

Lyman Beecher, *Autobiography, Correspondence, etc.,* edited by Charles Beecher (New York, Harper & Brothers, 2 vols., 1864, 1865).

C. S. Braden, *These Also Believe* (New York, The Macmillan Co., 1949, pp. xv, 491). A careful study of various religious groups and movements in the United States on the fringes of Protestantism.

F. M. Brodie, *No Man Knows My History. The Life of Joseph Smith, Mormon Prophet* (New York, A. A. Knopf, 1945, pp. ix, 476, xix). Well written, critical of Smith.

J. A. Burns, *The Principles, Origin, and Establishment of the Catholic School System in the United States* (Cincinnati, Benziger Brothers, 1912, pp. 415). Based chiefly on well-known printed material, but in part upon manuscript sources.

J. A. Burns, *The Growth and Development of the Catholic School System in the*

United States (Cincinnati, Benziger Brothers, 1912, pp. 421). A continuation of the preceding book, covering the period from about 1840 onward.

H. Bushnell, *Christian Nurture* (New York, Charles Scribner's Sons, 1861, pp. vi, 407).

M. A. Cheney, *Life and Letters of Horace Bushnell* (New York, Harper & Brothers, 1880, pp. x, 579).

E. H. Cherrington, editor, *Standard Encyclopedia of the Alcohol Problem* (Westerville, Ohio, American Issue Publishing Co., 6 vols., 1925–1930). Compiled under forces working for prohibition, to aid in the fight against alcohol.

E. T. Clark, *The Small Sects of America* (New York and Nashville, Cokesbury Press, 1937, pp. 311). Based upon extensive research, often through personal visitation.

J. B. Clark, *Leavening the Nation. The Story of American Home Missions* (New York, The Baker & Taylor Co., 1903, pp. 362). An excellent survey.

W. R. Cross, *The Burned-Over District. The Social and Intellectual History of Enthusiastic Religion in Western New York, 1800–1850* (Cornell University Press, 1950, pp. xiii, 383). Extremely well done.

E. F. Dakin, *Mrs. Eddy. The Biography of a Virginal Mind* (New York, Charles Scribner's Sons, 1930, pp. x, 563). Based on solid research, critical of Mrs. Eddy.

Dictionary of American Biography (New York, Charles Scribner's Sons, 22 vols., 1928–1937). The standard work. A monument of careful research.

J. H. Dubbs, *History of the Reformed Church, German* (New York, Christian Literature Society, 1895, pp. 213–423).

W. E. B. DuBois, editor, *The Negro Church* (Atlanta, The Atlanta University Press, 1903, pp. viii, 212).

H. O. Dwight, *Centennial History of the American Bible Society* (New York, The Macmillan Co., 2 vols., 1916). By a secretary of the society.

W. Elliott, *The Life of Father Hecker* (New York, The Columbus Press, 1894, 2d ed., pp. xvii, 428). Warmly sympathetic.

H. W. Foote, *Three Centuries of American Hymnody* (Harvard University Press, 1940, pp. x, 418). A competent survey.

R. H. Gabriel, *The Course of American Democratic Thought. An Intellectual History Since 1815* (New York, The Ronald Press Co., 1940, pp. xi, 452). A standard survey.

C. B. Goodykoontz, *Home Missions on the American Frontier. With Particular Reference to the American Home Missionary Society* (Caldwell, Idaho, The Caxton Printers, 1939, pp. 460). Based upon extensive research.

P. Guilday, *The Life and Times of John Carroll, Archbishop of Baltimore (1735–1815)* (New York, The Encyclopedia Press, 1922, pp. xiv, 864). Well and sympathetically done.

Charles Hodge, *Systematic Theology* (New York, Charles Scribner's Sons, 3 vols., 1872, 1873).

C. H. Hopkins, *History of the Y.M.C.A. in North America* (New York, Association Press, 1951, pp. xii, 818). Based upon prolonged and competent research in the sources.

C. H. Hopkins, *The Rise of the Social Gospel in American Protestantism, 1865–1915* (Yale University Press, 1940, pp. xxii, 352). A standard work.

W. S. Kennedy, *The Plan of Union: or a History of the Presbyterian and Congregational Churches of the Western Reserve; with Biographical Sketches of the Early Missionaries* (Hudson, Ohio, Pentagon Steam Press, 1856, pp. iv, 262). Drawn from the original sources.

K. S. Latourette, *A History of the Expansion of Christianity. Volume IV, The Great Century,* A.D. *1800–1914. Europe and the United States of America* (New York, Harper & Brothers, 1941, pp. viii, 516).

W. A. Linn, *The Story of the Mormons from the Date of their Origin to the year 1901* (New York, The Macmillan Co., 1902, pp. xxv, 637). Based on extensive research and antagonistic to the Mormons.

W. W. Manross, *A History of the American Episcopal Church* (New York, Morehouse-Gorham, Inc., 2d ed., 1950, pp. xiv, 415). Except for chaps. 1, 2, and 8, based upon original sources.

B. Mathews, *John R. Mott, World Citizen* (New York, Harper & Brothers, 1934, pp. xiii, 469). A warmly appreciative biography by a personal friend, based upon data provided by Mott.

H. F. May, *Protestant Churches in Industrial America* (New York, Harper & Brothers, 1949, pp. x, 297). Covers the period from 1828 to 1895.

T. Maynard, *The Story of American Catholicism* (New York, The Macmillan Co., 1941, pp. xviii, 694). With official ecclesiastical imprimatur.

W. R. Moody, *D. L. Moody* (New York, The Macmillan Co., 1930, pp. 556). By a son.

H. N. Morse, editor, *Home Missions Today and Tomorrow. A Review and Forecast* (New York, Home Missions Council, 1934, pp. xvi, 419). An official study by the Home Missions Council.

H. R. Niebuhr, *The Kingdom of God in America* (New York, Harper & Brothers, 1937, pp. xvii, 215). A discerning interpretation of the religious history of the United States.

H. R. Niebuhr, *The Social Sources of Denominationalism* (New York, Henry Holt and Co., 1929, pp. viii, 304). Brilliantly conceived and written.

O. M. Norlie, *History of the Norwegian People in America* (Minneapolis, Augsburg Publishing House, 1925, pp. 602). Packed with information, but without footnote references to the sources.

J. H. O'Donnell, *The Catholic Hierarchy of the United States* (Washington, The Catholic University of America, 1922, pp. xiv, 223). A doctoral dissertation. Contains brief biographies of the bishops and extensive bibliographies.

T. O'Gorman, *A History of the Roman Catholic Church in the United States* (New York, The Christian Literature Co., 1895, pp. xviii, 515).

W. Rauschenbusch, *Christianity and the Social Crisis* (New York, The Macmillan Co., 1907, pp. xv, 429).

B. H. Roberts, *A Comprehensive History of the Church of Jesus Christ of Latter Day Saints* (Salt Lake City, Deseret News Press, 6 vols., 1930). An official history.

I. D. Sankey, *Sankey's Story of the Gospel Hymns and Sacred Songs and Solos* (Philadelphia, The Sunday School Times Co., 1906, pp. vii, 272).

D. S. Schaff, *The Life of Philip Schaff, in Part Autobiographical* (New York, Charles Scribner's Sons, 1897, pp. xv, 526).

C. E. Schneider, *The German Church on the American Frontier. A Study of the Rise of Religion among the Germans of the West* (St. Louis, Eden Publishing House, 1939, pp. xx, 579). Detailed, scholarly, based upon extensive research.

G. Shaughnessy, *Has the Immigrant Kept the Faith? A Study of Immigration and Catholic Growth in the United States 1790–1920* (New York, The Macmillan Co., 1925, pp. 289). By a Roman Catholic, learned and optimistic.

C. P. Shedd, *Two Centuries of Student Christian Movements, Their Origin and Intercollegiate Life* (New York, Association Press, 1934, pp. xxii, 466). The standard account.

J. H. Snowden, *The Truth about Mormonism* (New York, George H. Doran Co., 1926, pp. xix, 369). A history of origins and developments, based on careful research, critically objective.

G. M. Stephenson, *The Religious Aspects of Swedish Immigration. A Study of Immigrant Churches* (University of Minnesota Press, 1932, pp. viii, 542). Competent.

G. M. Stephenson, *The Puritan Heritage* (New York, The Macmillan Co., 1952, pp. 282). A semi-popular account of Protestantism in the United States, mostly on the colonial period and the first half of the nineteenth century.

P. L. Stewart, *Sheldon Jackson* (New York, Fleming H. Revell Co., 2d ed., 1908, pp. 488).

A. P. Stokes, *Church and State in the United States* (New York, Harper & Brothers, 3 vols., 1950). The standard work in its field.

A. H. Strong, *Systematic Theology* (Rochester, N. Y., E. R. Andrews, 1886, pp. xxix, 758).

W. W. Sweet, *Religion on the American Frontier. The Baptists, 1783–1830. A Collection of Source Material* (New York, Henry Holt and Co., 1931, pp. ix, 652).

W. W. Sweet, *Religion on the American Frontier. Vol. II, The Presbyterians, 1783–1840, a Collection of Source Materials* (New York, Harper & Brothers, 1936, pp. xii, 939).

W. W. Sweet, *Religion on the American Frontier, 1783–1850, Vol. III, The Congregationalists. A Collection of Source Materials* (University of Chicago Press, 1939, pp. xi, 435).

W. W. Sweet, *The Story of Religion in America* (New York, Harper & Brothers, 2d rev. ed., 1950, pp. ix, 492). A useful survey.

D. G. Tewksbury, *The Founding of American Colleges and Universities before the Civil War. With Particular Reference to Religious Influences Bearing upon the*

College Movement (Teachers College, Columbia University, 1932, pp. x, 254). Based upon extensive reading in primary and secondary sources.

R. S. Walker, *Torchlights to the Cherokees. The Brainerd Mission* (New York, The Macmillan Co., 1931, pp. xii, 339).

L. A. Weigle, *American Idealism* (Yale University Press, 1928, pp. 356). An excellent survey of the religious history of the United States in the form of comments on pertinent illustrations.

A. B. Wentz, *The Lutheran Church in American History* (Philadelphia, The United Lutheran Publication House, 2d ed., 1933, pp. 465). An authoritative survey.

A. S. Will, *Life of Cardinal Gibbons, Archbishop of Baltimore* (New York, E. P. Dutton & Co., 2 vols., 1922). Based upon personal acquaintance and extensive research in the letters and journals of Gibbons.

C. G. Woodson, *The History of the Negro Church* (Washington, D. C., The Associated Publishers, 2d ed., 1921, pp. x, 330).

G. F. Wright, *Charles Grandison Finney* (Boston, Houghton Mifflin Co., 1893, pp. vi, 329).

G. J. Zeilinger, *A Missionary Church with a Mission. A Memoir of the Seventy-fifth Anniversary of the Evangelical Synod of Iowa and Other States* (Chicago, Wartburg Publishing House, 1929, pp. 115). Published under the authority of the Synod.

BRITISH NORTH AMERICA
AND GREENLAND

Scale of Miles

0   200   400   600   800

HAGSTROM CO. N.Y.

MEXICO, CENTRAL AMERICA
AND THE WEST INDIES

SOUTH AMERICA

Chapter LI

CHRISTIANITY IN BRITISH AND LATIN
AMERICA IN THE NINETEENTH CENTURY

Christianity in the Americas was by no means confined to the United States. It was also present in every other country in the Western Hemisphere. In none other was it exactly like that of the United States. In most it was very different. Yet in general the course of Christianity in the Western Hemisphere was characterized by the same problems. The population was predominantly from Western Europe, either of the pre-nineteenth century or the nineteenth century immigration. It faced some of the same forces making for de-Christianization. In almost every land there were representatives of the aboriginal Indian peoples whose inherited cultures had either disintegrated or were disintegrating under the impact of Western civilization. In several countries there were larger or smaller numbers of Negroes. Originally slaves, by the end of the nineteenth century legal emancipation had come to all of them, but they still were faced with problems arising from their earlier servile status. For the most part the Americas outside the United States fell into two categories, those portions where the political and dominant cultural connexions were with the British Isles, and those where they were with Latin Europe. For a variety of reasons, chiefly because it did not have so prominent a place in the world scene, we need not give as much space to the Christianity of these lands as we have to that of the United States. We must, however, trace its course, even though more briefly than we have that of the latter.

BRITISH NORTH AMERICA

For those portions of North America which in the nineteenth century were part of the British Empire, the period opened, not in 1815 but in 1763 and 1783. By the peace of Paris, in 1763, which ended the Seven Years' War, the exclusion of France from North America which had been begun earlier was all but completed. Except for two small islands, St. Pierre and Miquelon, off the Newfoundland coast, and, from 1801 to 1803, a brief renewal of power in the vast region including and reaching northward from Louisiana, French rule was at an end. North of what soon became the United States, the British supplanted it. The secession of the Thirteen Colonies, formally acknowledged in 1783, removed from the British Empire the most populous portion of its North American possessions. However, in the course of the nineteenth century expansion to the north of the United States completed the incorporation into the Empire of an area which was slightly larger than that country. By the fourth quarter of the century all of it except Newfoundland and Labrador came together to form, under a federal form of government, the Dominion of Canada.

Largely because much of the territory was sub-arctic in climate, the population of Canada remained smaller than that of the United States. In 1914 the total for Canada and Newfoundland was about eight millions. Its growth was very rapid. Most of it was near the southern border. In 1914 its chief elements were French, descendants of settlers from the pre-British period, a large immigration from the British Isles, and thousands from the United States. That from the United States was made up, first, of those loyal to the Empire who would not or could not remain in the seceding Thirteen Colonies, and, second, of those who in the nineteenth century sought homes on the great prairies of the Canadian West. Immigration also came from the Continent of Europe, but by no means as large as that which poured into the United States. There were scattered minorities of Indians and, in the far North, of Eskimoes. Negroes were present but were by no means as prominent as in the great republic on the south.

Proportionately the Roman Catholic Church was stronger and more compact than in the United States. It constituted about two-fifths of the population. It was predominantly of French descent, but in it there were a substantial Irish contingent and smaller elements from Germany, Italy, Poland, Austria-Hungary, and Belgium. The bulk of the French were in the province of Quebec. Most of them were rural and they had large families and multiplied rapidly. In spite of the anti-Roman Catholic temper of Great Britain in the eighteenth and the fore part of the nineteenth century, from its outset British rule was tolerant of the Roman Catholic Church in Canada. To no small degree this was because of the desire to prevent the French from siding with the United States in its war of independence and in its second war with Great Britain. To the French Canadians the Roman Catholic Church was the symbol and bond of their nationalism as against the British. They looked with intense dislike upon the anti-Roman Catholic actions of the French Revolution and upon the anti-clericalism which characterized much of France in the nineteenth century. They deemed France apostate. Very few of them became Protestants or drifted into secularism. From an earlier Gallican attitude of administrative independence of the Holy See, in the course of the nineteenth century they became more and more ultramontane. In few countries did the Roman Catholic Church have so firm a hold on all phases of the lives of its members as it did on the French in Canada. The non-French elements, mainly Irish, were mostly outside the province of Quebec, the French stronghold, and did not mix easily with their French fellow-believers. Between the French and the Irish Roman Catholics, indeed, tensions existed, somewhat similar to those which were found in the Roman Catholic Church in the United States between the various national groups. There were Roman Catholic missions among the Indians and Roman Catholics shared in the settlement of the Western frontier.

Canada had very few from the Orthodox Churches. Several thousand Dukhobors came from Russia, seeking refuge from persecution, but they did not have a large place in the religious life of the country.

The Protestantism of Canada was both like and unlike that of the United States. Like the latter, it had denominations of British origin—Anglicans, Presbyterians, Methodists, Congregationalists, and Baptists. However, Congregationalists played no such large rôle as in the United States and, in contrast with the United States, where they were the largest denominational family, Baptists were a small minority. Methodism was prominent, but not as much so as in the great republic to the south. It entered partly through contacts with the United States and partly because of its rapid growth in contemporary England. The Church of England and Presbyterianism were much stronger in Canada than in the United States. This was due to the dominance of the English and Scottish elements in the nineteenth century immigration. De-Christianization made no such initial inroads as in the United States. In 1911 95 per cent. of the population of Canada professed to have a church connexion as against 43.5 per cent. in the United States in 1910. There was, accordingly, no mass conversion of a partially de-Christianized population and revivalism was not as prominent as in the latter country. As in the United States, by the end of the century no church was established by law. However, for many years financial aid was given the Church of England by the governments of Upper and Lower Canada, approximately the later provinces of Ontario and Quebec. This was in the form of government lands which were set aside as clergy reserves. Other denominations protested against what they deemed to be discriminatory preference. The Presbyterians were especially vocal, coming as most of them did from Scotland, where the state church was of their faith. Eventually portions of the clergy reserves were commuted for a permanent endowment.

Substantial aid in nurturing Protestantism among the white population and in missions to the Indians was given from the British Isles. The Society for the Propagation of the Gospel in Foreign Parts was represented by hundreds of missionaries, some to the whites and some to the Indians. The Society for Promoting Christian Knowledge assisted in the erection of Anglican churches and in establishing colleges and universities. The Church Missionary Society sent missionaries and substantial sums of money for both whites and Indians. Some societies were founded by Anglicans, especially for Canada or Newfoundland. Famous among the Anglican missionaries was Charles James Stewart (1775–1837). A younger son of the Earl of Galloway and a graduate of Oxford, he lived simply, devoted his private means and his stipend to nurturing the Church of England in Canada, travelled widely founding new churches, and in his later years was (Anglican) Bishop of Quebec. The Church of Scotland, the Free Church of Scotland, and the Irish Presbyterian Church aided Presbyterianism with funds and personnel. The London Missionary Society and the Colonial Missionary Society helped Canadian Congregationalism. In 1837 the Baptist Canadian Missionary Society was organized in England. One of the outstanding missionaries from the British Isles was Wilfred Grenfell (1865–1940). A physician and surgeon, greatly impressed by Moody and some of Moody's converts, he gave himself first to the fishermen of the North Sea and then, beginning in 1891, to the fishermen and other dwellers on the bleak coast of Labrador. Through hospital ships, schools, coöperatives, and other devices, and with assistance in money and personnel from Britain and the United States, he did much to transform wholesomely the life of a widely scattered and hard-pressed community.

As the century wore on Protestantism in Canada became sufficiently strong to assume more and more of the responsibility for the founding and support of churches, for recruiting and training the ministry for them, and for making itself felt in the new settlements on the western frontier. It also began to share in the world-wide missionary enterprise and to that end organized its own societies. Here was a vigorous Protestant Christianity which by the end of the century largely dispensed with help from abroad and began to reach out beyond the borders of the Dominion to other lands.

Greenland, the British, Danish, and Dutch West Indies, British and Dutch Guiana, and British Honduras

In addition to British North America, there were several islands and island groups near to the Americas and three pieces of territory on the mainland of Central and South America which belonged to predominantly Protestant powers. In most of them, as was to be expected, Protestantism was the prevailing form of Christianity. In almost all it made substantial progress in the nineteenth century. Since the populations involved were not large, they must be dismissed with only passing mention.

On Greenland the Christianity which had been re-planted by Scandinavian Lutheran and German Moravian missionaries in the eighteenth century continued to gain and by 1914 had won all but a few of the scanty Eskimo, Danish, and mixed Danish and Eskimo inhabitants. Most of the Christians had been taught to read and write. The missionaries responsible for this achievement under the adverse climate were still Moravians and Danish Lutherans. In 1900 the Moravians deemed their mission accomplished and withdrew, leaving the Danish Lutheran state church in sole charge.

In most of the West Indies the peoples were predominantly Negroes. Long before the end of the nineteenth century emancipation had been accomplished. In the Dutch West Indies the majority of the Negroes were Roman Catholics and in the nineteenth century that form of the faith continued to gain. Protestantism was confined chiefly to the ruling Dutch minority. In contrast, the Danish West Indies, also predominantly Negro, were prevailingly Protestant, partly Moravian and partly Church of England.

Of the British West Indies the largest was the island of Jamaica and with a population at the end of the century of about 800,000, the large majority of them Negroes. From the British occupation (1655) until 1870 the Church of England was established and received financial support from the state. Several Anglican missionary societies were represented and after the emancipation of the slaves sought to help the freedmen to make the best use of their new status. Next to the Church of England, the Baptists and Methodists had the largest constituencies, but there were as well other denominations, not only Protestant but also the Roman Catholics. By 1914 almost all the population had a connexion with some church, although for many this was very tenuous.

The second largest of the British West Indian islands, Trinidad, did not come into British hands until late in the eighteenth century. It had previously belonged to Spain and, in consequence, the Roman Catholic Church was strong. Under British rule Protestant missionaries of several denominations entered, including notably the Church of England, which until 1870 had the support of the state.

In most of the others of the British West Indies the Church of England was dominant, but the Methodists usually also had constituencies gathered through earnest missionary efforts. In a few of the islands Roman Catholics were in the majority.

On the mainland, British Honduras, flanked as it was by Spanish America, with a culturally backward population of Negroes, Indians, and whites of Spanish or British blood was much more Roman Catholic than Protestant. By

1914, due to faithful missionary effort, largely by Jesuits, Roman Catholics constituted about two-thirds of the whole, a substantial growth in the nineteenth century. Thanks also to heroic missionaries, there were Anglicans, Methodists, and Baptists.

In Dutch Guiana (Surinam), predominantly Negro, but with Indian, Chinese, Javanese, and white minorities, Protestants were the most numerous of the religious groups. This was due chiefly to the Moravians who, entering in 1735 and persisting in spite of peculiarly difficult conditions, by 1914 had gathered a very considerable membership. British Guiana, taken from the Dutch during the Napoleonic Wars, was larger in both area and population than Surinam. In 1914 about two-fifths of its population were Negroes and another two-fifths were from India and Ceylon, largely Tamils, brought in as labourers on the plantations. Most of the Roman Catholic minority were Portuguese, originally labourers from Madeira. Several Protestant denominations sent missionaries. Of these the Anglicans, assisted by the state, attracted the largest numbers of converts.

Nineteenth Century Latin America: The General Setting

What was known collectively as Latin America embraced Mexico, almost all of Central and South America, and several islands in the West Indies, including the largest, Cuba and Haiti. In 1789, at the outbreak of the era of the French Revolution and the Wars of Napoleon, all of it was in a colonial status, governed from the Old World. By 1815 that position had begun to change. In the island of Haiti French rule was overthrown by an insurrection of the Negro majority. To escape the Napoleonic armies the Portuguese ruling house shifted its residence to Brazil. In Spanish America, during the French occupation of the mother country, local governments were set up, in part by American-born whites, the *creoles,* which professed to rule on behalf of the King of Spain.

By the year 1914 all of Latin America had become fully independent politically of Europe except French Guiana and some islands in the West Indies which remained in French hands. With the exception of Puerto Rico, which was ceded to the United States by Spain as a result of war in 1898, all of autonomous Latin America had republican forms of government. In the several countries this status had been reached at widely different times. In the largest of the lands, Brazil, Portuguese by language and inheritance, it was not attained until 1889. From the severing of the ties with Portugal in 1822 until that year Brazil had been governed as an empire under a branch of the Portuguese royal family. In Spanish America, except for Puerto Rico, Cuba, and adjacent islands, political independence from the mother country was achieved before 1850, partly through war and often through marked internal disorder.

Political independence did not mean political stability. Although the governments were nominally republics and democracies, many of them were in fact military dictatorships. As a rule, dictators were overthrown only by revolutions, and while few of these were costly in life, they brought recurrent disorder. In some lands upsurging movements of the submerged majority with demands for true democracy added to the revolutions.

In most Latin American lands independence of the mother countries did not immediately greatly alter the social and economic structure inherited from colonial days. To be sure, in Haiti it was accomplished by uprisings which brought the former Negro slaves into power, and in Mexico the desire of the Indian majority for release from exploitation by the whites and for more voice in the government and larger opportunity for the good things of life was a complicating factor. In general, however, the white minority remained in power. For the most part independence came as a revolt of American-born whites and mestizos against paternalistic rule from Europe under European-born officials. Modern industries were slow in arriving and the economy was still based upon agriculture, cattle-raising, fruit-growing, mining, and, latterly in some countries, petroleum. Exports were of fruits and foods of various kinds, coffee, and minerals and were exchanged for the products of the industries of Europe and the United States.

Latin America: The Difficult Situation of the Roman Catholic Church

The new age brought grave difficulties for the Roman Catholic Church. Some of these were from the heritage of the past. We have seen (Chapter XLI) the striking successes of Roman Catholic missions in Spanish and Portuguese America in the sixteenth, seventeenth, and eighteenth centuries. Through them the immigrants from Europe had been held to the faith, the vast majority of the Indians and a large proportion of the Negroes had been won to at least a formal acceptance, schools and universities had been created, and laws had been enacted and to some degree enforced to protect the Indians from selfish exploitation by the whites. A beginning had been made towards recruiting and training an indigenous clergy.

Yet the Spanish and Portuguese American churches were still parasitic. Like the civil governments, they were paternalistically controlled and directed from the mother countries. The bishops were appointed by the crown. Rome had little or no voice in the administration and, while the churches were emphatically orthodox in doctrine, Papal decrees could be promulgated only with the consent of the crown. Most of the missionaries and bishops were not American-born but were from the Old World. Moreover, the expulsion of the Jesuits from the Spanish and Portuguese domains in the second half of the eighteenth century had deprived the missions of numerous and able personnel. Although other orders, notably the Franciscans, took over their responsibilities, the transition had made for loss of momentum. At best, under the new conditions of political independence the Roman Catholic Church, accustomed to depend on the Old World, would have been seriously handicapped.

The struggle for political independence brought additional and grave problems. As we have seen, it was to no small degree a revolt of the native-born whites against European-born officials. In this European-born clergy were involved. Many of the latter perished or left the country, and the parishes, missions, and dioceses staffed by them suffered. Some of the schools in which missionaries were prepared were closed. In large areas missions and their flocks were taken from the regular and put in charge of the secular clergy. The transfer was usually followed by decline, especially since on the average the seculars were inferior in character to the regulars. Moreover, the Church became the victim of a contest between the Spanish crown and the new governments for control of the appointments to the episcopate. The Spanish crown insisted on exercising its traditional power of naming the bishops. In view of the historic administrative autonomy of the Church in Spain as against Rome and the rising tide of anti-clericalism in that land, the Vatican did not dare openly to dissent, or its authority in Spain and in the Church in that country might further suffer. The new governments insisted on assuming the authority formerly granted the crown and upon naming the bishops. This Rome was slow to concede. As a result, in 1826 only 10 of the 38 bishoprics in Spanish America were occupied and of these only 5 were being actively administered. In 1847 Venezuela, which had been a special sufferer, had about 200 fewer priests than at the end of the colonial period.

Added to these difficulties were anti-clerical and anti-Christian currents from Europe. As was to be expected, the cultural ties of Latin America were primarily with Latin Europe. France was especially influential. It was natural, therefore, that the anti-clericalism and the secular, rationalistic revolt against Christianity which were striking features of Latin Europe in the nineteenth century and particularly of France had repercussions in Latin America. The movement for political independence in Spanish America was profoundly shaped by the ideas and example of the French Revolution. It was inevitable that the religious aspects of that upheaval would have repercussions in America and that the continuation of the Revolution throughout the nineteenth century would also be a persistent factor in Spanish and Portuguese America.

Comte and his Positivism won many followers among the intellectuals. While outward conformity to the Church might be continued, for a large proportion of the upper classes the Roman Catholic faith and therefore Christianity were a waning influence. The more conservative among the wealthy who clung to their special privileges inherited from the old order often supported the Roman Catholic Church as a bulwark against change, but those wishing to improve the lot of the masses regarded it as an obstacle.

In almost every Latin American country the struggle between the clericals, who backed the Church, and the anti-clericals, who sought to subordinate it to the state, was chronic. First one would be in control and then the other. Thus from 1860 to 1875 Ecuador was dominated by García Moreno, a highly educated aristocrat who was convinced by what he saw of the fruits of liberalism in Europe that the only alternative to anarchy was the moral discipline and the national unity given by the Roman Catholic faith. He therefore accorded great power to the Church and Rome. His assassination (1875) was followed by an anti-clerical reaction. The pendulum then swung again towards the Church, but from 1897 to 1914 anti-clericals were in power. For the most part compromises were reached in the Latin American republics by which the Roman Catholic Church was the official religion of the state, but religious liberty was professedly granted, for each vacancy in the episcopate the state and Rome joined in naming the new incumbent, civil marriage as well as that by the Church was accorded recognition by the state (although in Brazil late in the century civil marriage was made compulsory), and the state increased its control and support of education as against the Church.

As a result of these various factors, in 1914 the Roman Catholic Church in Latin America was distinctly weaker than in 1815. Many of the upper classes and of the masses had drifted from it. It did not possess sufficient vitality to recruit enough priests from its indigenous constituency to give adequate pastoral care to its nominal children. New cults entered or sprang up, including spiritualism in one or another form. Among many of the Indians and the Negroes superstitions and pagan rites and customs persisted from the pre-Christian past. Throughout the masses there were ignorance, poverty, and deplorable distortions of the faith, and both among the educated and the masses Christian standards of morals, especially in sex relations, were widely ignored. The Latin American Church continued to be parasitic, depending in part on Europe for its clergy, taking almost no share in the world-wide propagation of the faith, doing little to reach the pagan Indians who existed in the mountain fastnesses and in the tropical jungles of its river valleys, and giving rise to no major new monastic orders or creative theological thinking. This was all the more serious in view of the fact that Latin America held the largest body of nominal Roman Catholics outside of Europe and that the emergence of this body through immigration and the conversion of the Indians and the Negroes had been the major achievement of the great forward surge of Roman Catholic missions which accompanied and followed the Catholic Reformation. Taken together with the losses in Europe, it seemed to bode ill for the future of that form of the Christian faith.

The problem was aggravated by fresh immigration from Europe, chiefly of Roman Catholics and mainly to Southern Brazil, Uruguay, Argentina, and Chile. Much of it was from Italy and, while nominally Roman Catholic, in contrast with the Irish and Germans of that faith in the United States, it showed little religious zeal.

LATIN AMERICA: ATTEMPTS TO REVIVE AND STRENGTHEN THE ROMAN CATHOLIC CHURCH

Rome and the Roman Catholics of Europe did not supinely accept the grim condition of their Church in Latin America. They sought to come to the rescue. Partly as a result, by the year 1914 the Church registered some improvement. It reached its low point in the first half of the century and thereafter achieved gains.

The Papacy was able to exert more influence than had been permitted it by the Spanish and Portuguese governments before independence. It now had a voice, even if not complete control, in the naming of bishops. It had apostolic delegates in the region. In 1858, with the endorsement of Pope Pius IX, who had been apostolic delegate in Chile, the *Collegio Pio-Latino-Americano Pontificio* was opened in Rome for the education of clergy for Latin America. In 1899 a plenary council of the clergy of that area was held in the college.

To reinforce the Church in its ministry to nominal Roman Catholics and to staff its missions to non-Christians, clergy, mostly regulars, and lay brothers and sisters came to Latin America from Europe. They were of many orders and congregations and from several countries. There were Lazarists from Portugal and Spain, Capuchins from the Tyrol and Italy, Mercedarians from Italy, Franciscans from Italy, Germany, and the Netherlands, Dominicans from France, Redemptorists from Austria and the Netherlands, German Missionaries of the Holy Family, Barnabites, Salesians of Don Bosco, Pallottines, Benedictines, Missionaries of the Holy Ghost, and members of the Society of the Divine Word. Undiscouraged by their earlier expulsion from the Spanish and Portuguese domains, the Jesuits reëntered, coming from several countries. Barred from time to time from more than one of the republics, they usually contrived to gain readmission. In 1899 a college was founded at Burgos, Spain, to train clergy for Latin America. Sisters of several congregations came from

Canada and the United States. At least one teaching brotherhood conducted schools. Through the assistance from Europe not only were many existing parishes staffed, but also several missions to non-Christian Indians which had lapsed were renewed and new ones were founded. The geographic frontiers of Christianity were again pushed forward in the mountains of Mexico, in the Andes, in the Gran Chaco, in Patagonia, and in the vast and steaming valley of the Amazon and its tributaries. Clergy and teachers were provided for some of the nineteenth century immigration from Europe. The Pious Society of Missions, usually known as the Pallottines, founded in Italy in 1835 by Vincent Mary Pallotti to serve immigrants to America, staffed a number of enterprises. Some provision was made for reaching the large Japanese contingents in Brazil. Clerical ministration was given to thousands of Uniates who migrated to the southern portions of South America.

In spite of all the assistance from abroad and although some recovery had been achieved from the low point reached in the first half of the nineteenth century, in 1914 the Roman Catholic Church in Latin America was far from healthy. It was still parasitic, dependent upon continuing infusions of life from the Old World, and taking little more than a negative rôle in the world-wide extension of its branch of the Christian faith.

Latin America: The Coming of Protestantism

In view of its low vitality, it was not to be expected that any indigenous movement as vigorous as Protestantism would emerge from the Roman Catholic Church in Latin America. In the course of the nineteenth century Protestantism appeared, flourished, and put down such firm rootage that after 1914 much of its growth was without help from the outside. However, at the outset Protestantism was entirely from abroad. It came partly through immigration and partly through extensive missions, some from the British Isles but chiefly from the United States.

The Protestantism which entered through immigration was of varied origin. Some was from the British Isles. Through the world-wide extension of their trade and investments in the nineteenth century, British merchants established themselves in Latin American ports, notably in Buenos Aires, the largest city in South America, and thousands of British sailors had shore leave. To meet their needs Anglican chapels and chaplains were provided, at first with financial assistance from the British Government but later chiefly by the British residents. There were a few Presbyterian churches for the Scottish colonists and merchants. Contingents of Italian Waldensees entered Uruguay and Argentina and their clergy not only served their own congregations but also conducted missions for Roman Catholics. After the Civil War, settlers took refuge in

Brazil from the defeated South of the United States, among them Baptists, Methodists, and Presbyterians, and became nuclei for missions to their Roman Catholic neighbours. There were other Protestant immigrant churches, mostly small, among them Swedish Lutherans and Swiss, Boers, and Dutch of the Reformed faith. The largest Protestant immigration was from Germany. It began in the first half of the nineteenth century and settled chiefly in Brazil. German colonists also found homes in Uruguay, Argentina, and Chile. While, failing clerical ministrations from their faith, some of the German Protestants had their children baptized by Roman Catholics, the majority were gathered into Protestant churches. Here, as in the United States, during at least the first generation the services were in German and the congregations drew their strength from the fact that they were social as well as religious associations bound together by the common tie of nationality and language. At the outset in Brazil stipends for the pastors of the larger German communities were provided by the government. Missionaries and financial assistance came from Europe. Some of the former were from Basel and Barmen. The largest of the resulting denominations was one in which both Lutherans and Reformed joined, but several others were represented and in 1900 the Missouri Synod began an enterprise which ultimately gathered several thousands into its fellowship.

British Protestants early began missions, some among non-Christian Indians and others among Roman Catholics. The most extensive among non-Christians were by the South American Missionary Society, an Anglican enterprise which arose out of the efforts of Allen Francis Gardiner (1794–1851). Gardiner, a former commander in the British navy, selected Patagonia because it was difficult, and in an attempt to inaugurate a mission perished, with his companions, on bleak Tierra del Fuego. Partly because of the inspiration of his heroism, the society attracted recruits and funds and conducted missions, chiefly in Patagonia and the Chaco. There were other British missions, but less extensive, for non-Christian Indians in several parts of Latin America. The South American Missionary Society also had missions among Roman Catholics. Beginning in the 1820's the British and Foreign Bible Society entered Latin America, stimulated the formation of local Bible societies, and distributed Bibles in Spanish and Portuguese. Although most of the local societies were ephemeral, the mother society persisted in its programme and maintained scores of sub-depots for the circulation of the Scriptures. Several British missions, largely conservative theologically and of the Evangelical type, and including the Plymouth Brethren, were active in Latin American countries. In Brazil, partly as the outcome of one of them, Congregational churches arose akin to Baptists in practice, and early in their history became self-supporting and self-propagating.

It was through missions from the United States that the major spread of Protestantism in Latin America was achieved. The missions were directed mainly to the nominally Roman Catholic population, but to a lesser extent were also among non-Christian Indians. They began soon after 1815 but did not attain significant dimensions until the second half of the century. They then grew rapidly, came to 1914 on an ascending scale, and continued to mount after that year. Ultimately they were operating in each of the Latin American republics. They were mainly from the larger denominations of the older white stock—Methodists, Baptists, Presbyterians, Episcopalians, Congregationalists, and Disciples of Christ—but they also were from some of the younger, enthusiastic movements, notably the Seventh Day Adventists, the Christian and Missionary Alliance, the Church of the Nazarene, and the Central American Mission. The American Bible Society was active almost from its inception.

The numerical strength of Protestantism varied from country to country. Because of the proximity of the United States, it was marked in Mexico. It was greatest in Brazil. That was partly because Brazil was the largest of the Latin American countries, both in population and in area. To some degree it was because of the weakness of the Roman Catholic Church, in part it was because of the presence of large bodies of Protestant immigrants (although only a small minority of them sought to win their non-Protestant neighbours), and it was also through the weakening of the old patterns of life and the striking increase in wealth and population in the south of the country, the area in which Protestantism became strongest. It was especially in Brazil that Protestants drawn from former Roman Catholic constituencies early became self-propagating. In general, Latin American Protestants tended to be sharply critical of Roman Catholicism and conservative theologically. By 1914 Protestant communicants in Latin America totalled well over half a million. By the middle of the twentieth century they had more than doubled and what could be counted as the Protestant community was still larger. Protestantism was making more substantial gains from a nominally Roman Catholic population than anywhere else in the world. They were several times greater than those being made by the Roman Catholic Church from professedly Protestant constituencies the world around.

SUMMARY

In their formal profession the populations of British and Latin America were overwhelmingly Christian. The Christianity of Canada, both Roman Catholic and Protestant, was vigorous and by 1914 was beginning to reach out beyond the borders of the country and share in the world-wide spread of the faith. That of the British, Danish, and Dutch West Indies, mainly among Negroes who were not emancipated until the nineteenth century, left much to be desired. In Latin America, where at the outset of the century the large majority were professedly Roman Catholic but where the Church was drawing most of its leadership and missionaries from Europe and was only slowly developing its own clergy, independence and intellectual currents from Europe which were undermining Christianity made for a serious reverse. In the latter part of the century some recovery was accomplished, but this was chiefly by personnel from Europe. Latin American Roman Catholic Christianity was anemic and depended for its continuing life upon transfusions from abroad. Protestantism had been introduced and was making rapid strides, but in 1914 was still a minority movement.

SELECTED BIBLIOGRAPHY

E. Braga and K. G. Grubb, *The Republic of Brazil. A Survey of the Religious Situation* (London, World Dominion Press, 1932, pp. 164). Competent, by Protestants.

W. H. Calcott, *Church and State in Mexico 1822–1857* (Duke University Press, 1926, pp. 327). Ably done.

W. H. Calcott, *Liberalism in Mexico, 1857–1929* (Stanford University Press, 1931, pp. xiii, 410). A careful piece of work.

G. B. Camargo and K. G. Grubb, *Religion in the Republic of Mexico* (London, World Dominion Press, 1935, pp. 166). A pro-Protestant able survey.

K. G. Grubb, *Religion in Central America* (London, World Dominion Press, 1937, pp. 147). By a Protestant, an expert in missionary surveys.

K. S. Latourette, *A History of the Expansion of Christianity. Volume V, The Great Century in the Americas, Australasia, and Africa, A.D. 1800–1914* (New York, Harper & Brothers, 1943, pp. ix, 526).

L. Lemmens, *Geschichte der Franziskannermissionen* (Münster i.W., Aschendorffschen Verlagsbuchhandlung, 1929, pp. 376). Carefully done, by a Franciscan.

C. Lindsey, *Rome in Canada. The Ultramontane Struggle for Supremacy over the Civil Authority* (Toronto, Lovell Brothers, 1877, pp. 398).

J. A. Mackay, *The Other Spanish Christ. A Study of the Spiritual History of Spain and South America* (London, Student Christian Movement Press, 1932, pp. xv, 288). By a scholarly Protestant, long a missionary in Peru.

J. L. Mecham, *Church and State in Latin America* (University of North Carolina Press, 1934, pp. viii, 550). Objective. Based largely on printed sources.

E. A. Peers, *Spain, the Church and the Orders* (London, Eyre & Spottiswoode,

1939, pp. xi, 219). By an Anglican, sympathetic, from long residence and much reading.

E. Ryan, *The Church in the South American Republics* (New York, The Bruce Publishing Co., 1932, pp. viii, 119). By a Roman Catholic priest, popular in style, but scholarly.

[E. Ryerson], *"The Story of My Life." By the Late Rev. Egerton Ryerson, D.D., LL.D. (Being Reminiscences of Sixty Years' Public Service in Canada)*, edited by J. G. Hodgins (Toronto, William Briggs, 1883, pp. 613).

A. Shortt and A. G. Doughty, editors, *Canada and Its Provinces* (Toronto, Glasgow, Brook and Co., 23 vols., 1914–1917). A standard work of reference.

C. W. Vernon, *The Old Church in the New Dominion. The Story of the Anglican Church in Canada* (London, Society for Promoting Christian Knowledge, 1929, pp. viii, 215). Semi-popular.

M. Watters, *The History of the Church in Venezuela, 1810–1930* (University of North Carolina Press, 1933, pp. ix, 260). Carefully done; based upon the sources.

R. Young, *From Cape Horn to Panama. A Narrative of Missionary Enterprise among the Neglected Races of South America, by the South American Missionary Society* (London, 2d ed., South American Missionary Society, 1905, pp. xii, 212).

AUSTRALIA, NEW ZEALAND,
THE EAST INDIES,
AND THE PHILIPPINE ISLANDS

Scale of Miles

0   400   800   1200

Chapter LII

THE RAPID SPREAD OF CHRISTIANITY IN AUSTRALASIA

West of the Americas stretches the Pacific Ocean. In it are thousands of islands large and small. A collective name applied to a large number of them but with somewhat vague boundaries is Australasia. We will here employ it in its most inclusive sense and will embrace under it Australia, New Zealand, the island groups known as Polynesia, Melanesia (including New Guinea and the neighbouring islands on the east and south), Micronesia, and Hawaii. We will not regard it as extending as far to the north-west as the East Indies and the Philippines. In the nineteenth century it possessed similarities to the Americas of a slightly earlier day. Here, as in the Americas, were tribes in "primitive" stages of culture with animistic religions. Upon them, also as in the Americas, came Western man and his civilization with disintegrating effects. At times the pioneers of the impact were traders, at other times settlers, and at still others missionaries. The Occident would have come and the disintegration would have followed had never a Christian missionary arrived. What the latter did was to modify the impact by seeking to win the islanders to his faith and, that accomplished, to assist them in building a society which would embody Christian ideals. As in the Americas, but not as extensively, immigration from Europe gave rise to new nations. Here the challenge to Christianity was to hold the immigrants to their hereditary faith and to make that faith effective in the new societies.

AUSTRALIA

The larger of the nations that arose from white colonization was Australia. Here was a land which was too huge to be called an island and which did not quite rank unquestionably as a sixth continent. In 1815 only sparsely populated and that chiefly by one of the most "primitive" groups of mankind, and in its southern portions lying well within the temperate zone, in an age when

Western European peoples were flooding into the vacant spaces of the earth it constituted an invitation and a temptation to white settlement.

As we have seen (Chapter XLIV), that settlement had begun late in the eighteenth century and by the involuntary transportation of convicts from the British Isles. While the sending of convicts to Australia did not entirely cease until the 1860's, before the nineteenth century was well advanced free settlers were pouring into the land. In 1914 they and their descendants constituted the overwhelming majority of the population. They established their homes mainly on the south-east coast and in the neighbouring Tasmania and in distinct colonies which did not come together as states in a federal government until 1901. The new nation was prevailingly urban, and organized labour became powerful.

In Australia as in British North America where another self-governing dominion arose, also largely by nineteenth century immigration, Christianity was confronted with the challenge of holding the colonists and their descendants to their historic faith, and of doing so in the face of currents which seemed to be working against it. Among them were the weakening of Old World patterns of life in the fresh environment, the growth of cities and large bodies of labour in industry, absorption in acquiring the material goods of life in a new country, and the intellectual movements of the nineteenth century Occident which were adverse to the faith. In addition to these conditions, shared with other new commonwealths of the British Empire, in Australia in its earlier years Christianity faced the handicap of dealing with a convict population.

Although slightly less so than in Canada, in Australia Christianity was strikingly successful in weaving itself into the warp and woof of the new nation. In spite of the obstacles peculiar to the country, in 1914 the proportion of those professing a connexion with one or another of the churches was almost the same as in Canada. In this, as in Canada, Christianity was assisted by the rising tides of life in the British Isles.

More than in Canada and much more than in the United States, the white population was from the British Isles. There was not the problem, as in Canada, of a large non-British element which had gained rootage before the advent of British rule: Australia had no French enclave or anything corresponding to it. There was only slight immigration from the Continent of Europe, and the adamant policy of a "white Australia" kept out all but very small contingents from the islands which bordered the country on the east and north and from the teeming millions of Asia and its fringing islands. This meant that except for small Lutheran minorities of German ancestry the Christianity of Australia was overwhelmingly from the British Isles.

In proportion to the total church constituency of the country, the Roman Catholic Church was only about half as strong in Australia as in Canada and the United States. It was almost entirely from the Irish immigrants and their descendants. It was not until 1819 that uninterrupted services of the clergy began. In 1842 Australia was given a comprehensive hierarchy.

In 1914 the Church of England had twice as many constituents as the Roman Catholics. For years it received assistance from England in the form of clergy and funds through several missionary societies. For a time financial aid was given by the colonial governments, and before many years this was also accorded to some other churches. Eventually, for the most part in the 1860's and 1870's, it was discontinued, and the Church of England, along with the other denominations, became dependent upon voluntary contributions. Increasingly the initiative and support were from the Australians. The first clergy arrived before 1815, but it was not until 1836 that a Bishop of Australia was consecrated. He was William Grant Broughton. Able, energetic, sympathetic with the Oxford or Tractarian movement, he travelled widely in his vast see, recruited clergy, and obtained the creation of additional bishoprics. He became the first metropolitan of the ecclesiastical province of Australia, and died (1853) while in England attempting to gain greater freedom of the Church of England in Australia from state control under an autonomous ecclesiastical structure in which the clergy and laity would share.

The Presbyterians, with not quite an eighth of the population in 1914, were mainly of Scottish and Scotch-Irish origin. Several branches of Presbyterianism were represented, but eventually some of them coalesced. As was true of the Anglicans, for many years assistance in clergy and money came from the British Isles, but in time self-support was achieved. The outstanding pioneer was John Dunmore Lang. Of Scottish birth and education, he came to Australia in 1823 with the express purpose of promoting Presbyterianism. Of great physical and mental vigour, an ardent advocate of the financial independence of the Church from the state, he encouraged Protestant immigration, recruited clergy from the British Isles, and fostered education.

In 1914 Methodists had about the same numbers as the Presbyterians. The first class meeting was gathered in 1812 and the pioneer missionary reached the country in 1815. Aid came from British Methodism, but in 1855 the first Australian Conference assembled and formulated a plan for the Australian Wesleyan Connexion, partly independent of the mother church.

Baptists, Congregationalists, and some other British denominations gathered churches in Australia, but were much less numerous than Roman Catholics, Anglicans, Presbyterians, or Methodists.

The aborigines were not forgotten. Under the initial impact of the white man their numbers, estimated to have been about 250,000 or 300,000 in 1788, by the fore part of the twentieth century dwindled to about 50,000 pure bloods and

25,000 mixed bloods. By 1914 they were mostly in the western and northern portions of the country, regions where white population was small. They were served by several missions, some Roman Catholic and some Protestant, some from abroad and others maintained by Australian Christians.

Long before 1914 Australian Protestants began reaching out beyond their borders to propagate their faith. They regarded themselves as having peculiar obligations to the primitive peoples in the islands to the east and north and also sent missionaries to Asia.

Here was a vigorous Christianity which was holding the immigrant, was doing much to shape the ideals, morals, and education of the new nation, and was beginning to share in the world-wide spread of the faith.

New Zealand

Much smaller in area than Australia, the group of islands known collectively as New Zealand had in 1914 only about a million people, slightly over a fourth of that of the commonwealth on its north. At the outset of the nineteenth century the population was made up of Maoris, the descendants of Polynesians who had arrived a few hundred years earlier. White immigration did not begin on a large scale until the 1840's. It was then overwhelmingly from the British Isles, with a proportionately much smaller contingent from Ireland than in Australia.

Christianity first entered New Zealand in the form of Protestant missions to the Maoris. This was at the instance of Samuel Marsden whom we have already met (Chapter XLIV) as one of the earliest clergymen of the Church of England in Australia. The initial party of Anglican missionaries landed in 1814. Partly at the instance of Marsden, Methodists also came. Their pioneer station was opened in 1822. The first Roman Catholic mass in New Zealand was said by a French missionary in 1838. Christianity spread rapidly, mainly through the representatives of the Church Missionary Society. The first Anglican bishop, George Augustus Selwyn, arrived in 1842. Able, devoted, with an iron physical constitution, a high churchman, he had a large share in establishing his church among the Maoris and the white settlers and in inaugurating Anglican missions in several of the island groups to the north and east of Australia. In 1854 it was said that all but about 1 per cent. of the Maoris were at least nominally Christian.

The Church Missionary Society sought to prevent the coming of white colonists, for it believed, correctly as the event proved, that it would lead to the exploitation of the Maoris and to war. In spite of its opposition, in the 1840's whites began to pour in.

White settlement was to some extent from religious motives. Edward Gibbon

Wakefield, impressed with the way in which earnestly Christian minorities had contributed to the shaping of the Thirteen Colonies which later became the United States, sought to bring similar elements into the founding of what he dreamed of as the future nation of New Zealand. He himself appears to have had little interest in religion and to have valued it simply as a means to attracting colonists of a high type. Partly through the impulse given by him in the 1850's an Anglican colony was founded around Christchurch, on the South Island. Slightly earlier, in the 1840's a similar contingent of Scottish Presbyterians, hoping to create an ideal Christian community, established a centre which they called Dunedin, an old Celtic designation of Edinburgh, at Otago, also on the South Island.

The majority of the white colonists came from other than a religious impulse. Yet in 1914 all but a small fraction of them claimed a church connexion. More than two-fifths were Anglicans. The Church of England in New Zealand owed its organization chiefly to Selwyn. He called its first synod in 1844. In 1858 he was made metropolitan and had under him four bishoprics. In 1857 a constitution was framed for the Church and the first general synod assembled in 1859. Presbyterians constituted about a fourth of the population, nearly twice their proportion in Australia. Methodists were the third largest of the denominations, and Roman Catholics, mainly of Irish stock, ranked fourth. Baptists, Congregationalists, both small in numbers, and a few other denominations were represented.

THE OTHER ISLANDS OF THE PACIFIC

It is a temptation to go at length into the nineteenth century spread of Christianity among the aboriginal populations of the many islands and groups of islands that stud the Pacific east and north of New Zealand and Australia. On each island or island cluster it had a distinct history. Deeds of heroism abounded, mass conversions were common, and often within less than a generation almost the entire island or island group became professedly Christian. However, the population total, even of all the vast expanse, was not large, and we must content ourselves with a few generalizations and three concrete thumb-nail sketches.

The generalizations must be briefly given. The larger part of the missions were by Protestants, mostly Congregational, Anglican, Methodist, and Presbyterian from the British Isles, Australia, and New Zealand. Congregationalists from the United States were prominent in Hawaii and Micronesia. The Roman Catholics were chiefly from France. The usual but not the invariable course of Christianity was the arrival of the first missionaries, initial resistance, possibly prolonged and aggravated in the native mind by unhappy memories of cruelties and exploitation by white traders, next a few conversions, then the conversion of the chief, that event followed by a mass conversion of the island, and finally the slow process of instruction to make the nominal faith actual and to build a group life which would be somewhere nearly worthy of the designation Christian. In the process the language would be reduced to writing, part or all of the Bible translated into it, school books and other literature prepared, schools inaugurated and conducted, and, on some islands, simple handicrafts taught. Often, perhaps from the first generation of Christians, some went as missionaries to distant islands, facing the perils both of the sea and of a hostile reception. Long before 1914 most of Polynesia, the eastern fringe of islands stretching from Hawaii to New Zealand, all of Micronesia, and part of Melanesia had accepted the faith. Progress was being registered in some of the larger groups of Melanesia and on the fringes of formidable New Guinea.

It will be remembered that it was on Tahiti of the Society Islands that eighteen, the chief contingent of the initial enterprise of the London Missionary Society on *The Duff,* had landed in 1796. In 1798 eleven of the eighteen, discouraged, sought haven in Australia and two others, taking native wives, were cut off by the mission. In 1808 the paramount chief of Tahiti, while in close association with the missionaries on a neighbouring island from which he had taken refuge from a rebellion, asked for baptism. This was not at once granted him, but when, in 1815, he returned to Tahiti and reëstablished his power, he toured the island urging his subjects to accept the new faith. The population complied, a printing press was set up, the Bible was translated, schools were organized, and a code of laws based on Christian ideals was promulgated by the chieftain. The faith and its associated code of laws quickly spread to others of the Society Islands.

Some of *The Duff* party were landed on the Tonga or Friendly Islands. However, within about four years three were killed, one acquired a native wife and abandoned his faith, and the others fled to Australia. Partly through interest aroused by contacts with these last, British Methodists took up the enterprise, before 1840 mass conversions had brought most of the islands into the Christian fold, and the chief of one of the islands had proclaimed a code of laws based on Christian principles.

Hawaii had been frequented by white traders for about a generation before the first missionaries arrived. Because of that contact the population had declined by more than half, the disintegration of its culture was far advanced, and a chieftain, utilizing fire-arms obtained from the traders, had brought all the islands under his rule. Then, in 1820 there landed the first group of a succession of Congregational missionaries from New England. Within twenty years the language was reduced to writing, parts of the Bible were translated, thousands were enrolled in schools, laws were enacted by the native government against prostitution, gambling, drunkenness, and the profanation of Sunday, and a mass movement brought about a sixth of the population into the membership of the Church. In 1863 the American Board of Commissioners for Foreign Missions, under which the missionaries had come, deeming that its task had been accomplished and that the churches were ready for self-government, greatly reduced its aid. In the latter part of the century the scene was complicated by an extensive immigration, most of them labourers on the plantations, a minority of them Roman Catholic Spaniards, Portuguese, and Filipinos, and the majority non-Christian Japanese, Chinese, and Koreans. Some advance was made among the Asiatics by several denominations.

SUMMARY

In the nineteenth century Christianity became the dominant religion in the Pacific. This was chiefly through the emergence of two new nations, Australia and New Zealand, by immigration from the British Isles and through success in holding it to its hereditary faith. It was also through the conversion of a large proportion, although as yet only a minority, of the indigenous peoples.

SELECTED BIBLIOGRAPHY

R. Anderson, *History of the Sandwich Islands Mission* (Boston, Congregational Publishing Co., 1870, pp. xxiv, 408). By an official of the American Board of Commissioners for Foreign Missions.

H. N. Birt, *Benedictine Pioneers in Australia* (London, Herbert & Daniel, 2 vols., 1911).

J. W. Burton, *The Call of the Pacific* (London, Charles H. Kelley, 1912, pp. xiv, 286). A study book for the churches.

W. W. Burton, *The State of Religion and Education in New South Wales* (London, J. Cross and Simpkin and Marshall, 1840, pp. vii, 321, cxxxvi). By a judge with a strong Anglican bias.

J. Cameron, *Centenary History of the Presbyterian Church in New South Wales* (Sydney, Angus and Robertson, 1905, pp. xxii, 449). An official history based on documents.

R. A. Giles, *The Constitutional History of the Australian Church* (London, Skeffington & Son, 1929, pp. 320). Scholarly.

G. Goodman, *The Church in Victoria during the Episcopate of the Right Reverend Charles Perry, First Bishop of Melbourne* (London, Seeley & Co., 1892, pp. xxiv, 476). By a clergyman who served under Perry. Quotes extensively from documents.

R. Hamilton, *A Jubilee History of the Presbyterian Church in Victoria . . . from the Foundation of the Colony to 1888* (Melbourne, M. L. Hutchinson, 1888, pp. xx, 495, xxx). Based largely on church records.

H. Jacobs, *New Zealand. Containing the Dioceses of Auckland, Christchurch, Nelson, Waiapu, Wellington, and Melanesia* (London, Society for Promoting Christian Knowledge, 1887, pp. xvi, 480). Deals chiefly with the development of the structure of the Church of England in New Zealand.

K. S. Latourette, *A History of the Expansion of Christianity. Volume V, The Great Century* A.D. *1800–1914 in the Americas, Australasia and Africa* (New York, Harper & Brothers, 1943, pp. ix, 526).

D. MacDougall, *The Conversion of the Maoris* (Philadelphia, Presbyterian Board of Publication and Sabbath-School Work, 1899, pp. viii, 216).

J. S. Needham, *White and Black in Australia* (London, Society for Promoting Christian Knowledge, 1935, pp. 174). By a former missionary among the blacks.

D. M. Stewart, *The Presbyterian Church of Victoria . . . 1859–1899* (Melbourne, D. W. Paterson & Co., pp. vi, 129). An official history.

H. W. Tucker, *Memoir of the Life and Episcopate of George Augustus Selwyn* (London, William Wells Gardner, 2 vols., 1879). Based on original sources.

W. Ullathorne, *The Catholic Mission in Australasia* (London, Keating & Brown, 3d ed., pp. 58).

F. T. Whitington, *William Grant Broughton, Bishop of Australia* (Sydney, Angus & Robertson, 1936, pp. xiv, 300).

AFRICA
AND THE ADJACENT ISLANDS

Scale of Miles

0   200   100   600   800   1000

HAGSTROM CO., N.Y.

Chapter LIII

THE PENETRATION OF MADAGASCAR AND AFRICA SOUTH OF THE SAHARA

From Australasia and the islands of the Pacific we move, appropriately, westward to Madagascar and Africa south of the Sahara. Here, too, the white man and his culture impinged upon "primitive" man; here, too, in the temperate zone extensive white immigration led to the emergence of a new nation; here, also, "primitive" cultures began to disintegrate through the infiltration of white civilization; and here Christianity had a striking advance which continued after 1914 at an accelerated pace.

MADAGASCAR

Madagascar, one of the largest islands of the world and separated from Africa by a strait which at its narrowest point is about 250 miles wide, ethnically was quite distinct from the neighbouring continent. In language and race its population, known collectively as the Malagasy, was more akin to the Malays, Polynesians, and Melanesians than to the Africans. The most active and most nearly dominant of its many tribes were the Hòva, with their home in the central plateau from 4,000 to 6,000 feet above sea level and so more conducive to vigour than the enervating tropical lowlands. At the dawn of the nineteenth century the Malagasy and especially the Hòva were beyond the "primitive" stage of culture but were not yet highly civilized. Some time before 1800 the highlands had become politically united under the Hòva. In the first decade of the nineteenth century one of the Hòva chieftains began the acquisition of fire-arms and through them extended his rule.

It was under this chieftain that Christianity was effectively introduced and entered on what was to be a dramatic course. It had first been brought by Roman Catholics during the sixteenth and seventeenth centuries but had not gained a firm foothold and had disappeared. The chieftain was eager to employ European methods and tools to enlarge his domains and render them more prosperous. To this end he made diplomatic and commercial overtures to the

British and encouraged the coming of teachers. He therefore showed favour to representatives of the London Missionary Society. Under him and his immediate successor the Bible and a hymn book were translated and printed, schools were opened, and a number of the Hòva were baptized. Then, from 1836 to 1861, an anti-foreign and anti-Christian reaction was led by the reigning chieftainess. The missionaries were ordered out and Christians were persecuted. Yet the faith spread and Roman Catholic missionaries entered. Late in the 1860's a new chieftainess and her leading aids were baptized, as Protestants, and Christianity began a rapid spread. Additional societies entered, some of them Protestant and some Roman Catholic. Most of the Protestants were British, with the London Missionary Society leading, and in 1868 the Madagascar Congregational Union came into being as a means towards an autonomous Malagasy church. Lutherans from Norway and the United States came. By 1890 Christians numbered about a third of a million. In 1895 France annexed the island. French officials were both anti-clerical and anti-British and for a time missions, especially those of British Protestants, found conditions adverse. French Protestants came to the rescue and took over numbers of the schools and hundreds of the congregations associated with the London Missionary Society. Additional Roman Catholic orders entered from France. By 1914 Protestants, both baptized and adherents, totalled about 400,000 and Roman Catholics over 200,000. Together the Protestant and Roman Catholic constituencies were between a fifth and a fourth of the population.

Africa South of the Sahara: The Penetration of the Interior by Europeans

In the nineteenth century Africa south of the Sahara contained the largest population of "primitive" cultures to be found anywhere on the planet. Except in a few places, largely on or near its northern borders, it had no continuing states or kingdoms. For the most part its organization was tribal. The vast majority were not only illiterate but also spoke languages which had never been given a written form. Religion was chiefly animism in one or another of its protean manifestations.

The nineteenth century witnessed the penetration of this congeries of "primitive" peoples by the white man, the partition of the land among European powers, and the beginning of a disintegration of the inherited patterns of life which was to proceed at an accelerated pace after 1914. In 1815 that penetration had only barely begun. Here and there on the coast were trading posts, most of them having the slave trade as a main cause of their existence. For three centuries vessels freighted with their tragic cargoes of involuntary emigrants had been sailing from them to provide labourers for the plantations of the New World. The "black ivory" had been obtained by the attack of one tribe on another and for every slave delivered to the white trader two or three dead were left somewhere along the tracks of the raiders. Exploration of the interior began in earnest late in the eighteenth century and was continued from the early years of the nineteenth century by numbers of intrepid adventurers. It was not completed until after 1900, but most of its startling disclosures were in the third quarter of the nineteenth century. In it several missionaries had a part. Indeed, the two most famous explorers were David Livingstone, of whom we must say more in a moment, and Henry M. Stanley who, although not a missionary, became involved in his African journeys through his successful effort to find Livingstone.

In the 1880's and 1890's earth-hungry European powers divided most of the Africa which had been revealed and by arrangement among themselves delimited the boundaries of the possessions thus acquired. At a conference in Berlin in 1884–1885 they agreed upon general principles and also set up the Congo Free State under the King of Belgium with the provision that it was to be "perpetually neutral." In the partition Great Britain, France, Portugal, and Germany obtained the major shares and in 1905 Belgium annexed the Congo Free State, thus formally making it what it had increasingly actually been, the Belgian Congo.

Exploration and the setting up of colonial regimes combined with the effects of foreign commerce and traders and the labours of missionaries to bring about the weakening of old customs and institutions. That weakening proceeded more rapidly in some areas than in others and, gathering momentum and accelerated by events after 1914, in the twentieth century became general.

Could Christianity minister to the millions of individuals thus become accessible? As the old society disappeared, partly because of the missionary impact, could Christianity help protect the Africans from the evils brought by the new day and assist in building a structure which would make for a richer life for the otherwise deracinated and often bewildered multitude?

In seeking to answer these questions we must not take the space to record in detail the spread of Christianity in Africa. That would lengthen this chapter to several volumes. All that we can attempt is to formulate a few generalizations and to deal rapidly with the course of the faith in a few sections of the continent.

THE SPREAD OF CHRISTIANITY IN AFRICA SOUTH OF THE SAHARA:
INCLUSIVE GENERALIZATIONS

The main characteristics of the spread of Christianity in Africa south of the Sahara can be quickly summarized. It was seen in all the political units into which European powers had divided the region by the end of the nineteenth century, but it was more rapid in some than in others. It was more by Protestants than by Roman Catholics. In 1914 the former outnumbered the latter two to one, but by 1914 the latter were taking an increasing part and in some sections after that year were to forge ahead of the other. Both branches of the faith were represented in all the European possessions, but in general, as was to be expected, Protestants were stronger in the British territories and Roman Catholics in the French, Portuguese, and Belgian colonies. Missionaries fought slavery and the slave trade, reduced scores of languages to writing, in the tongues thus given a literary form began the preparation of Christian literature, including the translation of part or all of the Bible, inaugurated and maintained the vast majority of the schools which sought to prepare the Africans for the white man's world, were pioneers in bringing Occidental medicine to deal with the diseases of the African, sought to inculcate Christian standards of morals and, sometimes clumsily, sometimes skilfully, encouraged the Africans to adjust their inherited mores to them. Above all, they won Africans to the faith, brought them into churches, and began recruiting and training Africans to lead them, thus seeking to give Christianity permanent rootage.

THE COMPLEX STORY OF CHRISTIANITY IN SOUTH AFRICA

It was in South Africa that by 1914 Christianity made a more rapid and extensive advance than in any other part of the continent in the nineteenth century. There in that year, with the possible exception of Ethiopia (Abyssinia), Christians constituted a larger proportion of the population than in any other African country.

By 1914 there had emerged in the southern extremity of the continent, predominantly in the temperate zone, a new nation, the Union of South Africa, as a self-governing dominion within the British Empire. It presented an extraordinarily complex ethnic picture with multiple and intense cleavages and frictions along racial and national lines. The whites were the governing group, but they were in the minority, although a substantial minority, and were divided between the Boers or Afrikanders of mixed Dutch and French Huguenot ancestry and the British. Afrikander-British relations, long tense, had recently been further embittered by a war (1899–1902) after which the British, technically the victors, had sought to heal the sting and solve the problem by giving the region dominion status (1909–1910). Yet the two groups remained apart, distinct in language, religion, and, to some extent, in outlook and customs. The Africans were divided among the Bushmen, a dwindling minority, the Hottentots, also a minority, and the Bantus, consisting of many tribes and who, migrating from the North, had begun filtering into the area not far from the time of the first arrival of the whites. In addition there were what were known as the Coloured, a mixed stock, mostly at the Cape, descendants of slaves and convicts from the East, mostly Malays commingled with Hottentots and with some admixture of white blood. There was an Indian minority, chiefly in Natal. There were also several thousand Chinese.

The Afrikanders, largely rural, multiplying rapidly with their large families of children, speaking their own language, Afrikaans, from the inherited Dutch, tended to be clannish, much as were the French in another British dominion, Canada, and for the same reason. The vast majority were members of the Dutch Reformed Church in one or another of its several branches. As the French Canadians found in the Roman Catholic Church a symbol and tie of their nationality as against the ruling power and the immigrant British and abhorred the liberalism of revolutionary and post-revolutionary France, so the Afrikanders were loyal to the Dutch Reformed Church as a bond and a feature of their distinctive life and culture and that church was theologically very conservative.

Into the Dutch Reformed Church there entered a strong infusion of the Pietistic strain of the Evangelical awakening. This was chiefly through a Scot, Andrew Murray, who came to South Africa early in the nineteenth century in response to a plea, reinforced by the British governor, for clergy to meet the dearth of pastors for the Dutch churches. His sons, John and Andrew, Jr., after their education in Scotland, where they were in close touch with a revival movement, and in Utrecht, where they were members of a little circle which, reacting against eighteenth century rationalism, were symptoms of a rising tide of faith, returned to South Africa and became ministers in the Dutch Reformed Church. John Murray became prominent as a teacher in the leading theological seminary and Andrew Murray, Junior (1828–1917), became extremely influential as a pastor and as the author of devotional books which had a wide circulation not only in South Africa but also through much of that wing of world-wide Protestantism which was committed to revivals and the Evangelical movement.

The British elements entered after the occupation by their mother country during the Napoleonic Wars and the subsequent annexation. They were mainly English, Scotch, and Irish. Most of them seem to have held at least nominally to their hereditary faith. The Roman Catholics were predominantly Irish. Proportionately the Church of England was stronger among the British element than in Canada, Australia, or New Zealand, and the Presbyterians less so. As was to be expected after what we have found in the other dominions, Methodism was prominent and the Baptists and Congregationalists, the other large British denominations, were present but far behind these others in size.

The outstanding place held by the Anglicans was in part due to the leadership given by the first resident bishop, Robert Grey, who was appointed in 1847 to the See of Cape Town, was in sympathy with the Oxford movement, travelled indefatigably over his huge diocese, built churches, recruited and trained clergy, and initiated missions to non-Christians. When he died, in 1872, he was Metropolitan of the (ecclesiastical) Province of South Africa with other bishops under him.

Christianity spread rapidly among the non-Europeans of South Africa. By 1914 about 30 per cent. of that element were accounted as Christian. The proportion varied from section to section. It was highest in the Orange Free State, next highest in the Cape Province, where contact with the white man and the missionary had been longest, and lowest in Natal. The total mounted rapidly in the latter part of the century. The non-European Christians were overwhelmingly Protestant. The Dutch Reformed Church had a share in their conversion, especially after the impetus given by the younger Andrew Murray, but was not as active as the British and tended to treat them in a paternalistic fashion.

The leading pioneer in British missions to the non-Europeans was the London Missionary Society. As its first representative it sent the Dutchman, John Theodore Vanderkemp, whom we have met as the one chiefly responsible for the formation of the Netherlands Missionary Society. He died in 1811 and in 1820 there came to head the London Missionary Society's enterprise John Philip, who served until 1850. Vigorous, courageous, and characterized by marked initiative, Philip championed the cause of the Africans, fought slavery, furthered treaties with native chiefs to end the wars on the frontiers of white settlement, worked to have native states set up from which all whites except missionaries and those approved by missionaries would be excluded, and encouraged the entrance of other Protestant societies. British Methodist missionaries won more converts than the London Missionary Society, the Scottish Presbyterians specialized on Christian schools for the Africans, the Anglicans had extensive enterprises, and some other British missions came. French, Scandinavian, Swiss, and German Protestants shared in spreading the Christian faith. Americans arrived chiefly through the American Board of Commissioners for Foreign Missions and the African Methodist Episcopal Church. Roman Catholics were present but were a small minority. To these denominations of foreign origin were added a rapidly mounting number of African origin, mostly among the Bantus. Yet the multiplicity of the varieties of Christianity did not make for as much confusion as might have been expected. Some of the denominational missions were confined to particular areas. For example, the French Protestants centered their efforts on Basutoland and Barotseland, and the Hermannsburg Mission in a section of the Transvaal.

David Livingstone and What Issued from His Vision and Labours

The most famous missionary to Africa, David Livingstone (1813–1873), began his labours in South Africa but moved on to an even wider sphere and was a powerful stimulus and inspiration to the initiation of missions in several areas. A Scot of mixed Highland and Lowland descent, the son of humble and deeply religious parents, he was born in a tenement at Blantyre, a small factory community near Glasgow. He went to work in a cotton mill at the age of ten, but, avid for learning, he attended night school, read such books on science and travel as he could obtain, and, after a deep religious experience, decided to become a medical missionary to China and acquired an education in theology and medicine. With sympathies which could not be confined to any one denomination, he applied to the London Missionary Society, for its undenominational character appealed to him. Since war between Great Britain and China kept him from the land of his first choice, he went to South Africa, lured by the challenge of Robert Moffat, a missionary on the frontier in that country who said that from where he lived on any clear morning the smoke of a thousand villages could be seen where the name of Christ had never been heard. Livingstone joined Moffat and married his daughter. However, he could not long be content in any one place. The urge to travel and discovery which had been with him from boyhood, transmuted by his Christian faith, drove him to journey after journey to parts of the interior never before seen by a European. His purpose was to open the way for the Gospel, for the righting of wrongs, and the healing of social sores. He dreamed of the benefits which Western civilization could bring to Africa. He loved the Africans, dealt with them tactfully and selflessly, and won their confidence. Fearless and with an indomitable will, he drove his body, often racked and spent with fever and dysentery, to incredible exploits. A keen observer, he made voluminous records of what he saw. His Christian faith sustained him, kept him humble, and in the end mellowed the native asperity of his character. In his later years he severed his connexion with the London Missionary Society, not because he had changed his purpose, but because he believed that he could best fulfill it as an agent of the British Government.

The fame of Livingstone's journeys and his appeals led to the inauguration of a number of missions in the areas which he revealed to the European world. In a lecture at Cambridge (1857) his challenge: "Do you carry on the work which I have begun. I leave it with you," called forth (1858) the Universities'

Mission to Central Africa, an Anglican enterprise. It had as its initial goal Lake Nyasa and the valley of the river which drained it, the Shiré. What looked like disaster met its first efforts, but, establishing headquarters at Zanzibar, it gradually made its way to Lake Nyasa from the east rather than the south and expanded its activities to other areas as well. Stirred by the life and death of Livingstone, both the Free Church of Scotland and the Church of Scotland began missions in the neighbourhood of Lake Nyasa, the one with head-quarters at a station called Livingstonia and the other at a centre to which the name Blantyre was given. Through them languages were reduced to writing, numbers of schools opened, and thousands of converts gathered into churches.

Due to the impulse given by Livingstone, there arose a very important centre of Christianity in Uganda, in the highlands of equatorial Africa. Here dwelt a vigorous people, the Baganda, Bantus with an intermixture of Hamitic blood, under a ruling dynasty which may have been in power since the fifteenth century. They were first brought into effective contact with Christianity through Henry M. Stanley. Stanley, a newspaper correspondent sent by Bennett of *The New York Herald* to find Livingstone, from whom the outer world had not heard for some time, during their few days together was tremendously impressed by the intrepid traveller-missionary. After the death of Livingstone, alone in the interior to which he had given his life, Stanley felt constrained to take up the unfinished task of exploration. In 1874 he reëntered Africa on an expedition which brought him to Uganda. There he taught the principles of the Christian faith to the king of the Baganda, the half-pagan half-Moslem Mtesa, and translated part of the Bible for him. Convinced of the truth of the white man's religion by the superiority of the mechanical inventions of the Europeans and by the assertion (by that time substantially true) that, in con-trast with the Arabs, Christians did not enslave Africans, Mtesa professed him-self a Christian. Stanley gave publicity to what had transpired and called for missionaries to follow up what he had begun. To enter the opening there came, first representatives of the Church Missionary Society (1877), and then, in 1879, White Fathers despatched by their founder, Lavigerie. In spite of persecu-tion instigated by Mtesa's successor from fear that the acceptance of Christianity would be followed by annexation by some European power, both the Anglicans and the Roman Catholics had striking numerical success. In 1894, the year that Uganda became a British protectorate, a section of the country was assigned by Rome to an English society, the Mill Hill Fathers. By 1914 Christians totalled more than 200,000, about 40 per cent. of them Anglicans and about 60 per cent. Roman Catholics. Each church had an extensive system of schools and was recruiting and training an indigenous clergy.

SOME OTHER CENTRES OF RAPID CHRISTIAN EXPANSION

The Congo Free State, by 1914 reconstituted as the Belgian Congo, was another area of the rapid growth of Christianity. Here, with the possible exception of Nigeria, was the largest African population of any political unit south of the Sahara. The majority were Bantus of many tribes. Into the Congo Free State, beginning in the 1870's, challenged by the information about the region given by Stanley, came many Protestant societies, some of them interdenominational "faith" missions and some denominational. They were mostly from Great Britain and the United States. Simultaneously there entered an increasing number of Roman Catholic orders. Some of these were French, such as the White Fathers, and some were German, but more and more they were Belgian. Belgian Roman Catholics, predominant in their native land, became progressively more active in missions and centered most of their attention upon this, their one colonial possession. Stressing the fact that they were Belgians as against the Protestants, who were non-Belgians, they asked, often successfully, for preferential treatment by the government. Both Protestants and Roman Catholics attracted large numbers of converts, but the latters' growth was peculiarly spectacular.

Nigeria, British-administered in the partition of Africa, appealed to the consciences of British Christians. In it, especially in the animistic South rather than in the North, for the latter was more distant from the sea and was penetrated by Islam, Presbyterians from Scotland, the Church Missionary Society, and Methodists, as well as some others from the British Isles were active. Here Samuel Adjai Crowther, rescued as a lad from a slave ship and later the first African to become an Anglican bishop, had his diocese. Southern Baptists from the United States were also represented and there were some Roman Catholics.

SUMMARY

Long a victim of the greed of the white man, in the nineteenth century Africa south of the Sahara, penetrated partly from imperial ambition, partly from the spirit of adventure and insatiable curiosity, and partly from the motive of spreading the Christian faith, was covered, in places thinly, by a network of Christian missions. In the fore part of the century these were mostly Protestant. By the year 1914 Roman Catholics were rapidly increasing their participation. Missionaries were reducing languages to writing, translating and distributing the Bible, founding and conducting hundreds of schools, fighting the retreating remnants of slavery, and gathering Christian communities. Numerically Christianity was strongest in South Africa, where a new nation dominated by whites was emerging. There were other centres, notably Uganda, where Christians were becoming a considerable proportion of the population. The momentum given before 1914 mounted after that year and by the middle of the twentieth century a mass conversion was well under way.

SELECTED BIBLIOGRAPHY

W. G. Blaikie, *The Personal Life of David Livingstone* (New York, Fleming H. Revell Co., preface 1880, pp. 508). The best popular biography.

J. Bouniol, editor, *The White Fathers and Their Missions* (London, Sands & Co., 1929, pp. 334). A popular account.

R. J. Campbell, *Livingstone* (New York, Dodd, Mead & Co., 1930, pp. x, 295). More critical than the biography by Blaikie.

J. Du Plessis, *The Evangelisation of Pagan Africa. A History of Christian Missions to the Pagan Tribes of Central Africa* (Cape Town and Johannesburg, J. C. Juta & Co., 1930, pp. xii, 408). By a competent scholar, but with few references to sources.

J. Du Plessis, *A History of Christian Missions in South Africa* (London, Longmans, Green & Co., 1911, pp. xx, 494). Well done, but with few references to the sources.

J. Du Plessis, *The Life of Andrew Murray of South Africa* (London, Marshall Brothers, 1919, pp. xvi, 553). Not only the standard biography, but also virtually a history of the Dutch Reformed Church in South Africa in the nineteenth and the early part of the twentieth century.

W. Ellis, *The Martyr Church: A Narrative of the Introduction, Progress, and Triumph of Christianity in Madagascar* (London, John Snow & Co., 1870, pp. x, 404). By one with first-hand knowledge of the events.

C. P. Groves, *The Planting of Christianity in Africa. Volume One, to 1840* (London, Lutterworth Press, 1948, pp. xiii, 330). Carefully done.

K. S. Latourette, *A History of the Expansion of Christianity. Volume V, The Great Century in the Americas, Australasia and Africa,* A.D. *1800–1914* (New York, Harper & Brothers, 1943, pp. ix, 526).

J. Page, *The Black Bishop, Samuel Adjai Crowther* (New York, Fleming H. Revell Co., no date, pp. xv, 440).

J. Richter, *Geschichte der evangelischen Mission in Afrika* (Gütersloh, C. Bertelsmann, 1922, pp. 813). The standard comprehensive account of the history of Protestant missions in Africa, written with a German bias.

H. M. Stanley, *Through the Dark Continent* (New York, Harper & Brothers, 2 vols., 1878).

E. Stock, *The History of the Church Missionary Society: Its Environment, Its Men, and Its Work* (London, Church Missionary Society, 4 vols., 1899–1916). The standard history, by a secretary of the society.

A. E. Tucker, *Eighteen Years in Uganda & East Africa* (London, Edward Arnold, 2 vols., 1908). Autobiographical, by a distinguished Anglican bishop in that region.

F. D. Walker, *The Romance of the Black River. The Story of the C.M.S. Nigeria Mission* (London, Church Missionary Society, 1930, pp. xvi, 267). A popular account.

INDIA, BURMA
and CEYLON

Scale of miles
0 100 200 300 400

FRENCH INDO-CHINA,
SIAM and the
MALAY PENINSULA

Scale of miles
0   100   200   300

THE CHINESE EMPIRE,
JAPAN, KOREA
and SIBERIA

Scale of miles
0 100 200 300 400 500

Chapter LIV

THE NINETEENTH CENTURY SPREAD OF THE FAITH IN SOUTH, SOUTH-EAST, AND EAST ASIA AND THE FRINGING ISLANDS

As we move from the islands of the Pacific and Africa south of the Sahara to South, South-east, and East Asia and the fringing islands we come into a different world. We are no longer in an area of great, relatively unoccupied, salubrious lands into which peoples of European blood poured to found new nations as they did in the Americas, Australia, New Zealand, and South Africa. Nor are we where the pre-white population was prevailingly of "primitive" cultures, as in the Pacific islands which we have seen and in Africa south of the Sahara. We are, rather, in a region of teeming populations, where more than half of the earth's inhabitants were crowded into less than a fourth of the land surface of the globe and where the latter part of the nineteenth century saw the total mount rapidly and the pressure on subsistence become increasingly intense. Moreover, the region was one of ancient, high civilizations. There were also millions of "primitive" peoples, but they were in the minority and were usually dominated by their "civilized" neighbours. These civilizations were more resistant to the impact of the Occident than were the "primitive" cultures of the American Indians, the Pacific islanders, and the Africans south of the Sahara.

However, here as in these other regions the Europeans became dominant politically and their culture and their commerce effected a progressive penetration. Under the pressure cultural and political revolutions set in. They were slower in beginning than among the "primitives" with whom we have thus far had to do and for the most part were only well under way by 1914. They were to continue after that year, and with startling developments.

In these areas in the nineteenth century Christianity was almost everywhere present and the numbers of Christians were growing. Here were the large majority of the missionaries, both Roman Catholic and Protestant. However, the numerical gains were chiefly among those of "primitive" or near-"primitive" cultures. Only small minorities were gathered from the more highly civilized elements. Yet Christianity was having an increasing effect on the region and was making its impress upon the changing cultures.

Here, even more than in most of our chapters, we must be tantalizingly brief, not even mentioning some of the most radiant and heroic lives which issued from the Christian Gospel. Nor can we attempt to give to the region the space which the dimensions and importance of its populations would seem to demand. We must content ourselves with only such a condensed account as the size of the Christian communities seems to permit. We have earlier (Chapter XLIX) dealt with Western Asia to the borders of India and with the reaches of Asia under Russian rule. We will therefore now begin with India and move eastward.

CHRISTIANITY PENETRATES ALL INDIA

In India Christianity was confronted by what in extent and separate existence is a continent. In many ways it resembled Europe. Both India and Europe are peninsulas jutting out from the land mass of Eurasia. The great mountains which separate India from the rest of Eurasia are a much more formidable barrier than are the Urals, the range which is considered the landward border of Europe. Both regions are varied in language and race, India even more so than Europe. In both a dominant culture was associated with a religion, that of Europe with Christianity and that of India with Hinduism. Both had minority religions, but these were more numerous in India than in Europe, and in India Islam was more prominent than in Europe. Neither had ever been completely united politically under one rule, but each had seen empires which had had that as their goal.

The outstanding new feature of nineteenth century India was British rule. Beginning early in the seventeenth century through their purely commercial East India Company, as a means of protecting their persons and their trade the British had felt themselves forced to control some of the land surface of India. Having once begun to occupy territory, the British, to make secure what they held, believed themselves to be under the necessity of extending their rule to the natural borders of the country. The conquest is usually regarded as having begun in the 1750's and as having been completed in the 1850's with the suppression of what was remembered as the Mutiny, an attempt by Indian troops in the British armies to unseat their masters. With the post-Mutiny settlement Great Britain ceased to administer India through the East India Company and put the vast country directly under the crown.

The British brought in much of Western civilization. They criss-crossed the land with railways and telegraph lines, instituted a postal service, and developed a system of education in which English was the medium of instruction in the higher grades and the subjects studied were prevailingly Occidental. They built up a series of courts which administered impartial justice. They fought famine and disease and eliminated domestic war, giving India more than a generation of profound peace, the *pax Britannica*.

Yet even Great Britain did not bring all of India under one rule. In 1914 the Portuguese and French still had enclaves, albeit small ones, and a large minority of the population were governed indirectly through what were called native states, in which the historic princely families were permitted to reign under British supervision.

Some years before 1914 a movement began, chiefly under the Indian National Congress, which was to win independence for India less than a century after the completion of the British conquest.

At the dawn of the nineteenth century Christianity had been present in India continuously for many centuries. In 1815 it was represented by three main wings. There was the ancient Syrian Church, professiong to trace its origin to the Apostle Thomas, and with connexions with the Jacobites in Syria. The Roman Catholic Church had had communities in India since the closing years of the fifteenth century. The majority of the population in the Portuguese possessions, the chief of which was Goa, were of that faith, and Portugal claimed through its historic padroado, or right of patronage, the control over all Roman Catholic enterprise, including especially the naming of bishops, not only in its territories, but elsewhere in India. Many thousands of the Syrian community had long been joined to Rome as Uniates. There were some Roman Catholics outside the Portuguese territories, including those in the much less extensive French enclaves and in and around such centres of missionary activity as Madura. Protestants had been making converts in India since the beginning of the Danish-Halle mission early in the eighteenth century. However, they were much less numerous than either the Syrian Christians or the Roman Catholics.

The English East India Company had long opposed missions within its territories from the fear that by stirring up religious animosities among non-Christians they would make its rule more difficult and cut into its profits. Friends of missions had done much to relax the restrictions by writing favouring changes into the Company's charter, notably at the time of its renewal by Parliament in 1793 and 1813. Indeed, by the alterations in the latter year provision was made for the creation of an Anglican episcopate in India and what amounted to permission was obtained for missionaries to live and work in the Company's territories.

The vast majority of the Christians of all three wings of the faith were in South India. The North had scarcely been touched. Moreover, due to the adverse factors which affected Christianity in Europe in the second half of the eighteenth century, Roman Catholics were declining in morale and numbers. Their number was said to have fallen off more than half from the estimated 2,000,000 or 2,500,000 of 1700.

The nineteenth century witnessed an amazing growth of Christianity. This was achieved chiefly by the Roman Catholic Church and Protestantism. The Syrian Church did not experience much expansion, for it had long been what in effect was a caste, a closed community neither losing many to non-Christian faiths nor gaining many from them. Through revivifying contacts with Protestants, especially through the Church Missionary Society, in the nineteenth century a large minority, seeking to purify the Church, withdrew from the Syrian body and formed themselves into the Mar Thoma Church.

The Roman Catholic missionary body was greatly augmented. Some of this was by the restoration of the Jesuits and the coming of new orders and societies. Much was by the reinforcement of orders already represented. The Portuguese padroado was a chronic irritant and handicapped Rome both in providing needed episcopal jurisdiction in territories newly entered and in dealing with abuses in areas which were clearly Portuguese. Agreements between Portugal and the Holy See in the latter half of the century, while not entirely removing it, eased the tension and gave Rome a free hand in most of the country. In 1884 Rome appointed an apostolic delegate to represent it in India and in 1886 it created a hierarchy for the country. The land was divided into seven ecclesiastical provinces and various vicariates and prefectures apostolic were given the rank of bishoprics. More provision was made for the preparation of an Indian clergy. Here and there mass movements brought thousands into the Church. They were largely among hill tribes of "primitive" cultures and the depressed or outcaste classes, the lowest rung in the caste ladder. There were also conversions among the middle castes and even from the highest caste, the Brahmins. In some places missionaries undertook measures to raise the economic level of the chronically destitute Christians by coöperative stores, rice banks, industrial schools, cottage industries, and improved methods of agriculture. Tracts of land were obtained and on them Christian colonies were developed from outcaste or low caste groups. In the half century between 1861 and 1911 the total number of Roman Catholics is reported to have more than doubled, from slightly over a million to nearly two millions and a quarter.

Protestant Christianity had an even more striking increase. Its numbers were not as great. In 1914 it counted about one million baptized adherents. This, however, was an increase from only a few thousand in 1815. The advance was achieved through hundreds of missionaries. In 1914 the Protestant missionary staff totalled 5,465, which was more than that of the Roman Catholics. It came from many denominations and from the British Isles, the United States, and the Continent of Europe, especially Germany, Switzerland, and Scandinavia. The Serampore Trio, Carey, Marshman, and Ward, did some of their most notable translating of the Bible into Indian tongues after 1815, and Carey lived until 1834.

Partly with government sanction, the Anglican communion gradually developed a structure which embraced the large part of India. The foreign personnel was mostly provided and supported by organizations which depended upon members of the Church of England, among them the Church Missionary Society, the Society for the Propagation of the Gospel in Foreign Parts, the Church of England Zenana Missionary Society, and the Cambridge and Oxford Missions. Famous among its bishops was Reginald Heber (1783–1826), best remembered for such hymns as "Holy, Holy, Holy," "The Son of God Goes Forth to War," "From Greenland's Icy Mountains," and "Brightest and Best of the Sons of the Morning," and who died, deeply lamented, after less than three years in India. Notable also was the sturdy Evangelical, Daniel Wilson (1778–1858), who gave more than a quarter of a century to that country. Towards the end of the period, in 1912, an Indian, V. Z. Azariah (1874–1945), was consecrated bishop, the first of his countrymen to be given that rank by Anglicans. He proved to be an inspiring leader both in his own diocese and in world-wide Protestantism.

Next to the Roman Catholics and the Anglicans in numbers of missionaries and in the area covered was the Methodist Episcopal Church of the United States. Its outstanding pioneer in extending its lines not only in India but also to Burma and the Malay Peninsula was James Mills Thoburn (1836–1922). He was reinforced by the itinerant William Taylor (1821–1902), who through years in California soon after its annexation to the United States, then in Australia (from which he sent the eucalyptus seeds which introduced that tree to its extensive use in California) and New Zealand in the formative years of those countries, next in the British Isles, then in India, then on the west and east coasts of South America, and finally as missionary bishop in Africa, did more than any other one man to effect the broad geographic spread of American Methodism.

Most of the numerical gains of Protestantism, even more than of the Roman Catholic Church, were through mass conversions of the animistic tribes and the depressed or outcaste groups.

Protestantism's approach to India was varied. Much of it was through mass conversions, although at the outset these came almost unexpectedly. Some of it was through schools. In time these were assisted by grants-in-aid from the Government of India, not because they were Christian but because they helped the British programme of education. They ranged from village schools which to members of the depressed classes were doors of hope to a world of larger opportunity, through secondary schools, to colleges of university grade. A notable pioneer in Christian higher education was Alexander Duff (1806–1878) who, kindled by the Evangelical Awakening and Thomas Chalmers and coming to India in 1829 as the first foreign missionary of the Church of Scotland, sought to win the Brahmins and through them, presumably the natural leaders of the land, all India, by schools in which the best of Western learning, superbly taught, would be combined with an ardent Christian faith. At the Disruption he went with the Free Church of Scotland. His method became largely that of the Scottish Presbyterians and greatly influenced other Protestant missions. Protestant missions also furthered the education of women and girls. They did much for medicine, pioneered in some forms of agriculture, and cared for lepers.

Although the large majority of the Protestants were from the hill tribes and the depressed classes, numbers were won from the castes, including the Brahmins. Among the upper class converts were those who sought to acclimatize Christianity in India. Thus N. V. Tilak, a Brahmin, attempted to fuse the Christian message with the Hindu *bhakti,* religious devotion directed towards a particular deity, and composed Christian hymns after the Indian manner. Sundar Singh, from a wealthy Sikh family, a mystic, endeavoured to embody Christian ideals in the guise of a *sadhu,* or Indian holy man. There were others from the higher castes who were not so concerned to give Christianity an Indian garb, but who, each in his or her own way, were notable examples of Christian living. One of them was Pandita Ramabai (1858–1922). Of Brahmin parentage, educated by her father, a learned Hindu teacher, early orphaned and then widowed, she gave herself to her fellow-widows, became a Christian, and was led by her faith to a deeper devotion to widows, particularly those of low caste.

Christianity began to have effects outside the circles of the churches and their constituencies. Thus the Brahmo Samaj, organized in 1828 in an attempt to reform Hinduism, was clearly due to contacts with Protestant missionaries. The Ramakrishna Mission, also from within Hinduism, was founded on a Christmas Eve after the telling of the story of Jesus.

CHRISTIANITY MAKES READJUSTMENTS AND GROWS IN CEYLON UNDER BRITISH RULE

In Ceylon, separated from India by a shallow narrow strait, the dominant religion was Buddhism. The Portuguese rule of the sixteenth century had been accompanied by the planting and growth of the Roman Catholic Church. The displacing of the Portuguese by the Dutch in the seventeenth century brought Protestantism, and as we have seen, Dutch pressure led to defections from the Roman Catholic fold and the seeming prosperity of Protestantism. The British occupation during the Napoleonic Wars and the formal annexation by Great Britain were followed by the extension of British rule over the entire island. The expulsion of the Dutch and the religious toleration granted by the British led to the rapid decline of the Protestant communities. Thousands joined the Roman Catholics, presumably because of an hereditary attachment, and other thousands returned to their ancestral Buddhism and Hinduism.

Then were seen recovery and advance. Scores of missionaries from Europe furthered the Roman Catholic cause and in 1911 the census showed 339,300 of that faith as against a count of 66,830 in 1806. Protestant missionaries came, mostly British Baptists, Methodists, and Anglicans, but also a few American Congregationalists. Protestantism was not as strong numerically as in Dutch days, but it was in a much healthier condition. In 1911 the government census showed Christians to be more than one-tenth of the population of the island, a much larger proportion than in India and than in any country in South-east or East Asia or its fringing islands except the Philippines.

BURMA

In Burma the dominant group, the Burmese proper, were solidly Buddhist. The country also contained several other peoples, largely animistic in religion. The numerically strongest of these were the Karens. British rule was extended over the country in three successive wars, in 1824–1826, 1852, and 1885. At the outset of the century there were almost no Christians, and such few as existed were Roman Catholics.

The nineteenth century saw a rapid growth of Christianity. Most of it was among the Karens and was chiefly through American Baptists, with Adoniram Judson (1788–1850), whom we have already met (Chapter XLIV), as the great pioneer. Some other Protestant groups were represented, and also Roman Catholics.

THE MALAY PENINSULA AND SINGAPORE

Jutting out between Burma and Siam, athwart the sea lanes between India and the Far East, is the Malay Peninsula, its tip the southernmost point of Asia. Successive waves of seafarers from the West had seized points along its coast— the Arabs, from whom came the Islam which was dominant from the fifteenth century onward, then the Portuguese, who left a small deposit of Roman Catholicism, next the Dutch, and finally, during the Napoleonic Wars, the British. The British built Singapore and in the course of the nineteenth century extended their control over all the lower part of the peninsula. Chinese and Indians came, attracted by the economic opportunities. Eventually there were far more Chinese than Indians. It was among these two peoples that Christianity achieved such gains as it registered. Almost no converts were made from the Malays who constituted the majority of the population, for they were solidly Moslem. Both Roman Catholicism and Protestantism were propagated, the latter mainly by Anglicans and American Methodists, and substantial Christian minorities were gathered.

Siam (Thailand)

Siam, or Thailand, to give it its alternative name, maintained its political independence. It was more solidly Buddhist than the neighbouring Burma, with a much smaller percentage of animistic folk. It was probably for these reasons that Christianity made much less progress than in Burma. The Roman Catholic wing of the faith continued to be represented by the Society of Foreign Missions of Paris, as it had been since the seventeenh century, but in 1912, even after some accessions in the preceding century, it counted only about 36,000 adherents. Protestantism entered in the fore part of the nineteenth century and was spread mainly by American Presbyterians. Numerically it was weaker than Roman Catholicism.

Striking Growth in Indo-China

The story was far otherwise in what was collectively known as Indo-China, made up of Cambodia, Cochin-China, Tonkin, Annam, and Laos. Here the French gradually extended their rule, beginning with footholds in the South in 1787.

Before 1914 the spread of Christianity was almost entirely through the Roman Catholic Church. At the dawn of the nineteenth century this was chiefly by the Society of Foreign Missions of Paris, the Spanish Dominicans, and a large body of native priests. Christians then were said to number 310,000. The first two-thirds of the nineteenth century were punctuated by recurring persecutions, with the execution of hundreds of priests and catechists and of thousands of lay Christians. In spite of persecution the faith continued to thrive and in the intervals of peace had a rapid growth. France made the persecutions the excuse for extending her rule and with the completion of the conquest in the last quarter of the century they virtually stopped. Under these favouring conditions Christians multiplied and in 1914 totalled slightly less than a million. Many were gathered into villages which were purely of their faith and, thanks to the tutelage of the missionaries and the native clergy, were generally more prosperous than their non-Christian neighbours.

THE SPREAD OF THE FAITH IN THE EAST INDIES

South and east of Asia stretched the vast congeries of islands, large and small, known collectively to nineteenth century Europeans as the East Indies. As we have reminded ourselves (Chapter XLI), the inhabitants were predominantly of one or another variety of Malay stock and language. In the course of the millenniums several waves of culture had flooded in, each leaving a deposit of religion. Hinduism and Buddhism had once been dominant and in the nineteenth and twentieth centuries one of the smaller islands, Bali, was still Hindu. Islam had arrived, borne by the Arabs, and had become the religion of the majority. As we have also noted (Chapter XLI), in the sixteenth century the Portuguese had brought Roman Catholic Christianity. In the nineteenth century it persisted in the small areas which remained to that people in the Little Sunda Islands. In the seventeenth century Protestantism had been introduced by the Dutch. Under Dutch auspices a state church of the Reformed faith had arisen and had attracted substantial numbers, chiefly on the smaller islands. In 1815 it counted between 65,000 and 200,000 members.

In the nineteenth century the Dutch extended their rule over almost all the archipelago. The exceptions were the British territories on the north-eastern coasts of Borneo and the Portuguese section, now confined to the eastern part of Timor.

With the expansion of Dutch rule missionary activity increased. Most of it was Protestant and by Dutch societies. Some Protestant missions were German. The Dutch missions were the fruitage of the religious awakenings of the nineteenth century and of the sense of responsibility which issued from them for the welfare of the peoples of this largest of the Dutch colonial possessions. The state church, the so-called Protestant Church of the East Indies, also grew. Roman Catholic missions revived, in part from the Netherlands and in part from Germany, and by 1914 were mounting.

The main gains of Christianity were among the animists. They were chiefly in the island of Celebes, notably the northern peninsula, Minahassa, where a mass movement into the state church occurred, and from the Bataks, a vigorous folk in Sumatra among whom the Rhenish Missionary Society had an extensive enterprise. A few thousand Moslems were won, chiefly on the most populous of the islands, Java. By 1914 there were over a half million baptized Protestants in the Dutch portions of the East Indies. To these must be added those in the British portions of Borneo, the fruits of British missions, and the Roman Catholics.

The results of Christianity were striking, not only numerically, but also in other ways. Scores of languages were reduced to writing and the beginnings of a Christian literature were made in them. Hundreds of schools were begun. Medical care was given. The status of women was improved. Due to the pressure on the Dutch Government of the Christian conscience, organized into parties and led by Abraham Kuyper, whom we have previously met (Chapter XLVII), much of the earlier exploitation of the inhabitants through what was known as the "culture" system was reduced and what was called the "ethical policy" was adopted. More significant still, churches were growing with an increasing number of indigenous leaders.

Drastic Changes in the Philippines

As we have seen, in the Philippines under Spanish rule the majority of the population became Roman Catholics. The non-Christians consisted of animists, mostly in the mountains, the immigrant Chinese minorities, and the large Moslem contingent, the Moros, in the South. Until the coming of the Americans the islands were, in general, tranquilly somnolent, only slightly disturbed by outside currents until the eve of the American conquest.

Occupation by the United States (1898) was quickly followed by marked changes. The American educational system was introduced and beginnings were made in training the Filipinos in the kind of democratic political life and institutions which were standard in the United States.

Marked stirrings of religious life were seen. Protestantism was introduced by missionaries from the United States and made rapid strides, chiefly among the nominally Roman Catholic elements. As a phase of the nationalist movement which had arisen in the 1890's, the Independent Catholic Church of the Philippines, or the Filipino Independent Church, came into being as a secession from the Roman Catholic Church. All the Roman Catholic bishops and most of the leading Roman Catholic clergy had been Spaniards. Many Filipinos wished Rome to appoint Filipino bishops. Since Rome would not assent, hundreds of thousands broke away. A Roman Catholic Filipino priest, Aglipay, was elected archbishop and several other Filipino priests were elected bishops. Through the influence of a Filipino who had been in touch with liberal thought in Europe, the new church sought fellowship with the Unitarians. However, the civil courts denied it the possession of the church buildings which it had sought to take over from the Roman Catholics and it experienced difficulty in obtaining an able, educated clergy.

Faced with Protestantism, the Aglipay secession, and disestablishment, the Vatican took drastic measures. Numbers of priests came from the United States, American Archbishops of Manila were appointed, several Filipino priests were raised to the episcopate, hundreds of the more obnoxious Spanish friars who had battened off the land left, not to return, and the effort was made to provide better training for candidates for the priesthood. Some of the irritation against the landlordism of the friars was removed by the purchase by the civil government of over 400,000 acres of the land held by the orders. Several non-Spanish European orders sent missionaries. Fresh reinforcements arrived from Spain. Existing Roman Catholic schools altered their courses of study to meet the new conditions and new schools were begun.

By these several measures the Christianity of what was still the only predominantly Christian people in the Far East was reinvigorated.

THE RENEWED PENETRATION OF CHINA BY CHRISTIANITY

In the year 1815 the outlook for Christianity in the Chinese Empire seemed very bleak. That realm, the most populous of any on the globe, was all but hermetically sealed against the foreigner. The Portuguese retained a slight toe-hold at Macao, near Canton. The Russians were permitted a tenuous semi-political, semi-ecclesiastical mission in Peking. Western merchants were allowed a strictly limited commerce through one port, Canton, and in that port were confined to a narrow strip of land, the "Thirteen Factories," along the river. Diplomatic and even consular relations on terms of equality were not permitted, nor was travel within the empire possible for foreigners. A few Roman Catholic communities continued, the fruits of heroic missions of earlier, less adverse days. Roman Catholics may have totalled 200,000, and were widely scattered. They were served surreptitiously by a few Chinese and still fewer foreign priests. In Canton the sole Protestant missionary, Robert Morrison, maintained a precarious residence as a translator for the East India Company, devoting himself chiefly to the preparation of Christian literature. The one colleague sent him before 1815 was compelled to leave China and sought contacts with the Chinese through their overseas emigrants in the British-owned Malacca.

China's doors were forced open by the Western world, led at first by the major commercial power of the nineteenth century, Great Britain. However, not until late in the century did Chinese culture really begin to crumble. Then the revolution set in which continued to mount and in the middle of the twentieth century seemed to be still far from completed. The main successive stages of the impact can be quickly described, together with such of their features as made for the spread of Christianity.

First was a war from 1839 to 1842 through which the British sought to obtain larger commercial privileges and consular relations based upon equal status with the Chinese officials. Unfortunately for the good name of Great Britain it was precipitated by British resistance to the efforts of the Chinese Government to prevent the importation of opium, the chief commodity in British sales to China. By the ensuing treaty, a treaty which was supplemented by ones with the United States and some other Western powers, five ports were opened to foreign residence, the island of Hongkong was ceded to Britain, foreigners were accorded extraterritorial status, a fixed tariff was scheduled, and official intercourse was based on the principle of equality. Following these treaties, in the 1840's the Chinese Government granted toleration to Christianity, but forbade missionaries to propagate it outside the five treaty ports. The Chinese viewed the treaties as conceding too much, the foreigners as granting too little.

An uneasy truce was succeeded, in 1856–1860, by a second war in which the French joined the British. The treaties which followed, most of them signed in 1858, opened additional ports to foreign trade and residence, provided for the establishment of legations of the powers in the capital, Peking, permitted foreigners to travel anywhere in the Empire, assured missionaries the right to propagate their faith, and promised protection to both missionaries and Chinese Christians in the practice of their faith. Then came nearly a generation of penetration by missionaries and other foreigners but with no basic changes in the inherited structure of Chinese life.

In 1894–1895 a war with Japan in which China was defeated and forced to cede Formosa to the victor and to acknowledge the independence of Korea was followed in the late 1890's by the acquisition of leaseholds, spheres of influence, and concessions for the building of railways which seemed to presage the partition of China among Western powers; by attempts, in 1898, at reforms and changes which would enable China to escape her doom; by the Boxer movement in 1900 which sought to expel the foreigner and which was suppressed by foreign troops and climaxed by punitive measures and the stationing of foreign troops in Peking and Tientsin to guard the legations; and by a war between Russia and Japan in 1904–1905 which, to the humiliation of the Chinese, was mostly fought on their soil while they stood by, helpless.

As a result, in an attempt to preserve their political independence the Chinese sacrificed their cultural independence. In 1905 the civil service examinations were abolished which had been based upon the Confucian Classics and through which the civil bureaucracy had been recruited. Simultaneously drastic changes were made in the educational system which demoted Confucian literature from its historic supremacy and introduced Western subjects. In 1911–1912 the Confucian monarchy was swept aside and China entered upon the experiment of a republic made perilous by her complete lack of experience with it and by the vast dimensions of the country. Confucianism, long the basis of Chinese life, was fatally weakened and a fundamental revolution in Chinese life and institutions began.

Under these circumstances, could Christianity be so effectively presented that

it would be built into the warp and woof of the new China which was emerging? By the year 1914 great strides were made by both Roman Catholic and
Protestant Christianity and it seemed that the answer would be in the affirma-
tive.

The body of Roman Catholic missionaries was progressively augmented. The
staffs of orders and societies already present were greatly enlarged and new
orders and congregations entered. They were almost entirely from the Continent of Europe. The French led, especially through the Society of Foreign
Missions of Paris, but Germans, Italians, Spaniards, and some others were also
represented. In 1914 the total foreign staff was not far from 2,500. Roman
Catholic missionaries placed their chief emphasis upon winning converts and
building the Church. In this they persisted in spite of chronic persecutions and
a tragic loss of life through the Boxer madness. In 1912 the total number of
Roman Catholics was reported to be 1,431,258, approximately a seven-fold
increase in a hundred years. That the Church was taking root was seen in the
growing numbers of Chinese who were entering the priesthood or becoming
lay brothers or sisters, and the many organizations of Chinese Christians which
were springing up. In addition to building the Church, the Roman Catholics
had schools, although not as many in the middle and higher grades as Protestants, they engaged in famine relief, maintained many orphanages and homes
for the aged, and in Inner Mongolia had Christian colonies on lands owned by
the mission.

Protestants increased their missionary staffs even more rapidly. In 1914 the
total was said to be 5,462. The missionaries were from scores of societies and
many denominations. In 1895 about two-thirds were from the British Isles,
approximately one-third were from the United States, and between two and
three per cent. were from the Continent of Europe. In 1914 about half were
from the United States, about two-fifths from the British Isles, and nearly one-
tenth from the Continent of Europe. The organization having the largest number of missionaries was the China Inland Mission. It was begun in 1865 by J.
Hudson Taylor. Conservative theologically after the Evangelical pattern, it
accepted "willing, skilful workers" regardless of their denominational affiliation. As its name indicates, it sought to reach the regions untouched by other
Protestant missions. It promised no fixed salaries but distributed among its
members what came in. It was adamantly opposed to going into debt and it
never directly solicited gifts. It depended on prayer for recruits and funds, and
such Biblical words as *Ebenezer* and *Jehovah Jireh*, carrying the assurance,
"hitherto hath the Lord helped us" and "the Lord will provide," were prominent. In 1914 it had over 1,000 missionaries on its rolls.

Protestant converts rapidly increased. In 1914 communicants totalled over

250,000 and the baptized more than a third of a million. While these figures were much less than those of Roman Catholics, they represented a larger proportional increase.

Protestants adopted a wide variety of methods and sought to make the Gospel effective in many different although not unrelated ways. As did the Roman Catholics, they endeavoured to found and nourish churches. In contrast with the Roman Catholic Church, these were not knit into one ecclesiastical structure, but until after 1914 even the Roman Catholics had little sense of cohesion except through distant Rome, and, as we are to see in the next chapter, in China as in some other areas where Protestantism was being newly planted, coöperation among Protestants was increasing. Protestants also had as an aim familiarizing all Chinese with the Gospel. That was the major purpose of the China Inland Mission and it was shared by other groups. Towards it contributed not only personal contacts and preaching in streets and in halls open to the street, but also the preparation and widespread distribution of literature, especially of translations of the Bible. Millions of copies of portions of the Scriptures were circulated. Protestants founded most of the best secondary and higher schools through which before 1914 the Western learning desired by the Chinese in the two decades before that year could be obtained without leaving the country. They pioneered in the introduction of Western medicine, in public health education, and in the creation of medical and nursing professions which would apply the rapidly advancing medical skills of the Occident. They led in the care of the insane and the blind. They engaged in famine relief. They sought to prevent famines by introducing or developing improved methods of agriculture and forestry, ways of fighting plant and animal diseases, and increasing the yields of grains and fruits. Largely under the leadership of Timothy Richard (1832–1919) through the Christian Literature Society, in the 1890's and the early 1900's they provided literature by which the Chinese could learn of the history and institutions of the Occident. In other words, through many channels they were striving to prepare the Chinese for the vast changes which were inevitable and to make the impact of the Occident a blessing and not a curse to the millions of that great realm.

In its early days in China Protestantism shared in the responsibility for a tragic uprising. It centered around a leader who had received Christian instruction through Protestant literature and a Protestant missionary. It took over some features of Christianity, but its resemblance was only superficial. It sought to displace the reigning dynasty with its own, which it designated hopefully T'ai P'ing, "Great Peace." It was also a revolt of the underprivileged masses and in some respects was the abortive first stage of the revolution which in the twentieth century swept away the old order. It first clashed with the existing government in 1848 and was not finally suppressed until 1865. In the intervening years it laid waste much of the lower Yangtze Valley.

CHRISTIANITY IN HELPLESS AND UNHAPPY KOREA

By geographic position Korea was foredoomed to the unhappy role of being a bone of contention among powerful neighbours. A peninsula commanding the sea approaches to North China, Manchuria, much of Japan, and Eastern Siberia, China, Japan, and latterly Russia sought either to dominate it or to prevent it from falling into the hands of one of the others. From time to time across the centuries China had controlled part or all of Korea. Japan had intermittently possessed footholds in the South and on one occasion had over-run all the country. At the dawn of the nineteenth century Korea was tributary to China and had drawn much of its culture from that empire. In the 1870's Japan began to take a renewed interest in the peninsula. In the 1880's Korea reluctantly opened its doors to the Occident and entered into treaty relations with Western powers. In 1894 China and Japan went to war over the question of the control of the country. China was defeated and eliminated. Then Russia entered the scene as the chief rival of Japan. The result was the Russo-Japanese War of 1904–1905, the defeat of Russia, and the annexation of Korea by Japan (1910).

Christianity appears first to have been introduced to Korea in the 1590's in connexion with the Japanese invasion, carried by Christians in the Japanese army. It seems to have made no converts among the Koreans and to have vanished with the evacuation of the Japanese forces.

It was not until 1784 that Christianity began a continuing life in the land. Late in 1783 a Korean in the annual embassy to Peking, one of a circle who since the preceding decade had been studying Christian books prepared by Roman Catholic missionaries in China, sought out Roman Catholic missionaries in the Chinese capital. He asked baptism and was given it. Returning to Korea in the spring of 1784, he won converts, largely in scholarly and official circles. Persecution soon followed. In the course of the next ninety years several priests, Chinese and Europeans, made their way into the country, but they were either executed or driven out. Yet the faith persisted, and that in spite of recurring persecutions, the last severe one in 1866, which took toll of thousands of lives.

After treaty relations were established with Western powers serious persecution ceased for over a generation. Roman Catholic missionaries increased, all of them from the Continent of Europe and most of them from France. Converts multiplied and candidates for the priesthood were recruited and trained.

It was in the 1870's that Protestant missionaries began to have some touch with Koreans through Manchuria, but it was not until the 1880's that they established continuous residence in the country. The first to do so were Presbyterians and Methodists from the United States and it was through these American denominations that Protestantism had its chief growth. By 1914 Protestants outnumbered Roman Catholics, both in missionary staffs and in converts. The increase of converts was striking after 1894 and particularly so between 1906 and 1910. Among the reasons for the Protestant growth was the early adoption of the principles of insisting on early self-support, of encouraging each Christian to seek to win his neighbours, of setting aside some Christians, as the churches were prepared to support them, for spreading the faith, and of church structures in Korean style built only as the Koreans paid for them. Many Bible classes were developed to train the laity to share in the propagation of the faith.

THE RE-INTRODUCTION OF CHRISTIANITY TO JAPAN

We have seen (Chapter XLI) how Christianity was introduced to Japan in the sixteenth century, made rapid headway, and then, early in the seventeenth century, was proscribed and driven underground. We have also noted that, to keep the empire uncontaminated by Christianity, Japan's rulers closed the country against all contacts with the Western world except for a strictly limited and tightly regulated trade with the Dutch through one port, Nagasaki. Edict boards denouncing Christianity were posted throughout the realm, but several thousand Christians, mostly in the island of Kyushu, transmitted their faith in secret from generation to generation, maintained baptism, the one sacrament which could be administered by lay folk, and, without priests, continued their prayers.

Until the 1850's Japan remained all but hermetically sealed against the Western world and rebuffed several attempts to induce her to alter her policy. After the beginning of the opening of China and the rapid increase of Occidental commerce and shipping in the Pacific, Japan could scarcely expect to maintain her isolation. It was in 1853 that at the insistent invitation of the United States through Commodore Perry her doors became slightly ajar. Later in that decade she entered into her first commercial treaties, the initial one with the United States. In the 1860's there began the rapid adoption of much of Occidental institutions, culture, and industrial methods. It continued at a mounting pace throughout the rest of the century.

Some of the basic traditions and institutions of the past were strengthened rather than weakened, notably the reverence paid to the emperor, the nourishing of patriotism through the state cult, Shinto, and the prominence of the military. Buddhism persisted, more vigorous than in China or Korea, and many Shinto cults flourished.

Yet great innovations were made. The prevailing feudalism was abolished, telegraph lines, railways, and a commercial marine were built, industrialism was begun, an army and navy were created on Western models, codes of law and law courts inspired by the Occident were brought into being, a constitution with a diet or parliament and a cabinet was framed and put into force, and an educational system of a Western type was developed based upon universal, compulsory primary education and culminating in universities. Population was mounting and the standard of living was rising. Hard work, intelligence, and intense national pride and ambition were outstanding characteristics. By 1914 Japan was on the way to becoming one of the major world powers.

It was into this changing yet conservative Japan that, in the late 1850's, Christianity was re-introduced. It came, almost simultaneously, through the Roman Catholic Church, the Russian Orthodox Church, and various forms of Protestantism. At the outset progress was slow, for the old distrust and hostility survived, and it was only in 1873 that the anti-Christian edict boards throughout the realm were ordered removed. Fairly rapid increase in the Christian communities was seen in the 1870's, and in the 1880's the growth was so startling that some among the missionaries and their supporters were hoping that a mass conversion would soon sweep the nation into the Christian fold. In the 1890's a reaction occurred and gains were much slower. They again became marked after 1900, but not as much so as in the 1880's.

The Roman Catholic missionaries were mostly from France, Spain, and Germany and were of several orders and societies, including those, the Jesuits, Dominicans, and Franciscans, which had had the major part in planting the faith in the sixteenth and seventeenth centuries. In the 1860's the hidden surviving Christian communities were uncovered. The government renewed its persecution, although not in so severe a form as in the seventeenth century, and discontinued it only because of pressure from the Western powers. Many of the hidden Christians resumed their ancestral connexion with the Roman Catholic Church. Several thousand did not do so but, cherishing the variations which had developed during the centuries, maintained an existence separate from any form of Christianity from the West. In 1912 Roman Catholics are said to have totalled 66,134, most of them from the humbler walks of life.

The Russian Orthodox Church came in as a phase of the eastward movement of the Russian Empire, for in the latter part of the nineteenth century the tsars were extending their domains on and near the Pacific at the expense of the Chinese Empire and were threatening Japan. However, the planting and growth of the Russian mission were due primarily to one man, Ivan Kasatkin, better known as Nicolai. Coming in 1861 as a chaplain to the Russian consulate at Hakodate in the northern island, Hokkaido, at first he only slowly won converts. As they increased, he moved his headquarters to Tokyo. He received substantial financial aid and some personnel from Russia. He was made successively bishop and archbishop and at the time of his death, 1912, more than 30,000 were of his faith. Here was numerically the most successful mission of the Russian Orthodox Church among non-Christians outside the Russian Empire.

Of the three main branches of Christianity it was Protestantism that had the most extensive growth in Japan and which exerted the greatest influence. In 1913 the membership of Protestant churches was 102,790, or more than that of the combined totals of the Roman Catholics and Russian Orthodox. Nor was that figure a true measure of the extent of Protestantism. There were an undetermined number who thought of themselves as Christians and had become such through Protestants, but who had no formal church connexion. Many of them arose from the lectures, Bible-teaching, and writings of Kanso Uchimura (1861–1930) who, earnestly Christian, out of conviction did not associate himself with any ecclesiastical body. The Protestant missionaries were overwhelmingly although not entirely from the United States. Many denominations were represented, but the largest were the Congregationalists, Presbyterians, Methodists, and Anglicans. Protestantism was mostly urban. It was recruited mainly from the professional and middle classes and numbers of its leaders were from the *samurai,* what might be called the knightly class or minor aristocracy of the feudal hierarchy which had controlled the country before the formal abolition of feudalism in the 1870's. Many Japanese Protestants early wished their churches to be independent financially and administratively of the foreigners. For instance, he who is best known as Joseph Hardy Neesima (1843–1890), a radiant, devoted spirit of *samurai* stock, educated in America, had as his major achievement the founding of the Doshisha, a Christian university in the ancient capital, Kyoto, a stronghold of conservatism, and while welcoming in it foreign funds and personnel, insisted that it be controlled by Japanese. Protestantism approached Japan from several angles, but it stressed education and most of its more prominent leaders came into the faith through contacts with teachers, either in mission or government schools.

Rapid though the growth of Christianity was, in 1914 missionaries had been continuously in the country only slightly more than a half century. While Christians, and especially Protestant Christians, were more influential in the nation's life than their numbers would have led the casual observer to expect, in 1914 less than one in two hundred were of that faith.

SUMMARY

By the year 1914 Christianity had come full circle about the globe. By moving westward it had been firmly planted on the west coast of the Americas and in some of the islands of the Pacific. Carried chiefly from the British Isles and Western Europe, it had been equally well established in Australia, New Zealand, and South Africa. Entering from both directions, namely, from the British Isles and Western Europe on the one hand and from the Americas on the other, it had expanded its existing footholds and established new ones in the islands of the Pacific, Africa south of the Sahara, and the south and east of Asia and the fringing islands. This was almost entirely through Roman Catholics and Protestants, in proportion to the situation at the outset of the century more by the latter than the former. In most of Asia and Africa Christianity was only beginning to take root and was dependent on personnel and funds from the Occident. Moreover, in South, South-east, and East Asia and the fringing islands, with the exception of Ceylon, Indo-China, some of the East Indies, and the Philippines, Christians were still very small minorities, constituting not more than 1 per cent. of the population and usually less. In several lands even these gains had been made chiefly not from the ruling groups, but from the lowest rungs of the social scale, from those of animistic or near-animistic faith. Striking though the advances had been, most of them were very recent, mainly in the second half of the century. In 1914 they were on the momentum of a rising tide, but it was not yet clear whether they would be permanent. Christianity was much stronger in Africa south of the Sahara, South, South-east, and East Asia and the neighbouring islands than it had ever been, but the historian remembered that it had twice before vanished from the most populous of these lands, China, and had all but been extinguished in Japan. He might well find himself wondering whether it would again disappear. That was one of the questions which he was to pose to the twentieth century. As we are soon to see, the gains continued in that century and in every land the faith put down deeper roots and more and more had indigenous leadership. However, as old adversaries weakened, new ones emerged and in the middle of the twentieth century in most lands the position of Christianity was still precarious. Yet we need to remind ourselves that this had been the condition of the faith since its beginning, from the days of the lowly birth in a manger in Bethlehem and the crucifixion in Jerusalem.

SELECTED BIBLIOGRAPHY

M. Broomhall, *The Jubilee Story of the China Inland Mission* (London, Morgan & Scott, 1915, pp. xvi, 386). An official history, well written.

The Capuchin Mission Unit, Cumberland, Maryland, *India and Its Missions* (New York, The Macmillan Co., 1923, pp. xxi, 315). A useful survey of Roman Catholic missions in India, for the most part based on excellent authorities.

O. Cary, *A History of Christianity in Japan* (New York, Fleming H. Revell Co.,

2 vols., 1907). The standard account in English, especially of Protestant missions. The first volume is on Roman Catholic and Russian Orthodox missions, the second on Protestant missions. The author, a Protestant, attempts to be objective.

E. R. Clough, *Social Christianity in the Orient. The Story of a Man, a Mission and a Movement* (New York, The Macmillan Co., 1914, pp. xiii, 409). Important for the light shed on one of the early mass movements to Christianity in India.

J. N. Farquhar, *Modern Religious Movements in India* (New York, The Macmillan Co., 1915, pp. xv, 471). A standard work, valuable for what it says of the influence of Christianity on other faiths.

G. G. Findlay and W. W. Holdsworth, *The History of the Wesleyan Methodist Missionary Society* (London, The Epworth Press, 5 vols., 1921–1924). An official history, based largely on the manuscript records of the society.

W. J. Hail, *Tsêng Kuo-fan and the Taiping Rebellion* (Yale University Press, 1927, pp. xvii, 422). A standard account, carefully done.

M. H. Harper, *The Methodist Episcopal Church in India. A Study of Ecclesiastical Organization and Administration* (Lucknow, The Lucknow Publishing House, 1936, pp. vii, 222). A doctoral dissertation at the University of Chicago, by a Methodist missionary.

R. L. Howard, *Baptists in Burma* (Philadelphia, The Judson Press, 1931, pp. 168). By a former missionary in Burma.

D. J. B. Kuruppu, *The Catholic Church in Ceylon. A Brief Account of Its History and Progress* (Colombo, "The Messenger" Press, 1923, pp. 24).

K. S. Latourette, *A History of Christian Missions in China* (New York, The Macmillan Co., 1929, pp. xii, 930). Comprehensive.

K. S. Latourette, *A History of the Expansion of Christianity. Volume VI, The Great Century in Northern Africa and Asia,* A.D. *1800–1914* (New York, Harper & Brothers, 1944, pp. vii, 502).

A. Launay, *Histoire Générale de la Société des Missions-Étrangères* (Paris, Pierre Tequi, 3 vols., 1894). By a member of the society. Based on the archives.

G. B. McFarland, editor, *Historical Sketch of Protestant Missions in Siam 1828–1928* (Bangkok Times Press, 1928, pp. xvii, 386).

F. Marnas, *La "Religion de Jésus" (Iaso Ja-kyō) Ressuscitée au Japon dans la Seconde Moitié de XIX* e *Siècle* (Paris, Delhomme et Briquet, 2 vols., c.1897).

L. G. Paik, *The History of Protestant Missions in Korea 1832–1910* (Pyeng Yang, Union Christian College Press, 1929, pp. v, 438, xiii). A Yale doctoral dissertation, carefully documented.

J. W. Pickett, *Christian Mass Movements in India. A Study with Recommendations* (New York and Nashville, Abingdon-Cokesbury Press, 1933, pp. 382). Based upon prolonged, objective study.

J. Rauws, H. Kraemer, F. J. F. Van Hasselt, and N. A. C. Slotemaker de Bruine, *The Netherlands Indies* (London, World Dominion Press, 1935, pp. 186). A survey and study of missions in the Netherlands Indies, by experts.

J. Richter, *Indische Missionsgeschichte* (Gütersloh, C. Bertelsmann, 2d ed., 1924, pp. vi, 570). The standard history of Protestant missions in India. There is an English translation of an earlier edition.

J. Richter, *Die evangelische Mission in Fern- und Südost-Asien, Australien, Amerika* (Gütersloh, C. Bertelsmann, 1932, pp. xii, 488). Readable. Few references to sources, but occasional bibliographies.

J. Richter, *Die evangelische Mission in Niederländisch-Indien* (Gütersloh, C. Bertelsmann, 1931, pp. 167). The only general history, except in Dutch, of missions in the Netherlands Indies.

J. Richter, *Das Werden der christlichen Kirche in China* (Gütersloh, C. Bertelsmann, 1928, pp. xvi, 584). A readable and comprehensive account, chiefly of Protestantism.

J. Schmidlin, translated from the German, with additions and modifications by M. Braun, *Catholic Mission History* (Techny, Ill., Mission Press, 1933, pp. xiv, 862). A standard survey.

F. Schwager, *Die katholische Heidenmission der Gegenwart in Zusammenhang mit ihrer grossen Vergangenheit* (Steyl, Missionsdruckerei, 1907, pp. 446). A standard work.

J. M. Thoburn, *My Missionary Apprenticeship* (New York, Phillips and Hunt, 1887, pp. 425).

H. St. G. Tucker, *The History of the Episcopal Church in Japan* (New York, Charles Scribner's Sons, 1938, pp. 228). By a bishop of that church who served in Japan.

H. G. Underwood, *The Call of Korea. Political-Social-Religious* (New York, Fleming H. Revell Co., 3d ed., 1908, pp. 204). By a distinguished Protestant missionary to Korea.

S. R. Warburton, *Eastward: The Story of Adoniram Judson* (New York, Round Table Press, 1937, pp. xi, 240). The standard life.

A. W. Wasson, *Church Growth in Korea* (New York, International Missionary Council, 1934, pp. xii, 175). A scholarly study, chiefly of the part of the Korean Church related to the Methodist Episcopal Church, South.

Chapter LV

THE EXCEEDING GREATNESS OF THE POWER: WHERE SIN ABOUNDED GRACE MUCH MORE ABOUNDED

As we look back across this survey of Christianity in the nineteenth century, what can be said of the effect of the faith upon the human scene? To answer that question we must view the world as a whole and not confine our attention to any one segment of it. If, as Christian faith affirms, God was in Christ reconciling the world unto Himself, if He sent His son into the world that the world might be saved through him, was that purpose nearer to accomplishment in 1914 than in 1815? Here is essentially a global question and it requires a global answer.

In the preceding ten chapters (Chapters XLV–LIV, especially Chapter XLV) we have repeatedly seen something of the challenge with which Christianity was confronted. Vast movements were in progress in the historic Christendom, where the faith had longest been supposedly dominant, which threatened the very existence of Christianity. It was sobering that most of these were in part the fruits of Christianity, some more, some less. The scientific approach, the utilization of science and man's ingenuity in such fashion that the nineteenth and twentieth centuries became the age of the machine, forms of philosophy which either repudiated the faith outright or seemed to supersede it, the application of historical methods to the Bible with the result that that collection of documents which had been revered as inspired was declared to be imperfect and abounding in errors of fact and opinion, the rise of social theories and programmes which, while owing much to Christianity, either ignored or rejected it, the pressure of supposedly Christian peoples upon non-Christian peoples the world over with the danger, real or latent, of wholesale exploitation of the latter in the presumed interest of the former—these and many other trends and movements were a menace to Christianity. Some were perverting to man's hurt what had come through Christianity. Sin, collective and individual, was

1334

abounding on a vast scale. Could Christianity rise to the occasion? Was it the channel of a power so "exceeding great" that grace would much more abound?

Something of the answer to these questions must have been sensed in the narrative in the preceding chapters. All that we need take the space to do here is to summarize what has been given piecemeal and to add some facts and movements that have not thus far been mentioned.

In the first place it must be clear that in the nineteenth century Christianity became more widely spread geographically than it or any other faith had ever been. This spread was in connexion with the expansion of European peoples. Although Christianity was in part the cause of that expansion, it by no means followed automatically that it would be propagated with it. Only an abounding vigour could have held to their ancestral faith so large portions of the European emigrants who created the new nations and could have won contingents from most of the peoples who heretofore had been touched slightly or not at all.

Among non-European peoples the Christianity thus planted had a much more extensive influence than the size of the churches which were called into being would have led one to expect. These churches were of first-class importance. Presumably it was primarily upon them that the perpetuation and continued spread of the faith among their respective peoples would depend. In them, moreover, were lives in which were seen the characteristic "fruits of the Spirit" which Paul described in the first century of the Christian faith. In addition, usually but not always more or less closely related to them, were other contributions through the missionaries who spread the Christian faith. Hundreds of languages were for the first time given a written form, the Bible was translated into them in whole or in part, other Christian literature was prepared, and schools of a Western type were opened, often the pioneers of the kind of education which was to prevail as governments, either colonial or indigenous and independent, undertook an educational system for the new day. Orphanages were conducted in which thousands of children were cared for who would otherwise have perished. Famine relief was undertaken and attempts were made to introduce improvements in agriculture and forestry which would reduce or eliminate famine. Hospitals were founded and steps were taken to initiate medical and nursing professions trained in the science and techniques which were making rapid strides in the Occident. Public health education was inaugurated. Efforts were made to raise the status of women. All this, and more, was accomplished through a body of missionaries, men and women, which never numbered more than a quarter of a million and which was usually much less and which was not concentrated in one country but was distributed thinly over more than half the land surface of the globe and among much more than half the earth's population.

In addition the Christian conscience fought the selfish exploitation of non-white peoples by the dominant white race. Sometimes it found expression in missionaries. Even more often it stirred to action Christians who were not missionaries. It brought about the abolition of Negro slavery. It sought to curb the production and sale of opium and opium derivatives. It opposed any form of forced labour. The empire which ruled over the most people and the widest area was that of Great Britain. In the nineteenth century the quality of the British colonial official showed a marked improvement over the eighteenth century. The official might still regard himself as belonging to a superior race and culture and speak contemptuously of those whom he ruled as "lesser breeds without the law" and as "half devil and half child," but towards them he felt an obligation to give devoted and honest service, to bear what in the latter part of the century a poet who grew up in that atmosphere called "the white man's burden." This improvement seems to have been due, at least in part, to the Evangelical Awakening, the revivals which followed it, and the general rise in the level of Christian living which were their products.

Among the traditionally Christian peoples in Europe, the Americas, and Australasia, the faith also had striking effects. We have noted the fashion in which it was the stimulus and the sustaining impulse in the successful struggles for prison reform, for better care of the insane, and for legislative measures shortening the hours of labour, safeguarding the health of labourers, protecting women and children in mines and industry, and obtaining improved housing. This was especially important in an age and countries in which the industrial revolution was bringing together aggregations of labour, some of them vast, in the mining and factory towns and cities which were springing up almost over-night. Moved by their faith, Christians devised new methods and programmes for the education of the masses. They brought into being hundreds of colleges and universities, even though some of these later departed from the Christian principles of their founders. Christians also were the initiators and supporters of measures and movements to reduce the sufferings attendant on wars and to eliminate war by devising and operating institutions and measures for the peaceful adjustment of friction between nations and for international coöpera-tion for the welfare of mankind. By its symbol and name the Red Cross bore witness of its Christian origin. It came into being through the efforts of a Protestant layman of Geneva, Henri Dunant.

The hundreds of hospitals begun and maintained by various religious orders and churches were evidence of the continuing care for the sick which had been a feature of Christianity since its beginning. The new nursing profession which arose in the nineteenth century, largely from Protestant sources, further attested to the power of their faith to impel Christians to give themselves to the care of the sick and the wounded which had earlier again and again been displayed in orders, congregations, and confraternities in the Roman Catholic Church and which continued to find expression through them. The devout Roman Catholic, Louis Pasteur (1822–1895), by his research contributed immeasurably to advances in man's age-old struggle against disease.

Christianity helped to mould philosophy, even philosophies which did not acknowledge it or which rejected it.

Christianity's contributions to literature were so multiform and so numerous that to single out a few authors as examples seems invidious. Among the many thousands who showed its impress in accepting it, in struggling with the issues which it raised, or in paying tribute to it by repudiating it were the Russians N. V. Gogol (1809–1852) and T. M. Dostoievski (1821–1881), the Norwegian Ibsen, the German Goethe, the French Victor Hugo (1802–1885), the Scottish Thomas Carlyle, the English George Eliot, Alfred Tennyson, and Robert Browning, and the Americans Nathaniel Hawthorne, H. W. Longfellow, and J. R. Lowell.

Christian faith moulded and sustained such statesmen and shapers of nations as Abraham Lincoln and W. E. Gladstone.

Increasingly the churches and their benevolences were maintained by the voluntary contributions of their members rather than by compulsory taxation, thus attesting the loyalty of the rank and file of their constituencies. Gifts to a multitude of services for the public good, most of them moved by a sense of responsibility springing from the Christian faith, were an outstanding feature of the century, especially in the British Isles and the United States. Of this the large number of philanthropic agencies supported by private subscriptions were striking evidence. Some of the giving was on a princely scale. Most of it was in modest sums from millions with only moderate incomes.

Fully as important as any of these effects was the direct operation of the faith in millions of men and women. Many were lifted from moral defeat and degradation to enduring victory. Others, nurtured in the faith from childhood, either with or without some inner crisis grew into radiant spirits. Millions, notably in the partially de-Christianized elements of the population of the United States, were brought into a vital religious experience. Still others, nominally Christian, found that to them the faith became alive and thrilling. We must always remember, moreover, that Christian conviction holds that what follows beyond the gate of death and in the realm which the historian cannot penetrate is of even more importance than what is within the scope of the historian's craft.

To most of these effects we have already called attention. It was clear that Christianity came to 1914 and entered the twentieth century on a rising tide.

Another set of movements, an outcome of the Christian faith which partly began and partly was given an added impulse in the nineteenth century and which mounted rapidly after that year, was that by which Christians were coming together across denominational barriers and were achieving unity in ways which were essentially novel. It was significant that these movements issued from the most divided branch of Christianity, Protestantism, and at the outset from extreme forms of Protestantism, namely, those springing from the Evangelical awakening, which by pushing towards their full implications the distinctive Protestant convictions of salvation by faith and the priesthood of all believers seemed to make for unmitigated individualism and endless fissiparousness. It is also significant that they were mounting in a day when because of improved means of transportation and communication which had their origin in Christendom the inhabited world was rapidly shrinking in time-distances and all men were geographically becoming neighbours. The world was a neighbourhood, but it was a neighbourhood which suffered from frictions and tensions which threatened to make it a shambles. Could it be transformed into a coöperative brotherhood? If so it must be by spiritual and moral more than material forces. Christianity, rapidly becoming world-wide, more so than any other religion, by its professed major emphasis upon love of God and love of neighbour would seem to be the source to which men would most hopefully look for such a unifying tie. Yet the Christian Church was divided, apparently hopelessly so. Attempts at unity had been followed by fresh divisions. Especially after the rise and growth of Protestantism, even the largest of the Christian bodies, the Roman Catholic Church, drew into its fold a decreasing proportion of those who bore the Christian name. Although that church stoutly maintained that unity could rightly be found only by submitting to its head and entering its fellowship, an increasing proportion of Christians were refusing to respond to the repeated Papal invitations to conform. Now a fresh approach was being made, and with growing although still far from complete success. Here was a manifestation of the exceeding greatness of the power, so that where sin, collective, national, and individual, threatened the human race with added woes, grace was manifesting itself through fresh and unexpected channels.

The growing unity emanating from Protestant Christianity expressed itself in a number of ways, all interrelated and each contributing to the others. Eventually it came to be known as the Ecumenical Movement.

Among the earliest methods of attaining unity and one which persisted and had increasing manifestations and ramifications was coöperation in planning and action across denominational lines by individuals and groups but without the official participation of ecclesiastical bodies. Originally the organizations and conferences of this kind were drawn primarily from those committed to the Evangelical Awakening and kindred circles, such as the Pietists on the Continent of Europe and those in the United States in sympathy with the revivals. Eventually some of the movements drew in individuals from other traditions, including Anglo-Catholics, Roman Catholics, and communicants of the Orthodox and other Eastern Churches.

Coöperation by individuals rather than officially by ecclesiastical bodies had so many expressions that we must content ourselves with only a few examples. Among the first were the London Missionary Society, formed, it will be remembered, in 1795, the Religious Tract Society, begun in 1799, the British and Foreign Bible Society, founded in 1804, and the American Bible Society, organized in 1816. The Sunday Schools were another such movement. After various world gatherings, as we have noted, in 1907 the World's Sunday School Association was formally organized. The Young Men's Christian Associations belonged in this category. As we have seen, from their humble beginning in 1844 they multiplied rapidly and in 1855 the World's Alliance of the Young Men's Christian Associations was organized. Eventually the Associations, while remaining predominantly Protestant, also attracted members of the Roman Catholic Church and of some of the Eastern Churches who remained in full communion in their denominations. Similar were the Young Women's Christian Associations. In 1894 their various national coördinating bodies joined in forming the World's Young Women's Christian Association. The Young People's Society of Christian Endeavour, inaugurated in a Congregational Church in New England, proved contagious, and in 1895 the World's Christian Endeavour Union was launched. Partly out of the Young Men's and Young Women's Christian Associations and the Student Volunteer Movement for Foreign Missions came, in 1895, the World's Student Christian Federation, made up of various national movements which recruited students from many different denominations while encouraging them to remain loyal to their respective churches. Outstanding in its formation and early leadership was John R. Mott, whom we have already met and are to meet again and again in connexion with various expressions of the Ecumenical Movement.

What was known as the Evangelical Alliance made important contributions to the movement towards Christian unity. It had its origin partly in 1845 in a collective effort of clergy of several denominations to counteract the Tractarian or Oxford movement and to strengthen Protestantism. It was followed by a gathering in London in 1846 of over eight hundred from several countries of Europe and America. At the London meeting the Evangelical Alliance was founded. It had as its purpose "the advancement of Evangelical Protestantism

. . . and the counteraction of infidelity, Popery, and other forms of superstition, error, and profaneness, especially the desecration of the Lord's Day." It confessed the reality of the one Church, recognized what it deemed the essential unity of the Church, deplored the divisions, and sought to join in cultivating brotherly love. It adopted a doctrinal basis which was that of most Evangelicals of the day, regardless of denomination. Branches were formed in several countries and from time to time world meetings were held. Among the latter was one in Berlin in 1857 at the invitation of the King of Prussia and which bishops of the Church of England, including the Archbishop of Canterbury, and English Nonconformists joined in endorsing. Another was held in Geneva in 1861, and still another in Amsterdam in 1867. As we have seen, the most notable of the series of world gatherings of the Evangelical Alliance convened in New York in 1873, largely through the initiative and driving energy of Philip Schaff, and in it the trend was more towards the union of Evangelicals than opposition to Catholicism. Later world meetings were held, but with the emergence of other forms of coöperation, some of them partly from the stimulus given by the Evangelical Alliance, they gradually ceased to attract wide attention. Yet in its heyday the Evangelical Alliance had marked repercussions. From 1886 to 1898 the Congregational clergyman Josiah Strong (1847–1916) was the general secretary of the American branch. One of the leaders in the Social Gospel movement, he urged that the churches coöperate in helping to Christianize the social order and to bring to realization the kingdom of God on earth. However, in general the Evangelical Alliance did not follow him.

Another approach to Christian unity was through proposals for the federation or actual union of churches. Here pioneer documents were the *Fraternal Appeal to the American Churches* (1838) by S. S. Schmucker, the Lutheran whom we have already met (Chapter L), which offered a *Plan for Protestant Union*, followed in 1845 by the *Overture for Christian Union* drafted by Schmucker and signed by fifty clergymen from several denominations. The *Overture* proposed a concrete procedure and structure for the formation by the churches of what was called the Apostolic Protestant Union. The suggested programme was not adopted by the churches, but it helped to prepare the way for later coöperation.

Anglicans were active in approaching the Eastern Churches, the Roman Catholic Church, and Protestant Churches in efforts to encourage fellowship and to explore bases of union. Successive Lambeth Conferences of the bishops of the Anglican Communion devoted much attention to that subject. The Conference of 1888 adopted as a basis the proposal made in 1886 by the General Convention of the Protestant Episcopal Church and which came to be known as the Lambeth Quadrilateral. In the form given it in 1888 it read:

The Holy Scriptures of the Old and New Testament as containing all things necessary to salvation, and as being the rule and ultimate standard of faith.

The Apostles' Creed as the baptismal symbol; and the Nicene Creed as the sufficient statement of the Christian faith.

The two Sacraments ordained by Christ himself—Baptism and the Supper of the Lord—ministered with the unfailing use of Christ's words of institution and the elements ordained by Him.

The historic episcopate, locally adapted in the method of its administration to the varying needs of the nations and peoples called of God into the unity of His Church.

Approaches made by Anglicans to other communions before and after the formulation of the Lambeth Quadrilateral did not lead to union. Indeed, conversations with Rome were given a note of finality when in 1896 Pope Leo XIII declared Anglican orders invalid.

Nor, except in the case of some closely related churches of the same denominational family, did the nineteenth century see the fusion of two or more denominations. That was to wait until after 1914. What may be regarded as a possible exception was the South India United Church, formed in 1908 by congregations connected with the United Free Church of Scotland, the Reformed Church in America, the London Missionary Society, and the American Board of Commissioners for Foreign Missions, but these were bodies which in theology came out of the Reformed tradition and had long regarded themselves as akin.

Several denominational families devised ways of furthering fellowship among their several branches. Such were the Lambeth Conferences for the Anglicans, the World Alliance of the Reformed Churches holding the Presbyterian System, organized in London in 1875, the International Congregational Council, which had its initial meeting in London in 1891, the Ecumenical Methodist Conferences, the first of which convened in London in 1901, and the Baptist World Alliance, organized in 1905.

Although no striking "organic union" of churches was achieved, coöperation among ecclesiastical bodies mounted as the century progressed. We have noted the Plan of Union through which in the fore part of the century the Congregationalists and the Presbyterians joined in planting the faith on the Western frontier of the United States. We have also seen that in its earlier years churches of several denominations contributed to the American Board of Commissioners for Foreign Missions. Similarly, from its formation in 1826 until the withdrawal of the New School Presbyterians in 1861, the American Home Missionary Society, predominantly Congregational, drew its support from more than one denomination. From 1840 until 1886 the Church of England and the Prussian Church shared in a Protestant episcopate at Jerusalem.

In the latter part of the century coöperation embracing a larger number of denominations began to appear. Several state councils and federations of churches came into being. Various movements, among them the National Federation of Churches and Christian Workers, officially formed in 1901, culminated in 1908 in the organization of the Federal Council of the Churches of Christ in America, by twenty-nine national denominational bodies, with the purpose of expressing "the fellowship and catholic unity of the Christian Church" and of exerting "a larger combined influence for the Churches of Christ in all matters affecting the moral and social conditions of the people." While made up of official representatives of its member churches, the Federal Council of Churches was forbidden to have any authority over its constituent bodies. It could simply offer counsel and recommend courses of action on matters of common interest. From the beginning, partly because of the influential place which Josiah Strong had in its formation, it gave much attention to encouraging joint action by the churches in bringing Christian principles to bear upon various aspects of human society. In 1892 a Free Church Congress met at Manchester, in England, and there followed, also in the 1890's, the National Council of the Evangelical Free Churches. Numbers of local councils of churches also sprang up in the British Isles.

Important developments, in some ways the major developments towards effecting Christian unity through Protestantism, came through the missionary outreach of the churches. This is not surprising. In regions to which Christianity was being introduced the divisions perpetuated from the lands where the faith had been longer planted often seemed anachronistic, irrelevant, and a handicap to the spread of the Gospel. In the new environment the impulse to a united approach, while often meeting obstacles, was strong. Moreover, in the countries and sections from which missionaries were sent, joint consultation appeared imperative.

Early in the nineteenth century conferences of missionaries in particular areas and countries across denominational barriers began to be held. As the century progressed they multiplied in numbers and size. Thus in 1825 the Bombay Missionary Union was formed by members of four societies and included Anglicans, Congregationalists, and Presbyterians. In the 1850's regional conferences of missionaries in North and South India were seen. In 1873 there convened the first of a series of decennial all-India missionary conferences. They increased in the numbers of societies represented. Indians were also included. In 1902 the Fourth Decennial Conference, following the precedent of the South India missionary conference of 1900, was made up, not of all individuals who cared to come, but of delegates officially appointed by their respective bodies. In Japan conferences of Protestant missionaries from the entire country began in 1872 and the third in the series, that of 1900, appointed a continuing standing committee which brought into being the Conference of Federated Missions in Japan which met annually beginning in 1907. The 1900 gathering also gave an impetus to what was later the Federation of Churches in Japan. In China missionaries joined in translating the Bible as early as 1843, but the first general missionary conference was not until 1877. It was followed by others in 1890 and 1907, each larger than its predecessor. The 1907 gathering gave much attention to the promotion of continuing and visible unity. Other national or regional missionary conferences were convened, beginning in Mexico in the 1880's and in the first decades of the twentieth century in South Africa and for the Moslem world.

In the lands from which missionaries were sent, regular and continuing consultation and coöperation were devised early. In 1819 the secretaries of foreign mission boards with headquarters in London formed an association for "mutual counsel and fellowship." Beginning in 1863 delegates from several Scandinavian missionary societies met in Northern Lutheran Missions Conferences. In 1866 the first of a series of Continental Missions Conferences was held with representatives of several societies. In 1885 what was known as *Der Ausschuss der deutschen evangelischen Missionen* was constituted, a standing committee of all the Protestant missionary societies of Germany. It grew in its scope and work. A general Dutch missionary conference met in 1887 and became an annual event. What was eventually called the Foreign Missions Conference of North America convened for the first time in 1895. It met annually thereafter, chiefly as a gathering where officials and board members of the several Protestant missionary societies exchanged views. In 1907 it arranged for more nearly continuous consultation by the appointment of a smaller Committee of Reference and Counsel.

Meetings on a world scale on behalf of Protestant missions also developed. Precursors with attendance from only one nation were held in New York and London in 1854. What is usually regarded as the first of the series convened at Liverpool in 1860, drawing almost entirely from the British Isles. There followed others in London in 1878 and 1888, both international, and then the Ecumenical Missionary Conference in New York in 1900, with attendance from the United States, the British Isles, and the Continent of Europe. Each was larger than its predecessor. The 1900 gathering was especially outstanding with delegates from 162 mission boards and huge public meetings which by their programmes gave impressive demonstration to the variety and extent of foreign missions.

The most notable in the succession of the international, inter-denominational assemblies was the World Missionary Conference, held in Edinburgh in 1910.

It became a landmark in the history of the Ecumenical Movement, for it influenced profoundly some of the most important developments of the next forty or more years. In several ways it was in contrast with its predecessors and was an advance beyond them. First, it was more strictly a delegated body, made up of official representatives of the missionary societies. Second, it was a deliberative body, seeking to formulate policy for the years ahead. While it possessed no legislative authority, it could suggest, and because it was composed of leaders of the various societies there was reason to hope that its recommendations would be followed by action. In the third place, as a preliminary to the deliberations prolonged and extensive studies were made of the several aspects of the missionary enterprise and in their preparation hundreds of correspondents were enlisted in many different parts of the world, thus stimulating widespread thought. In the fourth place, the gathering was more comprehensive ecclesiastically than its predecessors. The latter had, in general, enlisted only Evangelicals. At Edinburgh several Anglo-Catholics were present and took part. Moreover, members of what later came to be called "the younger churches," namely, those founded by eighteenth and nineteenth century Protestant missions, while few, were prominent. Of first-class importance, in the fifth place, was the fact that provision was made for carrying forward the work of the gathering. A Continuation Committee was appointed. Through it conferences were held in 1912 and 1913 in various centres in Asia preparatory to more permanent coöperative bodies, a comprehensive scholarly journal, *The International Review of Missions,* was inaugurated, and, after 1914, as we are to see later, the International Missionary Council emerged. In the sixth place, the Edinburgh gathering also was in part responsible for the two organizations, the World Conference on Faith and Order and the Universal Christian Council for Life and Work, the two bodies which, after 1914, merged to form the World Council of Churches.

A seventh feature of major significance was the fashion in which "Edinburgh 1910" either brought to the fore or enlisted men who were to have an outstanding part in the growth of the Ecumenical Movement. John R. Mott was active in the preparations for the conference, presided at most of its sessions, and became the chairman of the Continuation Committee and then of the International Missionary Council. Joseph Houldsworth Oldham (1874——), born in Scotland, the first full-time secretary of the Student Christian Movement of Great Britain and Ireland, was chiefly responsible for the preparations for Edinburgh, became the first secretary of the International Missionary Council, and had a large part in the development of the Universal Christian Council for Life and Work. Charles H. Brent (1862-1929), a bishop of the Protestant Episcopal Church, there caught the vision which made him one of the chief initiators of World Conference on Faith and Order. William Temple, present as a "steward" or "usher," was later a vice-chairman of the International Missionary Council and the first chairman of the provisional committee which brought into being the World Council of Churches. V. S. Azariah, whom we have already met as the first Indian Anglican bishop, and a Chinese, Chêng Ching-yi (1881–1940), had leading parts in the Ecumenical Movement. There were also present some other men whose names later became household words in the Ecumenical Movement.

By deliberate choice, the Edinburgh conference confined its attention to missions to non-Christians and therefore did not include Protestant missions among the Roman Catholics in Latin America. As an eighth result of the gathering, some who believed that this huge area should be covered in coöperative fashion in 1913 had the Foreign Missions Conference of North America call a meeting from which emerged the Committee on Coöperation in Latin America, a body which was to have a notable history.

Summary

Christianity came to the year 1914 on a rising tide and with mounting momentum. In spite of the many adversaries which it encountered and which seemed to threaten its existence, in 1914 it was more widely spread geographically than at any previous time, it had given rise to men and movements which were as outstanding as any in the history of the faith, and it was making its impress upon more of mankind than ever before. The chief channel of this vitality was Protestantism. In addition to its striking geographic spread, proportionately much greater than that of any other wing of Christianity, to the fresh and novel movements which issued from it, and to its creative thought and scholarship, Protestantism also devised ways of drawing Christians together which were beginning to meet with marked success.

Selected Bibliography

W. R. Hogg, *Ecumenical Foundations. A History of the International Missionary Council and Its Nineteenth-Century Background* (New York, Harper & Brothers, 1952, pp. xi, 466). The indispensable and definitive study of the subject.

K. S. Latourette, *A History of the Expansion of Christianity. Volumes IV, V, VI, The Great Century* (New York, Harper & Brothers, 1941–1944).

G. J. Slosser, *Christian Unity. Its History and Challenge in All Communions, in All Lands* (New York, E. P. Dutton & Co., 1929, pp. xix, 425). Comprehensive, detailed.

VIGOUR AMIDST STORM:
BEGINNING IN A.D. 1914

Chapter LVI

AN AGE OF STORM: THE GENERAL SETTING, THE CHALLENGE TO CHRISTIANITY, AND THE VIGOUR OF THE CHRISTIAN RESPONSE

The summer of 1914 ushered the entire world and with it Christianity into a new and tumultuous age.

We have seen that for what was still regarded as Christendom the century between 1815 and 1914 was one of comparative peace, of amazing increases in population and wealth, and of even more astounding geographic expansion. By 1914 all the inhabited world had been penetrated and for the most part mastered by peoples who had been traditionally known as Christian. In other cultures the impact of the "Christian" Occident and its culture had begun to bring either profound changes or complete disintegration.

In spite of rising threats in the Occident to its historic faith and increasing open dissent and departure from it on the part of many, Christianity came to 1914 on a rising tide, gathering momentum as it spread across the face of the planet. Vigour and geographic expansion characterized all three of the major forms of Christianity. While showing less of them than any of the others, the Orthodox, especially the Russian Orthodox, clearly displayed them. The Roman Catholic Church, which had suffered severely both in the period from 1750 to 1815 and from the secularizing currents of the nineteenth century, had been knit together more closely under the Pope, had put forth many fresh movements, and had spread more widely geographically than ever before. But it was Protestantism which had been the vehicle of the greatest vitality. From it had issued many movements, some of them novel and evidence of quite astounding creativity. From being confined almost entirely to North-western Europe and the British Isles and a narrow strip on the eastern seaboard of North America, it had become world-wide and the dominant faith of burgeoning new nations in both the Southern and the Northern Hemisphere. By its very genius seem-

ingly endlessly divisive and dividing, it was beginning to draw together, groping in fresh institutional ways towards the unity which all Christians in principle believed should characterize the followers of Christ. The main stream of
the faith was beginning to surge through the channels of Protestantism.

Now came, apparently abruptly, an age which from some of its aspects
seemed an ominous ebb in the Christian tide. Indeed, there were those who
spoke of the age as the "post-Christian era." From what had once been denominated Christendom issued wars and revolutions which threw the entire
world into disorder and set all humanity on the march. That march appeared
to many to be moving mankind away from Christianity. If only one set of facts
were taken into consideration here seemed to be another of the major recessions which had punctuated the course of the faith. Indeed, so serious did it
appear to be that pessimists and critics might proclaim it as the last of the recessions, certain to end in the disappearance of Christianity, or, if not its complete
disappearance, its decline to an inconspicuous and unimportant rôle in the life
of the race.

Two facets of the age differentiated the period from the earlier ones which
were indubitably recessions. One of these was the fact that the threats to the
faith arose in large part from Christianity and were a menace because they were
perversions of the gifts which had come to man through it. They seemed to be
spelling the doom of Christianity—as though Christianity itself had given birth
to enemies which were to destroy it.

In ages of retreat the enemies had come in some degree from distortions of
Christian contributions. Indeed, that had been progressively more prominent
with each of the successive recessions. In the first, that from A.D. 500 to A.D. 950,
the chief initial causes had been the internal decay of the Roman Empire and
the irruption of barbarians from the North. For neither of these was Christianity
a significant cause. The major later factor was the Arab invasion from the
South-east, given added dynamic and unity by Islam. It was Islam which by
A.D. 950 had become dominant in about half of what had been Christendom,
and Islam was indebted both to Judaism and Christianity, although more to the
former than the latter.

The second major recession, that from 1350 to 1500, arose in part from the
break-up of the Mongol Empire, for which Christianity was not responsible,
and from the blows dealt by the Black Death, or bubonic plague, of which
Christianity could not be counted as a source. More potent was the fresh surge
of Islam, born by Mongols and Turks. Presumably the exploits of Tamerlane
and the Ottoman Turks were not due as much to the fact that they were
Moslems as had been those of the Arabs in the earlier recession. Proportionately
to the geographic extent of Christianity the gains of Islam at its expense were

not as great as in the eighth and ninth centuries. But in so far as Islam was a factor, Christianity, as one of the formative although minor contributors to the birth of Islam, was a cause. More serious threats to Christianity in the period between 1350 and 1500 were from within Christendom. They arose partly from the failure of the Catholic Church, whether of the East or of the West, to purge itself of corruption and to allow itself to be a sufficiently effective channel for the "exceeding greatness of the power" of the Gospel. They were also from the passing of the medieval civilization of Western Europe which Christianity had done much to produce and with which it was intricately associated. The waning of that civilization was chargeable to a complex variety of developments. Not all of them are fully discernible, but to some Christianity contributed. One was the Renaissance and another the humanism which was closely associated with the Renaissance. Both could be ascribed in some degree to Christianity. Another was the rising prosperity with the growth of cities and the decay of feudalism, a process which Christianity had assisted by helping to discipline the rude barbarians who had overwhelmed much of South-western Europe and by making for an inclusive order in that region.

The fact that the period from 1750 to 1815 had brought serious crises for Christianity and in some areas was a recession was due almost entirely to forces at work within Western Christendom and for which Christianity was to some degree responsible. Such were the rationalism and the Deism of the era and the political ideas which inspired and largely shaped the French Revolution. They were in part from Christianity, even though only distorted expressions or perversions of it.

The age which began in the summer of 1914 was made distinct by movements all of which either issued from Western Europe or were profoundly influenced by contact with Western Europe. Whether Western Europe should still be called a part of Christendom was questionable, but it was there that Christianity had shown its chief vitality from the tenth into the nineteenth century, or for only a little less than a millennium. Moreover, most if not all of the features peculiar to the era bore the impress of Christianity, even when they were perversions of it and menaced its existence.

One of the most obvious of the features of the age was war. Within a little less than forty years two world wars devastated much of the earth's surface and several lesser ones were waged. Never before had so much of mankind been engaged simultaneously in war, war which might be called internecine because it was really a civil war within the totality of the human race. Never before had mankind massed such large armies or produced weapons which worked wholesale destruction on so gigantic a scale. The first of the two world wars originated in Western Europe and there took its greatest toll in life and property. The second had its first rumblings in the Far East in the "Mukden incident" between China and Japan in September, 1931, and in the large scale invasion of China by Japan in July, 1937, but it attained global proportions in the late summer of 1939 through Western Europe. Everywhere it was fought with the kind of organization and equipment which had first been developed by Western European peoples and it dealt even more severe blows to Western Europe than had World War I.

It was sobering to recall that the intense nationalism which was a major cause of the two wars was historically closely associated with the self-consciousness of the masses which could be traced in part to Christianity with its emphasis upon the dignity and worth of every individual. It was also provocative of thought that the science which made possible the weapons with which the wars were fought was indebted to Christianity through its emphasis upon an orderly and dependable universe and the initiative and courage which it had inspired in Western man since the heyday of the Middle Ages.

Another of the outstanding characteristics of the post-1914 world was revolution. Ancient monarchies were swept away. Outstanding in their collapse were those of China, Russia, Germany, and Italy. It was not simply that the ruling house toppled, discredited by lack of success in dealing with foreign foes, although this is a phase of the change. More important was the disappearance of the entire monarchical structure, centuries old, in China going back more than two thousand years, and the substitution of what were called republics. Usually a determined minority seized control and, asserting that it was acting on behalf of the masses, attempted to erect a new framework inspired and maintained by a body of ideas.

The ideologies varied from country to country. Some were democratic in the sense in which Anglo-Saxons and Western Europeans understood that term. One took the name of national socialism, another was fascism, and what vied in its dynamic force with the Anglo-Saxon type of liberal democracy was communism, the Marxist form of socialism. In some other countries, notably in India, Burma, and Indonesia, a Western regime founded on imperialistic expansion was discarded and a republic was substituted for it. Under whatever name or ideology, these regimes appealed to the masses, masses restless under age-long oppression and official exploitation and corruption and roused to a great hope, a hope of a better day for themselves and their children.

It was highly significant that all the ideologies that gained the mastery, with the possible exception of that which dominated Japan in the 1930's and the fore part of the 1940's and here and there a resurgent Islam, were originally formulated in Western Europe and, even when they were hostile to it, were to some degree indebted to Christianity. From time to time we have noted that debt (especially in Chapter XLV). It was particularly marked in the two most widely spread of the ideologies, democracy of the Anglo-Saxon and French types and the Marxist communism which was professed by the party which mastered Russia and which, spreading from Russia by a combination of physical force and extraordinarily skilful intrigue, political manipulation, and propaganda, by 1953 was dominant in most of Central Europe, Western Germany, Central Asia, North Korea, and China. Communism was a secularized version of the Christian understanding of history. Under the influence of Judaism and Christianity it believed that history moves to a climax. However, it declared that the climax is not to be reached by the power and under the direction of God, as the Jewish and Christian faiths held, but is to be from the inevitable course of nature, and the goal is not to be the perfected kingdom of God, but a classless society in which the nation state will fade away and each individual will contribute according to his ability and each is to have according to his need. In contrast with the Christian Gospel, based upon self-giving love, it inculcated hate, stimulated class conflict, and utilized lies in its propaganda when lies seemed to serve its ends. Here was a vast, some called it a demonic, perversion of Christianity which was frankly anti-Christian and which many regarded the most serious threat to Christianity since the rise of Islam.

It is also significant that the hopes and aspirations which these ideologies promised to fulfill were roused by contact with the West and to no small extent were due to the Christian elements in Occidental culture. Some of the outstanding men and movements that called them forth were either professedly Christian or were frank to admit that they were influenced by Christ. Thus much of the post-1914 restlessness among Africans south of the Sahara was fed and given hope by the Watch Tower Movement, another name for Jehovah's Witnesses. He who did most to shape the ideals of revolutionary China between 1911 and the late 1940's was Sun Yat-sen, an avowed Christian who owed most of his formal education to Christian schools. The chief architect of the foundations of the Republic of India and the main leader in seeking to erase the caste barriers which kept the depressed classes in hereditary squalor was M. K. Gandhi, who, while not a Christian, gladly affirmed the impress which Christ had made on him.

Still another feature of the era which began in 1914 was the decline of Western Europe in the total world scene. With an interruption in the fourteenth and the fore part of the fifteenth century, from as far back as the first of the Crusades Western European peoples had been expanding. In the nineteenth century they had grown strikingly in wealth and numbers and by the year 1914 they and their culture dominated the globe. Seen against the background of the total span of human history that hegemony was brief. In 1914 it began a rapid decline. The culture which had its rise in Western Europe continued to spread. Nations chiefly of Western European stock, notably the United States, loomed ever more prominently in the affairs of mankind. In spite of wars the population of Western Europe showed an increase. Yet Western European nations were not as masterful as they had been. Peoples whom they had governed rose in revolt and cast off their rule even when, as latterly had been true of several of the powers, especially Great Britain and the Netherlands, that rule had been benevolent and had prepared its subjects for autonomy. Many in Western Europe believed and loudly proclaimed that the region and its culture were victims of fatal illnesses. The optimism which had prevailed in the nineteenth century gave way to profound pessimism. The obvious causes of the decline and the pessimism were the two world wars and the subsequent revolutions which swept across Western Europe, but the conviction was held that these, while undoubtedly important, were symptoms of a much more basic malady. The fear and the pessimism were shared, although by no means as deeply, by nations which had arisen chiefly from the migrations of Western European peoples, including the United States, and that in spite of the fact that by the middle of the twentieth century the latter country was the wealthiest and the most powerful on the planet.

The decline, sickness, and pessimism of Western Europe took on added significance in view of the fact that the area was the heart of what had been "Christian" civilization. Here for nearly a thousand years most of the creative movements in Christianity had had their rise—the revivals in the Roman Catholic Church which had found expression in new monastic orders, the main ferment of creative theological thought, and various awakenings which had broken with the Roman Catholic Church, the chief of them Protestantism. Here the two forms of Christianity which had spread most vigorously since the fifteenth century, Roman Catholicism and Protestantism, had their historic centres. Was Christianity responsible for the illness of Western Europe, whether by contributing to the applied science and the ideologies which were working its doom or from inability to prevent or counteract the perversions of its good gifts which were at the root of the disease?

The situation was made the more grave by the contrast between the apprehensive gloom which covered what had been the heart of Christendom and the aggressive confidence which, at least outwardly, characterized communism and communists, an openly anti-Christian fruit of Western "Christian" civilization and to which Christianity had contributed. Was Christianity, as communists and many of its other critics declared, a waning force, to be left behind by the onward course of history? A somewhat similar hopefulness characterized the peoples of India and Pakistan after their achievement of independence from British rule in the latter part of the 1940's.

As if to confirm the dire prophecies of the demise of Christianity was the fact that the Christian churches were suffering numerical losses in Europe, and this in contrast with the mounting tide on which they had reached 1914. As we are to see somewhat more in detail later, the de-Christianization of great masses in Western Europe which had been begun at least as early as the eighteenth century and which had been partly obscured by the vigour displayed by that faith in the nineteenth century was making rapid strides.

The de-Christianization was all the more serious because it was most marked in what some of the contemporaries called "modern mass society," the urban centres which continued to grow as a result of industrialization. Christianity remained strongest in the rural districts, the small towns, and some of the suburbs where the older social patterns more nearly persisted and which by its earlier successes Christianity had permeated even when it had not transformed them. Christianity was finding it difficult to maintain footholds among the labourers in the mines and factories and among the shifting masses of population, some displaced by war, some by movements from country and small town to city, some in the new housing developments, and some by migration, often seasonal, from one occupation to another. It was sobering to reflect that the industrialization which brought this challenge and these losses was in part, as we have more than once reminded ourselves, a fruit of the science to which Christianity had contributed.

Disturbing also were the vast increases in population which continued in the twentieth century. These meant that in spite of the phenomenal geographic spread of Christianity, there were more non-Christians in the middle of the twentieth century than in 1815 or even in 1914. They also carried with them growing pressure upon subsistence, added physical suffering, and mounting dissatisfaction and restlessness which could easily become the seeds of new revolutions and more gigantic wars.

Over the entire human race hung the threat of wars to which the first two world holocausts of the century would be only preliminary. By mid-century the human race was being gathered into two camps around rival colossi. On the one hand, with the advantage of the possession of the heart-land of the largest of the continents, Eurasia, were Russia and her satellites and allies, inspired by a confident communism. On the other hand was the United States, the centre of a less closely bound congeries of states scattered over much of the rest of the globe. The two colossi were feverishly arming and, utilizing the science which had originated in the erstwhile Christendom, were developing ever more destructive weapons. The outlook seemed grim, both for the human race and for Christianity. There were many, even among intelligent and informed Christians, who could see only this side of the picture.

Yet there was another side, a second facet. It made the years which followed 1914 one of the greatest eras in the history of Christianity. Christians who knew the world scene as a whole were conscious that they and their fellow-believers were a minority set in a hostile world, but they were not content to be on the defensive. For them the figure of speech still held true with which at the outset Christ had described his Church. That Church was like a besieging army against a foe who was on the defensive, ensconced in a beleaguered city, and they believed the promise that the gates of hell which the Church was attacking would not prevail against it. They were mindful of their Lord's parting commission to the apostles to make disciples of all nations, baptizing them and teaching them to observe all that he had commanded them, assured of his continuing presence to whom all authority had been given. In the face of the many threats and challenges, after 1914 Christianity was putting forth fresh movements, was becoming more widely spread, more deeply rooted among more peoples, and more nearly united on a world scale, and was having growing constructive effects which were at least partly offsetting the perils. In the succeeding chapters we are to see this somewhat more in detail, although even then necessarily only in cursory fashion.

In Europe, long the traditional stronghold of the faith, the proportion of those who called themselves Christians declined, and the percentage of those who regularly attended church services seems to have fallen off even more. Yet fresh and vigorous new movements issued from Christianity in worship, thought, and action. In the United States, in contrast, the mass conversion of the non-Christian and partially de-Christianized elements of the population continued. For instance, in the twenty-four years between 1926 and 1950 the membership of all religious bodies, including the Jewish congregations, increased 59.9 per cent. as against a growth of 28.6 per cent. in the population. The percentage increase of Protestants was 63.7, of Roman Catholics 53.9, and of Judaism 22.5. In other words, Judaism was losing, and if the totals of membership had included only Christians the gains would have been above 60 per cent. In the rest of the Americas and in Australasia the percentage of church membership did not greatly alter, except that in Latin America, particularly in Brazil, Protestantism mounted rapidly in numbers and vitality. In North Africa and Western Asia the shrinkage of the ancient churches persisted and was accelerated as against the nineteenth century, but in Africa south of the Sahara the mass conversion proceeded, in some areas spectacularly. In India and Indonesia and to a lesser extent in most of the lands of South-east Asia the proportion of Christians in the population multiplied. In China and Japan, in spite of foreign wars, invasions, and domestic stress, the numerical strength of the Church grew, although not as markedly as in India. While still represented by small minorities in Asia, at the mid-century mark Christians were more nearly evenly distributed the world around than in 1914. The growth was by both Roman Catholics and Protestants.

Even more significant of the mounting strength of Christianity in the entire human scene was the fashion in which Christianity was taking root and on its newer geographic frontiers in Asia and Africa was becoming less dependent on missionaries from the Occident. Both Roman Catholics and Protestants stressed the recruiting and training of indigenous leaders and were transferring administrative responsibility to them. An increasing proportion of Roman Catholic nuns, priests, and bishops were of native stock and the same was true of the corresponding personnel in Protestant churches and institutions. In time of stress, when Occidental missionaries were compelled to withdraw or were interned, many although not all of the indigenous bodies displayed the ability not only to survive but also to grow. Indigenous forms of Christian art and music were appearing.

The movement towards Christian unity which was issuing from Protestantism and expressing itself through novel channels and which we noted as beginning before 1914 gained in momentum. By mid-century it had not drawn all Protestantism together, but in one way or another it was bringing the large majority of Protestants into a growing fellowship and was making friendly contacts with thousands in other branches of Christianity.

Moreover, in a distraught world in which colossal suffering and frustrating fears mingled with daring aspiration, Christianity was the major impelling motive in healing and relief on a larger scale than had ever before been seen. Sometimes through frankly Christian channels, such as aid to prisoners of war by the Young Men's Christian Associations in World War I, the American Friends Service Committee, Church World Service during and after World War II, Hilfswerk in Germany, and scores of other agencies, sometimes through organizations which had their origins in Christian faith and sacrifice but did not bear the Christian name, such as Near East Relief in and after World War I and the International Red Cross, aid and hope were brought to sufferers. The League of Nations and its successor, the United Nations, with their departments for the peaceful settlement of disputes between nations and for human welfare, and their dream of an international structure based on law and coöperation rather than the near-chaos of the day, had as their initial and chief architects men and women who were moved and sustained by Christian faith.

By the middle of the twentieth century the age which opened in 1914 was still too near its beginning for adequate appraisal. It was not clear whether it was one of recession or advance in the Christian tide. Evidence could be adduced to support either judgement. Here, as from the beginning of the course of the Christian faith, the words which Paul used to describe himself were applicable to Christianity: ". . . unknown and yet well known, as dying and behold we live." The Christian could find a basis for Paul's confident assertion, "Where sin abounded, grace did much more abound."

To that story we now turn. It must sometime be told in detail. Here we can give it only in inadequate summary.

EUROPE
1919 - 1939

Scale of Miles
0   200   400   600   800

ICELAND

NORWAY

SWEDEN

FINLAND

Leningrad

RUSSIA

°Moscow

Volga

ASIA

CASPIAN SEA

Stockholm

BALTIC SEA

ESTONIA

LATVIA

LITHUANIA

EAST PRUSSIA

POLAND

UKRAINE

Kiev

Dnieper R.

GEORGIA

BLACK SEA

Istanbul
(Constantinople)

NORTH SEA

SCOTLAND

Newcastle

GREAT BRITAIN

ENGLAND

WALES

NORTH IRELAND

EIRE

Maynooth

Liverpool

London

DENMARK

HOLLAND

THE NETHER-LANDS

Amsterdam

Utrecht

BELGIUM

Paris

FRANCE

Berlin°

GERMANY

BAVARIA

WÜRTEM-BERG

Rhine R.

Basel

SWITZER-LAND

Geneva

CZECHOSLOVAKIA

AUSTRIA

HUNGARY

RUMANIA

Danube R.

JUGOSLAVIA

SERBIA

MONTE-NEGRO

BULGARIA

ALBANIA

GREECE

TURKEY

ITALY

Rome°

CORSICA

SARDINIA

SICILY

SPAIN

PORTUGAL

M E D I T E R R A N E A N   S E A

AFRICA

Lund

Chapter LVII

STORM, TESTING, LOSSES, AND VITALITY
IN TRADITIONAL CHRISTENDOM AFTER
A.D. 1914

As we have suggested, the wars and revolutions which began in the summer of 1914 bore especially heavily on the historic stronghold of Christianity, Europe and Western Asia. Here World War I broke out. Here the revolutions began and the revolutionary ideologies were developed which swept across much of the rest of the world. As was to be expected, they were particularly potent in the region of their origin. Here World War II had its strategic centre and wrought much of its devastation. Here were the scenes of the origin of the main forms of Christianity, whether of the various Eastern Churches, the Roman Catholic Church, or the major expressions of Protestantism. Here had been the chief theological activity and here almost all the varieties of monasticism had had their birth. In Europe and Western Asia, accordingly, after 1914, Christianity faced one of the greatest challenges of its history. In Western Asia it was already suffering from the centuries-long erosion of Islam. In Europe, and particularly in Western Europe, it was being subjected to the continued attrition of the intellectual currents and the industrialization of society which we have noted as menaces in the nineteenth century and earlier.

Would Christianity survive the combination of these older attacks and the added threats of the twentieth century? If it perished or even seriously dwindled in Europe and Western Asia, would it continue on its geographic periphery, where it had displayed so striking an expansion since the fifteenth and especially since the eighteenth century? If it were fatally or even seriously wounded at what had been the centres from which it had spread, would it persist and continue to grow at its extremities? By the middle of the twentieth century it was clear that it was suffering numerical losses in Europe and Western Asia and that in some quarters there were indications of a failure of nerve. On the other hand, fresh expressions of vitality were appearing in all three major branches of Christianity, most strikingly in the one which had displayed the greatest vigour in the nineteenth century, Protestantism, but also in the Roman Catholic Church, and, to a much less extent, in some of the Eastern Churches. Nor did Protestants and Roman Catholics cease their efforts to spread the faith throughout the world. Rather, they redoubled them, and with the result that the momentum seen on the eve of 1914 continued and issued in what we hinted near the close of the preceding chapter.

THE ROMAN CATHOLIC CHURCH IN EUROPE AFTER 1914

Following the order which we adopted in our account of the nineteenth century, we turn first of all to the record of the Roman Catholic Church in Europe after 1914. We must remember, however, that simultaneously the developments were in progress in Protestantism and the Eastern Churches which we are to summarize a little later. The three main branches of Christianity did not interact on one another as closely as had the Roman Catholic and the Eastern Churches before 1350 or as had the Roman Catholic Church and Protestantism in the sixteenth and seventeenth centuries. They had about as much influence on one another as in the nineteenth century, perhaps slightly more than then. Protestantism especially affected the other two. Yet they tended to go their separate ways. We will first note, in comprehensive outline, the series of blows to which the Roman Catholic Church was subjected after 1914 and then describe, although with what must be tantalizing brevity, what took place in certain phases of the life of that church and in particular countries and areas.

To those who are at all familiar with the stage in the history of Europe which was ushered in by the events of the summer of 1914, the main blows dealt the Roman Catholic Church in its traditional heart-land require only the briefest mention. First was World War I. It entailed the destruction of what had long been a bulwark of the Roman Catholic Church, the Hapsburg-ruled Austria-Hungarian Empire, serious damage to Belgium, an almost solidly Roman Catholic land, exhausting drains on France, from which more Roman Catholic missionaries had come in the nineteenth century than from any other country, the defeat of Germany, whose Catholic constituency had been increasingly active in the latter part of the nineteenth century, and debilitating efforts by Italy, where was the headquarters of the Roman Catholic Church. There followed, as an aftermath of the war, the triumph of fascism in Italy, with its demand for complete control over the lives of Italians, particularly of youth, with objectives which were not-too-covertly anti-Christian, the domination of Germany and Austria by the Nazis, equally intent upon a totalitarian regime which demanded the subservience of the Church and the complete possession of the minds and souls of youth, and the growing menace of Russian communism, as yet only on the periphery of the Roman Catholic citadel. Civil war in Spain brought further complications, as did the fascist adventure in Ethiopia. Then came World War II with physical destruction and spiritual exhaustion which wounded Europe much more deeply than had World War I and which was followed by the advance of the iron curtain of vigorously totalitarian, emphatically anti-Roman Catholic Russian communism over lands with Roman Catholic majorities and with the threat of a farther westward movement of that curtain into traditionally Roman Catholic territory.

In Europe in general the Roman Catholic Church emerged from World War I with an enhanced prestige and vigour that carried through the troubled period which much of mankind was despairingly hoping would be an introduction to permanent peace but which proved to be a prelude to an even more gigantic war. The Papal throne was occupied by a succession of able men, Benedict XV (Giacomo della Chiesa), who reigned from 1914 to 1922, Pius XI (Achille Ratti), of middle class stock, scholar, mountaineer, and courageous and skilful administrator, who wore the tiara from 1922 to 1939, and Pius XII (Eugenio Pacelli), a scion of the Papal nobility who succeeded him, the first Papal secretary of state to be elevated to that high office since Hildebrand (Gregory VII). Men of experience and initiative, they were vigorous and usually astute.

During and after World War I Benedict XV again and again addressed the world, calling to its attention principles for establishing peace and urging the belligerents to compose their differences. He used the facilities of his church to alleviate the sufferings from the war through negotiating the exchange of prisoners and civilians in occupied countries, aiding the sick, furthering the repatriation of prisoners of war and the correspondence of prisoners with their families, and promoting the relief of devastated areas.

After the war there was a decided revival in the Roman Catholic Church. Youth organizations sprang up, additional episcopal sees were organized, numbers of monastic, educational, and charitable institutions flourished, frequent communion was emphasized, Eucharistic Congresses in various parts of the world stimulated and focused the devotion of clergy and laity, and Catholic Action, begun in the nineteenth century, enlisted more and more of the laity.

The study of theology was quickened. True to the impetus given by Leo XIII, it stressed Thomas Aquinas, and thinkers appeared who commanded respect not only within but also outside Roman Catholic circles. Some of the intellectuals who had regarded Christianity as not worthy of consideration were again willing to examine the claims of Roman Catholic philosophy and theology. Among those who won their attention was Jacques Maritain

(1882——), a Frenchman of Protestant antecedents, a convert in his twenties, who from his personal experience as well as his observation came to believe that the course of the stream from Descartes through Rousseau, Kant, Hegel, Darwin, and Freud had led the modern man away from God to atheism and futility. He found what seemed to him to be the answer in Catholic faith as expressed by Aquinas, sought to interpret it in fresh ways, and hoped that through those who accepted it growing islands of Christian life and sanity would emerge in a culture which he regarded as disintegrating through its abandonment of the principles on which the great spirits of the Middle Ages had sought to build civilization. Étienne Henry Gilson (1884——), another Frenchman, reared a Roman Catholic and not a convert as was Maritain, a specialist on the thought of the Middle Ages, was not so exclusively attached to Aquinas, but regarded him as one of the eminent formulators of Christian theology. The Jesuit Erich Przywara (1889——), of Slavic descent but working in Germany and in German, in opposition to recent and current philosophy which rejected or belittled Christianity, held that logically the only possible metaphysics is Catholic and argued that Aquinas had shown how the Christian revelation apprehended by faith had met the problem of the contradiction between God and the world and had bridged the gap between them.

The trends in Roman Catholic theology, like those which we are to see in Protestant and Orthodox theology, obviously reflected an awareness of the parlous state of the world and especially of Western civilization as revealed by the wars and revolutions of the day. There was a deep conviction that the Occident must have been proceeding on false premises, that the error was in a lack of understanding and in a faulty conception of man and the universe, and that the truth was in the historic Christian faith.

A revival of Roman Catholic piety was furthered by the liturgical movement. Having its inception, as we have seen (Chapter XLVI), in the nineteenth century, it was given a marked impetus in 1914 in the monastery of Maria Laach in Germany and continued to spread. As we have noted, it was an attempt to deepen and strengthen the corporate life of the Church through a return to the practice of the early centuries of the faith in the intelligent participation of the congregation in the Eucharist. Instead of the members of the congregation being simply spectators and hearers of what was done in the mass by priest and choir, it would have them share in it. The liturgical movement took many forms. In one of its aspects it encouraged the wide distribution of missals, with translations into the vernaculars to enable the congregation to follow what was done at the altar. As a further step it taught the members of the congregation to give the responses to what was said by the priest. In some places it encouraged the congregation to join in singing the mass, often stressing the Gregorian music which had gained fresh favour in the nineteenth century through Papal initiative. In a few localities, notably after World War II, it put the liturgy into the vernacular except for the central formulæ, which were kept in Latin. The movement sought to make of the Roman Catholic Church not merely a huge administrative structure but also and primarily a living organism and wished to penetrate and inspire Catholic Action with a growing sense of the reality of the central mystery of the faith and to reawaken the Church as a community of faith in which both priests and laity had a part. The liturgical movement gained momentum, grew in various countries in Europe, was made a means of winning some from the de-Christianized industrial labourers, and became especially prominent after World War II.

Both the theological developments and the liturgical movement were manifestations of the trend which we noted in the nineteenth century that tended to make the Roman Catholic Church a self-conscious minority in a hostile world and increasingly under centralized control by the Papacy. By the mid-twentieth century that trend was by no means carried through to its logical conclusion. In some countries the traditional particularism continued, even though weakened. In many lands the Roman Catholic faith was officially that of the state and the nation and was accepted by the masses as a social heritage without much intelligent conviction. Yet more and more the Roman Catholic Church was becoming an hierarchical structure directed by the Pope, supported by a loyal, hard-working body of clergy, monks, and nuns, and maintained by an instructed and disciplined laity.

A demonstration of the power of the Supreme Pontiff was given in the proclamation by Pius XII on November 1, 1950, of the bodily assumption to heaven of the Virgin Mary as a dogma to be believed by all the faithful. It was the first instance of a solemn definition of dogma by the Pope since that of the immaculate conception of the Virgin Mary in 1854 and also the first since Papal infallibility had been affirmed by the Vatican Council in 1870. Unlike the action of 1870, it was accepted by the clergy and laity without serious dissent.

The Roman Catholic Church was still the largest of the sects or divisions in the Christian Church. The Popes were unwavering in their insistence that the only true unity of Christians was through obedience to them as the successors of Peter and as therefore entrusted by Christ with the direction of his Church. In face of the growing Ecumenical Movement among Protestants and of invitations from the latter to join in it and thus tacitly or openly to consent to being one among several churches, none with priority over the others or the exclusive possessor and guardian of Christian truth, the Pope (June 5, 1948) forbade Catholics to take part in public discussions of religious questions without the permission of the Holy See. Pius XII, as had others in his office, invited all

Christians to come to what he declared to be the one fold and the one shepherd.

Nor was the Roman Catholic Church content to be on the defensive. Recognizing the hostility of the world and glorying in its heritage of a long line of those who had suffered martyrdom for the faith, it continued to seek to win all men. Never had it had Popes who were more zealous supporters of its global missions than were those of the twentieth century. Increasingly Rome expanded its direction and control of missions. This was partly through able leadership in the Congregation for the Propagation of the Faith. In 1922 the Society for the Propagation of the Faith, an organization French in origin and long French in leadership, was placed more immediately under Papal direction and its headquarters were moved to Rome. Contributions to foreign missions mounted and the staffs of missionaries increased. Moreover, the Popes emphasized the importance of training and recruiting an indigenous clergy and raised to the episcopate more and more natives of Asia and some Negroes of Africa. Thus they sought to root the Church in these areas and to give vivid demonstration of the mankind-embracing scope of the Roman Catholic Church. The number of Roman Catholics mounted in South and East Asia and in Africa south of the Sahara. The growth was especially phenomenal in the Belgian Congo and, until the adverse political conditions which came late in the 1930's, it was very marked in China. While support in personnel and money for the world-wide mission from the United States and Canada mounted rapidly, in the middle of the twentieth century most of it was still from Europe. Beleaguered though it was in Europe, from that, its ancient centre, the Roman Catholic Church continued to push forward its geographic frontiers in all possible quarters of the planet.

In Italy, strangely enough, for both the Roman Catholic Church and the fascist government which came to power in 1922 aspired to control all aspects of the nation's life, the tension was eased which had existed between Church and state since the triumph of the unified Kingdom of Italy in the preceding century. It will be recalled that following the French Revolution and the Napoleonic era anti-clericalism had been prominent. Although almost all Italians were nominally Roman Catholics, the politically united liberal Italy eliminated the Papal States and confiscated the properties of many of the monastic houses. The Popes, in protest, considered themselves "prisoners of the Vatican" and forbade the faithful to take part in the government. Now, by formal agreements, a partial reconciliation was effected between Pius XI and Mussolini, the head of the Fascist regime. At the very outset of his reign Pius XI conferred his initial blessing *urbi et orbi* from the front balcony of St. Peter's, thus breaking the precedent set by his immediate predecessors who, since the absorption of the Papal States in 1870, had given it from within the Vatican. In 1929 by the Lateran Treaty the Pope's temporal power was restored by the creation of the state of Vatican City, a small domain of 109 acres centering about St. Peter's, and by the recognition of the Supreme Pontiff's status as a sovereign prince. The Pope was paid an indemnity to compensate for his loss of revenues from his former domains. A concordat (also in 1929) regularized the relations between the Vatican and the Kingdom of Italy. By it the state recognized the religious ceremony as giving civil status to marriage, and the teaching of the Roman Catholic religion was made obligatory in secondary education, supplementing an earlier act (1923) which introduced religious instruction in the elementary schools. The clergy were accorded special privileges. In return the state was to have a voice in the appointment of clergy and the boundaries of dioceses were to be altered to make them correspond as nearly as possible with those of the civil provinces.

Yet the ink was scarcely dry on these documents when conflict arose, largely over the control of youth and over social and economic issues. Mussolini ordered the church organizations of boys and girls absorbed into the fascist structure and commanded that the young men's organizations connected with Catholic Action be dissolved. The fascists also sought to extend the control of the state over church schools. On his side, the Pope claimed the right to make pronouncements on social and economic issues. This he did in *quadragesimo anno,* May 15, 1931, issued on the fortieth anniversary of Leo XIII's famous *rerum novarum,* in which he sought to apply its principles to current conditions. A partial and uneasy compromise was reached by which the fascists agreed to the renewal of the Roman Catholic youth organizations and the Pope assented to limitations on the functions of those bodies.

When, in 1935, Italy invaded Ethiopia, although Pius XI incurred the displeasure of the fascist press by declaring wars of conquest unjust, the Roman Catholic Church made no clear-cut protest but sought to take advantage of the situation to extend Papal authority over the Ethiopian Church.

World War II and the collapse of the fascist regime and the Kingdom of Italy followed by the coming of a republican form of government worked no basic changes in the relations of Church and state. During World War II Pius XII laboured for peace and sought to protect the suffering. In May, 1940, he incurred the wrath of Mussolini by expressing his sympathy with Belgium, Luxembourg, and the Netherlands at the time of the German invasion. After Italy became a belligerent he exerted himself to have Rome declared an open city by both sides and thus to save it from bombing and pillage. He was so far successful that until the later days of the conflict Rome was spared and then was not as heavily bombed as were several other major cities of Europe. When, in 1946, the monarchy was overturned, the Holy See, true to its established policy of uncompromising condemnation of communism, sought to rouse Italian Catholics to oppose the communists in the elections. In 1948 it mobilized the parish priests, Catholic Action, youth groups, and women's societies and aided in the victory of the Christian Democrats. Already, in 1947, the Lateran Treaty of 1929 had been written into the constitution of the republic. The Pope sought to undercut communism by encouraging measures to improve the conditions of tenant-farmers and other low-income groups.

We must note the revival of Roman Catholic thought among Italians. Papal encyclicals, monastic orders, teachers in the expanding Catholic universities, and various laymen helped to reduce the gap between science and religion and formulated Roman Catholic economics, sociology, political science, and psychology.

Inevitably the Roman Catholic Church was involved in the welter of Spanish politics. In 1931 the monarchy gave way to a republic. The republican government nationalized ecclesiastical property but left it in the hands of the Church. It disestablished the Church, discontinued the salaries paid by the state to the clergy, ordered the Jesuits expelled, and forbade Roman Catholic teaching orders and congregations to continue their educational activities. In several cities mobs destroyed churches and convents. While for a time the moderates were in power and the anti-clerical measures were relaxed, in 1936 radicals again resorted to violence and priests were killed and churches were burned. In 1936 civil war broke out between a confused combination of liberals and radicals, including communists, on the one hand and conservatives on the other. In general Russia supported the radicals and the Nazis the conservatives. The struggle, which did not end until March, 1939, became a prelude to the European phase of World War II. The conservatives were headed by Franco and the *Falange Española Tradicionalista*. Franco, supported by his army, became dictator. Franco's government was an uneasy alliance of the army, the landowners, capitalists, and the Roman Catholic Church. The Roman Catholic faith was again made the state religion, ecclesiastical property was restored to the Church, religious bodies were once more permitted, and religious instruction was resumed in the schools. In general, the support of the Church by the state was continued into the 1950's. The pendulum which in the nineteenth century had swung violently from anti-clericalism to clericalism and again to anti-clericalism, was now pronouncedly at a clerical extreme.

Portugal had a somewhat similar record, although not punctuated by quite as much violence. In its early years the republic which in 1910 had supplanted the monarchy was anti-clerical. Church and state were separated and the religious orders were expelled. The course of the republic was stormy and varied.

A measure of peace was established in 1926 when Carmona became president. He continued in that post into the 1950's. In 1933 Salazar, as prime minister, began what in effect was a dictatorship. A devout Roman Catholic, his regime was pro-clerical. While in principle liberty of worship was assured, by a concordat of 1940 its property was restored to the Roman Catholic Church. In other ways the Salazar regime favoured that church.

In some ways the Roman Catholic Church sank to its nadir in France with its disestablishment in the first decade of the twentieth century. World War I and its immediate aftermath saw a partial recovery. For a variety of reasons the Roman Catholic faith gained in prestige. Several of the most popular generals were known to be devout Catholics and numbers of priests gained fame by their heroism. Diplomatic relations with the Vatican were resumed and religious orders and congregations were permitted to renew their labours. The de-Christianization which had begun in the eighteenth century and which had been proceeding at unequal pace from the time of the Revolution appeared to have been halted. The theological revival and the espousal of the faith by some of the intellectuals of which we spoke a few moments ago continued. The liturgical movement made itself felt.

However, in the 1940's various studies seemed to show that de-Christianization, if halted, was still marked. Slightly more than three-fourths of the population were said to be baptized in the Catholic faith, and it was reported that even in Paris four-fifths of the children born between 1930 and 1943 had been given the rite, but it was contended that for the majority baptism was merely a social convention inherited from earlier ages. It was declared that only about a fourth of the population had regular contact with the Church, and that at most only a tenth could be counted as "observing" Catholics, faithful to their duties to the faith. The "observants" were estimated to vary from 2 per cent. in the cities to 38 per cent. in rural districts. In some cities de-Christianization was comparatively recent and remnants of Christian culture and attitudes survived. In others it had been accomplished so many years before that scarcely a memory of Christian mentality could be found. As part of the aftermath and the sufferings of World War II a form of "existentialism" appeared which was indebted to Kierkegaard but which, with Sartre as its outstanding spokesman, was frankly non-Christian. It enjoyed a wide vogue among intellectuals and pseudo-intellectuals.

Yet after World War II active missionary efforts to win the de-Christianized were noted and here and there priests were working as manual labourers in factories to make understanding contacts with members of the classes who had drifted furthest from the faith.

Belgium remained predominantly Roman Catholic and made surprisingly

rapid recovery from the German invasions of the two world wars. All faiths
were tolerated and the state paid the salaries not only of Roman Catholic
priests but also of Protestant clergy and Jewish pastors. Religious instruction
was given in the primary schools. Advanced social legislation was continued.
While an anti-clerical trend was sometimes seen in the government, in general
Belgium was spared the extremes which were seen in Spain and earlier in
France, Italy, and Portugal.

Because of their high birth rate, the proportion of Roman Catholics mounted
in the once predominantly and still traditionally Protestant Netherlands.

The decades which followed World War I brought severe trials to the Roman
Catholic Church in Germany. The years immediately following the war did
not prove as adverse as those of the national socialist (Nazi) regime. Roman
Catholics were prominent in the government under the republic which was
set up after the overthrow of the Hohenzollern monarchy. Several of the chan-
cellors were of that faith. Communism, for a time a serious threat, ceased to be
formidable. A concordat favourable to the Church was entered into between
the Vatican and Bavaria. Many schools and monasteries were founded and
new parishes were created. The advent to power of Hitler, in 1933, brought
increasing adversity. The Centre Party, predominantly Roman Catholic, disbanded in 1933, but the national socialists were distrustful of Catholic Action,
fearing that it was the Centre Party under another guise. In 1933 the Vatican
entered into a concordat with the German Government which seemed to assure
the Church of the large degree of freedom which it had enjoyed under the
preceding regime. However, conflicts soon broke out. In 1934 the Nazi state
began to act against Roman Catholic labour organizations. Repressive measures
were taken against the Roman Catholic press. In 1935 efforts were instituted to
indoctrinate children in Roman Catholic schools with the Nazi world view and
other attempts followed to curtail Roman Catholic education and to wean
youth from the Church and capture it for Hitler. Government officials accused
religious houses of being centres of currency smuggling and of sexual irregularities.

The annexation of Austria by Germany in 1938 brought problems to the
Church in that prevailingly Roman Catholic country. It was followed by the
secularization of most of the schools, the closing of numbers of Church educational institutions, the dissolution of several monasteries and theological
seminaries, the imprisonment of many priests, the extensive confiscation of
ecclesiastical properties, and the renunciation of the faith by thousands.

In the face of these attacks the German bishops spoke out against the violations of the concordat and against restrictions on freedom and the euthanasia

of the insane and incurables. Here and there Roman Catholics united with Protestants in resistance to the Nazi regime.

World War II brought distress, partly through the concentration camps and partly through the destruction by enemy bombing of thousands of civilians and many church buildings. Roman Catholics and Protestants often shared the use of such churches as escaped. After the war the Church rose to the task of relief of the sufferers and the repair and reconstruction of its physical equipment. In the portions of Germany which remained outside the Russian Zone about half the population was Roman Catholic. Better organized than the divided Protestantism, the Roman Catholic Church was making gains and was winning converts.

THE ROMAN CATHOLIC CHURCH AND COMMUNISM IN EUROPE

It was in communism that the Roman Catholic Church discerned its major enemy in the decades which followed World War I and to it that church, led by the Popes, presented sturdy resistance. Communism and the government of the U.S.S.R. paid the Roman Catholic Church the compliment of taking its opposition seriously and seeking in every way in their power to undermine it, either by destroying it completely or by severing its national units from their administrative allegiance to Rome and making them completely submissive to the communist state. Communism could bring to the contest a coherent ideology spread by all the devices of modern propaganda with no regard for the truth and supported by the might of a totalitarian regime. The Roman Catholic Church had as weapons simply its faith and its ecclesiastical organization unsupported by police or armies. The Church entered the struggle handicapped by the losses which it had already suffered and was hampered by the other adverse forces which we have repeatedly described as operating in the nineteenth and twentieth centuries. The contest appeared uneven. The Roman Catholic Church was dealt severe blows, but by the mid-century its main citadels were unshaken. Here was an epic struggle of world-embracing scope which had only begun by the mid-twentieth century and which would require volumes fully to narrate. All that we can hope to do is to mention a few of the main features of its European phases. We must later note it in other parts of the world.

We have already seen the fashion in which the Roman Catholic Church was confronted by communism, usually in association with other movements, in Germany after World War I, in Spain between the two world wars, and in Italy after World War II. Communism was also to be seriously reckoned with in France, especially after World War II. It was, however, in Russia itself and in Central Europe that the Roman Catholic Church chiefly felt the full force of communism. In Russia the Communist Party seized power in 1917, here, in the guise of the U.S.S.R., it fully consolidated itself, and here communism espoused the traditional Russian imperialism, but in new, camouflaged, and more potent forms. In the U.S.S.R. itself Roman Catholics were small minorities. Although the Kremlin took vigorous action against the Roman Catholic Church within what had been its post World War I borders, the numerical losses could not be large. It was in the border lands, especially Hungary, Czechoslovakia, Poland, Latvia, Estonia, and Lithuania, which were brought within the iron curtain, particularly by World War II and its aftermath, that the numerical threat was the most pronounced.

As a consequence of World War I and the break-up of the Hapsburg empire, Hungary became a republic. In it Roman Catholics were a majority, with Protestants constituting substantial minorities. In 1918 that republic was under the communists, led by a Jew, Bela Kun. Many priests and bishops were killed and much ecclesiastical property was confiscated. Roman Catholics and Protestants joined forces, defeated the communists, and in 1920 a monarchical form of government was instituted, but without the Hapsburgs. The former religious situation was largely restored, with Roman Catholics constituting more than two-thirds of the population. In 1928 a concordat was reached with the Vatican and a diplomatic representative was sent to the Holy See. In 1944 German forces occupied the country and set up a regime favourable to the Nazis. The following year Russian troops drove out the Germans, in 1946 a republic was proclaimed, and in February, 1947, a peace treaty was signed with the United Nations. In August, 1946, diplomatic relations were restored with the Vatican. Early in 1949 what was called the People's Independent Front was formed of several parties, with the communists clearly dominant. While the constitution of 1949 separated the Church from the state "to ensure freedom of conscience and the free practice of religion," twice that year the British and American Governments formally declared that the peace treaty was being violated by the denial of human rights and fundamental freedoms. In 1949, in spite of emphatic protests from the Vatican, the primate of the Roman Catholic Church in Hungary, Cardinal Mindszenty, was sentenced to life imprisonment on the charge of treason. The following year fifty-nine orders with more than ten thousand monks and nuns were dissolved and their properties were confiscated. Most church schools, then comprising more than half of the educational institutions, were nationalized in 1948, and in 1950 only eight licensed Roman Catholic schools remained, staffed by members of teaching orders.

In Czechoslovakia, which in 1918 emerged from World War I as an independent republic, nearly three-fourths of the population were Roman Catholics. The first government tended to be socialist and anti-clerical and only strong

Roman Catholic opposition prevented the confiscation of Church property and making civil marriage compulsory. Between 1918 and 1930 several hundred thousand Roman Catholics separated themselves from Rome and, while preserving much of the faith, had a married clergy and a liturgy in the vernacular. More thousands broke entirely with the Church and called themselves agnostics. In the 1920's adjustments were effected between the state and the Vatican through which much of its sequestered land was restored to the Church, the teaching of religion was included in the programmes of the schools, the state was to have a voice in naming the bishops and was to provide the salaries of the clergy, the latter were to be citizens and take the oath of allegiance to the republic, and part of the Church services were to be in the vernacular. In 1939 came the German annexation, but by the outcome of World War II the country was freed from Nazi rule. Then, in 1948, the National Front was formed of several parties, the familiar device by which the communists sought to achieve control, and obtained possession of the government. The orientation was increasingly towards Moscow. In 1949 the state adopted the policy of administering all the churches through a department of ecclesiastical affairs and of paying the salaries of the clergy. By 1950 more than nine-tenths of the clergy were said to have taken the oath of allegiance to the government. Here was an attempt, largely successful, to nullify the administrative control by the Pope of a branch of the Roman Catholic Church.

For the Roman Catholic Church the outcome of World War I brought gains in Poland, gains which were threatened by World War II and its sequel and by ties with Communist Russia. World War I was followed by the independence and re-integration of Poland after its dismemberment in the eighteenth century by its strong neighbours, Russia, Prussia, and Austria. Since Poland was overwhelmingly Roman Catholic, this carried with it the appearance of a strong, unified Roman Catholic bloc, reinforced by nationalist loyalties. In 1925 relations between Poland and the Vatican were regularized by a concordat. With the approval of the Church a dictatorship was set up in Poland and parliamentary government was discontinued. The new Poland had many Orthodox Ukrainians within its borders. The Poles attempted by force to assimilate the Ukrainians and this entailed the attempt to win them to Roman Catholicism by depriving them, by imprisonment, of their Orthodox clergy and the execution of many.

With the coming of World War II to Europe in September, 1939, Poland was invaded from the west by the Germans and from the east by the Russians. Polish resistance was quickly crushed and both the conquerors took measures to erase Polish nationalism, measures which included restraints on the Roman Catholic Church. That church was obviously their enemy, especially since the

Pope maintained close and friendly ties with the Polish government-in-exile and during the latter part of that struggle accorded its ambassador asylum in the Vatican. For nearly four years, from June, 1941, when the Nazi armies moved against Russia, until the fore part of 1945, when the Russians drove them out, the Germans occupied the country and Roman Catholics suffered, although not as much as the Jews.

After the Nazis were expelled, with Russian assistance a Polish government was set up, obviously friendly to Russia and communism. A constitution was adopted for the Republic of Poland. By the standard device of a coalition with friendly groups and parties, in 1947 the communists obtained full control. The coming of the new regime boded ill for the Roman Catholic Church. The Vatican did not give it formal recognition but continued relations with the Polish government-in-exile. The communists attempted to convince the Poles that while they were under the Nazis the Pope had abandoned them. The Ruthenian Uniates, former Orthodox, whom the pressure of the Polish king and nobility had brought into union with Rome in 1596 by the Synod of Brest (Chapter XL), were now encouraged by the Russians to renounce the tie with Rome. Many of their bishops were deported, imprisoned, or killed, a synod of 216 priests seceded from the Union of Brest, praised Stalin for bringing them back into the Orthodox fold, and their church was put under the Patriarch of Moscow. The communist regime attempted to separate the Roman Catholics in Poland from the administrative control of Rome and in 1950 representatives of the episcopate signed an agreement with the government which, while guaranteeing freedom of worship, religious instruction, and participation in charitable activities, was so worded that it could be interpreted by the communists in their favour.

The little countries, Estonia, Latvia, and Lithuania, which had been given their independence as a result of World War I, were forcibly incorporated into the U.S.S.R. in 1940. A considerable proportion of their population was Roman Catholic. Under Soviet rule the Roman Catholic Church was gravely weakened by deportations, many of them to Siberia, and by other measures. The Pope attempted to aid those who had fled to Western Europe and in 1946 set up the Lithuanian Ecclesiastical Institute for exiled Lithuanian priests.

In Rumania, after World War II formally independent but under communist control, action was also taken against Roman Catholics. In 1948 the Uniate priests were constrained to petition the Orthodox Patriarch for readmission to the Orthodox Church. Roman Catholics of the Latin rite were put under pressure and almost all the hierarchy were imprisoned.

The lines continued to be ever more sharply drawn between the Roman Catholic Church and the communists. In July, 1948, a Pan-Orthodox conference held in Moscow in celebration of the five hundredth anniversary of the independence of the Orthodox Church of Russia from Constantinople formally denounced the Pope for his "participation in fratricidal wars against democracy in defense of fascism." On July 1, 1949, Pius XII, through a decree published by the Supreme Congregation of the Holy Office, a body established in 1542 with substantially the same powers as the Spanish Inquisition, declared that it was not permitted to any Catholic to become a member of a communist party or to support or circulate publications which defended the doctrines and practice of communism, and denied the sacraments to those who disobeyed.

Although it broke with Moscow, the communist regime of Tito in Jugoslavia embarrassed the Roman Catholic Church. For centuries the territory embraced by Jugoslavia had been divided between Roman Catholics and Orthodox. Croatia was prevailingly Roman Catholic, the Serbs Orthodox. Under the Italo-German occupation during World War II there were attempts at the forcible conversion of the Orthodox by the puppet regime, although the Vatican formally stood against any form of external pressure and insisted that conversion must be by voluntary adherence to the faith. When Tito drove out the Italians and Germans the tables were turned. The head of the Roman Catholic hierarchy, Archbishop Stepinac, was tried and sentenced to sixteen years of hard labour for alleged collaboration with the invaders and the forcible conversion of Orthodox Serbs. Even after he had severed his ties with the Kremlin, Tito refused to release the archbishop. By the end of 1949 over 4,000 Roman Catholic places of worship had been closed, scores of priests had been executed or imprisoned, and hundreds had gone into exile. As the years passed restrictions were somewhat abated.

THE TESTING OF PROTESTANTISM ON THE CONTINENT OF EUROPE

Serious as were the problems which were presented to the Roman Catholic Church by the post-1914 Europe, they were not as grave as those which Protestantism had to meet. Protestantism had its origin in Germany. Here was the historic centre of Lutheranism. Here the Reformed Churches were also strong. Here the creative ferment in nineteenth century Protestant theology and Biblical scholarship was the most marked. From Germany thousands of Protestant missionaries had gone out to many parts of the world. Yet it was Germany which bore the main brunt of defeat in World War I, it was in Germany that national socialism and Hitler sought to make the Church come to heel in the period between the two wars and during World War II, it was Germany which was crushed and divided by the outcome of World War II, and after that division it was chiefly Protestant portions of Germany which were in the Russian zone and subject to communist pressure. Moreover, millions of the Germans who were forcibly displaced by the westward movement of Poland's boundary at the end of World War II were predominantly Protestant. The

German occupation during World War II of the Netherlands, Denmark, and Norway, all with Protestant majorities, the last two overwhelmingly so, for the time being presented a sharp challenge. The deep involvement of predominantly Protestant Great Britain in the two world wars had repercussions on the Christianity of that realm which were, in general, adverse. We are first of all to sketch the record on the Continent of Europe and then are to summarise that in the British Isles.

Early effects of the defeat in World War I on Germany were spiritual shock and efforts on the part of many to seek the rebirth and strengthening of the nation's life through religion. Several movements arose with this objective, mostly through Protestantism. Some boldly departed from Christianity. The more radical, endeavouring to return to the Teutonic spirit which they asserted had given might to the Germans before the advent of Christianity, declared that the country had been weakened by Jewish-Christian influence. In general they were frankly pagan, and added incentive to the anti-semitism which under the Nazis broke out in the most wholesale persecution of those of Jewish blood which the world had seen in centuries.

Some movements were channelled through the churches. The outcome of World War I with the fall of the Hohenzollern empire loosened the historic bond between Church and state. Under the Republic which followed, Church and state were separated. The state became religiously neutral and while it protected the churches it gave them independence in their inner government. Protestants greatly multiplied their youth organizations and extended their works of charity. In general the financial undergirding of the churches came from a percentage of the members' income collected by the churches or through government agencies on behalf of the churches. There were also subsidies from the civil authorities in return for ecclesiastical property confiscated during the Napoleonic era.

One of the post-war movements sought to mobilize the resources of the churches by uniting the several Landeskirchen, the territorial bodies which were a survival of the pre-nineteenth century political divisions. In 1921–1922 it drew together twenty-eight of these churches and the Moravians in the German Evangelical Church Federation. That federation was what its name implied and permitted its members to preserve their autonomy.

The coming to power in 1933 of national socialism under Hitler was even more a menace to Protestantism than to the Roman Catholic Church. The latter was more nearly united and accustomed to oppose itself to the state. Protestants were divided, could not act together, and the Lutheran majority had a tradition of subserviency to the state which boded ill for the future under a totalitarian regime. National socialism, with its emphasis upon the German volk, strengthened the hands of those who would accommodate Christianity to what they conceived to be the German spirit or would return to pre-Christian German paganism.

What was called the German Faith Movement attracted several groups who in one way or another expressed this trend. With Jacob Wilhelm Hauer, a former missionary and pastor and a professor of comparative religion in one of the universities as an outstanding representative, it sought the emancipation of the German nation from Christianity. However, it disavowed any intention of restoring the cults of the old German gods.

Much less extreme and having the support of Hitler was the Faith Movement of German Christians. It confined its membership to those of Aryan descent, cut off all Masonic connexions, denounced communism, stressed what it declared to be the spirit of Germany and Luther, and sought, by a nation-wide organization, to make of the Church a united body to parallel national socialism. For a time it seemed successful and effected a centralized nation-wide organization embracing both Lutheran and Reformed which had as its head an ardent supporter of Hitler.

Opposition arose, with the courageous and outspoken Martin Niemöller, a former submarine officer and now pastor of a prominent church in Berlin, as a prominent leader. In 1934 it crystallized in the Confessional Synod, or Church, in which Reformed, Lutherans, and United (Lutheran and Reformed) joined. A complicated struggle ensued. A large proportion of the pastors and a minority of the laity held to the Confessional Church, although rifts appeared in the latter between the Lutheran and Reformed. They stood out against the state. The sales of Bibles mounted.

The government was stern, imprisoned many of the pastors, and, in spite of his release by the court with a comparatively small fine, put Niemöller into a concentration camp. In an effort to win and indoctrinate the rising generation, church youth groups were ordered dissolved and the youth were enrolled in Nazi organizations.

World War II added to the difficulties of Protestants. The national socialist state, embarked on a life and death struggle, strove to crush all opposition, including that in the churches. Church publications were curtailed. Many pastors and laymen were arrested, some for protesting against the cruelties against the Jews, some for opposition to the euthanasia of the aged and infirm and the glorification of the unmarried mother, and some for other criticisms of the government. Further difficulties were placed in the way of giving religious instruction to children and youths. It is said that 85 per cent. of the pastors of the Confessional Church were taken into the armies. As the war progressed, enemy bombings destroyed many church buildings. Fuel shortage reduced the number of services in the structures which survived.

As we have suggested, World War II and its immediate aftermath brought to Protestantism heavy territorial losses in some regions and in several other sections and countries imposed severe handicaps. The blows dealt by the German occupation in the Netherlands, Denmark, and Norway, while serious at the time, were not lasting. However, the Russian annexation in 1940 of Estonia, Latvia, and Lithuania, in each of which Lutherans were in the majority, made for substantial reductions in the Protestant bodies in these lands which the end of the war did not repair. The forced migration of Germans, most of them Protestants, from the territories annexed to Poland on the border between that country and Germany was a major loss. The majority of those who were thus displaced moved into Germany and there for a time constituted undigested, poverty-stricken enclaves. The descent of the iron curtain over Hungary, Czechoslovakia, and much of Eastern Germany brought problems to the Protestants in these areas. Their churches were put under varying restraints and disabilities.

Yet Protestantism, like Roman Catholicism, not only persisted. It also displayed remarkable vigour. The Confessional Church attracted many moderates who were alienated from the state by its anti-Christian actions. Some relief was given to prisoners of war. In German-occupied countries, notably the Netherlands and Norway, much of the opposition was spearheaded by church leaders. In the Netherlands the Reformed Church denounced the Nazi treatment of the Jews and the Nazi view of the soul and the world. The Reformed Church achieved a national synodical structure more effective than it had possessed for several generations. At times Roman Catholics and Protestants coöperated in their resistance. In Germany after World War II hundreds of church buildings wrecked by enemy bombings were repaired or rebuilt, and Protestants did much for relief, especially through *Hilfswerk*. In 1948 and 1949 a national federation of the churches (but not a union, for it respected the autonomy of its members) was achieved under the name of the Evangelical Church in Germany which embraced all but one of the *Landeskirchen,* thus renewing and continuing what had been begun in 1921–1922 and 1933 and making unnecessary the Confessional Synod. For at least the time being, one result of the years of suffering was to lower the barriers that had divided the "liberals" from the "orthodox."

THE GROWTH OF THE ECUMENICAL MOVEMENT AND ITS RELATION TO THE CONTINENT

Between the two world wars and notably during and after World War II the Ecumenical Movement grew. More and more it drew into fellowship with one another the Protestants in Europe and outside Europe, thus strengthening

European Protestantism. To this several agencies contributed. One of them was the World's Committee of the Young Men's Christian Associations, aided by the enlarged activities in Europe of the North American Young Men's Christian Associations. Especially outstanding were the formation and growth of the International Missionary Council and the World Council of Churches.

As we have suggested (Chapter LV), the International Missionary Council was a result of the World Missionary Conference held at Edinburgh in 1910. That gathering had taken steps looking towards the formation of such an organization, but the early coming of World War I delayed it. With the war came a rift between the Protestants of Germany and those of the countries which had fought Germany. Several years were required to heal it and it had not been effaced when, in 1921, a gathering at Lake Mohonk, in New York State, brought the International Missionary Council into being. The International Missionary Council chiefly had as members national and regional bodies, among them at the outset the Foreign Missions Conference of North America and the Conference of Missionary Societies of Great Britain and Ireland, and, eventually, the German Protestant Missions Committee (*Ausschuss*), although this last did not send delegates to Lake Mohonk. Rapidly there were formed such bodies as the National Christian Council of India (1923), the National Christian Council of China (1922), the National Christian Council of Japan (1923), the Congo Protestant Council (1924), and the Near East Christian Council for Missionary Coöperation (1929) which became members of the International Missionary Council. John R. Mott was the first chairman and J. H. Oldham one of the first secretaries. Various functions were undertaken, including the continued publication of *The International Review of Missions* and assistance to German missions and missionaries. Conferences were held at Jerusalem in 1928, late in 1938, on a still larger scale, at Tambaram, on the outskirts of Madras, and with smaller attendances, at Whitby, Ontario, in 1947, and Willingen, Germany, in 1952, which did much to help Protestants in coöperative planning for pursuing their world mission. They were especially significant for the wide range of ecclesiastical and theological convictions represented and for the mounting participation of the "younger churches," a now general designation for the bodies planted by Protestant missions in Latin America, Asia, and the Pacific.

At this particular point in our story, however, we are primarily concerned with the fashion in which during and after World War II the International Missionary Council came to the rescue of most of the Protestant missions of the Continent. The outbreak of the European phase of the war in September, 1939, at once cut off German missionaries from financial support from the Fatherland. An initial gift of £250 was made by a donor in Scotland, a country then at war with Germany. Before long aid was sent from other countries and churches. When in 1940 the German "lightning war" brought France, Belgium, the Netherlands, Denmark, and Norway under the Nazi yoke, the missionaries from these lands were also left without contact with their home constituencies. The International Missionary Council assembled what was soon called the "Orphaned Missions Fund." Contributions came from several countries and denominations, including some of the "younger churches," but were mostly from the United States. Close *liaison* was established with American Lutherans, for they gave generously to maintain the missions of their Continental brethren. Assistance continued after the war. So far as the officers of the International Missionary Council knew, not a single unit of the Continental missionary enterprises was suspended because of lack of funds. Here was a solidarity of mutual help by a Christian fellowship which transcended denominational, national, and warring lines which was unprecedented in all the history of Christianity. It showed a striking gain over the divisions that had marred the Protestant fellowship because of World War I.

The World Council of Churches was slightly younger than the International Missionary Council and grew out of the union of two other bodies, the World Conference on Faith and Order and the Universal Christian Council for Life and Work. The first of these, as we have said (Chapter LV), was in part sprung from the World Missionary Conference of 1910. It was for the purpose of bringing together the representatives of the churches to discuss the issues which had traditionally divided them and to explore the possibility of agreement. It held major conferences at Lausanne in 1927 and at Edinburgh in 1937. The other had as its chief creator Nathan Söderblom (1866-1931), primate of the Church of Sweden, and drew part of its inspiration from the 1910 gathering. It was for the purpose of stimulating thought and action on the application of Christian faith and principles to social and international problems. Its chief meetings were at Stockholm in 1925 and at Oxford in 1937. Before Oxford Söderblom had died and J. H. Oldham had become the leading promoter. It seemed to many that a more inclusive organization was advisable to bring the churches together. In May, 1938, representatives of numbers of these bodies convened in Utrecht and drafted a constitution for the World Council of Churches. This had as its nucleus what were called briefly Faith and Order and Life and Work. It was officially described as "a fellowship of churches which accept our Lord Jesus Christ as God and Saviour." In contrast with the International Missionary Council, whose members were regional and national bodies, its members were churches and it was, accordingly, ecclesiastical in structure and outlook. It could not legislate for the churches, but it was intended to facilitate common study and action. Headquarters were established at Geneva, Switzerland. Although the coming of World War II delayed its formal organization, it began functioning in 1938 under the caption of "the World Council of Churches in process of formation." It was officially constituted in a great assembly at Amsterdam in 1948. By that time well over a hundred churches had become members. They included almost all the major Protestant bodies of the Continent of Europe and the British Isles, the majority of those of the Americas and Australasia, and most of the larger "younger churches" of Asia and Africa. It also embraced several of the Orthodox and Old Catholic Churches. Close working ties were established with the International Missionary Council and the two bodies were officially described as "in association with" each other. Looser, but also friendly relations were had with what were described as "other ecumenical movements," such as the several world denominational or confessional associations, the World Council of Christian Education (formerly the World's Sunday School Association), the World's Student Christian Federation, and the World's Young Men's Christian Association.

We shall later have more to say of the World Council of Churches and the other phases of the Ecumenical Movement. Here we must note that during World War II the World Council of Churches, although still only "in process of formation," did much to cement bonds between churches on both sides of the warring lines and to care for sufferers from the struggle, and that after the fighting ceased it was the major coördinating agency for the extensive relief given by the Protestant Churches of the British Isles, the United States, and other countries to the Christians of the Continent of Europe and their churches.

The Ecumenical Movement made great strides. Here was the new form of unity among Christians which had been begun before 1914 and which had mounted in phenomenal fashion after World War I. Although obtaining most of its financial support and much of its leadership from the United States and drawing in "younger churches" of Latin America, Asia, and Africa and most of the branches of historical Protestant communions in the Dominions of the British Commonwealth, it had its major centre in Europe. This European orientation was especially marked in the World Council of Churches. Here was a body which, with headquarters in Continental Europe, the heart of Christendom, was bringing together in fellowship almost all the hitherto sundered branches of the Protestantism of that part of the world. It embraced not only representatives of all the main and several of the minor families of Protestantism. In one way or another the Ecumenical Movement also took in many non-Protestants. Thus the Young Men's Christian Associations in Poland were predominantly Roman Catholic in membership and in Greece they were overwhelmingly Orthodox. As we have said, the World Council of Churches had in its membership several of the Eastern and Old Catholic bodies. This was accomplished without weakening allegiance to these non-Protestant bodies. Indeed, a concomitant of the Ecumenical Movement was a renewal of confessional consciousness.

CHANGING CURRENTS IN PROTESTANT SCHOLARSHIP AND THOUGHT ON THE CONTINENT OF EUROPE

The Protestantism of Europe could scarcely pass through the storms which swept over the Continent in the era which began in the summer of 1914 without profound changes in its thought. Had it failed to respond to the stimulus the presumption would have been that it was moribund. That fresh streams of thought issued from it was evidence of continued vitality.

A sobering but quite understandable development was the waning of the leadership which Germany had held in the nineteenth century. This was to be expected, for Germany was defeated in both wars, between them fell victim to the Nazi madness, and in the second suffered not only from exhaustion by reason of the efforts put forth in that struggle, but also from enemy bombing. Following World War II came the political division between the Eastern and the Western Zones, the advance of the Russian-communist iron curtain over Eastern Germany, the "cold war" between Russia and the West, of which Germany was a chief centre, and the long delay in the writing of a peace treaty.

The waning of German leadership did not mean the complete disappearance of theological ferment. Down to the capture of Germany by the national socialists in the 1930's the universities saw an attenuated continuation of the mental activity which had made them outstanding in the nineteenth century. The post World War II years witnessed something of a renewal. Many Germans, some of whom had taken refuge in other countries, commanded the attention and respect of Protestant intellectuals the world over. Yet the number of outstanding German scholars was declining, by mid-century most of them were middle-aged or older, and few younger men were emerging as successors. Much of the theological activity on the Continent which attracted the attention of world-wide Protestantism was in lands which had succeeded in preserving their neutrality during the two wars, Switzerland and Sweden.

In Biblical scholarship a method which gained wide currency was what was known as *Formgeschichte,* or form criticism. It held that records of the life and teaching of Christ in the Four Gospels were largely shaped by the purposes of those who had preserved and handed down what was contained in these brief accounts. These purposes were declared to be missionary and didactic. They were to proclaim the Christian Gospel to non-Christians and instruct catechumens and converts. It was held that they determined to a marked degree the arrangement of what had been transmitted in fragmentary fashion through oral tradition and to some extent modified the phrasing of the incidents and sayings which were reported. So, too, early liturgical use was considered to have modified the accounts of the Last Supper and the interpretations of the meaning of the Eucharist. Form criticism is usually said to have had its inception in *Die Formgeschichte des Evangeliums* by Martin Dibelius (1883–1947), which appeared in 1919, but some of the basic presuppositions were of earlier origin. The method was not universally accepted and those who were more or less committed to it did not fully agree on conclusions reached through it.

Next to form criticism in its influence on the study of the New Testament was the emphasis upon the importance of eschatology in the teachings of Jesus and the letters of Paul. It began before 1914, but was stressed in the period which followed that year. A classic formulation was by Albert Schweitzer (1875——) in the book translated into English under the title *The Quest of the Historical Jesus* and which in its original German edition was published in 1906. An Alsatian, later to become famous as musician, philosopher, theologian, and medical missionary to Africa, in this study Schweitzer held that Jesus had conceived himself as not the founder but the announcer of the kingdom of God and had believed that the kingdom was to be in the future and to be established by the intervention of God. Schweitzer maintained that Jesus regarded "the end of all things" as being close at hand and that he believed that it would be followed by the appearance of himself as Son of Man and the coming of the kingdom. The ethics which Jesus taught, so Schweitzer said, was not intended as universally and always binding on all men, but simply as a "transition-ethics" in preparation for the early climax of history in the coming of the kingdom. Schweitzer also emphasized the eschatological aspects in Paul. Since the death of Jesus was not followed immediately by the intervention of God, so Schweitzer went on to affirm, the Early Church reconstructed its eschatology, or conception of the "last things," the termination of history, and its conviction about Christ. Some other scholars did not accept this view and believed that Jesus expected that the climax of history would be long delayed. However, while by no means fully agreeing with all the conclusions of Schweitzer, a considerable number of scholars saw in the Gospels and Paul more of an expectation of an early end of history than had been often noted. Obviously they ran counter to the assumptions underlying the Social Gospel movement, that the kingdom of God could be built gradually within history by the efforts of man in coöperation with God.

The trend in Protestant thought which attracted the most attention was what was variously known in one or another of its aspects as the theology of crisis, dialectical theology, and neo-orthodoxy. In large part it was at the outset a product of a state of mind induced by World War I and its aftermath. Especially in Germany and the lands immediately around it, men were impressed with the tragedy of life. They saw themselves caught in gigantic forces which were sweeping them to destruction and with which individuals and even nations were unable to cope. They felt themselves powerless in the colossal agony of the years. Sin and evil became real. Did life have meaning? If so, what was it? Where was it to be found? Yet helpless though the individual was to alter the vast and demonic currents about him, he must make decisions. He must say "yes" or "no." He could not be content with abstract, disinterested speculation which had no immediate effect upon him. He could not be merely a spectator. He must make choices between alternatives, between "either" and "or." Those choices might mean for him the difference between life and death.

The results of the struggle were varied. As we have seen, for many the ferment brought the repudiation of Christianity and the search for another answer, often with the dogmatic affirmation of a non-Christian faith. For others who remained within the churches a profound distrust of pre-war philosophy and theology arose. They tended to repudiate the optimism of the nineteenth century and its confidence in the competence of reason and human effort. They lost faith in the idealism which was associated with Kant and Hegel and which saw all the universe, including man, as set in a framework of controlling ideas. They regarded as unsatisfying the theology of Schleiermacher which found validity in the religious experience of the individual, for this was too subjective, and longed for some objective word from God which was not dependent on human feeling. They repudiated the Ritschlianism of the late nineteenth century which believed in the progressive achievement of the kingdom of God through collaboration of men with the divine purpose. Troeltsch himself was badly shaken by the war. Numbers of Christians discovered Kierkegaard (Chapter XLVII). His existentialism and his dialectical paradoxes spoke to their condition. Many turned again to Luther with renewed interest and found in him, if not the full answer to their quest, at least basic convictions which proved a guide in their darkness.

The theologian who stood out most pronouncedly in this trend and who spoke with a volume and a vigour which commanded the widest hearing, sometimes with assent and sometimes with sharp dissent, was Karl Barth (1886——). Barth was German Swiss by birth, the son of a theological lecturer at Basel. He studied in several German universities and sat at the feet of some of the leading Ritschlians. For a time he was a pronounced liberal. In 1911 he became pastor of a small Reformed church in North-west Switzerland, in that politically neutral land but close to the embattled Germany which was so largely his spiritual home. From that vantage he watched Western Europe pass through the agony of World War I. It was during these years, preaching Sunday after Sunday to a congregation almost within sound of the big guns, that he was forced to think through his faith afresh. It was there that he began the writing which brought him fame. After the war he was in Germany successively on the faculties of Göttingen, Münster, and Bonn. Then, in 1935, because he could not stomach the Nazi regime, he returned to Switzerland and taught at Basel.

The first of his books which brought Barth to the attention of the world was his *Commentary on the Epistle to the Romans,* published in 1918. Coming as it did not far from the climax of World War I and speaking in bold paradoxes and uncompromising denunciation of liberalism and of existing religion and the churches, it provoked controversy. In some quarters it was hailed with enthusiastic approval and in others was emphatically rejected. This and other works which flowed fast from the prolific pen of Barth were the chief source of what became known as the "theology of crisis" or "dialectical theology." By "crisis" was meant what was happening to theology and civilization and also what inevitably overtakes every man and the institutions which man creates when, confident in his own ability, he attempts to solve his problems and finds himself confounded by God. "Dialectical" was intended to signify that man can never by his own reason reach God. When he tries to do so he sees contradictions in his results and can only say "yes" and "no" and wait for a direct word from God, a word which comes not because man deserves it, for this he does not and cannot do, but only through God's grace. Barth maintained that Schleiermacher and those influenced by him had succumbed to subjectivism and that Ritschl, Troeltsch, and others of their ilk had made Christian doctrine contingent on history and therefore as relative to its time and environment and having no absolute, dependable truth. He declared that what we must do is to heed not what other men say about God, but what God has to say to men. Men must listen to the word of God. That word reaches us through the Bible but is not bound by it. He stressed the sinfulness of man. All man's achievements, including religion, so he maintained, are tainted and made worse than futile by man's pride. Man and his works stand under the judgement of God. The world is lost and of themselves men can never find the word which God speaks to it. But, so Barth went on to say, that word has come to us by the direct, sovereign act of God, by revelation through Jesus Christ and his cross and resurrection. Man must humbly accept this revelation. Yet Barth would not have Christians withdraw from the world, but act in it.

Barth thought of himself as formulating nothing new, but as simply again putting into words the unchanging Gospel. In his major work, his several volume *Kirchliche Dogmatik,* he endeavoured to set it forth in full, systematic form. He clearly belonged in the Reformed tradition, with its emphasis upon the sovereignty of God. For a time he was strongly influenced by Kierkegaard, but as the years passed the gloomy Dane was less important in his thinking. However, his orthodoxy was not entirely a repetition of what had gone before. It was "neo-orthodoxy."

Barth was an ardent and often vehement controversialist. Much of his polemic he directed against a fellow and slightly younger Swiss, Emil Brunner (1889——). Brunner was near enough like Barth to be classified with the neo-orthodox, but he differed from him in making a place for "natural theology," namely, man's ability by his searching to arrive at some phases of the truth about God. Born near Zürich, a student there and in Berlin before World War I, for several years a pastor, for a year a student in the United States, during most of his active life Brunner was on the faculty of the University of Zürich. For a time he seemed to agree with Barth, but he came to the conviction that the latter was mistaken in regarding the divine image in man as having been completely destroyed by the fall, in denying that there is a general revelation of God in nature, conscience, and history, and in declaring that there is nothing in human nature which responds to the appeal of God's grace. He affirmed that something of God's will in the "law of nature" is to be found in human institutions. To this Barth made a violently angry retort and from time to time returned to the attack.

Barth's theology helped to give backbone to the Confessional Church in its contest with the Nazi state. A German theologian, Karl Heim (1874——), a native of Württemberg, and for a time secretary of the German Student Christian Movement, led in the intellectual battle against that German Faith Movement which was a frankly pagan and anti-Christian development in the years between the two world wars. He centered his theology around three convictions, namely, Christ as Lord and Leader (the latter in conscious contrast with Hitler and others who were called *Führer,* or leader), Christ as saviour from sin, and Christ as deliverer from the powers of darkness and death.

Differing in many ways from Barth and Heim was Paul Tillich (1886——). Prussian by birth, a chaplain in the German army in World War I, he was successively on the faculties of five German universities, and then, because of his opposition to the Nazis, went to the United States (1933) to the staff of Union Theological Seminary, in New York City. While in Germany, in addition to his writing and teaching in philosophy and theology, he was active in politics. In his later years his thought was especially influential in the United States. Impressed with the urgency of the time and the revolutionary movements, he sought to apply in fresh ways the basic distinctive Protestant principles.

In Sweden, neutral during both world wars, religious life had a somewhat distinct course, by no means indifferent to the storms in the world about it, but without such drastic changes as in Germany. Nathan Söberblom (1866–1931), a distinguished scholar and teacher, who died as Archbishop of Uppsala and thus as primate of the Church of Sweden, in the years which immediately followed World War I was the outstanding personality in Scandinavian religious life. He was best known for his share in the Ecumenical Movement and especially for his part in calling into being the Universal Christian Council for Life and Work and his guiding hand during its earlier years. There was a continuation of the liturgical revival which had become marked in the nineteenth century. In theology two names were especially prominent, Gustaf Emanuel Hildebrand Aulén (1879——) and Anders Nygren (1890——), members of the faculty of the University of Lund. Both men were influenced by Barth and criticized much of the liberalism of nineteenth century German theology from Schleiermacher to Ritschl and Harnack. However, they did not go as far to the extreme of rejecting human reason and its product, natural theology, as did Barth. Moreover, in contrast with Barth, who was clearly in the Reformed tradition, and loyal to their Lutheran rearing and associations, while deploring some of the developments in Lutheranism after Luther, they stressed what they believed that they found in him. They tended to go back to the great theologians of the early Christian centuries and to restore what they regarded as classical Christianity. They did not care for Barth's paradoxes and put in the foreground the wonder and joy of the incarnation of Christ as victor. Nygren especially emphasized *agape,* the self-giving love of God, as central and distinctive in Christianity.

The reaction against nineteenth century liberalism spread to the Reformed Churches in the Netherlands and France, but in neither did it win universal acceptance and in the Netherlands it produced fresh divisions. However, in France reunion was achieved between the two wings of the Reformed Church which had separated in the nineteenth century.

Contrasting Loss and Vigour in Continental Protestantism

Seen from some angles, after 1914 Protestantism on the Continent of Europe appeared to be declining. The mounting vitality which had been exhibited by many churches in the latter part of the nineteenth century had partly obscured the indifference and even the defection of many which were especially marked in the cities and industrial communities, the storm centres and focal points of the new age. After 1914, accelerated by the world wars and the revolutions which began in that year, the drift away from Christianity continued. The large majority still outwardly conformed to patterns which had become traditional as social customs. They were baptized and confirmed, and usually were married in the Church and buried from it. Yet for the majority active participation in the Church declined. In Germany it was estimated that about 95 per cent. of the population had a formal church membership. Yet, while the proportion varied greatly from section to section and city to city, in the mid-century it was said that only between 5 and 10 per cent. of the Protestants were regular attendants at church.

In the Netherlands an increasing proportion of the population, especially in the cities, was reported to be without a vital church connexion. Even in Sweden, neutral in both wars and where religious instruction was part of the curriculum in the schools, where the overwhelming majority were supposed to be members of the Church of Sweden, and where the tie between Church and state continued, in the 1940's only a small minority, said to be from 4 to 7 per cent., were regular attendants at the services of the Church.

This was only one side of the picture. A minority were deeply committed to the Christian faith and from them new currents of life issued. We have spoken of the Ecumenical Movement and the fashion in which much of the resistance to Nazi domination, both in Germany and in neighbouring lands overrun by the Nazis, came from earnest Christians. Simply as additional instances, by no means exhaustive, we can note that at Sigtuna, in Sweden, there was a folk school which brought together hand workers and brain workers in an effort to further understanding between them on the basis of Christianity, and that in France there came into being in 1939 what was known as CIMADE (*Comité Inter-Mouvements Auprès des Evacués*), a Protestant youth lay movement which began before the German occupation and persisted through and after the occupation to engage in relief and evangelism, first among the refugees and other sufferers from war, and later among the de-Christianized proletariat. After World War II, fresh efforts at evangelism were made in Germany and France, some of them in unique ways, in Germany more laymen became active in the Church, and in the Eastern Zone, behind the iron curtain, church life was maintained in the face of grave hardships and perils.

In the Netherlands in the 1940's an active movement, *Kerk en Wereld* ("Church and World"), was set on foot to effect the re-Christianization of the de-Christianized. Moreover, in 1951, in succession to an *ad interim* organization begun in 1945, the Netherlands Reformed Church achieved a more integrated structure as a means towards reform and renewal. In Continental Protestantism, as in the Roman Catholic Church, the trend appeared to be towards a situation in which convinced Christians were a self-conscious minority set in a pagan and de-Christianized world, but were seeking to reach out into it, serve its needs, and win at least some in it.

In the British Isles the course of events was not unlike that on the neighbouring Continent. Britain was deeply involved in the two world wars, an active belligerent throughout the course of the first and from the beginning to the end of the European phase of the second. During World War I she paid a terrific toll in hundreds of thousands of the flower of her young manhood, an incalculable loss in future leadership in Church and state. In World War II the cost in life, although serious, was not as great as in its predecessor. However, in the second, enemy bombings wrought more material damage, and exhaustion from concentrating individual and national effort on the struggle was more marked.

Between the two wars a partial recovery was effected. The churches sought to reinforce their depleted missionary staffs abroad, and at home endeavoured to reach the masses and to permeate the nation's life. A striking example of the latter was what was known as COPEC (Conference on Christian Politics, Economics, and Citizenship), held in 1924, and in which most of the churches joined. There were union movements, part of a wide trend in Protestantism. In 1929 the Church of Scotland and the United Free Church of Scotland came together, thus healing the breach which had existed since the Disruption of 1843. This was the more easily achieved since the practices which had led the Free Church to withdraw had ceased. In 1932 the largest groups of British Methodism were united.

Encouraging symptoms of fresh life were seen. In Scotland a clergyman of aristocratic lineage, George F. MacLeod, inaugurated a movement which had as its object the quickening of the religious life of the country and reaching the unchurched masses through a community enterprise which had as a centre and symbol Iona, the island from which, centuries before, Columba had led in winning much of Scotland and England. There were those who spoke for the life of the spirit. The Keswick conferences continued, a stimulus and fellowship of the theologically conservative Evangelicals of the several denominations. Anglican monastic orders flourished. Evelyn Underhill (1875–1941) wrote extensively on the way of the mystic and with growing feeling and understanding. Congregationalists and Baptists admitted women to their ministry, and at least one of these, Agnes Maude Royden (1876——), became favourably known on both sides of the Atlantic.

Theological thought and Biblical scholarship were vigorous. Neither the Scots nor the English moved as far from nineteenth century patterns as did the Germans and the Swiss. In general they continued, with modifications, late nineteenth century trends. As in the nineteenth century, great variety was seen. Some of the outstanding figures of the period immediately before World War I lived through that struggle, but their principal contributions had been made before it broke out. Thus early in the century the Congregationalist, Peter Taylor Forsyth (1848–1921), wrote books on the place of Christ which some of the next generation held to have made Barth and neo-orthodoxy unnecessary for them. Like Barth, but with less bluntness in repudiating man's natural ability, he emphasized the divine initiative in Christ. The Anglo-Catholic, Charles Gore (1853–1932), in his later years Bishop of Oxford, did much to combine the social message of the Church with theology. In his maturity he is said to have exerted more influence on the theological thought of the Church of England than any other of his contemporaries. After World War II there was a revival of interest in F. D. Maurice. In the evangelical tradition there were liberals and conservatives, and between the two wings much discussion was heard, but not of the dimensions of the "fundamentalist-modernist" controversy which we shall find in the United States of that period. Extreme liberalism was represented by the Unitarian, L. P. Jacks (1860——), editor of *The Hibbert Journal*. Platonism within the Church of England was associated with W. R. Inge (1860——), Dean of St. Paul's Cathedral in London, who, partly because of his Platonic and Neoplatonic bent, contributed to the literature of mysticism. He also took delight in exposing and flaying what he deemed contemporary slogans and shibboleths both among laity and clergy and earned the sobriquet of "the gloomy dean." F. R. Tennant (1866——) of Cambridge, trained in the natural sciences, like Inge an Anglican clergyman, rejected intuition as a road to knowledge, and built his theology on an empirical basis of observed fact through the use of reason. In a sense his was a continuation of the eighteenth century natural theology and he stood in the succession of Butler and Paley.

It is a temptation to give a long list of names, for there were many, Scottish and English, who made what to their contemporaries seemed outstanding contributions, some in theology and some in Biblical studies. In general, the majority conformed to a trait which was said to be characteristically British and did not go to extremes. They stated the historic Christian faith ably and in the language of their day. Much effort was devoted, both in England and Scotland, to putting Christian belief in such a manner that it would be intelligible and convincing to the intellectuals as well as the masses. While recognizing form criticism and eschatology, Biblical experts were not carried away by either school. One of them, the Congregationalist Charles Harold Dodd (1884——), professor of divinity at Cambridge, put forth and persuasively argued for the position known as "realized eschatology," holding that Jesus believed that in his day the kingdom of God had already begun to arrive. Yet to list all the important men in a book as comprehensive and as limited in dimensions as this would issue in a mere catalogue, the chief impression of which would only be the wealth of competent scholars which the churches of Great Britain possessed in these years.

One who rose to prominence in the years between the wars must be more than mentioned, William Temple (1881–1944). He was not to be remembered primarily as a theologian, although he was competent in both philosophy and theology and wrote fairly extensively in those areas, notably in his *Nature, Man and God* (1934). Moving philosophically from an earlier idealism to what he called "dialectical realism," he held to the essential core of the Christain faith as maintained in the Church of England and without aligning himself fully with any one of the particular schools within that communion. He was known, too, as a man of prayer and his *Readings in St. John's Gospel* (1939, 1940), the fruit of many years of meditation, published in his later years, were evidence of a profound devotional life. However, he was noted chiefly for the wide range of his interests and an integrity of character which eventually made him the outstanding British churchman of the 1930's and 1940's and one of the most eminent Englishmen of the century. Born in the palace of the Bishop of Exeter, the son of a man who died as Archbishop of Canterbury, he went, quite naturally, to Rugby and Oxford, had a fellowship in Queen's College, Oxford, and was ordained in the Church of England. Then came the headmastership of a school and a parish in London. He was a leader of the Life and Liberty Movement, designed to inject new life in the Church of England, to free it from some of its encumbrances and abuses, and, while retaining its tie with the state, to give it greater liberty to control its affairs without the interference of government. There followed a canonry at Westminster Abbey (1919), appointment to be Bishop of Manchester (1921), and translation to the Archbishopric of York (1929) and (1942) to the Archbishopric of Canterbury. Temple endeavoured to make the Church a growing force in the nation's life. Born to privilege, he sought to give opportunity to the masses for education and the other good things of life. He was sympathetic with the Labour movement, joined the Labour Party (1918), and worked to eliminate the contrasts, so marked in highly industrialized Britain, between squalor and luxury. Caught up in his youth in the Student Christian Movement, which rose above denominational barriers, he became outstanding in the Ecumenical Movement. He was chairman of COPEC and was prominent in Faith and Order, Life and Work, and the International Missionary Council. He was chairman of the Provisional Committee of the World Council of Churches and laboured until (1942) the British Council of Churches came into being, embracing the Church of England, the Church of Scotland, and the Nonconforming Churches. On his enthronement as Archbishop of Canterbury he declared that the great new fact of the era was that "as though in preparation for such a time as this," God had been building up a Christian fellowship which now extended into every nation, and bound "citizens of them all together in true unity and mutual love." He exerted himself to make that fellowship a growing reality.

The Church of England continued to be inclusive, with a wide range of theological and ecclesiastical convictions. These were all the way from an ultra-conservative Evangelicalism, akin to the fundamentalism of the United States and intensely Protestant, to an Anglo-Catholicism which hoped for "reunion" of the severed branches of the Catholic Church under the Pope, but with the Pope, as Bishop of Rome, being simply *primus inter pares* in the episcopate, without the infallibility and the administrative absolutism which had accrued to him in the Roman Catholic Church.

Various attempts were made to find accord with Catholics of different shades on the one hand and Nonconforming Protestants on the other. From 1921 to 1926 what were known as the Malines Conversations were carried on intermittently between several Anglo-Catholics on the one hand and, on the other, Cardinal Mercier of Belgium and some other members of the Roman Catholic Church. However, they caused uneasiness on both sides, broke down after the death of Mercier, and later (1928) Papal action made their position impossible. More hopeful relations were established with the Orthodox. In 1922 the Ecumenical Patriarch and the Holy Synod of Constantinople declared Anglican orders to have the same validity as those of Rome, the Old Catholics, and the Armenians, a declaration in which two other Orthodox Patriarchs eventually joined. The *Appeal to all Christian People* issued by the Lambeth Conference of 1920 led to extensive conferences with representatives of the Nonconformist Protestant bodies in England, but without the results for which the Anglicans had hoped. An overture of the Archbishop of Canterbury in the 1940's was no more successful, but, in one way and another, friendlier relations were cultivated with the Nonconforming Protestants as well as the Orthodox.

An issue which for a time jeopardized the tie between the state and the Church arose over the revision of the Book of Common Prayer. It was associated with the effort to obtain greater liberty for the Church of England, partly in permitting a variety in public worship which would allow room for those of Catholic as well as Protestant convictions, partly by setting up effective ecclesiastical courts, and partly by allowing the people of the parish an effective voice in choosing their pastor. What was known as the Enabling Act passed by Parliament in 1919 looked in this direction. In 1921 what was known as the Church Assembly came into being, with both lay and clerical membership. It constituted the legislative body for the Church of England. Even before 1914 there had been efforts at a revision of the familiar Book of Common Prayer. During World War I the Eucharist became more prominent. Some Anglo-Catholics used the Roman canon of the mass, either secretly or openly. After long discussion and by actions which represented a substantial majority of the bodies and officials which could speak for the Church of England, a revised prayer book was submitted to Parliament, for that body had the final authority to present it for royal approval. It did not please all in the Church of England. To the extreme Evangelicals it seemed to go too far in the Catholic direction. To the Anglo-Catholics it did not go far enough, especially in restrictions placed on the reserved sacrament which were designed to limit it to giving the communion to the sick and to prevent its adoration. The revised book was approved by the House of Lords but in 1927 was defeated in the House of Commons. The argument against it which proved most potent was that it represented a movement away from Protestantism towards Rome. Some changes were made by the Church to mitigate this objection, but in vain. The House of Commons again (1928) refused its approval. However, the bishops permitted the use of variations from the Book of Common Prayer which did not go beyond those proposed in 1927–1928.

In the 1920's, 1930's, and 1940's a number of factors contributed to bring serious losses to Christianity in the British Isles. One was the continuation of the intellectual trends which, as we have noted, in the nineteenth century questioned Christianity or dismissed it as untenable or irrelevant. For example, the writers who were said to have exerted the widest popular influence in the first half of the century, G. B. Shaw, D. H. Lawrence, and H. G. Wells, all rejected traditional Christian morals. Another adverse factor was the progressive industrialization of the nation with growing aggregations of labourers in factories and mines. There the routine, the attitudes, the conditions of work, the housing conditions, and other patterns of life tended to wean from the faith those caught up in them and presented grave obstacles to those who attempted to reach with the faith either the youth or the elders. The forms of worship and parish organization and activity which had been developed in a different social structure were ill adapted to these phases of an industrialized society. A threat to Christianity, in part related to this last, was the shifts of population. Some suburbs mounted in size, new ones arose, the cities stretched out into the country, and millions changed their places of residence. If they had church connexions in their old homes, effort was required to establish fresh ones in their new ones, and for the majority religious conviction was too mild to provide the needed stimulus. Nor did the churches display sufficient initiative to hold and win more than a minority of the deracinated multitudes. The great depression which began in the United States in 1929 and which spread to the British Isles, as to the larger part of the world, brought other serious problems in unemployment, loss of morale, and declining giving to churches and philanthropic enterprises. The growth of the "welfare state" with its socialistic programme severely handi-capped the classes upon which the churches had heavily depended. The hitherto underprivileged were benefited, but the cost was largely defrayed by income and inheritance taxes which bore especially heavily on the middle and upper classes. Other developments also hit these erstwhile privileged groups and reduced their ability to support the churches and the missionary and other organizations related to these bodies.

As if these were not enough, World War II dealt further blows. Many church structures were damaged or destroyed by enemy bombing and because of the difficulty of obtaining building materials after the war were repaired only slowly if at all. Thousands were evacuated from the cities to escape air raids and thus were out of touch with whatever church connexions had once been theirs. Young men were called to the colours and the numbers preparing for the ministry sharply declined. Civilians were caught up in home defense and other war activities on Sundays as well as week days and habits of church at-tendance were weakened or broken. The prolonged strain of the war left multitudes weary, including the conscientious from whom came much of the leadership of the churches. The impoverishment and the austerity which accompanied and followed the war were additional obstacles. In waging the two wars Britain used up much of the capital accumulated in the halcyon days when it led the world in industry, trade, and finance, and became a debtor rather than a creditor nation. Thus the ability to give to the churches and their agencies was impaired. Moreover, there were the coarsening of morals, the increase in the consumption of alcohol, and the neglect of religion which have been the usual accompaniments of war.

The British Empire which had reached its proud climax in the nineteenth century seemed to be going to pieces. Soon after World War II India, Pakistan, Burma, and Ceylon either became fully independent or self-governing. Increas-ing restlessness was seen in the African possessions. Young men could no longer be assured of a career in the colonial service. The British West Indies were an economic liability rather than an asset. To be sure, the British Commonwealth, composed of nations bound together by the symbolic tie of the crown, was unique and had strength, but in it the British Isles were not as prominent as formerly and "imperial preference" which gave them a favoured position in the commerce of the dominions was threatened. The larger part of Ireland withdrew from the empire and became an independent republic. Great Britain accorded it dominion status in 1921, and in 1948 and 1949 the last constitutional links were severed between it and the United Kingdom.

Under these circumstances it was not strange that active church membership and church attendance declined. Not far from 1937 it was said that of the potential Protestant constituency in England only about 14 per cent. were communicant members, that only 5 to 10 per cent. were regular attendants at church, and that scarcely one-fourth went to church as often as once in three months. This seems to have been a distinct decline from the beginning of the century. Efforts at mass evangelism of the de-Christianized, some on a local and some on a national scale, yielded only scanty returns. The figures appear to have fallen further by the end of World War II, but to have shown a slight recovery in the years immediately after that struggle. There was reported to be much criticism of the morals and integrity of church members by non-church-goers and disdain for the clergy.

A falling-off in the clergy in numbers and quality from the high point reached on the eve of 1914 was also marked and increasing difficulty was experienced, especially after World War II, in recruiting enough men to fill the vacancies. Part of the cause was the deadening of any inclination towards the ministry by the months and years of service in the armed forces. A few found their vocation to the ministry while in uniform, and immediately after the war there was a sudden and sharp increase in the numbers of those applying for theological training. However, soon after 1950 there was again the cry of a dearth of clergy. Another cause of the shortage of clergy was economic. Stipends did not keep pace with the cost of living and fell behind those of artisans and even, in some instances, of unskilled labourers. The large incomes and pluralism which had been a scandal even as late as the fore part of the nineteenth century had passed, especially after World War II. The huge rectories and episcopal residences which were inherited by the Church of England from an earlier age became a burden which taxed the resources and the energies of those who lived in them. Difficulty was experienced in obtaining funds and personnel to maintain the overseas enterprises which had been an outstanding feature of nineteenth century British Protestantism. Moreover, it was noted that while some of the bishops of the Church of England were national figures with a marked influence in public affairs and on the life of the nation as a whole, and although there were still distinguished preachers and scholars both in England and Scotland, fewer of the clergy of the Non-conformist churches and of the Church of Scotland commanded the attention and respect of the country than in the half century and more before 1914.

Grim though these aspects of the picture undoubtedly were, British Protestantism was by no means dead. Indeed, it displayed marked vigour. We have noted the partial recovery made in the 1920's, after World War I. Although thousands who thought of them at all regarded the churches as irrelevant and as not speaking to their day, little antagonism to Christianity as such was seen. In its ethical standards the nation gave evidence of a Christian heritage, even though that heritage might be fading. In many communities, some of them in the cities, church services were well attended and numbers of congregations maintained an active life. Women constituted a majority of the faithful in the churches, but laymen were not lacking. Among the latter were some in high position in government, business, and education. There was a noticeable hunger for satisfying answers to the riddles of life, with a wistful hope that they might be found in the Christian faith. It was a matter of comment that not a few of the children of nineteenth century agnostics and sceptics were becoming Christians, and from deep conviction. Several outstanding intellectuals, formerly without faith or even scoffers, were converts and in their writing were setting forth Christian convictions and wrestling with the challenge presented by the Gospel to the de-Christianized members of their generation. In the 1950's both faculty members and students in at least some of the universities were increasingly interested in Christianity. The Education Act of 1944 made religious instruction compulsory in the schools, and measures were taken in preparing syllabi and teachers to render the legislation effective. The Religious Affairs Department of the British Broadcasting Corporation arranged programmes which were heard by a larger proportion of the population than attended church and the majority of the listeners were said to be non-church-goers of the working classes. Several of the outstanding intellects among Protestants dealt courageously with the issues presented by the new age with its colossal evils, by the minority position of Christians in what had once been regarded as Christendom, and by what looked like a retreating wave of faith. Out of their straitened resources, British Protestants gave generously to the relief of the suffering on the neighbouring Continent, maintained many of the philanthropies which had been begun at home by their predecessors in a prosperous age, continued the major proportion of their foreign missions, and contributed to the foreign missions of their even more hardly pressed brethren across the Channel. Not only William Temple, but also many men and women of lesser but still significant stature promoted the Ecumenical Movement. British Protestantism was following not only tried methods and historic traditions, but was reaching out in new ways.

PROSPERING ROMAN CATHOLICISM IN THE BRITISH ISLES

In contrast with the severe blows dealt Protestantism in the British Isles by the events which followed 1914, the Roman Catholic Church prospered.

In England, Scotland, and Wales the advance of the Roman Catholic Church which began in the nineteenth century continued. It will be remembered (Chapter XLVIII) that at the dawn of the nineteenth century there were Roman Catholics, chiefly in Yorkshire, Lancashire, and the Highlands of Scotland, who represented a continuity of the faith from pre-Reformation days. They suffered under political disabilities which were removed in the first half of the century. To them were added, mostly in England, converts, largely from the Anglo-Catholic wing of the Church of England. However, by the year 1914 the large majority of the Roman Catholics in Great Britain were Irish immigrants and their descendants. They or their fathers had come mainly as unskilled labourers to the coal mines of Wales and around Newcastle and to the manufacturing and commercial cities—Liverpool, London, Birmingham, Manchester, Glasgow, and smaller similar centres.

After 1914 this Irish constituency continued to provide the large majority of the Roman Catholics of England, Scotland, and Wales. Converts were made, mainly by marriage, but the gain was chiefly by the excess of births over deaths. In England and Wales the total of Roman Catholics rose from 1,870,000 in 1914 to 2,650,000 in 1950. While there was said to have been some leakage, in general the children of Roman Catholics remained true to the faith of their parents and their attendance at the services of the Church was maintained. No dearth of clergy was experienced. Priests totalled 3,835 in 1910, 5,642 in 1940, and 6,643 in 1950. As the Irish were longer in England, many of them prospered and became members of the middle and professional classes. The rank and file benefited from the social legislation of the period. As a result, funds were obtained, churches and chapels multiplied, and schools, theological seminaries, and monasteries grew. The movements of population to the suburbs in the 1930's and 1940's and the dispersals from the hearts of the cities during World War II brought a wider geographic distribution of the Roman Catholic population and new churches and chapels were erected to care for the Diaspora.

In the Republic of Ireland (Eire) Roman Catholics were predominant. The small Protestant minorities declined after Irish independence. While religious liberty was granted to other denominations, the Roman Catholic Church was officially recognized as the guardian of the faith. As a neutral in World War II, Eire was spared many of the hardships which constituted problems for the churches in Great Britain and on the Continent. The population was enthusiastically Roman Catholic. This may have been because, as earlier, that branch of the faith was identified with Irish nationalism. In the mid-twentieth century almost the entire population were said to be regular in their attendance at church. Priests, monks, and nuns increased, and many went to Great Britain, to the Irish in the Americas and Australasia, and as missionaries to non-Christians. From Maynooth, the Roman Catholic university, were graduated many who became bishops either in Eire or in the Irish communities abroad.

THE COMMUNIST TEST TO RUSSIAN CHRISTIANITY

In 1917, under the stress of World War I, the tsar's regime in Russia collapsed. For a few months the moderate revolutionaries, headed by Kerensky, were in power. Late in 1917 they were swept out by the radicals, and the Bolsheviki, a wing of the communists, took control. Eventually the Union of Soviet Socialist Republics (U.S.S.R.) came into being, with the Communist Party in power, first under Lenin and then under Stalin.

The revolution brought the most searching test that Christianity had known in Russia since the Mongol invasion. In some ways the trial was more severe. To be sure, Christianity was better rooted in Russia in 1917 than in the thirteenth century, but the communists were far more aggressively anti-Christian than the Mongols had been.

The first effect of the liberal stage of the revolution of 1917 was to give the Church greater freedom. In August of that year an all-Russian Sobor, or Synod, of the Russian Orthodox Church met in Moscow, made up of ecclesiastics and laity. In the autumn the Sobor voted to restore the Patriarchate, discontinued under Peter the Great more than two centuries earlier, and in November elected to that post Tikhon, the Metropolitan of Moscow. The Patriarch was made subject to the Sobor and was not much more than its chief executive.

Before the Church could fairly find itself under its new organization the communist storm broke upon it. In December, 1917, the Soviet declared all land to be national property. Ecclesiastical monastic holdings were explicitly included and the Church was deprived of the larger part of its income. That same month all schools, among them theological seminaries and academies, were ordered to be turned over to the state's Commissariat of National Education. Thus the education of youth and even of its own priesthood was taken from the Church. A few days later the state said that it would give legal status only to such marriages as were performed by civil ceremonies and transferred to its bureaus the registration of births and deaths, formerly ecclesiastical functions. Within a few weeks, in January, 1918, the Church was formally separated from the state, state payment of the salaries of the clergy was ordered discontinued, religious vows and oaths were abrogated, instruction in religion was forbidden in both government and private schools, compulsory collection of funds for the support of ecclesiastical institutions was outlawed, the right to hold property was denied to religious associations, and religious rites were no longer to accompany state functions. Citizens were permitted to hold religious convictions or to renounce them, and religious rites might be continued if they did not interfere with public order.

These acts of a communist-dominated government can be easily understood. Communism regarded religion as the "opiate of the people," hindering their full emancipation. Moreover, in the eyes of the communists, who had long been proscribed and hunted down by the old regime, the Church was a tool of the hated oppressor.

It was not to be expected that the Church would tamely submit to the radical changes in its status. Tikhon and the Sobor denounced (January, 1918) the confiscation of ecclesiastical property and appealed to Christians to resist it. Popular outbreaks followed, but they were suppressed and hundreds were shot or otherwise punished.

For a few months the state did not enforce all its ecclesiastical decrees, but in July, 1918, it reaffirmed its position of the preceding December and January, and in the constitution specifically guaranteed to all citizens the right of anti-religious as well as religious propaganda. Associations of citizens might be granted the use of church buildings for worship, but structures not so utilized were ordered seized.

As the resistance of many churchmen continued and a church council of *émigrés* called for the restoration of the Romanovs, the communist regime, still fighting for its life against the "white" armies which sought to overthrow it, stiffened its anti-Christian measures. Priests and bishops were classified with non-productive elements in the population and were disfranchised. Education for the priesthood was made almost impossible. Divisions in the Church were fomented. About forty bishops and a thousand priests are said to have perished in the civil wars waged with the anti-communist forces. Religious instruction of youths under eighteen years of age in groups of more than four was forbidden. In 1922 church articles were confiscated with the ostensible purpose of applying the proceeds of their sale to famine relief. A Union of the Godless was organized and anti-religious literature was issued.

A five-year programme adopted in 1929 for the progressive conversion of Russia to a communist state included drastic measures against religion. The publication of religious books was made more difficult. Religious societies were forbidden to engage in any social services such as coöperatives, sanatoriums, medical care, relief to their indigent members, associations for recreation, or even meetings for religious instruction. Special theological courses were still allowed, but only by express permission of the state. No believer was permitted to teach in a state school. Itinerant preaching, such as that in which Baptists and Evangelicals engaged, was forbidden. Many of the clergy were arrested and sentenced to hard labour in the North and Siberia. Numbers of church buildings were transformed into moving picture houses. A five-day and then a six-day week was substituted for the seven-day week, and thus the Christian cycle of work and worship was broken. Many church buildings were diverted from their original purpose by the simple expedient of placing on the congregations unbearable burdens for repairs, taxes, rental, and insurance. It is said that in the first year of the five-year plan about two thousand churches were closed, or about as many as had been liquidated in the preceding eleven years. At least two cathedrals in prominent cities were turned into museums of religion which in effect were anti-religious, and other museums were set up to exalt science and defame religion. Anti-religious plays, literature, radio broadcasts, motion pictures, and lectures were employed, and by May, 1932, it is said that the Godless Union numbered 7,000,000 members besides 1,500,000 children who were counted as Godless.

The growth of the cities militated against Christianity. No new churches could be erected and clergy were few, and in the urban environment those coming from the rural districts and the small towns where more of the faith persisted found it difficult to make contact with the Church.

The Russian Orthodox Church was further weakened by divisions within its ranks. What was known as the Living Church was organized, made up of those more in sympathy with the government than was Tikhon. Some of its bishops were from the married clergy rather than the monks, as had been the tradition. In several regions, notably in the Ukraine and Georgia, regional autonomous Orthodox Churches were set up and the one in the Ukraine suffered from additional rifts. Peter, who succeeded to the Patriarchate after the death of Tikhon (1925), was exiled to Siberia and another schism developed.

Beginning in 1936 the anti-religious programme became less severe. Bell-ringing and the collection of funds for churches were permitted. In 1940 the seven-day week was restored and Sunday was made a compulsory holiday. Workers were no longer penalized for absences during the Christmas and Easter festivals. The showing of anti-Christian plays and anti-Christmas and anti-Easter carnivals were prohibited. The franchise was restored to the clergy.

Yet anti-religious measures by no means ceased. Several bishops were shot on the charge of espionage, and more churches, as well as synagogues and mosques, were closed. In 1940 it was estimated that about 90 per cent. of the churches in use in 1917 had been converted to secular purposes or destroyed, that the number of bishops had declined 75 per cent., the number of deacons 80 per cent., and of priests 90 per cent.

Christian bodies outside the Orthodox Church also suffered. This was true of Roman Catholics, the Old Believers, several other sects which had separated from the former state church, and the Baptists and Evangelicals.

In spite of these adversities Christianity persisted. In the 1930's the militant anti-Christian campaign began to decline. It was said that secret monasteries existed and that the training of priests continued, even though surreptitiously. It was reported that numbers of women memorized the New Testament and portions of the prayer book and went from home to home, baptizing the children and giving religious instruction. A substantial proportion of the population, especially in the rural sections, were believers.

In the 1940's relations between Church and state improved. This seems in the first instance to have been because of the need of unity in the face of the German invasion of 1941. The Russian Orthodox Church stood staunchly with the nation and the government in the resistance to the alien armies. In 1943 the state gave permission to the "Old Church," as distinguished from the "New Church," sprung from the Living Church movement, to elect a Patriarch. This it did in September of that year. The following month the government set up a council to maintain official contacts between itself and the Russian Orthodox Church. It also created a council which was to deal with all other religious cults. Another reason for the declining hostility between the Church and the state was said to have been the rise of a generation which had not known the Church in the days of the tsars and so did not share the bitter hostility of the older revolutionaries who had regarded it as an ally of the hated monarchical regime. It was reported, too, that with mounting nationalism there was an awareness of Russian history and of the important part in it which the Church had played. Then, too, it was conjectured that the state regarded the Russian Orthodox Church as useful in cementing relations with the Balkan countries, especially Rumania and Bulgaria, where the Orthodox Churches were strong. Perhaps, too, the Church was deemed to have been sufficiently weakened to be no longer a menace.

Whatever the reasons, at mid-century the antagonism between Church and state was not as acute as in the first years of the communist regime. The Communist Party was still officially antagonistic to religion and called the Church a tool and ally of exploiters, but did not engage in as active persecution as formerly. The episcopate of the Russian Orthodox Church endorsed the peace plans put forward by the communists in their war of nerves with the West and denounced the Central Committee of the World Council of Churches for supporting the action of the United Nations in Korea in the summer of

1950. The Russian Orthodox Church would have no fellowship with the Ecumenical Movement but, presumably in accord with the Kremlin, regarded it as the religious front of Western imperialism and capitalism.

It was clear that at mid-twentieth century Christianity was still very much alive in Russia. In 1945 it was estimated that there were about 20,000 Orthodox churches, 30,000 priests, 10 theological seminaries, 2 theological academies, and 87 monasteries and nunneries. In 1951 it was reported that several famous churches had been restored and were being used for religious purposes, and that the Holy Trinity Monastery near Moscow, long an outstanding centre of the Russian Orthodox Church, had been refurbished and was thronged with pilgrims. There could be no doubt that in at least some of the main cities Orthodox Church services attracted large numbers and that the throngs on the high festivals, notably Easter, were especially large and devout. Some other Christian groups of tsarist days also continued. For example, the Popovsty, or Old Believers who had priests, possessed a supreme council. The Lutherans in Estonia, Latvia, and Lithuania had synods. Those called Baptists, a designation which included Baptists, Evangelicals, and Pentecostals, were numerous and their meetings in Moscow were largely attended. In 1950 they were said to number 3,200,000.

Here and there outside of the U.S.S.R. larger and smaller bodies of Russian Orthodox Christians were found. Some, as in the United States, had been in existence before the Revolution of 1917. Others were made up chiefly of refugees. A major centre of Russian Orthodox thought arose in Paris after World War I. There the most distinguished figure was Nikolai Alexandrovitch Berdyaev (1874–1948). Born in Kiev, of aristocratic and cultured parentage, in his younger days Berdyaev attempted to combine idealistic and Marxist views, but he was never an orthodox Marxist and could not accept the dialectical determination of that ideology. Exiled for a time in his student days for his antagonism to the tsarist regime and his sympathy with the working classes, he early attracted attention in literary and socially radical circles. His wife, deeply mystical and eventually a Roman Catholic, was the daughter of a wealthy lawyer who was religiously a complete sceptic. Berdyaev was much influenced by Soloviev, before World War I was active in religious-philosophical societies, returned to the Church, and had contacts with groups of mystics who wished to see the kingdom of God realized on earth. Grieved by the socially reactionary strain in the Russian Orthodox Church, he criticized it and was threatened with exile to Siberia. When the Revolution brought its adherents to power he was also a critic of Marxism. Yet for a time he held a chair in the University of Moscow and not until 1921 was he deported by the Soviet authorities. In Germany and France he was associated with the Young Men's

Christian Association and the World's Student Christian Federation. It was in the 1920's and 1930's that his writings began to attract wide attention among intellectuals, especially Christian intellectuals, in Western Europe and America. He opposed both the tyranny of the communist regime in Russia and the reactionary attitudes of the Russian *émigrés* and Western *bourgeois* capitalism.

Always courageously independent in his thinking and writing, Berdyaev had his own kind of personalism and existentialism. Never one to conform, he held that knowledge is an activity of a free spirit, that man is a spiritual being, that God is spirit, that spirit is activity, and that God has breathed spirit into man. He maintained that both philosophy and theology must start with the God-man Christ. He believed profoundly in the incarnation. As he saw it, the Trinity, with the historic conviction that the Son was "begotten and not made," showed that while God and man are distinct they are not wholly alien, that there is in God the eternal face of man, and that God is to be known only through Christ, as the God-man through whom He touches man. In the activity of God Berdyaev saw the clue to history, and especially in the liberation of the spirit of man by Christ. He believed that the decay of Western civilization had begun with the Renaissance, when Western man, taking advantage of the freedom and exaltation of man which had come through Christianity, affirmed himself, exalted his reason, ignored the tie between God and man which had brought him this freedom, and paved the way to scepticism and a loss of faith in man's reason. This movement, so he held, culminated in the mechanical age in which the humanism of the Renaissance ended in anti-humanism, making man a mere cog in the machine. History, so he contended, is to be given its final significance by the second coming of Christ.

More limited in his influence, but more nearly in the pattern of the Russian Orthodox Church, was Sergius Bulkagov (1871-1944). The son of a priest, in his youth he was a Marxist and for a time was professor of political economy. Partly through the influence of Soloviev, he returned to the Church, in 1918 was ordained priest, and in 1922 was banished. He became a founder of the Orthodox Theological Institute in Paris and occupied its chair of dogmatic theology. Holding to the Orthodox faith, he wrote extensively.

STORMS IN THE BALKANS

In the twentieth century what in its most inclusive sense was the Balkan Peninsula was the scene of storm after storm. The first broke out in 1912 with a war which before it ended in 1913 involved all the countries of the region—Serbia, Montenegro, Bulgaria, Rumania, Greece, and the remnants of the once large possessions of Turkey in Europe. That war was the immediate preliminary to World War I. As a sequel to World War I Greece was defeated in a struggle with Turkey (1921–1923) and nearly a million and a half Greek Orthodox refugees from Anatolia and Asia Minor deluged the country. The Balkans were also engulfed in World War II, with an Italian-German invasion of Greece and Albania, a German invasion of Jugoslavia, the later advance of the Russian armies, the post-war inclusion of Bulgaria and Rumania within the Russian iron curtain, the setting up of the communist regime under Tito in Jugoslavia, and the break of Tito with Moscow. These developments could not but affect the religious scene.

Although they contained Roman Catholic and Moslem minorities, in 1914 in all the Balkan countries except Albania and the remnant of European Turkey through one or another of its branches the Orthodox faith was professed by a majority of the population. This, obviously, was the heritage of the history which we have sketched in earlier chapters. Amid the vicissitudes of the tempestuous post-1914 years the Orthodox Churches continued. They also gave indications of vigour. After World War I the *Zoe* movement enlisted and inspired a number of choice spirits in Greece. Lay initiative was seen in the Orthodox Church both in Greece and Rumania. In Bulgaria the government improved the theological education out of which came the clergy. There was more reading of the Bible than formerly. Several thousand Uniates returned to the Orthodoxy of their fathers.

World War II and its aftermath brought fresh complications. In Greece in the Italian-German invasion and the subsequent civil war in the North hundreds of priests succumbed and many parishes were left vacant. Yet the Orthodox Church remained strong. For a time after 1944 its primate was regent of the country. *Zoe* revived, as did a lay movement, and some of the vacant parishes were re-supplied with priests. The Orthodox Church of Greece adhered to the World Council of Churches and representatives, both lay and clerical, were active in the Ecumenical Movement. In Jugoslavia the Patriarchate which had been suppressed by the Turks in 1766 was reconstituted. Numbers of the clergy, including some of the bishops and the *locum tenens* of the Patriarchate, were imprisoned on the charge of opposition to the Tito regime, but they were subsequently released and in 1952 the churches which had escaped destruction or confiscation were reported to be crowded. In February, 1945, the schism which had separated the Bulgarian Orthodox Church from the Ecumenical Patriarch of Constantinople was healed. In 1949, in accordance with the communist pattern, the Orthodox Church of Bulgaria, while still described as "the traditional Church of the Bulgarian People," was disestablished, churches were forbidden to conduct schools except theological seminaries, or to have youth movements, and their hospitals and relief institutions were taken over by the state. The new constitution of the Bulgarian Orthodox Church provided for a Patriarch to head it, but delay was experienced in filling the post. In Rumania the law of 1948 "concerning the freedom of all religions" placed religions and religious teaching under the control of the state. The Orthodox Church was headed by a Patriarch and a Holy Synod. In 1948 about a million and a third Uniates severed their connexion with Rome and returned to the Orthodox Church.

THE WANING OLDER CHURCHES IN WESTERN ASIA AND NORTH-EASTERN AFRICA

The years after 1914 witnessed the further decline of the older churches in Western Asia and North-eastern Africa which had been in process since the Arab and the subsequent Turkish conquests.

In Turkey, shortly before 1914 a quite secular government came into power. It was intent upon making Turkey a strong, unified, Westernized state. To that end it wished to free the nation not only from what it deemed the incubus of Islam but also from the religious minorities, most of them Christian, which by long Turkish policy were distinct political entities. The protection of the Christian minorities had furnished occasion for the intervention of Western governments, a fact intolerable to the nationalists. During and soon after World War I tens of thousands of Armenians and Greek Orthodox perished, many of them massacred, and thousands of Roman Catholics and hundreds of Protestants also succumbed. Early in the 1920's what was euphemistically called on "exchange" moved a few thousand Turks from Greece to Turkey and, as we have seen, a much larger number of Greeks from Asia Minor to Greece. At the mid-century, Turkey, confined by the outcome of World War I and its aftermath to Asia Minor and a slight foothold, including Istanbul (Constantinople), in Europe, had very few Christians. Asia Minor, the first large region to be fairly solidly Christian by faith, now contained only a few of that religion. The constituency over which the Ecumenical Patriarch exercised direct jurisdiction shrank to very small proportions and that office, once vying with the Papacy in power, now had little but the tantalizing memory of a great past.

The Armenian (Gregorian) Church suffered from the communist rule over the portion of its constituency which was in Russian territory south of the Caucasus. The number of monks declined and there was difficulty in electing a successor to the Catholicos who was assassinated in 1937.

During World War I thousands of Nestorians, Chaldeans (Nestorians who had submitted to Rome), Jacobites, and Syrian Uniates in Iran (Persia) and what was later Iraq lost their lives. Turks, Kurds, and Moslem Persians took the occasion to fall on them, minorities which were now all but defenseless. The Church of the East, as the Nestorians preferred to be called, dwindled almost to the vanishing point in scattered remnants in Iran, Iraq, the United

States, and a few other lands. A great church which had once been represented from Mesopotamia to South India and the China Sea had all but perished.

The coming into being of the state of Israel in 1948 and the ensuing war with the Arabs led to the death of numbers of the Christian Arab minority and to the displacement from their homes of many of the survivors.

In Egypt the Coptic Church continued to suffer from the slow leakage to the dominant Islam which for centuries had been weakening it. Yet because of its birth rate it probably increased in numbers. In the neighbouring Ethiopia the Italian invasion of the 1930's could not but work damage to the church of that land. The Italian masters severed the traditional administrative connexion between the Ethiopian and the Coptic Church and after the restoration of native rule the tie was only in part renewed.

Throughout most of Western Asia and Northern Africa Protestant and Roman Catholic missions persisted. Both drew their converts chiefly from the older Eastern Churches, but to each came a few from Islam. Protestants especially won a few hundred Moslems in Iran and Arabia. The Vatican continued to make much of the Uniate bodies and to enhance their dignity it created (1917) for their special supervision the Congregation for Oriental Churches. Wherever political conditions permitted, both Protestants and Roman Catholics maintained their educational and medical institutions. Both gave extensive relief to the sufferers from the recurrent wars and massacres.

Yet the numerical gains of the Roman Catholic and Protestant communities were not sufficient to offset the losses experienced in the decline of the ancient Eastern Churches. The enterprise of Christians from the West did not halt the slow decline of Christianity which had been under way for over a thousand years in the land of its birth and the region of its initial greatest strength.

SUMMARY

The period of history which opened in the tragic summer of 1914 bore hard on the traditional Christendom and its churches. To the adverse forces which had been present in the nineteenth century and earlier there were added devastating wars and sweeping revolutions, the major one of the latter openly and the others tacitly anti-Christian. In several countries survivals existed from the ages when Christianity was the professed faith of the entire nation and when Church and state were complementary but often rival aspects of an inclusive structure of society. Increasingly, however, the tie between Church and state was either loosened or completely severed. Christians were seemingly in the process of becoming minorities in a frankly or covertly non-Christian society. To many, especially to those whose attention was focused mainly on Europe, mankind appeared to be moving into what some called the post-Christian era.

This interpretation was an over-simplification which ignored other and quite contrary aspects of the world scene. Christianity was by no means dead in what had once been called Christendom. Far from being moribund, it was displaying vigour, especially in its Roman Catholic and Protestant expressions. Moreover, as we have suggested and are to see further in the following chapters, it was gaining outside of Europe, whether in the Americas, Africa, Asia, or the islands which fringe these continents. The gains were partly numerical and partly in the vitality of the churches. Moreover, Protestantism, the most rapidly expanding form of Christianity, was developing a capacity for achieving world-wide unity in ways new in the history of religion. By the mid-century mark that unity by no means included even all Protestants and had drawn in only minorities from Roman Catholics and members of the Eastern Churches. However, it seemed merely at its beginnings. Moreover, in a variety of ways Christianity was making an impression on more of mankind, including those who did not bear the Christian name, than ever before.

The contrast could not help but be provocative to all who sought to understand the history of the race and the place of the Christian Gospel in the course of mankind on the planet.

SELECTED BIBLIOGRAPHY

P. B. Anderson, *People, Church and State in Modern Russia* (New York, The Macmillan Co., 1944, pp. vii, 240). By an expert.

T. Andræ, *Nathan Söderblom,* translated from the Swedish by E. Groening and A. Völklein (Berlin, Alfred Töpelmann, 1938, pp. 232).

K. Barth, *Dogmatics in Outline,* translated by G. T. Thomson (New York, Philosophical Library, 1947, pp. 155). Barth's own summary of his theology.

G. A. Beck, editor, *The English Catholics 1850–1950* (London, Burns, Oates & Washbourne, 1950, pp. xix, 640). Contains some excellent special studies.

G. K. A. Bell, *Randall Davidson, Archbishop of Canterbury* (Oxford University Press, 2 vols., 1935). By a close friend. Valuable not only as a biography but also as a history of the Church of England during Davidson's lifetime.

D. A. Binchy, *Church and State in Fascist Italy* (Oxford University Press, 1941, pp. ix, 774). Excellent. Carefully documented.

W. A. Brown, *Toward a United Church. Three Decades of Ecumenical Christianity* (New York, Charles Scribner's Sons, 1946, pp. xvi, 264). By one long active in the Ecumenical Movement.

R. P. Casey, *Religion in Russia* (New York, Harper & Brothers, 1946, pp. viii, 198). Chiefly on religion under the Communist regime.

O. F. Clarke, *Introduction to Berdyaev* (London, Goeffrey Bles, 1950, pp. 192). Excellent.

J. S. Curtiss, *Church and State in Russia. The Last Years of the Empire 1900–1917* (Columbia University Press, 1940, pp. ix, 442).

A. S. Duncan-Jones, *The Struggle for Religious Freedom in Germany* (London, Victor Gollancz, 1938, pp. 319). By the (Anglican) Dean of Chichester.

C. C. Eckhardt, *The Papacy in World Affairs as Reflected in the Secularization of Politics* (University of Chicago Press, 1937, pp. xiv, 310).

W. C. Emhardt, *Religion in Soviet Russia. Anarchy* (Milwaukee, Morehouse-Gorham, Inc., 1929, pp. xix, 383). By an Episcopalian; well documented.

N. F. S. Ferré, *Swedish Contributions to Modern Theology, with Special Reference to Lundensian Thought* (New York, Harper & Brothers, 1939, pp. x, 250). By a specialist.

P. Guilday, editor, *The Catholic Church in Contemporary Europe, 1919–1931. Papers of the American Catholic Historical Association,* Vol. II (New York, P. J. Kenedy & Sons, 1932, pp. xiv, 354).

O. Halecki, *Eugenio Pacelli: Pope of Peace* (Farrar, Straus & Young, 1951, pp. viii, 355). Sympathetic.

R. d'Harcourt, *The German Catholics,* translated by R. J. Dingle (London, Burns, Oates & Washbourne, 1939, pp. xiii, 274). By a French Roman Catholic cleric.

W. Hauer, K. Heim, and K. Adam, *Germany's New Religion. The German Faith Movement,* translated by T. S. K. Scott-Craig (New York and Nashville, Abingdon-Cokesbury Press, 1937, pp. 168).

S. W. Herman, *It's Your Souls We Want* (New York, Harper & Brothers, 1943, pp. xv, 315). A description of the contemporary religious scene in Germany by one who had been pastor of an American church in Berlin.

W. R. Hogg, *Ecumenical Foundations: A History of the International Missionary Council and Its Nineteenth-century Background* (New York, Harper & Brothers, 1952, pp. viii, 466). The definitive account.

W. M. Horton, *Contemporary Continental Theology. An Interpretation for Anglo-Saxons* (New York, Harper & Brothers, 1938, pp. xxi, 246). By an American specialist.

W. M. Horton, *Contemporary English Theology* (New York, Harper & Brothers, 1936, pp. xix, 186). By a specialist.

F. A. Iremonger, *William Temple, Archbishop of Canterbury, His Life and Letters* (Oxford University Press, 1948, pp. xv, 663). Carefully done.

L. P. Jacks, *The Confessions of an Octogenarian* (London, G. Allen & Unwin, 1942, pp. 272).

A. Keller and G. Stewart, *Protestant Europe: Its Crisis and Outlook* (New York, Harper & Brothers, 1927, pp. 385). By experts.

K. S. Latourette, *A History of the Expansion of Christianity. Volume VII, Advance Through Storm A.D. 1914 and After, with Concluding Generalizations* (New York, Harper & Brothers, 1945, pp. xiii, 542).

H. Lilje, *The Valley of the Shadow,* translated by O. Wyon (Philadelphia, The Muhlenberg Press, 1950, pp. 128). The autobiographical account of the imprisonment of a German Protestant clergyman under the Nazis.

R. B. Lloyd, *The Church of England in the Twentieth Century* (New York, Longmans, Green & Co., 2 vols., 1947, 1950). By a clergyman of the Church of England. Contains excellent material. Brings the story to 1939.

N. O. Lossky, *History of Russian Philosophy* (New York, International Universities Press, 1951, pp. 416). From a Russian Orthodox viewpoint.

G. MacLeod, *We Shall Rebuild. The Work of the Iona Community on Mainland and on Island* (Glasgow, The Iona Community, 1944, pp. 129).

F. McCullagh, *The Bolshevik Persecution of Christianity* (London, John Murray, 1924, pp. xxi, 401).

A. Manhattan, *The Vatican in World Politics* (New York, Gaer Associates, 1949, pp. 444). Carefully done. Critical of the Vatican.

N. Micklem, *National Socialism and the Roman Catholic Church* (Oxford University Press, 1939, pp. xi, 243). By an English Nonconformist Protestant scholar.

C. Pichon, translated from the French by J. Misrahi, *The Vatican and Its Rôle in World Affairs* (New York, E. P. Dutton & Co., 1950, pp. 382). Very sympathetic.

O. Piper, *Recent Developments in German Protestantism* (London, Student Christian Movement Press, 1934, pp. xvi, 159). By a distinguished German Protestant theologian, an exile from the Hitler regime.

M. Power, *Religion in the Reich* (London, Longmans, Green & Co., 1939, pp. viii, 240). Based largely on visits to Germany. Critical of the Nazis.

J. D. Regester, *Albert Schweitzer, The Man and His Work* (New York and Nashville, Abingdon-Cokesbury Press, 1931, pp. 145). A sympathetic, competent summary.

B. S. Rowntree, *English Life and Leisure. A Social Study* (New York, Longmans, Green & Co., 1951, pp. xvi, 482). An account of contemporary life in England, based upon careful case studies.

A. Schweitzer, *The Quest of the Historical Jesus. A Critical Study of Its Progress from Reimarus to Wrede,* translated by W. Montgomery (2d enlarged ed., London, Adam and Charles Black, 1911, pp. x, 410).

M. Spinka, *The Church and the Russian Revolution* (New York, The Macmillan Co., 1927, pp. xii, 330). By a church historian, competent in Slavic studies.

G. S. Spinks, *Religion in Britain since 1900* (London, Andrew Dakers, 1952, pp. 256). Mostly by Spinks, but with chapters by J. Parkes and E. L. Allen.

N. S. Timasheff, *Religion in Soviet Russia, 1917-1942* (New York, Sheed & Ward, 1942, pp. xii, 171). From a Roman Catholic standpoint. Well documented and, in general, objective.

E. Underhill, *Worship* (New York, Harper & Brothers, 1937, pp. xxi, 350).

M. A. C. Warren, *The Truth of Vision* (London, The Canterbury Press, 1948, pp.

159). Valuable as showing the fashion in which one sensitive, thoughtful English Christian wrestled with the problem presented by the scene in the late 1940's.

The First Assembly of the World Council of Churches, Held at Amsterdam August 22d to September 4th, 1948, edited by W. A. Visser 't Hooft (New York, Harper & Brothers, 1949, pp. 271). The official report.

Chapter LVIII

THE EXPANDING FAITH IN THE LARGER OCCIDENT: THE AMERICAS AND AUSTRALASIA AFTER A.D. 1914

What did the post-1914 age mean for Christianity in the larger Occident, namely, those nations of European stock which had grown up in the Americas and Australasia in the preceding four centuries? Predominantly Christian by heredity, and, in general, having been held to a profession of the faith, they were also part of what had once been called Christendom. Was the twentieth century course of the faith the same as in the older portion of Christendom?

There could not fail to be similarities. The world was now too closely bound together to permit the complete isolation of one section from another. All but one of the forces which we have noted (Chapter LVI) as moulding Western Europe also affected the Americas and Australasia. That one was significant. It was the decline of Western Europe. As a corollary by mid-century the larger Occident, especially the United States, was much more prominent than in 1914. Indeed, by 1950 the United States was generally regarded as the most powerful nation on the planet and its weight was being felt everywhere on the globe. Moreover, in consequence, the pessimism in Western Europe which accompanied the decline of that region was much less marked in the larger Occident.

Since most of the movements which beginning in 1914 shook the world originated in Europe, they had greater effects there than in the Americas and Australasia. Almost all the larger Occident was drawn into the world wars of the century, but they were not fought on its soil and it did not experience physical destruction or as great a loss of life as did Europe. The revolutions which swept across most of that continent, while not without repercussions in the Americas and Australasia, did not plow as deeply in these regions as in the older part of Christendom. Indeed, some were saying that there must be a reversal of traditional designations, that instead of being the Old World, Europe was now the New World, and that the Americas, accustomed to regarding themselves as the New World, were in reality the Old World, for they preserved more of the characteristics of the nineteenth century than did Europe.

Under these circumstances, in the larger Occident Christianity was not dealt as severe blows as it was in Europe. In some ways its course in the one region differed strikingly from that in the other. Several trends knew no boundaries. For instance, the Ecumenical Movement was seen in both, and theological currents in each affected those in the other. Yet in several ways the contrasts were so marked that it became difficult for Christians, particularly Protestant Christians, on the two sides of the Atlantic to understand each other.

We turn, first of all, to the United States, for it was by far the most populous and wealthiest of the countries of the larger Occident. From there we will move on, but more briefly, to the other lands of that region.

The Mounting Vigour of Christianity in the United States of the Twentieth Century: General Movements

The phenomenal growth in population and the even more amazing increase in wealth of the United States in the twentieth century were paralleled by mounting vigour in the Christianity of that country. In this there was a similarity to the British record of the nineteenth century, when the abounding prosperity and power of Great Britain were accompanied by a rising tide in the churches. Here seems to have been more than a coincidence, but in neither land was it certain that the advance of Christianity was chiefly due to that in the other aspects of life or that the latter could be ascribed to the former.

In one respect the gains of Christianity in the United States outstripped those in other phases of the nation's life. Proportionately the increase of church membership was much larger than that of the population as a whole. In 1910 the percentage of the population who were members of some religious body was said to have been 43.4. In the next decade, perhaps because of World War I, it remained stationary. In 1940 it seems to have risen to 47.1. Between 1926 and 1950 the population of Continental United States increased about 28.6 per cent. In the same period the membership of the larger religious bodies grew by 59.8 per cent. In 1950 church membership was about 57 per cent. of the population. This growth was overwhelmingly that of the Christian churches, for the only other religious bodies included in the statistics were Jewish and in 1950 these were only slightly more than 5 per cent. of the whole. Indeed, since from 1926 to 1950 the Jewish congregations increased only about 20 per cent., had they not been included in the figures of religious bodies the gains of the Christian churches would have been seen to have been even greater than 59.8 per cent. What we have called the mass conversion of the population of the United States was obviously continuing, for the percentage of church membership in 1800 has been estimated as 6.9 per cent., in 1850 at 15.5 per cent., and in 1900 at 35.7 per cent. Some of the mass conversion was among previously non-Christian segments, mostly Negroes, Indians, and Asiatics. Most of it was among the partially de-Christianized elements of Christian ancestry.

Whether mass conversion was accompanied by a lowering of the intelligent and whole-hearted commitment of the average church member to the Christian faith would be difficult either to prove or disprove. Nor were there dependable nation-wide figures to disclose whether attendance at church services was increasing or declining. In some sections of the country, mostly in the North and West, the Sunday evening preaching services and the mid-week meetings which in the nineteenth century had been customary among most Protestants were progressively dropped. Life was becoming more complex and the competition of other interests, especially commercialized amusements and various forms of outdoor recreation, proved serious. The older patterns of Protestant church life more nearly survived in the South.

The several aspects of the mass conversion which we have noted (Chapter L) as characterizing the course of Christianity in the United States in the nineteenth century continued, but with modifications.

The westward movement of population persisted, with the problem of holding to the Church those of its members who were caught up in it and of winning the un-churched. Except for a few pockets, the frontier as such was said to have disappeared late in the nineteenth century, but millions swelled the populations of the westernmost states, especially the three on the Pacific coast. It was clear both that progress was being made and that full success had not been achieved. The proportion of church members remained highest in the older states and while substantial in the newer states was smaller the farther west one went. In 1926 it was 62 and 63 per cent. on the Atlantic seaboard, 51 and 52 per cent. in the central states, 44 per cent. in the Rocky Mountain states, and 35 per cent. on the Pacific coast. The situation varied from locality to locality, but in general these averages gave what seems to have been a correct figure. The churches had been strikingly energetic in dealing with the frontier, but they had not entirely caught up with it.

After 1914 the situation presented by immigration was greatly altered. The coming of World War I all but cut off the stream of immigration which had been pouring across the Atlantic, latterly at the rate of more than a million a year. Following the war drastic legislation kept it from attaining anything approaching its former dimensions. Yet it was still flowing. The numbers of Jews rose sharply, augmented especially by refugees from the ruthless programme of extermination carried out by the Nazis in the 1930's and 1940's. By mid-century more than half the Jews of the entire world were in the United States. After World War II hundreds of thousands of various faiths who had been displaced by that struggle were permitted to enter. More than a million Mexicans, most of them unskilled labourers of the lowest income groups, made their way across the border into the South-west. The hysterical removal of Japanese from the Pacific coast states to what were euphemistically called "relocation camps" after the outbreak of war between the United States and Japan in December, 1941, constituted a further challenge to the churches. For the most part, as before 1914, the immigrants either remained true to the religion of their fathers or drifted away from it into secularism. Not until the second and third generations of their American-born descendants was there much shifting from one denomination to another. Of the effects of the changes in immigration upon the religious history of the United States we shall have something to say when we seek to summarize the developments in the main branches of Christianity.

The Indians, a small minority of the population, tended to fade out of the consciousness of most Americans. In the 1940's only 360,000 were counted as in that category. Yet both Protestant and Roman Catholic mission agencies still sought to serve them. Protestants spent more on them per capita than upon any other racial group. From 1914 to 1939 the proportion of Christians among them rose from between a third and a half to nearly three-fifths.

Negroes constituted a much larger proportion of the population than did the Indians. Although their percentage of the whole slightly declined, in 1950 they were still approximately one-tenth of the total. In general their condition improved, both educationally and economically. They were moving from the farms to the cities, from the South to the North, and from the old South to the South-west. White Protestant churches continued to assist them, mainly through schools. In 1932 they spent more on the Negroes than on any other one group of the population outside their own congregations. Roman Catholics also conducted missions among Negroes.

The large majority of Negro church members were still in purely Negro denominations. This was chiefly by the choice of the Negroes themselves, for here were institutions of which they were in complete control and which were not dominated by the white man. The proportion of Negroes who were church members was slightly larger than that of the whites. As among the whites, more women than men had church membership, but the percentage of women was higher and of men was lower among Negroes than among whites. Baptists still predominated, about two-thirds of the whole, with Methodists second, a little less than a fourth of the total. Roman Catholics remained a small minority, but were growing, especially in the cities.

The movements of population were not confined to those from east to west or of the Negroes. Much of the nation was involved. Villages, towns, and cities continued to grow at the expense of the farming population. In the cities, particularly after the advent of the automobile, suburbs expanded rapidly and in the North-east and parts of the Middle West were made up largely of the older American stock, predominantly Protestant by tradition. Apartment houses multiplied, especially in the centres of the large cities, and in the 1930's, 1940's, and 1950's huge "housing projects" arose, often on sites which had formerly been slums. Migratory elements of the population, subsisting by seasonal employment, were swelled by the great depression of the 1930's, by a devastating drought in the 1930's from the Dakotas southward in what at the time was called the "dust bowl," and by the demand for labour in the "defense industries" of World War II and the rearmament of the 1950's. Many of the migrants were in automobile "trailer camps."

The shifts in population were a threat and a challenge to the churches. Could these largely uprooted and often rootless elements be reached and held? Protestantism had its main strength in the suburban areas and the villages and towns rather than in the hearts of the larger cities, the purely farming areas, and the chronically migratory. In general it lost ground in the congested older sections of the cities. Roman Catholics still seemed to have more success in the crowded portions of the cities, but that was probably because the newer immigration, much of it of that faith and on a lower economic level than the older stock, largely dwelt there. In general, a higher proportion of the city than of the rural population had membership in the churches. In 1926 it was 58 per cent. for the former and 52 per cent. for the latter. Those living on isolated farms were more difficult to gather into congregations than those in villages and towns, where a sense of community was more easily developed.

Ever present were currents of life and thought which were adverse to Christianity. The fevered prosperity of the 1920's led to a neglect of religion. Even after the depression of the 1930's, World War II, and the perilous aftermath of that struggle sobered the nation, the secular spirit was widespread. The sceptical intellectual movements which had been prominent in the nineteenth century and which mounted in the latter part of that period continued. They were reinforced by the philosophy of John Dewey which dominated much of education and penetrated some Protestant circles.

In the United States, displaying as it did more variety than Christianity had ever done elsewhere, in the years following 1914 each main branch of the faith was vigorous and experienced growth.

The Mounting Vigour of Christianity in the United States:
The Eastern Churches

The Eastern Churches, planted firmly in constituencies which had sought haven and opportunity in the United States and which were predominantly urban, grew in numbers and wealth. They were a minority and won almost no converts, but they multiplied and were increasingly well-rooted with clergy more and more of whom were American-born. The Patriarch of the Church of the East (Nestorian) found refuge in the United States and there were also congregations of some of the other small Eastern Churches.

The Orthodox were especially prominent. Before 1914 they had been mostly within the structure of the pioneer of their wing of the faith on American soil, the Russian Orthodox Church. After 1914 several churches of national origin achieved distinct ecclesiastical organizations and ultimately became autonomous. They included the Albanian Orthodox Church, the Bulgarian Orthodox Church, the Rumanian Orthodox Church, the Greek Orthodox Church (Hellenic), the Serbian Orthodox Church, and the Ukrainian Orthodox Church. The largest of these was the Greek Orthodox (Hellenic), which in 1943 was said to have 675,000 members. It was dependent on the Ecumenical Patriarch of Constantinople (Istanbul). After 1917 the unity of the Russian Orthodox constituency was broken over the issue of the communist regime and of loyalty to the Patriarchate in Moscow. Several of the other national groups also suffered from fissiparousness. In the 1940's a federation was formed of most of the Orthodox Churches in the United States.

The Mounting Vigour of Christianity in the United States:
The Roman Catholic Church

The Roman Catholic Church prospered but was confronted by grave problems. As we have hinted, the stream of immigration to which it owed most of its growth was greatly reduced after 1914. That meant that it was enabled to catch up with its task. We have earlier noted (Chapter L) the extraordinary record of the nineteenth century. In spite of the extreme poverty of the large majority of its constituency, newly arrived, and primarily through clergy recruited and funds contributed in the United States, the Roman Catholic Church held to its faith the large majority of its hereditary constituency. It erected thousands of churches and chapels, built a vast educational system of parochial and secondary schools, universities, and theological seminaries, developed hundreds of monasteries, and knit very diverse national elements into one national ecclesiastical structure fully loyal to Rome. In 1914 it was by far the largest denomination in the country. Yet this achievement was only by dint of great effort. Now, with the annual immigration only a fraction of what it had been, the Roman Catholic Church consolidated its position, sought to win converts from the population in which it was set, and took an increasing share in foreign missions.

In numbers the Roman Catholic Church registered striking advances. In 1906 its members were said to total 14,210,755, in 1916 15,721,815, in 1926 18,605,003, and in 1950 28,634,878. The increase was due predominantly to immigration and the excess of births over deaths. Several organizations were active in seeking to win converts. Among them were the Paulist Fathers, the Catholic Unity League, the National Converts League, the Catholic Missionary Union, and the League for Prayer for the Conversion of America. In the year 1949 the number of conversions was reported as being 117,130. Many, perhaps the majority of these were through marriage.

Even more marked was the growth of the Roman Catholic Church in material possessions. As its constituency was longer in the United States, it shared more and more in the wealth of the country. By the middle of the century most of its members were still in the lower income groups. Yet Roman Catholics were increasingly in a position to contribute to the various enterprises of the Church and did so. Many new church and school buildings were constructed, numbers of them in much better architectural form than earlier had been general, hundreds of hospitals and orphanages were maintained, enlarged, or founded, and increasing sums were contributed to the Society for the Propagation of the Faith and to other foreign missionary agencies.

Additional organizations were developed and old ones enlarged. In 1919 the National Catholic Welfare Conference was constituted in succession to the National Catholic War Council which had been formed primarily to further the interests of the Church among the members of the armed services. Every bishop in the United States had a voice in it, and it possessed departments and committees which covered a wide range of activities and interests. It was administered by a board of ten bishops elected at the annual meeting of the hierarchy. That annual meeting was in itself a means of achieving a sense of national unity in the Church. The National Catholic Welfare Conference was the chief means of stimulating and coördinating Catholic Action.

Participation in foreign missions rapidly mounted. Some of it was through American provinces of existing orders, such as the Franciscans, the Lazarists, the Jesuits, and the Society of the Divine Word. Much was through new organizations. Notable among the latter was the Catholic Foreign Mission Society of America, better known as Maryknoll from its headquarters on a hill above the Hudson River. It was founded in 1911 and was in close association with the Foreign Mission Sisters of St. Dominic. The Catholic Students' Mission Crusade was begun in 1918, for much the same purpose as the (Protestant) Student Volunteer Movement for Foreign Missions. Indeed, it owed its origin largely to the example given by the latter. Until World War II the region to which the Roman Catholics of the United States directed most of their missionary energy was the Far East, especially China. They also extended their efforts into other areas, among them India and Africa. After World War II they sent more missionaries to Latin America than to any other region.

The growth in numbers, wealth, and participation in the world-wide missions of their church encouraged Roman Catholics, especially the clergy. Official pronouncements and the Roman Catholic press had a note of confidence.

However, the church was confronted by problems, some transient and others persistent. One of its passing perplexities was presented to it by a priest, Charles E. Coughlin (1891——), who rose to nation-wide influence while in charge of the church of the Shrine of the Little Flower at Royal Oak, Michigan, on the outskirts of Detroit. He was among those who early appreciated radio as a vehicle for reaching a wide audience. He began broadcasting in 1926. He addressed himself largely to economic and political issues and, professing to be applying the principles of the *Rerum novarum* (1891) of Leo XIII to the current situation, endeavoured to inject Christianity into the economic system. For several years he won only local attention. Then came the depression which began late in 1929 and which deepened in the 1930's. Millions were unemployed and multitudes lost their savings. They were prepared to listen to a voice which confidently offered a solution. Coughlin quickly attracted a nation-wide radio audience which was most numerous in the Middle West and the North-east. He attacked capitalists and bankers, urged paying off interest-bearing government bonds with non-interest-bearing currency, and was vigorous against national prohibition. From 1932 to 1934 he supported Franklin D. Roosevelt under the slogan, "Roosevelt or ruin," then turned against him and his New Deal, labeling him a "liar" and a "scab President." Becoming more and more violent, he declared that Jewish bankers had made possible Russian communism, advocated the reorganization of the government as a corporate state, and encouraged the formation (1938) of the "Christian Front." To many he seemed to be fomenting a revolt akin to fascism and Nazism. At first some of his superiors defended him, but he became increasingly embarrassing to the hierarchy, was rebuked by the Vatican, and ultimately lapsed into silence.

More chronic and serious were some other problems. One was the fact that, being strongest in the cities, the Roman Catholic Church suffered from the declining birth rate which was a feature of urban life. This was in spite of its vigorously expressed opposition to contraceptive devices. Another was the inroads of secularism. The attraction of the material side of the nation's life diverted many from the claims of the faith. There were also losses to Protestantism. Precisely how large these latter were no one knew. They probably exceeded the gains from Protestantism. Not many were won to the congregations gathered by Protestants specifically for converts from Roman Catholicism. However, many Roman Catholics slipped away through marriage. Numbers became Protestants as part of their assimilation to American life, especially in communities which were predominantly of that wing of the faith. Others sought membership in a Protestant church from profound religious conviction. In New York City there was a mission maintained by former priests to assist priests who wished to leave the Roman Catholic Church.

In general after 1914 the Roman Catholicism of the United States displayed the features which had characterized it in the decades immediately preceding that year. It was activistic. In scholarship it was still behind some Roman Catholic circles in Europe and in academic quality its universities did not yet rank with the best of those on Protestant foundation or supported by the state. No outstanding mystics had emerged from it and no new monastic orders had been formed comparable in size with those which had originated in Europe.

Also as a continuation of nineteenth century trends, the Roman Catholic Church was served by a body of priests and of sisters who were, on the average, well trained, hard-working, and devoted. It had large numbers of bishops and archbishops who were able administrators. So many were there of the latter that even to name the more prominent would unduly lengthen our pages, and to single out two or three for special mention would be to ignore others who were of equal importance.

Skill was shown in utilizing the radio. Through it more than one preacher acquired a national reputation which, while not as spectacular as that of Coughlin, was more nearly in accord with the traditions of the church. Notable among them was Fulton John Sheen (1895——). Highly trained in philosophy and theology in the United States and Europe, he was a member of the faculty of the Catholic University of America, an eloquent preacher, a prolific author, a persuasive apologist and expounder of the Roman Catholic faith, and was eventually honoured with the title of bishop. Through the radio his voice was carried across the nation.

Movements of a novel character were evidence of a vigour which broke out in new ways. Such was that of the Christophers, which sought to enlist both Catholics and non-Catholics in intelligent efforts to "change the world" by making their faith effective in the various lay professions and occupations. The liturgical movement gained headway. Although by the mid-century, as we have seen, only one American had been canonized, and she not native-born, there was much of the kind of prayer and radiant devotion which might well be producing others to whom their church would later accord that recognition.

THE MOUNTING VIGOUR OF CHRISTIANITY IN THE UNITED STATES: PROTESTANTISM

If mounting vigour characterized the Eastern Churches and the Roman Catholic Church in the United States in the generation after 1914, it was even more striking in the Protestantism of the country. As had been true since its beginning, so far as it was affected by any religion the United States was predominantly Protestant. In spite of the secularism which had been present from the inception of the nation, Protestant Christianity had entered decisively into the ideals of the country and continued to do so. The mass conversion to the faith which had been in process in the nineteenth and twentieth centuries was still more through Protestantism than the other two main branches of Christianity. Between 1906 and 1926 the membership of Protestant churches is said to have increased 46 per cent. compared with 25 per cent. in the Roman Catholic Church. Between 1926 and 1950, as against a growth in the population of the country of about 28.6 per cent., Roman Catholic membership seems to have gained 53.9 per cent. and the membership of Protestant denominations 59.7 per cent. The percentage increase in the Eastern Churches in that twenty-four-year period appears to have been very much larger, but that may have been in part because of obviously imperfect estimates. At the most in 1950 these bodies included only a little more than 2 per cent. of the church membership of the country and their growth was due to increasing effectiveness in gathering into their fold their hereditary constituency rather than to conversions. The proportionate gains of Protestantism varied from denomination to denomination. For the most part between 1926 and 1950 the percentage increase of the older and larger denominations, such as the Methodists, the Presbyterians, the Congregationalists, and the Disciples of Christ, was not as large as that of the Roman Catholics, and it was the younger, smaller Protestant bodies which had the most spectacular growth. However, the totals of the three major Baptist bodies, namely, the Southern Baptist Convention and the two main Negro conventions, with a total reported membership in 1950 of over 14,000,000, had risen more than 100 per cent. in that twenty-five year period, and in the three leading Lutheran churches the rise was slightly over 60 per cent. It will be remembered that Baptists were the largest of the denominational families and Lutherans the third largest.

In their general outlines the methods by which the mass conversion and the striking growth of the Protestant bodies were achieved after 1914 did not differ essentially from those employed in the nineteenth century. The Sunday Schools were still the main dependence for the religious education of children and youths. To supplement them more and more moving pictures were filmed. "Evangelistic campaigns" were, as formerly, customary among Baptists, Methodists, and a number of smaller denominational families. Hundreds of itinerant "evangelists" were used in these "special meetings." A few rose to national prominence. Among them was William Ashley ("Billy") Sunday (1863–1935), a Presbyterian, a former professional baseball player, who not far from 1900 began to attract wide attention by his spectacular, informal pulpit mannerisms and by his "sawdust trail" along which converts made their way from their seats to the front of the "tabernacles" which were erected for him. As the radio came into use, it was employed by hundreds of preachers, several of them with nation-wide coverage. Some, notably Harry Emerson Fosdick (1878————), a Baptist, had their audiences chiefly among the educated. The one with the widest hearing was also a Baptist, Charles E. Fuller (1887————), who appealed to the rank and file. He began broadcasting in 1925 and through what he called "The Old-fashioned Revival Hour" by 1942 had what he believed to be a world-wide audience. Soon after World War I a movement grew up around Frank N. D. Buchman (1878————) which was said to have spread to more than sixty countries. By novel means under fresh terminology it sought to win individuals, especially among students, intellectuals, the wealthy, and those influential in political life and labour. Long called "the groups" or the "Oxford groups," a name given it at Christ Church, Oxford, in 1921, in 1938 it was re-named Moral Re-armament, usually "M.R.A."—as "a race in time to re-make men and nations" and sought to effect "personal, social, racial, national, and supernatural change." The Youth for Christ Movement, strong in the 1940's, spread to other countries. It was addressed primarily to those of teen age.

Evangelism was accompanied by a prolific composition of hymns. Most of them were akin to the spirituals, white and Negro, and the Gospel hymns of the previous century and had a widespread popular appeal. They were evidence that the Protestant form of the Christian faith had vitality among the masses.

Theological activity among Protestants was marked. The currents of thought were many and varied. The most widely influential were three. One was the "liberalism" which rose to a crescendo on the eve of 1914. A second was "neo-orthodoxy." The third was "fundamentalism," which repudiated both "liberalism" and "neo-orthodoxy."

"Liberalism" had many and able exponents. They differed among themselves, but in general they had confidence in human reason, applied it to the study of the Bible, using the historical methods that had acquired wide vogue in the nineteenth century, tended to believe that essential Christian doctrines could either be demonstrated by rational processes or could be shown not to be contrary to them, and were hopeful that a society could be achieved by man's effort which would progressively conform to Christian standards. The preacher who did most through the pulpit and pen to present to a wide constituency Christianity as understood by "liberals" was Harry Emerson Fosdick, who exerted his greatest influence while pastor of the Riverside Church in New York City. Earnest, clear, persuasive, stating convictions held by Evangelicals in fresh ways and in terms which took account of current scholarship, he aided many thoughtful souls who in the midst of the challenges of the age were seeking a firm footing to face unafraid and honestly the questions hurled at them by critics and the crises of individual and collective life. He enabled them not only to retain their Christian faith but also to discover that it was richer and more valid than they had once thought possible. A great "liberal" who was best known for his expert knowledge and personal experience in the way of the Christian mystic was the Quaker philosopher, Rufus Matthew Jones (1863–1948). Having a large share in initiating the American Friends Service Committee and serving as its chairman and then its honorary chairman from its inception until his death, he illustrated what had often been earlier demonstrated, that the Christian mystic, by the vision and strength derived from his intimate fellowship with the Unseen, often becomes a man or woman of intense action. The list of outstanding "liberals" in theology, Biblical and historical studies, and action could be greatly prolonged.

"Neo-orthodoxy" had strong kinship with the corresponding movement in Europe. Like the latter, it was in part a reaction against the optimism which was dominant in Western civilization in the latter part of the nineteenth century. It was also a reaffirmation of the uniqueness of the action of God in the revelation of Himself as recorded in the Scriptures and which culminated in what He did through Christ. It was given additional impetus by the financial depression and the deterioration of the international situation in the 1930's with their proof of the insecurity of the civilization which had been so hopefully acclaimed by many in the feverishly prosperous 1920's. It was also a protest against the non-theistic humanism, the confidence in man's ability, which had flourished in the decade after World War I. While willing to accept much of the methods and results of the historical approach to the Scriptures which prevailed in "liberal" circles, "neo-orthodoxy" revolted against a great deal of the theology which went with them. Like "liberalism," it displayed marked variety. Its most prominent exponent and formulator was Reinhold Niebuhr (1892———). He decried what he deemed the utopianism of "liberalism" and its belief that man could achieve an ideal society. He stressed the chronic sinfulness of man and the fashion in which all man's efforts at improvement for himself and his fellows are tainted with sin and therefore can never attain perfection. He made much of the crucifixion as God's way of dealing with man. He thought and spoke in terms of paradoxes. While pouring scorn on utopianism, he laboured prodigiously through many organizations to combat evil and promote righteousness.

The "fundamentalists," many of whom preferred to be called "conservatives" or "evangelicals," denounced what they called "modernism." They sought to maintain the inerrancy of the Bible and the convictions long held by Evangelicals. Among the latter were the deity and virgin birth of Christ, Christ's atoning and substitutionary death, his bodily resurrection, his second coming, the work of the Holy Spirit in the conversion and the sanctification of the sinner, the eternal blessedness of those accounted by God as righteous because of their faith in Christ, and the eternal punishment of the wicked. In doing so they attacked those in the churches who seemed to them to be compromising or corrupting the faith. To many of them Harry Emerson Fosdick became a symbol of what they abhorred. In 1919 the World's Christian Fundamentals Association was organized.

Within several denominations conflicts arose out of the efforts of the "fundamentalists" to obtain the adoption of their convictions and to eliminate those who disagreed with them. In some this led to open division. A redoubtable champion of "fundamentalism" was the intellectually able John Gresham Machen (1881–1937). The failure to retain him on the faculty of the Princeton Theological Seminary became the occasion of a bitter fight and eventual schism in the Presbyterian Church in the U.S.A.

"Evolution" was obnoxious to the "fundamentalists," for it seemed to them to deny the authority of the Scriptures. They attempted to have the states enact legislation to prevent the teaching of it in the schools. In Tennessee, where they succeeded, the trial of a teacher, John Thomas Scopes, in 1925, on the charge of violating the law, attracted world-wide attention, especially since among the attorneys for the prosecution was William Jennings Bryan, former Democratic nominee for the Presidency of the United States and at one time Secretary of State. "Fundamentalist" and "conservative" views were taught in a rapidly growing number of Bible schools and theological seminaries and many evangelists reinforced them through the pulpit, the platform, and the radio.

In spite of the diversity and theological conflicts, Protestantism in the United States moved in the direction of a more conscious and visible unity. Here were some of the most striking phases of the global trend towards Christian unity which was one of the outstanding features of the faith in the post-1914 years.

One of these phases was the fusion of two or more ecclesiastical bodies, sometimes called "organic union." The unions were of churches which were either of the same denominational family or were closely related in polity, creed, and constituency. The largest was that consummated in 1939 through which the Methodist Episcopal Church, the Methodist Episcopal Church, South, and the Methodist Protestant Church came together to form the Methodist Church, which in 1950 numbered nearly 9,000,000 members. Not so large, but totalling approximately 2,000,000 members in 1950, was the United Lutheran Church which, as we have seen (Chapter L), was formed in 1918 by three groups. In 1919 it was joined by the Slovak Zion Synod. Still smaller, but substantial, was the Norwegian Lutheran Church of America, which came into being in 1917 after a generation or more of negotiation and which in 1946 was re-named the Evangelical Lutheran Church of America. In 1930 the American Lutheran Church resulted from the union of three synods which were chiefly of German stock. In 1934 two other bodies of German origin and of very similar polity and faith, the Evangelical Synod of North America and the Reformed Church in the United States, drew together in the Evangelical and Reformed Church. In the year 1946 there was the union of two denominations of Methodist temper and polity and chiefly of German stock, the Evangelical Church and the United Brethren in Christ, in the Evangelical United Brethren. In 1931 the Congregational Churches and the General Convention of the Christian Church, which was largely congregational in polity, became the Congregational Christian Churches. This partial list embraces the largest of the united bodies, but smaller ones also came into being.

By mid-century attempts at the union of churches of quite distinct polities and traditions had not come to fruition. In two important instances they seemed to be frustrated. These were the prolonged negotiations between the Presbyterian Church in the U.S.A. and the Protestant Episcopal Church and the proposed merger of the Congregational Christian Churches with the Evangelical and Reformed Church.

Looser associations of similar churches were part of the scene, among them the Synodical Conference, of which the Missouri Synod was the main constituent, and the American Lutheran Conference, which embraced the Augustana Lutheran Church, the Lutheran Free Church, the United Evangelical Lutheran Church, the American Lutheran Church, and the Evangelical Lutheran Church. The American Lutheran Conference churches were drawn into a larger but still looser National Lutheran Council which also included the United Lutheran Church and the Finnish and Danish Lutheran Churches.

By the year 1950 there were conversations among outstanding leaders which looked towards an inclusive association and even union of leading denominations.

Much more notable than the progress of organic union was the growth of coöperation among the churches. In 1951 there were said to be over 900 local and state councils of churches, about 2,000 ministerial associations, and over 1,800 councils of United Church Women. Late in 1950 there was formally launched the National Council of the Churches of Christ in the United States of America. By the year 1952 into it had merged twelve bodies through which the majority of Protestants and some of the Orthodox coöperated. These were the Federal Council of the Churches of Christ in America, the Home Missions Council of North America, the Foreign Missions Conference of North America, the Missionary Education Movement, the International Council of Religious Education, the National Protestant Council on Higher Education, the United Council of Church Women, the United Stewardship Council, Church World Service, the Interseminary Committee, the Protestant Radio Commission, and the Protestant Film Commission. In 1951 the National Council could point to a membership of twenty-nine churches which embraced about two-thirds of the Protestant and Orthodox membership of the country. Several other denominations were represented on one or another of the divisions or other units of the National Council.

A still more inclusive organization of Protestant origin was the National Conference of Christians and Jews which came into being between World War I and World War II. It was not made up of religious bodies, but was an association of individuals. Its purpose was to further understanding and remove friction among Protestants, Roman Catholics, and Jews.

Americans were also active in the several world organizations which were global expressions of the Ecumenical Movement. The financial support of these bodies came chiefly from the United States, and while by no means dominant, Americans were prominent in the leadership.

Not all Protestants joined in these coöperative movements. A substantial minority believed that the Federal Council of Churches and its successor, the National Council of the Churches of Christ in the U.S.A., were hopelessly tainted with "modernism." Some of the opposition formed a fellowship called the National Association of Evangelicals. Conservative in theology, it stressed evangelism. Another body which had a Presbyterian core and placed its chief emphasis on doctrine was the American Council of Christian Churches. Each of these reached out to form a global organization, the one the World Evangelical Fellowship and the other the International Council of Christian Churches. There were bodies, several of them large, among them the Southern Baptist Convention and some of the Lutheran churches, which coöperated either very little or not at all with any of these interdenominational organizations.

In spite of dissent and tensions among Protestants there was a growing unity. This was seen not only in organic unions and coöperation but also in other ways. Forms of worship spread from one denomination to another. Among several of the churches which had been opposed to liturgy traditional features of dignified worship began to be taken over from the Catholic (but not necessarily the Roman Catholic) heritage. "Divided chancels" which accorded a central place to the altar or communion table were substituted for the arrangement which focused attention on the pulpit. Ministers and choirs donned vestments. Books of prayer for use in the public services became common, most of them with forms for the communion which were adaptations of the historic liturgies. More and more hymnals, even of the least coöperative denominations, drew from authors who ranged all the way from Unitarians to Roman Catholics. The observance of Lent, Holy Week, Good Friday, and Whitsunday which a generation earlier would have been shunned as "Popery" spread among churches on the extreme wing of Protestantism. Methods of reaching children, young people, and the laity, including summer assemblies, tended to be the same, regardless of the denomination. From time to time, chiefly on the initiative of Protestants, limited coöperation among Protestants, Roman Catholics, and Jews was achieved on special projects.

However, tensions continued between Roman Catholics and Protestants and at times became acute. They were aggravated in the 1940's and in the 1950's by Protestant opposition to proposals for giving aid from the funds of the Federal Government to church schools, which meant primarily Roman Catholic schools, and to the diplomatic representation of the United States Government at the Vatican.

The Protestants of the United States increasingly made their weight felt in questions of global concern and shared in the world-wide spread of the faith. Either through official church channels or through undenominational agencies organized for special emergencies, they contributed hundreds of millions of dollars to the relief of suffering during and after World War I and World War II. This relief was on an ascending scale: it was decidedly greater in the 1940's and 1950's than it had been earlier. Much of it went to former enemy peoples, especially to Germans and Japanese. Such organizations as Near East Relief, which was brought into existence in World War I, the American Friends Service Committee, also an outgrowth of World War I but attaining much larger proportions as the years passed, and Church World Service, through which numbers of churches coöperated during and after World War II, were only a few of the many agencies. With the impoverishment of Western Europe and Britain, the Protestant Churches of the United States undertook an increasing share in the foreign missions of their branch of the faith, and, as we have seen, maintained not only their own representatives, but also because of the vicissitudes of World War II assumed the support of some of the Continental missionaries. For a time after World War I when there was a return to isolationism and what was mistakenly termed "normalcy," a sharp falling off of giving to missions and other benevolences was experienced. The decline was accentuated by the failure of the Interchurch World Movement, an attempt to capitalize on the interest developed in World War I and permanently to increase the contributions to charitable enterprises. The depression which began late in 1929 and which deepened during the fore part of the 1930's brought a further decline of church incomes, and in 1935 the per capita contributions of Protestants to church enterprises, congregational, national, and foreign, was only about half what it had been in 1930. By 1940 it was beginning to recover and in 1951 it was larger by nearly a third than in 1930.

The depression of the 1930's and World War II were not as devastating in the United States as they were across the Atlantic. After the first sharp blow of the depression, the wealth of the United States again mounted. The effect of these two crises proved a stimulus to the Protestantism of the United States. Millions were shocked out of the complacency which had characterized the country in the 1920's and which had so affected impressionable youth that a large proportion of those who were adolescents in that decade were, from the standpoint of the Christian faith, "the lost generation." Realizing the basic and terrifying insecurity of the human race, many turned to the Christian faith for an answer. After World War II, in contrast with what was taking place in Great Britain, hundreds of young men flocked into the ministry of the Protestant churches. Theological seminaries were crowded, and, in general, in native ability and seriousness as well as in numbers the student bodies of these institutions surpassed anything that had been known in the century and possibly in the history of the country.

THE MOUNTING VIGOUR OF THE CHRISTIANITY OF THE UNITED STATES: Its Effect on the Country and the World

What effect did this mounting vigour of the Christianity of the United States have upon the United States and upon the world? The answer to that question, important though it is, cannot be fully determined. Nor can we even take the space to summarize all that is known. We can mention only a few facts and be content to regard them as examples of what a full account would disclose.

It was clear that the post-1914 era saw a grave decline in some aspects of the nation's morals which Christianity had not been able to prevent. This was probably the almost inevitable accompaniment and sequel of the wars in which the country engaged and of the deceptive prosperity which it experienced in the 1920's and the 1940's. The prohibition of the manufacture and sale of alcoholic beverages which was written into the Constitution of the United States in 1919 was annulled in the 1930's and subsequently the consumption of alcohol and with it alcoholism reached alarming proportions. The use of narcotics and the attendant addiction to drugs were causes of concern. The divorce rate mounted and the instability of the family was heightened. Psychiatrists rapidly increased in numbers and their offices were thronged with patients. In the 1920's gangsters terrified some of the cities. Corruption was rife in municipal, state, and national governments. In their propaganda communists rang the changes on racial discrimination against the Negroes. The pessimist could easily find evidence to support the thesis that in spite of the progressive mass conversion of the country Christianity was waning in its effect upon the country and its people.

This, however, as often in the past, was only one side of the picture. As heretofore, the scene was one of stark contrasts. Christians were by no means giving up the struggle to make their faith count in the nation and the world. When the divorce rate is mentioned, we must immediately recall the millions of marriages blessed by the Church which were successful amid the strains of a complex and stormy age. When attention is called to political corruption, in the same breath there must be mentioned the thousands of honest, conscientious public servants who were held to integrity by what had come to them through the churches. Race relations, although by no means ideal, were not as bad as formerly, and in no small degree the gain was due to the Christian conscience and initiative. The chief organization for the relief of suffering from natural emergencies, the Red Cross, through its name and symbol witnessed to its Christian origin. In addition to the large sums contributed by individuals for the alleviation of the distresses brought by the wars of the period, vast appropriations were made and disbursed through the national government. Much of this was for former enemies. Never before had a nation given so lavishly for the amelioration of the lot of other peoples. Some was through international organizations, such as UNRRA (United Nations Relief and Rehabilitation Administration), and some through its own bureaus, such as ECA (Economic Coöperation Administration). Much was for prudential reasons, but much was stimulated by the Christian conscience. It was partly because of the pressure put on the Congress by churches and church organizations, for instance, that in 1951 that body voted a large sum to send grain to help cope with famine in India. The chief architect of the League of Nations was Woodrow Wilson, and his vision and persistent labours to make the dream a reality were from his Christian faith. Prolonged education and agitation through the churches had a large share in nullifying the isolationism which kept the United States out of that body and prepared the way for the leadership of that country in the formation of the United Nations. President Franklin D. Roosevelt had a simple but sincere faith about which he said little but which sustained him in the heavy burdens which he bore. During World War II the Federal Council of Churches created a Commission on the Bases of a Just and Durable Peace which was headed by John Foster Dulles. Dulles later declared that his share in that undertaking and his Christian faith were determinative in his negotiation of the peace treaty between the United States and Japan (signed in September, 1951) which was in principle not retaliatory and vindictive, but was intended to make for reconciliation. It was largely from the United States that the impulse came for the Churches Commission on International Affairs, a joint agency of the World Council of Churches and the International Missionary Council, and one of the American officers of the Commission had an outstanding part in the framing of the Declaration of Human Rights and the correlated Covenant of Human Rights put forward through the United Nations.

THE VIGOUR OF CANADIAN CHRISTIANITY

In Canada after 1914 Christianity continued to display the vigour which had marked its course in the nineteenth century. There is space to mention only four of its manifestations.

One of these was the growth of the Roman Catholic Church. This was through a high birth rate rather than immigration or conversions. As we have seen (Chapter LI), the major strength of that church was along the French elements of the population. In contrast with the Roman Catholics of the United States, who were mostly urban and therefore with a declining birth rate, they were predominantly rural and had large families. The Canadian Protestants were increasingly urban and their birth rate reflected that fact. The proportion of Roman Catholics in the population rose from about 40 per cent. in 1911 to approximately 43.8 per cent. in 1941. Between 1931 and 1941 the population of the country mounted by 10.5 per cent., but Roman Catholics added to their numbers by over 16 per cent. Now that immigration from Protestant Great Britain had declined from its nineteenth century dimensions, Roman Catholic leaders were confident that before the century was out they would constitute a majority in the nation. It was not merely in numbers that French Roman Catholicism was increasingly vigorous. In it organizations emerged to deal with social and labour issues. The liturgical movement had adherents. A growing share was taken in the foreign missions of the church.

There were several hundred thousand Orthodox in Canada divided into national churches.

The trend towards unity within Protantism made itself felt. Its most striking expression was the creation, in 1925, of the United Church of Canada, a merger of the Methodists, Congregationalists, and a majority of the Presbyterians. It and the Church of England were the largest non-Roman Catholic bodies in the Dominion. One of the chief reasons for its formation was to reach more effectively with the faith the burgeoning communities in the West, for these could be better approached unitedly than by divided and competing churches. In 1944 the Canadian Council of Churches was constituted by bringing together several coöperative interdenominational bodies. In 1951 five Canadian churches had membership in the World Council of Churches. Canadians were also active in the International Missionary Council and other phases of the Ecumenical Movement.

In Canada as in the United States churches which by their enthusiastic, emotional evangelism, the informality of their meetings, and their confidence in the inerrancy of the Scriptures appealed to the lower income groups had a spectacular growth. They were evidence that the larger and older churches, with their tendency towards dignity in worship and intellectual content in their preaching, did not meet the needs of the underprivileged elements of the population.

Weakness and Strength in Latin America

The course of Christianity in Latin America following 1914 was, in the main, one of advance. However, it was advance which was chiefly due to what was injected from abroad rather than to the inherent strength of the Christian communities of the area.

It will be recalled (Chapter LI) that from the beginning the Christianity of the region had been dependent upon continuous infusions of blood from the outside. Until the nineteenth century that Christianity had been Roman Catholic. In Spanish America the Roman Catholic Church had suffered severely from the disturbances which accompanied the achievement of political independence from the mother country. In general it had sided with the elements which sought to preserve the economic and social *status quo*. The struggle between clericals and anti-clericals was a factor in the politics of most Latin American lands. While in the nineteenth century the majority of the clergy were of native stock, their average in character and education left much to be desired. Their numbers were inadequate and they did little for the conversion of the non-Christian Indians who still existed on the fringes of European settlement. Most of the missions to the Indians and some of the care of the nominally Christian population were by clergy from Europe. Protestantism was introduced in the first half of the nineteenth century but did not have much growth until the second half of the century. Then its increase was chiefly through immigration and missionaries from Great Britain and the United States. The Eastern Churches were slimly represented by immigrants.

After 1914 the Roman Catholic Church advanced. This was partly through conversions from non-Christian Indians and chiefly through clergy from Europe and the United States. Until World War II the missionaries were mainly from Europe. That cataclysm cut off much of the help from that continent. It also obstructed the flow of missionaries from the United States to the Far East, until then the area to which had been directed most of the recently awakened missionary interest of the Roman Catholics of that country. Attention was diverted to Latin America and by 1950, as we have seen, that region became the major foreign field of the Roman Catholics of the United States. Some of the missionaries went to non-Christian Indians. Most of them, however, served the nominally Christian population.

In spite of the aid from the outside, the Roman Catholic Church did not fully rid itself of the weaknesses which had plagued it. Many of its nominal adherents and others who had drifted completely away from it sought satisfaction for their religious longings in positivism, theosophy, or one form or another of spiritualism. Many were without religion. A few became communists. In the 1920's and 1930's the Roman Catholic Church was subjected to severe attacks in Mexico by anti-clericals and, latterly, by anti-Christians. By 1935 fourteen states had forbidden priests and had made saying mass or giving the sacraments a criminal offense. However, a reaction occurred, and in the 1940's conditions became less unfavourable.

In some Latin American republics there were indications of fresh vitality in the Roman Catholic Church. Here and there the quality of the indigenous clergy showed improvement. In more than one country Catholic Action enlisted the laity. The revival of the study of Thomas Aquinas came by contagion from Europe and won the respect of some of the intellectuals.

The Eastern Churches were still small and were the result of immigration.

Protestantism displayed more vigour in Latin America than did any other branch of Christianity. It owed its growth chiefly to missionaries from the United States, but by mid-century it was spreading of its own momentum, strikingly so in Brazil. Protestantism increased in numbers in every Latin American country, but was strongest in the largest of them, Brazil, and, next to Brazil, in Mexico. In spite of its many divisions, it showed the trend towards coöperation which it manifested in other regions. Conferences for all Protestants and their missions were held in 1916, 1925, 1929, and 1948. That of 1948 was predominantly indigenous in its initiation and leadership, and this was symptomatic of a general trend. In several of the republics there were national councils and in Brazil there was a Federation of Evangelical Churches. In 1949

Protestant communicants were said to total a million and a third as against about half that in 1938 and less than a fourth that in 1914. In 1949 the Protestant community was estimated as being four and a half millions.

Continued Vigour in Australasia

We can pause for only the briefest of notices of the post-1914 course of Christianity in the predominantly Anglo-Saxon and Protestant nations of Australia and New Zealand. The churches of Australia were less and less dependent for clergy upon the British Isles. They were developing more missions for those of their own land whose connexion with the faith was only nominal and were taking increased responsibility for spreading the Gospel among the aborigines on their frontiers and on the islands in the Pacific to their east and north. Australian Protestants were also showing the trend towards unity which was seen in other countries. Through the National Missionary Council formed in 1927 they had memberhip in the International Missionary Council. Several of their churches were in the World Council of Churches.

Much the same development characterized the post-1914 Christianity of New Zealand. Shifts of population, especially to the cities, were accompanied by the erection of new church buildings. New Zealand Protestants were drawn into the Ecumenical Movement, including both the International Missionary Council and the World Council of Churches. They also reached outside the country in missions in the Pacific.

The vast expanse of islands to the east and north of Australia and New Zealand, all under white control but with predominantly non-white populations, continued to feel the impact of Occidental culture. By 1914, as we have seen (Chapter LI), most of the Polynesians and Micronesians and some of the Melanesians had become Christian. After that year the faith, both Roman Catholic and Protestant, continued its spread among the Melanesians and the Papuans.

Summary

After 1914 in contrast with the de-Christianization of large elements of the populations of what had long been the heart of Christendom, Europe, Christianity was advancing in the nations of European stock in the Americas and Australasia. This was especially notable in the largest of these lands, the United States. It was true of the Eastern Churches and the Roman Catholic Church, but it was even more marked in Protestantism. Protestantism was gaining among the de-Christianized elements and the non-Christian Negroes, Indians, and Orientals in the United States. It was also having a striking growth among the nominally Roman Catholic constituencies in Latin America. Protestants of the United States and Canada were taking an ever larger share in the world outreach of their branch of the faith. They were tending to come together in new expressions of Christian unity and were prominent in the Ecumenical Movement.

SELECTED BIBLIOGRAPHY

A. Abel, *Protestant Home Missions to Catholic Immigrants* (New York, Institute of Social and Religious Research, 1933, pp. xi, 143). Based largely upon careful field work.

P. Blanshard, *American Freedom and Catholic Power* (Boston, The Beacon Press, 1949, pp. 350). Factual, critical of the Roman Catholic Church.

E. Braga and K. G. Grubb, *The Republic of Brazil. A Survey of the Religious Situation* (London, World Dominion Press, 1932, pp. 184).

E. de S. Brunner, *Immigrant Farmers and Their Children* (Garden City, N. Y., Doubleday & Co., 1929, pp. xvii, 277). Carefully done.

E. de S. Brunner, G. S. Hughes, and M. Patten, *American Agricultural Villages* (New York, George H. Doran Co., 1927, pp. 326).

J. W. Burton, *Missionary Survey of the Pacific Islands* (London, World Dominion Movement, 1930, pp. v, 124). By the general secretary of the Methodist Missionary Society of Australia.

La Canada Ecclésiastique. Annuaire du Clergé . . . 1932 (Montreal, Librairie Beauchemin, 1932, pp. 963).

E. T. Clark, *The Small Sects in America* (New York and Nashville, rev. ed., Abingdon-Cokesbury Press, 1949, pp. 256). A standard survey.

W. H. Clark, *The Oxford Group, Its History and Significance* (New York, Bookman Associates, 1951, pp. 268). A doctoral dissertation.

J. J. Considine, *Call for Forty Thousand* (New York, Longmans, Green & Co., 1946, pp. 319). By a Roman Catholic specialist on missions, a survey of the Roman Catholic Church in Latin America with a plea for missionaries from the United States.

H. P. Douglass, *Church Unity Movements in the United States* (New York, Institute of Social and Religious Research, 1934, pp. xxxviii, 576). A careful study based upon extensive research.

Evangelical Handbook of Latin America, 1937 Edition (New York, Committee on Coöperation in Latin America, pp. 119).

H. E. Fosdick, *The Modern Use of the Bible* (New York, The Macmillan Co., 1924, pp. 291). A good example of the writings and general position of the author.

C. L. Fry, *Diagnosing the Rural Church* (New York, Harper & Brothers, 1924, pp. 234).

C. L. Fry, *The U.S. Looks at Its Churches* (New York, Institute of Social and Religious Research, 1930, pp. xiv, 183).

J. T. Gillard, *Colored Catholics in the United States* (Baltimore, The Josephite Press, 1941, pp. x, 298).

W. Halich, *Ukrainians in the United States* (The University of Chicago Press, 1937, pp. xiii, 174). Based upon extensive research and personal knowledge.

D. Hinshaw, *Rufus Jones, Master Quaker* (New York, G. P. Putnam's Sons, 1951, pp. xi, 306). Warmly appreciative, based upon research and personal acquaintance.

J. H. Kolb and E. de S. Brunner, *A Study of Rural Society. Its Organization and Changes* (Boston, Houghton Mifflin Co., 1935, pp. xiv, 642). Objective, scholarly.

K. S. Latourette, *A History of the Expansion of Christianity. Volume VII, Advance Through Storm* A.D. *1914 and After, with Concluding Generalizations* (New York, Harper & Brothers, 1945, pp. xiii, 542).

R. S. and H. M. Lynd, *Middletown. A Study in Contemporary American Culture* (New York, Harcourt, Brace and Co., 1929, pp. x, 550). A survey of a midwestern city.

J. G. Machen, *Christianity and Liberalism* (New York, The Macmillan Co., 1930, pp. 189). An excellent example of the author's convictions.

J. A. Mackay, *The Other Spanish Christ. A Study in the Spiritual History of Spain and South America* (London, Student Christian Movement Press, 1932, pp. xv, 288). By a distinguished Protestant scholar and administrator, long a missionary in Latin America.

P. R. Martin, *The First Cardinal of the West. The Story of the Church in the Archdiocese of Chicago under the Administration of His Eminence, George Cardinal Mundelein, Third Archbishop of Chicago and the First Cardinal of the West* (The New World Publishing Co., 1934, pp. 215).

B. E. Mays and J. W. Nicholson, *The Negro's Church* (New York, Institute of Social and Religious Research, 1933, pp. xiii, 321). A dependable, scholarly study.

J. F. Moore, *Will America Become Catholic?* (New York, Harper & Brothers, 1931, pp. x, 252). Objective, by a Protestant.

H. N. Morse, editor, *Home Missions Today and Tomorrow. A Review and Forecast* (New York, Home Missions Council, 1934, pp. xvi, 419). An official study by the Home Missions Council.

R. Niebuhr, *The Nature and Destiny of Man* (New York, Charles Scribner's Sons, 2 vols., 1941, 1943). The major work of a prolific author.

W. Parsons, *Mexican Martyrdom* (New York, The Macmillan Co., 1936, pp. vi, 304). A description of the anti-Catholic movement, by a Jesuit with experience in Mexico.

L. Pope, *Millhands and Preachers. A Study of Gastonia* (Yale University Press, 1942, pp. xvi, 369). A brilliant, competent study of the churches in a Southern mill town.

G. C. Powers, *The Maryknoll Movement* (Maryknoll, Catholic Foreign Mission Society of America, 1920, pp. xix, 167). By a member of the society.

W. S. Rycroft, *On This Foundation. A Study of the Evangelical Witness in Latin*

America (New York, The Friendship Press, 1942, pp. xiii, 210). By a secretary of the Committee on Coöperation in Latin America.

C. E. Silcox, *Church Union in Canada* (New York, Institute of Social and Religious Research, 1933, pp. xvii, 493). Authoritative.

United States Department of Commerce, Bureau of the Census, *Religious Bodies: 1926* (Washington, United States Government Printing Office, 2 vols., 1929).

United States Department of Commerce, Bureau of the Census, *Religious Bodies: 1936* (Washington, United States Government Printing Office, 2 vols., 1941). Not as reliable in its statistics as the one for 1926.

THE AMERICAS AND AUSTRALASIA AFTER A.D. 1914   1493

Chapter LIX

THE CRUCIAL TEST: THE COURSE OF CHRISTIANITY OUTSIDE THE OCCIDENT AFTER A.D. 1914

While Christianity was facing an extraordinarily formidable combination of enemies in the historic geographic centre of its strength, in the vast portions of the world outside the Occident it was confronted by what in some ways was the most crucial of its tests of the post-1914 era. In the Occident, Christianity, although challenged, was unquestionably vigorous. To be sure, in Europe it was losing in numbers and in fact, although not nominally, convinced Christians were a minority. Yet within that minority there was the vitality which had again and again been displayed by Christians in times of unusual adversity. In the larger Occident, the Americas and Australasia, notably in the most populous and most powerful of its countries, the United States, with some exceptions the Church was gaining. Critics might call this "social lag," and declare that on the geographic periphery of what had once been Christendom the faith was still being carried forward by a momentum gathered in earlier centuries and had not yet felt the full impact of the forces which were so sombrely potent in Europe. Yet advance was being registered.

The situation was different outside the Occident. Here dwelt more than half of mankind. Here, in India and China, were the most populous nations. Here, except on the shores of the Mediterranean, Christians had never been more than a small minority. Christianity had more than once been planted across Asia, but aside from the western fringe of that continent only in India had it gained a continuing foothold, and until late in the nineteenth century the Syrian Christians who there represented it had long ceased to seek to win their non-Christian neighbours. As we have seen, Christianity had been spreading in Asia and Africa south of the Sahara since the latter part of the fifteenth century, but this had been in connexion with European trade and empire-building. Down to 1914 its tide had been mounting, but so also had been that of

European commercial and colonial imperialism. In that year the churches and their associated educational and philanthropic institutions which had been planted in Asia and Africa had been predominantly controlled and financed by missionaries from Europe and North America.

After 1914 the picture rapidly changed. By 1952 burgeoning nationalism had conspired with the declining strength of Western Europe to liquidate Occidental colonial rule from most of Asia and its few remnants might not long be retained. In much of Africa unrest was seething, either openly or under the surface. Russian communism, frankly anti-religious, had taken over China and North Korea, was threatening much of the rest of Asia, and was to be reckoned with in Africa. In some other areas, notably Turkey, secularism was in control of the government, and in India the dominant leader, Nehru, wished to achieve a secular state. Elsewhere secularism was a pervading force.

Under these circumstances could the "younger churches" survive? For the most part they were small minorities. Would they go the way of their predecessors in Asia? The issue was crucial. Christianity had at its heart a Gospel which professed to be for all men. Thus far it had been so largely confined to the Occident that the two had been identified with each other. Were it now to fade in Asia and Africa, the phenomenal spread of the preceding four centuries, and especially of the nineteenth century, would have been ephemeral. Christianity would again be regional, identified with one culture, and that culture and the position of Christianity within it were being so challenged that many observers despaired of them both.

In 1952, when these pages were being composed, the answer was by no means demonstrable. However, in almost every land in Africa south of the Sahara and in South and East Asia and its fringing islands advances were being made in numerical strength, in a firmer rootage through indigenous leadership, and in knitting the Christian communities into the reinforcing strength of one or the other of two world-wide fellowships, the one Roman Catholic and the other Protestant. To a brief summary of these advances and of the menacing forces in the face of which they were made we must now turn.

MADAGASCAR AND AFRICA SOUTH OF THE SAHARA

In that largest congeries of peoples of "primitive" cultures, on the island of Madagascar and in Africa south of the Sahara, the generation which followed 1914 witnessed acceleration in the disintegration of the indigenous cultures which was due to the impact of the Occident. It was also marked by rising restlessness against the white man's rule. At the same time it saw a striking numerical increase of the Christian churches. So rapid was the growth that it might be truthfully said that a mass conversion was in progress which could be compared with that of the Roman Empire in the first five centuries of the faith and of Western Europe between the fifth and twelfth centuries. Indigenous leadership and sects were also emerging, evidence that Christianity was taking root and was not entirely dependent upon continuing stimulus from the churches of Europe and America.

As we have seen (Chapter LIII), Christianity, both Roman Catholic and Protestant, had gained a foothold in Madagascar in the nineteenth century and after an initial period of persecution had spread rapidly. Its chief strength was among the Hòva, the enterprising folk whose home was the high interior plateau. After 1914 the numerical growth of both main wings of the Church continued. The proportion of Christians in the population rose from about a fourth in 1914 to about a third in 1950. In the latter year the Protestant and Roman Catholic communities were of about equal size. The latter seems to have increased more than the former. Among the Protestants there were hundreds of Malagasy clergy and still more hundreds of lay preachers, both men and women. In 1925 nine Malagasy were ordained as Roman Catholic priests and in 1939 a Malagasy was consecrated as bishop and appointed to a vicariate apostolic which was entrusted to Malagasy clergy. World War II cut off part of the contacts between missionaries and their home constituencies, but Malagasy Christians rose to meet the emergency. They took a larger share in propagating their faith. Founded by missionaries from several denominations and countries, Protestantism drew together, and in 1934 the majority of the societies agreed to give to the congregations connected with them the common designation "the United Protestant Church of Madagascar."

The wars and revolutions of the twentieth century could not but have repercussions in Africa south of the Sahara. While the region was the scene of little actual fighting, many Africans saw combat service in Europe and Asia. All the area except Liberia was politically under Europeans and administered by them, but German territories passed into other hands and in some sections, notably British, where colonial policy nurtured self-government, there was much restlessness under white rule.

The continued spread of Christianity was furthered by the growing cultural and religious vacuum left by the dissolution of traditional African life. It was more rapid in some sections than in others. In it both Protestants and Roman Catholics shared, but unequally under different political regimes. The Roman Catholic increase was largest in equatorial Africa. In general the Roman Catholic advance was greater than the Protestant. That was in part because Roman Catholics added to their missionary staffs more extensively than did Protestants. Both Roman Catholics and Protestants paid much attention to recruiting and training African leadership for the Church. By mid-century about one-seventh of the priests, more than a fourth of the brothers, and nearly a third of the sisters of the Roman Catholic Church were Africans. In 1952 there were four African bishops. Protestants were also increasing their African ministry. In several colonies Protestants were moving towards a closer integration of their forces. Councils were formed, at least two of which had membership in the International Missionary Council.

As in our description of the course of Christianity in Africa south of the Sahara in the nineteenth century, so for the post-1914 years we must content ourselves with a few brief notes on some of the areas, principally those in which Christianity was making its greatest advances.

In the complex racial structure of the Union of South Africa with its many and growing tensions, Christianity continued its numerical gains in the non-European population. Those bearing the Christian name increased from about one-third of the whole in 1914 to more than half of the whole at the mid-century mark. Although Roman Catholics multiplied their missionaries about fourfold during the period and their constituency grew, in 1950 the large majority of the Christians were still Protestants.

One of the striking developments of the years was the proliferation of Protestant divisions among the Africans. In 1906 what were sometimes called Bantu sects and sometimes separatist churches were said to number fifteen or more, in 1922 sixty-five, in 1932 over three hundred, and in 1947 about one thousand. In the last two years they totalled well over a million members. Nowhere else on the planet was there such a multiplication of independent ecclesiastical bodies. For this fissiparousness several causes were ascribed. One was the desire to be independent of the white man, seen in the fact that several of the separatist churches were secessions from denominations founded and to a greater or less degree controlled by missionaries. The majority of the Bantu sects were fresh divisions from existing separatist bodies. All had African leadership and most of them were the creations of individual "prophets" or preachers. It was suggested that, in a region where the white man was dominant and the Africans were strictly segregated and denied participation in government and many of the professions and occupations, these churches provided an outlet for those ambitious for leadership and were a modern, partly Christian counterpart of the tribe and its chief. Some made much of ritual. Many professed to supply physical healing, and the trend seemed to be towards a syncretism of Christianity with animism.

Just north of the Union of South Africa were Southern and Northern Rhodesia. Here after 1914 the proportion of Christians mounted more rapidly than in the Union of South Africa, but by 1950 it was only about a sixth of the total population.

In Portuguese East and West Africa, or Mozambique and Angola, Roman Catholics were given preference by the colonial administration and accordingly far outnumbered the Protestants. In 1940 about 30 per cent. of the population were classed as Christians, of whom about three-fourths were Roman Catholics and a fourth Protestants.

In Nyasaland, which less than a century earlier had been entered by missionaries in response to the appeal of Livingstone, by 1950 approximately a third of the population were Christians, about half of them Protestants and about half Roman Catholics.

The neighbouring Tanganyika, the former German East Africa, did not have so large a proportion of Christians. Yet here, too, the increase was marked and by mid-century they were about a sixth of the whole, slightly more than half of them Roman Catholics.

Christianity was first introduced to Uganda in the 1870's. There on the relatively salubrious highlands it had flourished. In 1950 more than 40 per cent. of the population were regarded as Christians, about a third of them Protestants and two-thirds Roman Catholics.

In the Belgian Congo and the territory mandated to Belgium after World War I, Ruanda-Urundi, the numerical progress of Christianity after 1914 was phenomenal. Because of the favour shown by the government, which professed to regard them as national and the Protestants as foreign, Roman Catholic missions made much greater gains than did the latter. In 1950 Roman Catholics totalled about 3,500,000, an increase from about 100,000 in 1914. Protestantism also flourished, and in 1946 counted in its community over 1,100,000. This meant that by mid-century about one in three of the population were thought of as Christian.

French Equatorial Africa was made famous in the post-1914 years by the labours of Albert Schweitzer, whom we have already met (Chapter LVII) as a distinguished New Testament scholar. Extraordinarily versatile, noted as an organist, an authority on Bach, and a philosopher, from a sense of mission, impelled by the teachings of Jesus, in his late youth, although already on the road to a distinguished career in Europe, Schweitzer studied medicine and went to Africa to devote his skill to the relief of suffering. Dominant in him was reverence for life.

Nigeria, under British rule, and with a population much larger than that of the Belgian Congo, in the mid-1940's counted only slightly more than six out of a hundred of its people as Christians. Of these about two-thirds were Protestants and a third Roman Catholics. The contrast with the Belgian Congo and Uganda was partly due to the fact that, carried across the Sahara on the caravan routes, Islam had preceded Christianity and had won much of the northern portions of the country.

On the Gold Coast, made prosperous by the cacao which was its chief export, the numbers of Christians mounted, mainly in the animistic South rather than the Islam-penetrated North. By 1950 slightly more than 10 per cent. were regarded as Christians, two-fifths of them Roman Catholics and three-fifths Protestants.

In spite of growth in government institutions, Christian schools continued to offer the Africans most of such opportunities as existed to acquire an education of an Occidental kind to prepare them for the white man's world. Christian missionaries also gave much of such medical care and public health safeguards as was available.

It was not only in the Union of South Africa that Christianity was beginning to reflect its environment and thus to root itself in the cultural soil. In some other parts of Africa evidence was appearing of somewhat similar developments. Prophets arose, all bearing the impress of Christianity, some more and some less. Several of them led nationalist or racial movements which gave the white colonial authorities anxious days. At least one, Harris, who came to prominence about 1913, was primarily a Christian itinerant evangelist and prepared the way for mass movements to the Christian faith on the Ivory Coast, the Gold Coast, and in Nigeria. In some areas the Watch Tower Movement, sprung from Jehovah's Witnesses, whom we have met in the United States, took root and stirred thousands of Africans to hope for the day when white supremacy and exploitation would be no more.

THE STRIKING GROWTH OF CHRISTIANITY IN INDIA

In the generation after 1914 revolutionary political change swept across India. At the outbreak of World War I India was still under British rule. Indians were only beginning to have a share in the higher offices of the government. In 1947 as a result of several decades of nationalistic agitation, in which M. K. Gandhi (1869-1948) was the outstanding leader, two self-governing dominions came into being—India, soon to become the Republic of India, and Pakistan. They remained within the Commonwealth to which the name British was usually prefixed, but for all practical purposes were independent nations. The Republic of India was predominantly Hindu, and Pakistan prevailingly Moslem. Although an exodus of Moslems from India to Pakistan and of Hindus from Pakistan to India was accompanied with loss of life, the transition to independence was accomplished with little fighting. By mid-century no such basic cultural revolution was seen as was occurring in China.

In these stirring years the two largest of the Christian communities, the

Roman Catholics and the Protestants, continued to grow, the latter more rapidly than the former. In 1911 the former numbered a little over two and a half millions and in 1950 about three millions. In 1914 the number of baptized Protestants was about one million and in 1936 about two and a half millions. In 1946 the number of Protestant communicants was reported as being 1,865,000. This was an increase from 1,042,000 in 1936, ten years earlier. If in 1946 the proportion of baptized to communicants was the same as in 1936, in that year baptized Protestants totalled nearly four and a half millions. The Christian community—Roman Catholic, Protestant, Syrian, and Mar Thoma—rose from about 1 per cent. of the population in 1914 to about 2½ per cent. in 1950, and that in spite of the fact that the total population of the country had mounted and that the Syrian and Mar Thoma Churches did not have as marked an increase as the Roman Catholics and Protestants. As before 1914, so after that year the majority of Christians were south of an imaginary line from Bombay to Madras.

The Protestant increase was, as earlier, mainly from the depressed classes and the animistic hill tribes and to a large degree by mass movements. Although the overwhelming majority of Protestants were from the lowest rungs of the social and economic ladder, their average death rate was less than that of Moslems and Hindus and their percentage of literacy higher than for India as a whole. Drunkenness, divorce, and polygamy practically disappeared among them.

Among both Roman Catholics and Protestants the growth of Indian leadership was marked. Rome transferred more and more dioceses from foreign to Indian bishops and clergy. Protestants showed a similar trend and some Indians rose high in the Ecumenical Movement. Prominent among the latter was V. S. Azariah (1874-1945), whom we have already met as the first Indian bishop of the Anglican communion, who made his diocese, Dornakal, a model in the quality of its Christian life and its outreach to the non-Christians, and who was a vice-chairman of the International Missionary Council. Outstanding also was Sarah Chakko, as a college president and as a secretary and then a president of the World Council of Churches.

The movement towards unity within Protestantism had striking manifestations in India. This was all the more notable because of the great variety of denominations and nationalities represented in the missionary body. The two most prominent expressions were the National Christian Council and the Church of South India. The National Christian Council was organized in 1923, succeeding the National Missionary Council. The dropping of the word "Missionary" was significant, for it made evident the transition from foreign to indigenous leadership. Missionaries had an important share in the new body, but from the first Indians collaborated and before long were in the fore. The National Christian Council, like its predecessor, was based upon regional councils and through them made for greater coöperation on the local level.

The Church of South India, constituted in 1947, was a union of the South India United Church, which had come into being in 1908 as a fusion of bodies connected with Reformed, Presbyterian, and Congregational churches in Britain and the United States, with Methodists and Anglicans. The Anglicans were the most numerous element. It was the first time that a section of that communion had been drawn into so comprehensive a union. In doing so it had the consent of the Church of India, Burma, and Ceylon, which was the Anglican body in that part of the world. However, led by the Church of England, the Anglican fellowship did not enter into communion with it. The reason for the reluctance was the fact that, while the Church of South India had an episcopate which was regarded by Anglicans as having apostolic succession, some of its clergy, ordained in denominations without that succession, were given full status in the new body. Yet that body, over a million strong, succeeded in establishing a high degree of harmony among its diverse elements and became a member of the World Council of Churches.

One of the features of the course of Christianity in India after 1914 was the growing influence exerted upon the country. Christians were a small, even though rapidly growing minority of the population, yet the Christian faith had effects far outside their circles. These were seen in education, medicine, rural life, and the position of women. Sometimes less tangible but probably more pervasive were the repercussions on religion and morals. Thousands of individuals who had been in Christian schools or who in other ways had come under Christian influence had their beliefs and practices modified, sometimes basically. True to the Hindu tradition, they were quite willing to honour Christ and even to regard him as the greatest of the incarnations of the Divine. Also in accord with their Hindu background, they refused to grant that Christ was uniquely, as the Church firmly declared, *the* way to the Father, rather than one of several ways, all about equally good, to the ultimately Unknowable. Nor were they willing, by being baptized, to sever their connexion with the Hindu community and openly to become members of the Church.

The outstanding single example of the influence of Christianity was in and through Gandhi. Gandhi would not call himself a Christian, but declared himself to be a Hindu. Yet from his student days he was in intimate touch with Christians, mostly Protestants. He had a profound reverence for Christ, was deeply moulded by the Sermon on the Mount, and in such times of crisis as entering upon or concluding one of his fasts would have a Christian as well as a Hindu hymn sung. A favorite of his was: "When I survey the wondrous cross on which the Prince of Glory died." When he was assassinated, the saying was common among non-Christians that he had died a Christ-like death. Thus, perhaps unwittingly, Christ was regarded as the supreme standard. Gandhi had a greater effect on India than any of his fellow-countrymen of his generation. Through him, therefore, the influence of Christ, while by no means dominant, became more widespread in that land than at any previous time. Through Gandhi the teaching and example of Jesus made for non-violent resistance, greater opportunity to the depressed classes, and the positive meaning of un-selfish service rather than the traditional negative connotation to the ancient Indian term *ahimsa*, which may be loosely translated "harmlessness."

THE CHEQUERED COURSE OF CHRISTIANITY IN SOUTH-EAST ASIA

In Ceylon the course of Christianity was but little affected by the wars and revolutions of the first half of the twentieth century. The island saw no fighting, and after World War II the transition to dominion status (1948) within the (British) Commonwealth was made peacefully and without the preliminary conflicts with the British authorities which punctuated Indian history after 1914. Both Roman Catholics and Protestants increased in num-bers, the former about 60 per cent., slightly more rapidly than the rate of growth of the population. Protestants more than doubled their communicant membership. Christians were about one in ten of the population. The Roman Catholic Church, having been on the island much longer than Protestantism, had about five times as many adherents as the latter. Protestants were active in the Ecumenical Movement and at mid-century the three major denominations, Anglicans, Methodists, and Baptists, were in process of merging into one united church. A revival of Buddhism, the dominant religion of Ceylon, and connected with the rising tide of nationalism, brought some anxiety to the Christians, but seemed not greatly to have retarded the latter's growth.

In storm-tossed Burma the course of Christianity was more troubled. Until 1942 it went on much as it had in the latter part of the nineteenth century. Protestants, mainly Baptists, the result of missions from the United States, were more numerous than Roman Catholics. Both had very small constit-uencies among the dominant race, the Burmese, and were strongest among the largest racial minority, the Karens. Until 1942 the numbers of both mounted proportionately much more rapidly than the population as a whole. In-digenous leadership increased and the Baptist churches especially became au-tonomous and progressively less dependent on foreign funds and personnel.

Then, in 1942, the Japanese drove out the British and professed to encourage Burmese independence. The three years of Japanese rule were marked by much fighting. When, in 1945, the Japanese were expelled, the country did not donesian Christianity was largely dependent upon its inherent vigour for survival and growth. Yet under these difficult circumstances both Protestants and Roman Catholics registered substantial increases. In the 1940's the Batak Protestants added several scores of thousands to their numbers. Between 1942 and 1948 Roman Catholics were reported to have grown by about 150,000. In 1950 Protestants organized a national council of churches which was a kind of federation of thirty autonomous churches. Contacts were made with both the International Missionary Council and the World Council of Churches.

Storm and Vigour in the Philippines

The record in the Philippines from 1914 until 1942 was one of growth. Protestants multiplied about six-fold, mainly by converts from a nominal Roman Catholicism. Through membership in the International Missionary Council they entered into the Ecumenical Movement. The Roman Catholic Church rapidly increased its Filipino clergy and appointed Filipinos to the majority of its episcopal sees, including the Archbishopric of Manila, its highest ecclesiastical post in the islands. The Philippine Independent Church, the child of Filipino nationalism with Aglipay as its first head, grew slowly, but suffered from inadequate leadership.

The Japanese conquest brought disruption of much of the nation's life. Destruction of life and especially of property accompanied it and the fighting which expelled the Japanese. In 1946 full political independence from the United States came according to a schedule agreed upon before the Japanese invasion, but close ties were maintained with that country.

Following World War II the churches demonstrated by their actions that the vigour displayed before that struggle had not been seriously impaired. Roman Catholics rebuilt or repaired many of their structures and institutions and were active in the relief of suffering. Protestants rebuilt churches, reopened schools, and had more students for the ministry than at any earlier time. In 1948 the United Church of Christ of the Philippines was formed by a fusion of the Presbyterians, Congregational-Christians, Evangelical United Brethren, and some Methodists and Disciples of Christ. That same year the Philippine Independent Church obtained apostolic succession for its episcopate by the consecration of three of its bishops by bishops of the Protestant Episcopal Church. The majority element also adjusted its creeds to eliminate their Unitarian elements and make them conform to the Anglican tradition.

Recurrent and Mounting Storm in China

After 1914 China was the scene of as severe a series of trials as Christianity experienced anywhere in those years. That vast country with the largest population of any land on the globe was in the throes of a prolonged revolution which was due to the impact of the Occident. The revolution began in the latter half of the nineteenth century and by the middle of the twentieth century seemed to be only in its early stages. The inherited Chinese culture in all of its aspects was shaken to its foundations and much of it was disappearing. Especially shattering were the blows dealt to Confucianism, the ideology which had been dominant in Chinese civilization. The liquidation of the Confucian monarchy in 1911–1912 was followed by what essayed to be a republic. Civil strife brought increasing chaos. Then, in 1926 and 1927, the Kuomintang, or Nationalist Party, with the teachings of Sun Yat-sen as its ostensible programme and with Chiang Kai-shek as its outstanding leader, brought unity to most of the land. That unity was disputed by the communists and a long struggle ensued between them and the Kuomintang which for a time limited them first to the South-east and then to a section of the North. The Japanese invasion which began in Manchuria in September, 1931, and attained full scale dimensions in July, 1937, by 1941 brought almost all the eastern portions of the country under Japanese-controlled puppet regimes. The defeat of Japan in 1945 was followed by the attempt of the Kuomintang-dominated Nationalist Government to consolidate all the country under its rule. This attempt was contested by the communists and in 1949 they succeeded in taking possession of the entire mainland. With Mao Tse-tung as their outstanding figure, they set up what they called the People's Republic of China. Chiang Kai-shek and the main body of such of the Kuomintang forces as survived took refuge on Formosa, where they were protected by the United States navy. The communists had close ties with Russia and these were strengthened. They set about a comprehensive and resolute campaign for the mass conversion of China to communism through the intensive "re-education" of its millions and their leaders in the Marxist-Lenin interpretation of history and principles of life and action. It was the most gigantic effort at a drastic transformation of the outlook and mores of an entire people that the world had ever seen.

Through all the vicissitudes of these years until the communist triumph Christianity more than held its own. Both the Roman Catholic Church and Protestantism gained in numbers and made rapid progress in developing Chinese leadership. For a brief time after the Revolution of 1911–1912 Christianity was almost popular and seemed to be moving in to fill the vacuum left by the disintegration of Confucianism. In 1914 Roman Catholics were said to number 1,581,430, and in 1924 2,208,880. In 1914 the Protestant communicant membership was reported as being 257,431, and in 1924 402,539. In both years the Protestant constituency was much larger. In the 1920's, beginning in 1922 and coming to a climax in 1926 and 1927, ostensibly an anti-religious but actually anti-Christian movement swept the country. It was encouraged by the communists and was fed by Chinese nationalism, resentful as it was of the "unequal treaties" with their restrictions on China's full autonomy. Missionaries were accused of being "imperialists" and Chinese Christians of being "running dogs" of the foreigners. Many missionaries left the country, government control was extended over Christian educational institutions, and Chinese were given the dominant share in the administration of Christian schools. Late in the 1920's the pressure somewhat abated, but in the 1930's and 1940's the Japanese placed serious restrictions on churches and other Christian institutions in the sections under their rule. Moreover, after the United States and Great Britain entered the war against Japan (December, 1941) American and British missionaries in Japanese-controlled areas were interned. The prolonged fighting of the decades after 1914 brought destruction to much church property and in many regions banditry was a chronic menace.

In spite of all these adversities, Christians increased in numbers and the Church became more deeply rooted. In 1929 Roman Catholics were said to number 2,486,841, in 1937 2,934,175, in 1941 3,262,678, and in 1947 3,251,347. The Chinese clergy multiplied and in 1926 six Chinese priests were consecrated bishops by the Pope himself in a great ceremony in St. Peter's. In later years still more were raised to the episcopacy, and eventually a Chinese was created a cardinal and a hierarchy was created for China (1946). In 1914 a national organization was given the Roman Catholic Church in China. In subsequent years this was strengthened. Catholic Action and other lay activities were encouraged and prospered.

Protestantism also flourished. Between 1924 and 1936 its communicant membership is said to have risen to 567,390, a 40 per cent. increase and proportionately a more rapid growth than that of the Roman Catholic Church. In the next ten years, disturbed by the Japanese occupation as it was, the total continued to mount, but not so strikingly. As heretofore, Protestantism approached the Chinese in a wide variety of ways, seeking to assist them in the time of their painful transition. The most influential Chinese of the century until the triumph of communism, Sun Yat-sen, was a Protestant, and had received most of his formal education through Protestant missionaries. Chiang Kai-shek was baptized by a Protestant after he became master of most of China and seemed to be sincere in his purpose of being true to the faith. Several other outstanding men and women in the Kuomintang regime were Protestants or had been educated in Protestant schools. The majority of Protestants coöperated in the National Christian Council, formed in 1922, and through it were associated with the International Missionary Council. For a brief time a Chinese was one of the presidents of the World Council of Churches. In 1927 what was called the Church of Christ in China came into being. In it were eventually fused the Presbyterians, the United Brethren, the churches associated with the United Church of Canada, and some of the Congregationalists and Baptists. Increasingly Chinese came to the fore as leaders in Protestant churches and institutions. Several indigenous movements akin to churches arose, but not as numerous or as syncretistic as the separatist churches of South Africa.

The triumph of communism brought the greatest reverse which Christianity had suffered in China for at least a century and a half. If threatened the very existence of the faith in that country. Ostensibly the communists granted religious liberty, but only in their sense of that term. They strove to eradicate from the churches all traces of what they deemed foreign imperialism. By the end of 1952 almost all missionaries, Roman Catholic and Protestant, had either voluntarily left the country or had been forcibly expelled. Most of the few who remained were either in prison or were confined to their homes and could not carry on their normal activities. Not for nearly a hundred years had there been so few missionaries in China. The communists sought, but with only scant success, to induce Chinese Roman Catholics to break off all connexions with the Holy See and to form a Chinese Catholic Church. They compelled Protestants to sever all ties with the Occident. Under the specious slogans of self-support, self-government, and self-propagation they constrained Protestant churches and institutions to cease to receive funds and personnel from abroad. After they entered the Korean war against the United Nations the communists required the churches to join in the nation-wide campaign to "resist America" and "aid Korea." Church leaders and Christian constituencies were subjected to indoctrination in communist ideology. The communists sought to constrain all Protestants to join the Church of Christ in China and the National Christian Council, bodies now under the control of those committed to communist theory.

CHRISTIANITY IN BELLIGERENT AND DEFEATED JAPAN

In the 1930's and 1940's Christianity in Japan was submitted to drastic testing, but survived and entered upon a day of opportunity.

From 1914 until early in the 1930's Christians, although a small minority, continued to grow in numbers and were not molested. Between 1912 and 1936 Roman Catholics increased by about a half, to a little over 100,000, and Protestant communicants more than doubled. In the latter year they were more than 200,000. The much smaller Orthodox body suffered from the Russian revolution, for financial aid from Russia ceased and the staff of the mission was reduced. In these years a Japanese, Toyohiko Kagawa (1888———), rose to world-wide fame in Protestantism. Won to the faith in his student days, he received a theological training in Japan and the United States, for a time lived in

Franciscan-like love and poverty in one of the worst slums in the country, espoused the cause of organized labour, encouraged coöperatives, and wrote prolifically. Before many years he became an itinerant preacher, and at one time had as his goal a million converts. Protestants were drawn into the Ecumenical Movement. The National Christian Council was organized in 1923 and had membership in the International Missionary Council.

In the 1930's the government exerted increasing pressure on Christian organizations. Beginning with the Japanese coup in Manchuria in 1931, the condemnation of Japan by the League of Nations in 1933, and the withdrawal of Japan from that body (March, 1933), the war spirit in Japan mounted and nationalism became more and more fevered. When, in 1937, the full scale invasion of China was launched, chauvinism rose to a shrill crescendo. Foreigners, including missionaries, found residence embarrassing and most of them eventually left the country. As a way of reinforcing patriotism the government emphasized state Shinto and required all Japanese, including Christians, to observe its ceremonies. Since the government declared that the ceremonies were purely patriotic and not religious, the Roman Catholic Church permitted its members to comply and the large majority of Japanese Protestants took a similar attitude. The Roman Catholic Church quickened the pace of developing an indigenous clergy and placing administration in the hands of Japanese bishops. A similar process had long been under way among Protestants. In 1940 the Japanese government brought pressure upon all churches to become independent of financial aid from abroad and to complete the transfer of places of responsibility to Japanese. Early in 1941, realizing that if they did not do so voluntarily the government would compel it, the large majority of the Protestants brought about a fusion of the several denominations into what was called the Church of Christ in Japan, in Japanese *Nippon Kirisuto Kyodan,* usually abbreviated as the *Kyodan.*

The outbreak of war with the United States and the British Empire in December, 1941, meant further hardship for the Christians. The pace of the war and of the manufacture of munitions quickened and pastors as well as laymen were forced to join in it. Such British and American missionaries as remained were interned. Christians were urged and some of them were persuaded to establish friendly ties with Christians in lands overrun by the Japanese forces and to induce them to join in building what was euphemistically declared to be the "co-prosperity sphere of East Asia." As the tide turned against Japan, enemy bombing wrought havoc in the cities and a large proportion of the church buildings shared in the general holocaust. Christians, along with non-Christians, came out of the war depleted physically and nervously.

With the defeat and occupation of Japan the door of opportunity once more opened for Christianity. Japanese were willing to listen to the Christian message, for they were spiritually adrift and many wondered whether the reason for the debacle of the empire had not been a false ideology and asked whether the secret of the American victory was to be found in what they deemed the religion of the United States. Both Roman Catholics and Protestants, especially of the United States, sought to take advantage of the opportunity. Numbers of former missionaries returned and hundreds of new ones arrived. Roman Catholics sent more than Protestants. The Orthodox were given an American archbishop for their head. Many church buildings were repaired or rebuilt and new ones were erected. Thousands of converts were gathered, but not as many as the sanguine had hoped. The Church of Christ in Japan continued to have the majority of Protestants, even though the Anglicans, Lutherans, and some others withdrew from it. Contacts were again made by Protestants with the Ecumenical Movement.

TRAGEDY IN KOREA

For Korea and Christianity in Korea the two decades which followed 1914 were comparatively peaceful. The Japanese authorities were suspicious of the Protestant churches as possible centres of disaffection, especially since most Protestant missionaries were from the United States and were known to be critical of Japanese rule. However, in that interval both Roman Catholics and Protestants nearly doubled in numbers.

The 1930's and 1940's brought tragedy. When, in the 1930's, the Japanese embarked on their invasion of China and the opinion of much of the world hardened against them, they became increasingly fearful of possible rebellion in Korea and sought to assimilate that country so far as possible to Japan. Koreans, including Christians, were required to conform to the ceremonies of state Shinto. To Roman Catholics and to some Protestants this did not prove especially embarrassing, but many of the largest Protestant denomination, the Presbyterians, refused to comply. In 1940 most missionaries, especially American Protestant missionaries, left the country.

The defeat of the Japanese was hailed by the Koreans as liberation and an opportunity for national independence. Some missionaries returned and reinforcements were sent. Church life revived.

Disillusion soon came, followed by greater suffering than the nation had known since the Japanese invasion of the sixteenth century. The country was divided at the thirty-eighth parallel between the Russian and the American forces. In the North a communist regime was soon set up and adverse pressure was brought on Christian organizations. In the South under the republic organized through the auspices first of the United States and then of the United Nations, Christians had full liberty. One of their number, a Protestant, was president of the republic and there were Christians in some other high posts in the state. Many Christian refugees from the persecution in the North built churches. Then, in June, 1950, came the invasion from the North which sought to unite the land under communist rule. At first the communist armies seemed triumphant and overran most of the South. Resistance by the United Nations, depending chiefly on the United States, soon rolled back the attackers, but Chinese intervention late that year and Russian supplies led to the establishment of an uneasy front only slightly north of the thirty-eighth parallel. The ebb of the tide of battle to and fro meant intense distress to millions. Yet Christians maintained worship and were active in seeking to win others. Many converts were made among the prisoners taken by the United Nations' forces. Christianity was deeply rooted and vigorous.

SUMMARY

In the brief summaries with which we have had to content ourselves in this chapter statistics, usually dreary, may have seemed too prominent. However, they are indications, even if imperfect ones, of the amazing growth of Christianity in the non-Occidental world in the stormy generation which came on the scene in 1914. Vast revolutions were sweeping across the majority of mankind which lived outside the Occident. The revolutions were largely because of the impact of the Occident. The idealisms and ideologies which they embodied, whether nationalism, liberal democracy of the Anglo-Saxon kind, or communism, were of Occidental origin and were indebted to Christianity, even though in some instances only to a minor degree. In them and in the weakening of the hitherto dominant Western Europe, Christianity faced a major threat and challenge. In general by mid-century it was making striking progress towards meeting it. What the future had in store the historian could not tell. However, as in 1952 he looked back over the little more than a third of a century which covered the tempestuous years since 1914, he could say that, while still minorities, in most countries small ones, Christians had rapidly gained in numbers, leadership was emerging from them, and the churches were being knit into world-wide Christian fellowships. Within the "younger churches" the Gospel was beginning to bear its distinctive fruits in transformed and ennobled lives. Moreover, the Gospel was having effects far outside the circles of those who bore the Christian name. It was by no means dominant but it was more widely potent than at the beginning of the century.

Selected Bibliography

Agenzia Internationale Fides, *Le Missioni Cattoliche* (Rome, Consiglio Superiore della Pontificia Opera della Propagazione della Fide, 1950, pp. xxi, 548). Especially valuable for its statistics.

C. F. Andrews, editor, *Mahatma Gandhi. His Own Story* (New York, The Macmillan Co., 1931, pp. 372). Autobiographical, edited by an Anglican missionary, a close and warmly sympathetic friend of Gandhi.

W. Axling, *Kagawa* (New York, Harper & Brothers, rev. ed., 1946, pp. vii, 195). By a close friend and admirer. Contains selections from Kagawa's writings.

R. T. Baker, *Darkness of the Sun. The Story of Christianity in the Japanese Empire* (New York and Nashville, Abingdon-Cokesbury Press, 1947, pp. 254). An account of Protestant Christianity in Japan from 1941 to 1945.

H. P. Beach and C. H. Fahs, *World Missionary Atlas* (New York, Institute of Social and Religious Research, 1925, pp. 252). A competent statistical survey, mostly of Protestant missions.

B. Chaturvedi and M. Sykes, *C. F. Andrews, a Narrative* (London, George Allen & Unwin, 1949, pp. xiv, 334). A careful biography, by warm admirers, of a unique Anglican missionary to India.

J. J. Considine, *Across a World* (New York, Longmans, Green & Co., 1942, pp. xvi, 400). A popular travelogue of a Maryknoller describing Roman Catholic missions in several lands.

Fides News Service (Rome, c.1926 ff.). News releases on current happenings in Roman Catholic missions. Compiled in close coöperation with the Society for the Propagation of the Faith.

C. Graham, *Azariah of Dornakal* (London, Student Christian Movement Press, 1946, pp. 128). A warmly sympathetic biography.

K. G. Grubb and E. J. Bingle, editors, *World Christian Handbook* (London, World Dominion Press, 1949, pp. xv, 405). A competent statistical survey, mostly of Protestant missions, with interpretative articles.

The International Review of Missions (London, 1912 ff.). The official organ of the International Missionary Council. The standard Protestant journal on foreign missions. Especially valuable for its annual surveys of events in missions, both Protestant and Roman Catholic.

K. S. Latourette, *A History of Christian Missions in China* (New York, The Macmillan Co., 1929, pp. xii, 930).

K. S. Latourette, *A History of the Expansion of Christianity. Volume VII, Advance Through Storm A.D. 1914 and After, with Concluding Generalizations* (New York, Harper & Brothers, 1945, pp. xiii, 542).

Laymen's Foreign Missions Inquiry, O. A. Petty, editor (New York, Harper & Brothers, 7 vols., 1933). Selections from the factfinders' reports and the appraisers' reports of a comprehensive and elaborate investigation of American Protestant missions in India, Burma, China, and Japan. Contains much valuable information.

J. Mackenzie, editor, *The Christian Task in India* (London, Macmillan & Co., 1929, pp. xvii, 297). By various authors.

N. Macnicol, *India in the Dark Wood* (London, Edinburgh House Press, 1930, pp. 224). A popularly written book by an authority on India and missions in India.

J. I. Parker, *Interpretative Statistical Survey of the World Mission of the Christian Church* (New York, International Missionary Council, 1938, pp. 323). A competent statistical survey of Protestant missions, with interpretative articles.

R. E. Phillips, *The Bantu are Coming. Phases of South Africa's Race Problem* (London, Student Christian Movement Press, 1930, pp. 238). By an American Protestant missionary who devoted his life to the race problem in Johannesburg.

J. W. Pickett, *Christian Mass Movements in India. A Study with Recommendations* (New York and Nashville, Abingdon-Cokesbury Press, 1933, pp. 382). Based upon careful, objective investigation reaching over some years.

J. Rauws *et al., The Netherlands Indies* (London, World Dominion Press, 1935, pp. 186). Authoritative survey of missions in that land.

A. Schweitzer, *Out of My Life and Thought* (New York, Henry Holt and Co., 1933, pp. 288).

B. G. M. Sundkler, *Bantu Prophets in South Africa* (London, Lutterworth Press, 1948, pp. 344). A thoroughly competent study of the Bantu Christian sects in South Africa.

Testo-Atlante Illustrato delle Missioni (Novara, Istituto Geografico de Agostini, 1932, pp. 160). An official atlas and statistical study of Roman Catholic missions.

A. W. Wasson, *Church Growth in Korea* (New York, International Missionary Council, 1934, pp. xii, 175). A scholarly study, chiefly of the part of the Korean Church related to the Methodist Episcopal Church, South.

Chapter LX

VIGOUR IN AN AGE OF STORM: CONTRASTING WEAKNESS AND STRENGTH

In a famous letter of a Christian of the first century there is the affirmation: "The weakness of God is stronger than men." It is there applied specifically to Christ crucified, but if it was true the demonstration is to be partly seen in what followed from the crucifixion. The entire course of Christianity since that first Good Friday must be considered if we are to seek to determine whether Paul's triumphant claim is verified by history.

Never was the testing more severe and searching than in the era which opened in the summer of 1914. There then began, in the very heart of the traditional stronghold of Christianity, in the centre of what had been called Christendom, a conflagration which swept across the world. The conflagration did not end with the stilling of the guns in November, 1918. It seemed to die down and men hoped that it had been extinguished, but here and there in the next twenty years it flared up afresh, and that in spite of well-intentioned efforts to guard against it. Outbursts in the 1930's were followed by a holocaust which proved to be even more widespread and devastating than the stage which had its inception in 1914. While this, too, subsided in 1945, in the early 1950's mankind viewed the future with fearful apprehension, wondering whether worse was not still to come. Wars were accompanied and followed by revolutions. Centuries-old forms of government and ruling houses were overthrown. In several countries, including one of the largest and most powerful, Russia, and the most populous on the planet, China, totalitarian regimes more tyrannical than the old took their place. Hundreds of millions of the underprivileged of mankind were stirring to a fierce new hope and demanded access to the good things of life heretofore enjoyed by only the few. The might of Western Europe which had been mounting since at least the fifteenth century and which on the eve of 1914 dominated most of Africa and much of Asia was being shattered. In the midst of these vast forces the very existence of Christianity seemed threatened. War was notoriously destructive of the moral and spiritual values associated with the faith. Some of the revolutionary movements, including the most extensive, communism, were openly anti-religious and specifically anti-Christian. Geographically even more extensive than communism was a secularism which was undercutting all religions and making them seem irrelevant and outmoded. Whether in Europe, the Americas, Australasia, Africa, Turkey, India, China, or Japan, it was weakening existing faiths and leading to the discontinuance of historic cults and ceremonies. It sprang from a number of sources and was compounded of several elements. To it contributed the scientific method, intellectual currents associated with science and rationalism and which made for religious scepticism, the modern industrial system, the rapid growth of cities and a new type of urban life, and absorption in acquiring the material goods of life accentuated by the exhilarating prospect of obtaining them through the processes made possible by the application of science. Secularism was closely associated with an exaggerated nationalism which for many became a substitute for religion.

It appeared ominous for the future of Christianity that the forces which were menacing Christianity had their rise in Christendom. As we have seen, in varying degree at least some of them were attributable to Christianity. This was true of communism, the scientific method, the machine, the industrial processes of the age, and even of secularism. They would seem, accordingly, to be more destructive of Christianity than of the other religions of mankind.

Moreover, to one not prejudiced in its favour, Christianity appeared singularly handicapped as it was confronted by these foes. The churches which were its vehicles had less backing from armies and governments than at any time since the fourth century. The separation of Church and state which had been in process in the nineteenth century went on more rapidly after 1914. In several lands what had once been support of the faith by civil rulers, even though that had meant control by the government, was supplanted by covert or open hostility. For the most part the churches now depended, not upon taxation levied on all, but upon voluntary contributions. In what had once been Christendom, Christians were increasingly finding themselves moving towards the position of being minorities. As had been true throughout their history, the churches were by no means perfect embodiments of the Gospel. In all of them were features and characteristics which seemed to be a denial of the Gospel.

Here undoubtedly was weakness. Was it simply human weakness? Or was it what Paul called the weakness of God? Would it prove stronger than men and their institutions? Was there what Paul believed to be "the exceeding greatness of His power" and was it, as Paul confidently anticipated, to make Christ 'far above all principality, and power, and might, and dominion and every name that is named . . . in this world," and had God "put all things under" Christ's "feet"? In the first century of the faith *The Epistle to the Hebrews* had said, "We see not yet all things put under him." In the twentieth century that was still true. Was there any indication that progress was being made?

As in attempting to answer these questions we seek to draw together and summarize what has been mentioned in the preceding four chapters we do well to remind ourselves, as we did at the outset of our study of this period, that 1952, when these lines were written, was quite too early to give a final appraisal. In that year the period which opened in 1914 appeared only to have begun. Our narrative must, perforce, pause with a comma or at most a semicolon. At least a generation would need to elapse before perspective could be obtained. Much longer might be required. Yet even as early as 1952 some facts appeared to stand out as significant.

One which we have repeatedly noted was the continued world-wide spread of the faith. Although convinced Christians were becoming a minority in Europe, and in Russia even nominal Christians were far less than half the population, in the United States, the most populous Occidental country outside Europe, the proportion of church members continued the rise which had been in progress since the eighteenth century. It had not declined in most of the rest of the Americas or in Australasia. In all but a few of the non-Occidental parts of the world the numbers of those bearing the Christian name were still mounting. More nearly than at any previous time Christianity was being planted among all the peoples of the globe.

We have also called attention again and again to the fact that in the non-Occidental portions of the earth the faith was rapidly taking root in indigenous leadership and was spreading from the new Christian communities which were springing up. While missionaries were still coming from the Occident, more and more they were assisting rather than directing the "younger churches." As was being said in Protestant circles, they regarded themselves as "colleagues," not masters, and as "partners in obedience" to the command of Christ to make disciples of all nations. In other words, Christianity was ceasing to be as nearly identified with the Occident and Western civilization as it had been for a thousand years or more and was becoming universal.

In a day when through mechanical inventions time distances were shrinking and all men were being drawn into close propinquity with one another, progress was being seen towards a world-wide unity of Christians. This was being achieved through Protestantism, the form of Christianity which by its distinctive principles, salvation by faith and the priesthood of all believers, seemed the most hopelessly divided wing of Christianity.

Here was no sudden or transient movement. It had begun at least as far back as the eighteenth century and had mounted in the nineteenth century. After 1914 it went forward at an accelerated pace. It did not spring from religious indifferentism or from those who had no stake in the distinctive convictions which separated the denominations. Most of its leaders were men and women who were prominent in their respective churches. Nor did it have its source primarily or chiefly in the fear of the forces arrayed against Christianity. It arose, rather, from the desire to spread the faith and to make it more effective in the life of mankind.

The movement towards Christian unity had a multiplicity of expressions. Yet there was a common pattern which was seen in most countries where Protestantism was represented and which had global fellowship as its crowning feature. It was correctly called ecumenical, for it cherished the dream of spreading throughout all mankind and was making headway towards that goal. In some of its expressions individuals coöperated regardless of their denominational affiliations. Others were fusions, or "organic unions," of hitherto distinct denominations. Still others were what were sometimes called "world confessional organizations," global fellowships of denominational families. More numerous were those manifestations through which ecclesiastical bodies, usually churches but many of them missionary societies, coöperated and in doing so found an inclusive fellowship. The organization which loomed largest in 1952 was the World Council of Churches. In that year it had 158 member churches in 43 countries. In close association with it was the International Missionary Council, and in looser association the "world confessional organizations" and what were called "other ecumenical organizations."

The Ecumenical Movement was a new approach towards the attainment of the unity in love which had been the dream of Christians since the very outset of the faith. By the mid-twentieth century it was by no means all-inclusive. Although thousands of Roman Catholic laity were drawn into some of its expressions, notably the Young Men's Christian Associations, officially the Roman Catholic Church held aloof. Some Protestants and the majority of the Eastern Churches did not enter it. Yet the vast majority of Protestants and some of the Eastern Churches were embraced in it. Never before had Christians developed so ecclesiastically inclusive and varied a fellowship. Once before, as we saw near the beginning of our story, a somewhat similar unity had been achieved, but this had been within an existing political structure, that of the Roman Empire. Now it was being made actual in a world which was politically divided and atomistic. At times it was effective across barriers erected by war.

What was this world-wide Christianity doing? What was being accomplished because of the faith, whether through the Ecumenical Movement, the Roman

Catholic Church, the Eastern Churches, or through Christians who were not in any of these bodies? That in the post-1914 world with its wars, revolutions, and blatant display of stark material power Christianity was expanding geographically and was becoming rooted in more peoples than ever before, and that progress was being made towards a fellowship of Christians of unprecedented inclusiveness was evidence of vigour. It could be adduced as proof that the weakness of God was stronger than men and that what to the "wise and the prudent" seemed folly—Christ's course which appeared to end on the cross— was wiser than men.

Was this all? Were there other indications of "the exceeding greatness of His power"? Were these growing, keeping pace or more than keeping pace with the expanding world-wide extent of the visible organizations which bore the Christian name? As we have attempted to follow the course of Christianity across the centuries, we have repeatedly reminded ourselves that much of such evidence could well escape our notice. Even to see the kingdom of God, the indications of God's sovereignty and His "mighty power," we were warned at the very outset of the Good News, requires so drastic a reorientation that it is described as a new birth, a complete "change of mind."

Yet in the preceding four chapters we have here and there called attention to deeds, institutions, and movements which owed their existence at least in part to Christ and which but for him would probably never have been. We have noted the relief given to sufferers from wars and "natural" disasters, such as floods and droughts. Some of it was through churches and bodies connected with churches and clearly bearing the name of Christ. Much was through private organizations, notably the Red Cross, which had their inception in those moved by the Christian faith. More was by governments, in the later years of the period chiefly that of the United States which gave lavishly of its vast resources. State aid was obviously partly from motives of self interest. Much of it, however, was because of pressure from churches or other avowedly Christian organizations, or because of goodwill traceable to Christian sources. We have also seen how, in continuation of what was begun before 1914, thousands of hospitals were founded and maintained both in countries long under Christian influence and in lands where Christianity was a relatively recent arrival. Likewise as a continuation of what had been inaugurated before 1914, the foundations were laid of the modern medical and nursing professions and public health services in China. More important than the technical skills imparted was the inculcation of ideals of self-denying service derived from the Christian faith. In region after region Christian missionaries and those trained in Christian institutions continued to be pioneers in the new forms of education demanded by the age and in better methods of agriculture. In many lands contributions were made to improving the status of women, to the sanctity of marriage, and to the family. Through the Gospel hope of access to more of the good things of life was brought to thousands of the underprivileged, notably among the depressed classes and the animistic hill tribes of India and the Negroes of the United States and Africa. What seems to have been the decisive impulse in calling into being the League of Nations and its successor, the United Nations, was given by the Christian faith operating through some of the creators of these institutions for the achievement of an orderly world. Yet in many of these instances the contribution of Christianity, while undoubted, was difficult to ascertain with precision.

Even less amenable to statistical measurement but, at least from the Christian standpoint, of greater importance was the direct impress of the Gospel upon individuals. In millions who bore the Christian name the effects were slight. Yet in them Christianity was by no means unimportant in providing ethical standards and in giving some gleams of the goal which the Gospel set forth for the individual in maturing as a son of the eternal God. Others whose number no man could know were transformed. To some the change came with dramatic suddenness. In others it was wrought more slowly. Whether abruptly or gradually, it was marked by the appearance of what Paul called the fruits of the Spirit—love, joy, peace, longsuffering, kindness, goodness, faithfulness, meekness, and self-control. In such lives there was a distinctive radiance. They were "the light of the world." That they were found in an increasing number of countries and peoples was of major significance for mankind.

All these were effects within history which the historian could note even if he could not adequately appraise them. The Christian faith holds that of greater consequence were results which transcend history and reach beyond the grave. These the skills of the historian cannot prove. If he is not a Christian he will dismiss them, perhaps wistfully, perhaps impatiently. If he is a Christian he will rejoice in them but only as apprehensible through faith.

BY WAY OF INCLUSIVE
RETROSPECT

Chapter LXI

BY WAY OF INCLUSIVE RETROSPECT

Our story is told. It is not completed. As we suggested in the last chapter, it pauses with a comma, for it still goes on. Indeed, it may barely have begun. What we have narrated covers a scant nineteen and a half centuries. This is only a small fraction of the course of mankind on the planet and is merely the latest fifth or sixth of the span thus far of what we call civilization. Because of the date at which these lines must be written, we are discontinuing our narrative when for the first time Christianity was becoming genuinely world-wide, adding universality in fact to what from the beginning had been universality in principle. Yet the historian as historian cannot peer into the future and we have come to the last section to which the scroll has thus far been unrolled.

It may be of help to take a backward glance over what has been traversed. To the reader to whom this book has been the first introduction to the history of Christianity the sixty chapters through which he has made his toilsome way will probably seem so crowded with details, persons, and movements that he comes to their end with a bewildered sigh of relief. Although from time to time we have attempted to pause for perspective, it may be of help to conclude with an attempt at a comprehensive summary which, from the vantage of the mid-twentieth century, will survey the whole road over which we have travelled, point out its main stages, and essay some suggestions of its significance for our knowledge of man and of the universe.

The beginnings of Christianity, it will be remembered, seemed singularly unpromising. To be sure, Jesus had back of him the long religious development which had issued in the Judaism of his day and from which, humanly speaking, he was sprung. Moreover, his brief life was spent in a section of the Mediterranean world at the beginning of a period when the *pax Romana* was bringing administrative unity and material prosperity to that portion of mankind and when a profound and widespread religious ferment gave opportunity for the successful dissemination of a new faith. However, in the few months of his public career Jesus wrote no book and created no elaborate organization to perpetuate his message and his work. His crucifixion appeared to mean complete frustration and his proclamation of the imminence of the kingdom of God seemed to be the futile dream of a well-meaning but quite unpractical visionary. At the outset his followers constituted merely one out of several Jewish sects and one of the feeblest of the many faiths which were competing in the Græco-Roman world. Moreover, the Roman Empire occupied but a small fraction of the earth's surface and embraced only a minority of even the civilized portion of mankind. By the time that Christianity had begun to gain headway, the realm was giving indications of the illnesses which brought its demise. Its inhabitants were ceasing to say or to do much that was really new. The creative impulse seemed to be dying.

Within its first five centuries Christianity won the professed allegiance of the large majority of the population of the Roman Empire and spread beyond it, chiefly but not entirely in contiguous territory. Christianity centered around Christ, but its theology, its organization, and its worship were developments which in part reflected the environment in which they took shape. Without Jesus Christianity would not have been, and while some forms of the faith, especially those known collectively as Gnosticism, tended to belittle his historicity, the one which ultimately prevailed cherished the records of his earthly life and sought to make its theology take full account of it. So much creative vigour did Christianity possess that from it came the various churches. In theory there was only one Church, the "body of Christ," but in actuality there were several churches. One of them, which claimed to be catholic and the custodian of the faith as taught by Jesus and the apostles, was the largest.

There was that about Jesus, his life, teachings, death, and resurrection which stirred men to intense intellectual activity in an attempt to see their meaning and which, while inescapably utilizing some of the thought patterns of the day, issued in conclusions which were essentially new. Christian worship took much from Judaism, but at its core, especially in the Eucharist, it was a fresh creation. By its discipline the Catholic Church as well as some of the bodies which dissented from it attempted to bring the conduct of its members towards an approximation of what Jesus had taught. As hundreds of thousands flocked into the Church and, in spite of the efforts of many zealous clergy, the lives of most Christians were not much if any better than those of the adherents of the surviving remnants of paganism, monasticism arose. Negatively it was a protest against the laxity of the main body of Christians and positively it claimed to offer a way of becoming perfectly conformed to the teachings of Jesus. Although at first the monks on the one hand and many of the bishops and clergy on the other tended to look askance at each other, monasticism soon became an integral part of the life of the Church.

Christianity did not save the Roman Empire. In its first five centuries, except in the area of religion, it did not greatly alter the life and customs of the Græco-Roman community. Nor did it reshape civilization. Death came slowly to the empire. Indeed, it never really arrived. There were prolonged illness and weakness and then transition to later stages of culture which continued much of the Græco-Roman heritage. The decline of the empire was due to internal decay and to invasions from without. Christianity did not prevent either.

From the Christian standpoint the most disastrous of the invasions was that of the Arabs. Inspired by a new religion, Islam, to which both Judaism and Christianity contributed, in the seventh and eighth centuries the Arabs made themselves masters of about half of Christendom, from Syria southward and westward to the Pyrenees. In that stretch of territory Islam was dominant, and while Christianity did not quickly disappear and in most places survived as the faith of a minority, the churches dwindled. In proportion to the area which it covered, through Islam Christianity suffered the greatest defeat in its history. Only in Spain, Portugal, and Sicily did it regain the ground then lost.

For some centuries it seemed that a similar fate might be overtaking Christianity in the territories which remained to it north of the Mediterranean. During five hundred years or more wave after wave of invaders, mostly non-Christian barbarians, poured in from the north and east.

Because of the decay of the realm and the culture with which it had become closely identified—the Roman Empire and its Græco-Roman civilization—Christianity seemed to be on the way out. The churches which were its vehicles were dwindling in numbers and suffering from a loss in morale. A bulwark remained in the remnant of the empire which clustered around Constantinople and in the West Rome was the rallying centre of another wing of the faith. In the East, the Nestorians, although a minority, first under Zoroastrian and then under Moslem rulers, propagated the faith as far as the China Sea and South India. Yet the period roughly bounded by the years 500 and 950 was the most discouraging since the unpromising beginning in the first century. In the West the revival under the Carolingians in the eighth and ninth centuries was followed by a relapse which brought the Church of Rome to the lowest point it had thus far known and by 950 Nestorianism had died out on its easternmost frontier, China.

Out of what looked like hopeless disaster and chiefly in what in the sixth century must have seemed the most unpromising areas and congeries of peoples came fresh achievements which were the preparation for the world-wide rôle which Christianity had in later centuries. The barbarian invaders of Western Europe were won, some of them during the darkest hours of the dark ages. From this apparently discouraging material and in a section of the world from which it seemed most unlikely that light would emerge, a civilization arose on which Christianity made a more profound impress and in which it had a larger creative part than it had had on that of Rome. In the formation of that civilization Christianity was by no means the only element. Pre-Christian Græco-Roman culture, the Moslem Arabs, and Teutonic tradition all had a share. Nor was that civilization fully Christian. Yet it was continually challenged by Christianity and in it were many who were radiant because of the Gospel, who were honoured for their Christlikeness, and who were at once an inspiration and a rebuke to those about them. From Christianity came great theologies, vigorous new monastic movements, universities, noble art and architecture, daring political theories, and haunting ideals of peace. But much in the life of Western Europe from 950 to 1350, as later, was palpably, almost stridently non-Christian and in stark contrast to the faith to which almost all gave lip service.

While this culture was developing in Western Europe, Christianity persisted in the continuation of the Roman Empire which had Constantinople as its capital. From there it permeated some of the barbarians who had settled in the Balkans and spread into the vast plains of the later Russia. However, perhaps because the break with the Græco-Roman past was not as marked, Christianity did not as nearly inform the eastern remnant of the Roman Empire as it did Western Europe, nor did as much creativity issue from it in the Balkans and Russia as in the West.

During the four centuries between 950 and 1350 the faith spread once more across Asia to the China coast, but, as before, it was represented only among small minorities.

There followed, approximately between 1350 and 1500, a period when Christianity again seemed moribund. In Asia it died out except westward from Persia to the Mediterranean and in South India. The Ottoman Turks, bearers of Islam, overwhelmed the remnants of the Byzantine Empire, long the bulwark of Christianity in Eastern Europe and Asia Minor, and turned the chief cathedral of the Greek Orthodox Church, Saint Sophia, into a mosque. They carried the crescent to the very walls of Vienna, threatening Western Europe. In Western Europe, the chief remaining stronghold of Christianity, the major official representative of the faith, the Roman Catholic Church, long suffered from debilitating division between rival Popes, and its hierarchy from the Popes down was shot through and through with moral corruption. The Renaissance came, in part having its source in Christianity. Yet in some of its aspects, notably in phases of humanism, it was in fact even though not ostensibly a departure from the faith. Towards the end of the period Western Europe entered on a breath-taking geographic expansion which at the outset was ruthless in its treatment of non-European peoples and upon which the professed faith of the explorers and conquerors appeared to have little effect.

Then, beginning not far from 1500, there pulsed forth a great resurgence of life. It showed itself first in Western Europe, almost simultaneously in the Protestant and Roman Catholic Reformations. The Protestant Reformation was predominantly in North-western Europe, including the British Isles. It displayed great variety, but in general had as its distinctive principle salvation by faith. The Roman Catholic Church rejected it and Western Christendom was permanently divided. The Roman Catholic Reformation began slightly before the Protestant Reformation. While to a large degree it was independent of the latter, it directed much of its energy against it, defined the position of the Roman Catholic Church on the issues at stake in such fashion as to leave no room for Protestantism, and sought, in some areas with success, to win back the territory which had been lost. By the middle of the seventeenth century it was clear that reconciliation between these two wings of Western Christianity was impossible, and that neither would eliminate the other. While neither was content to accept it as final, thereafter the geographic boundary between the two changed but little.

Somewhat later came movements in Russian Christianity which were indications of rising vigour, but at the outset they were quite distinct from those in Western Europe, nor did they have as widespread repercussions.

The fresh burst of life in European Christianity was followed by a territorial expansion of the faith which for magnitude had never been equalled, either by Christianity or by any other religion. It was closely associated with the amazing geographic discoveries, commerce, conquests, and migrations of European peoples. Precisely to what degree Christianity was responsible for these phenomena has never been determined. Similarly we do not know how far if at all the movements which we call the Protestant and Catholic Reformations and the abounding daring and vitality which led to this spread of European power were due to some factor or factors which were common to them all. However, in the sixteenth, seventeenth, and eighteenth centuries Christianity was planted in the Americas, on the fringes of Africa south of the Sahara, across the northern reaches of Asia, and in much of South and East Asia and its bordering islands. Most of this was by Roman Catholics, chiefly because predominatingly Roman Catholic lands, Spain and Portugal, were the main colonizing powers of the time. Some of it was by Protestants in connexion with the colonies of Protestant peoples, and across Northern Asia it was by the Russian Orthodox.

The Christian communities which arose from this expansion varied greatly in vigour. The largest, in Spanish and Portuguese America, proved anemic and their continued life depended to no small degree upon unremitting transfusions of blood from Europe in the form of clergy and lay brothers. That in Canada, Roman Catholic, maintained itself even after the ties with France were severed. The one in Japan, also Roman Catholic, driven into hiding by persecution and cut off from the outside world, survived for about two hundred and fifty years with no contact with Christians of other lands. The Russian Orthodox communities, while spread over a large area, were small. The largest new Protestant communities, those in the British colonies in North America, were conspicuous for their vitality and propagating power. The small Protestant community in South Africa was also persistent and later experienced a rapid growth. Protestantism in the West Indies, India, Ceylon, and the East Indies, like the Roman Catholicism of Spanish and Portuguese America, was dependent upon that of Europe for its continued existence. In land after land, the presence of Christianity helped to soften the impact of European upon non-European peoples and to make the coming of the Occident a blessing rather than a curse.

The latter part of the eighteenth century brought a combination of adversities which to many of the intellectuals seemed to sound the death knell of Christianity. They were all the more serious because they largely centered in Western Europe, where Christianity had for several centuries shown its greatest vigour and because they bore especially heavily upon the Roman Catholic Church, through which most of the territorial expansion had been accomplished during the preceding several centuries. The dissolution of the Society of Jesus, the body through which much of the spread of the faith in the preceding two centuries had been made, was crippling. The growth of rationalism, partly sprung from a one-sided view of the conception of the dignity of man which had been derived from Christianity, but in which man's creatureliness and salvation through the act of God in Christ were ignored or discounted, undercut or destroyed the faith of many. A series of devastating wars and, above all, the French Revolution and the Wars of Napoleon shook Europe.

Yet, even while thousands were prepared to hail the demise of Christianity, movements were under way in Great Britain and the United States which were to issue in one of the most potent revivals that the faith had known. They were in Protestantism and were to rise to major proportions in the following century.

The nineteenth century presented a combination of contrasts. On the one hand, much of the traditional Christendom was more prosperous than any large group of mankind had ever been. Science and the industrial revolution, to an undetermined degree outgrowths of Christianity, were enriching Western Europe and North America beyond anything previously seen. Compared with earlier eras, the age was peaceful. Knowledge of man's physical universe was expanding by breath-taking leaps and bounds. Optimism was mounting. Revolutionary ideas, partly derived from Christianity, envisioned a human society in which the humblest would share in the good things of life. These ideas contributed to revolutions which from time to time shook much of Christendom. European peoples were continuing at an accelerated pace the expansion which had begun at least as early as the fifteenth century. In that intoxicating atmosphere there were Christians who dreamed and planned for the complete remaking of mankind and civilization to bring them into conformation with the standards of their faith.

On the other hand, some features of the age appeared to threaten the very existence of Christianity. The materialism and secularism which were reinforced by the scientific and mechanical advances of the day dominated thousands and seemed to make Christianity irrelevant or a pleasant but optional adjunct to the good life. The patterns of the burgeoning industrial communities gave little room for the worship and parish life of the churches through which Christianity was perpetuated. At the outset they were a means of exploiting the labourers, with features which were a flat contradiction of Christian precepts and ideals. Some of the programmes offered for the reorganization of society, notably communism, were anti-Christian. Many who worked for better conditions of the labouring classes regarded the Church as one of the bulwarks of entrenched privilege and were critical of it and of the faith which it represented. Numbers of intellectuals and others who followed them believed, some regretfully, some gladly, that science had made Christianity untenable. The association of Christianity with Western imperialism proved a handicap: peoples upon whom that imperialism bore heavily either were critical because of the connexion or were moved by it to look favourably upon Christianity, thus failing to understand the true genius of the faith.

In the face of these adverse factors Christianity displayed striking vitality and came to the end of the century more vigorous and more potent in the affairs of mankind than it had been at the outset of the century or at any previous time. This was true of all three of the main branches of the faith.

The Roman Catholic Church displayed notable resilience in recovering from the blows dealt it in the eighteenth century and especially during the French Revolution and the Napoleonic Wars. Old monastic orders renewed their strength and the Society of Jesus was revived and again became potent. Many new orders came into being. Anti-clericalism led to the separation of Church and state in France and in several other countries brought the confiscation of much ecclesiastical property and various restrictions on the Church. Partly because of the hostility of the governments of states which had once been friendly but which had sought to control the Church within their borders, the

Roman Catholic Church became more tightly integrated under the Popes than ever before. The Pope was now formally declared to be infallible in matters of faith and morals. Administratively his power was markedly enhanced. The Papacy set itself against some of the major trends of the day. This also was in the direction of making the Roman Catholic Church, especially its hierarchy, its monks and nuns, and its more loyal laity as distinguished from those to whom the connexion was mainly a social convention, a self conscious minority in an alien world and closely knit around the Pope. Yet the Roman Catholic Church was not merely on the defensive. It was expanding, both by emigration to the Americas and Australasia and through missions in Asia, Africa, and the Americas.

It was Protestantism which showed the greatest vigour of any of the branches of Christianity. From it issued many new movements and organizations. Within it there was a ferment of theological thought, a large proportion of it fresh and creative. There was also intensive study of the Bible, much of it courageously applying the new methods of historical scholarship. Protestantism moved in on the growing manufacturing and commercialized centres of industrialized Britain. Proportionately it spread more rapidly and widely than either the Roman Catholic Church or the Orthodox Churches. At the outset of the nineteenth century confined almost entirely to North-western Europe and the Atlantic seaboard of North America, by the dawn of the twentieth century it had spanned North America, was making a rapid growth in Latin America, was the dominant religion in Australasia, and had been planted in most of the countries of Africa and Asia.

The Orthodox Churches, especially that of Russia, were also on a rising tide, although not so strikingly as were the Roman Catholic Church and Protestantism. In the Balkans they emerged from under the Moslem Turkish yoke. In Russia there was access of vigour. While geographic expansion was not as spectacular as in the case of the other two major branches of the faith, it took place through migration to the Americas and Siberia and through a notable mission in Japan.

The year 1914 opened a new and stormy stage in the course of Christianity. The contrasts were even greater than in the nineteenth century and the threats to the faith rose to larger proportions. Yet Christianity gave evidence of amazing vigour and continued its geographic spread.

The challenges to Christianity were many. Some were continuations of those of the nineteenth century, among them absorption in the pursuit of wealth, the growing industrialization of society, some of the programmes advocated for collective welfare, and adverse intellectual currents. To them were added two world wars and several lesser wars, the decline of Western Europe, revolutions which destroyed forms of government, social structures, and inherited ethical and religious convictions for at least a third of mankind, rebellion against the supremacy of Western European nations, the advance of pronouncedly anti-Christian communism, and a great groundswell among the masses in many lands demanding more of the good things of life. Significantly, and in the eyes of many observers ominously, most of these challenges originated and attained their most formidable dimensions in what had been regarded as the historic heart of Christendom.

Although it suffered losses, some of them serious, in general Christianity rose to the challenge. The Roman Catholic Church displayed features which had characterized it in the nineteenth century. Many of its hereditary constituency had their allegiance weakened or dissolved, but those who remained were more nearly consolidated under the Papacy. The See of Peter had a succession of able, upright men. There was fresh intellectual activity, especially in theology. The liturgical movement, Eucharistic congresses, and other developments stimulated piety. Catholic Action enlisted more and more of the laity. The geographic spread in Africa and Asia mounted. Also as in the nineteenth century, proportionately Protestantism flourished more pronouncedly than did the Roman Catholic Church. It experienced numerical decline in Europe, but it continued to gain in the United States, in Latin America (where its advance was chiefly among the nominally Roman Catholic population), in Africa, and in South and East Asia and its fringing islands. Even more than the Roman Catholic Church, it was stirred by theological ferment. Through the Ecumenical Movement it developed an expanding fresh approach towards Christian unity. The Eastern Churches were hard hit, especially the Russian Orthodox Church, but none of them died, and some exhibited sturdy vitality in the face of what looked like overwhelming disaster, especially from communism. Christianity came to the mid-twentieth century more nearly world-wide in its extent and influence than either it or any other religion had ever been.

In the relatively brief nineteen and a half centuries of its existence, in spite of its seemingly unpromising beginning, Christianity had spread over most of the earth's surface and was represented by adherents in almost every tribe and nation and in nearly every inhabited land. It had gone forward by pulsations of advance, retreat, and advance. Measured by the criteria of geographic extent, inner vigour as shown by new movements from within it, and the effect on mankind as a whole, each major advance had carried it further into the life of the world than the one before it and each major recession had been less severe than its predecessor. In spite of this spread, in the middle of the twentieth century Christianity was still the professed faith of only a minority of men, in some of the largest countries only a small minority. Of those who bore the

Christian name, especially in lands where they were in the majority, only a minority made the thoroughgoing commitment required by the genius of the faith.

What effect had Christianity had across the centuries, operating as it did through this minority? Again and again in the preceding chapters we have sought to give data towards the answer. Often we cannot know whether Christianity was at all an element in a particular movement or action. In many other instances we can be reasonably sure that it entered as a factor, but so compounded with other causes that we cannot accurately appraise the extent of its responsibility. Among these were the emergence of universities in the Middle Ages, the Renaissance, the rise of the scientific method, the geographic discoveries by Europeans in the fifteenth, sixteenth, and seventeenth centuries, democracy of the Anglo-Saxon kind, and communism. Whether in any of these it was determinative, so that but for it they would not have come into being, we are not and probably cannot be sure. We can be clear that in some movements Christianity was dominant. Such were the appearance and development of the various churches, monasticism in its several manifestations, the Protestant and Catholic Reformations, the formulation of the great creeds of the first few centuries, and the construction of most of the systems of theology. Yet in none of these was Christianity the only cause. Indeed, what we call Christianity changed from time to time. In most of its forms what came from Jesus and his apostles was regarded as primary and determinative, but other contributions entered, among them the cultural background of individuals and groups, the personal experiences of outstanding leaders, and inherited religions and philosophical conceptions.

In spite of these uncertainties and complicating factors, we can be fully assured of some of the fruits of what constitutes the core of the Christian faith and of Christianity, namely, the life, teachings, death, and resurrection of Jesus. We can, of course, be clear that without this core Christianity and the churches would not have been. It is by no means responsible for all that was done in the guise of Christianity or under the ægis of the churches, and much was performed in its name which was quite contrary to it. However, the perversion of the Gospel is one of the facts of which an appraisal of the results of Christianity must take account. It is incontestable that from Christ issued unmeasured and immeasurable power in the life of mankind. We know that because of him across the centuries untold thousands of individuals have borne something of his likeness. Thousands have been so reared in the knowledge of him that from childhood and without striking struggle they have followed him and have increasingly shown the radiance of the faith, hope, and self-giving love which were in him. Other thousands have come to the same path and goal through deep sorrow, initial moral defeat, and soul-wrenching struggles. Some have been famous and have passed on to other thousands the light which has come from him. More have been obscure and have been known only to a limited circle, but within that circle they have been towers of strength.

Through Christ there has come into being the Church. The Church is never fully identical with ecclesiastical organizations. It is to be found in them, but not all of their members belong to it and it is greater than the sum of them all. Yet, though never fully visible as an institution, the Church has been and is a reality, more potent than any one or all of the churches. "The blessed company of all faithful people," it constitutes a fellowship which has been both aided and hampered by the churches, and is both in them and transcends them.

From individuals who have been inspired by Christ and from the Church has issued movement after movement for attaining the Christian ideal. That ideal has centered around the kingdom of God, an order in which God's will is done. It sets infinite value upon the individual. Its goal for the individual is to become a child of God, to "know the love of Christ which passeth knowledge" and to "be filled unto all the fulness of God"—God Who is Creator and Father, Who revealed His true nature, self-giving love, by becoming incarnate in Jesus Christ and permitting the seeming defeat and frustration of the cross, and Who is ever active in history in individuals and the collective life of mankind. Its goal for the individual cannot be completely attained this side of the grave, but is so breath-taking that within history only a beginning is possible. Nor can it be reached in isolation, but only in community. In Christ's teaching love for God, as the duty and privilege of man, is inseparably joined with love for one's neighbour.

The ideal and the goal have determined the character of the movements which have been the fruits of Christianity. Although men can use and often have used knowledge and education to the seeming defeat of the ideal, across the centuries Christianity has been the means of reducing more languages to writing than have all other factors combined. It has created more schools, more theories of education, and more systems than has any other one force. More than any other power in history it has impelled men to fight suffering, whether that suffering has come from disease, war, or natural disasters. It has built thousands of hospitals, inspired the emergence of nursing and medical professions, and furthered movements for public health and the relief and prevention of famine. Although explorations and conquests which were in part its outgrowth led to the enslavement of Africans for the plantations of the Americas, men and women whose consciences were awakened by Christianity and whose wills it nerved brought about the abolition of Negro slavery. Men and women similarly moved and sustained wrote into the laws of Spain and

Portugal provisions to alleviate the ruthless exploitation of the Indians of the New World. Wars have often been waged in the name of Christianity. They have attained their most colossal dimensions through weapons and large scale organization initiated in Christendom. Yet from no other source have there come as many and as strong movements to eliminate or regulate war and to ease the suffering brought by war. From its first centuries the Christian faith has caused many of its adherents to be uneasy about war. It has led minorities to refuse to have any part in it. It has impelled others to seek to limit war by defining what, in their judgement, from the Christian standpoint is a "just war." In the turbulent middle ages of Europe it gave rise to the Truce of God and the Peace of God. In a later era it was the main impulse in the formulation of international law. But for it the League of Nations and the United Nations would not have been. By its name and symbol the most extensive organization ever created for the relief of the suffering caused by war, the Red Cross, bears witness to its Christian origin. The list might go on indefinitely. It includes many another humanitarian project and movement, ideals in government, the reform of prisons and the emergence of criminology, great art and architecture, and outstanding literature. In geographic extent and potency the results were never as marked as in the nineteenth and twentieth centuries.

What meaning does this history of Christianity have? What does it indicate of the nature of man and of the environment in which man finds himself? The answer cannot be given on the basis of facts ascertained by observation and appraised by human reason. It can come only as an act of faith. Yet it need not contradict observation and reason and in it what has been ascertained through them can have a place and intelligibility be given to what otherwise seems confusing and contradictory. The historian is vividly aware that any suggestion which he may essay will not win universal assent. He has seen too many diverse replies given across the centuries, some of them boldly and some hesitantly, to be confident that any which he can offer will have a different fate. He recalls that it was said long ago that "whether there be knowledge it shall be done away" and that we know only in part. Yet the historian owes it to any who may read his pages to state whatever answers his study of the records has brought to him.

First of all, as a conclusion of faith supported by what is deemed to be fact interpreted by reason, is the conviction that we live in a universe which is not unintelligible confusion but is orderly, and that it is created and sustained by One Whom we call God. Next is the conviction, reached in similar fashion, that man, as a part of that universe, is also created by God. The ancient record declares that "God created man in His own image," and that He did so out of the dust of the ground, breathing into him the breath of life. That, too, is partly a conclusion of faith, but it also explains the contradiction of which thoughtful men have long been painfully aware—on the one hand their aspirations to transcend time and space and to have fellowship with God, and on the other hand their earthiness in physical and moral frailty and in their imperfect knowledge.

Faith and reason combine to declare that since God has created man in His own image, He must design him for fellowship with Himself. This means that He desires men to be creatures who are not automata, for robots could not be in His image. They must have freedom of choice, and that freedom must be sufficient to permit them either to rebel against God or voluntarily to seek to know God's will and do it. It is clear that from as far back as men know their own history and presumably further, men have used that freedom to rebel against their Creator and to seek to follow their own, misdirected wills.

Faith declares, and believes that in doing so it rightly interprets the evidence, that God judges men, that through what we may call laws or patterns which He has built into the universe, men's rebellion and perversion of their freedom bring on them misery, corruption of character, and what is painfully obvious in the course of human history—hatred, strife between individuals, classes, races, and nations, physical degeneracy, and moral slavery, so that men, meant to be higher than the animals about them, sink lower than the brutes. Yet faith, also supported by fact, insists that this judgement is in love and mercy and is for the purpose of bringing men back from the perversion of their wills to the purpose which God has for them.

Christian faith declares that because of what Christians call His grace, the love which men can never earn or deserve but can only accept in humble, wondering gratitude, God acted to redeem men and reconcile them to Himself. Still respecting men's wills, He did this by a long preparation through the lawgivers and prophets of Israel and then by the astounding act, without precedent and with no need of repetition, in the incarnation in Jesus of Nazareth, who was both "very God of very God, begotten, not made" and also true man.

The incarnate Word lived, taught, announced the kingdom of God, and was crucified through the self-interest and stupidity of representatives of as high a religion and as good a government as men had thus far known. Thus God at once passed judgement on men's best achievement and sought to save the world which had committed the crime.

Christian faith goes on to declare that the cross did not end all, that through God's power Christ rose, triumphant, and ever lives in what to men is the mystery of his unity with God the Father. Moreover, Christian faith asserts that after these events in history, God continued to act, in enhanced fashion, through what it calls the Holy Spirit, Spirit Who is also God and Who, always present, came in a fresh way because Christ was no longer bodily with men. Christian faith also affirms that in those who "receive Christ" a new birth is wrought by God through His Spirit, that Christ dwells in their hearts by faith, and that they are transformed, becoming lights in a dark world.

The historian, if he shares this faith, believes that in the pattern thus disclosed the facts fit into place. He is certain that, judged by his effect, Jesus Christ has been the most influential life lived on this planet. He sees coming from him the many fruits at which we have hinted in the preceding pages. He believes Christ's influence to be mounting. Yet the historian must also recognize that what has issued from Christ has been the occasion for greater perversions of man's free will than had been witnessed before Christ's appearance. That was seen spectacularly in the crucifixion, in which men whose predecessors had persecuted those of their fellows who had spoken for God now killed the Son Himself. It has been apparent in the centuries since the crucifixion—in the corruption which we have noted in the churches themselves, in the large scale exploitation of other peoples by those bearing the Christian name, in the enslavement of Negroes by nominal Christians, in the slums of the industrial and mining towns and cities which in Christendom were a result of the industrial revolution, in the application of science to mass destruction in war, most highly developed among peoples long under Christian influence, and in the emergence and spread of such tyrannical ideologies as national socialism and communism, both of which arose in Christendom. These and other instances have been the turning of the good gifts of God, in part the fruits of the Gospel, to the misery of men. All of these perversions, however, have been challenges to which earnest Christians have responded. They have been stimulated by them and their faith to use them as an occasion for bringing about a greater good than would have come had they not been stung to action by them. This does not mean that God is responsible for the demonic twistings of His bounty to men's hurt. It may well be evidence, in contrast, that God is sovereign and that, having given men free will, He does not permit its misdirection to defeat His benign purpose. Indeed, it is conceivable that He never allows the abuse of free will to get completely out of hand, but has placed such resources at the disposal of those who, also of their free will, respond to the promptings of His Spirit that they bring good out of evil.

What is to be the end of the story? That the course of Christianity on the planet has only recently begun is evident. Is it only at its beginning? Is history to go on until all human society, within history, and all individuals within it fully conform to God's ideal for men? Or is God to bring history suddenly to an end, perhaps at an early date? Here Christians have not been agreed. Earnest.

intelligent, and devout men, honestly seeking to know God's purpose, have taken what look like diametrically opposing views and have held them with conviction. That was true of the writers of the New Testament, even at times of the same writer. Thus Paul, in his *Letter to the Romans,* speaks of some men as "vessels of wrath fitted to destruction" and declares that God has "mercy on whom He will have mercy and whom He will He hardeneth," and also says that "God hath shut them all up together in unbelief that He might have mercy upon all." Even Jesus both spoke solemnly of the path which leads to destruction and which many enter and in one of his parables pictures the good shepherd as leaving the ninety-nine sheep who are safe in the fold and seeking the one which had gone astray, declaring that it was not the will of God "that one of these little ones should perish." *The Gospel according to John* is emphatic that "God sent not his Son into the world to condemn the world, but that the world through him might be saved." Jesus believed that there would be a dramatic end of history and that until then both the wheat and the weeds would grow together, but for that event he refused to set a date. He advised his disciples to be ready for it at any moment, but warned them, in the parable of the wise and foolish virgins, that it might be long delayed. Here, obviously, we are dealing with a future for which history does not provide a precedent and where the historian must tread humbly and by faith and not by what he has seen.

Yet they who have learned of Jesus reach out in faith and affirm that God is not only sovereign but that He is also love, love as seen in the seeming weakness of the babe in Bethlehem's manger and of the cross, but love which because of "the exceeding greatness of His Power . . . which He wrought in Christ when he raised him from the dead" cannot and will not be defeated. As they are stirred to the depths by the mystery of evil and cry out in anguish "My God, why?" they affirm with Paul that while "the whole creation groaneth and travaileth in pain" God subjected the creation to frustration "in hope," and that it "shall be delivered from the bondage of corruption into the glorious liberty of the children of God." They are convinced that the full course of the Gospel is not and cannot be contained within history, that God has made Christ lord not only in this age but also in that which is to come, and that it is the purpose of God through Christ to reconcile all things unto Himself, whether things upon the earth or things in the heavens. Those who have been taught of Christ have that hope and that faith because of what they know of the love of God in Christ and because that love has been poured into their hearts through His Holy Spirit Whom God has given them.